Communications
in Computer and Information Science 17

Tiziana Margaria Bernhard Steffen (Eds.)

Leveraging Applications of Formal Methods, Verification and Validation

Third International Symposium, ISoLA 2008
Porto Sani, Greece, October 13-15, 2008
Proceedings

Volume Editors

Tiziana Margaria
Universität Potsdam
August-Bebel-Str. 89
14482 Potsdam, Germany
E-mail: margaria@cs.uni-potsdam.de

Bernhard Steffen
Technische Universität Dortmund
Otto-Hahn-Str. 14
44227 Dortmund, Germany
E-mail: steffen@cs.tu-dortmund.de

Library of Congress Control Number: 2008937454

CR Subject Classification (1998): D.2.4, D.4.5, F.3, I.2.2, D.4.7

ISSN	1865-0929(Communications in Computer and Information Science)
ISSN	0302-9743(Standard)
ISBN-10	3-540-88478-5 Springer Berlin Heidelberg New York
ISBN-13	978-3-540-88478-1 Springer Berlin Heidelberg New York

Springer is a part of Springer Science+Business Media

springer.com

Printed in Germany

Typesetting: Camera-ready by author, data conversion by Scientific Publishing Services, Chennai, India
Printed on acid-free paper SPIN: 12546602 06/3180 5 4 3 2 1 0

Preface

This volume contains the conference proceedings of ISoLA 2008, the Third International Symposium on Leveraging Applications of Formal Methods, Verification and Validation, which was held in Porto Sani (Kassandra, Chalkidiki), Greece during October 13–15, 2008, sponsored by EASST and in cooperation with the IEEE Technical Committee on Complex Systems.

Following the tradition of its forerunners in 2004 and 2006 in Cyprus, and the ISoLA Workshops in Greenbelt (USA) in 2005 and in Poitiers (France) in 2007, ISoLA 2008 provided a forum for developers, users, and researchers to discuss issues related to the **adoption and use** of rigorous tools and methods for the specification, analysis, verification, certification, construction, test, and maintenance of systems from the point of view of their different application domains. Thus, the ISoLA series of events serves the purpose of bridging the gap between designers and developers of rigorous tools, and users in engineering and in other disciplines, and to foster and exploit synergetic relationships among scientists, engineers, software developers, decision makers, and other critical thinkers in companies and organizations. In particular, by providing a venue for the discussion of common problems, requirements, algorithms, methodologies, and practices, ISoLA aims at supporting researchers in their quest to improve the utility, reliability, flexibility, and efficiency of tools for building systems, and users in their search for adequate solutions to their problems.

Additionally to regular and poster sessions, the program of the symposium consisted of:

- Two invited talks, by Manfred Broy (TU Munich, Germany) and Dimitrios Georgakopoulou (Telcordia Technologies, Austin, USA)
- A keynote by Jifeng He (East China Normal University, Shanghai, China)

Special tracks and thematic sessions were devoted to the following hot and emerging topics:

- Service Engineering in a Converging Telecommunications / Web 2.0 World (joint with SEW-32)
- Tools and Applications in Industrial Software Quality Control
- Introduction of Multi-Core Systems in Automotive Applications
- Model-Driven SOA
- Applications of Formal Approaches to Service-Oriented Computing
- Trustworthy Computing: Theories, Methods, Tools, and Experience in China and South East Asia
- Non-Functional Requirements in Embedded Systems
- Processes, Methods and Tools for Developing Educational Modules to Support Teaching and Technology Transfer
- Ubiquitous and Context-Aware Systems

- Formal Methods for Analyzing and Verifying Very Large Systems
- Tools for Service-Oriented Discovery of Knowledge
- Tackling the Challenges of Software Development Process for SMEs with Rigorous Support and Open Source

There were also two co-located events:

- *SEW-32*, the 32nd Software Engineering Workshop, in cooperation with NASA and IEEE
- jABC Workshop with the jABC/jETI Developer and User Group meeting

We thank the Track and Session organizers and the members of the Program Committee and their subreferees for their effort in selecting the papers to be presented.

Special thanks are due to the following organizations for their endorsement: EASST (European Association of Software Science and Technology), Fraunhofer FOKUS (Berlin, Germany), and our own institutions – the TU Dortmund and the University of Potsdam.

We are also grateful to Holger Willebrandt, Christian Winkler, and Zoi Choselidou for their very appreciated help in preparing this volume.

August 2008

Tiziana Margaria
Bernhard Steffen

Organization

General Chair	Bernhard Steffen (TU Dortmund, Germany)
Program Chair	Tiziana Margaria (Universität Potsdam, Germany)
Organization and Finance Chair	Petros Stratis (Cyprusisland, Nicosia, Cyprus)

Program Committee

Tom Ball
Francine Ellen Barbosa
Karin Breitman
Ruth Breu
Jean-Pierre Briot
Maura Cerioli
Song Jin Dong
Schahram Dustdar
Stefania Gnesi
Karl M. Göschka
Hermann Edward Haeusler
Axel Hahn
Mike Hinchey
Antti Huima
He Jifeng
Raimund Kirner
Jens Knoop
Joost Kok
Bernd Krämer
Nada Lavrac
Björn Lisper
Zhiming Liu
Jian Lu
José Carlos Maldonado
Christian Metzler
Alexander K. Petrenko
Enrico Pittaluga
Peter Puschner
Christian Schallhart
Jörn Schneider
Markus Schordan
Hong-Linh Truong
Helmut Veith
Ji Wang
Martin Wechs
Uwe Zdun
Dirk Ziegenbein

Table of Contents

Invited Talks

Keynote

Tools and Applications in Industrial Software Quality Control

Introduction of Multi-core Systems in Automotive Applications

Model-Driven SOA

Applications of Formal Approaches to Service-Oriented Computing

Trustworthy Computing: Theories, Methods, Tools and Experience in China and South East Asia

Non-functional Requirements in Embedded Systems

Processes, Methods and Tools for Developing Educational Modules to Support Teaching and Technology Transfer

Ubiquitous and Context Aware Systems

Formal Methods for Analysing and Verifying Very Large Systems

Tools for Service-Oriented Discovery of Knowledge

Tackling the Challenges of Software Development Process for SMEs with Rigorous Support and Open Source

Regular Papers

Architecture Based Specification and Verification of Embedded Software Systems
(Work in Progress)

Manfred Broy

Institut für Informatik, Technische Universität München
D-80290 München Germany
broy@in.tum.de
http://wwwbroy.informatik.tu-muenchen.de

Abstract. Large scale embedded software intensive systems as we find them, for instance, in cars today need structured techniques in terms of comprehensive architectures for mastering their specification, development, and verification. Comprehensive system architectures provide the appropriate levels of abstraction separating logical from technical views. We show how logical architecture provides a systematic focal point for specification and refinement based development with early verification.

Keywords: Large Scale Embedded Software Systems, Comprehensive Architecture, Specification, Verification.

1 Introduction

Modern software systems and software-intensive systems offer to their users large varieties of different functions, in our terminology called *services* or *features*. We speak of *multi-functional distributed interactive systems*. Such systems typically are *embedded* within technical devices or organizational processes to support, control as well as enhance those. They are *mobile*, *dynamic*, and accessed *concurrently* via families of independent, often multi-modal user interfaces. They are not only connected to such user interfaces but also to sensors and actuators.

For instance, in premium cars we find thousands of functions based on embedded software systems. These functions are technically realized by networks of processing units (CPUs).

Systems of the described type are typically *deployed* and *distributed* over large networks of computing devices; they are based on software infrastructure such as operating systems and communication services in terms of communication protocols and busses. They exploit the services of middleware such as, for instance, object request brokers.

To master their complexity, large software systems are better constructed in a modular fashion and decomposed into components. These components are grouped together in software architectures. Today the concept of software architecture is recognized as a key contribution in software design. Ideas to structure systems along

T. Margaria and B. Steffen (Eds.): ISoLA 2008, CCIS 17, pp. 1–13, 2008.

these lines go way back to the early concepts of "*structured programming*" due to Dijkstra (see [14]) and the ideas of "*modularization*" due to Parnas (see [15]).

In the following we give an overview over the ongoing research at the Technical University of Munich aiming at a comprehensive, model-based, architecture driven, verification based approach to system evolution. This work covers a broad spectrum of foundational and practical research. At the Technical University of Munich we are working in the field of systematic development of software intensive systems for more than 10 years. We are following an approach where we combine quite foundational research with practical transfer work. The foundational research concentrates on system modelling, system specification, verification in terms of a system modelling theory, which gives the mathematical framework for describing systems, their refinement, their specification and verification in a way that important properties like modularity, transitivity of refinement and flexible ways to change levels of abstractions are supported. Furthermore, based on the foundational approach, we develop concepts and notations that scale and that can be used in industrial engineering environments and that are targeted towards the practical needs. To support and evaluate our approach, we carry out a number of experimental pilot developments in cooperation with industrial partners where on the one hand we try to understand which are the most crucial challenges in industry and on the other hand apply our approach aiming at proof of concept.

To be able to do such medium size experiments we need tool support. Therefore we are working in prototyping tools for quite some years for several reasons. First of all it is important to understand how tools can support the engineering approaches and whether they are appropriate for a comprehensive tool support.

Second, the tool support is very important to be able to apply our approaches to larger size applications. Moreover, we study the situations in practise and analyze, which are the most pressing needs around. This helps us also to determine the direction of our more foundational research.

Finally, we do a number of ambitious experiments to see how the methods scale and how they can be applied to industrial applications. A very typical example here is what we did in the VERISOFT project (see [2], [3], [4]), where we carried out the verification of a function in a car – actually the emergency call function – which brings in all the technical problems in real life systems how we typically find them today.

It is a goal of this paper to show the philosophy of our approach to work out a professional engineering methodology, based on a proper theory, supported by tools and capable to scale up with the needs of industrial processes. As a result this paper gives just overviews and shows a few of the most important properties that we require from theory and sketch how a development that is driven by specification, refinement, and verification concepts could look like. Details to what is presented here can be found in many papers that are referenced at the end of this contribution.

2 Seamless Model-Based Development

Seamless model-based development promises to lift software development and programming onto higher levels of abstraction providing a seamless chain of models covering all phases from requirements to integration and system verification. As long as model-based development mainly aims at generating code from models, modelling languages are nothing but a kind of higher level programming languages. However, in seamless model-based development modelling is not just an implementation method. It is a paradigm that is capable to provide support throughout the entire development and evolution life cycle (for more details, see [13]).

Modelling ideally has to start with requirements engineering. Actually it can be a very important help in requirements engineering when informal requirements are turned into models step by step such that at the end, the requirements engineering produces a functional model capturing the functional requirements and a quality model that describes the quality profile. Based on the model we can check the completeness and the consistency of the requirements, which is impossible for natural language requirements specifications. In turn, the systems architecture and subsequently models can describe the software architecture. Provided these models are chosen carefully enough and based on a proper theory then the architecture model can be verified to guarantee the compliance to the functional requirements (see section 3). Furthermore, a careful tracing is possible between the functional requirements and the architecture model.

In particular, the quality model can be used to evaluate and validate the architecture. To be able to do that a carefully structured model of architecture has to be worked out, not just describing a system at the technical implementation level but also describing carefully chosen useful abstractions such as logical architectures or function hierarchies. A seamless and comprehensive model-based development is a key to a much more systematic development process with significantly higher possibilities for automation.

To be able to carry out such an approach a number of ingredients are required.

- **A sound and appropriate theoretical basis (see section 4):** An appropriate **modelling theory** that provides
  - the needed modelling concepts such as the **concept of a system** and that of a **user function**, with
    - a concept for structuring the functionality by **functional hierarchies**,
    - concepts to establish **dependency relationships** between these functions,
    - techniques to **model the functions** with their **behaviour** in isolation including **time** behaviour and to connect them, according to their dependency relations into a comprehensive functional model for the system.
  - a concept of **composition** and **architecture** to capture
    - the **decomposition** of the system into **components**, that cooperate and interact to achieve the system functionalities,
    - the interfaces of the components including not only the **syntactic interfaces** but also the **behaviour interfaces**
    - a notion of **modular composition**, which allows us to define the interface behaviour of a composed system from the interface behaviours of its components.

    This provides a hierarchical notion of a logical architecture.
  - a modelling theory that is strong and expressive enough to capture issues of the technical architecture such as questions of structuring software deployment, of tasks and threads, as well as modelling behaviour aspects of hardware.

  - **A comprehensive system architecture model:** The modelling theory must be strong enough and expressive enough to model all relevant aspects of hardware and software architectures of a system. These aspects and properties of architecture should be modelled in a very direct and explicit way. The modelling theory should be able to express very directly properties of the architecture and its components. A comprehensive architecture model of an embedded system and its functionality is a basis for a system meta-model that comprises all the content needed to describe a distributed embedded system.
- **Product Model:** The product model provides a data model to capture all the modelling artefacts. Its structure is described by a meta-model. The meta-model is not only of interest from a theoretical point of view. Much more important, it is the basis for a data model that allows to capture all the contents that describe an embedded system inside a computer, forming a product model which can be used at the backbone for the development. In the product model the dependencies and relationships between the modelling artefacts should be identified, which are a key to extensive tool support. In the end all artefacts produced throughout the development should be part of the meta-model and all the parts should be related in a semantic way such that tracing, impact analysis or consistency checks are possible.
- **Extensive Development Automation by Tool Support:** Automation can only be achieved if the models and their theory support this kind of automation. In fact, the support in automation has to address the capturing and working out of models, the analysis of models, in particular, towards their consistency and with respect to important properties as well as techniques for generating further development artefacts from models. Tooling should be based completely on the artefact model such that tools that carry out the steps of capturing models and creating models, analyzing models and generating new artefacts from existing ones basically only manipulate and enhance the product model. The whole development should be seen as an incremental and iterative process with the goal to work out the comprehensive artefact model.
- **Process Model:** A comprehensive process model is needed that refers to the modelling artefacts and to the activities that are needed to complete the architecture model step by step. In particular, according to the consistency notions of the artefact model, the checking of consistency but also the generating of consistent parts has to be based on the artefact model. Typically, examples of at least semi-automatic generation of parts of the model are the generation of component behaviour from scenarios, synthesis of state machines from interaction diagrams, generation of test cases from requirement models, verification of architecture models, generation of code.
- **Process Support:** On the artefacts model, beside the relationships that form the structure of the product model, a careful version and configuration management has to be established. In the end all artefacts will exist in versions and certain subsets of the artefacts form consistent configurations describing a system.

It is clear that such a comprehensive approach using modelling cannot be introduced into practical development processes in one step. Therefore transition and migration scenarios are needed.

Nevertheless we believe that it is important to develop a long-term vision and based on this long-term vision to show the benefits of a seamless development process and to indicate how steps are possible that result in earlier wins when following such a road map.

3 Comprehensive System Architectures

A comprehensive architecture provides a structured view onto a system. We are in particular interested in structuring a system in terms of its comprehensive architecture into a logical and a technical architectural view (see [12]).

3.1 The Logical View

The logical system architecture defines the decomposition of the system into a set of sub-systems (the components); it constitutes the logical design of the system.

We are interested to provide a formal model for the comprehensive architecture and all of its views (see Fig. 1). In this paper we concentrate on the logical view onto modelling the architecture and its foundation.

3.1.1 Functionality: Usage View by Functional Feature Hierarchies

The usage view models the overall functionality of a software (intensive) system. Such a system offers, in general, a large set of functions, often for a number of different classes of users. These functions can be modelled in isolation and later composed into a comprehensive system functionality. Another issue is the relationship between this service taxonomy and the logical architecture. The functionality in terms of the usage/service view is modelled as follows:

- Feature hierarchies describe multi-functional systems by a directed acyclic graph where each node represents a function (a "functional feature") and the arcs represent the subsystem relation. They represent the logical decomposition of the functionality of a system into sub-functions.
- Additional arcs in the feature hierarchy represent functional dependencies also called feature interaction.
- The leaves in the hierarchy represent the "atomic" functions that are not further decomposed.

The usage view sees the system as a hierarchy of functions (features, services) that are offered by the system to its users.

The function hierarchy, also called service taxonomy is to be specified in the requirements engineering. It comprises (models) all functional requirements. The dynamic modelling and specification of atomic functions can be done by specifying assertions, by state machines, or by interaction diagrams. They describe interaction patterns given by partial functions on streams.

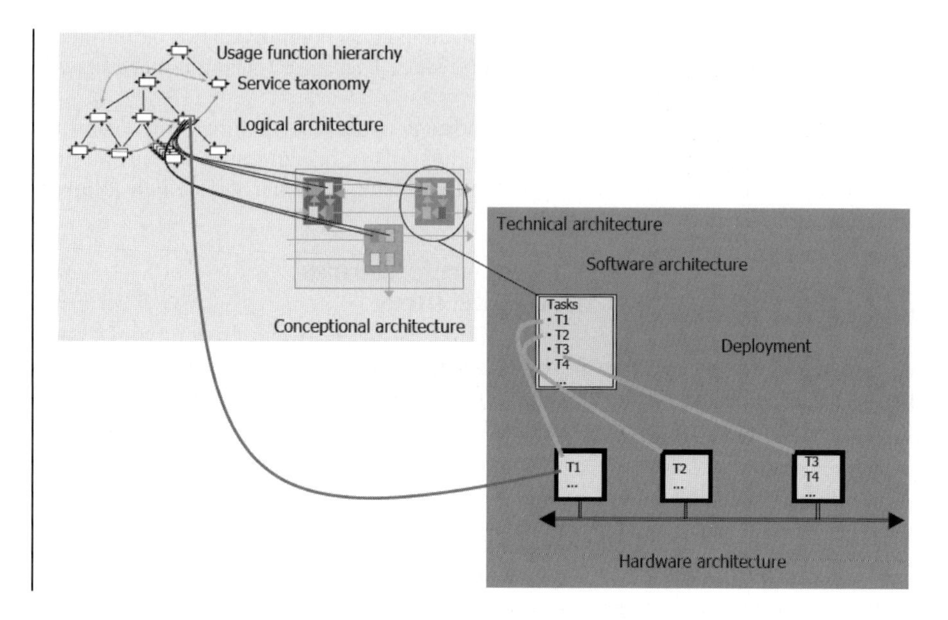

Fig. 1. Comprehensive System Architecture

3.1.2 Logical System Architecture

The logical system architecture captures the design view:

- A set of components that interact by exchanging messages over channels,
- By their co-operation the components generate the behaviour as modelled by the usage view (if the architecture is correct),
- Components can be further decomposed; this leads to a hierarchical logical component architecture.

The logical system architecture has to be worked out in the design phase. It comprises the decomposition of the systems into a set and hierarchy of sub-systems (logical components) fixing their logical roles.

3.2 The Technical Architecture

The technical architecture describes how the system is implemented technically by a system of hardware and software.

3.2.1 Software Architecture

The software architecture consists of the design time software architecture that describes the design classes in terms of the software components and how they work together. It comprises the application software as well as the software platform (OSEK, bus systems).

The run time software architecture decomposes a system into tasks and defines their scheduling.

3.2.2 Hardware Architecture

The hardware architecture consists of controllers (CPUs), the communication devices, the sensors and actuators as well as the devices of the user interface.

3.2.3 Deployment

The deployment defines the mapping from software units onto the hardware devices.

4 Modeling Systems and Their Architectures

For a comprehensive modeling of the structural and dynamic properties of systems and their architectures we need a basic system model. It allows us to model systems and their components, and to construct systems by composition. It should allow us to work out system specifications, to define logical architectures, to construct implementations and to carry out verifications.

4.1 A Universal System Model

In the following we outline the framework of the theory of system specification, refinement and verification without going into technical or formal details. Such details can be found in [6] and [9].

4.1.1 Specifying Systems, Its Functions and Their Refinement

We aim at a black box view onto systems. This requires a system model capturing the system interface. A system interface has a static and a dynamic part. We assume that we can both describe the static and dynamic properties by a logical formula called system specification. Let SysSpec be the set of system specifications.

A system function is a partial system behavior that is a "slice" of the system specification. Like a system a system function has a static and a dynamic specification. Again, we assume that we can describe both by a logical formula. Let FunSpec be the set of system functions. A system specification is a special case of a system function specification.

$$\text{SysSpec} \subseteq \text{FunSpec}$$

A system may offer a set of system functions. For a system specification $S \in$ SysSpec and system function $F \in$ FunSpec we write

$$S \ \textbf{offers} \ F$$

to express that the system specified by S offers the function specified by F. This concept is the basis for the service taxonomy and function hierarchy.

On system functions and system specifications $F1, F2 \in$ FunSpec we assume a refinement relation; the formula

$$F1 \ \textbf{refinesto} \ F2$$

expresses that the function specification F2 is a refinement of F1. The refinement relation is assumed to be a partial order. In the simplest case refinement corresponds to reverse implication. More precisely, since we assume that specifications F1 and F2 are represented by predicates, then we define:

$$\text{F1 } \mathbf{refinesto} \text{ F2} \Leftrightarrow (\text{F1} \Leftarrow \text{F2})$$

This shows that refinement is a transitive and reflexive relation. Assuming that the logical content of a specification describes it uniquely, refinement is antisymmetric and thus a partial order.

In more sophisticated cases a function specification F2 ∈ FunSpec is a simulation of the function specification F1 ∈ FunSpec. To capture simulations formally we need the mathematical concept of simulations Ψ ∈ SysSim which can be modeled by mappings

$$\Psi: \text{SysFun} \rightarrow \text{SysFun}$$

We assume that we generalize refinement using simulations by the rule that for all simulations Ψ ∈ SysSim we have:

$$\text{F1 } \mathbf{refinesto} \text{ F2} \wedge \text{F3} = \Psi(\text{F2}) \Rightarrow \text{F1 } \mathbf{refinesto} \text{ F3}$$

This rule shows that the functional composition of simulations Ψ_1, Ψ_2 ∈ SysSim to a mapping Ψ: SysFun → SysFun defined by

$$\Psi(\text{F}) = \Psi_2(\Psi_1(\text{F}))$$

leads to a refinement again if we assume that the refinement relation is transitive. Conversely, if we assume that the functional composition of simulations yields simulations the transitivity of refinement via simulation follows.

4.1.2 Composition

Both system specifications and system function specifications can be composed. We assume a composition operator

$$\otimes: \text{SysFun} \times \text{SysFun} \rightarrow \text{SysFun}$$

We assume that composition is monotonic for refinement as shown by the following rule

$$\text{F}_1 \mathbf{\ refinesto\ } \text{G}_1 \wedge \text{F}_2 \mathbf{\ refinesto\ } \text{G}_2 \Rightarrow \text{F}_1 \otimes \text{F}_2 \mathbf{\ refinesto\ } \text{G}_1 \otimes \text{G}_2$$

This rule is very essential, as we will see later.

We assume that ⊗ is a partial composition operator. Only systems and function specifications that fit (syntactically) together can be composed. Given $S_1, S_2, \ldots, S_n \in$ SysSpec such that the term

$$\text{S}_1 \otimes \text{S}_2 \otimes \ldots \otimes \text{S}_n$$

denotes a well-defined system specification again, a system architecture is specified. Note that $S_1 \otimes S_2 \otimes \ldots \otimes S_n$ is a system specification (and leads to a defined composition) again. Note that the system architecture is given by the specification $S_1 \otimes S_2 \otimes \ldots \otimes S_n$ of the sub-systems and by the term $S_1 \otimes S_2 \otimes \ldots \otimes S_n$ that shows the structure of the architecture.

4.2 Implementation

An implementation of a system can be given at the model level by a state machine or by program code. Let SysImp be the set of system implementations. For P ∈ SysImp and S ∈ SysSpec we write

$$S \textbf{ refinesto } P$$

to express that P is a correct implementation. We assume that SysImp ⊆ SysSpec. In other words, an implementation is a special case of an "operational" system specification.

5 Specification and Verification Driven System Evolution

In this section we sketch how a system can be constructed in a specification and verification driven way based on the concept of a logical architecture.

5.1 Requirements Engineering: Specifying the System Functionality

In the course of requirements engineering a system specification F ∈ SysSpec is worked out that represents the formal specification of the functional requirements. This represents the overall system specification. We can specify F by specifying sub-functions $F_1, \dots, F_m$ ∈ SysFun such that

$$F \textbf{ offers } F_i$$

holds for all i, $1 \le i \le m$. The $F_1, \dots, F_m$ form the function hierarchy – note that for some i and j, $1 \le i, j \le m$, we have

$$F_j \textbf{ offers } F_i$$

This shows that the relation offer defines a partial order on the sub-functions $F_1, \dots, F_m$ with F as its upper bound.

5.2 Specifying and Verifying the Architecture

In the course of system evolution the system is decomposed into a set of sub-systems, called components. We specify $S_1, S_2, \dots, S_n$ ∈ SysSpec are the specifications of these components such that

$$S_1 \otimes S_2 \otimes \dots \otimes S_n$$

forms an architecture of the system.

The architecture is correct if

$$F \textbf{ refinesto } S_1 \otimes S_2 \otimes \dots \otimes S_n$$

Showing correctness requires the proof of the formula

$$F \Leftarrow S_1 \otimes S_2 \otimes \dots \otimes S_n$$

Since we assume that the specifications of S and $S_1, S_2, \ldots, S_n$ are given by logical formulas and the **refinesto**-relation basically is reverse implication the verification is equivalent to the proof of a logical statement in predicate logic.

5.3 Implementing the Components

In the next step we have to construct implementations $P_1, P_2, \ldots, P_n \in$ SysImp for each of $S_1, S_2, \ldots, S_n \in$ SysSpec such that for all $k = 1, \ldots, n$

$$S_k \ \textbf{refinesto} \ P_k$$

holds. To prove the correctness of the implementation we have to prove these relations. Since we assume that the specifications $S_1, S_2, \ldots, S_n$ of the components are given by logical formulas and the **refinesto**-relation basically is reverse implication the verification is again equivalent to the proof of a logical statement, if we are able to prove logical formulas

$$S_k \Leftarrow P_k$$

for the implementations $P_1, P_2, \ldots, P_n \in$ SysImp.

5.4 Integration and Verification

In the next step we integrate the system component implementations $P_1, P_2, \ldots, P_n \in$ SysImp into the composed system $P \in$ SysImp by

$$P = P_1 \otimes P_2 \otimes \ldots \otimes P_n$$

By integration we obtain the implementation P of the overall system defined by the composition of the sub-systems into the implementation $P_1 \otimes P_2 \otimes \ldots \otimes P_n$. The correctness of the implementation is expressed by the proposition

$$S_1 \otimes S_2 \otimes \ldots \otimes S_n \ \textbf{refinesto} \ P$$

This proposition is actually a theorem by the monotonicity of composition for refinement provided all components are correctly implemented.

5.5 Overall System Verification

Finally by integration we have obtained a system that should offer the required functionality as specified by the system requirement specification F. This is a theorem, however, since the proposition

$$F \ \textbf{refinesto} \ P$$

follows straightforward from

$$F = S_1 \otimes S_2 \otimes \ldots \otimes S_n \wedge P = P_1 \otimes P_2 \otimes \ldots \otimes P_n$$

and from

$$S_1 \otimes S_2 \otimes \ldots \otimes S_n \ \textbf{refinesto} \ P_1 \otimes P_2 \otimes \ldots \otimes P_n$$

by transitivity of refinement and monotonicity of composition.

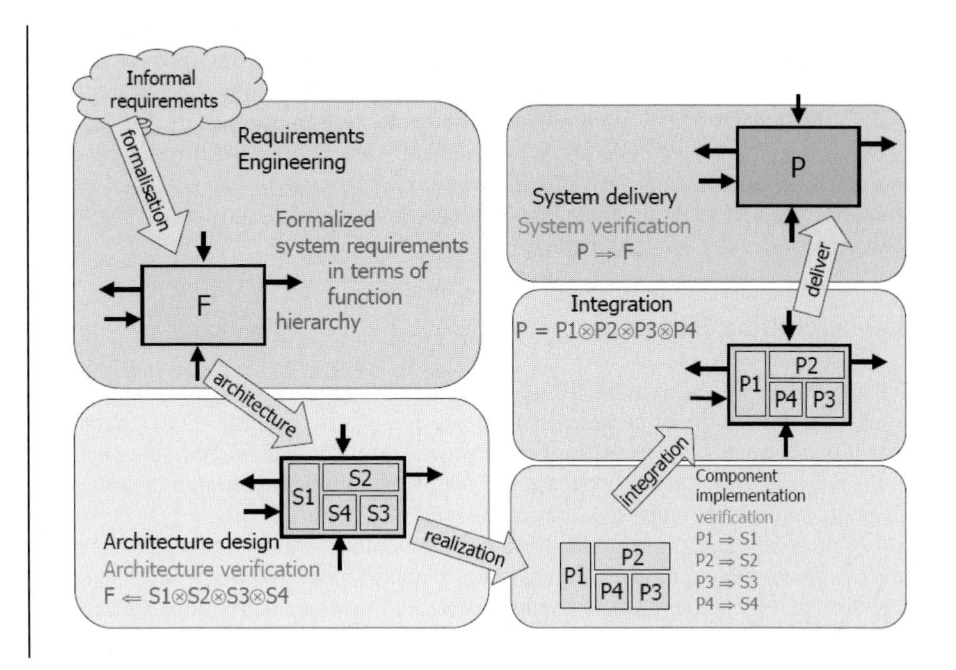

Fig. 2. The Specification, Refinement, and Verification Process

5.6 Conclusion

Our simple consideration shows that in principle it is possible to specify architectures in such a precise and formal way that they can be verified before they are implemented. What we have presented is a very idealistic approach where we assume complete specifications both for the overall system and its architecture on which a verification proof can be based. In practice, of course, we might use more pragmatic techniques where we give more prototyping-like descriptions of architectures, perhaps describing the behaviour of the subcomponents by state machines. This allows us, in contrast to logical verification, an early verification by simulation, a partial verification by model checking, or at least to generate test cases. This could also have the benefit that from this we can derive quite a number of integration tests that are used in practice.

What we have described is very much in contrast to what we usually observe in industry, where architectures are not sufficiently precisely described, in general. As a result, all the further development work going on that should be based on architectures cannot be done in a sufficiently precise way. Architectures are not precisely specified and therefore cannot be verified before implementing the sub-systems. Implementations have to be produced although the specifications are not properly worked out and although it is not clear whether the specifications together form a correct system when we compose them into the architecture. This is only discovered very late in the integration phase.

As a result in the integration phase a lot of problems arise that are difficult to deal with because they have to be handled by complex processes between the producers of the subsystems – in case of the automotive industry often suppliers – and the OEMs that do the integration. Even corrections of bugs in the components are not so simple because as long as there is no precise architecture description also it is not clear how to correct the components such that they work properly together. As a result integration goes through trial and error, many iterations are needed and lots of bugs might still remain after the integration phase.

6 Concluding Remarks

What we have presented looks for the first moment only as a very rough and perhaps superficial description of approaches to the design of software intensive system. Nevertheless, all what is presented has a very precise and in detail worked out counterpart in the ongoing research in our group. We believe it is important to point out the overall philosophy of the approach that at the same time aims at progress in the formal foundations of system development and makes sure that what is produced there can be practically used in engineering. In any case, to achieve that we have to work at several scientific levels including theory, engineering and practice at the same time what is certainly difficult and needs a large group of researchers but on the other hand might be the only way to get progress towards a more systematic, formally sound development process supported by tools. The feedback between the foundational work und the practical evaluation and experimentation provides fruitful insights at both for theory and practice.

What is needed is a deep theoretical understanding and a theory which has all the required properties, an understanding of engineering issues and ways how to work out a basis on which the theory can be applied in practice. Finally we need an understanding of the engineering practice and its needs and how it relates to industrial practices. On this basis experiments can be worked out that on the long run help to transfer the concepts of such an approach into practice.

Acknowledgements

It is a pleasure for me to thank my colleagues from our research group and our industrial partners for many useful discussions. David Trachtenherz provided a number of helpful remarks about the manuscript.

References

1. Abrial, J.-R.: Formal methods: Theory becoming practice, vol. 13(5), pp. 619–628 (May 2007)
2. Botaschanjan, J., Gruler, A., Harhurin, A., Kof, L., Spichkova, M., Trachtenherz, D.: Towards Modularized Verification of Distributed Time-Triggered Systems. In: Misra, J., Nipkow, T., Sekerinski, E. (eds.) FM 2006. LNCS, vol. 4085, pp. 163–178. Springer, Heidelberg (2006)

3. Botaschanjan, J., Kof, L., Kühnel, C., Spichkova, M.: Towards Verified Automotive Software. In: SEAS 2005: Proceedings of the Second International ICSE Workshop on Software Engineering for Automotive Systems, pp. 1–6. ACM Press, New York (2005)
4. Botaschanjan, J., Broy, M., Gruler, A., Harhurin, A., Knapp, S., Kof, L., Paul, W., Spichkova, M.: On the Correctness of Upper Layers of Automotive Systems. Formal Aspects of Computing, FACS (to appear)
5. Broy, M., Krüger, I.H., Meisinger, M.: A Formal Model of Services. ACM Transactions on Software Engineering and Methodology (TOSEM) 16(1), 5 (2007)
6. Broy, M.: Model-driven architecture-centric engineering of (embedded) software intensive systems: modeling theories and architectural milestones, vol. 3(1), pp. 75–102 (2007)
7. Broy, M.: The Grand Challenge in Informatics: Engineering Software-Intensive Systems. IEEE Computer, 72–80 (2006)
8. Bauer, A., Broy, M., Romberg, J., Schätz, B., Braun, P., Freund, U., Mata, N., Sandner, R., Ziegenbein, D.: Auto-MoDe—Notations, Methods, and Tools for Model-Based Development of Automotive Software. In: Proceedings of the SAE 2005 World Congress, Detroit, MI. Society of Automotive Engineers (April 2005)
9. Broy, M.: Two Sides of Structuring Multi-Functional Software Systems: Function Hierarchy and Component Architecture. In: Kim, H.-K., Tanaka, J., Malloy, B., Lee, R. (eds.) Proceedings 5th ACIS International Conference on Software Engineeering Research, Management & Applications (SERA 2007), August 20 – 22, pp. 3–10. IEEE Computer Society, Los Alamitos (2007)
10. Broy, M., Krüger, I.H., Pretschner, A., Salzmann, C.: Engineering Automotive Software. In: Proceedings of the IEEE, vol. 95(2), pp. 356–373 (February 2007)
11. Pretschner, A., Broy, M., Krüger, I.H., Stauner, T.: Software Engineering for Automotive Systems: A Roadmap. In: Future of Software Engineering (FOSE 2007). IEEE Computer Soceity, Los Alamitos (2007)
12. Broy, M., Feilkas, M., Grünbauer, J., Gruler, A., Harhurin, A., Hartmann, J., Penzenstadler, B., Schätz, B., Wild, D.: Umfassendes Architekturmodell für das Engineering eingebetteter Softwareintensiver Systeme, Modellierungstheorien und Architekturebenen. Technical Report. Technische Universität München
13. Broy, M., Feilkas, M., Herrmannsdoerfer, M., Merenda, S., Ratiu, D.: Seamless Model-based Development: from Isolated Tools to Integrated Model Engineering Environments. IEEE (to appear)
14. Dijkstra, E.W.: Notes on Structured Programming. In: Dahl, O.-J., Hoare, C.A.R., Dijkstra, E.W. (eds.) Structured Programming. Academic Press, New York (1972)
15. Parnas, D.: On the criteria to be used to decompose systems into modules. Comm. ACM 15, 1053–1058 (1972)

Information System Engineering Supporting Observation, Orientation, Decision, and Compliant Action

Dimitrios Georgakopoulos

Telcordia, USA

The majority of today's software systems and organizational/business structures have been built on the foundation of solving problems via long-term data collection, analysis, and solution design. This traditional approach of solving problems and building corresponding software systems and business processes, falls short in providing the necessary solutions needed to deal with many problems that require agility as the main ingredient of their solution. For example, such agility is needed in responding to an emergency, in military command control, physical security, price-based competition in business, investing in the stock market, video gaming, network monitoring and self-healing, diagnosis in emergency health care, and many other areas that are too numerous to list here. The concept of Observe, Orient, Decide, and Act (OODA) loops is a guiding principal that captures the fundamental issues and approach for engineering information systems that deal with many of these problem areas. However, there are currently few software systems that are capable of supporting OODA. In this talk, we provide a tour of the research issues and state of the art solutions for supporting OODA. In addition, we provide specific examples of OODA solutions we have developed for the video surveillance and emergency response domains.

T. Margaria and B. Steffen (Eds.): ISoLA 2008, CCIS 17, p. 14, 2008.

Modelling Coordination and Compensation

He Jifeng*

Shanghai Key Laboratory of Trustworthy Computing
East China Normal University, China

Abstract. Transaction-based services are increasingly being applied in solving many universal interoperability problems. Exception and failure are the typical phenomena of the execution of long-running transactions. To accommodate these new program features, we extend the Guarded Command Language [10] by addition of compensation and coordination combinators, and enrich the standard design model [15] with new healthiness conditions. This paper shows that such an extension is conservative one because it preserves the algebraic laws for designs, which can be used to reduce all programs to a normal form algebraically. We also explore a Galois link between the standard design model with our new model, and show that the embedding from the former to the latter is actually a homomorphism.

1 Introduction

With the development of Internet technology, web services play an important role to information systems. The aim of web services is to achieve the universal interoperability between different web-based applications. In recent years, in order to describe the infrastructure for carrying out long-running transactions, various business modelling languages have been introduced, such as XLANG, WSFL, BPEL4WS (BPEL) and StAC [25,16,9,7].

Coordination and compensation mechanisms are vital in handling exception and failure which occur during the execution of a long-running transaction. Butler *et al.* investigated the compensation feature in a business modelling language StAC (Structured Activity Compensation) [6]. Further, Bruni *et al.* studied the transaction calculi for StAC programs, and provided a process calculi in the form of Java API. [4]. Qiu *et al.* have provided a deep formal analysis of the coordination behaviour for BPEL-like processes [23]. Pu *et al.* formalised the operational semantics for BPEL [22], where bisimulation has been considered. The π-calculus has been applied in describing various compensable program models. Lucchi and Mazzara defined the semantics of BPEL within the framework of the π-calculus [19]. Laneve and Zavattaro explored the application of the π-calculus in the formalisation of the compensable programs and the standard pattern of composition [17]. We introduced the notation of design matrix to describe various irregular phenomena of compensable programs in [12,13].

* This work was supported by the National Basic Research Program of China (Grant No. 2005CB321904) and Shanghai Leading Academic Discipline Project B412.

T. Margaria and B. Steffen (Eds.): ISoLA 2008, CCIS 17, pp. 15–36, 2008.

This paper is an attempt at taking a step forward to gain some perspectives on long-running transactions within the design calculus [15]. Our novel contributions include

- an enriched design model to handle exception and program failure.
- a set of new programming combinators for compensation and coordination
- an algebraic system in support of normal form reduction.
- a Galois link between the standard design model with our new model

The paper is organised as follows: Section 2 provides a mathematical framework to describe the new program features. Section 3 extends the Guarded Command Language by addition of compensation and coordination combinators to synchronise the activity of programs. It also investigates the algebraic properties of our new language. We introduce normal form in Section 4, and show that all programs can be reduced to a normal form algebraically. Section 5 establishes a Galois link between the standard design model with our new model, and prove that the embedding from the former to the latter is a homomorphism. The paper concludes with a short summary.

2 An Enriched Design Model

In this section we work towards a precise characterisation of the class of *designs* [15] that can handle new programming features such as program failure, coordination and compensation.

A subclass of designs may be defined in a variety of ways. Sometimes it is done by a syntactic property. Sometimes the definition requires satisfaction of a particular collection of algebraic laws. In general, the most useful definitions are these that are given in many different forms, together with a proof that all of them are equivalent. This section will put forward additional healthiness conditions to capture such a subclass of designs. We leave their corresponding algebraic laws in Section 3.

2.1 Exception Handling

To handling exception requires a more explicit analysis of the phenomena of program execution. We therefore introduce into the alphabet of our designs a pair of Boolean variables $eflag$ and $eflag'$ to denote the relevant observations:

- $eflag$ records the observation that the program is asked to start when the execution of its predecessor halts due to an exception.
- $eflag'$ records the observation that an exception occurs during the execution of the program.

The introduction of error states has implication for sequential composition: all the exception cases of program P are of course also the exception cases of $P;Q$. Rather than change the definition of sequential composition given in [15], we enforce these rules by means of a healthiness condition: if the program Q is asked to start in an exception case of its predecessor, it leaves the state unchanged

$(\mathbf{Req_1})\ Q \;=\; II \lhd eflag \rhd Q$

when the design II adopts the following definition

$$II \;=_{df}\; true \vdash (s' = s)$$

where s denotes all the variables in the alphabet of Q.

A design is $\mathbf{Req_1}$-healthy if it satisfies the healthiness condition $\mathbf{Req_1}$. Define

$$\mathcal{H}_1(Q) =_{df} (II \lhd eflag \rhd Q)$$

Clearly $\mathcal{H}_1$ is idempotent. As a result, Q is $\mathbf{Req_1}$ healthy if and only if Q lies in the range of $\mathcal{H}_1$.

The following theorem indicates $\mathbf{Req_1}$-healthy designs are closed under conventional programming combinators.

Theorem 2.1

(1) $\mathcal{H}_1(P \sqcap Q) \;=\; \mathcal{H}_1(P) \sqcap \mathcal{H}_1(Q)$

(2) $\mathcal{H}_1(P \lhd b \rhd Q) \;=\; \mathcal{H}_1(P) \lhd b \rhd \mathcal{H}_1(Q)$

(3) $\mathcal{H}_1(P; \mathcal{H}_1(Q)) \;=\; \mathcal{H}_1(P); \mathcal{H}_1(Q)$

2.2 Rollback

To equip a program with compensation mechanism, it is necessary to figure out the cases when the execution control has to rollback. By adopting the technique used in the exception handling model, we introduce a new logical variable $forward$ to describe the status of control flow of the execution of a program:

- $forward' = true$ indicates successful termination of the execution of the forward activity of a program. In this case, its successor will carry on with the initial state set up by the program.
- $forward' = false$ indicates it is required to undo the effect caused by the execution of the program. In this case, the corresponding compensation module will be invoked.

As a result, a program must keep idle when it is asked to start in a state where $forward = false$, i.e., it has to meet the following healthiness condition:

$(\mathbf{Req_2})\ Q \;=\; II \lhd \neg forward \rhd Q$

This condition can be identified by the idempotent mapping

$$\mathcal{H}_2(Q) \;=_{df}\; II \lhd \neg forward \rhd Q$$

in the sense that a program meets $\mathbf{Req_2}$ iff it is a fixed point of $\mathcal{H}_2$.

We can charecterise both $\mathbf{Req_1}$ and $\mathbf{Req_2}$ by composing $\mathcal{H}_1$ and $\mathcal{H}_2$. To ensure that their composition is an idempotent mapping we are going to show that

Theorem 2.2

$\mathcal{H}_2 \circ \mathcal{H}_1 \;=\; \mathcal{H}_1 \circ \mathcal{H}_2$

Proof: From the fact that

$$\mathcal{H}_1(\mathcal{H}_2(Q)) \;=\; II \lhd eflag \vee \neg foward \rhd Q \;=\; \mathcal{H}_2(\mathcal{H}_1(Q))$$

Define $\mathcal{H} =_{df} \mathcal{H}_1 \circ \mathcal{H}_2$..

Theorem 2.3

A design is healthy (i.e., it satisfies both $\mathbf{Req}_1$ and $\mathbf{Req}_2$) iff it lies in the range of $\mathcal{H}$.

The following theorem indicates that healthy designs are closed under the conventional programming combinators.

Theorem 2.4

(1) $\mathcal{H}(P \sqcap Q) \;=\; \mathcal{H}(P) \sqcap \mathcal{H}(Q)$

(2) $\mathcal{H}(P \lhd b \rhd Q) \;=\; \mathcal{H}(P) \lhd b \rhd \mathcal{H}(Q)$

(3) $\mathcal{H}(P; \mathcal{H}(Q)) \;=\; \mathcal{H}(P); \mathcal{H}(Q)$

In the following sections, we will confine ourselves to healthy designs only.

3 Programs

This section studies a simple programming language, which extends the Guarded Command Language [10] by adding coordination constructs. The syntax of the language is as follows:

$$\begin{aligned} P \;::=\; & \texttt{skip} \mid \texttt{fail} \mid \texttt{throw} \mid \bot \mid x := e \mid \\ & P \sqcap P \mid P \lhd b \rhd P \mid P; P \mid b *_{\mathcal{H}} P \mid \\ & P \;\texttt{cpens}\; P \mid P \;\texttt{else}\; P \mid P \;\texttt{catch}\; P \mid P \;\texttt{or}\; P \mid P \;\texttt{par}\; P \mid \end{aligned}$$

In the following discussion, v will represent the program variables referred in the alphabet of the program.

3.1 Primitive Commands

The behaviour of the chaotic program $\bot$ is totally unpredictable

$$\bot \;=_{df}\; \mathcal{H}(\mathbf{true})$$

The execution of `skip` leaves program variables intact.

$$\texttt{skip} \;=_{df}\; \mathcal{H}(\mathbf{success})$$

where $\mathbf{success} \;=_{df}\; true \vdash ((v' = v) \wedge forward' \wedge \neg eflag')$

The execution of `fail` rollbacks the control flow.

$$\texttt{fail} \;=_{df}\; \mathcal{H}(\mathbf{rollback})$$

where $\mathbf{rollback} \;=_{df}\; true \vdash ((v' = v) \wedge \neg forward' \wedge \neg eflag')$

An exception case arises from the execution of `throw`

$$\texttt{throw} =_{df} \mathcal{H}(\mathbf{error})$$

where $\mathbf{error} =_{df} true \vdash ((v' = v) \wedge eflag')$

3.2 Nondeterministic Choice and Sequential Composition

The nondeterministic choice and sequential composition have exactly the same meaning as the corresponding operators on the single predicates defined in [15].

$$P; Q =_{df} \exists m \bullet (P[m/s'] \wedge Q[m/s])$$

$$P \sqcap Q =_{df} P \vee Q$$

The change in the definition of $\bot$ and `skip` requires us to give a proof of the relevant laws.

Theorem 3.1

(1) $\texttt{skip}; P = P = P; \texttt{skip}$

(2) $\bot; P = \bot$

(3) $\bot \sqcap P = \bot$

Proof: Let $s = (v, forward, eflag)$.

$$\begin{aligned}
&(1)\ \texttt{skip}; P && \{\text{Theorem 2.4(3)}\}\\
&= \mathcal{H}(\mathbf{success}; P) && \{\mathcal{H}(Q) = \mathcal{H}((forward \wedge \neg eflag)^\top; Q)\}\\
&= \mathcal{H}((true \vdash (s' = s)); P) && \{(true \vdash (s' = s); D = D\}\\
&= \mathcal{H}(P) && \{P \text{ is healthy}\}\\
&= P
\end{aligned}$$

Besides the laws presented in [15] for composition and nondeterministic choice, there are additional left zero laws for sequential composition.

Theorem 3.2

(1) $\texttt{throw}; P = \texttt{throw}$

(2) $\texttt{fail}; P = \texttt{fail}$

Proof:

$$\begin{aligned}
&(1)\ \texttt{throw}; P && \{\text{Theorem 2.4(3)}\}\\
&= \mathcal{H}(\mathbf{error}; P) && \{\text{Def of } \mathbf{error}\}\\
&= \mathcal{H}(\mathbf{error}; (eflag)_\bot; P) && \{P = \mathcal{H}(P)\}\\
&= \mathcal{H}(\mathbf{error}; (eflag)_\bot; \mathcal{H}(P)[true/eflag]) && \{\text{Def of } \mathcal{H}\}\\
&= \mathcal{H}(\mathbf{error}; (eflag)_\bot) && \{\text{Def of } \texttt{throw}\}\\
&= \texttt{throw}
\end{aligned}$$

3.3 Assignment

Successful execution of an assignment relies on the assumption that the expression will be successfully evaluated.

$$x := e \;=_{df}\; \texttt{skip}[e/x] \lhd \mathcal{D}(e) \rhd \texttt{throw}$$

where the boolean condition $\mathcal{D}(e)$ is true in just those circumstances in which e can be successfully evaluated [21]. For example we can define

$$\begin{aligned}
\mathcal{D}(c) &=_{df} true \;\text{ if } c \text{ is a constant} \\
\mathcal{D}(e_1 + e_2) &=_{df} \mathcal{D}(e_1) \wedge \mathcal{D}(e_2) \\
\mathcal{D}(e_1/e_2) &=_{df} \mathcal{D}(e_1) \wedge \mathcal{D}(e_2) \wedge e_2 \neq 0 \\
\mathcal{D}(e_1 \lhd b \rhd e_2) &=_{df} \mathcal{D}(b) \wedge (b \Rightarrow \mathcal{D}(e_1)) \wedge (\neg b \Rightarrow \mathcal{D}(e_2))
\end{aligned}$$

Notice that $\mathcal{D}(e)$ is always well-defined, i.e., $\mathcal{D}(\mathcal{D}(e)) = true$.

Definition 3.1

An assignment is *total* if its assigning expression is well-defined, and all the variables of the program appear on its left hand side.

3.4 Conditional

The definition of conditional and iteration take the well-definedness of its Boolean test into account

$$P \lhd b \rhd Q \;=_{df}\; (\mathcal{D}(b) \wedge b \wedge P) \vee (\mathcal{D}(b) \wedge \neg b \wedge Q) \vee \neg\mathcal{D}(b) \wedge \texttt{throw}$$

$$b *_{\mathcal{H}} P \;=_{df}\; \mu_{\mathcal{H}} X \bullet (P; X) \lhd b \rhd \texttt{skip}$$

where $\mu_{\mathcal{H}} X \bullet F(X)$ stands for the weakest **Req**− healthy solution of the equation $X = F(X)$.

The alternation is defined in a similar way

$$\mathbf{if}(b_1 \rightarrow P_1, .., b_n \rightarrow P_n)\mathbf{fi} \;=_{df}\; \begin{pmatrix} \bigvee_i (\mathcal{D}(b) \wedge b_i \wedge P_i) \vee \\ \mathcal{D}(b) \wedge \neg b \wedge \bot \vee \\ \neg\mathcal{D}(b) \wedge \texttt{throw} \end{pmatrix}$$

where $b =_{df} \bigvee_i b_i$.

The following theorem illustrates how to convert a conditional into an alternation with well-defined boolean guards.

Theorem 3.3

$P \lhd b \rhd Q \;=$

$\mathbf{if}((b \lhd \mathcal{D}(b) \rhd false) \rightarrow P,\; (\neg b \lhd \mathcal{D}(b) \rhd false) \rightarrow Q,\; \neg\mathcal{D}(b) \rightarrow \texttt{throw})\mathbf{fi}$

A similar transformation can be applied to an assignment.

Theorem 3.4

$$x := e \;=\; (x, y, ..z := (e, y, .., z) \lhd \mathcal{D}(e) \rhd (x,\, y, .., z)) \lhd \mathcal{D}(e) \rhd \mathtt{throw}$$

The previous theorems enable us to confine ourselves to well-defined expressions in later discussion. For total assignment, we are required to reestablish the following laws.

Theorem 3.5

(1) $(x := e; x := f(x)) \;=\; (x := f(e))$

(2) $x := e; (P \lhd b(x) \rhd Q) \;=\; (x := e; P) \lhd b(e) \rhd (x := e; Q)$

(3) $(x := e) \lhd b \rhd (x := f) \;=\; x := (e \lhd b \rhd f)$

(4) $(x := x) \;=\; \mathtt{skip}$

The following laws for alternation will be used in later normal form reduction.

Theorem 3.6

Let $\underline{G}$ denote a list of alternatives.

(1) $\mathbf{if}(b_1 \rightarrow P_1, ...\, P_2, \,..\, b_n \rightarrow P_n)\mathbf{fi} \;=\; \mathbf{if}(b_{\pi(1)} \rightarrow P_{\pi(1)}, .., b_{\pi(n)} \rightarrow P_{\pi(n)})\mathbf{fi}$

where π is an arbitrary permutation of $\{1, .., n\}$.

(2) $\mathbf{if}(b \rightarrow \mathbf{if}(c_1 \rightarrow Q_1, .., c_n \rightarrow Q_n)\mathbf{fi},\, \underline{G})\mathbf{fi} \;=$

$\mathbf{if}(b \wedge c_1 \rightarrow Q_1, .., b \wedge c_n \rightarrow Q_n,\, \underline{G})\mathbf{fi}$

provided that $\bigvee_k c_k \;=\; true$

(3) $\mathbf{if}(b \rightarrow P,\, b \rightarrow Q,\, \underline{G})\mathbf{fi} \;=\; \mathbf{if}(b \rightarrow (P \sqcap Q),\, \underline{G})\mathbf{fi}$

(4) $\mathbf{if}(b \rightarrow P,\, c \rightarrow Q,\, \underline{G})\mathbf{fi} \;=\; \mathbf{if}(b \vee c \rightarrow (P \lhd b \rhd Q) \sqcap (Q \lhd c \rhd P),\, \underline{G})\mathbf{fi}$

(5) $\mathbf{if}(b_1 \rightarrow P_1, .., b_n \rightarrow P_n)\mathbf{fi}\,;\, Q \;=\; \mathbf{if}(b_1 \rightarrow (P_1; Q), .., b_n \rightarrow (P_n; Q))\mathbf{fi}$

(6) $\mathbf{if}(b_1 \rightarrow P_1, .., b_n \rightarrow P_n)\mathbf{fi} \sqcap Q \;=\; \mathbf{if}(b_1 \rightarrow (P_1 \sqcap Q), .., b_n \rightarrow (P_n \sqcap Q)\mathbf{fi}$

(7) $\mathbf{if}(b_1 \rightarrow P_1, .., b_n \rightarrow P_n)\mathbf{fi} \wedge Q \;=\; \mathbf{if}(b_1 \rightarrow (P_1 \wedge Q), .., b_n \rightarrow (P_n \wedge Q))\mathbf{fi}$

provided that $\bigvee_k b_k \;=\; true$

(8) $\mathbf{if}(false \rightarrow P,\, \underline{G})\mathbf{fi} \;=\; \mathbf{if}(\underline{G})\mathbf{fi}$

(9) $\mathbf{if}(b_1 \rightarrow P_1, .., b_n \rightarrow P_n)\mathbf{fi} \;=\; \mathbf{if}(b_1 \rightarrow P_1, .., b_n \rightarrow P_n,\, \neg \vee_i b_i \rightarrow \bot)\mathbf{fi}$

(10) $\mathbf{if}(true \rightarrow P)\mathbf{fi} \;=\; P$

3.5 Exception Handling

Let P and Q be programs. The notation P `catch` Q represents a program which runs P first, and if its execution throws an exception case then Q is activated.

$$P \;\mathtt{catch}\; Q \;=_{df}\; \mathcal{H}(P; \phi(Q))$$

where $\phi(Q) \;=_{df}\; II \lhd \neg eflag \rhd Q[false,\, true/eflag,\, forward]$

Theorem 3.7

(1) $P\ \texttt{catch}\ (Q\ \texttt{catch}\ R)\ =\ (P\ \texttt{catch}\ Q)\ \texttt{catch}\ R$

(2) $(\texttt{throw catch}\ Q)\ =\ Q\ =\ (Q\ \texttt{catch throw})$

(3) $P\,\texttt{catch}\,Q\ =\ P$ if $P \in \{\bot,\ \texttt{fail},\ (v := e)\}$

(4) $\textbf{if}(b_1 \rightarrow P_1, .., b_n \rightarrow P_n)\textbf{fi}\ \texttt{catch}\ Q\ =$
$\textbf{if}(b_1 \rightarrow (P_1\ \texttt{catch}\ Q), .., b_n \rightarrow (P_n\ \texttt{catch}\ Q))\textbf{fi}$

(5) $(P \sqcap Q)\ \texttt{catch}\ R\ =\ (P\ \texttt{catch}\ R) \sqcap (Q\ \texttt{catch}\ R)$

(6) $P\ \texttt{catch}\ (Q \sqcap R)\ =\ (P\ \texttt{catch}\ Q) \sqcap (P\ \texttt{catch}\ R)$

Proof:

(1) LHS $\{\text{Def of } \texttt{catch}\}$

$= \mathcal{H}(\mathcal{H}(P; \phi(Q)); \phi(R))$ $\{\text{Def of } \mathcal{H}\}$

$= \mathcal{H}((forward \wedge \neg eflag)^\top;$
$\mathcal{H}(P; \phi(Q)); \phi(R))$ $\{Q \lhd false \rhd P\ =\ P\}$

$= \mathcal{H}(P; \phi(Q); \phi(R))$ $\{\phi(Q); \phi(R)\ =\ \phi(Q; \phi(R))\}$

$= \mathcal{H}(P; \phi(Q; \phi(R)))$ $\{\phi(S)\ =\ \phi(\mathcal{H}(S))\}$

$= \mathcal{H}(P; \phi(\mathcal{H}(Q; \phi(R))))$ $\{\text{Def of } \texttt{catch}\}$

$= \mathcal{H}(P; \phi(Q\,\texttt{catch}\,R))$ $\{\text{Def of } \texttt{catch}\}$

$= RHS$

(2) $\texttt{throw}\,\texttt{catch}\,Q$ $\{\text{Def of } \texttt{catch}\}$

$= \mathcal{H}(\texttt{throw}; \phi(Q))$ $\{\text{Def of } \texttt{throw}\}$

$= \mathcal{H}(Q[false,\ true/eflag,\ forward])$ $\{\text{Def of } \mathcal{H}\}$

$= \mathcal{H}(Q)$ $\{Q\ =\ \mathcal{H}(Q)\}$

$= Q$ $\{\phi\texttt{throw}\ =\ \texttt{skip}\}$

$= Q\,\texttt{catch}\,\texttt{throw}$

(3) LHS $\{\text{Def of } \texttt{catch}\}$

$= \mathcal{H}((v := e); \phi(Q))$ $\{\text{Def of } \mathcal{H}\}$

$= \mathcal{H}((forward \wedge \neg efalg)^\top; (v := e); \phi(Q))$ $\{e \text{ is well-defined}\}$

$= \mathcal{H}((forward \wedge \neg efalg)^\top; (v := e);$
$(forward \wedge \neg eflag)_\bot; \phi(Q))$ $\{\text{Def of } \phi\}$

$= \mathcal{H}((forward \wedge \neg efalg)^\top; (v := e);$
$(forward \wedge \neg eflag)_\bot)$ $\{(v := e) = \mathcal{H}(v := e)\}$

$= RHS$

(5) LHS $\{\text{Def of } \texttt{catch}\}$

$= \mathcal{H}(\mathbf{if}(b_1 \to P_1,\ b_n \to P_n)\mathbf{fi}\,;\ \phi(R))$ $\{\text{Theorem 3.6(5)}\}$

$= \mathcal{H}(\mathbf{if}(b_1 \to (P_1; \phi(R),$

$b_n \to (P_n; \phi(R))\mathbf{fi}$ $\{\text{Theorem 2.4(2)}\}$

$= RHS$

3.6 Compensation

Let P and Q be programs. The program $P\,\mathtt{cpens}\,Q$ runs P first. If its execution fails, then Q is invoked as its compensation.

$$P \ \mathtt{cpens}\ Q \ =_{df} \ \mathcal{H}(P; \psi(Q)$$

where $\psi(Q) =_{df} (II \lhd forward \vee eflag \rhd Q[true/forward])$

Theorem 3.8

(1) $P\ \mathtt{cpens}\ (Q\ \mathtt{cpens}\ R) \ = \ (P\ \mathtt{cpens}\ Q)\ \mathtt{cpens}\ R$

(2) $P\ \mathtt{cpens}\ Q \ = \ P$ if $P \in \{\mathtt{throw}, \bot, (v := e)\}$

(3) $(\mathtt{fail}\,\mathtt{cpens}\,Q) \ = \ Q \ = \ (Q\ \mathtt{cpens}\ \mathtt{fail})$

(4) $\mathbf{if}(b_1 \to P_1, .., b_n \to P_n)\mathbf{fi}\,\mathtt{cpens}\,Q \ =$

$\mathbf{if}(b_1 \to (P_1\,\mathtt{cpens}\,Q), .., b_n \to (P\,\mathtt{cpens}\,Q))\mathbf{fi}$

(5) $(P \sqcap Q)\,\mathtt{cpens}\,R \ = \ (P\,\mathtt{cpens}\,R) \sqcap (Q\,\mathtt{cpens}\,R)$

(6) $P\,\mathtt{cpens}\,(Q \sqcap R) \ = \ (P\,\mathtt{cpens}\,Q) \sqcap (P\,\mathtt{cpens}\,R)$

(7) $(v := e; P)\,\mathtt{cpens}\,Q \ = \ (v := e); (P\,\mathtt{cpens}\,Q)$

Proof:

Let $B \ =_{df} \ (forward \wedge \neg eflag)$.

(1) RHS $\{\text{Def of } \mathtt{cpens}\}$

$= \mathcal{H}(\mathcal{H}(P; \psi(Q)); \psi(R))$ $\{\text{Def of } \mathcal{H}\}$

$= \mathcal{H}(B^\top; \mathcal{H}(P; \psi(Q)); \psi(R))$ $\{Q \lhd false \rhd P \ = \ P\}$

$= \mathcal{H}(P; \psi(Q); \psi(R))$ $\{\psi(Q; \psi(R) \ = \ \psi(Q; \phi(R))\}$

$= \mathcal{H}(P; \psi(Q; \psi(R)))$ $\{\psi(Q) \ = \ \psi(\mathcal{H}(Q))\}$

$= \mathcal{H}(P; \psi(\mathcal{H}(Q; \psi(R))))$ $\{\text{Def of } \mathtt{cpens}\}$

$= LHS$

$$\begin{array}{lr}
(7)\ LHS & \{\text{Def of } \texttt{cpens}\} \\
= \mathcal{H}(v := e; P; \psi(Q)) & \{B^\top; (v := e) \ = \ B^\top; (v := e); B_\perp\} \\
= \mathcal{H}(v := e; B_\perp; P; \psi(Q)) & \{\text{Def of } \mathcal{H}\} \\
= \mathcal{H}(v := e; B_\perp; \mathcal{H}(P; \psi(Q))) & \{B^\top; (v := e) \ = \ B^\top; (v := e); B_\perp\} \\
= \mathcal{H}(v := e; \mathcal{H}(P; \psi(Q))) & \{\text{Theorem 2.4(3)}\} \\
= RHS &
\end{array}$$

3.7 Coordination

Let P and Q be programs. The program $P \, \texttt{else} \, Q$ behaves like P if its execution succeeds. Otherwise it behaves like Q.

$$P \ \texttt{else} \ Q \ =_{df} \ (P; forward^\top) \vee (\exists t' \bullet P[false/forward'] \wedge Q)$$

where t denotes the vector variable $< ok,\ eflag,\ v >$.

Theorem 3.9

(1) $P \ \texttt{else} \ P \ = \ P$

(2) $P \ \texttt{else} \ (Q \, \texttt{else} \ R) \ = \ (P \ \texttt{else} \ Q) \, \texttt{else} \ R$

(3) $P \ \texttt{else} \ Q \ = \ P$ if $P \in \{\perp, (v := e), (v := e; \texttt{throw})\}$

(4) $(x := e \ \texttt{fail}) \ \texttt{else} \, Q \ = \ Q$

(5) $\textbf{if}(b_1 \rightarrow P_1, ..., b_n \rightarrow P_n)\textbf{fi} \ \texttt{else} \ R \ =$
$\textbf{if}(b_1 \rightarrow (P_1 \ \texttt{else} \ R), .., b_n \rightarrow (P_n \ \texttt{else} \ R))\textbf{fi}$

(6) $P \ \texttt{else} \ \textbf{if}(c_1 \rightarrow Q_1, ..., c_n \rightarrow Q_n)\textbf{fi} =$
$\textbf{if}(c_1 \rightarrow (P \ \texttt{else} \ Q_1), .., c_n \rightarrow (P \ \texttt{else} \ Q_n))\textbf{fi}$

provided that $\bigvee_k c_k \ = \ true$

(7) $(P \sqcap Q) \ \texttt{else} \ R \ = \ (P \ \texttt{else} \ R) \sqcap (Q \ \texttt{else} \ R)$

(8) $P \ \texttt{else} \ (Q \sqcap R) \ = \ (P \ \texttt{else} \ Q) \sqcap (P \ \texttt{else} \ R)$

Proof:

$$\begin{array}{lr}
(1)\ LHS & \{\text{Def of } \texttt{else}\} \\
= P; forward^\top \vee \exists t' \bullet P[false/forward'] \wedge P & \{\text{predicate calculus}\} \\
= (\exists t' \bullet P[false/forward'] \vee \neg\exists t' \bullet P[false/forward'] \wedge \exists t' \bullet P[true/forward'])\wedge & \\
\quad (P; forward^\top) \ \vee \exists t' \bullet P[false/forward'] \wedge P & \{forward^\top \vee II \ = \ II\} \\
= (\neg\exists t' \bullet P[false/forward'] \wedge \exists t' \bullet P[true/forward']) \wedge (P; forward^\top) \vee & \\
\quad \exists t' \bullet P[false/forward'] \wedge P & \{P; II \ = \ P\} \\
= (\neg\exists t' \bullet P[false/forward'] \wedge \exists t' \bullet P[true/forward']) \wedge P \vee & \\
\quad \exists t' \bullet P[false/forward'] \wedge P & \{\text{predicate calculus}\} \\
= (\exists t' \bullet P[true/forward'] \vee \exists t' P[false/forward']) \wedge P & \{\exists t',\ forward' \bullet P \ = \ true\} \\
= RHS &
\end{array}$$

$$
\begin{aligned}
&(6)\ LHS && \{\text{Def of } \mathtt{else}\}\\
&= P; forward^{\top} \vee \exists t' \bullet P[false/forward'] \wedge \\
&\quad \mathbf{if}(c_1 \rightarrow Q_1, .., c_n \rightarrow Q_n)\mathbf{fi} && \{\text{Theorem 3.6(7)}\}\\
&= P; forward^{\top} \vee \mathbf{if}(c_1 \rightarrow \exists t' \bullet P[false/forward'] \wedge Q_1, ...\\
&\quad c_n \rightarrow \exists t' \bullet P[false/forward'] \wedge Q_n)\mathbf{fi} && \{\text{Theorem 3.6(6)}\}\\
&= \mathbf{if}(c_1 \rightarrow (P; forward^{\top} \vee \exists t' \bullet P[false/forward'] \wedge Q_1), ..\\
&\qquad c_n \rightarrow (P; forward^{\top} \vee \exists t' \bullet P[false/forward'] \wedge Q_n))\mathbf{fi} && \{\text{Def of } \mathtt{else}\}\\
&= RHS
\end{aligned}
$$

The choice construct $P \,\mathtt{or}\, Q$ selects a successful one between P and Q. When both P and Q succeed, the choice is made nondeterministically.

$$P \ \mathtt{or}\ Q \ =_{df} \ (P \ \mathtt{else}\ Q) \sqcap (Q \ \mathtt{else}\ P)$$

Theorem 3.10

(1) $P \,\mathtt{or}\, P \ = \ P$

(2) $P \,\mathtt{or}\, Q \ = \ Q \,\mathtt{or}\, P$

(3) $(P \,\mathtt{or}\, , Q) \,\mathtt{or}\, R \ = \ P \,\mathtt{or}\, (Q \,\mathtt{or}\, R)$

(4) $\mathbf{if}(b_1 \rightarrow P_1, .., b_n \rightarrow P_n)\mathbf{fi} \,\mathtt{or}\, Q \ = \ \mathbf{if}(b_1 \rightarrow (P_1 \,\mathtt{or}\, Q), ..., b_n \rightarrow (P_n \,\mathtt{or}\, Q))\mathbf{fi}$

provided that $\bigvee_k b_k \ = \ true$

(5) $(P \sqcap Q) \,\mathtt{or}\, R \ = \ (P \,\mathtt{or}\, R) \sqcap (Q \,\mathtt{or}\, R)$

Proof:

(1) From Theorem 3.9(1)

(2) From the symmetry of $\sqcap$

(3) From Theorem 3.9(2)

(4) From Theorem 3.9(7) and (8)

(5) From Theorem 3.9(9) and (10)

Let P and Q be programs with disjoint alphabets. The program $P \,\mathtt{par}\, Q$ runs P and Q in parallel. It succeeds only when both P and Q succeed. Its behaviour is described by the *parallel merge* construct defined in [15]:

$$P \ \mathtt{par}\ Q \ =_{df} \ (P \|_M Q)$$

where the parallel merge operator $\|_M$ is defined by

$$P \|_M Q \ =_{df} \ (P[0.m'/m'] \| Q[1.m'/m']); M(ok, 0.m, 1.m, m', ok')$$

where m represents the shared variables $forward$ and $eflag$ of P and Q, and $\|$ denotes the disjoint parallel operator

$$(b \vdash R) \| (c \vdash S) \ =_{df} \ (b \wedge c) \vdash (R \wedge S)$$

and the merge predicate M is defined by

$$M \; =_{df}$$

$$true \vdash \begin{pmatrix} (eflag' = 0.eflag1 \vee 1.eflag) \wedge \\ (\neg 0.eflag \wedge \neg 1.eflag) \Rightarrow (forward' = 0.forward1 \wedge 1.forward) \wedge \\ (v' = v) \end{pmatrix}$$

We borrow the following definition and lemma from [15] to explore the algebraic properties of par.

Definition 3.2 (valid merge)

A merge predicate $N(ok,\, 0.m,\, 1.m,\, m',\, ok')$ is valid if it is a design satisfying the following properties

(1) N is symmetric in its input $0.m$ and $1.m$

(2) N is associative

$$N3(1.m,\, 2.m,\, 0.m/0.m,\, 1.m,\, 2.m] \;=\; N3$$

where $N3$ is a three-way merge relation

$$N3 \;=_{df}\; \exists x, t \bullet N(ok,\, 0.m,\, 1.m,\, x,\, t) \wedge N(t,\, x,\, 2.m,\, m',\, ok')$$

(3) $N[m,\, m,\, /0.m,\, 1.m] \;=\; true \vdash (m = m') \wedge (v' = v)$

where m represents the shared variables of parallel components.

Lemma 3.1

If N is valid then the parallel merge $\|_N$ is symmetric and associative.

From the definition of the merge predicate M we can show that M is a valid merge predicate.

Theorem 3.11

(1) $(P \texttt{ par } Q) \;=\; (Q \texttt{ par } P)$

(2) $(P \texttt{ par } Q) \texttt{ par } R \;=\; P \texttt{ par } (Q \texttt{ par } R)$

(3) $\bot \texttt{ par } Q \;=\; \bot$

(4) $\mathbf{if}(b_1 \rightarrow P_1, ..., b_n \rightarrow P_n)\mathbf{fi} \texttt{ par } Q \;=$

$\quad \mathbf{if}(b_1 \rightarrow (P_1 \texttt{ par } Q), ..., b_n \rightarrow (P_n \texttt{ par } Q))\mathbf{fi}$

(5) $(P \sqcap Q) \texttt{ par } R \;=\; (P \texttt{ par } R) \sqcap (Q \texttt{ par } R)$

(6) $(v := e; P) \texttt{ par } Q \;=\; (v := e); (P \texttt{ par } Q)$

(7) $\texttt{fail par throw} \;=\; \texttt{throw}$

(8) $\texttt{fail par fail} \;=\; \texttt{fail}$

(9) $\texttt{throw par throw} \;=\; \texttt{throw}$

(10) $\texttt{skip}_A \texttt{ par } Q \;=\; Q_{+A}$

$$(b \vdash R)_{+\{x, .., z\}} \;=_{df}\; b \vdash (R \wedge x = x' \wedge .. \wedge z' = z)$$

Proof:

(1) and (2): From Lemma 3.1.

(3) From the fact that $\bot \| Q \; = \; \bot$ and $\bot ; M \; = \; \bot$

(4) From Theorem 3.6(5) and the fact that

$$\mathbf{if}(b_1 \to P_1, ..., b_n \to P_n)\mathbf{fi} \| Q \; = \; \mathbf{if}(b_1 \to (P_1 \| Q), .., b_n \to (P_n \| Q))\mathbf{fi}$$

(5) From the fact that $(P \sqcap Q) \| R \; = \; (P \parallel R) \sqcap (Q \parallel R)$

(6) From the fact that $(v := e; P) \| Q \; = \; (v := e); (P \| Q)$

4 Normal Form

The normal form we adopt for our language is an alternation of the form:

$$\mathbf{if}(b1 \to \sqcap_{i \in S1}(v := e_i),\; b2 \to \sqcap_{j \in S2}(v := f_j; \texttt{fail}),\; b3 \to \sqcap_{k \in S3}(v := g_k; \texttt{throw})\mathbf{fi}$$

where all expressions are well-defined, and all assignments are total, and all the index sets S_i are finite. The objective of this section is to show that all finite programs can be reduced to normal form. Our first step is to prove that normal forms are closed under the programming combinators defined in the previous section.

Theorem 4.1

Let $P \; = \; \mathbf{if}\,(b1 \to P1,\, b2 \to P2,\, b3 \to P3)\,\mathbf{fi}$

and $Q \; = \; \mathbf{if}\,(c1 \to Q1,\, c2 \to Q2,\, c3 \to Q3)\,\mathbf{fi}$, where

$P1 = \sqcap_{i \in S1}(v := e1_i)$ $\qquad$ $Q1 = \sqcap_{i \in T1}(v := f1_i)$

$P2 = \sqcap_{j \in S2}(v := e2_j); \texttt{fail}$ $\qquad$ $Q2 = \sqcap_{j \in T2}(v := f2_j); \texttt{fail}$

$P3 = \sqcap_{k \in S3}(v := e3_k); \texttt{throw}$ $\qquad$ $Q3 = \sqcap_{k \in T3}(v := f3_k); \texttt{throw}$

Then $P \sqcap Q \; =$

$$\mathbf{if}\begin{pmatrix} (b1 \wedge c \vee c1 \wedge b) \to \\ \quad \sqcap_{i \in S1,\, j \in T1}(v := (e1_i \lhd b_1 \rhd f1_j)) \sqcap (v := (f1_j \lhd c_1 \rhd e1_i)) \\ (b2 \wedge c \vee c2 \wedge b) \to \\ \quad \sqcap_{i \in S2,\, j \in T2}(v := (e2_i \lhd b_2 \rhd f2_j)) \sqcap (v := (f2_j \lhd c_2 \rhd e2_i)); \texttt{fail} \\ (b3 \wedge c \vee c3 \wedge b) \to \\ \quad \sqcap_{i \in S3,\, j \in T3}(v := (e3_i \lhd b_1 \rhd f3_j)) \sqcap (v := (f3_j \lhd c_1 \rhd e3_i)); \texttt{throw} \end{pmatrix}\mathbf{fi}$$

where $b =_{df} \; b_1 \vee b_2 \vee b_3$ and $c =_{df} \; c_1 \vee c_2 \vee c_3$

Proof: LHS {Theorem 3.6(6)}

$$= \textbf{if}(b1 \to (P1 \sqcap Q),\ b2 \to (P2 \sqcap Q),\ b3 \to (P3 \sqcap Q))\textbf{fi}$$

{Theorem 3.6(6)}

$$= \textbf{if}\begin{pmatrix} b1 \to \textbf{if}(c1 \to (Q1 \sqcap P1),\ c2 \to (Q2 \sqcap P1),\ c3 \to (Q3 \sqcap P1))\textbf{fi} \\ b2 \to \textbf{if}(c1 \to (Q1 \sqcap P2),\ c2 \to (Q2 \sqcap P2),\ c3 \to (Q3 \sqcap P2))\textbf{fi} \\ b3 \to \textbf{if}(c1 \to (Q1 \sqcap P3),\ c2 \to (Q2 \sqcap P3),\ c3 \to (Q3 \sqcap P3))\textbf{fi} \end{pmatrix}\textbf{fi}$$

{Theorem 3.6(2) and (9)}

$$= \textbf{if}\begin{pmatrix} (b1 \wedge c) \to P1, & (b2 \wedge c) \to P2, & (b3 \wedge c) \to P3, \\ (b \wedge c1) \to Q1, & (b \wedge c2) \to Q2, & (b \wedge c3) \to Q3 \end{pmatrix}\textbf{fi}$$

{Theorem 3.6(4)}

$$= \textbf{if}\begin{pmatrix} (b1 \wedge c \vee b \wedge c1) \to (P1 \lhd b1 \rhd Q1) \sqcap (Q1 \lhd c1 \rhd P1) \\ (b2 \wedge c \vee b \wedge c2) \to (P2 \lhd b2 \rhd Q2) \sqcap (Q2 \lhd c2 \rhd P2) \\ (b3 \wedge c \vee b \wedge c3) \to (P3 \lhd b3 \rhd Q3) \sqcap (Q3 \lhd c3 \rhd P3) \end{pmatrix}\textbf{fi}$$

{Theorem 3.5(3)}

$$= RHS$$

Let

$$W =_{df} \textbf{if}(b1 \to (x := e1),\ b2 \to (x := e2); \texttt{fail},\ b3 \to (x := e3); \texttt{throw})\textbf{fi}$$

$$R =_{df} \textbf{if}(c1 \to (x := f1),\ c2 \to (x := f2); \texttt{fail},\ c3 \to (x := f3); \texttt{throw})\textbf{fi}$$

Theorem 4.2

$$W; R =$$

$$\textbf{if}\begin{pmatrix} (b1 \wedge c1[e1/x]) \to (x := f1(e1)) \\ (b2 \wedge (\neg b_1 \vee c[e1/x]) \vee b1 \wedge c2[e1/x]) \to \\ \quad (x := (e2 \lhd b2 \rhd f2[e1/x]) \sqcap x := (f2[e1/x] \lhd c2[e1/x] \rhd e2)); \texttt{fail} \\ (b3 \wedge (\neg b1 \vee c[e1/x]) \vee b1 \wedge c3[e1/x]) \to \\ \quad (x := (e3 \lhd b3 \rhd f3[e1/x]) \sqcap x := (f3[e1/x] \lhd c3[e1/x] \rhd e3)); \texttt{throw} \end{pmatrix}\textbf{fi}$$

Proof:

LHS {Theorem 3.6(5)}

$$= \textbf{if}(b1 \to (x := e1); R,\ b2 \to (x := e2); \texttt{fail},\ b3 \to (x := e3); \texttt{throw})\textbf{fi}$$

{Theorem 3.5(2)}

$$= \textbf{if}\begin{pmatrix} b1 \to \textbf{if}\begin{pmatrix} c1[e1/x] \to (x := f1[e1/x]), \\ c2[e1/x] \to (x := f2[e1/x]); \texttt{fail}, \\ c3[e1/x] \to (x := f3[e1/x]); \texttt{throw} \end{pmatrix}\textbf{fi} \\ b2 \to (x := e2); \texttt{fail} \\ b3 \to (x := e3); \texttt{throw} \end{pmatrix}\textbf{fi}$$

{Theorem 3.6(2) and (3)}

$$= \mathbf{if} \begin{pmatrix} b1 \wedge c1[e1/x] \rightarrow (x := f1[e1/x]), \\ b1 \wedge c2[e1/x] \rightarrow (x := f2[e1/x]); \texttt{fail}, \\ b2 \wedge \neg(b1 \wedge \neg c[e1/x]) \rightarrow (x := e2); \texttt{fail} \\ b1 \wedge c3[e1/x] \rightarrow (x := f3[e1/x]); \texttt{throw}, \\ b3 \wedge \neg(b1 \wedge \neg c[e1/x]) \rightarrow (x := e3); \texttt{throw} \end{pmatrix} \mathbf{fi}$$

{Theorem 3.6(4)}

$= RHS$

Theorem 4.3

$W \,\texttt{catch}\, R =$

$$\mathbf{if} \begin{pmatrix} (b1 \wedge (\neg b3 \vee c[e3/x]) \vee b3 \wedge c1[e3/x]) \rightarrow \\ \quad (x := (e1 \lhd b1 \rhd f1[e3/x]) \sqcap x := (f1[e3/x] \lhd c1[e3/x] \rhd e1)) \\ (b2 \wedge (\neg b3 \vee c[e3/x]) \vee b3 \wedge c2[e3/x]) \rightarrow \\ \quad (x := (e2 \lhd b2 \rhd f2[e3/x]) \sqcap x := (f2[e3/x] \lhd c2[e3/x] \rhd e2)); \texttt{fail} \\ (b3 \wedge c3[e3/x]) \rightarrow (x := f3[e3/x]); \texttt{throw} \end{pmatrix} \mathbf{fi}$$

Proof:

LHS {Theorem 3.7(2) and (3)}

$= \mathbf{if}(b1 \rightarrow (x := e1),\ b2 \rightarrow (x := e2); \texttt{fail},\ b3 \rightarrow (x := e3); R)\mathbf{fi}$

{Theorem 4.6(2)}

$$= \mathbf{if} \begin{pmatrix} b1 \rightarrow (x := e1), \\ b2 \rightarrow (x := e2); \texttt{fail}, \\ b3 \rightarrow \mathbf{if} \begin{pmatrix} c1[e3/x] \rightarrow (x := f1[e3/x]), \\ c2[e3/x] \rightarrow (x := f2[e3/x]); \texttt{fail}, \\ c3[e3/x] \rightarrow (x := f3[e3/x]); \texttt{throw} \end{pmatrix} \mathbf{fi} \end{pmatrix} \mathbf{fi}$$

{Theorem 4.6(2) and (3)}

$$= \mathbf{if} \begin{pmatrix} b1 \wedge (\neg b3 \vee c[e3/x]) \rightarrow (x := e1), \\ b3 \wedge c1[e3/x] \rightarrow (x := f1[e3/x]), \\ b2 \wedge (\neg b3 \vee c[e3/x]) \rightarrow (x := e2); \texttt{fail} \\ b3 \wedge c2[e3/x] \rightarrow (x := f2[e3/x]); \texttt{fail}, \\ b3 \wedge c3[e3/x] \rightarrow (x := f3[e3/x]); \texttt{throw} \end{pmatrix} \mathbf{fi}$$

{Theorem 3.6(4)}

$= RHS$

Theorem 4.4

$$W\ \mathtt{cpens}\ R\ =$$
$$\textbf{if}\begin{pmatrix}(b1 \wedge (\neg b2 \vee c[e2/x]) \vee b \wedge c1[e2/x]) \rightarrow \\ \quad (x := (e1 \lhd b1 \rhd f1[e2/x]) \sqcap x := (f1[e2/x] \lhd c1[e2/x] \rhd e1)) \\ (b2 \wedge c2[e2/x]) \rightarrow (x := f2[e3/x]); \mathtt{fail} \\ (b3 \wedge (\neg b2 \vee c[e3/x]) \vee c3[e2/x] \wedge b) \rightarrow \\ \quad (x := (e3 \lhd b3 \rhd f3[e2/x]) \sqcap x := (f3[e2/x] \lhd c3[e2/x] \rhd e3); \mathtt{throw}\end{pmatrix}\textbf{fi}$$

Proof: Similar to Theorem 4.3.

Theorem 4.5

$$W\ \mathtt{else}\ R\ =$$
$$\textbf{if}\begin{pmatrix}(b1 \wedge c \vee b \wedge c1) \rightarrow (x := (e1 \lhd b1 \rhd f1) \sqcap x := (f1 \lhd c1 \rhd e1)) \\ (b2 \wedge c2) \rightarrow (x := f2); \mathtt{fail} \\ (b3 \wedge c \vee c3 \wedge b) \rightarrow (x := (e3 \lhd b3 \rhd f3) \sqcap x := (f3 \lhd c3 \rhd e3)); \mathtt{throw}\end{pmatrix}\textbf{fi}$$

Proof: LHS {Theorem 4.9(2) and (3)}

$$= \quad \textbf{if}(b1 \rightarrow (x := e1),\ b2 \rightarrow R,\ b3 \rightarrow (x := e3); \mathtt{throw})\textbf{fi}$$

{Theorem 4.6(2)}

$$= \quad \textbf{if}\begin{pmatrix}b1 \wedge (\neg b2 \vee c) \rightarrow (x := e1), \\ b2 \wedge c1 \rightarrow (x := f1), \\ b2 \wedge c2 \rightarrow (x := f2); \mathtt{fail}, \\ b2 \wedge c3 \rightarrow (x := f3); \mathtt{throw}, \\ b3 \wedge (\neg b2 \vee c) \rightarrow (x := e3); \mathtt{throw}\end{pmatrix}\textbf{fi}$$

{Theorem 3.6(4)}

$$= \quad RHS$$

Theorem 4.6

$$W \lhd d \rhd R\ =$$
$$\textbf{if}\begin{pmatrix}(\hat{d} \wedge b1 \vee \hat{\neg d} \wedge c1) \rightarrow \\ \qquad (x := (e1 \lhd b1 \rhd f1) \sqcap x := (f1 \lhd c1 \rhd e1)) \\ (\hat{d} \wedge b2 \vee \hat{\neg d} \wedge c2) \rightarrow \\ \qquad (x := (e2 \lhd b2 \rhd f2) \sqcap x := (f2 \lhd c2 \rhd e2)); \mathtt{fail} \\ (\hat{d} \wedge b2 \vee \hat{\neg d} \wedge c2 \vee \neg \mathcal{D}(d)) \rightarrow \\ \qquad (x := ((e3 \lhd b3 \rhd f3) \lhd \mathcal{D}(d) \rhd x) \sqcap \\ \qquad x := ((f3 \lhd c3 \rhd e3) \lhd \mathcal{D}(d) \rhd x)); \mathtt{throw}\end{pmatrix}\textbf{fi}$$

where $\hat{d} \ =_{df} \ d \lhd \mathcal{D}(d) \rhd false$

Proof: LHS {Theorem 3.3}

$$= \quad \mathbf{if}(\hat{d} \rightarrow W,\ \neg\hat{d} \rightarrow R,\ \neg\mathcal{D}(d) \rightarrow \mathtt{throw})\mathbf{fi}$$

{Theorem 3.6(2) and (3)}

$$= \quad \mathbf{if}\begin{pmatrix} \hat{d} \wedge b1 \wedge c \rightarrow (x := e1), & \neg\hat{d} \wedge c1 \wedge b \rightarrow (x := f1), \\ \hat{d} \wedge b2 \wedge c \rightarrow (x := e2); \mathtt{fail}, & \neg\hat{d} \wedge c2 \wedge b \rightarrow (x := f2); \mathtt{fail}, \\ \hat{d} \wedge b3 \wedge c \rightarrow (x := e3); \mathtt{throw}, & \neg\hat{d} \wedge c3 \wedge b \rightarrow (x := f3); \mathtt{throw}, \\ \neg\mathcal{D}(d) \rightarrow \mathtt{throw} & \end{pmatrix}\mathbf{fi}$$

{Theorem 3.6(4)}

$$= \quad RHS$$

Theorem 4.7

$$(x := e)\ \mathtt{par}\ R\ = \mathbf{if}\begin{pmatrix} c1 \rightarrow (x,\, y\ :=\ e,\, f1), \\ c2 \rightarrow (x,\, y := e,\, f2); \mathtt{fail}, \\ c3 \rightarrow (x,\, y\ :=\ e,\, f3); \mathtt{throw} \end{pmatrix}\mathbf{fi}$$

Proof:

LHS {Theorem 4.11(4)}

$$= \mathbf{if}\begin{pmatrix} c1 \rightarrow ((x := e)\,\mathtt{par}\,(y := f1)), \\ c2 \rightarrow ((x := e)\,\mathtt{par}\,(y := f2; \mathtt{fail})), \\ c3 \rightarrow ((x := e)\,\mathtt{par}\,(y := f3; \mathtt{throw})) \end{pmatrix}\mathbf{fi}$$

{Theorem 4.11(6) and (10)}

$$= RHS$$

Theorem 4.8

$$(x := e; \mathtt{fail})\ \mathtt{par}\ R\ =$$

$$\mathbf{if}\begin{pmatrix} c1 \vee c2 \rightarrow \\ \quad (x,\, y\ :=\ (e,\, f1) \lhd c1 \rhd (e,\, f2) \sqcap x,\, y := (e,\, f2) \lhd c2 \rhd (e,\, f1)); \mathtt{fail} \\ c3 \rightarrow (x,\, y\ :=\ e,\, f3); \mathtt{throw} \end{pmatrix}\mathbf{fi}$$

Proof: Similar to Theorem 4.7.

Theorem 4.9

$$(x := e; \mathtt{throw})\ \mathtt{par}\ R\ =$$

$$\mathbf{if}\begin{pmatrix} c1 \vee c2 \vee c3 \rightarrow \\ \quad \begin{pmatrix} (x,\, y\ :=\ ((e,\, f1) \lhd c1 \rhd (e,\, f2)) \lhd c1 \vee c2 \rhd (e,\, f3)) \sqcap \\ (x,\, y\ :=\ ((e,\, f2) \lhd c2 \rhd (e,\, f1)) \lhd c1 \vee c2 \rhd (e,\, f3)) \sqcap \\ (x,\, y\ :=\ (e,\, f3) \lhd c3 \rhd ((e,\, f1) \lhd c1 \rhd (e,\, f2))) \sqcap \\ (x,\, y\ :=\ (e,\, f3) \lhd c3 \rhd ((e,\, f2) \lhd c2 \rhd (e,\, f1))) \end{pmatrix}; \mathtt{throw} \end{pmatrix}\mathbf{fi}$$

Proof: Similar to Theorem 4.7

Now we are going to show that all primitive commands can be reduced to a normal form.

Theorem 4.10

$\texttt{skip} \;=\; \mathbf{if}(true \rightarrow (v := v))\mathbf{fi}$

Proof: $\texttt{skip}$ $\{\text{Theorem 3.5(4)}\}$

$= \quad v := v$ $\{\text{Theorem 4.6(10)}\}$

$= \quad \mathbf{if}(true \rightarrow v := v)\mathbf{fi}$

Theorem 4.11

$\texttt{fail} \;=\; \mathbf{if}(true \rightarrow (v := v); \texttt{fail})\mathbf{fi}$

Proof: Similar to Theorem 4.10.

Theorem 4.12

$\texttt{throw} = \mathbf{if}(true \rightarrow (v := v); \texttt{throw})\mathbf{fi}$

Proof: Similar to Theorem 4.10.

Theorem 4.13

$\bot \;=\; \mathbf{if}()\mathbf{fi}$

Proof: From Theorem 4.6(10).

Theorem 4.14

$x := e \;=\; \mathbf{if}(\mathcal{D}(e) \rightarrow (x, y, .., z \;:=\; (e \lhd \mathcal{D}(e) \rhd x), y, .., z), \; \neg\mathcal{D}(e) \rightarrow \texttt{throw})\mathbf{fi}$

Proof: From Theorem 4.4.

Finally we reach the conclusion.

Theorem 4.15

All finite program can be reduced to a normal form.

Proof: From Theorem 4.1–4.14.

5 Link with the Original Design Model

This section explores the link between the model of Section 2 with the original design model given in [15].

For any design P and **Req**-healthy design Q we define

$$\mathcal{F}(P) =_{df} \mathcal{H}(P; \texttt{success})$$

$$\mathcal{G}(Q) =_{df} Q[true, false/forward, eflag]; (forward \wedge \neg eflag)_{\bot}$$

Theorem 5.1

$\mathcal{F}$ and $\mathcal{G}$ form a Galois connection:

(1) $\mathcal{G}(\mathcal{F}(P)) \;=\; P$

(2) $\mathcal{F}(\mathcal{G}(Q)) \sqsubseteq Q$

Proof: $\mathcal{G}(\mathcal{F}(P))$ $\qquad\{\text{Def of } \mathcal{F} \text{ and } \mathcal{G}\}$

$$= \quad P; \texttt{success}; (true \vdash (v' = v)) \lhd forward \wedge \neg eflag \rhd \bot) \qquad \{\text{Def of } \texttt{success}\}$$

$$= \quad P; (true \vdash (v' = v)) \qquad \{\text{unit law of } ;\}$$

$$= \quad P$$

$\mathcal{F}(\mathcal{G}(Q))$ $\qquad\{\text{Def of } \mathcal{F} \text{ and } \mathcal{G}\}$

$$= \mathcal{H}(Q[true, \neg false/forward, eflag];$$
$$(true \vdash (v' = v) \lhd forward \wedge \neg eflag \rhd \bot); \texttt{success})$$
$$\{\text{Def of } \mathcal{H},\;\; (P \lhd b \rhd Q); R \;=\; (P; R) \lhd b \rhd (Q; R)\}$$

$$= Q; (\texttt{success} \lhd forward \wedge \neg eflag \rhd \bot) \qquad \{\text{Def of } \texttt{sucess}\}$$

$$= Q; ((true \vdash (v' = v \wedge forwared' = forward \wedge eflag' = eflag))$$
$$\lhd forward \wedge \neg eflag \rhd \bot) \qquad \{\bot \sqsubseteq D\}$$

$$\sqsubseteq Q; (true \vdash (v' = v \wedge forwared' = forward \wedge eflag' = eflag)) \qquad \{\text{unit law of } ;\}$$

$$= Q$$

$\mathcal{F}$ is a homomorphism.

Theorem 5.2

(1) $\mathcal{F}(true \vdash (v' = v)) \;=\; \texttt{skip}$

(2) $\mathcal{F}(true \vdash (x' = e \wedge y' = y \wedge z' = z)) \;=\; (x := e)$

provided that e is well-defined.

(3) $\mathcal{F}(true) \;=\; \bot$

(4) $\mathcal{F}(P1 \sqcap P2) \;=\; \mathcal{F}(P1) \sqcap \mathcal{F}(P2)$

(5) $\mathcal{F}(P1 \lhd b \rhd P2) \;=\; \mathcal{F}(P1) \lhd b \rhd \mathcal{F}(P2)$

provided that b is well-defined.

(6) $\mathcal{F}(P1; P2) \;=\; \mathcal{F}(P1); \mathcal{F}(P2)$

(7) $\mathcal{F}(b * P) \;=\; b *_{\mathcal{H}} \mathcal{F}(P)$

Proof:

$$
\begin{array}{ll}
(6)\ \mathcal{F}(P1;P2) & \{\text{Def of } \mathcal{F}\} \\
= \mathcal{H}(P1;P2;\texttt{success}\} & \{\texttt{success}; P2; \texttt{success} = \\
 & P2; \texttt{success}\} \\
= \mathcal{H}((P1;\texttt{success};P2;\texttt{success})) & \{(forward \wedge \neg eflag)^{\top}; \texttt{success}; Q = \\
 & (forward \wedge \neg eflag)^{\top}; \texttt{success}; \mathcal{H}(Q)\} \\
= \mathcal{H}((P1;\texttt{success});\mathcal{H}(P2;\texttt{success})) & \{\text{Theorem 2.4}\} \\
= \mathcal{H}(P1;\texttt{success});\mathcal{H}(P2;\texttt{success}) & \{\text{Def of } \mathcal{F}\} \\
= \mathcal{F}(P1)\,;\,\mathcal{F}(P2) &
\end{array}
$$

$$
\begin{array}{ll}
(7)\ LHS & \{\text{fixed point theorem}\} \\
= \mathcal{F}((P; b * P) \lhd b \rhd (true \vdash (v' = v))) & \{\text{Conclusion (1), (5), (6)}\} \\
= (\mathcal{F}(P); LHS) \lhd b \rhd \texttt{skip} &
\end{array}
$$

which implies that $LHS \sqsupseteq RHS$

$$
\begin{array}{ll}
\quad \mathcal{G}(RHS) & \{\text{fixed point theorem}\} \\
= \mathcal{G}((\mathcal{F}(P); RHS) \lhd b \rhd \texttt{skip}) & \{\mathcal{G} \text{ distributes over } \lhd b \rhd\} \\
= \mathcal{G}(\mathcal{F}(P); RHS) \lhd b \rhd \mathcal{G}(\texttt{skip}) & \{\text{Def of } \mathcal{G}\} \\
= (\mathcal{F}(P)[true,\, false/forward,\, eflag]; RHS; & \\
\quad (foward \wedge \neg eflag)_{\perp}) \lhd b \rhd (true \vdash (v' = v)) & \{\text{Def of } \mathcal{F}\} \\
= (P; \textbf{success}; RHS; & \\
\quad (forward \wedge \neg eflag)_{\perp}) \lhd b \rhd (true \vdash (v' = v)) & \{\text{Def of } \textbf{success}\} \\
= (P; RHS[true,\, false/forward,\, eflag]; & \\
\quad (forward \wedge \neg eflag)_{\perp}) \lhd b \rhd (true \vdash (v' = v)) & \{\text{Def of } \mathcal{G}\} \\
= (P; \mathcal{G}(RHS)) \lhd b \rhd (true \vdash (v' = v)) &
\end{array}
$$

which implies

$$
\begin{array}{ll}
\quad \mathcal{G}(RHS) \sqsupseteq (b * P) & \{\mathcal{F} \text{ is monotonic}\} \\
\Rightarrow \mathcal{F}(\mathcal{G}(RHS)) \sqsupseteq LHS & \{\text{Theorem 5.1(2)}\} \\
\Rightarrow RHS \sqsupseteq LHS &
\end{array}
$$

6 Conclusion

This paper presents a design model for compensable programs. We add new logical variables $eflag$ and $forward$ to the standard design model to deal with the features of exception and failures. As a result, we put forward new healthiness conditions $\mathbf{Req_1}$ and $\mathbf{Req_2}$ to characterise those designs which can be used to specify the dynamic behaviour of compensable programs.

This paper treats an assignment $x := e$ as a conditional (Theorem 4.1). After it is shown that `throw` is a new left zero of sequential composition, we are allowed to use the algebraic laws established for the conventional imperative language in [15] to convert finite programs to normal form. This shows that the model of Section 2 is really a conservative extension of the original design model in [15] in the sense that it preserves the algebraic laws of the Guarded Command Language.

Acknowledgement

The ideas put forward in this paper have been inspired from the discussion with Tony Hoare, and the earlier work of my colleagues.

References

1. Abadi, M., Gordon, A.D.: A calculus for cryptographic protocols: The spi calculus. Information and Computation 148(1), 1–70 (1999)
2. Alonso, G., Kuno, H., Casati, F., et al.: Web Services: Concepts, Architectures and Applications. Springer, Heidelberg (2003)
3. Bhargavan, K., et al.: A Semantics for Web Service Authentication. Theoretical Computer Science 340(1), 102–153 (2005)
4. Bruni, R., Montanari, H.C., Montannari, U.: Theoretical foundation for compensation in flow composition languages. In: Proc. POPL 2005, 32nd ACM SIGPLAN-SIGACT symposium on principles of programming languages, pp. 209–220. ACM, New York (2004)
5. Bruni, R., et al.: From Theory to Practice in Transactional Composition of Web Services. In: Bravetti, M., Kloul, L., Zavattaro, G. (eds.) EPEW/WS-EM 2005. LNCS, vol. 3670, pp. 272–286. Springer, Heidelberg (2005)
6. Bulter, M.J., Ferreria, C.: A process compensation language. In: Grieskamp, W., Santen, T., Stoddart, B. (eds.) IFM 2000. LNCS, vol. 1945, pp. 61–76. Springer, Heidelberg (2000)
7. Bulter, M.J., Ferreria, C.: An Operational Semantics for StAC: a Lanuage for Modelling Long-Running Business Transactions. LNCS, vol. 2949, pp. 87–104. Springer, Heidelberg (2004)
8. Butler, M.J., Hoare, C.A.R., Ferreria, C.: A Trace Semantics for Long-Running Transactions. In: Abdallah, A.E., Jones, C.B., Sanders, J.W. (eds.) Communicating Sequential Processes. LNCS, vol. 3525, pp. 133–150. Springer, Heidelberg (2005)
9. Curbera, F., Goland, Y., Klein, J., et al.: Business Process Execution Language for Web Service (2003), `http://www.siebei.com/bpel`
10. Dijkstra, E.W.: A Discipline of Programming. Prentice Hall, Englewood Cliffs (1976)
11. Gordon, A.D., et al.: Validating a Web Service Security Abstraction by Typing. Formal Aspects of Computing 17(3), 277–318 (2005)
12. Jifeng, H., Huibiao, Z., Geguang, P.: A model for BPEL-like languages. Frontiers of Computer Science in China 1(1), 9–20 (2007)
13. Jifeng, H.: Compensable Programs. In: Jones, C.B., Liu, Z., Woodcock, J. (eds.) Formal Methods and Hybrid Real-Time Systems. LNCS, vol. 4700, pp. 349–364. Springer, Heidelberg (2007)

14. Hoare, C.A.R.: Communicating Sequential Language. Prentice Hall, Englewood Cliffs (1985)
15. Hoare, C.A.R., Jifeng, H.: Unifying theories of programming. Prentice Hall, Englewood Cliffs (1998)
16. Leymann, F.: Web Service Flow Language (WSFL1.0). IBM (2001)
17. Laneve, C., et al.: Web-pi at work. In: De Nicola, R., Sangiorgi, D. (eds.) TGC 2005. LNCS, vol. 3705, pp. 182–194. Springer, Heidelberg (2005)
18. Jing, L., Jifeng, H., Geguang, P.: Towards the Semantics for Web Services Choreography Description Language. In: Liu, Z., He, J. (eds.) ICFEM 2006. LNCS, vol. 4260, pp. 246–263. Springer, Heidelberg (2006)
19. Lucchi, R., Mazzara, M.: A Pi-calculus based semantics for WS-BPEL. Journal of Logic and Algebraic Programming (in press)
20. Milner, R.: Communication and Mobile System: the π-calculus. Cambridge University Press, Cambridge (1999)
21. Morris, J.M.: Non-deterministic expressions and predicate transformers. Information Processing Letters 61, 241–246 (1997)
22. Geguang, P., et al.: Theoretical Foundation of Scope-based Compensation Flow Language for Web Service. LNCS, vol. 4307, pp. 251–266. Springer, Heidelberg (2006)
23. Qiu, Z.Y., et al.: Semantics of BPEL4WS-Like Fault and Compensation Handling. In: Fitzgerald, J.S., Hayes, I.J., Tarlecki, A. (eds.) FM 2005. LNCS, vol. 3582, pp. 350–365. Springer, Heidelberg (2005)
24. Tarski, A.: A lattice-theoretical fixpoint theorem and its applications. Pacific Journal of Mathematics 5, 285–309 (1955)
25. Thatte, S.: XLANG: Web Service for Business Process Design. Microsoft (2001)

Animating Event B Models by Formal Data Models

Idir Ait-Sadoune and Yamine Ait-Ameur

LISI / ENSMA - Téléport 2 - 1, avenue Clément Ader - B.P. 40109,
86960 Futuroscope Cedex - France
{idir.aitsadoune,yamine}@ensma.fr

Abstract. We present a formal approach allowing to animate event B formal models. Invariants, deadlock freeness properties are expressed and proved on these models. This paper presents an approach that suggests to complete the proof activity in the event B method by animation activity. The obtained animator may be used to check if the event B models obtained fulfill user requirements, or to provide a help to the developer when describing its formal event B models and particularly in defining event B invariants and guards. More precisely, event B models are translated into data models expressed in the EXPRESS formal data modeling technique. The obtained data models are instantiated and provide an animation of the original B models. Following this approach, it becomes possible to trigger event B models, which themselves trigger entity instantiation on the EXPRESS side. As a further step, we show that the B models can be used as a monitoring system raising alarms in case of incorrect systems behavior. The proposed approach is operationally implemented in the B2EXPRESS tool which handles animation of event B models. It has been experimented for the validation of multimodal human interfaces in the context of VERBATIM project[1].

1 Introduction

Formal developments of programs or systems based on refinement and proof consist in defining a succession of models M_i, where M_{i+1} is a refinement of M_i. These models introduce gradually the elements describing the system to be designed starting from the informally expressed requirements. Properties corresponding to requirements, expressed by pre-conditions, post-conditions, invariants, etc. are checked and maintained during this development process. In addition, the correctness of refinement is ensured by a gluing invariant which preserves the properties established at the previous refinement. To guarantee the correctness of such developments, a set of proof obligations is associated to each operation (preservation of the invariant, correctness of refinement, etc). Discharging these proof obligations is performed either with an automatic prover (model checkers, theorem provers or type systems) or interactively with a semi-automatic one.

[1] Project funded by the French research agency. http://iihm.imag.fr/nigay/VERBATIM/

T. Margaria and B. Steffen (Eds.): ISoLA 2008, CCIS 17, pp. 37–55, 2008.

The B method [1,2], in particular the event B method, used in our developments, is one of the development methods that supports the proof activity, refinement and code production, but it does not support, in particular, models animation for requirements validation. Properties related to the requirements are translated into B expressions and the only way to establish them is by proving the generated proof obligations. We get a proof based validation.

The possibility of animating event B models at any abstraction level, in a refinement chain, would enrich the development process by other validation techniques, offering other possibilities of validating not only the informal requirements, but also the development itself. The interest of such a validation is double.

- On the one hand, it makes it possible to control if the requirements are taken into account in the various models. The capability to describe scenarios of use and to animate the models according to these scenarios is offered to a user.
- On the other hand, it guides the developer in the proof process. For example checking if the gluing invariant is satisfied in a given refinement or not. Offering the possibility of combining both animation of models and formal proof of their proof obligations provides assistance to a developer.

Both activities help the developer and increase development quality.

There are many event B models animators. We quote ProB [3] based on the model checking technique. Sequences of events are produced by exploring the states of the model which causes a combinatorial explosion of explored states and indeterminism is managed by evaluating finite sets of values. This article describes the B2EXPRESS animator for event B models. It has been developed on the basis of a data modeling technique. The animation principle consists in translating every event B model to a formal data model expressed in the EXPRESS formal data modeling language [4,5]. The animation process consists in instantiating EXPRESS model entities. The generation of instances is guided by a process algebra expression and indeterminism is managed in interaction with the developer who can choose its values arbitrarily in a finite or potentially infinite set. EXPRESS instances can be, also, produced by an external running application and sent to B2EXPRESS. In this case, B can be used as a monitoring system. This capability is not offered with ProB.

We have structured this paper as follows. First, we present a brief description of the two formal techniques used in this paper: event B and EXPRESS. Then, next sections are devoted to the description of the designed animator and the approach we have proposed. Finally, last section relates our proposal to related work and focuses on the two B animators Brama [6] and ProB [3].

2 Formal Techniques Implementations

Two formal techniques are put into practice : the event B method which supports our developments and validation by proof, and the second is the technique of

EXPRESS data modeling used as a support of the definition of the animator of event B models and thus of validation by animation. For each technique, only the major elements needed to understand this article are given.

2.1 Event B Method

Let us briefly describe the B formal method [1,2] in its event version. A model is defined as a set of variables, defined in the **VARIABLES**, clause that evolve thanks to events defined in the **EVENTS** clause. The notion of Event B model encodes a state transition system where the variables represent the state and the events represent the transitions from one state to another. Moreover, the refinement capability offered by Event B allows to decompose a model (thus a transition system) into another transition system with more and more design decisions moving from an abstract level to a less abstract one. Refinement technique allows to preserve the proved properties and therefore it is not necessary to prove them again in the refined transition system (which is usually more complex). The structure of an Event B model is given on figure 1.

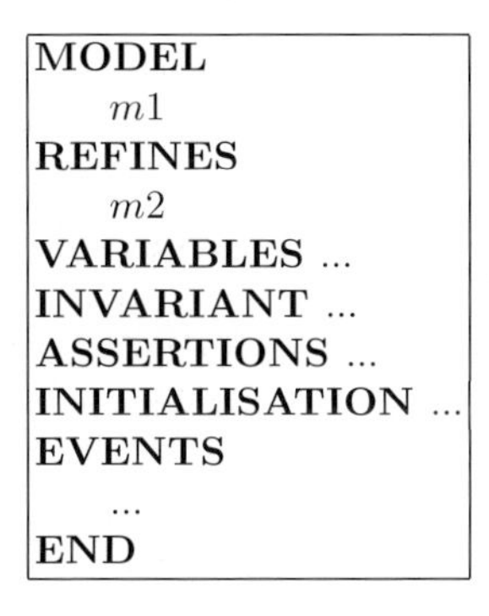

Fig. 1. The structure of an Event B model

A model *m1* is defined by a set of clauses. It may refine another model *m2*. Briefly, the clauses mean:

- **VARIABLES** clause represents the variables of the model of the specification. Refinement may introduce new variables in order to enrich the described system.
- **INVARIANT** clause describes, thanks to first order logic expressions, the properties of the attributes defined in the clause **VARIABLES**. Typing information and safety properties are described in this clause. These properties shall remain true in the whole model and in further refinements. Invariants need to be preserved by the initialisation and events clauses.
- **ASSERTIONS** are logical expressions that can be proved from the invariants. They do not need to be proved for each event like for the invariant. Usually, they contain properties expressing that there is no deadlock no live lock.

- **INITIALISATION** clause allows to give initial values to the variables of the corresponding clause. They define the initial states of the underlying transition system.
- **EVENTS** clause defines all the events that may occur in a given model. Each event is described by a body thanks to generalized substitutions defined below. Each event is characterized by its guard (i.e. a first order logic expression involving variables). An event is fired when its guard evaluates to true.

The semantics of the effect of the initialisation and the events occurring in a B model on states so described thanks to generalized substitutions. Generalized substitutions are based on the weakest precondition calculus of Dijkstra [7]. Formally, several substitutions are defined in B. If we consider a substitution S and a predicate P representing a post-condition, then *[S]P* represents the weakest precondition that establishes P after execution of S. The substitutions occurring in Event B models are inductively defined by the following expressions [1,2] :

$$[\textbf{SKIP}]\, P \Leftrightarrow P \tag{1}$$

$$[S_1 \,||\, S_2]\, P \Leftrightarrow [S_1]\, P \wedge [S_2]\, P \tag{2}$$

$$[\textbf{ANY}\ v\ \textbf{WHERE}\ G\ \textbf{THEN}\ S\ \textbf{END}]\, P \Leftrightarrow \forall v (G \Rightarrow [S]\, P) \tag{3}$$

$$[\textbf{SELECT}\ G\ \textbf{THEN}\ S\ \textbf{END}]\, P \Leftrightarrow G \Rightarrow [S] P \tag{4}$$

$$[\textbf{BEGIN}\ S\ \textbf{END}]\, P \Leftrightarrow [S]\, P \tag{5}$$

$$[x := E]\, P \Leftrightarrow P(x/E) \tag{6}$$

P(x/E) represents the predicate P where all the free occurrences of x are replaced by the expression E.

Substitutions 1, 2, 5 and 6 represent respectively the empty statement, the parallel substitution expressing that *S1* and *S2* are performed in parallel, the block substitution and the affectation. Substitutions 3 and 4 are the guarded substitutions where S is performed under the guard G.

In all the previous substitutions, the predicate G represents a guard. Each event guarded by a guard G is fired if the guard is true and when it is fired, the post-condition P is established (feasibility of an event). The guards define the feasibility conditions given by the *Fis* predicate defined in [1].

Semantics of Event B Models. The events of a model are atomic events. The associated semantics is an interleaving semantics. Therefore, the semantics of an Event B model is trace based semantics with interleaving. A system is characterized by the set of licit traces corresponding to the fired events of the model which respects the described properties. The traces define a sequence of states that may be observed by properties. All the properties will be expressed on these traces.

This approach has proved to be able to represent event based systems like interactive systems. Moreover, decomposition (thanks to refinement) allows building of complex systems gradually in an incremental manner by preserving the initial properties thanks to the gluing invariant preservation.

Refinement of Event B Models. Each Event B model can be refined. A refined model is defined by adding new events, new variables and a gluing invariant. Each event of the abstract model is refined in the concrete model by adding new information by expressing how the new set of variables and the new events evolve. All the new events appearing in the refinement refine the *skip* event of the refined model. Each new event corresponds to an $\epsilon - transition$ in the abstract model.

The gluing invariant ensures that the properties expressed and proved at the abstract level (in the **ASSERTIONS** and **INVARIANTS** clauses) are preserved in the concrete level. Moreover, **INVARIANT, ASSERTIONS** and **VARIANT** clauses allow to express deadlock and live lock freeness.

1. They shall express that the new events of the concrete model are not fired infinitely (no live lock). *A decreasing variant is introduced for this purpose.*
2. They shall express that at any time an event can be fired (no deadlock). *This property is ensured by asserting (in the* ***ASSERTIONS*** *clause) that the disjunction of all the abstract events guards implies the disjunction of all the concrete events guards.*

A Simple Example. Let us consider on the figure 2.a, the specifications of the clock example [8]. The abstract specification *Clock* uses one variable h describing the hours of the clock. Two events are described. The first (*incr* event) allows to increment the hour variable. The second event is the *zero* event. It is fired when $h = 23$ to initialize the hour variable.

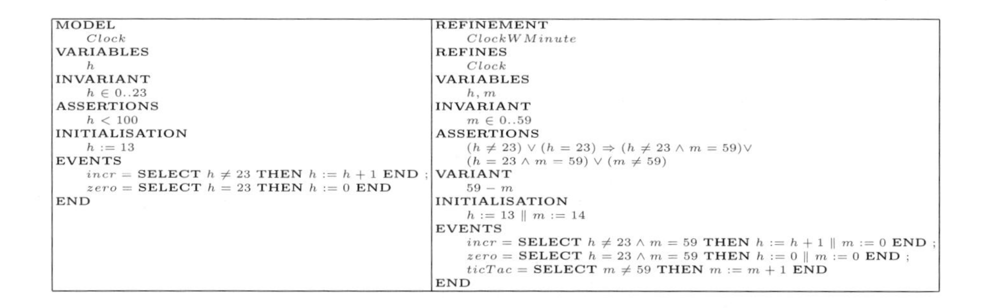

Fig. 2. (a) Example of a B event model. (b) Example of a B event refinement.

In the refinement specification *ClockWMinute* (figure 2.b), we introduce a new variable m and a new event *ticTac*. We enhance the guards of the *incr* and *zero* events in introducing the description of minutes. **ASSERTIONS** clause allows to ensure that the new events of the description system can be fired.

2.2 The EXPRESS Data Modeling Language

EXPRESS [4,5] is an object oriented data modeling language, normalised as ISO 10303-11. It was originally defined to represent data models in the engineering area and it is now widely used in several other data modeling domains. The major advantage of this language is its capability to describe structural, descriptive and procedural concepts in a common data model and semantics. This integration avoids the use of several models and languages that require bridging over the gap between all the defined models (like in UML). A data model in EXPRESS is represented by a set of schemas that may refer to each other. Each schema contains two parts. The first part is a set of entities that are structured in an object oriented approach (supporting multiple inheritance). The second part contains procedures, functions and global rules used to express constraints.

Entity definition. Entities are named and defined by a set of attributes (may be an empty set) assigned to each entity. Each attribute has a domain (where it takes its values) defining a data type. It can be either a simple domain (integer, string ...) or a structured domain (lists, sets, bags ... hard encoded in EXPRESS) or an entity type meaning that an attribute is of type another entity.

Figure 3.a shows the entity *B* with three attributes: a real, a list of strings and a relation with another entity *A* which has only one integer attribute. *att_I* is an inverse attribute of entity *A*, corresponding to the inverse link defined by attribute *att_3* in entity *B*.

Entities may have instances. Each entity has an identifier. The attribute values are either literal values of the EXPRESS simple or structured built-in types or they are references to other entity instances. An example of a model extension associated to the previous entity definitions is shown (figure 3.b). The #2 instance of the entity *B*, where *att_1* evaluates to 4.0, *att_2* is the list ('*hello*', '*bye*') and *att_3* points the particular instance #1 of the entity A where its *att_A* attribute evaluates to 3.

(a)	(b)

SCHEMA *Foo1*;
 	
ENTITY *A*;
    att_A : *INTEGER*;
INVERSE
    att_I : *B* FOR *att_3*;
END_ENTITY;
 	
ENTITY *B*;
    att_1 : *REAL*;
    att_2 : *LIST* [0 :?] *OF STRING*;
    att_3 : *A*;
END_ENTITY;
 	
END_SCHEMA;
	# 1=A(3);
	# 2=B(4.0, ('hello','bye'), #1);

Fig. 3. (a) Entity definition. (b) Entity instance.

Multiple inheritance. Inheritance (single and multiple) is introduced by the **SUPERTYPE** and **SUBTYPE** EXPRESS keywords. The **SUBTYPE** clause occurring in an entity *E* is followed by the enumeration of the set of entity names representing the superclasses of *E*.

Constraining entities. It is possible to limit the allowed set of instances of the data models to those instances that satisfy some stated constraints. EXPRESS uses first order logic which is completely decidable since the set of instances is finite. Constraints are introduced thanks to the **WHERE** clause that provides for instance invariant, and to the global **RULE** clause that provides for model invariant.

Let us assume that the allowed values for *att_A* in *A* are [1..10] and that exactly only two instances of entity A shall have an attribute value equals to 1.

These constraints are respectively described by the *wr1* local rule in entity *A* and by the *Card* global rule both defined on figure (4.a). **SELF** plays the same role as *this* in the C++ or Java Languages.

Derivations and constraints are the only places where functions may occur. They are inherited. Set inclusion defines the semantics of the EXPRESS inheritance mechanism.

```
ENTITY A;
    att_A : INTEGER;
  WHERE
    wr1 : (SELF.att_A >= 1)
  AND
    (SELF.att_A <= 10);
END_ENTITY;
```

```
RULE Card FOR A;
  WHERE
    SIZEOF(QUERY(inst <* A|
    (inst.att_A = 1))) = 2;
END_RULE;
```

```
FUNCTION F (x : typ_1; y : typ_2) : typ_3;
    (*Function_Body; *)
END_FUNCTION;
```

Fig. 4. (a) EXPRESS local and global constraints. (b) EXPRESS function declaration.

Functions and procedures. Functions can be used to associate rules to data. These rules may be either derivation or (local or global) constraints. Figure (4.b) shows the function declaration in EXPRESS. This declaration introduces a function interface with two parameters (x and y) of types *typ_1* and *typ_2* respectively. The result is of type *typ_3*. *Function_Body* represents the body of the defined function. Assignment, sequence and control structures (if statements, loops and recursion) may be used in the function body. These features give the same expression possibilities as other recursive specification languages.

2.3 Graphical Representation

To help a user in understanding EXPRESS data models, the EXPRESS-G graphical representation has been defined. It represents the structural and descriptive constructs of the EXPRESS language (classes and attributes) but the procedural constructs (derivation and rules) are not represented. The example of figure 5

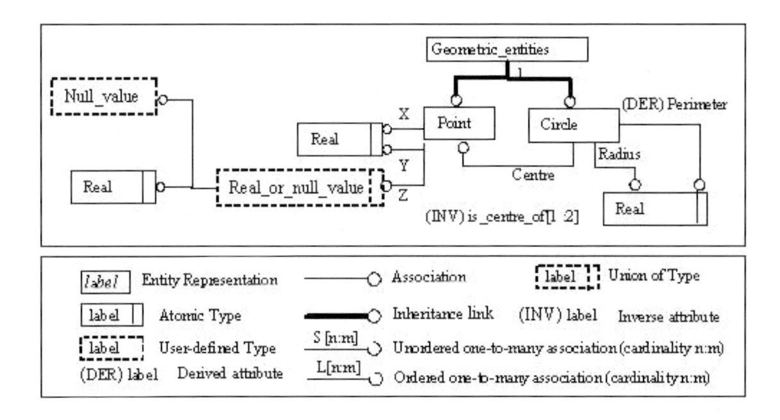

Fig. 5. EXPRESS-G representation of geometric entities

illustrates an EXPRESS-G representation of a simple data model related to geometrical entities.

In this example *geometric_entity* can be either a *circle* or a *point*. A *circle* has a *center* and a *radius*, and a derived attribute perimeter. A *point* has coordinates *X, Y, Z* but *Z* may have either a real value or a null value introduced by the **SELECT** (sum of types) type *real_or_null_value*. Finally in this model, a *point* can be the *center* of two *circles* at the maximum. This is specified by the inverse attribute *is_center_of*.

We described above the concepts necessary for understanding the remainder of this paper. For more information on the EXPRESS language, the reader may consult [4,5].

3 Validation by Animation

This section addresses the animation of event B models. Based on a model transformation, we have built the B2EXPRESS animator. It allows a developer to validate the behavior of an event B model through the expression of scenarios encoded by event traces.

3.1 From Event B Models to EXPRESS Data Models

The proposed transformation from B to EXPRESS starts from the observation that an event B model can be seen as a transition system. So, we consider that animating an event B model consists in traversing the underlying transition system and building traces. Therefore, as a first step, we have defined an EXPRESS meta-model for:

- transition systems with states and guarded transitions;
- describing the traces that result from the traversal of this transition system.

This model defines a set of generic resources shared by every event B model. Each translated event B model into an EXPRESS data model subtypes these generic resources for each particular B model. This process is detailed below.

Transition Systems Meta-Model. The transition systems meta-model of figure (6.a) is composed of :

- states described by the STATE entity with no attributes;
- transitions of the TRANSITION entity with two attributes of STATE type. They represent the source (*DepState*) and target (*ArrState*) states of this transition;
- an initial state of the system described in the BEGIN entity by the *InitState* attribute.

The abstract entity EVENTS is introduced to gather events. It is abstract and thus does not have instances.

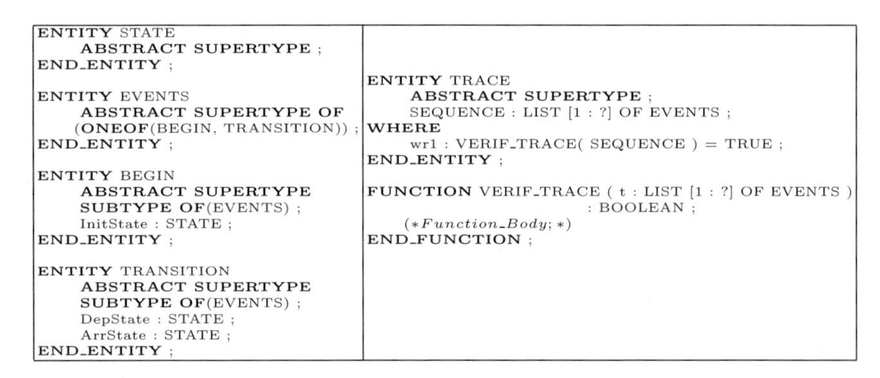

```
ENTITY STATE
    ABSTRACT SUPERTYPE ;
END_ENTITY ;

ENTITY EVENTS
    ABSTRACT SUPERTYPE OF
   (ONEOF(BEGIN, TRANSITION)) ;
END_ENTITY ;

ENTITY BEGIN
    ABSTRACT SUPERTYPE
    SUBTYPE OF(EVENTS) ;
    InitState : STATE ;
END_ENTITY ;

ENTITY TRANSITION
    ABSTRACT SUPERTYPE
    SUBTYPE OF(EVENTS) ;
    DepState : STATE ;
    ArrState : STATE ;
END_ENTITY ;
```

```
ENTITY TRACE
    ABSTRACT SUPERTYPE ;
    SEQUENCE : LIST [1 : ?] OF EVENTS ;
WHERE
    wr1 : VERIF_TRACE( SEQUENCE ) = TRUE ;
END_ENTITY ;

FUNCTION VERIF_TRACE ( t : LIST [1 : ?] OF EVENTS )
                        : BOOLEAN ;
  (*Function_Body; *)
END_FUNCTION ;
```

Fig. 6. (a) EXPRESS transition systems meta-model. (b) EXPRESS traces meta model.

The Meta Model of Traces. In order to support animation, the previous schema is enriched by the TRACE EXPRESS entity containing the animation sequence represented by an ordered list of transitions. It represents one possible sequence of interleaved events. A local constraint (**WHERE** rule *wr1* on figure (6.b)) ensures that, for each sequence, for two consecutive transitions T_i and T_{i+1}, the target state of T_i is the source state of T_{i+1}. This constraint also checks that the sequence starts from the initial state.

Transformation of an Event B Model into an EXPRESS Transition System. Once the generic resources are defined, we are able to describe the transformation rules from B to EXPRESS. These rules are defined on the structure of event B models. The transformation process is inductively defined on the structure of the B models. It is based on the following rules defined for the representation of the:

- **a-** state variables of the B model (**VARIABLES** clause) by new attributes in a new EXPRESS entity that subtypes the entity *STATE* of the transitions systems meta-model. The B invariant is examined and analysed in order to type these attributes;
- **b-** logical properties expressed in the **INVARIANT** and **ASSERTIONS** clauses by global EXPRESS rules (**RULE**) defined on the *STATE* entity;
- **c-** **INITIALISATION** clause by an entity inherited from the BEGIN of the transitions system meta-model;
- **d-** events in the B clause **EVENTS** by entities inherited from the EXPRESS entity TRANSITION of the transitions systems meta-model.

Next, we show how these rules are formally defined.

a- The VARIABLES clause and the typing part of the INVARIANT. State variables are issued from the **VARIABLES** clause and their type from the **INVARIANT** clause. Each variable is represented by an attribute of the same name typed by an EXPRESS type. The attributes are defined in the VARIABLES EXPRESS entity inherited from STATE entity (see figure 7 for an example).

```
VARIABLES
      Var1,
      Var2,
...
INVARIANT
      Var1 ∈ INTEGER ∧
      Var2 ∈ BOOL ∧
...
```

```
ENTITY VARIABLES
      SUBTYPE OF (STATE);
      Var1 : INTEGER;
      Var2 : BOOLEAN;
...
END_ENTITY;
```

Fig. 7. Example of processing the VARIABLES clause and the typing part of the INVARIANT

b- The INVARIANT and ASSERTIONS event B clauses. First the invariant is re-written in a conjunctive normal form. This form allows the animator to check precisely the parts of the invariant or assertion that are violated and thus to localize potential errors precisely in the invariant or assertion. The variables typing expressions are not taken into account here, they are already processed when declaring the state.

Each logical sub-expression of the invariant is transformated into global EXPRESS **RULE** (see figure 8 for an example). The EXPRESS iterator **QUERY**$(x < *E|P(x))$ returning the bag of instances x of E satisfying the predicate $P(x)$ is used.

```
INVARIANT
      Var1 ∈ {0,1} ∧
      Var1 ≠ Var3 ∧
...
```

```
RULE INVARIANT01 FOR (VARIABLES) ;
WHERE
      QUERY (x < * VARIABLES |
      NOT (x.Var1 IN [0,1]) ) = [] ;
END_RULE ;

RULE INVARIANT02 FOR (VARIABLES) ;
WHERE
      QUERY (x < * VARIABLES |
      NOT (x.Var1 <> x.Var3) ) = [] ;
END_RULE ;
...
```

Fig. 8. Example of a transformation of the INVARIANT clause

c- The INITIALISATION event B clause. An INITIALISATION entity is derived from the transitions system meta-model by subtyping the entity BEGIN. Each substitution of the event B **INITIALISATION** clause is encoded by a local constraint (**WHERE** clause in an entity) on the *InitState* attribute of the INITIALISATION entity. This constraint expresses the attributes values obtained after applying the different substitutions (figure 9).

```
INITIALISATION
      Var1 := 1 ||
      Var2 := TRUE ||
...
```

```
ENTITY INITIALISATION
SUBTYPE OF (BEGIN) ;
WHERE
(InitState.Var1 = 0) AND
(InitState.Var2 = TRUE) AND
...
END_ENTITY ;
```

Fig. 9. Example of a transformation of the INITIALISATION event B clause

d- The EVENTS event B clause. Each event of the **EVENTS** event B clause is transformed into an entity subtyping the entity TRANSITION of the transitions systems meta-model. The *DepState* and *ArrState* are inherited. The guard and the substitutions of the body of each event are translated into local constraints attached to the transitions.

Event B	EXPRESS
Event1 = SELECT Var1 = 1 THEN Var1 := 0 END ;	ENTITY Event1 SUBTYPE OF (TRANSITION) ; WHERE Guard : DepState.Var1 = 1 ; Sub : ArrState.Var1 = 0 ; Const : ArrState.Var2 = DepState.Var2 ; END_ENTITY ;

Fig. 10. Example of a transformation of the EVENTS event B clause

The guard is associated to the transition source state (*DepState*) and the substitutions of the body of the event are associated to the transition target state (*ArrState*). Finally, additional constraints guarantee that the state variables that have not been affected by the event substitutions remain the same in the *ArrState*. Figure 10 shows an example of a simple event transformation.

At this level, we have defined the transformation rules for the elements of B which have their corresponding EXPRESS constructs defined in the EXPRESS language, such as simple types (INTEGER, BOOLEAN, NATURAL) and the basic operation like the assignment, arithmetic and logical operations.

In parallel to the translation of a B model to an EXPRESS data model, Java classes used to browse and to instantiate the EXPRESS data model are generated. These classes are used by the B2EXPRESS tool, described in section 5, to instantiate the EXPRESS data model in order to animate the translated B model. The generated Java classes can be seen as an implementation of the given B model, so, this approach can also be used as a Java code generator for B models. The principle of generating such classes is not addressed in this paper.

3.2 An Example

We discuss an example of an intermediate B refinement *Ref_1*(see figure 11). It consists of querying a database system by giving the name and address of a person. The system retrieves from the database the results of the query. The *Query* event defines different manners of querying the system. It is decomposed to take into account different interaction possibilities of entering name and address. Name and address input events are interleaving events. Finally, the *Search* event retrieves from a database the results of the query and the *ResultQuery* is devoted to display the result to the user. This interacting scenario is described by the expression:

"$Query = (InputName^{*}||InputAddress^{*}); Search; ResultQuery$"
where $*$ is the iteration, ; indicates the sequence and $||$ defines the interleaving operator. The *Query* event is encoded in the refinement *Ref_1* of figure 11.

REFINEMENT Ref_1 ... **SETS** $string$ **VARIABLES** $querySending, ev1, nn, na,$ $name, address$ **INVARIANT** $ev1 \in 0..3 \wedge nn \in \mathbb{N} \wedge na \in \mathbb{N} \wedge$ $name \in string \wedge$ $address \in string \wedge$ $querySending \in \{0, 1\} \wedge$ $(querySending = 1 \Leftrightarrow ev1 \neq 0)$ ... **INITIALISATION** $querySending := 0 \parallel$ $nn, na := 1, 1 \parallel$ $ev1 := 3 \parallel$ $name, address :\in string, string$ **EVENTS** $NameAddress =$ **SELECT** $EV1 = 3$ **THEN** $ev1 := ev1 - 1 \parallel nn :\in \mathbb{N} \parallel na :\in \mathbb{N}$ **END** ;	$InputName =$ **SELECT** $ev1 = 2 \wedge nn \neq 0$ **THEN** $nn := nn - 1 \parallel name :\in string$ **END** ; $InputAddress =$ **SELECT** $ev1 = 2 \wedge na \neq 0$ **THEN** $na := na - 1 \parallel address :\in string \wedge$ **END** ; $Search =$ **SELECT** $ev1 = 2 \wedge nn = 0 \wedge na = 0$ **THEN** $ev1 := 1$ **END** ; $Query =$ **SELECT** $ev1 = 1$ **THEN** $querySending, ev1 := 1, 0$ **END**; $ResultQuery = ...$ **END**

Fig. 11. Example of an event B model

The *name* and *address* variables of *string* type define the values of the name and of the address. The *nn* and *na* integer variables indicate the arbitrary numbers of iterations (corresponding to $*$). They are initialized in the *NameAddress* event. Finally, the *ev1* variable (decreasing integer variable) initialized to three is a variant that describes the sequence order of events trigging.

The **EVENTS** clause on Figure 11 describes the events of *Ref_1* refinement. The *NameAddress* event initializes the *nn* and *na* iterator whereas *InputName*, *InputAddress* and *Search* events decompose (refine) the *Query* abstract event. When these three events are triggered ($ev1 = 0$), they return the control to the *Query* abstract event which ends the sequence.

The application of the transformation rules of section 3.1 to the B model of figure 11 leads to the EXPRESS code presented in figure 12. The state variables are represented by a set of attributes in the VARIABLES entity. The invariant is described in a conjunctive normal form and contains two subexpressions represented in the global rules INVARIANT_0 and INVARIANT_1. The **INITIALISATION** clause is encoded in the INITIALISATION entity. The substitutions of this clause are defined by a local constraint, *INIT* on the *InitState* attribute, expressing the values affected to the state variables (e.g. $querySending := 1$ becomes $InitState.querySending = 1$). The event *NameAddress* is encoded by the entity NameAddress inherited from TRANSITION. The event guard is represented by the local constraint *GUARD* (where $ev1 = 3$ becomes $DepState.ev1 = 3$). Similarly, the substitution are encoded by the *SUB* local constraint (e.g. $ev1 := ev1 - 1$ becomes $ArrState.ev1 = DepState.ev1 - 1$). The unchanged variables remain unchanged from *DepState* to *ArrState*. It is expressed by the local constraints $(cst1, .., cst4)$. The other events have not been introduced to keep this paper in a reasonable length.

The EXPRESS models are checked by providing a set of instances. The consistency of this set is ensured by data type, unicity, local and global constraints. The checking ECCO Toolkit tool [9] supports such checks and provides a Java

```
ENTITY VARIABLES
    SUBTYPE OF (STATE) ;
    querySending : INTEGER;
    ev1 : INTEGER;
    nn : INTEGER;
    na : INTEGER;
    adress : STRING;
    name : STRING;
END_ENTITY ;

RULE INVARIANT_0 FOR (VARIABLES) ;
    WHERE
    QUERY(s < *VARIABLES|TRUE) =
    QUERY(s < *VARIABLES|
       (s.ev1 >= 0) AND (s.ev1 <= 3));
END_RULE ;

RULE INVARIANT_1 FOR (VARIABLES) ;
    WHERE
    QUERY(s < *VARIABLES|TRUE) =
    QUERY(s < *VARIABLES|
       ((s.querySending = 1) AND (s.ev1 <> 0))
       OR NOT(((s.querySending = 1) AND (s.ev1 <> 0))));
END_RULE ;
```

```
ENTITY INITIALISATION
    SUBTYPE OF (BEGIN);
    WHERE
    INIT : (InitState.QuerySending = 1) AND
    ('STRING' IN TYPEOF(InitState.name) ) AND
    ('STRING' IN TYPEOF(InitState.adress) ) AND
    (InitState.nn = 1) AND
    (InitState.na = 1) AND
    (InitState.ev1 = 3);
END_ENTITY;

ENTITY NameAddress
    SUBTYPE OF (TRANSITION);
    WHERE
    GUARD : (DepState.ev1 = 3);
    SUB : (ArrState.ev1 = DepState.ev1 − 1) AND
    ('INTEGER' IN TYPEOF(ArrState.nn) ) AND
    ('INTEGER' IN TYPEOF(ArrState.na) );
    cst1 : ArrState.name = DepState.name;
    ...
    cst4 : ArrState.address = DepState.address;
END_ENTITY ;
...
```

Fig. 12. Translation of a B model in Figure 11 into an EXPRESS model

```
DATA;
#1=VARIABLES(0,3,1,1,.NULL.,.NULL.);
#2=VARIABLES(0,2,2,1,.NULL.,.NULL.);
#3=VARIABLES(0,2,1,1,.NULL.,.DAVID.);
#4=VARIABLES(0,2,0,1,.NULL.,.LIONEL.);
#5=VARIABLES(0,2,0,0,.RENNES.,.LIONEL.);
#6=VARIABLES(0,1,0,0,.RENNES.,.LIONEL.);
#7=VARIABLES(1,0,0,0,.RENNES.,.LIONEL.);
#8=VARIABLES(0,3,1,1,.NULL.,.NULL.);
#19=INITIALISATION(#1);
#20=NAMEADDRESS(#1,#2);
#21=INPUTNAME(#2,#3);
#22=INPUTNAME(#3,#4);
#23=INPUTADDRESS(#4,#5);
#24=SEARCH(#5,#6);
#25=RESULTQUERY(#6,#7);
#26=QUERY(#7,#8);
#37=VAL_TRACE((#19,#20,#21,#22,#23,#24,#25,#26))
ENDSEC;
```

Fig. 13. Instances corresponding to the EXPRESS model of figure 12

interface allowing to exploit the EXPRESS models and the instances of these models.

Figure 13 shows a set of instances corresponding to the EXPRESS model of figure 12. We observe that:

- there are 8 states identified by the instances #1 to #8 and 8 events have been triggered;
- initialisation is defined by instance #19;
- the events leading from state #1 to state #8 are given by instances #19 to #26. They correspond to the defined test sequence;
- the trace is described by the instance #37 which defines the sequence in the order of execution.

4 Processing Higher Order Objects

The transformation process we described above is based on the transitions systems meta-model and on the EXPRESS language capabilities. However, some B constructs do not have their corresponding EXPRESS construction (e.g. a function, an injective function, a domain restriction etc.) and higher order objects cannot be manipulated in the EXPRESS language. In this case, like for transition systems, it is required to define a meta-model for higher order objects. Instead of describing the whole proposed meta-model, we show how a function is defined from a relation. Figure 14 shows the EXPRESS-G model associated

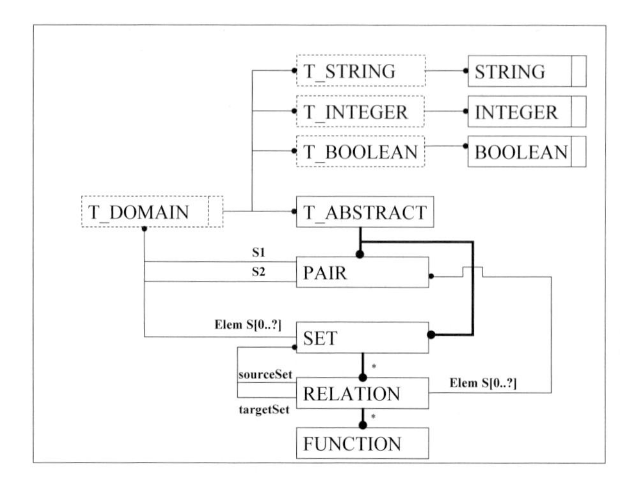

Fig. 14. EXPRESS-G representation of higher order objects meta-model

to this description corresponding to the EXPRESS meta model we have written to describe such objects.

The data type domain is extended to contain any abstract data type (T_ABSTRACT) more the ones available in EXPRESS (integer, boolean, string). From the T_ABSTRACT type, we introduce, by subtyping the notions of set and pairs. These notions are themselves used to describe relations (a set of pairs in the *Elem* attribute) and functions as specialised relations. The whole B constructs have been modeled using this approach.

5 The B2EXPRESS Tool

The B2EXPRESS tool implements the previously described transformation process. It takes the event B model as input and generates the corresponding EXPRESS model. It offers several options and opportunities to animate the event B models based on the EXPRESS obtained model. Animation consists in instantiating the different entities of the obtained EXPRESS model which is hidden to the user.

This section describes the various possibilities offered by B2EXPRESS for animating event B models.

5.1 Triggering Events

Events are triggered on the graphical user interface (see figure 15) by mouse clicks. Figure 15 shows the list of events in ①, the state variables and their current values in ②, the trace of events in ④ and the potential error messages in ⑤. In the case of an **ANY** substitution, a dialog box appears, it asks for potential values for the local variables introduced by this substitution.

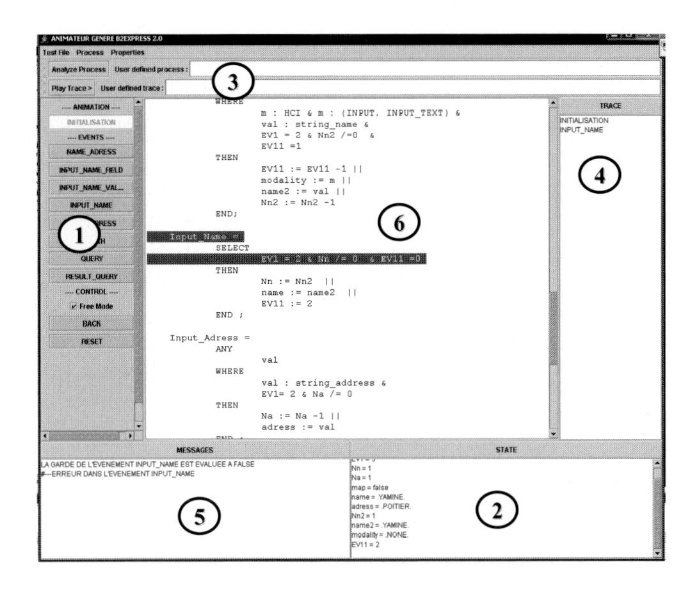

Fig. 15. B2EXPRESS interface

Each time an event is triggered, B2EXPRESS produces instances of the corresponding EXPRESS schema. B2EXPRESS, using the ECCO API [9], checks if the instances are correct and fulfill all the local and global EXPRESS constraints. Error messages (deadlock, invariant violation, ...) are returned and spied by B2EXPRESS in order to localise the errors on the source event B code (⑥ on figure 15).

In order to offer various validation possibilities, two animation modes are offered by B2EXPRESS:

– *the guarded mode* where only those events, whose guard evaluates to true, can be triggered. They are in green color (① on figure 15) and those that cannot be triggered are in red.
– *the free mode*, which leaves freedom to the user to trigger any event even if its guard evaluates to false. This mode is useful when a developer wants to check invariants, to detect deadlocks or to check if some suitable behaviors are excluded from the model.

In addition to the different invariants and assertions, the event B model traces can be controlled by a process algebra expression (with interleaving semantics) to define the behavior expected for this model (③ on figure 15). For example, we define for the model in Figure 11, the following behavior: *"NameAddress ; InputName ; InputAddress ; Search ; ResultQuery ; Query"* (";" indicates the sequence). Thus, if the event *InputAdress* is triggered before *InputName*, an error will be detected. This possibility allows a developer to validate requirements expressed by either suited or unsuited behaviors.

5.2 Tracing Process Algebra Expressions

B2EXPRESS offers the possibility to instantiate EXPRESS entities by triggering events corresponding to traces of a process algebra expressions with interleaving semantics. The suited event B model traces may be defined by the user (③ on figure 15). For example, we define for the model in Figure 11, the following expression : *"NameAddress ; (InputName || InputAddress) ; Search ; ResultQuery ; Query"* (";" indicates the sequence and "||" defines the interleaving operator). From this expression, B2EXPRESS generates EXPRESS entity instances corresponding to the two possible sequences *"NameAddress ; InputName ; InputAddress ; Search ; ResultQuery ; Query"* and *"NameAddress ; InputAddress ; InputName ; Search ; ResultQuery ; Query"*. This possibility allows a developer to validate requirements expressed by behaviors.

5.3 B2EXPRESS as a Monitoring System

B2EXPRESS accepts an input set of EXPRESS instances. These instances may be generated by an external running application for which we want to validate properties. When this application runs, it generates instances corresponding to the various EXPRESS entities. B2EXPRESS reads these instances and verifies whether they preserve the consistency of the event B models corresponding to the specification of the application. In this case, B2EXPRESS can be used as a monitoring system where B models are used to monitor the application they specify.

In the context of the VERBATIM project, this option has been used to check different properties of running multimodal user interfaces (CARE properties [10]). The *InputName* event, described in figure 11, is refined by two events *InputNameByVoice* and *InputNameByKeyBoard* to take into account voice and keyboard modalities available in the application that describes this model [11].For example, when the user has used the voice and the keyboard at the same time to enter the name, the application has generated instances of EXPRESS entities corresponding to this scenarios *"NameAddress ; **InputNameByVoice ; InputNameByKeyBoard** ; InputName ; InputAddress"*. We have been able to check the *redundancy* property [10].

This possibility allows a developer to monitor a running application and to a posteriori check relevant properties available in B models and absent from the running application code.

6 Comparison with Related Work

Traditionally, the tools associated with the B method are AtelierB [12], B ToolKit [13] and more recently the Rodin platform [14]. These tools support representation of B models, generation of proof obligations and a theorem prover to discharge them. In order to equip proof based developments with validation and animation techniques, several approaches have emerged and the recent years have seen the birth of two main B animators : ProB [3] and Brama [6].

The ProB animator is based on the model checking technique. To perform the model checking procedure, abstract sets of B are valued by small finite sets and integer variables are associated with intervals of integers. A transition system is built from the B model to be animated.

Sequences of events, violating the invariant, are produced by exploration of the states of the model, and visualized when the model is incoherent. This exploration is driven by the properties of the invariant. Moreover, ProB allows the user to visualize the state of the model (all variables of the clause **VARIABLES**) and evaluates the invariant at each step. The user can also limit the number of the explored states.

Brama is the other animator we have studied. It is developed by ClearSY. It allows a developer to realize graphical animations representing the transition system associated with a B model. The animation can be viewed on the states of the graph. The animation, visualized on the graphical representation is linked to various events and variables of the B model.

The B2EXPRESS animator, we have developed, consists in producing an EXPRESS data model whose instances describe traces of events of the B model. The EXPRESS models are checked by providing a set of instances. The consistency of this set is checked by controlling the types of data, the unicity, local and global constraints. The ECCO Toolkit tool [9] supports such checking and provides a Java interface allowing to exploit the EXPRESS models and the instances of these models.

Compared to other tools, B2EXPRESS offers the ability to run scenarios not conform to the model and makes it possible to locate the nature of the error caused by these scenarios, thanks to free mode (section 5).

To manage the indeterminism, ProB proposes small finite sets whereas B2EXPRESS offers to the user the possibility to introduce the desired value. The ProB approach is powerful and provides with an efficient model checking. The B2EXPRESS tool does not offer automatic state exploration but it allows to choosing any specific input value.

In addition, B2EXPRESS accepts an input set of EXPRESS instances that can be issued from an external running application. In this case, B2EXPRESS can be used as a monitoring system. It also offers the possibility of introducing a process algebra expression that allows to expressing a desired behavior. When the trace of triggered events is not conform to the described expression, then the tool signals it. This last validation is useful to check if the user requirements expressed as scenarios are supported by the written B model. This last capability was at the origin of this approach, because we have been applying B for validating Human Computer Interfaces where these scenarios are frequently defined as preliminary specifications.

7 Conclusion: Combining Proof and Animation

Originally, the event B method has been defined to describe a stepwise refinement. The development is a sequence of event B models linked by a refinement relation. The method relies on the proof of a set of generated proof obligations to ensure the models and refinement correctness. When these proof obligations are proved, the development is said to be correct.

However, the event B method does not support animation. Animation is used to check some user requirements expressed by scenarios. The animation can play these scenarios and decide whether the event B model satisfies the user requirements.

Moreover, it may happen that the written event B models are difficult to prove because of complex proof obligations, missing of guard strengthening, incomplete invariants and so on. In this case, the developer is not aware about the source of this problem. Animation provides the developer with some help in designing their event B models and conducting their proof process. The developer can animate his models and check whether the invariant, or the guards are correct by giving some input values to the animator. He also can write observers for the proof obligations he considers as difficult to prove. Proceeding this way in a development, process shows the possibility to combine both animation and proof. The first helps the second. As shown in this paper B2EXPRESS also offers the possibility to define traces of events that can be defined, at the requirement level, for validating the model and constraining the behavior.

As further work, we plan to equip B2EXPRESS with animation of temporal logic properties verification. Since we have explicitly shown the event traces. The idea to follow is close to the one of Lustre where traces are flows of data.

Finally, the reader may refer to *"http://www.lisi.ensma.fr/members/idir/"* for some videos running the B2EXPRESS tool.

References

1. Abrial, J.: The B Book. Assigning Programs to Meanings. Cambridge University Press, Cambridge (1996)
2. Abrial, J.R.: Extending b without changing it (for developing distributed systems). In: Habrias, H. (ed.) First B Conference, Putting Into Pratice Methods and Tools for Information System Design, Nantes, France, p. 21 (1996)
3. Leuschel, M., Butler, M.: ProB: A model checker for B. In: Araki, K., Gnesi, S., Mandrioli, D. (eds.) FME 2003. LNCS, vol. 2805, pp. 855–874. Springer, Heidelberg (2003)
4. IS010303.02: Product data representation and exchange - part 2: Express reference manual. ISO (055) (1994)
5. Schenck, D., Wilson, P.: Information Modelling The EXPRESS Way. Oxford University Press, Oxford (1994)
6. ClearSy: BRAMA, un nouvel outil d'animation graphique de modèles B. ClearSy - Conférence B (2007)
7. Dijkstra, E.: A Discipline of Programming. Prentice-Hall, Englewood Cliffs (1976)
8. Cansell, D.: Assistance au développement incrémental et à sa preuve. Habilitation à diriger les recherches, Université Henri Poincaré (2003)
9. Staub, G., Maier, M.: ECCO Tool-Kit, An Environnement for the Evaluation of EXPRESS Models and the Development of STEP based IT Applications. User Manual (1997)

10. Coutaz, J., Nigay, L., Salber, D., Blandford, A., May, J., Young, R.: Four easy pieces for assessing the usability of multimodal interaction: the CARE properties. In: Proceedings of Human Computer Interaction - Interact 1995, pp. 115–120. Chapman and Hall, Boca Raton (1995)
11. Ait-Ameur, Y., Ait-Sadoune, I., Baron, M., Mota, J.: Validation et vérification formelles de systèmes interactifs multimodaux fondées sur la preuve. In: 18 Conférence Francophone sur l'Interaction Homme-Machine (IHM 2006), Montréal, Canada, vol. 1, pp. 123–130. ACM Press, New York (2006)
12. ClearSy: Atelier B - version 3.5 (1997)
13. Limited, B.C.U.: B-toolkit, `http://www.b-core.com`
14. ClearSy: Rodin (2006), `http://www.clearsy.com/rodin/industry_day.html`

Automated Formal Testing of C API Using T2C Framework

Alexey V. Khoroshilov, Vladimir V. Rubanov, and Eugene A. Shatokhin

Institute for System Programming of Russian Academy of Sciences (ISPRAS),
B. Communisticheskaya, 25, Moscow, Russia
{khoroshilov,vrub,spectre}@ispras.ru
http://ispras.ru

Abstract. A problem of automated test development for checking basic functionality of program interfaces (API) is discussed. Different technologies and corresponding tools are surveyed. And T2C technology developed in ISPRAS is presented. The technology and associated tools facilitate development of "medium quality" (and "medium cost") tests. An important feature of T2C technology is that it enforces that each check in a developed test is explicitly linked to the corresponding place in the standard. T2C tools provide convenient means to create such linkage. The results of using T2C are considered by example of a project for testing interfaces of Linux system libraries defined by the LSB standard.

Keywords: Formal testing, compliance testing, parameterized tests, medium-quality tests.

1 Introduction

Verification of a complex software system, checking its correctness in each situation is a very important but an extremely difficult task. Automated testing is often used for software verification and when considering developing such tests we have to deal with the trade-off between thoroughness of the tests and the resources needed to develop, use and maintain these tests.

The optimal solution depends on many factors specific to a particular project. In this paper we consider development of tests that check program interfaces for C language ("C API") for compliance with a standardized specification (and actually for other kinds of mature developers documentation) for program interfaces. Such problem statement suggests taking the following factors into account:

- The tests need to be maintained as the standard evolves.
- The existence of a standard means assuming that the behaviour of the system under test is described in enough detail. Nevertheless, it may not be the case for fast evolving standards.
- More often than not, the inconsistencies found by the tests will be analyzed not by the tests' developer but rather by the experts from the companies that wish to check their products for compliance with the standard. So it can be crucial to facilitate analysis of such failures.

T. Margaria and B. Steffen (Eds.): ISoLA 2008, CCIS 17, pp. 56–70, 2008.

These factors lead to several requirements for test suites and thus for an approach taken to develop test suites. But they impose no restrictions on the trade-off between available resources and the thoroughness of the tests.

As far as compliance testing is concerned, testing of basic functionality is a rather common choice. To check basic functionality means to verify behaviour of the system in its several common use cases probably including some scenarios when the system must report an error (error scenarios). This path is quite attractive for verification of industrial software because it often gives a guarantee of revealing all significant violations of the standard for reasonable cost.

When it is crucial to ensure strict compliance of a software system with a standard and there are enough resources available, more thorough ("deep") testing is chosen. For instance, the deep tests may strive to check each class of test situations possible for each aspect of functionality of each interface function. Deep tests of this kind that still remain maintainable can be created using the tools based, for example, on UniTesK technology [1] that, among other things, suggests using special model-based testing techniques. This technology is used, for instance, in CTesK tools [2]. The following features of CTesK allow to go through all the test situations and to facilitate analysis of test coverage:

- the means for formal description of the requirements for the system under test;
- support for automatic generation of test action sequences by dynamic creation of a test system behaviour model;
- support for a wide range of test quality metrics in terms of a requirement model with automated gathering of data concerning the achieved coverage.

There are alternatives, of course. When it is necessary to cover a large amount of functions in a short period of time, the decision can be made in favour of less thorough testing. Sometimes its purpose is to ensure that each of these functions can just be called with correct arguments and does not lead to a crash. One of the approaches to development of such tests ("shallow tests"), AZOV technology is described in [15].

The purpose of T2C tools described in this paper is to facilitate development of tests that check basic functionality of a software system. These tools, while being inferior to CTesK in respect of test thoroughness, allow achieving a reasonable balance between the quality of the tests and the resources needed to develop and maintain these tests. T2C tools support basic recommendations for dealing with requirements in formal testing for compliance with a standard such as creating a catalog of elementary requirements specified in the standard, ensuring traceability of the requirements in the tests and measuring test quality in terms of covered elementary requirements. T2C technology enforces that each check in a developed test is explicitly linked to the corresponding place in the standard and T2C tools provide convenient means to create such linkage.

This paper is organized as follows. In the first part several approaches to similar problems are considered and their advantages and disadvantages with respect to testing basic software functionality are discussed. Then basic features of T2C tools are described as well as the work flow they support. After that the results of applying T2C for a real-world problem are discussed, namely the experience of using this technology to develop tests for several libraries from GTK+ stack and fontconfig for compliance with the Linux Standard Base (LSB) [3]. The future directions of T2C development as well as its integration with other tools from UniTesK family are presented in the conclusion.

2 Technologies and Tools for the Development of Basic Functionality Tests for Program Interfaces

2.1 MANUAL

Test systems that ensure the functionality is checked thoroughly usually need a range of services of underlying operating system. That is why when the very operating system is under test, it is required to be relatively stable for these tests to operate properly.

To mitigate this problem and to minimize unintentional influence of test system on the target system, distributed architecture is often used in test development. This implies that most of the tasks are performed on an auxiliary ("instrumental") machine, while only a small test agent is working on the target machine. But even in this case interaction between the test agent and the instrumental machine requires some components of the system under test to be operational.

That is why it is important to make sure that the key components of the target system are operational before proceeding to thorough testing of its program interfaces.

An approach for creating tests of basic operation system's functionality named MANUAL was developed in software engineering department of ISPRAS for the project that involved testing of a POSIX-compliant real time operating system for embedded devices. These tests verified that the key components of the operating system are operational before the beginning of deeper testing by the system developed using CTesk tools.

A test in MANUAL is in fact code in C programming language using macros and functions of MANUAL support library. Each test is a separate function beginning with `TC_START("name of the test")` macro and ending with `TC_END()` macro. The body of the test consists of three parts:

- preparation of data and of the environment;
- test action itself and checking its results;
- deallocation of resources.

Checking the system under test for correctness is done with the function `tc_assert(expression_to_check, "text describing the failure")`. If the expression to check is false, it is assumed that an failure has been detected and a message is output that describes this failure. Besides, the system automatically catches exceptional situations that appear during the execution of the test and treats them like failures.

MANUAL system supports hierarchical composition of tests into the packages. There are two modes for running the tests: automatic and interactive. In the automatic mode the system executes the specified set of tests or packages and stores execution log. In the interactive mode the user can navigate the package tree down to an individual test and execute the chosen test or package.

The main drawback of MANUAL system is its low scalability. The scalability problems result from the fact that each test is a function in C language which, as the test suite grows, requires either multiple duplication of the source code or a significant amount of a rather tedious manual work to structure the code.

Lack of test parametrization, while reasonable when implementing simple operability checks for basic functionality of a target system, is a significant obstacle for applying this approach to development of more thorough test suites.

2.2 Check

Check system [4] is designed in the first place for unit testing of software during the development process. Nevertheless, Check can also be used for testing program interfaces for compliance with the standards.

Check provides the test developer with a set of macros and functions to perform checks in the tests, to combine the tests in suites, to manage output of the results, etc.

A test is code in C programming language enclosed between `START_TEST` and `END_TEST` macros. The requirements are checked in the tests using the following functions: `fail_unless(expression_to_check, "text describing the failure")` and `fail_if(expression_to_check, "text describing the failure")`.

Functions performing initialization and clean-up of used resources can be specified both for each particular test and for each test suite (so called *checked and unchecked fixtures*).

Advantages of Check system:

- support for running each test in a separate process, i.e. a kind of isolation of the tests from one another and from Check environment;
- automatic handling of exceptional situations in the tests;
- support for specifying maximum execution time for a test;
- special facilities for checking situations where execution of the function under test should result in sending a signal;
- integration of test building and test execution system with autoconf and automake the tools commonly used for automation of software building and installation [5].

Check, however, has several drawbacks that prevent using it in some cases:

- It is difficult to develop parameterized tests with Check. It is often the case that some function needs to be tested with different sets of its arguments' values while the code of the test remains almost the same. It could be reasonable to pass these sets of values to the test as parameters. However only

the number of the test can be explicitly passed to this test as a parameter which is not convenient.
- There is no linkage of the checks performed in a test to the places in the documentation (standard) where the corresponding requirements are stated.
- To add a new test in a suite, it is necessary to recompile the source of all the other tests of this suite too, which is not always reasonable.
- Common test results codes ("verdicts") listed in the standard for testing compliance to POSIX [6] are not supported which may make it more difficult to analyze test results.

2.3 CUnit

CUnit system [7] can be used in the same cases as Check [4], but is generally less powerful.

One of the most important drawbacks of CUnit compared to Check is the fact that all the tests as well as the harness that executes them and collects their results run in the same process. This means that a failure in a test may, for example, lead to corruption of memory used by CUnit harness or by some other test.

Also, unlike Check, there is no protection from test "hang-up": maximum execution time can not be specified for a test.

Still there are some advantages CUnit has over Check:

- Support for so called *fatal and non-fatal assertions*. In the first case if a check reveals that a requirement was violated, test execution stops and thus further checks are not performed in this test (this approach is always used in Check). One the other hand, if violation of a requirement has been detected in a non-fatal assertion, test execution continues. Further checks in this test can probably provide the developer with more detailed information about what was really happening in the system under test. This may help to discover the cause of the detected failure.
- A set of special functions and macros that facilitate commonly used checks such as equality and inequality of integers, floating-point numbers, strings, etc.
- Support for reporting the test results in several formats including those that can be displayed in a web browser (xml+xslt).

Nevertheless, the drawbacks pointed out for Check in the previous section apply to CUnit too. Test Environment Toolkit (TET) described below is free from some of these.

2.4 TET (Test Environment Toolkit)

TETware system (TET, TestEnvironmentToolkit) is quite widely used for testing various program interfaces. TET tools provide a common way to run different tests and to obtain a report of the test results in a common format [8]. Data concerning test execution including its result (test verdict) and the messages it outputs is accumulated in so called *TET journal.*

TET consists of the following basic components:

- test case controller (tcc) this component manages test execution and gathering information the tests output;
- application program interface (TET API) that should be used in the tests to be able to run them within TET harness. TET API is available for several programming languages including C and C++.

The most important advantages of TET are probably the following:

- a common environment for running the tests;
- handling exceptional situations in the tests (segmentation faults, for example) by the means of the test case controller;
- common test result codes (verdicts) that comply with the standard [6]: PASS, FAIL, UNRESOLVED, etc., along with the ability to define additional test result codes;
- an ability to add new tests to the suite without recompiling the remaining tests (using so called *TET scenarios*)
- a common format for a report of test execution (*TET journal*).

These TET's features make the analysis of test execution results easier. Particularly, the program tools processing TET journal may not take the specifics of the tests into account while collecting the statistics of test results, for example.

On the other hand, TET tools have something to do mostly with automation of test execution and collecting of test results. TET provides neither means to somehow automate test development nor the API for performing checks in the tests. Consequently, there are several reasons that make using "pure" TET (without any enhancements) rather inconvenient:

- Lack of means to link the checks performed in the tests to the corresponding parts of the standard.
- It is often necessary to create tests with almost the same source code and the difference is, for example, only in the parameters passed to the functions called in this test or, say, in element types of used arrays, etc. It seems reasonable to automate development of such tests so as to reuse common parts of the source code. Unfortunately, TET provides no special means for this.
- The test developer needs to manually add definitions of special functions, data structures, etc., required to run the tests within TET harness. This could be done automatically as well.
- The tests being executed by the test case controller are not always easy to debug. It could be helpful both for searching for errors in the test itself and for investigating the behaviour of the system under test to be able to avoid TET's influence on test execution. This could facilitate the use of debugger programs such as gdb and others.

Described below are two systems that have TET as their basis: GTKVTS and T2C. These systems manage to overcome TET's drawbacks to some extent.

2.5 Automation of TET-Compliant Test Development in GTK+-2.0 Verification Test Suite (GTKVTS)

An approach used in GTK+-2.0 Verification Test Suite (GTKVTS) for development of TET-compliant tests allows avoiding some of the TET's drawbacks [9].

First of all, GTKVTS uses so called parameterized tests. That is, the developer writes a template for the test source code in plain C language just marking in some special way the places where to put the values of test's parameters. Several sets of parameter's values can be specified for each test template of this kind. Almost anything can be a test parameter, not only parameters of tested functions or their expected returns values. Sometimes its is reasonable to consider types of used data as test parameters (like C++ templates) or even to make a statement calling the target function a parameter and so on.

The GTKVTS C code generator creates a single function in C language for each set of parameters' values based on the test source template (see Fig. 1).

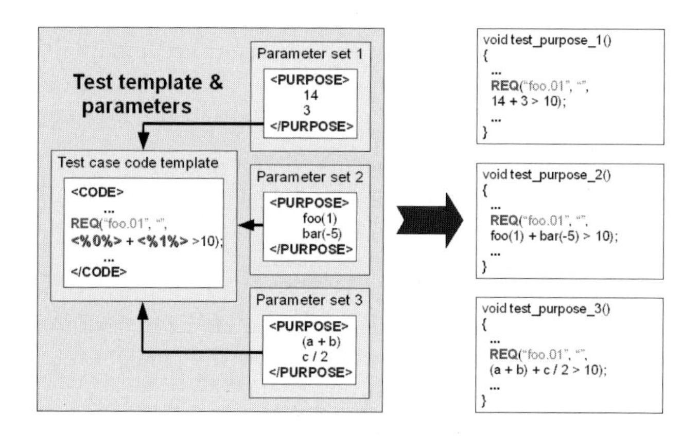

Fig. 1. Generating C code based on a template. "<%0%>" and "<%1%>" mark the places in the template where actual values of the parameters are to be inserted.

Second, GTKVTS tools automatically insert in the generated C source code definitions of special data structures and functions required to be able to run the test within TET harness, so the developer does not have to worry about this. Besides that, makefiles for building the tests and TET scenario files are also generated automatically which can be convenient.

The authors of GTKVTS also tried to encourage linking the checks in the tests with the relevant fragments of a standard: the test developer should specify the text of the requirements checked in this test in the comments before it. Unfortunately, this text is not used in the test itself and it is usually difficult to find out from the trace of the test, which requirements have been checked and which of them have been violated.

There are also some less significant drawbacks of GTKVTS tools, such as lack of support for debugging the test outside of TET harness and the fact that the tools are specialized for developing tests for the libraries from GTK+ stack only.

2.6 Comparison of Existing Approaches

Considered above are five approaches (and corresponding tools) for test development for program interfaces in C language. The summary of their advantages and disadvantages is given in Table 1.

Table 1. Comparison of existing approaches

	MANUAL	Check	CUnit	TET	GTKVTS
Test parametrization	-	-	-	-	+
Traceability of requirements	-	-	-	-	-
Execution of tests in separate processes	-	+	-	-	-
Automatic handling of exceptional situations	+	+	-	+	+
Restriction of test execution time	-	+	-	+	+
Hierarchical package organization	+	-	-	-	-
Convenience of debugging	+	+	+	-	-
Portability of the tests	-	+	+	+	-
Using standard test verdicts [6]	-	-	-	+	+

Each of the approaches considered above has some advantages. However all of them have one significant drawback from the point of view of testing program interfaces for compliance with standards, namely lack of support for linkage of the checks in the tests to the requirements of the standard ("traceability of requirements"). In addition, none of these approaches has all the advantages described above while there seems to be no contradiction between them.

When it was decided to develop T2C tools, a requirement was stated that these tools support (and enforce to some extent rather than just encourage) traceability of requirements while still keeping the advantages of existing approaches shown in table 1 except hierarchical organization of test packages. This exception is due to the fact that the possibility to hierarchically organize the test packages does not significantly affect the development and usage of compliance tests.

3 T2C ("Template-to-Code") System

3.1 General Information

T2C ("Template-to-Code") system facilitates the development of parameterized tests that can be executed both within and outside of TET harness.

The source code of the tests in C programming language is created based on a T2C-file that contains test templates along with the sets of parameter's values for these tests (the idea is the same as in GTKVTS - see Fig. 2). A fragment of a T2C-file is shown below.

The tests to be created based on a template presented in Fig. 2 have two parameters: `TYPE` and `INDEX`. `int` will be used as `TYPE` and `6` as `INDEX` in the first of the tests, `double` and `999`, respectively, in the second one.

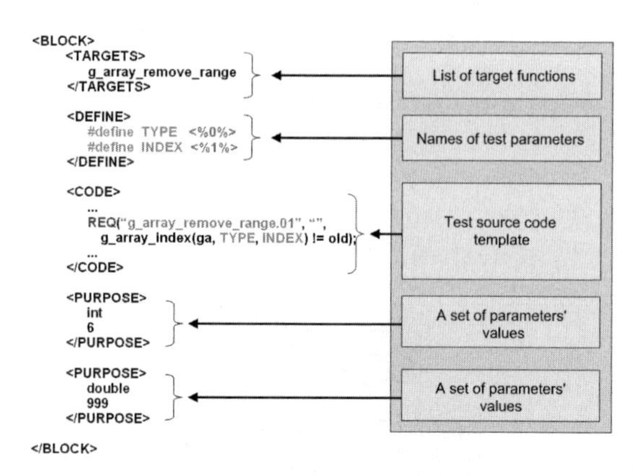

Fig. 2. A fragment of a T2C-file

Like in GTKVTS, definitions of data structures and functions required to run the tests within TET harness will be added to the source of the tests automatically. Necessary makefiles and TET scenario files will be created as well.

So T2C tools retain main advantages of GTKVTS system while supporting the recommendations for development of compliance tests stated, for instance, in [10]:

- creating a catalog of elementary requirements for program interfaces to be tested;
- linkage of the checks performed in the tests to the relevant places in the corresponding standard;
- testing quality measurement in terms of covered elementary requirements.

The following enhancements have been made in T2C compared to GTKVTS:

- The test developer is provided with a set of high level program interfaces (T2C API) to perform the checks in the tests. Now if a check in the test reveals violation of some requirement, the text of this requirement is output to the test's trace (TET journal) along with other useful information.
- It is possible to create a standalone version of a test in pure C/C++ without using any of TET's features. This can be rather convenient both for debugging the test and for thorough investigation of what happens in the system under test in case of a failure.
- Templates of T2C-files (do not confuse them with the test templates) are created automatically for a text of the standard with the requirements marked up in it in a special way.
- T2C-file can also contain the code needed for initialization and cleanup of the resources used by any the tests to be generated from this file as well as for deallocation of resources allocated in each particular test.
- Execution of each test in a separate process is supported as well as in a single process.
- Maximum execution time for a test can be specified. This is useful if some of the tests may hang.

3.2 Test Development with T2C Tools: The Workflow

Main stages of test development process with T2C tools are described in this section (see also Fig. 3).

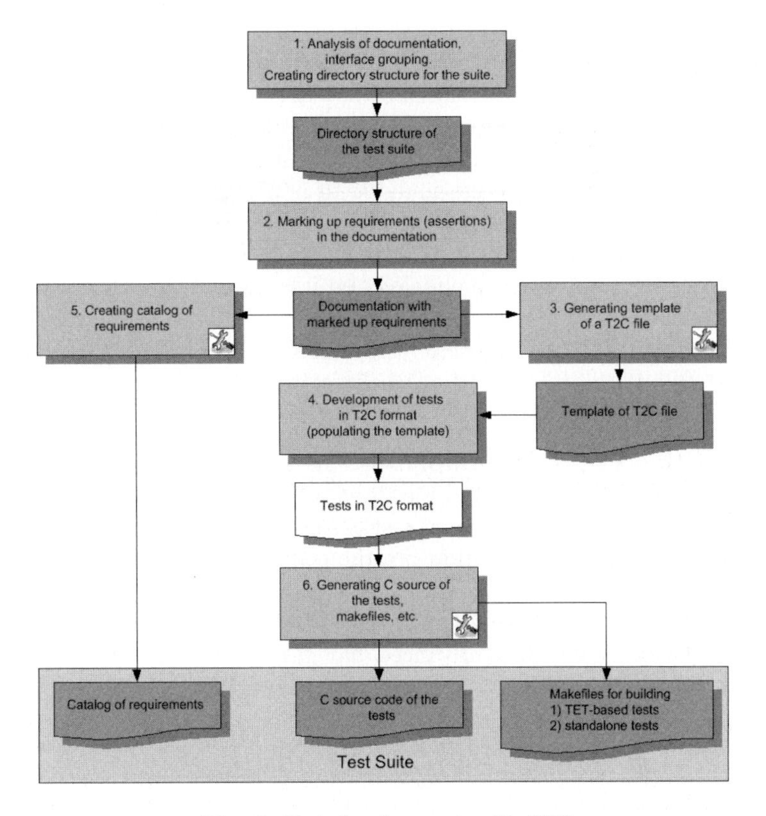

Fig. 3. Test development with T2C

Analysis of Documentation and Interface Grouping. First of all, before trying to write conformance tests for some interfaces one should examine the documentation of these interfaces to find out what is to be tested. During this analysis one should also split the interfaces to be tested into groups, each of which implements a coherent part of the system's functionality ("functional groups"). One should avoid the situations when some interfaces from group A are needed to check the interfaces from group B ("A depends on B") and in the same time interfaces from A are needed to test those from B (cyclic dependency).

Sometimes the grouping is already done in the documentation. For instance, a reference manual for Glib2 library [11] is divided in sections such as "Memory Allocation", "String Utility Functions", "Key-value file parser", etc. Interfaces described in each section usually form a single functional group.

During the test development one or more T2C-files are created for each functional group. It is often reasonable to create appropriate directory structure for the test suite at this stage too.

From now on it is assumed that the standard (documentation) for the interfaces to be tested is a set of HTML documents.

Requirement (Assertion) Markup in the Documentation. Elementary requirements for each of the interfaces to be tested are marked up in the documentation in a special way at this stage. Each elementary requirement is given a unique identifier [10]. The text of a requirement can be assembled from several parts if necessary or it can be reformulated to improve readability.

Markup of requirements is performed in HTML editor KompoZer (`www.kompozer.net`) enhanced with ReqMarkup tool that was developed during OLVER project [12] and then remodeled and integrated into T2C system.

Creating a Template of T2C-file. Once the requirements for a particular functional group of interfaces have been marked up, the ReqMarkup tool automatically creates a template for the corresponding T2C-file.

Populating the T2C File Template. This stage is the most important in the development of the tests. Now the developer should populate the template of a T2C-file adding the templates of test case source code along with the parameter's values for the tests. In addition, the code for initialization and cleanup of resources used by the tests should be specified in special sections of the file.

The T2C Editor tool a plugin for Eclipse IDE - can be helpful for visual editing of T2C files providing advanced navigation among the file's sections, convenient means for dealing with the parameters of the tests, etc.

Preparing Catalog of Elementary Requirements. Based on the documentation with the requirements marked up, ReqMarkup tool also creates a catalog of requirements for the corresponding group of interfaces. This catalog is used during the execution of the test: if it is detected that a requirement is violated, the text of the requirement with the particular identifier is loaded from the catalog and output to the test's trace for future analysis.

Generating the Source Code of the Tests, Makefiles and TET Scenarios. When the tests in T2C format are prepared and so is the catalog of elementary requirements, the developer should invoke T2C Code Generator that will create the files with source code of the tests (in C or C++ language), makefiles for building the tests from these sources, TET scenario files, etc.

Building, Executing and Debugging the Tests. At this stage the developer should build the test suite using the makefiles generated at the previous step. After that the test suite is ready. One may run the tests within TET harness or debug some of them outside of TET and so forth.

4 Applying T2C to Test Development for LSB Desktop

T2C system was used (and is used now) in development of tests for interface operations (*"interfaces"*) of Linux libraries, defined in the Linux Standard Base (LSB). For example, the tests for the following libraries were prepared using T2C tools:

- Glib (libglib-2.0);
- GModule (libgmodule-2.0);
- GThread (libgthread-2.0);
- GObject (libgobject-2.0);
- ATK (libatk-1.0);
- Fontconfig (libfontconfig).

Table 2 shows the results of testing these libraries. The descriptions of inconsistencies found by the tests are published in `http://linuxtesting.ru/results/impl_reports`.

Table 2. Results of testing several Linux libraries for compliance with LSB by the tests developed using T2C tools

Library	Version	Total interfaces	Tested interfaces	Problems found
libatk-1.0	1.19.6	222	222 (100%)	11
libglib-2.0	2.14.0	847	832 (98%)	13
libgthread-2.0	2.14.0	2	2 (100%)	0
libgobject-2.0	2.16.0	314	313 (99%)	2
libgmodule-2.0	2.14.0	8	8 (100%)	2
libfontconfig	2.4.2	160	160 (100%)	11
Total		**1553**	**1537(99%)**	**39**

Remark 1. The *"Version"* column shows the latest version of the corresponding library at the moment when the test suite was published. The number of errors found by the tests is shown for this very version of the library. There is an ongoing work on these errors in collaborations with the developers of respective libraries, so it is possible that some or even all of these errors are (or will be) fixed in newer versions.

Remark 2. The *"Total interfaces"* column shows total number of interface operations (*"interfaces"*) defined in the LSB for the particular library including undocumented ones. Almost all documented interfaces were tested.

The average costs for a full cycle of test development (from the analysis and markup of requirements to the debugged code of the tests) for a single interface are about 0.5 - 1 man-day.

It should also be mentioned that the interfaces from these libraries are not always described in detail in the documentation. In average, 2 - 3 elementary requirements were found for each interface.

Table 3. Coverage of requirements for LSB libraries

Library	Requirements	Checked requirements	Requirement coverage (%)
libatk-1.0	515	497	96%
libglib-2.0	2461	2290	93%
libgthread-2.0	2	2	100%
libgobject-2.0	1205	1014	84%
libgmodule-2.0	21	17	80%
libfontconfig	272	213	78%
Total	**4476**	**4033**	**90%**

Table 4. Code coverage data

Library	Lines of code (total)	Executed lines	Code coverage (%)
libglib-2.0	16263	12203	75.0%
libgthread-2.0	211	149	70.6%
libgobject-2.0	7000	5605	80.1%
libgmodule-2.0	270	211	78.1%
Total	**23744**	**18168**	**76.5%**

The information concerning the number of elementary requirements for tested interfaces is given in Table 3 as well as requirement coverage data.

It can be interesting to find out what portion the source code of the libraries under test the tests act upon. The code code coverage data for four libraries of glib2 group is shown in Table 4. The data was collected for glib2 package version 2.16.3 using gcov tool. The parts of these libraries not defined in the LSB were not taken into account.

5 Conclusion

The problem of testing program interfaces for compliance with their documentation (including standards) is very important for providing quality and interoperable software systems. Various technologies as well as corresponding tools are developed for this purpose that allow to somehow automate the work and make it more systematic. These approaches always have to deal with a trade-off between the quality of the tests and the cost of developing these tests. The choice is often made here based on some quite subjective factors. Meanwhile, the choice of target testing quality governs the choice of the optimal technology and tools as well, because different levels of cost and quality require different approaches. For instance, as far as deep (thorough) testing is concerned, UniTesK technology proved very useful [13], although the cost of learning the technology and of the actual test development is rather high.

This paper describes T2C technology which is oriented to efficient development of "medium level" tests checking basic functionality of program interfaces. The term "medium level" corresponds in this case to the common notion of industrial testing quality achieved in the most of the test suites analyzed by the authors (e.g., Open Group certification tests, LSB certification tests, OpenPosix tests and Linux Test Project). T2C allows raising the efficiency of development of such tests by providing the following basic features that reduce manual work for preparing the environment and duplicating the code that is not specific for a particular test:

- automatic generation of test templates based on the catalog of requirements;
- usage of named parameters in the source code of the tests with automated generation of a separate test instance for each set of parameters' values;
- a high-level API that can be used in the code of the test to check the requirements and output trace messages;
- generation of standalone tests, i.e. self-sufficient programs in C or C++ language which significantly simplifies debugging the tests as well as the tested system compared to debugging them within TET test execution environment or the like.

The execution environment for the tests created using T2C technology is based on widely used TETware tools, which facilitates integration of the tests into existing test suites and the environments that manage test execution and analysis of the results. Besides that, one of important features of T2C is systematic work with catalogs of elementary requirements and enforcing the explicit linkage of requirement checks in the tests to the relevant places in the standard and output of corresponding messages to the test execution report.

T2C technology was successfully used at the Institute for System Programming of Russian Academy of Sciences in the project [14] for development of certification tests for checking compliance of Linux libraries with the LSB standard. Presented in this paper are the statistical data concerning the developed tests, found errors in the libraries and the costs of development. The data allow concluding that the technology is efficient for development of tests of the particular quality level for various modules and libraries. The tools support C and C++ programming languages for the present, but there are no principal obstacles that prevent applying the technology to other general purpose programming languages such as C# and Java. It should be mentioned however that the availability of quite stable text of the requirements is essential for successful use of T2C because the stage of documentation analysis and preparing of the requirement catalog may require a lot more work when the quality of the documentation is low and/or when it is changed too actively.

It is planned to enhance integration of T2C tools with Eclipse IDE as well as provide means for using these tools from other popular development environments. The possibility of integration of T2C and CTesK systems will be also investigated.

References

1. Kuliamin, V.V., Petrenko, A.K., Bourdonov, I.B., Kossatchev, A.S.: UniTesK Test Suite Architecture. In: Eriksson, L.-H., Lindsay, P.A. (eds.) FME 2002. LNCS, vol. 2391, pp. 77–88. Springer, Heidelberg (2002)
2. CTESK web page, http://www.UniTesK.com/products/ctesk
3. The Linux Standard Base, http://www.linux-foundation.org/en/LSB
4. Check web page, http://check.sourceforge.net/doc/check.html/index.html
5. Autoconf and Automake web page, http://www.gnu.org/software/automake/
6. IEEE.2003.1-1992 IEEE Standard for Information Technology – Test Methods for Measuring Conformance to POSIX – Part 1: System Interfaces. IEEE, New York, NY, USA (1992) ISBN 1-55937-275-3
7. CUnit web page, http://cunit.sourceforge.net/
8. TETware User Guide, http://tetworks.opengroup.org/documents/3.7/uguide.pdf
9. GTKVTS Readme, http://svn.gnome.org/viewvc/gtkvts/trunk/README
10. Kuliamin, V.V., Pakulin, N.V., Petrenko, O.L., Sortov, A.A., Khoroshilov, A.V.: Formalization of requirements in practice, ISPRAS, Moscow (preprint, 2006) (in Russian)
11. Glib Reference Manual, http://www.gtk.org/api/2.6/glib/
12. Linux Verification Center, http://linuxtesting.ru/
13. UniTesK web site, http://UniTesK.com/
14. LSB Infrastructure project web page, http://ispras.linux-foundation.org/
15. AZOV Framework web page, http://ispras.linux-foundation.org/index.php/AZOV_Framework

Tailoring and Optimising Software for Automotive Multicore Systems

Torsten Polle and Michael Uelschen

Advanced Driver Information Technology GmbH
Robert-Bosch-Straße 200
31139 Hildesheim
{tpolle,muelschen}@de.adit-jv.com

Abstract. The software architecture of embedded systems is heavily influenced by limitations of the underlying hardware. Additionally, real-time requirements constrain the design of applications. On the other hand, embedded systems implement specific functionalities and hence give the designer the opportunity to optimize the system despite of limitations. Multicore systems compromise the predictability of real-time requirements. Again, with the knowledge of the application the software design can benefit from the multicore architecture. This paper discusses how to decide on software design based on use-cases and shows new avenues how to efficiently implement the design with an example.

Keywords: Multicore, Scheduling, Automotive Embedded Systems, Producer-Consumer Pattern.

1 Introduction

Starting with a multiprocessor architecture at the super computer and main frame classes in the 1970's and 1980's the technology process got improved, which enabled chipset manufacturers to layout several cores on one die. The year 2005 was the inflection point when the increase of the clock frequency got restricted around 4 GHz, primarily because of huge power consumption and it was then, when multicore technology hit the consumer market.

Now the multicore architecture is entering the embedded automotive domain. The first adopters are driver information systems followed by multicore systems for classical electronic control units (ECU). Head units like car navigation systems combine functionality from the consumer electronics market (like MP3 or video playback functionality) with increasing complexity as well as from the automotive domain (like CAN or MOST networking).

Therefore an ever-increasing demand for processing power has to be satisfied. Although a multicore architecture has the potential to sate this demand, the change of paradigm forestalls the efficient usage of the provided processing power. Certainly, embedded systems can borrow from the approaches taken in the consumer electronics market. But there are differences like priority-based scheduling and optimisation techniques, which have to be taken care of. Therefore it will be interesting to see if

T. Margaria and B. Steffen (Eds.): ISoLA 2008, CCIS 17, pp. 71–81, 2008.

and how already established principles to use parallelism can be re-used in the automotive domain.

This paper extends [1] by covering the entire software design process. The starting point is six "meta" use-cases. These use-cases are in contrast with those that describe what the developed software is doing; they rather describe how to change the software. A multicore architecture offers several cores, on which software can be executed. The question "Which parts of the software are executed where?" is a new aspect of software design. The use-cases offer criteria on such decisions. Finally, it is shown that well established optimisation techniques have to be replaced for multicore systems.

2 Use-Cases for Automotive Multicore Systems

For the investigation of use-cases it is assumed that a functional single-core system is already available. This means migration of legacy code is a major requirement. This is important especially for considerations outside the academic world since car makers and suppliers usually cannot afford to start such complex systems from scratch.

In this paper the focus is on homogenous multicore systems [2]. The shared access to the memory subsystem is symmetric and peripherals are identical from individual core point-of-view. Heterogeneous architectures, e.g. constituting core connecting with a DSP, are out of scope of following sections.

The major observed trends or use-cases for multicore in the automotive domain can be classified as:

2.1 Use-Case 1: Deployment of New Functions

For the realization of upcoming features additional computing power is required. This is to support technology advancement, on one hand (like the European satellite navigation system Galileo). On the other hand, more rigid laws and standards (like the European eCall) have to be implemented. The use case also covers the refactoring of existing application, e.g. in order to increase performance or precision.

2.2 Use-Case 2: Redundant Systems

For automotive control units that require high safety and reliability, the use of multicore is a cost-efficient approach. However a failure of the underlying hardware will affect the entire system. Further investigations are necessary to verify which application can be designed for this approach.

2.3 Use-Case 3: Concentrating of Functions

Since cars are equipped with up to 100 ECUs, the minimization of the amount is a strong objective. This is driven by many factors, hardware costs being one of them. Also the configuration management and therefore the test and release process gets less complex and time-consuming as the amount of possible combinations of software and hardware versions goes down.

2.4 Use-Case 4: Convergence of Domains

Beside the requirement to reduce the amount of devices in the car it turns out that the different automotive domains are getting closer to each other. In an example by Toyota [3] the availability of the current position as well as the calculated route to some destination can be used for other applications in the car like vehicle control. The domain of driver information gets closer to driver assistance or to the powertrain domain. Functionalities from the consumer electronics domain are getting into the car. This leads to several challenges since the consumer and automotive domain follow different rules, e.g. innovation cycles [4]. The requirements focus mainly on 2 fields: visualization (human-machine-interface) and connectivity (mobile phones, media player). Solutions known from the desktop world will be integrated in future infotainment systems [5].

2.5 Use-Case 5: Architecture Harmonization

The introduction of two or more identical cores reduces the need of specialized hardware like a DSP. This approach is based on the assumption that a harmonized hardware as well as software architecture increases flexibility. This also might simplify the usage of tools (as compilers and debuggers) and programming languages.

2.6 Use-Case 6: Parallel Algorithms

Often algorithms can be parallelized to solve some problem more natural. Having a hardware environment that supports parallelism avoids sequential refactoring of a parallel algorithm. In contrast to fields of high performance computing the nature of algorithms for car applications is different. For example it might be beneficial to parallelize the route calculation for getting shorter computation cycles in a navigation system. But analysis of the current devices has shown that the access to the external map data (e.g. on CD or DVD) rules the system performance.

Parallelism on control level utilizes (light-weight) threads, as provided by the underlying real time operating system (RTOS) to get computing done concurrently. In order to schedule these threads for execution on the individual cores, the kernel of the operating system has several options. It turns out that different mechanisms need to be considered for partitioning software on embedded systems compared to the desktop world.

3 Scheduling

Scheduling in desktop or server systems for user level programs is round-robin in nature, to give enough justice to all user programs under execution. This scheduling mechanism is non-deterministic as the operating systems (OS) steals control from threads to realize round-robin scheduling. In case of embedded systems, the scheduling is generally priority based pre-emptive. And in such scheduling schemes, an application may misbehave or lead to data race conditions if more than two threads of different priority go to RUN state at the same time.

3.1 Symmetric Multiprocessing

In case of priority-based, pre-emptive scheduling on SMP kernels, the kernel provides flexibility to decide, which thread runs on which core. Dynamic load balancing is one of the properties of SMP mode.

The advantages of symmetrical multiprocessing are:

- The operating system manages automatic dynamic load balancing. The OS decides how to distribute threads across processors/cores to assure effective usage of all processors/cores.
- Inter-core communication can be implemented very easily using inter-processor interrupts as memory is visible to all processors/cores. No explicit message passing mechanism is required.

The drawbacks of symmetrical multiprocessing are:

- Deterministic behavior gets degraded because of automatic load balancing. Also the load balancing algorithm consumes more CPU time as the number of processors/cores in the system, increases.
- Cache coherency, synchronization mechanisms and shared data, limits application scalability.
- Synchronization among threads compels execution across cores to become sequential.

3.2 Asymmetric Multiprocessing

SMP is the de-facto standard of multicore server and desktop operating systems [6]. For the embedded world also other architectures are under consideration. On systems with asymmetric multiprocessing (AMP) different operating systems or several instances of the same are executed in parallel sharing the same physical hardware.

In this case load balancing is not supported and the communication between the cores is costly. On the other hand porting of existing single-core applications is less difficult.

The usage of several operating systems on a multicore system requires a communication channel for the synchronization of shared resources (e.g. memory or I/O). After virtualization was successfully introduced to the server and workstation domain, there are initial attempts to apply similar concepts to embedded systems [7, 8].

3.3 Hybrid Multiprocessing

A promising approach is hybrid architecture: running just one RTOS but putting restrictions on the scheduling strategy. Such hybrid configuration is supported by the clever design of the scheduler logic and its associated data structures available as a part of the kernel:

- Single Core. A core is configured in the way that a set of threads is defined to run exclusively on a specific core. Neither migrating of threads from this, nor to this core is allowed. The scheduling strategy on this core is priority-based. Load balancing is not possible.

- Execution Order Preserving. Threads are pooled to a partition with dependencies. The scheduler assures that the execution order of the depending threads is kept. If two threads have no dependencies, the scheduler is allowed to run these in parallel for load balancing reasons.
- Core Affinity. A thread is bound to a specific core. The scheduler does not migrate the thread for execution even if a different core is idle. Other threads can migrate to this core and will be scheduled priority-based.

The most flexibility is given if the RTOS supports the combination of SMP and the described AMP modes. For example, on a three core system, the system designer can configure at boot-time one core as one scheduling unit and the remaining two cores together, as another scheduling unit.

Another configuration for a three core system could be that each core is treated as one scheduling unit. Here the situation tends to be like an AMP system. Such configuration gives flexibility to port existing legacy applications from single-core systems to multicore systems.

Currently there are no standards on scheduling for multicore available. Some RTOS like eT-Kernel [9] or Neutrino [10] support both these flavors of SMP and AMP.

4 Application Binding

Without detailed understanding of the system requirements no general rules can be given how to apply the different multiprocessing modes to the described use-cases. Therefore in this section only examples can be given how to bind an application to the cores. A major open issue is the predictability of real-time requirements.

Based on the different use-cases the software partitioning varies. In contrast to multi-purpose systems like desktop computers or the high performance computing domain the symmetric multiprocessing design may be inappropriate. Table 1 summarizes the mapping of the use-cases to different software partitioning.

A hybrid multiprocessing approach enables the designer to keep dependencies and timings of the existing application and combine new functions. If algorithms can be parallelized and a short execution time is required, then a pure symmetric scheduling strategy fits. A hybrid approach does not gain additional benefits.

Table 1. The symmetric multiprocessing approach is most beneficial for load-balancing reason or if an algorithm is following the single program-multiple data pattern

Use Case	Asymmetric	Symmetric	Hybrid
1: Deployment of new Functions		**	***
2: Redundant Systems	***		**
3: Concentrating of Functions	**		***
4: Convergence of Domains	**		***
5: Architectural Harmonization	*	**	***
6: Parallel Algorithms		***	

Rating: * suitable with restrictions; ** suitable; *** most benefial approach

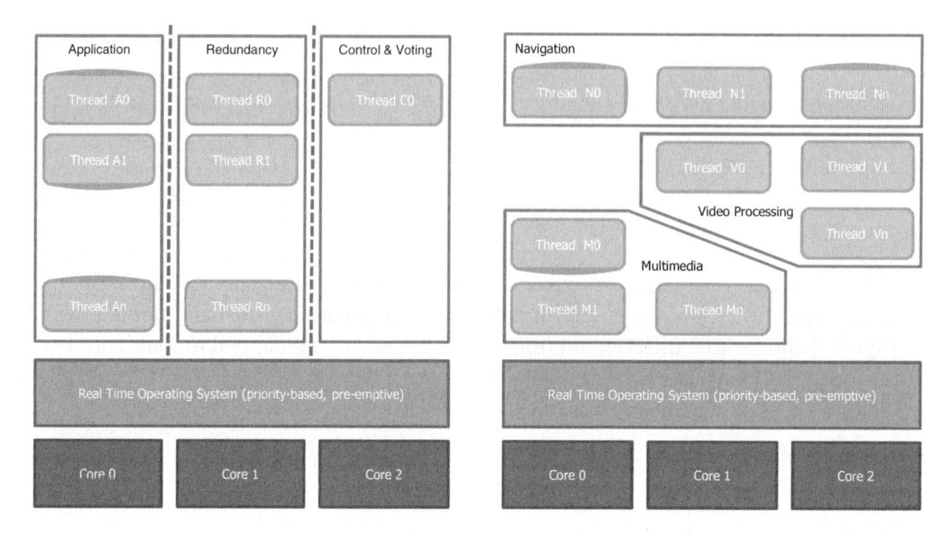

Fig. 1. For the implementation of a redundant system vertical partitioning of the software is appropriate, running each redundant application on a separate core and the control application on the third. For combining several legacy applications horizontal partitioning gives the flexibility of load balancing and preserving of execution order.

Usually redundant systems should be separated mutually. Therefore an asymmetrical partitioning minimizes the influence of a system to the other. Depending on the level of separation also single-core mode in a hybrid multiprocessing is appropriate (cf. figure 1).

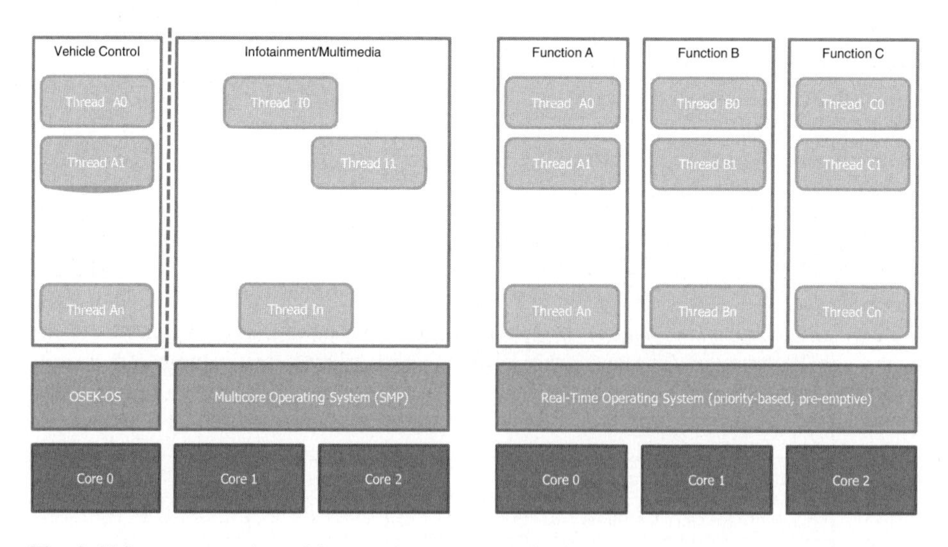

Fig. 2. Using asymmetric multiprocessing two operating systems are running in parallel representing different automotive domains (left). A real-time operating system that supports hybrid multiprocessing can bind functionalities to dedicated cores (right).

In case of replacing dedicated DSP functionality for harmonization reasons by a multicore architecture a hybrid approach can be applied. The ported DSP application can be moved in a hybrid environment running in single-core mode. But also an asymmetrical multiprocessing system may be appropriate as first step of a migration strategy. The drawback of asymmetrical multiprocessing is to have two operating systems running in parallel that need to get synchronized in an appropriate manner. But in specific cases this can be beneficial.

If pure computation power is required and the data can be arranged in a way that the calculation is symmetrical a pure symmetrical multiprocessing scheduling is the most appropriate. Again, the nature of automotive applications is usually not that way.

Figure 2 shows how different automotive domains can be mapped to multicore systems in different ways. Combining vehicle control functionality with the infotainment domain leads to the sketched architecture. On a single-core the OSEK operating system schedules threads (or tasks in OSEK nomenclature). Having a second symmetrical multiprocessing operating system both domains can run on a joint multicore hardware. Migrating different single-core applications to a multicore system can be achieved in single-core mode of a hybrid environment.

5 Design Patterns

The task to decide on the layout of an application across several cores is governed by the question to what degree the application can be parallelized. The challenge to get an application in an embedded device parallelized is as complex as on the desktop or server domain. No general guideline can be given since control parallelism always requires specific knowledge on the problem space. Design patterns are a well-accepted technique in software design. Some design patterns from the non-embedded world [11, 12] may also be applied for the embedded domain. But special attention has to be bestowed on the implementation.

5.1 Parallel Design

If a problem can be divided in the way that the algorithm can work in parallel and independent on separate chunks of data, then the master-worker pattern is an appropriate approach. A master thread controls a set of workers in a fork-join manner. For example sorting a large array can be implemented as parallel running worker threads quick-sorting sub-arrays. Merging the workers' output by the master thread finalizes the algorithm. Since the locality of the sub-arrays is very high, negative effects to the cache can be avoided. The speed-up is high. Other prominent examples are matrix calculations like multiplication or solving of linear equations on a mesh for fluid dynamics. Usually the nature of an embedded automotive application is not that way.

A central time-consuming algorithm of a navigation device is the route calculation. Finding the shortest path in a street network can be computed efficiently by Dijkstra's greedy algorithm [13]. Efficient parallelizing of such problem is much harder as the simple divide-and-conquer cannot be used easily. In order to achieve load balancing the pipelining programming pattern which works like an assembly line seems to be a more beneficial approach. In case of route calculation the data reading from some medium like DVD-Rom or SD-card can be arranged in the way that always a buffer of the next edges of the street network is available for the shortest path calculation. Using two threads on separate cores will speed-up the overall performance.

5.2 Efficient Implementations

Parallel design patterns require efficient implementations. The producer-consumer pattern is a well-known pattern and can be used for the communication between components. One component, the producer, generates data, which is used by another component, the consumer. A simple and efficient implementation can be achieved, when a ring buffer is used. As depicted in figure 3, the producer adds data at the position write pointer, and the consumer reads data at the read pointer.

The producer has to take care that the write pointer never overtakes the read pointer, while the consumer has to make sure that the read pointer does not overtake the write pointer.

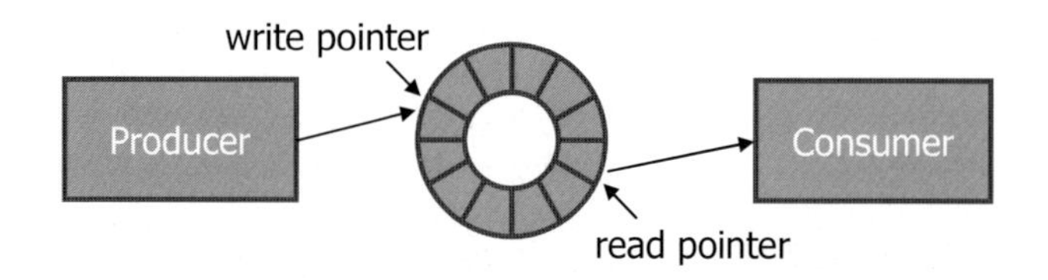

Fig. 3. The producer-consumer pattern is realised with a ring buffer

Although the implementation does not need further synchronisation mechanisms for just one producer and one consumer, the implementation does not work, if multiple producers or consumers enter the scene, because updates of the write pointer or read pointer are not atomic and therefore open to race conditions. In this case, e.g. a mutex must be used to protect the access to the ring buffer respectively the write and read pointer. The introduction of the mutex comes with the additional cost of a system call. In embedded systems these costs are often not acceptable. Therefore less "expensive" implementations are chosen. E.g. instead of using a mutex to protect the access to the ring buffer, CPU interrupts are masked as long as the access to the ring buffer is performed. But unfortunately in a multicore system, this approach does not work. When disabling interrupts for one core, another core is not prevented from accessing the ring buffer. To make the implementation work for multicore systems, the implementation can use a spinlock. If the spinlock is taken on a core, other cores cannot execute code in the critical section. They perform a busy wait until the lock is released. Alas, a simple spinlock is not sufficient, because the system might end in a dead lock. If the spinlock is taken and as many tasks as cores are available want to take the spinlock as well and these tasks have a higher priority than the task holding the spinlock, these tasks will on the one hand side wait for the lock to be released and on the other hand side prevent the task, which holds the lock, from releasing the lock. Therefore before the spinlock is taken, the task has to disable interrupts, in order not to be interrupted. The interrupts are enabled after the spinlock has been released.

The instructions to enable and disable interrupts are often privileged instructions, which only can be executed when the processor is in privileged mode. Often it is not desirable to run the processor in privileged mode. Instead user mode should be used whenever possible.

Therefore an implementation, which does not rely on masking interrupts, is necessary. To this end, atomic update operations like test and swap or load link and store can be used. But these operations cannot cover the entire access to the ring buffer. They can only be used to protect the update of the write and read pointer. First, a component reserves space in the ring buffer by updating the write pointer and then fills the ring buffer with data. Special care has to be taken, when a consumer wants to read data from the ring buffer. Since the write pointer is updated before the data in the ring buffer becomes ready, invalid data might be read by the consumer. If for example two components reserve space in the ring buffer, they will update the write pointer to hold first the value wp_i and then the value wp_{i+1} (cf. figure 4).

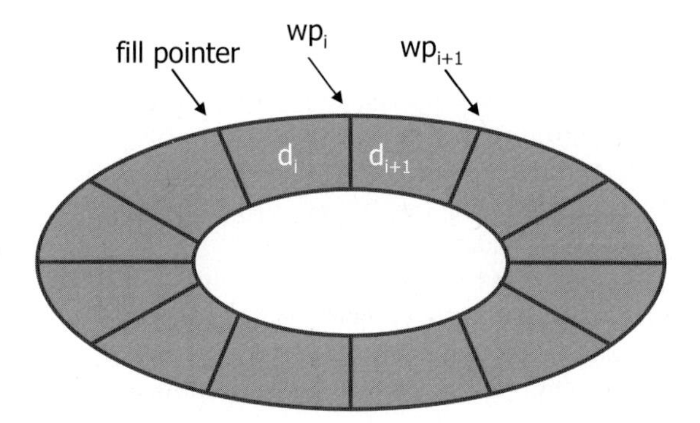

Fig. 4. Multiple Producers

Afterwards they each fill the reserved space with data d_i and d_{i+1}, respectively. At this point, it is not known which of the data is written first. To keep track of the point where data has been completely written, a fill pointer can be introduced. The fill pointer is updated after d_i has been written. In order to know whether the data d_{i+1} has already been written or not, an indicator is necessary. One way to realise such an indicator is to build up a list for the data, which has been filled, without updating the fill pointer. E.g. the element corresponding to data d_{i+1} holds the information wp_{i+1} and length(d_{i+1}) (see figure 5).

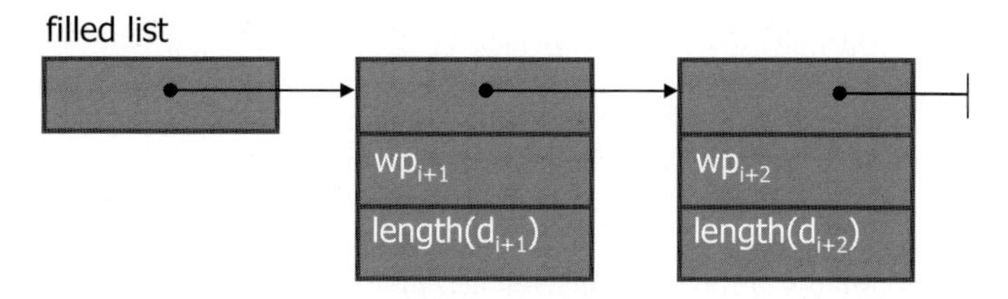

Fig. 5. Filled List

The elements are stored in ascending order of the write pointer value. The insertion of elements into the list has to be done by test and swap operations.

Although the algorithm presented comes with an overhead for the insertion into the filled list, the performance improvement is significantly compared to a solution using a mutex. On a system with a processor clock of 400 MHz, the operating system T-Kernel needs about 3μsecs for a system call. Whereas the implementation presented above takes only 100 nsecs, if no element is in the list. If there are already elements in the list when a new element is inserted, the traversal of each element takes 50 nsecs. Additionally, the algorithm is non-blocking, hence a producer can also run in the context of an interrupt.

Certainly, the optimisation can only be employed if the number of conflicting accesses to the ring buffer is an exception rather than the normal case.

6 Conclusion

Embedded systems are usually closed systems in the sense that user interaction is limited and any direct interference like installing user-defined applications is prohibited. This gives the opportunity to tune and optimise software. A multicore architecture takes away some optimisation techniques like efficient locking through interrupt masking, but at the same time offers new ways to gain performance like binding applications or threads to specific cores.

Based on use-cases this paper focuses on how to apply different operating system modes. However multicore systems compromise the predictability of real-time requirements. Further studies should focus on porting existing applications in order to get more evidence that hybrid multiprocessing is a feasible approach to support keeping such real-time conditions.

References

1. Das, B., Polle, T., Uelschen, M.: A Note on Software Partitioning for Embedded Homogenous Multicore Systems. In: Informatik 2008, München (2008) (accepted as conference submission)
2. Polle, T., Uelschen, M.: Softwareentwicklung für eingebettete Multi-Core-Systeme iX 3, 124–131 (2008)
3. Takei, T.: Toyota Works on Own OS for Automotive Terminals. Nikkei Electronics Asia (2006), http://techon.nikkeibp.co.jp/article/HONSHI/20061026/122752/
4. Lucke, H., Schaper, D., Siepen, P., Uelschen, M., Wollborn, M.: The Innovation Cycle Dilemma. In: Koschke, R., Herzog, O., Rödiger, K., Ronthaler, M. (eds.) Informatik 2007. LNI, vol. 110, pp. 526–530. Gesellschaft für Informatik, Bonn (2007)
5. Microsoft Auto 3.0, http://www.mircosoft.com/windowsautomotive
6. Kleidermacher, D.: Is symmetric multiprocessing for you? Embedded Systems Design Europe, January-February, 28–31 (2008)
7. Widmann, P.: Multi-Core-Systeme sinnvoll nutzen. Elektronik 13, 66–69 (2008)
8. Domeika, M.: Software Development for Embedded Multi-Core Systems: A Practical Guide Using Embedded Intel Architecture. Butterworth Heinemann (2008)

9. Gondo, M.: Blending Asymmetric and Symmetric Multiprocessing with a Single OS on ARM11 MPCore. Information Quarterly 4, 38–43 (2006)
10. Leroux, P.N., Craig, R.: Easing the Transition to Multi-Core Processors. Information Quarterly 4, 34–37 (2006)
11. Akhter, S., Roberts, J.: Multi-Core Programming. Intel Press (2006)
12. Rauber, T., Rünger, G.: Multicore: Parallele Programmierung. Springer, Heidelberg (2008)
13. Smith, J.D.: Design and Analysis of Algorithms. PWS-KENT Publishing, Boston (1989)

Fault Handling Approaches on Dual-Core Microcontrollers in Safety-Critical Automotive Applications

Eva Beckschulze, Falk Salewski, Thomas Siegbert, and Stefan Kowalewski

Embedded Software Laboratory, RWTH Aachen University, Germany
surname@cs.rwth-aachen.de

Abstract. The number of safety-critical applications is increasing in the automotive domain. Accordingly, requirements given by recent safety standards have to be met in these applications. These requirements include a demonstration of sufficient measures for the handling of permanent and transient hardware faults. Moreover, a consideration of software faults is required. In this work, approaches based on dual-core microcontrollers are investigated with respect to their fault handling capabilities. Therefore, *function monitoring architectures* that are based on a supervision of the implemented function and *generic architectures*, which monitor the hardware executing the application, are compared. This comparison is then further illustrated by an application example. Summarizing, both approaches come with their specific advantages and disadvantages, which should be considered during the development of the functional safety concept.

1 Introduction

Modern automobiles include an increasing amount of functionalities and most of these functionalities are implemented in software to allow flexible and complex applications. Faults in most of these functions could lead directly or indirectly to serious accidents which makes the majority of functions implemented in today's automobiles safety-critical. Most popular examples are driver assistance systems for stability control and crash avoidance, which typically require access to at least the brake system. However, even comparably simple applications as the electronic locking of the steering wheel require extensive safety measures, as a malfunction easily results in an accident.

The consideration of safety aspects in automobiles is complicated by two major aspects. First of all, most of these systems are real-time systems which require a completed computation of tasks before a given deadline. This requirement includes the execution of all required safety measures. The second aspect is that high requirements for low costs and low power lead to controllers with restricted resources. These requirements result in restricted memory sizes and computation power, but also in the need to apply general purpose devices whenever possible.

T. Margaria and B. Steffen (Eds.): ISoLA 2008, CCIS 17, pp. 82–92, 2008.

The advent of dual-core microcontrollers might help to meet the mentioned challenges. Although these devices are not yet established in the automotive domain, different approaches to use them in safety critical applications were proposed already. This paper aims to compare these approaches for safety-critical applications with a safety integrity level of ASIL C (automotive safety integrity level according to ISO WD 26262 [6]). Therefore, the requirements for such an application are presented briefly in the following Section 2. Next, known approaches with dual-core microcontrollers are presented and compared in Section 3. Then, a dual-core approach is applied on an example automotive application presented in 4. Finally, a conclusion of these investigations is given in Section 5.

2 Requirements for ASIL C Application

Specific safety requirements have to be considered in safety-critical systems. In this regard, it is important that safety is a system property [10]. Thus, it has to be made sure that the **combination** of hardware and software never leads to an unsafe state. This property is typically achieved by implementing a sufficient *safety function*. A safety function is responsible for the detection and the handling of all faults which could lead to unsafe states of the overall system. One form of fault handling is to shut down the system as soon as a critical fault is detected (*fail-silent system*). Another option is to try a form of fault recovery. This recovery could include a simple reset of the system (could mitigate transient hardware faults and some software faults) or a more fine grained recovery (e.g. to defined recovery point in the system). During recovery, the actuators have to be put into a safe state to prevent potential hazards. Alternatively, the outputs might remain in their current state if fault handling can be achieved in a time shorter than the so-called *fault-tolerant time span* [6]. A disadvantage of these approaches is that the system cannot perform its service while the faults are handled. This disruption might be not acceptable for safety-critical systems that require permanent service (e.g. drive-by-wire system) and do not allow sufficiently fast recovery. A combination of two fail-silent units to one *fail-operational system* is one solution to this problem (see e.g. [15]).

For the automotive domain, a specific safety standard, namely the standard ISO WD 26262 [6] is currently developed[1]. The standard requires a comprehensive safety analysis, in which potential hazards are determined. These hazards are rated according to so-called automotive safety integrity levels (ASIL). They range from ASIL A to ASIL D with the latter representing the most demanding level. For each hazard, a safety goal is formulated that has to be assured by a suitable safety concept.

For applications rated as ASIL C, specific safety requirements are given in the ISO WD 26262. For the hardware parts of such a system, a sufficient handling of possible hardware faults has to be shown by the application of *fault metrics* and *coverage criteria* introduced in this standard. Accordingly, single point faults (faults that alone could violate a safety goal) are only permitted, if their risk

[1] As the standard is still a working draft, contents presented here might still change.

of occurrence is sufficiently low and special measures are taken to ensure this low occurrence. Moreover, only a limited fraction of single point faults is allowed according to the fault metrics. While a higher fraction of multiple point faults (faults that could lead to the violation of the safety goal only in combination with other faults) is allowed, measures are required to determine latent multiple faults during a given time (e.g. one power-up and power-down cycle). Therefore, extensive fault handling approaches are required in these systems. How the specific properties of dual-core microcontrollers could be used to apply fault handling approaches are described in the following section.

3 Safety Architectures with Dual-Core Microcontrollers

Dual-core architectures vary in the the kind of redundancy used for the second core (homogeneous or heterogeneous) and in the kind of program execution (symmetrical or asymmetrical). Regarding safety architectures of dual-core systems we distinguish *generic architectures* from *function monitoring architectures*. Whereas in generic architectures there is a monitoring function for each safety-related component, function monitoring architecture rely upon a simplified model of the safety-critical part of the application for detecting safety-critical failures. In the following the two different approaches are discussed.

3.1 Function Monitoring Architectures

The concept of function monitoring is shown in Fig.1. The function level with its sensors (S) and actuators (A) provides the functionality of the system. The shown monitoring level implements the safety function. It uses redundant safety-critical inputs and available additional independent sensors to determine the state of the system regarding potential violations of the safety goals. Thereupon, the monitoring function either enables or disables the safety-related actuators[2] of the system independently or makes the decision based upon a comparison with the result of the function level. For a comparison, tolerance ranges may have to be specified, as usually the simplified model only indicates the order of magnitude and does not compute exact values. Moreover, effects on reliability have to be considered carefully (see Section 3.3).

A function monitoring architecture is known from the method for controlling the drive unit of a vehicle [2]. This concept comprises three levels, where the first and the second level act as shown in Fig. 1. As in the proposed approach these two levels rely on the same hardware, a third level implemented by a different computation element is responsible for detecting common cause failures in the hardware of the first and second level via challenge response communication. Applying this concept to dual-core systems we propose to implement the function level (cp. Fig. 1) on the first core and the monitoring on the second core. In order to establish the independence of the two levels, we propose simple additional components off the shelf. These will be discussed in Section 3.4.

[2] In Fig.1, only the lower actuator is assumed to be safety-related.

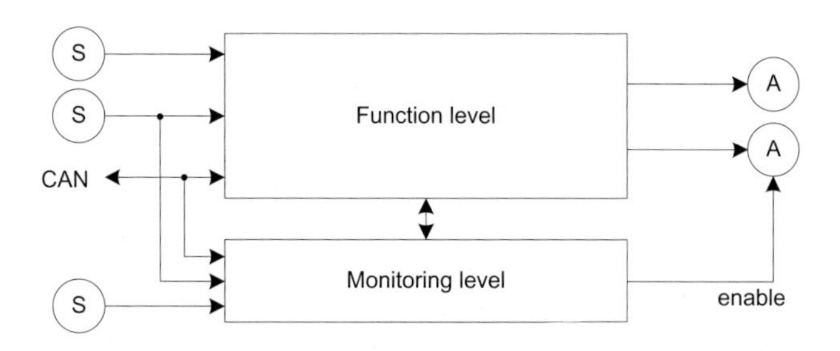

Fig. 1. Concept of function monitoring architectures

Provided that the monitoring function is simple, the second core is not used to capacity. A heterogenous dual-core system with a smaller and maybe slower second core could reduce logic overhead.

If the dual-core system is used to gain performance benefits, the function level is distributed to both cores and mutual monitoring can be applied. Again, there exists a concept of three levels [1]. Here, the third level is motivated by the limited communication capabilities of this approach (e.g. challenge response procedure is executed via CAN bus). In a dual-core system there is a more comfortable way of communication, as a so-called exchange RAM might be used to exchange data between the function level and the monitoring level. In order to guarantee as much hardware independence as possible, tasks should be assigned statically to the cores. The difficulty is that of finding a sensible distribution of both application and monitoring.

Function monitoring does not make special demands on the architecture of the dual-core architecture which allows the use of general purpose devices. A further advantage is the low complexity but at the same time the high fault coverage. It is not confined to safety-critical hardware faults, but may detect also certain software faults. Though, the crucial part of designing function monitoring architectures is hazard and risk analysis. The resultant specification of safety goals establishes the basis for the function monitoring. Therefore, a missing safety goal might result in a single point fault. On the other hand certification of the required safety integrity is considered as comparably easy, as a dedicated safety function is implemented on the second core for each safety goal.

Further on, if formal verification is applied to show the correctness of the implemented safety function, this verification can be reduced to the second core executing the safety function. As this function has typically a much lower complexity than the overall application, verification can be simplified this way. However, reuse of the safety function for other applications is limited and not every application is suitable for function monitoring.

3.2 Generic Architectures

Generic architectures require a careful analysis of all safety-related components. Fig. 2 illustrates the general concept, in which device supervision is responsible

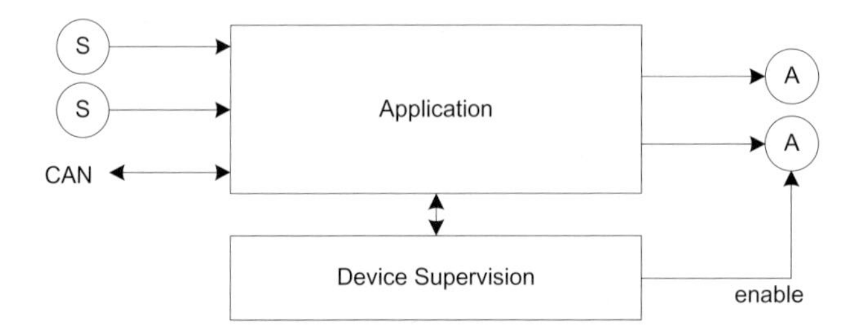

Fig. 2. Concept of generic architectures

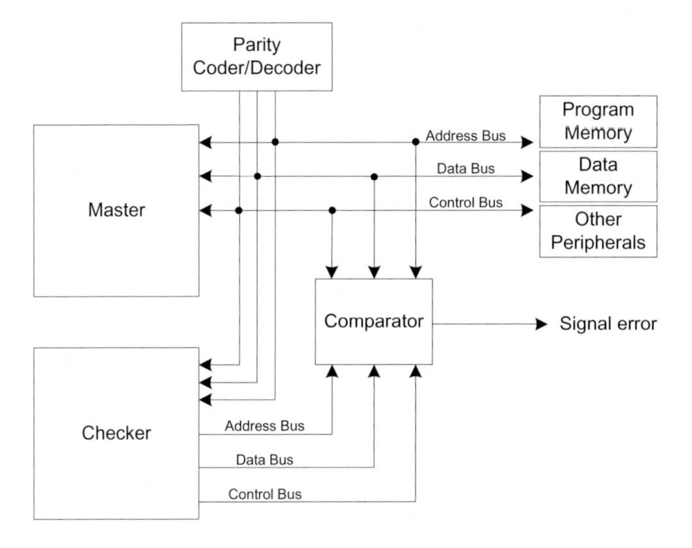

Fig. 3. Concept of lock step architecture

for detecting faults in the application hardware and disabling the safety-critical output, if necessary. While this consideration typically has to include all components of a microcontroller (e.g. I/O-blocks, memories, CPU, internal buses, on-chip peripherals), we focus our inspection on the most important components, processor and memory. Nevertheless, a brief discussion of fault handling for the remaining components can be found in Section 3.4.

A popular approach for detecting faults in the processor is to run a dual-core microcontroller in lock step configuration (symmetrical approach). Therefor, both processors receive the same input signals, execute the same software in parallel and the output signals (addresses, data or control signals) of the processors are compared to each other. This comparison requires additional hardware that detects discrepancies and disables the outputs if an error occurs. Fig. 3 illustrates the lock step principle.

Lock step configuration provides concurrent detection of transient and permanent processor faults. In order to avoid a common cause failure through electric disturbances affecting both cores in the same way, it is suggested to delay the clock signal for the second core by 1/2 cycle [7]. Though, as the second processor is exclusively used for redundancy, there is no performance advantage over a single core microcontroller. An elegant solution to use the second core more efficiently is presented in [9]. The proposed dual-core architecture provides two different modes of operation, which can be switched dynamically. In safety mode the system is run in lock step configuration while in performance mode the cores execute different programs independently to gain maximal performance. This requires a partition of the program into safety-critical and uncritical computations. Furthermore a switch to safety mode is required at least once in the fault-tolerant time span, in order to ensure that safety-related outputs do not violate the safety goals.

However, lock step configuration is limited to detect processor faults, whereas the handling of memory faults is not included yet. Indeed, in a lock step architecture, the handling of faults in the memories seems to be the crucial point for an ASIL C system. The use of parity with a diagnostic coverage of 60 % [6] for both data and instruction memory suggested in [8] and illustrated in Fig. 3 provides a weak protection. Alternatively, data error correction codes offer higher fault coverage, but the involved overhead, especially with respect to memory access time, is a problem [12]. In the Delphi Secured Microcontroller Architecture [5], the dual-core system is provided with a data stream monitor to enable concurrent error detection for nonvolatile memory. While that way no performance disadvantage is introduced, further additional logic is needed.

Another possibility to monitor the correct functioning of the first processor is a control flow checking algorithm executed by the second processor [3]. Fault injection experiments in [14] showed that in average about 78% of the faults induced by heavy-ion radiation and power supply disturbances resulted in control flow errors, whereas those can also origin from memory and bus transients. Even if all control flow errors are detected by the second processor, the so-called watchdog-processor, bit flips in registers that result in corrupted data or in the execution of a wrong instruction are not covered. Therefore it is doubtful, whether control flow checking provides sufficient coverage of single point faults for an ASIL C system.

In [4] an asymmetric dual-core system is proposed. The second core acts as a safety monitor performing a variety of extensive tests with respect to the processor, memory and different peripherals. As those tests cannot be executed concurrently and probably take longer than the fault-tolerant time span, they are not appropriate to the detection of single point faults. A high fault coverage is therefore achieved for latent multiple point faults only, for which the acceptable detection time span is more generous (10 hours for an ASIL C system). For concurrent detection of single point faults in all components low-level hardware support is demanded.

3.3 Comparison of Effects on Reliability

With respect to safety, it is often sufficient to switch over to a safe state as soon as an error is detected (fail-silent). Taking reliability and availability into consideration, a more sophisticated approach of fault handling is required. Comparing function monitoring architectures and generic architectures, safety interferes differently with reliability and availability.

Function monitoring states the set of safety-critical faults explicitly. This distinction between uncritical and safety-critical faults causes the system to switch to the safe state only if necessary. However, this decision might be a *false positive*. These describe the decision of the safety function that the system is in a safety-critical state, although the system's state is correct. There are two different causes of false positives. Possibly, the monitoring function does not define the safety-critical state sufficiently accurately. If this applies, a trade-off between reliability and safety is required. On the other hand, false positives can be caused by transient faults in the monitoring function. In order to increase the reliability of the monitoring function in event of a transient fault, it is possible to introduce error counters. The counter is increased each time the safety function detects an error but is reset if the safety function detects no error. Not until the counter reaches a predefined value, the safety function switches in the safe state and initiates further recovery procedures. Attention has to be turned to the fault-tolerant time spans of the safety goals. These may not be exceeded while increasing the counter.

In contrast, in generic architectures the safety function cannot distinguish between safety-critical and uncritical faults. In [3] the authors suggest to restrict the handling of memory faults to an application-specific set of safety-critical data. While this approach seems to be similar to function monitoring, there is a difference. It has to be considered that even a fault in a safety-critical variable may have no effect, e.g. if it is a bit-flip in the least significant bit of a variable. It is even more complex to determine whether a fault is safety-critical in the processor or in nonvolatile memory, as a wrong address in the program counter could cause a jump to an arbitrary instruction.

On the other hand, memory error correction codes provide sufficient redundant bits to correct single bit error (and detect some two bit errors) and are therefore useful to increase reliability. While in general in software implemented error correction codes introduce a high overhead with respect to memory and time, it might be a feasible solution if this task is executed by the second processor.

Taking into account the missing distinction between critical and uncritical faults in generic architectures, safety mechanisms must be able to handle all faults in safety-related components. If redundancy provided by the safety mechanism is only designed for error detection (no correction technique included), probability of failure is higher than in an one channel system. Therefore, reliability is more affected by the kind of recovery performed in a generic architecture. A traditional form of recovery is checkpointing in combination with rollback recovery. In order to avoid overhead with respect to time and memory, the program may be tested for a fixed point, where the program can be restarted without saving the system's state before. In [16], a more fine-grained approach for the lock step configuration is suggested, which enables the system to retry faulty instructions immediately. The most comprehensive action, a software reset may be performed after recovery failed.

Besides the interference of safety with reliability in generic architectures, it has to be considered that the comprehensive error detection in generic architectures provides the opportunity to increase the overall reliability of the system. This will be of increasing importance due to technology scaling and small supply voltage resulting in a high soft error rate for logic and memory [11].

3.4 Common Problems

Dual-core devices have a lack of sufficient independence between the two cores. A simple solution for several common cause failures is an external time-windowed watchdog [4]. In asymmetric dual-core architectures, the job of triggering the watchdog can be assigned to the second core executing the safety functions. If the system fails to trigger the watchdog in the specific time window, the watchdog initiates a reset. The smaller the time window, the higher is the probability that failures of the clock or faults caused by heat are detected. For detecting insufficient supply voltages, most watchdogs are provided with *brown-out*[3] detection. As the triggering of the watchdog requires a communication via the internal system bus, a complete failure of this bus can also be detected. On the other hand, not all transient faults in the internal bus system can be detected this way. However, these faults represent dual point faults[4], as the two cores do not use the system bus simultaneously. Moreover, most bus faults could be covered by a parity decoder as applied in the lock step approach.

It is difficult to design the safety architecture of a system completely independent from the application. Simple software techniques can reduce overhead and complexity of the overall system. Thus, to a certain extent, both types of architecture rely on hazard and risk analysis. In function monitoring architectures, safety-critical faults caused by input or output pins are detected by the monitoring function which has redundant inputs and outputs. In order to detect faulty I/O concurrently in generic architectures, the simplest way is also duplication, provided that no hardware measure is available to check the inputs and thus preserve independence of the application. In both types of architecture, redundant I/O should use different port registers to ensure maximal physical independence. Some applications receive safety-critical information via the CAN bus. In this case, the CAN controller represents a single point of failure. However, information redundancy in combination with message counters can be applied to detect faults in the CAN messages.

The interference of all further on-chip peripherals (e.g. timers, analog-to-digital conversion) has to be analyzed. Future hardware architectures could support the designer by including self-checking abilities for some components.

[3] The term *brown-out* describes an undesired lowering of the supply voltage for some period of time.

[4] The term *dual point fault* represents a special case of multiple point faults in which faults in two components are required to violate the safety goal.

4 Evaluation of Application Example

Within this section, the implementation of an application example, namely a controller for a convertible top, on a dual-core device is described briefly. The main task of this controller is to open or close the convertible top. However, potential hazards can occur during operation. As an example, the convertible top might break away if opened while driving at high speed and might injure or kill other road users. Another example could be that a person might shut a finger or other bodily parts in the mechanic of the convertible top and therefore receive an injury. Hence, it is necessary to establish safety goals and the corresponding safety function to prevent the occurrence of these hazards. For this application example, two safety goals have been defined:

1. The convertible top will not move if the vehicle is driving.
2. The convertible top will not move if this is not requested by the user.

In order to implement the main task of the controller, a lot of sensors (e.g. roof status, window status, trunk status, vehicle speed, user panel) and actuators (e.g. hydraulic pump and valves, electric motors) are required. However, for the implementation of the safety function, only few sensors and actuators (those that are safety-related) have to be considered. In the application example, the following information is required to determine a violation of the safety goals: vehicle speed, ignition status, and status of user request. The user request is received from a control panel which is connected to two of the controller's digital inputs. The current speed and ignition status of the vehicle are sent via CAN bus to the controller. Furthermore, only the hydraulic pump is responsible for moving the convertible top and is therefore the only actuator which could lead to a violation of the safety goals. Thus, the safety goals are achieved by the following safety requirement:

An activation of the hydraulic pump will be allowed if the current speed is 0 Km/h, the ignition has been turned on and either the open button or the close button is pressed.

In order to fulfill this safety requirement and to fulfill the requirements defined by ASIL C in Section 2, the safety architectures which are presented in Section 3 could be applied.

For this application example, a generic architecture will result in a lot of overhead. Each safety-related component has to be covered by a generic safety mechanism to ensure that the safety goal will not be violated. The generic architecture does not take into account the specific characteristics of the application, namely disabling the hydraulic pump.

In contrast, a function monitoring architecture is very easy to realize in this case. This approach takes advantage of the specific characteristics of the application. Therefore, the safety function does only check the boundary conditions given by the safety requirements (speed, ignition status, status control panel) and enables the hydraulic pump only if the conditions are fulfilled. Further safety mechanisms to detect latent multiple point faults can be implemented by additional measures easily and with a diagnostic coverage as high as required by [6]. Hence, the overhead is considered as lower in this architecture. Therefore, the function monitoring architecture is the preferred safety architecture.

Nevertheless, it is generally not possible to say which architecture should be used for other applications. In particular, it depends on the complexity of the safety function to be implemented. In this application example, the complexity of this function is very low. It has a size, measured in Lines of Code (LoC), of about 200 LoC while the application itself has a size of roughly 1500 LoC. Furthermore, the application example includes only one safety-related actuator. The more actuators have to be controlled by the function monitor, the higher will be the complexity of the function monitor itself. In case of a more complex safety function, it might be better to use a generic approach, which is mostly independent from the actual application. Since the complexity of generic architectures is also known, it is possible to estimate the costs for realizing the chosen generic architecture for an application. Such an estimation is generally harder to achieve for function monitoring architectures. However, the complexity of a function monitor can be predicted roughly in most instances, since the boundary conditions (and other safety functions used in the function monitor) are derived from the function safety requirements.

Usually, the decision for or against generic architectures and function monitoring architecture, respectively, can be made in a early development phase. Since the boundary conditions and other safety functions used in the function monitor are derived from the function safety requirements, it is usually possible to predict the complexity of the function monitor.

5 Conclusion

In this paper we presented different approaches for implementing safety architectures with dual-core systems. These approaches were categorized into *function monitoring architectures* and *generic architectures*. The concept of function monitoring can be implemented comparatively easy, if the complexity of the corresponding safety function is low, which is the case in several automotive applications (as in the application example described above). In opposite to generic architectures, coverage of both safety-critical hardware and software faults can be achieved with an acceptable hardware overhead. Moreover, if only the safety function is executed on the second core, (formal) verification of the correctness of the implemented safety function will be simplified. On the other hand, generic architectures are superior to function monitoring, if it is difficult to state the application's safety-critical states exactly. However, high fault coverage of the component-based safety mechanisms in these approaches comes along with a need for additional supporting hardware. Nevertheless, the comprehensive fault detection mechanisms available in generic architectures can be used to increase overall system reliability.

Moreover, the distinction between function monitoring architectures and generic architectures is not limited to dual core architectures. Further methods for comprehensive fault detection exist. A promising example is the platform-based hardware-centric approach presented in [13].

Summarizing, both approaches come with their specific advantages and disadvantages and the choice depends on the application as well as on the cost and the technical maturity of devices based on generic architectures.

References

1. Bauer, T.: Verfahren und Vorrichtung zur gegenseitigen Überwachung von Steuereinheiten. DE Patent n.19933086 by R.B. GmbH (2001)
2. Bederna, F., Zeller, T.: Verfahren und Vorrichtung zur Steuerung der Antriebseinheit eines Fahrzeugs. DE Patent 4438714 der Robert Bosch GmbH (1995)
3. Benso, A., Carlo, S.D., Natale, G.D., Prinetto, P.: A watchdog processor to detect data and control flow errors. Iolts, 144 (2003)
4. Brewerton, S.: Dual core processor solutions for IEC61508 SIL3 vehicle safety systems. In: Embedded World Conference (2007)
5. Fruehling, T.L.: Delphi secured microcontroller architecture. In: Design and Technologies for Automotive Safety-Critical Systems. SAE World Congress (March 2000)
6. ISO. ISO/WD 26262 - Road vehicles - Functional Safety. International Organization for Standardization, working draft (2007)
7. Kanekawa, N., Meguro, T., Isono, K., Shima, Y., Miyazaki, N., Yamaguchi, S.: Fault detection and recovery coverage improvement by clock synchronized duplicated systems with optimal time diversity. In: FTCS 1998: Proceedings of the The Twenty-Eighth Annual International Symposium on Fault-Tolerant Computing, Washington, DC, USA, p. 196. IEEE Computer Society Press, Los Alamitos (1998)
8. Kottke, T., Steininger, A.: A generic dual-core architecture. In: 7th IEEE International Workshop on Design and Diagnostics of Electronic Circuits and Systems (DDECS 2004) (April 2004)
9. Kottke, T., Steininger, A.: A reconfigurable generic dual-core architecture. In: DSN 2006: Proceedings of the International Conference on Dependable Systems and Networks, Washington, DC, USA, pp. 45–54. IEEE Computer Society Press, Los Alamitos (2006)
10. Leveson, N.G.: Safeware - System Safety and Computers. Addison-Wesley, Reading (1995)
11. Mariani, R.: Soft errors on digital components – an emerging reliability problem for new silicon technologies. In: Fault Injection Techniques and Tools for Embedded Systems Reliability Evaluation, vol. 23, pp. 49–60. Springer, Heidelberg (2004)
12. Mariani, R., Boschi, G.: A system-level approach for embedded memory robustness. Solid-State Electronics Journal 49, 1791–1798 (2005)
13. Mariani, R., Fuhrmann, P.: Comparing fail-safe microcontroller architectures in light of IEC 61508. In: 22nd Int. Symposium on Defect and Fault-Tolerance in VLSI Systems (DFT 2007), September 2007, pp. 123–131. IEEE Computer Society Press, Los Alamitos (2007)
14. Miremadi, G., Karlsson, J., Gunneflo, U., Torin, J.: Two software techniques for on-line error detection. In: Digest of Papers, 22nd Int. Symposium on Fault-Tolerant Computing, pp. 328–335 (1992)
15. Montenegro, S.: Sichere und fehlertolerante Steuerungen. Hanser Verlag (1999)
16. Salloum, C.E., Steininger, A., Tummeltshammer, P., Harter, W.: Recovery mechanisms for dual core architectures. In: DFT 2006: Proceedings of the 21st IEEE International Symposium on Defect and Fault-Tolerance in VLSI Systems, Washington, DC, USA, pp. 380–388. IEEE Computer Society Press, Los Alamitos (2006)

Timing Validation of Automotive Software

Daniel Kästner[1], Reinhard Wilhelm[2], Reinhold Heckmann[1], Marc Schlickling[1,2], Markus Pister[1,2], Marek Jersak[3], Kai Richter[3], and Christian Ferdinand[1]

[1] AbsInt GmbH, Saarbrücken, Germany
[2] Saarland University, Saarbrücken, Germany
[3] Symtavision GmbH, Braunschweig, Germany

Abstract. Embedded hard real-time systems need reliable guarantees for the satisfaction of their timing constraints. During the last years sophisticated analysis tools for timing analysis at the code-level, controller-level and networked system-level have been developed. This trend is exemplified by two tools: AbsInt's timing analyzer aiT, and and Symtavision's SymTA/S. aiT determines safe upper bounds for the execution times (WCETs) of non-interrupted tasks. SymTA/S computes the worst-case response times (WCRTs) of an entire system from the task WCETs and from information about possible interrupts and their priorities. A seamless integration between both tools provides for a holistic approach to timing validation: starting from a system model, a designer can perform timing budgeting, performance optimization and timing verification, thus covering both the code and the system aspects. However, the precision of the results and the efficiency of the analysis methods are highly dependent on the predictability of the execution platform. Especially on multi-core architectures this aspect becomes of critical importance. This paper describes an industry-strength tool flow for timing validation, and discusses prerequisites at the hardware level for ascertaining high analysis precision.

1 Introduction

Developers of safety-critical real-time systems have to ensure that their systems react within given time bounds. Tests and measurements help to detect violations of time bounds, but cannot prove their absence, unless all possible scenarios are covered. Face to the complexity of today's embedded software and the complexity of contemporary hardware architectures this is virtually impossible. Moreover, tests and measurements are only available late in the development cycle. Tools for static program analysis can obtain results valid for all possible system runs and inputs, even before the first real prototypes are available. Examples for such tools are AbsInt's timing analyzer aiT, and Symtavision's SymTA/S tool. aiT is a code-level analysis tool determining safe upper bounds for the execution times (WCETs) of non-interrupted tasks. SymTA/S works at the system level; it computes the worst-case response times (WCRTs) of an entire system from the task WCETs and from information about possible interrupts and their priorities.

T. Margaria and B. Steffen (Eds.): ISoLA 2008, CCIS 17, pp. 93–107, 2008.

A tool coupling between aiT and SymTA/S paves the path towards a holistic timing validation tool chain. The system developer creates a system model in SymTA/S, consisting of a task graph, information on task scheduling (priorities, time slots, etc.), and information on task activation (time tables, interrupts, etc.). To determine the WCRTs of the tasks with possible interrupts, the WCETs of the non-interrupted tasks are required. To obtain these WCETs, SymTA/S sends requests to aiT. Then aiT asks the developer for necessary information on hardware configuration and executables, determines the requested WCETs, and sends them back to SymTA/S. The coupling of SymTA/S with aiT allows SymTA/S to determine end-to-end timings in an early development phase, with automatic identification of problematic system configurations and automatic system optimization as a next step. In the EU projects INTEREST and INTERESTED the tool coupling is extended towards model-based code generation tools such as ASCET[8] and SCADE[7] to support the entire development process from the model till the implementation with formally verified timing behavior.

Static-analysis-based methods can give timing guarantees even for complex processor architectures exhibiting a huge execution-time variability and a strong dependency of the execution time on the initial execution state. Nevertheless, the efficiency and the precision of the result of timing analysis highly depends on the hardware architecture. As an example, a cache with a random replacement strategy does not allow for a cache analysis with good precision. The design of the internal and external buses, if done wrongly, leads to hardly analyzable behavior and great loss in precision. Multi-core architectures with shared caches, finally, will create a space of interleavings of interactions on these caches that will make sound and precise timing analysis practically infeasible at all.

The trend in automotive embedded systems is towards unifying frameworks like AUTOSAR. Such frameworks aim at managing the increasing functional complexity and allowing for better reconfigurability and maintainability. Standardized interfaces allow to compose components, independently developed by different suppliers, on ECUs. A runtime environment provides basic services, like intra- or inter-ECU communication between components. At a lower level AUTOSAR abstracts from the underlying hardware, the actually deployed ECUs. From a functional point of view this framework is appealing because of the gained compositionality.

The AUTOSAR timing model currently being developed concerns mainly the integration of scheduling requirements. The success of scheduling analysis depends on the predictability of the execution times of the AUTOSAR-"runnables", the basic building blocks of a software component. When multiple components are mapped to a hardware architecture where a high degree of interference between the components cannot be avoided (e.g., due to shared caches or buses) execution times of runnables may vary considerably and the possibilities to predict safe and precise execution time bounds can be rather limited. This limits the success of the scheduling analysis and this counteracts the idea of composing software components. Thus, the applicability of the AUTOSAR idea depends on availability of architectures on which software composition doesn't lead to unpredictable timing behavior.

In the following, we present a tool flow for validating timing behavior based on aiT and SymTA/S. In Sec. 2-Sec. 3 we discuss the influence of the hardware architecture on the timing validation process, based on experience with static timing-analysis in the embedded-systems industry [30,13] and theoretical insights [23,22,11]. Sec. 5 first address hardware issues that have to be respected both in single core and in multi-core architectures. Face to the increased complexity of multi-core designs, there these aspects become even more critical than they are in the single core domain. Sec. 5 concludes with discussing specific issues for multi-core architectures.

2 The System Level: Schedulability Analysis

Scheduling analysis is a systematic approach that automatically finds and evaluates critical timing situations resulting from function and system integration. Such *corner case identification* is the opposite of traditional test-based methods: instead of massive testing to try to find all corner cases, scheduling analysis systematically constructs scenarios leading to worst-case timing.

SymTA/S [14] is Symtavision's tool for timing and scheduling analysis and optimization for controllers, networks and entire systems. SymTA/S computes the worst-case response times (WCRTs) of tasks and the worst-case end-to-end communication delays. It takes into account the worst-case execution times of the tasks as well as information about RTOS scheduling, bus arbitration, possible interrupts and their priorities. The graphical user interface of SymTA/S offers ways to specify a system architecture, select scheduling on controllers and arbitration on buses, map functions to controllers and communication to busses, and to describe dataflow, activation conditions, deadlines and other timing constraints.

The analysis results are displayed in a variety of ways. The most powerful and easy to understand are *Gantt-Charts* that visualize to the designer why and under which conditions deadlines can be violated. There are two main use cases for SymTA/S:

1. *timing design / budgeting* during early design stages and
2. *timing verification* during later design stages.

The added value for verification is exemplified in Figure 1: the upper part of the diagram displays a typical timing trace, showing a response time of 6.9 ms for a task executed every 10 ms – well below the 10 ms deadline. In the lower part, SymTA/S scheduling analysis has constructed a worst-case schedule leading to a WCRT of 9 ms for the 10 ms task – still below the deadline, but much closer. The key message is that no other schedule will produce a longer WCRT. SymTA/S thus safeguards against deadline violations resulting from worst-case schedules. Furthermore, the Gantt-display enables the designer to check the reasoning of SymTA/S and thus to see if some important information has been omitted in the model.

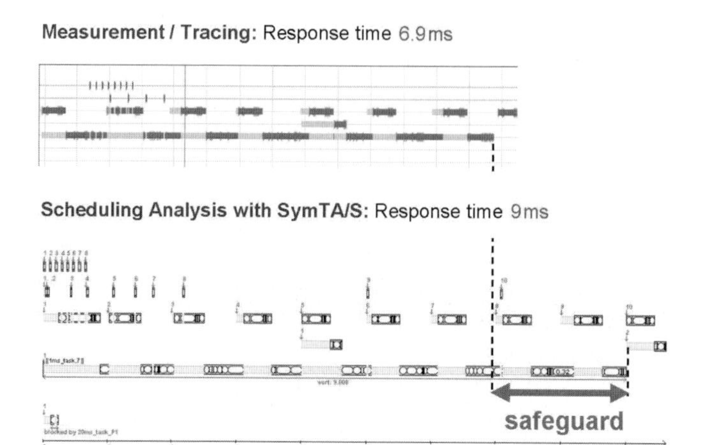

Fig. 1. Safeguarding timing using scheduling analysis (as compared to measurement)

Furthermore SymTA/S also supports the system design stage. With a *what-if* scheduling analysis it is easily possible to estimate how additional functions and their scheduling will influence overall system timing, and whether deadlines can be safely met for a specific design alternative. As a result, timing budgets for individual functions of sub-systems can be derived early on, and given to a designer as part of a requirements specification. Additionally, SymTA/S offers a plugin for *design-space exploration* allowing designers to automatically evaluate the strengths and weaknesses of alternative designs with respect to timing and performance. A plugin for *sensitivity analysis* allows users to automatically determine the amount of extra load (e.g., caused by additional functions) permissible without violating deadlines.

3 The Code Level: Static Timing Analysis

aiT computes safe upper bounds on the worst-case execution times (WCETs) of sequential tasks. For a precise computation of the WCET, aiT operates on the executable. If available, aiT can also read the source files for further information. The WCET is computed in several phases [9] (see Figure 2).

In the first step a *decoder* reads the executable and reconstructs its control flow [27]. Then, *value analysis* determines lower and upper bounds for the values in the processor registers for every program point and execution context, which lead to bounds for the addresses of memory accesses (important for cache analysis and if memory areas with different access times exist). Value analysis can also determine that certain conditions always evaluate to true or always evaluate to false. As consequence, certain paths controlled by such conditions are never executed. Thus value analysis can detect and mark some unreachable code.

WCET analysis requires that upper bounds for the iteration numbers of all loops be known. aiT tries to determine the number of loop iterations by *loop*

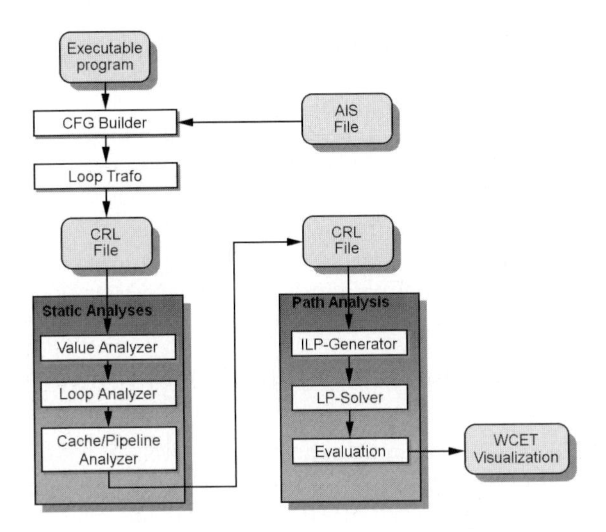

Fig. 2. Phases of WCET Computation

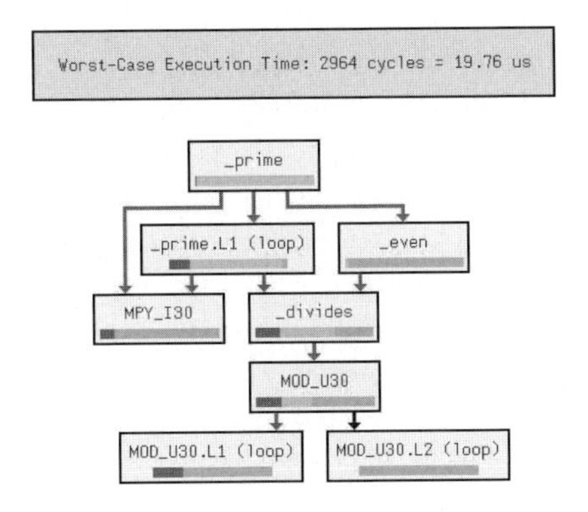

Fig. 3. Call graph with WCET result

bound analysis [10], but succeeds in doing so for simple loops only. Bounds for the remaining loops must be provided as specifications in a separate parameter file (.ais file) or annotations in the C source. The *micro-architectural analysis* [6,29,11] determines bounds on the execution time of individual basic blocks by performing an abstract interpretation of the program. It thereby takes into account the processor's pipeline, caches, and speculation concepts: static cache analyses determine safe approximations to the contents of caches at each program point. All accesses into main memory are classified into hits, misses, or accesses of unknown nature. A pipeline analysis analyzes how instructions pass through the pipeline accounting for occupancy of shared resources like queues and functional units etc., and for the classification of memory references by the cache analysis etc [26]. Ignoring these average-case-enhancing features would result in imprecise bounds. Using this information, *path analysis* determines a safe estimate of the WCET. The program's control flow is modeled by an integer linear program [16,28] so that the solution to the objective function is the predicted worst-case execution time for the input program.

After a successful analysis, aiT reports its results in several ways: aiT can produce a graphical output showing the call graph and control flow graph of the analyzed part of the application. Alternatively, aiT can write a text report meant to be human readable, and a more formal XML report. These reports contain detailed results for all analyzed routines in all calling contexts, including specific results for the first few iterations of loops vs. a result for the remaining iterations.

4 The Interaction between SymTA/S and aiT

Timing analysis is a novel domain, and the requirements for coupling code-level and system-level tools were not suitably covered by any existing exchange format. Therefore, the concept of "Timing Cookies" has been developed in the INTEREST project to avoid the duplication of the sophisticated user-interfaces of the tools. The information exchanged is stored in such a Timing Cookie in the first round of communication between the tools. During the next round of communication this information is retrieved from that cookie so that invariant parts do not have to be re-entered manually.

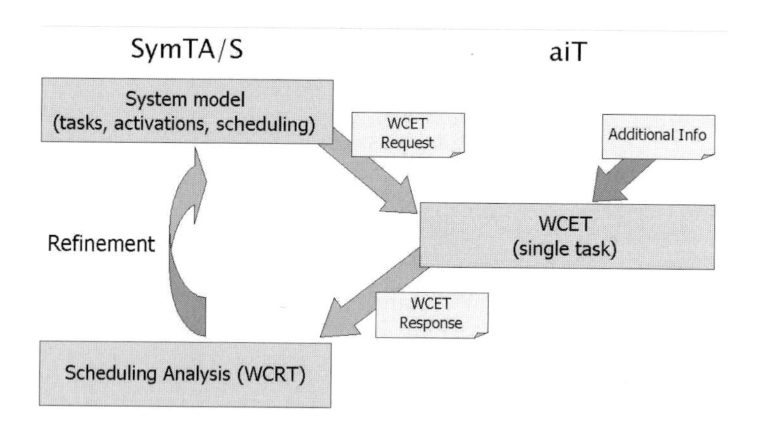

Fig. 4. Flow of requests and responses

The Timing Cookie Exchange Format XTC is defined as an XML schema. It is organized hierarchically since some information can be reused for different analyses. For instance, a CPU configuration can be reused for different runnables sharing the same CPU. The information in the common section is structured in four blocks: general, CPU, runnable (i.e., an atomic piece of software[1]), and mode (a specific control-flow path through the runnable).

[1] AUTOSAR [2] terminology has been adopted.

The interaction between SymTA/S and aiT follows the following pattern: From a system model, SymTA/S launches a request for WCET information for specific pieces of code (see Figure 4). This request is tagged with a unique ID and sent to aiT in an XTC. If necessary, aiT queries the user for all missing information required to service the request. For the first request issued for a system model, this typically includes the type of processor, the location of the executable code, the starting point of the analysis etc. When aiT answers the request by sending an XTC with a response back to SymTA/S, it stores this information in the private aiT-part of the cookie. This aiT-specific information will be included in subsequent requests so that aiT can use the information already gathered without the need to ask the user again.

5 Hardware and Predictability

In modern microprocessor architectures caches, pipelines, and all kinds of speculation are key features for improving (average-case) performance. Caches are used to bridge the gap between processor speed and the access time of main memory. Pipelines enable acceleration by overlapping the executions of different instructions. Multi-core designs combine two or more independent cores into a single die. Cores in a multi-core device may share a single coherent cache at the highest on-device cache level or may have separate caches. The processors also share the same interconnect to the rest of the system. Each core independently implements the typical hardware features described above for the single core domain.

The consequence is that the execution time of individual instructions, and thus the contribution of one execution of an instruction to the program's execution time can vary widely. This variation depends on the execution state, e.g., the contents of the cache(s), the occupancy of other resources, and thus on the execution history. It is therefore obvious that the attempt to predict or exclude timing accidents needs information about the execution history.

For WCET computation, the state space of input data and initial states is too large to exhaustively explore all possible executions in order to determine the exact worst-case execution times. Instead, bounds for the execution times of basic blocks are determined, from which bounds for the whole system's execution time are derived. Some abstraction of the execution platform is necessary to make a timing analysis of the system feasible. These abstractions lose information, and thus are in part responsible for the gap between WCETs and upper bounds. How much is lost depends both on the methods used for timing analysis and on system properties, such as the hardware architecture and the analyzability of the software.

Most of the problems posed to timing analysis are caused by the *interference on shared resources*. Resources are shared for cost, energy and performance reasons. Different users of a shared resource may often access the resource in a statically unknown way. Different access sequences may result in different states of the resource. The different sequences may already exhibit different execution times, and the resulting resource states may again cause differences in the future timing behavior. An out-of-order processor will execute an instruction stream in one sequential order. Exhaustive exploration could, in principle, identify this one sequence for each input and initial state, while in practice, this is infeasible. Thus, this order is assumed to be not statically known. This forces the analysis to consider all possible sequences. Different sequences may have different effects on the cache contents. Examples of shared resources with interferences are buses and memory: Buses are used by several masters, which may access the buses in unpredictable ways. On a multi-core system the interference on shared resources is significantly increased wrt a single core system. Memory and caches are shared between several processors or cores. One thread executed on one core does not know when accesses by another thread on another core will happen.

In the following we will first investigate the predictability of common elementary hardware features: pipelines, caches, and buses. This discussion applies both for single core and multi-core architectures, since they determine the "internal´´ behavior of each core in a multi-core design. In Sec. 5.4 we additionally discuss specific features of multi-core designs.

5.1 Pipelines

For non-pipelined architectures one can simply add up the execution times of individual instructions to obtain a bound on the execution time of a basic block. Pipelines increase performance by overlapping the executions of different instructions. Hence, a timing analysis cannot consider individual instructions in isolation. Instead, they have to be considered collectively – together with their mutual interactions – to obtain tight timing bounds. Superscalar- and out-of-order execution increase the number of possible interleavings. The larger the buffers (e.g., fetch buffers, retirement queues, etc.) are the longer lasts the influence of past events. Dynamic branch prediction, cache-like structures, and branch history tables increase history dependence even more.

The analysis of a given program for its pipeline behavior is based on an abstract model of the pipeline. All components that contribute to the timing of instructions have to be modeled conservatively. Depending on the employed pipeline features, the number of states the analysis has to consider varies greatly. To compute a precise bound on the execution time of a basic block, the analysis needs to exclude as many *timing accidents*, i.e., incidents that cause an increase of an instruction's execution time, as possible. Such accidents are data hazards, branch mispredictions, occupied functional units, full queues, etc.

Abstract states may lack information about the state of some processor components, e.g., caches, queues, or predictors. Transitions of the pipeline may depend on such missing information. Then the analysis must take all alternative scenarios into account. One could be tempted to design the analysis such that only the locally most expensive pipeline transition is chosen. However, in the presence of *timing anomalies* [17,23] this approach is unsound.

The notion of *timing anomalies* was introduced by Lundqvist and Stenström in [17]. In the context of WCET analysis, [23] presents a formal definition.

Intuitively, a timing anomaly is a situation where the local worst-case does not contribute to the global worst-case. For instance, a cache miss–the local worst-case–may result in a globally shorter execution time than a cache hit. A scenario where this can occur is when the cache miss penalty prevents the branch unit from misspeculating and prefetching along the wrong path. An especially severe timing anomaly is the so-called *domino effect* [17] that causes the difference in execution time of the same program starting in two different hardware states to become arbitrarily high. The existence of domino effects is undesirable for timing analysis. Otherwise, one could safely discard states during the analysis and make up for it by adding a predetermined constant. Unfortunately, domino effects show up in real hardware. In [25], Schneider describes a domino effect in the pipeline of the PowerPC 755. Another example is given by Berg [3] who considers the PLRU replacement policy of caches. Thus, in general, the analysis has to follow all possible successor states.

Architectures can be classified into three categories depending on whether they exhibit timing anomalies or domino effects.

- **Fully timing compositional architectures:** The (abstract model of) an architecture does not exhibit timing anomalies. Hence, the analysis can safely follow local worst-case paths only. One example for this class is the ARM7.
- **Compositional architectures with constant-bounded effects:** These exhibit timing anomalies but no domino effects. In general, an analysis has to consider all paths. To trade precision with efficiency, it would be possible to safely discard local non-worst-case paths by adding a constant number of cycles to the local worst-case path. The Infineon TriCore is assumed, but not formally proven, to belong to this class.
- **Non-compositional architectures:** These architectures, e.g., the PowerPC 755 exhibit domino effects and timing anomalies. For such architectures timing analyses always have to follow all paths since a local effect may influence the future execution arbitrarily.

5.2 Caches

To obtain tight bounds on the execution time of a task, timing analyses *must* take into account the cache architecture. The cache analysis tries to classify memory accesses as hits or misses. Memory accesses that cannot be safely classified as a hit or a miss have to be conservatively accounted for by considering both possibilities. The precision of a cache analysis is strongly dependent on the predictability of the cache architecture, especially on its replacement policy. The three most common replacement strategies are the following:

- The LRU(Least Recently Used) replacement strategy uses age bits to discard the least recently used cache line in case of a cache miss. When a cache hit occurs, the age information of all cache lines is updated. It is used in the FREESCALE PPC603E core and the MIPS 24K/34K.

- With the FIFOstrategy the cache is organized like a queue: new elements are inserted at the front evicting elements at the end of the queue. In contrast to LRU, hits do not change the queue. FIFO is used in the INTEL XSCALE and some ARM9 and ARM11 based processor cells.
- PLRU(Pseudo-LRU) is a tree-based approximation of the LRU policy. It arranges the cache lines at the leaves of a tree with $k-1$ "tree bits" pointing to the line to be replaced next. For an in detail explanation of PLRU consider [22,1]. It is used in the POWERPC 75X and the INTEL PENTIUM II-IV.

In [21] the influence of these three replacement strategies on the precision of static cache analyses is analyzed. The results show that LRU-replacement has the best predictability properties of all replacement policies. Employing other policies, like PLRU or FIFO, yields less precise WCET bounds, because fewer memory accesses can be classified as hits of misses. This also has the consequence that timing analysis has to explore more possibilities so that the efficiency is lower than with LRU.

Static cache analyses usually cannot make any assumptions about the initial cache contents. Cache contents on entrance depend on previously executed tasks. Even assuming a completely empty cache may not be conservative as shown in [3,21], the notable exception being LRU. FIFO and PLRU are much more sensitive to their state than LRU. Depending on its state, FIFO(k) may have up to k times as many misses and arbitrarily more hits, on the same access sequence. PLRU and LRU coincide at associativity 2. For greater associativities, the same access sequence under a PLRU strategy may incur arbitrarily many more misses for one starting state than for another. For PLRU(8), the number of hits of the same access sequence with different starting states may differ by a factor of 11. In [21] also the aggregated effect of the initial cache setting on WCET has been investigated for a realistic hardware setting. For a 4-way set-associative FIFO cache with a cache miss penalty of 50 cycles, the worst-case execution time may be a factor of 3 higher than the measured time of the same access sequence, only due to the influence of the initial cache state. If PLRU were used as a replacement policy the difference could be even greater.

This is especially detrimental for measurement-based approaches [18,4,32]. Measurement would trivially be sound if all initial states and inputs would be covered. Due to their huge number this is usually not feasible. Some measurement-based approaches consider distributions of execution times (execution time profiles) of program snippets, which are then composed according to the control flow. Each program fragment is measured with a subset of the possible initial states and inputs so that the maximum of the measured execution times is in general an underestimation of the worst-case execution time. Using corrective bounds for the so-called execution time profiles can introduce large pessimism since they don't exploit context and flow information [19].

Relatively simple architectures without any performance-enhancing features like pipelines, caches, etc., exhibit the same timing independently of the initial state. For such architectures, measurement-based timing analysis is sound [32].

[5] and [32] propose to lock the cache contents [20,31] and to flush the pipeline at program points where measurement starts. This is not possible on all architectures and it also has a detrimental effect on both the average- and the worst-case execution times of tasks.

5.3 Buses

A bus is a subsystem for transferring data between different components inside a computer, between a computer and its peripheral devices, or between different computers. Examples are system buses like the *60x-bus* [12], internal computer buses like *PCI* and external computer buses like *CAN* or *FlexRay*.

In general, busses are clocked with a lower frequency than the CPU. The number of possible displacements of phase between CPU- and bus-clock signal is bounded, i.e. at the start of a CPU cycle the bus cycle can only be in a finite number of states. For example, if the CPU operates at $f_{CPU} = 100$ MHz and the bus at $f_{BUS} = 25$ MHz, there are 4 different states. In general, the number of states is determined by $\frac{f_{CPU}}{\gcd(f_{CPU}, f_{BUS})}$.

Analyzing timing behavior of memory accesses is special because these accesses cross the CPU/bus clock boundary. Since the time unit for timing analyzes is one CPU cycle, the analysis needs to know when the next bus cycle begins. Otherwise it would have to account for the worst case: the bus cycle has just begun and the CPU needs to wait nearly a full bus cycle to perform a bus action. This pessimism would lead to less precise WCET bounds. Therefore, the displacement of phase has to modeled within a micro-architectural analysis so that the search space for the analysis is augmented by the number of different bus-clock-states.

Parallel buses (e.g., SCSI) introduce further complication. The execution of consecutive memory accesses can be overlapped, i.e. for two accesses, the address phase of the second access can be overlapped with the data phase of the first access (*bus pipelining*). Pipelined buses need to arbitrate the incoming bus requests, e.g. if there is an instruction fetch and a memory access at the same time, the arbitration logic needs to decide which bus request is issued first.

Asynchronous mechanisms such as *DMA* or *DRAM* refresh cannot be analyzed with the methods described so far. A DMA transmission and a DRAM refresh and their associated costs cannot be contributed to the execution of an instruction. The costs of a DRAM refresh must be amortized over time. A similar approach can be used if the frequency of DMA is statically known.

5.4 Multi-core Architectures

There is a tendency towards the use of multi-core architectures for their good energy/performance ratio. Shared memories (Flash, RAM) and peripherals are connected to the cores by shared buses or cross-bars. Conflicts when accessing shared resources are usually resolved by assigning fixed priorities. Depending on the architecture, conflicts on shared resources can be expected to happen frequently. For example, if the cores have no private RAM, a potential conflict might occur for each access (typically 20-30% of all executed instructions). Examples for current automotive multi-core architectures are the Infineon TriCore TC1797, the Freescale MC9S12X and the Freescale MPC5516. They consist of a powerful main processor and a less powerful co-processor. For future automotive multi-core architectures we see a design trend towards the use of identical cores mostly with shared memories.

Under the aspect of predictability, some existing and upcoming multi-core architectures are unacceptable because of the interference of the different cores on shared resources such as caches and buses. The execution time of a task running on one core typically depends on the activities on the other cores. Static worst-case execution time analysis usually assumes the absence of interferences. The additional time (or penalty) caused by interferences must be bounded for a scheduling analysis. For architectures with domino effects and timing anomalies inside the cores the additional inter-core interferences represent a huge obstacle to determining such a bound. Especially the unconstrained use of shared caches can make a sound and precise analysis of the cache performance impossible. The set of potential interleavings of the threads running on the different cores result in a huge state space to be explored resulting in poor precision.

There exist first approaches to the analysis of the cache performance of shared caches in multi-core systems. All approaches implicitly assume *fully timing compositional architectures* (see Sec. 5.1). They compute the cache footprint of preempted and preempting tasks, determine the intersection, and assume the rest as being eliminated (cf. [15]). This approach is neither context-sensitive nor flow-sensitive and therefore overly pessimistic. For a fully timing-compositional architecture, Schlieker, Ivers, and Ernst [24] determine upper bounds of the penalties by computing the number of potential conflicts when accessing shared memory by counting the number of memory accesses possibly generated on different cores. Thus it becomes apparent that in order to achieve good predictability results on a multi-core system choosing a fully timing compositional intra-core architecture combined with separate caches is of utmost importance.

6 Conclusion

Embedded hard real-time systems need reliable guarantees for the satisfaction of their timing constraints. In order to provide software and system designers with an efficient way to verify timing properties of ECU software, the code-level timing analysis tool aiT and the system-level timing analysis tool SymTA/S have been coupled. Starting from a system model, a designer can perform timing budgeting, performance optimization and timing verification, thus covering both the code and the system aspects. XML Timing Cookies (XTC) provide for a user-friendly, open, and efficient tool integration. SymTA/S communicates with aiT via XTC, sending analysis requests and receiving responses. While providing a holistic tool flow for timing validation to system designers, the precision of the results and the efficiency of the analysis methods depend on the predictability of the execution platform.

This is particularly important face to the trend towards unifying frameworks like AUTOSAR in automotive embedded systems. The goal is to establish a standard in which components, possibly independently developed by different suppliers, can be integrated on ECUs by standardized interfaces. To this end AUTOSAR abstracts from the underlying hardware, the actually deployed ECUs. The AUTOSAR timing model currently being developed concerns mainly the integration of scheduling requirements. However, the success of scheduling analysis depends on the predictability of the execution times of the AUTOSAR-"runnables". Thus, the applicability of the AUTOSAR idea depends on availability of architectures on which software composition doesn't lead to unpredictable timing behavior.

The experience with the use of static timing analysis methods and the tools based on it in the automotive and the aeronautics industries is positive. Static-analysis-based methods can give timing guarantees even for complex processor architectures exhibiting a huge execution-time variability and a strong dependency of the execution time on the initial execution state. However, when multiple components are mapped to a hardware architecture where a high degree of interference between the components cannot be avoided (e.g., due to shared caches or buses) execution times of runnables may vary considerably and the possibilities to predict safe and precise execution time bounds can be rather limited. This limits the success of the scheduling analysis and this counteracts the idea of composing software components. In contrast, choosing a fully timing compositional intra-core architecture combined with separate caches will lead to good predictability results. In consequence, the underlying hardware architecture has to be chosen with timing predictability in mind.

This paper discusses the most important hardware components affecting timing predictability and summarizes their effect on the applicability of measurement-based approaches and on the efficiency and precision of static analysis methods. An industry-strength tool flow for timing validation is presented, and the prerequisites at the hardware level for ascertaining high analysis precision are detailed.

References

1. Al-Zoubi, H., Milenkovic, A., Milenkovic, M.: Performance evaluation of cache replacement policies for the SPEC CPU2000 benchmark suite. In: ACM-SE 42: Proceedings of the 42nd Annual Southeast Regional Conference, pp. 267–272. ACM Press, New York (2004)
2. T. AUTOSAR Development Partnership. Automotive Open System Architecture (AUTOSAR) (2003), http://www.autosar.org
3. Berg, C.: PLRU cache domino effects. In: Proceedings of 6th International Workshop on Worst-Case Execution Time (WCET) Analysis (July 2006)
4. Bernat, G., Colin, A., Petters, S.M.: WCET analysis of probabilistic hard real-time systems. In: RTSS 2002: Proceedings of the 23rd IEEE Real-Time Systems Symposium (RTSS 2002), Washington, DC, USA, p. 279. IEEE Computer Society, Los Alamitos (2002)

5. Deverge, J.-F., Puaut, I.: Safe measurement-based WCET estimation. In: Wilhelm, R. (ed.) 5th Intl. Workshop on Worst-Case Execution Time (WCET) Analysis, Dagstuhl, Germany, Internationales Begegnungs- und Forschungszentrum für Informatik (IBFI), Schloss Dagstuhl, Germany (2005)
6. Engblom, J.: Processor Pipelines and Static Worst-Case Execution Time Analysis. PhD thesis, Dept. of Information Technology, Uppsala University (2002)
7. Esterel Technologies. SCADE Suite, http://www.esterel-technologies.com/products/scade-suite
8. ETAS Group. ASCET Software Products, http://www.etas.com/en/products/ascet_software_products.php
9. Ferdinand, C., Heckmann, R., Langenbach, M., Martin, F., Schmidt, M., Theiling, H., Thesing, S., Wilhelm, R.: Reliable and precise WCET determination for a real-life processor. In: Henzinger, T.A., Kirsch, C.M. (eds.) EMSOFT 2001. LNCS, vol. 2211, pp. 469–485. Springer, Heidelberg (2001)
10. Ferdinand, C., Martin, F., Cullmann, C., Schlickling, M., Stein, I., Thesing, S., Heckmann, R.: New developments in WCET analysis. In: Reps, T., Sagiv, M., Bauer, J. (eds.) Wilhelm Festschrift. LNCS, vol. 4444, pp. 12–52. Springer, Heidelberg (2007)
11. Ferdinand, C., Wilhelm, R.: Efficient and precise cache behavior prediction for real-time systems. Real-Time Systems 17(2-3), 131–181 (1999)
12. Freescale Semiconductor, Inc. PowerPC Microprocessor Family: The Bus Interface for 32-Bit Microprocessors, Rev. 0.1 (2004)
13. Heckmann, R., Langenbach, M., Thesing, S., Wilhelm, R.: The influence of processor architecture on the design and the results of WCET tools. IEEE Proceedings on Real-Time Systems 91(7), 1038–1054 (2003)
14. Henia, R., Hamann, A., Jersak, M., Racu, R., Richter, K., Ernst, R.: System level performance analysis – the SymTA/S approach. IEEE Proceedings on Computers and Digital Techniques 152(2) (March 2005)
15. Lee, C.-G., Hahn, J., Min, S.L., Ha, R., Hong, S., Park, C.Y., Lee, M., Kim, C.S.: Analysis of cache-related preemption delay in fixed-priority preemptive scheduling. In: RTSS 1996: Proceedings of the 17th IEEE Real-Time Systems Symposium (RTSS 1996), Washington, DC, USA, p. 264. IEEE Computer Society, Los Alamitos (1996)
16. Li, Y.-T.S., Malik, S.: Performance Analysis of Embedded Software Using Implicit Path Enumeration. In: Proceedings of the 32nd ACM/IEEE Design Automation Conference (1995)
17. Lundqvist, T., Stenström, P.: Timing anomalies in dynamically scheduled microprocessors. In: Proceedings of the 20th IEEE Real-Time Systems Symposium (RTSS 1999), pp. 12–21 (December 1999)
18. Petters, S.M.: Worst Case Execution Time Estimation for Advanced Processor Architectures. PhD thesis, Technische Universität München, Munich, Germany (September 2002)
19. Petters, S.M., Zadarnowski, P., Heiser, G.: Measurements or static analysis or both? In: Rochange, C. (ed.) WCET (2007)
20. Puaut, I., Decotigny, D.: Low-complexity algorithms for static cache locking in multitasking hard real-time systems. In: RTSS 2002: Proceedings of the 23rd IEEE Real-Time Systems Symposium (RTSS 2002), Washington, DC, USA, p. 114. IEEE Computer Society, Los Alamitos (2002)
21. Reineke, J., Grund, D.: Sensitivity of cache replacement policies. Reports of SFB/TR 14 AVACS 36, SFB/TR 14 AVACS (March 2008)ISSN: 1860-9821, http://www.avacs.org

22. Reineke, J., Grund, D., Berg, C., Wilhelm, R.: Timing predictability of cache replacement policies. Real-Time Systems 37(2), 99–122 (2007)
23. Reineke, J., Wachter, B., Thesing, S., Wilhelm, R., Polian, I., Eisinger, J., Becker, B.: A definition and classification of timing anomalies. In: Proceedings of 6th International Workshop on Worst-Case Execution Time (WCET) Analysis (July 2006)
24. Schliecker, S., Ivers, M., Ernst, R.: Integrated analysis of communicating tasks in MPSoCs. In: Proceedings of the 4th International Conference on Hardware/Software Codesign and System Synthesis, pp. 288–293. ACM Press, New York (2006)
25. Schneider, J.: Combined Schedulability and WCET Analysis for Real-Time Operating Systems. PhD thesis, Saarland University (2003)
26. Schneider, J., Ferdinand, C.: Pipeline Behavior Prediction for Superscalar Processors by Abstract Interpretation. In: Proceedings of the ACM SIGPLAN Workshop on Languages, Compilers and Tools for Embedded Systems, vol. 34, pp. 35–44 (May 1999)
27. Theiling, H.: Extracting Safe and Precise Control Flow from Binaries. In: Proceedings of the 7th Conference on Real-Time Computing Systems and Applications, Cheju Island, South Korea (2000)
28. Theiling, H., Ferdinand, C.: Combining abstract interpretation and ILP for microarchitecture modelling and program path analysis. In: Proceedings of the 19th IEEE Real-Time Systems Symposium, Madrid, Spain, pp. 144–153 (December 1998)
29. Thesing, S.: Safe and Precise WCET Determinations by Abstract Interpretation of Pipeline Models. PhD thesis, Saarland University (2004)
30. Thesing, S., Souyris, J., Heckmann, R., Randimbivololona, F., Langenbach, M., Wilhelm, R., Ferdinand, C.: An abstract interpretation-based timing validation of hard real-time avionics software systems. In: Proceedings of the 2003 International Conference on Dependable Systems and Networks (DSN 2003), June 2003, pp. 625–632. IEEE Computer Society, Los Alamitos (2003)
31. Vera, X., Lisper, B., Xue, J.: Data cache locking for higher program predictability. SIGMETRICS Perform. Eval. Rev. 31(1), 272–282 (2003)
32. Wenzel, I.: Measurement-Based Timing Analysis of Superscalar Processors. PhD thesis, Technische Universität Wien, Institut für Technische Informatik, Treitlstr. 3/3/182-1, 1040 Vienna, Austria (2006)

Towards Using Reo for Compliance-Aware Business Process Modeling

Farhad Arbab, Natallia Kokash, and Sun Meng

CWI, Kruislaan 413, Amsterdam, The Netherlands
firstName.lastName@cwi.nl

Abstract. Business process modeling and implementation of process supporting infrastructures are two challenging tasks that are not fully aligned. On the one hand, languages such as Business Process Modeling Notation (BPMN) exist to capture business processes at the level of domain analysis. On the other hand, programming paradigms and technologies such as Service-Oriented Computing (SOC) and web services have emerged to simplify the development of distributed web systems that underly business processes. BPMN is the most recognized language for specifying process workflows at the early design steps. However, it is rather declarative and may lead to the executable models which are incomplete or semantically erroneous. Therefore, an approach for expressing and analyzing BPMN models in a formal setting is required. In this paper we describe how BPMN diagrams can be represented by means of a semantically precise channel-based coordination language called Reo which admits formal analysis using model checking and bisimulation techniques. Moreover, since additional requirements may come from various regulatory/legislative documents, we discuss the opportunities offered by Reo and its mathematical abstractions for expressing process-related constraints such as Quality of Service (QoS) or time-aware conditions on process states.

1 Introduction

The Service-Oriented Computing (SOC) paradigm supports the idea of building distributed applications by composing self-contained and loosely-coupled services. Service-Oriented Architecture (SOA) is the main architectural concept within this paradigm designed to support the realization of cross-organizational business processes. In this kind of architecture, services are employed to accomplish certain activities within a process. Several specifications coordinate the collaboration of individual services. In the simplest case, known as orchestration, one business partner manages the order in which required services are executed. In a more complex scenario, called choreography, each partner is responsible for executing services that realize its own business logic as well as interacting with other partners to achieve a common goal.

A stack of protocols that defines how web services collaborate is currently established. In particular, WS-BPEL [1] and WS-CDL [2] are the most com-

T. Margaria and B. Steffen (Eds.): ISoLA 2008, CCIS 17, pp. 108–123, 2008.

monly recognized languages dealing with orchestration and choreography, respectively. However, these languages are implementation-level languages while business processes incorporate various aspects, both functional and non-functional, that may be difficult to capture and convert directly into executable code. Therefore, additional tools are used at the level of domain analysis and abstract process design. The Business Process Modeling Notation (BPMN) [3] is a standard and widely-accepted graphical notation for this purpose. According to this notation, the process can be represented in the form of activities produced either by humans or software applications, important events occurring in the process and control flow on the involved activities. One of the reasons why BPMN stands out among other notations for business process modeling is its ability to define concurrent tasks and sub-processes with exception handling and compensation associations, which have been proven to be useful even at the stage of early design. As a trade-off to its expressive power, BPMN lacks semantic precision.

Two attempts have been made at defining formal semantics for BPMN subsets [4,5]. In the first approach [4], a core subset of BPMN is mapped into Petri nets. However, this approach encounters problems with reflecting the behavior of multiple concurrent activities in presence of exception handling. The second approach [5] formalizes the BPMN semantics (including time-aware semantics [6]) in a more consistent way using Communicating Sequential Processes (CSP). The main drawback of this model is that it does not preserve the structure of BPMN diagrams which makes the mapping difficult to follow. Additionally to these approaches, a number of works provide insights and tools for automated translation of BPMN into BPEL processes [7,8]. Such translations bridge the gap between the process modeling and their implementation using web services technology. However, they pose significant restrictions on admissible BPMN patterns and do not prevent developers from implementing erroneous processes. Later on, BPEL processes can be verified using a wide range of formal techniques [9,10,11] and model checking tools [12], but this scenario shifts the process verification to the implementation phase and thus slows down the incremental process design.

A number of challenging issues need to be addressed before SOC becomes a mature approach for developing flexible business applications. Among such issues is the SOA adaptation to the ever changing business/legislative requirements and process evolution. Multitudes of regulations constantly emerge to shape businesses and incorporate the best practices into corresponding software applications. The aim of the recently started COMPAS (Compliance driven Models, Languages, and Architectures for Services) project[1] is to develop an infrastructure to ensure dynamic and ongoing compliance of services-oriented applications to business regulations. These regulations come from legislative documents such as Basel II1, IFRS2, MiFID3, LSF4, HIPAA, Tabaksblat5, and the Sarbanes-Oxley6 Act, just to name a few. In addition to external regulations, there are internal considerations of Quality of Service (QoS) which result in similar requirements. Currently, there are no well-established practices for representing and tracking compliance-related controls. At the early process development stages,

[1] `http://www.compas-ict.eu/`

they can be expressed by means of modeling languages like BPMN or UML with textual annotations. However, such specifications are often ambiguous and may result in erroneous process implementation. Therefore, a modeling notation with precise semantics is required. This notation should be powerful enough to represent the major structural and control/data flow elements of processes, as well as to express various compliance concerns.

In this paper, our objective is two-fold. Firstly, we consider the main business process modeling primitives as defined in BPMN and show how they can be represented using a semantically precise coordination language, Reo. Secondly, we discuss the potential of our formalism in expressing compliance concerns.

The rest of this paper is organized as follows. In Section 2, we sketch the main steps of our approach to compliance-aware business process modeling. Section 3 contains an overview of BPMN and in Section 4, we introduce Reo. In Section 5, we present the mapping from BPMN to Reo. In Section 6, we discuss compliance rule modeling from the perspective of Reo. Finally, in Section 7, we outline our conclusions and future work.

2 Overview

The overall vision of our framework is shown in Fig. 1. Business analysts may use traditional notations for creating business process models such as BPMN or UML Activity Diagrams (ADs) as well as more specific ones, e.g., BPEL Graphical Modeling Tools (GMT)[2]. At this level, compliance concerns can be expressed using Domain Specific Languages (DSL) or GMT extensions, see [13] and [14] for examples of such approaches. One of the goals of the COMPAS project is to develop DSLs capable of expressing major categories of compliance concerns. These models will not necessarily guarantee the level of precision sufficient for the direct process implementation. Therefore, we propose to introduce an intermediate layer on which the high-level models will be verified and refined. The basic semantics of this layer is defined by Reo.

Reo is a channel-based exogenous coordination language supported by a graphical tool, an animation engine and a model checker[3]. These tools allow us to use Reo both for graphical process modeling and for formal process verification before its actual implementation. There are several reasons why Reo seems appropriate in the context of the COMPAS project. First, using Reo connectors it is possible to represent both choreography and orchestration of process activities as well as internal and external behavior of involved services in a unified formalism [15]. Moreover, Reo patterns can be automatically translated into Constraint Automata (CA) which are suitable for representing service compositions with QoS guarantees [16] and time-aware processes [17]. CA are essentially variants of labeled transition systems where transitions are augmented with pairs $\langle N, g \rangle$ of synchronization and data constraints rather than action labels. The states of a CA stand for the network configurations (e.g., contents

[2] http://www.eclipse.org/bpel/

[3] http://homepages.cwi.nl/~koehler/ect/index.htm

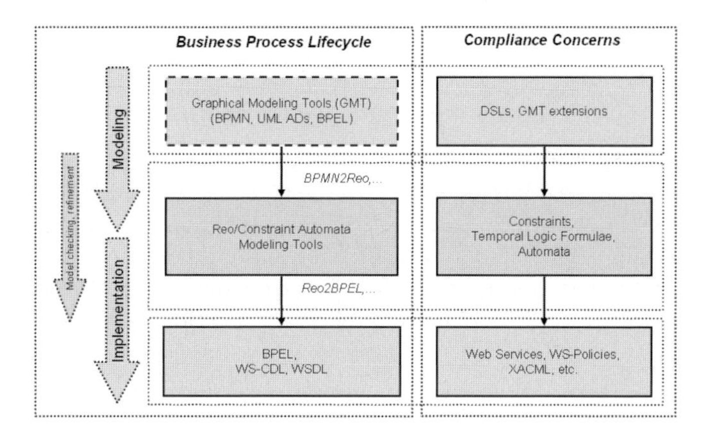

Fig. 1. Reo for business process modeling with compliance concerns

of the buffers) while transition labels $\langle N, g\rangle$ can be viewed as I/O operations performed in parallel (more precisely, sets of nodes where data flow is observed in parallel and boolean conditions on the data items observed on those models). Moreover, CA can be extended by associating various properties with states and transitions (e.g., QoS characteristics). We assume that at this step, compliance rules are converted into automata transition constraints, temporal logic formulae, or result into automata state reachability checking. After model checking and refinement, the Reo/CA process models can be automatically translated into executable SOC languages such as WS-BPEL, as well as to Java code.

This paper focuses on the first step of the proposed framework, namely, on the BPMN to Reo conversion. The choice of BPMN as a modeling notation is justified by the fact that it comes with a number of useful process concepts such as events, exception handling, transactions and message flow. BPMN is a de-facto standard for business process modeling supported by a number of software tools. Moreover, such a mapping is interesting from the research perspective since no efficient semantic model for BPMN currently exists. Nonetheless, generally the COMPAS project is not bound to this notation and we plan to develop similar mapping tools for translating other design languages, in particular, UML ADs and BPEL GMTs, into Reo models.

3 Business Process Modeling Notation (BPMN)

In this section we overview the main structural elements of BPMN.

The basic BPMN concepts are *flow objects*, *connecting objects*, *swimlanes* and *artifacts*. Flow objects are the main graphical elements defining the behavior of a business process. BPMN distinguishes three types of flow objects, namely, *events*, *activities* and *gateways*. These elements are linked according to well-defined syntactic rules by two *connecting objects*: *sequence flow* and *message flow*. A third

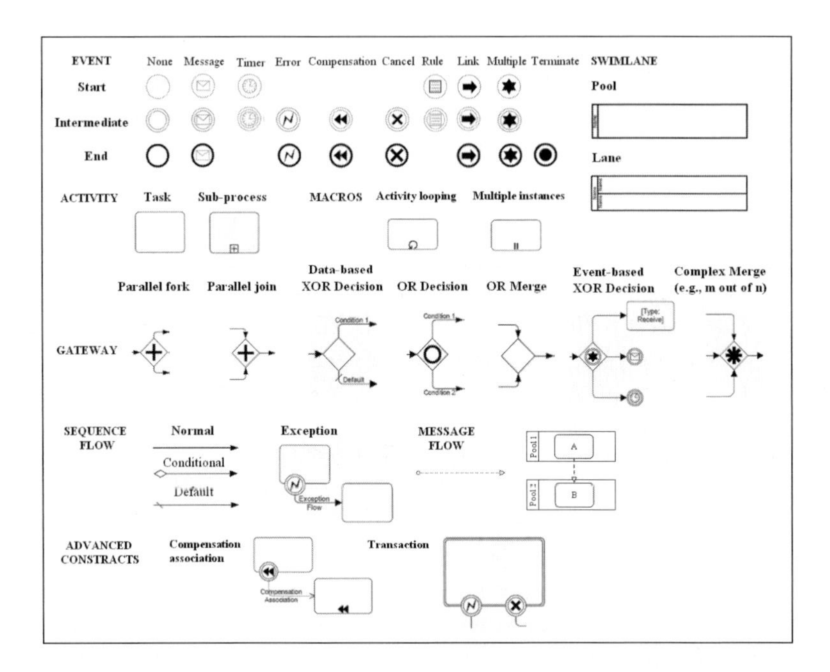

Fig. 2. Selected BPMN elements

connecting object is *association* and it is used to connect flow objects with text and non-flow elements. Two types of *swimlanes*, *pools* and *lanes*, arrange the main BPMN elements into groups. Finally, *artifacts* are introduced to provide additional information about a process. This concept is extendable and besides three standard artifacts, that is, *data objects*, *groups* and *annotations*, designers can introduce their own artifacts.

Figure 2 shows the selected BPMN elements that are essential for modeling process behavior. BPMN identifies three types of events: a *start event* signals the start of a process, an *end event* signals the end of a process and an *intermediate event* is an event occurring during a process. Different triggers such as *message, timer, rule, link, error, cancel, compensation, terminate and multiple trigger* can be associated with events. The detailed description of the triggers and their usage rules can be found in the BPMN specification [3].

An *activity* can be an *atomic task* or a *sub-process*. To each task a *type* can be assigned. Among the specific task types are *service*, *receive* and *send* tasks. A sub-process is a compound of other activities and a sequence flow on them. BPMN introduces two attributes that are commonly used to identify special types of activities (both tasks and sub-processes), namely, *looping* activities and *multiple concurrent instances* of the same activity.

A *gateway* is a construct used to control divergence and convergence of the sequence flows. A *parallel fork* gateway is used to split an incoming sequence flow into several concurrent branches, while a *parallel join* gateway synchronizes several concurrent sequence flows. A *data/event-based XOR decision* gateway selects one out of a set of mutually exclusive sequence flows according to some data-based condition or external event. An *OR decision* behaves similarly but it allows more than one alternative to be selected. An *OR merge* shows the convergence of several sequence flows into one sequence flow. Finally, *complex decision/merge* gateways are used to cover the advanced sequence flow control constructs that cannot be easily handled using other gateways. One such example is the so called *m out of n* choice when m arrived tokens out of n initiated parallel sequence flows are required to continue the process.

BPMN distinguishes two basic types of flow. The *sequence flow* prescribes the order of activities performed by one entity while the *message flow* regulates the flow between two communicating entities represented by separate *pools*. The sequence flow consists of a *normal flow* to which a transition guard can be assigned (uncontrolled, conditional or default flow) and *exception flow* that originates from some event and is used to handle exceptions. Finally, BPMN defines a number of advanced constructs such as *compensation association* and *transaction*. Due to space limits, we will not consider these constructs in this paper.

4 Reo

Reo [18] is a channel-based exogenous coordination model wherein complex coordinators, called *connectors*, are compositionally constructed from simpler ones. We summarize only the main concepts in Reo here. Further details about Reo and its semantics can be found in [17,18,19,20].

Complex connectors in Reo are formed as a network of primitive connectors, called *channels*, that serve to provide the protocol which controls and organizes the communication, synchronization and cooperation among the components/services that they interconnect. Each channel has two *channel ends* which can be of two types: *source* and *sink*. A source end accepts data into its channel, and a sink end dispenses data out of its channel. It is possible for the ends of a channel to be both sinks or both sources. Reo places no restriction on the behavior of a channel and thus allows an open-ended set of different channel types to be used simultaneously together. Figure 3 shows the graphical representation of basic channel types in Reo. A *FIFO1 channel* represents an asynchronous channel with one buffer cell which is empty if no data item is shown in the box (this is the case in Fig. 3). If a data element d is contained in the buffer of a FIFO1 channel then d is shown inside the box in its graphical representation. A *synchronous channel* has a source and a sink end and no buffer. It accepts a data

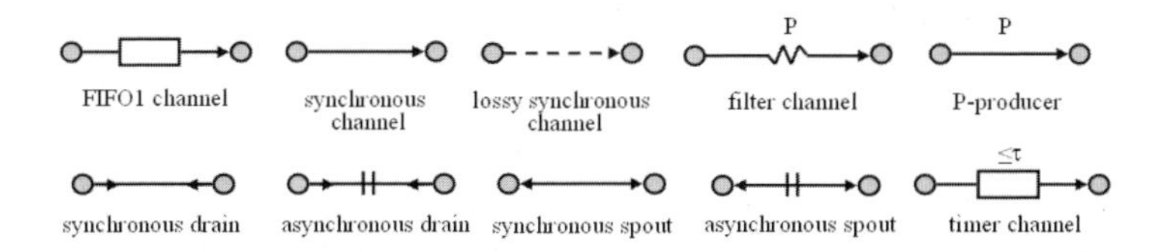

Fig. 3. Some basic channels in Reo

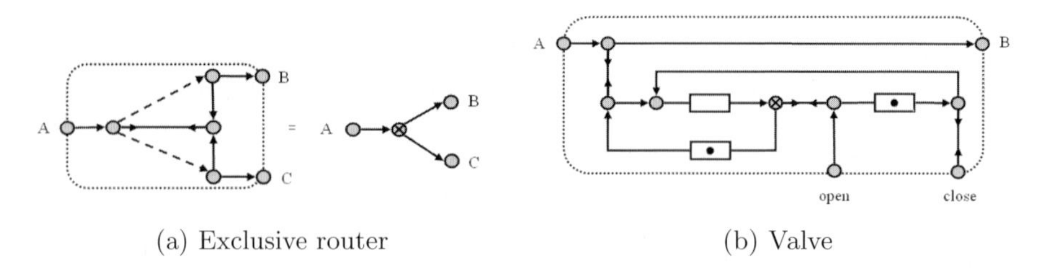

(a) Exclusive router (b) Valve

Fig. 4. Examples of Reo connectors

item through its source end iff it can simultaneously dispense it through its sink. A *lossy synchronous channel* is similar to synchronous channel except that it always accepts all data items through its source end. The data item is transferred if it is possible for the data item to be dispensed through the sink end, otherwise the data item is lost. For a *filter channel*, its pattern $P \subseteq Data$ specifies the type of data items that can be transmitted through the channel. Any value $d \in P$ is accepted through its source end iff its sink end can simultaneously dispense d; all data items $d \notin P$ are always accepted through the source end but are immediately lost. The P-producer is a variant of a synchronous channel whose source accepts any data item, but the value dispensed through its sink is always a data element $d \in P$.

There are some more exotic channels permitted in Reo: *(A)synchronous drains* have two source ends and no sink end. A synchronous drain can accept a data item through one of its ends iff a data item is also available for it to simultaneously accept through its other end as well, and all data accepted by this channel are lost. An asynchronous drain accepts data items through its source ends and loses them, but never simultaneously. *(A)synchronous Spouts* are duals to the drain channels, as they have two sink ends. A *timer channel with early expiration* allows the timer to produce its timeout signal through its sink end and reset itself when it consumes a special "expire" value through its source [17]. Complex connectors are constructed by composing simpler ones via the *join* and *hiding* operations, see [17] for more details.

Example 1. Figure 4(a) shows an implementation of an exclusive router by composing five synchronous channels, one synchronous drain and two lossy synchronous channels together. The connector provides three nodes A, B and C for other entities (connectors or component instances) to write to or take from. A data item arriving at the input port A flows through to only one of the output ports B or C, depending on which one is ready to consume it. The input data is never replicated to more than one of the output ports. If both output ports are ready to consume a data item, then one is selected non-deterministically. To avoid writing an exclusive router every time it is used, we introduce a notation similar to a node to represent this connector. We will also use XOR-nodes with more than two outputs. Such a connector can be defined by combining several two-output exclusive routers.

Additionally, it is useful to define a priority on the outputs of an exclusive router in such a way that the data item will always flow into the prioritized output if more than one output is enabled. Such a deterministic prioritized exclusive router can be implemented by connecting the input of an exclusive router with its non-prioritized outputs through valve connectors (see Fig. 4(b)). A valve connector is able to close and reopen the flow from A and B. Initially, the circuit is in the "open" state, i.e., a data item arriving at the input port A flows to the output B until the close command arrives. After that, the circuit goes into the "close" state, i.e., the flow remains blocked until the open command arrives. If the prioritized output of the exclusive router becomes ready to accept data, it can simultaneously close the valves thus making other outputs unavailable.

5 Mapping BPMN to Reo

In this section we use Reo to represent a comprehensive set of BPMN modeling primitives and common constructs.

5.1 Basic Objects: Tasks, Events, Gateways and Message Flow

Generally, BPMN tasks and sub-processes correspond to external components or black-boxes whose collaboration is coordinated by Reo. However, it is still possible to simulate the behavior of certain activities using Reo channels. For example, an atomic task with one input and one output can be represented by a simple FIFO1 or a timer channel while a sub-process can be modeled by a Reo connector that preserves the number of its incoming and outgoing flows.

An event with no trigger (start, end or intermediate) or an end event with a terminate trigger can be shown as a Reo node (source, sink or mixed). Other event triggers can be modeled using the basic Reo channels. Thus, (i) a timer event can be represented with the help of a timer channel, (ii) an incoming message event can be simulated by a synchronous drain whose first end is an input port and the second end is an internal process node (see Fig. 5(a)) while (iii) an event with a rule trigger corresponds to a filter channel with an appropriate transition condition. Other BPMN events such as outgoing messages, error, compensate, cancel or link events occurring as a part of the sequence flow correspond to the immediate transitions into required places of the process where they will be triggered and can be represented by means of synchronous channels. However, if a process or a subprocess that must react to such an event is not ready to accept it, the current sequence flow will be blocked. This problem can be resolved either by using a lossy synchronous channel which indicates that if an event is not picked up at the destination point it will be lost, or a FIFO1 channel which indicates that a message generated by an event will wait until it can be processed. Figure 5(b) shows the Reo connectors corresponding to these three message sending protocols. The composite conditions such as the case where the process execution continues when a required message has arrived or a certain deadline has been reached, can be modeled by the combination of several

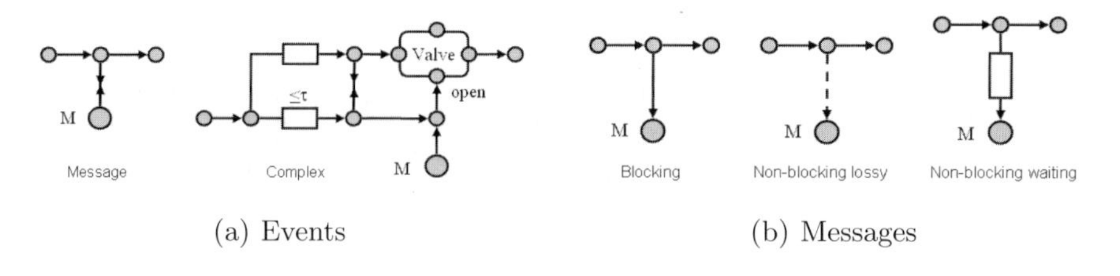

(a) Events (b) Messages

Fig. 5. Modeling BPMN events and messages in Reo

Reo channels. The Reo pattern for the aforementioned complex event is shown in Fig. 5(a). It uses a valve connector introduced in Fig. 4(b) to control the data flow from the start to the end nodes. We assume that initially in this circuit the valve is closed and reopens by a timer event or a message arrival.

Figure 6(a) shows the Reo connectors for the basic BPMN gateways, namely, data-based XOR decision, event-based XOR decision, XOR merge, parallel fork and parallel join. A data-based XOR decision is modeled using a synchronous channel which represents the incoming flow and two (or more) filter channels with a common source that represent the alternative outgoing flows. Filter transition conditions (guards) are defined by boolean expressions g_1 and g_2. The representation of an event-based XOR decision mainly depends on the semantics of the events that affect the decision. In our case, the lower branch is selected if a message arrives in a predefined period of time, and the higher branch is preferred otherwise. An XOR merge consists of two (or more) synchronous channels with a common sink. A parallel fork is composed of two (or more) diverging synchronous channels. A parallel join consists of two (or more) synchronous channels representing the incoming parallel sequence flows that are further synchronized with the help of a synchronous drain channel. Several lossy synchronous channels with a common sink are then used to get a single outgoing token. An OR decision gateway can be modeled in Reo similarly as the data-based XOR decision whose guards are not necessarily mutually exclusive. Additionally, using Reo, the designer can define various complex control gateways. For example, Fig. 6(b) shows a connector for an *m out of n* synchronizer pattern. This is a *lossy* version of the pattern, that is, the circuit loses its extra inputs before the next cycle. Alternatively, by substituting n lossy synchronous channels introducing the input data with n simple synchronous channels one can create a *sparing m out of n* pattern that delays to spare its extra inputs for the next cycle.

In BPMN a message flow is used to show the flow of messages between two entities that are prepared to send and receive them. Therefore, by default we can represent the BPMN message flow using synchronous channels. However, BPMN does not aim at specifying any further details about entity communication except perhaps in textual annotations. In contrast, the Reo syntax enables the process designers to model this aspect at a high level of abstraction. Thus, one can differentiate synchronous and asynchronous message exchanges. In the former case, the sequence flow is blocked until the reply message is received. In the latter case, other activities can be performed while waiting for a reply message.

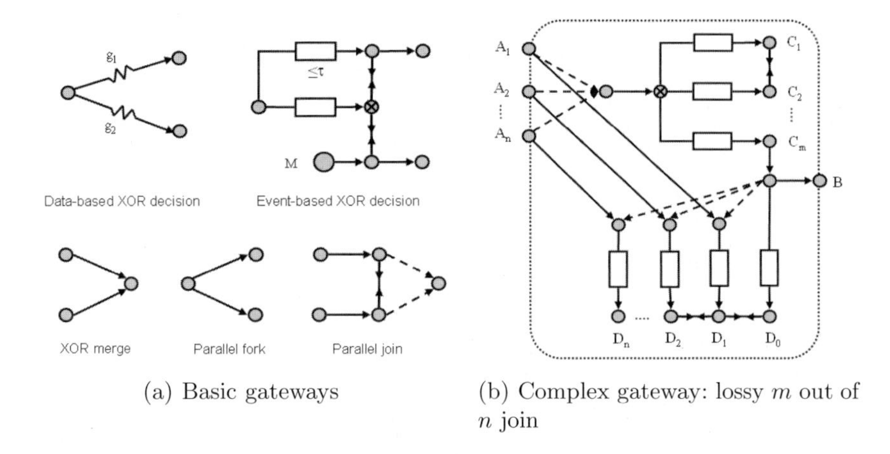

(a) Basic gateways

(b) Complex gateway: lossy m out of n join

Fig. 6. Modeling BPMN gateways in Reo

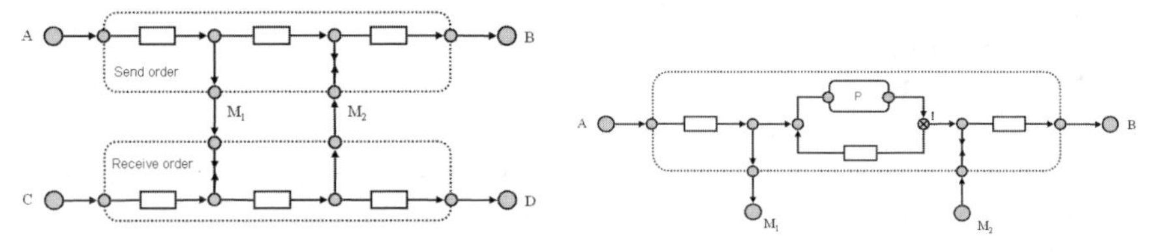

(a) Synchronous message exchange: Send/Receive Order Scenario

(b) Asynchronous message exchange

Fig. 7. Modeling BPMN message flows in Reo

Figure 7(a) shows a synchronous version of a Send/Receive Order scenario while Fig. 7(b) demonstrates how the asynchronous messaging can be represented in Reo: after sending a message M_1 the entity can perform activities of the subprocess P until a reply message M_2 is received. Here we assume that the output of the exclusive router being opened by the message M_2 has priority and a token will successfully leave the cycle. We use a small exclamation mark to show the prioritized output in the figure.

Despite the behavioral simplicity of the basic Reo channels, the issue of building Reo connectors with a desired behavior is not a trivial task. Therefore, in the following subsections we provide Reo connectors for the most tricky BPMN constructs, namely, sub-processes with exception handling and transactions.

5.2 Sub-processes and Exception Handling

Each sub-process can be seen as a separate BPMN process. The translation of BPMN processes without exception handling into Reo circuits is rather straightforward. However, the occurrence of an exception event within a sub-process interrupts the execution of the sequence flow and spawns the exception flow that

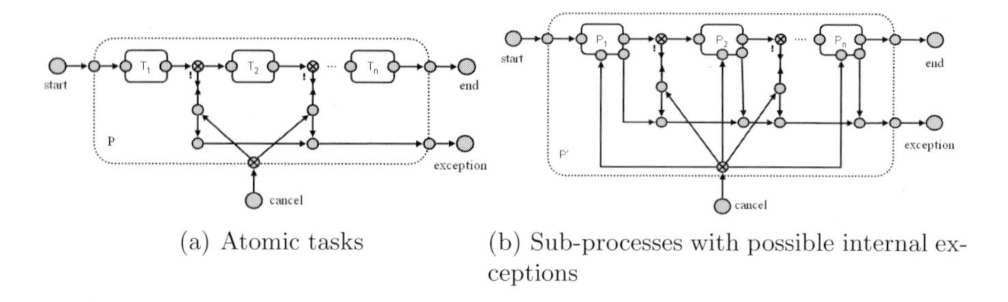

(a) Atomic tasks (b) Sub-processes with possible internal exceptions

Fig. 8. Exception handling in processes consisting of sequential activities

often affects other sub-processes and must be appropriately handled. There are two major issues here, namely, (i) to be able to interrupt a sub-process at any point of its execution and (ii) to clean all tokens/data in the circuit including those used to propagate exception events. The composition of Reo connectors implementing these issues depends on the structural aspects of sub-processes. We consider four basic constructs, namely, (i) sequential execution of atomic tasks, (ii) sequential execution of sub-processes, (iii) parallel execution of atomic tasks, and (iv) parallel execution of sub-processes.

Figure 8(a) depicts a Reo circuit that simulates the execution of a process P consisting of n serial atomic tasks. The normal flow traverses tasks $(T_1, T_2, ..., T_n)$ from the start to the end. Each two neighbor tasks are interconnected using an exclusive router with priority that is used to interrupt the process. Another exclusive router is used to direct a cancel message into the point where the execution token currently resides. The cancel message opens the output of the prioritized exclusive router and two tokens fire in the corresponding synchronous drain. Simultaneously, the cancel message is directed to the exception output which signals that the process has been interrupted.

In the above circuit we assumed that an atomic task, once invoked, always completes successfully. This may not be the case for some activities. Figure 8(b) depicts a Reo circuit that simulates the execution of a process P' consisting of n serial sub-processes $(P_1, P_2, ..., P_n)$. Each sub-process $P_i, 1 \leq i \leq n$, can be interrupted from outside by a cancel message or can generate an internal exception. The exception handling in the former case is analogous to the case of atomic tasks. In the latter case, the exception flow originating from a sub-process is redirected to the exception output of the process P'.

Figure 9(a) shows a process consisting of n parallel atomic tasks. This Reo circuit is essentially composed of a parallel fork and a parallel join gateways with n outgoing and n incoming branches, respectively. When a task $T_i, 1 \leq i \leq n$, is completed, the corresponding token waits in the FIFO1 channel until other tasks are completed as well. After that, the token flows to the circuit output. For interrupting the process, the cancel message is directed to each of the prioritized exclusive routers. FIFO1 channels are used to avoid synchronization of task cancelations. Indeed, the fact that some tasks were not completed when a cancel message has arrived should not prevent the interruption of the tasks in other

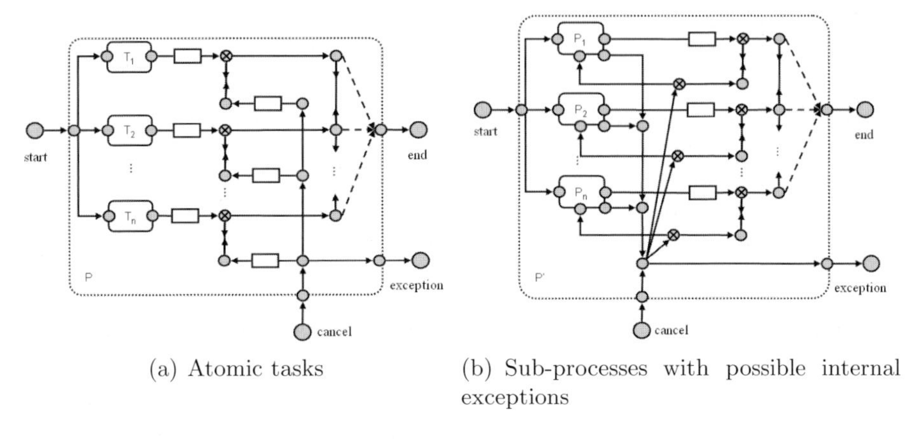

(a) Atomic tasks

(b) Sub-processes with possible internal exceptions

Fig. 9. Exception handling in processes consisting of parallel activities

branches. Additionally, the cancel message is directed to the exception output to signal the interruption of the process P.

If an internal exception occurs in a sub-process that is executed in parallel with other sub-processes within a process, this exception should be propagated to all other branches in order to interrupt them as well. Figure 9(b) shows how a Reo connector looks in this case. In each branch, an additional exclusive router is employed to propagate a cancel message (originating either from an internal or external event) to an executing sub-process or to the point where the token waits for a synchronization with other sub-processes.

In the Reo connectors for processes with sequential activities we assumed that once a process has been invoked it will not be invoked again until the first invocation has completed. Such mutual exclusion behavior can be ensured by a FIFO1 channel whose source end coincides with the start state of the process and whose sink end is connected using a synchronous drain with the end state of the process. When a process is invoked, one token flows into the FIFO1 channel and waits until the execution reaches the end state, thus, preventing other tokens from entering the circuit through the process input port. It is easy to see that this assumption can be relaxed without significant changes in the circuit behavior. The main difference is that in this case a cancel message will choose one of the executions non-deterministically and stop it without affecting the others. Observe also that if the previous invocation has been interrupted, the valve connectors (see Fig. 4(b)) used to implement prioritized exclusive routers may be closed. Before the next execution cycle, they must be reopened by means of messages sent to their open ports.

6 Reo Perspectives in Compliance Rule Modeling

In this section we outline our initial ideas about using Reo for modeling advanced compliance process requirements.

Legal, regulatory, and business requirements cause a vast number of organizations to make major changes in their business processes and supporting IT infrastructures. Currently, there are no well-established techniques to ensure the compliance of a process with regulations that may be relevant for it. Most of the regulatory/legislative acts are subject to domain-specific and process-specific interpretations. Often, these interpretations are not even properly documented. Moreover, there is no obvious notation or (semi-)formal modeling language for expressing compliance concerns.

Compliance policies are very broad in nature. Clearly, some policies relate to business processes, while others may only partially do or may not relate to them at all. Business process modeling languages and their graphical representations are relevant for capturing, describing, formalizing, executing and enforcing policies that can be expressed in a form of local or global *constraints* or *permissions* and *obligations* on control or data flow. Often, process definition languages are augmented with modal or temporal logic formulae to encode certain kinds of compliance rules such as that some condition will eventually be true or will not be true until another statement becomes true. Several frameworks exploit this approach for modeling legislative/regulatory compliance rules [14,21]. In particular, Liu et al. [14] introduce the Business Process Specification Language (BPSL) for expressing compliance concerns on top of BPEL processes. Then, BPSL constructs are automatically translated into Linear Temporal Logic (LTL) while BPEL processes are first translated into pi-calculus and finally into Finite State Machines to enable static process verification by means of model-checking techniques. Ghose and Koliadis [21] deal with BPMN processes that are further refined and represented in a form of semantically-annotated digraphs called Semantic Process Networks (SPNets). Compliance rules in this work are modeled using Computation Tree Logic (CTL). Giblin et al. [22] introduce REALM (Regulations Expressed as Logical Models), a metamodel and a method for modeling compliance rules over concept models in UML. Since the UML Object Constraint Language (OCL) does not support temporal predicates, REALM specifically focuses on time-based properties expressed in a specially designed Real-time Temporal Object Logic (RTOL). Several other approaches consider specific categories of compliance rules. For example, Governatori et al. [23] developed a Formal Contract Language (FCL) for representing compliance requirements extracted from service contracts. FCL expresses normative behavior of the contract signing parties by means of chains of permissions, obligations, and violations. Brunel et al. [24] use Labeled Kripke Structures (LKS) which are a state/event extension of LTL both for specifying system behavior and related security requirements, also defined in a form of permissions, obligations, and violations.

In this context, we see Reo and its underlying mathematical formalisms, in particular extended CA (e.g, quantitative CA [16], timed CA [17], resource-sensitive timed CA [25]), as a common operational semantics for unambiguous modeling of both process workflows and compliance rules. As mentioned in Section 2, Reo and CA have been successfully applied for service composition with end-to-end QoS guarantees [16] and for the construction of systems with real-time properties expressed by means of temporal logics [17]. Existing model-checking and bisimulation tools for Reo are able to automatically verify some important properties of process models such as the absence of deadlocks, reachability of certain states and proper completion, as well as to check the behavioral equivalence of Reo circuits [26]. Moreover, we believe that using the application of graph transformation theory to Reo [27] we will be able to guarantee process compliance with some structural requirements such as that "*any large loan must be approved by at least two authorized bank officers*".

Our intuition that Reo and its formal models can be used for representing and reasoning about (some kinds of) process-related compliance concerns is supported by a recent independent work in this direction. Brandt and Engel [28] apply Reo, Abstract Behavior Types, and algebraic graph transformations in addition to DSLs for secure modeling of distributed IT systems in a real-world banking scenario. The authors as well claim that security requirements can be modeled by graph constraints on the domain specific models. The mentioned formal methods in particular are used to control requirements originating from security compliance frameworks such as ISO 27001:2005, ISO 27002:2007, SOX or CobiT (e.g., firewall placement and secure connection).

7 Conclusions and Future Work

In this paper, we have presented a novel approach to semantically unambiguous modeling of business process workflows. We have used Reo channels as basic building blocks to model a comprehensive set of BPMN objects and advanced constructs such as sequential and parallel sub-processes with exception handling. The mapping of BPMN diagrams into Reo networks helps to unveil some process aspects that otherwise may remain underspecified (e.g. message synchronization). The resulting Reo models make it possible to formally analyze and compare business processes. In addition, we have discussed how Reo can cope with possible business process modeling extensions that aim at enforcing process-related compliance concerns.

Our approach has several advantages over existing efforts to formalize BPMN semantics, most notably [4,5]. In contrast to the Petri-net-based approaches [4] our model appropriately deals with exception handling and concurrency. In contrast to the CSP-based approaches [5], Reo is compositional and preserves the exact structure of BPMN diagrams by appropriate grouping of basic channels and finer-grained connectors into coarser-grained connectors. Similarly to [6], we can take into account the time-aware aspects of business processes by means of timer connectors. Moreover, in our work we have considered a significantly larger set of BPMN elements. However, part of our results, in particular, representation of compensation associations, transaction modeling and dynamic reconfiguration of Reo connectors to deal with multiple instances of the same activity, remain uncovered in this paper and are subjects for upcoming publications.

Our future work includes implementation of a BPMN to Reo convertor. We also plan to elaborate our initial ideas on applying Reo and CA for modeling and analyzing compliance-driven processes as discussed in this paper, both theoretically and on a number of practical examples illustrating how the proposed approach can be used to alleviate the problem of erroneous process implementation.

Acknowledgements

This work is part of the IST COMPAS project, funded by the European Commission, FP7-ICT-2007-1 contract number 215175, `http://www.compas-ict.eu/`

References

1. Curbera, F., Goland, Y., Klein, J., Leymann, F.: Business process execution language for web services. Technical report, IBM (2002), `http://www.ibm.com/developerworks/library/ws-bpel/`
2. Kavantzas, N., Burdett, D., Ritzinger, G.: Web services choreography description language (WS-CDL) version 1.0. Working draft, W3C (2004), `http://www.w3.org/TR/2004/WD-ws-cdl-10-20040427`
3. (OMG), O.M.G.: Business process modeling notation (BPMN) specification. Final adopted specification, OMG (2006), `http://www.bpmn.org/Documents/OMGFinalAdoptedBPMN1-0Spec06-02-01.pdf`
4. Dijkman, R.M., Dumas, M., Ouyang, C.: Formal semantics and analysis of BPMN process models. In: Information and Software Technology (IST) (2008)
5. Wong, P., Gibbons, J.: A process semantics for BPMN. Technical report, Queensland University of Technology (2007), `http://www.comlab.ox.ac.uk/publications/publication454-abstract.html`
6. Wong, P., Gibbons, J.: A relative timed semantics for BPMN. Technical report, Queensland University of Technology (2007), `http://www.comlab.ox.ac.uk/publications/publication1496-abstract.html`
7. Recker, J., Mendling, J.: On the translation between BPMN and BPEL: Conceptual mismatch between process modeling languages. In: Proc. of the Int. Conf. on Advanced Information Systems Engineering, pp. 521–532 (2006)
8. Ouyang, C., Dumas, M., ter Hofstede, A., van der Aalst, W.: Pattern-based translation of BPMN process models to BPEL web services. Int. Journal of Web Services Research (JWSR) 5(1), 42–61 (2007)
9. Ouyang, C., Verbeek, E., van der Aalst, W.M.P., Breutel, S., Dumas, M., ter Hofstede, A.H.M.: Formal semantics and analysis of control flow in WS-BPEL. Science of Computer Programming 67(2-3), 162–198 (2007)
10. Lohmann, N.: A feature-complete Petri net semantics for WS-BPEL 2.0. In: Dumas, M., Heckel, R. (eds.) WS-FM 2007. LNCS, vol. 4937, pp. 77–91. Springer, Heidelberg (2008)
11. Lucchia, R., Mazzara, M.: A pi-calculus based semantics for WS-BPEL. Journal of Logic and Algebraic Programming 70(1), 96–118 (2007)
12. Nakajima, S.: Model-checking behavioral specification of BPEL applications. Electronic Notes in Theoretical Computer Science (ENTCS) 151, 89–105 (2006)
13. McCarty, L.T.: A language for legal discourse. In: Proc. of the Int. Conf. on Artificial Intelligence and Law (ICAIL 1989), pp. 180–189. ACM Press, New York (1989)

14. Liu, Y., Müller, S., Xu, K.: A static compliance-checking framework for business process models. IBM Systems Journal 46(2), 335–361 (2007)
15. Meng, S., Arbab, F.: Web service choreography and orchestration in Reo and constraint automata. In: Proc. of the ACM Symposium on Applied Computing (SAC 2007), pp. 346–353. ACM Press, New York (2007)
16. Arbab, F., Chothia, T., Meng, S., Moon, Y.J.: Component connectors with QoS guarantees. In: Murphy, A.L., Vitek, J. (eds.) COORDINATION 2007. LNCS, vol. 4467, pp. 286–304. Springer, Heidelberg (2007)
17. Arbab, F., Baier, C., de Boer, F.S., Rutten, J.J.M.M.: Models and temporal logics for timed component connectors. Int. Journal on Software and Systems Modeling 6(1), 59–82 (2007)
18. Arbab, F.: Reo: A channel-based coordination model for component composition. Mathematical Structures in Computer Science 14(3), 329–366 (2004)
19. Arbab, F., Rutten, J.: A coinductive calculus of component connectors. In: Wirsing, M., Pattinson, D., Hennicker, R. (eds.) WADT 2003. LNCS, vol. 2755, pp. 34–55. Springer, Heidelberg (2003)
20. Baier, C., Sirjani, M., Arbab, F., Rutten, J.: Modeling component connectors in Reo by constraint automata. Science of Computer Programming 61, 75–113 (2006)
21. Ghose, A.K., Koliadis, G.: Auditing business process compliance. In: Krämer, B.J., Lin, K.-J., Narasimhan, P. (eds.) ICSOC 2007. LNCS, vol. 4749, pp. 169–180. Springer, Heidelberg (2007)
22. Giblin, C., Liu, A.Y., Müller, S., Pfitzmann, B., Zhou, X.: Regulations expressed as logical models (REALM). In: Proc. of the 18th Annual Conf. on Legal Knowledge and Information Systems, pp. 37–48 (2005)
23. Governatori, G., Milosevic, Z., Sadiq, S.: Compliance checking between business processes and business contracts. In: Proc. of the Int. Enterprize Distributed Object Computing Conf. (EDOC 2006), pp. 221–232. IEEE Computer Society Press, Los Alamitos (2006)
24. Brunel, J., Cuppens, F., Cuppens, N., Sans, T., Bodeveix, J.P.: Security policy compliance with violation management. In: Proc. of the Workshop on Formal Methods in Security Engineering (FMSE 2007), pp. 31–40. ACM Press, New York (2007)
25. Meng, S., Arbab, F.: On resource-sensitive timed component connectors. In: Bonsangue, M.M., Johnsen, E.B. (eds.) FMOODS 2007. LNCS, vol. 4468, pp. 301–316. Springer, Heidelberg (2007)
26. Blechmann, T., Baier, C.: Checking equivalence for Reo networks. In: Proc. of the Int. Workshop on Formal Aspects of Component Software (FACS) (2007)
27. Koehler, C., Lazovik, A., Arbab, F.: Connector rewriting with high-level replacement systems. Electronic Notes in Theoretical Computer Science (ENTCS) 194(4), 77–92 (2008)
28. Brandt, C., Engel, T., Braatz, B., Hermann, F., Ehrig, H.: An approach using formally well-founded domain languages for secure coarse-grained IT system modelling in a real-world banking scenario. In: Proc. of the Australasian Conf. on Information Systems (ACIS 2007), pp. 386–395 (2007)

On the Risk Management and Auditing of SOA Based Business Processes

Bart Orriens, Willem-Jan v/d Heuvel, and Mike Papazoglou

Dept. of Information Management, Tilburg University
PO Box 90153, 5000 LE Tilburg, The Netherlands
{b.orriens,wjheuvel,mikep}@uvt.nl

Abstract. SOA-enabled business processes stretch across many cooperating and coordinated systems, possibly crossing organizational boundaries, and technologies like XML and Web services are used for making system-to-system interactions commonplace. Business processes form the foundation for all organizations, and as such, are impacted by industry regulations. This requires organizations to review their business processes and ensure that they meet the compliance standards set forth in legislation. In this paper we sketch a SOA-based service risk management and auditing methodology including a compliance enforcement and verification system that assures verifiable business process compliance. This is done on the basis of a knowledge-based system that allows integration of internal control systems into business processes conform pre-defined compliance rules, monitor both the normal process behavior and those of the control systems during process execution, and log these behaviors to facilitate retrospective auditing.

1 Introduction

SOA is an integration framework for connecting loosely coupled software modules into on-demand business processes. Business processes form the foundation for all organizations, and as such, are impacted by industry regulations. Without explicit business process definitions, flexible rule frameworks, and audit trails that provide for non-repudiation, organizations face litigation risks and even criminal penalties. Compliance regulations, such as Basel II [3], HIPAA [7], Sarbanes-Oxley (SOX) [27] and others require all organizations to review their business processes and ensure that they meet the compliance standards set forth in the legislation. This can include, but is not limited to, data acquisition and archival, document management, data security, financial accounting practices, shareholder reporting functions and to know when unusual activities occur. In all cases, these control and disclosure requirements create auditing demands for SOAs.

Internal control constitutes a fundamental cornerstone in auditing, which is used to assure business process compliance, delivering objective and independent guarantees regarding virtually all accounting aspects of service-enabled business processes, including risk management, financial checks and governance processes (Rezaee, 2007). A typical financial reporting control might mitigate the risk of misstating revenue due to inadequate physical or electronic security over sales documents and electronic files.

T. Margaria and B. Steffen (Eds.): ISoLA 2008, CCIS 17, pp. 124–138, 2008.

This helps implement a compliance regulation act, such SOX section 404, which mandates that well-defined and documented processes and controls be in place for all aspects of company operations that affect financial information and reports. To achieve this functionality requires: (i) controlling and auditing who accesses financial information, (ii) controlling and auditing what financial information is accessed, and (iii) ensuring financial information is not compromised during transmission. Due to the inherent complexity present in compliance regulations, such as SOX, most companies cannot address these requirements without a strategy for automating the integration of the diverse business processes and their accompanying internal control systems throughout the enterprise.

Existing auditing solutions and tools are hopelessly outdated and not applicable in SOA environments [20]. These are tightly coupled to the controlled application, and assume that applications are homogenous and monolithic in nature. Moreover, solutions are typically reactive in nature (noted also in e.g. [25]). That is, their focus is to detect violations after they have occurred. However, in today's business environment a pro-active approach is required in which organizations are able to control their business processes such that violations are avoided; and in the event that violations do occur, an immediate response can be carried out; for example by triggering an automated procedure to resolve a compliance problem or by notifying the business process manager. Some initial work in the area of risk management has been done (e.g. [17] and [25]), however, current proposals are still preliminary in nature. This paper introduces a service compliance methodology (SCM) that is intended to be a first step towards filling this SOA risk management and auditing void for service-enabled business processes (henceforth referred to simply as business processes). Concretely, SCM is intended to enable external control systems to be integrated into business processes during execution conform pre-defined compliance rules, monitor the behavior of these control systems in order to react to compliance violations at the moment that they occur, and log the application and outcome of the control systems for auditing purposes.

2 Risk Management and Auditing for SOAs

To provide the ability to establish control and documentation, reduce risk and error potential, in cases where service-enabled processes impact financial reporting (e.g. in end-to-end sales cycles, payment cycles or production cycles), we propose the use of a methodology based on the concept of a risk management and auditing SOA. Such SOA combines SOA with risk management and auditing principles for business processes, and relies on: 1) a risk management strategy to integrate control systems into business processes and monitor their behavior; and 2) an auditing strategy to evaluate the effectiveness of these control systems. The first ensures that business processes are executed according to predefined regulatory policies and that violations can be promptly dealt with; while the second allows for providing explicit proof of compliance enforcement and violation mitigation ro facilitate auditing.

By checking the control systems, risks can be mitigated while safeguarding service-driven processes and increasing their reliability. Auditors rely on internal control systems as they provide audit evidence that helps reduce substantive testing. Assuring the quality of internal control systems to reduce the number of auditing activities has in fact been a proven strategy since the 1970s [29]. In addition, and perhaps more importantly, auditing the internal control systems of processes within or between organizations is a required practice.

Given this rationale, SCM adopts a risk management strategy that addresses those fragments of a business process that are exposed to the risk of control weaknesses, while fewer efforts need to be spent on those process fragments (and services on which they rely) with strong controls. These items become candidates for immediate evaluation and, where necessary, remediation. For example, handling salaries might be deemed a low-risk item since they are tightly controlled by a small group of people. Revenue recognition, on the other hand, might be deemed high risk because of loosely defined recognition procedures. This strategy becomes particularly significant in large, business-critical SOA-applications.

According to the standard control definition given by ISA 315 [14], control activities performed on business processes (and therefore part of any SOA-based solution) may fall into several classes forming SOA risk management tenets:

1. Performance reviews: include reviews and analyses of actual performance versus budgets, forecasts, and prior period performance; relating different sets of data (operating or financial) to one another, together with analyses of the relationships and investigative and corrective actions; comparing internal data with external sources of information; and review of functional or activity performance.
2. Information processing control procedures: encompass application controls, which apply to the processing of individual business processes. These controls help ensure that all transactions occurred are authorized, and are completely and accurately logged and processed.
3. Physical controls: encompass the network-level security of service end-points, including adequate safeguards such as secured access/control to services; measures against data availability threats (e.g., XML attacks), and data integrity.
4. Segregation of duties: intended to reduce the opportunities to allow any person to be in a position to both perpetrate and conceal errors or fraud in the normal course of the persons duties. This is achieved by assigning access roles along a business process, logging service execution trails, and maintaining custody of services. For example, if an employee has custody of services and also accounts for them, there is a high risk of that person using the services for personal gain and adjusting their logs to cover theft (Hayes, 2005).
5. Authorization: accounting controls need to check procedures of reviewing and approving specific operations or transactions, e.g., approving the invocation of purchase orders, or change orders.

In addition, from a legislative perspective, an analysis of current compliance regulations (like Basel II [3] and Sarbanes-Oxley [27]) reveals that compliance requirements affect not only the basic structure of business processes, but also more advanced concerns such as monitoring, privacy, quality, retention, security and transactionality. Appropriate business process control activities should be integrated into process models to address these risk management issues.

To monitor business process control activities, the service compliance methodology should accommodate the following SOA auditing tenets (derived from intersecting core SOA with basic auditing principles conform [13] and [14]):

1. Independent auditing: The auditor (which can be a human or automated agent) is to be independent, but may be either internal or external to the organization(s) where the service-enabled processes execute.
2. Policing the SOA behavior: requires the ability to monitor events or information produced by the services/processes, monitoring instances of business processes, viewing process instance statistics, including the number of instances in each state (running, suspended, aborted or completed), viewing the status, or summary for selected process instances, suspend, and resume or terminate selected process instances. Of particular significance is the ability to be able to spot problems and exceptions in the business processes and move toward resolving them as soon as they occur.
3. Real-time reporting: requires the ability to disclose in real-time material events such as significant write-downs or bad debt recognition. Alerts can be represented as alarms directed to a human administrator. Alternatively, they can be real-time electronic events that in turn are used to trigger an automated remediation event like service shut-down or policy change.
4. Logging execution trails: requires the ability to log business processes and transaction execution trails to provide auditing capability and non-repudiation. Audit in an SOA transaction could involve tracking any number of activities and incidents. It must provide evidence that a particular identity accessed a specific service resource; the service consumers request satisfied the service providers security policies (communication integrity, privacy, data cleanliness, etc.); and that the service providers response satisfied security and performance contracts established with the service consumer (particularly if an SLA is specified in the policy). Secure logging of what happened, when, by whom and under what terms in an SOA communication underpins any forensic audit of a transaction.
5. Continuous auditing: There is a critical need for continuous auditing replacing the semiannual audits, which has become even more evident through new governmental regulations regarding real-time reporting requirements (SOX), that allows independent auditors to provide written assurance on a subject matter using a series of auditors reports issued simultaneously with, or a short period after, the occurrence of events underlying the subject matter [5]. The fundamental philosophy is that business processes must perform in a predictable manner accurately and precisely around target performance limits.

3 Service-Enabled Process Compliance Methodology (SCM)

The SCM methodology supports integration of internal control systems into business processes to facilitate risk management and auditing, and that meets the desiderata and constraints that were defined in section 2. The methodology adopts a formal deductive inference approach to apply compliance policies and rules to business processes by integrating appropriate control systems in a monitorable manner. The methodology is grounded on an abstract compliance enriched process model and a corresponding compliance rule specification language. The abstract, compliance enriched process model defines the basic constructs for specifying the elementary interaction arrangements, relationships and behavior of individual services that are to be assembled in a business process. Compliance requirements are annotated to these constructs using control primitives, which describe a specific usage of particular control system functionalities (e.g. in relation to monitoring or security). This allows organizations to address the identified risk management SOA tenets by incorporating appropriate control systems into their business processes.

Since the decision of whether or not to apply certain control mechanisms is often context dependent, compliance rules can be selected to express under what circumstances particular control primitives must be enforced. For example, a sales manager may only be interested in being notified about high risk sales orders made by customers with bad credit history and above $500. These kinds of compliance rule are specified using a sophisticated compliance rule specification language and packaged into compliance policies that address particular compliance legislations (or parts thereof). Business managers can select one or more compliance policy from a control directory and associate it with a business process. As this process is being carried out conform its abstract process model, the selected compliance rules will be applied to enrich the model with appropriate control primitives. This is facilitated by the knowledge base, which allows formal derivation of which control primitives are to be annotated to the model; where decisions made based on the rules are logged so they are available for future inspection.

The abstract, compliance enriched process model is declarative in nature and as such can not be directly executed. Therefore, to cater for the actual execution of business processes the abstract process model and its annotated control primitives are translated into an executable model. Here we adopt the defacto BPEL for that purpose. The translation of the elementary service interactions in the abstract process model is done by mapping its elements to BPEL equivalent constructs. Control primitives are integrated into the BPEL model by placing WS-Policy assertions on the services that are participating in the process. This ensures that only services capable of meeting the compliance requirements are engaged. Also, appropriate control activities are inserted to ensure that the BPEL process and its services actually behave in accordance with the specified control primitives. These can for example pertain to authorization aspects, segregation of duties, information processing, enforcement of system security measures, and verification of financial information in order to support the SOA risk management tenets. The resulting BPEL process is subsequently executed as normal. Because the application of compliance rules is typically runtime dependent (e.g. depending on the exact order message that was received), this procedure is followed every time that the BPEL process enters an execution scope (that is, there are activities to be executed). That is, each time an execution scope is encountered, execution is paused and the current BPEL execution model is translated into its abstract counterpart. Compliance rules are then applied to this abstract process model as described before and execution is resumed in a normal manner.

To support SOA auditing tenets 2,3 and 4 both the normal process activities in a BPEL process as well as any inserted control activities can be monitored and logged. For normal activities this is done by abstractly annotating them with appropriate monitoring control primitives. During transformation into BPEL corresponding monitoring activities are then included to enable monitoring. To accommodate the same for control activities, the abstract process model allows control primitives to be applied to other control primitives. This allows for example to define that in case a security authentication control is not passed, the response must be that this failure is logged and a notification is send to a human manager. These activities can themselves be logged as well, as such establishing a clear audit trail of the behavior of both the business process and its integrated control systems. Moreover, automated handling of control related events can be facilitated by defining appropriate responses in compliance rules (just like normal compliance rules). Furthermore, the behavior of integrated control systems can be audited independent from particular business processes. This allows both external and internal auditors (SOA auditing tenet 1) to verify the functioning of these control systems, after which they can be assured of their proper behavior when integrated into a process; which in turn allows processes to be performed in a predictable manner in accordance with compliance rules. Also, given the runtime nature of the SCM continuous auditing becomes more feasible. Finally, audit trails as well as reasoning logs can be examined to distil trends such as controls that are repeatedly not applied successfully.

Fig. 1 illustrates the SCM methodology and its individual steps. The SCM methodology works as follows: as a first step business managers selects pre-defined compliance policies and rules from the **control repository** by indicating what legislative

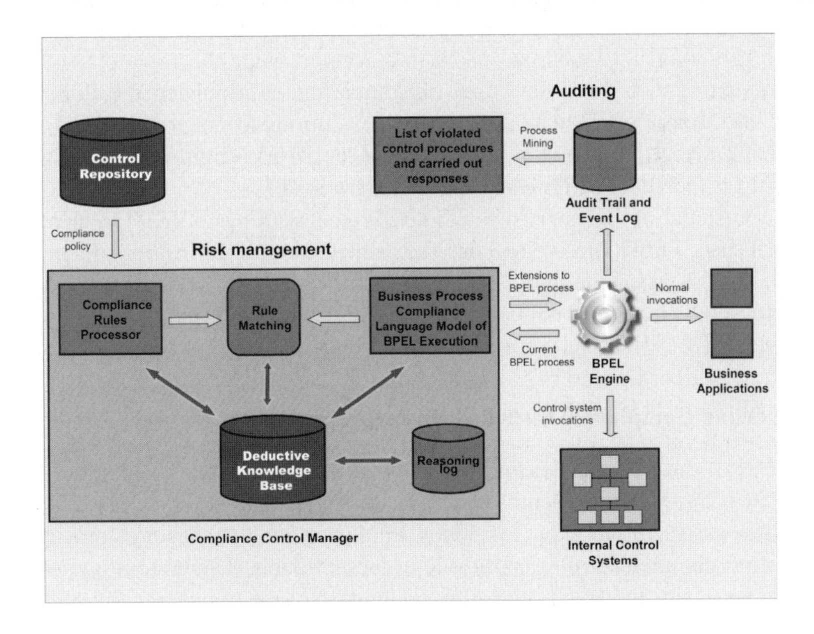

Fig. 1. SCM Methodology Overview

compliance requirements must be met by which particular business process. The **compliance control manager** receives the compliance rules collected by the **control directory** and assures that the targeted BPEL based business processes are executed in conformance to these rules. Concretely, what happens is that each time during execution that the **BPEL engine** enters an execution scope (i.e. one or more activities to be performed), the engine halts execution and sends its current execution model to the **compliance control manager**. The **compliance control manager** transforms the received execution model into a so-called Business Process Compliance Language (BPCL) based business process model. This BPCL model describes the prescriptive BPEL execution model in a declarative manner. The **compliance control manager** then carries out the rule matching activity to identify if and when certain compliance controls must be enforced based on the applicable compliance rules (also defined in terms of BPCL).

The rule matching activity is supported by the knowledge base which captures formalized models and rules and facilitates rule matching with logical inferences. Once reasoning has been completed, the **compliance control manager** contacts the **BPEL engine** in order to update its BPEL execution model by inserting control activities for enforcing any applicable control requirements, as well as adding constraints to the abstract services responsible for the process' normal activities. We adopt the WS-Policy standard for this purpose to express constraints as assertions. The **BPEL engine** then restarts execution, goes through the execution scope and carries out the activities it finds. Any added control activities are called in the same way as normal activities through service operation invocation; where these operations are implemented by special middleware services provided by **internal control systems** (e.g. offered via an enterprise service bus). Also, any constraints placed on the abstract services responsible for the execution of normal activities, are taken into account when the abstract services are bounded to actual services. This is done by comparing the stipulated WS-Policy assertions to those supported by available services (i.e. through standard service discovery and selection). As such, from the perspective of the **BPEL engine** the only thing that has changed is that more activities need to be performed.

In the remainder of this paper, we will discuss the workings of SCM in more detail. Because of space limitations we will only focus here on the specification of compliance enriched business process models, and compliance policies and rules; as such, our work on the actual application of compliance rules using the reasoning engine is omitted here. An overview of the BPCL in UML class diagram notation is shown in Fig. 2.

3.1 Modeling Compliance Enriched Business Processes

At the heart of the SCM methodology stands the Business Process Compliance Language (BPCL), which is currently under development. This language is intended to provide the constructs necessary to define compliance enriched business process models as well as compliance rules applicable to these models. The bottom part of Fig. 2 shows the portion of the BPCL that allows definition of the basic structure of business processes, and its annotation with control primitives. As can be seen a business process model is defined as a collection of process constructs. Such constructs represent building blocks from which a process model can be constructed. They are abstractly defined

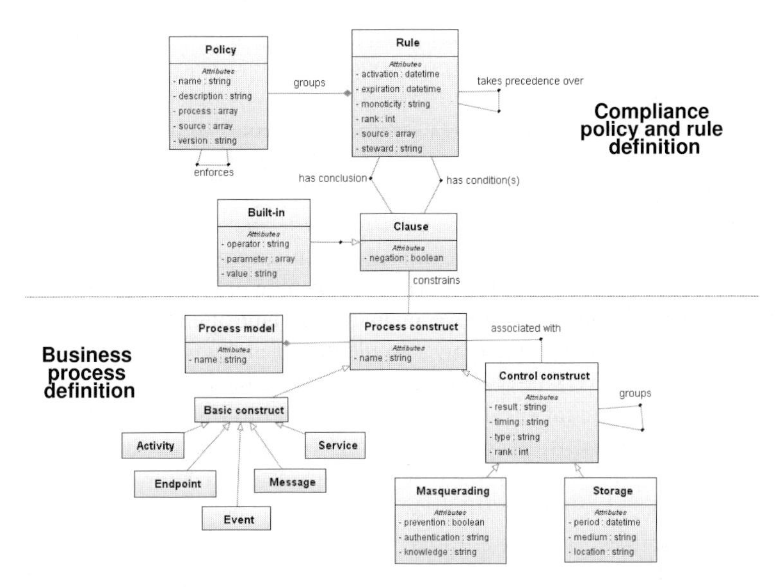

Fig. 2. Business Process Compliance Language (BPCL) Overview

in the **process construct** class. Each process construct has an unique name for identification and reference purposes. The **process construct** class has two subclasses, being **basic construct** and **control construct** class. Also abstract in nature, these classes demarcate the difference between the basic constructs making up business process models and the control primitives applicable to these constructs.

Basic process modeling constructs are themselves specialized into concrete classes representing 'standard' service enabled business process modeling constructs to capture the five viewpoints for business process modeling, being functional, locational, temporal, informational and participational view. Fig. 2 only shows the main classes in these viewpoints for reasons of clarity: **activity**, **endpoint**, **event**, **message** and **service** class. Messages represent containers of information consisting of meta-data and actual data. Meta-data comprises the information required to deliver the message and enable its processing, while payloads contain any content of the message not conveyed in its meta-data. Messages have a particular format (conform e.g. an XML schema), follow certain semantics (e.g. defined in an ontology), be in a certain language, and consist of message parts which represent snippets of information. Each message part has a name, type and value. Its type can be basic like double, integer, string, but also refer to a complex type (for example defined in the XML schema).

Messages function as the 'inputs' and 'outputs' of activities. Activities represent well-defined functions and can be dependent on one another. Activities can be complex in nature grouping other activities in parallel, loops or sequence (defined in appropriate activity class subclasses). Activities are 'carried out by' services. Services have properties like name and have associated classes capturing details concerning for example category and version. Services are 'found at' endpoints, which are related to classes capturing characteristics like network location, time zone, jurisdiction, and address information. Finally, events capture business process occurrences. Events are signaled by messages and are crucial for facilitating the monitoring of business processes. Events have an identifier, a time stamp, a severity indicating importance, and a causal vector identifying the events that caused it. The causal relations among events will follow the ordering of the activities generating the events. Also, events can be composite in nature aggregating other events; which will be conform how the activities generating events are structured into complex activities [18].

Control constructs annotate the basis process constructs with compliance related primitives. The basic characteristics of control constructs are comprised in the abstract **control construct** class. Control constructs are atomic or composite in nature. Atomic control constructs define exactly one compliance requirement, and share four attributes: 'timing', 'result', 'rank' and 'type'. The 'timing' attribute expresses when a compliance control must be enforced in relation to the normal process activities. It can be set to 'before', 'in place of' and 'after', and affects the manner in which control activities are integrated into the normal BPEL process. Timing is dependent on the type of control and the context in which it is used. For example, for an authorization control associated with an order approval activity the timing will be set to 'before'; as it does not make sense to perform authorization afterwards. The 'result' attribute of a control construct depicts the outcome of the control activity, and can be equal to 'success' or 'failure'. This attribute allows to consider the result of control activities and define appropriate responses in compliance rules.

The 'rank' attribute of the **control construct** class allows ordering in case multiple control constructs are associated with a process construct; e.g. to express that first notification of an event must be done and only then that the event is logged. To indicate that control constructs associated with the same process construct are to be carried out in parallel, their rank can be set to the same height. Lastly, the 'type' property contains the kind of control construct. We identify five main categories: *functional*, *informational*, *locational*, *participational* and *temporal* constructs, which are attached to activities, messages, endpoints, services, and events respectively. Individual control construct sub classes are then added to the BPCL to define specific control mechanisms. Fig. 2 shows two example control construct classes; e.g. the 'masquerading' control construct for a process activity, which can contain a property to depict that for authentication purposes an username/password combination must be provided as proof of knowledge. We are currently in the progress of developing a classification (and subsequent definition) of control construct for addressing a diverse range of compliance requirements. These concrete control constructs are all defined as sub-classes of the **control construct** class with appropriate attributes to define the exact requirements of the expressed control primitive (in addition to those defined in the **control construct** class). Due to space limitations we do not discuss this further here.

Different from atomic control constructs, the BPCL also facilitates definition of composite control constructs via 'groups' relations between control constructs. These constructs group other constructs (both atomic and/or composite) and apply their own control primitive to it. This allows for example to define that the notification and logging of an event must be done in an all-or-nothing manner (i.e. as an atomic transaction). Additionally, since control constructs are process constructs, they can themselves be annotated with control constructs. The interpretation of such annotation is that the control primitives expressed in the latter control constructs are applied to those with which they are associated. One important application of this is that it enables to attach monitoring constructs to other control constructs. This has the effect that the outcome of the application of these constructs is itself monitored. This empowers organizations to not only monitor the progress of their normal business process activities, but also those related to the effectuation of control mechanisms within these processes; e.g. allowing to define that if authentication for an activity fails, then a human manager must be notified. It also provides the means to express statement like that information must be stored in a secure manner; which can be captured by associating a storage control with an encryption control that itself is attached to a message. This has the effect that first the message is encrypted, after which the resulting (encrypted) message is stored.

3.2 Defining Compliance Rules and Policies

In the previous subsection we discussed the BPCL in relation to the definition of compliance enriched business process models; and explained how control constructs can be annotated to basic process modeling constructs. However, as observed in the introduction of section 3, the decision of whether or not to apply certain control mechanisms is often dependent on the specific business process conditions during execution. To accommodate for this the BPCL also provides the concepts for the definition of compliance rules and policies. Concretely, compliance rules can be specified in an expressive manner on top of the process modeling constructs. In Fig. 1, these rules are then matched against the BPCL representation of a running BPEL process to customize integration of control mechanisms into business processes. This is done with the help of the knowledge base inferencing capabilities. Both the BPCL model and the applicable compliance rules are translated into the knowledge base format, after which new facts constituting annotations of control constructs are deduced based on the current BPCL model. BPCL rules also have several attributes to facilitate their specification, categorization, application and management.

The central class in the BPCL for compliance rule definition is the **rule** class. Rules take the form `IF [conditions are satisfied] THEN [annotate control primitive]`. A rule has zero or more conditions and exactly one conclusion. Both are expressed as clauses based on the **clause** class. Clauses constrain process constructs and link compliance rules to business process models. A clause constrains a parameterized process construct. The **clause** class is specialized in the **built-in** class. Built-in clauses allow to express: 1) an evaluation of the value of a particular process construct attribute using a built-in operator and a set value; or 2) a derivation of a new value based on one or more process construct attributes (potentially from different parameterized process constructs) conform a built-in operator. Supported evaluation operators in BPCL include text and numerical comparison, membership evaluation, and, date and time operators. Derivation operators encompass addition, substraction, division and multiplication. An example is that `IF [customer order amount in an order is higher than $500], THEN [perform authentication using an username/password combination]`. To monitor the outcome of this control mechanism, another rule can then be that `IF [result of authentication equals failed], THEN [notify sales manager]`.

Rule conditions can be negated (via the clause 'negation' attribute). Negation empowers organizations to express both desired and undesired conditions. This allows for example to state that `IF [customer status is not equal to 'gold' and order amount is higher than $1000], THEN [do credit check]`. A relevant distinction in this regard is the intent of the negation. Strong, or classical, negation conveys the necessity to explicitly show that something is not true. In contrast, negation interpreted in a weak sense indicates that something is considered not true if it can not shown to be true. This is a subtle yet important difference for compliance, as in one case explicit proof is required of separation of duties whereas in the other case this is not necessary. At this point in time we only use negation in rule conditions; as we do not see direct application of compliance rules of the form "IF [conditions apply] THEN [do not annotate control primitive]". This also means that we restrict the usage of negation in rule conditions to weak negation (since no explicit negative conclusions can be drawn). This has the benefit that rules can be unambiguously be interpreted using perfect model semantics [28]; as such avoiding situations in which it is unclear which interpretation is correct.

Continuing, rules in BPCL can be monotonic or non-monotonic in nature as indicated in their 'monoticity' attribute. Non-monotonic rules (also known as defeasible rules) are common in business, for example to override standard rules with special-case exceptions, to incorporate more recent updates and etceteras [12]. In relation to compliance the matter of non-monoticity is of interest as it allows organizations to indicate to what extent it is important that a compliance rule is enforced; and consequently how grave the consequences are in case the rule is not satisfied. Monotonic compliance rules must always be met, but non-monotonic ones may be violated (albeit potentially at a cost). Monoticity also empowers organizations to prioritize their compliance rules in case they express conflicting requirements (e.g. the need for authentication contradicts with a demand for anonymity). Monotonic rules always take precedence over non-monotonic ones, while the latter can themselves be further ordered through the usage of the 'rank' property as well as 'relative prioritization' relations between rules. The effect of rule monoticity properties during inferencing is that it instructs the knowledge base to prioritize rules in case they care conflicting with one another.

Additionally, each rule has the attributes 'activation date', 'expiration date', 'source', and 'steward'. The first two express the period in which a rule is active. From a compliance point of view this is useful to ensure that rules are only enforced when appropriate. For example, the IFRS [24] requirements for financial reporting in 2007 likely differ from those of other years, and thus should not be applied for example in 2006 or 2008. Situations such as these prompt the need for some form of life cycle management to manage the status of compliance rules. The impact of activation and expiration dates is that rules will only be applied by the knowledge base if these rules are active given the internal clock of the knowledge base. In order to establish a link between a compliance rule and one or more compliance legislations, the origin(s) of a rule can be specified in the 'source' attribute. This will identify the name of a specific section/subsection of a legislation that the rule originates from (e.g. Sarbanes-Oxley section 402). This allows the categorization of compliance rules, enabling for example to select a subset of the Sarbanes-Oxley compliance rules and apply them to a business process. Finally, the delegation of responsibility for achieving particular compliance goals is another concern that is addressed in BPCL. Concretely, compliance rules have a 'steward' attribute to identify organizational actors. This allows the responsibility for compliance enforcement to be tied to the organization's management and operations structure.

Logically related compliance rules can be clustered into compliance policies using the **policy** class. Such policies are similar in nature to WS-Policy based policies [2], however they contain much more expressive rules than WS-Policy assertions. Currently policies can not contain multiple alternatives like in WS-Policy, though we will to include such support in the future if this is deemed useful. For identification purposes a policy has a name as well as a short textual description. Additionally, a policy has a 'source' property, which identifies by name to what compliance legislation(s) the policy is related (typically in more general terms than the source specified for a compliance rule). Potentially a single policy can be related to multiple legislations, e.g. supporting compliance of both Basel II and Sarbanes-Oxley at the same time. Each policy also has a 'process' property indicating to what type(s) of business process it is applicable (e.g. the purchase and payment process). Finally, there can be multiple versions of policies in existence. Differentiation between them is expressed using the 'version' property. Based on the source, process and version properties customized packaging of compliance policies and rules can be done by organizations when accessing their control directory. This increases intuition, as it enables managers to refer to particular legislative compliance issues (rather than manually collecting compliance rules and policies).

For example, if a sales process manager wishes to apply all 'Sarbanes-Oxley section 402' related compliance rules to the sales process, then he/she will define a request by stipulating the source (Sarbanes-Oxley section 402) and the type of process (the sales process). In response, the control directory will search its contents and retrieve the SoX compliance policy defined for the sales process by comparing against the 'source' and 'process' attributes of available policies. For each found policy, the control directory removes any rules not related to section 402. The control directory next groups the resulting rules into a compliance package. In case multiple versions of a Sox 402 policy were found, these are presented to the sales process manager for selection. Interestingly, this approach also allows specification of requests for compliance of a process to multiple regulations. To illustrate, the sales process manager can stipulate to apply all Sarbanes-Oxley 402 rules, as well as the Basel II related rules. The control directory will retrieve the appropriate rules for both types of legislation and merge these into a single compliance policy. In all cases, the resulting compliance policy is sent to the compliance control manager, who ensures that the contained rules will then be applied during business process execution conform the SCM methodology. Due to space limitations we do not discuss this further here.

4 Related Work

In the last years there has been an increase in attention paid to the role of compliance within business processes. A typical example is [21] which defines a formalization for internal controls and how they relate to operational processes. Similar works include [23] and [10]. Though these contribute to the insight in the relation between processes and compliance, they do not address how control mechanisms can be integrated in executable business processes. In the area of process control objectives works have chartered the implications of compliance for IT, most notably COSO [6] and COBIT [15]. COSO identifies several control activities (including authorizations, data verifications, reviews of operating performance, security of assets and segregation of duties), but does not define how to integrate them in business processes. Related, COBIT (short for Control Objectives for Information and related Technology) is useful as it identifies a large number of control objectives for business processes, which are subsequently refined into concrete application controls. However, like COSO, COBIT does not provide the means to integrate these objectives into business process models.

[25] presents a framework for the modeling of control objectives within business process structures based on a modal logic based approach using Formal Contract Language [11]. This is akin to the sketched BPCL, but we allow more expressive definition as control constructs can be associated with and/or grouped by other control constructs. [25] also advocates usage of a controls directory which holds the interpretation of com pliance regulations in the specific context of an organization (given the ambiguity of such regulations). Our approach will be able to facilitate this following [8], which attaches meta-data to compliance rules to depict the relationship between specific rules and compliance legislations. Finally, [25] hints at how the approach allows assessing the degree of process compliance; and how the usage of logic allows for analyzing why a particular decision in a business process was made. The SCM approach will be able to provide the same kind of reasoning via its formal knowledge base. Moreover, given the expressive nature of the BPCL (e.g. in terms of monoticity and prioritization), the SCM is planned to facilitate more sophisticated assessment and reasoning.

[26] proposes an aspect-oriented based approach for linking compliance to business protocols (i.e. abstract business processes). This is very similar to the usage of compliance rules in this paper, where rule conditions express aspect pointcuts and the rule conclusion defines the advice. The difference is that in our approach these are externalized and administered by a separate rule engine; positioning them better for analysis and management purposes. [17] sketches a model checking method in which business process models are expressed in the Business Process Execution Language (BPEL) [1], and then transformed into pi-calculus and finite state machines. At the same time compliance rules are expressed in a graphical Business Property Specification Language, which are next translated into linear temporal logic. Then, process models are verified against the resulting statements by means of model-checking technology. [9] proposes a similar approach using semantically annotated process models based on Business Process Modelling Notation (BPMN) [22] and Computational Tree Logic. Although useful in nature, our work extends these approaches by allowing for more rich annotation of control primitives.

[8] suggests to capture business processes and Canadian privacy related legislative requirements separately using the User Requirements Notation (URN) [16]). The paper also proposes to add documentation notes to the goal model capturing the privacy requirements , similar like what is done in this paper. [4] observes that often compliance objectives are delegated within the organizational hierarchy, where they are refined in a top-down manner. The described management is similar to the one proposed in this

paper. In this regard [4] also notes that in delegation compliance requirements are often refined; e.g. via goal refinement similar to for example what is proposed for security in [19] in relation to the Tropos methodology. Our work does not address this issue yet, but we plan to include this in the future.

5 Conclusions

Business processes form the foundation for all organizations and are subject to industry regulations. Without explicit business process definitions, flexible rules frameworks, and audit trails that provide for non-repudiation, organizations face litigation risks and even criminal penalties. To address such problems we have proposed a SOA compliance methodology (SCM) based on the concept of a risk management and auditing SOA - to oversee the compliance of business processes with internal accounting control for the purpose of risk management and auditing. The results that we have presented provide an initial basic theoretical foundation for addressing the raised SOA based business process risk management and auditing tenets. Significant extensions are needed in several directions to guarantee a practical methodology. Work is needed to realize runtime support in the form of interaction with the BPEL engine to achieve integration and enforcement of control requirements during execution. Also, validation of the approach (particularly in terms of the adopted architecture and BPCL) in the context of real life case studies has to be carried out. Moreover, for demonstration purposes illustrative compliance rules and policies should be developed that address certain compliance regulations.

References

1. Alves, A., Arkin, A., Askary, A., Barreto, C., Bloch, B., Curbera, F., Ford, M., Goland, Y., Guízar, A., Kartha, N., Liu, C., Khalaf, R., König, D., Marin, M., Mehta, V., Thatte, S., van der Rijn, D., Yendluri, P., Yiu, A.: Web services business process execution language version 2.0 (April 2007)
2. Bajaj, S., Box, D., Chappell, D., Curbera, F., Daniels, G., Hallam-Baker, P., Hondo, M., Kaler, C., Langworthy, D., Nadalin, A., Nagaratnam, N., Prafullchandra, H., von Riegen, C., Roth, D., Schlimmer, J. (eds.) Sharp, C., Shewchuk, J., Vedamuthu, A., Yalçýnalp, Ü., Orchard, D.: Web services policy 1.2 framework (April 2006)
3. Basel Committee on Banking Supervision. International convergence of capital measurement and capital standards (June 2006)
4. Breaux, T., Antón, A., Spafford, E.: A distributed requirements management framework for legal compliance and accountability. Technical Report 14, North Carolina State University Computer Science (2006)
5. Canadian Institute of Chartered Accountants. Continuous auditing: research report. CICA/AICPA (1999)
6. COSO. Internal control for financial reporting - guidance for smaller public companies (2006)
7. Department of Health and Human Services. Hipaa privacy rule. US Federal Register (December 2000)
8. Ghanavati, S., Amyot, D., Peyton, L.: A requirements management framework for privacy compliance. In: Proceedings of the Workshop on Requirements Engineering (2007)

9. Ghose, A., Koliadis, G.: Auditing business process compliance. In: Proceedings of the International Conference on Service-Oriented Computing (2007)
10. Goedertier, S., Vanthienen, J.: Designing compliant business processes with obligations and permissions. In: Eder, J., Dustdar, S. (eds.) BPM Workshops 2006. LNCS, vol. 4103, pp. 5–14. Springer, Heidelberg (2006)
11. Governatori, G., Milosevic, Z.: A formal analysis of a business contract language. International Journal of Cooperative Information Systems 15(4) (2006)
12. Grosof, B., Gruninger, M., Kifer, M., Martin, D., McGuinness, D., Parsia, B., Payne, T., Tate, A.: Semantic web services language requirements (February 2008)
13. Hayes, R., Dassen, R., Schilder, A., Wallage, P.: Principles of Auditing: An introduction to international standards on Auditing. Prentice Hall/Financial Times (2005)
14. International Federation of Accountants. Handbook of International Auditing, Assurance and Ethics Pronouncements. John Wiley, Chichester (2006)
15. IT Governance Institute. Framework for control objectives: Management guidelines and maturity models (cobit 4.1) (2007)
16. ITU-T. User requirements notation (urn) – language requirements and framework. ITU-T Recommendation Z.150 (February 2003)
17. Liu, Y., Müller, S., Xu, K.: A static compliance-checking framework for business process models. IBM Systems Journal 46(2), 335–362 (2007)
18. Luckham, D.: The Power of Events: An Introduction to Complex Event Processing in Distributed Enterprise Systems (Hardcover). Addison-Wesley Professional, Reading (2002)
19. Mouratidis, H., Giorgini, P., Manson, G.: An ontology for modelling security: The tropos approach. In: Proceedings of the 7th International Conference on Knowledge-Based Intelligent Information & Engineering Systems, Oxford, United Kingdom (September 2003)
20. Murthy, U., Groomer, S.: A continuous auditing web services model for xml-based accounting systems. Accounting Information Systems 5, 139–163 (2004)
21. Namiri, K., Stojanovic, N.: Towards a formal framework for business process compliance. In: Proceedings of the Multikonferenz Wirtschaftsinformatik (February 2008)
22. Object Management Group. Business process modeling notation (February 2006)
23. Padmanabhan, V., Governatori, G., Sadiq, S., Colomb, R., Rotolo, A.: Process modeling: The deontic way. In: Proceedings Of The Australia-Pacific Conference on Conceptual Modeling (2006)
24. PriceWaterhouseCoopers. Adopting ifrs first-time adoption of international financial reporting standards (June 2004)
25. Sadiq, S., Governatori, G., Naimiri, K.: Modeling control objectives for business process compliance. In: Alonso, G., Dadam, P., Rosemann, M. (eds.) BPM 2007. LNCS, vol. 4714, pp. 149–164. Springer, Heidelberg (2007)
26. Svirskas, A., Courbis, C., Molva, R., Bedzinskas, J.: Compliance proofs for collaborative interactions using aspect-oriented approach. In: Proceedings of the IEEE Congress on Services (2007)
27. US Congress. Sarbanes-oxley of 2002 (January 2002)
28. van Gelder, A., Ross, K., Schlipf, J.: The well-founded semantics for general logic programs. Journal of the ACM 38(3), 620–650 (1991)
29. Yu, S., Neter, J.: A stochastic model of the internal control system. Journal of Accounting Research 11, 273–295 (1973)

SCA and jABC: Bringing a Service-Oriented Paradigm to Web-Service Construction

Georg Jung[1], Tiziana Margaria[1], Ralf Nagel[2], Wolfgang Schubert[1], Bernhard Steffen[2], and Horst Voigt[1]

[1] Universität Potsdam, Chair Service and Software Engineering
{jung,margaria,schubert,voigt}@cs.uni-potsdam.de
[2] TU Dortmund, Chair Programming Systems
{ralf.nagel,steffen}@cs.tu-dortmund.de

Abstract. Extensibility, flexibility, easy maintainability, and long-term robustness are core requirements for modern, highly distributed information and computation systems. Such systems in turn show a steady increase in complexity. In pursuit of these goals, software engineering has seen a rapid evolution of architectural paradigms aiming towards increasingly modular, hierarchical, and compositional approaches. Object-orientation, component orientation, middleware components, product-lines, and - recently - service orientation.

We compare two approaches towards a service-oriented paradigm, the Service Component Architecture (SCA) and the jABC.

1 Introduction

The Service Component Architecture (SCA) [1,2] was developed recently as an industry standard for service-oriented development of complex, distributed, (web-based) applications.[1] Core of the SCA approach is the notion of the *service component*. Applications are built by arranging a cooperative network of service components which communicate through standardized interfaces.

In essence, SCA is an extensive set of specifications which describe an overall assembly model, implementation support for various programming and database languages, bindings to existing web-service-, messaging-, and middleware-standards, and policy and profiling mechanisms to access and customize infrastructure functionality. As such, SCA has proved effective and useful for building applications in practice.

By continuously emphasizing the service component, service architecture or service oriented development, SCA implicitly promotes a particular concept to be associated with the term "service". A *service* in the sense of SCA is a certain component that provides its functionality through a specific interface (the service interface, often directly identified with the service). Likewise, an *assembly* of services is merely a topology of components which are connected through

[1] The first SCA specification, version 0.9, dates from November 2005, version 1.0 from March 2007.

T. Margaria and B. Steffen (Eds.): ISoLA 2008, CCIS 17, pp. 139–154, 2008.

provide-use relations among their services or service interfaces. In other words, SCA associates service-orientation with a structural, interface-centric view in an assembly model which otherwise follows a component-oriented paradigm (similar to the one proposed in, e.g., [3,4]).

While this notion has its merits in terms of intuition and viability, it is by no means the only workable grounds to introduce a service-oriented paradigm into the practice of application development. An orthogonal view is offered by the service concept of jABC [5,6,7,8,9] a framework for model-driven and service-oriented development that originated in the early '90s (previously named METAFrame [10]). Originally it was applied to the model-driven development of advanced telecommunication services for Intelligent Networks [11,12]. Due to the ease of generalization of that service model, it meanwhile evolved into a flexible model-driven approach spanning both local and distributed (web-based) application development and customization [5,13].

In jABC the term "service" is used to denote functional building blocks (SIBs[2]), which are viewed as independent from their location, the program-entity, and hardware-platform which provides them. Instead, the defining quality of a SIB, which forms the core abstraction of jABC, is its interaction with the environment, which manifests in its behavioural semantics and its manipulations of a global context. The SIBs are assembled – or as one says, orchestrated – with their operational or behavioural semantics in mind. Concretely, this means that each SIB, once activated, executes its logic and upon termination triggers subsequent SIBs according to the outcome of this execution. This methodology of composition has been termed *lightweight process coordination* [9] and is closely related to the SIB model standardized by ITU [14].

The two approaches emphasize dual angles of the idea of a service, which can be characterized as:

- *resource-oriented* vs. *process-oriented*
- *architectural* vs. *behavioral*
- *static* vs. *dynamic*

In the following we will investigate these dual views for their potential to support a truly service-oriented development. We initiate the comparison of the SCA and jABC concepts, considering properties, structures, meta models [15], and semantics, using some examples to illustrate the different viewpoints.

The rest of this paper is organized as follows. Sect. 2 and 3 introduce the meta-models of SCA and jABC, respectively. Sect. 4 examines the common component-middleware paradigm and compares it with the SCA and jABC with respect to structural and computational properties. Sect. 5 discussed the characteristics of component flavored assembly. Sect. 6 evaluates both approaches along technical and pragmatic characteristics. Finally, we briefly discuss related work (Sect. 7), and summarize our findings so far in Sect. 8.

[2] SIB stands for *Service Independent Building Block*, a notion coined in the nineties in the Telecommunication area [14], where the notion of service was meant to denote whole service orchestrations [14,12]. SIBs were back then the atomic service-like entities of which those services were aggregations.

2 The Meta-model of SCA

In SCA, each service component implements some specific business logic and provides its functionality through standardized interfaces, described in SCA literature as service-oriented interfaces and shortly called *services*. To implement its business logic, each service component can rely on third-party functionality provided by other components by linking to their respective service interfaces through so called *references*. A reference interface can be linked to a service interface by means of a *wire*, which abstracts the communication infrastructure through which functionality of third-party service interfaces can be accessed remotely.

A given assembly of service components interconnected through a set of wires can be summarized as a *composite*, and service or reference interfaces of the components inside the composite can be *propagated* to be visible as interfaces of the composite itself. Thus, the composite as a whole shows similar characteristics as a single service component and can be used in the same way inside larger composites. This enables a straightforward hierarchy structure for SCA assemblies, distinguishing "atomic" components and composite components. Finally, a service component may feature property-interfaces which allow to customize its behavior and can be propagated to be visible as properties of a composite in the same way as interfaces.

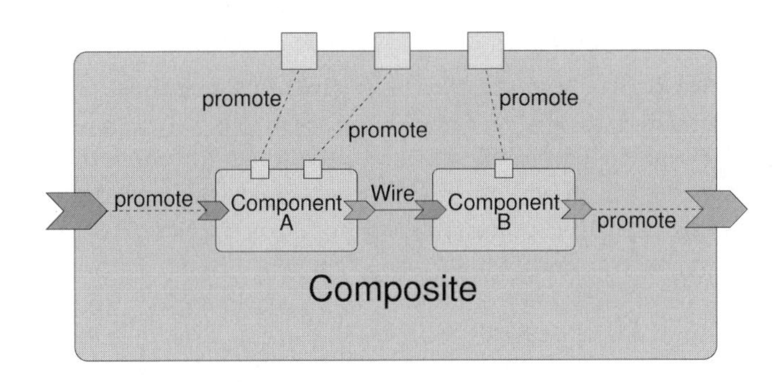

Fig. 1. Schematic of the SCA assembly-model

Fig. 1 shows a schematic of the SCA assembly model (see `www.osoa.org`). Other than what one might expect, the service interfaces are the incoming interfaces and the reference interfaces are the outgoing ones. This reflects a view from *inside* the component/composite, where services (of others) are used and the references to services (of oneself) are provided. It can therefore be described as a developer's view (as opposed to, e.g., a composer's view), which again emphasizes the idea that services are used to integrate third-party functionality into an application.

In [2], Edwards proposes a UML-model of the SCA assembly. The excerpt in Fig. 2 shows the essential part: concrete components with their component-properties, -references, and -services serve as implementation for component

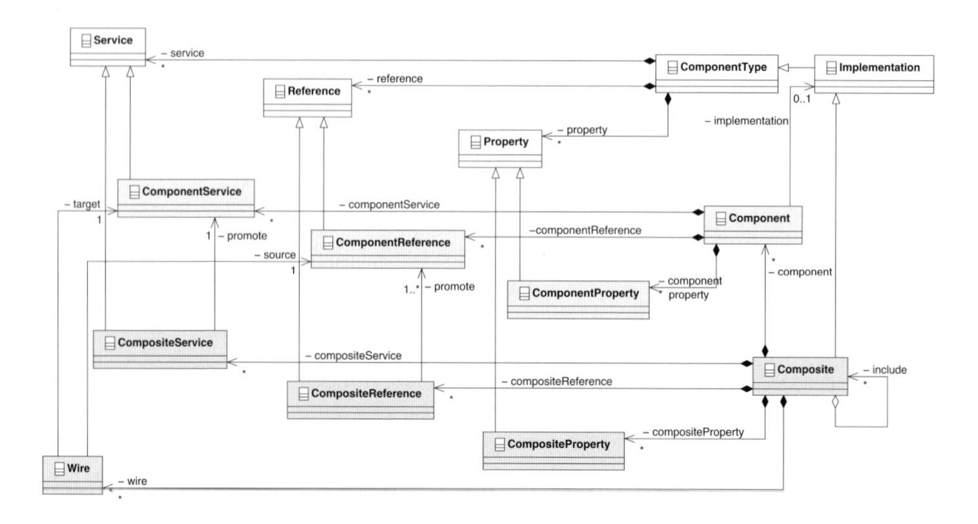

Fig. 2. An UML-model of the SCA-assembly

types. The composite on the other hand is a specific way to implement a component type (indicated by the inheritance relation to implementation), and can in turn contain multiple components. The wire as a part of the composite connects one reference with one service interface. Unfortunately, this model leaves out several crucial interrelation constraints, for example it shows that one service and one reference can be attached to one wire, but it glosses over how many wires can be attached to a single service or reference. E.g., a single wire per service interface and zero-to-many wires per reference interface seem reasonable connectivity constraints. Also, the model shows inheritance relations across different levels of abstraction (i.e., type–instance relations. Services on components *inherit* from services on component types in this model. Here an implementation/interpretation relation would seem more appropriate. Nevertheless, the model is clearly meant to expose *structural* or *static* interrelations of the SCA notions to enable implementations. To this aim it is certainly more helpful than a conceptional relationship model.

3 The Meta-model of jABC

jABC follows a completely different compositional paradigm, called lightweight process coordination [9], which - instead of structural properties - revolves around the operational aspects of its elementary building blocks (see Sect. 1). Concretely, a SIB is an executable entity, internally realized as a specifically annotated Java class.[3] As such, it intrinsically carries an arbitrarily fine-grained/precise operational semantics. A SIB can be a model placeholder for some functionality

[3] While jABC is currently implemented in Java, the core concept is independent of the programming language. Previous versions, for example, realized the same model in C++.

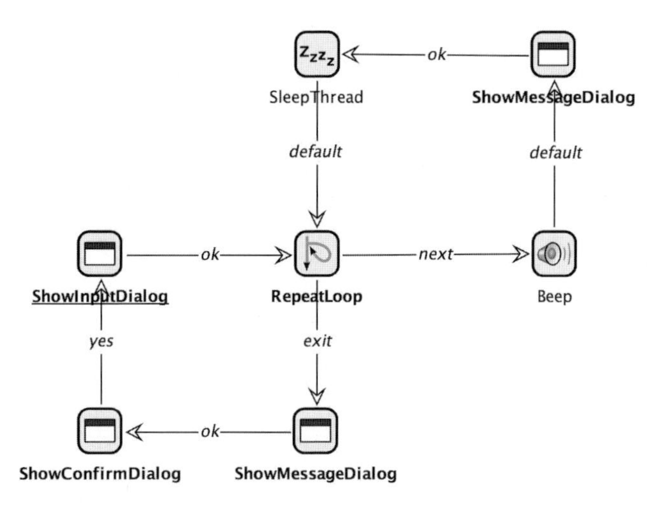

Fig. 3. Assembly of services in jABC: the SLG is a *process*

or a full implementation of that functionality, as well as any level of refinement/abstraction expressible by the (Java) programming language in between. Further, each SIB has one entry point, where the execution starts, and multiple exit points (called *branches*) which represent different outcomes of its execution at the model level.

SIBs can be arranged into topologies called *Service Logic Graphs* (SLG) which specify process behavior by connecting outgoing SIB branches to the entry points of other SIBs. Inside an SLG, the execution of a SIB starts whenever one of its incoming branches is *active*, which means that the SIB which governs the branch terminated its execution with an outcome associated with that branch. One SIBs inside an SLG can be assigned to be *start SIBs*, which means that its execution is started without an incoming active branch; start SIBs are the entry points of the process modelled by the respective SLG.

Fig. 3 shows a simple process, graphically modeled as SLG.[4] The labels of start SIBs, here **ShowInputDialog**, are underlined, those of possible exit SIBs (e.g., **ShowInputDialog**, **RepeatLoop**, ...) are printed in bold-font. In the basic, sequential case, each SIB terminates with one active branch which determines the next SIB to be executed. Parallel and concurrent structures are likewise possible, as used in the bioinformatics applications [16,17]. Hence, an SLG is a graphical, executable, node-action process description.

SLGs can be canonically wrapped into (*graph-*) SIBs to allow for a hierarchical organization of complex process models. Moreover, process models which follow a certain standard defined by jABC can be directly exported into (partial or complete) stand-alone applications, a feature which turns jABC from a modeling into a development tool. Finally, there are SIBs which serve as wrappers for outside

[4] The process model shown in Fig. 3 is one of the tutorial examples which come with the standard installation of jABC.

functionality (e.g., non-Java applications such as C++, C#, SOAP/WSDL Web services, etc.): this enables modeling and building of heterogeneous, distributed, applications.

The service concept as a compositional paradigm is particularly strong in jABC, since all visible business-logic in an SLG boils down to *orchestration* of the functionality abstracted within the SIBs. Each SIB independently and without interruption manipulates the global context, similar to what happens in blackboard systems [18], and upon its termination the jABC passes the control to the next SIB. As opposed to a component-oriented approach, SIBs never access or interact with other SIBs through channels or interfaces; instead, their functionality is local and self-contained.

4 Comparison with Component-Orientation

If one revisits the SCA meta-model with a regular, component oriented, architecture-methodology in mind (such as, e.g., the CORBA Component Model CCM [19], or Enterprise Java Beans [20]), many structural similarities surface. All of them support the concept of the *component*, accompanied by the notions of the *interface* which offers access to the component, and the *connector*, which allows composers to link components together. The variety of kinds of available connectors, components, and interfaces is sometimes associated with the term *architectural style*, depending on the communication capabilities it offers (e.g., publish-subscribe architecture, remote procedure-call RPC, broadcast, etc.).

These three fundamental concepts (colloquially: boxes, dots, and lines) generally appear in a middleware context or comparable setting, where a more or less fixed infrastructure with a given set of communication, persistence, execution, and similar capabilities is abstracted to be able to focus on business-level functionality and high-level assembly. Fig. 4 for example formalizes EJB in a two-part meta-model which distinguishes between general parts of a component-oriented paradigm (labeled platform independent model, PIM) and parts specific to the EJB model (labeled platform specific model, PSM).[5] Meta-models of various middleware-centric component frameworks can be built by simply exchanging the PSM with the specifics of a different platform.

SCA fits into this structural model too, if one considers the use of (previously existing, established) internet-communication protocols (HTTP, SMTP, etc.) to be comparable to more local approaches such as a CORBA RPC layer. In this case, a meta-model for SCA can be built by using the aforementioned PIM and complementing platform-specific parts and terms of SCA (Fig. 5).

Note that in middleware-centric architectural styles, the term "service" is often used for the capabilities of the middleware (e.g., persistence service, publish-subscribe service, etc.). These middleware services are again fundamentally distinct from the service concept of SCA. In high-level, and in particular business process level service oriented environments, middleware services have to

[5] The notions of PIM/PSM have been proposed in similar forms independently by various authors; see, e.g., [15], where the acronyms PIM and PSM appear first.

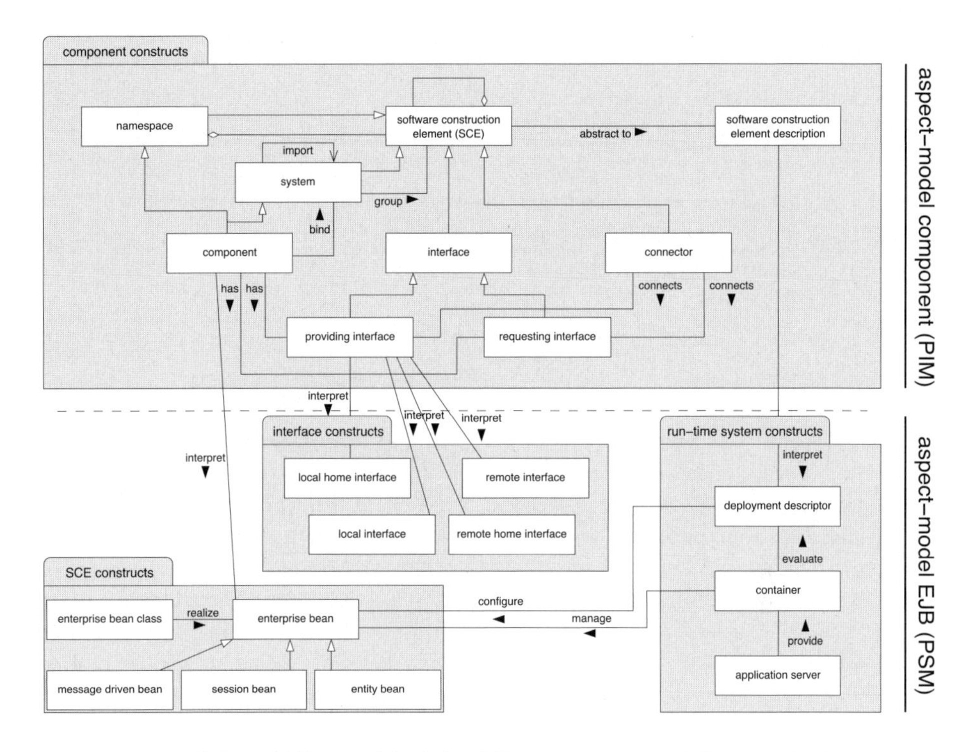

Fig. 4. A PIM/PSM model of the EJB component-middleware platform

be thoroughly abstracted so that they can be independently and mechanically configurable. This is because, to actually facilitate development instead of making it more complex, they have to support an agnostic developer (i.e., component integrator). For example in a CCM architecture [19], no matter where a component is located, it can use the RPC service, hence the service has to be location-agnostic. The middleware service is therefore not analogue to the service (interface) in SCA which is location-bound. Instead the wire in SCA is a much closer equivalent to the location-agnostic intuition of a service because it abstracts a ubiquitous communication service. In fact, keeping the complexity of the infrastructure and communication channels abstracted in SCA in mind, it seems reasonable to consider their entirety as some kind of middleware.

The assembly model of jABC follows an entirely different approach which is operation-centered, instead of structure-centered. As opposed to the SCA service interface it does also not consider location. It does not correspond in any way to the component-oriented, middleware-centric, paradigm. In fact, the notion of the global context in jABC contradicts the strict data-encapsulation which is required by the component methodology. There is, however, a close correspondence between the idea of the SIB and the (arbitrarily complex) middleware-service. Like the SIB, the middleware service does not consider a localized persistence feature in its definition, and like the SIB, it is defined rather through its functionality than its structure.

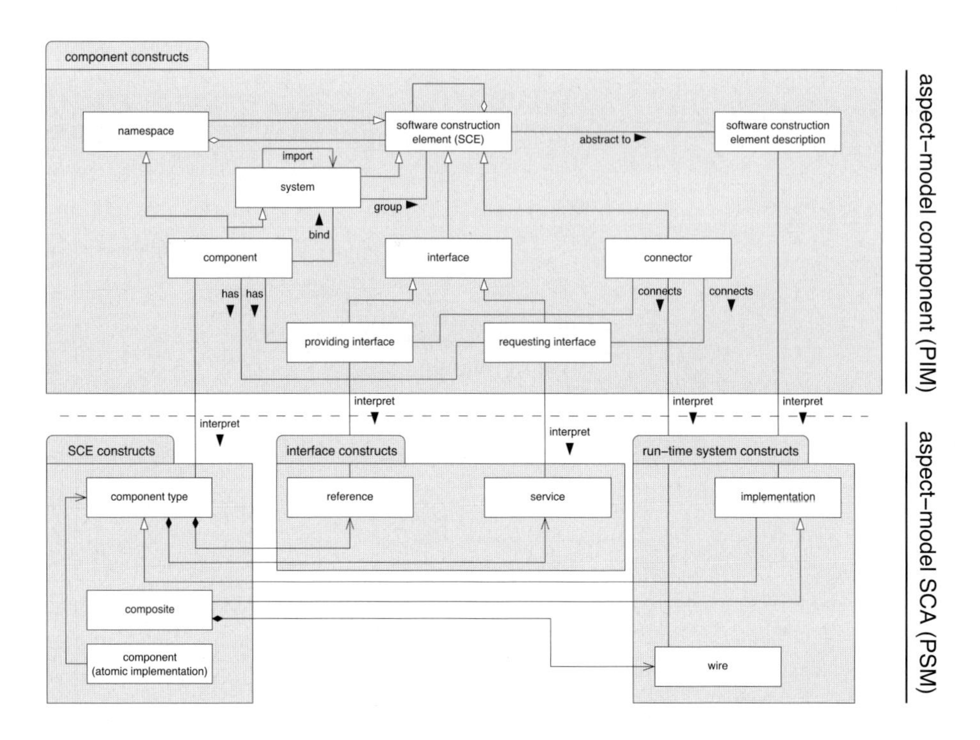

Fig. 5. SCA meta model, fitted into a component-middleware structure, cfr. Fig. 4

5 Characteristics of Component Flavored Assembly

We discuss here the two aspects that seem to us most prominent.

5.1 Complex, Fixed, Layer-Structures and the Service Concept

The two notions of service discussed in the previous section (the middleware/ infrastructure-layer service and the SCA service interface) fall short for the task of service composition. In both concepts (as opposed to the one of jABC) the service is only modeled through the structural properties of its access point, and if services are to be combined the developer has to resort to hand-coded business logic.

At the same time, even the complexity of the infrastructure layer itself suggests the necessity for a methodology for easy assembly of services. The fact that for example connectors in a component topology cannot be neglected as trivial was first pointed out by Shaw [21], and this realization subsequently found its way into literature about practical application of the component-oriented paradigm (e.g., in [3, *pp.* 429] Szypersky states that "A connector, when zooming in, can easily have substantial complexity and really ask for partitioning into components itself"). Nevertheless, discovering this "duality" between component and connector [3, *same page*] did not yet trigger a revisiting of terminology,

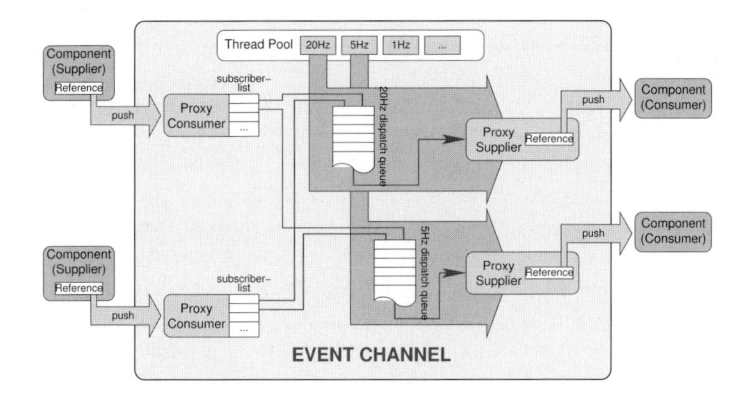

Fig. 6. Schematic view of the PRiSM Event-channel

paradigms, and abstractions of component-oriented architectural styles or an introduction of lightweight process coordination into the middleware concepts.

To illustrate the lack of expressiveness, consider the PRiSM real-time component middleware, which was developed by the Boeing company within the Bold Stroke effort for middleware-based aviation control systems [22]. PRiSM features, much like CCM, two main channels for communication: An asynchronous event notification service with very limited payload capability and a synchronous RPC connection which can be used to communicate data through the return values (but not to trigger computation, since it is not thread-safe). The implementation of the notification service called *event-channel* is intertwined with the middleware's thread handling mechanism (Fig. 6). A thread starts with a periodic timeout event (20Hz, 5Hz, 1Hz in Fig. 6, distributed through the event notification service) and runs until all events within its buffer (called the rate group's *dispatch queue*) are handled. The events trigger computation within the individual components and subsequent events can be queued within the same dispatch queue or dispatch queues of other threads. In other words, timeout events and dispatches drive the components of a rate group, and the buffering within the event channel serves for messages to cross rate groups.

To exchange data between different threads/rate-groups, systems on the PRiSM platform make heavy use of a so-called *control-push–data-pull* strategy. If new data has been generated (e.g., by a device-driver component such as a GPS), the generating component issues an event which notifies consumers of the data. This event is queued within the dispatch queues of the receiver's respective threads. At the time these threads become active and the event is dispatched, the receiving components actively fetch the announced data from the generating component through RPC-calls. This method guarantees that threads never execute out of turn, and data is only transmitted when both available and needed. The drawback is that two different middleware connectors are needed for one logical connection.

To avoid "cross-wiring" or other inconsistencies which can occur with these double connections it seems obvious that a new abstraction should be added

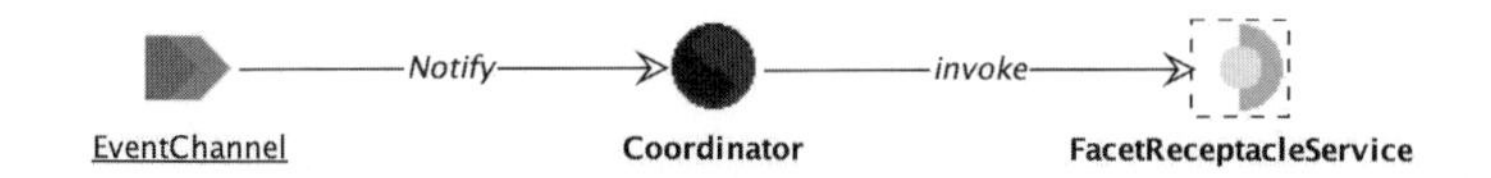

Fig. 7. Composing a non-blocking message service in jABC

to the middleware capabilities which denotes the double connection as a single connector of a new type. In a middleware-centric or generally in a tiered approach with emphasis on interface compatibility, we can certainly introduce the abstraction, but the semantics of the new connector can only be implemented "by hand", since the operational semantics of the different existing connectors are not captured by the model, even though the general push-pull strategy could have been understood without knowledge about the implementation details of the individual communication channels.

When using a lightweight process coordination methodology, as in the jABC, instead (applied to coordinating the middleware processes), the task of assembling a new (ubiquitous, semantically unambiguous, hierarchically constructed) communication service from existing ones becomes clear and simple. The two connectors are composed as a sequence, together with a control unit which handles possible data conversions if necessary (Fig. 7).

In the PRiSM middleware, the infrastructure services are necessarily simplistic due to the real-time aspects, with limited options to reasonably combine multiple services into orchestrated compounds. Yet, even in this constrained microcosm-setting the middleware would benefit from process coordination. In the macrocosm of a web-based, highly distributed, application, the variety of existing services increases: there are services which would be considered infrastructure (such as communication), and services provided on top of the infrastructure. Here the possibilities of assembling meaningful combinations multiply.

5.2 Perspective, Location, and Entry-Point: Topology vs. Coordination

Consider a composite service where a central unit C acts as the orchestrator and in turn relies on services provided by distinct units A and B. For example, for a list of authorized database-accesses, A authorizes the access, B offers it, and C orchestrates services A and B to allow its users to handle the authorization and the complete list of accesses via a single call to C.

The difference between a model of this situation in SCA and in jABC can be summarized as *perspective* or viewpoint (Fig. 8 (a) and (b)).

- SCA offers a model of the physical *topology*: C appears as the provider of the service that promotes a reference for service access. Through wires, C connects the service interfaces it needs to the respective references provided by A and B. The structural aspects of the example are captured and localized by the SCA model, but the operational aspects are hidden. In fact, SCA would require to integrate tailored business logic into C as their orchestration.

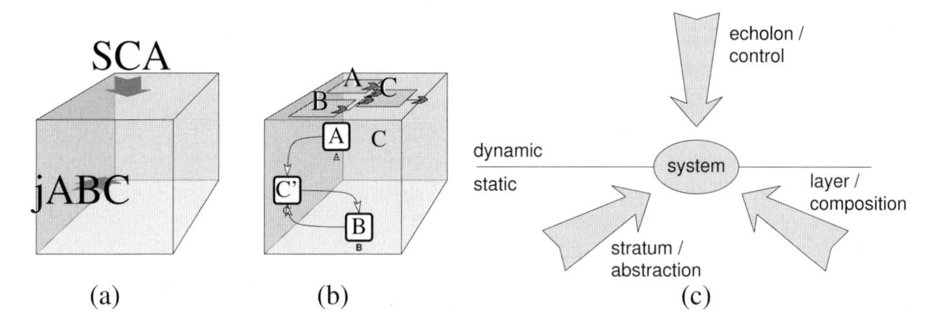

Fig. 8. Different perspectives: (a) SCA and jABC perspectives, (b) Topology or process coordination, (c) Perspectives according to Mesarovic

- jABC on the other hand abstracts all location aspects. Entry point of the operational model *through* the composite-service C is the start-SIB A, where the first operation happens (the authorization), then C' (the actual mediation service) is invoked, and subsequently a loop between C' and B performs the service until the list of authorized accesses is complete. The jABC model glosses over the actual topology of the involved units (components, or SIBs, or services).

Concerning executability and coding aspects, while the SCA-model only allows auto-generating code-stubs which handle the interconnection and communication aspects, but needs control and business logic to be added, the jABC model is designed to be sufficient to generate the complete system through the Genesys plugin [23]. As described in Sect. 3, given a sufficiently complete modeling of the individual SIBs, jABC acts as an intuitive, graphical, development tool rather than a modeling tool.

The need for multiple perspectives has been noted earlier. Most eminently in [24], Mesarovic et al. propose three perspectives which have to be consolidated for a complete system model. They coin the terms *echelon*, *layer*, and *stratum* which—in current terminology—denote control or behavior, composition or topology, and abstractions and data types respectively (Fig. 8(c)).

6 Evaluation

In this section we are going to investigate the appropriateness of the described specification styles for *service orientation* relative to the widely agreed upon characteristics of service orientation. Here, we consider a technical and a pragmatic side, both with three dimensions.

Technical characterization: as introduced in [7]

- (Extreme) loose coupling and self containment of the services.
- Virtualization: clear separation from implementation/realization details.
- Domain specificity: a service-oriented setup should seamlessly integrate into the setup of the considered domain.

Pragmatic characterization:

- Scalability, both for the successive 'assembly' of functionality, as well as for the number of users of developed artifacts.
- Participation: service-orientation aims at giving the domain expert access and control of the development and evolution of the artifacts.
- Agility: changes and adaptations should be easy and ideally be controllable at the (process) model level.

Despite their strong semantic differences, the SCA approach and jABC approach are quite similar when it comes to the technical characteristics: both support loose coupling and virtualization, and the organization in the virtualized components enables a domain-specific development.

The differences show up, however, when it comes to the pragmatic characteristics, which we will now consider individually.

6.1 Scalability

This first dimension is still supported quite similarly in the two approaches, by clean concepts of hierarchy. Both SCA and jABC offer conceptually similar options to assemble larger elements (service components or SIBs) out of topologies of smaller ones: In SCA the composite can act as component, in jABC an SLG can be packed into a SIB, and in either case it is necessary to propagate or mark interfaces of the internal structures to be visible on the external structure.

Concerning the scalability in the number of users, both approaches can make adequate use of standard technology like scalable application servers, which support growing sizes of users.

The real difference between the SCA and the jABC approach becomes apparent when looking at the remaining two dimensions.

6.2 Participation

Technically, we can regard service orientation as an 80/20 approach to application/process development. It aims at a maximal involvement of the application expert in order to avoid misunderstandings and to overcome communication hurdles. At the best, users should be able to directly influence, control, and adapt the services according to their needs. At least for typical day-to-day situations, this should be possible without IT knowledge. Thus, service orientation potentially has a disruptive impact on the current structures.

The jABC directly addresses this goal by putting the application/business process in the center of attention, while the architectural and resource-oriented SCA approach still addresses IT experts.

6.3 Agility

Agility can be regarded as a logical consequence of rigorous participation. Giving control (of the 80%) of system adaptation and evolution directly to the application expert eliminates time consuming and expensive multi-party interactions, with the misunderstandings and communication hurdles for the majority of tasks.

The One-Thing Approach supported by the jABC [25,26] is directly designed to establish this level of control: the user/application/business-level process remains part of the artifact, which gradually turns into the product along the development and which is maintained during the subsequent lifecycle. This allows the application experts in particular to redesign their processes, control permissions, and add business rules at the application/business process level, with the immediate consequence of enactment. Thus, essentially, the changes are implemented as soon as they were specified. Of course, more radical changes will still require IT support, but in our experience they are not as frequent. As before, the SCA approach can be seen here as a valid support for IT involvement. Thus it may well accelerate required modifications, but in a more 'classical' setting.

7 Related Work

Previous work in service oriented architecture research focusses mostly on standards, languages, and features of SCA [27,28], or on the assembly model (i.e., interface definitions) [29]. There is little work on classifying the architectural patterns or combining them with flexible behavioral semantics.

Among the approaches towards combining service orientation with general-purpose behavioral descriptions is the SENSORIA project [30] and [31,32]. SENSORIA aims at a comprehensive approach to service-oriented development with focus on specific problems of loose coupling and heterogeneous environments, raising issues in security, specification, and communication, at a technical level. In contrast, we focus on participation, meaning that we directly address and involve the application expert via the 'One-Thing Approach' [33,25], throughout the entire lifecycle.

8 Conclusions

Both SCA and jABC are frameworks with substantial practical merit. By emphasizing the term "service" within the basic modeling structures, they both also claim to move forward to a novel, service-oriented, software-development paradigm. Nevertheless, their notion of service is fundamentally different.

This paper presented a structural, concept oriented, comparison between these two approaches, focussing on the main characteristics and of service orientation. We showed that

- The SCA development paradigm is essentially *component-oriented*, and as such it treats its extensive infrastructure specification as analogous to a middleware layer. Therefore it builds on proven software construction methodologies which are established as best practice in industrial software development, and brings them into the realm of web-based application development.

– By elevating the required interface, called *service*, to be the core modeling entity, SCA deviates from the standard component-oriented paradigm, which instead puts the component itself into the center of consideration. It seems however questionable whether this shift of emphasis alone is sufficient to warrant the label "service-oriented" development.
– As common to other component-oriented approaches, the operational aspects of a software system are not captured within SCA models, which concentrate on their structural aspects. This could become a handicap when addressing problems as service orchestrations, where SCA can rely on strong capabilities of the comprehensive infrastructure (i.e., a vast body of specification and machinery, XML artifacts and ties to all major communication protocols, maintained by a large community), but still needs hand-tailored solutions to be supplied for control-flow.
– The jABC methodology on the other hand is entirely operation centered and it hides topology, location, and connection aspects. It appears as the better candidate when it comes to transcending the semantic gap, as even control structures exist as services. While the ties to web-communication protocols are not an essential part of jABC, they are provided through various plugins (most eminently through jETI).
– The service concept of jABC is very close to an intuitive understanding of service (which, e.g., manifests itself in the term "middleware service" and in various other domains) that requires the service to be ubiquitously accessible (location-agnostic) and mechanically configurable. In fact it seems that the lightweight process coordination offers an elegant way to recombine and enhance common platform services as well as complex web-based business services. Therefore, jABC is not only applicable to web-development or similar tasks, it also offers itself as the semantic underpinning for an operational modelling inside component-oriented methodologies.

Looking at the intent and main characteristics of service orientation, it became clear to us that the two dual specification approaches, although being semantically quite different, are quite similar concerning the first four criteria, namely loose coupling, virtualization, domain specificity, and scalability. In fact, both approaches are based here almost on the same means – only applied to frameworks that aim at covering different perspectives: SCA takes the architectural perspective, which focusses on a resource view, and jABC a behavioral perspective, which focusses on a process view.

The real impact of the choice of perspective, however, becomes apparent when looking at the remaining characteristics, namely participation and agility, and this essentially for one single reason: Whereas SCA is based on lower level, infrastructure-oriented modelling and design, which is accessible to typical domain experts, jABC puts the (user-level) process in the center of attention. This directly supports participation, and, due to the One-Thing Approach, it also provides a new level of agility: the majority of day-to-day change requests can be resolved directly at the application process level, without even involving IT support. Put figuratively, the jABC is a framework that support the slogan "Easy for the many, difficult for the few", in particular by enabling the *many*, whereas SCA addresses the *few*, and supports them in their role of solving difficult tasks.

References

1. Margolis, B., Sharpe, J.L.: SOA for the Business Developer. MC Press (June 2007)
2. The Open SOA Collaboration: SCA web-site, `http://www.osoa.org/display/Main/Service+Component+Architecture+Home`
3. Szyperski, C.: Component Software: Beyond Object-Oriented Programming, 2nd edn. ACM Press / Addison-Wesley (2002)
4. Heineman, G., Councill, B.: Component-Based Software Engineering: Putting the Pieces Together. Addison Wesley, Reading (2001)
5. Steffen, B., Margaria, T., Nagel, R., Jörges, S., Kubczak, C.: Model-Driven Development with the jABC. In: Bin, E., Ziv, A., Ur, S. (eds.) HVC 2006. LNCS, vol. 4383, pp. 92–108. Springer, Heidelberg (2007)
6. Homepage of the jABC framework, `http://www.jabc.de`
7. Margaria, T., Steffen, B.: Service engineering: Linking business and IT. IEEE Computer 39(10), 45–55 (2006)
8. Steffen, B., Narayan, P.: Full life-cycle support for end-to-end processes. IEEE Computer 40(11), 64–73 (2007)
9. Margaria, T., Steffen, B.: Lightweight coarse-grained coordination: a scalable system-level approach. STTT - Int. Journ. on Software Tools for Technology Transfer 5(2), 107–123 (2004)
10. Steffen, B., Margaria, T.: METAFrame in practice: Design of Intelligent Network Services. In: Olderog, E.-R., Steffen, B. (eds.) Correct System Design. LNCS, vol. 1710, pp. 390–415. Springer, Heidelberg (1999)
11. Steffen, B., Margaria, T., Claßen, A., Braun, V., Reitenspieß, M.: An environment for the creation of intelligent network services. In: Annual Review of Communication, Int. Engineering Consortium (IEC), Chicago, USA, pp. 919–935 (November 1996)
12. Margaria, T., Steffen, B., Reitenspieß, M.: Service-oriented design: The roots. In: Benatallah, B., Casati, F., Traverso, P. (eds.) ICSOC 2005. LNCS, vol. 3826, pp. 450–464. Springer, Heidelberg (2005)
13. Kubczak, C., Margaria, T., Steffen, B., Nagel, R.: Service-oriented Mediation with jABC/jETI. In: Petrie, C., Lausen, H., Zaremba, M., Margaria, T. (eds.) Semantic Web Services Challenge: Results from the First Year (Semantic Web and Beyond). Springer, Heidelberg (to appear, 2008)
14. ITU Geneva, Switzerland: Recommendation Q.1211 - General Recommendations on Telephone Switching and Signaling Intelligent Network: Introduction to Intelligent Network Capability Set 1 (March 1993)
15. Object Management Group: MDA guide version 1.0.1, `http://www.omg.org/cgi-bin/apps/doc?omg/03-06-01.pdf`
16. Lamprecht, A.L., Margaria, T., Steffen, B.: Seven variations of an alignment workflow – an illustration of agile process design/management in Bio-jETI. In: Măndoiu, I., Sunderraman, R., Zelikovsky, A. (eds.) ISBRA 2008. LNCS (LNBI), vol. 4983, pp. 445–456. Springer, Heidelberg (2008)

17. Lamprecht, A.L., Margaria, T., Steffen, B., Sczyrba, A., Hartmeier, S., Giegerich, R.: Genefisher-p: Variations of genefisher as processes in biojeti. BioMed Central (BMC) Bioinformatics 2008. In: Supplement dedicated to Network Tools and Applications in Biology 2007 Workshop (NETTAB 2007), April 25, vol. 9(Suppl. 4), p. 13 (2008)
18. Nii, H.: Blackboard systems. AI Magazine 7(2), 38–53, 7(3), 82–106 (1986)
19. Object Management Group: OMG formal/06-04-01 (CORBA Component Model Specification, v4.0) (April 2006)
20. Matena, V., Krishnan, S., DeMichiel, L., Stearns, B.: Applying Enterprise JavaBeans. Addison Wesley, Reading (2003)
21. Shaw, M.: Procedure calls are the assembly language of software interconnection: Connectors deserve first-class status. In: Lamb, D.A. (ed.) Selected papers from the Workshop on Studies of Software Design. LNCS, vol. 1078, pp. 17–32. Springer, Heidelberg (1993)
22. Hatcliff, J., Deng, W., Dwyer, M., Jung, G., Ranganath, V.P.: Cadena: An integrated development, analysis, and verification environment for component-based systems. In: Proc. 25th Int. Conf. on Software Engineering (ICSE 2003), May 2003, vol. 841, pp. 160–173. IEEE Computer Soceity Press, Los Alamitos (2003)
23. Jörges, S., Margaria, T., Steffen, B.: Genesys: Service-oriented construction of certified code generators. ISSE – Int. Journal on Innovations in Systems and Software Engineering – a NASA Journal (to appear)
24. Mesarovic, M., Macko, D., Takahara, Y.: Theory of Hierarchical, Multilevel, Systems. Mathematics in Science and Engineering, vol. 68. Academic Press, New York (1970)
25. Margaria, T., Steffen, B.: Business Process Modelling in the jABC: The One-Thing Approach. In: Handbook of Research on Business Process Modeling, IGI Global (2008)
26. Margaria, T.: Service is in the eyes of the beholder. IEEE Computer 40(11), 33–37 (2007)
27. Curbera, F.: Component contracts in service-oriented architectures. IEEE Computer 40(11), 74–80 (2007)
28. Zou, Z., Duan, Z.: Building business processes or assembling service components: Reuse services with bpel4ws and sca. In: ECOWS 2006, Proc. European Conference on Web Services, pp. 138–147 (2006)
29. Ding, Z., Chen, Z., Liu, J.: A rigorous model of service component architecture. ENTCS 207, 33–48 (2008)
30. Wirsing, M., Hölzl, M., Acciai, L., Banti, F., et al.: SENSORIA patterns: Augmenting service engineering with formal analysis, transformation and dynamicity. In: ISoLA 2008. CCIS, vol. 17, pp. 170–190. Springer, Heidelberg (This Volume) (2008)
31. Fiadeiro, J.L., Lopes, A., Bocchi, L.: Algebraic Semantics of Service Component Modules. In: Fiadeiro, J.L., Schobbens, P.-Y. (eds.) WADT 2006. LNCS, vol. 4409, pp. 37–55. Springer, Heidelberg (2007)
32. Fiadeiro, J.L., Lopes, A., Bocchi, L.: A Formal Approach to Service Component Architecture. In: Bravetti, M., Núñez, M., Zavattaro, G. (eds.) WS-FM 2006. LNCS, vol. 4184, pp. 193–213. Springer, Heidelberg (2006)
33. Hörmann, M., Margaria, T., Mender, T., Nagel, R., Steffen, B., Trinh, H.: The jabc approach to rigorous collaborative development of scm applications. In: ISoLA 2008. CCIS, vol. 17, pp. 724–737. Springer, Heidelberg (This Volume) (2008)

A Use-Case Driven Approach to Formal Service-Oriented Modelling*

Laura Bocchi[1], José Luiz Fiadeiro[1], and Antónia Lopes[2]

[1] Department of Computer Science, University of Leicester
University Road, Leicester LE1 7RH, UK
{bocchi,jose}@mcs.le.ac.uk
[2] Department of Informatics, Faculty of Sciences, University of Lisbon
Campo Grande, 1749-016 Lisboa, Portugal
mal@di.fc.ul.pt

Abstract. We put forward a use-case based approach for SRML – a formal framework that is being defined by the SENSORIA consortium for service-oriented modelling. We expand on the way SRML contributes to the engineering of software systems and we propose a number of extensions to the UML for supporting that approach. We use a mortgage brokerage scenario for illustrating our approach.

1 Introduction

This paper is about a new way of developing software, which we believe requires that we revisit the methods and techniques that software engineers have been using so far. This new approach is based on *Service-Oriented Computing* (SOC) over *Global Computers* (GC).

We view SOC as a new computing paradigm in which interactions are no longer based on fixed or programmed exchanges of *products* with specific parties – what is known as clientship in object-oriented programming – but on the provisioning of *services* by external providers that are procured on the fly subject to a negotiation of service level agreements (SLAs). More precisely, the processes of discovery and selection of services as required by an application are not programmed (at design time) but performed by the middleware according to functional and non-functional requirements (SLAs). The process of binding the client application and the selected service is not performed by skilled software developers, but also at run time, by the middleware. Because the set of available services changes as providers update their portfolios, and that service-level agreements may involve context-dependent conditions, different instances of the same application may bind to different services and operate according to different SLAs resulting from different negotiations.

Having said this, one has to recognise that these capabilities of SOC as a paradigm are not always fully exploited by current Web/Grid-based technologies. One of the

* This work was partially supported through the IST-2005-16004 Integrated Project *SENSORIA: Software Engineering for Service-Oriented Overlay Computers.*

T. Margaria and B. Steffen (Eds.): ISoLA 2008, CCIS 17, pp. 155–169, 2008.

aims of the SENSORIA project [17] is to provide a framework in which the promise of SOC can be captured and used for evolving existing software technologies and engineering methodology. In this context, several formal languages and techniques are being developed that address different aspect or phases of the envisaged development process. Among these is SRML – the SENSORIA Reference Modelling Language – aimed at supporting the more abstract levels of design specification, what we call 'business modelling'. Modelling in SRML is independent of the languages in which services are programmed and the platforms in which they are deployed.

SRML provides a minimalistic textual language that has been devised in order to facilitate the definition of a mathematical semantics for its constructs and the whole process of service discovery and binding [1,10]. In this paper, we focus mainly on methodological aspects, namely on a process that can be followed to arrive at (formal) service models in SRML starting from informal (or semi-formal) specifications in notations that are typical of the UML, including use-case diagrams to capture requirements. The paper proceeds as follows. In Section 2, we provide an overview of the engineering 'architecture' and processes that we see supporting SOC in GC. In Section 3, we provide a brief overview of SRML. In Section 4, we investigate use cases as a means of deriving the structure of SRML modules. In Section 5, we consider the use of statecharts for the definition of the orchestration of services. As a running example, we will use a mortgage brokerage service.

2 Service-Overlay Computers

Following the Global Computing EU initiative [12], 'global computers' are "computational infrastructures available globally and able to provide uniform services with variable guarantees for communication, co-operation and mobility, resource usage, security policies and mechanisms". The notion of 'service-overlay computer' explored by SENSORIA addresses precisely the development of highly distributed loosely coupled applications that can exploit services that are globally available.

In this setting, there is a need to rethink the way we engineer software applications, moving from the typical 'static' scenario in which components are assembled to build a (more or less complex) system that is delivered to a customer, to a more 'dynamic' scenario in which (smaller) applications are developed to run on such global computers and respond to business needs by interacting with services and resources that are globally available. In this latter setting, there is much more scope for flexibility in the way business is supported: business processes can be viewed globally as emerging from a varying collection of loosely coupled applications that can take advantage of the availability of services procured on the fly when they are needed.

The notion of 'system' itself, as it applies to software, also needs to be revised. If we take one of the accepted meanings of 'system' – *a combination of related elements organised into a complex whole* – we can see why it is not directly applicable to SOC/GC: services get combined at run time and redefine the way they are organised as they execute; no 'whole' is given *a priori* and services do not compute within a fixed configuration of a 'universe'. In a sense, we are seeing reflected in software engineering the trend for 'globalisation' that is now driving the economy.

SOC brings to the front many aspects that have already been discussed about component-based development (CBD) [8]. Given that different people have different perceptions of what SOC and CBD are, we will simply say that, in this paper, we will take CBD to be associated with what we called the 'static' engineering approach. For instance, starting from a universe of (software) components as 'structural entities', Broy et al view a service as a way of orchestrating interactions among a subset of components in order to obtain some required functionality – "services coordinate the interplay of components to accomplish specific tasks" [6]. As an example, we can imagine that a bank will have available a collection of software components that implement core functionalities such as computing interests or charging commissions, which can be used in different products such as savings or loans.

SOC differs from this view in that there is no such fixed system of components that services are programmed to draw from but, rather, an evolving universe of software applications that service providers publish so that they can be discovered by (and bound to) business activities as they execute. For instance, if documents need to be exchanged as part of a loan application, the bank may rely on an external courier service instead of imposing a fixed one. In this case, a courier service would be discovered for each loan application that is processed, possibly taking into account the address to which the documents need to be sent, speed of delivery, reliability, and so on. However, the added flexibility provided through SOC comes at a price – dynamic interactions impose the overhead of selecting the co-party at each invocation – which means that the choice between invoking a service and calling a component is a decision that needs to be taken according to given business goals. This is why SRML makes provision for both SOC and CBD types of interaction (through *requires* and *uses* interfaces as discussed in the next section).

To summarise, the impact that we see (and explore) SOC to have on software engineering methodology stems from the fact that applications are built without knowing who will provide services that may be required, and that the discovery and selection of such services is performed, on the fly, by dedicated middleware components. This means that application developers cannot rely on the fact that someone will implement the services that may be required so as to satisfy their requirements. Therefore, service-oriented 'clientship' needs to be based on shared ontologies of data and service provision. Likewise, service development is not the same as developing software applications to a costumer's set of requirements: it is a separate business that, again, has to rely on shared ontologies of data and service provision so that providers can see the services that they provide discovered and selected.

This view is summarised in Figure 1, where:

- *Activities* correspond to applications developed according to requirements provided by a business organisation, e.g. the applications that, in a bank, implement the financial products that are made available to the public. The *activity repository* provides a means for a run-time engine to trigger such applications when the corresponding requests are published, say when a client of the bank requests a loan at a counter or through on-line banking. Activities may be implemented over given components (for instance, a component for computing and charging interests) in a traditional CBD way, but they can also rely on services that will be procured on the fly using SOC (for instance, an insurance for protecting the customer in case he/she is temporarily prevented from re-paying the loan due to illness or job loss). Activities are typed by *activity modules*. As discussed in Section 3, these identify the components that activities need to be bound to when they are launched and the services (types) that they may require as they execute. Modules also include a specification of the workflow that orchestrates the interactions among all the parties involved in the activity.

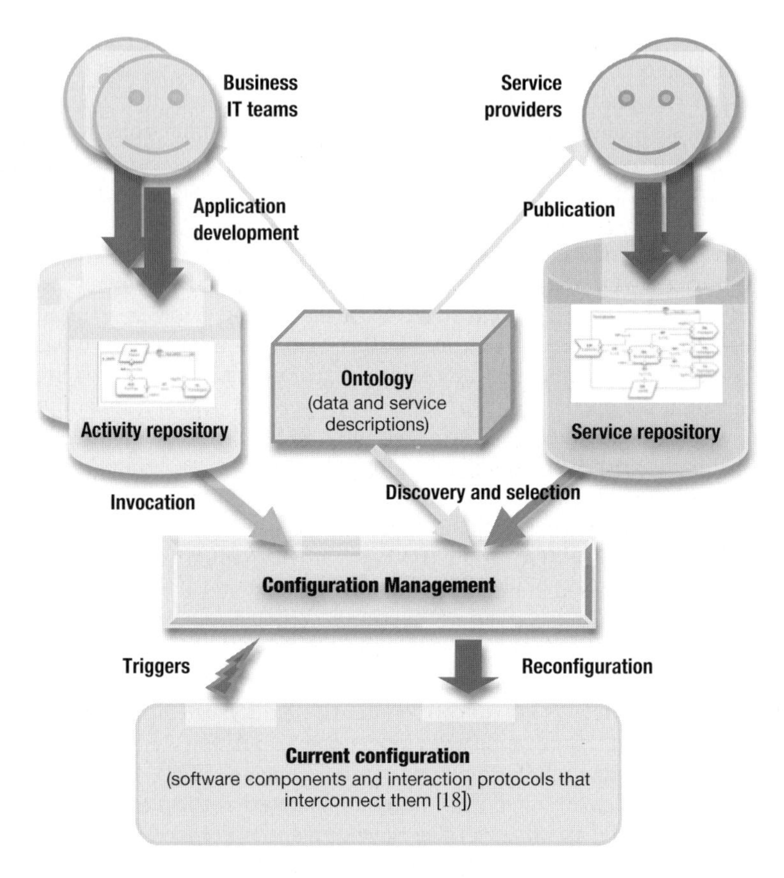

Fig. 1. Overall 'engineering' architecture and processes

- *Services* differ from activities in that they are not developed to satisfy specific business requirements of a given organisation but to be published (in service repositories) in ways that allow them to be discovered when a request for an external service is published in the run-time environment. As such, they are classified according to generic service descriptions – what in the next section we call 'business protocols' – that are organised in a hierarchical ontology to facilitate discovery. Services are typed by 'service modules', which, like activity modules, identify the components and additional services that may be required together with a specification of the workflow that orchestrates the interactions among them so as to deliver the properties declared in the service description – its 'provides-interface'. Modules also specify 'service-level agreements' that need to be negotiated during matchmaking and selection.

- The *configuration management* unit is responsible for the binding of the new components and connectors that derive from the instantiation of new activities or services. A formal model of this unit can be found in [11].
- The *ontology* unit is responsible for organising both data and service descriptions. In this paper, we do not discuss the classification and retrieval mechanisms per se. See, for instance, [14,16] for some of the aspects involved when addressing such issues. Notice that the 'business IT teams' and the 'service providers' can be totally independent and unrelated: the former are interested in supporting the business of their companies or organisations, whereas the latter run their own businesses. They share the ontology component of the architecture so that they can do business together.

3 The SENSORIA Reference Modelling Language

In this section, we provide an overview of SRML focusing on the concepts needed to understand the rationale for the use-case-based approach that is proposed in Section 4. The main modelling primitive offered by SRML is called a *module*, with two specialisations – activity and service modules – in the sense discussed in Section 2.

A module M consists of:

- A graph $graph(M)$, i.e. a set $nodes(M)$ of nodes and a set $edges(M)$ of M where each edge e is associated with two nodes – $e{:}n \leftrightarrow m$. Edges are also called 'wire interfaces'.
- A distinguished subset of nodes $requires(M) \subseteq nodes(M)$, called 'requires-interfaces'.
- A distinguished subset of nodes $uses(M) \subseteq nodes(M)$, called 'uses-interfaces'.
- In the case of service modules, a node $provides(M) \in nodes(M)$ distinct from $requires(M)$ and $uses(M)$, called the 'provides-interface'.
- In the case of activity modules, a node $serves(M) \in nodes(M)$ distinct from $requires(M)$ and $uses(M)$, called the 'serves-interface'.
- We denote by $components(M)$ the set of $nodes(M)$ that are not in $provides(M)$ or $serves(M)$, nor in $requires(M)$ or $uses(M)$ – these are called 'component interfaces'.
- A labelling function $label_M$ that assigns
  - o A 'business role' to every $n \in components(M)$
  - o A 'business protocol' to every $n \in provides(M) \cup requires(M)$
  - o A 'layer protocol' to every $n \in serves(M) \cup uses(M)$
  - o A connector $<\mu_A, P, \mu_B>$ to every edge $(e{:}n \leftrightarrow m)$ where P is an 'interaction protocol' with two 'roles' $roleA_P$ and $roleB_P$, and μ_A (resp. μ_B) is an attachment between $roleA_P$ and $label_M(n)$ (resp. $roleB_P$ and $label_M(m)$).
- An internal configuration policy (indicated by the symbol ⏱) consisting of
  - o For every node $n \in requires(M)$, a condition $trigger(n)$ that identifies the trigger of the external service discovery process.

  - o For *n*∈*components(M)*, two boolean functions *init(n)* and *term(n)* that determine initialisation and termination conditions, respectively.
- An external configuration policy (indicated by SLA) consisting of:
  - o A constraint system *cs(M)* based on a fixed c-semiring [4].
  - o A set *sla(M)* of constraints over *cs(M)*.
  - o For every variable in *cs(M)*, a *type*.
  - o A partial assignment *owner* of either a node or an edge of *M* to the variables of *cs(M)*.

Variables and constraints in *cs(M)* determine the quality profile to which the discovered services need to adhere. A precise account can be found in [11].

The formalisms used in SRML for defining business roles, business protocols, layer protocols and interaction protocols are discussed in [2,9]: business roles are (declarative) specifications of state transition systems in terms of state variables, triggers, guards, and publication of events; business protocols consist of temporal logic sentences (we are using a version of UCTL [3]) that specify properties of the (service-oriented) conversations held with external parties; interaction protocols are specifications of the way wires coordinate interactions between parties; layer protocols specify properties of the (component-based) interactions held with persistent components and top-level users.

An activity module (ACT), depicted using the diagrammatic notation adopted in SRML, is shown in Figure 2:

- The serves-interface (at the top-end of the module) identifies the interactions that should be maintained between the activity and the rest of the system in which it will operate.

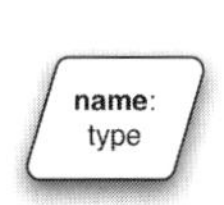

- Uses-interfaces (at the bottom-end of the module) are defined for those (persistent) components of the underlying configuration that the activity will need to interact with once instantiated. The corresponding layer protocols identify the views of those components that the activity will need to see supported, i.e. the behaviour required of the actual interfaces that need to be set up for the activity to interact with components that correspond to (persistent) business entities.
- Requires-interfaces (on the right of the module) are defined (in association with the configuration policies) for services that the activity will have to procure from external providers if and when needed. Typically, these reflect the structure of the business domain itself in the sense that they reflect the existence of business services provided outside the scope of the local context in which the activity will operate.

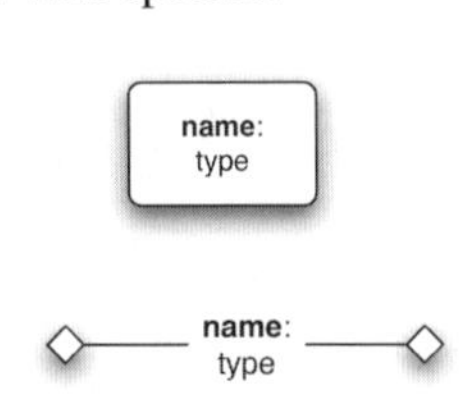

- Component and wire interfaces (inside the module) should be defined for orchestrating all these entities (actors) in ways that will deliver stated user requirements through the serves-interface. The actual choice of the component interfaces and corresponding business roles may also reflect the existence of predefined patterns of orchestration that are available to the designers or reflect business components that will be created in support of the activity.

- The choice of the internal architecture of the module (components and wires) should also reflect the nature of the communication and distribution network over which the activity will run.

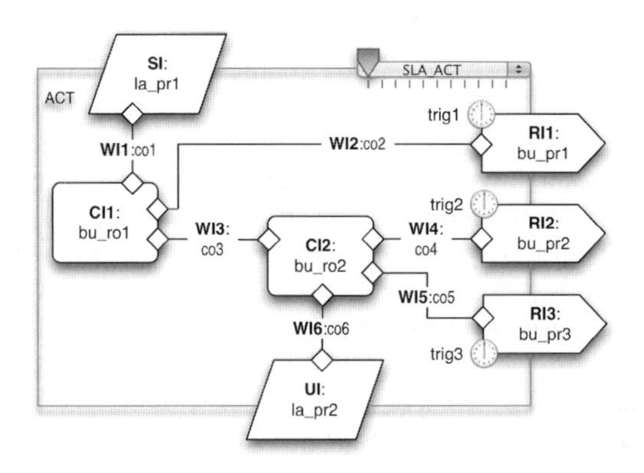

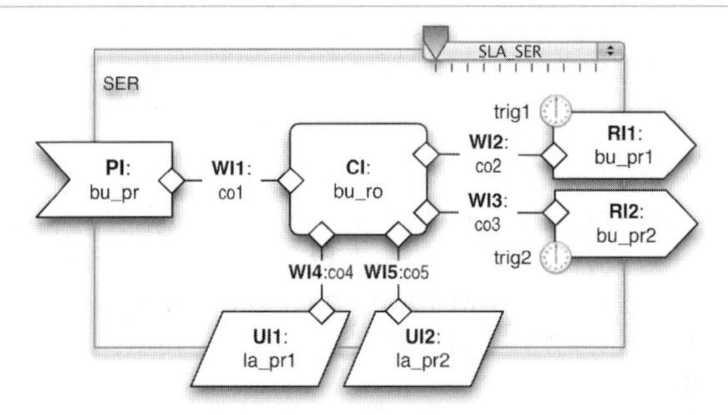

Fig. 2. Diagrammatic notation for activity (top) and service (bottom) modules

In the case of a service module, a similar diagrammatic notation is used except that a provides-interface is used instead of a server-interface, as shown at the bottom of Figure 2 (module SER). In this case:

- The provides-interface should be chosen from the hierarchy of standard business protocols because the purpose here is to make the service available to the wider market, not to a specific client.

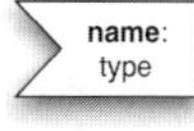

- Some of the component interfaces will correspond to standard components that are part of the provider's portfolio. For instance, these may be application domain dependent components that correspond to typical entities of the business domain in which the service provider specialises.
- Uses-interfaces should be used for those components that the service provider has for insuring persistence of certain effects of the services that it offers.

4 From Use-Case Diagrams to SRML

In this section, we propose an extension of use-case diagrams for service-oriented applications and discuss how to use these diagrams to obtain the skeleton of SRML modules. In order to illustrate our proposal, we will use a fragment of a financial case study. We consider the case of a financial services organisation that wants to develop a mortgage brokerage service *GetLoan* capable of binding a customer activity with a number of components with which it needs to interact to get a mortgage. This service involves the following steps: (1) proposing the best mortgage deal to the customer that invoked the service; (2) taking out the loan if the customer accepts the proposal; (3) opening a bank account associated with the loan if the lender does not provide one; and (4) getting insurance if required by either the customer or the lender.

The selection of lenders needs to be restricted to firms that are considered reliable. For this reason, we consider an *UpdateRegistry* activity supporting the management of a registry of reliable lenders. This activity relies on an external certification authority that may vary according to the identity of the lender. Reporting to Figure 1, notice that while the aim is to publish *GetLoan* in a service repository for being discovered and invoked by other services, the *UpdateRegistry* activity is driven by the requirements of the financial services organisation itself – it will be stored in an activity repository and will be invoked by internal applications (e.g., a web interface).

4.1 Use-Case Diagrams for Service-Oriented Applications

Traditionally, use-case diagrams are used for providing an overview of usage requirements for a system that needs to be built. As discussed in Section 2, our aim is to address a novel development process that does not aim at the construction of a 'system' but, rather, of two kinds of software applications – services and activities – that can be bound to other software components either statically (in a component-based way) or dynamically (in a service-oriented way).

The methodological implications of this view are twofold. On the one hand, services and activities have the particularity that each has a single usage requirement. Hence, they can be perceived as use cases. On the other hand, from a business point of view, the services and activities to be developed by an organisation constitute logical units. For instance, in our example, the *UpdateRegistry* activity and the *GetLoan* service can be seen to operate as part of a same business unit and, hence, it makes sense to group them together in the same use-case diagram. That is, use-case diagrams may become useful to structure usage requirements of units of business logic.

In order to reflect these methodological implications in the usage of use cases, we propose a number of extensions to the standard notation. Figure 3 illustrates our proposal using the mortgage example: the diagram represents a business logical unit with the two use cases identified before. The rectangle around the use cases, which in traditional use-case diagrams indicates the boundary of the system at hand, is used to indicate the scope of the business unit. Anything within the box represents functionality that is in scope and anything outside the box is considered not to be in scope.

For the *UpdateRegistry* service, the primary actor is *Registry Manager*; its goal is to control the way a registry of trusted lenders is updated. The registry itself is regarded as a supporting actor. The *Certification Authority* on which *UpdateRegistry* relies is also considered a supporting actor in the use case because it is an external service that needs to be discovered based on the nature of each candidate lender.

In the *GetLoan* activity, the primary actor is a *Customer* that wants to obtain a mortgage. The use case has four supporting actors: *Lender*, *Bank*, *Insurance* and *Registry*. The *Lender* represents the bank or building society that lends the money to the customer. Because only reliable firms can be considered for the selection of the lender, the use case involves communication with *Registry*. When the lender does not provide a bank account, the use case involves an external *Bank* for opening of a new account. Similarly, the use case involves interaction with an *Insurance* provider for cases where the lender requires insurance or the customer decides to get one.

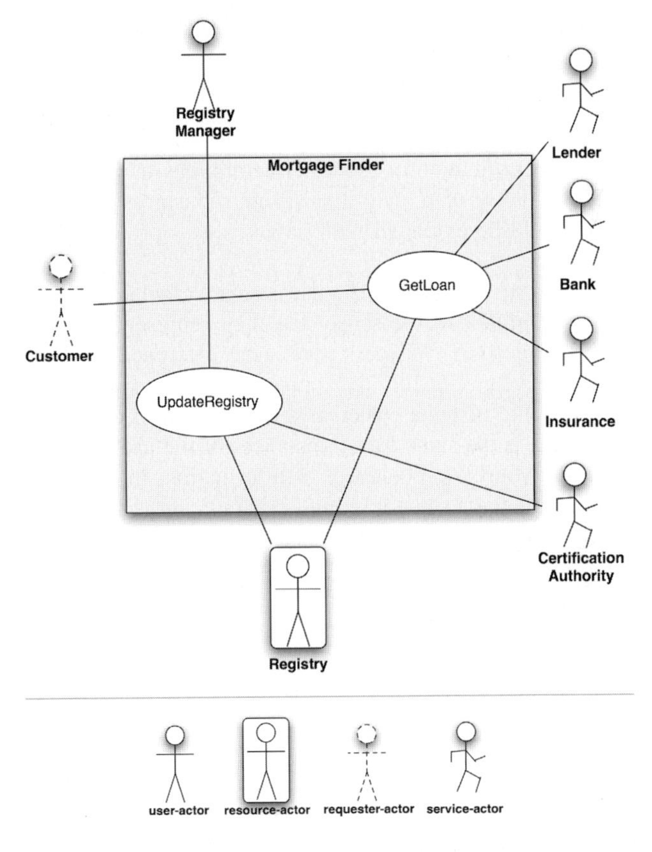

Fig. 3. Service-oriented use-case diagram for *Mortgage Finder*

As happens in traditional use cases, we view an actor as any entity that is external to the business unit and interacts with at least one of its elements in order to perform a task. As motivated above, we can distinguish between different kinds of actors, which led us to customise the traditional icons as depicted in Figure 3. These allow us to discriminate between *user/requester* and *resource/service* actors.

User-actors and *requester-actors* are similar to primary actors in traditional use-case diagrams in the sense that they represent entities that initiate the use case and whose goals are fulfilled through the successful completion of the use case. The difference between them is that a *user-actor* is a role played by an entity belonging to the business organisation that operates the activity triggered by the entity, while a *requester-actor* is a role played by any entity (usually belonging to a different business organisation) that triggers the discovery of (and binds to) the service.

For instance, the user-actor *Registry Manager* represents an interface for an employee of the business organisation that is running *Mortgage Finder* whereas the requester-actor *Customer* represents an interface for a service requester that can come from any external organisation. A requester-actor can be regarded as an interface to an abstract user of the functionality that is exposed as a service; it represents the range of potential customers of the service and the requirements typically derive from standard service descriptions stored in service repositories such as the UDDI. In SRML, and reporting to Figure 1, these descriptions are given by business protocols and organised in a shared ontology, which facilitates and makes the discovery of business partners more effective. The identification of requester-actors may take advantage of existing descriptions in the ontology or it may identify new business opportunities. In this case, the ontology would be extended with new business protocols corresponding to the new types of service.

Resource-actors and *service-actors* of a use case are similar to supporting actors in traditional use-case diagrams in the sense that they represent entities to rely on in order to achieve the underlying business goal. The difference is that a service-actor represents an outsourced functionality to be procured on the fly and, hence, will typically vary from instance to instance, whereas a resource-actor is an entity that is statically bound and, hence, is the same for all instances of the use case. Resource-actors are typically persistent sources/repositories of information. In general, they are components already available to be shared within a business organisation.

The user- and resource-actors, which we represent on the top and bottom of our specialised use-case diagrams, respectively, correspond in fact to the actors that are presented on the left and right-hand side in traditional use-case diagrams, respectively. In contrast, the 'horizontal dimension' of the new diagrams, comprising requester- and service-actors, captures the types of interactions that are specific to SOC.

We assume that every use case corresponds to a service-oriented artefact and that the association between a primary actor and a use case represents an instantiation/invocation. For this reason, in this context, we constrain every use case to be associated with only one primary actor (either a requester or a user).

4.2 Deriving the Structure of SRML Modules

The proposed specialisations of use-case diagrams allow us to derive a number of aspects of the structure of SRML modules. Each use case, representing either a service or an activity, is naturally modelled as either a SRML service module or activity module, respectively. The actors associated with a use case identify the interfaces used in the module. It is straightforward to model each actor type with a specific type of interface of the SRML module. Each user-actor, which represents the interface to the user that triggers the instantiation of an activity, is modelled as a SRML serves-interface.

Each requester-actor, which represents the interface to the entity that invokes a service, is modelled as a SRML provides-interface. Similarly, service-actors are modelled as requires-interfaces and resource-actors as serves-interfaces. Figure 4 presents the structure of the modules derived from the use-case diagram in Figure 3.

The definition of the internal structure of the module (i.e., the components and wires that define the internal workflow) may depend on the portfolio of components already available for reuse within the business organisation. In our case study, the orchestration of the modules relies on a single component. The definition of a complex internal structure from scratch, deriving from the decomposition of the orchestration in a number of coordinated units, can be done using traditional techniques for CBD. We leave this topic for further investigation and discussion.

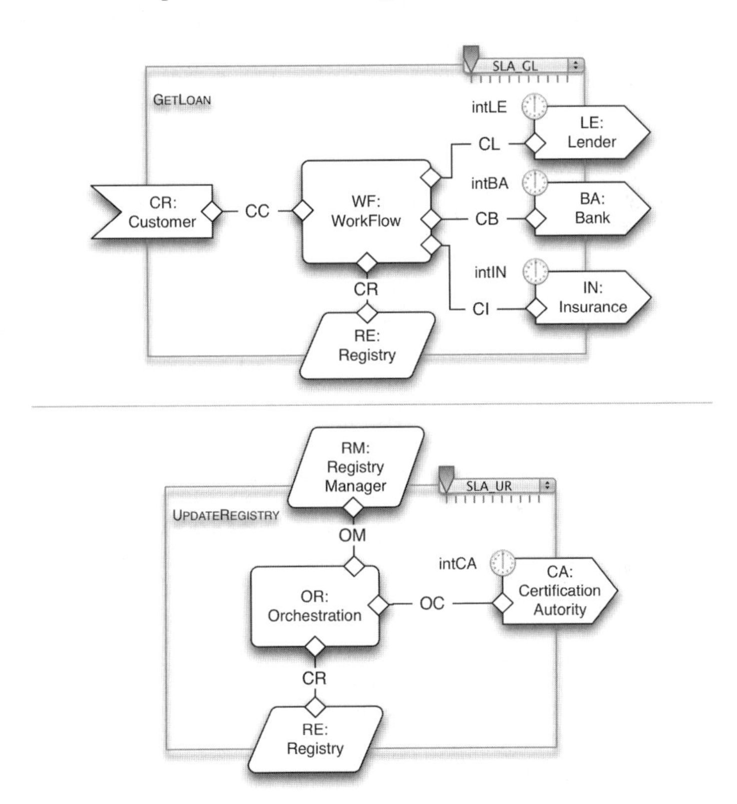

Fig. 4. The SRML modules for the service *GetLoan* and the activity *UpdateRegistry*

5 Using Statecharts for SRML Orchestration

Section 4.2 describes how to derive the structure of SRML modules corresponding to use cases. In this section, we discuss how in SRML we model the internal behaviour of a module in terms of a (possibly distributed) orchestration of a number of interactions among the identified partners. For this purpose, we adapt UML statechart diagrams to operate with the interaction primitives that are available in SRML.

We illustrate the method considering the orchestration of the SRML module *GetLoan*. Initially, the customer sends his/her profile and preferences for the mortgage. If the customer accepts the proposal, and depending on the services provided by the lender, some additional activities may be performed separately: opening a bank account and buying insurance. The workflow terminates when the customer rejects the proposal or the deal is signed off.

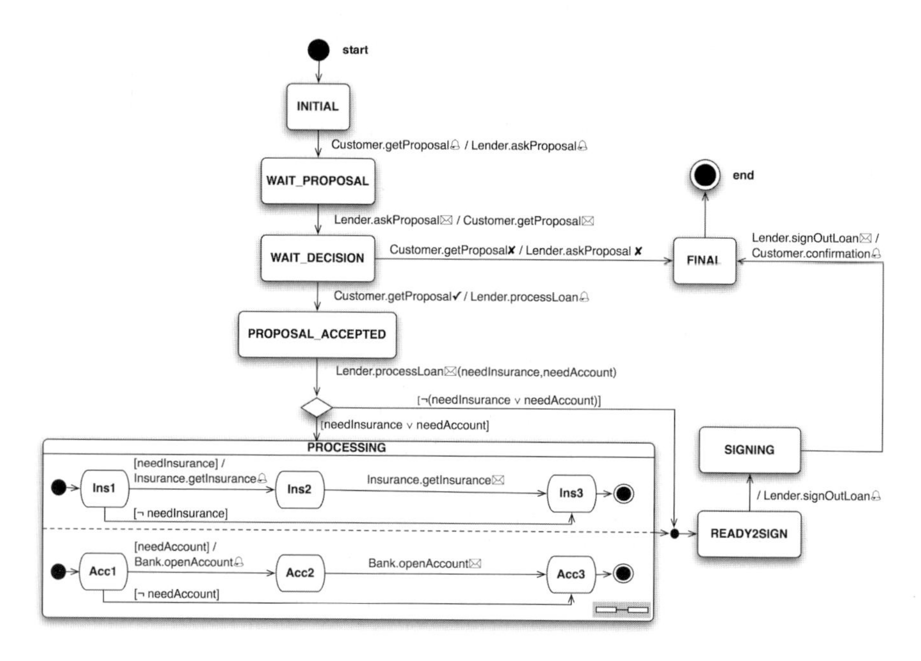

Fig. 5. Statechart diagram for *GetLoan*

Figure 5 presents the statechart corresponding to the orchestration of *GetLoan*. The labels of the transitions (triggers and effects) use the language of interaction events that is provided by SRML. SRML supports asynchronous one-way (*receive* and *send*) and conversational (*send&receive* and *receive&send*) interactions. A conversational interaction may involve a number of possible steps, which we call interaction events: the initiation of the interaction (e.g., *getProposal*🔔), the reply event (e.g., *getProposal*✉) sent by the co-partner, the confirmation and cancellation events (e.g., *getProposal*✓ and *getProposal*✗), and a revoke event (e.g., *getProposal*✞) that triggers a compensation process. A one-way interaction is associated with only one event. The language and semantics of this language is discussed in [1,2].

Such a statechart defines what in Section 3 we called a 'business role', i.e. the type of orchestration that every instantiation of the service will implement to coordinate the interactions among the parties involved in the provision of the service. SRML also offers a textual notation for business roles that consists of a declaration of the interactions in which the components can be involved and a specification of the state parameters and state transitions of the orchestration process.

Figure 6 presents the interactions supported by *WorkFlow*, the specification of the component *WF* of the module *GetLoan*.

```
BUSINESS ROLE WorkFlow is
INTERACTIONS
    r&s getProposal
        🔔 idData:usrdata
           income:moneyvalue
           partnerIncome:moneyvalue
           preferences:prefdata
        ✉ proposal:mortgageproposal
    s&r askProposal
        🔔 idData:usrdata
           income:moneyvalue
           partnerIncome:moneyvalue
        ✉ proposal:mortgageproposal
    s&r processLoan
        🔔 proposal:mortgageproposal
        ✉ loanData:loandatatype
           accountIncluded:bool
           insuranceRequired:bool
    s&r getInsurance
        🔔 idData:usrdata
           loanData:loaddatatype
        ✉ insuranceData:insurancedatatype
    s&r openAccount
        🔔 idData:usrdata
           loanData:loaddatatype
        ✉ accountData:accountdatatype
    s&r signOutLoan
        🔔 loanData:loandatatype
           insuranceData:insurancedatatype
           accountData:accountdatatype
        ✉ contract:loancontract
    snd confirmation
        🔔 contract:loancontract
```

Fig. 6. Interactions supported by *WF* in the SRML module *GetLoan*

Each transition in a business role is defined by: a *trigger*, typically the occurrence of an event, a *guard* enabling the transition, the *effects* over the local state and the events that are published with the corresponding parameter assignments. An extract of the transitions resulting from the statechart of *GetLoan* are presented in Figure 7.

An advantage of using the (formal) specification language of business roles over statecharts is that it supports underspecification (logical formulas are used for specifying effects and publication of events) and a refinement process that allows designers to start with loose requirements over states and transitions and add detail as more knowledge is gathered about the required behaviour. Another advantage is that is provides us a formal framework to which we can map specifications in other notations such as the ones available in workflow languages like BPEL [5]. More details and examples can be found in [9].

```
ORCHESTRATION
local s:[INITIAL, WAIT_PROPOSAL, WAIT_DECISION, PROPOSAL_ACCEPTED,
      PROCESSING, READY2SIGN, SIGN, FINAL], needAccount,needInsurance:bool
transition GetClientRequest
    triggeredBy getProposal🔔
    guardedBy s=INITIAL
    effects s'=WAIT_PROPOSAL
    sends askProposal🔔
        ∧ askProposal.idData=getProposal.idData
        ∧ askProposal.income=getProposal.income
        ∧ askProposal.partnerIncome=getProposal.partnerIncome
transition GetLenderProposal
    triggeredBy askProposal✉
    guardedBy s= WAIT_PROPOSAL
    effects s'= WAIT_DECISION
    sends getProposal✉
        ∧ getProposal.proposal=askProposal.proposal
```

Fig. 7. Fragment of *Workflow* in the SRML module *GetLoan*

6 Concluding Remarks and Further Work

We presented an approach for modelling service-oriented application based on (1) use-case diagrams and statecharts in order to capture requirements on units of business logic structured in terms of services and activities, and (2) the SENSORIA Reference

Modelling Language (SRML) to derive formal models of those services and activities. We proposed an extension of use-case diagrams in order to identify the relevant services and activities, and derive the structure of a SRML model for each of them. We also proposed a customisation of statechart diagrams in order to model the behaviour of the business processes executed by activities and services in terms of the basic interaction primitives available in SRML.

SENSORIA is also producing a more global approach to modelling service orchestrations in UML2 – called UML4SOA – and utilising these models for code generation (including BPEL code) [14,19]. This approach favours the use of activity diagrams. Our choice for statecharts reflects the way we organise the behaviour of each module in terms of (internal and external) partners: the idea is that the behaviour of each partner can eventually be described by one or more statecharts, and that the behaviour of the activity/service emerges from the concurrent execution of these statecharts. This is also the view that is supporting analysis through the use of model-checking techniques [3,13]. This is on-going joint research between Leicester and ISTI (Pisa).

The overall methodology that we have in mind for developing software for global computers was also discussed and illustrated through (a much simplified version of) the financial case study being investigated in SENSORIA, namely the aspects that relate to a mortgage brokering service and registry activity. A novel aspect of SRML is the separation that it provides for services in the sense of component-based development (CBD) and service-oriented computing (SOC). This separation is reflected in the use of different kinds of actors in the proposed extension of use-case diagrams and different modelling primitives in SRML.

The specific formal support that is available in SRML was deliberately omitted because of lack of space but it can be found in a number of publications [e.g. 1,2,9,10,11]. This includes a computational model and associated logic through which we can reason about the properties of provided services using model-checking techniques [13], and also a formalism for service-level agreements [7]. However, the integrated use of these techniques within the overall methodology is still being investigated, including the support for the classification of service descriptions within an ontology that can support dynamic discovery. We are also investigating how the decomposition of use-cases using <<*include*>>/<<*extend*>> relationships, usually used to indicate potential reuse, can suggest better ways of structuring the orchestration of services and activities, as well as facilitate the checking of the properties of SRML modules.

Acknowledgments

We would like to thank our colleagues in the SENSORIA project for many useful discussions on the topics covered in this paper, especially Reiko Heckel for his insights and suggestions on use cases. We are also indebted to Colin Gilmore from Box Tree Mortgage Solutions (Leicester) for taking us through the mortgage business.

References

1. Abreu, J., Fiadeiro, J.: A coordination model for service-oriented interactions. In: Lea, D., Zavattaro, G. (eds.) COORDINATION 2008. LNCS, vol. 5052, pp. 1–16. Springer, Heidelberg (2008)

2. Abreu, J., Bocchi, L., Fiadeiro, J.L., Lopes, A.: Specifying and composing interaction protocols for service-oriented system modelling. In: Derrick, J., Vain, J. (eds.) FORTE 2007. LNCS, vol. 4574, pp. 358–373. Springer, Heidelberg (2007)
3. ter Beek, M., Fantechi, A., Gnesi, S., Mazzanti, F.: An action/state-based model checking approach for the analysis of communication protocols for Service-Oriented Applications. In: Leue, S., Merino, P. (eds.) FMICS 2007. LNCS, vol. 4916, pp. 133–148. Springer, Heidelberg (2008)
4. Bistarelli, S., Montanari, U., Rossi, F.: Semiring-based constraint satisfaction and optimization. Journal of the ACM 44(2), 201–236 (1997)
5. Bocchi, L., Hong, Y., Lopes, A., Fiadeiro, J.: From BPEL to SRML: a formal transformational approach. In: Dumas, M., Heckel, R. (eds.) WS-FM 2007. LNCS, vol. 4937, pp. 92–107. Springer, Heidelberg (2008)
6. Broy, M., Krüger, I., Meisinger, M.: A formal model of services. ACM TOSEM 16(1), 1–40 (2007)
7. Buscemi, M., Montanari, U.: CC-Pi: A constraint-based language for specifying service level agreements. In: De Nicola, R. (ed.) ESOP 2007. LNCS, vol. 4421, pp. 18–32. Springer, Heidelberg (2007)
8. Elfatatry, A.: Dealing with change: components versus services. Communications of the ACM 50(8), 35–39 (2007)
9. Fiadeiro, J.L., Lopes, A., Bocchi, L.: A formal approach to service-oriented architecture. In: Bravetti, M., Núñez, M., Zavattaro, G. (eds.) WS-FM 2006. LNCS, vol. 4184, pp. 193–213. Springer, Heidelberg (2006)
10. Fiadeiro, J.L., Lopes, A., Bocchi, L.: Algebraic semantics of service component modules. In: Fiadeiro, J.L., Schobbens, P.-Y. (eds.) WADT 2006. LNCS, vol. 4409, pp. 37–55. Springer, Heidelberg (2007)
11. Fiadeiro, J.L., Lopes, A., Bocchi, L.: Semantics of Service-Oriented System Configuration (submitted, 2008), http://www.cs.le.ac.uk/jfiadeiro
12. Global Computing Initiative, http://cordis.europa.eu/ist/fet/gc.htm
13. Gnesi, S., Mazzanti, F.: On the fly model checking of communicating UML state machines. In: ACIS International Conference on Software Engineering Research, Management and Applications, pp. 331–338 (2004)
14. Mayer, P., Koch, N., Schröder, A.: A Model-Driven Approach to Service Orchestration. In: Proceedings of IEEE International Conference on Services Computing (SCC 2008). IEEE Press, Los Alamitos (in print, 2008)
15. Pahl, K.: An ontology for software component matching. International Journal on Software Tools and Technology Transfer 9, 169–178 (2007)
16. Rao, J., Su, X.: A survey of automated web service composition methods. In: Cardoso, J., Sheth, A.P. (eds.) SWSWPC 2004. LNCS, vol. 3387, pp. 43–54. Springer, Heidelberg (2005)
17. SENSORIA consortium, White paper (2007), http://www.sensoria-ist.eu/files/whitePaper.pdf
18. Shaw, M., Garlan, D.: Software Architecture: Perspectives on an Emerging Discipline. Prentice Hall, London (1996)
19. Wirsing, M., Clark, A., Gilmore, A., Hölzl, M., Knapp, A., Koch, N., Schröder, A.: Semantic-based development of service-oriented systems. In: Najm, E., Pradat-Peyre, J.-F., Donzeau-Gouge, V.V. (eds.) FORTE 2006. LNCS, vol. 4229, pp. 24–45. Springer, Heidelberg (2006)

SENSORIA Patterns: Augmenting Service Engineering with Formal Analysis, Transformation and Dynamicity*

Martin Wirsing[1], Matthias Hölzl[1], Lucia Acciai[2], Federico Banti[2], Allan Clark[3], Alessandro Fantechi[2], Stephen Gilmore[3], Stefania Gnesi[4], László Gönczy[5], Nora Koch[1], Alessandro Lapadula[2], Philip Mayer[1], Franco Mazzanti[4], Rosario Pugliese[2], Andreas Schroeder[1], Francesco Tiezzi[2], Mirco Tribastone[3], and Dániel Varró[5]

[1] Ludwig-Maximilians-Universität München, Germany
[2] Università degli Studi di Firenze
[3] University of Edinburgh, Scotland
[4] Istituto di Scienza e Tecnologie dell'Informazione "A. Faedo" of CNR
[5] Budapest University of Technology and Economics

Abstract. The IST-FET Integrated Project SENSORIA is developing a novel comprehensive approach to the engineering of service-oriented software systems where foundational theories, techniques and methods are fully integrated into pragmatic software engineering processes. The techniques and tools of SENSORIA encompass the whole software development cycle, from business and architectural design, to quantitative and qualitative analysis of system properties, and to transformation and code generation. The SENSORIA approach takes also into account reconfiguration of service-oriented architectures (SOAs) and re-engineering of legacy systems.

In this paper we give first a short overview of SENSORIA and then present a pattern language for augmenting service engineering with formal analysis, transformation and dynamicity. The patterns are designed to help software developers choose appropriate tools and techniques to develop service-oriented systems with support from formal methods. They support the whole development process, from the modelling stage to deployment activities and give an overview of many of the research areas pursued in the SENSORIA project.

1 Introduction

Service-oriented computing is a paradigm where services are understood as autonomous, platform-independent computational entities that can be described, published, categorised, discovered, and dynamically assembled for developing massively distributed, interoperable, evolvable systems and applications. These characteristics have been responsible for the widespread success that service-oriented computing enjoys nowadays: many large companies invest efforts and resources in promoting service delivery on a variety of computing platforms, mostly through the Internet in the form of Web services. Soon there will be a plethora of new services as required for e-government, e-business, and e-science, and other areas within the rapidly evolving Information Society.

* This work has been partially sponsored by the project SENSORIA, IST-2 005-016004.

T. Margaria and B. Steffen (Eds.): ISoLA 2008, CCIS 17, pp. 170–190, 2008.

However, service-oriented computing and development today is mostly done in a non-systematic, ad-hoc way. Full-fledged theoretical foundations are missing, but they are badly needed for trusted interoperability, predictable compositionality, and for guaranteeing security, correctness, and appropriate resource usage.

The IST-FET Integrated Project SENSORIA addresses the problems of service-oriented computing by building, from first-principles, novel theories, methods and tools supporting the *engineering of software systems for service-oriented overlay computers*. Its aim is to develop a novel comprehensive approach to the engineering of service-oriented software systems where foundational theories, techniques and methods are fully integrated into pragmatic software engineering processes. The SENSORIA approach to service-oriented software development encompasses the whole development process, from systems in high-level languages, to deployment and re-engineering, with a particular focus on qualitative and quantitative analysis techniques, and automatic transformation between different development artifacts.

However, the broad range and the depth of the methods developed as part of the SENSORIA project means that it may be difficult for developers to identify the technique or tool that solves a particular problem arising in the development process, unless the developers are familiar with the whole range of scientific results of the project. To ameliorate this problem we are developing a catalogue of *patterns* that can serve as an index to our results and that illustrates, in a concise manner, the advantages and disadvantages of the individual techniques.

The structure of the paper is as follows: after a short overview of the SENSORIA project we explain the reasons for using patterns to present the SENSORIA results. Patterns are referenced in the usual format, with the pattern name followed by the page number of the pattern in parenthesis, e.g., *Service Modelling* describes the pattern named "Service Modelling" on page 175.

We then introduce several patterns ranging from the early design stage to deployment: *Service Modelling*, *Service Specification and Analysis*, *Functional Service Verification*, *Sensitivity Analysis*, *Scalability Analysis*, *Declarative Orchestration*, *Declarative Service Selection*, and *Model-Driven Deployment*. The last section summarises other results of the SENSORIA project and concludes.

2 The SENSORIA Project

SENSORIA is one of the three Integrated Projects of the Global Computing Initiative of FET-IST, the Future and Emerging Technologies action of the European Commission. The SENSORIA Consortium consists of 12 universities, three research institutes and four companies (two SMEs) from seven countries[1].

[1] LMU München (coordinator), Germany; TU Denmark at Lyngby, Denmark; Cirquent GmbH München, S&N AG, Paderborn (both Germany); Budapest University of Technology and Economics, Hungary; Università di Bologna, Università di Firenze, Università di Pisa, Università di Trento, ISTI Pisa, Telecom Italia Lab Torino, School of Management Politecnico di Milano (all Italy); Warsaw University, Poland; ATX Software SA, Lisboa, Universidade de Lisboa (both Portugal); Imperial College London, University College London, University of Edinburgh, University of Leicester (all United Kingdom).

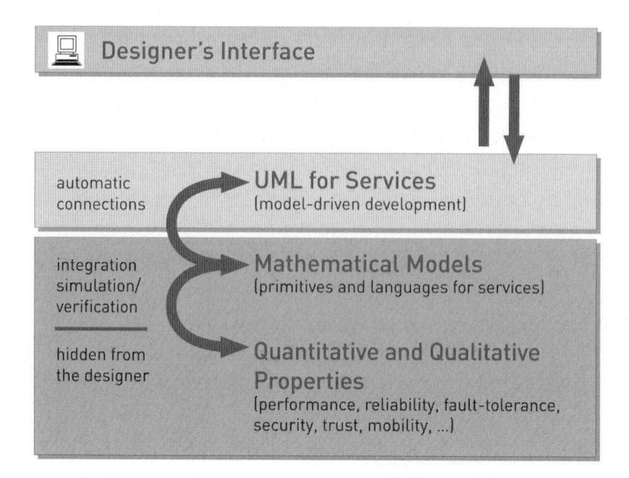

Fig. 1. SENSORIA approach: high-level models in UML4SOA are transformed into mathematical models based on the foundational calculi; qualitative and quantitative analsys can then be performed on these models

2.1 The SENSORIA Approach

SENSORIA is focusing on global services that are context adaptive, personalisable, and may require hard and soft constraints on resources and performance, and takes into account the fact that services have to be deployed on different, possibly interoperating, platforms, to provide novel and reusable service-oriented systems.

To this end, SENSORIA is generalising the concept of service in such a way that

- it is independent from the particular global computer and from any programming language;
- it can be described in a modular way, so that security issues, quality of service measures and behavioural guarantees are preserved under composition of services;
- it supports dynamic, ad-hoc, "just-in-time" composition;
- it can be made part of an integrated service-oriented approach to business modelling.

The results of SENSORIA include a comprehensive service ontology, and modelling languages for service-oriented systems based on UML [32] and SCA [21,40]. We have also defined a number of process calculi for service-oriented computing, such as SCC [6], a session-oriented general purpose calculus for service description; *Sock* [26], a three layered calculus inspired by the Web Services protocol stack; and COWS [30], the Calculus for the Orchestration of Web Services.

These foundational process calculi serve as a base for higher-level formalisms to specify and analyse service-oriented systems, such as process calculi and languages for coordination, quality of service and service-level agreements [10,13], or type systems for services, e.g., for data exchange [31] or resource usage [3].

SENSORIA is also addressing the important areas of languages, frameworks, tools and techniques for qualitative and quantitative analysis. Qualitative analysis methods are successfully applied, e.g., to the areas of cryptography, security and trust [4,35,37], whereas

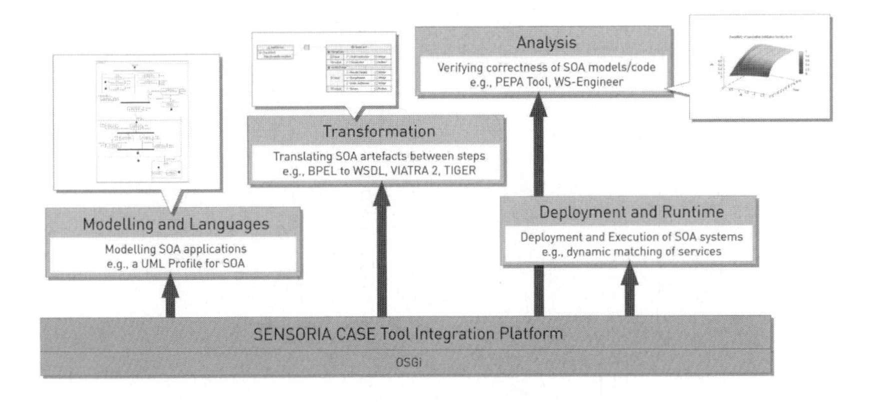

Fig. 2. SENSORIA tools, see [39] for the current list

calculi, logics and methods for quantitative analysis such as *StoKlaim* [16], *MoSL* [15], and *PEPA* [27] can be used in areas such as scalability or performance analysis [7].

Further work of SENSORIA concerns service contracts for checking the compliance of protocols and for automatic discovery and composition [8,9], new techniques for specifying and verifying the dynamic behaviour of services, including spatial logics and the verification of fault-tolerant systems [11,25], and programming- and modelling-level approaches to software architectures [22].

Moreover, SENSORIA is proposing a model-driven approach for service-oriented software engineering [41,32] that starts from high-level specifications in languages like SRML or UML4SOA and uses model transformation techniques [17,2] to generate both suitable input for the analysis tools, and executable services.

The development of mathematical foundations and mathematically well-founded engineering techniques for service-oriented computing constitutes a main research part of SENSORIA. Another important research direction focuses on making these foundations available for designers and developers by creating systematic and scientifically well-founded methods of service-oriented software development (cf. Fig. 1). The proposed approach is to build high-level models, e.g., in UML4SOA which can then be transformed into mathematical models based on the foundational calculi. Because of the precise definition of these calculi it is then possible to perform qualitative and quantitative analysis on the transformed models in order to gain valuable information about the quality, security, and performance of the system in the early stages of system development. Since the results of static analysis are transformed into annotations for the original high-level model, the designer does not have to be concerned with the formalisms used in the analysis process.

To facilitate the practical application of the results, SENSORIA is developing a service-based suite of tools (cf. Fig. 2) that support the new language primitives, the analysis techniques, re-engineering of legacy software into services [14] and other aspects of service development and deployment [23,34]. The tool suite gives continuous feedback on the usefulness and applicability of the research results; it is also a starting point for the design of new industrial support tools for service-oriented development.

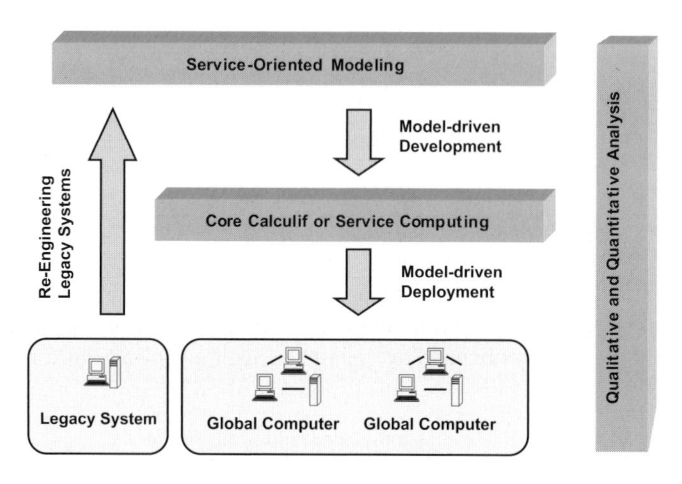

Fig. 3. SENSORIA research themes

Another main element of SENSORIA is the set of realistic case studies for different important application areas including telecommunications, automotive, e-university, and e-business. Most of the case studies are defined by the industrial SENSORIA partners to provide continuous practical challenges for the new techniques of Services Engineering and demonstrate the research results.

The interplay of the different research themes and activities of SENSORIA are illustrated in Fig. 3: Service-oriented modelling provides specifications and models which are transformed by model-driven development into the core calculi for service computing. Model-driven deployment is used for implementing services on different platforms. Legacy systems can be transformed into services using systematic re-engineering techniques. Qualitative and quantitative analysis back the service development process and provide the means to guarantee functional and non-functional properties of services and service aggregates.

The impact of SENSORIA on the development of services will be to bring mathematically well-founded modelling technology within the reach of service-oriented software designers and developers. By offering these techniques and tools, we hope to allow adopters to move to a higher and more mature level of SOA software development. In particular, we hope to contribute to an increased quality of service of SOA applications, measured both in qualitative and quantitative terms. As SENSORIA methods are portable to existing platforms, application of these methods is possible while keeping existing investments.

2.2 A Pattern-Based Approach to Service Engineering

The SENSORIA project is investigating many issues of engineering SOAs. One of the challenges is to make the research results available in a way that is useful not only as the basis for future research but also for software developers seeking to apply the research results. To this end we are developing a pattern language that describes which problems are addressed by the various SENSORIA tools and techniques, how they solve the problems they address, and which forces determine whether a technique is appropriate for a given situation or not.

The SENSORIA patterns are not limited to implementation issues, they encompass a wide range of abstraction levels, from implementation-oriented patterns in the spirit of [24] to architectural or process patterns. We structure the patterns in a way that approximately follows the "Pattern Language for Pattern Writing" presented in [33], but add some pattern elements that seem to be helpful for describing patterns specifically related to service-oriented software engineering. For readers familiar with the pattern community, it should be noted that we use the pattern format as an expository tool; our patterns are not necessarily obtained by "mining" existing applications for patterns.

Several elements have to be contained in each pattern: a pattern name; a context in which the pattern is applicable; a concise description of the problem solved by the pattern; the forces that determine the benefits and drawbacks of using the pattern; the solution proposed and the consequences resulting from the use of the solution. Furthermore each pattern has to be accompanied by examples. Several optional sections can be used to clarify the pattern, e.g., related patterns, code or model samples, or tools to support the pattern. For space reasons we have omitted some of the mandatory elements from some of the patterns in this paper.

3 Service Modelling

Context. Systems built on SOAs add new layers of complexity to software engineering, as many different artifacts must work together to create the sort of loosely coupled, adaptive, fault-tolerant systems envisioned in the service domain. It is therefore important to apply best practices already in use for older programming paradigms to services as well; in particular, modelling of systems on a higher level of abstraction should be used to get a general idea of the solution space. Modelling services should be possible in a language which is both familiar to software architects and thus easy to use, but also contains the necessary elements for describing SOA systems in a straightforward way.

You are designing a system which is based on a SOA. The system is intended to offer services to multiple platforms and makes use of existing services and artifacts on multiple hosts which must be integrated to work together in order to realise the functionality of the system.

Problem. When designing SOA systems, it is easy to get lost in the detail of technical specifications and implementations. Providing an overview of the service oriented architecture to realise is therefore crucial for effective task identification, separation, and communication in large projects. In this context, using a familiar, easy-to-understand, and descriptive language is a key success factor.

Forces

- The amount of specifications and platforms in the SOA environment makes it difficult to get a general idea of the solution space.

- Modelling the whole system in an abstract way gives a good overview of the tasks to be done, but does not directly yield tangible results. For small systems and projects, it is necessary to tailor this modelling task or even to skip it altogether.
- The model must be updated to reflect the architecture if it changes during implementation, or new requirements appear.
- The model is platform independent, and may be used to generate significant parts of the system. In case the system's target platform is not fixed or may experience changes, the workload involved in system re-implementation can be reduced considerably.
- Having a global architectural view eases the task of understanding the SOA environment considerably. This fact is of major significance if the SOA environment is to be extended by another team of software engineers or at a later date.
- The envisioned target platform(s) and language(s) should be supported by the modelling approach such that code generation may be used.

Solution. Use a specialised (graphical) modelling language to model the system and employ these models as far as possible for generating the system implementation. There are several languages which might be employed for this kind of task. One of the most widespread languages in the software engineering domain for modelling tasks is the Unified Modelling Language (UML). As UML itself however does not offer specific constructs for modelling service-oriented artifacts, it needs to be extended using its built-in profile mechanism. One profile for service oriented architectures is the UML4SOA profile [32], which enables modelling of both the static and the dynamic aspects of service-oriented systems. UML4SOA features specialised constructs for services, service providers and descriptions in its static part, as well as service interactions, long-running transactions, and event handling in its dynamic part. UML4SOA is also part of a model driven development approach for SOA, MDD4SOA, which in turn offers tools for generating code from UML4SOA models.

Consequences. A positive result of modelling a service-oriented system in a high-level way is that it gives a better idea of how the individual artifacts fit together. This is of particular importance in larger projects and for communication between developers and/or the customer. By using transformations, the models can also be employed for generating skeletons to fill with the actual implementation. However, the effort involved in creating readable models should not be underestimated. Also, care should be taken to only model aspects relevant on the design level instead of implementing the complete system on the modelling level.

A problem arising when specifying systems by models and applying model transformations to generate implementation fragments is the problem of model/implementation divergence. Therefore, special care must be taken that models are kept consistent with the implementation.

Tools. The use of a UML profile has the advantage that all UML CASE tools that support the extension mechanisms of the UML can be used, i.e. there is no need for the development of specific and proprietary tools. The UML4SOA profile may be provided already for the UML tool of choice, or may be defined by the means provided by the platform. In the SENSORIA project, the UML4SOA profile was defined for the Rational Software Modeler (RSM) and MagicDraw. MDD4SOA provides executable transformations for models from both UML tools to code skeletons of various target platforms, including the Web service platform and the Java platform. The transformers are integrated into the Eclipse environment.

Example. We illustrate the process by modelling an excerpt of a service-oriented eUniversity system: the management process of a student thesis, which is specified from the announcement of a thesis topic by a tutor to the final assessment and student notification. Figure 4 shows part of the orchestration process, namely the registration of the thesis and the compensation in case of cancellation.

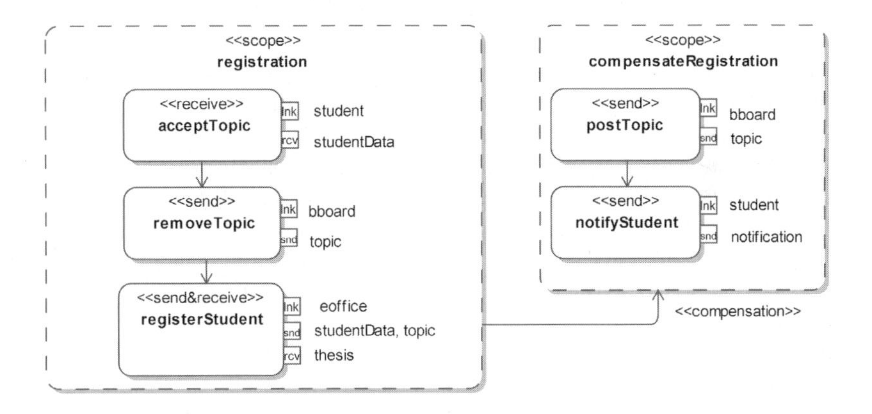

Fig. 4. UML4SOA activity diagram example

The UML2 activity diagram shows several stereotypes from the UML4SOA profile:

- A scope is a UML StructuredActivityNode that contains arbitrary ActivityNodes, and may have an associated compensation handler.
- Specialised actions have been defined for sending and receiving data. In particular, a send is an UML CallBehaviourAction that sends a message; it does not block. A receive is a UML AcceptCallAction, receiving a message, which blocks until a message is received.
- Service interactions may have interaction pins for sending or receiving data. In particular, lnk is an UML Pin that holds a reference to the service involved in the interaction, snd is a Pin that holds a container with data to be sent, and rcv is a Pin that holds a container for data to be received.
- Finally, specialised edges connect scopes with handlers. For example, compensation is a UML ActivityEdge to add compensation handlers to actions and scopes.

Our profile also contains elements for event- and exception handling; they are not included here for lack of space. For a complete overview see [32].

4 Service Specification and Analysis

Context. You are designing a service-oriented system that has to operate in an open-ended computational environment. The system is supposed to rely on autonomous and possibly heterogeneous services, hence different services may be implemented by different languages. Information about actual implementation of some services may be not accessible and only the services interactive behavior is known.

Problem. Specify a service-oriented system and verify that it guarantees some desirable behavioural properties.

Forces

- Process calculi have been proved able to define clean semantic models and lay rigorous methodological foundations for service-based applications and their composition.
- Process calculi enjoy a rich and elegant meta-theory and are equipped with a large set of analytical tools, such as e.g. typing systems, behavioural equivalences and temporal logics, that support reasoning on process specification.
- The additional cost and development effort incurred by using process calculi is only justified for systems with particularly high quality or security requirements.
- The use of process calculi requires highly trained personnel.

Solution. Use a service-oriented process calculus for formally specifying the system under consideration. Analyse the formal specification of the system by using suitable analytical tools.

Consequences. Process calculi, being defined algebraically, are inherently compositional and, therefore, convey in a distilled form the paradigm at the heart of service-oriented computing. On the other hand, a formal specification of service-oriented systems based on process calculi permits using powerful analysis tools to guarantee relevant properties.

Various kinds of typing systems, behavioural equivalences and temporal logics can be defined in order to deal with specific aspects of service-oriented systems. Thus, from time to time, the appropriate kind of reasoning mechanisms to work with should be chosen/defined depending on the property one intends to guarantee. As an example, to ensure that a system respects the expected behaviours, type systems can work in a complete statical manner or combine static and dynamic checks.

On the negative side, an analytical tool designed for a process calculus, in general, cannot be directly applied to a different one but has to be properly tailored.

Example. Two examples of process calculi suitable for modelling service-oriented systems are CaSPiS [5] and COWS [28]. Two classes of properties that, for example, can be verified on top of specifications defined by using the above calculi are *progress* (e.g. a client does not get stuck because of inadequate service communication capabilities) and *confidentiality* (e.g. critical data can be accessed only by authorised partners). Both properties can be verified by using the type systems introduced in [1], for CaSPiS, and in [29], for COWS, respectively.

Consider now a bank account service scenario where a client can ask for his balance. Specifically, upon receiving a balance request, the bank account service waits for the client's credentials and sends either the requested balance or an error message, depending on the validity of the credentials.

Code Example. Consider the following CaSPiS specification of the scenario:

$$\begin{aligned} BA &= bank\_account.(c : \mathsf{credts}).\mathbf{if\ is\_valid}(c)\ \mathbf{then}\ \langle balance \rangle\ \mathbf{else}\ \langle \mathbf{err} \rangle \\ C &= \overline{bank\_account}.\langle cred \rangle.(\ (b : \mathsf{int}).\uparrow \langle \mathbf{true}, b \rangle\ +\ (e : \mathsf{err}).\uparrow \langle \mathbf{false}, 0 \rangle) \\ Sys &= C \mid BA \end{aligned}$$

where **err** is a message with associated type err and the validity of credentials is checked by means of an auxiliary function, **is_valid**, that is private to the service $bank\_account$.

According to the safety result in [1], client progress is guaranteed in Sys. Indeed, supposing that $bank\_account$ has associated type $?\mathsf{credts}.(\ \tau.!\mathsf{int}\ +\ \tau.!\mathsf{err}\ )$, it can be inferred that client C is well-typed. More precisely, C's protocol has associated type $!\mathsf{credts}.(\ ?\mathsf{int} + ?\mathsf{err}\ )$, which is compliant with $bank\_account$'s type. Therefore, the whole system Sys is well-typed.

Consider now the new system Sys' defined below, where client C' does not comply with $bank\_account$ communication protocol:

$$\begin{aligned} C' &= \overline{bank\_account}.\ \langle cred \rangle.\ (b : \mathsf{int}).\uparrow \langle \mathbf{true}, b \rangle \\ Sys' &= C' \mid BA\ . \end{aligned}$$

C''s protocol has associated type $!\mathsf{credts}.?\mathsf{int}$, which clearly does not comply with $bank\_account$'s type. Therefore, client progress is not guaranteed in Sys'. Actually, Sys' can reduce to $[(b : \mathsf{int}).\uparrow \langle \mathbf{true}, b \rangle ||| \langle \mathbf{err} \rangle]$, where client protocol $(b\ :\ \mathsf{int}).\uparrow \langle \mathbf{true}, b \rangle$ is stuck.

The same scenario can be specified by using COWS as follows:

$$\begin{aligned} BA = &* [x_{client}, x_{credts}]\ bank\_account \bullet balance\_req?\langle x_{client}, x_{credts} \rangle. \\ &\quad [p, o]\ (\ p \bullet o!\langle \mathbf{is\_valid}(x_{credts}) \rangle \\ &\quad\quad \mid p \bullet o?\langle \mathbf{true} \rangle.\ x_{client} \bullet balance\_resp!\langle balance \rangle \\ &\quad\quad +\ p \bullet o?\langle \mathbf{false} \rangle.\ x_{client} \bullet balance\_resp!\langle \mathbf{err} \rangle\ ) \\ C = &\ bank\_account \bullet balance\_req!\langle client, cred \rangle \mid [x]\ client \bullet balance\_resp?\langle x \rangle \\ Sys = &\ C \mid BA\ . \end{aligned}$$

The type system for COWS introduced in [29] permits expressing and forcing policies regulating the exchange of data among interacting services and ensuring that, in that respect, services do not manifest unexpected behaviours. This permits checking confidentiality properties, e.g., that client credentials are shared only with the bank account service. The types can be attached to each single datum and express the policies for data exchange in terms of sets of partners that are authorised to access the data. Thus, the credentials $cred$, communicated by C to BA, gets annotated with the policy

$\{bank\_account\}$, that allows BA to receive the datum but prevents it from transmitting the datum to other services. The typed version of C is defined as follows

$$bank\_account \bullet balance\_req!\langle client, \{cred\}_{\{bank\_account\}}\rangle \\ \mid [x]\ client \bullet balance\_resp?\langle x\rangle$$

Once the static type inference phase ends, the BA's variable x_{credts} gets annotated with the policy $\{bank\_account\}$, which means that the datum that dynamically will replace x_{credts} will be used only by the partner $bank\_account$. In this way, the communication can safely take place.

Suppose instead that service BA (accidentally or maliciously) attempts to reveal the credentials through some "internal" operation such as $p_{int} \bullet o!\langle\{x_{credts}\}_r\rangle$, for some set r such that $p_{int} \in r$. Then, as result of the inference, we would get declaration of variable x_{credts} annotated with r', for some set r' such that $r \subseteq r'$. Now, the communication would be blocked by a runtime check because the datum sent by C would be annotated as $\{cred\}_{\{bank\_account\}}$ while the set r' of the receiving variable x_{credts} is such that $p_{int} \in r \subseteq r' \nsubseteq \{bank\_account\}$.

Related Patterns. The *Functional Service Verification* pattern is often useful to verify services specified according to this pattern.

5 Functional Service Verification

Context. You are designing a service-oriented system that has to operate in an open-ended computational environment. The system should perform its tasks and should not manifest unexpected behaviours in each state of the environment.

Problem. Current software engineering technologies for service-oriented systems remain at the descriptive level and do not support formal reasoning mechanisms and analytical tools for checking that systems enjoy desirable properties.

Forces

- The functionalities required of a service must be verified at design time.
- Properties to be insured by services should be expressed at a higher level of abstraction and therefore be independent from the technical details of the implementation.
- Logics have been since long proved able to reason about complex software systems as service-oriented applications are. In particular temporal logics have been proposed in the last twenty years, as suitable means for specifying properties of complex systems owing to their ability of expressing notions of necessity, possibility, eventuality, etc.
- The additional cost and development effort incurred by verification may only be justified for systems with particularly high quality or security requirements.
- Logic-based verification can only be performed by highly qualified developers.

Solution. Use a logical verification framework for checking functional properties of services by abstracting away from the environments in which they are operating. In particular, specify the properties of interest by using a temporal logic capable of capturing specific aspects of services, e.g. the logic SocL [20]. Define a formal specification of the system under consideration by using a process calculus, e.g. COWS [28], and, on top of this specification, define more abstract views by appropriately classifying system actions. Finally, verify the formulae over the abstract views of the system by using a model checker, e.g. the on-the-fly model checker CMC [20].

Consequences. The fact that the verification of properties is done over the abstract views of the system has many important advantages. On the one hand, it enables defining and working with many different abstract views of a system, thus reducing the complexity of the model of the system to be analysed. On the other hand, it enables defining service properties in terms of typical service actions (request, response, cancel, ...) and in a way that is independent of the actual specification of the service, both with regards to the process calculus used and with regards to the actual actions' names used in the specification. As a further consequence, it permits to identify classes of functional properties that services with similar functionalities must enjoy.

Example. Consider the following general properties that express two desirable attributes of services:

- *responsiveness*: the service under analysis always guarantees a response to each received request;
- *availability*: the service under analysis is always capable to accept a request.

Consider now a bank service scenario where a client can charge its credit card with some amount. Specifically, consider a client that tries to charge his credit card `1234` with two different amounts, Euros `100` and `200`, by performing two requests in parallel. An abstract view of the above system can be obtained by properly identifying the system actions corresponding to requests, responses and failure notifications of the interaction between the bank service and the client, and by specifying the system states where the service is able to accept a request. This way, the two general properties can be verified over the abstract system specification.

Code Example. The two properties presented in the previous section can be expressed as SocL formulae as follows:

- *responsiveness*: `AG(accepting_request(charge))`
- *availability*:
```
AG[request(charge,$id)]
    AF{response(charge,%id)
        or fail(charge,%id)} true
```

where `charge` indicates the interaction between the bank service and the client, while the variable `id` is used to correlate responses and failure notifications to the proper accepted requests.

A COWS specification of the scenario is

```
let
  Bank = * [CUST] [CC] [AMOUNT] [ID]
        bank.charge?<CUST,CC,AMOUNT,ID>.
        [p#][o#] (p.o!<>
              | p.o?<>. CUST.chargeOK!<ID>
            + p.o?<>. CUST.chargeFail!<ID>)

  Client = bank.charge!<client,1234,100,id1>
          | (client.chargeOK?<id1>.nil
            + client.chargeFail?<id1>.nil)
        | bank.charge!<client,1234,200,id2>
          | (client.chargeOK?<id2>.nil
             + client.chargeFail?<id2>.nil)
in
  Bank() | Client()
end
```

Once prompted by a request, the service `Bank` creates one specific instance to serve that request and is immediately ready to concurrently serve other requests. Two different correlation values, `id1` and `id2`, are used to correlate the response messages to the corresponding requests. Notably, for the sake of simplicity, the choice between approving or not a request for charging the credit card is here completely non-deterministic. An abstract view of the system can be obtained by applying the following rules:

```
Abstractions {
  Action charge<*,*,*,$1> -> request(charge,$1)
  Action chargeOK<$1>     -> response(charge,$1)
  Action chargeFail<$1>   -> fail(charge,$1)
  State  charge           -> accepting_request(charge)
}
```

The first rule prescribes that whenever the concrete actions `bank.charge!<client,1234,100,id1>` and `bank.charge!<client,1234,200,id2>` are executed, then they are replaced by the abstract actions `request(charge,id1)` and `request(charge,id2)`, respectively. Variables "`$n`" (with `n` natural number) can be used to defined generic (templates of) abstraction rules. Also the wildcard "`*`" can be used for increasing flexibility. The other rules act similarly. Notably, communications internal to the bank service are not transformed and, thus, become unobservable.

Related Patterns. The *Service Specification and Analysis* pattern is often useful to specify services that should be verified.

Tools. The tool CMC can be used to prove that the bank service specified above exhibits the desired characteristics to be available and responsive. A prototypical version of CMC can be experimented via a web interface available at the address `http://fmt.isti.cnr.it/cmc/`

6 Sensitivity Analysis

Context. You are analysing a service-oriented system in order to identify areas where the system performance can be improved with relatively little effort. There are many potential ways in which the system can be modified including optimising software components, purchasing new hardware or infrastructure, re-deploying existing hardware resources for other purposes, and many other possibilities.

Problem. Identify a low-cost method of improving system performance.

Forces
- The impact of changes on system performance can be hard to predict. Improving the efficiency of one component will not necessarily lead to an improvement overall. Optimisations which are applied in the wrong place may even lead to the overall performance being reduced.
- Some changes are expensive, others cheap. One change might require replacing a large part of the communication network, another might require rewrites of complex software, whereas one might require only reducing a delay such as a timeout.
- Given the many possible changes one could make it is infeasible to try each of them and compare the relative increase (or decrease) in performance.

Solution. Develop a high-level quantitative model of the service and experiment on the model in order to determine the changes which have the greatest positive impact. Of these, identify those which can be implemented with lowest cost, and carry out this implementation. The quantitative model can be evaluated using a modelling tool such as a simulator or a Markov chain solver computing the transient and passage-time measures which relate to user-perceived performance, together with the use of parameter sweep across the model to vary activity rates.

Consequences. The analysis has the potential to identify useful areas where optimisations can be applied. The numerical evaluation may be long-running but it is entirely automatic. The quantitative evaluation has the potential to generate many analysis results which need to be considered and assessed by a domain expert.

Example. This pattern is applied in [13] to investigate an automotive accident assistance service. A framework for experimentation and analysis allows many instances of a Markov chain solver to be executed and the results combined to identify how the service can most easily meet its required service-level agreement.

Related Patterns. The *Service Specification and Analysis* pattern is complementary in the sense that it uses similar methods to analyse behaviour.

Tools. The SENSORIA Development Environment hosts formal analysis tools which allow service engineers to perform parameter sweep across models of services expressed in the PEPA process algebra [27]. The PEPA model is automatically compiled into a continuous-time Markov chain and passage-time analysis is performed using the `ipclib` analysis tools [12].

7 Scalability Analysis

Context. You are a large-scale service provider using replication to scale your service provision to support large user populations. You need to understand the impact on your service provision of changes in the number of servers which you have available or changes in the number of users subscribed to your service.

Problem. Understanding the impact of changes on a large-scale system.

Forces

- Large user populations represent success: this service is considered by many people to be important or even vital. Scale of use is a tangible and quantifiable measure of value and being able to support large-scale use is an indicator of quality in planning, execution and deployment in service provision. Maintaining a large-scale system attracts prestige, attention and acclaim.
- Large user populations represent heavy demand. The service must be replicated in order to serve many clients. Replication represents cost in terms of hosting provision, hardware and electricity bills. Service providers would like to reduce service provision while continuing to serve large user populations.
- Modelling would help with understanding the system but large-scale systems are difficult to model. Conventional discrete-state quantitative analysis methods are limited by the the size of the probability distribution vector across all of the states of the system. Discrete-state models are subject to the well-known state-space explosion problem. It is not possible simply to use a very large Markov chain model to analyse this problem.

Solution. Develop a high-level model of the system and apply continuous-space analysis to the model. A continuous-space model can make predictions about a large-scale system where a discrete-state model cannot.

Consequences. TO DO

Related Patterns. The *Sensitivity Analysis* pattern is closely related in that it is possible to use the parameter sweep employed there to perform *dimensioning* for large-scale systems (i.e. determining whether a planned system has enough capacity to serve an estimated user population).

Tools. The SENSORIA Development Environment hosts analysis tools which allow service engineers to perform continuous-space analysis on models expressed in the PEPA process algebra [27]. The PEPA model is automatically compiled into a set of coupled ordinary differential equations and the initial value problem is evaluated using numerical integration. This predicts the number of users in different states of using the service at all future time points. Static analysis, compilation and integration are performed using the PEPA Eclipse Plug-in Project [36].

8 Declarative Orchestration

Context. You are designing a service-oriented system that has to operate in an open-ended, changing environment in which the presence of certain services cannot be guaranteed. The system should perform its tasks to the maximum extent possible in each state of the environment, possibly by utilising features of the environment that were not present when the system was designed.

Problem. Design a service-oriented system that can operate in an open-ended, changing environment.

Forces
- A pre-determined orchestration of services cannot adapt to significant, unforeseen changes in the environment.
- Specifying orchestrations for all possible changes is not feasible in some environments.
- Not having a pre-determined orchestration makes it more difficult to reason about the system.
- If the environment is too different from the one for which a system was originally designed it may no longer be possible to fulfil the system's function.
- Services have to provide a rich semantic description to be usable for declarative orchestrations.

Solution. Define an ontology for the problem domain that is rich enough to capture the capabilities of services. Specify the results of combining several services in a declarative manner, e.g., as plan components or logical implications. Use a reasoning component such as an planner, model checker, or a theorem prover to create orchestrations from these specifications and a description of the current environment.

Consequences. Declarative orchestrations can adapt to large changes in the environment without manual reconfiguration. They can easily incorporate information about new kinds of services and use them to fulfil their tasks.

On the negative side, declarative orchestration depends on an expressive domain model for which the reasoning process is often computationally expensive and time consuming, and also on the availability of rich semantic descriptions of unknown services. It is often difficult to control the behaviour of systems built on top of reasoning components and to ensure their correctness.

Related Patterns. Unless the environment is extremely unpredictable, a system designed according to *Declarative Service Selection* can often satisfy similar requirements while remaining easier to understand and analyse.

9 Declarative Service Selection

Context. You have designed an orchestration for a service-oriented system. During runtime, a number of services with similar functionality but different cost, reliability and quality trade-offs are available that can fulfil the requirements of the orchestration.

Problem. Find an optimal combination of services, taking into account the current situation and user preferences.

Forces

- The functionality required of the services is determined by the orchestration.
- The services available at run-time are not known during design-time.
- Different services with the same functionality can be differentiated according to other Quality of Service metrics.

Solution. Define a context-aware soft-constraint system that ranks solution according to their quality. Model user preferences using a partial order between the criteria described by individual soft constraints when possible, otherwise build a more complex mapping from the values of individual constraints to an overall result that describes the user preferences. A soft-constraint solver can the compute the optimal combination of services or a "good enough" combination of services computable in a certain time frame.

Consequences. The specification of the problem can be given without reference to a solution algorithm, thus the communication with domain experts and users is simplified. The computation of the quality of different combinations of services and the preference given to each individual characteristic are decoupled from each other. A soft-constraint solver provides a general mechanism to compute the desired combination of services.

On the other hand, the choice of evaluation functions is restricted by the theories that the soft-constraint solver can process. A general-purpose mechanism such as a solver is often less efficient than a well-tuned specialised implementation.

10 Model-Driven Deployment

Context. You are designing a service configuration where non-functional requirements (security, reliable messaging, etc.) play an important role. Models are designed in UML while the underlying standards-compliant platform have to be parametrised at a very low abstraction level (e.g. using specific APIs or XML formats).

Problem. There is a big semantical gap between the modelling and deployment concepts. Platforms and concepts are changing rapidly, interoperability is not guaranteed between low level models.

Forces. A service configuration is typically designed in high level modelling languages such as UML. The configuration of the underlying implementation platforms, however, needs the deep technical knowledge of related standards and product specific know-how. Services have to be redeployed, refactored and moved between runtime environments. Moreover, non-functional properties should be handled differently for different classes of users. It should be avoided to have the service designer specify the detailed technical requirements, he should rather work with predefined profiles.

Solution. We propose a multiple-step model driven workflow where separate model transformations implement the PIM2PSM and PSM2code mappings, as defined in the MDA approach. Services have to be modelled either in a specialised UML dialect or in a Domain Specific Editor. First, relevant parts of the model are filtered out and stored in a simplified representation format (neglecting e.g. tool-specific information). Then different Platform Independent Models are created for the different aspects of non-functional requirements, e.g. security, reliable messaging, component deployment, etc. Up to this step, platform requirements do not affect the process. Platform Specific Models contain implementation-specific attributes, taken from the PIM and predefined parameter libraries. Finally, structured textual code (e.g. XML descriptors) is generated.

Consequences. The method has the potential to connect high level models to low level runtime representations. Transformation chain targets server configurations with extensions for reliable messaging and security.

Example. Examples are the UML4SOA for modelling, VIATRA2 framework for transformation and Apache Axis (using Rampart and Sandesha modules) and IBM WebSphere as relevant industrial platforms. The method is used in different scenarios of the project.

Tools. The input of transformation is UML2 models in UML4SOA (designed e.g. in Rational Software Architect (RSA)). The transformation is integrated in the SENSORIA Development Environment while the output consist of descriptor files and client stubs.

11 Related Work

The idea of using patterns to describe common problems in software design and development was popularised by the so-called "Gang of Four" book [24]. Since its publication a wide range of patterns and pattern languages for many areas of software development has been published, see, e.g, the Pattern Languages of Programs (PLoP) conferences and the associated Pattern Languages of Program Design volumes, or the LNCS Transactions on Pattern Languages of Programming.

The area of patterns for SOA has recently gained a lot of attention, and several collections of design patterns for SOA have been recently published or announced [19,38]. The article [18] provides a short introduction. However these patterns address more general problems of SOA, while our patterns are focused on the formally supported techniques provided by SENSORIA. Therefore, our patterns can serve as an extension of, rather than as a replacement for, other pattern catalogues.

12 Conclusions and Further Work

In this paper, we have presented some results of the IST-FET EU project SENSORIA, in the form of a pattern language. The patterns address a broad range of issues, such as modelling, specification, analysis, verification, orchestration, and deployment of services. We are currently working on systematising and extending the collection of patterns in these areas, and we will also be developing patterns for areas which are not currently addressed, e.g., business process analysis and modelling.

This pattern catalogue is a useful guide to the research results of the SENSORIA project: as already mentioned in Section 2.1, we are investigating a broad range of subjects and without some guidance it may not be easy for software developers to find the appropriate tools or techniques.

However, the patterns presented in this paper only present a very brief glimpse at the research of the SENSORIA project. Important research areas include a new generalised concept of service, modelling languages for services based on UML and SCA, new semantically well-defined modelling and programming primitives for services, new powerful mathematical analysis and verification techniques and tools for system behaviour and quality of service properties, and novel model-based transformation and development techniques. The innovative methods of SENSORIA are being demonstrated by applying them to case studies in the service-intensive areas of e-business, automotive systems, and telecommunications.

By integrating and further developing these results SENSORIA will achieve its overall aim: a comprehensive and pragmatic but theoretically well founded approach to software engineering for service-oriented systems.

References

1. Acciai, L., Boreale, M.: A Type System for Client Progress in a Service-Oriented Calculus. In: Degano, P., De Nicola, R., Meseguer, J. (eds.) Concurrency, Graphs and Models. LNCS, vol. 5065, pp. 642–658. Springer, Heidelberg (2008)
2. Balogh, A., Varró, D.: Advanced Model Transformation Language Constructs in the VIATRA2 Framework. In: ACM Symposium on Applied Computing — Model Transformation Track (SAC 2006), pp. 1280–1287. ACM Press, New York (2006)
3. Bartoletti, M., Degano, P., Ferrari, G., Zunino, R.: Types and effects for Resouce Usage Analysis. In: Seidl, H. (ed.) FOSSACS 2007. LNCS, vol. 4423, pp. 32–47. Springer, Heidelberg (2007)
4. ter Beek, M.H., Moiso, C., Petrocchi, M.: Towards Security Analyses of an Identity Federation Protocol for Web Services in Convergent Networks. In: Proceedings of the 3rd Advanced International Conference on Telecommunications (AICT 2007). IEEE Computer Society Press, Los Alamitos (2007)
5. Boreale, M., Bruni, R., Nicola, R.D., Loreti, M.: Sessions and Pipelines for Structured Service Programming. In: Barthe, G., de Boer, F.S. (eds.) FMOODS 2008. LNCS, vol. 5051, pp. 19–38. Springer, Heidelberg (2008)
6. Boreale, M., Bruni, R., Caires, L., De Nicola, R., Lanese, I., Loreti, M., Martins, F., Montanari, U., Ravara, A., Sangiorgi, D., Vasconcelos, V., Zavattaro, G.: SCC: a Service Centered Calculus. In: Bravetti, M., Núñez, M., Zavattaro, G. (eds.) WS-FM 2006. LNCS, vol. 4184, pp. 38–57. Springer, Heidelberg (2006)
7. Bravetti, M., Gilmore, S., Guidi, C., Tribastone, M.: Replicating web services for scalability. In: Barthe, G., Fournet, C. (eds.) TGC 2007 and FODO 2008. LNCS, vol. 4912, pp. 204–221. Springer, Heidelberg (2008)
8. Bravetti, M., Zavattaro, G.: A Theory for Strong Service Compliance. In: Murphy, A.L., Vitek, J. (eds.) COORDINATION 2007. LNCS, vol. 4467, pp. 96–112. Springer, Heidelberg (2007)

9. Bravetti, M., Zavattaro, G.: Contract based Multi-party Service Composition. In: Arbab, F., Sirjani, M. (eds.) FSEN 2007. LNCS, vol. 4767, pp. 207–222. Springer, Heidelberg (2007)
10. Buscemi, M.G., Montanari, U.: CC-Pi: A Constraint-Based Language for Specifying Service Level Agreements. In: De Nicola, R. (ed.) ESOP 2007. LNCS, vol. 4421, pp. 18–32. Springer, Heidelberg (2007)
11. Ciancia, V., Ferrari, G.: Co-Algebraic Models for Quantitative Spatial Logics. In: Quantitative Aspects of Programming Languages (QAPL 2007) (2007)
12. Clark, A.: The ipclib PEPA Library. In: Harchol-Balter, M., Kwiatkowska, M., Telek, M. (eds.) Proceedings of the 4th International Conference on the Quantitative Evaluation of SysTems (QEST), September 2007, pp. 55–56. IEEE Computer Society Press, Los Alamitos (2007)
13. Clark, A., Gilmore, S.: Evaluating quality of service for service level agreements. In: Brim, L., Leucker, M. (eds.) Proceedings of the 11th International Workshop on Formal Methods for Industrial Critical Systems, Bonn, Germany, pp. 172–185 (August 2006)
14. Correia, R., Matos, C., Heckel, R., El-Ramly, M.: Architecture migration driven by code categorization. In: Oquendo, F. (ed.) ECSA 2007. LNCS, vol. 4758, pp. 115–122. Springer, Heidelberg (2007)
15. Nicola, R.D., Katoen, J.-P., Latella, D., Loreti, M., Massink, M.: Model checking mobile stochastic logic. Theor. Comput. Sci. 382(1), 42–70 (2007)
16. Nicola, R.D., Katoen, J.-P., Latella, D., Massink, M.: STOKLAIM: A Stochastic Extension of KLAIM. Technical Report 2006-TR-01, ISTI (2006)
17. Ehrig, K., Taentzer, G., Varró, D.: Tool Integration by Model Transformations based on the Eclipse Modeling Framework. EASST Newsletter 12 (June 2006)
18. Erl, T.: Introducing soa design patterns. SOA World Magazine 8(6) (June 2008)
19. Erl, T.: SOA Design Patterns. Prentice Hall/Pearson PTR (to appear, 2008)
20. Fantechi, A., Gnesi, S., Lapadula, A., Mazzanti, F., Pugliese, R., Tiezzi, F.: A model checking approach for verifying COWS specifications. In: Fiadeiro, J.L., Inverardi, P. (eds.) FASE 2008. LNCS, vol. 4961, pp. 230–245. Springer, Heidelberg (2008)
21. Fiadeiro, J.L., Lopes, A., Bocchi, L.: A Formal Approach to Service Component Architecture. In: Bravetti, M., Núñez, M., Zavattaro, G. (eds.) WS-FM 2006. LNCS, vol. 4184, pp. 193–213. Springer, Heidelberg (2006)
22. Foster, H., Kramer, J., Magee, J., Uchitel, S.: Towards Self-Management in Service-oriented Computing with Modes. In: Proceedings of Workshop on Engineering Service-Oriented Applications (WESOA 2007), Vienna, Austria, Imperial College London (September 2007)
23. Foster, H., Mayer, P.: Leveraging integrated tools for model-based analysis of service compositions. In: Proceedings of the Third International Conference on Internet and Web Applications and Services (ICIW 2008), Athens, Greece. IEEE Computer Society Press, Los Alamitos (2008)
24. Gamma, E., Helm, R., Johnson, R., Vlissides, J.: Design patterns: elements of reusable object-oriented software. Addison-Wesley Longman Publishing Co., Inc., Boston (1995)
25. Gönczy, L., Varró, D.: Modeling of Reliable Messaging in Service Oriented Architectures. In: Proc. of the International Workshop on Web Services - Modeling and Testing (2006)
26. Guidi, C., Lucchi, R., Gorrieri, R., Busi, N., Zavattaro, G.: SOCK: A Calculus for Service Oriented Computing. In: Dan, A., Lamersdorf, W. (eds.) ICSOC 2006. LNCS, vol. 4294, pp. 327–338. Springer, Heidelberg (2006)
27. Hillston, J.: A Compositional Approach to Performance Modelling. Cambridge University Press, Cambridge (1996)
28. Lapadula, A., Pugliese, R., Tiezzi, F.: A Calculus for Orchestration of Web Services. In: De Nicola, R. (ed.) ESOP 2007. LNCS, vol. 4421, pp. 33–47. Springer, Heidelberg (2007)

29. Lapadula, A., Pugliese, R., Tiezzi, F.: Regulating data exchange in service oriented applications. In: Arbab, F., Sirjani, M. (eds.) FSEN 2007. LNCS, vol. 4767, pp. 223–239. Springer, Heidelberg (2007)
30. Lapadula, A., Pugliese, R., Tiezzi, F.: A Calculus for Orchestration of Web Services. In: De Nicola, R. (ed.) ESOP 2007. LNCS, vol. 4421, pp. 33–47. Springer, Heidelberg (2007)
31. Lapadula, A., Pugliese, R., Tiezzi, F.: Regulating data exchange in service oriented applications. In: Arbab, F., Sirjani, M. (eds.) FSEN 2007. LNCS, vol. 4767, pp. 223–239. Springer, Heidelberg (2007)
32. Mayer, P., Schroeder, A., Koch, N.: A Model-Driven Approach to Service Orchestration. In: Proceedings of the IEEE International Conference on Services Computing (SCC 2008). IEEE Computer Society Press, Los Alamitos (2008)
33. Meszaros, G., Doble, J.: Metapatterns: A pattern language for pattern writing (1996)
34. Mukhija, A., Dingwall-Smith, A., Rosenblum, D.S.: QoS-Aware Service Composition in Dino. In: Proceedings of the 5th European Conference on Web Services (ECOWS 2007), Halle, Germany. IEEE Computer Society Press, Los Alamitos (2007)
35. Nielson, F., Nielson, H.R.: A flow-sensitive analysis of privacy properties. In: 20th IEEE Computer Security Foundations Symposium, CSF 2007, Venice, Italy, 6-8 July 2007, pp. 249–264. IEEE Computer Society Press, Los Alamitos (2007)
36. Web site for the pepa eclipse plugin (last accessed 2008-06-24), `http://homepages.inf.ed.ac.uk/mtribast/plugin/download.html`
37. Probst, C.W., Nielson, F., Hansen, R.R.: Sandboxing in myKlaim. In: The First International Conference on Availability, Reliability and Security, ARES 2006 (2006)
38. Rotem-Gal-Oz, A.: SOA Patterns. Manning (to appear, 2009)
39. Tools integrated into the SENSORIA Development Environment, `http://svn.pst.ifi.lmu.de/trac/sct/wiki/SensoriaTools`
40. Wirsing, M., Bocchi, L., Clark, A., Fiadeiro, J.L., Gilmore, S., Hölzl, M., Koch, N., Pugliese, R.: SENSORIA: Engineering for Service-Oriented Overlay Computers, ch. 7. MIT Press, Cambridge (submitted, 2007)
41. Wirsing, M., Clark, A., Gilmore, S., Hölzl, M., Knapp, A., Koch, N., Schroeder, A.: Semantic-Based Development of Service-Oriented Systems. In: Najm, E., Pradat-Peyre, J.-F., Donzeau-Gouge, V.V. (eds.) FORTE 2006. LNCS, vol. 4229, pp. 24–45. Springer, Heidelberg (2006)

Safety and Response-Time Analysis of an Automotive Accident Assistance Service

Ashok Argent-Katwala[1], Allan Clark[2], Howard Foster[1], Stephen Gilmore[2], Philip Mayer[3], and Mirco Tribastone[2]

[1] Imperial College, London, England
[2] The University of Edinburgh, Scotland
[3] Ludwig-Maximilians-Universität, Munich, Germany

Abstract. In the present paper we assess both the safety properties and the response-time profile of a subscription service which provides medical assistance to drivers who are injured in vehicular collisions. We use both timed and untimed process calculi cooperatively to perform the required analysis. The formal analysis tools used are hosted on a high-level modelling platform with support for scripting and orchestration which enables users to build custom analysis processes from the general-purpose analysers which are hosted as services on the platform.

1 Introduction

Service providers who sell services which are concerned with human health and human safety have a responsibility to assess the quality of the service which they provide in terms of both its correctness of function and its speed of response. One way to carry out such an assessment is to construct a precise formal model of the service and perform the analysis on the model to shed light on the behaviour of the service itself. Such an assessment exercises the ability to apply both qualitative methods (such as model-checking) and quantitative methods (such as transient analysis) in service evaluation. The service providers delivering these critical services may not themselves have the technical skills to apply methods such as these. Further, even if they are able to source the necessary skills from expert users elsewhere, they may not be happy to take advantage of this because they would then risk revealing information about their current service provision which they might be unwilling to disclose to anyone outside their organisation.

One possible way in which the stakeholders of formal analysis methods can contribute to alleviating this problem is by embedding their analysers in modelling environments which lower the barrier to use of the methods. These environments can then be adopted and applied by the service providers in-house, allowing them to evaluate their service provision without revealing sensitive information about their current service. The SENSORIA Development Environment (SDE) assists us in the goal of bringing state-of-the-art analysis methods closer to the service providers who need to apply them.

T. Margaria and B. Steffen (Eds.): ISoLA 2008, CCIS 17, pp. 191–205, 2008.

The SDE brings together analysis tools for process calculi and allows users to combine them using scripting. In particular the SDE includes analysis tools for the two process calculi which we use in the present work:

- Finite State Processes (FSP), and
- Performance Evaluation Process Algebra (PEPA).

Specifically, the SDE hosts the following tools:

- the LTSA model-checker for FSP, and
- the `ipclib` response-time analyser for PEPA.

We describe the use of the SDE on an analysis problem which is of particular interest to one of the industrial partners in our current research project. The partner in question is a consultancy providing advice to a major Bavarian car manufacturer. They have been asked to consult on a subscription service which uses the on-board diagnostic and communication systems in high-end cars to provide an accident assistance service. In this paper we use the SDE and other tools to assess the accident assistance service against both safety properties (using model-checking over labelled transition systems) and response-time properties (using transient analysis of continuous-time Markov chains).

2 Service Design

Our model of the Accident Assistance Service details the events which are the area of responsibility of the service itself. That is, those activities which occur between an accident report being received and the service discharging its responsibility to act on the accident report. In some cases this will lead to an ambulance being sent, and in other cases not. Our model does not require us to know – or allow us to predict – anything about activities which happen before or after these events. For example, we do not estimate how often accidents occur and we do not calculate how long ambulances take to arrive. Both of these many be interesting to know, but our model here does not speak of them.

The activity diagram shown in Figure 1 provides a high-level view of the events in the scenario. Events are triggered by an incoming accident report which the service begins to process (*Process Accident Data*). From this incoming report is obtained all of the available information about the status of the vehicle. Multiple attempts are made to contact the driver (*Contact Driver*) and the service must then respond (*Classify Severity*). In the cases when the accident has been classified as critical medical assistance is dispatched (*Dispatch Ambulance*). Events are logged in a central log for audit purposes, whether an ambulance was dispatched or not.

The service needs to take two major decisions during its realm of responsibility. First, whether to continue to attempt to contact the driver, or assume that they are injured. Second, to classify this accident as critical or not.

Considering the accident assistance service at a lower level of detail we note that the service is triggered by any impact or collision which causes the car

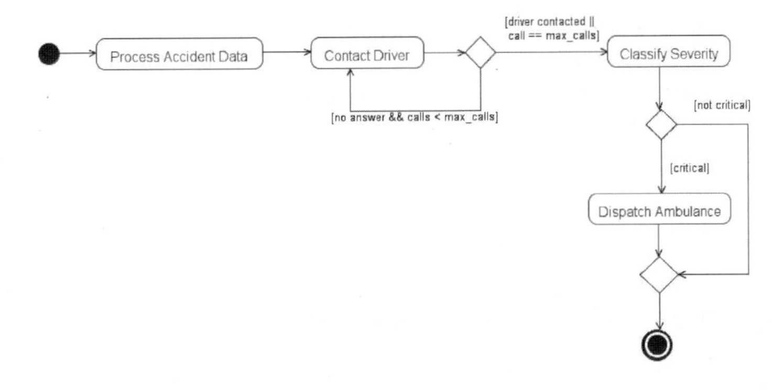

Fig. 1. UML2 Activity Diagram of Accident Assistance Service

airbag to deploy. Immediately after the airbag has deployed the on-board communication module transmits to the assistance service a report with as much information as it can obtain from the car's diagnostic system. This report includes information about the state of the car itself obtained from sensors in the engine and the braking system. The report also specifies the speed of the car at the moment of impact and, most importantly, the geographical location of the car as obtained from the on-board GPS.

On receipt of such a report, the subscription service attempts to contact the registered driver of the car by mobile telephone. If the driver answers the telephone and confirms that they are unhurt then no further action needs to be taken. If they instead say that they have been hurt in the accident then the service will dispatch an ambulance to the reported location to assist them.

The third case to consider occurs when the service cannot get confirmation from the driver that they do not need assistance. It might seem that the obvious course of action should be to consider not getting an answer to be a critical case but there is evidently a possibility that the service will send an ambulance when it is not needed. That is, the driver is unhurt but did not have their mobile telephone with them, or it had no battery charge, or they had no signal from their telephone service provider, or many other similar reasons. Because critical services should not be deployed without good reason, the accident assistance service would like to reduce the number of occasions when an ambulance is dispatched in error.

The information on the car status and the speed of the car at the moment of impact sent with the accident report become significant in the case where we have no answer from the driver. The service needs to classify this accident as critical or not and many factors will influence the classification of an accident. Speed at the time of impact is a major factor, as is degree of damage to the car, but the geographical location and the time of day also impact on the classification. The reason for this is that the injured driver is less likely to get help from passing motorists if the car accident happens in a remote location late at night than if the accident happens in a heavily-populated area during the day.

In the case of no answer and car diagnostics which point to very little damage (say, the car was stationary at the time of impact, and the engine, brakes, lights and other critical functions seem to be functioning normally) then the service will decide not to send an ambulance to prevent sending one when it could be needed elsewhere.

3 Safety Analysis of the Assistance Service

In this section we discuss the safety analysis of the Accident Assistance Service. Safety Analysis is concerned with assuring that properties of the service behaviour are upheld and in particular, that there are no undesirable behaviour traces exhibited given the various constraints of the service. The nature of this service exhibits various specified conditions of progress, for example, if the driver answers his or her cellphone within a number of attempts, then the progress is different to that if he or she does not. Such conditions need to be examined for behaviour consistency. For this reason, we focus on the behaviour process of the service rather than data analysis, given the design of the service specified in section 2 and an implementation written in some software process language. For the purpose of our analysis, we translate the service process workflow in to the Finite State Process (FSP) notation to concisely and formally model the workflow states and transitions.

3.1 FSP, LTS and Behaviour Models

The FSP notation [1,2] is designed to be easily machine readable, and thus provides a preferred language to specify abstract processes. FSP is a textual notation (technically a process calculus) for concisely describing and reasoning about concurrent programs. FSP supports a range of operators to define a process model representation.

A summary of the operators for FSP is given as follows.

Action prefix "->": `(x->P)` describes a process that initially engages in the action `x` and then behaves as described by the auxiliary process `P`;

Choice "|": `(x->P|y->Q)` describes a process which initially engages in either `x` or `y`, and whose subsequent behaviour is described by auxiliary processes `P` or `Q`, respectively;

Recursion: the behaviour of a process may be defined in terms of itself, in order to express repetition;

Sequential composition ";": `(P;Q)` where `P` is a process with an `END` state, describes a process that behaves as `P` and when it reaches the `END` state of `P` starts behaving as the auxiliary process `Q`;

Parallel composition "||": `(P||Q)` describes the parallel composition of processes `P` and `Q`;

Relabelling "/": Re-labelling is applied to a process to change the names of action labels. The general form of re-labelling is `/ {newlabel/oldlabel}`;

The hiding, trace equivalence minimisation, and weak semantic equivalence minimisation operators of FSP are not used here. We omit their descriptions for brevity.

3.2 Translation of Service Design to FSP

The Accident Assistance Service design illustrated in Figure 1 specifies a number of activity transitions linked either as a sequence or through decisions. To translate these to the FSP notation, and a formal model, we traverse the workflow and build a series of FSP processes composed to build a complete process architecture model. To begin with we start with the *initial node*. The initial node specifies a transition to the *Process Accident Data* activity, which represents a report from the on-board vehicle diagnostics system. Additionally at this step, we need to determine and store a variable which holds a report status. In the FSP (listed below), we represent these actions by creating a process (PROCESSACCIDENTDATA) and a sequence for the choice of status reported from the vehicle diagnostics. The VEHDIAGCHOICE process has two options, one for a normal status or one for a critical status. Note that we need to look ahead to see which activity follows this to determine whether this process composition is complete. In this case the next activity is again a simple transition.

```
// Diagnostics Composition
DIAGCHOICE =
 ( vehicle.emergsrv.diags_normal->emergsrv.diag.write[0]->END
 | vehicle.emergsrv.diags_critical->emergsrv.diag.write[1]->END ).
REQUESTDIAGS = (emergsrv.vehicle.requestdiags->END).
REQUESTDIAGSEQ = REQUESTDIAGS; DIAGCHOICE; END.
||DIAGNOSTICS = (REQUESTDIAGSEQ).
```

Immediately following the *Process Accident Data* activity is the *Contact Driver* activity. This activity is linked with two steps in the workflow. Firstly the activity itself is linked with a decision step, to determine if either the driver was successfully contacted or a maximum number of calls has been reached. The composition for this therefore is the action of calling the driver, and then a choice of either proceeding to the next step of the workflow (because the call was successful or maximum call attempts reached) or the action is repeated.

```
// Call Attempts Composition
const Max = 3 // no of calls before automatic dispatch
range Int = 0..2 // 0 - not critical, 1 - critical, 2 - unknown

CALLATTEMPT(N=0) = CALL[N],
CALL[v:Int] = (emergsrv.driver.callphone->ANSWER[v]),
ANSWER[v:Int] =
  ( driver.emergsrv.noanswer->CALL[v+1]
  | driver.emergsrv.answer->ANSWEREDACTION ),
ANSWEREDACTION =
  ( emergsrv.phone.write[0]->END
  | emergsrv.phone.write[1]->END ),
CALL[Max] = (emergsrv.phone.write[2]->END).

set ACTSET = {emergsrv.driver.callphone,
                 driver.emergsrv.noanswer, driver.emergsrv.answer}
TERMS = (ACTSET->TERMS).
||CALLATTEMPTS = (TERMS || CALLATTEMPT(0)).
```

Lastly, two processes are built to represent the *Classify Severity* and *Dispatch Ambulance* activities. In the first activity again the workflow specifies a decision point. The classification activity represents a choice of transition depending on the status of both the accident data report and contacting the driver. To represent this in FSP we recall the values assigned as part of the two previous compositions (*Process Accident Data* and *Contact Driver*). The choice of process transition is represented using a conventional structured construct of IF..THEN..ELSE. The FSP below represents the conditional operation of the diagnostics status reported by the vehicle. A similar model is built to represent the result of calling the driver and then these two choice models are composed. The comparison of whether the status is critical determines if the *Dispatch Ambulance* is undertaken.

```
// check phone answered
QUERYPHONESTATUS = (emergsrv.phone.read[i : 0..2]->QUERYPHONESTATUS[i]),
QUERYPHONESTATUS[i : 0..2] -
    if (i==2) then QUERYDIAGSTATUS; END
    else if (i==1) then DISPATCH; END
         else LOGREPORT; END.

// check diagnostic information received
QUERYDIAGSTATUS = (emergsrv.diag.read[i : 0..1]->QUERYDIAGSTATUS[i]),
QUERYDIAGSTATUS[i : 0..1] =
    if (i==1) then DISPATCH; END
    else LOGREPORT; END.
```

A simple sequence process represents the actual *Dispatch Ambulance* activity, which is triggered if the status is critical. In preparation for analysis a complete architecture model – representing the sequence composition of the workflow processes we have defined – is also summarised in the code below.

```
// Dispatch Ambulance
SENDAMBULANCE = (emergsrv.station.send_ambulance->END).
||DISPATCH = (SENDAMBULANCE).

// Dispatch Report (Final Action)
LOG = (emergsrv.log.result->END).
||LOGREPORT = (LOG).

// Service Main sequence
set PHONE_ALPHABET = {emergsrv.phone.{read,write}.[0..2]}
MAINSEQ = ACCIDENT; AIRBAG; GETSTATUS; QUERYPHONESTATUS; END
        + {PHONE_ALPHABET}.
```

3.3 Analysis Using LTSA

The constructed FSP can be used to model the exact transition of workflow processes through a modelling tool such as the Labelled Transition System Analyzer (LTSA) [1], which compiles an FSP model into a state machine and provides a resulting Labelled Transition System (LTS). LTSA is made available as a component of the SDE. The LTSA tool has an inbuilt safety check to determine whether a specified process is deadlock free. Deadlock analysis of a model involves performing an exhaustive search of the LTS for deadlock states (i.e. states with no outgoing transitions). A default deadlock check of the service process results in no violations being found (i.e. that there are no deadlock states in the model).

However, we need to check properties of the service to meet the requirements in operation. For example, that an ambulance is dispatched only when requested by the driver or, (in the case of no answer) when the car diagnostics indicate severe damage. We add this property to the model through a further FSP statement using the keyword **property** and specifying that both the driver asked for an ambulance (`emergsrv.phone.read[1]`) or did not answer but the diagnostic information on the car indicated severe damage (`emergsrv.diag.read[1]`). The formal statement of this property is listed below.

```
// FSP Property to check only critical status leads to dispatch
property PROP =
 ( emergsrv.phone.read[2] ->
       emergsrv.diag.read[1] ->
            emergsrv.station.send_ambulance -> END
 | emergsrv.phone.read[1] ->
       emergsrv.station.send_ambulance -> END
 ).
```

Using this property specification language we were able to apply model-checking to uncover errors in our original model which we corrected before going on to response time analysis of the model.

4 Response-Time Analysis of the Assistance Service

Response-time analysis considers the timed behaviour of the system under study in the context of a particular workload and a particular sequence of activities which must take place. It is possible to think of this as a sub-scenario with a distinguished start activity which starts a clock running and a distinguished stop activity which stops it. The analysis will determine the probability of completing the work needed to take us from the start activity to the stop activity, via any possible path through the system behaviour. This probability value can be plotted against time to give a complete picture of the response-time distribution. With respect to the accident assistance service we will consider the response-time from the airbag being deployed until the assistance service logs that it has completed its investigation and has discharged its duty to send an ambulance if one was required (or it has determined that an ambulance was not required).

For this aspect of the work we require a timed process algebra (FSP is untimed). We will use Performance Evaluation Process Algebra (PEPA) [3], a stochastically-timed Markovian process algebra. The PEPA language is supported by the Sensoria Development Environment and by formal analysis tools on the SDE such as the PEPA Eclipse Plug-in project [4] and the `ipclib` tool suite [5].

4.1 PEPA, CTMCs and Response Time

Many of the combinators of the PEPA language resemble the operators of FSP seen in Section 3. The most significant difference is that all activities in PEPA are timed. We provide a brief summary of the language here, referring the reader to [3] for the full formal details.

Prefix: $(\alpha, r).P$ describes a process which will first perform the activity α at an exponentially-distributed rate r and then evolve to become P.

Choice: $(\alpha, r).P + (\beta, s).Q$ describes a process which either performs activity α at rate r and evolves to become P, or it performs activity β at rate s and evolves to become Q. The two activities α and β are simultaneously enabled and whichever completes first will determine the continuation of the process.

Cooperation: In $P \underset{\mathcal{L}}{\bowtie} Q$ the processes P and Q cooperate over all of the activities in the set $\mathcal{L}$, meaning that they must synchronise on these activities. Activities not in $\mathcal{L}$ are performed independently, without any synchronisation. We write $P \parallel Q$ if $\mathcal{L}$ is empty.

Hiding: The process $P/\mathcal{L}$ is identical to P except that any uses of the activities in the set $\mathcal{L}$ have been renamed to τ (the silent activity) and no other process may cooperate with these activities. The duration of the activity is unchanged so that, for example, (β, s) becomes (τ, s).

Because an exponentially-distributed random variable is associated with the rate of each activity a PEPA model gives rise to a stochastic process, specifically a continuous-time Markov chain (CTMC). The generator matrix, Q, of this CTMC is "uniformised" with: $P = Q/q + I$ where $q > \max_i |Q_{ii}|$ and I is the identity matrix. This process transforms a CTMC into one in which all states have the same mean holding time $1/q$. The required computation for the response-time distribution is to compute the probability of reaching a set of designated target states from a set of designated source states. This rests on two key sub-computations. First, the time to complete n hops ($n = 1, 2, 3, \ldots$), which is an Erlang distribution with parameters n and q. Second, the probability that the transition between source and target states occurs in exactly n hops. After generating the state-space of the model to derive the generator matrix of the CTMC the required response-time distribution can be computed by uniformisation [6,7].

4.2 Analysis Using `ipclib`

Because of the strong similarity between FSP and PEPA translating our existing FSP model into the PEPA language was straightforward. We checked the consistency of the PEPA model against the FSP model by translating the FSP logical propositions into PEPA stochastic probes [8] and confirmed that (the translations of) these propositions held for (the translation of) the model.

We analysed the PEPA model with the `ipclib` [5] tool suite. We investigated the response time of the model across a range of feasible rates for each of the activities performed. Each of the rates can vary independently of the others and to cover all of the cases being considered we generated more than 300 experimental runs of the `ipclib` tools with different parameter values. We performed sensitivity analysis of response-time profiles for the possible parameter values.

We varied the three rates corresponding to the rates at which each subsequent call attempt is ended either by the customer answering the phone or a timeout.

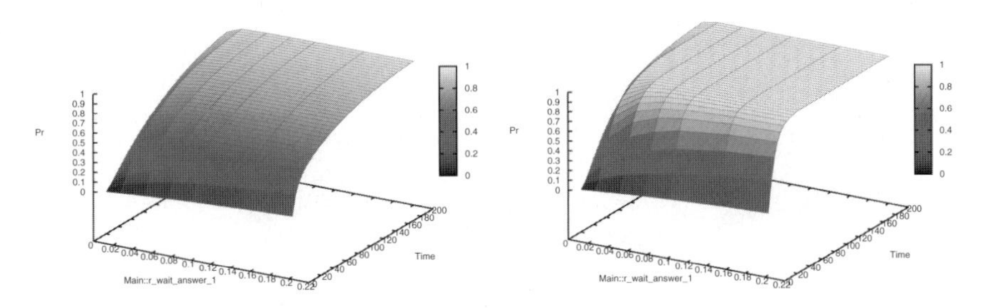

Fig. 2. Response-time graphs for the accident assistance service

These are the rates *r_wait_answer_1*, *r_wait_answer_2* and *r_wait_answer_3*. The analysis tool then produces a group of sensitivity-analysis graphs for each of the three rates. Each graph in the first group plots the cumulative distribution function of completing the passage against the varying rate of *r_wait_answer_1* while the other two rates are kept constant. There is one such graph in the first group for all possible combinations of the two rates *r_wait_answer_2* and *r_wait_answer_3*. Each graph in group one relates the effect that varying the rate *r_wait_answer_1* will have on the completion of the passage. There must be one for every combination of the other two rates because the effect that *r_wait_answer_1* has on the outcome depends upon the values of the other two rates.

Figure 2 shows two graphs in the first group of sensitivity graphs. In the graph on the left rates *r_wait_answer_2* and *r_wait_answer_3* are at low values while in the graph on the right the two rates are held at high values. We see that in either case the rate of *r_wait_answer_1* does have an effect on the probability of completion. We can see this because each line in the graph is different resulting in a 'warped' surface plot. The graph on the left is less warped than the graph on the right. This suggests that varying the rate of *r_wait_answer_1* has more effect whenever the two other rates are at high values. This is because when those rates are high, the bottleneck in completing the passage becomes the activities performed at rate *r_wait_answer_1*. When the other two rates are lower they become the bottleneck and indeed we see that by time $t = 15$ there is not yet a probability of approximately 1.

Figure 3 shows two graphs in the third group of sensitivity graphs. These look similar to the graphs in Figure 2 but we see that they are less warped. This tells us that *r_wait_answer_3* has less effect on the probability of completing the passage. This confirms our intuition because the activities which occur at rate *r_wait_answer_3* are not always performed at all in a successful completion of the passage. In some cases the driver will answer the phone call at the first or second attempt. The graph on the left shows the sensitivity of *r_wait_answer_3* when the rates *r_wait_answer_1* and *r_wait_answer_2* are held at low values and in the graph on the right those rates are held at high values. As before we see that the varied rate has more effect when the unvaried rates are held high. Again this confirms our intuition; all of the rates measured here are performed along the passage and increasing any one of them has a positive effect on the

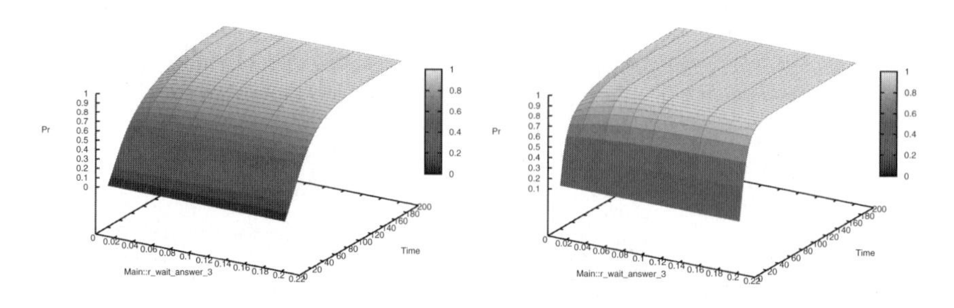

Fig. 3. Response-time graphs for the accident assistance service

probability of completion, therefore we expect that when one rate is the slowest rate varying that rate will achieve more of a performance gain than varying the already faster rates. Overall from these sensitivity-analysis graphs we can surmise that if one wishes to increase the performance then it is of most benefit to increase the rate of the first rate (*r_wait_answer_1*) before the others and the second rate (*r_wait_answer_2*) before the final rate (*r_wait_answer_3*). However if any of the rates are significantly slower than the others then that is the rate which should be increased even if it is *r_wait_answer_3*.

We also obtain summary information about all of the experiments performed. The graph (Figure 4, left) shows best case, worst case, median and the 20-80 percentiles over all response-time graphs. From this we can see that we need to wait until time 80 to be over 50% confident that the passage will have completed regardless of the configuration. However at this time the median is above 95% meaning that in half of the configurations we are very confident that the passage will have completed. Also at this time removing the worst performing 10% of the configurations gives us over 80% confidence of completing the passage. Also from this graph we can see that at time 120 the median begins to approximate 100% confidence that the passage has completed (meaning that in half of the configurations we can be sure that the passage has completed).

Probability of completion at a time bound can be plotted across the more than 300 experiments which we performed, leading to a different summary (Figure 4, right) from which we can make conclusions such as "the probability of service being completed by $t = 195$ seconds is at least 90%, even if all calls to the driver take the longest time which has been allocated for them". We can also see from both styles of summary graphs that the difference between the best and lowest performing configurations starts off small at low time bounds where there is little probability of completing the passage regardless of the configuration. As the time increases the gap grows wider until at some point the worst performing configuration begins to close the gap until eventually there is a near 100% probability of completing the passage for all configurations. For the modeller if this peak in the difference occurs at an important time the configuration of the real system is very important. On the other hand the modeller may be given more confidence if this peak occurs before a time bound in which (for whatever reason) they are particularly interested.

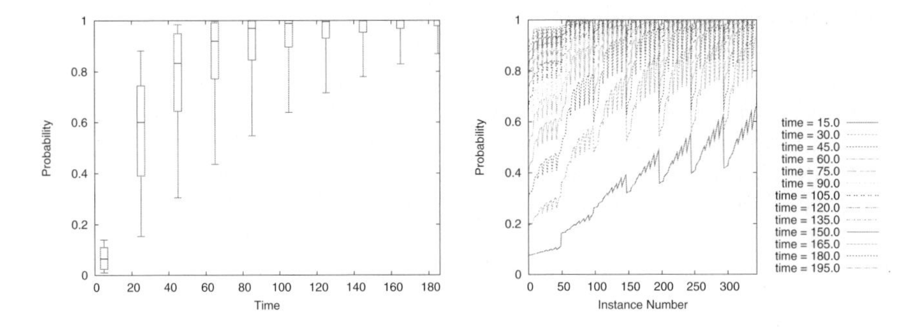

Fig. 4. Summary information for all response-time calculations

5 SENSORIA Development Environment

The previous sections have described qualitative and quantitative methods with corresponding tools for performing safety and response-time analysis of services. In order to make these tools available to software engineers in the field, they have been integrated into the SENSORIA Development Environment (SDE). The SDE is a modelling, simulation and analysis platform which supports the integrated evaluation of both functional and non-functional aspects of systems and services. Based on Eclipse, the SDE may also be integrated with various other tools available for this platform.

5.1 SDE Features

Being based the OSGi platform underlying Eclipse, the SDE is itself built in a service-oriented way. Upon installation, tools register themselves in the SDE core, thereby offering their functionality to all other installed tools, including orchestrators. Through various integrated tools, the SDE currently offers functionality which falls into these major categories:

- **Modelling functionality.** This includes graphical editors for familiar modelling languages such as UML, as supported by industry-standard tools such as the Rational Software Architect, which allow for intuitive modelling on a high level of abstraction. However, there are also text- and tree-based editors for process calculi.
- **Formal analysis functionality.** The SDE offers model checking and numerical solvers for stochastic methods based on process calculi code defined by the user or generated by model transformation.

The tools presented in this paper offer functionality which falls into the second category. In particular, the PEPA tools including the SRMC extensions [4] as well as LTSA and WS-Engineer have been made available as services in the SDE. They offer the follow functionality:

- **Simulators and Single-Step Navigators** which allow the user to investigate a model and look for modelling errors in the input and unexpected behaviour in execution related to liveness or reachability problems.
- **Model-Checkers** which check consistency between the model and an interesting property. In case of errors, a (graphical) violation trace is generated.
- **Steady-State and Transient Analysers** for performance analysis. These analysers provide simulation traces showing variation in the states of the model components over time, and utilisation charts, cumulative distribution plots and other visualisations which represent graphically the numerical results computed.

Through scripting, these analyses can be combined, as will be outlined in the next section.

5.2 Orchestrating Tools with the SDE

During software development and analysis of software systems, it is often desirable to run several analyses as a suite, perhaps passing input from one tool to the other, and gathering and presenting the output in a single place – in other words, orchestrating tools to perform as a whole.

To enable such orchestrations, the SDE offers the ability to compose installed tools by means of arbitrary orchestration mechanisms. In particular, we offer the ability to script such orchestrations by means of JavaScript. An orchestration may be written as a set of annotated JavaScript functions, thus in effect creating a new service orchestrating the referenced tools.

As an example, we consider the orchestration of the tools for the methods presented in the previous sections to perform analysis on the Automotive Accident

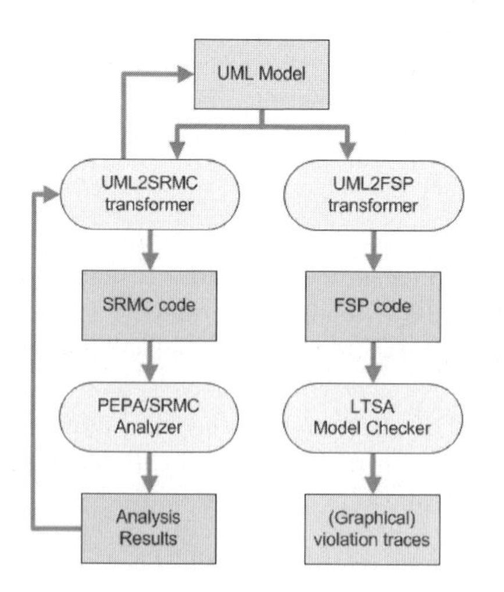


```
function checkUML(umlSource) {

        // transform to PEPA
        uml2pepa = sCore.findToolById("uml2pepa");
        pepaModel = uml2pepa.transform(umlSource);

        // perform analysis with PEPA tool
        pepa = sCore.findToolById("pepa");
        markovChain = pepa.getMarkovChain(pepaModel);
        distribution = pepa.getSteadyState(markovChain);
        throughput = pepa.getThroughput(markovChain);

        // back annotation
        uml2pepa.reflect(umlSource, distribution, throughput);

        // transform to LTSA FSP (input to WS-Engineer)
        uml2ltsa = sCore.findToolById("uml2ltsa");
        fspModel = uml2ltsa.uml2fsp(umlSource);

        // perform analysis with WS-Engineer
        wse = sCore.findToolById("wsengineer");
        result = wse.analyse(fspModel);

        if (result.hasErrors())
                return ltsa.mscFromLTSATrace(result.getTrace());

        return umlSource;

}
```

Fig. 5. Orchestration of the four tools together with JavaScript orchestration code

Assistance Service. As the orchestration is intended to be used by developers not too familiar with formal methods, we will start with a UML model and, at the end, provide back-annotated UML for showing results of the quantitative analysis with PEPA/SRMC as well as a (graphical) violation trace in case of errors during the qualitative analysis with LTSA.

The JavaScript code for this orchestration is concise (Fig. 5, right). In the beginning, we retrieve the tools by unique identifiers, invoke the functions involved, and finally return the combined output to the user. Within the SDE, a generic wizard handles this call such that users are able to select the input model graphically using a file open wizard, and also get the results opened in appropriate editors inside the Eclipse workbench or externally. Thus, it is easy for developers to employ such orchestrations as part of their work.

6 Related Work

We have considered performance aspects of the accident assistance service previously [9]. Our work in that earlier paper did not incorporate any model-checking aspects and dealt only with a simpler version of the accident assistance service without priority classifications.

Other authors have applied model-checking to analyse automotive safety services. In [10] the authors use high-level UML specification that makes use of domain-specific extensions The on-the-fly model checker UMC [11] is subsequently used to verify a set of correctness properties formalized in the action- and state-based temporal logic UCTL. Subsequently to the authors writing this paper the UMC model-checker has been made available as a service on the SDE, opening the possibility of conjoined use with the methods deployed in this paper.

In [12] an on-road assistance scenario is considered where the authors treat the process of obtaining assistance for a car subsequent to a breakdown (which is not necessarily a life-threatening accident). The authors formalise the problem in the COWS process calculus and give a formal treatment of fault and compensation handling.

Formal model-checking of service compositions has been undertaken mostly on their implementation, rather than the design of the service itself. For example, as a result of new standards to define and execute service compositions (such as the Web Services Business Process Execution Language), model-checking these has included translation to Finite State Machines, graphs and simulation models. We have already considered analysing these models in [13], whilst more recently in [14] using UML Deployment Models to analyse service compositions with deployment constraints. There has also been some similiar work on UML to Finite State Machines, particularly Activity Diagrams in [15]. These works also define a formal semantics for UML Activity Diagrams, but do so with a differing focus of aligning activities as two or more distributed processes and structure of roles within activities.

7 Conclusions

In this paper we presented a co-ordinated analysis of safety properties and the response-time profile of an automotive accident assistance scenario. We used the untimed process calculus FSP to express our model of the scenario and model-checked critical properties using the WS-Engineer tool in the SDE. We added rate information to convert the FSP model into one in the stochastically-timed process calculus PEPA. We next converted the FSP logical properties into stochastic probes on the PEPA model. We then used the PEPA Eclipse Plug-in to check that the PEPA model which was obtained by translation from FSP respected the stochastic probes which were obtained by translation from the FSP logic. The PEPA Eclipse Plug-in confirmed that this was the case. We then used the `ipclib` tool suite to perform many response-time evaluations leading to the quantitative results seen.

Our overarching goal in this work has been to make the outputs from the formal analysis tools open to inspection by users who are not experts in process calculi. To this end, reports are often returned in a graphical form such as a message sequence chart or a graph. Our next goal is to streamline the modelling process by allowing users to express their initial model in a language with widespread acceptance, such as UML. We have made some progress on this, and have a scripting infrastructure in place to allow such conversions to be performed automatically but more remains to be done in this area.

Acknowledgements. The authors are supported by the EU FET-IST Global Computing 2 project SENSORIA ("Software Engineering for Service-Oriented Overlay Computers" (IST-3-016004-IP-09)) and the EPSRC PerformDB project (EP/D054087/1). The ipc/Hydra tool chain has been developed in co-operation with Bradley, Knottenbelt and Dingle of Imperial College, London.

References

1. Magee, J., Kramer, J.: Concurrency - State Models and Java Programs, 2nd edn. John Wiley, Chichester (2006)
2. Magee, J., Kramer, J., Giannakopoulou, D.: Analysing the behaviour of distributed software architectures: a case study. In: 5th IEEE Workshop on Future Trends of Distributed Computing Systems, Tunisia (1997)
3. Hillston, J.: A Compositional Approach to Performance Modelling. Cambridge University Press, Cambridge (1996)
4. Tribastone, M.: The PEPA Plug-in Project. In: Harchol-Balter, M., Kwiatkowska, M., Telek, M. (eds.) Proceedings of the 4th International Conference on the Quantitative Evaluation of SysTems (QEST), pp. 53–54. IEEE Computer Society Press, Los Alamitos (2007)
5. Clark, A.: The ipclib PEPA Library. In: Harchol-Balter, M., Kwiatkowska, M., Telek, M. (eds.) Proceedings of the 4th International Conference on the Quantitative Evaluation of SysTems (QEST), pp. 55–56. IEEE Computer Society Press, Los Alamitos (2007)

6. Grassmann, W.: Transient solutions in Markovian queueing systems. Computers and Operations Research 4, 47–53 (1977)
7. Gross, D., Miller, D.: The randomization technique as a modelling tool and solution procedure for transient Markov processes. Operations Research 32, 343–361 (1984)
8. Argent-Katwala, A., Bradley, J., Dingle, N.: Expressing performance requirements using regular expressions to specify stochastic probes over process algebra models. In: Proceedings of the Fourth International Workshop on Software and Performance, Redwood Shores, California, USA, pp. 49–58. ACM Press, New York (2004)
9. Clark, A., Gilmore, S.: Evaluating quality of service for service level agreements. In: Brim, L., Leucker, M. (eds.) Proceedings of the 11th International Workshop on Formal Methods for Industrial Critical Systems, Bonn, Germany, pp. 172–185 (2006)
10. ter Beek, M.H., Gnesi, S., Koch, N., Mazzanti, F.: Formal verification of an automotive scenario in service-oriented computing. In: Proceedings of the 30th International Conference on Software Engineering (ICSE 2008), Leipzig, Germany, pp. 613–622. ACM Press, New York (2008)
11. UMC model checker (2008), http://fmt.isti.cnr.it/umc/
12. Lapadula, A., Pugliese, R., Tiezzi, F.: Specifying and analysing SOC applications with COWS. In: Degano, P., De Nicola, R., Meseguer, J. (eds.) Concurrency, Graphs and Models. LNCS, vol. 5065, pp. 701–720. Springer, Heidelberg (2008)
13. Foster, H., Uchitel, S., Magee, J., Kramer, J.: Model-based Verification of Web Service Compositions. In: Proc. of the 18th IEEE Int. Conference on Automated Software Engineering, pp. 152–161. IEEE Computer Society Press, Los Alamitos (2003)
14. Foster, H., Emmerich, W., Magee, J., Kramer, J., Rosenblum, D., Uchitel, S.: Model Checking Service Compositions under Resource Constraints. In: The European Software Engineering Conference and ACM SIGSOFT Symposium on the Foundations of Software Engineering (ESEC/FSE 2007) (2007)
15. Badica, C., Badica, A., Litoiu, V.: Role activity diagrams as finite state processes. In: Second International Symposium on Parallel and Distributed Computing (2003)

A Framework for Analyzing and Testing the Performance of Software Services

Antonia Bertolino[1], Guglielmo De Angelis[1], Antinisca Di Marco[2], Paola Inverardi[2], Antonino Sabetta[1], and Massimo Tivoli[2]

[1] ISTI-CNR, Pisa, Italy
{antonia.bertolino,guglielmo.deangelis, antonino.sabetta}@isti.cnr.it
[2] Università dell'Aquila
Dipartimento di Informatica, via Vetoio, L'Aquila, Italy
{adimarco,inverard,tivoli}@di.univaq.it

Abstract. Networks "Beyond the 3rd Generation" (B3G) are characterized by mobile and resource-limited devices that communicate through different kinds of network interfaces. Software services deployed in such networks shall adapt themselves according to possible execution contexts and requirement changes. At the same time, software services have to be competitive in terms of the Quality of Service (QoS) provided, or perceived by the end user.

The PLASTIC project proposes an integrated model-based solution to the development and maintenance of services deployable over B3G networks. Notably, the PLASTIC solution includes formal techniques that combine predictive and empirical evaluation of QoS-aware services.

In this paper we provide an overview of the PLASTIC approach to the assessment of QoS properties. Referring to a complex eHealth service, we first generate and analyze performance models to establish requirements for stand-alone services. Then we use an empirical technique to test the QoS of an orchestration of services even when the actual implementations of the orchestrated services are not available.

1 Introduction

The promise of the Service Oriented Architecture (SOA) paradigm is to enable the dynamic integration between applications belonging to different, globally distributed enterprises, connected through heterogeneous B3G (Beyond 3rd Generation) networks. B3G service-oriented applications, as well as communication networks and embedded systems [1], require to consider extra-functional characteristics as a critical aspect of software development [2].

The openness of the B3G environments naturally leads the SOA paradigm to pursue mechanisms for specifying the provided levels of *Quality of Service* (QoS) and for establishing *Service Level Agreements* (SLAs) on them.

In addition, context-awareness and adaptation are key features for B3G services that are to be deployed in different environments and on hardware platforms with different characteristics. Applications must be able to react to context changes and to adapt

T. Margaria and B. Steffen (Eds.): ISoLA 2008, CCIS 17, pp. 206–220, 2008.

themselves to continue to provide services within the levels of QoS that were previously agreed.

Let us consider the typical case of a service provider who is to offer a certain service (S^*) to their clients according to QoS levels ratified in form of SLAs. In order to do so, the service provider could orchestrate a number of other services ($S_1 \ldots S_n$), which may be either under their direct control, or may be provided by third parties. However, usually the life-cycle of service S^* is independent of the life-cycle of the aggregated services S_i. For example, the actual implementation of some S_i could not be used during the development or the testing of S^* because they are developed concurrently with S^* or because using them would imply additional costs or undesired side-effects (e.g., undesired writes on a DB). Furthermore, the binding between S^* and S_i is defined at run-time. Therefore, assessing the properties of a service out of the properties of its constituents is a complex task, which limits the possibility to define SLAs for the developed service.

Traditional approaches applied to the development, the deployment and the maintenance of SOAs do not provide adequate support to these needs in terms of languages, methods, and tools. Nevertheless, in recent years much research has been devoted to methodologies for QoS evaluation, including *predictive* and *empirical* techniques [3].

In this respect, the main target of the PLASTIC project [4] is an integrated model-based solution supporting both the development of services deployable over B3G networks, and the definition of their related SLAs. The key idea of the project is that the QoS characteristics of the network and of the devices should be visible at the level of services. The solution proposed in PLASTIC includes formal techniques for both predictive and empirical evaluation of QoS-aware services.

Predictive techniques span methodologies and tools that can be exploited by service providers to guide the design starting from the earliest phases of the service development. These methodologies can provide predictive assessments on whether the proposed software solution is likely to meet the expected performance goals.

Also, in order to construct an efficient and effective application, developers should test it in advance in all possible network scenarios. However, at development time it is difficult to anticipate all possible configurations in which a service will be executed. An empirical solution for the off-line validation consists in providing a testbed in which the behavior of the underlying platform and of the network can be simulated in a realistic way. In particular, starting from the performance requirements of the services orchestrated to form a composite service, it is possible to automatically validate the performance requirements of the resulting composite service hence making it possible to define appropriate SLAs for it.

In this paper we provide an overview of the PLASTIC approach to the assessment of QoS (performance) properties. We describe the predictive technique to assess the QoS properties for stand-alone services under development, and the empirical technique to test an orchestration of these services when their actual implementations are not yet available. The combination of such techniques is illustrated through the design and the implementation of an eHealth service that satisfies performance requirements.

The remainder of the paper is structured as follows: Sect. 2 introduces the PLASTIC development process; Sect. 3 describes how to model an eHealth Service within

PLASTIC; Sect. 4 and Sect. 5 respectively describe the predictive and empirical approaches used to assess the QoS of the modeled eHealth example. Conclusions and future work are given in Sect. 6.

2 Development Process

In order to address in a comprehensive way the challenges in the development of B3G applications, a new development process model has been devised [5] in the context of the PLASTIC project (see Figure 1).

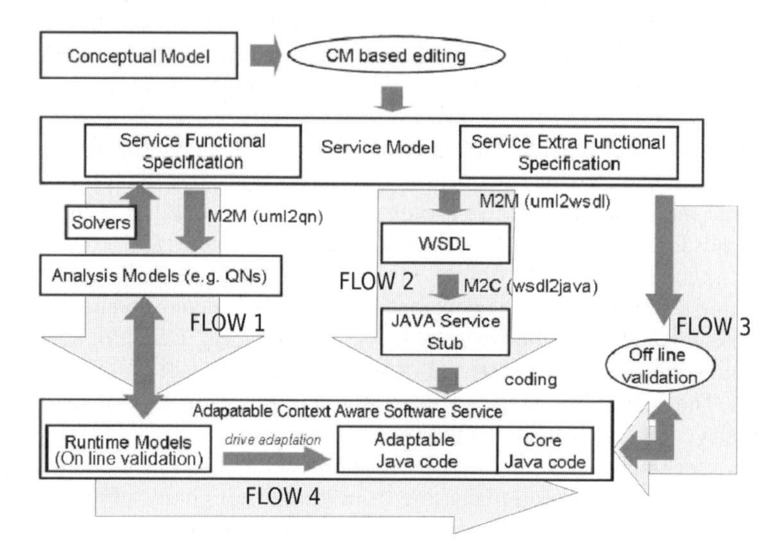

Fig. 1. The PLASTIC development process

All the activities in this process originate from the PLASTIC Conceptual Model [4,6], which provides a shared conceptual foundation for the construction of a Service Model. A Service Model involves the specification of both functional and extra-functional aspects[1] (see *Functional Service Specification* and the *Extra-Functional Service Specification* in Figure 1).

Based on such a service model, the PLASTIC process is structured into four main flows of activities (see Figure 1).

Flow 1 shows the generation of analysis models [8,9,10,11], which enable the *QoS analysis* of the service under development. This flow consists in the performance analysis process executed starting from the early phases of the software lifecycle. The aim of this activity is twofold: *(i)* to verify the service model with respect to QoS requirements, and (ii) to generate QoS models that the service can use later, at run time, in order to monitor the desired QoS and trigger adaptation when, e.g., the QoS level degrades due to possible context changes. The model-to-model (M2M) generation and

[1] We use the term *extra-functional*, as opposed to *non-functional*, following the terminology of [7].

the evaluation of the QoS models are automated and executed through a combination of tools (e.g. UML to Queueing Networks transformations engine – uml2qn), whereas the interpretation of results and feedback provision is still a human activity.

Flow 2 represents the automated generation of the skeleton implementation of the service from both M2M, and model to code (M2C) transformation engines. Specifically, this flow concerns the development of both the core code and the "adaptable" code of a service. The core code is the frozen unchanging portion of a self-adapting service (e.g., its required/provided interface). On the contrary, the adaptable code embodies a certain degree of variability making it capable to evolve (e.g., the logic of a service operation that depends on available resource constraints). This code portion is evolving in the sense that, based on contextual information, the variability can be solved with a set of alternatives (i.e., different ways of implementing a service) each of them suitable for a particular execution context. An alternative can be selected by exploiting the analysis models available at run-time.

Flow 3 on the right-hand side of the figure represents the *off-line* validation, which concerns validation at development time. In this phase services are tested in a simulated environment that reproduces functional and/or extra-functional run-time conditions.

Flow 4 concerns the *on-line* validation that consists in testing a service when it is ready for deployment and final usage. In particular, the PLASTIC validation framework supports validation during live usage stage, in which service behaviours are observed during real execution to reveal possible deviations from the expected behaviour. *On-line* validation can cover both functional and extra-functional properties.

All these four flows heavily rely on model-to-model and model-to-code automatic transformations.

The final result of this process is a deployable service code [12,13,14] that, through the support of the analysis models, has the capability to adapt to heterogeneous devices while still providing the previously agreed level of QoS. The service modeling is based on a UML profile that we have defined as a partial concrete implementation of the PLASTIC Conceptual Model.

3 Application Scenario: The eHealth Service

In this section we describe how to model an eHealth Service using the PLASTIC profile. In the following, we focus on the modelling views that contain useful information (i.e., stereotypes and tagged values) for performance analysis and testing methodologies [9,15] as we will introduce later.

We will focus on the specification of a Panic Button Scenario (PBS): the alarm is triggered when a patient's panic button is pressed in case of emergency. The eHealth Service (eHS) is in charge of handling the PBS work flow, response time and interaction among the different parties (i.e., patient, relatives or doctors) that are involved. Critical decisions, such as establishing the severity of the emergency, are taken by health specialists. An eHealth (sub-)service deployed on the patient's side monitors the vital parameters of the patient. When the patient presses the panic button, the system registers the patient's vital parameters into the eHealth database. At the same time, at the patient's side, a beeper is turned on to notify the patient that the alarm is being handled by the Service Manager. An internal counter is started to handle an "unknown" event. The eHealth database is scanned to search the most suitable supervisor to attend the patient, and a request is sent to the call center. Depending on the response of the call center, an alternative supervisor is requested or the event is assigned. The authorized supervisor is driven to set up the severity of the event by means of phone call. In some cases, the supervisor can also interact with the patient by means of cameras (e.g. the call fails, the patient cannot interact with the voice). Once the severity is set, an appropriate service must be composed to provide both, medical attention and response time according to the specific request, illness or accident.

The PLASTIC Service Model for eHS is composed of several views used to structure the UML design in packages. These views span from *requirement* view to *implementation* (i.e., component-oriented implementation) and *deployment* views, through the *service* view. Due to the lack of space, in the following we detail only the views that allow performance analysis and testing. For further details we refer to [4] where the service model is completely described with minor modifications.

Service View. The definition of the services that build up the PLASTIC application is given from both the structural and the behavioral perspectives. In particular, a Structural View is given by means of Service Description Diagrams (SDescrD) that show the *ServiceDescriptions* (e.g., ServiceManager, Patient Interactor Service) that may be combined on demand (*ServiceComposition* or *ServiceUsage* dependency from composite client to composite supplier services) and collaborate to provide the mobile eHealth Service, as illustrated in Figure 2.

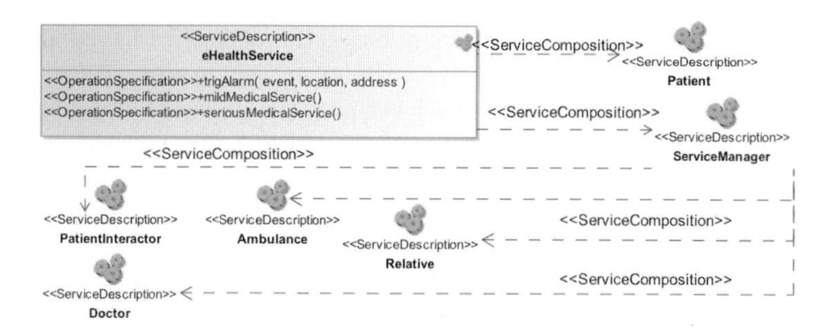

Fig. 2. The eHealth Service Description Diagram

The key concept is the *ServiceDescription*, which is the base structural unit for the description of PLASTIC applications at service level. It is a stereotype extending the UML2 Interface meta class. It provides some *OperationSpecifications* that, together, define what the user can request from its PLASTIC enabled device (e.g., doctors' or call center staff's laptop or PDA). For the sake of clarity, in Figure 2, we show the *OperationSpecifications* only for *eHealthService* and omit the ones for the other *ServiceDescriptions*.

Once all *ServiceDescriptions* have been specified, a number of business process descriptions have to be provided. Each of them describes the interactions (i.e., service orchestration) between the *ServiceDescriptions* identified in the SDescrD. These interactions model the behavior of a composite service operation. The composite service is the one obtained by composing the services in the SDescrD as specified by the set of business process descriptions. In particular, for each usage scenario of a composite service (e.g., the AlarmHandling use case of the PLASTIC eHealth service application), a Business Process Description Diagram (BPDD) has to be specified to describe the interactions (as Actions that refer to the already specified *OperationSpecification*) among the involved *ServiceDescriptions*.

As introduced above, one of the role played by the BPDD is describing the orchestration of different services. In this sense, the BPDD acts as the BPEL specification [16]. Nevertheless, BPDD also defines a well-structured set of annotations and tags that can be used in order to stereotype the elements described into the models. Differently from BPEL, such annotations can be instantiated at design time and then exploited for extra-functional analysis (e.g. performance or reliability analysis).

In Figure 3 the *ConversationSpecification* that realizes the behavior of the AlarmHandling use case is shown. At the bottom of Figure 3 there are two behaviors, Serious and Mild Medical services, that refer to two corresponding (sub-)BPDDs.

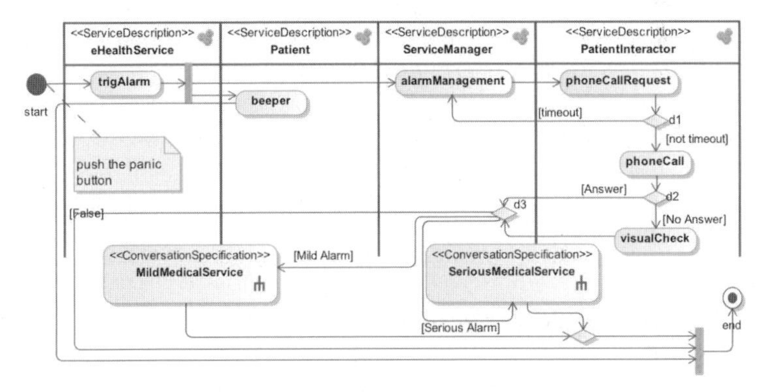

Fig. 3. The BPDD representing the service orchestration

Component View. In PLASTIC, a service can be implemented by one or more software components and, in turn, a software component can be used to implement one or more services. The PLASTIC Profile provides modeling constructs aimed at describing the component-based software architecture that implements a given service. Such description is organized in a Component View in turn distinguished into Structural View and Behavioral View.

Service Specification Diagrams (SSD) are introduced for defining the components implementing a *ServiceDescription*. Such diagrams are extensions of UML2 Class Diagrams and a number of new modeling constructs are provided, as detailed in Figure 4. The *ServiceRealization* stereotype is introduced to link *ServiceDescription* stereotyped interface and *ComponentSpecification* stereotyped components to describe how services are implemented in terms of software components. Moreover, by means of the SSD the designer can specify the contexts in which the service will be able to adapt. In particular *DeviceContextSpecification* elements are used to describe the possible devices (e.g., doctor's mobile or laptop). Each tag of such stereotypes refers to an available resource

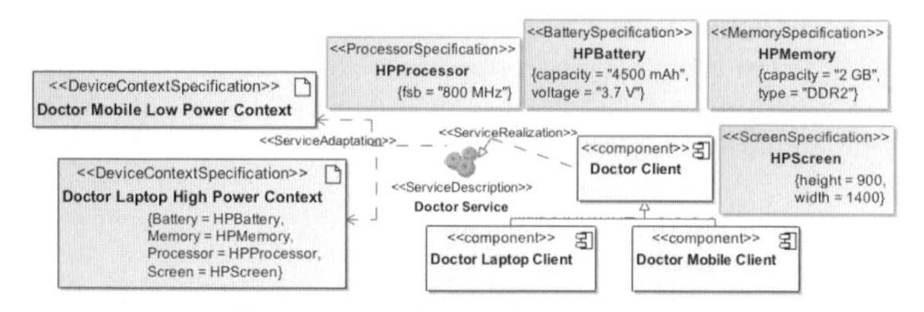

Fig. 4. The Service Specification Diagram for the Doctor Service

specification of the Resource package. The *DeviceContextSpecification* is then linked to adaptable services by means of *ServiceAdaptation* relationships.

Once the *ComponentSpecifications* of the components implementing the service being modeled have been given, their interactions have to be specified. The PLASTIC profile provides the designer with Elementary Service Dynamics Diagrams (ESDD) to model the interactions among the involved components (specified in the structural view by means of *ComponentSpecification* elements). Each ESDD is a suitably stereotyped UML sequence diagram annotated with information useful for performance analysis purposes, e.g., *latency*, *worst-case execution time*, *reliability (probability of failure)*, or *maximum number of simultaneous invocations* of a component operation.

Figure 5 shows the Elementary Service Dynamics Diagram, i.e., the interaction between component instances providing the AlarmManagement uml.Action defined in Figure 3. Additional information (i.e., stereotypes with their own tags) is introduced for the sake of performance analysis.

4 Performance Model Generation and Analysis

In PLASTIC a service can be either a composition of other services or a basic one implemented by an assembly of components. For a composite service, the performance analysis can be conducted both at the service composition level (abstract view of the service) and at the component level (detailed view of the service). For a stand-alone service, instead, the analysis can be only conducted at the component level.

The analysis process is composed by three steps: *(i)* generation of performance models from the Service Model through Model-to-Model transformation; *(ii)* evaluation of the generated performance models through solvers to obtain performance indices (e.g., response time); *(iii)* interpretation of the performance indices and possible production of feedbacks on the Service Model to improve the performance. The performance model that the service may use at run time is the last one generated during the analysis process.

In the following we first briefly recall what the SAP•one methodology [9] is (see Sect. 4.1) and then we show how to use it to analyze service performance at the component level. On the result of this analysis a provider might base the definition of the SLA of a service operation. In Sect. 4.2 we describe the analysis process of the alarmManagement operation of the ServiceManager service.

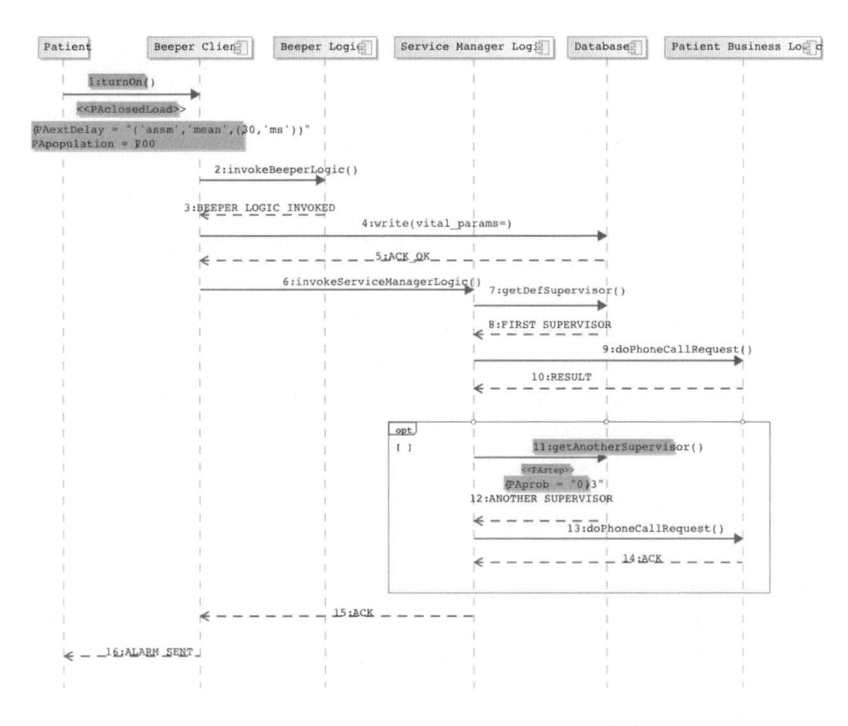

Fig. 5. The Elementary Service Dynamics Diagram for the Alarm Management

We used the approach several times to define the SLA concerning the mean response time for the operations of the services that have been composed (see Figure 3) into the *PLASTIC eHealth composite service* in order to implement the AlarmHandling functionality.

4.1 The Used Analysis Approach and Tools

The performance analysis is carried out by means of two tools: MOSQUITO and WEASEL.

MOSQUITO (MOdel driven conStruction of QUeuIng neTwOrks) [17] is a *model transformation* tool that generates Queuing Networks (QNs) starting from the PLASTIC Service Model. The model creation in MOSQUITO is based on two different methodologies: SAP•one [9] and Prima-UML [8]. In this work we use only the SAP•one methodology, hence details on the Prima-UML approach are omitted.

The SAP•one methodology, implemented by MOSQUITO, defines translation rules that map UML architectural patterns (identified in the Component View) into QN patterns. The target model is generated by composing the identified QN patterns suitably instantiated according to the particular scenario. To carry on the performance analysis, additional information generally missing in the software architecture description needs to be annotated on the software system model. Such data are strictly related to the performance aspects and are used both in the QN parameterization and in the workload definition. They are: the operational profile of the system that models the way the system will be used by the users (i.e. the distribution of frequencies of invocation of service's use cases by the service consumer); the workload entering the system as the estimated number of requests made to system components (modelled as service centers); the service demand of a request to the system components; the performance characterization of the system components represented by attributes such as service rate, scheduling policy, waiting queue capacity.

SAP•one associates each QN service center to a software component, and the QN customers represent the different requests that users make to the software system. The QN topology reflects the one of the Service Specification Diagram. Each ESDD is processed to lump the behavior that it represents into a class of jobs of the QN (i.e. a chain). In other words, a job traverses the network following the behavior described by the diagram it comes from. The workload of each chain is extracted from the annotations in the Use Case Diagram.

After that, by using MOSQUITO (hence following the SAP•one methodology), a QN model has been built, the WEASEL tool is used to solve the generated QN model in order to predict performance indexes. WEASEL [18] (a WEb service for Analyzing queueing networkS with multiplE soLvers) offers a Web Service that solves QN models specified in PMIF [19] format, using several off-the-shelf QN solvers (e.g., MVA-QFP [20] and SHARPE [21]). The performance measures are presented to the client as a text file in the original output format of the selected tool.

4.2 Performance Analysis of the alarmManagement

The alarmManagement action in Figure 3 must satisfy the following performance requirement[2]: *the average response time of alarmManagement must not exceed 10 seconds when the triggered alarms in the system are less than 100.*

To perform the analysis, we have used the SAP•one methodology. This means that the service has been considered at the component level where the alarmManagement action is implemented by components' interactions as specified in the Component View of the service model [4].

We generated the performance model (at the software architecture level) of the alarmManagement design by means of MOSQUITO using the SAP•one approach.

The obtained queuing network has been then evaluated via WEASEL where the selected solution technique was Exact MVA implemented in the MVA Queuing Formalism Parser [20].

For the *FirstDesign*, we analyze the mean response time as the number of alarm requests arriving to the system grows from 50 to 300. The proposed design did not satisfy the requirement. The system response time reaches 10 seconds with only 65 alarms. Moreover, the analysis highlighted that a database component is the bottleneck of this system design, hence to improve the system response time we should lighten the load offered to the database.

We produced the second design alternative by modifying the alarmManagement design as follows. In the dynamics model of Figure 5, the *Service Manager Logic* accesses the database twice to retrieve information on the two supervisors of the patient in trouble. This can be optimized by introducing in the database interface a new method that

[2] This requirement has been agreed by the customer together with the domain experts.

retrieves the information of all the supervisors of the patient. The call of this method substitutes the first call of the method used to get information about only one single supervisor, while the second call can be removed. In this way we reduce the load to the database.

On this design alternative, i.e., *SecondDesign*, we repeated the analysis and the requirement was satisfied since for the *alarmManagement* and the *visualCheck* operations we predicted a mean response time respectively equal to $7.25s$ and to $4.83s$ when the number of triggered alarms is 100. On the other hand, the mean system response time was 10 seconds when the *alarmManagement* operation handles 126 concurrent alarms.

5 Performance Testing

Following the design and analysis stages described above, the subsequent step in developing B3G services consists in early testing them within a simulated environment, which we referred to in Figure 1 as *off-line* validation. When developing a service orchestration, the composition of the external services must be tested both to validate that the implementation respects the functional contracts in place, and to evaluate if it actually meets the expected quality levels. Clearly the QoS offered by a composition not only depends on its implementation, but is also affected by the quality levels of the composed services. Furthermore, when the interaction happens through complex middlewares, the application of analytical techniques such as the one described above to derive the exposed extra-functional properties is not always feasible, since the modeling of such infrastructures is particularly difficult and error prone. This task becomes even harder when the analytical models of the platform have to be defined from scratch.

Testers may rely on empirical approaches when all the composed services are available, and can be also arbitrarily accessed at development time for testing purposes. However, in general this solution is applicable only in few lucky cases. In fact, commonly at least some of the external services are either not available at all (for instance simply not implemented, yet), or their usage comes along with unwanted side-effects (for instance utilization fees or database modifications). To circumvent this problem, in PLASTIC we provide support to the automatic derivation of testbeds to be used in the place of the real composed service.

In the following we present the proposed approach for the empirical evaluation of QoS properties of a composite B3G service and its application to the eHealth example described in Sect. 3. The approach relies on the specification of reasonable agreements on the extra-functional properties.

In a global view of the PLASTIC process, the performance bounds expected at design time, as derived by the analytic approach presented in Sect. 4.2, are exploited to infer the agreements used for testing the implementation of the orchestration described in Figure 3.

5.1 Puppet

As discussed in Sect. 4, predictive approaches are crucial during the design and the development of a software system, to shape the quality of the final product [22]. But increasingly modern applications are deployed over complex platforms (i.e., the middleware), which introduce many factors influencing the QoS and not always easy to model in advance. In such cases, empirical approaches, i.e., evaluating the QoS via runtime measurement, could help smoothing platform-dependent noise. However, such approaches require the development of expensive and time consuming prototypes [23], on which representative benchmarks of the system in operation can be run.

For example, testers may be interested in assessing that a specific service implementation can afford the required level of QoS (e.g., latency and reliability) when playing one of the roles in a specified choreography or when used in composition with other services (orchestration).

As we discussed in [15], there is large room for the adoption of empirical approaches when model-based *code-factories* can be used to automatically generate a running prototype from a given specification. In particular, as we argued in [15,24,25], given the high availability of standardized computer processable information, Web Services (WSs) and related technologies (e.g. WSDL, WS-BPEL, WS-CDL, WS-Agreement, WSLA) yield very promising opportunities for the application of empirical approaches to QoS evaluation.

In this direction, PUPPET (Pick UP Performance Evaluation Testbed) [15] is a *code-factory* which realizes the automatic derivation of testbeds for evaluating the desired QoS characteristics for a service under development, before it is deployed.

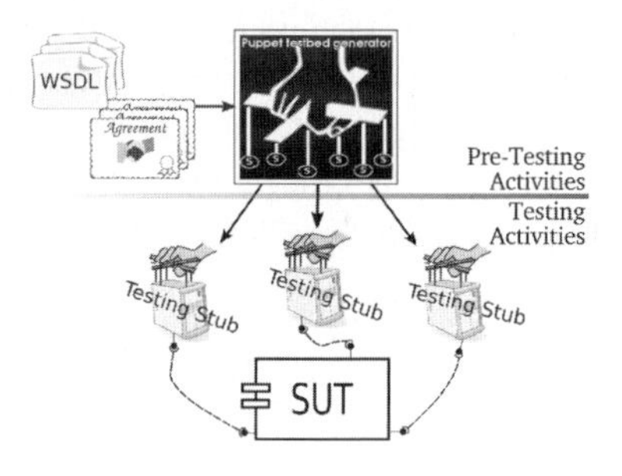

Fig. 6. PUPPET: The approach

PUPPET relies on the availability of the QoS specification of both the service under evaluation and the interacting services. Such assumption is in line with the increasing adoption of formal contracts to establish the mutual obligations among the involved parties and the guaranteed QoS parameters, which is referred to as the SLA for the WSs. For example, Figure 6 depicts the case when 3 different stubs are generated during pre-testing activities. Each stub is derived from a model describing the public interface of the remote services (WSDL), and the contracted SLA. During the testing activities, testers can bind the resulting stubs to the Service Under Test (SUT) using them as a testbed.

In [24], PUPPET was extended with a module able to include into the stubs also the emulation of the supposed functional behavior. In this case, the functional behavior of a service is described by means of the *Symbolic Transition System* (STS) models as described in [26]. Specifically, for each received invocation, the service stub can query the STS model and choose one of the possible functionally correct results, sending it back to answer the service client request.

Also, possible dynamic transformation of the network topology and, consequently, of the configuration of the environment must be taken into account when developing a networked service, especially in the off-line testing phase. In B3G, the most typical context change is due to the movement of nodes hosting services. Correspondingly, latest work extends PUPPET adding a module that plugs into the generated stubs the mobility emulation of the node hosting the service. The detailed description of this module is given in [25].

5.2 Performance Testing of the eHealth Service

Let us consider again the BPDD in Figure 3, and let us assume that the orchestration it describes is going to be implemented in parallel with the development of the four services it composes (i.e. eHealthService, Patient, ServiceManager, PatientInteractor). The problem that we want to solve here is how to test the performance of the orchestrated service even when just *models* of the composed services are available but the actual implementations are not (or we do not want to access to avoid undesired side-effects).

A possible solution to this problem is to use PUPPET to build stubs of the orchestrated services. As mentioned in Sect. 5, PUPPET ensures by construction that the extra-functional behavior exhibited by each generated stub conforms to the guaranteed levels expressed in a SLA.

```
1   ...
2   <wsag:GuaranteeTerm ... wsag:Obligated="
        ServiceProvider">
3    <wsag:ServiceScope wsag:ServiceName="
         ServiceManager">
4     <puppetScope:PuppetScope>
5      <puppetScope:Method>
6       <NameMethod>alarmManagement</
           NameMethod>
7      </puppetScope:Method>
8     </puppetScope:PuppetScope>
9    </wsag:ServiceScope>
10   ...
11   <wsag:ServiceLevelObjective>
12    <puppetSLO:PuppetSLO>
13     <puppetSLO:Latency>
14      <value>14500</value>
15      ...
16     </puppetSLO:Latency>
17    </puppetSLO:PuppetSLO>
18   </wsag:ServiceLevelObjective>
19  ...
```

–A–

```
1   ...
2   public class ServiceManagerSoapBindingImpl {
3   ...
4    public void alarmManagement ( ...
5   ...
6     Density D = new Density();
7     Double sleepValue = D.gaussian(14500-(
          System.currentTimeMillis()-
          cOmMoNinvocationTime));
8     if (sleepValue >= 0)
9      try {
10      Thread.sleep(sleepValue.longValue());
11     } catch (InterruptedException e) {}
12  ...
```

–B–

Fig. 7. `alarmManagement` : SLA and Generated Code into the Service Stub

Figure 7.A shows an example on how the QoS indexes obtained by the performance analysis prediction can be instantiated in an SLA. Specifically, `line 2` asserts that the term of the SLA is a service-side constraint that is applicable to the service ServiceManager (`line 3`) on the operation `alarmManagement` (`line 6`). Figure 7.B depicts the portion of the stub that PUPPET automatically generates with respects to the given SLA. The operational semantic we give in PUPPET to emulate the clauses on latency is defined in terms of a random and normally distributed sleeping period drawn in the range between 0 and the maximum expected time by the operation [15,24]. In this example, the stub emulates a service guaranteeing that its mean elapsed time conforms to the index defined in Sect. 4. Thus in Figure 7.A at `line 14` we imposed the max elapsed time as $14500ms$ which means emulating the mean response time in $7250ms$.

Note that in the stubs either the combined emulation of different QoS properties (e.g. latency with reliability), or the emulation of other aspects of the service (e.g. the functionality or the mobility) may affect the emulation of the latency clause. PUPPET solves these issues reducing at run-time the maximum latency time with the time elapsed emulating other aspects. Such delta is calculated as the difference between the timestamp executing instructions at `line 7` of Figure 7.B and the timestamp marked when the operation is called.

The goal of the approach presented here is limited to evaluating technical constraints that form the basis on which a SLA can be defined. However, in a more general setting, a SLA is more than just (a set of) technical constraints. Indeed, a number of non-technical aspects (legal clauses, penalties for violations, business strategies) play an important role in making contractually-agreed service provision a viable solution. A more general discussion of the problems related to establishing and enforcing a SLA as a *legal contract* is beyond the scope of this work, but can be found in [27].

6 Conclusion

B3G networks are characterized by a distributed, heterogeneous and mutable nature, which poses difficult problems in developing service-oriented systems. An additional challenge arises when such systems must meet precise QoS requirements.

Several European research projects, such as ASG [28], COMET [29], MADAM [30], MUSIC [31], SeCSE [32], recognized that it is certainly no longer possible to propose solutions without adequate specification and validation of QoS features, especially in heterogeneous and networked services contexts.

In particular, the SeCSE project exploits service specifications describing semantics and QoS information in order to guide the test phase, proposing tools for the automatic generation and execution of test cases. The exploitation of QoS-awareness in the context of highly dynamic systems is also a key feature of the MADAM project. The objectives of the project include the development of an adaptation theory and a set of reusable adaptation strategies and mechanisms to be enacted at run-time. Context monitoring is used as the basis for decision making about adaptation, which is managed to a large extent by generic middleware components.

The PLASTIC project tackled these challenges by defining a platform and introducing a comprehensive process for developing lightweight and QoS-aware services. This process spans the design, the predictive analysis and the validation of services, taking into account both functional and extra-functional characteristics.

With respect to the problem of the assessment of QoS properties, this paper shows how to fruitfully combine predictive and analytical approaches with empirical ones. In particular, it described how to link the results of those phases that are typical of the earliest stages of the service development process (i.e. performance model generation and analysis) with the input of those phases that characterized the latest parts of the development process (i.e. testing techniques and testing support tools).

It is important to remark that such integration was possible because all the common entities, the relations among the entities, as well as the artifacts and the extra-functional properties they model were formally defined and structured in the PLASTIC conceptual model [4,6]. In such a way it is ensured that the information captured and defined starting from the early phases of the software lifecycle can be referred and reused at each stage of the software development.

The application of the described approaches to a real world case study will further permit to refine and validate the whole framework. Specifically, in collaboration with the industrial partners of the PLASTIC project, we are applying the PLASTIC development process on wider and more complex case studies.

Acknowledgements. The authors wish to thank Andrea Polini for his contribution to the research on PUPPET, and Luca Berardinelli for his contribution in modeling the eHealth example. This work was supported in part by the PLASTIC Project (EU FP6 STREP n. 26955) and in part by the TAS^3 Project (EU FP7 CP n. 216287).

References

1. Bertolino, A., Bonivento, A., De Angelis, G., Sangiovanni Vincentelli, A.: Modeling and Early Performance Estimation for Network Processor Applications. In: Proc. of 9th MoDELS. Springer, Heidelberg (2006)
2. Ludwig, H.: WS-Agreement Concepts and Use – Agreement-Based Service-Oriented Architectures. Technical report, IBM (2006)
3. Woodside, M., Franks, G., Petriu, D.: The future of software performance engineering. In: FOSE 2007: 2007 Future of Software Engineering, pp. 171–187. IEEE Computer Society Press, Los Alamitos (2007)
4. PLASTIC Project: (EU FP6 STREP n. 26955), `http://www.ist-plastic.org`
5. Autili, M., Berardinelli, L., Cortellessa, V., Di Marco, A., Di Ruscio, D., Inverardi, P., Tivoli, M.: A development process for self-adapting service oriented applications. In: Krämer, B.J., Lin, K.-J., Narasimhan, P. (eds.) ICSOC 2007. LNCS, vol. 4749, pp. 442–448. Springer, Heidelberg (2007)
6. Autili, M., Cortellessa, V., Di Marco, A., Inverardi, P.: A conceptual model for adaptable context-aware services. In: WS-MaTe 2006 (2006)
7. Bass, L., Clements, P., Kazman, R.: Quality Attributes. In: Software Architecture in Practice, ch. 4, pp. 75–91. Addison-Wesley, Reading (1998)
8. Cortellessa, V., Mirandola, R.: PRIMA-UML: a Performance Validation Incremental Methodology on Early UML Diagrams. Science of Computer Programming 44(1), 101–129 (2002)
9. Di Marco, A.: Model-based Performance Analysis of Software Architectures. PhD thesis, University of L'Aquila (2005)
10. Di Marco, A., Mascolo, C.: Performance Analysis and Prediction of Physically Mobile Systems. In: ACM WOSP, Buenos Aires (Argentina) (2007)
11. Cortellessa, V., Singh, H., Cukic, B.: Early reliability assessment of UML based software models. In: ACM WOSP, pp. 302–309 (2002)

12. Inverardi, P., Mancinelli, F., Nesi, M.: A declarative framework for adaptable applications in heterogeneous environments. In: ACM SAC (2004)
13. SEA Group: (The Chameleon Project), http://www.di.univaq.it/chameleon/
14. Autili, M., Di Benedetto, P., Inverardi, P., Mancinelli, F.: A resource-oriented static analysis approach to adaptable Java applications. In: Proc. of CORCS 2008 (IEEE/COMPSAC 2008). IEEE Computer Society Press, Los Alamitos (to appear, 2008)
15. Bertolino, A., De Angelis, G., Polini, A.: A QoS Test-bed Generator for Web Services. In: Baresi, L., Fraternali, P., Houben, G.-J. (eds.) ICWE 2007. LNCS, vol. 4607, pp. 17–31. Springer, Heidelberg (2007)
16. IBM: BPEL4WS, Business Process Execution Language for Web Services, v.1.1 (2003)
17. MOSQUITO: (User manual), http://sealabtools.di.univaq.it/SeaLab/MosquitoHome.html
18. WEASEL: (User manual), http://sealabtools.di.univaq.it/SeaLab/Weasel/
19. Smith, C.U., Llado, C.M.: Performance model interchange format (pmif 2.0): XML definition and implementation. In: QEST 2004 Proceedings, pp. 38–47. IEEE Computer Society Press, Los Alamitos (2004)
20. Chereddi, C.: Mean Value Analysis for Closed, Separable, Multi Class Queueing Networks with Single Server & Delay Queues (2006)
21. Sahner, R.A., Trivedi, K.S.: SHARPE: Symbolic Hierarchical Automated Reliability and Performance Evaluator, Introduction and Guide for Users (2002)
22. Smith, C., Williams, L.: Performance Solutions: A practical Guide To Creating Responsive, Scalable Software. Addison Wesley, Reading (2001)
23. Liu, Y., Gorton, I.: Accuracy of Performance Prediction for EJB Applications: A Statistical Analysis. In: Gschwind, T., Mascolo, C. (eds.) SEM 2004. LNCS, vol. 3437, pp. 185–198. Springer, Heidelberg (2005)
24. Bertolino, A., De Angelis, G., Frantzen, L., Polini, A.: Model-based Generation of Testbeds for Web Services. In: Suzuki, K., Higashino, T., Hasegawa, T., Ulrich, A. (eds.) TestCom/-FATES 2008. LNCS, vol. 5047, pp. 266–282. Springer, Heidelberg (2008)
25. Bertolino, A., De Angelis, G., Lonetti, F., Sabetta, A.: Let The Puppets Move! Automated Testbed Generation for Service-oriented Mobile Applications. In: Proc. of the 34th €μ-SEAA, Parma, Italy. IEEE Computer Society Press, Los Alamitos (to appear, 2008)
26. Frantzen, L., Tretmans, J., Willemse, T.A.C.: A Symbolic Framework for Model-Based Testing. In: Havelund, K., Núñez, M., Roşu, G., Wolff, B. (eds.) FATES 2006 and RV 2006. LNCS, vol. 4262, pp. 40–54. Springer, Heidelberg (2006)
27. Skene, J., Skene, A., Crampton, J., Emmerich, W.: The Monitorability of Service-Level Agreements for Application-Service Provision. In: Proc. of WOSP 2007, pp. 3–14 (2007)
28. ASG: (EU IST FP6), http://asg-platform.org/
29. COMET: (EU IST FP6), https://www.comet-consortium.org/
30. MADAM: (EU IST FP6), http://www.ist-madam.org
31. MUSIC: (EU IST FP6), http://www.ist-music.eu/
32. SeCSE: (EU IST FP6), http://secse.eng.it

A Framework for Contract-Policy Matching Based on Symbolic Simulations for Securing Mobile Device Application *

Paolo Greci[1], Fabio Martinelli[1], and Ilaria Matteucci[1,2]

[1] IIT CNR, Pisa, via Moruzzi, 1 - 56125 Pisa, Italy
[2] CREATE-NET, Trento, Italy
fabio.martinelli@iit.cnr.it, ilaria.matteucci@iit.cnr.it

Abstract. There is a growing interest on programming models based on the notion of contract. In particular, in the security realm one could imagine the situation where either downloaded code or software service exposes their security-relevant behavior in a contract (that must to be fulfilled). Assuming to have already a mechanism to ensure that the program/service adheres to the contract, it just remains to check that the contract matches with the user security policy. We refer to this testing procedure as *contract-policy matching*.

We specialize this framework in the ambit of mobile devices. The contract and the user policy are formally expressed by using (symbolic) transition systems.

Then, *contract-policy matching* amounts to simulation checking, *i.e.*, a contract transition system is simulated by a policy one. This means that we check if for each transition corresponding to a certain security action of the contract (and so possibly performed by the program), the policy system has a similar transition and resulting contract system is again simulated by the resulting policy one.

Showing some running examples, we eventually present an implementation of simulation-matching algorithm, developed in J2ME and suitable to run also on smart phones.

Keywords: Contract-policy matching, simulation relation, symbolic transition systems, mobile application.

1 Introduction

Over the last few years the amount of users that download from the net programs or applications (*e.g.*, Java Midlets) for smart phones and other mobile devices has been growing. However, in many cases, either the identity of developers of the applications is unknown to the user or those developers could not be trusted. Thus, the execution of these programs is possibly unsafe. For this reason, the study of mechanisms and techniques that permit to safely execute programs has been increased.

In this paper we exploit the security *contract* concept that lies at the core of the approach for securing mobile services developed in the S3MS project ([1]). A *contract*

* Work partially supported by EU project "Software Engineering for Service-Oriented Overlay Computers"(SENSORIA), Artist2 "Network of Excellence on Embedded Systems Design" and "Secure Software and Services for Mobile Systems" (S3MS).

T. Margaria and B. Steffen (Eds.): ISoLA 2008, CCIS 17, pp. 221–236, 2008.

(see [2]) is a specification of the intended security-relevant behavior of the program by the producer. The use of contracts allows the program developer to declare which are the security-relevant actions the program might perform at run-time. Then, users that plan to download and execute such programs might just check that 1) the program adheres to the contract 2) the contract matches their local security *policy*, *i.e.*, a policy that specifies the set of acceptable executions (*e.g.*, see [3,4]) w.r.t. the local user.

Both steps are necessary to ensure safe program execution. For the first point, program-contract compliance, one could use static verification techniques and, in the following, we assume this can be solved (*e.g.*, see [1] for an overview of the possible techniques). When the code is available, as in the case of mobile applications, these techniques allow the user to directly inspect the code-contract compliance. Clearly, in service oriented architectures, where the code implementing the service is usually not available the phase of code-contract cannot be directly checked by the service user and different tools must be applied as run-time monitoring or reputation mechanisms.

As a whole, this contract-based framework enables very interesting business models that empower users with full control on the applications executed on their devices. The user may decide whether to execute an application even if the program developer is not trusted, provided that the code-contract-policy compliance phases are satisfied. Indeed, in this case the application is harmless (actually will adhere to the security policy).

If one restricts the attention to the *contract-policy matching* phase, than one might note that the same idea also works when dealing with service oriented architectures. Indeed services might declare the usage of the security-sensible resources on performing a given service. For instance, an user could choose a service only of this service declares not to disclose any private information acquired during service execution (or to communicate this information only to a specific partner).

In this paper we mainly focus on the second phase of the framework, *i.e.*, *contract-policy matching* phase, by presenting an appropriate theory and implementation for mobile devices.

Both the contract and the policy specification are given in ConSpec language (see [5]) strongly inspired by the policy specification language PSLang which was developed by Erlingsson and Schneider in [6] for runtime monitoring. We also use the notion of *symbolic transition systems* in order to deal with infinite state systems.

The basic idea underlying *contract-policy matching* is that any sequence of security relevant actions allowed by the contract is also allowed by the policy. Trace inclusion is thus a suitable candidate for the contract-policy matching. However, for generic contract and policy, the complexity is PSPACE complete, even for finite state systems.

Our main idea is to use the simulation relation (see [7]) as a formal compliance relation between contracts and policies. This relation can be efficiently checked on finite state systems. In addition, there exists a semi-decision procedure for checking similarity between symbolic transition systems. We have already studied in [4,8] a simulation-based approach for the guarantee that a system results secure by describing mechanisms for enforcing security property at run-time. Here we present a framework for using simulation relation for doing contract-policy matching. In particular, contract transition system is simulated by a policy one, if, for each transition corresponding to a certain security action of the contract (and so possibly performed by the program), the policy has a similar transition and resulting contract system is yet simulated by the resulting policy one.

When the algorithm reports that the contract is simulated by the policy then one is sure that the contract matches the policy and so the program can be safely executed on the device.

We have also implemented this algorithm for the J2ME Platform. The tool takes as input a contract and a policy specified in ConSpec language. Then, using a parser, we translate the ConSpec specification into symbolic transition systems syntax and so we obtain two objects of type `Policy`. Once we have the two symbolic systems, we check if they are similar. Moreover, our implementation is developed in order to run also on smart-phones, PDAs and other devices with a limited computation and storage resources.

This document is organized as follows: Section 2 recalls some notion about the ConSpec language and symbolic transition system. Section 3 presents the contract-policy matching algorithm and Section 4 describes our developed tool. Section 5 shows as example of how the presented algorithm, and consequently our tool, works and Section 6 concludes the paper.

2 Background

In this section we recall some notions about the ConSpec language for contract and policy specification (see [5]) and symbolic transition systems (see [9,10]), that are useful for the rest of the paper.

2.1 Contracts, Policies and Their Specification Language ConSpec

Firstly, according to [11], we give the following definition of a contract and a policy.

Definition 1. *A* contract *is a formal complete and correct specification of the behavior of the application for what concerns relevant security actions (* e.g., *Virtual Machine API call, Operating System Calls). It defines a subset of the traces of all possible security actions.*

For instance, a contract could be composed by the following list of relevant security actions:

- The application does not send MMS messages
- The application only sends messages to determined numbers
- The application sends only text (or binary) messages

Definition 2. *A* policy *is a formal complete specification of the acceptable behavior of applications to be executed on the platform for what concerns relevant security actions (*e.g., *Virtual Machine API call, Operating System Calls). It defines a subset of the traces of all possible security actions.*

For example, a policy could contain the following relevant security actions:

- The application only receives SMS messages on a specific port
- The application does not use Bluetooth or IrDA connections
- The application doesn't use local socket connections (like 127.0.0.1 or localhost)

Both the contract and the policy are syntactically described by exploiting the ConSpec language that is introduced in [5,12] for contract and policy specification. ConSpec formal specification defines the contract that is guaranteed by the application and the policy that is desired/enforced by the platform (see Figure 1 for the syntax).

The ConSpec language is strongly inspired by the policy specification language PSLang which was developed by Erlingsson and Schneider in [6] for runtime monitoring. However, even if ConSpec is a more restricted language than PSLang, it is expressive enough to write policies on multiple executions of the same application, and on executions of all applications of a system. In addition to policies on a single execution of the application and of a certain class object lifetime according to the *scope* of the policy.

A ConSpec policy, after the declaration of the integer range (MAXINT) and string length (MAXLEN) that are used, specified its *scope* definition that reflects at which scope the specified contract will be applied. If the SCOPE is `Object` than only object are modified. If the requirements are on a single run of the application, then we talk about a SCOPE `Session` and if the policy talks about multiple runs of the same application the SCOPE is `Multisession`. Moreover there is also a `Global` scope for monitoring all the applications on a system.

The tag `RULEID` identifies the *area* of the contract (which security-relevant actions the policy concerns, for example "files" or "connections").

After the specification of the scope, the policies in ConSpec are composed of the *declaration of the security state* followed by *event clauses* that state the conditions for the effect of security relevant actions.

```
SCOPE <Object ClassName | Session | MultiSession> [RuleID] [VersionID]

SECURITY STATE
    <bool | int | string> VarName1 = <DefaultValue1>
        ...
    <bool | int | string> VarNameN = <DefaultValueN>

<BEFORE | AFTER> EVENT MethodSignature_1 PERFORM
    condition_1 -> update_1
            ...
    <condition_M1> -> update_M1
                ...
<BEFORE | AFTER > EVENT MethodSignature_K PERFORM
    condition_1 -> update_1
            ...
    <condition_MK> -> update_MK
```

Fig. 1. Syntax of ConSpec

Because the primitive types of the language are `int`, `boolean` and `string`, the *state declaration* is a series of variables declarations of the primitive types.

An *event clause* is composed by a *security relevant action* (the event) and a *event modifier* which states when update to the state is performed w.r.t. the execution of the event.

Events are method invocations, *e.g.*, system calls or methods provided by an API. Event clauses define the allowed transitions of the ConSpec automaton. The security relevant action is fully specified by the *signature* which consists of the name of the method belongs and the types of its arguments. For each security relevant action, there exists at most one event clause in ConSpec.

The modifier is followed by a sequence of guard-update block pairs. The available modifiers are BEFORE and AFTER which indicate when the guards must be evaluated and the update block must be executed (or program aborted in case no guard applies) before or after the event.

The update specifies how a state is updated for the security relevant action while the guard select the states, which the particular update will apply, as a subset of states. The guards are consider from the top to the bottom and, if none of them are matched there is no transition for that command from the current state. For the sake of simplicity, we here assume that all the guards are mutually disjointed, so that the order of evaluation does not matter.

The event specification of ConSpec also contains names to formal arguments. The scope of these identifiers is the sequence of guard and update blocks that follow. The guard is a side-effect free boolean expression which can mention only the set argument values and the security state. Guards may also use decidable predicates on variables, *e.g.*, "url.startsWith("sms://")" in Example 1 that ensures the parameter *url* is a string that starts with "sms://".

The update is specified using a simple imperative language. The update block begins with local variable declarations. The scope of these variables is limited to the current block. The update block consists of a list of assignments. The variables that can occur on the left hand of assignments are restricted to local variables and security state variables. As requirement we have that there exists at least one statement in each update block (at least `skip`). In this way we consider both cases: in the case the value of a local variable is not changed then the statement `skip` is used, on the contrary, if the statement is different to `skip`, the variable's value is update.

Example 1. Let us specify the policy: "The maximum number of SMSs that can be sent in a session is 3" A ConSpec specification of this policy is presented at Figure 2.

Example 2. Let us consider the following policy: "Only network connections with `www.google.it` and `www.yahoo.it` can be opened, but after a connection with `www.yahoo.it` no connection with `www.google.it` can be opened". The ConSpec specification for this policy is in Figure 3. The ConSpec specification of the considered policy said that, initially the security state is characterized by a state variables `yahoo` set to false. Before the execution of the action `open`, there is a check: If the URL's name starts with `http://www.google.it` and the `yahoo` boolean variable is set to false then once is allowed to open the URL without doing other actions (url.startsWith("http://www.google.it") && (!yahoo) -> skip). On the other hand, if

```
SCOPE Session *

SECURITY STATE
    int smsno = 0

BEFORE javax.io.microedition.Connector.open(String url) PERFORM
    url.startsWith("sms://") -> skip

BEFORE javax.wireless.messaging.MessageConnection.send(String msg)PERFORM
    (smsno <3) ->smsno=smsno+1
```

Fig. 2. A ConSpec specification of the policy from Example 1

```
SCOPE Session *

SECURITY STATE
    boolean yahoo = false

BEFORE javax.io.microedition.Connector.open(String url) PERFORM
    url.startsWith("http://www.google.it") && (!yahoo) -> skip
    url.startsWith(" http://www.yahoo.it") -> yahoo = true
```

Fig. 3. A ConSpec specification of the policy from Example 2

the URL's name starts with `http://www.yahoo.it`, the URL is open and the flag `yahoo` is set to true (url.startsWith(" http://www.yahoo.it") -> yahoo = true).

It is possible to note that one clause exclude the other.

2.2 Symbolic Transition System

We recall here the process algebra language introduced in [9,10] and its formal semantics in terms of symbolic transition systems that we will use later to give formal semantics to ConSpec language.

The language consists of a syntactic category $DExp$ of data expressions, ranged over by e, e' etc. This includes, at least, an infinite set Val of values, ranged over by v, v' etc. and a countably infinite set of variables Var of data variables, ranged over by x, y etc. which is disjointed from Val. There is also a syntactic category $BExp$ of boolean expressions, ranged over by b, b', etc. with the usual set of boolean operators (*true, false*, $\wedge$, $\vee$ and $\rightarrow$). Furthermore, for every pair of data expressions e, e' we assume that $e = e'$ is a boolean expression. Moreover, each data expression e and each boolean expression b has associated to it a set of free data variables, $fv(e)$ and $fv(b)$ respectively, and that only data variables can occur free in these expressions.

We need the notion of *evaluation* ρ which is the total mapping from Var to Val. We assume that an application ρ to data expression e denoted $[\![e]\!]_\rho$, always yields a value from Val and similarly for boolean expressions, $[\![b]\!]_\rho$ is either $true$ or $false$. Moreover, the notion $\rho \models b$ indicates that $[\![b]\!]\rho = true$ and $b \models b'$ indicates that for every evaluation ρ, $\rho \models b$ implies $\rho \models b'$.

Let t be a term of the language, and P a process identifier, the syntax of the language is the following:

$$t ::= \mathbf{0} \mid a.t \mid t + t \mid \texttt{if}\ b\ \texttt{then}\ t \mid t[f] \mid P(\bar{e})$$
$$a ::= \tau \mid c?x \mid c!e$$

where c is a channel name,f a relabelling function and $P(\bar{e})$ is a process which is defined recursively by associating to each identifier P and equation of the form $P(\bar{x}) \Leftarrow t$ and $\bar{x}$ and $\bar{e}$ are vectors of variables or expressions respectively.

The operational semantics of process algebra languages is usually given by using the notion of *labelled transition system* that is triple $\langle S, Act, \rightarrow \rangle$ where S is the set of *states*, Act is the set of action names and $\rightarrow \subseteq S \times Act \times S$ is a *transition relation*. Usually the notation $s_1 \xrightarrow{a} s_2$ is used in place of $(s_1, a, s_2) \in \rightarrow$.

The PRE operator means that a (closed) term $a.P$ represents a process that performs an action a and then behaves as P. The operator $COND$ means that if the guards b holds than the transition is allowed. $SUM1$ and $SUM2$ are the non-deterministic choice between the terms t and u. Choosing the action of one of the two components means dropping the other. REN is the relabelling operators: The term $t[f]$ behaves like t, but its actions are renamed through relabelling function f. Finally REC permits the definition of recursive terms.

In order to deal more easily with infinitely branching transition systems, one could use the notion of *symbolic transition systems* (see again [9,10]). This is a labelled transition system in which there is a *symbolic transition relation*, in place of $\rightarrow$, which has the form $\xrightarrow{b,a}$ where b is a boolean expression and a is a symbolic action, namely:

$$a \in Act^{Symb} = \{c!e, c?x | e \in DExp, x \in Var\}$$

where $c!e$ and $c?x$ means the output and input actions respectively.

Intuitively, $t \xrightarrow{b,a} u$ means that, if b holds, t can perform a and thereby evolve into u. Hence it is possible abbreviate $\xrightarrow{true,a}$ as $\xrightarrow{a}$. The set of bound variables of a symbolic action is defined thus: $bv(c?x) = \{x\}$.

Now it is possible to give the following formal definition.

Table 1. Symbolic Transitional Semantics

$$PRE\ \frac{-}{a.t \xrightarrow{true,a} t} \qquad COND\ \frac{t \xrightarrow{b',a} t'}{\texttt{if}\ b\ \texttt{then}\ t \xrightarrow{b' \wedge b,a} t'}\ fv(b) \cap bv(a) = \emptyset$$

$$SUM1\ \frac{t \xrightarrow{b,a} t'}{t+u \xrightarrow{b,a} t'} \qquad SUM2\ \frac{u \xrightarrow{b,a} u'}{t+u \xrightarrow{b,a} u'}$$

$$REN\ \frac{t \xrightarrow{b,a} t'}{t[f] \xrightarrow{b,f(a)} t'[f]} \qquad REC\ \frac{t[\bar{e} \backslash \bar{x}] \xrightarrow{b,a} t'}{P(\bar{e}) \xrightarrow{b,a} t'}\ P(\bar{x}) \Leftarrow t$$

Definition 3. *A* symbolic transition system *is a n-tuple $\langle Q, BExp, Act^{Symb}, \rightarrow \rangle$, where Q is the set of states, $BExp$ is a set of boolean expressions Act^{Symb} is the set of symbolic actions and $\rightarrow \subseteq Q \times (BExp \times Act^{Symb}) \times Q$ as defined in Table 1.*

A symbolic transition system is said to be deterministic *when, whenever, given a state q and an symbolic transaction $\xrightarrow{b,a}$ there exists one and only one q' s.t. $q \xrightarrow{b,a} q'$. This means that if there exist two state q' and q'' s.t. $q \xrightarrow{b,a} q'$ and $q \xrightarrow{b,a} q''$ then $q = q''$.*

3 Contract-Policy Matching

In this section we are going to show the technical machinery for formal contract-policy matching. In particular, we first show how to give formal semantics to ConSpec and then how to perform contract-policy matching through simulation checking.

3.1 From ConSpec Language to Process Algebra

To map a ConSpec language into the language we have recalled in Section 2.2 we restrict ourselves to consider policy and contract with only one RuleID. We take the following steps.

First we consider a process constant $S(\boldsymbol{x})$ with as many variables as the state variables. Basically, when instantiated, this represents an actual state of the ConSpec automaton.

Then, each BEFORE event clause:

```
<BEFORE > EVENT MethodSignature1 PERFORM
    condition1 -> update1
              ...
    <conditionM1> -> updateM1
```

is mapped into the corresponding process

$$\begin{array}{l} \text{EC(u)=}\texttt{if}\ \textit{condition}_1\ \texttt{then}\ \textit{MethodSignature}_1.\text{S}(\boldsymbol{e_1})+ \\ \qquad \dots \\ \qquad \texttt{if}\ \textit{condition}_{M_1}\ \texttt{then}\ \textit{MethodSignature}_1.\text{S}(\boldsymbol{e_n}) \end{array}$$

where, $\boldsymbol{u}$ is the set of parameters of the method *MethodSignature*$_1$ and $\boldsymbol{e_j}$, with $j = 1, \dots, M_1$, corresponds to the new assignment of each variable, if any. For instance, if *update*$_1$ is $x := x + 1$ and x is the i_{th} variable in the state, then e_1 is the vector of expression where i_{th} expression is $x + 1$. We also note that parameters in u cannot be assigned.

Now let us consider an event clause with AFTER as modifier as follows:

```
<AFTER > EVENT MethodSignature1 PERFORM
    condition1 -> update1
              ...
    <conditionM1> -> updateM1
```

It can be encoded in the following process:

$$\begin{aligned}\text{MethodSignature1}(\boldsymbol{r}).(\texttt{if } \textit{condition}_1 \texttt{ then } \mathrm{S}(\boldsymbol{e_1})+ \\ \dots \\ \texttt{if } \textit{condition}_{M_1} \texttt{ then } \mathrm{S}(\boldsymbol{e_n}))\end{aligned}$$

where conditions can also mention the return values in $\boldsymbol{r}$.

Then, the final process description is the summation of the corresponding processes for each clause and its initial state is the process constant with parameters the initial values in the security state. Hence, a ConSpec specification can be seen as a symbolic process.

Example 3. Considering again the policy in Figure 3 that informally says "Only network connections with `www.google.it` and `www.yahoo.it` can be opened, but after a connection with `www.yahoo.it` no connection with `www.google.it` can be opened".

Let $\mathrm{S}(yahoo)$ be the process constant state with the boolean variable $yahoo$. The initial security state is $\mathrm{S}(false)$. This specification corresponds to the following process:

$$\begin{aligned}\mathrm{E(url)}{=}\texttt{if } b(google) \wedge(\neg\, \mathrm{yahoo}) \texttt{ then } m(url)!.\mathrm{S}(false)+ \\ \texttt{if } b(yahoo) \texttt{ then } m(url)!.\mathrm{S}(true)\end{aligned}$$

where $b(google)$=*url.startsWith("http://www.google.it")*, $b(yahoo)$= *url.startsWith(" http://www.yahoo.it")* and $m(url)!$=*javax.io.microedition.Connector.open(String url)*. The graphical representation of this policy is depicted in Figure 4.

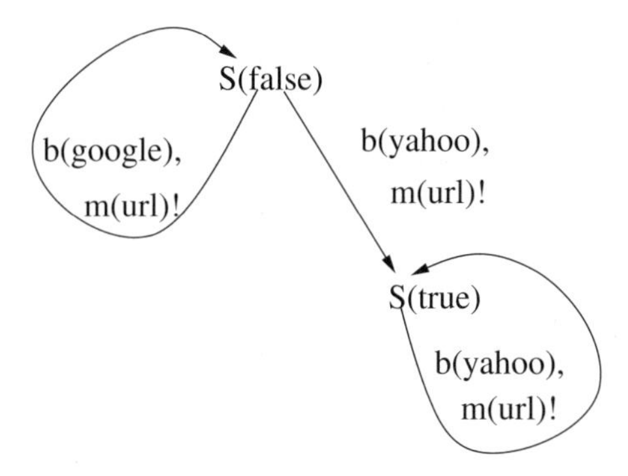

Fig. 4. The graphical representation of the symbolic process that specifies the policy in Figure 3

3.2 Contract-Policy Matching as Simulation Checking

Contract-policy matching should ensure that any security relevant behavior allowed by the contract is also allowed by the policy. A natural candidate relation among contracts and policies, when specified formally through transition systems, is language inclusion and as a matter of fact, such an approach has been advocated in [13].

In our previous work (*e.g.*, [8,14,15]), we successfully used the simulation relations for security policies enforcement. We thus decided to use also in the S3MS project this notion that has several nice features. In particular, we consider simulation relation because checking language inclusion for non-deterministic (finite) automata is $PSPACE$-complete while simulation relation on finite automata can be checked in polynomial time. In addition, since the simulation relation is a stronger relation than language inclusion, we are on the safe side when we use this relation. (It is also a congruence w.r.t. process algebras operators.)

We thus recall the notion of simulation in symbolic transition systems (*e.g.*, see [16]).

A set of boolean expressions B is called a *b-partition* if $\bigvee B = b$. Semantically B can be regarded as a partition of the value space represented by b, or more precisely, for any evaluation ρ, $\rho \models b$ iff $\rho \models b'$ for some $b' \in B$.

In the following we write $a =^b a'$ to mean that if $a \equiv !e$ then a' has the form $!e'$ with $b \models e = e'$ and $a \equiv a'$ otherwise.

Definition 4. *A $BExp$-indexed family of relations $\mathcal{R} = \{R^b | b \in BExp\}$ is a* strong symbolic simulation *if it satisfies: $(t, u) \in R^b$ implies that*

if $t \xrightarrow{b,a} t'$ with $bv(a) \cap fv(b,t,u) = \emptyset$, then there is a $b \wedge b_1$-partition B s.t. for each $b' \in B$ there exist b_2, a' and u' with $b' \models b_2$, $a =^{b'} a'$, $u \xrightarrow{b_2,a'} u'$ and $(t', u') \in R^{b'}$.

We write $t \prec^b u$ if $(t, u) \in R^b \in \mathcal{R}$ for some symbolic simulation $\mathcal{R}$.

This definition offers a method to check when one process is simulated by another one. We illustrate this through the following example.

Example 4. Let us consider again the policy in Example 3 with its mapping into the following symbolic process:

$$\text{E(url)=}\texttt{if } b(google) \wedge (\neg \text{ yahoo}) \texttt{ then } m(url)!.\text{S}(false)+$$
$$\texttt{if } b(yahoo) \texttt{ then } m(url)!.\text{S}(true)$$

where $b(google)$=url.startsWith("http://www.google.it"), $b(yahoo)$= url.startsWith(" http://www.yahoo.it") and $m(url)$!=javax.io.microedition.Connector.open(String url).

Now let us consider the following ConSpec contract specification:

MAXINT 10 MAXLEN 10
RULEID Rule5
VERSION 1.0

SCOPE SESSION
SECURITY STATE

BEFORE javax.io.microedition.Connector.open(String myurl) PERFORM
myurl.equals("http://www.google.it") → skip;

This contract means that the application only has access to the URL that is equal to "http://www.google.it".

Since there is no state variable, here the constat process S does not depend on any variable. The contract is also represented by the process:

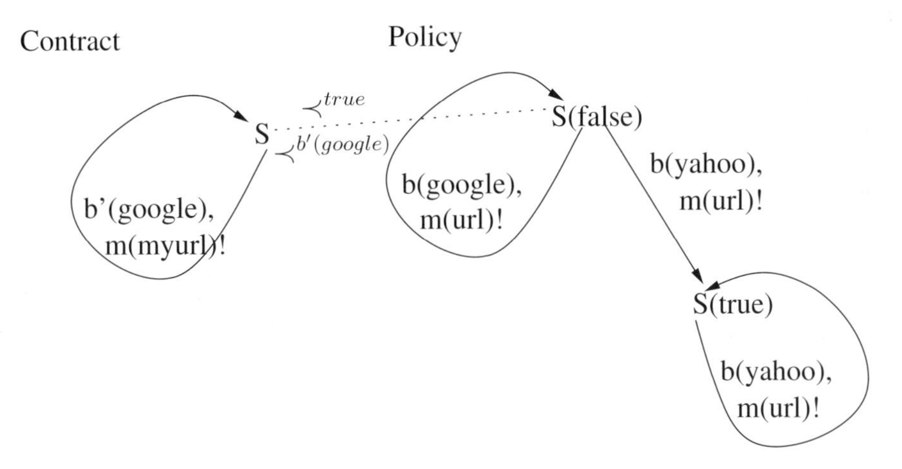

Fig. 5. The graphical representation of the symbolic process that specified the policy and the contract

`if` $b'(google)$ `then` $m(myurl)$!.S

where $b'(google)$= *myurl.equals("http://www.google.it")*.

In Figure 5 there is a graphical representation of the two symbolic processes that specify the policy and the contract respectively. In order to prove that the contract and the policy are in simulation relation we start to consider the couple (S, S($false$)) $\in R^{true}$. Now we have that S$\stackrel{b'(google),m(url)}{\longrightarrow}$S. Let B=$\{b'(google)\}$ be the $b'(google)\wedge true$-partition, we have to prove that there exist b, a' and S' s.t. $b(google) \models b$, $m(url) =^{b'(google)} a'$ and (S,S') $\in R^{b'(google)}$. These conditions hold by taking $b = b(google) \wedge \neg yahoo$, $a' = m(myurl)$ and S'=S($false$). Indeed it remains to prove that (S,S') $\in S^{b(google)}$ but this follows from the fact that the only transition from S is $\stackrel{b(google),m(url)}{\longrightarrow}$ to S itself and $b'(google) \wedge b(google) \equiv b'(google)$.

In [16], a sound and complete proof systems for simulation has been provided. It assumes the decidability of implication and equivalence among boolean expressions.

In order to simplify the computation steps, one could consider deterministic policies. In this case, finding the appropriate partition on the second process becomes much easier. We use this simplifying assumption in the actual implementation of the simulation checking tool.

4 A Tool for Simulation Checking on Mobile Device

Here we describe the structure and performances of the tool that we developed for the simulation contract-policy matching. It has been implemented on Java 2 Micro Edition (J2ME) and may actually run on smart-phones.

4.1 Architecture of the Tool

The architecture of the tool can be schematically represented as in Figure 6.

According to Figure 6, at the beginning there are a policy and a contract described by using ConSpec language. In order to obtain two transition systems from the ConSpec specification, the method `parseFile()` of the `ConSpecParse`is used. It takes in input "file.pol" and gives as output the symbolic system. Hence we have two transition systems, one for the contract and one for the policy.

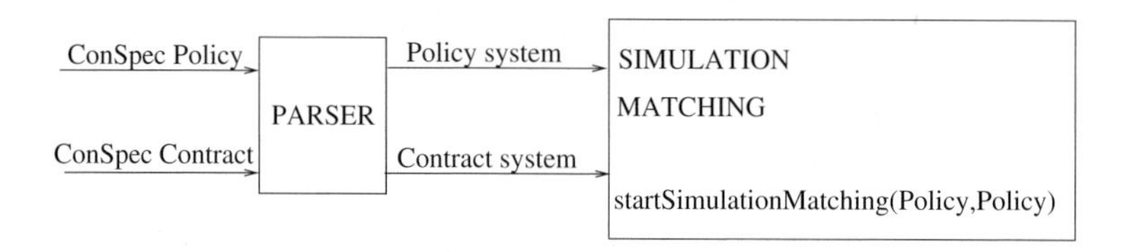

Fig. 6. The architecture of the tool

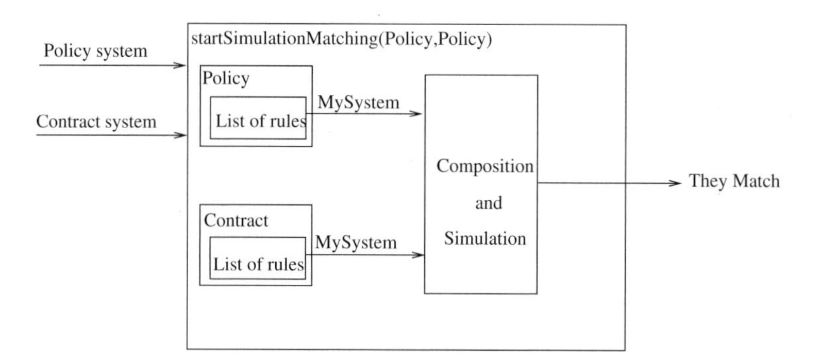

Fig. 7. Zoom of the Simulation Matching part

From the applicative point of view, the most important class of the tool is the class `utilSimulMatch` whose behavior is represented in Figure 7. This class contains among its methods the method `startSimulationMatching(Policy,Policy)` that is the main method of the class. As a matter of fact, once it receives in input two objects of the type `Policy` it checks if they are similar.

4.2 Performance

For our experiments we used HTC Universal (as also know as IMATE JASJAR or QTEK 9000) with the PhoneME Java platform that runs on Linux OpenMoco distribution, Kernel 2.6.21, CPU Intel XScale PXA270, CPU Clock 520 MHz, ROM type Flash EEPROM, ROM capacity 128 MiB, including 43.5 MiB user-accessible non-volatile storage, RAM type SDRAM and RAM capacity 64 MiB, 50MiB accessible.

We tested several couples contract-policy of different number of states and we noticed that the amount of time spent from the machine to generate the symbolic systems and to do the matching is directly proportional to the number of states of the generated symbolic systems.

The results we observed are summarize in Table 2.

Table 2. Performance of the simulation contract-policy matching tool on device

Policy $\sqcup$ Contract states number	System time
60	100-120ms
120	320-370ms
350	3000-4000ms

5 Some Examples

Because the tool must run on mobile devices, or, in general, on devices with a little amount of available memory, the policies that we have studied are very simple.

Let us consider to have a smart-phone on which is set the policy of the Example 2: "Only network connections with `www.google.it` and `www.yahoo.it` can be opened, but after a connection with `www.yahoo.it` no connection with `www.google.it` can be opened"[1].

As we have already said, our tool takes in input a ConSpec specification for the policy which, as we can see in Fig 8 and Example 2, is the following:

```
MAXINT 50 MAXLEN 20
RULEID Rule5
VERSION 1.0

SCOPE SESSION
SECURITY STATE
boolean yahoo=false;

BEFORE javax.io.microedition.Connector.open(String url) PERFORM
url.startsWith("http://www.google.it")&&!yahoo → skip;
url.startsWith("http://www.yahoo.it")→ yahoo=true;
```

Let us suppose to consider an application with the following ConSpec contract specification (see Figure 8).

```
MAXINT 10 MAXLEN 10
RULEID Rule5
VERSION 1.0

SCOPE SESSION
SECURITY STATE
```

[1] Even if tests were made on a real device, the images that we present in this section are screen shots obtained by using an emulator given by the Sun Java Wireless Toolkit 2.5.1.

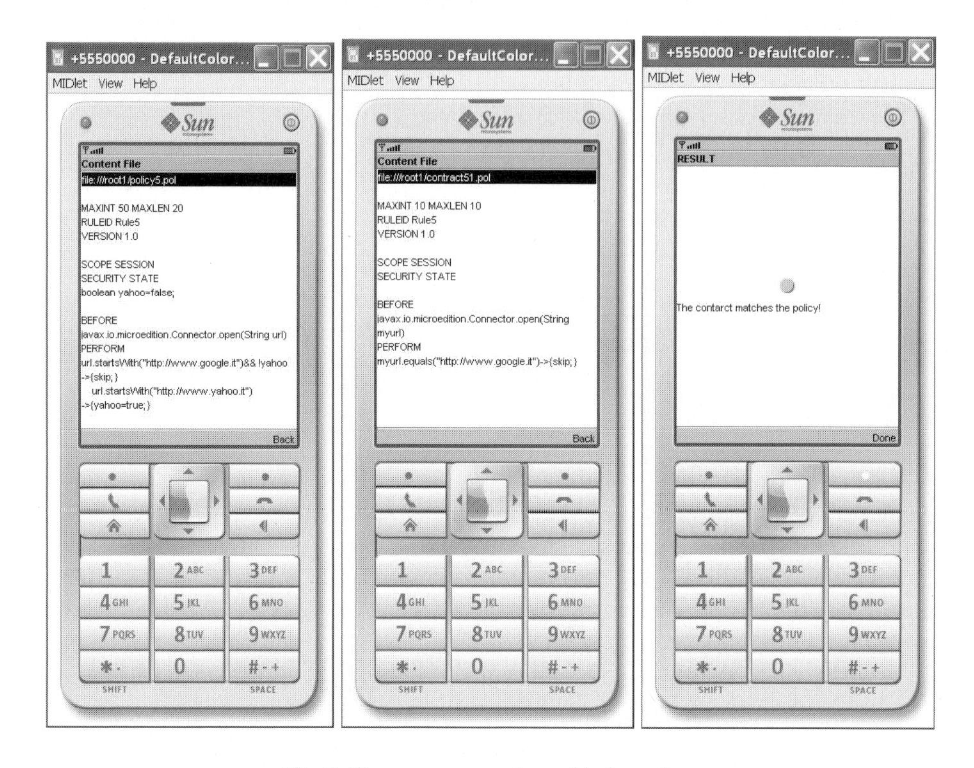

Fig. 8. The contract matches with the policy

BEFORE javax.io.microedition.Connector.open(String myurl) PERFORM
myurl.equals("http://www.google.it") → skip;

Running our tool we obtain that this contract matches our policy (see Figure 8). As a matter of fact, it means that the application has access to URLs equal to "http://www.google.it". Hence, it never accesses to URLs starting with "http://www.yahoo.it", it is allowed to open URLs equal to "http://www.google.it" whenever it wants.

On the other hand, if the application has the following contract (see also Figure 9):

MAXINT 50 MAXLEN 20
RULEID Rule5
VERSION 1.0

SCOPE SESSION
SECURITY STATE
boolean ya=false;

BEFORE javax.io.microedition.Connector.open(String urlx) PERFORM
urlx.startsWith("http://www.yahoo.it")→ ya=true;
urlx.startsWith("http://www.google.it") → skip;

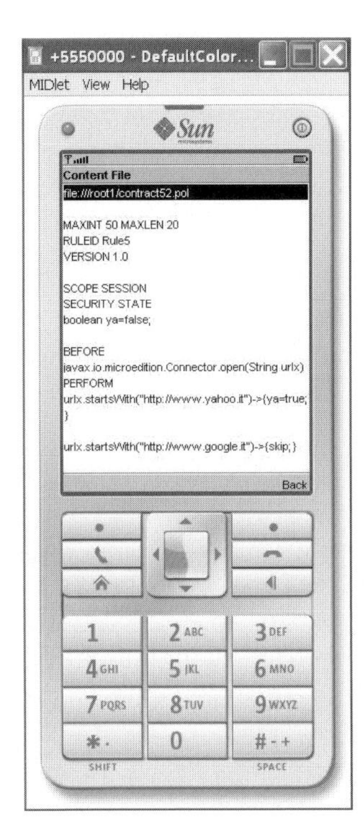

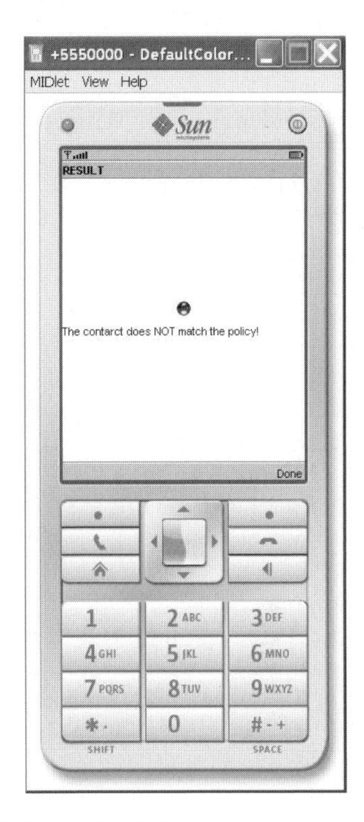

Fig. 9. A contract that does not match

In this case the response of our tool is negative. Indeed, by analyzing the contract, it is easy to see that it is allowed to access to google also after an access to yahoo but this is forbidden by our policy (see Figure 9).

6 Conclusion and Future Work

The paper presents a framework on symbolic simulation based contract-policy matching. We have shown how contract and policies can be formally expressed through (symbolic) process algebras terms. Then we advocated the usage of symbolic simulation as the notion of contract-policy matching.

Moreover, we also described our tool, developed in J2ME, that permits us to do the contract-policy matching also on smart phone and small devices.

As future work, we aim to apply this framework also to service oriented architectures. This would be useful both to allow secure service composition as well as to negotiate services based on their security relevant behavior. The technology developed till now, working also on devices with limited resources could be instrumental for enhancing usage of pervasive service applications.

Acknowledgments

We would like to thank the reviewers for their helpful comments.

References

1. Dragoni, N., Martinelli, F., Massacci, F., Mori, P., Schaefer, C., Walter, T., Vetillard, E.: Security-by-contract (SxC) for software and services of mobile systems. In: At your service: Service Engineering in the Information Society Technologies Program. MIT Press, Cambridge (2008)
2. Dragoni, N., Massacci, F., Naliuka, K., Siahaan, I.: Security-by-contract: Toward a semantics for digital signatures on mobile code. In: López, J., Samarati, P., Ferrer, J.L. (eds.) EuroPKI 2007. LNCS, vol. 4582, pp. 297–312. Springer, Heidelberg (2007)
3. Schneider, F.B.: Enforceable security policies. ACM Transactions on Information and System Security 3(1), 30–50 (2000)
4. Martinelli, F., Matteucci, I.: An approach for the specification, verification and synthesis of secure systems. Electr. Notes Theor. Comput. Sci. 168, 29–43 (2007)
5. Aktug, I., Naliuka, K.: Conspec – A formal language for policy specification. Electr. Notes Theor. Comput. Sci. 197(1), 45–58 (2008)
6. Erlingsson, Ú., Schneider, F.B.: Sasi enforcement of security policies: a retrospective. In: NSPW 1999: Proceedings of the 1999 workshop on New security paradigms, pp. 87–95. ACM, New York (2000)
7. Milner, R.: Communicating and mobile systems: the π-calculus. Cambridge University Press, Cambridge (1999)
8. Martinelli, F., Matteucci, I.: Through modeling to synthesis of security automata. Electr. Notes Theor. Comput. Sci. 179, 31–46 (2007)
9. Hennessy, M., Lin, H.: Symbolic bisimulations. In: MFPS 1992: Selected papers of the meeting on Mathematical foundations of programming semantics, Amsterdam, The Netherlands, pp. 353–389. Elsevier Science Publishers, Amsterdam (1995)
10. Hennessy, M., Lin, H.: A Symbolic Approach to Value-Passing Processes. In: Handbook of Process Algebra. Elsevier, Amsterdam (2001)
11. Dragoni, N., Massacci, F., Naliuka, K., Siahaan, I., Quillinan, T., Matteucci, I., Schaefer, C.: Deliverable 2.1.4-Methodologies and tools for contract matching- S3MS European Project (2007)
12. Aktung, I.: Syntax and semantics of conspec (last visited 09/07/2008) (2007), `https://trinity.dit.unitn.it/bscw/bscw.cgi/d33953/ConSpec`
13. Desmet, L., Joosen, W., Massacci, F., Philippaerts, P., Piessens, F., Siahaan, I., Vanoverberghe, D.: Security-by-contract on the.net platform, vol. 13, pp. 25–32. Elsevier Advanced Technology Publications, Oxford (2008)
14. Matteucci, I.: Automated synthesis of enforcing mechanisms for security properties in a timed setting. Electr. Notes Theor. Comput. Sci. 186, 101–120 (2007)
15. Martinelli, F., Matteucci, I.: Partial model checking, process algebra operators and satisfiability procedures for (automatically) enforcing security properties. Technical report, IIT-CNR (2005) Presented at the International Workshop on Foundations of Computer Security (FCS 2005)
16. Ingolfsdottir, A., Lin, H.: Handbook of Processes Algebra. In: A Symbolic Approach to Value-passing Processes, ch. 7. Elsevier, Amsterdam (2001)

ASERE: Assuring the Satisfiability of Sequential Extended Regular Expressions*

Naiyong Jin and Huibiao Zhu

Shanghai Key Laboratory of Trustworthy Computing, East China Normal University
{nyjin,hbzhu}@sei.ecnu.edu.cn

Abstract. One purpose of Property Assurance is to check the satisfiability of properties. The Sequential Extended Regular Expressions (SEREs) play important roles in composing PSL properties. The SEREs are regular expressions with repetition and conjunction. Current assurance method for LTL formulas are not applicable to SEREs.

In this paper, we present a method for checking the satisfiability of SEREs. We propose an extension of Alternating Finite Automata with internal transitions and logs of universal branches (IAFA). The new representation enables *memoryful* synchronization of parallel words. The compilation from SEREs to IAFAs is in linear space. An algorithm, and two optimizations are proposed for searching satisfying words of SEREs. They reduce the stepwise search space to the product of universal branches' guard sets. Experiments confirm their effectiveness.

Keywords: Alternating Automata, Satisfiability, Memoryful Synchronization.

1 Introduction

The correctness of functional specifications is important. Conflicting properties will put design and verification effort into vain. Property Assurance [4] [20] aims at a methodology for checking the existence of behaviors which satisfy a set of properties, and the satisfaction of given properties for all possible behaviors of a system. With property assurance, designers can develop a better understanding and have stronger confidence in their specifications.

PSL [11] is an industry standard specification language (IEEE-1850) for circuit and embedded system design. The core logic of PSL is an extension of LTL with the Sequential Extended Regular Expressions (SEREs). SEREs are operands of PSL's LTL operators. Therefore, the satisfiability of SEREs is critical to the correctness of PSL specifications. Bloem *et al.* have addressed the satisfiability problem of LTL in [20]. In this paper, we present a method for Assuring the satisfiability of clocked SEREs [9] (ASERE).

* This paper is supported by the "863" project (2007AA01302) of Ministry of Science and Technology of China, and the "Dengshan Project"(067062017) of the Science and Technology Commission of Shanghai Municipality.

T. Margaria and B. Steffen (Eds.): ISoLA 2008, CCIS 17, pp. 237–251, 2008.

Related Work

The automata-theoretic approach for proving the satisfiability (SAT) of regular expressions starts with converting an expression r into an automaton A_r, then checks the non-emptiness of the language L accepted by A_r, that is $L(A_r) \neq \phi$. The formula holds if we can find a word w such that $w \in L(A_r)$.

The topic of automata construction for intersection-extended regular expressions (IERE) was carefully studied by Ben-David *et al.* in [1]. Firstly, they transform an IERE r into an *Alternating Finite Automaton* (AFA), then to a *Non-deterministic Finite Automaton* (NFA). The state complexity of such a transformation is $2^{O(|r|)}$, where $| r |$ refers to the size of r. The construction from SEREs to AFA is linear. The exponential increase takes place in transforming the AFA of $r_1\&\&r_2$ to NFA. $r_1\&\&r_2$ requires that words of r_1 and r_2 should both start and terminate simultaneously. One important reason that forces them to further transforming AFA to NFA is due to the fact that the acceptance of $r_1\&\&r_2$ depends on the universal activeness of the accepting states of r_1 and r_2. However, a traditional AFA does not have the accepting states for universal branches.

Vardi *et al.* gave a systematic analysis on the time complexity of the language emptiness problem by automata-theoretic approach in [22] [15] [13]. For traditioanl alternating automata, their time complexity is in exponential time. In the last ten years, the progress was driven by the LTL model checking [2] [17] [10]. The expressiveness of LTL is equivalent to that of the star-free ω-regular expressions. Runs of the alternating automata for LTL are *memoryless* [13]. But SEREs are not *memoryless*. They can repeat infinitively, and conjunct with other SEREs to form new ones, like $r_1\&\&r_2$. Therefore, we must explore new methods for the SAT problem of SEREs.

Contribution

In summary, the contribution of this paper includes:

1. An extesion of Alternating Finite Automata with internal transitions and universal branching logs. The new representation enables *memoryful* synchronization of parallel words. The construction from SEREs to IAFA is in linear space.
2. An algorithm for proving the satisfiability of SEREs by IAFA. Two optimization methods are proposed. They reduce the stepwise search space to the product of universal branches' guard sets.

The rest of this paper is organized as follows. Section 2 presents the syntax and the semantics of SERE. Section 3 reviews the evolution of Alternating Automata, and justifies their use in representing SEREs. The new features to be enhanced for the satisfiability problem of SERE are explored. Section 4 introduces the Internal-transition-enhanced AFA (IAFA) as the operating representation of SEREs. In Section 5, we develop a DPLL-like stepwise search algorithm and use zchaff [18] as the building block in each step. After that, we propose two optimizations which are able to reduce the search space of each step from exponential to linear. Experiments and analysis are presented in Section 6. And Section 7 discusses our future works.

We leave the detailed proofs, the automaton constructions and the diagrams in a technical report which, in along with the source code of ASERE, is available at [23].

2 SERE: Syntax and Semantics

The syntax of SEREs supported by ASERE is defined recursively as follows:

Definition 2.1. *(SEREs)*

$r ::= \epsilon$ *empty expression*
$\mid b$ *Boolean expression*
$\mid \{r\}$ *bracketed SERE*
$\mid r;\ r$ *sequential concatenation*
$\mid r\&\&r$ *length – matching conjunction*
$\mid r\&r$ *non – length – matching conjunction*
$\mid r \mid r$ *disjunction*
$\mid r[*]$ *repeating r for zero or more times*
$\mid r[*k]$ *repeating r for k times*
$\mid r[*n : m]$ *repeating r for n to m times, n can be* 0, *and m can be infinitive*

In accordance with [7], we define the semantics of *SERE* with finite and infinite words over $\Sigma = 2^V \cup \{\epsilon\}$, where V refers to the predicate variable set, and ϵ refers to an empty word. We denote by $Bool_V$ the set of Boolean expressions over V, $Bool_V = 2^{2^V}$.

We denote a letter from Σ by l, and a word by w. $\sharp w$ denotes the length of w. The empty word ϵ has length 0, a finite non-empty word $w = l_0 l_1 \ldots l_n$ has length $n+1$, and an infinite word has length ∞. We denote the $(i+1)$th letter of w by w^i, the suffix of w starting at w^i by $w^{i\ldots}$, and the finite sequence of letters starting from w^i and ending in w^j by $w^{i..j}$. If $i > \sharp w$, then $w^i = \epsilon$. $w_1 w_2$ denotes the sequential concatenation of w_1 and w_2. If w_1 is infinite, then $w_1 v = w_1$. W^* denotes finite words whose letters are from W. For the empty word ϵ, $w\epsilon^* = \epsilon^* w = w$.

$l \Vdash b$ denotes that the letter l satisfies the Boolean expression b. The Boolean satisfaction relation $\Vdash \subseteq \Sigma \times Bool_V$ behaves in the usual manner.

Definition 2.2. *(Boolean Satisfaction) For letter $l \in \Sigma$, atomic proposition $p \in V$, and Boolean expressions $b, b_1, b_2 \in Bool_V$, then*

1. $l \Vdash p$ **iff** $p \in l$
2. $l \Vdash \neg b$ **iff** $l \nVdash b$
3. $l \Vdash$ **true** $\wedge\, l \nVdash$ **false**, *4)*
4. $l \Vdash b_1 \wedge b_2$ **iff** $f \Vdash b_1 \wedge f \Vdash b_2$

$w \models r$ denotes that the word w satisfies the SERE r tightly.

Definition 2.3. *(SERE Tight Satisfaction)*

$w \models \epsilon$ **iff** $\sharp w = 0$
$w \models b$ **iff** $\sharp w = 1 \wedge w^0 \Vdash b$
$w \models \{r\}$ **iff** $w \models r$
$w \models r_1;\ r_2$ **iff** $\exists w_1, w_2 \bullet w = w_1 w_2 \wedge w_1 \models r_1 \wedge w_2 \models r_2$
$w \models r[*]$ **iff** $w \models \epsilon \vee \exists w_1 \neq \epsilon, w_2 \bullet w = w_1 w_2 \wedge w_1 \models r \wedge w_2 \models r[*]$
$w \models r[*k]$ **iff** $w \models \overbrace{r;\ \ldots;\ r}^{k\ times}$
$w \models r[*n : m]$ **iff** $w \models \overbrace{r;\ \ldots;\ r}^{n\ to\ m\ times}$
$w \models r_1\ \&\&\ r_2$ **iff** $w \models r_1 \wedge w \models r_2$

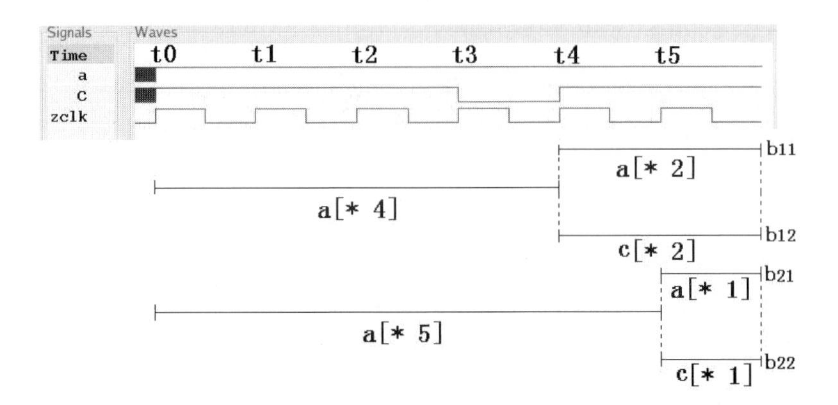

Fig. 1. Runs of $a[*4:5];\ \{a[*1:2]\&\&c[*1:2]\}$

$w \models r_1 \mid r_2$ **iff** $w \models r_1 \vee w \models r_2$
$w \models r_1 \& r_2$ **iff** $w \models \{r_1 \&\& \{r_2;\ \mathbf{true}[*]\}\} \mid \{\{r_1;\ \mathbf{true}[*]\} \&\& r_2\}$

SERE can describe non-deterministic behaviors succinctly [16]. One may have different interpretations of a SERE over a finite word. For instance, **Fig.1** illustrates two interpretations of

$$a[*4:5];\ \{a[*1:2]\&\&c[*1:2]\}$$

over the word given in the wave form. For the first interpretation, after 4 clocks of a, it branches at t_4, and its branches, $a[*2]$ (b_{11}) and $c[*2]$ (b_{12}), last two clocks. For the second interpretation, after 5 clocks of a, it branches at t_5, and its branches, $a[*1]$ (b_{21}) and $c[*1]$ (b_{22}), last only one clock cycle. Though b_{12} and b_{22} all reach their accepting states, b_{11} should length-match with b_{12}, not b_{22}. This example tells us that word length is not sufficient enough for us to synchronize words of parallel SEREs.

3 A Review of Alternating Automata

By **Definition 2.3**, we know that SERE supports two types of branches. They are the existential branch, $r_1 \mid r_2$, and the universal branch, $r_1 \&\& r_2$. No cooperation takes place between spawned processes in both types of branches, until the time comes to decide the acceptance of the input. That kind of concurrency is termed as *weak concurrency* [12].

NFA is the counterpart of *existential* branching in the automaton world. AFA further enrich NFA with universal branches. An *AFA on finite words* is a tuple of $A =< \Sigma, S, s_0, \rho, F >$, where Σ is the input letter set, S is a finite set of states, s_0 is the initial state, and F is a finite set of accepting states. $\rho : S \times \Sigma \rightarrow 2^{2^S}$ is a transition function. The target of a transition is not a state of S, but a subset of S. A state may transit to multiple target sets to express non-deterministic behavior. For instance, a transition $\rho(s, l) = \{\{s_1, s_2\}, \{s_3, s_4\}\}$ states that A accepts a letter l from state s, and it activates both s_1 and s_2, or both s_3 and s_4. Chandra *et al.* [5] have proved that AFA is doubly exponentially more succinct than Deterministic Finite Automata (DFA). Thus, we have the following observation.

Observation 3.1. *AFA is a promising representation of SERE.*

Traditionally, runs of AFAs are expressed in terms of trees [22] [13]. A finite tree is a finite non-empty set $T \subseteq \mathbb{N}^*$ such that forall $x \cdot c \in T$, with $x \in \mathbb{N}^*$ and $c \in \mathbb{N}$, we have $x \in T$. The elements of T are called nodes, and the empty word ϵ is the root of T. The level of a node x, denoted $\mid x \mid$, is x's distance from the root ϵ. Particularly, $\mid \epsilon \mid= 0$. A run of A on a finite word $w = l_0 \cdot l_1 .,. l_{n-1}$ is a S-labelled tree $< T_R, R >$, where T_R is a tree and $R : T_R \rightarrow S$ maps each node of T_R to a state in S. For $< T_R, R >$, the followings hold:

- $R(\epsilon) = s_0$
- Let $x \in T_R$ with $R(x) = s$ and $\rho(s, l_{|x|}) = \mathbb{S}'$. There is a (possible empty) set $S_K = \{s_1, \ldots, s_k\}$ such that there exists a $S_y \subseteq S_K$ with $S_y \in \mathbb{S}'$, and for all $1 \leq c \leq k$, we have $x \cdot c \in T_R$ and $R(x \cdot c) = s_c$

A word W is accepted iff there is an *accepting* run on it. A run is *accepting* if all nodes at depth n are labelled by states in F.

By the above two statements, we can imply that in AFA, there is no accepting state for universal branches. Usually, there should be certain extra-mechanism which monitors whether the acceptance condition holds or not. This method is not elegant in addressing expressions like $\{\{r_1\&\&r_2\};\ r_3\}$, where r_3 starts after an accepting run of $\{r_1\&\&r_2\}$. A better ways seems to be setting a special state whose activeness indicates a successful synchronization of r_1 and r_2. With the state, we can concatenate the automata of $\{r_1\&\&r_2\}$ and r_3 by usual approaches. Those acceptance states are internal. They are not activated by input letters.

Observation 3.2. *The synchronization states for universal branches are necessary for keeping the elegance of automata-theoretic approach.*

Another weakness of tree-represented AFA is that AFA do not constrain the breadth of a level. An active state will move to sets of target states whenever an input letters satisfy some corresponding guards. So with the verification process continuing, the memory grows without restrictions.

Kupferman and Vardi [14] [13] proposed to merge *similar* target states of transitions into a single one. That results in representing runs of AFAs by Directed Acyclic Graphs (DAG). For two nodes x_1 and x_2, they are *similar* iff $\mid x_1 \mid=\mid x_2 \mid$ and $R(x_1) = R(x_2)$. Recently, the DAG approach [8] [3] is accepted in static verification (model checking) for LTL properties. The intuition is that the LTL formulas are equivalent to star-free words. For AFAs converted from LTL formulas, they do not have loops other than self loops. Hence, runs of traditional LTL-AFAs are *memoryless* [13]. During verification, one only needs to look in the future, but never the past. In other words, *similar* states correspond to the same future mission: to accept the suffixes which satisfy a common property.

Kupferman *et al.* represent a *memoryless* run $< T_R, R >$ by a DAG $G_R =< V, E >$, where

1. $V \subseteq S \times \mathbb{N}$ is such that $< s, l >\in V$ iff there exists $x \in T_R$ with $\mid x \mid= l$ and $R(x) = s$. For example, $< s_0, 0 >$ is the only vertex of G_R in $S \times \{0\}$.

2. $E \subseteq \bigcup_{l \geq 0}(S \times \{l\} \times (S \times \{l+1\}))$ is such that $E(< s, l >, < s', l+1 >)$ iff there exists $x \in T_R$ with $| x |= l$, $R(x) = s$ and $R(x.c) = s'$ for some $c \in \mathbb{N}$.

Configurations $C_i \subseteq S$ are sets of active states, where i refers to the level of a DAG. It is evident that, by DAG, every configuration contains at most $| S |$ states which are roots of different subtrees. A DAG is acceptable if $C_i \subseteq F$ holds.

The branches of AFA's DAGs resemble the requirements of universal choices [8]. A DAG is just a single path through the existential choices of an AFA. One may have to try breadth-first search, depth-first search or backward search [6] in looking for an accepting run. That is why the *EXPTIME* complexity of AFA is unavoidable [21].

We find that if a memory can distinguish different universal branching histories, then the runs with different branching histories will not be able to activate the synchronization states. Thus a *memoryful* DAG with synchronization states can enable concurrent runs of both *existential* and *universal* branches.

Observation 3.3. *A* memoryful *DAG can accommodate all possible runs of an AFA.*

4 Representing SEREs by IAFA

We formalize the Internal-transition-enhanced AFA (IAFA) as follows

Definition 4.1. *An IAFA is a tuple of* $A = (V, \Sigma_A, S, \mathbf{H}, s_0, \rho, F)$*, where*

• V is a set of variables of the SERE under assuring.
• S is a set of states.
• $\mathbf{H} = 2^{2^{\mathbb{N}^*}}$ is a set of historical log sets. A historical log $h \in \mathbb{N}^*$, namely $h = t_0t_1 \ldots t_{n-1}t_n$, is a finite sequence of time-stamps. It records the important timing information of runs which make a state active. We have H range over the sets of historical logs.
• $\Sigma_A = Bool_V \cup FOP_{SH}$ is the letter set of A. FOP_{SH} refers to the first order predicates over $S \cup S \times \mathbf{H}$. We distinguish $\mathbf{true}_V$ and $\mathbf{true}_{SH}$. $\mathbf{true}_V$ stands for logic **true** over V and $\mathbf{true}_{SH}$ stands for logic **true** over $S \cup S \times \mathbf{H}$.
• s_0 is the initial state.
• F is the set of states for tight acceptance.
• In IAFA, a transition ρ is in type of $S \times \Sigma_A \times U \times 2^S$, where
  • Σ_A specifies the guarding conditions.
  • U is a set of assignments which update historical logs whenever a transition takes place.
  • The target of a transition is a subset of S. All elements of the subset should be active after the transition.

We classify IAFA transitions into *external* and *internal* ones. Our SEREs are synchronous. The external transition can be triggered only on clock events. Therefore the guarding conditions of external transitions are in form of $Bool_V \wedge clock\_event$. For conciseness, we do not attach the *clock_event* in reasoning external transitions. The guarding conditions of *internal* transitions are in type of FOP_{SH}. We call a special type of internal self-loop transitions as τ transitions. τ-typed transitions are in form like

$(s, g_s, u_s, \{s\})$. A τ transition keeps a state active between two external transitions. We have ρ_e, ρ_i and ρ_τ to represent the set of *external*, *internal* and τ transitions. Notation $s.\tau$ denotes s's τ transition.

A configuration C gives out the status and historical logs of active states. Configurations are in type of $2^{S \times \mathbf{H}}$. Notation $C.ST$ denotes the set of active states in C, that is $C.ST = \{s \mid (s, H) \in C\}$. In a configuration, a state can have only one set of historical logs. That is if $(s, H_1) \in C$ and $(s, H_2) \in C$, then $H_1 = H_2$. Therefore, we represent the historical log set of s by $s.H$. For two active states s_1 and s_2, they are synchronizable if and only if they share common historical logs. That is $s_1.H \cap s_2.H \neq \phi$

A predicate $g \in FOP_{SH}$ holds under the configuration C, if there exists some pairs $(s, s.H) \in C$ which make g **true**. We represent the case by $C \models g$.

Definition 4.2. *Let* $A = (V, \Sigma_A, S, H, s_0, \rho_A, F)$ *be a IAFA, runs of A over a word* $w = w_0 w_1 w_2 \ldots w_k$ *is a sequence of configurations* $\Delta = C_0 C_1 \ldots C_n$, *where*

1. $C_0 = \{(s_0, \phi)\}$
2. *Given a letter* w_i, *if* $\exists s \in C_i.ST, (s, g, u, S') \in \rho_e$, *and* $w_i \Vdash g$, *then* $S' \subseteq C_{i+1}.ST$
3. *Given a state* $s \in C_i.ST$, *if* $(s, g, u, S') \in \rho_i$, *and* $C_i \models g$, *then* $S' \subseteq C_{i+1}.ST$.
4. *Given a state* $s \in C_i.ST$, *if* $s.\tau \in \rho_\tau$, *and* $s \in C_{i+1}.ST$, *then for all* $(s, g, u, S') \in \rho_i$, $C_i \models \neg g$ *holds.*

The second and the third clause of **Definition 4.2** state that for external and internal transitions, whenever their guarding conditions hold, they should take place immediately. That amounts to an identical treatment towards both universal and existential branches. However, such a treatment will not impact the correctness of assuring SEREs. Because in SEREs, the acceptance of universal branches asks for synchronization of peers. For $r_1 \&\& r_2$, if the branches of r_1 and r_2 are not able to synchronize on their termination, then the condition for the tight satisfaction of $r_1 \&\& r_2$ will fail.

Due to the existence of clock events, the external and internal transitions take place interleavingly. An external transition increases the word length. However, an internal

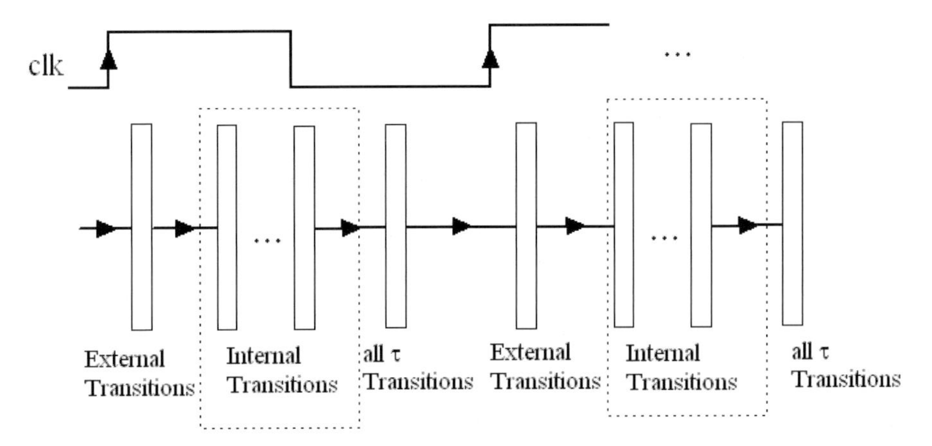

Fig. 2. Transitions of IAFAs

transition resembles the empty letter ϵ. The last clause of **Definition 4.2** says that a τ transitions are triggered only when the corresponding states do not have other enabled internal transitions. **Fig.2** illustrates the running patterns of IAFAs. Supposing the clock events of external transitions are the posedges of clk, then on each *posedge(clk)*, an IAFA will sample the values of V and trigger enabled external transitions. After that, there comes a sequence of internal transitions until all states have only τ transitions enabled.

Proposition 4.3. *For each SERE r, there is an IAFA A_r, such that $w \models r$ **iff** $w \in L(A_r)$ and A_r has $O(|\ r\ |)$ states.*

Proof: In [23].

Here, we give out the IAFA construction for r_1 && r_2, as illustrated in **Fig. 3**. Given $A_i = (V, \Sigma, S_i, \mathbf{H_i}, s0(r_i), \rho_i, \{ss(r_i)\})$ are IAFAs of r_i, then

$S(r_1\&\&r_2) = S(r_1) \cup S(r_2) \cup \{s_0, s_f\}$

$s_0(r_1\&\&r_2) = s_0$

$\rho_A(r_1\&\&r_2)$

$= \rho_A(r_1) \cup \rho_A(r_2)$

$\quad \cup\{(s_0,\ \mathbf{true}_{LV}, u_i, \{s_0(r_i)\}) \mid$

$\qquad u_i = \{l\_s\_0(r_i).H.include(push(l\_s\_0.H, t))\}\}$

$\quad \cup\{(ss(r_1), g, u, \{s_f\}), (ss(r_2), f\_ss\_1, \phi, \phi)\}$

$F(r_1\ \&\&\ r_2) = \{s_f\}$

$\quad$ where, $g = f\_ss\_r\_2 \wedge (f\_ss\_r\_1.H \cap f\_ss\_r\_2.H \neq \phi)$

$\qquad u = \{T := f\_ss\_r\_1.H \cap f\_ss\_r\_2.H;$

$\qquad\quad f'\_s\_f := 1;\ f'\_s\_f.H.include(T.pop);\ \}$

In the above clause, all target states of s_0 inherit s_0's history logs, and have a new universal branching time as the last time stamp of their history logs. s_f is the tight accepting state of $r_1\&\&r_2$. Before reaching s_f, we shall synchronize on the tight accep-

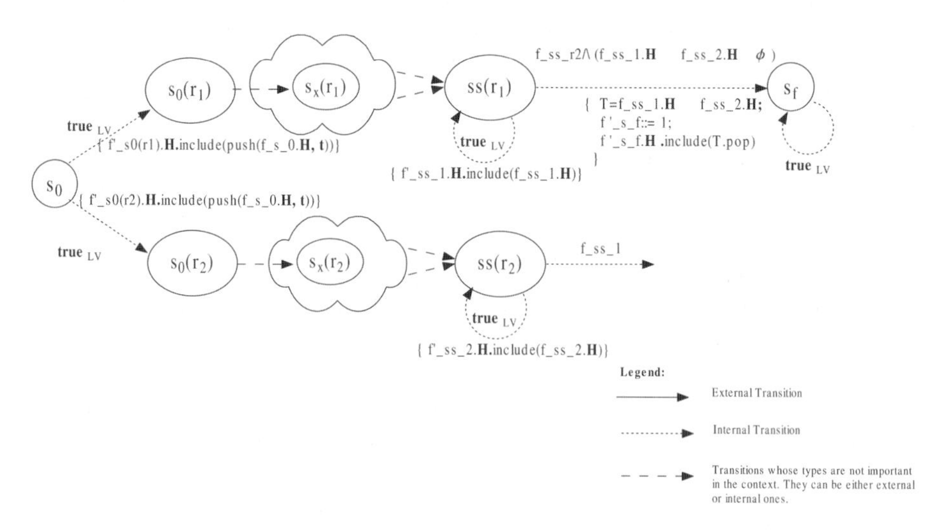

Fig. 3. The IAFA of $r_1\&\&r_2$

tance of both r_1 and r_2. For the transition from $ss(r_1)$, the guarding condition
$f\_ss\_r\_2 \wedge (f\_ss\_r\_1.H \cap f\_ss\_r\_2.H \neq \phi)$
conveys the idea that for a successful synchronization, both $ss(r_1)$ and $ss(r_2)$ shall be active and both of them have common histories of universal choices. The update part activates s_f and assigns the $T.pop$ as histories to s_f. T is a temporary variable. It is just the common histories of $ss(r_1)$ and $ss(r_2)$. $T.pop$ removes the branching time which is pushed into logs on leaving s_0. Once the automata reaches s_f, both $ss(r_1)$ and $ss(r_2)$ are deactivated.

By this example, we can see the effect of the τ transitions. According to the semantics of PSL [7], The length of a clocked SERE is counted on clock events. Internal transitions within two external transitions do not take time. It may takes different numbers of internal transitions to reach $ss(r_1)$ and $ss(r_2)$. With the τ transition, $ss(r_1)$ will not miss the synchronization with $ss(r_2)$ only if $ss(r_2)$ could be active in the current clock cycle.

Proposition 4.4. *The time complexity of the satisfiability problem of SERE is* $O(2^{d \cdot |V|})$, *where* $|V|$ *is the number of variables in V and d is the search depth.*

Proof: In [23].

5 The Implementation and Optimization

The search process of ASERE follows the classic DPLL algorithm [19], which is the base of most Boolean SAT solvers. For SAT solvers, a *conflict* is an implied assignment in which some variables are assigned both **true** and **false** . If no conflict is detected in the preprocessing, a DPLL SAT solver starts by assigning a value to an unassigned variable. If all variables are assigned, a solution is found. Otherwise, the solver will *deduce* values of other variables through a process called *Boolean Constraint Propagation* (BCP). If a conflict is detected, it will perform *backtrack* to undo some decisions. If all decisions have to be undone, then one can conclude the unsatisfiability of a boolean expression. The *deduce* and *backtrack* processes form the inner loop. It stops if no more deduction is possible and the deductions do not imply conflicts. After that, the solver will decide the next branch provided that there are still unassigned variables.

Our `ASERE` algorithm is similar. The target of each decision is to find a letter which can trigger the *external* transitions such that the IAFA can move forward. The *internal* transitions take the role of BCP. The search process of `ASERE` is illustrated in **Fig.4**.

1. Line 1 says that `ASERE` will initially try for internal transitions.
2. If an internal trial returns `TRIAL_PASS`, `ASERE` will commit the trial by *configuration_update()*. If in `sat_check`, no states of *F* becomes active, `ASERE` will continue for more internal transitions.
3. The codes from line 13 to line 20 state that if `ASERE` finds that all internal transitions are τs, it shifts to external trials. Before the next external trial, `ASERE` will check whether it reaches the maximal search depth. If so, `ASERE` *backtrack*s to the previous configuration for the last external trial by *configuration_retreat()*.

```
 1 trial_type = INTERNAL_TRIAL;
 2 while( !terminate ){
 3     cont = false;
 4     trial_ret = TRY_STEP_FORWARD(trial_type);
 5     switch ( trial_ret ){
 6       case EXTERNAL_FAIL:
 7               if (current_search_depth == 0)
 8                 terminate = true;
 9               else configuration_retreat();
10               cont = true;
11               break;
12
13       case INTERNAL_TAO:
14               configuartion_update(trial_type);
15               if ( reach_max_search_depth )
16                 configuration_retreat();
17
18               trial_type = EXTERNAL_TRIAL;
19               cont = true;
20               break;
21
22       case INTERNAL_FAIL:
23               if (current_search_depth == 0)
24                 terminate = true;
25               else configuration_retreat();
26
27               cont = true;
28               break;
29
30       case TRIAL_PASS:
31       default        :;
32     }
33
34     if ( cont )
35       continue;
36
37     configuration_update(trial_type);
38     satisfied = sat_check();
39     if ( !satisfied ){
40       if ( reach_max_search_depth )
41         configuration_retreat();
42
43       trial_type = INTERNAL_TRIAL;
44     } else return SAT;
45 }
46 return UNSAT;
```

Fig. 4. The Algorithm of ASERE

4. For the external trials, ASERE calls a SAT solver to find a letter l which should satisfy the disjunction of the guarding conditions of the active states. That is

$$l \Vdash \bigvee_k g_k \ \ with \ \ (s, g_k, u, S') \in \rho_e \wedge s \in C_i.ST \tag{1}$$

If such a l does exist, the external trial will return TRIAL_PASS and some external transitions of active states take place. Accordingly, ASERE updates the configuration as specified in line 37.
5. However, if the external trial returns EXTERNAL_FAIL and the search depth is greater than 0, ASERE will *backtrack* as well. That amounts to the deduction that the prefix word after the last external trial can not lead to a satisfying word. Then, ASERE continues with external trials for other words.
6. The codes from lines 38 to line 44 state that after updating a configuration, if some states of F become active, then a tight satisfying word is found. Otherwise, ASERE will try all possible internal trials to propagate the influence of the last letter. As in 3, *backtrack*ing is necessary if ASERE reaches the maximal search depth.

Proposition 4.4 tells us that the time complexity of SERE's satisfiability problem is $(2^{|V|})^d$. The base $2^{|V|}$ gives the search space of each *external trial*. The complexity increases exponentially along with the search depth. The exponent d is unavoidable. Our optimization effort focuses on reducing the step-wise search space by extra constraints. We propose 2 optimization methods, they are the the *Post-Trial Check* and the *No-Repeated-Transition Check*.

Opt.1(*Post-Trial Check*)

The motivation is to utilize the structure information of SEREs. For instance, to the *length-matching conjunction* $r_1 \&\& r_2$, whenever an external transition of r_1 (r_2) takes place, then at least one external transition of r_2 (r_1) has to take place as well. If a branch has no more active states after a trial, it is impossible for further runs to synchronize. And we can halt the search process earlier. Therefore, we must ensure the simultaneous activeness of universal branches' states. That criteria applies to *internal trials* too.

Given a temporary configuration C and an IAFA A_r generated from r, predicate $PTC(C, A_r)$ holds if C passes the *Post-Trial Check*. We setup a temporary configuration C_i' for the result of C_i after the current trial. Only when C_i' passes PTC, can *configuration_update()* commits the trial by assigning C_i' to C_{i+1}. We define $PTC(C, A_r)$ as follows.

Definition 5.1.

- For $r = \epsilon$, $r = b$, $r = r_1[*n]$, $r = r_1[*n : m]$ and $r = r[*]$
  $PTC(C, A_r) =_{df} \bigvee_{s \in S(r)} s \in C.ST$
- For $r = r_1;\ r_2$ and $r = r_1 \mid r_2$
  $PTC(C, A_r) =_{df} PTC(C, A_{r_1}) \vee PTC(C, A_{r_2}) \qquad \bigvee_{s \in S(r) - S(r_1) - S(r_2)} s \in C.ST$
- For $r = r_1 \&\& r_2$ and $r = r_1 \& r_2$[1]

[1] Please refer the automata construction of $A_{r_1 \ \&\& \ r_2}$ and $A_{r_1 \ \& \ r_2}$ for s_0, s_f, s_{f1} and s_{f2}.

$$PTC(C,A_r) =_{df} s_0 \in C.ST \vee s_f \in C.ST$$
$$\vee((PTC(C,A_{r_1}) \vee s_{f1} \in C.ST) \wedge (PTC(C,A_{r_2}) \vee s_{f2} \in C.ST))$$

Now, let us have a look at the time complexity of Opt.1. Suppose r_1 and r_2 are two concurrent SEREs, C is a configuration, and $CG_1(C)$ and $CG_2(C)$ are the *candidate guard* sets of A_{r1} and A_{r2}.

$$CG_i(C) = \{g \mid \exists u, S, s \in C.ST \cap S(r_1) \bullet (s, g, u, S) \in \rho(r_i)\}$$

Let $LET(C)$ be the set of letters which can trigger external transitions of C's active states and the resulting C' can pass the *Post-Trial Check*. Then,

$$LET(C) = \{l \mid \exists g_{1i} \in CG_1(C), g_{2j} \in CG_2(C) \bullet l \Vdash g_{1i}g_{2j}\}$$
$$= \bigcup_{g_{1i}, g_{2j}} \{l \mid l \Vdash g_{1i}\} \cap \{l \mid l \Vdash g_{2j}\}$$

Let $size(g)$ be the size of the letter set whose elements satisfy g. Then,

$$\mid LET(C) \mid \leq \sum_{g_{1i}, g_{2j}} min(size(g_{1i}), size(g_{2j})) \qquad (2)$$

Formula (2) gives the upper bound of the letter space restricted by Opt.1 in each external trial. The letter set characterized by g is a subset of 2^V. Though the exponent in $size(g)$ is not removed, if the biggest $size(g)$ are small, then $\mid LET(C) \mid$ will be small.

Opt.2(*No-Repeated-Transition Check*)

Opt.1 reduces the search space from 2^V to $LET(C)$. It is observed that there is still redundancy in $LET(C)$. It is possible for different letters to trigger an identical bunch of external transitions which lead to identical suffix words. It is reasonable to cancel a trial if it does not contribute new transitions. That is the motivation of our second optimization (Opt.2), the *No-Repeated-Transition Check*. Opt.2 reduces the search space to the product of the guard sets of universal branches. In terms of Opt.1, the search space of Opt.2 is $CG_1(C) \times CG_2(C)$. Consequently, its size is $\mid CG_1(C) \mid \times \mid CG_2(C) \mid$. Now, we get an algorithm whose time complexity is linear in each external trial. However, Opt.2 may not always reduce the number of external trials. Because, the check is applied after external trials.

6 Experiments and Analysis

By **Proposition 4.3**, the size of A_r is linear to $\mid r \mid$, our experiment focuses on the time aspect in concluding an unsatisfiable SERE and searching finite words of a satisfiable one. We carry out the algorithm comparison on a ThinkPad with dural 1.83GHz CPUs, and 2GB RAM. The parallel feature of the machine is not exploited. We adopt *zchaff* [18] (version 2007.3.12) as the engine for external trials. Currently, there is no standard benchmark for the satisfiability of SEREs. We forge the test cases with the object as covering as many SERE constructs as possible.

Table.1.2.3.4 demonstrate some test results. In those tests, the minimal search depth is 1, the maximal search depth is 22, and the upper bound for external trials is 100,000. If the value is reached before finding any satisfying word, we can not conclude on the satisfiability of the SEREs Under Assuring (SUA).

The performance of our optimizations is encouraging. If a SUA has abundant features of concurrency, as in experiment 1 and 2, the performance promotion is significant. It confirms our prediction on the algorithm complexity. The effect of *Opt.2* is dominant in experiment 3 and 4. It is rather quick in concluding the unsatisfiability of the SUAs. And the joint use of *Opt*.1 and *Opt*.2 is preferable if satisfiability is the only pursuit.

It is interesting to investigate **Table.2**, which aims at the first 30 satisfying words. We find that if we turn off *Opt*.2, the ratio of *external trial* against *internal trial* is less than 1. But it is greater than 1 when *Opt*.2 = 0. That means quite a number of *external trials* are not committed if they do not bring new transitions. Consequently, turning on *Opt*.2 can work out more diversified words.

Table 1. Experiment 1

SERE	$\{\{\{a\ xor\ b\}[*1:4]\}\&\&\{\{b\ xor\ c\}[*2:5]\};\ \{\{[*2:4];\ !a[*2:5]\}[*2]\}\&\{[*5];\ a[*4]\}\}$				
Target	To find the first satisfying word				
Opt. 2	Opt. 1	NO. External-Trial	NO. Internal-Trial	Time(s)	NO. Found
0	0	100000	11145	64.79	0
0	1	59	97	0.09	1
1	0	1357	759	0.78	1
1	1	32	82	0.07	1

Table 2. Experiment 2

SERE	$\{\{\{a\ xor\ b\}[*1:4]\}\&\&\{\{b\ xor\ c\}[*2:5]\};\ \{\{[*2:4];\ !a[*2:5]\}[*2]\}\&\{[*5];\ a[*4]\}\}$				
Target	To find the first 30 satisfying words				
Opt. 2	Opt. 1	NO. External-Trial	NO. Internal-Trial	Time(s)	NO. Found
0	0	100000	11145	65.15	0
0	1	106	420	0.36	30
1	0	49632	29066	29.19	30
1	1	3588	2743	2.78	30

Table 3. Experiment 3

SERE	$\{[*10];\ \{a\}\&\&\{!a\}\}$				
Target	To find the first satisfying word				
Opt. 2	Opt. 1	NO. External-Trial	NO. Internal-Trial	Time(s)	NO. Found
0	0	100000	33431	16.94	0
0	1	6141	9210	2.45	0
1	0	99	65	0.03	0
1	1	33	43	0.01	0

Table 4. Experiment 4

SERE	$[*10];\ \{a[*3]\}\&\&\{b;\ TRUE;\ !a\}$				
Target	To find the first satisfying word				
Opt. 2	Opt. 1	NO. External-Trial	NO. Internal-Trial	Time(s)	NO. Found
0	0	100000	20057	22.96	0
0	1	100000	103598	22.08	0
1	0	256	104	0.09	0
1	1	62	52	0.03	0

7 Future Works

In this paper, we have presented the algorithms behind the tool kit ASERE for assuring the satisfiability of SEREs. We have formalized the IAFA as the representation of SERE. Essentially, the IAFA conception is a *memoryful*, *synchronization-enabled* and *multi-tape* computing model.

We have proposed a DPLL-like search process and discussed two optimizations aiming at reducing the number of external trials. Experiments have confirmed our prediction on their performance.

In the future, we will carry out our research in the following directions.

- Enabling the fusion operator : (overlapping concatenation) in ASERE.
- Extending ASERE to LTL so that we can solve the assurance problem for formulas in PSL's simple subset. A possible solution is to combine the alternating automaton approach with the SNF approach [4] [20]. The SNF addresses the LTL constructs and the alternating automaton addresses the embedded SEREs. The challenging work lies in searching the satisfying words of r **until** b, which requires a new search for r on each clock event until the assertion of b. However, the length of the satisfying words of r is so non-deterministic that it is rather hard to decide the depth at which we can assert b .

References

1. Ben-David, S., Bloem, R., Fisman, D., Griesmayer, A., Pill, I., Ruah, S.: Automata construction algorithm optimized for PSL. Technical Report Delivery 3.2/4, PROSYD (July 2005)
2. Benedetti, M., Cimatti, A.: Bounded model checking for past ltl. In: Proceedings of the International Conference on Tools and Algorithms for the Construction and Analysis of Systems, pp. 18–33 (2003)
3. Bloem, R., Cimatti, A., Pill, I., Roveri, M., Semprini, S.: Symbolic implementation of alternating automata. In: H. Ibarra, O., Yen, H.-C. (eds.) CIAA 2006. LNCS, vol. 4094, pp. 208–218. Springer, Heidelberg (2006)
4. Bloem, R., Cavada, R., Esiner, C., Pill, I., Roveri, M., Semprini, S.: Manual for property simulation and assurance tool. Technical Report Deliverable D1.2/4-5, PROSYD (2005)
5. Chandra, A., Kozen, D., Stockmeyer, L.: Alternation. Journal of ACM 28(1), 113–114 (1981)
6. Feikbeiner, B., Sipma, H.: Checking finite traces using alternating automata. Formal Methods in System Design 24(2), 101–127 (2004)
7. Fisman, D., Eisner, C., Havlicek, J.: Formal syntax and Semantics of PSL: Appendix B of Accellera's Property Specification Language Reference Manual, 1.1 edn. Accellera (March 2004)
8. Hammer, M.: Linear Weak Alternating Automata and The Model Checking. PhD thesis (2005)
9. Havlicek, J., Fisman, D., Eisner, C.: Basic results on the semantics of accellera PSL 1.1 foundation language (2004)
10. Heljanko, K., Junttila, T.A., Keinänen, M., Lange, M., Latvala, T.: Bounded model checking for weak alternating büchi automata. In: Proceedings of the 18th International Conference on Computer Aided Verification, pp. 95–108 (2006)
11. IEEE. IEEE 1850-2005 Standard for Property Specification Language (PSL) (2005)
12. Kupferman, O., Ta-Shma, A., Vardi, M.Y.: Concurrency counts (2001)

13. Kupferman, O., Vardi, M.Y.: Weak alternating automata and tree automata emptiness. In: Proceedings of the Thirtieth Annual ACM Symposium on the Theory of Computing, pp. 224–233 (1998)
14. Kupferman, O., Vardi, M.Y.: Weak alternating automata are not that weak. ACM Transactions on Computational Logic (TOCL) 2(3), 408–429 (2001)
15. Kupferman, O., Vardi, M.Y., Wolper, P.: An automata-theoretic approach to branching-time model checking. Journal of the ACM 47(2), 312–360 (2000)
16. Lange, M.: Linear time logics around PSL: Complexity, expressiveness, and a little bit of succinctness. In: Caires, L., Vasconcelos, V.T. (eds.) CONCUR 2007. LNCS, vol. 4703, pp. 90–104. Springer, Heidelberg (2007)
17. Latvala, T., Biere, A., Heljanko, K., Junttila, T.: Simple is better: Efficient bounded model checking for past LTL. In: Cousot, R. (ed.) VMCAI 2005. LNCS, vol. 3385, pp. 380–395. Springer, Heidelberg (2005)
18. Moskewicz, M.W., Madigan, C.F., Zhao, Y., Zhang, L., Malik, S.: Chaff: Engineering an efficient sat solver. In: Proceedings of the 38th Design Automation Conference (DAC 2001), pp. 530–535 (2001)
19. Prasad, M.R., Biere, A., Gupta, A.: A survey of recent advances in sat-based formal verification. International Journal on Software Tools for Technology Transfer 7, 156–173 (2005)
20. Roveri, M.: Novel techniques for property assurance. Technical Report Deliverable D1.2/2, PROSYD (2004)
21. Vardi, M.Y.: Alternating automata and program verification. In: van Leeuwen, J. (ed.) Computer Science Today. LNCS, vol. 1000, pp. 471–485. Springer, Heidelberg (1995)
22. Vardi, M.Y.: An automata-theoretic approach to linaer temporal logic. In: Moller, F., Birtwistle, G. (eds.) Logics for Concurrency. LNCS, vol. 1043, pp. 238–266. Springer, Heidelberg (1996)
23. http://sites.sei.ecnu.edu.cn/Teachers/nyjin/e/asere_e.html

Computing Must and May Alias to Detect Null Pointer Dereference*

Xiaodong Ma, Ji Wang, and Wei Dong

National Laboratory for Parallel and Distributed Processing, P.R. China
{xd.ma,wj,wdong}@nudt.edu.cn

Abstract. This paper presents a novel algorithm to detect null pointer dereference errors. The algorithm utilizes both of the must and may alias information in a compact way to improve the precision of the detection. Using may alias information obtained by a fast flow- and context- insensitive analysis algorithm, we compute the must alias generated by the assignment statements and the must alias information is also used to improve the precision of the may alias. We can strong update more expressions using the must alias information, which will reduce the false positives of the detection for null pointer dereference. We have implemented our algorithm in the SUIF2 compiler infrastructure and the experiments results are as expected.

1 Introduction

Null pointer dereference is a kind of common errors in programs written in C. If a pointer expression (including a pointer variable) which points to NULL is dereferenced, the program will fail. If a pointer expression is uninitialized or freed, we call it an invalid pointer expression. Dereferencing an invalid pointer expression may not crash the program, but will get a wrong datum. Therefore, dereferencing a NULL pointer or an invalid pointer are regarded as null pointer dereference errors in this paper.

Alias information is needed to detect the null pointer dereference error. For example, dereferencing $*e$ after statement $e = NULL$ or $free(e)$ will cause an error. It should be noticed that dereferencing any expression which may be alias of $*e$ also possibly causes a null pointer dereference error. Thus a conservative algorithm needs the *may alias* information. Of course, we know that although a conservative algorithm does not miss any real error, it may produce many false alarms. This paper makes attempt to find much information to improve the precision of static analysis for null pointer dereference. Statement $e = malloc()$ assigns e with a non-NULL value, thus e can be dereferenced and $*e$ can be written after this statement under the condition that the l-value of e is not changed. If e' is the alias of e before every possible execution of this statement

* This work is supported by National Natural Science Foundation of China(60725206, 60673118 and 90612009), National 863 project of China(2006AA01Z429), Program for New Century Excellent Talents in University under grant No. NCET-04-0996.

T. Margaria and B. Steffen (Eds.): ISoLA 2008, CCIS 17, pp. 252–261, 2008.

and its l-value cannot be changed, then we can say that dereferencing e' or write $*e'$ is also a valid operation. If we do not have the *must alias* information, we may report errors, which could be false alarms actually.

Figure 1 illustrates the usage of must and may alias information. Statement 3 will not cause error because $*z$ is the must alias of $*y$. Statement 7 may cause error because y is the may alias of $*x$ and $*x$ has been nulled at statement 6. It is clear that must alias information can make the detection algorithm more precise. However, the must alias information has not been well used in the existing error finding techniques.

```
int **x, *y, *z;
...
1. y = malloc();
2. z = y;
3. *z = 5;
4. if(...)
5.    x = &y;
6. *x = NULL;
7. *y = 5;
```

Fig. 1. Usage of must and may alias

There are some null pointer dereference detection tools, such as [13], [2] and [9]. But they have not exploited the must alias information. There is a little work about computing and exploiting the must alias information in C programs. To the best of our knowledge, the only work is [1]. It defines an extended form of must alias and uses the result to improve the precision of def-use computation. In this paper, our algorithm computes the must and may alias information of a set of k-limiting expressions [7] from the result of a fast flow- and context- insensitive alias analysis algorithm and the must alias information is used to detect the null pointer dereference errors. A tool prototype has been implemented and the initial experimental results are as expected.

This paper is organized as follows. We first introduce the points-to graph and the method for computing l-values of expressions in Section 2, then the details of our must alias computation algorithm in Section 3 and null pointer dereference detection algorithm in Section 4. Section 5 gives the experimental results. The related work and conclusions are in Section 6.

2 Points-to Graph

We suppose the result of the flow- and context- insensitive alias analysis algorithm is a points-to graph. In this section, we introduce the definition of points-to graph and describe how to compute the l-value of an expression in a points-to graph. Then we introduce the concept of may alias and define the must alias used in this paper.

A *location set* is an abstraction of the memories. It is a pair of the form $(name, offset)$ where $name$ describes a memory block and $offset$ is the offset within that block. Notice that for a variable we just use its name as the *name* and for the dynamically allocated heaps we use the allocation-site abstraction. We consider an array as a variable with the type of its elements.

A *points-to graph* is a directed graph with the location sets as nodes. There is a directed edge from one node to another if one of the memory locations represented by the first node may point to one of the memory locations represented by the second one.

Figure 2 is a segment of C code and its corresponding flow-insensitive points-to graph. *heap_1* denotes all the memory locations allocated at line 1. *heap_2.32* is the "next" field of the structure allocated at line 2. Different fields of a structure are represented by different location sets.

```
struct list{
  int d;
  struct list *n;
};
struct list *x, *y;
1.   x = malloc();
2.   x->n = malloc();
```

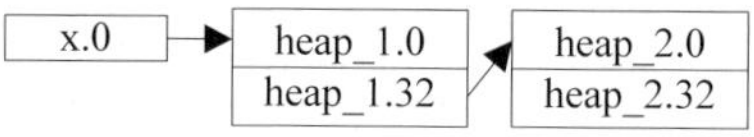

x.0 → heap_1.0 | heap_1.32 → heap_2.0 | heap_2.32

Fig. 2. An example segment of C code and the points-to graphs

Given a points-to graph, we can compute the l-value of an expression, which is a set of the possible location sets used to store its value. Besides all the location sets occurring in the points-to graph, we introduce another kind of location set called "virtual location set". It is in the form of "$\&l$" where l is a location set. We define the l-value of an expression e on the points-to graph G by a function $ll(e, G)$ as following.

$$ll(const, G) = \emptyset \quad ll(null, G) = \emptyset \quad ll(x, G) = \{x.0\}$$
$$ll(\&e, G) = \{\&l \mid l \in ll(e, G)\} \quad ll(e.f, G) = \{n.f \mid n.0 \in ll(e, G)\}$$
$$ll(*e, G) = \quad \{l' \mid \&l' \in ll(e, G) \text{ or } ((l, l') \in G, l \in ll(e, G))\}$$
$$ll(e{\rightarrow}f, G) = \{n.f \mid (l, n.0) \in G, l \in ll(e, G)\}$$

May alias is discussed widely, such as [6], [8], [10] and [12]. Alias information is computed at the control flow graph vertex, that is, before the execution of each statement–we call it program point. It is obvious that there may be more than one path through each program point. At a program point, if the l-value of expression e_1 and e_2 may be the same, then e_1 and e_2 have may alias relationship. It is possible that the l-value of e_1 in some execution path is the same as that of e_2 in another execution path. In this case, e_1 and e_2 may not be alias actually.

In order to make the definition of must alias clear, we use the postfix form of an expression e, which is defined by a function $pf(e)$ in the following, where x is a variable.

$pf(const) = const \quad pf(x) = x \quad pf(\&e) = e\& \quad pf(*e) = e* \quad pf(e.f) = e.f$
$pf(e{\rightarrow}n) = e * .n$

We say that e_1 is the must alias of e_2 at a program point p if e_1 and e_2 have the same l-value at every possible execution of p. But in some cases, the l-value of e_1 or e_2 may not be defined. For example, $x{\rightarrow}n{\rightarrow}n$ does not have l-value before the execution of statement 2 in Figure 2.

Let $e_1 = e_1'\omega$, $e_2 = e_2'\omega$, where ω can be empty. If e_1' and e_2' have the same l-value, then we think e_1 and e_2 have must alias relationship.

3 Computing Must Alias

3.1 Must Alias Data Flow Fact

Based on a flow- and context- insensitive may alias analysis, we compute the fixpoint of data flow fact of must alias at the program point before each statement. The must alias relation is an equivalence relation, that is, it is reflexive, symmetric and transitive. For example, if e_1 is the must alias of e_2 and e_2 is the must alias of e_3, then e_1 is the must alias of e_3. May alias relation is also reflexive, symmetric, but not transitive, because two may alias pairs may be generated in different execution paths. Supposing r is a must alias relation on the expression set E, we can get $E \backslash r = \{C_r^1, C_r^2, ..., C_r^n\}$.

The data flow fact of must alias used in our algorithm is a tuple (r, M) where r is a must alias relation on E and M is a map from the equivalence class with respect to r to the location sets in the points-to graph. In other words, $M(C_r^i)$ denotes all the possible l-values of the expressions in C_r^i.

Let r_1, r_2 be must alias relation on E, we define $r_1 \preceq r_2$ if and only if $\forall e_1 \in E, \forall e_2 \in E, < e_1, e_2 > \in r_1 \Rightarrow < e_1, e_2 > \in r_2$. Thus the partial order of the data flow fact is defined as $(r_1, M_1) \sqsubseteq (r_2, M_2)$ if and only if $r_1 \preceq r_2$ and $\forall e \in E$, $M_1([e]_{r_1}) \supseteq M_2([e]_{r_2})$. Two special elements are also defined: the top element $\top$ and the bottom element $\bot$. For any data flow fact d, we have $d \sqsubseteq \top$ and $\bot \sqsubseteq d$.

May alias information can be deduced from the data flow fact. If $M([e_1]_r) \cap M([e_2]_r) \neq \emptyset$, then we say that $\forall e_x \in [e_1]_r$, $\forall e_y \in [e_2]_r$, e_x and e_y have the may alias relation. If two data flow facts d_1 and d_2 satisfy $d_1 \sqsubseteq d_2$, then the must alias pairs in d_2 is a superset of that in d_1. Because the possible l-values of each expression in d_1 is also a superset of that in d_2, it is easy to prove that the may alias pairs deduced from d_2 is a subset of that from d_1. d_2 has more must alias pairs and less may alias pairs than that of d_1, thus d_2 is more precise than d_1.

We use data flow analysis to compute the data flow fact at each program point. Initially, the data flow fact at each program point is $\bot$. "join" operation "$\sqcup$" is defined to compute the fixpoint of the data flow fact at each program point. In order to define the join operation of the data flow fact, we define that of the equivalence relation. Join operation $\vee$ of two equivalence relations r_1 and r_2 is defined as the transive closure of the union of r_1 and r_2, that is, $r_1 \vee r_2 = closure(r_1 \cup r_2)$. Thus $r_1 \vee r_2$ is also an equivalence relation.

The join operation of data flow fact is defined as:

$(r_1, M_1) \sqcup (r_2, M_2) = (r_1 \vee r_2, M')$, M' satisfies $M'(C^i_{r_1 \vee r_2}) = (M_1([e_1]_{r_1}) \cap M_2([e_1]_{r_2})) \cap ... \cap (M_1([e_n]_{r_1}) \cap M_2([e_n]_{r_2}))$ where $C^i_{r_1 \vee r_2} = \{e_1, ..., e_n\}$.

Of course, for any data flow fact d, we have $\top \sqcup d = \top$, $\bot \sqcup d = d$.

3.2 Must Alias Analysis

In this subsection, we will show the effect of statements on data flow facts, that is, how a statement produces a new data flow fact from an input data flow fact.

Some auxiliary functions need to be defined first.

$deref(e) = stars(e) - addr(e)$. Where $stars(e)$ is the number of character '*' in e and $addr(e)$ is the number of character '&'. The result of $deref(e)$ is the dereference depth of e. It is easily to know that $\forall e \in E, deref(e) \geq -1$.

$may(e, (r, M)) = \{e' | M([e']_r) \cap M([e]_r) \neq \emptyset, e' \in E\}$ is the set of expressions which are the may aliases of e.

$lchg(e, (r, M)) = \{e'\omega | e' \in may(e, (r, M)), deref(ew) > deref(e), e'w \in E\}$. The result of this function is all the expressions whose l-value may be changed to different location sets by a statement which assigns a value to e.

We use a transfer function to define the effect of a statement. Three kinds of statements are considered: the allocation statement $e = malloc()$; the free statement $free(e)$ and the assignment statement $e_0 = e_1$. Note that we think $free(e)$ has the same effect as that of $e = NULL$, so e_1 in the assignment statement is supposed not to be NULL.

The transfer function for $e = malloc()$.

$[e = malloc()](r, M) = (r', M')$ where r' satisfies the following condition.

(1) $\forall e_0 \notin lchg(e, (r, M))$, $\forall e_1 \notin lchg(e, (r, M))$: $< e_0, e_1 > \in r \Rightarrow < e_0, e_1 > \in r'$;

(2) $\forall e_0 \in may(e, (r, M)), e_0 \notin lchg(e, (r, M))$ and $\forall e_1 \in may(e, (r, M)), e_1 \notin lchg(e, (r, M))$, $< e_0, e_1 > \in r \Rightarrow < e_0\omega, e_1\omega > \in r'$ whenever $deref(e_0\omega) > deref(e_0)$ and $e_0\omega \in E$, $e_1\omega \in E$.

(3) there are no more relation pairs in r' other than that generated by rules (1) and (2).

It can be proved that r' is also an equivalence relation.

M' is defined on the equivalence class with respect to r'.

$M'([e_x]_{r'}) = M([e_x]_r)$ if $[e_x]_{r'} \cap lchg(e, (r, M)) = \emptyset$

For the equivalence class which contains expression whose l-value may be changed, we write it in the form of $[e_y\omega]_{r'}$ where $e_y \notin lchg(e, (r, M))$ and $e_y \in may(e, (r, M))$. The possible l-value of this set of expressions is defined as:

$$M'([e_y\omega]_{r'}) = \begin{cases} heap\_i.f_x & : \text{ if } e\omega \in [e_y\omega]_{r'} \text{ and } deref(e_y\omega) = deref(e_y) + 1 \\ heap\_i.f_x \cup M([e_y\omega]_r) & : \text{ if } e\omega \notin [e_y\omega]_{r'} \text{ and } deref(e_y\omega) = deref(e_y) + 1 \\ \emptyset & : \text{ if } e\omega \in [e_y\omega]_{r'} \text{ and } deref(e_y\omega) > deref(e_y) + 1 \\ M([e_y\omega]_r) & : \text{ if } e\omega \notin [e_y\omega]_{r'} \text{ and } deref(e_y\omega) > deref(e_y) + 1 \end{cases}$$

heap_i is the abstract heap allocated at the current statement. The suffix f_x depends on the types of expression $e_y\omega$. If the l-value of an equivalence class is allocated definitely at the current statement, then we use $heap\_i.f_x$ as its l-value, else we add $heap\_i.f_x$ to the original l-value set to make our computation of l-value conservative. It is clear that the currently allocated heap cannot be dereferenced-which explains why $\emptyset$ occurs in the definition.

The transfer function for $free(e)$.

$[free(e)](r, M) = (r', M')$.

Because we regard the effect of $free(e)$ as assigning NULL to e, the rules for generating r' are the same as that of statement $e = malloc()$.

The definition of M' is divided into two cases.

For the equivalence class $[e_x]_{r'}$ which does not contain any expression in $lchg(e, (r, M))$, we get $M'([e_x]_{r'}) = M([e_x]_r)$.

For the equivalence classes which contains expression in $lchg(e, (r, M))$, we can write it as $[e_y\omega]_{r'}$ where $e_y \in may(e, (r, M))$ and $e_y \notin lchg(e, (r, M))$.

$$M'([e_y\omega]_{r'}) = \begin{cases} \emptyset & : \text{ if } e\omega \in [e_y\omega]_{r'} \text{ and } deref(e_y\omega) > deref(e_y) \\ M([e_y\omega]_r) : & \text{ if } e\omega \notin [e_y\omega]_{r'} \text{ and } deref(e_y\omega) > deref(e_y) \end{cases}$$

The transfer function for $e_0 = e_1$.

$[e_0 = e_1](r, M) = (r', M')$.

The effect of this statement can be divided into two parts: it first destroys the old value of e_0 and then assigns a new value to it. In other words, we replace it with two statements: $e_0 = NULL; e_0 = e_1$. The generation of r' can also be divided into two steps: the generation of equivalence relation r'' after the execution of $e_0 = NULL$ and that of r' after $e_0 = e_1$. We can get r'' by applying the same rules as that for the $e = malloc()$ statement. The generation of r' is defined in the following.

$$r' = \begin{cases} closure(r'' \cup \{< e_0\omega, e_1\omega > \mid deref(e_0\omega) > deref(e_0)\}) & : \text{if } (1) \\ r'' & : \text{else} \end{cases}$$

where $(1) \equiv e_0 \notin lchg(e_0, (r, M)), e_1 \notin lchg(e_0, (r, M))$.

The definition of M' is as following.

$M'([e_x]_{r'}) = M([e_x]_r)$ if $[e_x]_{r'} \cap lchg(e_0, (r, M)) = \emptyset$.

For the equivalence class $[e_y\omega]_{r'}$ which satisfies $[e_y\omega]_{r'} \cap lchg(e_0, (r, M)) \neq \emptyset$, $e_y \in may(e_0, (r, M))$ and $e_y \notin lchg(e_0, (r, M))$, we can have:

$$M'([e_y\omega]_{r'}) = \begin{cases} M([e_1\omega]_r) & : \text{ if } (2) \\ M([e_1\omega]_r) \cup M([e_y\omega]_r) : & \text{ if } (3) \\ bottom & : \text{ else} \end{cases}$$

In the above definition, $(2) \equiv e_1 \notin lchg(e_0, (r, M)) \wedge e_0\omega \in [e_y\omega]_{r'} \wedge \forall\omega' : deref(e_1) < deref(e_1\omega') < deref(e_1\omega) \Rightarrow e_1\omega' \notin lchg(e_0, (r, M))$. If (2) is satisfied, we are sure that the l-value of $e_y\omega$ is changed and the corresponding l-value of the source equivalence class is not changed. Thus we can replace the l-value of $[e_y\omega]_{r'}$ with that of $[e_1\omega]_r$. (3) $\equiv e_1 \notin lchg(e_0, (r, M)) \wedge e_0\omega \notin [e_y\omega]_{r'} \wedge \forall\omega' : deref(e_1) < deref(e_1\omega') < deref(e_1\omega) \Rightarrow e_1\omega' \notin lchg(e_0, (r, M))$. In this case, the l-value of the source equivalence class is not changed, too. But we are not sure whether $[e_y\omega]_r$ is the target equivalence class. So we use the union operation to make our algorithm conservative. In the third case, *bottom* denotes all the possible location sets of $e_y\omega$. This value is used because the l-value of the source class may be changed and the target class may not be assigned with the l-value of the source class.

In the inter-procedural analysis phase, we add a sequence of statements which assign the formal parameters with the corresponding real arguments before stepping into the called procedure. After exiting from the called procedure p, we clean the must information of the local expressions of p. That is, there is no expression which is the must alias of a local expression except itself.

4 Null Pointer Dereference Detection

The null pointer dereference detection algorithm which will be presented is based on the results of the must alias analysis. The strong updates derived from the must alias information can make the detection algorithm more precise. In this section, we suppose the data flow fact of must alias information has already been computed at the program point before each statement.

In order to detect null dereference error, we use a data flow fact to describe the allocation information. It is a function $A : E \rightarrow \{true, false\}$. $A(e) = true$ denotes that the pointer expression e points to a valid memory location. $A(e) = false$ means that e points to $NULL$ or other invalid memory location, such as an uninitialized or freed one.

As in the computing of must alias, there is a function describing the allocation information at each program point. We compute its fixpoint. The top value of the allocation information $A_\top$ is defined as: $\forall e \in E(A_\top(e) = true)$ and the bottom $\forall e \in E(A_\bot(e) = false)$. $A_1 \sqsubseteq A_2$ iff $\forall e \in E(A_1(e) = false \vee A_2(e) = true)$. $A_1 \sqcup A_2 = A'$ where $\forall e \in E(A'(e) = A_1(e) \vee A_2(e))$. The initial allocation information at each program point is $A_\bot$.

Each type of statements can be regarded as a transfer function which takes a must alias data flow fact (r, M) and an allocation data flow fact A as inputs and outputs allocation data flow fact A'.

The transfer function for $e = malloc()$.
$[e = malloc()]_A((r, M), A) = A'$ where:

$$A'(e_y) = \begin{cases} false: & \text{if } e_y \in lchg(e, (r, M)) \\ true: & \text{if } e_y \notin lchg(e, (r, M)) \text{ and } < e_y, e > \in r \\ A(e_y): & \text{else} \end{cases}$$

The transfer function for $free(e)$.
$[free(e)]_A((r, M), A) = A'$ where:

$$A'(e_y) = \begin{cases} false: & \text{if } e_y \in may(e,(r,M)) \text{ or } e_y \in lchg(e,(r,M)) \\ A(e_y): & \text{else} \end{cases}$$

The transfer function for $e_0 = e_1$.
$[e_0 = e_1]_A((r, M), A) = A'$.

The definition of A' is divided into two parts. The first is for the expressions which are not in $lchg(e_0, (r, M))$ and the second is for the other expressions. We also rewrite expressions in the second part in the form of $e_y\omega$ where $e_y \in may(e_0, (r, M))$ and $e_y \notin lchg(e_0, (r, M))$.

$A'(e_x) = A(e_x)$ if $e_x \notin lchg(e_0, (r, M))$.

$$A'(e_y\omega) = \begin{cases} A(e_1\omega) & : \text{ if (2)} \\ A(e_1\omega) \wedge A(e_y\omega) : & \text{ if (3)} \\ false & : \text{ else} \end{cases}$$

The inter-procedural analysis is in the similar way as that in the must alias analysis. A sequence of statements which assign real arguments to the corresponding formal parameters are inserted at the entry of the called procedure. $A(e)$ is assigned with $false$ after exiting from procedure p if e is the local expression of p.

Using the allocation information, we can decide whether an expression causes null pointer dereference. If an expression $e\omega$ is read or written and the following conditions are satisfied: (1) $A(e) = false$; (2) $deref(e\omega) > deref(e)$, then we say that a null pointer dereference may occur.

5 Experiment

We have implemented the prototype of our algorithm in the SUIF2 compiler infrastructure and evaluated it with the test cases from samate [11]. The description of the test cases and the results of our experiment are listed in Table 1.

NPD stands for "Null Pointer Dereference" in Table 1. From the results of the experiment, we can see that our method has a good precision. It should be

Table 1. Experiment with the test cases from samate

Case IDs	Reports	Bugs	Description
1760	1	1	Ordinary NPD.
1875	1	1	NPD through array element.
1876	1	1	NPD through array element in branch condition.
1877	1	1	NPD within branch of switch statement.
1879	1	1	NPD caused inter-procedurally.
1880	0	0	Dereferencing inter-procedurally without NPD.
1934	0	0	NPD within unreachable branch of if statement.

noticed that in the program No. 1394, there is a dereference of a null pointer in the branch of an if statement, but the condition cannot be satisfied. Our tool uses the allocation information to decide whether some simple condition expressions can be satisfied. For example, if $A(e) = true$, then we can know the value of $e \neq NULL$ is true.

6 Related Work and Conclusions

Must alias information is very useful for many analysis like constant propagation, register allocation and dependence analysis [3]. However, not much work has been done for must alias analysis [5]. In most cases, it is the side effect of a may alias analysis and is used during the process of may alias analysis in order to improve the precision. [6] defines must alias in an optimistic manner: if during the analysis a pointer only points to one object, then it is treated as a must alias. This definition may miss the must alias information between some expressions which have heap locations in their access path. [1] introduces an extended must alias analysis to handle dynamically allocated locations and this result is used to improved def-use information. CALYSTO [2] can detect null pointer dereference errors. It embraces the ESC/Java [4] philosophy of combining the ease of use of static checking with the powerful analysis of formal verification. It is fully automatic, performing inter-procedural analysis. PSE [9] is also a null pointer dereference detection tool. It tracks the flow of a single value of interest from the point in the program where the failure occurred back to the point in the program where the value may have originated. In other words, it can work in a demand-driven fashion.

In this paper, we propose a novel must alias analysis algorithm. Using the result of a fast, imprecise may alias analysis, it can compute the must alias relation between complex expressions and improve the precision of the may alias at the same time. Exploiting the must alias information, a precise null pointer dereference detection algorithm is also proposed. In the futrue, we will improve the scalability of our tool and use it to check some real world applications.

References

1. Altucher, R.Z., Landi, W.: An extended form of must alias analysis for dynamic allocation. In: POPL 1995: Proceedings of the 22nd ACM SIGPLAN-SIGACT symposium on Principles of programming languages, pp. 74–84. ACM, New York (1995)
2. Babić, D., Hu, A.J.: Calysto: Scalable and Precise Extended Static Checking. In: Proceedings of 30th International Conference on Software Engineering (ICSE 2008), May 10–18 (2008)
3. Emami, M.: A practical interprocedural alias analysis for an optimizing/parallelizing c compiler. Master's thesis, McGill University (1993)
4. Flanagan, C., Leino, K.R.M., Lillibridge, M., Nelson, G., Saxe, J.B., Stata, R.: Extended static checking for java. In: PLDI 2002: Proceedings of the ACM SIGPLAN 2002 Conference on Programming language design and implementation, pp. 234–245. ACM, New York (2002)

5. Hind, M.: Pointer analysis: haven't we solved this problem yet? In: PASTE 2001: Proceedings of the 2001 ACM SIGPLAN-SIGSOFT workshop on Program analysis for software tools and engineering, pp. 54–61. ACM, New York (2001)
6. Hind, M., Burke, M., Carini, P., Choi, J.-D.: Interprocedural pointer alias analysis. ACM Transactions on Programming Languages and Systems 21(4), 848–894 (1999)
7. Jones, N.D., Muchnick, S.S.: Flow analysis and optimization of lisp-like structures. In: POPL 1979: Proceedings of the 6th ACM SIGACT-SIGPLAN symposium on Principles of programming languages, pp. 244–256. ACM, New York (1979)
8. Liang, D., Harrold, M.J.: Efficient points-to analysis for whole-program analysis. In: ESEC / SIGSOFT FSE, pp. 199–215 (1999)
9. Manevich, R., Sridharan, M., Adams, S., Das, M., Yang, Z.: Pse: Explaining program failures via postmortem static analysis. In: Richard, N. (ed.) Proceedings of the 12th International Symposium on the Foundations of Software Engineering (FSE 2004)November 2004. ACM, New York (2004)
10. Rugina, R., Rinard, M.: Pointer analysis for multithreaded programs. In: PLDI 1999: Proceedings of the ACM SIGPLAN 1999 conference on Programming language design and implementation, pp. 77–90. ACM Press, New York (1999)
11. Samate test cases, `http://samate.nist.gov`
12. Steensgaard, B.: Points-to analysis in almost linear time. In: Symposium on Principles of Programming Languages, pp. 32–41 (1996)
13. Xie, Y., Aiken, A.: Saturn: A scalable framework for error detection using boolean satisfiability. ACM Trans. Program. Lang. Syst. 29(3), 16 (2007)

A Partial Order Reduction Technique for Parallel Timed Automaton Model Checking

Zhao Jianhua, Wang Linzhang, and Li Xuandong*

State Key Laboratory of Novel Software Technology
Dept. of Computer Sci. and Tech. Nanjing University
Nanjing, Jiangsu, P.R. China 210093
zhaojh@nju.edu.cn

Abstract. We propose a partial order reduction technique for timed automaton model checking in this paper. We first show that the symbolic successors w.r.t. partial order paths can be computed using DBMs. An algorithm is presented to compute such successors incrementally. This algorithm can avoid splitting the symbolic states because of the enumeration order of independent transitions. A reachability analysis algorithm based on this successor computation algorithm is presented. Our technique can be combined with some static analysis techniques in the literate. Further more, we present a rule to avoid exploring all enabled transitions, thus the space requirements of model checking are further reduced.

1 Introduction

Timed automata, and their parallel compositions, can be used to model realtime systems. A timed automaton[1] is derived by extending a conventional finite state automaton with clock variables and time guards. A (concrete) state of a timed automaton is a tuple composed of a concrete control location and clock values, which are real numbers. The concrete state space of a timed automaton is infinite. So the model checking on timed automata is performed by enumerating symbolic states. Each symbolic state is a tuple of a control location and a clock constraint. It represents a set of concrete states on the same location, of which the clock values satisfying the constraint. Nowadays, powerful timed automata model checking [2][3] tools have succeeded in verifying many industrial systems. However, the state space explosion problem still remains a challenge to researchers.

In the domain of model checking for temporal systems, partial order reduction methods are proved to be efficient. Such methods try to avoid exhaustive state space exploration by avoid enumerating all interleaves of independent transitions. Intuitively speaking, two transitions a, b are independent to each other implies that, the sequence ab is a transition sequence from a state s to another state s' if and only if ba is also a sequence from s to s'. One of these two sequences can be selected as the representative of them. Checking one sequence is equivalent to checking all these sequences.

* This paper is supported by the National Grand Fundamental Research 973 Program of China (No.2002CB312001).

T. Margaria and B. Steffen (Eds.): ISoLA 2008, CCIS 17, pp. 262–276, 2008.

However, in the domain of real time systems, the clock values should also be considered. Even if two transition does not interfere with each other, different orders of these transitions lead to different successive states. Considering the case that a, b respectively reset the clocks $c1$ and $c2$ to 0. Given a symbolic state s, the symbolic state enumeration algorithm used in tools like UPPAAL and Kronos generally gets two different symbolic successors with respect to the sequences ab and ba. So these two transitions is considered to be dependent to each other if such symbolic analysis algorithms are employed.

In the paper [4] and [5], a *local time semantics* is proposed to decouple the transitions of different component of a parallel composition of timed automaton. Each component has its local time. Under such semantics, the transitions a and b are independent if they are from two different components. However, only for a specific class of timed automata, the symbolic state spaces are finite.

In the paper [6], D. Dams, etc. proposed that only a subset of the enabled transitions should be explored if the transitions in this subset covers all other transitions. However, such covering relations are restrictive.

In the paper [7], D. Lugiez, P. Niebert, and S. Zennou presented a method to avoid symbolic state splitting. They compute symbolic successors with respect to the infinite index Myhill-Nerode congruence, but test whether a state should be further explored by a finite index preorder. In their algorithm, the symbolic states is called 'event zones', which are conjunctions of difference bounds on clock variables and a set of auxiliary variables.

In this paper, we propose a partial order reduction technique for parallel timed automaton model checking. Using such a technique, the symbolic successors are computed w.r.t. partial order paths, instead of single transitions. Thus, we avoid splitting the symbolic state because of the enumeration order of transitions. An efficient algorithm which can compute the successors incrementally is presented in this paper. This technique can be combined with some static analysis techniques in the literate. Also, we present a rule to avoid exploring all enabled transitions.

This paper is organized as follows. We give a brief introduction to parallel timed automata in Section 2. In Section 3, we give the definitions of a transition independence relation and partial order paths. We also show that the successor of a symbolic state w.r.t. a partial order path is also a symbolic state. In Section 4, we present an incremental algorithm to compute the successors w.r.t. partial order paths. The reachability analysis algorithm employing this successor computation algorithm is presented Section 5. A rule to avoid exploring all enabled transitions is presented in Section 6. The Section 7 presents some case studies. We conclude this paper in Section 8.

2 Background

2.1 Parallel Timed Automata

Let C be a finite set of clock variables. We use $\mathcal{G}(C)$ to denote the set of time guards, which are conjunctions of the formulas of the form $c \backsim n$, where $c \in C$, $\backsim \in \{<, \leq, =, \geq, >\}$, and n is a non-negative integer.

A timed automaton can be viewed as a conventional finite state automaton equipped with clock variables and time guards. These clock variables and time guards are used to constrain the time distance between the occurrence of transitions. A finite set of timed automata can be composed through synchronization channels or shared variables to model concurrent systems. We use parallel timed automata, which are defined as follow, to describe such parallel compositions.

Definition 1. *A parallel timed automaton A is a tuple $(S, s_0, C, \Sigma, \rightarrow, F, I)$, where*

1. *S is a finite set of locations;*
2. *$s_0 \in S$ is the initial location;*
3. *C is a finite set of clock variables;*
4. *$\Sigma \subseteq \mathcal{G}(C) \times 2^C$ is a finite set of transitions. Given a transition $e = (g, r)$, we say g is the time guard of e, and e resets the clocks in r;*
5. *$\rightarrow \subseteq S \times \Sigma \times S$ is a finite set of edges. We write $l \xrightarrow{e} l'$ if $(l, e, l') \in \rightarrow$.*
6. *$F \subseteq S$ is the set of acceptance locations.*
7. *$I \subseteq S \mapsto \mathcal{G}(C)$ assigns each location in S a location invariant. Each location invariant is a conjunction of formulas of the form $c < n$ or $c \leq n$, where $c \in C$ and n is a non-negative integer.*

Using this definition, we can avoid details such as shared variable assignments and guards, synchronization channels, and so on. Thus we can discuss about partial order reduction on an abstract level.

Given a location l, a transition e is *enabled* at l, denoted as $\texttt{Enable}(l, e)$, if $l \xrightarrow{e} l'$ for some location l'. A transition may take place many times during the evolution of a timed automaton. So there may be many occurrences of a transition during the evolution. Given a transition occurrence o, we use $\underline{o}$ to denote the corresponding transition. A *path* leaving from a location l to another location l' is a sequence of transition occurrences $o_1, o_2, \ldots, o_n$ satisfying that there exists a sequence of locations $l_0, l_1, l_2, \ldots, l_n$ such that $l_0 = l$, $l_n = l'$, and $l_i \xrightarrow{\underline{o_{i+1}}} l_{i+1}$ for $i = 0, 1, 2, \ldots, n-1$. We say l' is the *final location* of p. Let (g_i, r_i) be the transition of o_i for $i = 1, 2, \ldots, n$. We define

$$R(p, i, c) = \begin{cases} 0 & \nexists k.(k < i) \wedge (c \in r_i) \\ j & j \text{ is the bigest integer satisfying that } (c \in r_j) \wedge (j < i) \end{cases}$$

Intuitively speaking, if $R(p, i, c) > 0$, it is the index of the last transition occurrence resetting the clock c before o_i; $R(p, i, c) = 0$ means that there is no transition occurrence resetting c before o_i.

A *state* of the timed automaton A is a tuple (l, v), where $l \in S$, v is a clock valuation which maps each clock in C to a non-negative real value, and v satisfies the time guard $I(l)$, i.e. the location invariant of l.

Let $p = o_1, o_2, \ldots, o_n$ be a path from l to l'. A sequence of time-stamped transition occurrences $\alpha = (\varepsilon, t_0), (o_1, t_1), (o_2, t_2), \ldots, (o_n, t_n)$ is said to be an *execution* starting from a state (l, v) to another state (l', v') following p, denoted as $(l, v) \xrightarrow{\alpha} (l', v')$ if the following conditions hold.

1. **(Transition occurrence order).** For each $i(0 \leq i \leq n-1)$, $t_i \geq t_{i+1}$.
2. **(Transition time guards).** For each integer $i(1 \leq i \leq n)$ and each atomic formula $c \backsim m$ of the time guard of $\underline{o_i}$, $t_{R(p,i,c)} - t_i \backsim m$ if $R(p,i,c) > 0$; $v(c) + t_0 - t_i \backsim m$ if $R(p,i,c) = 0$.
3. **(Location invariants).** Let $l_0, l_1, l_2, \ldots, l_n$ be a sequence of locations satisfying that $\forall k(1 \leq k \leq n).l_{k-1} \stackrel{o_k}{\Rightarrow} l_k$, $l_0 = l$ and $l_n = l'$. For each integer $i(1 \leq i \leq n)$ and each atomic formula $c \backsim m$ of the location invariant of l_{i-1}, $t_{R(p,i,c)} - t_i \backsim m$ if $R(p,i,c) > 0$; $v(c) + t_0 - t_i \backsim m$ if $R(p,i,c) = 0$.
4. **(Final state).** The clock valuation v' is defined as follow. For each clock c, $v'(c) = t_{R(p,n+1,c)}$ if $R(p,n+1,c) > 0$; $v'(c) = v(c) + t_0$ if $R(p,n+1,c) = 0$. The clock valuation v' must satisfy the location invariant of l_n,

In this paper, an execution is viewed as a history of evolution. The time stamp of a transition occurrence represents the time elapsed since the transition occurred. The time guards and location invariants constraint the difference between time stamps.

A transition $e = (g, r)$ is said to be *invariant-irrelevant* w.r.t. a clock c if and only if for any two locations l_1, l_2 such that $l_1 \stackrel{e}{\rightarrow} l_2$, the constraints about c of $I(l_1)$ and $I(l_2)$ are same. Otherwise, it is said to be *invariant-relevant.*

Now considering the condition about location invariants. Notice that $t_{i-1} \geq t_i$, it is unnecessary to check the location invariant about a clock c on l_{i-1} if the atomic formulas about c in $I(l_{i-1})$ and the ones in $I(l_i)$ are same and $\underline{o_i}$ does not reset c. So the third condition can be changed to the following one.

3′ **(Location invariants).** For any integer $i(1 \leq i \leq n)$ such that either $\underline{o_i}$ is invariant-relevant to a clock c, or $\underline{o_i}$ resets c, and $c \backsim m$ ($\backsim \in \{<, \leq\}$) is an atomic formula of $I(l_{i-1})$, we have that $t_{R(p,i,c)} - t_i \backsim m$ holds if $R(p,i,c) > 0$; $v(c) + t_0 - t_i \backsim m$ holds if $R(p,i,c) = 0$.

2.2 Symbolic States and the Symbolic Successors w.r.t. Paths

Because the value of clocks are real numbers, the state space of a parallel timed automaton is generally infinite. Model checking for timed automata can be performed by enumeration of symbolic states. A symbolic state is a tuple (l, D), where l is a location, and D is a conjunction of atomic formulas of the form $x - y \backsim m$, where $x, y \in C \cup \{0\}$, and m is an integer. A symbolic state (l, D) represents the set of states $\{(l, v) | v(c) \backsim m$ holds for each formula $x \backsim m$ of $D\}$. We say a state (l, v) is in a symbolic state (l, D), denoted as $(l, v) \in (l, D)$, if and only if (l, v) is in this set.

Let (l, D) be a symbolic state, $p = o_1, o_2, \ldots, o_n$ be a path from l to l'. The set of concrete states reachable from a state in (l, D) through an execution following p can also be represented as a symbolic state. We call this state as the symbolic successor of (l, D) w.r.t. p, denoted as $sp(p, (l, D))$. The set of reachable concrete states is as follow.

$$\left\{ (l', v') \middle| \begin{array}{l} \exists\, (l, v), \alpha.((l, v) \in (l, D)) \wedge ((l, v) \stackrel{\alpha}{\longrightarrow} (l', v')) \\ \wedge(\alpha \text{ is an execution following } p) \end{array} \right\}.$$

Let $\{c_1, c_2, \ldots, c_k\}$ be the clock set of a parallel timed automaton A. We introduce the following auxiliary time variables: $t_{c_1}, t_{c_2}, \ldots, t_{c_k}$, t_0, $t_{o_1}, t_{o_2}, \ldots, t_{o_k}$. We define $V(p, i, c)$ as follows.

$$V(p,i,c) = \begin{cases} t_{o_j} & \text{where } j = R(p,i,c) \text{ if } R(p,i,c) > 0 \\ t_c & \text{if } R(p,i,c) = 0 \end{cases}$$

A time variable x is said to be *active* after o_i if and only if either $x = V(p, i+1, c)$ for some clock c, or $x = t_{o_i}$.

The above set of concrete successive state can be expressed as a conjunction of difference bounds of these auxiliary variables. The way we used here is similar to the one in the paper [7].

The condition that the sequence $\alpha = (\varepsilon, t_0), (o_1, t_{o_1}), (o_2, t_{o_2}), \ldots, (o_n, t_{o_n})$ is an execution following p starting from (l, v) to (l', v'), where $\forall c \in C.v(c) = t_c - t_0$ if and only if

1. $\texttt{ORDER}(p) \wedge \texttt{GUARDS}(p) \wedge \texttt{INV}(p)$ and
2. $\forall c \in C.v'(c) = V(p, n+1, c)$ and v' satisfies the location invariant of l'.

Here, the formulas $\texttt{ORDER}(p)$, $\texttt{GUARDS}(p)$ and $\texttt{INV}(p)$ are defined according to the conditions of the definition of executions. All of them are conjunctions of difference bounds of the form $x - y \sim m$, where x, y are auxiliary time variables, $\sim \in \{<, \leq\}$, and m is an integer. The condition which specifies that (l, v) is in a symbolic (l, D) can also expressed as a conjunction of difference bounds. We use $\texttt{IN}(D)$ to denote this condition.

The set of concrete states reachable from a state in (l, D) through an execution following p is as follow.

$$\left\{ (l', v') \;\middle|\; \begin{array}{l} \exists\, t_{c_1}, t_{c_2}, \ldots, t_{c_k}, t_0, t_{o_1}, t_{o_2}, \ldots, t_{o_n} . \\ (\; \texttt{IN}(D) \wedge \texttt{ORDER}(p) \wedge \texttt{GUARDS}(p) \wedge \texttt{INV}(p) \\ \;\wedge (\forall c \in C.v_n(c) = V(p, n+1, c))) \\ \;\wedge (v' \text{ satisfies the location invaraint of } l') \end{array} \right\}$$

3 Independent Transitions and Partial Order paths

In this section, we first define an independence relation on transitions. If two transitions e_1, e_2 are independent to each other, the occurrence of e_1 does not disable or enable e_2, and vice versa. Further more, as we will show later, changing their occurrence order in a path does not change the conditions about the time guards and location invariants.

Definition 2. *Given two transitions $e_1 = (g_1, r_1)$ and $e_2 = (g_2, r_2)$, we say e_1 and e_2 are independent to each other, denoted as* $\texttt{Indep}(e_1, e_2)$*, if and only if the following conditions hold.*

1. *For any two locations l, l' such that $l \xrightarrow{e_1} l'$,* $\texttt{Enable}(l, e_2) \Leftrightarrow \texttt{Enable}(l', e_2)$*; and vice versa.*
2. *For any two given locations l, l', there exists a location l_1 such that $l \xrightarrow{e_1} l_1$ and $l_1 \xrightarrow{e_2} l'$, iff there exists a location l_2 such that $l \xrightarrow{e_2} l_2$ and $l_2 \xrightarrow{e_1} l'$.*

3. $r_1 \cap r_2 = \emptyset$.
4. *For any atomic formula* $c \backsim n$ *in* g_1 *(or* g_2*),* c *is not in* r_2 *(or* r_1 *respectively).*
5. *For any clock* c*, either* e_1 *or* e_2 *is invariant-irrelevant to* c*.*

We can exchange two adjacent transition occurrences of a path to derive another path, if the corresponding transitions are independent to each other. The derived path and the original one start from same location, and also arrive at same location. Notice that the conditions corresponding to time guards and location invariants constrain the time distance between a pair of transition occurrences: the first one resets a clock c and the second one tests c. Exchanging two independent transition occurrence does not changing such occurrence pairs. So we have the following conditions.

Proposition 1. *Let* $p = o_1, o_2, \ldots, o_n$ *be a path of a timed automaton from* l *to* l'*, and* o_i, o_{i+1} *are two adjacent transition occurrences of* p *and* $\mathtt{Indep}(\underline{o_i}, \underline{o_{i+1}})$*. We have the following conclusions.*

1. $p' = o_1, o_2, \ldots o_{i-1}, o_{i+1}, o_i, o_{i+2}, \ldots, o_n$ *is also a path form* l *to* l'*.*
2. $\mathtt{GUARDS}(p')$ *and* $\mathtt{INV}(p')$ *are respectively same as* $\mathtt{GUARDS}(p)$ *and* $\mathtt{INV}(p)$*.*
3. *For each clock* c*,* $V(p, n+1, c)$ *is same as* $V(p', n+1, c)$*.*

Definition 3. *A* partial order path (POP) *of a timed automaton* A *is a tuple* $(p, <)$*, where* $p = o_1, o_2, \ldots, o_n$ *is a path of* A *from* l *to* l'*, and* $<$ *is a partial order on the set* $\{o_1, o_2, \ldots, o_n\}$ *satisfying that for any two integer* i, j*, (1)* $o_i < o_j \Rightarrow i < j$*, and (2)* $(i < j) \wedge \neg\mathtt{Indep}(o_i, o_j) \Rightarrow o_i < o_j$*.*

Let $p' = o'_1, o'_2, \ldots, o'_n$ be an arbitrary topological sort of the POP $(p, <)$. Notice that p' can be derived from p by repeatedly exchanging adjacent independent transition occurrences, from Proposition 1, p' is also a path.

We say an execution α *conforms* to $(p, <)$ iff the corresponding path of α is a topological sort of $(p, <)$. The set of states which are reachable from a state in (l, D) through an execution conforming to $(p, <)$ can be expressed as follow.

$$\left\{ (l', v) \;\middle|\; \begin{array}{l} \exists\, t_{c_1}, t_{c_2}, \ldots, t_{c_k}, t_0, t_{o_1}, t_{o_2}, \ldots, t_{o_n}, p'.(\\ \quad (p' \text{ is a topological sort of } (p, <))\wedge \\ \quad \mathtt{IN}(D) \wedge \mathtt{ORDER}(p') \wedge \mathtt{GUARDS}(p') \wedge \mathtt{INV}(p')\wedge \\ \quad \forall c \in C.v(c) = V(p', n+1, c)\ ) \\ \wedge\ (v \text{ satisfies the location invariant of } l_n) \end{array} \right\}.$$

Notice that all topological sorts of $(p, <)$ can be derived by repeatedly exchanging adjacent independent transition occurrences. From Proposition 1, the formulas $\mathtt{GUARDS}(p')$, $\mathtt{INV}(p')$, $V(p', n+1, c)$ are respectively same as $\mathtt{GUARDS}(p)$, $\mathtt{INV}(p)$, $V(p, n+1, c)$. The condition $\exists p'.((p' \text{ is conforming to } (p, <)) \wedge \mathtt{ORDER}(p'))$ is equivalent to $\mathtt{ORDER}((p, <))$, which is defined as follow.

$$(\bigwedge_{i=1}^{n} 0 - t_{o_i} \le 0) \wedge (\bigwedge_{i=1}^{n} t_{o_i} - t_0 \le 0) \wedge (\bigwedge_{\text{for each } o_i, o_j \text{ such that } o_i < o_j} t_{o_j} - t_{o_i} \le 0)$$

So the set can be rewritten as follow.

$$\left\{ (l,v) \;\middle|\; \begin{array}{l} \exists\, t_{c_1}, t_{c_2}, \ldots, t_{c_k}, t_0, t_{o_1}, t_{o_2}, \ldots, t_{o_n}.(\\ \quad \mathtt{ORDER}((p,<)) \wedge \mathtt{IN}(D) \wedge \mathtt{GUARDS}(p) \wedge \mathtt{INV}(p) \wedge \\ \quad \forall c \in C.v(c) = V(p, n+1, c)\ ) \\ \wedge\ (v \text{ satisfies the location invariant of } l_n) \end{array} \right\}.$$

In our implementation of the reachability analysis algorithm, the partial order $<$ is represented using a directed acyclic graph G which induces $<$. We also write the POP $(p,<)$ as (p,G). The condition $\mathtt{ORDER}((p,<))$ is equivalent to the following condition, denoted as $\mathtt{ORDER}((p,G))$.

$$(\bigwedge_{i=1}^{n} 0 - t_{o_i} \leq 0) \wedge (\bigwedge_{i=1}^{n} t_{o_i} - t_0 \leq 0) \wedge (\bigwedge_{(o_i, o_j) \text{ is an edge of } G} t_{o_j} - t_{o_i} \leq 0)$$

We use $\mathcal{S}_I((p,<),(l,D))$, or $\mathcal{S}_I((p,G),(l,D))$, to denote the set of concrete states which are reachable from a state in (l,D) through an execution conforming to $(p,<)$. From the above discussion, we have the following proposition.

Proposition 2. *For two POPs $(p,<)$ and $(p,<')$ from l satisfying that $<\subseteq<'$, $\mathcal{S}_I((p,<'),(l_0,D_0)) \subseteq \mathcal{S}_I((p,<),(l_0,D_0))$.*

4 Compute Symbolic Successors w.r.t. POPs

In this subsection, we will present a method to compute a symbolic state representing the set $\mathcal{S}_I((p,G),(l,D))$ for a given symbolic state (l,D) and a given POP (p,G). We first present a basic method to compute symbolic successors w.r.t. POPs. This method employs a well-known data structure called difference bound matrixes (DBM). Then we will present an optimized algorithm to compute such successors incrementally.

4.1 Difference Bound Matrixes and the Basic Successor Algorithm

A difference bound matrix (DBM)[9] over a set of variables is a matrix of which each row and column corresponding to a variable or the constant 0. Each element is a tuple $(\backsim, m)$ or $(<, +\infty)$, where $\backsim \in \{<, \leq\}$ and m is an integer or $+\infty$. Given a conjunction of atomic formulas of the form $x - y \backsim m$, the DBM M representing this conjunction is as follow. For each atomic formula $x - y \backsim m$, $M[x,y] = (\backsim, m)$, where $M[x,y]$ represents the element at the cross of the row corresponding to x and the column corresponding to y. All the other elements are set to $(<, +\infty)$.

The operator + over the elements of a DBM is defined as follow. $(\prec, m) + (\prec', m') \triangleq (\prec'', m + m')$, where $\prec'' \in \{<, \leq\}$, and $\prec''$ is $\leq$ if and only if both $\prec$ and $\prec'$ are $\leq$ and $m', m \neq +\infty$. Here we define $+\infty + n = n + (+\infty) = +\infty$.

We say $(\prec, m)$ is smaller than $(\prec', m')$, denoted as $(\prec, m) < (\prec', m')$, if either $m < m'$, or $(m = m') \wedge (\prec = <) \wedge (\prec' = \leq)$.

Let M be a DBM over a set of variables. A sequence of these variables $x_1, x_2, \ldots, x_k$ is said to be a *chain* of M from x_1 to x_n if $M[x_i, x_{i+1}]$ is not $(<, +\infty)$ for $i = 1, 2, \ldots, k-1$. The length of this chain is defined as $M[x_1, x_2] + M[x_2, x_3] + \ldots + M[x_{k-1}, x_k]$. A DBM M is said to be *canonical* if and only if for any two variables x, y, either $M[x, y] = (<, +\infty)$ and there is no chain from x to y, or the chain x, y is (one of) the shortest chain from x to y.

Given a non-empty DBM M, for any two variables x, y such that there is a chain from x to y, there must be a shortest chain from x to y and no time variable appears in the chain more than once.

Given a DBM M over a variable set $\mathcal{V}$, there is a canonical DBM M' such that the conjunctions represented by M and M' are equivalent. Let D be the conjunction represented by M. Let $\{x_1, x_2, \ldots, x_k\}$ be a subset of $\mathcal{V}$. The formula $\exists x_1, x_2, \ldots, x_k.D$ is equivalent to a conjunction represented by the DBM derived by removing from M' all the columns and rows corresponding to $x_1, x_2, \ldots, x_k$.

Given a symbolic state (l, D), and a partial order path (p, G) from l, the formulas $\texttt{ORDER}((p, G))$, $\texttt{IN}(D)$, $\texttt{GUARDS}(p)$, and $\texttt{INV}(p)$ are conjunctions of atomic formulas of the form $x - y \backsim m$, where $\backsim \in \{<, \leq\}$, and x, y are time variables or 0. So the conjunction of these four formulas can be represented as a DBM over time variables and 0. We use $\mathcal{M}((p, G), (l, D))$ to denote this DBM.

Without loss of generality, suppose $\{t_{c_1}, t_{c_2}, \ldots, t_{c_{k'}}, t_{o_1}, t_{o_2}, \ldots, t_{o_{n'}}\}$ $(0 \leq k' \leq k, 0 \leq n' \leq n)$ be the set of variables which are active after o_n. The set of concrete states which are reachable from a state in (l, D) through an execution conforming to (p, G) can be expressed as follow.

$$\left\{ (l', v') \left| \begin{array}{l} \exists\, t_{c_1}, t_{c_2}, \ldots, t_{c_{k'}}, t_{o_1}, t_{o_2}, \ldots, t_{o_{n'}}.(\\ \quad \exists\ \ t_{c_{k'+1}}, t_{c_{k'+2}}, \ldots, t_{c_k}, t_0, t_{o_{n'+1}}, t_{o_{n'+2}}, \ldots, t_{o_n}. \\ \qquad (\, \texttt{ORDER}((p, G)) \wedge \texttt{IN}(D) \wedge \texttt{GUARDS}(p) \wedge \texttt{INV}(p)\,) \\ \quad \wedge\ \ \forall c \in C.v'(c) = V(p, n+1, c)\ \ ) \\ \wedge\ \ (\ \ v' \text{ satisfies the location invariant of } l_n) \end{array} \right. \right\}.$$

Here, the formula $\exists t_{c_{k'+1}}, t_{c_{k'+2}}, \ldots, t_{c_k}, t_0, t_{o_{n'+1}}, t_{o_{n'+2}}, \ldots, t_{o_n}.(\texttt{ORDER}(p, <) \wedge \texttt{IN}(D) \wedge \texttt{GUARDS}(p) \wedge \texttt{INV}(p))$ is equivalent to a conjunction represented by a DBM derived by removing all the columns and rows corresponding to variables which are not active after o_n from the canonical form of $\mathcal{M}((p, G), (l, D))$. We use $\mathcal{S}_A((p, G), (l, D))$ to denote this DBM. Let D_A be the conjunction represented by $\mathcal{S}_A((p, G), (l, D))$, the above set can be written as follow.

$$\left\{ (l', v') \left| \begin{array}{l} (\ \exists\ t_{c_1}, t_{c_2}, \ldots, t_{c_{k'}}, t_{o_1}, t_{o_2}, \ldots, t_{o_{n'}}. \\ \quad (\ \ D_A \wedge \forall c \in C.v'(c) = V(p, n+1, c))\ ) \wedge \\ (\ v' \text{ satisfies the location invariant of } l_n) \end{array} \right. \right\}.$$

The above set can be represented by a symbolic state $(l', D \wedge I(l'))$, where $I(l')$ is the location invariant of l', and D is a conjunction derived as follows. For any two clocks c_1, c_2, $c_1 - c_2 \sim m$ is an atomic formula of D if and only if $V(p, n+1, c_1) - V(p, n+1, c_2) \sim m$ is an atomic formula of D_A.

From the above discussion, the symbolic successor of (l, D) w.r.t. (p, G), i.e. $\mathcal{S}_I((p, G), (l, D))$, can be computed as follow.

Step 1. Construct the DBM $\mathcal{M}((p,G),(l,D))$ according to the definition, and compute the canonical form of this DBM. Then compute $\mathcal{S}_A((p,G),(l,D))$ by removing the columns and rows corresponding to the non-active variables.

Step 2. Compute $\mathcal{S}_I((p,G),(l,D))$ based on $\mathcal{S}_A((p,G),(l,D))$ as above.

The first step is time-consuming when the path p is composed of many transition occurrences. The second step is efficient and the time complexity is independent to the length of p. In the next subsection, we will present a method to compute $\mathcal{S}_A((p,G),(l,D))$ incrementally.

4.2 An Incremental Algorithm to Compute Successors w.r.t. POPs

Let (p,G) be a POP from l to l', where $p = o_1, o_2, \ldots, o_n$. Let (l,D) be a symbolic state. For each $i = 1, 2, \ldots, n$, (p_i, G_i) is a POP defined as $p_i = o_1, o_2, \ldots, o_i$, and for any two transition occurrences o_j, o_k where $j, k \leq i$, (o_j, o_k) is an edge of G if and only if (o_j, o_k) is an edge of G_i. M_i is used to denote the DBM $\mathcal{S}_A((p_i, G_i),(l,D))$, M_0 is used to denote the canonical DBM representing D. In this subsection, we will show that M_n can be computed efficiently based on $M_0, M_1, M_2, \ldots, M_{n-1}$.

$\mathcal{V}_i$ is used to denote the set $\{t_{c_1}, t_{c_2}, \ldots, t_{c_k}, t_0, t_{o_1}, t_{o_2}, \ldots, t_{o_i}\}$ for $i = 1$ to n. A chain of $\mathcal{M}((p,<),(l,D))$ is said to be an *i-chain* if and only if all of the time variables are in the set $\mathcal{V}_i$. From the definition of (p_i, G_i), `ORDER`, `IN`, `GUARDS` and `INV`, M_i can be derived by removing from M_n the columns and rows corresponding to variables in $\mathcal{V}_n - \mathcal{V}_i$. So a sequence of variables is an i-chain of $\mathcal{M}((p,G),(l,D))$ if and only if it is a chain of $\mathcal{M}((p_i,G_i),(l,D))$. So, for any two variables x, y which are active after o_i, $M_i[x,y]$ equals to the length of the shortest i-chain of $\mathcal{M}((p,G),(l,D))$ from x to y.

Let x, y be two variables in the set $\mathcal{V}_n$, we say y is later than x if either $x \in \{t_{c_1}, t_{c_2}, \ldots, t_{c_k}, t_0\}$ and $y \in \{t_{o_1}, t_{o_2}, \ldots, t_{o_n}\}$, or $x = t_{o_i}, y = t_{o_j}$ and $i < j$.

From the definition of `ORDER` and `IN`, for any atomic formula $x - y \sim m$ of `ORDER`$((p,G))$ and `IN`(D), y is not later than x. For any two variables x, y such that y is later than x and $\mathcal{M}((p,G),(l,D))[x,y] = (\backsim, m) \neq (<, +\infty)$, $x - y \backsim m$ must be an atomic formula of `GUARDS`(p) or `INV`(p). According to the definition of `GUARDS` and `INV`, let y be t_{o_j} for some j, x must be the variable $V(p,j,c)$ for some clock c. So for any integer m such that $R(p,j,c) \leq m < j$, x is active after o_m. So we have the following proposition.

Proposition 3. *Let $x_1, x_2, \ldots, x_m$ be a time variable chain of $\mathcal{M}((p,G),(l,D))$, and i, j be two integers such that (1) t_{o_i} is the latest variable satisfying that x_1 is active after o_i; (2) x_n is active after o_j; (3) t_{o_j} is later than $t_{o_i}, x_1, x_2, \ldots, x_m$. We have the following conclusion. Either $x_1, x_2, \ldots, x_m$ is an i-chain of the DBM $\mathcal{M}((p,G),(l,D))$; or there is a variable x_k $(1 < k \leq n)$ such that x_k is active after o_i, x_{k+1} is later than t_{o_i} and $x_1, x_2, \ldots, x_k$ is an i-chain if $k > 1$.*

Notice that $\mathcal{S}_A((p,G),(l,D))$ is derived by removing some columns and rows from the canonical form of $\mathcal{M}((p,G),(l,D))$. Given two variables x_1, x_2 which are active after o_n, $\mathcal{S}_A((p,G),(l,D))[x_1,x_2]$ is the length of the shortest chain of $\mathcal{M}((p,G),(l,D))$ from x_1 to x_2.

Let $\{x_1, x_2, \ldots, x_m, t_{o_n}\}$ be all the variables which are active after o_n. All the x_is are also active after o_{n-1}. If the shortest chain from x_i to x_j does not contains t_{o_n}, this chain is also an $(n-1)$-chain. So the length of this chain is $M_{n-1}[x_i, x_j]$. If the shortest chain from x_i to x_j passes through t_{o_n}, the chain can be divided into two parts: the shortest chain from x_i to t_{o_n}, and the shortest chain from t_{o_n} to x_j. The length of the shortest chain from x_i to x_j equals to the sum of the length of these two parts.

Let $y_1, y_2, \ldots, y_k, t_{o_n}$ be the shortest chain from y_1 to t_{o_n} such that y_1 is active after o_{n-1} and no variable appears in this chain twice. Because t_{o_n} is later than y_k and $\mathcal{M}((p, G), (l, D))$ is not $(<, +\infty)$, y_k is also active after o_{n-1}. Further more, $y_1, y_2, \ldots, y_k$ is an $(n-1)$-chain. So the length of the chain $y_1, y_2, \ldots, y_k, t_{o_n}$ is $M_{n-1}[y_1, y_k] + \mathcal{M}((p, G), (l, D))[y_k, t_{o_n}]$.

Let $t_{o_n}, y_1, y_2, \ldots, y_m$ be the shortest chain from t_{o_n} to y_m such that y_m is active after o_{n-1}. There are two cases: none of $y_1, y_2, \ldots, y_{m-1}$ is active after o_{n-1}; and otherwise.

In this first case, from Proposition 3, we can separate $y_1, y_2, \ldots, y_m$ into following segments.

$$y_1, y_2, \ldots, y_{m_1}, \; y_{m_1+1}, y_{m_1+2}, \ldots, y_{m_2}, \; \ldots, \; y_{m_{j-1}+1}, y_{m_{j-1}+2}, \ldots, y_{m_j} (= y_m)$$

such that for a set of integers $n_1 < n_2 < \ldots < n_j$, the following conditions hold for $i = 1, 2, \ldots, j$. (Here, we set m_0 to 0.)

1. The time variable $t_{o_{n_i}}$ is the latest one such that $y_{m_{i-1}+1}$ is active after o_{n_i}.
2. Either $m_i = m_{i-1} + 1$; or $y_{m_{i-1}+1}, y_{m_{i-1}+2}, \ldots, y_{m_i}$ is an n_i-chain of the DBM $\mathcal{M}((p, G), (l, D))$ and y_{m_i} are active after o_{n_i}.
3. y_{m_i} is later than $t_{o_{n_{i-1}}}$.

For any DBM M and a variable x, we can set $M[x, x]$ to $(\leq, 0)$ and get an equivalent DBM. If we set $M_i[x, x]$ to $(\leq, 0)$, the length of the ith segment is $M_{n_i}[y_{m_{i-1}+1}, y_{m_i}]$. So the length of this chain equals $\mathcal{M}[t_{o_n}, y_1] + M_{m_1}[y_1, y_{m_1}] + \mathcal{M}[y_{m_1}, y_{m_1+1}] + M_{m_2}[y_{m_1+1}, y_{m_2}] + \mathcal{M}[y_{m_2}, y_{m_2+1}] + \ldots + M_{m_j}[y_{j-1+1}, y_j] + \mathcal{M}[y_{m_j}, x_i]$, where $\mathcal{M} = \mathcal{M}((p, G), (l, D))$. Notice that t_{o_n} is later than y_1 and y_1 is not active after o_{n-1} and $\mathcal{M}[t_{o_n}, y_1]$ is not $(<, +\infty)$, $t_{o_n} - y_1 \sim m$ must be an atomic formula of the condition $\texttt{ORDER}((p, G))$, where $\mathcal{M}[t_{o_n}, y_1] = (\sim, m)$.

From the above discussion, the algorithm depicted in Figure 1 compute the shortest lengths of chains from t_{o_n} to variables through a set of variables which are not active after o_{n-1}. When this algorithm returns, the value $Length(x)$ is the length of the shortest chain of the first case from t_{o_n} to x. The time complexity of DistanceFromTon( ) depends on the length of p. However, it is efficient in real applications if the directed acyclic graph is constructed carefully.

In the second case, the chain can be divided into two parts: $t_{o_n}, y_1, y_2, \ldots, y_k$ and $y_k, y_{k+1}, \ldots, y_m$, where k is the least integer such that y_k is active after o_{n-1} and $k < m$. The first part is a path in the first case while the length of the second part is $M_{n-1}[y_k, y_m]$.

From the above discussion, for any variable x which is active after o_n, the length of the shortest chain from x to the time variable t_{o_n} is $M_{n-1}[x, y] +$

DistanceFromTon((p,G))
{ $S :=$ the set of transition occurrences o of p such that (o, o_n) is an edge of G;
  for each x in S, set $Length(x) = (\leq, 0)$;
  while $(S \neq \emptyset)$ do
  { $v :=$ a time variable in S; $S := S - \{v\}$;
    Let t_{o_j} be the latest time variable such that v is active after o_j.
    for each time variable x which is active after o_j do
      for each y which is later than t_{o_j} and $\mathcal{M}[x, y] \neq (<, +\infty)$ do
      { if $Length(y)$ is undefined, or $\mathcal{M}[x, y] + M_J[v, x] + Length[v] < Length(y)$
        { Set $Length(y)$ to $\mathcal{M}[x, y] + M_J[t_{o_I}, x] + Length[t_{o_I}]$
          if (y is not active after o_{n-1}) $S := S \cup \{y\}$
        }
      }
  }
  return $Length$.
}

Fig. 1. The algorithms compute the distance from t_n to other variables

$\mathcal{M}[y, t_{o_n}]$ for a variable y active after o_{n-1} (y may be identical to x). The length of the shortest chain from t_{o_n} to x is $Length(x) + M_{n-1}[x, y]$ for a variable y active after o_{n-1} (y may be identical to x). For any two variables x, y (x, y are not t_{o_n}) which are active after o_n, they must also be active after o_{n-1}. The length of the shortest chain from x to y may be $M_{n-1}[x, y]$, or $l_1 + l_2$, where l_1 and l_2 are respectively the lengths of the shortest chain from x to t_{o_n}, and the one from t_{o_n} to y. So $\mathcal{S}_A((p, G), (l, D))$ can be computed as follow. First, use the algorithm depicted in Figure 1 to compute the map $Length(x)$; then compute the shortest length between two variables which are active after o_n as described above.

5 A Reachability Analysis Algorithm Using Partial Order Path

In this section, we will present a reachablity analysis algorithm which explores the state space in a depth-first method. Let the $p = o_1, o_2, \ldots, o_n$ be the current path being explored, this algorithm compute successor of the initial symbolic state w.r.t. the POP $(p, <_p)$, where $<_p$ is defined as $\{(o_i, o_j) | (i < j) \wedge \neg\texttt{Indep}(\underline{o_i}, \underline{o_j})$.

This algorithm represent the relation $<_p$ as a directed acyclic graph. During the exploration, each time the current POP $(p, <_p)$ is appended with a new transition occurrence o, o is added to the graph as a node. An arc from o_i to o is added if and only if $\neg\texttt{Indep}(\underline{o_i}, \underline{o})$ and there is no occurrence o_j such that (o_i, o_j) and (o_j, o) are two arcs of the directed acyclic graph.

This reachability analysis algorithm uses the incremental algorithm presented in the previous section to compute the symbolic successors w.r.t. POPs.

The algorithm is depicted in Figure 2. It checks whether the parallel timed automaton can reach a location in F. The function $Backtracking()$ removes the last elements of p and $NodeList$, and restore the directed acyclic graphs inducing $<_p$ after the last elements of p is removed.

Proposition 4. *All the locations generated by this algorithm is reachable. Further more, if no location in F is reachable, the algorithm generates all the reachable control locations of the parallel timed automaton.*

Proposition 5. *In the algorithm depicted in Figure 2, the relation $\subseteq_K$ can be replaced by a simulation relation $\sqsubseteq$ between symbolic states if for any two symbolic states (l, D) and (l, D'), $(l, D) \subseteq (l, D') \Rightarrow (l, D) \sqsubseteq (l, D')$.*

From this proposition, we can using some static analysis techniques in the literate in our algorithm. These techniques, for example the technique in [8], have been proved to be successful.

$NodeList = \ll (l_0, D_0) \gg$, where (l_0, D_0) is the initial symbolic state;
$p = \ll\gg$; $ReachableStateSet = \emptyset$;
while(TRUE){
  Let $EnableSet = \{e|Enable(l, e)\}$ where l is the final location of p.
  if (all transitions in $EnableSet$ are explored for the current path p){
    if ($p = \varepsilon$) return FALSE;
    Backtracking( );
  } else {
    $e :=$ an unexplored transition in $EnableSet$;
    Mark e as explored for the current path p;
    $p := po$, where $\underline{(o)} = e$;
    Compute the new directed acyclic graph which induces $<_p$;
    Compute $\mathcal{S}_A((p, <_p), (l_0, D_0))$ and $\mathcal{S}_I((p, <_p), (l_0, D_0))$ incrementally;
    if ($\mathcal{S}_I((p, <_p), (l_0, D_0))$ is not empty){
      if $l' \in F$ return TRUE;
      if $(\exists(l', M'') \in ReachableStateSet.\mathcal{S}_I((p, <_p), (l_0, D_0)) \subseteq_K M'')$
        Backtracking( );/*because of contained successor*/
      else
        $ReachableStateSet := ReachableStateSet \cup (l', \mathcal{S}_I((p, <_p), (l_0, D_0)))$
    }else
      Backtracking( );/*because of empty successor */
  }/*end of if (all transitions ...*/
}/*of while*/

Fig. 2. The reachablity analysis algorithm

6 A Rule to Avoid Exhaustive Exploration

The algorithm in Figure 2 can avoid splitting symbolic states because of the enumeration order of independent transitions. However, all enabled transitions are explored in that algorithm. In this section, we will present a rule to cut off some enabled transitions.

A transition e is called *invisible* if for any two locations l and l' such that $l \xrightarrow{e} l'$, $l \in F \Leftrightarrow l' \in F$.

A set of transitions $\{e_1, e_2, \ldots, e_n\}$ is called *inevitable* after a location l if the following conditions hold.

1. For $i = 1, 2, \ldots, n$, $Enable(l, e_i)$.
2. Let $p = o_1, o_2, \ldots, o_k$ be an arbitrary path from l, either $\exists i, j.\underline{o_i} = e_j$, or $\forall i, j.\mathtt{Indep}(\underline{o_i} = e_j)$.

Intuitively speaking, one of these transitions eventually takes place after l if the time constraints are not considered.

Suppose that at a time during the state space exploration using the algorithm in Figure 2, p is the current path being explored, and e is an explored transition which is enabled at the last node of the $NodeList$. We say e is *exposed* at p if the algorithm has backtracked because of empty successor or contained successor, when the current path is $poo_1o_2 \ldots o_n$, where $\underline{o} = e$, and $\mathtt{Indep}(e, \underline{o_i})$ for $i = 1, 2, \ldots n$.

Proposition 6. *During the state space exploration, let p be the current path being explored. Let l be the last locations. Let* $\{e_1, e_2, \ldots, e_n\}$ *be a set of transitions enabled on l and all of these transitions are explored on p. The algorithm can avoid exploring the transitions not in this set if all the following conditions hold.*

1. *This set is inevitable after l.*
2. *All the transitions are invisible.*
3. *All of them are explored but not exposed.*

7 Case Studies

We have implemented an experimental tool which employs the partial order reduction technique in this paper. This tool can also use the static analysis technique presented in the paper [8]. We have applied our algorithm to several examples including the artificial Diamond example from the paper [7], CSMA/CD protocol, and Fischer's mutual protocol. The CSMA/CD protocol checked by our algorithm is slightly modified. The collision is broadcasted to all the stations through a commit location and one channel, instead of a set of channels.

We have applied our experimental tool to these cases using an IBM Z60t ThinkPad with an Intel Pentium 1.86G processor and 512M memory. The space

Systems	Basic	POP	RIF	POP+RIF	PSET
DIAMOND 2	24	11	11	11	7
DIAMOND 3	91	19	19	19	10
DIAMOND 4	344	29	29	29	13
DIAMOND 5	1309	41	41	41	16
DIAMOND 6	5017	55	55	55	19
Fischer 2	21	20	18	18	18
Fischer 3	166	152	65	65	65
Fischer 4	1753	1580	220	220	220
Fischer 5	23016	20652	727	727	727
CSMA 4	929	755	531	531	258
CSMA 5	7468	5023	2878	2878	850
CSMA 6	61143	31631	15197	15197	2594
CSMA 7	N/A	N/A	78032	78032	7490

Fig. 3. The numbers of symbolic states generated for difference cases

requirement is expressed as the number of states generated. These data are depicted in Figure 3. The columns DIAMOND n, CSMA n, and Fischer n respectively stand for Diamond example with $2n$ clocks, CSMA/CD protocol with n stations, and Fischer protocol with n processes. The row Basic, POP, RIF, POP+RIF, PSET respectively stand for the basic reachability analysis algorithms, the algorithm depicted in Figure 2, the algorithm with 'removing irrelevant formulas' optimization as described in the paper [8], the algorithm with both RIF and PO, and the algorithm with all above techniques and the technique to avoid exhaustive exploration described in the section 6. The cpu time used by the algorithm with POP reduction is generally 1-2 times as the time used by the reachability algorithm without POP reduction.

These data shows that the POP successor algorithm results in some space reduction. When both the POP technique and the RIF technique are applied to these cases, the POP technique results in no further reduction. However, this does not means that RIF technique always outperforms the POP reduction. We have changed the DIAMOND example slightly, the RIF technique results in no reduction for the new DIAMOND example, but the POP technique works well.

It is also shown that the rule in Section 6 can reduce the space requirement further.

8 Conclusions

In this paper, we proposed a partial order reduction technique for parallel timed automaton model checking.

We first define an independence relation on transitions. Then, we present a reachability analysis algorithm which explores the state space by generating successors w.r.t. partial order paths. A partial order path is composed of a set of transition occurrences and a partial order on this set. The order of two independent transition occurrences may be unspecified by the partial order. All topological sorts of this partial order are paths of the parallel timed automaton. Further more, we show that a symbolic state can be used to represent the set of all the concrete states reachable from some concrete states in a symbolic state through any one of these paths.

We present an algorithm to compute such symbolic successors incrementally. A reachability analysis algorithm based on this successor algorithm is presented. These algorithm can avoid splitting symbolic states because of the occurrence order of independent transitions.

One advantage of our partial order technique is that our technique can be combined with some static analysis technique in the literate.

Further more, we presented a rule to compute persistent transition set. Under some conditions, the reachability analysis algorithm needs only explore a subset of the enabled transitions.

References

1. Alur, R., Dill, D.: A theory of timed automata. Theoretical Computer Science 126(2), 183–235 (1994)
2. Larsen, L., Pettersson, Y.: Compact Data Structures and State-space Reduction for Model-Checking Real-Time Systems. Real-time system 25, 255–275 (2003)
3. Daws, C., Olivero, A., Tripakis, S., Yovine, S.: The tool Kronos. In: DIMACS Workshop on Verification and Control of Hybrid Systems, October 1995. LNCS, vol. 1066. Springer, Heidelberg (1995)
4. Bengtsson, J., Jonsson, B., Lilius, J., Yi, W.: Partial order reductions for timed systems. In: Sangiorgi, D., de Simone, R. (eds.) CONCUR 1998. LNCS, vol. 1466, pp. 485–500. Springer, Heidelberg (1998)
5. Minea, M.: Partial order reduction for verification of timed systems, Ph.D. thesis, Carnegie Mellon University (1999)
6. Dams, D., Gerth, R., Knaack, B., Kuiper, R.: Partial-order reduction techniques for real-time model checking, Formal Methods for Industrial Critical Systems, Amsterdam, vol. 10, pp. 469–482 (May 1998)
7. Lugiez, D., Niebert, P., Zennou, S.: A Partial Order Semantics Approach to the Clock Explosion Problem of Timed Automata. In: Jensen, K., Podelski, A. (eds.) TACAS 2004. LNCS, vol. 2988, pp. 296–311. Springer, Heidelberg (2004)
8. Zhao, J., Li, X., Zheng, T., Zheng, G.: Removing Irrelevant Atomic Formulas for Checking Timed Automata Efficiently. In: Larsen, K.G., Niebert, P. (eds.) FORMATS 2003. LNCS, vol. 2791. Springer, Heidelberg (2004)
9. Bengtsson, J., Yi, W.: Timed Automata: Semantics, Algorithms and Tools. In: Desel, J., Reisig, W., Rozenberg, G. (eds.) Lectures on Concurrency and Petri Nets. LNCS, vol. 3098, pp. 87–124. Springer, Heidelberg (2004)

Program Verification by Reduction to Semi-algebraic Systems Solving*

Bican Xia[1], Lu Yang[2], and Naijun Zhan[3]**

[1] LMAM & School of Mathematical Sciences, Peking University
[2] Shanghai Key Lab. of Trustworthy Computing, East China Normal University
[3] Lab. of Computer Science, Institute of Software, Chinese Academy of Sciences
znj@ios.ac.cn

Abstract. The discovery of invariants and ranking functions plays a central role in program verification. In our previous work, we investigated invariant generation and non-linear ranking function discovering of polynomial programs by reduction to semi-algebraic systems solving. In this paper we will first summarize our results on the two topics and then show how to generalize the approach to discovering more expressive invariants and ranking functions, and applying to more general programs.

Keywords: Program Verification, Ranking Functions, Invariants, Polynomial Programs, Semi-Algebraic Systems, Quantifier Elimination.

1 Introduction

The discovery of invariants and ranking functions plays a central role in program verification, and is therefore thought as the most challenging problem of program verification. In recent years, due to the advance of computer algebra, various approaches to non-linear invariant generation and termination analysis of polynomial programs have been established, based on computer algebra. These approaches have widely been applied to program verification and made tremendous success. However, almost each of these approaches has its limitations, e.g. some of them are limited to linear (affine) systems, some of them suffers from high complexity, some of them can only generate weak invariants or ranking functions and so on.

In order to overcome the weakness of the well-established approaches, following the line of [14], by exploiting our results on solving semi-algebraic systems (SASs), we proposed more practical and efficient approaches to polynomial invariant generation and ranking function discovering of polynomial programs respectively in [5] and [4]. In this paper, we will first summarize the results reported in [4,5] and correct mistakes in Example 7 in [5]. Then we will extend

* This work is supported in part by NKBRPC-2002cb312200, NKBRPC-2004CB318003, NSFC-60493200, NSFC-60721061, NSFC-60573007, NSFC-90718041, and NSFC-60736017 and NKBRPC-2005CB321902.

** The corresponding author: South Fourth Street, No. 4, Zhong Guan Cun, Beijing, 100080, P.R. China.

T. Margaria and B. Steffen (Eds.): ISoLA 2008, CCIS 17, pp. 277–291, 2008.

the approach such that it can not only be applicable to more general classes of programs and show how to synthesize more expressive invariants and ranking functions. We will investigate to extend the approach to general multivariate polynomial systems and even fractional polynomial systems. We also study to extend the approach to synthesizing invariants that can be represented by a general polynomial formula, even a fractional polynomial formula, and ranking functions that could be either a polynomial or a fractional polynomial.

1.1 Related Work

Up to now, most of well-established invariant generation methods either based on abstract interpretation [10,2,18,9], or on quantifier elimination [7,14], or on polynomial algebra [15,16,19,20,21].

The basic idea of the approaches based on abstract interpretation is to perform approximate symbolic execution of a program until an assertion is reached that remain unchanged by further executions of the program. However, in order to guarantee termination, the method introduces imprecision by the use of an extrapolation operator called *widening/narrowing*. This operator often causes the technique to produce weak invariants. Moreover, proposing widening/narrowing operators with certain concerns of completeness is not easy and becomes a key challenge for abstract interpretation based techniques [10,2].

In contrast, [15,16,19,20,21] exploited the theory of polynomial algebra to discover invariants of polynomial programs. The technique of linear algebra to generate polynomial equations of bounded degree as invariants of programs with affine assignments was applied in [15]. In [19,20], it was first proved that the set of polynomials serving as loop invariants has the algebraic structure of an ideal, then was proposed an algorithm to obtain a finite base of the ideal by using fixpoint computation. Finally an algorithm by using Gröbner bases and the elimination theory was given. The approach is theoretically sound and complete in the sense that if there is an invariant of the loop that can be expressed as a conjunction of polynomial equations, applying the approach is guaranteed to generate it. A similar approach to finding polynomial equation invariants whose form is priori determined (called templates) by using an extended Gröbner basis algorithm over templates was presented in [21].

Compared with polynomial algebra based approaches that can only generate invariants represented as polynomial equations, the approach from [7] can generate linear inequalities as invariants for linear programs, which based on *Farkas' Lemma* and non-linear constraint solving. In [14], a very general approach for automatic generation of more expressive invariants was proposed, which is based on the technique of quantifier elimination, and applied the approach to Presburger Arithmetic and quantifier-free theory of conjunctively closed polynomial equations. Theoretically speaking, the approach can also be applied to the theory of real-closed fields, but it was pointed out in [14] that this is impractical in reality because of the high complexity of quantifier elimination, which is at least double exponential [12].

Following the line of [14], a very general and efficient approach to ranking function discovery and invariance generation of linear and polynomial programs was presented in [9]. However, the approach of [9] is incomplete in the sense that, for some program that may have ranking functions and invariants of the predefined form, applying the approach may not be able to find them, as Lagrangian relaxation and over-approximation of the positive semi-definiteness of a polynomial are used.

Likewise, inspired by [14], by exploiting our results on solving semi-algebraic systems (SASs), we proposed more practical and efficient approaches to polynomial invariant generation and ranking function discovering of polynomial programs respectively in [5] and [4]. Comparing with other well-established invariant generation methods, the advantages of the approach of [5] include: Can generate more expressive invariants, which are represented as a semi-algebraic systems consisting of polynomial equations, inequations and inequalities; Has lower complexity, compared with the methods directly based on Gröbner Base or first-order quantifier elimination. The complexity of the approach in [5] is singly exponential in the number of program variables plus doubly exponential in the number of parameters approximately, while the latter with double exponential in the number of program variables and parameters; Still is complete, compared with the approach of [9] in the sense that whenever there exist invariants of the predefined form, our approach can indeed synthesize them.

On the other hand, compared to other well-established termination analysis approaches, the advantages of [4] include: Firstly, it can be applied to non-linear programs and discover non-linear ranking functions, whereas most of other well-established can only be applicable to linear programs and synthesize linear ranking functions, such as [11,8,17]; Secondly, the approach is complete compared with [9] in the sense that if there exist ranking functions of the predefined template, it can indeed discover them. But, our approach is just a sufficient method for termination analysis, not a sufficient and necessary one like [22,1] which focuses on a special subclass of linear programs; Furthermore, the complexity of our approach is still very high comparing with the approaches of [9,3].

1.2 Basic Notions

Let $\mathcal{K}[x_1, ..., x_n]$ be the ring of polynomials in n indeterminates, $X = \{x_1, \cdots, x_n\}$, with coefficients in the field $\mathcal{K}$. Let the order of the variables be $x_1 \prec x_2 \prec \cdots \prec x_n$. Then, the *leading variable* (or *main variable*) of a polynomial p is the variable with the greatest index which indeed occurs in p. If the leading variable of a polynomial p is x_k, p can be collected w.r.t. its leading variable as $p = c_m x_k^m + \cdots + c_0$ where m is the *degree* of p w.r.t. x_k and c_is are polynomials in $\mathcal{K}[x_1, ..., x_{k-1}]$. We call $c_m x_k^m$ the *leading term* of p w.r.t. x_k and c_m the *leading coefficient*. For example, let $p(x_1, \ldots, x_5) = x_2^5 + x_3^4 x_4^2 + (2x_2 + x_1)x_4^3$. The leading variable, term and coefficient of $p(x_1, \ldots, x_5)$ are x_4, $(2x_2 + x_1)x_4^3$ and $2x_2 + x_1$, respectively.

An *atomic polynomial formula* over $\mathcal{K}[x_1, ..., x_n]$ is of the form $p(x_1, \ldots, x_n) \rhd 0$, where $\rhd \in \{=, >, \geq, \neq\}$. A *polynomial formula* is a boolean combination of atomic polynomial formulae. We will denote by $PF(\mathcal{K}[x_1, \ldots, x_n])$ the set of polynomial formulae over $\mathcal{K}[x_1, ..., x_n]$ and by $CPF(\mathcal{K}[x_1, \ldots, x_n])$ the set of conjunctive polynomial formulae over $\mathcal{K}[x_1, ..., x_n]$, which only contain logical connective $\wedge$, respectively.

An *atomic fractional polynomial formula* over $\mathcal{K}[x_1, ..., x_n]$ is of the form $\frac{p(x_1,\ldots,x_n)}{q(x_1,\ldots,x_n)} \rhd 0$, where $p(x_1, \ldots, x_n) \neq 0$ is relative prime to $q(x_1, \ldots, x_n)$, both of them are in $\mathcal{K}[x_1, \ldots, x_n]$, and $\rhd \in \{=, >, \geq, \neq\}$. A *fractional polynomial formula* is a boolean combination of atomic fractional polynomial formulae. We will denote by $FPF(\mathcal{K}[x_1, \ldots, x_n])$ the set of fractional polynomial formulae over $\mathcal{K}[x_1, ..., x_n]$.

It is easy to prove the following theorem that indicates $FPF(\mathcal{K}[x_1, \ldots, x_n])$ is as expressive as $PF(\mathcal{K}[x_1, \ldots, x_n])$.

Theorem 1

i) *$PF(\mathcal{K}[x_1, \ldots, x_n]) \subseteq FPF(\mathcal{K}[x_1, \ldots, x_n])$;*
ii) *For any $\phi \in FPF(\mathcal{K}[x_1, \ldots, x_n])$, there exists $\phi' \in PF(\mathcal{K}[x_1, \ldots, x_n])$ such that $\phi \Leftrightarrow \phi'$.*

In what follows, we will use $\mathbb{Q}$ to stand for rationales and $\mathbb{R}$ for reals, and fix $\mathcal{K}$ to be $\mathbb{Q}$. In fact, all results discussed below can be applied to $\mathbb{R}$.

In the following, the n indeterminates are divided into two groups: $\mathbf{u} = (u_1, ..., u_t)$ and $\mathbf{x} = (x_1, ..., x_s)$, which are called parameters and variables, respectively, and we sometimes use "," to denote the conjunction of atomic formulae for brevity.

Definition 1. *A semi-algebraic system is a conjunctive polynomial formula of the following form:*

$$\begin{cases} p_1(\mathbf{u}, \mathbf{x}) = 0, \ldots, p_r(\mathbf{u}, \mathbf{x}) = 0, \\ g_1(\mathbf{u}, \mathbf{x}) \geq 0, \ldots, g_k(\mathbf{u}, \mathbf{x}) \geq 0, \\ g_{k+1}(\mathbf{u}, \mathbf{x}) > 0, \ldots, g_l(\mathbf{u}, \mathbf{x}) > 0, \\ h_1(\mathbf{u}, \mathbf{x}) \neq 0, \ldots, h_m(\mathbf{u}, \mathbf{x}) \neq 0, \end{cases} \tag{1}$$

where $r > 0, l \geq k \geq 0, m \geq 0$ and all p_i's, g_i's and h_i's are in $\mathbb{Q}[\mathbf{u}, \mathbf{x}] \setminus \mathbb{Q}$. An SAS of the form (1) is called parametric *if $t \neq 0$, abbreviated as PSAS, otherwise* constant, *written as CSAS.*

An SAS of the form (1) is usually denoted by a quadruple $[\mathbb{P}, \mathbb{G}_1, \mathbb{G}_2, \mathbb{H}]$, where $\mathbb{P} = [p_1, ..., p_r], \mathbb{G}_1 = [g_1, ..., g_k], \mathbb{G}_2 = [g_{k+1}, ..., g_l]$ and $\mathbb{H} = [h_1, ..., h_m]$.

For a CSAS S, interesting questions are how to compute the number of real solutions of S, and if the number is finite, how to compute these real solutions. For a PSAS, the interesting problem is so-called *real solution classification*, that is to determine the condition on the parameters such that the system has the prescribed number of distinct real solutions, possibly infinite.

2 Discoverer

Theories on how to classify real roots of PSASs and isolate real roots of CSASs were developed in [26,25,24,27]. The core of the theories is the generalized *Complete Discrimination System* (CDS). A computer algebra tool named DISCOVERER [23] has been developed in Maple to implement these theories. Comparing with other well-known computer algebra tools like REDLOG [13] and QEPCAD [6], DISCOVERER has two distinct features as follows.

Real Solution Classification of PSASs: For a PSAS T of the form (1) and an argument N of the following three forms:

- a non-negative integer b;
- a range $b..c$, where b, c are non-negative integers and $b < c$;
- a range $b.. + \infty$, where b is a non-negative integer,

DISCOVERER provides the functions **tofind** and **Tofind**, which determine the conditions on $\mathbf{u}$ such that the number of the distinct real solutions of T equals to N if N is an integer, otherwise falls in the scope N.

Real Solution Isolation of CSASs: For a CSAS T of the form (1) only with a finite number of real solutions, DISCOVERER can determine the number of distinct real solutions of T, say n, and find out n disjoint cubes with rational vertices in each of which there is only one solution. In addition, the width of the cubes can be less than any given positive real. The two functions are realized by calling **nearsolve** and **realzeros**, respectively.

3 Invariants and Ranking Functions

We use transition systems to represent programs.

Definition 2. *A transition system is a quintuple $\langle V, L, T, \ell_0, \Theta \rangle$, where V is a set of program variables, L is a set of locations, and T is a set of transitions. Each transition $\tau \in T$ is a quadruple $\langle \ell_1, \ell_2, \rho_\tau, \theta_\tau \rangle$, where ℓ_1 and ℓ_2 are the pre- and post- locations of the transition, the transition relation ρ_τ is a first-order formula over $V \cup V'$, and θ_τ is a first-order formula over V, which is the guard of the transition. The location ℓ_0 is the initial location, and the initial condition Θ is a first-order formula over V.*

Only if θ_τ holds, the transition can take place. Here, we use V' (variables with prime) to denote the next-state variables.

If all formulae of a transition system are from $CPF(\mathcal{K}[x_1, \ldots, x_n])$, the system is also called semi-algebraic transition system *(SATS). Similarly, a system is called* polynomial transition system *(PTS) (resp.* fractional polynomial transition system *(FPTS)), if all its formulae are in $PF(\mathcal{K}[x_1, \ldots, x_n])$ (resp. $FPF(\mathcal{K}[x_1, \ldots, x_n])$).*

According to Theorem 1, it is easy to see that

Theorem 2. *For each fractional polynomial transition system, there is a polynomial transition system such that the two transition systems are equivalent in the sense that any property holds on one of them iff the property holds on the other either.*

A state is a valuation of the variables in V. The space of states is denoted by $Val(V)$. Without confusion we will use V to denote both the variable set and an arbitrary state, and use $F(V)$ to mean the (truth) value of function (formula) F

under the state V. The semantics of transition systems can be explained through state transitions as usual.

We denote the transition $\tau = (l_1, l_2, \rho_\tau, \theta_\tau)$ by $l_1 \overset{\rho_\tau, \theta_\tau}{\rightarrow} l_2$, or simply by $l_1 \overset{\tau}{\rightarrow} l_2$. A sequence of transitions $l_{11} \overset{\tau_1}{\rightarrow} l_{12}, \ldots, l_{n1} \overset{\tau_n}{\rightarrow} l_{n2}$ is called *composable* if $l_{i2} = l_{(i+1)1}$ for $i = 1, \ldots, n-1$, and written as $l_{11} \overset{\tau_1}{\rightarrow} l_{12}(l_{21}) \overset{\tau_2}{\rightarrow} \cdots \overset{\tau_n}{\rightarrow} l_{n2}$. A composable sequence is a *transition circle* at l_{11}, if $l_{11} = l_{n2}$. For any composable sequence $l_0 \overset{\tau_1}{\rightarrow} l_1 \overset{\tau_2}{\rightarrow} \cdots \overset{\tau_n}{\rightarrow} l_n$, it is easy to show that there is a transition of the form $l_0 \overset{\tau_1;\tau_2;\cdots;\tau_n}{\rightarrow} l_n$ such that the composable sequence is equivalent to the transition, where $\tau_1; \tau_2 \cdots; \tau_n$, $\rho_{\tau_1;\tau_2;\cdots;\tau_n}$ and $\theta_{\tau_1;\tau_2;\cdots;\tau_n}$ are the compositions of $\tau_1, \tau_2, \ldots, \tau_n$, $\rho_{\tau_1}, \ldots, \rho_{\tau_n}$ and $\theta_{\tau_1}, \ldots, \theta_{\tau_n}$, respectively. The composition of transition relations is defined in the standard way, for example, $x' = x^4 + 3; x' = x^2 + 2$ is $x' = (x^4 + 3)^2 + 2$; while the composition of transition guards have to be given as a conjunction of the guards, each of which takes into account the past state transitions. In the above example, if the guard of the first transition is $x + 7 = x^5$ and that of the second is $x^4 = x + 3$, then guard of the composition is $x + 7 = x^5 \wedge (x^4 + 3)^4 = (x^4 + 3) + 3$.

3.1 Invariants

Informally, an *invariant* of a program at a location is an assertion that holds on any program state reaching the location. An invariant of a program can be seen as a mapping to map each location to an assertion which has inductive property, that is, *initiation* and *consecution*. *Initiation* means that the image of the mapping at the initial location holds on the loop entry; while *consecution* means that for any transition the invariant at the pre-location together with the transition relation and its guard implies the invariant at the post-location. In many cases, people only consider an invariant at the initial location and do not care about invariants at other locations. In this case, we can assume the invariants at other locations are all *true* and therefore *initiation* and *consecution* mean that the invariant holds on the loop entry, and is preserved by any transition circle at the entry point.

Definition 3 (Invariant at a Location). *Let $P = \langle V, L, T, l_0, \Theta \rangle$ be a transition system. An invariant at a location $l \in L$ is a first-order formula ϕ over V such that ϕ holds on all states that can be reached at location l.*

Definition 4 (Invariant of a Program). *An* assertion map *for a transition system $P = \langle V, L, T, l_0, \Theta \rangle$ is a map associating each location of P with a first-order formula. An assertion map η of P is said to be* inductive *iff the following conditions hold:*

Initiation: $\Theta(V_0) \models \eta(l_0)$.
Consecution: *For each transition $\tau = \langle l_i, l_j, \rho_\tau, \theta_\tau \rangle$,*

$$\eta(l_i)(V) \wedge \rho_\tau(V, V') \wedge \theta_\tau(V) \models \eta(l_j)(V').$$

It is well-known that if η is an inductive mapping of P, then $\eta(l)$ is an invariant of P at l. Therefore, an inductive mapping of P forms an invariant of P.

3.2 Ranking Functions

Definition 5 (Ranking Function). *Assume $P = \langle V, L, T, l_0, \Theta \rangle$ is a transition system. A ranking function is a function $\gamma : Val(V) \to \mathbb{R}^+$ such that the following conditions are satisfied:*

Initiation: $\Theta(V_0) \models \gamma(V_0) \geq 0$.
Decreasing: *There exists a constant $C \in \mathbb{R}^+$ such that $C > 0$ and for any transition circle $l_0 \stackrel{\tau_1}{\to} l_1 \stackrel{\tau_2}{\to} \cdots \stackrel{\tau_{n-1}}{\to} l_{n-1} \stackrel{\tau_n}{\to} l_0$ at l_0,*

$$\rho_{\tau_1;\tau_2;\cdots;\tau_n}(V, V') \wedge \theta_{\tau_1;\tau_2;\cdots;\tau_n}(V) \models \gamma(V) - \gamma(V') \geq C \wedge \gamma(V') \geq 0.$$

Condition 1 says that the ranges of all the initial states satisfying the initial condition under the ranking function is nonnegative; Condition 2 expresses the fact that the value of the ranking function decreases by at least C as the program moves back to the initial location along any transition circle, and is still nonnegative.

In Definition 5, if γ is a polynomial, then it is called a *polynomial ranking function*.

Remark 1

- According to Definition 5, for any transition system, if a ranking function exists, then the system will not go through l_0 infinitely often.
- Ranking functions can be seen as loop invariants at the entry point.

In the subsequent two sections, we will summarize the results of [5,4], where all formulae are in $CPF(\mathcal{K}[x_1, \ldots, x_n])$ and ranking functions are polynomial.

4 Generating Polynomial Invariants

Given an SATS S, the procedure of generating polynomial invariants with the approach of [5] includes the following 4 steps:

1. **Predefine Parametric Invariants.** Predefine a template of invariants at each of the underlining locations, which is a PSAS. All of these predefined PSASs form a parametric invariant of the program.
2. **Derive PSASs from Initial Condition and Then Solve.** According to Definition 4, we have $\Theta \models \eta(l_0)$ which means that each real solution of Θ must satisfy $\eta(l_0)$. In other words, $\Theta \wedge \neg\eta(l_0)$ has no common real solutions. This implies that for each atomic polynomial formula ϕ in $\eta(l_0)$, $\Theta \wedge \neg\phi$ has no real solutions. Note that $\eta(l_0)$ is the conjunction of a set of atomic polynomial formulae and therefore $\Theta \wedge \neg\phi$ is a PSAS according to the definition. Thus, applying the tool DISCOVERER to the resulting PSAS $\Theta \wedge \neg\phi$, we get a necessary and sufficient condition such that the derived PSAS has no real solutions. The condition may contain the occurrences of some program variables. In this case, the condition should hold for any instantiations of these variables. Thus, by universally quantifying these variables (we usually

add a scope to each of these universally quantified variables according to the program) and then applying QEPCAD, we can get a necessary and sufficient condition only on the presumed parameters.

Repeatedly apply the procedure to each atomic polynomial formula of the predefined invariant at l_0 and then use the conjunction of all the resulting conditions.

3. **Derive PSASs from Consecutive Condition and Then Solve.** From Definition 4, for each transition $\tau = \langle l_i, l_j, \rho_\tau, \theta_\tau \rangle$, $\eta(l_i) \wedge \rho_\tau \wedge \theta_\tau \models \eta(l_j)$, so $\eta(l_i) \wedge \rho_\tau \wedge \theta_\tau \wedge \neg\eta(l_j)$ has no real solutions, which implies that for each atomic polynomial formula ϕ in $\eta(l_j)$,

$$\eta(l_i) \wedge \rho_\tau \wedge \theta_\tau \wedge \neg\phi \tag{2}$$

has no real solution. It is clear that (2) is a PSAS. By applying the tool DISCOVERER, we obtain a necessary and sufficient condition on the parameters for (2) to have no real solution. Similarly to Step 2, we may need to use quantifier elimination in order to get a necessary and sufficient condition only on the presumed parameters.

4. **Generate Invariants.** According to the results obtained from Steps 1, 2 and 3, we can get the final necessary and sufficient condition only on the parameters of each of the invariant templates. If the condition is too complicated, we can utilize the function of PCAD of DISCOVERER or QEPCAD to prove if or not the condition is satisfied. If yes, the tool can produce the instantiations of these parameters. Thus, we can get an invariant of the predetermined form by replacing the parameters with the instantiations, respectively.

Note that the above procedure is *complete* in the sense that for any given predefined parametric invariant, the procedure can always produce the corresponding concrete invariant, if it exists. Therefore, we can also conclude that our approach is also *complete* in the sense that once the given polynomial program has a polynomial invariant, our approach can indeed find it theoretically, because we can assume parametric invariants in program variables of different degrees, and repeatedly apply the above procedure until we obtain a polynomial invariant.

Remark 2. In Steps 2 and 3, we can also apply DISCOVERER for first-order quantifier elimination in a special manner. We will illustrate this point by the following example.

4.1 Example

In this subsection, we will illustrate the above procedure by revising Example 7 from [5] which contains some mistakes in the resulting conditions because of incorrect use of the tools DISCOVERER and QEPCAD.

Example 1. The code of the program is on Fig.4 (a).

```
Integer (x, y) := (0, 0);
l0 : while x ≥ 0 ∧ y ≥ 0 do
        (x, y) := (x + y^2, y + 1);
end while
```

(a)

$$P = \{ \quad V = \{x, y\} \quad L = \{l_0\} \quad T = \{\tau\} \ \}$$

where

$$\tau = \langle l_0, l_0, x' - x - y^2 = 0 \wedge y' - y - 1 = 0, x \geq 0 \wedge y \geq 0 \rangle$$

(b)

Fig. 4.

The corresponding SATS is on Fig.4 (b).

Firstly, we predefine a parametric invariant at l_0 as

$$eq(x, y) = a_1 y^3 + a_2 y^2 + a_3 x - a_4 y = 0, \tag{3}$$

$$ineq(x, y) = b_1 x + b_2 y^2 + b_3 y + b_4 > 0 \tag{4}$$

where $a_1, a_2, a_3, a_4, b_1, b_2, b_3, b_4$ are parameters. Therefore, $\eta(l_0) = (3) \wedge (4)$.

Secondly, according to *Initiation* of Definition 4, $\Theta \models \eta(l_0)$ is equivalent to neither of the following two PSASs having real solutions.

$$x = 0, y = 0, eq(x, y) \neq 0 \tag{5}$$

$$x = 0, y = 0, ineq(x, y) \leq 0 \tag{6}$$

By calling **tofind**$(([x, y], [\,], [\,], [eq(x, y)], [x, y], [a_1, a_2, a_3, a_4], 0)$ we get that (5) has no real solutions iff *true*. While calling **tofind**$([x, y], [-ineq(x, y)], [\,], [\,], [x, y], [b_1, b_2, b_3, b_4], 0)$ we get that (6) has no real solutions iff $b_4 > 0$.

Thirdly, consider Consecution w.r.t. the transition τ. We have

$$eq(x, y) = 0 \wedge x' - x - y^2 = 0 \wedge y' - y - 1 = 0 \models eq(x', y') = 0 \wedge ineq(x', y') > 0. \tag{7}$$

This means that the following two PSASs both have no real solutions.

$$eq(x, y) = 0 \wedge x' - x - y^2 = 0 \wedge y' - y - 1 = 0 \wedge x \geq 0 \wedge y \geq 0 \wedge eq(x', y') \neq 0 \tag{8}$$

$$ineq(x, y) > 0 \wedge x' - x - y^2 = 0 \wedge y' - y - 1 = 0 \wedge x \geq 0 \wedge y \geq 0 \wedge ineq(x', y') \leq 0 \tag{9}$$

By calling **tofind**$([x' - x - y^2, y' - y - 1, eq(x, y)], [x, y], [\,], [eq(x', y')\ ], [x', y', x], [y, a_1, a_2, a_3, a_4], 0)$, we obtain that (8) has no real solutions if and only if

$$a_3 y^2 + 3a_1 y^2 + 2y a_2 + 3a_1 y - a_4 + a_2 + a_1 = 0 \vee \tag{10}$$

$$a_3 = 0.^1 \tag{11}$$

Further by Basic Algebraic Theorem, (10) holds for all y iff

$$-a_4 + a_2 + a_1 = 0 \wedge 3a_1 + 2a_2 = 0 \wedge a_3 + 3a_1 = 0, \tag{12}$$

while (11) leads to a trivial result.

[1] This resulting condition on a_1, a_2, a_3, a_4 from Consecution is different from the one given in [5], as there happened a mistake in calling **tofind** in [5]. But the final condition in [5] is correct, same as here.

For (9), by calling **tofind**($[x'-x-y^2, y'-y-1], [-ineq(x',y'), x, y], [ineq(x,y)], [\,]$, $[x',y'], [x,y,b_1,b_2,b_3,b_4], 0$), we obtain that (9) has no real solutions iff

$$b_4 + b_3 + b_2 + 2b_2y + b_3y + b_2y^2 + b_1x + b_1y^2 > 0. \tag{13}$$

Then, we have to perform quantifier elimination on (13) under the premise that $x \geq 0, y \geq 0, ineq(x,y) > 0$. Here, we use DISCOVERER in a complicated way[2], and get the following sufficient and necessary condition[3]

$$\begin{aligned} b_1 > 0 \wedge b_4 > 0 \wedge b_2 + b_3 + b_4 > 0 \wedge ((b_2 \geq 0 \wedge b_2 + b_3 \geq 0) \vee \\ (b_1 + b_2 \geq 0 \wedge 2b_2 + b_3 \geq 0) \vee d_1 \leq 0 \vee d_2 < 0 \vee (f_1 \leq 0 \wedge f_2 \geq 0)) \end{aligned} \tag{14}$$

where

$$\begin{aligned} d_1 &= -4b_1b_3 - 4b_1b_2 + 4b_2^2 \\ d_2 &= -4b_1b_2 - 4b_1b_3 - 4b_4b_1 + b_3^2 - 4b_4b_2 \\ f_1 &= 2b_4b_1^2 + 2b_4b_1b_2 - 2b_2^2b_1 - 4b_1b_2b_3 - b_1b_3^2 + 2b_2^3 \\ f_2 &= b_2^4 - 2b_2^2b_1b_4 + b_4^2b_1^2 - 4b_4b_1b_3b_2 - b_2^2b_3^2 + 4b_2^3b_4 + b_1b_3^3 + b_1b_2b_3^2 \end{aligned}$$

Remark 3. We also applied QEPCAD to the above formula and obtained a different formula, though equivalent formula.

It is easy to see that the invariant given in [5] is still an invariant of the program with the predefined template, i.e.

$$\begin{cases} -2y^3 + 3y^2 + 6x - y = 0, \\ x - y^2 + 2y + 1 > 0 \end{cases}$$

is an invariant of P, where

$$(a_1, a_2, a_3, a_4) = (-2, 3, 6, 1), (b_1, b_2, b_3, b_4) = (1, -1, 2, 1).$$

Furthermore,

$$\begin{cases} -2y^3 + 3y^2 + 6x - y = 0, \\ \frac{4}{3}x - y^2 + \frac{1}{4}y + 3 > 0 \end{cases}$$

is another invariant of P , where

$$(a_1, a_2, a_3, a_4) = (-2, 3, 6, 1), (b_1, b_2, b_3, b_4) = (\frac{4}{3}, -1, \frac{1}{4}, 3).$$

However, the latter invariant does not satisfy the formula (17) in [5].

5 Discovering Non-linear Ranking Functions

As we explained in Remark 1, a ranking function can be represented as a special loop invariant of a loop at the entry point. Therefore, the above procedure still

---

[2] The procedure is so involved, as we need to apply the tool multiple times, so we here omit the detailed discussion.

[3] The formula (17) in [5] is not correct because of a mistake when using QEPCAD.

works for non-linear ranking function discovering subject to appropriate modifications. Roughly speaking, The approach to discovering non-linear ranking functions in [4] consists of the following 4 steps:

Step 1–Predefine a Ranking Function Template. Predetermine a template of ranking functions.

Step 2– Encode Initial Condition. According to the initial condition of ranking function, we have $\Theta \models \gamma \geq 0$ which means that each real solution of Θ must satisfy $\gamma \geq 0$. In other words, $\Theta \wedge \gamma < 0$ has no real solution. It is easy to see that $\Theta \wedge \gamma < 0$ is a PSAS according to Definition 1. Therefore, by applying DISCOVERER, we get a necessary and sufficient condition for the derived PSAS to have no real solutions. The condition may contain the occurrences of some program variables. In this case, the condition should hold for any instantiations of the variables. Thus, by introducing universal quantifications of these variables (we usually add a scope to each of the variables according to different situations) and then applying QEPCAD or DISCOVERER, we can get a necessary and sufficient condition in terms of the parameters only.

Step 3–Encode Decreasing Condition. From Definition 5, there exists a positive constant C such that for any transition circle $l_0 \xrightarrow{\tau_1} l_1 \xrightarrow{\tau_2} \cdots \xrightarrow{\tau_n} l_0$,

$$\rho_{\tau_1;\tau_2;\cdots;\tau_n} \wedge \theta_{\tau_1;\tau_2;\cdots;\tau_n} \models \gamma(V) - \gamma(V') \geq C \wedge \gamma(V') \geq 0, \tag{15}$$

equivalent to

$$\rho_{\tau_1;\tau_2;\cdots;\tau_n} \wedge \theta_{\tau_1;\tau_2;\cdots;\tau_n} \wedge \gamma(V') < 0, \tag{16}$$

$$\rho_{\tau_1;\tau_2;\cdots;\tau_n} \wedge \theta_{\tau_1;\tau_2;\cdots;\tau_n} \wedge \gamma(V) - \gamma(V') < C \tag{17}$$

both have no real solutions. Obviously, (16) and (17) are PSASs according to Definition 1. Thus, by applying DISCOVERER, we obtain some conditions on the parameters. Subsequently, similarly to Step 2, we may need to use QEPCAD or DISCOVERER to simplify the resulting condition in order to get a necessary and sufficient condition in terms of the parameters only.

Step 4–Solve Final Constraints. According to the results obtained from Steps 1, 2 and 3, we can get the final necessary and sufficient condition only on the parameters of the ranking function template. Then, by utilizing DISCOVERER or QEPCAD, prove if or not the condition is satisfied and produce the instantiations of these parameters such that the condition holds. Thus, we can get a ranking function of the predetermined form by replacing the parameters with the instantiations, respectively.

Remark 4. Note that the above procedure is *complete* in the sense that for any given template of ranking function, the procedure can always synthesize a ranking function of the give template, if there indeed exist such ranking functions.

5.1 Discussions: Generating Invariants vs. Discovering Ranking Functions

We have shown how to reduce the discovery of invariants and ranking functions to directly solving SASs by exploiting the inductive property of invariants and ranking functions. Although invariants and ranking functions both have such a property, the former is inductive w.r.t. a small step, i.e. each of single transitions of the given loop in contrast that the latter is inductive w.r.t. a big step, that is each of transition circle at the initial location of the loop. The difference entails that the approach from [5] can be simply applied to single loop programs as well as nested loop programs, without any change; but regarding the discovery of ranking functions, we have to further develop the approach of [4] in order to handle nested loop programs, although it works well for single loop programs.

6 Complexity Analysis

Assume given an SATS $P = \langle V, L, T, l_0, \Theta \rangle$, we obtain k distinct PSASs in order to generate its polynomial invariants or ranking functions with the approach. W.l.o.g., suppose each of these k PSASs has at most s polynomial equations, and m inequations and inequalities. All polynomials are in n indeterminates (i.e., variables and parameters) and of degrees at most d.

For a PSAS S, by CAD (*cylindrical algebraic decomposition*) based quantifier elimination on S has complexity $\mathcal{O}((2d)^{2^{2n+8}}(s+m)^{2^{n+6}})$ according to the results of [12], which is double exponential w.r.t. n. Thus, the total cost is $\mathcal{O}(k(2d)^{2^{2n+8}}(s+m)^{2^{n+6}})$ for directly applying the technique of quantifier elimination to generate invariants and ranking functions of a program as advocated by Kapur [14].

In contrast, the cost of our approach includes two parts: one is for applying real solution classification to generate condition on the parameters possibly still containing some program variables; the other is for applying first-order quantifier elimination to produce condition only on the parameters (if necessary) and further exploiting PCAD to obtain the instantiations of these parameters. According to the complexity analysis in [5], the cost for the first part is singly exponential in n and doubly exponential in t, where t stands for the dimension of the ideal generated by the s polynomial equations. The cost for the second part is doubly exponential in t. So, compared to directly applying quantifier elimination, our approach can dramatically reduce the complexity, in particular when t is much less than n.

7 Beyond Semi-Algebraic Transition Systems

In this section, we will discuss how to generalize the above approach to more general programs beyond SATSs.

Polynomial Transition Systems. A PTS can be transformed into an equivalent SATS by adding additional transitions. The basic idea is as follows: First, given a PTS P, we rewrite all guards and transitions relations in disjunctive normal form. Let P' be the resulting PTS; Second, if there is a transition of the form $\tau = \langle i, j, \rho_\tau, \theta'_\tau \vee \theta''_\tau \rangle$, then we replace τ by $\tau_1 = \langle i, j, \rho_\tau, \theta'_\tau \rangle$ and $\tau_2 = \langle i, j, \rho_\tau, \theta''_\tau \rangle$;

if there is a transition of the form $\tau = \langle i, j, \rho'_\tau \vee \rho''_\tau, \theta_\tau \rangle$, then we replace τ by $\tau_1 = \langle i, j, \rho'_\tau, \theta_\tau \rangle$ and $\tau_2 = \langle i, j, \rho''_\tau, \theta_\tau \rangle$; Repeat the second step until all guards and transition relations are conjunctive polynomial formulae. Finally, we obtain an SATS that is equivalent to P.

The following theorem guarantees that we can reduce the problem of discovery of invariants and ranking functions of a PTS to that of the resulting SATS.

Theorem 3. *Let P be a PTS, and P' be the resulting SATS from the above procedure. Then, P and P' have the same invariants and ranking functions.*

Fractional Polynomial Transition Systems. According to Theorem 2 and the above discussion, it is easy to see that the problems of invariant generation and ranking function discovering for FPTSs can be reduced to those of SATSs too.

8 More Expressive Invariants and Ranking Functions

In this section, we will discuss how to extend the approach to synthesizing more expressive invariants and ranking functions. According to the results of the above section, for simplicity, here we only need to consider to extend the approach to synthesize more expressive invariants and ranking functions of SATSs.

General Polynomial Formula as Invariant. Given an SATS, we will extend the approach presented in Section 4 in the following way: In first step, we allow to predefine a template of invariant ϕ, which is a parametric polynomial formula rather than a PSAS. Then, we rewrite the parametric polynomial formula into a conjunctive normal form $\phi_1 \wedge \phi_2 \wedge \cdots \wedge \phi_n$, where each ϕ_i is a disjunction of some atomic polynomial formulae. In the second step, according to Initiation, we have $\Theta_0 \models \bigwedge_{i=1}^n \phi_i$. This means that $\Theta_0 \wedge \bigvee_{i=1}^n \neg\phi_i$ has no real solutions. This entails that for $i = 1, \cdots, n$, $\Theta_0 \wedge \neg\phi_i$ has no real solutions. It is easy to see that $\Theta_0 \wedge \neg\phi_i$ is a PSAS, therefore, Initiation case is reduced to solving SASs. Applying the technique used in Section 4, we can obtain a condition on the parameters only. In the third step, similarly to the above, we can show that Consecution can also be reduced to solving SASs either, and therefore, we can get another condition on the parameters. Finally, similarly to Section 4, we can instantiate the parameters according to the resulting condition on them and generate invariants with the predefined template.

Fractional Polynomial Formula as Invariant. For this case, in the first step, we predefine a template of invariant that is a parametric fractional polynomial formula. According to Theorem 1, the parametric fractional polynomial formula is equivalent to a parametric polynomial formula. So, the rest steps are reduced to those of the above case.

Fractional Polynomial as Ranking Function. By Theorem 1, similarly to the previous discussion, it is quite easy to extend the approach of [4] to synthesize a ranking function represented by a fractional polynomial.

9 Conclusions

In this paper, we first summarized our previous work on synthesizing polynomial invariants and ranking functions reported in [4,5] by reduction to solving SASs, and redid Example 7 from [5] by correcting some mistakes. Then, we investigated the issue to generalize the approach in two directions: one is applicable to more general programs, beyond SATSs, to PTSs, even to FPTSs; the other is to synthesize more expressive invariants and ranking functions.

How to further improve the efficiency of the approach is still a big challenge as well as our main future work, since the complexity is still single exponential w.r.t. the number of program variables, and doubly exponential w.r.t. the number of parameters (at least). It is worth investigating how to further extend the approach to handle more general programs with more complicated data. The potential solution could be to integrate different decision procedures. Here, we only focus on Tarski's Algebra, so we can only deal with real variables.

Acknowledgements

We are so grateful to Prof. Chaochen Zhou and Yinhua Chen for their contributions to the previous joint work. We also thank Prof. Chaochen Zhou for many fruitful discussions with him on this work and his valuable comments on the draft of this paper. We thank Dr. Dimitar P. Guelev for his proof-reading and comments to improve the presentation of this paper so much.

References

1. Braverman, M.: Termination of integer linear programs. In: Ball, T., Jones, R.B. (eds.) CAV 2006. LNCS, vol. 4144, pp. 372–385. Springer, Heidelberg (2006)
2. Besson, F., Jensen, T., Talpin, J.-P.: Polyhedral analysis of synchronous languages. In: Cortesi, A., Filé, G. (eds.) SAS 1999. LNCS, vol. 1694, pp. 51–69. Springer, Heidelberg (1999)
3. Bradley, A., Manna, Z., Sipma, H.: Terminaition of polynomial programs. In: Cousot, R. (ed.) VMCAI 2005. LNCS, vol. 3385, pp. 113–129. Springer, Heidelberg (2005)
4. Chen, Y., Xia, B., Yang, L., Zhan, N., Zhou, C.: Discovering non-linear ranking functions by solving semi-algebraic systems. In: Jones, C.B., Liu, Z., Woodcock, J. (eds.) ICTAC 2007. LNCS, vol. 4711, pp. 34–49. Springer, Heidelberg (2007)
5. Chen, Y., Xia, B., Yang, L., Zhan, N.: Generating polynomial invariants with DISCOVERER and QEPCAD. In: Jones, C.B., Liu, Z., Woodcock, J. (eds.) Formal Methods and Hybrid Real-Time Systems. LNCS, vol. 4700, pp. 67–82. Springer, Heidelberg (2007)
6. Collins, G.E., Hong, H.: Partial cylindrical algebraic decomposition for quantifier elimination. J. of Symbolic Computation 12, 299–328 (1991)
7. Colón, M., Sankaranarayanan, S., Sipma, H.B.: Linear invariant generation using non-linear constraint solving. In: Hunt Jr., W.A., Somenzi, F. (eds.) CAV 2003. LNCS, vol. 2725, pp. 420–432. Springer, Heidelberg (2003)
8. Colón, M., Sipma, H.B.: Synthesis of linear ranking functions. In: Margaria, T., Yi, W. (eds.) TACAS 2001. LNCS, vol. 2031, pp. 67–81. Springer, Heidelberg (2001)

9. Cousot, P.: Proving program invariance and termination by parametric abstraction, Langrangian Relaxation and semidefinite programming. In: Cousot, R. (ed.) VMCAI 2005. LNCS, vol. 3385, pp. 1–24. Springer, Heidelberg (2005)
10. Cousot, P., Halbwachs, N.: Automatic discovery of linear restraints among the variables of a program. In: ACM POPL 1978, pp. 84–97 (1978)
11. Dams, D., Gerth, R., Grumberg, O.: A heuristic for the automatic generation of ranking functions. In: Workshop on Advances in Verification (WAVe 2000), pp. 1–8 (2000)
12. Davenport, J.H., Heintz, J.: Real Elimination is Doubly Exponential. J. of Symbolic Computation 5, 29–37 (1988)
13. Dolzman, A., Sturm, T.: REDLOG: Computer algebra meets computer logic. ACM SIGSAM Bulletin 31(2), 2–9
14. Kapur, D.: Automatically generating loop invariants using quantifier llimination. In: Proc. IMACS Intl. Conf. on Applications of Computer Algebra (ACA 2004), Beaumont, Texas (July 2004)
15. Müller-Olm, M., Seidl, H.: Polynomial constants are decidable. In: Hermenegildo, M.V., Puebla, G. (eds.) SAS 2002. LNCS, vol. 2477, pp. 4–19. Springer, Heidelberg (2002)
16. Müller-Olm, M., Seidl, H.: Precise interprocedural analysis through linear algebra. In: ACM SIGPLAN Principles of Programming Languages, POPL 2004, pp. 330–341 (2004)
17. Podelski, A., Rybalchenko, A.: A complete method for the synthesis of linear ranking functions. In: Steffen, B., Levi, G. (eds.) VMCAI 2004. LNCS, vol. 2937, pp. 239–251. Springer, Heidelberg (2004)
18. Rodriguez-Carbonell, E., Kapur, D.: An abstract interpretation approach for automatic generation of polynomial invariants. In: Giacobazzi, R. (ed.) SAS 2004. LNCS, vol. 3148, pp. 280–295. Springer, Heidelberg (2004)
19. Rodriguez-Carbonell, E., Kapur, D.: Automatic generation of polynomial loop invariants: algebraic foundations. In: Proc. Intl. Symp on Symbolic and Algebraic Computation (ISSAC 2004) (July 2004)
20. Rodriguez-Carbonell, E., Kapur, D.: Generating all polynomial invariants in simple loops. Journal of Symbolic Computation 42, 443–476 (2007)
21. Sankaranarayanan, S., Sipma, H.B., Manna, Z.: Non-linear loop invariant generation using Gröbner bases. In: ACM POPL 2004, pp. 318–329 (2004)
22. Tiwari, A.: Termination of linear programs. In: Alur, R., Peled, D.A. (eds.) CAV 2004. LNCS, vol. 3114, pp. 70–82. Springer, Heidelberg (2004)
23. Xia, B.: DISCOVERER: A tool for solving semi-algebraic systems. In: Software Demo at ISSAC 2007, Waterloo, July 30 (2007); ACM SIGSAM Bulletin, 41(3), 102–103 (2007)
24. Xia, B., Yang, L.: An algorithm for isolating the real solutions of semi-algebraic systems. J. Symbolic Computation 34, 461–477 (2002)
25. Yang, L.: Recent advances on determining the number of real roots of parametric polynomials. J. Symbolic Computation 28, 225–242 (1999)
26. Yang, L., Hou, X., Zeng, Z.: A complete discrimination system for polynomials. Science in China (Ser. E) 39, 628–646 (1996)
27. Yang, L., Xia, B.: Real solution classifications of a class of parametric semi-algebraic systems. In: Proc. of Int'l Conf. on Algorithmic Algebra and Logic, pp. 281–289 (2005)
28. Yang, L., Zhan, N., Xia, B., Zhou, C.: Program verification by using DISCOVERER. In: Proc. VSTTE 2005. LNCS, vol. 4171, pp. 528–538. Springer, Heidelberg (2005)

Debugging Statecharts Via Model-Code Traceability

Liang Guo and Abhik Roychoudhury

School of Computing, National University of Singapore
{guol,abhik}@comp.nus.edu.sg

Abstract. Model-driven software development involves constructing behavioral models from informal English requirements. These models are then used to guide software construction. The compilation of behavioral models into software is the topic of many existing research works. There also exist a number of UML-based modeling tools which support such model compilation. In this paper, we show how Statechart models can be validated/debugged by (a) generating code from the Statechart models, (b) employing established software debugging methods like program slicing on the generated code, and (c) relating the program slice back to the Statechart level. Our study is presented concretely in terms of dynamic slicing of Java code produced from Statechart models. The slice produced at the code level is mapped back to the model level for enhanced design comprehension. We use the open-source JSlice tool for dynamic slicing of Java programs in our experiments. We present results on a wide variety of real-life control systems which are modeled as Statecharts (from the informal English requirements) and debugged using our methodology. We feel that our debugging methodology fits in well with design flows in model-driven software development.

Keywords: Statecharts, Traceability, Debugging, Slicing.

1 Introduction

Model-driven software development is becoming increasingly popular. There exist many tools which enable design specification in terms of Unified Modeling Language (UML) diagrams. Subsequently code is generated from these diagrams either semi-automatically (as in Rhapsody from I-Logix [1] which compiles Statechart models into C/C++/Java code) or manually using the UML diagrams as guidance. Irrespective of whether the code is generated automatically or manually, some of the testing/dynamic analysis is done at the code level. At the UML level, usually verification methods like model checking are employed to check critical properties about the design.

If the testing/debugging of a piece of model-driven software reveals/explains an "unexpected program behavior" how do we reflect it at the model level? This requires us to maintain associations between model elements and code (which are built during code generation), and then exploit these associations to highlight the appropriate model elements which are responsible for the so-called unexpected behavior. We advocate such a method for debugging model-driven software in this paper. The benefits of relating the results of debugging model-driven software to the model level are obvious — it enables design comprehension and debugging at the model level. Since most debugging tools

T. Margaria and B. Steffen (Eds.): ISoLA 2008, CCIS 17, pp. 292–306, 2008.

work at the code level, this forms an important step in enabling model-driven software development.

To make our study concrete, we fix a modeling langauge and a debugging method — Statecharts [2] as the modeling language and dynamic slicing [3,4] as the debugging method.[1] Given a program P and input I, the programmer provides a slicing criterion of the form (l, V), where l is a control location in the program and V is a set of program variables referenced at l. The purpose of slicing is to find out the statements in P which can affect the values of V at l via control/data flow, when P is executed with input I. Thus, if I is an offending test case (where the programmer is not happy with the observable values of certain variables), dynamic slicing can be performed and the resultant slice can be inspected (at the code level). However, at this stage, it might be important to reflect the results of slicing at a higher level, say at the model level — to understand the problem with the design. We address this issue in this paper.

We consider the situation where the design is modeled using class diagrams and Statecharts i.e. the behavior of each class is given by a Statechart and these Statecharts are *automatically compiled* into code in a standard programming language like Java. We present experimental results on a number of *real-life control systems* drawn from various application domains such as avionics, automotive and rail-transportation. These control systems are designed as Statecharts from which we automatically generate Java code (into which associations between model elements and lines of code are embedded). Subject to an observable error, the generated Java code is subjected to dynamic slicing. The resultant slice is mapped back to the model level, while preserving the Statechart's structure, orthogonality (multiple processes executing concurrently) and hierarchy.

One could argue that, if the models are executable and automatic compilation of models to code is feasible (as is the case for Statecharts) — the debugging should be done at the model level. Indeed, we could build a dynamic slicing tool directly for Statecharts.[2] However, to popularize such tools for debugging model-driven software will require a bigger shift in mind-set of programmers who are accustomed to debugging code written in standard programming languages. Moreover, debugging the implementation is a more focused activity, since it allows us to ignore the bugs in the model which do not appear in the implementation (since the implementation may have lesser behaviors than the model, as is the case when we compile Statecharts to sequential code).

In summary, this paper proposes a methodology for debugging model-driven software, in particular, code generated from executable models like Statecharts. Our proposed methods/tools focus on generating code with tags (to associate models and code), using existing tools and algorithms to debug the generated code and exploiting the model-code tags to reflect the debugging results at the model level. We feel that it is important to develop backward links between the three layers in software development — requirements, models and code. This article constitutes a step in this direction where we relate results of debugging at code level to the model level.

[1] The reason for choosing a *dynamic* analysis technique as the debugging method is obvious — it corresponds more closely to program debugging by trying out selected inputs.

[2] Static slicing of Statecharts has been studied in [5]. Direct simulation of statecharts has been discussed in [6].

2 State-of-the-Art in Statechart Compilation

Compilation of Statecharts for generating code has been studied in many research articles. Some of these works, specifically those focusing on embedded system designs, give importance to generating efficient C/SystemC code from State diagrams [7,8]. Certain other works (*e.g.*, [9] and, to a lesser extent, [10]) generate Java code from full-fledged UML designs consisting of Class Diagrams, State Diagrams and Collaboration Diagrams. *None* of these works support full-fledged model-code association, so lines of generated code cannot be easily mapped back to model elements. In fact, as we illustrate in the following via an example, even the commercial tools for Statechart modeling and code generation do not properly support association between Statechart models and generated code.

Rhapsody and Stateflow are two of the successful tools released by I-Logix[1] and MathWorks[11] respectively, which can generate code from Statechart models. Rhapsody supports all Statechart features and is capable of generating C, C++, and Java code. Stateflow supports Statechart models as part of a complete embedded system design. It supports most of the Statecharts' features, and can generate C code from Statecharts. Given a Statechart with sufficient details, all three tools (Rhapsody, Stateflow and our tool) are able to generate executable code supporting AND/OR-states and event broadcasting. Meanwhile, all three tools provide model-code association to some extent. All tools tag pieces of code with the corresponding Statechart elements information.

However, tags maintained by Rhapsody and Stateflow are not sufficient for supporting full model-code association. The purpose of tags in Rhapsody is to help users refer to model elements automatically while editing the generated code. The tags only associate actions (in transitions and states) and conditions (in transitions). *The code corresponding to events and transition firings is not tagged, and hence there is no direct association for these elements.* Stateflow generates tags on model structure for reference purpose only. Only state entry and state exit are tagged before and after each transition firing. *There is no association existing for events, transitions, actions and conditions.* When a transition is entering or leaving a composite state, all levels of states entered/exited are tagged, instead of the target/source (sub-)state only. Although it shows clearly the execution behavior of a composite state, it increases the difficulty in understanding the triggered transition as well as its source and target states.

The problem with incomplete tags for model element is, we cannot construct a complete trace of the Statechart execution, and hence no systematic analysis method can be applied. After the code is generated, we can perform debugging when an error is found. To enable a comprehensive understanding of the bug report at model level, the code-level bug report should be mapped back to model level. In both Rhapsody and Stateflow, since some model elements are not tagged for model-code association, the model-level bug report becomes incomplete. Our tool is able to build a full model-code association, and it maps bug report from code-level back to model-level.

In the following, we capture the capabilities of the existing tools as far as maintaining code to model backward associations is concerned. We use the popular Rail-car example developed by David Harel and Eran Gery in [12] to illustrate the differences. The example is drawn from the rail-transportation domain and has been widely used as a case study of UML-based system behavior modeling. In this example, there are a fixed

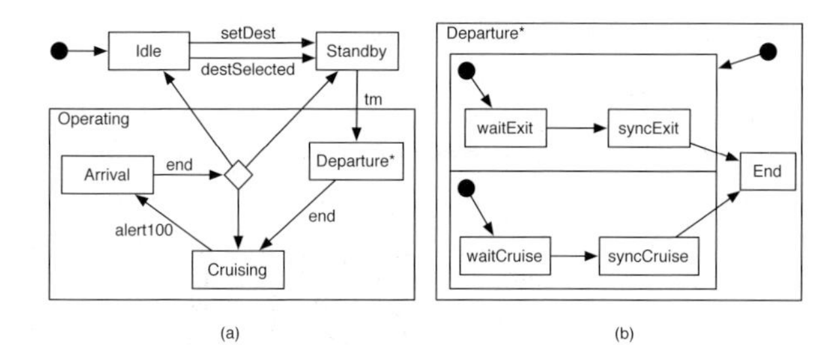

Fig. 1. Statechart fragment corresponding to `car` object. (a) the top-level Statechart, and (b) the details of composite state `Departure`. State `Arrival` is also a composite state, the details of which is not shown.

Our Tool		Rhapsody		Stateflow	
Element Type	Element Name	Element Type	Element Name	Element Type	Element Name
T_action	initial	T_action	initial	------	------
E	destSelected	------	------	------	------
T_fire	Idle2Standby	------	------	------	------
E	tm	------	------	------	------
T_fire	standby2departure	------	------	T_fire	standby2departure
⋮	⋮	⋮	⋮	⋮	⋮
S_entry	DepartureEnd	S_entry	DepartureEnd	S_entry	DepartureEnd
E	end	------	------	------	------
T_fire	departure2cruising	------	------	T_fire	departure2cruising
E	alert100			------	------
T_action	cruising2arrival	T_action	cruising2arrival	------	------
T_fire	cruising2arrival	------	------	T_fire	cruising2arrival
⋮	⋮	⋮	⋮	⋮	⋮
S_entry	ArrivalEnd	S_entry	ArrivalEnd	S_entry	ArrivalEnd
E	end	------	------	------	------
T_action	arrival2cond	T_action	arrival2cond	------	------
T_condition	arrival2idle	T_condition	arrival2idle	------	------
T_fire	arrival2idle	------	------	T_fire	arrival2idle
(a)		(b)		(c)	

Fig. 2. Model-level slices based on the code generated from (a) our tool, (b) Rhapsody, and (c) Stateflow. A dashed line shows a missing model element in the slice resulting from Rhapsody or Stateflow. "E", "T", and "S" appearing in "Element Type" denote "Event", "Transition", and "State". Model elements for `CarHandler` and details inside the states `Departure` and `Arrival` of `Car` are omitted for the ease of understanding.

number of terminals located along a cyclic path. Each adjacent pair of these terminals is connected by two rail tracks, one of which is for clockwise travel and another for anti-clockwise travel of the rail cars. There are several (a fixed number of) rail cars available for transporting passengers between the terminals. There is a control center which receives, processes and communicates data between various terminals and railcars. Each terminal has several car handlers to process transactions between the terminal and cars. More details about the example along with the class diagrams and Statecharts for each class appears in [12].

In particular, we consider the Statechart of a `car` object (shown in Figure 1). Suppose we have a car moving from a terminal to a neighboring terminal (its destination). In terms of the Statechart behavior, the car object is expected to visit states `Idle`, `Standby`, `Departure`, `Cruising`, `Arrival`, and back to `Idle`. Here we use slicing as the debugging method to study how the car finally comes back to state `Idle`. We set the last occurrence of `Idle` [3] as the slicing criterion and perform slicing based on the car object. As shown in Figure 2, the model-level slice on column (a) is produced by mapping the code-level slice backward using our approach, while the slices on column (b) and (c) are from code generated by Rhapsody and Stateflow. Although code from all three tools have almost identical behavior, our tool is able to produce a complete model-level slice. More specifically, all events and transition-firings are missing in the slice resulting from Rhapsody, which contains only a sequence of actions executed and conditions checked. For example, since the transition between states `Idle` and `Standby` is missing, we have no idea which event - `setDest` or `destSelected` - triggers the car object transiting from `Idle` to `Standby`. In the slice resulting from Stateflow, the transition-firings are only reconstructed from state entry/exit information as well as the model structure. Here also, we cannot determine the transition triggered from state `Idle` to `Standby`. Note that the missing event here (`setDest` or `destSelected`) could be broadcast to other objects (running concurrently), thereby triggering transitions in other objects. Thus, not tracking these events hampers our understanding of the overall system behavior (and not just the behavior of the `car` object in question).

In summary, the existing tools do not maintain detailed model-code associations while generating code from Statecharts. Rhapsody only tags actions (which are executed as an effect of states/transitions) and conditions (which serve as the guard of transitions). Stateflow only tracks the states through which the Statechart moves. *None of the tools track the events which trigger the transitions and are broadcasted resulting in non-trivial communication patterns across the different concurrent objects represented by a Statechart.* These events are often responsible for "unexpected behaviors"; without considering them in our debugging methods (and bug reports) it would be impossible to comprehend concurrent system designs represented by Statecharts.

3 Overall Methodology

In this section, we present the methodology to trace design information between models and code. Specifically, our work consists of the following steps.

- *Forward code generation.* We automatically generate Java code from Statecharts while using appropriate tags to store model-code association information. The Java code can then be used to perform code-level analysis (*e.g.*, debugging via dynamic slicing).
- *Backward code-to-model mapping.* With the debugging result (bug report) from code analysis and the association information obtained, we perform a mapping to produce a model-level bug report, which is more tightly related to the Statechart and also smaller.
- *Hierarchical analysis result.* Although the model-level bug report is easier to understand than code-level report, it may still be large and complex. We utilize the important features of Statecharts (hierarchy/orthogonality) to re-structure the model-level bug report. Furthermore, we separate out the flow of different active objects (from the same class) whose behavior is captured by the same Statechart.

[3] We assume that the execution of Statechart model can be finished by entering an "End" state eventually.

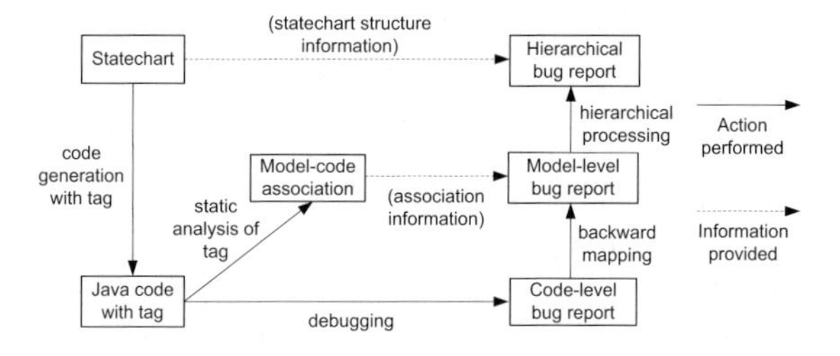

Fig. 3. Maintaining the traceability between model and code

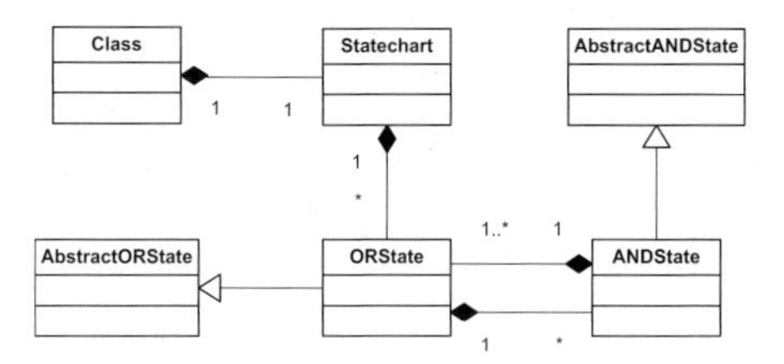

Fig. 4. Class diagram of Java code generated from Statecharts

The whole methodology is summarized in Figure 3. When a Statechart model is available[4], we can generate code automatically. Since the code is generated completely from the model, we know exactly which part of code results from a particular model element. By tagging this piece of code with the corresponding model element information, we are able to derive the association between model and code. If we encounter an observable error while executing the code, we can use methods (such as slicing) to debug it. With the debugging result (code-level bug report), we can map the bug report backward to model-level by changing statements in code-level bug report to the corresponding model elements. To fully regain the structure of Statecharts, the model-level bug report can be re-organized. The re-organized hierarchical bug report maintains both the structure of Statechart as well as the elements in the original model-level bug report. We now elaborate the intricacies involved in each of these steps.

4 Code Generation

First we discuss how we can maintain tags between model elements and generated code during the process of code generation. It is worthwhile to note that, *we always translate a Statechart to a single-threaded Java program. Thus, event communication at the Statechart level gets translated to method calls at the code level.*

For each class of active objects in the system model, the corresponding Statechart is realized at the software level via several Java classes. As shown in Figure 4, a Statechart contains a set of OR-state classes. Meanwhile, an OR-state class may have several AND-state classes — where each AND-state class corresponds to a concurrently

[4] The states and transitions must be defined, and all appropriate triggers/conditions/actions must be available — such that the system is executable after generating code.

```
1.  public void trigger(Events event)
2.  {
3.        switch(event) {
4.              <% for each (transition t in current state) { %>
5.              case Events.<% transtion t's event %>:
6.                    <% if (transition t has condition) { %>
7.                    if(<% transition name %>_Condition()) {
8.                    <% } %>
9.                    <% if (transition t has action) { %>
10.                   <% transition name %>_Action(event);
11.                   <% } %>
12.                   <% transition name%>_Fire();
13.                   <% if(transition t has condition) { %>
14.                   }
15.                   <% } %>
16.                   break;
17.             <% } //end for each %>
18.             default:
19.                   for each (AND-State as contained) {
20.                         as.trigger(event);
21.                   }
22.       }
23. }

24. <% for each (transition t in current state) { %>
25. <% if(transition t has action) { %>
26. /**
27. * @model type=transition_action name=<% transition name %>
28. */
29. private void <% transition name %>_Action(Object parameter) {
30.       <% transition t's action %>
31. }
32. <% } %>

33. <% for each (transition t in current state) { %>
34. /**
35. * @model type=transition_fire name=<% transition name %>
36. */
37. private void <% transition name %>_Fire() {
38.       Create target state object;
39.       make transition;
40. }
41. <% } %>
```

Fig. 5. A fragment of template used in code generation

executing component. Each AND-state class may again contain different classes corresponding to the possible (OR-)states in which the system component (corresponding to the AND-state) can be in. The design of OR-states within an AND-state follows the State design pattern [13].

While generating code from Statechart models, we mark the lines of code corresponding to specific model elements with the model element name and type. The usual model element types correspond to events, states, transitions, conditions, actions and etc. Note that while generating Java code, each method only contains code for at most one model element. These markers or tags are inserted as *Javadoc* comments in the generated code in the form of: `@model type=`*type* `name=`*name* For example, if a method $meth$ in code corresponds to state $S2$ in a Statechart model, we insert the following comment before $meth$:

```
/**
*@model type=state name=S2
*/
```

The code generation mechanism is implemented using Eclipse framework, which is capable of emitting text files w.r.t. a set of templates and inputs to the templates. Figure 5 shows a fragment of a template used in generating an *ORState* class as in Figure 4, which is writing in pseudo code for ease of understanding. Line 1 - 23 represents the method to dispatch event, and line 24 - 32 and line 33 - 41 represents two methods for transition's action and transition firing respectively. Note that text contained in "<%" and "%>" is to be substitute with the real input - e.g. transition name, code for transition action, and etc. Other text is emitted as is. Each element is written as a method. For example, line 30 will be replaced with the code of transition action during generation. The tag for model element is written in the template as well, with appropriate names to be substitute. Line 26 - 28 shows such a tag for transition's action. Inserting tags as *Javadoc* comments at method level serves several purposes: (a) instead of inserting tag to every statement related to a model element, we greatly reduce the space overhead for tags; (b) Javadoc is a standard documentation format in Java program, and thus the generated tags can be easily processed by other design tools for their own analysis, and (c) it allows us to incrementally change the code, for minimal changes in the Statechart model.

Note that the tags in the generated code cannot be efficiently used for relating code-level bug reports to the model level. Indeed this is the main motivation of our work — debugging model-driven software such that the results of debugging can be shown and communicated to the designers at the model level. Since the tags are embedded inside the generated code as plain text, relating the lines in bug-reports to the model-level will involve expensive file accesses. Consequently, we use the tags in the generated code to build an in-memory representation of the model-code association. The association consists of tuples of the following form: `(Model element name, Element type, Java class file, Line numbers)` indexed by `(element name, type)` and `(class file, line numbers)` separately. Maintaining the model-code associations in-memory as well as in the file for generated code allows us to avoid regenerating the code for minor changes in the model.

Effect of incremental changes. The process of maintaining tags during code generation and building the in-memory model-code association is important for model-level debugging. Once the bugs are found and fixed at the model level, the changes need to be propagated to the generated code. This can be done automatically using the tags, provided the fixes at the model level do not add/remove any model elements. We note that often the bug-fixes involve correcting a wrong condition or a wrong action in the Statechart model. Such changes in the model level only *modify* model elements. These changes do not affect the tags, and thus do not require re-generating code from the modified model. In fact, as long as the structure of the Statechart model (the structure resulting from states and transitions) is not affected, there is no need to re-generate code from the Statechart. Instead we can use existing tags, to directly (and automatically) propagate the changes from the model level to the code level. The in-memory model-code associations can then be re-built on demand from the modified code.

5 Mapping Code-Level Bug Reports to Statechart-Level

We now elaborate the method for mapping the debugging results of the generated code back to the Statechart model level. Most debugging methods report a list of statements (the *bug report*) that are potentially related to the observable "error". These statements are at the level of the generated code. Recall that our model-code association stored in-memory contains tuples of the form

```
(Model element name, Element type, Java class file, Line #).
```

Thus, we can map a set of statements in the generated code to a set of model elements at the Statechart model level. This constitutes our preliminary model level bug report. The model-level bug report is smaller and more compact than the code-level bug report.

Take the example in Figure 1, where the "car" object visits states `Idle`, `Standby`, `Departure`, `Cruising`, `Arrival`, and back to `Idle` (the states inside composite states are not mentioned here). Suppose we set the last occurrence of `Idle` state as the slicing criterion, which is essentially translated to a number of lines in generated code passed to JSlice. The code-level bug report will consist of a set of `(Java class file, line number)` tuples. Apparently, a number of entries in the bug report corresponds to one model element. By utilizing the model-code association, we can get a set of model elements as the model-level bug report. For this example, we will have:

```
State Idle, Transition Idle → Standby, State Standby,
        ..., State waitExit, State syncExit, ...
```

Note that in the model-level bug report, all related model elements are reported as a simple set. The hierarchy structure of Statechart is totally disregarded. The designer cannot figure out those more important (more suspicious) elements quickly from the element set. Thus, we need to further re-organize the model-level bug report.

Separating flows from different objects in a class. We observe that debugging program generated from Statechart models differs in one significant way from normal debugging of sequential programs. A Statechart model M for a process class can capture the communication and control flow of *several* active objects running concurrently. This is because there might be several active objects in the class whose behavior is captured by M. Consequently, in the model-level bug report, it is important to separate out the relevant control flows of these different objects — so that the designer can trace the source of the observable "error". For example, if a state $S2$ appears in the model-level bug report, it might capture the visit of several active objects of the same class to the state $S2$ (each possibly multiple times). To separate out the control flows of the different objects, we can let our code-level debugging method return *a sequence of statement instances* rather than a *set of statements*. This is possible for popular debugging methods such as dynamic slicing [4,3,14] and fault localization [15]. The sequence of statement instances (call it σ_{code}) gets mapped to a sequence of model element instances (call it σ_{model}) using model-code associations. These model element instances may come from different objects; we can project σ_{model} to get the sequences of model element instances for the *different* active objects.

Hierarchical Bug reports. Even after we project the model-level bug report for each active object, the bug report for objects are still sets of model elements, which may be huge compared to the entire model for the designer to inspect. In fact, we can go beyond the projection of model level bug report for active objects. Since a Statechart model has a hierarchy structure, the parent-children relationship of states can be formed as a tree automatically. Nodes in this hierarchy tree correspond to *OR-states* in Statechart. Children of a node n are OR-states directly contained by n's AND-states. Note that in the hierarchy tree we do not include AND-states. Usually the model designers are interested in how the model is executed - that is, how transitions are fired between OR-states. Building hierarchical bug report at code-level is studied in [16]. However, the organization of code-level hierarchical bug report may not correspond to the structure of Statechart. Thus, we need to build hierarchical bug report at model-level w.r.t the Statechart organization.

Given a model-level bug report (as a sequence of model element instances), we first project the report to get the sequence of model element instances for every object of

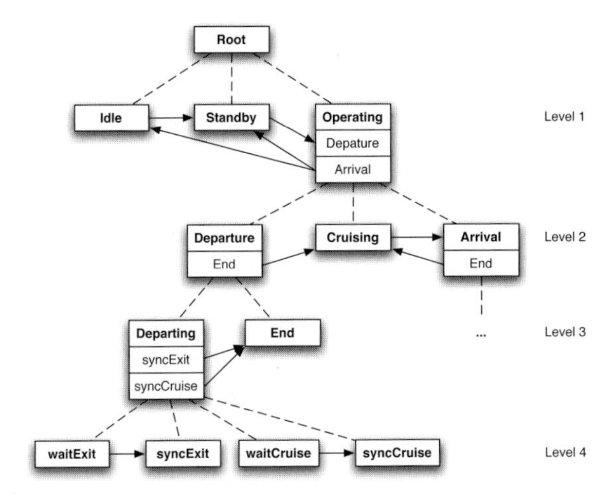

Fig. 6. Hierarchical bug report for the example in Figure 1

class C. This sequence is projected further for each node of the hierarchy tree of Statechart model M for class C. This leads to a bug report which contains the structure of the Statechart model and enables greater design comprehension. Figure 6 shows the hierarchical bug report (as a hierarchy tree) of Statechart example as in Figure 1. As the top level states in the statechart are `Idle`, `Standby`, and `Operating`, we have three nodes representing these three states at Level 1 in Figure 6. The node `Operating` can be further divided into three nodes as in Level 2, corresponding to the three OR-states contained by state `Operating`, and so on. At each level, we shows transitions (in bug reports) across nodes only. That is, transitions within a composite state is hided for current level, and can be examined by zooming into the composite state. Furthermore, each node (state) may selectively show *sub-states* where there exist cross-node transitions connecting them. For example, at Level 1 in Figure 6, we have transition connecting `Standby` and `Departure` (in `Operating`).The hierarchical bug report can be constructed as follows.

1. project model-level bug report to get the sequence of model element instances for every active object o (object-level bug report R_o);
2. build the hierarchy tree of states T_o for every active object o;
3. prune the hierarchy tree - for a sub-tree rooted at node n, if all nodes in the sub-tree are not in R_o, and no transition connecting them, we can prune this sub-tree in T_o;
4. connect nodes in T_o with all transitions in R_o, and expand node to show sub-states if any transition connects to them. In particular, for each transition $t \in R_o$, we connect it to two states/nodes s_1 and s_2, where
   - $parent(s_1) = parent(s_2)$, and
   - $ancestor(source\_state(t)) = s_1$, and
   - $ancestor(target\_state(t)) = s_2$.

By presenting this hierarchical bug report, the model designer can determine which model state is potentially buggy at higher level, and navigate inside to see the detailed transitions reported for that state, and so on. This approach is more effective to designer than being presented a *long* list of model elements.

6 Experimental Setup

In order to experimentally evaluate our methodology, we adopt and construct four statechart models. These models used are shown in Table 1. The third column shows the number of elements in the statechart model, counting OR-states, AND-states, transitions, actions, and conditions. Except for the RailCar example discussed in section 2, the other three models are based on real-life systems. The automated shuttle system [17] consists of several shuttles running on a railway network. They bid to transport passengers between two stations and earn money upon the completion of the transportation; meanwhile, the shuttles have to pay for the rail network usage. The weather control system is part of the Center TRACON Automation System (CTAS) [18] developed by NASA. It is used to control the air traffic at large airports. The weather controller contains a weather control panel dispatching weather status, a communication manager, and several clients receiving weather information. Such an update may succeed or fail and clients must respond with correct actions. The Media Oriented Systems Transport (MOST) [19] is a networking standard for multi-media devices (such as CD player) communicating in a car network. The network may contain up to 64 nodes, and each node corresponds to a multimedia device. These nodes are known as Network Slaves in MOST terminology. There is a special node called Network Master responsible for maintaining the network information in a central registry. The Network Master scans the whole network upon a change in the network status. Network Slaves may reply with valid or invalid information and further action must be performed (e.g. a re-scan). The MOST standard is currently maintained by the "MOST Cooperation", an umbrella organization consisting of various automotive companies and component manufacturers like BMW, Daimler-Chrysler and Audi.

Table 1. Statechart models used in our experiment

Statechart	Description	# model elements
RailCar	A rail car system from [12]	121
ShuttleSystem	Shuttles transporting passengers between stations [17]	117
WeatherControl	Updating weather status to clients [18]	202
MOST	Networking standard of multimedia system in cars [19]	277

For each of the above four models, we manually inject four to five bugs, resulting in four to five buggy versions (from each of which code is subsequently generated). These bugs can be categorized as follows.

- *Wrong control flow* - The bug affects states visited, including transition pointing to a wrong state, a condition is tightened or relaxed, or the event trigger of a transition is wrong. These correspond to "branch errors" in the generated code.

- *Wrong action* - The assignment to a variable in the action corresponding to a Statechart state/transition may be wrong. These correspond to "assignment errors" in the generated code.
- *Missing element* - The bug results from a missing transition, condition, or action. These correspond to "code missing errors" in the generated code. For bugs of this type, we define the bug in terms of elements existing in the Statechart model. Thus, if a condition or action is missing we mark the corresponding transition as buggy, and so on.

For each buggy version, we manually generate five to ten test cases which are failing runs with observable errors. In other words, the executions of these test cases are different w.r.t the correct version and the buggy version.

We choose *dynamic slicing* [3,4] as the debugging method to produce code-level bug reports and perform backward mapping to model-level. Given a program P, input I, line of code l and set of variables V — dynamic slicing can find the statements/statement-instances of P which (directly or transitively via control or data flow) affect the value of V at l in the execution trace corresponding to I.

We modify and exploit the dynamic Java slicing tool JSlice [20,21] from our previous work [14] to produce code-level slices. JSlice is an open-source tool which performs backwards dynamic slicing of sequential Java programs. Since backwards slicing requires storing of the execution trace, JSlice performs online compression during trace collection. The compressed trace representation is traversed without decompression during slicing. The program slices produced by JSlice are mapped back to model elements using the association between model entities and the generated code. The model-level slice is then further processed to produce hierarchical slices which correspond to the structure of the Statechart.

7 Experimental Results

We employ our tool on nineteen buggy program versions (for the four Statecharts in Table 1) to evaluate the efficiency and effectiveness of the methodology.

7.1 Code Generation

Given a Statchart model, we automatically generate a *single-threaded* Java program. While generating code from Statechart model, we also insert tags in generated Java files; the tags are processed to construct an in-memory structure representing association between model and code. Thus it is important to make sure the overhead of tags and building the in-memory association is small enough.

Figure 7(a) shows the time to generate code for the four models. For each model, it shows the time to generate code without tags, the time to generate code and tags, and the time to generate tagged code as well as the in-memory model-code association. The time overhead of tags in code generation is mainly for emitting into files (and writing to disk) and is largely system dependent. Among all models, the time required to generate code with tags increases 3% - 13%, compared with generating code without tag. From the figure, the time for generating code and tags is 34% - 45% of the total

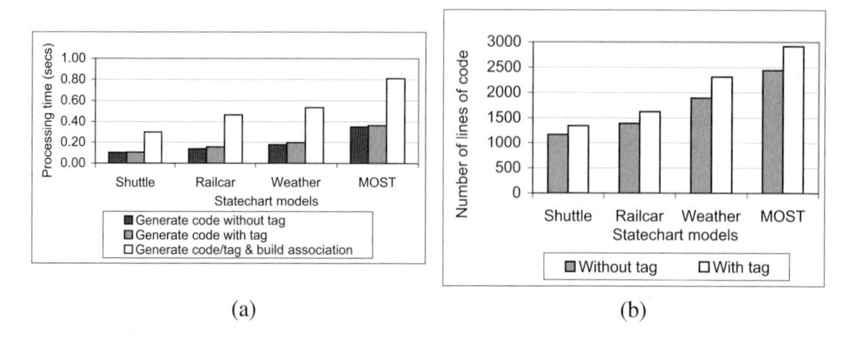

Fig. 7. (a) Time to generate code and build model-code association. It compares the time to generate code without tag, time to generate code with tag, and time to generate code/tag and build association; and (b) The number of lines of code for four models.

time. The remaining time is spent in building the in-memory associations. We recall that modifications to Statecharts which only modify model elements do not require re-generation of code. Thus, the overhead of code generation is usually incurred only once across several runs of debugging.

The size of generated code is shown in Figure 7(b). The increase in code size due to tags is low — 15% - 22%.

7.2 Dynamic Slicing

After we have the Java code and the model-code association information, we perform dynamic slicing on each of the nineteen buggy programs (corresponding to the four Statechart models). At the model level, we specify the slicing criterion as the last "wrong" state visited by a particular object (which gives the observable "error"). Since we actually perform slicing at code level, we specify the criterion as the corresponding state entry point (not necessarily the state entry action) in the code.

As mentioned earlier, each Statechart model has several buggy versions, and in each buggy version the slicing criterion is set based on the observable error. However, for dynamic slicing, apart from the slicing criterion, we also need inputs which exhibit the observable error in question. Hence corresponding to each buggy version, (at least) five test cases are chosen. *The experimental results (shown in Table 2) report all quantities corresponding to a buggy version as the average over all the test cases for that buggy version.* The goal for choosing different inputs for the slicing was to get rid of (or at least reduce) the influence of any specific program input on the overall results. Furthermore, the same bug may manifest itself as different observable errors for different inputs (leading to different slicing criteria).

The columns with heading "Slice Size" in Table 2 show the comparison of slice sizes. For all the buggy versions, the size of model-level slice is 12% to 25% of corresponding code-level slice. This is not surprising since a single model element may require a couple of lines of code to implement. The model-level slice is 27% to 47% compared with the total number of model elements, while the corresponding ratio for code-level slices is 17% to 30%. The larger ratio for model-level slices (as compared to

Table 2. Summary of Experimental Results. Column 2 shows the type of bug, 1 - wrong control flow, 2 - wrong action, and 3 - missing element. The four columns under the heading "Slice Size" represent average size of code-level slices, total lines of code, average size of model-level slices, and total number of statechart elements. The two columns under the heading "Time" show the average dynamic analysis time, including time to map slice from code level and to build hierarchical slice.

Model	Bug Type	Slice Size				Time (secs)	
		Code-level Slice	LOC	Model-level Slice	Total Elements	Map from Code-level	Build Hierarchy Slice
Shuttle System	1	316.2	1167	42.7	117	0.046	0.691
	1	334.8		43.5		0.039	0.609
	3	331.8		43.5		0.036	0.604
	2	282.0		37.5		0.027	0.591
	1	286.3		37.7		0.031	0.599
Railcar	2	412.8	1389	49.2	121	0.053	0.639
	3	405.3		47.0		0.044	0.613
	1	411.9		49.0		0.053	0.620
	1	414.0		48.4		0.045	0.607
Weather Control	1	353.7	1889	89.7	202	0.092	0.963
	1	324.8		78.2		0.090	0.985
	3	338.8		84.0		0.094	1.018
	1	376.4		94.6		0.097	1.016
	2	356.5		88.8		0.099	0.996
MOST	1	447.0	2440	74.3	277	0.118	1.009
	3	454.0		76.8		0.113	0.985
	1	491.1		92.0		0.194	1.058
	2	494.6		85.8		0.172	1.037
	1	466.0		81.3		0.133	1.028

code-level slices) is due to the same reason as above - when an element is included in the model-level slice, it is common that only a portion of corresponding code appears in the code-level slice.

The time to map code-level slice to model-level is shown in the first column under the heading "Time" in Table 2. We did not find significant differences across buggy versions of the same model. The average time to build hierarchical slice is shown in the second column under the heading "Time" in Table 2. It includes analyzing and constructing hierarchy tree for the Statechart and projecting the dynamic slice corresponding to the different nodes of the hierarchy tree. The time is almost same for each model, because reading the Statechart structure and constructing the tree needs a large amount of time.

Note that not all bugs can be found in dynamic slices. In our experiment, three of the nineteen buggy program versions (corresponding to the four Statecharts considered) had slices that do not contain the bug. For example, none of the dynamic slices contained the bug for the second buggy version of Shuttle System. Here, the condition of a choice transition was wrong and the corresponding transition never got fired. Thus, the error here occurred due to some portion of the model *not* being executed. Such errors cannot be located via dynamic slicing, and we need to employ techniques such as "relevant slicing" [22,14].

8 Discussion

More and more software is not being produced in a hand-written manner. Indeed, in certain safety-critical domains (*e.g.*, avionics), developers are strongly encouraged to generate code from behavioral models. Consequently, we need new debugging methodologies. In this article, we have suggested the use of software debugging methods (such as dynamic slicing) on the code generated from behavioral models. The bug-report is then played back at the model level by exploiting the associations between program fragments and model elements, thereby achieving model debugging.

Acknowledgments. This work was partially supported by a NUS research grant R252-000-321-112, and a Public Sector Funding research grant from A*STAR, Singapore.

References

1. Rhapsody tool. I-logix, inc. website, `http://www.ilogix.com`
2. Harel, D.: Statecharts: A visual formalism for complex systems. Science of Computer Programming 8(3), 231–274 (1987)
3. Agrawal, H., Horgan, J.: Dynamic program slicing. In: ACM SIGPLAN Conference on Programming Language Design and Implementation (PLDI) (1990)
4. Korel, B., Laski, J.W.: Dynamic program slicing. Information Processing Letters 29(3), 155–163 (1988)
5. Heimdahl, M.P.E., Whalen, M.W.: Reduction and slicing of hierarchical state machines. In: Intl. Symp. on Foundations of Software Engineering (FSE) (1997)
6. Feldman, Y.A., Schneider, H.: Simulating reactive systems by deduction. ACM Transactions on Software Engineering and Methodology (TOSEM) 2(2) (1993)
7. Nguyen, K.D., Sun, Z., Thiagarajan, P.S., Wong, W.-F.: Model-driven SoC design via executable UML to systemc. In: IEEE Real-time Systems Symp (RTSS) (2004)
8. Wasowski, A.: On efficient program synthesis from statecharts. In: Intl. Conf. on Languages, Compilers and Tools for Embedded Systems (LCTES) (2003)
9. Kohler, H.J., Nickel, U., Niere, J., Zundorf, A.: Integrating UML diagrams for production control systems. In: Intl. Conf. on Software engineering (ICSE) (2000)
10. Harrison, W., Barton, C., Raghavachari, M.: Mapping UML designs to Java. In: Intl. Conf. on Object-oriented Prog. Sys. and Languages (OOPSLA) (2000)
11. Stateflow tool. The MathWorks, inc. website, `http://www.mathworks.com`
12. Harel, D., Gery, E.: Executable object modeling with statecharts. IEEE Computer 30(7) (1997)
13. Gamma, E., Helm, R., Johnson, R., Vlissides, J.: Design Patterns. Addison-Wesley, Reading (1995)
14. Wang, T., Roychoudhury, A.: Using compressed bytecode traces for slicing Java programs. In: Intl. Conf. on Software Engineering (ICSE) (2004)
15. Guo, L., Roychoudhury, A., Wang, T.: Accurately choosing execution runs for software fault localization. In: Mycroft, A., Zeller, A. (eds.) CC 2006. LNCS, vol. 3923, pp. 80–95. Springer, Heidelberg (2006)
16. Wang, T., Roychoudhury, A.: Hierarchical dynamic slicing. In: International Symposium on Software Testing and Analysis (ISSTA) (2007)
17. Shuttle_Control_System. New rail-technology Paderborn, `http://www.cs.uni-paderborn.de/cs/ag-schaefer/CaseStudies/ShuttleSystem`
18. CTAS. Center TRACON automation system, `http://www.ctas.arc.nasa.gov`
19. MOST Cooperation, `http://www.mostcooperation.com`
20. JSlice: dynamic slicing tool for Java. T. Wang and A. Roychoudhury, National University of Singapore, `http://jslice.sourceforge.net`
21. Wang, T., Roychoudhury, A.: Dynamic slicing on Java bytecode traces. ACM Transactions on Programming Languages and Systems (TOPLAS) 30(2) (2008)
22. Gyimóthy, T., Beszédes, Á., Forgács, I.: An efficient relevant slicing method for debugging. In: 7th ACM SIGSOFT International Symposium on Foundations of Software Engineering, pp. 303–321 (1999)

Model Checking CSP Revisited: Introducing a Process Analysis Toolkit

Jun Sun, Yang Liu, and Jin Song Dong

School of Computing,
National University of Singapore
{dongjs,liuyang,sunj}@comp.nus.edu.sg

Abstract. FDR, initially introduced decades ago, is the *de facto* analyzer for Communicating Sequential Processes (CSP). Model checking techniques have been evolved rapidly since then. This paper describes PAT, i.e., a *p*rocess *a*nalysis *t*oolkit which complements FDR in several aspects. PAT is designed to analyze event-based compositional system models specified using CSP as well as shared variables and asynchronous message passing. It supports automated refinement checking, model checking of LTL extended with events, etc. In this paper, we highlight how partial order reduction is applied to improve refinement checking in PAT. Experiment results show that PAT outperforms FDR in some cases.

1 Introduction

Hoare's classic Communicating Sequential Processes (CSP [7]) has been a rather successful event-based modeling language for decades. Theoretical development on CSP has advanced formal methods in many ways. Its distinguishable features like alphabetized parallel composition have proven to be useful in modeling a wide range of systems.

FDR (Failures-Divergence Refinement) [12] is the *de facto* analyzer for CSP, which has been successfully applied in various domains. Based on the model checking algorithm presented in [12] and later improved with other reduction techniques presented in [15], FDR is capable of handling large systems. Nonetheless, since FDR was initially introduced, model checking techniques have evolved a lot in the last two decades. Quite a number of effective reduction methods have been proposed which greatly enlarge the size the systems that can be handled. Some noticeable ones include partial order reduction, symmetry reduction, predicate abstraction, etc. Moreover, verification based on temporal logic properties has gathered much attention. In this work, we present a process analysis toolkit named PAT[1], which is designed to incorporate advanced model checking techniques to analyze event-based compositional system models. PAT complements FDR in a number of ways. The following is a list of PAT's main functionalities.

– refinement checking. Refinement checking in FDR has been proved useful [16,14]. Given a process representing the implementation and another representing the specification, PAT (like FDR) automatically verifies whether there is a refinement relationship between them. Refinement checking in FDR replies on normalizing the

[1] Available at http://www.comp.nus.edu.sg/~liuyang/pat

T. Margaria and B. Steffen (Eds.): ISoLA 2008, CCIS 17, pp. 307–322, 2008.

specification before hand, which has proven to be very effective for some systems [15]. Nonetheless, normalization is computational expensive in general. In PAT, an alternative approach which brings normalization on-the-fly is adopted.
- temporal logic based model checking. An LTL model checker is embedded in PAT. Users are allowed to specify properties using standard LTL (extended with events, refer to Section 4.4). An on-the-fly explicit model checking algorithm is then used to produce counterexamples (if there is) or to conclude true.
- simulation. PAT supports various ways of system simulation, e.g., random simulation, user-guided step-by-step simulation, system graph generation, etc.

Besides, dedicated algorithms have been developed to analyze specialized properties, e.g., deadlock-freeness, divergence-freeness, invariants, LTL properties under weak or strong fairness assumptions, etc. In order to handle systems with large number of states, partial order reduction has been realized in PAT to enhance LTL model checking, refinement checking as well as other dedicated verification algorithms. Previous works on partial order reduction have only been applied to refinement checking in limited ways (refer to *diamond reduction* presented in [15]). Based on previous theoretical works [18,19], novel reduction techniques have been developed in PAT to enhance refinement checking. In this paper, the algorithms for partial order reduction as well as its soundness are discussed in detail. Other features of PAT are briefly introduced.

The remainder of the paper is organized as follows. Section 2 reviews PAT's input language. We briefly introduce FDR and its refinement checking in Section 3. Section 4 presents FDR's refinement checking algorithm and the refined one with partial order reduction. Section 5 concludes the paper and reviews related works and future works.

2 Communicating Sequential Processes with Extensions

In this section, we introduce our extended CSP language, i.e., its operational semantics as well as the definitions of the trace refinement, stable failure refinement and failure/divergence refinement.

Definition 1 (Process). *A process is defined as follows,*

$$\begin{aligned} P ::= & \; Stop \mid Skip \mid e \rightarrow P \mid c!exp \rightarrow P \mid c?x \rightarrow P \\ \mid & \; P; \, Q \mid P \Box Q \mid P \sqcap Q \mid P \lhd b \rhd Q \mid [b] \bullet P \mid P \bigtriangleup Q \mid P \setminus X \\ \mid & \; P_1 \parallel P_2 \parallel \cdots \parallel P_n \mid P_1 \mid\mid\mid P_2 \mid\mid\mid \cdots \mid\mid\mid P_n \end{aligned}$$

where c is a channel with bounded buffer size, b is a Boolean expression, X is a set of events, exp is an expression and e is an event. Event e may be a simple abstract event or a compound one (e.g., $e.x.y$) with an optional sequence of assignments.

We support most of the CSP language constructs. The two most noticeable extensions are shared variables and asynchronous message passing. It has long been known (see [7] and [13], for example) that one can model a variable as a process parallel to the one that uses it. The user processes then read from, or write to, the variable by CSP communication. Similarly, one can model a (bounded) message channel as a process. Nonetheless, these 'syntactic sugars' are mostly welcomed. Supporting them explicitly allows us to avoid generating multiple parallel processes and hence verify more efficiently in some cases[2]. Most of the operators (as explained in [7]) are well-understood. We briefly review the extended ones as well as ones whose semantics needs clarification. The operational semantics is presented in Appendix A.

Let Σ denote the set of all visible events and τ denote an invisible action. Let Σ^* be the set of finite traces. Let Σ_τ be $\Sigma \cup \{\tau\}$. Event prefixing $e \rightarrow P$ performs e and behaves as P afterward. If e is attached with assignments, the valuation of the global variables is updated accordingly. For simplicity, assignments are restricted to update only global variables.$Skip = \checkmark \rightarrow Stop$ where $\checkmark$ is the termination event. Sequential composition, $P_1;\ P_2$, behaves as P_1 until its termination and then behaves as P_2. An external choice is solved only by the engagement of an visible event. A choice depending on the truth value of a Boolean expression is written as $P_1 \lhd b \rhd P_2$. If b is true, the process behaves as P_1, otherwise P_2. State guard $[b] \bullet P$ is blocked until b is true and then proceeds as P. $P_1 \bigtriangleup P_2$ behaves as P_1 until the first visible event of P_2 is engaged, then P_1 is interrupted and P_2 takes control. Process $P \setminus X$ hides all occurrences of events in X. One of the key features of CSP is the alphabetized multi-threaded parallel composition. Let αP be the alphabet of P which excludes τ and $\checkmark$. In PAT, alphabets can be manually set or derived from the events constituting the process expression. Parallel composition of processes is written as $P_1 \parallel P_2 \parallel \cdots \parallel P_n$, where shared events must be synchronized by all processes whose alphabet contains the event. The indexed interleaving is written as $P_1 \mid\mid\mid P_2 \mid\mid\mid \cdots \mid\mid\mid P_n$, in which all processes run independently except communication through shared variables and message channel (and synchronization upon termination, i.e., rule ter). Recursion is allowed by process referencing. The semantics of recursion is defined as Tarski's weakest fixed-point. Processes may be parameterized (see examples later).

For simplicity, we focus on the operational semantics in this work, i.e., the semantics of a model is associated with a labeled transition system. Due to the global variables and channels, configuration of a given system is composed of three parts (P, V, C) where P is the current process expression, V is the current valuation of the global variables which is a set of mappings from a name to a value, and C is the current status of the channels which is a set of mappings from a channel name to a sequence of items in the channel. A transition is of the form $(P, V, C) \xrightarrow{e} (P', V', C')$, which means (P, V, C) evolves to (P', V', C') by performing event e.

Example 1. The following models the classic dining philosophers [7],

$$\begin{aligned}
Phil(i) &= get.i.(i+1)\%N \rightarrow get.i.i \rightarrow eat.i \rightarrow \\
&\quad \rightarrow put.i.(i+1)\%N \rightarrow put.i.i \rightarrow think.i \rightarrow Phil(i) \\
Fork(i) &= get.i.i \rightarrow put.i.i \rightarrow Fork(i) \ \Box \\
&\quad get.(i-1)\%N.i \rightarrow put.(i-1)\%N.i \rightarrow Fork(i) \\
Pair(i) &= (Phil(i) \parallel Fork(i)) \setminus \{get.i.i, put.i.i, think.i\} \\
College &= (\|_{i=0}^{N-1} Pair(i)) \setminus \bigcup_{i=0}^{N-1} \{get.i.(i+1)\%N, put.i.(i+1)\%N\}
\end{aligned}$$

where N is a global constant (i.e., the number of philosophers), $get.i.j$ ($put.i.j$) is the action of the i-th philosopher picking up (putting down) the j-th fork and fc is a global

[2] Refer to [13] for cases in which this is not true in the world of FDR.

variable recording the amount of food that has been consumed. The system is composed of N philosopher-fork-pairs running in parallel. The following is the transition system of *College* with $N = 2$. All events except the bolded ones are invisible. □

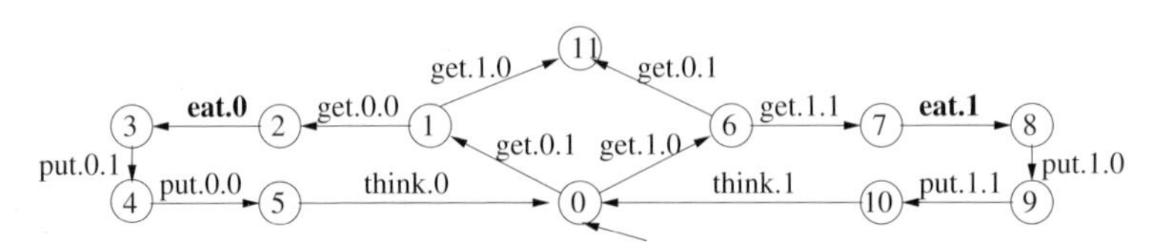

3 FDR and Refinement Checking

Failures-Divergence Refinement (FDR [12]) is a well-established model checker for CSP. Different from temporal logic based model checking, using FDR, safety, liveness and combination properties can be verified by showing a refinement relation from the CSP model of the system to a CSP process capturing the properties. In addition, FDR verifies whether a process is deadlock-free or not. In the following, we review the notion of different refinement/equivalence relationship in terms of labeled transition systems.

Definition 2 (Labeled Transition System). *An LTS is 3-tuple* $L = (S, init, T)$ *where* S *is a set of states,* $init \in S$ *is the initial state and* $T : S \times \Sigma_\tau \times S$ *is a labeled transition relation. Let* s, s' *be members of* S*.*

- $s \overset{e_1, e_2, \cdots, e_n}{\rightarrow} s'$ *if and only if there exists* $s_0, \cdots, s_n \in S$ *such that for all* $0 \leq i \leq n$ *such that* $s_i \overset{e_i}{\rightarrow} s_{i+1}$ *and* $s_0 = s \wedge s_n = s'$*.*
- *Let* $tr : \Sigma^*$ *be a sequence of visible events.* $s \overset{tr}{\Rightarrow} s'$ *if and only if there exists* $e_1, e_2, \cdots, e_n$ *such that* $s \overset{e_1, e_2, \cdots, e_n}{\rightarrow} s'$ *and* $tr = \langle e_1, e_2, \cdots, e_n \rangle \upharpoonright \{\tau\}$ *is the trace with invisible actions filtered.*
- $s \rightarrow^* s'$ *if and only if there exists* $e_1, \cdots, e_n$ *such that* $s \overset{e_1, e_2, \cdots, e_n}{\rightarrow} s'$*. In particular,* $s \rightarrow^* s$*.*
- $enabled(s) = \{e : \Sigma_\tau \mid \exists s' \bullet s \overset{e}{\rightarrow} s'\}$*. A state is stable if and only if* $\tau \notin enabled(S)$*.*
- $mrefusal(S) = \Sigma \setminus enabled(S)$ *is the maximum refusal set, i.e., the maximum set of events which can be refused.*
- $s \overset{\tau *}{\rightarrow} s'$ *if and only if* $s \overset{\tau, \cdots, \tau}{\rightarrow} s'$*.* $\tau^*(s) = \{s' : S \mid s \overset{\tau *}{\rightarrow} s'\}$ *is the set of stable states reachable from* s *by performing zero or more* τ *transitions.*
- *A state is a divergence state* $div(s)$ *if and only if* $\tau \in enabled(s) \wedge s \in \tau^*(s)$*.*

The set of traces of L is $traces(L) = \{tr : \Sigma^* \mid \exists s' : S \bullet init \overset{tr}{\Rightarrow} s'\}$. The set of divergence traces of L, written as $divergence(L)$, is $\{tr : \Sigma^* \mid \exists tr' \bullet tr'$ is a prefix of $tr \wedge \exists s : S \bullet init \overset{tr'}{\rightarrow} s \wedge div(s)\}$. Note that if some prefix of a given trace is a divergence trace, the given trace is too. The set of failures of L, written as $failures(L)$, is $\{(tr, X) : \Sigma^* \times 2^\Sigma \mid \exists s : S \bullet init \overset{tr}{\rightarrow} s \wedge X \subseteq \Sigma \setminus enabled(s)\} \cup \{(tr, \Sigma) : \Sigma^* \times 2^\Sigma \mid tr \in divergence(L)\}$. Note that the system state reached by a divergence state may refuse all events. Given a model composed of a process P and a valuation V and a set of channels C, we may construct an LTS $(S, init, T)$ where $S = \{s \mid (P, V, C) \rightarrow^* s\}$, $init = (P, V, C)$ and $T = \{(s_1, e, s_2) : S \times \Sigma_\tau \times S \mid s_1 \stackrel{e}{\rightarrow} s_2\}$ using the operational semantics. However, S can be infinite due to several reasons. The first one is that the variables may have infinite domains or the channels may have infinite buffer size. We require (syntactically) that the sizes of the domains and buffers are bounded. The second is that P may allow unbounded recursion or replication, e.g., $P = (a \rightarrow P;\ c \rightarrow Skip) \Box b \rightarrow Skip$ or $P = a \rightarrow P \mid\mid\mid P$. In this paper, we focus on LTSs with finite number of states for practical reasons. The following defines refinement and equivalence.

Definition 3 (Refinement and Equivalence). *Let $L_{im} = (S_{im}, init_{im}, T_{im})$ be an LTS representing an implementation. Let $L_{sp} = (S_{sp}, init_{sp}, T_{sp})$ be an LTS representing a specification. L_{im} refines L_{sp} in the trace semantics, written as $L_{im} \sqsupseteq_T L_{sp}$, if and only if $traces(L_{im}) \subseteq traces(L_{sp})$. L_{im} refines L_{sp} in the stable failures semantics, written as $L_{im} \sqsupseteq_F L_{sp}$, if and only if $failures(L_{im}) \subseteq failures(L_{sp})$. L_{im} refines L_{sp} in the failures/divergence semantics, written as $L_{im} \sqsupseteq_D L_{sp}$, if and only if $failures(L_{im}) \subseteq failures(L_{sp})$ and $divergence(L_{im}) \subseteq divergence(L_{sp})$. L_{im} equals L_{sp} in the trace (stable failures/failures divergence) semantics if and only if they refine each other in the respective semantics.*

Different refinement relationship can be used to establish different properties. Safety can be verified by showing a trace refinement relationship. Combination of safety and liveness is verified by showing a stable failures refinement relationship if the system is divergence-free or otherwise by showing a failures/divergences refinement relationship. The readers shall refer to [14] for a discussion on the expressiveness of CSP refinement. In the following, we write $Im \sqsupseteq Sp$ to mean $L_{Im} \sqsupseteq L_{Sp}$ whenever it will not cause confusion. Internally, equivalence relationships may be used to simplify process expressions, e.g., $P \Box P$ is replaced by P for simplicity.

Example 2. Assume that the following process is used to capture the property for the dining philosophers: $Prop \mathrel{\widehat{=}} \|_{i=0}^{N-1} Eat(i)$ where $Eat(i) = eat.i \rightarrow Eat(i)$. It can be shown that $College$ trace-refines $Prop$ (given a particular N). Informally speaking, that means it is possible for each philosopher to eat, i.e., $\{eat.0, \cdots, eat.(N-1)\}^*$ are traces of $College$. In order to show that it is *always* possible for him/her to eat, we need to establish $College \sqsupseteq_F Prop$, which is not true, i.e., assume $N = 2$, $(\langle get.0.1, get.1.0\rangle, \{eat.0, eat.1\})$ is in $failures(College)$ but not $failures(Prop)$. □

In order to check refinement, every state of the implementation reachable from the initial state via some trace must be compared with every state of the specification reachable via the same trace. There may be many such states in the specification due to nondeterminism. In FDR, the specification is firstly normalized so that there is exactly one state corresponding to each possible trace. A state in the normalized LTS is a set of states which can be reached by the same trace from the initial state. For instance, The following shows the normalized LTS of the one presented in Example 1.

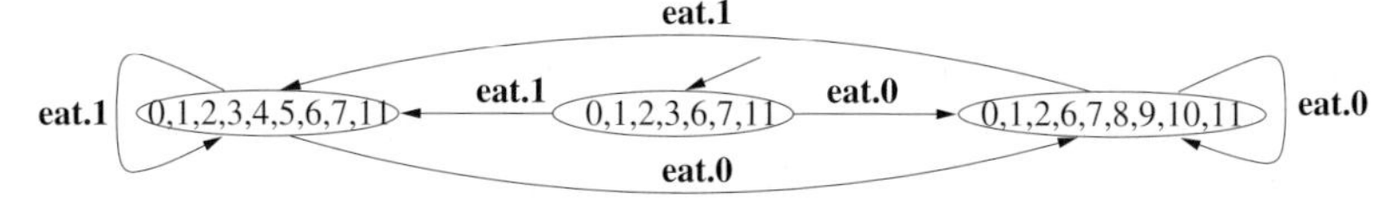

Definition 4 (Normalized LTS). *Let* $(S, init, T)$ *be an LTS. The normalized LTS is* $(NS, Ninit, NT)$ *where* NS *are subsets of* S, $Ninit = \tau^*(init)$ *and* $NT = \{(P, e, Q) \mid Q = \{v : S \mid \exists v_1 : P \bullet v_1 \xrightarrow{e} v_2 \wedge v \in \tau^*(v_2)\}\}$. *Given a normalized state* $s \in NS$,

- $enabled(s)$ *is* $\bigcup_{x \in s} enabled(x)$,
- $mrefusal(s)$ *is* $\{mrefusal(x) \mid x \in s\}$, *which is a set of maximum refusal sets,*
- $div(s)$ *is true if and only if there exists* $x \in s$ *such that* $div(x)$ *is true.*

Given an LTS constructed from a process, the normalized LTS corresponds the normalized process. A state in the normalized LTS groups a set of states in the original LTS which are all connected by τ-transitions. Given a trace, exactly one state in the normalized LTS is reached. FDR then traverses through every reachable states of the implementation and compare them with the corresponding normalized states in the specification (refer to the algorithm presented in [12]).

4 Verification

This section is devoted to algorithms for refinement checking. We start with reviewing a slightly modified on-the-fly checking algorithm based on the one implemented in FDR and then improve it with partial order reduction. Lastly, we review an alternative approach for verification that has been implemented in PAT, i.e., LTL-based verification.

4.1 On-the-Fly Refinement Checking Algorithm

Let *Spec* be the specification and *Impl* be the implementation. In FDR, *Spec* is firstly normalized. Refinement checking is then reduced to reachability analysis of the product of the *Impl* and the normalized *Spec*. It has been shown that such an approach works well for certain models [15]. Nonetheless, because normalization in general is computational expensive, it may not be always desirable. Thus, we adopted an alternative approach. Figure 1 presents the on-the-fly refinement checking algorithm which is modified and implemented in PAT. The algorithm similarly performs a reachability analysis in the product of the implementation and the normalized specification. The different is that normalization is brought on-the-fly as well.

Details of the following procedures are skipped for brevity. Procedure $tau(S)$ explores all outgoing transition of S and returns the set of states reachable from S via a τ-transition. We remark that this procedure will be refined later. Procedure $tauclosure(S)$ implements $\tau^*(S)$ using a depth-first-search procedure. The set of states reachable from S via only τ transitions is returned. For instance, given the LTS in Example 1, $tauclosure(0)$ returns $\{0, 1, 2, 6, 7, 11\}$. The procedure $tau(S)$ is applied repeatedly until all τ-reachable states are identified. Procedure $existSuperSet(x, Y)$ where x is a set and Y is a set of sets returns true if and only if there exists y in Y such that $x \subseteq y$.

Depending on the type of refinement relationship, the algorithm performs a depth-first search for a pair (Im, NSp) where Im is a state of the implementation and NSp is a state of the normalized specification such that, the enabled events of Im is not a subset of those of NSp (`C1`), or Im is stable and there does not exist a state in NSp which refuse all events which are refused by Im (`C2`), or Im diverges but not NSp (`C3`). The

```
procedure refines(Impl, Spec)
0. checked := ∅
1. pending.push((Impl, tauclosure(Spec)));
2. while pending ≠ ∅
3.     (Im, NSp) := pending.pop();
4.     checked := checked ∪ {(Im, NSp)};
5.     if ¬(enabled(Im) \ {τ} ⊆ enabled(NSp))                                    – C1
6.        ∨ (τ ∉ Im ∧ ¬ existSuperSet(mrefusal(Im), mrefusal(NSp)))            – C2
7.        ∨ (¬ div(NSp) ∧ div(Im))                                              – C3
8.          return false;
9.     else
10.         foreach (Im', NSp') ∈ next(Im, NSp)
11.             if (Im', NSp') ∉ checked
12.                 pending := pending ∪ {(Im', NSp')}
13.             endif
14.         endfor
15.     endif
16. endwhile
17. return true;
```

Fig. 1. Algorithm: $refines(Impl, Spec)$

algorithm returns true if no such pair is found. Note that if C1 is satisfied, a counterexample is found for any refinement checking; if C2 is satisfied, a counterexample is found for stable failures refinement checking or fairlure/divergence refinement checking; if C3 is satisfied, a counterexample is found for fairlure/divergence refinement checking only. The procedure for producing a counterexample is skipped for simplicity. Producing the shortest counterexample requires a breath-first-search after identifying the faulty state. Line 10 to 14 of algorithm *refines* explores new states of the product and pushes them into the stack *pending*. The procedure *next* is presented in Figure 2. Given a pair (Im, NSp), it returns a set of pairs of the form (Im', NSp') for each enabled event in Im. If the event is visible, NSp' is a successor of NSp via the event and Im' is the successor of Im via the same event. Otherwise, Im' is a successor of Im via a τ-transition and NSp' is Sp. Because normalization is brought on-the-fly, it is sometimes possible to find a counterexample before the specification is completely normalized. The soundness of the algorithm follows the soundness discussion in [12].

4.2 Partial Order Reduction

As any model checking algorithm, refinement checking suffers from state space explosion. A number of attempts have been applied to reduce the search space [15]. This section describes the one implemented in PAT based on partial order reduction. Our reduction realizes and extends the early works on partial order reduction for process algebras and refinement checking presented in [18] and [19]. The inspiration of the reduction is that events may be independent, e.g., $think.i$ is mutually independent of each other. Given $P = P_1 \parallel \cdots \parallel P_n$ and two enabled events e_1 and e_2, e_1 is dependent of e_2, written as $dep(e_1, e_2)$, and vice versa only if one of the following is true,

```
procedure next(Im, NSp)
0. toReturn := ∅
1. foreach e ∈ enabled(Im)
2.     if e = τ
3.         foreach Im′ ∈ tau(Im)
4.             toReturn := toReturn ∪ {(Im′, NSp)};
5.         endfor
6.     else
7.         NSp′ := {s | ∃ x : NSp • x -e-> x′ ∧ s ∈ tauclosure(x′)};
8.         foreach Im′ such that Im -e-> Im′
9.             toReturn := toReturn ∪ {(Im′, NSp′)};
10.         endfor
11.     endif
12. endfor
13. return toReturn;
```

Fig. 2. Algorithm: $next(Im, NSp)$

- e_1 and e_2 are from the same process P_i.
- $e_1 = e_2$ so that they may be synchronized, e.g., $get.i.i$ of process $Phil(i)$ and $get.i.i$ of process $Fork(i)$.
- e_1 updates a variable which e_2 depends on or vice versa, e.g., because $eat.i$ updates a global variable, all $eat.i$ are inter-dependent.

Two events are independent if they are not dependent. Because the ordering of independent events may be irrelevant to a given property, we may deliberately ignore some of the ordering so as to reduce the search space. Partial order reduction may be applied to a number of places in algorithm $refines$, namely, the procedure $tau(S)$ (and therefore $tauclosure$) and $next$. Since indexed parallel composition (and indexed interleaving) is the main source of state space explosion, we assume that Im is of the form $((P_1 \parallel P_2 \parallel \cdots \parallel P_n) \setminus X, V, C)$ in the following and show how it is possible to only explore a subset of the enabled transitions and yet preserve the soundness.

We start with applying partial order reduction to the procedure tau. Note that tau is applied to the specification or implementation independently. Thus, as long as we guarantee that the reduced state space (of either $Impl$ or $Spec$) is failures/divergence equivalent to the full state space, we prove that there is a refinement relationship in the reduced state space if and only if there is one in the full state space. Figure 3 show our algorithm for selecting a subset of the τ-transitions. The soundness proof is presented in Appendix B. In the algorithm tau', we try to identify one set of τ-transitions which are independent of the rest. If such a subset is found (i.e., the algorithm $stubborn\_tau$ returns a non-empty set of successors), only the subset is explored further. Otherwise (i.e., $stubborn\_tau$ returns an empty set), all possible τ-transitions are explored. In $stubborn\_tau$, the idea is to identify one process P_i such that all τ-transitions from P_i are independent of those from other processes. Note that this approach is most effective with τ-transition generated from one process only. It is possible to handle τ-transition generated from multiple processes with a slightly more complicated procedure (which we skip for brevity). The details of the following simple

procedure $tau'(Im)$
0. $nextmoves := stubborn\_tau(Im)$;
1. **if** $(nextmoves \neq \varnothing)$ **then return** $nextmoves$; **else return** $tau(Im)$;

procedure $stubborn\_tau(Im)$
0. **foreach** P_i
1. $por := enabled_{P_i}(Im) \subseteq \{\tau\} \cup X \wedge enabled_{P_i}(Im) = current(P_i)$
2. **foreach** $e \in enabled_{P_i}(Im)$
3. $por := por \wedge \neg\, loop(e) \wedge \forall\, e' : \Sigma_j \bullet j \neq i \Rightarrow \neg\, dep(e, e')$
4. **endfor**
5. **if** por **then**
6 **return** $\{(((\cdots \parallel P_i' \parallel \cdots) \setminus X), V, C') \mid (P_i, V, C) \xrightarrow{e} (P_i', V, C')\}$;
7. **endif**
8. **endfor**
9. **return** $\varnothing$;

Fig. 3. Algorithm: $tau'(Im)$ and $stubborn\_tau(Im)$

procedures have been skipped. Given $Im = (P, V, C)$, $enabled_{P_i}(Im)$ is the set of enabled event from component P_i, i.e., $enabled(Im) \cap enabled((P_i, V, C))$. For instance, given *College* with $N = 2$, $enabled(Pair(0))$ is $\{get.0.1\}$. $current(P_i)$ is the set of events that could be enabled in process P_i given the most cooperative environment. For instance, $current(Phil(i)) = \{get.i.(i + 1)\%N\}$ despite whether the fork is available or not. $loop(e)$ is true if and only if performing this event results in a state on the search stack, i.e., forming a cycle.

A process P_i is considered a candidate only if all enabled events from P_i result in τ-transitions (i.e., $enabled_{P_i}(Im) \subseteq \{\tau\} \cup X$) and no other transition could be possibly enabled given a different environment (i.e., $enabled_{P_i}(Im) = current(P_i)$). The former is required because we are only interested in τ-transitions. The latter (partly) ensures that no disabled event from P_i is enabled before executing an event from P_i. Furthermore, all enabled events from P_i must not form a cycle (so that an enabled event is not skipped for ever) or dependent on an enabled event from some other component. For detailed discussion on the intuition behind these conditions, refer to [4].

Example 3. Assume that $N = 2$ and the following is the current process expression,

$$((think.0 \rightarrow Phil(0) \parallel put.1.0 \rightarrow Fork(0)) \setminus \{get.0.0, put.0.0, think.0\}) \parallel$$
$$(((get1.1 \rightarrow eat.1 \rightarrow put.1.0 \rightarrow put.1.1 \rightarrow think.1 \rightarrow Phil(1)) \parallel Fork(1))$$
$$\setminus\{get.1.1, put.1.1, think.1\}) \setminus \{get.0.1, get.1.0, put.0.1, put.1.0\}$$

where the first philosopher has just put down both forks while the second one has just picked up his first fork. Two τ-transitions are enabled, i.e., one due to $think.0$ and the other due to $get.1.1$. The algorithm tau' would return only the successor state after performing $get.1.1$ (assuming it is not on the stack). This is the only event enabled for the second component of the outer parallel composition is the τ transition due to $get.1.1$ (and thus the condition at line 1 of $stubborn\_tau$ is satisfied). Because $get.1.1$ is local to the component, por is true after the loop from line 2 to line 4. □

procedure $next'(Im, Sp)$
0. **if** $\tau \in enabled(Im)$
1. $\quad nextmoves := stubborn\_tau(Im)$;
2. $\quad$ **if** $(nextmoves \neq \varnothing)$ **then return** $nextmoves$;
3. **else**
4. $\quad$ **foreach** $e \in enabled(Im)$
5. $\quad\quad por := stubborn\_visible(Im, e)$;
6. $\quad\quad$ **foreach** $S \in Sp$
7. $\quad\quad\quad por := por \wedge stubborn\_visible(S, e)$;
8. $\quad\quad$ **endeach**
9. $\quad\quad$ **if** por **then return** $\{(Im', tauclosure(Sp')) \mid Im \xrightarrow{e} Im' \wedge Sp \xrightarrow{e} Sp'\}$
10. $\quad$ **endeach**
11. **return** $next(Im, Sp)$;

procedure $stubborn\_visible(Im, e)$
0. $por := \neg\, loop(e) \wedge \forall\, e' : \Sigma_j \bullet e' \neq e \Rightarrow \neg\, dep(e, e')$;
1. **foreach** $P_i \in processes(e)$
2. $\quad por := por \wedge enabled_{P_i}(Im) = current(P_i) = \{e\}$;
3. **return** por;

Fig. 4. Algorithm: $next'(Im, Sp)$ and $stubborn\_visible(Im, e)$

The above algorithms apply partial order reduction to τ-transitions only. $tauclosure$ is refined as well since it is based on tau'. Unlike FDR, PAT is capable of applying partial order reduction to visible events. Because both *Impl* and *Spec* must make corresponding transitions for a visible event, reduction for visible events is complicated. A conservative approach has been implemented in PAT. Figure 4 present the algorithm, i.e., the refined $next$. If Im is not stable, we apply the algorithm $stubborn\_tau$ to identify a subset of τ-transitions (line 1). If no such subset exists, the pair (Im, Sp) is fully expanded (line 11). An algorithm $stubborn\_visible$ similar to $stubborn\_tau$ is used to check if a given visible event e is a candidate for partial order reduction. Function $processes(e)$ returns all process components (of the parallel composition) whose alphabet contains e. Firstly, we choose a possible candidate from Im using the algorithm $stubborn\_visible$. Event e is chosen if and only if, for each process in $processes(e)$, e is the only event from the process which can be enabled and all other enabled events are independent of e and performing e does not result in a state on the stack. Next, we check if e satisfies the same set of conditions for each state in the normalized state of the specification. If it does, e is used to expand the search tree at line 9 (and all other enabled events are ignored). In order to find such e efficiently, the candidate events are selected in a pre-defined order, i.e., events which have the least number of associated processes are chosen first. The soundness of the algorithm is presented in Appendix B.

Example 4. Let $P(i) = a.i \rightarrow b.i \rightarrow P(i)$. Assume the specification and implementation is defined as: $Spec = \|_{i=0}^{2} P(i)$ and $Impl = \|_{i=0}^{1} P(i)$. Assume we need to show that *Impl* trace-refines *Spec*. Initially, two events are enabled in *Impl*, i.e., $a.0$ and $a.1$. Assume that $a.0$ is selected first, because $loop(a.0)$ is false and $a.0$ is independent of all other enabled events (i.e., $a.1$), the condition at line 0 of algorithm $stubborn\_visible$

is satisfied. Because $a.0$ is the only event that would possibly be enabled from $P(0)$, the condition at line 2 is satisfied too. Thus, $a.0$ is a possible candidate for partial order reduction for $Impl$. Similarly, it is also a candidate for $Spec$ (which is the only state in the normalized initial state). Therefore, we only need to explore $a.0$ initially. □

4.3 Refinement Checking Experiments

We compare PAT with FDR using benchmark models for refinement checking. For the sake of a fair comparison, all models use only standard CSP features which are supported by both. The following table shows the experiment results for three models, obtained on a 2.0 GHz Intel Core Duo CPU and 1 GB memory.

model	N	property	result	PAT	FDR
Dining Philosophers	5	P [T= S	true	0.28125	0.067
Dining Philosophers	6	P [T= S	true	0.8593	0.069
Dining Philosophers	8	P [T= S	true	13.78	0.076
Dining Philosophers	10	P [T= S	true	430.28	0.107
Dining Philosophers	12	P [T= S	true	-	0.319
Reader/Writers	12	P [T= S	true	< 1	0.812
Reader/Writers	14	P [T= S	true	< 1	6.906
Reader/Writers	16	P [T= S	true	< 1	81.247
Reader/Writers	18	P [T= S	true	< 1	-
Reader/Writers	50	P [T= S	true	1.097	-
Reader/Writers	100	P [T= S	true	9	-
Reader/Writers	200	P [T= S	true	77.515	-
Milner's Cyclic Scheduler	11	P [T= S	true	< 1	19.011
Milner's Cyclic Scheduler	13	P [T= S	true	< 1	419.021
Milner's Cyclic Scheduler	14	P [T= S	true	< 1	-
Milner's Cyclic Scheduler	50	P [T= S	true	2.406	-
Milner's Cyclic Scheduler	100	P [T= S	true	9.765	-
Milner's Cyclic Scheduler	200	P [T= S	true	60.453	-

The first example is the classic dining philosopher problem, where N is the number of philosophers and forks. Because of the modeling, partial order reduction is not effective for this example. As a result, PAT handles about 10^7 states (about 11 philosophers and forks) in a reasonable amount of time. FDR performs extremely well for this example because of the strategy discussed in [15]. Namely, it builds up a system gradually, at each stage compressing the subsystems to find an equivalent process with (for this particular example) many less states. Notice that with manual hiding (to localize some events), PAT performs much better. The second example is the classic readers/writers problem, in which the readers and writers coordinate to ensure correct read/write ordering. N is the number of readers/writers. Reduction in PAT is very effective for this example. As a result, PAT handles a few hundreds readers/writers efficiently, whereas FDR suffers from state space explosion quickly (for $N = 18$). The third example is the Milner's cyclic scheduling algorithm, in which multiple processes are scheduled in a cyclic fashion. Partial order reduction is extremely effective for this model. As a result, PAT handles hundreds of processes, whereas FDR handles less than 14 processes. The experiment results show our best effort by far on automated model checking of an extended version of CSP. It by no means suggests the limit of our tool. We believe that by incorporating more reduction techniques (e.g., symmetry reduction) as well as fine-tuning the implementation, the performance of PAT can be improved significantly.

4.4 Temporal Logic Based Verification

Verification of CSP models has been traditionally based on refinement checking. CSP refinement is expressive enough to cover a large class of properties [14]. Nonetheless, temporal logic formulae have been proved effective as well as intuitive. Verification based on temporal logic has gathered much, evidenced by the rich set of theories and tools developed for CTL/LTL based verification [3,8]. In this section, we briefly discuss the LTL model checker embedded in PAT. We adopt an automata-based approach for explicit LTL model checking as Spin [8]. Because we are dealing with an event-based formalism, we extend standard Linear Temporal Logic (LTL) with events so that properties concerning both states and events can be stated and verified. For instance, the following specifies a desirable property of process *College*: $\Box\Diamond eat_0 \wedge \Box\Diamond eat_1 \cdots \Box\Diamond eat_{N-1}$ where $\Box$ reads as "always" and $\Diamond$ reads as "eventually". The property states that every philosopher will always eventually eat, i.e., no one starves.

Definition 5. *Let Pr be a set of propositions. An extended LTL formula is*[3]*,*

$$\phi ::= p \mid a \mid \neg\phi \mid \phi \wedge \psi \mid \Box\phi \mid \Diamond\phi \mid \phi U \psi$$

where p ranges over Pr and a ranges over Σ. Let $\pi = \langle P_0, x_0, P_1, x_1, \cdots\rangle$ be an infinite sequence of events. Let π^i be the suffix of π starting from P_i.

$$\begin{array}{ll}
\pi^i \models p & \Leftrightarrow P_i \models p \\
\pi^i \models a & \Leftrightarrow x_{i-1} = a \\
\pi^i \models \neg\phi & \Leftrightarrow \neg(\pi^i \models \phi) \\
\pi^i \models \phi \wedge \psi & \Leftrightarrow \pi^i \models \phi \wedge \pi^i \models \psi \\
\pi^i \models \Box\phi & \Leftrightarrow \forall j \geq i \bullet \pi^j \models \phi \\
\pi^i \models \Diamond\phi & \Leftrightarrow \exists j \geq i \bullet \pi^j \models \phi \\
\pi^i \models \phi U \psi & \Leftrightarrow \exists j \geq i \bullet \pi^j \models \psi \wedge \forall k \mid i \leq k \leq j-1 \bullet \pi^j \models \phi
\end{array}$$

The simplicity of writing formulae concerning events as in the above example is not purely a matter of aesthetics. It may yield gains in time and space (refer to examples in [2]). Given an extended LTL formula, PAT internally constructs a trace equivalent Büchi automaton using the state-of-the-art conversion proposed in [6]. For efficient reasons, the Büchi automata are transition-labeled (instead of state-labeled). Let $B^{\neg\phi}$ be the Büchi automaton constructed from property $\neg\phi$. The product of $B^{\neg\phi}$ and the model is generated. Two different algorithms (e.g., nested depth first search and strongly

[3] The next operator is not supported purposely because of partial order reduction.

connected component search based on Tarjan's algorithm) are then used to determine the emptiness of the product, i.e., explore on-the-fly whether the product contains a loop which is composed of at least one accepting state. Finite traces are extended to infinite ones in a standard way. In the presence of a counterexample, on-the-fly model checking usually produces a trace leading to a bad state or a loop quickly (refer to Section 4.3). Partial order reduction (similar to the one implemented in Spin) is applied for LTL verification. One unique feature of LTL verification in PAT is that we allow fairness assumptions to be associated with individual events and then verify the system under the fairness assumptions. For details, refer to [9].

5 Conclusion and Future Works

We present PAT, a process analysis toolkit, designed to apply model checking techniques to verify event-based compositional models. A number of verification algorithms have been implemented. This paper is related to works on developing tool support for CSP and process algebras, works on heuristics for partial order reduction and works on model checking in general. ARC (Adelaide Refinement Checker [11]) is a refinement checker based on ordered binary decision diagrams (BDD). It has been shown that ARC outperforms FDR in a few cases [11]. PAT adapts an explicit approach for model checking. It has long been known there are pros and cons choosing an explicit approach or a BDD approach (refer to comparisons between SPIN and SMV). Nonetheless, in the future, we may incorporate partial order reduction and BDD to achieve better performance. ProBE [1] is a simulator developed by Formal Method Europe to interactively explore traces of a given process. The simulator embedded in PAT has the full functionality of Probe. Though we have shown cases where PAT outperforms FDR, we believe that a full comparison is yet to be carried out with more experiments. A number of algorithms have been previously proposed for partial order reduction which is trace/failures/divergence preserving, e.g., [18,19]. The algorithms presented in the paper may be considered as lightweight realization and extension of those presented in [18,19]. In addition, this work is related to the huge amount of works dedicated to theories and tools development for model checking.

We are actively developing PAT. There are a number of directions to pursue in the future. Firstly, based our framework, more languages features will be incorporated, e.g., higher-order processes, broadcasting communication, integrated data operations as in integrated languages [10,5,17], etc. Secondly, more advanced reduction techniques will be incorporated. Lastly, a broad range of experiments and case studies must be performed to not only fully compare PAT with FDR but also to make PAT as a reliable and extensible framework for developing model checking techniques.

Acknowledgement

This work is partially supported by the research project "Sensor Networks Specification and Validation" (R-252-000-320-112) funded by Ministry of Education, Singapore.

References

1. Formal Systems (Europe) Ltd. Process Behaviour Explorer (2003), http://www.fsel.com/probe_download.html
2. Chaki, S., Clarke, E.M., Ouaknine, J., Sharygina, N., Sinha, N.: State/Event-Based Software Model Checking. In: Boiten, E.A., Derrick, J., Smith, G.P. (eds.) IFM 2004. LNCS, vol. 2999, pp. 128–147. Springer, Heidelberg (2004)
3. Cimatti, A., Clarke, E.M., Giunchiglia, E., Giunchiglia, F., Pistore, M., Roveri, M., Sebastiani, R., Tacchella, A.: NuSMV 2: An OpenSource Tool for Symbolic Model Checking. In: Brinksma, E., Larsen, K.G. (eds.) CAV 2002. LNCS, vol. 2404, pp. 359–364. Springer, Heidelberg (2002)
4. Clarke, E.M., Grumberg, O., Peled, D.A.: Model Checking. MIT Press, Cambridge (2000)
5. Dong, J.S., Hao, P., Qin, S., Sun, J., Yi, W.: Timed Patterns: TCOZ to Timed Automata. In: Davies, J., Schulte, W., Barnett, M. (eds.) ICFEM 2004. LNCS, vol. 3308, pp. 483–498. Springer, Heidelberg (2004)
6. Gastin, P., Oddoux, D.: Fast LTL to Büchi Automata Translation. In: Berry, G., Comon, H., Finkel, A. (eds.) CAV 2001. LNCS, vol. 2102, pp. 53–65. Springer, Heidelberg (2001)
7. Hoare, C.A.R.: Communicating Sequential Processes. International Series in Computer Science. Prentice-Hall, Englewood Cliffs (1985), www.usingcsp.com/cspbook.pdf
8. Holzmann, G.J.: The Model Checker SPIN. IEEE Trans. on Soft. Eng. 23(5), 279–295 (1997)
9. Sun, J.S.D.J., Liu, Y., Wang, H.H.: Specifying and Verifying Event-based Fairness Enhanced Systems. In: Proceedings of the 10th International Conference on Formal Engineering Methods (ICFEM 2008) (accepted, 2008)
10. Mahony, B., Dong, J.S.: Timed Communicating Object Z. IEEE Transactions on Software Engineering 26(2) (February 2000)
11. Parashkevov, A., Yantchev, J.: ARC - a Tool for Efficient Refinement and Equivalence Checking for CSP. In: Proceedings of the IEEE International Conference on Algorithms and Architectures for Parallel Processing (ICA3PP 1996), pp. 68–75 (1996)
12. Roscoe, A.W.: Model-checking CSP, pp. 353–378 (1994)
13. Roscoe, A.W.: Compiling Shared Variable Programs into CSP. In: Proceedings of PROGRESS workshop 2001 (2001)
14. Roscoe, A.W.: On the expressive power of CSP refinement. Formal Aspects of Computing 17(2), 93–112 (2005)
15. Roscoe, A.W., Gardiner, P.H.B., Goldsmith, M., Hulance, J.R., Jackson, D.M., Scattergood, J.B.: Hierarchical Compression for Model-Checking CSP or How to Check 10^{20} Dining Philosophers for Deadlock. In: Brinksma, E., Steffen, B., Cleaveland, W.R., Larsen, K.G., Margaria, T. (eds.) TACAS 1995. LNCS, vol. 1019, pp. 133–152. Springer, Heidelberg (1995)
16. Roscoe, A.W., Wu, Z.Z.: Verifying Statemate Statecharts Using CSP and FDR. In: Liu, Z., He, J. (eds.) ICFEM 2006. LNCS, vol. 4260, pp. 324–341. Springer, Heidelberg (2006)
17. Sun, J., Dong, J.S.: Design Synthesis from Interaction and State-Based Specifications. IEEE Transactions on Software Engineering 32(6), 349–364 (2006)
18. Valmari, A.: Stubborn Set Methods for Process Algebras. In: Proceedings of the Workshop on Parital Order Methods in Verification (PMIV 1996). DIMACS Series in Discrete Mathematics and Theoretical Computer Science, vol. 29, pp. 213–231 (1996)
19. Wehrheim, H.: Partial order reductions for failures refinement. Electronic Notes in Theoretical Computer Science 27 (1999)

Appendix A: Operational Semantics

The following Structural Operational Semantics (SOS) rules. We remark that $\Box$, $\sqcap$, $\|$ and $|||$ are symmetric and associative. $eval(V, exp)$ evaluates the value of the exp given valuation V. Notice that for any P, $\checkmark \in \Sigma_P$.

$$\frac{}{(Skip, V, C) \xrightarrow{\checkmark} (Stop, V, C)} \qquad \frac{(P, V, C) \xrightarrow{e} (P', V', C'), e \neq \checkmark}{(P \mid\mid\mid Q, V, C) \xrightarrow{e} (P' \mid\mid\mid Q, V', C')} [\, int_1 \,]$$

$$\frac{}{(e\{x = exp\} \rightarrow P, V, C) \xrightarrow{e} (P, V[x/eval(V, exp)], C)} [\, ass \,]$$

$$\frac{\neg\, full(C[c])}{(c!exp \rightarrow Q, V, C) \xrightarrow{c!eval(V, exp)} (Q, V, C[c/C[c] ^\frown \langle c!eval(V, exp)\rangle])} [\, output \,]$$

$$\frac{\neg\, empty(C[c])}{(c?x \rightarrow Q, V, C) \xrightarrow{c?C[c].head} (Q, V, C[c/C[c].tail])} [\, input \,]$$

$$\frac{(P, V, C) \xrightarrow{e} (P', V', C')}{(P;\ Q, V, C) \xrightarrow{e} (P';\ Q, V', C')} \qquad \frac{(P, V, C) \xrightarrow{\checkmark} (P', V', C')}{(P;\ Q, V, C) \xrightarrow{\tau} (Q', V', C')} [\, seq_2 \,]$$

$$\frac{(P, V, C) \xrightarrow{e} (P', V', C'), e \neq \tau}{(P \Box Q, V, C) \xrightarrow{e} (P', V', C')} [\, ex_1 \,] \qquad \frac{(P, V, C) \xrightarrow{\tau} (P', V', C')}{(P \Box Q, V, C) \xrightarrow{\tau} (P' \Box Q, V', C)}$$

$$\frac{}{(P \sqcap Q, V, C) \xrightarrow{\tau} (P, V, C)} \qquad \frac{(P, V, C) \xrightarrow{e} (P', V', C'), V \models b}{(P \lhd b \rhd Q, V, C) \xrightarrow{e} (P', V', C')} [\, con_1 \,]$$

$$\frac{(Q, V, C) \xrightarrow{e} (Q', V', C'), V \not\models b}{(P \lhd b \rhd Q, V, C) \xrightarrow{e} (Q', V', C')} \qquad \frac{(P, V, C) \xrightarrow{e} (P', V', C'), V \models b}{([b] \bullet P, V, C) \xrightarrow{e} (P', V', C')} [\, grd \,]$$

$$\frac{(P, V, C) \xrightarrow{e} (P', V', C')}{(P \triangle Q, V, C) \xrightarrow{e} (P' \triangle Q, V', C')} \qquad \frac{(Q, V, C) \xrightarrow{e} (Q', V', C'), e \neq \tau}{(P \triangle Q, V, C) \xrightarrow{e} (Q', V', C')} [\, int_2 \,]$$

$$\frac{(Q, V, C) \xrightarrow{\tau} (Q', V', C')}{(P \triangle Q, V, C) \xrightarrow{\tau} (P \triangle Q', V', C')} \qquad \frac{(P, V, C) \xrightarrow{e} (P', V', C'), e \notin X}{(P \setminus X, V, C) \xrightarrow{e} (P' \setminus X, V', C')}$$

$$\frac{(P, V, C) \xrightarrow{e} (P', V', C'), e \in X}{(P \setminus X, V, C) \xrightarrow{\tau} (P' \setminus X, V', C')} \qquad \frac{(P, V, C) \xrightarrow{e} (P', V', C') \land e \notin \Sigma_Q}{(P \parallel Q, V, C) \xrightarrow{e} (P' \parallel Q, V', C')}$$

$$\frac{(P, V, C) \xrightarrow{e} (P', V, C) \land (Q, V, C) \xrightarrow{e} (Q', V, C)}{(P \parallel Q, V, C) \xrightarrow{e} (P' \parallel Q', V, C)} [\ syn\ ]$$

Appendix B: Soundness of the Partial Order Reduction

We prove the soundness in two steps. Firstly, because the algorithm tau' applies to one model only (whereas $next'$ must coordinate both the implementation and the specification), it is sufficient to show that the reduction regarding τ-transitions (i.e., the algorithm $stubborn\_tau$) preserves failures/divergence equivalence. Secondly, we show that the reduction regarding visible events (i.e., the algorithm $next'$) is sound.

In [18], a set of sufficient conditions has been proved to preserve CSP failures divergence equivalence. It is thus sufficient to prove that the reduction regarding τ-transitions satisfies the sufficient conditions. In the following, let E be the reduced set of successors (i.e., the stubborn set as in [18]) and F be the full set. Notice that the result returned by algorithm $stubborn\_tau$ is returned by algorithm tau' or $next'$ if and only if it is not empty (line 1 of tau' and line 2 of $next'$). Thus, as long as F is not empty, E is not empty. By line 3 of algorithm $stubborn\_tau$, transitions other than those selected in E are all independent of those in E. By line 1 of $stubborn\_tau$, because the set of possibly enabled events must be the same of the set enabled event from the component, a transition from the component must remain disabled unless a transition from the components has been taken. By theorem 3.2 of [18], $\ddot{A}_0$, $\ddot{A}_1$, $\ddot{A}_2$, $\ddot{A}_3$ hold. Because only τ-transitions are reduced in tau', condition $\ddot{A}_4$ is trivial. By the condition $\neg\, loop(e)$ at line 3 of $stubborn\_tau$, no action will be ignored forever, and thus $\ddot{A}_5$ holds. $\ddot{A}_6$ is trivial for the same reason as for $\ddot{A}_4$. By theorem 4.2 and 5.3 in [18], the reduction regarding τ-transitions preserves trace/failures/divergence equivalence and thus is sound.

In order to prove that algorithm $next'$ is sound, we need to prove (in addition to the above) that the reduction regarding visible events are sound as well. We reuse the results which have been proved in [19] and show that the sufficient conditions proposed in [19] have been full-filled. Firstly, C1 and C3 in [19] are trivial true. Because of line 0 and 2 of $stubborn\_visible$, an action dependent (say e) on an action selected can only be executed after some action selected has been executed. There are two cases in which this might be violated. In both of these cases, some transition (say a) independent of e are executed, eventually enabled a transition that is dependent on e. In the first case, if a belongs to some other components. A necessary condition for this to happen is that a is dependent on e. This is prevented by line 1. In the other case, a belongs to the same component of e, which is not possible because we require that $current(P_i) = \{e\}$. The same argument applies to line 6 to 8 which guarantees that no action dependent on e is executed before e is executed (and there C1in [19] is proved). C2 in [19] is guaranteed by the condition $\neg\, loop(e)$. Therefore, we conclude the reduction is sound.

Formal Use of Design Patterns and Refactoring*

Long Quan[1], Qiu Zongyan[1], and Zhiming Liu[2]

[1] LMAM & Dept. of Informatics, School of Math. Peking University, Beijing 100871, China
[2] IIST, United Nations University, Macao, China
{longquan,qzy}@math.pku.edu.cn, lzm@iist.unu.edu

Abstract. Design patterns *has been used very effectively in object-oriented design for a long time.* Refactoring *is also widely used for producing better maintainable and reusable designs and programs. In this paper, we investigate how design patterns and refactoring rules are used in a formal method by formulating and showing them as* refinement laws *in the calculus of refinement of component and object-oriented systems, known as* rCOS*. We also combine refactoring and design patterns to provide some big-step rules of* pattern-directed refactoring.

Keywords: Object-Orientation, Design Pattern, Refactoring, *rCOS*, Refinement.

1 Introduction

Design pattern is widely accepted as a very useful OO technique to produce designs which are maintainable and reusable, as well as to reduce time and cost of development [9]. *Refactoring* is another important techniaue for improving existing designs or programs [20,8,21]. These techniques are also related that design patterns can be used to guide refactoring. In [8], Fowler collected 68 refactoring rules, where an example shows how the *State Pattern* is used to guide transformations of a program step by step using refactoring rules. Kerievsky discussed in [13] the *pattern-directed refactoring*, which can be seen as big-step refactoring rules toward patterns. However, there has been little investigation on how the techniques of design patterns and refactoring can be used in a formal method until recently when a few attempts are published.

Roberts [18] defined refactoring rules as program transformations, but there is no formal semantic-based proof to ensure that such transformations preserve the behavior of programs. M. Cornélio *et al.* [6] formalized and proved some of Fowler's refactoring rules as refinement laws in ROOL [2]. However, ROOL takes a copy semantics defined by weakest precondition transformers. Without references, some important and interesting laws of OO programs do not hold in ROOL [19]. More recently in [7], refactoring rules are defined and automated as model transformations for models at different abstraction levels including platform independent models, platform specific models and implementation specific models. Also in [17], refactoring of UML class diagrams is studied using the standard Object Constraint Language (OCL).

In this paper, we investigate how design patterns and refactoring rules can be both formulated as program refinement laws in rCOS [12,3]. The advantage of using rCOS is

* Supported by NNSF of China (No. 60718002), and Projects on HighQSofD and HTTS funded by Macao S&T Fund.

T. Margaria and B. Steffen (Eds.): ISoLA 2008, CCIS 17, pp. 323–338, 2008.

that it takes a reference semantic model with rich OO features, including *subtypes, visibility, inheritance, dynamic binding* and *polymorphism*. Also a UML profile is defined for rCOS [22,5] in a component-based model driven development process.

Similar to the idea in [6], we formulate refactoring rules as rCOS refinement laws of OO specification and programs. Take the advantage of the relational semantics of rCOS, the formulation of the refactoring rules and their proofs are better comprehensive compared with the approach of predicate transformers. We go one step further to formulate the pattern-directed refactoring rules suggested in [13]. Sketches of proofs are given in this paper, leaving the full details in a technical report [15].

We will briefly introduce rCOS in Section 2, and give the rCOS definition of the refactoring rules in Section 3, and the pattern-directed refactoring rules in Section 4. Ideas and sketches of proofs are given in Section 5. An example is used to illustrate the formal use of refactoring and pattern directed refactoring is presented in Section 6. Finally, we summarize the conclusions and discuss some future work.

2 Basics of rCOS

A program in rCOS is of the form *cdecls* • *P*, where *P* is the main program playing the role as *main method* in Java programs. P takes the form (gbv, c), where gbv denotes *global variable declarations* and c is a command. *cdecls* is a sequence of class declarations $cdecl_1; \ldots; cdecl_k$, where each $cdecl_j$ declares a class in the form :

$$
\begin{array}{l}
[\texttt{private}]\ \texttt{class}\ N\ [\texttt{extends}\ M]\ \{ \\
\quad \texttt{private} \quad U_1\ u_1 = a_1, \ldots, U_m\ u_m = a_m; \\
\quad \texttt{protected}\ V_1\ v_1 = b_1, \ldots, V_n\ v_n = b_n; \\
\quad \texttt{public} \quad W_1\ w_1 = c_1, \ldots, W_k\ w_k = c_k; \\
\quad \texttt{method} \quad m_1(\underline{T}_{11}\ \underline{x}_1, \underline{T}_{12}\ \underline{y}_1, \underline{T}_{13}\ \underline{z}_1)\{c_1\}; \cdots ; m_\ell(\underline{T}_{\ell 1}\ \underline{x}_\ell, \underline{T}_{\ell 2}\ \underline{y}_\ell, \underline{T}_{\ell 3}\ \underline{z}_\ell)\{c_\ell\} \\
\}
\end{array}
$$

where we use $\underline{x}$ to denote a sequence of x. Here are some explanations:

- A class can be declared as `private`, but public by default. Only public classes and primitive types can be used in global variable declarations.
- *N* is a class name, and *M* is its direct superclass.
- Initial values of attributes are given in declarations.
- A method can have value parameters $(\underline{T}_{i1}\ \underline{x}_i)$, result parameters $(\underline{T}_{i2}\ \underline{y}_i)$, and value-result parameters $(\underline{T}_{i3}\ \underline{z}_i)$. We often use $m(\underline{paras})\{c\}$ to denote method m, with $\underline{paras}$ its parameter list and c its body command which will be defined below.
- Following the Java convention, we assume an attribute `protected` when it is not tagged with an accessible modifier.

The issues of visibility are omitted here for the simplicity of the theory. We assume that all methods in a public class are public and and accessible in the main method, and all methods in a private classes are protected.

rCOS supports typical OO constructs, as will as some special "statements" for the specification and refinement:

$$
\begin{array}{rl}
c ::= & S \mid skip \mid chaos \mid \mathbf{var}\ T\ x = e;\ c;\ \mathbf{end}\ x \mid c; c \mid c \lhd b \rhd c \mid \\
& c \sqcap c \mid b * c \mid le.m(\underline{e}, \underline{v}, \underline{u}) \mid le := e \mid C.new(le)[\underline{e}]
\end{array}
$$

Here S is a specification statement in the form of a *framed design* $f : p \vdash R$ in UTP, b a Boolean expression, e an expression, and le an *assignable expression* of the form $le ::= x \mid le.a$,where x is a variable name and a an attribute name. We have sequential composition $c; c$, conditional $c \lhd b \rhd c$, and iteration $b * c$, while $\mathbf{var}\ T\ x = e;\ c;\ \mathbf{end}\ x$ is a command within a local declaration scope. The nondeterministic choice $c \sqcap c$, $skip$, $chaos$ and S are introduced only for the specification and refinement.

We use $le.m(\underline{e}, \underline{v}, \underline{u})$ to denote a call to method m of the object denoted by le, with value arguments $\underline{e}$, result arguments $\underline{v}$ for return values, and value-result arguments $\underline{u}$. Command $C.new(x)[\underline{e}]$ creates a new object of class C with initial attribute values from expressions $\underline{e}$ and assigns the object to variable x, which should be of the type C or its supertype. The form of expressions e is standard.

rCOS adopts an observation-based relational semantics and extends UTP to deal with the OO features. As in UTP, the semantics of a program is defined as a *design* $D = (\alpha, P)$, where α is the *alphabet* of the program consisting of its input and output variables, denoted as $\underline{x}$ and $\underline{x}'$ respectively, and P is a specification in the form $pre(\underline{x}) \vdash post(\underline{x}, \underline{x}')$ with semantics defined by predicate:

$$(ok \wedge pre(\underline{x})) \Rightarrow (ok' \wedge post(\underline{x}, \underline{x}'))$$

where $pre(\underline{x})$ and $post(\underline{x}, \underline{x}')$ are predicates describing the effect of the program based on the pre- and post-states of the alphabet, ok and ok' are auxiliary Boolean variables denoting the successful startup and termination of the program, $\underline{x}, \underline{x}'$ denote values of variables $\underline{x}$ in the initial and final states, respectively. This convention will be used throughout the paper. The difference from UTP is that variables can also hold objects.

For defining semantics of a command, a *framed design* D is often used in which specification P is of the form $\beta : pre(\underline{x}) \vdash post(\underline{x}, \underline{x}')$, meaning that D only changes variables in the subset β of α.

For OO programs, the semantic definition of a command makes use of the *static structure information* given by the class declarations for dynamic binding and visibility control. These structure details are represented by a group of logical variables, where variable $\mathbf{cname}$ of the set of declared class names, $\mathbf{attr}$ of a function returning the attributes of each class, $\mathbf{op}$ of a function returning the method set of each class, $\mathbf{superclass}$ of a function returning the direct superclass. In addition to the global variables gbv in the main program, we need a variable $\mathbf{\Sigma}$ representing the set of currently existing objects during the execution. The commands in the program make changes to these variables. For example, an object creation command changes $\mathbf{\Sigma}$ by adding in the new created object; when an attribute of object o is modified, this change is reflected in $\mathbf{\Sigma}$ accordingly. For the details of the model we refer the reader to paper [12].

rCOS has a powerful theory of refinement developed from the refinement of design in UTP. We first recall definitions of design refinement and data refinement in UTP [11].

Definition 1 (Refinement). *Design $D_2 = (\alpha, P_2)$ is a* refinement *of $D_1 = (\alpha, P_1)$, denoted by $D_1 \sqsubseteq D_2$, if P_2 entails P_1, i.e. $\forall \underline{x}, \underline{x}', ok, ok' \cdot (P_2 \Rightarrow P_1)$, where $\underline{x}$ are the variables contained in α.* □

Definition 2 (Data refinement). *Suppose ρ be a mapping from alphabet α_2 to alphabet α_1. Design $D_2 = (\alpha_2, P_2)$ is a* data refinement *of design $D_1 = (\alpha_1, P_1)$ under ρ, denoted by $D_1 \sqsubseteq_\rho D_2$, if $(P_1; \rho) \sqsubseteq (\rho; P_2)$. Here ρ is called a refinement mapping.* □

Note in the the definition, the refinement mapping ρ can be specified as a design.

In rCOS, we define the notions of *OO system refinement* and *OO structure refinement* (also known as *class refinement*) [12,22].

Definition 3 (System refinement). *For* $S_1 = (cdecls_1 \bullet P_1)$ *and* $S_2 = (cdecls_2 \bullet P_2)$ *with the same global variables gbv in* P_1 *and* P_2*, we say that* S_2 *is a* refinement *of* S_1*, denoted by* $S_1 \sqsubseteq_{sys} S_2$*, if the behavior of* S_2 *is less nondeterministic than that of* S_1*:*

$$\forall \underline{x}, \underline{x}', ok, ok' \cdot (S_2 \Rightarrow S_1)$$

where $\underline{x}$ *are the variables declared in gbv.* □

$S_1 \sqsubseteq_{sys} S_2$ requires that S_2 is less nondeterministic that S_1 with regards to the states of the global variables.

Definition 4 (Structure refinement). *Let* $cdecls_1$ *and* $cdecls_2$ *be two class declaration sections,* $cdecls_1$ *is a* refinement *of* $cdecls_2$*, denoted by* $cdecls_2 \sqsubseteq_{class} cdecls_1$*, if the former can replace the later in any object system:*

$$cdecls_2 \sqsubseteq_{class} cdecls_1 \widehat{=} (cdecls_2 \bullet P \sqsubseteq_{sys} cdecls_1 \bullet P)$$

holds for all main programs $P = (gbv, c)$*.* □

Intuitively, $cdecls_1$ provides the same or refined services as $cdecls_2$ can.

In [12], we studied the basic refinement laws that capture the nature of incremental development in OO programming, including the laws for adding a class into the declarations, introducing inheritance, functionality delegation, class decomposition, and encapsulating data, etc. Our work in [22] uses a graph theory for further study of the structure refinement where the soundness and completeness are established. We will study a set of special refinement laws that formalize the refactoring rules here.

3 Refactoring Rules in rCOS

In Fowler's book [8], refactoring rules are described via examples. Here we formulate them as rCOS refinement rules in order for their correctness to be provable. Fowler classifies refactoring rules into six categories. We show here the formalization for one rule from each category as a representative, leaving the others in our report [15].

In general, a refactoring rule should be formalized as a refinement law of the form $cdecls_0 \bullet P_0 \sqsubseteq cdecls_1 \bullet P_1$, where the left hand side is the original program and the right is the refactoring result. However, all rules presented here only involve structure refinement, except for rule **Parameterize Method** which needs modifications of main program. Thus, most of the rules take the form of $cdecls_0 \sqsubseteq cdecls_1$, where $cdecls_0$ and $cdecls_1$ are the class declarations involved.

We will use $N[M, pri, prot, pub, ops]$ to denote a class N with M as its direct superclass, *pri*, *prot*, and *pub* its private, protected and public attributes, respectively, and *ops* its methods. When no confusion, we will only give explicitly the parameters involved in a rule. For example, $N[ops]$ denotes a class with method set *ops*, and $N[prot, ops]$ for a class with protected attribute set *prot* and method set *ops*. In the rest of this section, the six refactoring rules are also presented with UML diagrams for illustration.

Rule *Extract Method* allows us to replace a piece of code in a method body with a call to a newly introduced method, which has the replaced code as its body.

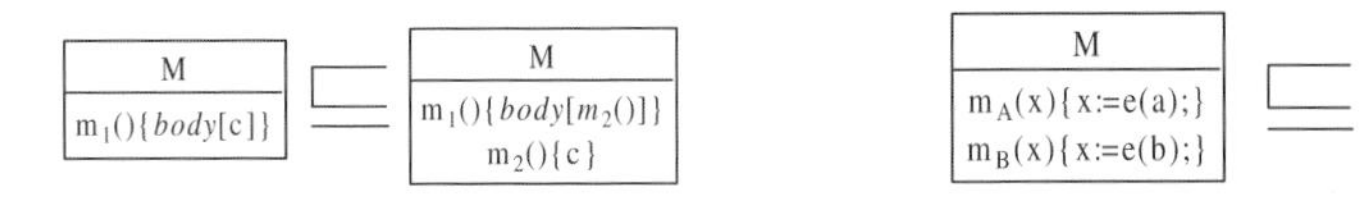

Fig. 1. Extract Method

Fig. 2. Parameterize Method

Rule 1 (Extract Method). *Assume that M has method set* $\{m_1()\{body[c]\}\} \cup ops$*. If c is part of the body of* m_1 *that does not modify any local variables of* m_1 *outside the scope*[1] *of c. We have*

$$\begin{aligned} & cdecls; M[\{m_1()\{body[c]\}\} \cup ops] \\ \sqsubseteq\ & cdecls; M[\{m_1()\{body[m_2()]\}, m_2()\{c\}\} \cup ops] \end{aligned} \quad (1)$$

where m_2 *is a new method name that is not used in cdecls or ops.*

This rule is illustrated in Fig. 1 where the program command c in the body of method m_1 and it is extracted as a method $m_2()$. Actually this is a special case of the general *Extract Method* rule. In the general case, c may refer to local variables that can be passed as arguments to the extracted method, with adequate parameter passing mechanisms.

If several methods do similar work with different values in their bodies, the following rule permits using only one method with an extra parameter for different values.

Rule 2 (Parameterize Method). *Let ops be a set of methods,* c *a command, and* m *a name not used in ops or cdecls. We have below rule where* x *is a result parameter of* m*:*

$$\begin{aligned} & cdecls; M[ops \cup \{m_a(x)\{x := e(a)\}, m_b(x)\{x := e(b)\}\}] \bullet P(c) \\ \sqsubseteq\ & cdecls'; M[ops' \cup \{m(r, x)\{x := e(r)\}\}] \bullet P(c') \end{aligned}$$

where

$$\begin{aligned} cdecls' &\mathrel{\widehat{=}} cdecls[m(a,x)/m_a(x), m(b,x)/m_b(x)] \\ ops' &\mathrel{\widehat{=}} ops[m(a,x)/m_a(x), m(b,x)/m_b(x)] \\ c' &\mathrel{\widehat{=}} c[m(a,x)/m_a(x), m(b,x)/m_b(x)] \end{aligned}$$

The idea of this rule is depicted in Fig. 2, where the two similar methods are replaced by the parameterized one. As said before, this is a system refinement rule.

Rule *Move Method* says that if a method of a class M only refers to attributes of another class N, we can move the method to class N.

Rule 3 (Move Method). *Let* N *b an attribute of class M, ops* $\cup \{m()\{c\}\}$ *the method set of* M*, where* m *is only used locally in* M*. And* ops_1 *the method set of N such that* $m()$ *is not in* ops_1*. If c only refers to an attribute* $b.x$ *of N and a method* $b.n()$ *of b for theoretical neatness*[2]*. Define*

$$\begin{aligned} ops' &\mathrel{\widehat{=}} ops[b.m()/m()] - \{m()\} \\ c' &\mathrel{\widehat{=}} c[x/b.x, n()/b.n()] \end{aligned}$$

where $F[a/b]$ *stands for the substitution of all occurrences of b. We have*

$$\begin{aligned} & cdecls; M[N\ b, ops \cup \{m()\{c\}\}]; N[ops_1] \\ \sqsubseteq\ & cdecls; M[N\ b, ops']; N[ops_1 \cup \{m()\{c'\}\}] \end{aligned}$$

provided that $m()$ *is not called from outside of M on the left hand side of the rule.*

[1] This means local variables declared outside c.

[2] It can be the case that c refers to a number of attributes and a number of methods of *N*.

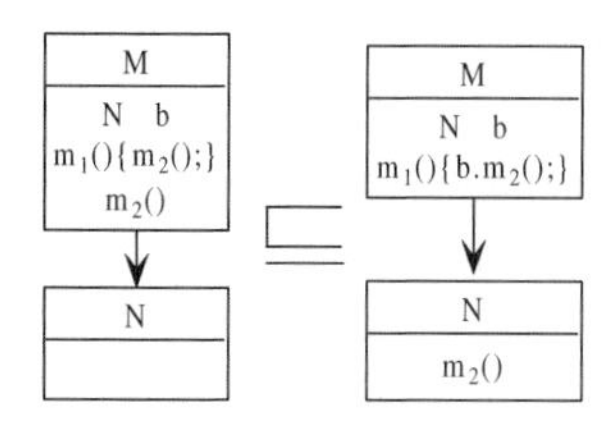

Fig. 3. Move Method

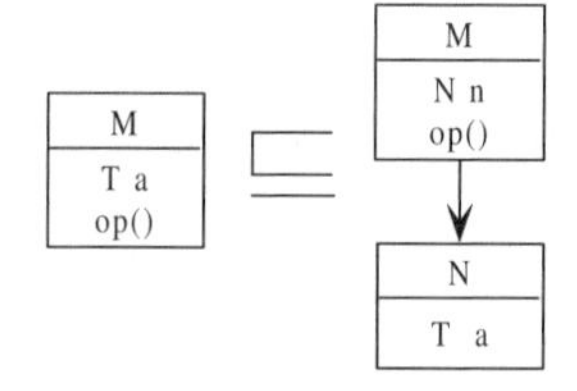

Fig. 4. Replace Data Value with Object

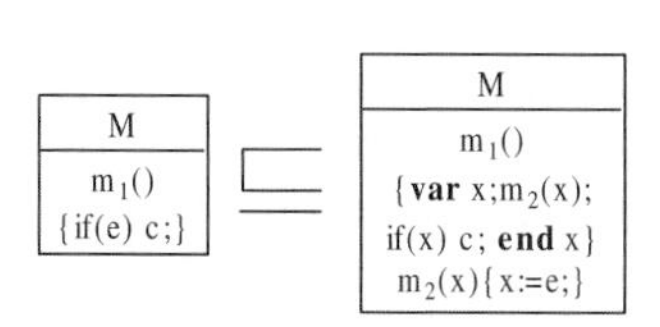

Fig. 5. Decompose Conditional

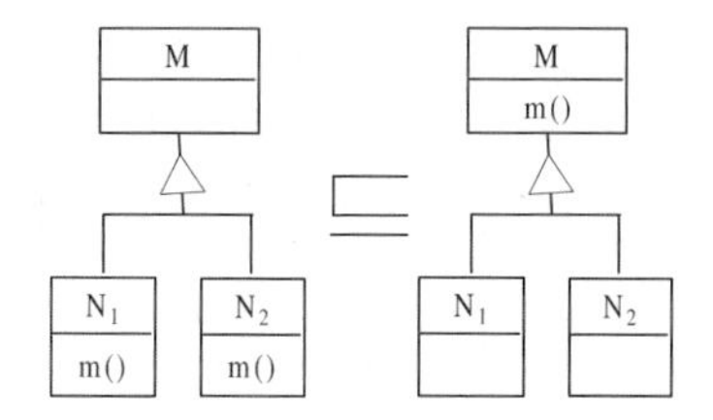

Fig. 6. Pull Up Method

A special case of this rule is shown in Fig. 3, where a arrow from M to N denotes that M has an N attribute. The combination of the rules for extracting and moving methods allows us to decompose a class for low coupling and high cohesion [14].

When we have a data item that needs additional data or behavior, the following rule allows us to define a new class to turn the data item into an object.

Rule 4 (Replace Data Value with Object). *Assume M is a class with attribute a of some primary data type T and methods ops, we have a refinement law:*

$$cdecls; M[T\ a, ops] \sqsubseteq cdecls; N[T\ a]; M[N\ n, ops']$$

Here N is a fresh class name not used in $cdecls$. If a is not public, we can define accessing methods $geta()$ and $seta()$. Further, ops′ is the same as ops except the references to a are replace by suitable "get" or "set" method calls when necessary.

This rule is shown in Fig. 4. One can see that the attribute $T\ a$ is replaced by an object in the refactorred program which encapsulates the data.

When there is a complicated conditional (if-then-else) statement, we can extract a method from the condition, and use the result of the method in the conditional instead.

Rule 5 (Decompose Conditional). *Assume e is a boolean expression, then*

$$\begin{aligned} &cdecls; M[ops \cup \{m_1()\{c_1 \lhd e \rhd c_2\}\}] \\ \sqsubseteq\ &cdecls; M[ops \cup \{m_1()\{\mathbf{var}\ bool\ x; m_2(x); c_1 \lhd x \rhd c_2; \mathbf{end}\ x\}, m_2(; bool\ y)\{y := e\}\}] \end{aligned}$$

where m_2 is a name that does not occur in ops, x is a new variable that is not in the body of m_1, and y is a result parameter of m_2.

In the general cases, the conditional is only a part of the body of m_1. This rule is illustrated in Fig. 5, where condition e is replaced by a variable which might make the program clearer.

When a method presents in each of several subclasses of a class, we can move it to the superclass. The rule below shows a special case with only two subclasses involved.

Rule 6 (Pull Up Method). *Assume M is the super class of N_1 and N_2, method $m()$ are declared with the same definition in both N_1 and N_2, and all attributes used in $m()$ are in M. Let ops be the operations declared in M which does not include $m()$. Then*

$$\begin{array}{l} \mathit{cdecls}; M[\mathit{ops}]; N_1[M, \{m()\} \cup \mathit{ops}_1]; N_2[M, \{m()\} \cup \mathit{ops}_2] \\ \sqsubseteq\ \mathit{cdecls}; M[\mathit{ops} \cup \{m()\}]; N_1[M, \mathit{ops}_1]; N_2[M, \mathit{ops}_2] \end{array}$$

As shown in Fig. 6, the duplicated method $m()$ is pulled up to the superclass.

4 Pattern-Directed Refactoring Rules

Design Patterns [9] are widely accepted as good practice in OO development. We focus on how to transform a program to make it conforming design patterns, i.e. the transformation from a naiver program to a design pattern styled program. The formal rules for these transformations are more effective and relatively more complex. We would like to keep the term *design pattern directed refactoring rules* for these transformations.

Different from basic refactoring rules, many design patterns directed rules are contextually sensitive, which require a change in the class declarations to be related to the corresponding modification of the main program. Therefore, they need to be defined as *program refinement*. We formalize each of these rules as a refinement law of the form:

$$\mathit{Cds}; \mathit{cdecls} \bullet P[c_0] \sqsubseteq \mathit{Cds}_d; \mathit{cdecls} \bullet P[c/c_o]$$

where

- Cds are some class declarations in the original naive program, Cds_d for the corresponding classes in the result, while *cdecls* for the classes unchanged,
- $P[c_0]$ and $P[c/c_0]$ are the main programs before and after the refinement, containing c_0 and c respectively, which will be called as *protocols* of the rule.

We call touple $\langle \mathit{Cds}, \mathit{Cds}_d, c_0, c\rangle$ the *frame* of a rule, and give each rule by defining its frame.

Some pattern-directed rules require tedious side-conditions. A fully formal definition requires to specify these conditions so that the rules can be proved and the conditions can be checked when the rules are applied or automated. For simplicity of the presentation, however, we assume that all the new methods and attributes on the right hand side of a rule use fresh names. The correctness issues of the rules are discussed in the next section, and more details are left in the technical report [15].

In the Gang-of-Four book [9], design patterns are classified into three categories: *Creational*, *Structural* and *Behavioral* patterns. We will take one representative pattern from each of these categories in this paper.

Abstract Factory: It is a creational pattern providing an interface for creating a family of related objects without explicitly invoking the class-specific constructors, thus enhancing extensibility and adaptability. The following rule shows how to refactor a piece of program with constructor invocations to *Abstract Factory* pattern-style program.

The classes and their relations for this rule corresponding to this pattern is depicted in Fig. 7, where we use methods named as *constructor* in classes $\mathit{ConcreteA}_0$, $\mathit{ConcreteB}_0$,

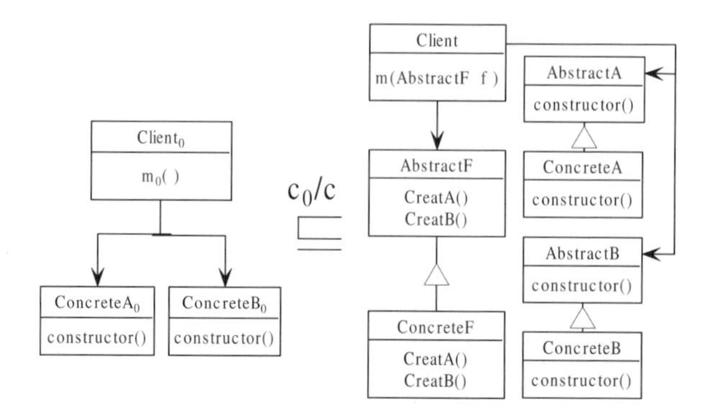

Fig. 7. Abstract Factory

ConcreteA and *ConcreteB* to explicitly show their constructor methods, that are generally assumed for all classes *C* and invoked by $C.new(x)$ in rCOS.

The class declarations *Cds* that will be refactored are shown on the left. The protocol c contains an invocation to method $m_0()$ which makes calls to the constructors of the associated two "concrete classes" $ConcreteA_0$ and $ConcreteB_0$

$$m_0()\{ConcreteA_0.new(a); ConcreteB_0.new(b)\}$$

The classes after refactoring are shown on the right of the figure that includes the new classes *AbstractF*, *AbstractA* and *AbstractB* and the *concreteF*. Also in the class declarations, the original $ConcreteA_0$ and $ConcreteB_0$ are changed to *ConcreteA* and *ConcreteB*, where the original constructor methods keep unchanged. In the new protocol c, method $m_0()$ is replaced by m in which the object creations *ConcreteA* and *ConcreteB* are carried out indirectly via its associated factory object *ConcreteF*. This is formalized in the following rule. Besides, new classes *AbstractA* and *AbstractB* are added with signatures for the constructor methods of corresponding concrete classes.

Rule 7 (Abstract Factory). *The frame of this rule is defined as:*

- *For the parts of the frame on the left hand side of the rule (in the program to be refactored)*

$$\begin{aligned} Cds &\mathrel{\widehat{=}} Client_0[\,]; ConcreteA_0[\,]; ConcreteB_0[\,]; \\ c_0 &\mathrel{\widehat{=}} \{\mathbf{var}\ Client_0\ x; Client_0.new(x); x.m_0(); \gamma; \mathbf{end}\ x\} \\ m_0() &\mathrel{\widehat{=}} m_0()\{ConcreteA_0.new(a); ConcreteB_0.new(b)\} \end{aligned}$$

  where γ is an arbitrary statement.
- *For the classes and protocol on the right hand side (the refactoring result)*

$$\begin{aligned} Cds_d &\mathrel{\widehat{=}} Client[\,]; AbstractF[\,]; ConcreteF[AbstractF]; AbstractA[\,]; AbstractB[\,]; \\ &\quad ConcreteA[AbstractA]; ConcreteB[AbstractB]; \\ c &\mathrel{\widehat{=}} \{\mathbf{var}\ Client\ x, ConcreteF\ cf; Client.new(x); \\ &\quad ConcreteF.new(cf); x.m(cf); \gamma; \mathbf{end}\ cf, x\} \end{aligned}$$

  where
  - *class AbstractF declares two method signatures $CreateA(, AbstractA\ x_a,)$ and $CreateB(, AbstractA\ x_b,)$ where x_a and x_b are result parameters.*

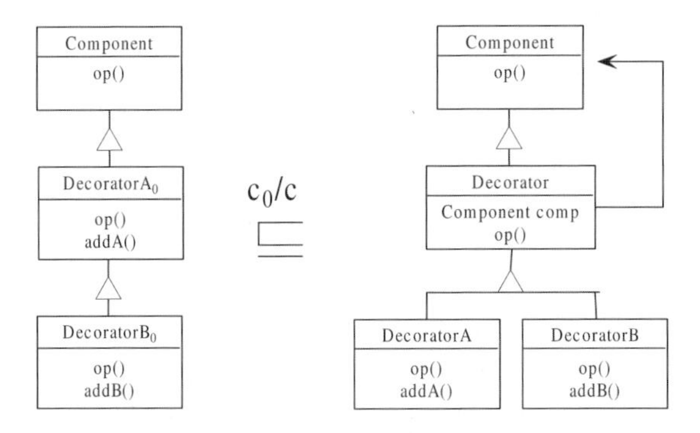

Fig. 8. Decorator

- *the two are defined in class ConcreteF:*

$$\textit{CreateA}(, \textit{AbstractA}\ x_a,)\{\textit{ConcreteA.new}(x_a)\}$$
$$\textit{CreateB}(, \textit{AbstractA}\ x_b,)\{\textit{ConcreteB.new}(x_b)\}$$

- *in the client class Client, the new method* $m()$ *is defined as*

$$m(\textit{AbstractF}\ f)\{f.\textit{CreateA}(a); f.\textit{CreateB}(b)\}$$

Concrete creation methods are encapsulated in the factory object. Because no concrete class is mentioned in the client program explicitly, the same program can be used to manipulate objects produced by other concrete factories without any modification. □

Decorator: Designers often need to add new functions to existing programs for various reasons. An example is given in Fig. 8, where the naive structures is shown on the left. Here are two classes *DecoratorA*$_0$ and *DecoratorB*$_0$ to decorate class *Component* with additional functions *addA* and *addB* injected into method *op* sequentially. This solution is not flexible enough. For example, it does not support the object with only *addB* added to *op* but not *addA*. *Decorator* is a structural pattern to provide a flexible solution for adding functionalities. The corresponding pattern style program is shown in Fig. 8 (right). The following rule describes the details of this refactoring.

Rule 8 (Decorator). *The frame of this rule is defined as:*

$$\begin{array}{lcl} Cds & \widehat{=} & \textit{Component}[\,]; \textit{DecoratorA}_0[\textit{Component}]; \textit{DecoratorB}_0[\textit{DecoratorA}_0] \\ Cds_d & \widehat{=} & \textit{Component}[\,]; \textit{Decorator}[\textit{Component}]; \\ & & \textit{DecoratorA}[\textit{Decorator}]; \textit{DecoratorB}[\textit{Decorator}] \\ c_0 & \widehat{=} & \{\textbf{var}\ \textit{DecoratorB}_0\ \textit{comp}; \textit{DecoratorB}_0.\textit{new}(\textit{comp}); \textit{comp.op}(); \textbf{end}\ \textit{comp}\} \\ c & \widehat{=} & \{\textbf{var}\ \textit{Component}\ \textit{comp}_1, \textit{DecoratorA}\ \textit{comp}_2, \textit{DecoratorB}\ \textit{comp}; \\ & & \textit{Component.new}(\textit{comp}_1); \textit{DecoratorA.new}(\textit{comp}_2)[\textit{comp}_1]; \\ & & \textit{DecoratorB.new}(\textit{comp})[\textit{comp}_2]; \textit{comp.op}(); \textbf{end}\ \textit{comp}, \textit{comp}_1, \textit{comp}_2\} \end{array}$$

Here the actual parameters $comp_1$ *and* $comp_2$ *are used to initialize attribute comp, and*

- *In class DecoratorA*$_0$ *and DecoratorB*$_0$*, the definitions of method op are given as follows:*

$$\textit{op}()\{\textit{Component.op}(); \textit{addA}()\} \quad \text{// in } \textit{DecoratorA}_0$$
$$\textit{op}()\{\textit{DecoratorA}_0.\textit{op}(); \textit{addB}()\} \quad \text{// in } \textit{DecoratorB}_0$$

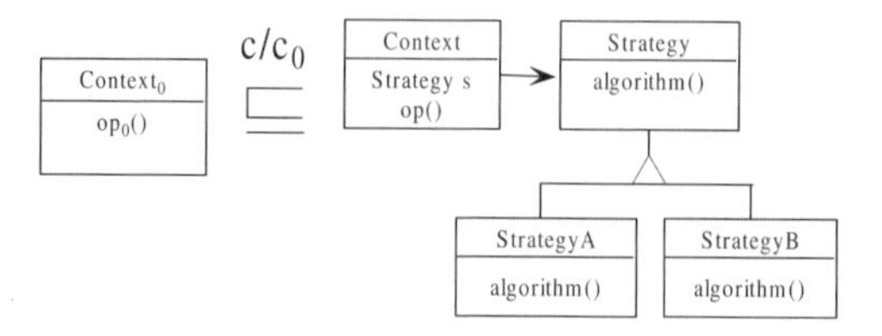

Fig. 9. Strategy

– *In Decorator, DecoratorA and DecoratorB, we have the following definitions:*

$$op()\{comp.op()\} \quad \text{// in } Decorator$$
$$op()\{Decorator.op(); addA()\} \quad \text{// in } DecoratorA$$
$$op()\{Decorator.op(); addB()\} \quad \text{// in } DecoratorB$$

The new program supports the flexible function-extension. □

Originally, the client obtains the results of *addA*() and *addB*() by invoking *op*() of the lowest sub-class $DecoratorB_0$. After refactoring, the client still invokes *addA*() and *addB*(), in turn via the reference *comp* in *Decorator*. So the behavior is preserved.

Strategy: Sometimes we have a family of algorithms, and want to make them interchangeable during executions. *Strategy* pattern allows the context to select the algorithms dynamically without using conditionals that may make a program hard to read and maintain. We use this pattern as an example for the last category, *behavioral* patterns. This rule also shows how to refactor a program containing a conditional statement to a pattern-style program. This pattern is shown in Fig. 9.

Rule 9 (Strategy). *The frame of this rule is defined as follows:*

$$\begin{array}{lcl} Cds & \widehat{=} & Context_0[\,]; \\ Cds_d & \widehat{=} & Context[\,]; Strategy[\,]; StrategyA[Strategy]; StrategyB[Strategy]; \\ c_0 & \widehat{=} & \{\mathbf{var}\ Context_0\ con; Context_0.new(con)[\,]; con.op_0(); \mathbf{end}\ con\} \\ c & \widehat{=} & \{\mathbf{var}\ Strategy\ s; (StrategyA.new(s) \lhd b \rhd StrategyB.new(s)); \\ & & \ \mathbf{var}\ Context\ con; Context.new(con)[s]; con.op(); \mathbf{end}\ s, con\} \end{array}$$

where

– *In classes $Context_0$ and Context, we have the method definitions:*

$$op_0()\{c_A \lhd b \rhd c_B\} \text{ // in } Context_0, \text{ use conditional to make choice}$$
$$op()\{algorithm()\} \text{ // in } Context, \text{ call an algorithmaccording to the object}$$

where b is a global variable for the choice between specific algorithms c_A and c_B.

– *In class Strategy, StrategyA and StrategyB*

$$algorithm() \quad \text{// in } Strategy, \text{ no implementation}$$
$$algorithm()\{c_A\} \quad \text{// in } StrategyA$$
$$algorithm()\{c_B\} \quad \text{// in } StrategyB$$

where c_A and c_B are the same sequence of commands as above. □

In the naive program, the context will execute c_A (or c_B) if b is *true* (or *false*). Correspondingly, in the pattern style program, it will create an object *StrategyA* (or *StrategyB*) if b is *true* (or *false*) for the reference s, and then execute c_A (or c_B) via the reference. So the behavior is preserved.

5 The Proofs

In this section we give the basic idea and the general proof procedure for the refinement laws, and illustrate the procedure via an example.

5.1 Class Refinement Laws

As shown above, each class refinement law is of the form

$$LHS \sqsubseteq RHS$$

According to Definition 4 (Class Refinement), to prove the law, we have to check

$$LHS \bullet P \sqsubseteq RHS \bullet P, \quad \text{For any } P = (gbv, c)$$

According to the definition, for each *class refinement* law, we need to prove that, for any $P = (gbv, c)$,

$$\forall stateV, stateV' \bullet (RHS; init; c) \Rightarrow \forall stateW, stateW' \bullet (LHS; init; c)$$

where $(stateV, stateV')$ and $(stateW, stateW')$ represent the initial and final states of the alphabets of the systems, respectively.

Using the definition of sequence composition in [11], we can prove that the following statement is equivalent to the above one,

$$\begin{array}{l} \forall stateV, stateV' \bullet (\exists stateV_0 \bullet \{RHS; init\} \\ \qquad (stateV \cup gbv, stateV_0 \cup gbv) \wedge\ c(stateV_0 \cup gbv, stateV' \cup gbv')\ ) \\ \Rightarrow \\ \forall stateW, stateW' \bullet (\exists stateW_0 \bullet \{LHS; init\} \\ \qquad (stateW \cup gbv, stateW_0 \cup gbv) \wedge\ c(stateW_0 \cup gbv, stateW' \cup gbv')\ ) \end{array}$$

As in UTP, $c(x_1, x_2)$ here stands for a predicate for the meaning (semantics) of command c, where x_1 is the state before execution of c, and x_2 the state after the execution. Further, $c_1(x, x_0) \wedge c_2(x_0, x')$ denotes that the final state after the execution of command c_1 is the same as the initial state of c_2, that is the middle state described by x_0.

We use $\mathcal{WS}$ to denote the state space of original design, and $\mathcal{VS}$ for the state space of corresponding refined design, thus $stateW, \ldots \in \mathcal{WS}$, and $stateV, \ldots \in \mathcal{VS}$. Now what we need to do is to find the corresponding states $stateW, stateW_0, stateW'$ in $\mathcal{WS}$ according to the states $stateV, stateV_0, stateV' \in \mathcal{VS}$.

To get the corresponding states, the proof goes through following steps:

1. In the first, take $stateW = stateV$.
2. Find a refinement mapping ρ which maps the refined state space to the original state space[3], then take $stateW_0 = \rho(stateV_0)$.

[3] Please note that the alphabet of the state spaces is the alphabet given in section 2.2.

3. Prove the existence of *stateW′* by showing that for any command c in rCOS, the commuting diagram Fig. 10 holds. With structural induction, we need to show that the commuting diagram holds for all primitive commands. The compound ones can be proved by the structure induction easily. It is easy to check that if this commuting diagram holds, then state *stateW′* exists.

As an example, we show here the proof skeleton for **Rule 1 (Extract Method)** in Section 3. For the work, we need to give first a refinement mapping from the state space of the alphabet of our system (the seven element tuple) to itself. The mapping ρ for this rule is as follows:

$$\rho \mathrel{\widehat{=}} id \oplus \{\mathbf{op}(M) \mapsto \mathbf{op}(M) \backslash \{m_2()\}\}$$

where id stands for the identity mapping. Informally, ρ modifies only $\mathbf{op}(M)$ and keeps all the others unchanged.

Finally, we need to check that for all primitive commands, the commuting diagram in Fig. 10. holds. In this rule, we only add a method $m_2()$ and change the body of $m_1()$, so only $le.m()$ in Section 2.1 should be checked. In the proof, we need to use accessorial mappings Set, $Reset$ and ϕ. The exact definitions of these mappings can be found in [12]. Here are some informal explanations:

- $Set(\cdot)$ and $Reset$ are adjuvant *designs* for initiating and recovering the state environments when the system enters and leaves the local environment of a method call. They can be nested and act as commands to maintain the status of local variables. Although acting as "commands", they are not allowed to use explicitly in programs, but can only be used in semantic definitions and reasoning about programs.
- ϕ defines the semantics of method calls as well as any potential recursive structures. It is useful when we need to expand the semantics of a nested method call.

The proof is as follows.

- If $c = o.m_1()$ where o is an object of M, then we compute the semantics of $m_1()$. On the right hand side

  $$[\![o.m_1()]\!] = \phi_M(m_1()) = Set(M); \phi_M(c); Reset$$

  And on the left hand side we have

  $$\begin{aligned} [\![o.m_1()]\!] &= \phi_M(m_1()) \\ &= Set(M); \phi_M(m_2()); Reset \\ &= Set(M); Set(M); \phi_M(c); Reset; Reset \\ &= Set(M); \phi_M(c); Reset \end{aligned}$$

  This command does not have affect on $\mathsf{op}(M)$, so here ρ acts as id. Thus

  $$\rho; c \sqsubseteq c; \rho$$

- If $c = o.m_2()$, then the right hand is not well formed. This makes the design on the right hand become *false*. Thus the law holds.

From the above example, one can see that once the refinement mapping ρ is given, the checking of the commuting diagram is straightforward by using the evaluation function. Other rules can be proved in the similar manner.

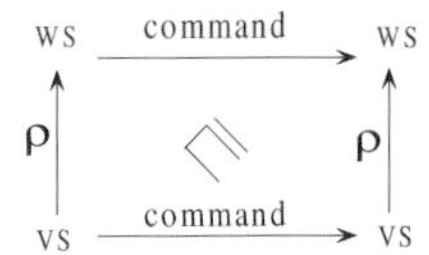

Fig. 10. Comm. Diagram for Class Ref.

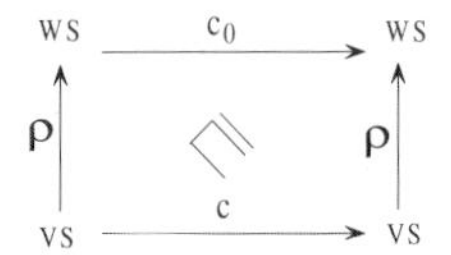

Fig. 11. Comm. Diagram of Program Ref.

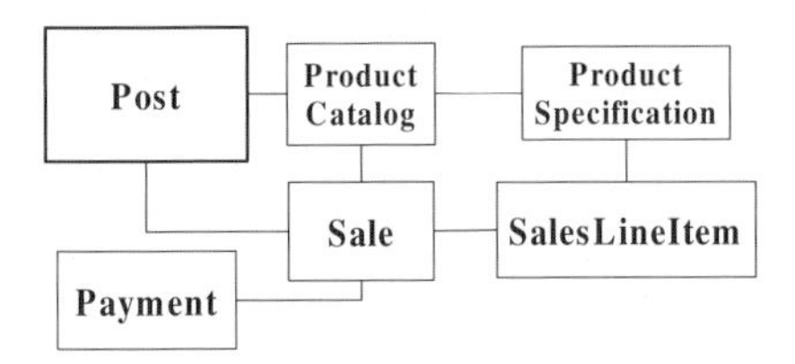

Fig. 12. Initial Structure of POST

5.2 System Refinement Laws

For *System refinement* laws, the strategy is almost the same as for the *Class refinement*. The only difference is in the third step, where we should check c and c_0 of the corresponding *protocol* rather than relative primitive commands, i.e., we have to prove

$$\rho; c_0 \sqsubseteq c; \rho$$

where c and c_0 are the given protocols in the refinement law.

The commuting diagram to be checked is illustrated in Fig. 11. Please notice that what on the arrows here are the original protocol c_0 and new protocol c rather than the primitive commands. We have given the refinement mappings and detailed proofs as well for all of our three pattern-directed rules in the report [15]. The proofs go almost the same manner as shown in Section 5.1. We omit the details here for the space.

6 A Case Study

rCOS is designed to support development of no-trivial software in an incremental way. Here we present a case study for the development of the *POST* system which is originally discussed in [14,5]. We give only an overview of this complicated case study.

POST (Point-Of-Sale Terminal) is a system used to record sales and handle payments, which is typically used in retail stores or supermarkets. It includes several hardware components such as a bar code scanner and a printer, and also a software part. We work on the software part only here. With the refinement laws for OO development, we can incrementally design the system, and finally, implement it on some platform, e.g., Java, or Visual C#.Net, etc.

In the initial design, the class structures of the program is modeled by the class diagram shown in Fig. 12.

In the refinement-based development process, supported by the relatively simple refinement laws in [12], we transform the system by steps, and finally have its *Design Model* depicted in Fig. 13, which is already very close to an executable program.

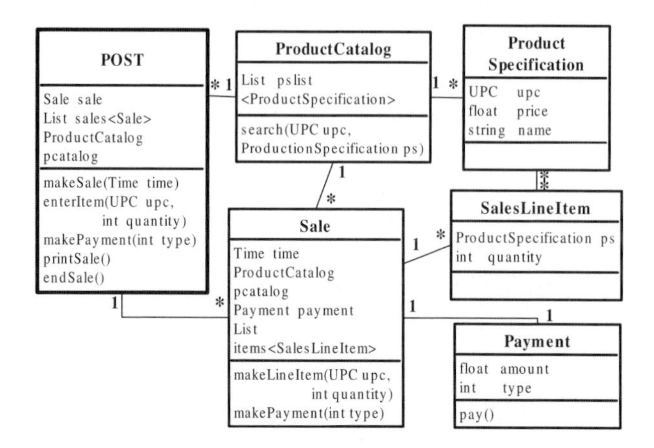

Fig. 13. Design Model of POST

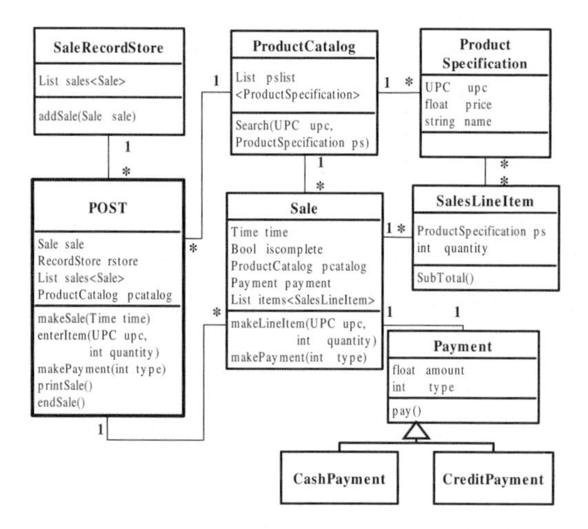

Fig. 14. Refactorred Final Model of POST

However, with a carefully analysis, we see that there are many poor-structured parts in this design model, such as:

1. Class *Post* has an attribute *sales* which is a list to record all the finished sales. It is not suitable to let the interface class maintain such a long list. In fact, this list can be considered as a database for the records. There may be several instances of *Post* working in parallel and need to share the same list. We would better use another class to maintain the list. From this consideration, we may extract a new class *RecordStore*.
2. There may be several ways to make the payment. This fact should be reflected in the design. Thus, in method *pay*() of *Payment*, we use a flag to direct the behavior of the method[4]. This kind of flag-directed code is thought a bad design for lack of flexibility and maintainability. Use the *Strategy Pattern*, we refactor it to a program with polymorphism.

[4] Please refer to [16] for the details.

3. For method *makePayment*() in class *Sale* to computer the total payment, it use now directly the attributes of *SalesLineItem*. It is better if the computation happens in the *SalesLineItem* objects to reduce the coupling between classes. So we would like to extract a method in class *Sale* and then move it to *SalesLineItem*.

Motivated by the feeling of the "bad smells", we use refactoring and pattern-directed refactoring rules to refine the system step by step. The development, or refinement, process is composed of six phases and each phase is done within several steps. The refactoring rules used include, for examples, the **Extract Method**, **Move Method**, and **Strategy** patterns etc. Here we only present the skeleton of the result of the last phase, as Fig. 14. We ignore the code of all the methods in Fig. 13 and Fig. 14..

7 Conclusions and Future Work

Refactoring and Design Pattern are both important concepts and powerful techniques in OO software development [8,13]. However, the definition of them are informal, based on intuition. Formalization of design patterns and refactoring rules is useful for scaling up the tradition refinement calculi, and it is important for tool support to correct by construction of software systems. This is the primary motivation of this work.

Based on rCOS, we present the work on formalization of refactoring rules given in [8], as well as a set of pattern-directed refactoring rules. Proving these rules and patterns precisely requires a formalism that defines object references and sharing. For example, with **Rule** 7, clients can create objects via a reference to a factory rather than invoke a constructor explicitly. This transformation improves the flexibility, reusability and maintainability of the system. In other two pattern-directed refactoring rules presented (**Rule** 8 and **Rule** 9), we also use reference type to support the implicit up-cast. This justifies the use of rCOS which is a refinement calculus with the needed features.

We include also here a detailed discussion on the skeleton of formal proofs of refactoring rules, and a proof example to illustrate the whole procedure. At last, we presented briefly a case study to show the formal development process based on these rules.

Our future work will aim at the automation of these rules and patterns and to integrate them into the rCOS tool for component-based and model driven design [4]. There exist some environments claiming to support refactoring [1]. However, a closer look at them reveals that what they do are only modifying the code rudely under people's command. There is no support to ensure that the modification is semantics-reserved.

In our current work, the proofs of the rules are based on the semantic model of rCOS. We would also like to develop an algebraic proof system for the refactoring and pattern-directed ones, so that many rules can be proved algebraically from a small set of refactoring rules. This will provide calculus of patterns and factoring rules to allows us to relate and compose patterns and rules.

References

1. Refactoringtools, `http://www.refactoring.com/tools.html`
2. Cavalcanti, A.L.C., Naumann, D.: A weakest precondition semantics for refinement of object-oriented programs. IEEE Trans. on Software Engineering 26(8), 713–728 (2000)

3. Chen, Z., He, J., Liu, Z., Zhan, N.: A model of component-based programming. In: Arbab, F., Sirjani, M. (eds.) FSEN 2007. LNCS, vol. 4767, pp. 191–206. Springer, Heidelberg (2007)
4. Chen, Z., Liu, Z., Stolz, V.: The rCOS tool. In: Cuellar, J., Maibaum, T.S.E. (eds.) FM 2008. LNCS, vol. 5014. Springer, Heidelberg (2008)
5. Chen, Z., Liu, Z., Ravn, A.P., Stolz, V., Zhan, N.: Refinement and verification in component-based model driven design. Technical Report 388, UNU/IIST, Macao SAR, China, Science of Computer Programming (submitted, 2008)
6. Cornélio, M.L., Cavalcanti, A.L.C., Sampaio, A.C.A.: Refactoring by Transformation. In: Pro. of REFINE 2002. ENTCS, vol. 70. Elsevier, Amsterdam (2002) (invited Paper)
7. Favre, L., Pereira, C.: Formalizing mda-based refactorings. In: 19th Australian Software Engineering Conference, pp. 377–386. IEEE, Los Alamitos (2008)
8. Fowler, M.: Refectoring, Improving the Design of Existing Code. Addison-Wesley, Reading (2000)
9. Gamma, E., Helm, R., Johnson, R., Vlissides, J.: Design Patterns, Elements of Reusable Object-Oriented Software. Addison Wesley, Reading (1994)
10. He, J., Liu, Z., Li, X., Qin, S.: A relational model for object-oriented designs. In: Chin, W.-N. (ed.) APLAS 2004. LNCS, vol. 3302, pp. 415–436. Springer, Heidelberg (2004)
11. Hoare, C.A.R., He, J.: Unifying Theories of Programming. Prentice-Hall, Englewood Cliffs (1998)
12. Jifeng, H., Li, X., Liu, Z.: rCOS: A refinement calculus for object systems. Theoretical Computer Science 365, 109–142 (2006)
13. Kerievsky, J.: Refactoring to Patterns. Addison-Wesley, Reading (2004)
14. Larman, C.: Applying UML and Patterns. Prentice-Hall International, Englewood Cliffs (2001)
15. Long, Q., He, J., Liu, Z.: Refactoring and pattern-directed refactoring: A formal perspective. Technical Report 318, UNU/IIST, Macao SAR, China (2005)
16. Long, Q., Qiu, Z., Liu, Z., Shao, L., He, J.: POST: A case study for an incremental development in rCOS. In: Van Hung, D., Wirsing, M. (eds.) ICTAC 2005. LNCS, vol. 3722, pp. 498–513. Springer, Heidelberg (2005)
17. Markovic, S., Baar, T.: Refactoring OCL annotated UML class diagrams. Journal Software and Systems Modeling 7, 25–47 (2008)
18. Roberts, D.B.: Practical Analysis for Refactoring. PhD thesis, University of Illinois at Urbana Champain (1999)
19. Silva, L., Sampaio, A., Liu, Z.: Laws of object-orientation with reference semantics (submitted for publication)
20. Tokuda, L.A.: Evolving Object-Oriented Designs with Refactoring. PhD thesis, University of Texas at Austin (1999)
21. Wake, W.C.: Refactoring Workbook. Pearson Education, London (2004)
22. Zhao, L., Liu, X., Liu, Z., Qiu, Z.: Graph transformations for object-oriented refinement. Formal Aspects of Computing (2008) doi:10.1007/s00165-007-0067-y

A Component-Based Access Control Monitor

Zhiming Liu, Charles Morisset, and Volker Stolz

United Nations University
International Institute for Software Technology
P.O. Box 3058, Macau SAR, China
{lzm,morisset,vs}@iist.unu.edu

Abstract. A control of access to information is increasingly becoming necessary as the systems managing this information is more and more open and available through non secure networks. Integrating an access control monitor within a large system is a complex task, since it has to be an "all or nothing" integration. The least error or mistake could lead to jeopardize the whole system. We present a formal specification of an access control monitor using the calculus of refinement of component and object systems (rCOS). We illustrate this implementation with the well known Role Based Access Control (RBAC) policy and we show how to integrate it within a larger system. Keywords: Component, Access Control, RBAC, Composition

1 Introduction

In the design of most information systems, security issues are usually considered as a secondary task. Roughly speaking, the first objective is to design a "working" system and then, if it is possible within the time and budget constraints, try to inject some security mechanisms. As a result of this approach, these mechanisms are often poorly designed and their lack of integration in the global system can cause major flaws. A classical example is when one can find, on a public server, both an SSH server (quite secure) and a Telnet server (usually non secure). This is often due to the fact that the telnet server is installed first, while the server is not public yet and the SSH server is only installed afterwards. The consequence is that not only the server is subject to simple attacks due to the weakness of Telnet, but the server administrator thinks he is protected because he has installed an SSH server and so will not enforce other security mechanisms.

Of course, there exist some domains where security issues are highly considered, usually because human beings or important sums of money are at stake. This is particularly true for the military field, where many security mechanisms have been created, including cryptographic techniques and access control models. In these fields, the question of security is addressed from the beginning, as a part of the global system, which usually ensures a greater confidence in the system.

The component-based approach in rCOS allows us to integrate the security aspect closer into the software engineering process instead of trying to add

T. Margaria and B. Steffen (Eds.): ISoLA 2008, CCIS 17, pp. 339–353, 2008.

it later. Some works already combine UML modeling and security issues, like UMLsec [15]. However, the latter focuses more on the cryptographic problematics while we try to address access control. Basically, the access control problematics consists in defining a policy, that is the set of granted (or denied) accesses to a system by subjects (users, processes, etc) over some objects (files, resources, processes, etc). An access control monitor (or reference monitor) is a program enforcing the policy, that filters all the accesses to grant only the ones allowed and to deny the ones forbidden.

The concept of access control can be split into the *interface* to the access control monitor and its actual *implementation*. As the rCOS software development methodology of component systems uses the familiar features of UML for the development process, we expect that a formalisation of monitoring will make this important aspect more accessible to practitioners and students.

But not only allows this to talk about security in familiar terms to software engineers, it also eliminates the disconnect between the software and reasoning about security aspects that might introduce additional errors when both were handled in different formalisms.

By using the notion of rCOS component interfaces, we can make sure that the monitor component is at least used syntactically correct and according to its protocol, that is the sequence of possible traces. Even the implementation of a monitor profits from being modeled in rCOS: we can give a high-level, mathematical specification and use the rCOS refinement techniques to obtain an executable implementation [4,19]. Additionally, the available formal methods for rCOS, like the verification of component composition through process algebra and model checking, allows reasoning about the correctness and properties of the composition of components realising access control with components providing the system behaviour that is to be protected.

From a normative point view, according to the Common Criteria [2], which is one of the authoritative references in the domain of safety and security systems, a reference monitor is an abstract machine which enforces the access control policies in a system and it should have the three following properties:

- unsafe subjects cannot interfere with it,
- unsafe subjects cannot circumvent its controls,
- it is simple enough to be analyzed and its behaviour understood.

We present here an approach addressing these properties. The main contributions of this paper are:

- the implementation of an access control model based on a recent formalization, which clearly separates the notion of policy and the one of implementation of a policy, and introduces some new concepts, such as the semantics of requests,
- another case study of the rCOS tool, showing how its features can be successfully applied to the access control problematics.

We first introduce in section 2 a formalisation of access control policies and models, with the example of the Role Based Access Control (RBAC) policy.

This formalisation, together with the different proofs, ensures that the monitor behaviour is understood and could be analyzed. It also guarantees that unsafe subjects cannot interfere with it, at least on the design level. Indeed, our approach, as most of classical software engineering approaches, does not ensure that the implementation will not be modified at run-time, or that the hardware the system is running on is safe. Then, in section 3, we outline the main features of rCOS and section 4 gives a description of a specification of the access control monitor within rCOS. Thanks to the component-based approach, it is possible to ensure that the monitor cannot be circumvented by hiding the non secure interfaces and integrating the monitor directly into the system. Finally, we present in this section a way to integrate such a monitor in a larger system.

2 Defining Access Control Models

In this section, we present a way to define access control systems, based on two main concepts: policy and model. Due to space limitation, we only give here an overview, a complete definition can be found in [14,21]. The *policy* is the description of the system on which it is enforced, defined as a state machine together with the notion of secure states. Hence, an access control policy is considered here as a functional property that a state machine must satisfy. Of course, the definition of the policy also includes all the information relevant to the definition of the system, such as subjects, objects, security information, etc. At this point, a policy can be seen as "static", since it is expressed over states, and a state is a snapshot of the system. We then introduce the notion of the *model*, which is basically a policy together with a set of requests (and, as we will see later, the semantics of these requests). These requests are a way for subjects to access objects. Lastly, it is possible to define an implementation (or several) for a model, through a transition function and a set of initial states. Intuitively, this implementation corresponds to a reference monitor and should be proved correct with respect to the security policy, that is, returning a secure state for any secure state and any request.

2.1 Access Control Policy

We first define the main entities of a system: $\mathcal{S}$ is the set of subjects (active entities initiating actions in the system), $\mathcal{O}$ is the set of objects (passive entities on which actions are made) and $\mathcal{A}$ is the set of access modes (read, write, append, etc). In this paper, we represent an access by a triple (s, o, a) expressing that a subject s accesses an object o according to the access mode a. Hence, we define the set of accesses $\mathbb{A}$ as the Cartesian product $\mathcal{S} \times \mathcal{O} \times \mathcal{A}$. Other approaches are possible to represent accesses. For example, in order to deal with "joint access" of a group of subjects over an object, as in [20], $\mathbb{A}$ can be defined as $(\wp(\mathcal{S})\backslash\{\emptyset\}) \times \mathcal{O} \times \wp(\mathcal{A})$.

Then we can define an access control policy $\mathbb{P}[\rho] = (\mathcal{S}, \mathcal{O}, \mathcal{A}, \Sigma, \Omega)$, where ρ is the security parameter (that is all the information needed to define the policy),

$\mathcal{S}$ the set of subjects, $\mathcal{O}$ the set of objects, $\mathcal{A}$ the set of access modes, Σ the set of states and Ω the security predicate, characterizing the secure states.

Role-Based Access Control models are a set of fairly new models first introduced in the nineties. The key concept of theses models is the notion of a role, which can be seen as an abstraction of the one of subject. Intuitively, a subject can have many roles and an object can be accessed by many roles. This indirection eases the management of subjects within a system, since the authorizations are related to roles (which are supposed not to change a lot) rather than subjects (who can change a lot). We give here a version of RBAC based on the RBAC92 model [7], in order to simplify the presentation, but some more complex versions can be found, as RBAC96 [24] extends RBAC92 with the addition of users (different from the subjects) and a roles hierarchy defined as a partial order. We write $\rho_{\mathsf{rbac}} = \mathsf{R}$ for the security parameter of RBAC, where R is the set of roles. A state $\sigma \in \Sigma_{\mathsf{rbac}}$ is a tuple $\sigma = (m, \mathsf{UA}, \mathsf{PA}, \mathit{roles})$ where m is the set of current accesses, $\mathsf{UA} \subseteq \mathcal{S} \times \mathsf{R}$ is the relation specifying which subject can activate which roles, $\mathsf{PA} \subseteq (\mathcal{O} \times \mathcal{A}) \times \mathsf{R}$ is the relation associating permissions (i.e. pairs $(o, a) \in \mathcal{O} \times \mathcal{A}$) to roles, and $\mathit{roles} : \mathcal{S} \to \wp(\mathsf{R})$ specifies the set of roles that have been activated by a subject. Hence, a subject may endorse many roles, as defined by UA, but does not have to activate all of them at the same time. The RBAC policy is specified by the predicate Ω_{rbac} as follows. Given a state $\sigma = (m, \mathsf{UA}, \mathsf{PA}, \mathit{roles})$, $\Omega_{\mathsf{rbac}}(\sigma)$ holds iff the two following properties are satisfied.

$$\forall s \in \mathcal{S} \quad \{(s, r) \mid r \in \mathit{roles}(s)\} \subseteq \mathsf{UA}$$
$$\forall s \in \mathcal{S}\ \forall o \in \mathcal{O}\ \forall a \in \mathcal{A} \quad (s, o, a) \in m \Rightarrow \exists r \in \mathsf{R}\ (r \in \mathit{roles}(s) \wedge ((o, a), r) \in \mathsf{PA})$$

We write $\mathbb{P}_{\mathsf{rbac}}[\rho_{\mathsf{rbac}}] = (\mathcal{S}, \mathcal{O}, \mathcal{A}, \Sigma_{\mathsf{rbac}}, \Omega_{\mathsf{rbac}})$ for the RBAC policy.

2.2 Access Control Model

As we said previously, a language of requests provides to the subjects of a system a way to access to objects. We write $\mathcal{R}$ for the set of requests. Most access control models consider at least the set $\mathcal{R}^{acc} = \{\langle +, s, o, a\rangle, \langle -, s, o, a\rangle\}$ allowing to express that the subject s asks to get (+) or to release (-) an access over the object o according to the access mode a. Depending of the access control model, there can also exist some "administrative" requests allowing to modify security functions of a state. We introduce here the requests allowing to change the active roles of a subject: $\mathcal{R}^{adm} = \{\langle +, s, r\rangle, \langle -, s, r\rangle\}$. The set of requests considered is then $\mathcal{R}^{rbac} = \mathcal{R}^{acc} \cup \mathcal{R}^{adm}$. We make here a clear distinction between accesses and requests. An access is the internal representation of actions currently done in the system and is authorized or not according to the security policy. A request is an action that a subject has to submit and is granted or not by an implementation. However, requests are usually strongly related to accesses, and to make explicit this relation, we introduce a notion of "weak" semantics of requests as a relation $[\![\mathcal{R}]\!]_\Sigma \subseteq \mathcal{R} \times \Sigma$. Given a request R and a state σ, the statement $(R, \sigma) \in [\![\mathcal{R}]\!]_\Sigma$ characterizes the properties that a state σ must satisfy when it is obtained by applying (in a successful way) the request R over another state. For $\mathcal{R}^{rbac}$, we can define $[\![\mathcal{R}^{rbac}]\!]_\Sigma$ as follows:

$$
\begin{array}{l}
(\langle +, s, o, a\rangle, \sigma) \in [\![\mathcal{R}^{rbac}]\!]_\Sigma \Leftrightarrow (s, o, a) \in \Lambda(\sigma) \\
(\langle -, s, o, a\rangle, \sigma) \in [\![\mathcal{R}^{rbac}]\!]_\Sigma \Leftrightarrow (s, o, a) \notin \Lambda(\sigma) \\
(\langle +, s, r\rangle, (m, \mathsf{UA}, \mathsf{PA}, roles)) \in [\![\mathcal{R}^{rbac}]\!]_\Sigma \Leftrightarrow r \in roles(s) \\
(\langle -, s, r\rangle, (m, \mathsf{UA}, \mathsf{PA}, roles)) \in [\![\mathcal{R}^{rbac}]\!]_\Sigma \Leftrightarrow r \notin roles(s)
\end{array}
$$

where $\Lambda(\sigma)$ denotes the set of all current accesses in σ. Note that such an approach to express a part of the semantics of requests only specifies the properties that a state must satisfy but does not describe how such a state has been changed. We introduce in [14,21] a semantical characterisation of such modifications. Due to space limitation, we omit here this technical part which is not essential at this level of specification.

Given a security parameter ρ, an access control model $\mathbb{M}[\rho]$ is defined by a tuple $\mathbb{M}[\rho] = (\mathbb{P}[\rho], [\![\mathcal{R}]\!]_\Sigma)$ where $\mathbb{P}[\rho] = (\mathcal{S}, \mathcal{O}, \mathcal{A}, \Sigma, \Omega)$ is an access control policy, $\mathcal{R}$ is a set of requests, and $[\![\mathcal{R}]\!]_\Sigma \subseteq \mathcal{R} \times \Sigma$ is a relation specifying the semantics of requests. For example, we write $\mathbb{M}_{\mathsf{rbac}}[\rho_{\mathsf{rbac}}] = (\mathbb{P}_{\mathsf{rbac}}[\rho_{\mathsf{rbac}}], [\![\mathcal{R}^{rbac}]\!]_{\Sigma_{\mathsf{rbac}}})$ for the RBAC model.

Implementing a model $\mathbb{M}[\rho]$ consists in defining both a set Σ_I of *initial states* and a *transition function* $\tau : \mathcal{R} \times \Sigma \to \mathcal{D} \times \Sigma$ (where $\mathcal{D} = \{\mathsf{yes}, \mathsf{no}\}$ are the answers) which allows moving from a state to another state of the system according to a request in $\mathcal{R}$. We write (τ, Σ_I) for such an implementation and $\Gamma_\tau(E)$ for the set of reachable states by τ from states occurring in E. For example, given the set of initial states $\Sigma_I^{\mathsf{rbac}} = \{\sigma \in \Sigma_{\mathsf{rbac}} \mid \Lambda(\sigma) = \emptyset\}$, we introduce the implementation $(\tau_{\mathsf{rbac}}, \Sigma_I^{\mathsf{rbac}})$ of $\mathbb{M}_{\mathsf{rbac}}[\rho_{\mathsf{rbac}}]$ where τ_{rbac} is defined in table 1 and where we use the following denotations:

$$
(roles \oplus (s', r))(s) = \begin{cases} roles(s) \cup \{r\} & \text{if } s = s' \\ roles(s) & \text{otherwise} \end{cases}
$$

$$
(roles \ominus (s', r))(s) = \begin{cases} roles(s) \setminus \{r\} & \text{if } s = s' \\ roles(s) & \text{otherwise} \end{cases}
$$

Due to the huge number of states, we do not draw here the corresponding automaton. In [21,10], this implementation is proved to be correct according to both the policy and the semantics of requests. More formally, we prove that each state reachable from an initial state is secure (i.e. $\Gamma_\tau(\Sigma_I) \subseteq \{\sigma \in \Sigma \mid \Omega(\sigma)\}$) and that for all $\sigma_1, \sigma_2 \in \Sigma$, and $R \in \mathcal{R}$, if $\tau(R, \sigma_1) = (\mathsf{yes}, \sigma_2)$, then $(R, \sigma_2) \in [\![\mathcal{R}]\!]_\Sigma$.

This definition of the RBAC model within our formal framework ensures that when a request is authorized, then the security policy is not violated. An implementation of this model is defined in Focal [10], which is a IDE combining a functional language, a specification language and a theorem prover. We now want to implement it following a component-based approach, and we use the rCOS methodology, which we introduce in the next section.

Table 1. Implementation of the RBAC Model

$$\tau_{\mathsf{rbac}}(R, (m, \mathsf{UA}, \mathsf{PA}, roles))$$

$$= \begin{cases} (\mathsf{yes}, (m \cup \{(s,o,a)\}, \mathsf{UA}, \mathsf{PA}, roles)) \\ \text{if } R = \langle +, s, o, a\rangle \\ \wedge\ \exists r \in \mathsf{R} \quad r \in roles(s) \wedge ((o,a), r) \in \mathsf{PA} \\ \\ (\mathsf{yes}, (m \setminus \{(s,o,a)\}, \mathsf{UA}, \mathsf{PA}, roles)) \\ \text{if } R = \langle -, s, o, a\rangle \\ \\ (\mathsf{yes}, (m, \mathsf{UA}, \mathsf{PA}, roles \oplus (s,r))) \\ \text{if } R = \langle +, s, r\rangle \\ \wedge\ (s,r) \in \mathsf{UA} \\ \\ (\mathsf{yes}, (m, \mathsf{UA}, \mathsf{PA}, roles \ominus (s,r))) \\ \text{if } R = \langle -, s, r\rangle \\ \\ (\mathsf{no}, (m, \mathsf{UA}, \mathsf{PA}, roles)) \quad \text{otherwise} \end{cases}$$

3 Models and Their Refinement and Composition

For a formal method and its tool support to be practically effective, it will have to be integrated with a *development process* and CASE tools, such as MasterCraft [26,18]. For these purposes, the rCOS semantic theory defines the important concepts and artifacts in the domain of object-oriented and component-based software engineering, like *classes, objects, components, interfaces, contracts, composition* (*connectors*), *coordination* and *glue*. It provides the behavioral semantics of these concepts with high level rules for refinement and verification.

Interfaces, Contracts and Components. Component-based software engineering creates new software by combining prefabricated components with programs that provide both glue between the components, and new functionality [5]. Furthermore, there seems to be no disagreement on the following interrelated properties that *components* enjoy.

1. *Black-box composability*, *substitutability* and *reusability*: "a component is a unit of composition with contractually specified interfaces and fully explicit context dependencies that can be deployed independently and is subject to third party composition" [25].
2. *Independent development*: components can be designed, implemented, verified, validated and deployed independently.
3. *Interoperability*: components can be implemented in different programming languages and paradigms; but they can be composed, be glued together and cooperate with each other. These features require that a component has a black-box specification of what it provides to and what it requires from its environment [25].

Components and Processes. We distinguish *service components* from *process components* [12,3]. A service component, simply called a component, provides computational services to the environments through their *provided interfaces.* However, the implementation of a provided service may also require services from other components. Thus, a component can have *required interfaces*, and a component with required interfaces is called an *open components* and one without required interfaces is called a *closed component.* A distinct feature of the rCOS definition of a component is that contracts are associated to the provided interfaces and the required interfaces separately. This separation makes the specification of a component a *truly black-box specification*, even without the need to know the information about the temporal dependency between a provided service and a required service.

A process component, simply called a process, does not provide services to other components. Instead it *coordinates* and *glues* components so that the service components become suitable for a specific application. Therefore, a process only has *required interfaces* and it *actively* invokes services of other components. A component on the other hand, though it may contain coordinating processes inside it, is passive and only interacts with the outside when a provided service is requested. We will see that compositions among components are different from their compositions with processes and compositions of processes [3]. We also proved in [3] the composition of a component and a process is a component.

In rCOS, a process is used to model programs that coordinate and schedule services of components, programs that are used to *glue* components together to make new components, and to model application tasks that are realized by requesting services from components.

Contracts of Interfaces. An *interface* provides the *syntactic type information* for an interaction point of a component. It consists of two parts: the *fields declaration section*, that introduces a set of variables with their types, and the *method declaration section*, that defines a set of method signatures. Each signature is of the form $m(T_1\ in; T_2\ out)$, where T_1 and T_2 are type names, *in* stands for an input parameter, and *out* stands for an output parameter.

Current practical component technologies provide syntactical aspects of interfaces only and leave the semantics to informal conventions and comments. This is obviously not enough for rigorous verification and validation. For this, we define the notion of *contracts* of interfaces.

The *contracts* of the interfaces of a component describe what is needed for the component to be *used* in building and maintaining software systems. The description of an interface must contain information about the viewpoints among, for example *functionality*, *behavior*, *protocols*, *safety*, *reliability*, *real-time*, *power*, *bandwidth*, *memory consumption* and *communication mechanisms*, that are needed for composing the component in the given architecture for the application of the system. However, this description can be incremental in the sense that newly required properties or view points can be added when needed according to the application [11].

In the current version of rCOS, a *contract of an interface* specifies the semantics of the interface:

- The *initial condition* defines the allowable starting states.
- The *functionality specification* of each method *op* is a *reactive design* of the form $g\&p \vdash R$. In Hoare and He's UTP [13], g is called the *guard* for a *synchronization* with the environment, p is called the *precondition* and R the *postcondition* of the design. An invocation to *op* when the guard is false will be blocked. When the guard is true, the execution will take place and terminate in a state satisfying the postcondition R if the precondition p holds, otherwise the execution diverges.
- The *interaction protocol*, specifies traces of method invocations, for the environment to follow when interacting with component via the interface.

The *domain of the reactive designs* forms a complete lattice with the predicate implication as the partial order, and it is closed under the convention programming compositions of sequential composition, condition choice, non-deterministic choice and the fixed point of iteration. These compositions are also monotonic.

A contract has a *failure-divergence* semantics with that the refinement relation between contracts is defined in the same way as CSP refinement under this semantics [22]. A complete proof technique using upwards and downwards simulation is established [3].

We can divide the fields (that are the state variables) of an interface into *data variables* and *control flow variables*, the reactive designs can be decomposed into *design* of the synchronisation control the design of *data functionality*. The designs of the flow of control are *reactive designs* about the change of control states, and the designs of the data functionality are simply pre and post conditions.

4 Access Control Component

Defining a reference monitor component from the previous formalisation requires a slight adaptation. Indeed, most of the concepts introduced in section 2 are defined in a formal way, using a set-based denotation and a functional approach. Since rCOS follows an object-oriented approach, we need to adapt these concepts. Roughly speaking, we first introduce a new class for every set, as described in figure 1. Rather than defining functions to associate roles to a subject, we use the object-oriented approach by defining a UML association between the class `Subject` and the class `Role`, with the target `roles: Role[*] {unique}`. Note that we define the relation `UA` as an attribute of the class `Subject` rather than as another association, to clarify the presentation. We define the permissions by introducing the method `pa(r:Role, m:Mode ; ret:`*boolean*`)`, where `r` and `m` are input parameters and `ret` is the output parameter, in the class `Object`: `o.pa(r,m;ret)` will set `ret` to `true` if the role `r` can access the object `o` according to the access mode `m`.

Moreover, a class is defined for every kind of request and as a direct consequence, the reference monitor contains four different methods, that we will refer

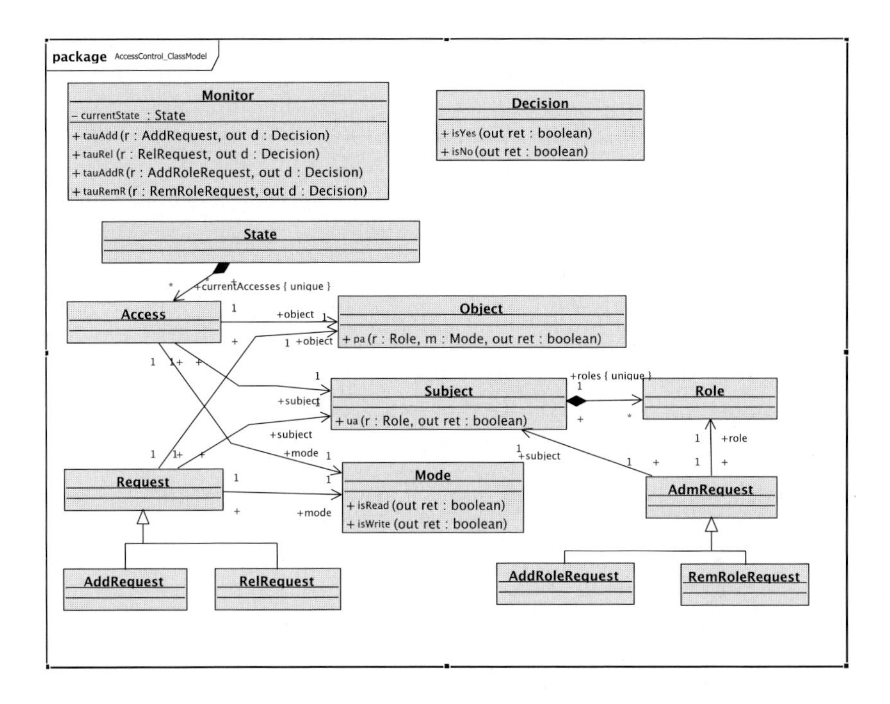

Fig. 1. Class Diagram in the rCOS Modeler

to below as the τ methods, each one of them treating a different type of request. The set of current accesses belongs to the internal state of the monitor and so we remove the reference to states in the parameters of the τ methods, which take a request `r` and return a decision `d`.

To stick more to the formal definition, we would have to also define a global method τ, which would take any type of request and would call the appropriate method according to the type. Such a method is however not necessary, so we do not include it in the interface `ValReq`.

```
component Monitor {
  provided interface ValReq {
    public tauAdd(AddRequest r ; Decision d);
    public tauRel(RelRequest r ; Decision d);
    public tauAddR(AddRoleRequest r ; Decision d);
    public tauRemR(RelRoleRequest r ; Decision d); }}
```

The controller class of this component (i.e. the class implementing the interface) is the class `Monitor`, which contains the current state, itself containing the set of current accesses. The security predicate is expressed as a class invariant, which ensures that the set of current accesses is always correct.

```
public class Monitor {
  public State currentState;
  invariant :   ∀ Subject s,  ∀ Role r ∈ s.roles: s.ua(r)
              ∧ ∀ Access a ∈ currentState.currentAccesses:
                ∃ Role r ∈ a.subject.roles: a.object.pa(r, a.mode);
```

Note that we use here the simplified notation of rCOS about output parameters: when there is only one output parameter, it can be considered as a return parameter like in usual programming languages. In the same way, to ease the reading of this paper, we use mathematical denotations for the logical connectors and the set operations instead of the rCOS keywords.

We are now in position to specify in the class `Monitor` the four τ methods defined in the interface `ValReq`. We specify them to respect the semantics of requests.

```
public tauAdd(AddRequest r ; Decision d) {
[ ⊢ d'.isYes() ⇒ ∃ Access a ∈ currentState'.currentAccesses:
                r.subject = a.subject ∧ r.object = a.object ∧ r.mode = a.mode]
}
```

where `d'` denotes the value of the variable `d` after the evaluation of the method.

```
public tauRel(RelRequest r ; Decision d) {
[ ⊢ d'.isYes() ⇒ ∀ Access a ∈ currentState'.currentAccesses:
                r.subject ≠ a.subject ∨ r.object ≠ a.object ∨ r.mode ≠ a.mode]
}
```

```
public tauAddR(AddRoleRequest r ; Decision d) {
[ ⊢ d'.isYes() ⇒ r.role ∈ r.subject.roles']
}
```

```
public tauRemR(RemRoleRequest r ; Decision d) {
[ ⊢ d'.isYes() ⇒ r.role ∉ r.subject.roles']
}
```

The notation $[\vdash p]$ stands for the design with the precondition `true` and the postcondition p. This specification ensures that the methods `tauAdd`, `tauRel`, `tauAddR` and `tauRemR` behave correctly according to the requests. Moreover, the separation of the definition of the security policy from the specification of these methods eases the reusability of the component. Indeed, it is possible to modify the security policy without changing this specification, if the considered requests are the same. This approach introduces a level of indirection, since these methods are not specified to respect the security policy, but rather to change the set of current accesses according to the requests, and this set is required to respect the security policy by the invariant.

Note that we present here a simple design for a reference monitor, in the sense that there is no need for defining a protocol between these methods. However, it is possible to define several global τ functions, each one of them applied in a different "security mode".

For instance, let us consider that our component relies upon an authentication mechanism (as a login/password system). If an attack is detected against this mechanism, like a brute-force attack, where an opponent tries every possible password for a given login, the system could decide to prevent any risk by denying any access asked by non-root subjects (we consider here that the root user cannot connect from the outside and so it is less prone to a brute force attack). In this case, a special mode "brute-force attack detected" could be switched on, and the method used to authorize accesses would be a more restrictive one. Such an approach would imply to define a protocol for the interface, corresponding to the several modes that could be switched on. Here again, specifying the policy as an invariant helps, since it is defined only once, and as long as the different methods `tau` respect the semantics of requests, they also respect the policy.

The definition of the different methods in the rCOS tool according to the formal definition given in table 1 and both refining the previously defined design and respecting the class invariant could be the following one.

```
public tauAdd(AddRequest r ; Decision d) {
  for (Role ro : r.subject.roles){
      if (r.object.pa(ro, r.mode))
      then {
        currentState.currentAccesses.add(r.subject, r.object, r.mode);
        return yes;
      }
  }
  return no;
}


public tauRel(RelRequest r ; Decision d) {
  currentState.currentAccesses.remove(r.subject, r.object, r.mode);
  return yes;
}


public tauAddR(AddRoleRequest r ; Decision d) {
  if (r.subject.ua(r.role)){
     r.subject.roles.add(r.subject);
     return yes;
   }
  return no;
}


public tauRemR(RemRoleRequest r ; Decision d) {
  r.subject.roles.remove(r.subject);
  return yes;
}
```

These implementations have been obtained using the rCOS refinement techniques [4,19]. They are proved to be correct by showing that the predicate corresponding to their semantics logically implies the previous specifications. Current work in the rCOS tool consists in integrating a theorem prover, in order to formally prove this implication.

Since we do not require the monitor to be complete, that is, to accept every correct request, the statement `return no` is also a valid implementation for each of the previous methods.

Integration. The reference monitor component described in the previous subsection acts as an oracle: its interface allows submitting a request which is either granted or denied. The set of current accesses stored in the internal state is only used to describe the policy. Indeed, some policies (e.g. Bell and LaPadula [16] or the Chinese Wall [1]) are defined according to the current accesses, to avoid some forbidden flows of information between objects. But in most of the cases, the interface of the reference monitor is not directly called by the user of the system. For instance, let us consider a Database Management System (DBMS), where the subjects of the monitor are the users of the database and the objects are the tables. It is also possible to consider an object as a tuple, but it can raise some problems with polyinstantiation [23]. A user executes an SQL query, which should be translated in a request $\langle +, s, o, a \rangle$, where s is the subject associated with the user (usually known in the environment from the connection), o is the concerned table and a is defined according to the query.

A DBMS can be described as the following component (we consider here only the SQL queries `INSERT, SELECT, UPDATE`).

```
component DBMS {
  provided interface SQLQuery {
    public connect (string id, string password; string con);
    public select (string con, string query; boolean ok);
    public insert (string con, string query; boolean ok);
    public update (string con, string query; boolean ok);
    public disconnect (string con);
  }
}
```

The method `connect` allows a user to connect to the DBMS using his login/password, and get a connection identifier, the methods `select, insert` and `update` allow to respectively execute a `SELECT`, an `INSERT` and an `UPDATE` SQL query over a connection identifier and `disconnect` closes a connection identifier.

The problem is the following one: we want to keep this interface for the user, in order to be transparent, and at the same time filter the SQL queries in order to grant only the ones respecting the security policy. We introduce a component `Proxy` as described in figure 2, which composes the `Monitor` and `DBMS` components (and hides their interfaces) and provides the same interface as `DBMS`.

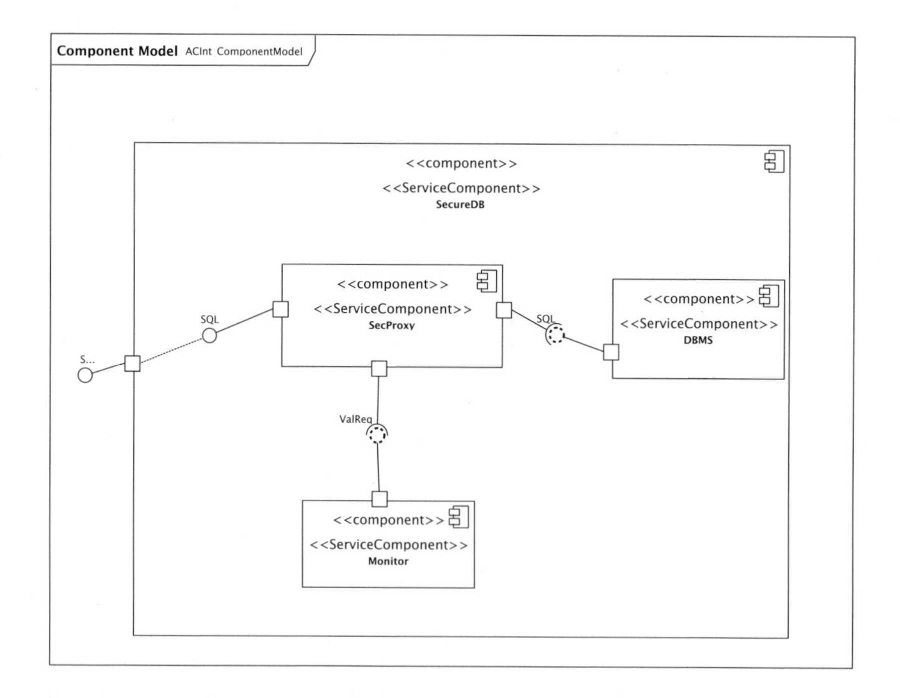

Fig. 2. Integration of a monitor in a database

```
component Proxy {
  provided interface SQLQuery { ... }
  composition : (Monitor || DBMS) \ { DBMS.SQLQuery, Monitor.ValReq }
}
```

The controller class of `Proxy` implements the interface `SQLQuery` and the pseudo-code for the method `select` is the following one.

```
public select(string con, string query; boolean ok) {
  Subject s := subject associated with the user;
  Object o := table concerned by the query;
  if (Monitor.valReq.tauAdd(⟨+, s, o, r⟩) = yes)
  then return DBMS.SQLQuery.select(con, query)
  else return false;
}
```

The method `insert` (resp. `update`) is defined in a similar way, except that the request passed to `tauAdd` is $\langle +, s, o, \mathsf{w} \rangle$ (resp. both $\langle +, s, o, \mathsf{r} \rangle$ and $\langle +, s, o, \mathsf{w} \rangle$).

With the previous definition, the accesses are never released, which is not a problem with the usual RBAC model, but which could be one with other policies such as the one of Bell and LaPadula. To address this issue, it is possible to release the accesses either at the end of the method, after the call to the DBMS or when the user disconnects from the DBMS.

5 Conclusion

By following a component-based approach to design and implement an access control reference monitor, we address some major issues as stated by the Common Criteria. Indeed, the mechanisms of composition and interfaces hiding allow to have a real black-box component, thus preventing unsafe subjects to interfere with it or to circumvent its controls. Moreover, the definition of a `Proxy` component makes its use transparent and easily integrable in a larger system, as a Database Management System. Our development relies upon a sound formal definition, which guarantees the correctness of the specification, since the rCOS tool allows integrating the formal aspect and will, in the future, use external tools, like model-checking or theorem proving, to verify and validate that the implementation meets the specification. Indeed, the proof of the correctness of the monitor is currently only done "on the paper", by induction over the reachable states. However, an objective of the rCOS Tool is to generate JML [17] specifications, and by using a tool like Krakatoa [8], which generates the proof obligations related to pre- and post-conditions and to class invariants, we could prove the correctness of the monitor with a theorem prover.

We have implemented here the RBAC policy, but thanks to the formal framework our work is based on, this approach could be used to define other policies, some of them are even already defined within this framework (e.g. Bell and LaPadula, the Chinese Wall, RBAC96, Delegation-Based, Lampson, ACL, Capabilities).

There are several ways to extend this work. For instance, nothing is said about the way to associate subjects and objects with roles in the example. Though it is not possible to define them in the most general case, it could be possible to determine them from use cases [6].

Finally, from a more practical point of view, a library of access control components could be defined. Such a library could allow software engineers with no experience in security and/or formal methods to easily use and enforce certified reference monitors.

Acknowledgements

Many thanks to Julien Blond and Mathieu Jaume for their precious help on this subject. This work was supported by the project HTTS funded by the Macao Science and Technology Development Fund and by the projects NSFC-60673114 and 863 of China 2006AA01Z165.

References

1. Brewer, D.F.C., Nash, M.J.: The Chinese wall security policy. In: Proc. IEEE Symposium on Security and Privacy, pp. 206–214 (1989)
2. Common Criteria for Information Technology Security Evaluation, `http://www.commoncriteriaportal.org/`
3. Chen, X., He, J., Liu, Z., Zhan, N.: A model of component-based programming. In: Arbab, F., Sirjani, M. (eds.) FSEN 2007. LNCS, vol. 4767, pp. 191–206. Springer, Heidelberg (2007)
4. Chen, Z., Liu, Z., Stolz, V.: The rCOS tool. In: Fitzgerald, et al. (eds.) [9]
5. de Alfaro, L., Henzinger, T.: Interface automata. In: Proc. of the 9th Annual Symposium on Foundations of Software Engineering, pp. 109–120. ACM press, New York (2001)
6. Fernandez, E.B., Hawkins, J.C.: Determining role rights from use cases. In: RBAC 1997: Proc. of the second ACM workshop on Role-based access control, pp. 121–125. ACM, New York (1997)
7. Ferraiolo, D.F., Kuhn, D.R.: Role-based access control. In: Proceedings of the 15th National Computer Security Conference (1992)
8. Filliâtre, J.-C., Marché, C.: The Why/Krakatoa/Caduceus platform for deductive program verification. In: 19th International Conference on Computer Aided Verification. Springer, Berlin (2007)
9. Fitzgerald, J., Larsen, P.G., Sahara, S. (eds.): Modelling and Analysis in VDM: Proceedings of the Fourth VDM/Overture Workshop, number CS-TR-1099 in Technical Report Series. Newcastle University (May 2008)
10. Habib, L.: Formalisation, comparaison et implantation d'un modèle de contrôle d'accès à base de rôles. Master's thesis, UPMC, Paris, France (2007)
11. He, J., Li, X., Liu, Z.: Component-based software engineering. In: Van Hung, D., Wirsing, M. (eds.) ICTAC 2005. LNCS, vol. 3722, pp. 70–95. Springer, Heidelberg (2005)
12. He, J., Li, X., Liu, Z.: A theory of reactive components. Electr. Notes Theor. Comput. Sci. 160, 173–195 (2006)
13. Hoare, C., He, J.: Unifying Theories of Programming. Prentice-Hall, Englewood Cliffs (1998)
14. Jaume, M., Morisset, C.: On specifying, implementing and comparing access control models. A Semantical Framework. Technical report, Univ. Paris 6, LIP6 (2007)

15. Jürjens, J.: UMLsec: Extending UML for secure systems development. In: Jézéquel, J.-M., Hussmann, H., Cook, S. (eds.) UML 2002. LNCS, vol. 2460, pp. 412–425. Springer, Heidelberg (2002)
16. LaPadula, L., Bell, D.: Secure Computer Systems: A Mathematical Model. Journal of Computer Security 4, 239–263 (1996)
17. Leavens, G.T.: Jml's rich, inherited specifications for behavioral subtypes. In: Liu, Z., He, J. (eds.) ICFEM 2006. LNCS, vol. 4260, pp. 2–34. Springer, Heidelberg (2006)
18. Liu, Z., Mencl, V., Ravn, A.P., Yang, L.: Harnessing theories for tool support. In: Intl. Symp. on Leveraging Applications of Formal Methods, Verification and Validation (ISoLA 2006), full version as UNU-IIST Technical Report 343 (August 2006), http://www.iist.unu.edu
19. Liu, Z., Stolz, V.: The rCOS method in a nutshell. In: Fitzgerald, et al. (eds.) [9]
20. McLean.: The algebra of security. In: Proc. IEEE Symposium on Security and Privacy, pp. 2–7. IEEE Computer Society Press, Los Alamitos (1988)
21. Morisset, C.: Sémantique des systèmes de contrôle d'accès. PhD thesis, Université Pierre et Marie Curie - Paris 6 (2007)
22. Roscoe, A.: Theory and Practice of Concurrency. Prentice-Hall, Englewood Cliffs (1997)
23. Sandhu, R., Chen, F.: The multilevel relational (mlr) data model. ACM Trans. Inf. Syst. Secur. 1(1), 93–132 (1998)
24. Sandhu, R.S., Coyne, E.J., Feinstein, H.L., Youman, C.E.: Role-based access control models. IEEE Computer 29(2), 38–47 (1996)
25. Szyperski, C.: Component Software: Beyond Object-Oriented Programming. Addison-Wesley, Reading (1997)
26. Tata Consultancy Services. Mastercraft, http://www.tata-mastercraft.com/

Navigating the Requirements Jungle*

Boris Langer[1] and Michael Tautschnig[2]

[1] Diehl Aerospace GmbH
An der Sandelmühle 13, 60439 Frankfurt, Germany
[2] Institut für Informatik
Technische Universität Darmstadt
Hochschulstr. 10, 64289 Darmstadt, Germany

Abstract. Research on validation and verification of requirements specifications has thus far focused on functional properties. Yet, in embedded systems, functional requirements constitute only a small fraction of the properties that must hold to guarantee proper and safe operation of the system under design.

In this paper we try to shine some light on the kinds of requirements occurring in current embedded systems design processes. We present a set of categories together with real-life examples. For each of them, we briefly describe possible approaches towards formal modeling and automated verification of the respective properties.

1 Introduction

Control systems deployed in commercial aircrafts, emergency systems installed in nuclear power plants, remote-controlled surgery robots in hospitals, and automated braking assistants in automobiles are just a few examples of modern safety-critical systems. During the last decades, humans are increasingly poised to hand the responsibility for their lives over to electronic systems.

The growing complexity of these systems, and the fact that a failure of a single subsystem may have fatal consequences for the users, forces the industry to reconsider the underlying development process to obtain products of the required quality.

The large scale of the systems inevitably requires a great number of stakeholders. Communication of needs and constraints is thus fundamentally complex, both because of the sheer amount, and even more because of different—domain specific—vocabularies. Ambiguities in early specifications (Figure 1) then yield costly changes at later project phases.

To overcome such issues, *requirements* based approaches (cf. [1]) are used in systems development. Requirements describe properties of a system. They give specifications of varying precision of the system to be developed, and later provide means to judge whether the product meets the goals.

The IEEE Standard 830 [2] lists desirable characteristics of requirements: (a) correct, (b) unambiguous, (c) complete, (d) consistent, (e) ranked in importance and/or stability, (f) verifiable, (g) modifiable, and (h) traceable. Further, each requirement shall be uniquely identified.

* Supported by DFG grant FORTAS – Formal Timing Analysis Suite for Real Time Programs (VE 455/1-1).

T. Margaria and B. Steffen (Eds.): ISoLA 2008, CCIS 17, pp. 354–368, 2008.

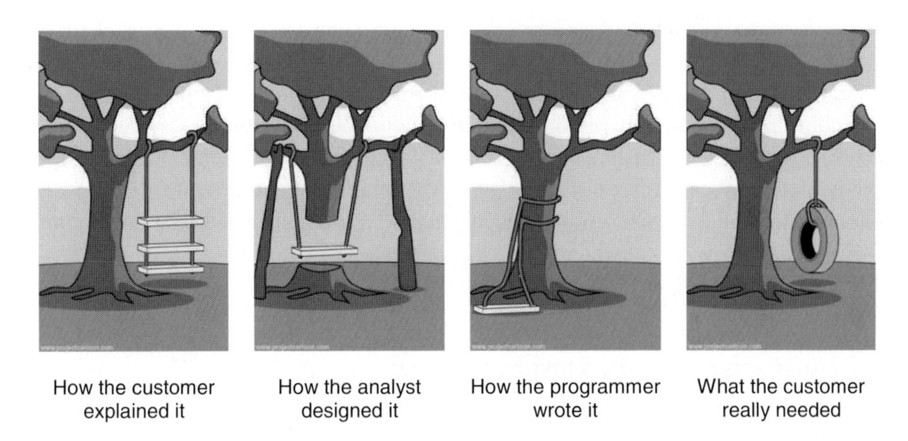

How the customer explained it
How the analyst designed it
How the programmer wrote it
What the customer really needed

Fig. 1. Well known misunderstandings in a project

Requirements Engineering in Avionics Industry

Because of the background of the authors, our view on the development process is inherently biased towards *avionics industry*. The term "avionics" is a synthesis of *aviation* and *electronics*. Starting in the early 1970s, the number of systems in an aircraft has grown in orders of magnitude. Thus it was necessary to emphasize integration of subsystems. It was primarily driven by the change from mechanical instruments to electronic instruments. This gave birth to avionics industry. Nowadays more than half of the budget of a new aircraft is spent on avionics systems.

Diehl Aerospace is one of the largest avionics suppliers in Europe. We deliver systems for Airbus and Boeing. Typical products are control systems for flaps, display systems, and cabin systems.

The avionics industry has been successful since around 30 years in developing highly reliable systems. Traveling by aircraft is safer than in any other vehicle. This might be due to a good understanding of the typical problems that can occur during a flight, but also because of the huge amount of money that is spent during the analysis phases of each newly developed program. As we expect air traffic to triple in the next 20 years, sustaining the quality and safety becomes a huge challenge for the existing infrastructure and new systems will need to be developed.

To guarantee quality and safety, regularities and guidelines controlled by official authorities must be adhered to. At systems level this is the international standard SAE-4754 [3], and for the software sub-systems DO-178B / ED-12B [4] applies. All guidelines are built on consensus of all players in industry. Most of these standards are based on older international standards like [5]. Further, many manufacturers compile internal standards based on existing ones to tailor them towards their typical projects (cf. [6]).

As we focus on software in this paper, we are primarily concerned with the objectives laid out in DO-178B / ED-12B. It delineates verification constraints to detect and report errors that may have been introduced during the software development processes. Software verification objectives are satisfied through a combination of reviews and analysis, the development of test cases and procedures, and the subsequent execution of those test procedures.

Contribution. In all such assessments, requirements specified earlier are checked. Not only the ability to assess varies largely among the set of requirements, but also the techniques used to describe the requirements are non-uniform. In this paper we we give a taxonomy of the kinds of requirements typically found in avionics system design, and take a short glance at possibilities of verifying that a requirement is met by an implementation. We therefore wade through the jungle of requirements along several paths: Requirements are first grouped according to their occurrence in the development process in Section 2.1, and then following our categorization in Section 3. We give examples from our domain to illustrate the abstract terms.

2 Requirements in the Design Process

Abstraction is a key concept in dealing with large scale system designs. Successive refinement keeps complexity local and manageable. Requirements follow this schema and occur at all levels of abstraction. For example, requirements coming from the customer are very high level and implementation independent, whereas the requirements for a specific software module are as detailed as necessary to directly derive source code based on them.

2.1 Hierarchy of Requirements

In Figure 2 the hierarchy of requirements is illustrated as a pyramid. The top level process in the aircraft development cycle includes the identification of aircraft functions and the requirements associated with these functions ([3] §5.1). As a result the purchaser technical specification (PTS) is the first document that describes the need of a new program. Each of the potential suppliers must explain to the purchaser how they intend to satisfy the requirements.

High Level Requirements. Specifications given in the PTS are also known as *high level requirements* (HLR). These are then refined to more detailed requirements. It is up to the systems design department to decide which of the requirements to allocate to a software modules or to a hardware modules.

Low Level requirements. The refinements of HLRs are called *low level requirements*. These describe software and hardware components in further detail. In the implementation phase, the low level requirements will be directly linked to parts of the system, i.e., source code or software architecture artifacts.

Derived Requirements. The class of *derived requirements* contains all specifications that do *not* stem from any design decision and thus cannot be traced backwards the requirements hierarchy. They are, however, essentially linked towards lower level requirements. As an example, consider the use of a specific scheduler (derived requirement), which dictates the least possible sampling rate (low level requirement).

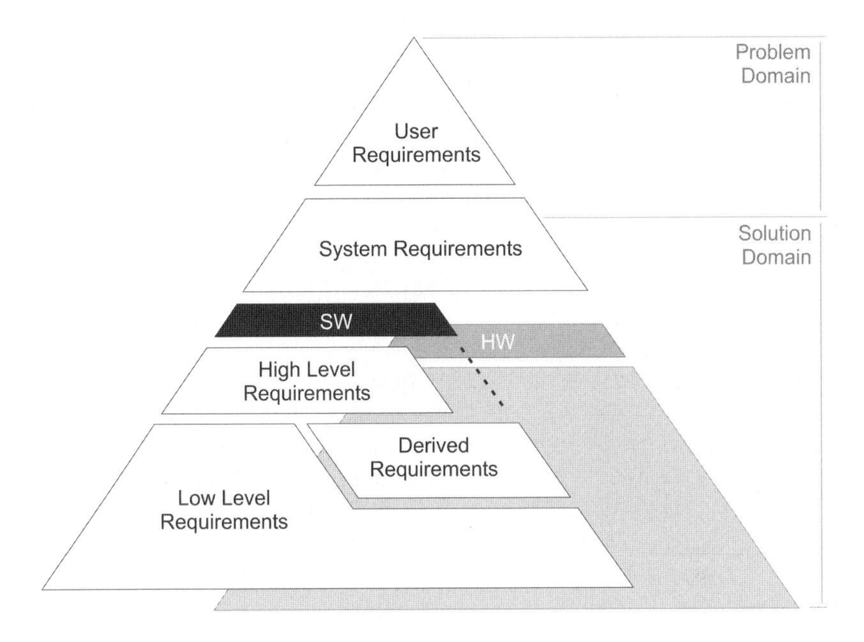

Fig. 2. The requirements pyramid

2.2 Assessment of Requirements

Requirements present the *necessary* conditions for quality and safety. Achievement, and thus the *sufficient* conditions thereof, must be checked in all phases of systems design. Therefore several principal processes of assessment are linked to requirements, which are detailed next. An overview of all activities in the development process is given in Figure 3.

Validation. In avionics, [3] §7 defines the process of *validation* as follows:

> Validation of requirements and specific assumptions is the process of ensuring that the specified requirements are sufficiently correct and complete so that the product will meet applicable airworthiness requirements. Validation is a combination of objective and subjective processes.

Thus, in Figure 3, the arrows labeled "validation" are drawn backwards to preceding phases. In each phase, all requirements must be validated against the requirements of the previous phases before a project can proceed.

Traceability. The key to validation of requirements is *traceability* [7], i.e., the existence of links between requirements, with the exception of derived requirements, as laid out in Section 2.1. Traceability enables later validation of the entire design and guarantees correspondence of the customer's high level requirements down to implementation details. DO-178B / ED-12B [4] §5.1.3 states this as follows:

> Each system requirement allocated to software should be traceable to one or more software high-level requirements.

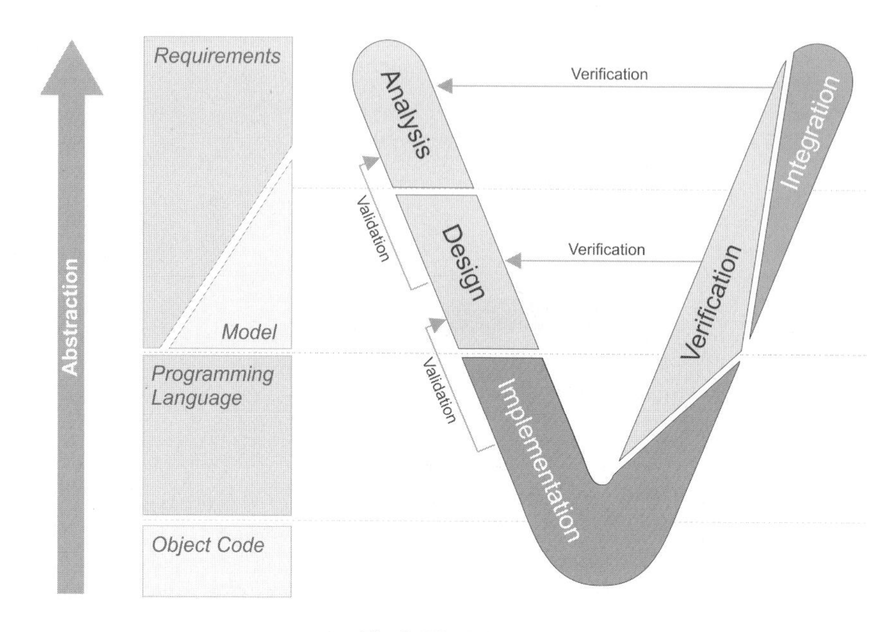

Fig. 3. The V-Model

Verification. While validation and traceability are only concerned with requirements themselves, *verification* links requirements and implementation. It is the process of assessing correctness of the implementation according to given requirements derived during analysis phase [3] §8.

Because of the complexity of requirements involved in large scale systems design, this calls for tool support (cf. [8]). While this is available using tools like Telelogic's Doors and Rhapsody, and Mathworks' MATLAB, *qualification* as required by DO-178B / ED-12B restricts the set of tools applicable in a DO-178B / ED-12B conforming process.

Qualification of a tool is needed when processes of DO-178B / ED-12B are eliminated, reduced or automated by the use of a software tool without its output being verified. Only deterministic tools may be qualified, that is, tools which produce the same output for the same input data when operating in the same environment. The tool qualification process may be applied either to a single tool or to a collection of tools.

Formal Methods. Proper *formal verification* requires the use of formal methods, both in requirements specification and in the process of verification itself. Further, [3] states:

> Any attempt to justify that a complex or highly integrated system is sufficiently error free, solely by means of testing, quickly becomes impractical as the system complexity increases.

DO-178B / ED-12B §12.3.1 explicitly states that formal methods may be applied to software requirements that (a) are safety-related, (b) can be defined by discrete mathematics, and (c) involve complex behavior, such as concurrency, distributed processing, redundancy management, and synchronization.

Current considerations for the successor of DO-178B / ED-12B take further formal methods into account. This means that future avionic programs can and/or must benefit from the power of mathematical techniques for validation and verification.

Nevertheless, there is a certain gap in practical applicability. In general, the benefits of formal methods are well acknowledged in avionics industry and several ongoing projects work on the introduction of related tools. From a system engineers perspective, however, there is a hurdle of fear to be overcome. The anxiety is twofold: First, a loss of control because of the involved complexity and lack of understanding is feared. Second, costs have not been fully understood, not even investigated, yet. Therefore, acceptance of formal methods is still lacking in many areas.

3 Categorizing Requirements

In the following we try to establish a sensible taxonomy for requirements found in real avionics projects. We also list possibilities for formal modeling and verification of the respective requirements. These listings will emphasize some gaps between the often idealized academic view and industrial requirements found in our projects. The examples of requirements are taken from an assessment of six recent projects conducted by Diehl Aerospace:

- The Onboard Airport Navigation System (OANS) for the A380
- The Doors and Slides Control System (DSCS) for the A350
- The Doors Control and Management Unit (DCMU) for the A380
- The Smart MultiFunction Display for the NH90 (SMD88)
- The Loader Software for the A400M
- The Display System of for Sikorsky S76

To avoid issues with intellectual property, however, in the given examples we have replaced the original names referring to these projects by *MODULE*, *SYSTEM*, etc.

3.1 Towards a Taxonomy

Obtaining a common taxonomy has proved to be very difficult. Even in the projects analyzed there were inconsistencies and heterogeneous categories. We decided to choose the main categories proposed by [9] and consider all other categories as sub-categories that can be assigned to one main category. The main categories are:

- Functional
  - behavior of the system
  - inputs, outputs and the functions it provides to the user
- Non-Functional
  - express attributes of the system
  - attributes of the environment
  - usability
  - reliability
  - performance
  - supportability

- Design Constraints
  - impose limits on the design of the systems
  - do not affect the external behavior of the system
  - must be fulfilled to meet technical, business or contractual obligations

To contrast some current trends, we will focus on non-functional requirements and design constraints in this document. Functional properties are already well supported by several modeling toolkits. The verification then focuses on simulation-based techniques, but formal methods like model checking [10] are in use as well.

Our focus on non-functional properties is also due to the fact that non-functional requirements are more generic than application-specific functional properties. Additionally, the ratio between functional and non-functional requirements in the programs under consideration was significantly towards the non-functional requirements (approximately 70 percent).

3.2 Non-functional Requirements

Non-functional requirements are also known as *qualities* of a system. We define *non-functional requirements* as the set of properties specifying in detail *how* to perform the intended functionality, in contrast to *functional properties* that state *what* the system under scrutiny shall do.

Safety Requirements. We refer to *safety* as described in [3]:

> Safety is defined as the state in which risk is lower than the boundary risk. The boundary risk is the upper limit of the acceptable risk. It is specific for a technical process or state.

Safety requirements should be determined by conducting a functional hazard assessment consistent with the processes in [11]. Safety can be considered as the most important aspect in avionics systems. Even though closely related, the *security* aspect currently is under consideration, but has less impact. This will change due to the fact that a system that is not secure cannot be safe (due to malicious persons). We distinguish *qualitative* and *quantitative safety*, as defined by [6]:

> Qualitative Safety is the compliance with requirements associated with hazard reduction principles, (common cause failure avoidance, requirement for segregation or fail safe at item of equipment level, requirements for particular type of function, monitoring, type of failure detection, requirement associated with components, requirement of Development Assurance Level, etc.).

> Quantitative Safety is the compliance with requirements for occurrence rate associated to particular functioning mode or to particular mal-functioning repercussions (failure conditions at item of equipment level).

We consider the following examples as representatives of safety requirements typically occurring in our projects:

Req 1. *Neither run-time errors, nor non-deterministic constructs the consequence of which includes processor halt, nor data corruption, nor security breaches, shall remain in the software.*

Req 2. *The code in use shall assure that no undesired or unscheduled events can be generated by the software itself.*

Formal correctness according to such requirements may be shown through static analysis [12] or model checking [10]. Both approaches may be fully automated, but require specifications to be expressed using specific logics and implementations to be translated or rewritten. To make the specification accessible to the system engineer, approaches such as SALT [13] may be followed. Recently, software model checking [14,15,16] has emerged as a sub-discipline of model checking, where implementations provided as C or Java code may be checked directly. Specifications may be given within the source code, using assertions and dedicated labels. The effective applicability of model checking depends upon the expressibility and availability of requirements in the specification dialect in use. We will, in the following, refer to model checking as one possible approach in several requirement categories, but note the dependency on usable formal specifications.

At this point it should be noted that the term *safety* is used for a specific class of specifications in this community. While at an abstract level qualitative safety may be expressed using *safety properties* (as used in formal verification), this does not hold for all examples of requirements listed here, as seen below.

Further formal and semi-formal techniques include automated and interactive theorem proving [17,18], Simulation [19], and Testing [20,21]. Most notably, both simulation and testing can be performed without any explicit specifications at hand and may thus see frequent use in development processes; but conversely, guarantees of correctness are a lot harder to obtain there.

In all of the above listed approaches, scalability to large scale systems is still an issue. Furthermore, purchaser and supplier must establish a level of trust that verification has been applied [22].

Req 3. *The safety relevant items/functions should provide adequate isolation; i.e., failure of one component/sub-function shall not cause a failure of another one.*

Req 4. *It shall be demonstrated where practical that all possible combinations of input signals independent of their sequence will not lead to abnormal system operation or status indication.*

Requirements describing interaction between components may be formally modeled using interface automata [23], or in certain cases also using type- and effect systems [24]. Whereas the latter has seen frequent practical applications [25], interface automata have not been widely adopted in industry thus far.

Req 5. *Inadvertent activation of the MODULE shall be less than* 1×10^{-5}.

Req 6. *The SYSTEM equipment shall be designed to minimize the potential for human errors that would significantly reduce safety.*

Whenever requirements do not fully prohibit errors, but instead constrain error rates by certain bounds, probabilistic models [26,27] and failure mode and effect analysis (FMEA) [28] is called for. This may be combined with model checking [29,30].

Req 7. *Special care shall be taken by the supplier and the purchaser to avoid display of ambiguous and/or meaningless information and messages.*

Even though clearly a safety requirement, the lack of metrics for such a requirement make the application of formal methods impossible in Req. 7.

Reliability Requirements. Reliability is the probability that an item will perform a required function under specified conditions, without failure, for a specified period of time [5].

Req 8. *The possibility of common mode faults that significantly reduce the reliability should be avoided.*

Req 9. *The reliability of monitoring functions shall be better (at least one order of magnitude) than the reliability of the corresponding monitored systems.*

The aspect of *availability* is closely tied to reliability. Availability is the "probability that an item is in a functioning state at a given point in time [6]" or the "Continuity of function [3] §5.2.1". Since some aircraft systems are required to perform a safe landing (e.g., the primary flight display in the cockpit) they have very high availability requirements. Example requirements for availability are:

Req 10. *The equipment should continue to operate correctly and continue to meet the safety requirements when subjected to several simultaneous fault conditions.*

Req 11. *Total loss of the MODULE functions shall be less than* 1×10^{-6}.

Both, reliability and availability requirements may be modeled and checked using FMEA techniques and probabilistic systems, as detailed for Req. 5 and 6. It shall be noted, however, that for software systems numbers analogous to MTBF (mean time before failure), which constitute the core of assessment in hardware systems, have not been established yet. Further, probabilistic reasoning generally is applied on abstract models, and not on an effective implementation.

Performance Requirements. Performance requirements define attributes of the function or system that make it useful to the aircraft and the customer. In addition to defining the type of performance expected, performance requirements include function specifics such as accuracy, fidelity, range, resolution, speed and response time [3] §5.2.2.3. This means that performance requirements do not cover only the aspect of processing speed, but also consider operational aspects and usability. Nevertheless, the worst case execution time (WCET) is often assessed during requirement analysis and has to demonstrated on the final product.

Req 12. *If the mechanism has no strictly predictable time behavior, as e.g., main loops applying polling mechanism, additional design precautions and verification measures shall be taken to fulfill the real time requirements of the system.*

It should be noted that in real-time systems *time* likely affect proper function, and thus must also be considered to be a *functional requirement* in some cases:

Req 13. *The maximum response time between MODULE commands available on NETWORK receiver and availability on NETWORK transmitter shall not exceed 50ms.*

Req 14. *The MODULE shall draw the reference format in a maximum time of 20 ms.*

Execution time analysis has traditionally been based on informal testing of the system under scrutiny on the effective target platform or using a simulator of the platform [31,32]. Formalizations of testing based approaches are presented in [33]. Safe upper bounds on WCET may be computed using static analysis [34].

Examples of performance requirements not related to execution time are:

Req 15. *The SYSTEM shall ensure that A/C position accuracy is not degraded by more than 0.5 m.*

Req 16. *The MODULE shall process only a single operation at a time.*

Again, probabilistic models and (probabilistic) model checking may be applied. As above, the translation of Req. 15 and 16 to specifications usable in model checking may be difficult and is very specific to the techniques used in the implementation. If it is applicable, however, the specifications used in model checking may become part of the software model. This would cater for support within the software engineering process, which is essential in cases where timing behavior affects proper function (see above).

Physical and Installation Requirements. We consider two sub-categories of physical requirements: *environmental* and *equipment specific*. The former deal with the location and surroundings of the avionics system, which is located in a special room called *avionics bay*. This room has an air conditioning system available that produces an optimal climate for electronic components. In case the air conditioning system fails, the electronic equipment has to perform the functionalities for a certain amount of time without degrading. Another problem arises when the air conditioning is powered down and the aircraft is parked in a hot location. Thus temperatures in the avionics bay can climb up to $80°C$. Even in this situation the equipment has to perform its tasks after power up without problems.

One of the issues coming up recently in avionics is the *single event upset* (SEU). With a higher integration of electronic circuits the probability of a neutron hitting a memory cell has increased. Especially for aircrafts flying at high altitudes this has become a real issue. To guarantee safe operations some measures have to be taken.

Req 17. *The hardware and software implementation solutions shall consider the possibility of atmospheric radiation effect. E.g., SEU (single event upset) and MBU (multiple bit upset, specifically MBUs leading to single word multiple upset) due to particle environment (radiations as for example: neutrons, protons, heavy ions, etc.) at high flight altitude (see also ABD0100.1.2 §4, also applicable for MBU).*

Both at software and hardware level (using models of the processing units), model checking and other formal methods listed for safety requirements may be applied. Specifications, however, will be highly involved and must be tailored towards each implementation. A more generic method would thus be desirable.

Req 18. *Each equipment of the SYSTEM shall be compliant with the conditions specified in document RTCA/DO-160 §13 "Fungus Resistance" with category depending on the component's installation location.*

Equipment specific requirements deal with all physical onboard pieces. Each piece of equipment adds up to the total weight of an aircraft. The airlines demand an efficient fleet and therefore the aircraft manufacturers try to minimize weight and power consumption on every single component.

Req 19. *The maximum weight of the complete SYSTEM shall be less than 35 kg.*

Req 20. *The maximum power consumption of the system/equipment shall be 80 VA.*

Mathematical modeling of Req. 18–20 may be based on computer aided design (CAD) tools, possibly with specific annotations. Statistic analysis of the modules in each design then yield the desired numbers. This technique is referred to as *computer aided engineering* (CAE) and tool support is widely available.

Maintainability Requirements. In [5] *maintainability* is defined as follows:

> Maintainability is the capability of the [...] product to be modified. Modifications may include corrections, improvements or adaptions of the software to changes in environment, and in requirements and functional specifications.

This category includes scheduled and unscheduled maintenance requirements, and any links to specific safety related functions. Factors such as the percent of failure detection or the percent of fault isolation may also be important. Provisions for external test equipment signals and connections should be defined in these requirements [3] §5.2.2.5.

Req 21. *The supplier shall comply with ABD0100.1.14 and GRESS module 1.8 for Obsolescence Management requirements.*

Req 22. *Fault tolerance principles or components intrinsic reliability shall be adopted where appropriate to achieve operational reliability targets and minimizes line maintenance work.*

Req 23. *SYSTEM software in-field loading shall not exceed 15 minutes.*

At best, annotated CAD models or module lists may be used to check such requirements. Maintainability, however, essentially involves business processes and thus would require formal models of the development processes as well.

3.3 Design constraints

Design constraints can be considered as special non-functional requirements. In fact, these requirements restrict the designer in choosing their architecture. Although requirements should be implementation independent, these special requirements are often used to enforce a certain design to conform with other developments. Design constraints are usually found in the lower level requirements specifications.

Architectural Requirements. Architectural requirements cope with the structure of a software module, and the way components are tied together. In the last years, the architecture of a system has become more and more important. Since most software systems are part of a larger system, interface design becomes crucial, and the chosen structure must be easily integrated into the next level of abstraction.

Req 24. *Software modularity shall be considered in order to improve the efficiency of future function evolutions.*

Req 25. *A modular programming style with clear predefined module interfaces shall be introduced in the operational software in order to layer the whole software package in a hardware dependent part and in a hardware independent part.*

Req 26. *Functional independent software parts shall be segregated in different software modules.*

Req 27. *The SYSTEM shall be able to support slight modifications with a minimum impact on the software and without needing a new architecture definition.*

Req 28. *The SYSTEM function software shall be designed to be highly re-usable and to optimize hardware/software independence. In particular, the software design shall ensure:*

- *Independence of the SYSTEM functions related to the aircraft environment (such as HMI or I/O functions).*
- *Independence of the different SYSTEM software functions between themselves to ensure efficient future evolutions of these functions.*
- *Independence of the SYSTEM software related to the hardware (for portability on PC host unit).*

Req 29. *The breakdown of the software shall be the same as the one used by the purchaser to produce the application detailed specification. To achieve this objective a procedure shall be mutually defined so that the purchaser specification integrates the supplier's wishes.*

From a formal point of view, Req. 24–29 describe syntactic properties of the implementation. Checking such specification thus is tied to the languages and modeling formalism used in the implementation. Further, metrics to measure progress and fulfillment of the requirements must be defined (cf. [35]).

Development Requirements. This class of requirements is also referred to as *coding guidelines*. Most important are those requirements that restrict the usage of dynamic memory allocation. Almost all of the projects under analysis contained one of these requirements.

Req 30. *The use of pointers is allowed provided the supplier applies specific coding standard rules and review check lists to restrict and manage its use. These rules shall be agreed upon by the supplier and the purchaser, shall forbid the dynamic memory allocation, and shall be applied for the new software and C++ reused software.*

Req 31. *Features with dynamic run-time behavior shall be avoided. No dynamic objects shall be created or destroyed during run-time.*

Req 32. *The MODULE shall not use dynamic memory allocation. All the memory shall be allocated at startup. The update by copy of the pre-allocated memory is allowed but the boundaries shall be checked.*

Other development requirements are:

Req 33. *The policy for the intended use of IEEE floating point computation shall be described in the Plan for Software Aspects of Certification (PSAC) and detailed in Software Design and Code Standards.*

Req 34. *The instrumented code shall only be used for demonstration of structural coverage, timing behavior, etc. Subsequently, the target executable object code shall be compiled and linked from the non-instrumented source code. Requirements based testing shall be repeated at the same level of testing and documented for the non-instrumented software package to demonstrate equivalence of functional and runtime-behavior for both instrumented and non-instrumented code.*

Req 35. *For validation purposes, the equipment shall allow to simulate internal failure.*

An analysis of approaches towards formal verification yields three groups here: (i) Static properties of source code. Here, syntactic checks as proposed for architectural requirements apply. (ii) Dynamic properties of the implementation. Model checking and static analysis may be used, as suggested for Req. 1. (iii) Business process related. Formal methods at software level do not apply.

HW/SW Interface Requirements

Req 36. *If the status returned by a MODULE register access function call is not RESULT_OK, then an application error shall be raised.*

This reachability property is best modeled and verified using model checking tools. Even though it may involved interaction with hardware, abstract models enable checking of the combined system.

Req 37. *The software design shall not compromise the hardware failure tolerance.*

The lack of metrics makes the formal analysis of such a requirement infeasible. Establishing appropriate metrics would be highly desirable, however, and enable probabilistic modeling and analysis of such requirements.

Req 38. *If the supplier uses the cache memory of a processor, they shall demonstrate as part of the verification plan the deterministic behavior of their solution.*

Req 39. *Usage of special software dependent resources (e.g., usage of CPU-registers for special purposes or cache memory) shall be justified and mentioned within the Software Accomplishment Summary.*

Req. 38 and 39 involve parts of the business process and thus cannot be formally checked at the implementation level.

4 Conclusions

Requirements form the basis of all systems developments processes in avionics industry. The large scale systems, however, yield a vast amount of requirements that must be managed and communicated. Based on our ongoing projects, we have presented a taxonomy to categorize the occurring requirements.

Focusing on non-functional properties and design constraints, we have given a set of examples of effectively occurring requirements and tried to elaborate formal means of verifying the respective properties.

The list of requirements and possibly applicable formal methods emphasizes the gap between an idealized mathematical model and practical applicability in an industrial context. While we do acknowledge the progress in fundamental research, we also hope that our work stimulates the development of tools that can be applied in our industrial context to further improve quality and safety in airborne traffic.

References

1. Nuseibeh, B., Easterbrook, S.: Requirements engineering: A roadmap. In: Finkelstein, A.C.W. (ed.) The Future of Software Engineering, Companion volume to ICSE (2000)
2. IEEE New York, NY, USA: IEEE Recommended Practice for Software Requirements Specifications (June 1998)
3. Society of Automotive Engineers, Inc. Warrendale, PA, USA: SAE ARP 4754, Certification Considerations For Highly-Integrated Or Complex Aircraft Systems (November 1996)
4. RTCA Inc. / EUROCAE: DO-178B / ED-12B, Software Considerations in Airborne Systems and Equipment Certification (December 1992)
5. International Organization for Standardization: ISO/IEC 9126-1:2001, Software engineering – Product quality – Part 1: Quality model (2001)
6. Airbus Industries Blagnac Cedex, France: Equipment – Design – General Requirements For Suppliers (December 1996)
7. Eide, P.L.H.: Quantification and Traceability of Requirements. Technical report, NTNU Norwegian University of Science and Technology (2005)
8. Kornecki, A.J., Hall, K., Hearn, D., Lau, H., Zalewsi, J.: Evaluation of software development tools for high assurance safety critical systems. In: HASE (2004)
9. Leffingwell, D., Widrig, D.: Managing Software Requirements. Addison-Wesley, Reading (2003)
10. Clarke, E.M., Grumberg, O., Peled, D.A.: Model Checking. MIT Press, Cambridge (1999)
11. Society of Automotive Engineers, Inc. Warrendale, PA, USA: SAE ARP 4754, Guidelines and Methods for Conducting the Safety Assessment Process on Civil Airborne Systems and Equipment (December 1996)
12. Nielson, F., Nielson, H.R., Hankin, C.: Principles of Program Analysis, 2nd edn. Springer, Heidelberg (2005)
13. Bauer, A., Leucker, M., Streit, J.: SALT—structured assertion language for temporal logic. In: Liu, Z., He, J. (eds.) ICFEM 2006. LNCS, vol. 4260, pp. 757–775. Springer, Heidelberg (2006)
14. Henzinger, T.A., Jhala, R., Majumdar, R., Sutre, G.: Software Verification with BLAST. In: Ball, T., Rajamani, S.K. (eds.) SPIN 2003. LNCS, vol. 2648, pp. 235–239. Springer, Heidelberg (2003)

15. Clarke, E.M., Kroening, D., Lerda, F.: A Tool for Checking ANSI-C Programs. In: Jensen, K., Podelski, A. (eds.) TACAS 2004. LNCS, vol. 2988, pp. 168–176. Springer, Heidelberg (2004)
16. Khurshid, S., Pasareanu, C.S., Visser, W.: Generalized Symbolic Execution for Model Checking and Testing. In: Garavel, H., Hatcliff, J. (eds.) TACAS 2003. LNCS, vol. 2619, pp. 553–568. Springer, Heidelberg (2003)
17. Robinson, J.A., Voronkov, A. (eds.): Handbook of Automated Reasoning, vol. 2. Elsevier and MIT Press (2001)
18. Nipkow, T., Paulson, L.C., Wenzel, M.: Isabelle/HOL—A Proof Assistant for Higher-Order Logic. Springer, Heidelberg (2002)
19. Wall, A., Andersson, J., Norström, C.: Probabilistic simulation-based analysis of complex real-times systems. In: ISORC (2003)
20. Tretmans, J., Brinksma, E.: TorX: Automated model-based tesing. In: ECMDSE (2003)
21. Holzer, A., Schallhart, C., Tautschnig, M., Veith, H.: FShell: Systematic Test Case Generation for Dynamic Analysis and Measurement. In: CAV, pp. 209–213 (2008)
22. Chaki, S., Schallhart, C., Veith, H.: Verification Across Intellectual Property Boundaries. In: Damm, W., Hermanns, H. (eds.) CAV 2007. LNCS, vol. 4590, pp. 82–94. Springer, Heidelberg (2007)
23. de Alfaro, L., Henzinger, T.A.: Interface Automata. In: FSE, pp. 109–120 (2001)
24. Pierce, B.C.: Types and programming languages. MIT Press, Cambridge (2002)
25. Kühnel, C., Bauer, A., Tautschnig, M.: Compatibility and reuse in component-based systems via type and unit inference. In: SEAA, pp. 101–108 (2007)
26. Vesely, W.E., et al.: Fault tree handbook. Technical Report NUREG-0492, Systems and Reliability Research, Office of Nuclear Regulatory Research, U.S. Nuclear Regulatory Commission, Washington, DC (1981)
27. Kemeny, J.G., Snell, J.L.: Finite Markov Chains. Van Nostrand Reinhold, New York (1960)
28. Stamatis, D.H.: Failure Mode and Effect Analysis: FMEA from Theory to Execution, 2nd edn. ASQ Quality Press (2003)
29. Vardi, M.Y.: Automatic verification of probabilistic concurrent finite-state programs. In: FOCS, pp. 327–338 (1985)
30. Kwiatkowska, M., Norman, G., Parker, D.: PRISM 2.0: A tool for probabilistic model checking. In: QEST, pp. 322–323 (2004)
31. Kirner, R., Lang, R., Freiberger, G., Puschner, P.: Fully automatic worst-case execution time analysis for Matlab/Simulink models. In: ECTRS, pp. 31–40 (2002)
32. Wang, Z., Haberl, W., Kugele, S., Tautschnig, M.: Automatic Generation of SystemC Models from Component-based Designs for Early Design Validation and Performance Analysis. In: WOSP (2008)
33. Kirner, R., Veith, H.: Formal timing analysis suite for real-time programs. Technical Report 58, Technische Universität Wien, Vienna, Austria (2005)
34. Ferdinand, C., Heckmann, R., Langenbach, M., Martin, F., Schmidt, M., Theiling, H., Thesing, S., Wilhelm, R.: Reliable and precise WCET determination for a real-life processor. In: Henzinger, T.A., Kirsch, C.M. (eds.) EMSOFT 2001. LNCS, vol. 2211, pp. 469–485. Springer, Heidelberg (2001)
35. Lakos, J.: Large Scale C++ Software Design. Addison-Wesley, Reading (1996)

Non-functional Avionics Requirements

Michael Paulitsch[1], Harald Ruess[2], and Maria Sorea[3]

[1] Honeywell Aerospace, Golden Valley, MN 55422, USA
Michael.Paulitsch@honeywell.com
[2] IABG, Ottobrunn, Germany
Ruess@iabg.de
[3] EADS Innovation Works, Munich, Germany
Maria.Sorea@eads.net

Abstract. Embedded systems in aerospace become more and more integrated in order to reduce weight, volume/size, and power of hardware for more fuel-efficiency. Such integration tendencies change architectural approaches of system architectures, which subsequently change non-functional requirements for platforms. This paper provides some insight into state-of-the-practice of non-functional requirements for developing ultra-critical embedded systems in the aerospace industry, including recent changes and trends. In particular, formal requirement capture and formal analysis of non-functional requirements of avionic systems – including hard-real time, fault-tolerance, reliability, and performance – are exemplified by means of recent developments in SAL and HiLiTE.

Keywords: Non-functional requirements, avionics, integrated modular avionics.

1 Introduction

Sometimes a clear separation between functional requirements (FR), which specify behavior, and non-functional requirements (NFR) consisting of constraints and qualities is suggested [24]. Hereby, qualities are properties of the system that its stakeholders care about and, hence, will affect their degree of satisfaction with the system; in contrast, constraints are not subject to negotiation and, unlike qualities, are off-limits during design trade-offs.

In the context of avionics systems we are arguing that such a clear separation between FR and NFR is often not possible as such a classification depends on the given context and the level of abstraction. Indeed, Paech et al. [29] propose an integrated view of NFRs, FRs, and architecture. This view is shared by the authors as will be illustrated in the avionics, and in particular the integrated modular avionics (IMA), domain.

The paper starts with related work in the field, followed by a general discussion of a selected set of NFRs in avionics. In particular, we discuss the impact of aerospace electronic system integration on NFR. In the remainder, we exemplify the formal capture and analysis of NFR in integrated modular avionics (IMA) architectures.

T. Margaria and B. Steffen (Eds.): ISoLA 2008, CCIS 17, pp. 369–384, 2008.

2 Related Work

There are multiple papers describing nonfunctional requirements (NFR) and functional requirements (FR) similar to this paper's overview on NFR. E.g., Glinz provides a detailed overview and discussion on NFR and FR and their differences [17].

The second class of related papers describes approaches of formally capturing and analyzing NFRs. Srivastava and Narasimhan [43] describe architectural support for FR and NFR of software exhibiting different mode-driven fault tolerance while considering quality of service properties. AADL (Architecture Analysis and Design Language) is an architecture description language (based on the MetaH developed by Binns et al. [12]) and standardized by the SAE [39]. AADL aims to provide support for domain-specific architectural styles and software patterns on distributed processor platforms. Heitmeyer et al. [20] formally analyze requirements specifications for type errors, completeness, circular definitions and non-determinism and apply these to examples in avionics. Morris and Koopman [26] present a technique to visualize system-level non-functional properties of embedded systems. Xu et al. [53] transform dependability requirements and architectural patterns into software architecture. Bate et al. [8] provide an approach to capture and model functional and non-functional properties in safety-critical systems. Owens et al. [27] present an integrated safety-oriented methodology for system development that combines the four state-of-the-art techniques intent specification, STAMP, STAMP-based hazard analysis (STPA), and state analysis. This methodology helps managing NFR especially safety-related aspects of NFRs. Bhatt et al. [10,11] address FR and NFR for the model-based development (MBD) of avionics systems. MARTE, a UML Profile for Modeling and Analysis of Real-time and Embedded Systems [27], allows capturing of NF properties.

3 Background: The Evolution of Avionics Platforms

The ongoing trend to even more integration and modular architecture approaches for avionics with Integrated Modular Architectures (IMA) influences the NFR for avionic platforms. Accompanied with trends of ever-decreasing design cycles and life expectancy of consumer electronics, NFRs are changing as do FRs with additional performance, pilot, and safety enhancements, such as synthetic vision, electronic flight bag, and required navigation performance. This document discusses aspects of integration of different subsystems into a common avionics platform characterized by a general compute platform and I/O interfaces and its impact on non-functional properties. I/O and computers are connected by a shared system network. The benefits of an IMA, like scalability, and obsolescence, have been widely recognized and are discussed with other NFR and properties in this paper.

Drivers for integration are reduction of size/volume, weight, and power needs (main theme is weight!); also some functional aspects, pilot workload reduction and convenience, and safety enhancements are direct or indirect drivers for integration (e.g. paperless cockpit). The term avionics comprises different systems depending on target market (commercial or military) or even for different markets (air transport, regional, and general aviation). Hence, integrated avionics can have a different meaning across various business segments. At the point of writing this paper, integration level reached in air transport commercial avionics is characterized by a common open system bus ARINC664 [1], with interfaces to different systems including flight control, engine control, passenger entertainment. Future integration efforts could stretch to include flight control electronics and engine control electronics into "traditional" avionic systems, such as display, navigation, communication, management, even for air transport category aircraft. In the military domain ASAAC (Allied Standard Avionics Architecture Council) is an emerging standard, which includes health-monitoring and in-flight reconfiguration capabilities.

4 Non-functional Avionics Requirements

This section presents multiple different avionics NFRs, related to dependability, performance, development, and operation.

4.1 Security

Security is a NFR that gains importance in integrated avionics as described by Jacob [21], Johnson [22] and Royalty [33] for the commercial airplanes sector. For example, recent approaches of connecting aircraft management networks, passenger entertainment, and avionic system in combination with the deployment of well-known COTS technology such as Ethernet and variants of internet protocols have led to increased security considerations as indicated by a recent FAA inquiry for Boeing's 787 [54].

In a federated architecture each subsystem is physically separate with minimal interaction and largely independent failure behavior from a security perspective. Traditionally, avionics systems address security requirements by using *system high* (operating at the highest classification of data entering the system) or by deploying an "air gap" (physical separation). Integrated avionics require partitioning for security (partitioned kernels and support for MILS – Multiple Independent Levels of Security/Safety) [21]. MILS is a process-oriented security architecture based on mathematical verification that draws from ARINC-653 [384] and ensures trusted foundations. Integration of functions has led to size, weight, and power reduction while maintaining or increasing functionalities (like software loading).

4.2 Maintenance

Traditionally commercial aircraft maintenance has followed very cyclic and scheduled maintenance approaches with multiple levels of maintenance actions depending on service. This is largely driven by the requirement for operational schedules of aircraft and crews as well as passenger satisfaction demanding high on-time departure and arrival. Clear quantitative metrics like schedule interruption indexes are designed to and tracked for an aircraft and its subsystems like avionics.

There is always an effort in significantly reducing requirements for maintenance. For example, parts management in avionics is very rigid and each part requires a separated number in case hardware or software load (firmware) is slightly different. In order to streamline maintenance and reduce inventory cost, there is a strong desire towards common parts. In IMA systems, this leads to generic I/O or general purpose compute cards and sometimes even one module having multiple software loads stored with mechanical pin strap selection schemes for functionality selection (e.g. via backplane connectors) dependent on its position in the rack.

Another effort underway is the extension of electronic distribution of software as defined in the ARINC report 666 [2, 3]. This should enable correction of problems within original specifications, resolve conflicts with emerging, preferred media-less operations, incorporate standards for digital signatures and web services, and set the stage for enhanced A/C software delivery, load, and management [6].

A significant effort is the extension of condition-based maintenance and prognostics in avionics as, e.g. described in [19, 40]. The reason for this development lays in the expanding role of electronics in aircraft and increased wear-out phenomena of silicon observed at smaller feature sizes and the imperfection of built-in local test and diagnostic test capability. Use of prognostics optimizes aircraft dispatch ability due to two major factors. One is the higher likelihood of available parts and/or personnel once prognostics and part supply management are interlinked. The second is that indication of failure cause reduces maintenance personnel time. Prognostic helps decreasing the equipment where no faults are found. Obstacles to deployment of prognostics are the multitude of failure modes and mechanisms, large number of parts with small failure probability, and missing signatures of failure mechanisms [19].

A very progressive approach towards maintenance is taken by engine electronics. Recognizing the mechanical wear-out dominance in turbine engines due to the severe environment and the superior performance of redundant electronics with respect to faults, extended operation and dispatch despite faults in electronics have been introduced. The methodology described in [38] is a good publicly available description and background for a time-limited dispatch process for redundant Full Authority Digital Engine Controllers (FADECs). Basically, the aircraft is allowed to continue operation for a specified period after detection of a fault dependent on the severance of potential fault effects.

Avionics equipment (e.g., flight, display, navigation, and environmental control as well as passenger comfort and utilities) have clearly established guidelines regarding dispatch requirements often referred to as Minimum Equipment Lists (MELs).

4.3 Safety, Availability, and Integrity

Dependability as NFR – especially related to safety – can be divided in two major classes. One class addresses the requirements of operation in the system environment in case of component failures. Requirements of this class often directly manifests in the architecture of avionics. An example of this class would be the success of a mission despite faulty components. The second class concerns the development process of the system itself and its implication of performance in the environment. Such NFRs may or may not show up in the avionics architecture. The second class comprises all efforts undertaken to assure the correctness of the design and efforts addressing requirements correctness as related to safety. Such non-functional requirements of design assurance have their roots – amongst others – in the impossibility of being able to purely test to the required levels of life-critical designs [14].

Availability and integrity (in relation to safety) is hard to distinguish from safety as any impact of availability or integrity loss of systems could directly impact safety, where availability is continuity of function and integrity is correctness of behavior

[36]. From a development perspective, safety of aircraft and, hence, IMA is governed by the Federal Aviation Regulations (FAR) and Joint Airworthiness Requirements (JAR) Part 25 for transport category aircraft and guidance material is presented in ARP4754 [36], and ARP4761 [37]. An important aspect for understanding NFR of avionics related to safety is the understanding of aircraft-level functions of avionics, which traditionally have been mainly implemented with separate equipment and, hence, have been able to be certified separately – to a certain extent. ARP4754 discusses certification-aspects of highly integrated and complex avionics systems where the term "highly-integrated" refers "to systems that perform or contribute to multiple aircraft-level functions". The term "complex" refers "to systems whose safety cannot be shown solely by test and whose logic is difficult to comprehend without the aid of analytical tools." Aircraft level functions are e.g. flight control, flight management system, situational awareness functions, and navigation. During certification, safety does not only need to be assessed with respect to avoidance of spare exhaustion but with respect to common mode influences, assurance of configuration and process (see e.g. DO178B [35]).

An important derived NFR of IMA architectures is the separation of different "chapters" (namely airplane-level functions) for the purpose of the easier analyses of the impact of faults on safety of the aircraft. As a consequence, aircraft-level shared components (like data concentrators or common compute platforms) of highly integrated complex systems, will likely be implemented in a high integrity manner (for example, using self-checking components) for transport category aircraft, so that a single device faults have a fail passive behavior and the impact of a highly shared device do not lead to failure effects that are hard to analyze as they would "stretch" into interaction of multiple aircraft level functions. Such high-integrity compute platforms also have a significant effect on the platform architecture and actuator redundancy approaches (due to reduced need for voting in end effector).

Typical process-related requirements are that any function in an IMA needs to be hosted on a platform with the same or higher development assurance level. Also the integrity of a function is determined by its failure condition impact (e.g. catastrophic impact would require level A assurance). The process also considers configuration management and common mode analysis, such as fault tree analysis (cut set), and zonal safety, in addition to verification and validation to ensure safe operation.

An interesting example of an NFR that is often discussed regarding its effectiveness is the use of dissimilarity. Dissimilar designs alone (at least for software) is believed to not yield the required availability and integrity requirements [23] and assumed to be impractical or may even provide a barrier between efficient communication between the software and the requirements team [25]. An example of successful application of dissimilarity (at hardware level) is the architectural design of the flight control computers in the Airbus A320/A330/A340. Dissimilar design on the platform level (not application level) is uncommon to take credit for (see e.g. comments in ARP4761 on dissimilarity or [13]), yet can be helpful to require on an informal level. The A320 flight control incurred a loss of cooling failure and all ELACs (ELevator and Aileron Computers) incurred a common mode fault due a batch of components not meeting its temperature operating range [13]. Due to SECs (Spoiler and Elevator Computers) different design from ELACs, SECs did not incur the fault and the affected plane landed safely. If the process would have been fully trusted,

SEC and ELAC had not had to be dissimilar. Dissimilarity on the system-level (e.g. different ways to display essential flight data via independent backup instruments) is often required and successfully implemented. Similar controversy underpins the use of signature-based approaches [30].

Typical NFRs of availability and integrity addressing redundancy-based techniques of compensating for failing hardware due to physical effects (permanent faults) are the well-known 10^{-9} failures per hour (or sometimes per mission) with respect to safety at the aircraft level.

In order to achieve such high levels of integrity and availability, typical reliability estimations not only need to consider reliability during mission, but also built-in test coverage or coverage of protection functions (scrubbing). Protection functions to ensure availability and integrity can have latent errors. Such errors would defeat the sole purpose of existence of protection functions, namely protection in case of fault of other systems. An example of a protection function for a network is the enforcement of bandwidth allocations in networks (guardian functions).

Transient faults are becoming more and more likely due to the decreased feature size in electronics [9]. NFR to tolerate transient faults are an important aspect in the design of IMA addressed e.g. in error detection or correction schemes for memories or other especially vulnerable components. Transient faults traditionally do not show up in fault tree analysis, but need analysis and design approaches depending on magnitudes. Transients can be a reliability hit and impact no-fault-found rates. The recent move towards composite airframe led to potentially increase transient upset rates of (as well as lightning effects to) electronics due to decreased shielding.

4.4 Temporal Performance Aspects

IMA uses powerful processors to optimize size, weight and power. Yet, increasing use of pipeline approaches and caches for performance reasons make worst-case execution time analyses harder. Dual-processor approaches with shared resources (like caches and memory busses) may exacerbate this even further.

With the increasing gap between worst-case and best-case processor performance, ARINC653 Operating System (OS) approaches [5] can get even more inefficient due to static allocation of time slots. Honeywell's OS DEOS, as used on the PRIMUS EPIC platform, allows slack management, which basically allows a managed approach of unused execution time for other "performance hungry" processes with the advantage of reduced response times (in single-core systems), but loss of ability of sub-frame scheduling. Timing requirements of platforms are often application-related end-to-end maximum requirements considering control and/or human factors. A very demanding application to host on an integrated platform is audio. MOPS (Minimum Operational Performance Standards) [34] requires end-to-end absolute audio delay of 10ms, which can lead to demanding platform requirements. Interesting for audio is also a differential output maximum delay to minimize interferences and audio cancellation effects between different cockpit audio outputs, which translate to maximum of multiple tens of microsecond synchronization between audio outputs resulting in a need of synchronization of the audio platform components.

Wittenmark et al. [52] describe impact of timing problems (jitter, delay, transient errors) on control applications and application or platform related treatment and mitigation of impact of communication delays, which can increase in integrated communication approaches. A special effect of asynchronous communication approaches like ARINC664 part 7 [1] is the possibility of oscillatory latency variations – also referred to as "beating" – due to variations of clocks of asynchronous end systems and resulting effects of queuing. While in ARINC629 [4] such effects have been avoided by special bus access approaches, asynchronously switched networks cannot prevent such effects, which may lead to application-level requirements for mitigation.

4.5 Testing and Diagnosis

In addition to built-in test and latent error scrubbing tests described above, integration and flight test and potentially diagnosis can require special architecture and NFR. Especially in IMAs, flight test requires observation of a significant amount of data flowing over the network. In addition, end systems send data on the network especially for testing purposes. All test data may need to be selectively evaluated. Given the amount of data, this requires special network bandwidth considerations and other performance and scheduling considerations.

4.6 Obsolescence

COTS electronics refresh cycles get shorter and shorter resulting in potential earlier redesign of avionics platforms. As this is often not financially viable, obsolescence aspects become an important non-functional design aspect of avionics.

Wilkinson et al. [51] describe this aspect in more details and propose a modular architecture approach with special interconnects (network, north bridge for processors) for electronics that become obsolete quickly (e.g. processors and memories). An example for a glue component that is not immediately affected by obsolescence is AFDX™ (ARINC664 part 7) network as it has been especially designed for aerospace. Honeywell addressed obsolescence and low production volume by deploying the MAC (Modular Aerospace Control) architecture for engine control.

4.7 Schedulability

Since the IMA approach allows multiple applications of different criticality levels to share common computing resources, it is important to keep individual applications away from potential interference. The main way for protecting integrated applications and system resources is via temporal and spatial partitioning. Spatial partitioning guarantees that an application has exclusive control over its own data and state information. With spatial partitioning, an application can be protected from any erroneous behaviors of other applications while sharing same physical resources. Temporal partitioning guarantees that an application or communication server has temporal exclusive access to its pre-allocated resources. With guaranteed pre-scheduled temporal partitioning, an application can meet their timing requirements.

For enforcing temporal partitioning, shared resources have to be scheduled while guaranteeing timing constraints of the application. When considering ARINC-based IMA systems, composed of several communicating applications that are connected by a fault tolerant time division multiplexing (TDM) bus, one has to take into account not only the constraints imposed by the applications but also the characteristics and efficient usage of the underlying communication bus [31,46,49]. Temporal partitioning also requires careful design when leveraging hardware-based data movement acceleration schemes (like DMAs) in that they do not interfere with partition-based accounting of timing.

In order to extent platforms with minimum interference of existing applications, an incremental scheduling approach should ideally be supported, where platform properties like communication latency and jitter are maintained for applications even after adding of additional applications or boxes to the platform. This is sometimes also referred to as delta-mode scheduling capability.

5 Exemplary Formal Requirements Capture and Analysis

The development of integrated modular avionics systems is subject to strong requirements for optimality in the use of resources, and correctness with respect to non-functional properties, as well as requirements for time-to-market and low cost through reuse and easy customization. For early design error detection, application of validation and analysis techniques is essential, especially to guarantee NFR and properties.

Several research projects deal with the aspects of non-functional requirements. The OMEGA project (http://www-omega.imag.fr/) extended a subset of UML with formal modeling and analysis methods for non-functional requirements, in particular, schedulability, time and performance. The SPEEDS project addresses the integration of heterogeneous components (http://www.speeds.eu.com). Its main goal is to develop a meta-model, which defines rich-component models to represent both functional and non-functional aspects in a uniform way and which allows the construction of complete virtual system models. COMBEST (http://www.combest.eu) extends the modeling methodology established in SPEEDS by developing a design theory for complex embedded systems, fully covering components heterogeneity, interface specifications, composability, compositionality, and refinement for functional and non-functional properties. A first step in this direction is realized by the BIP (Behavior, Interaction, Priority) framework that provides a methodology for modeling heterogeneous real-time components [41]. BIP allows for analyzing functional and non-functional requirements in an integrated manner, through composition of functional system models with the architecture of the underlying execution platform, where the platform architecture is described by non-functional characteristics, such as tasks, resources, and scheduling policies.

The SAE AADL standard [39] provides formal modeling concepts for the description and analysis of application systems architecture in terms of distinct components and their interactions. AADL supports the early prediction and analysis of critical system qualities—such as performance, schedulability, and reliability. For example, in specifying and analyzing schedulability, AADL-supported thread components include the predeclared execution property options of periodic, aperiodic (event-driven), background (dispatched once and executed to completion), and sporadic (paced by an upper rate bound) events. AADL specifications may be compiled into BIP and SAL, thereby serving as an application-specific language front-end to these verification-oriented systems.

Automated analysis of time-triggered bus protocols and architectures is challenging since it requires modeling timing aspects in a precise manner, dealing with very large state spaces, and taking failure models into account. A way for addressing this challenge is through model-based analysis (MBA). MBA is based on a four steps approach. In a first step, a model of the protocol/system under consideration is constructed, the so-called nominal system model. The second step involves the construction of a fault model that basically describes all possible faults that can affect the system, under the given fault hypothesis. Both system and faults models are usually represented as state machines or variants thereof, for expressing timings or probabilities. These state machines are usually expressed in convenient special-purpose languages such as Simulink or SCADE. In a third step, the desired requirements (functional and non-functional) are specified in some formal notation to support automated analysis. There are several candidate notations, including temporal logics like CTL or LTL and various extensions thereof. Once the extended system model, which consists of both the nominal system model and the fault model, is obtained, the forth step, analysis, involves verifying whether the system requirements hold in the presence of the faults defined in the model. Consequently, given a system model M, a fault hypothesis FH, and a NFR, the analysis problem may formally be expressed as the well-known model-checking problem M || FH |= NFR; here, M || FH denotes the combination of the system under consideration and the associated fault hypothesis. Using state-of-the-art model-checking tools such as SAL (http://sal.csl.sri.com) [15], all possible behaviors in the presence of faults within the scope of the specified fault hypothesis, may be analyzed. Therefore, these techniques may be used both for exhaustive fault injection and for verification.

5.1 Dependability

Model-checking techniques have been proven as efficient for analyzing the robustness of time-triggered communication protocols in the presence of faulty components during design [44]. The main approach here is model-based fault injection. It is essential to the utility of model checking for exploration and verification of fault-tolerant, distributed systems to be able to consider a large number of different kinds of faults—ideally, the fault model should be exhaustive, meaning that every kind of fault is described and that the model checker injects these in all possible ways in the considered model. Several classifications of failure modes in distributed systems can be found in literature [32,7]. A classification of component and system level failure modes for time-triggered communication networks, such as TTP and FlexRay is given in [42]. There, various failure modes, particularly related to time-triggered buses are distinguished and classified within the faults categories fail-silent, fail-omission, fail-invalid, fail-incorrect, and fail-untimely. A dependable time-triggered protocol has to ensure that the services it provides, such as, startup or re-integration are not flawed, even in presence of faulty components.

The most accurate representation of a faulty component can be obtained by placing the fault injector at the node module describing the component [45]. On the other hand, modeling faulty communication links is realized by injecting faults in the module specifying the communication. Faults vastly increase the state space that must be explored in model checking, since they introduce genuinely different behaviors. This aspect is considered in SAL by introducing a *fault degree*, as illustrated in [44]. A fault degree classifies the possible outputs of a faulty component, according to the failure modes identified above. For covering all failure modes related to time-triggered communication based on TTP, a fault degree of six is necessary. For example, a fault degree of 1 allows a faulty node only to fail silent, while fault degree 6 allows a node to send an arbitrary combination of frames with correct or incorrect semantics, noise, or nothing on each channel (i.e., Byzantine node failures). This scenario covers all failure modes from [42]. The following guarded command is used to inject into a node module a fault with a degree greater or equal 2.

```
[] state = faulty AND degree >= 2 →
    msg_out' = [[j:channels] IF j = 0 THEN cs_frame ELSE quiet ENDIF];
    time_out' = [[j:channels] IF j = 0 THEN S2 ELSE S1 ENDIF];
    state' = state;
```

Here, a faulty node sends a message (here cs_frame) on one channel and quiet on the other. Moreover, on the first channel the faulty node masquerades as node S2 (by sending the ID of node S2 in its time slot, here identified by S2).

Model-based fault injection techniques are used for assessing the robustness and fault-tolerance properties of systems. For example, in case of the startup service in time-triggered networks evaluating the robustness amounts to checking the safe startup of the system even if faulty components are present. The informal safe startup requirement "whenever there are two nodes in active state, these two nodes have synchronized local clocks (will agree on the slot time)" is specified in SAL as:

```
safety: LEMMA system |- G(FORALL (i,j: index):
            (states[i]=active AND states[j]=active) => (time_out[i]=time_out[j]));
```

Here, G denotes the always or $\Box$ modality of linear temporal logic (LTL), and system denotes the extended system model, consisting of the nominal models of the components, the nominal model of the redundant communication links, and the corresponding fault models.

5.1.1 Timings and Worst-Case Execution

Non-functional requirements include timeliness, that is, the ability of the considered system to provide response to events (e.g., originated in an external controlled environment) which must be functionally correct and furnished within precise and predictable timing constraints (e.g., deadlines). To ensure a system development compliant with timing requirements, the use of formal tools is mandatory.

SAL allows for expressing timing properties with respect to minimum timeouts, or the time required to stabilize after an upset. For instance, the requirement that a time-triggered system should start up within 10ms, as imposed on the TTP startup when deployed in safety-critical systems is formulated in SAL as the following lemma:

```
timely_startup: LEMMA system |- G(startup_time <= 10);
```

The variable *startup_time* measures the startup time of the system. It is initialized with zero and increased in every step until the components have reached the synchronous state. Here, the variable startup_time can be increased either discrete, in 1ms steps, or continuous, depending on the chosen modeling paradigms [42]. In the discrete paradigm time is encoded by finite data-types, resulting in a finite state space that can be analyzed using symbolic model checking techniques.

Systems involving continuous time can be efficiently represented in SAL using an explicit real-time model, called calendar automata [16]. The model includes a set of state variables and a set of timeout variables ranging over the reals. Additionally, there is a real-value variable time that denotes the current time. These variables control when discrete and time-progress transitions are enabled. Discrete transitions are enabled when the current time reaches the value of a timeout. Such a transition must increase the timeout to a new value strictly greater than its current value. In time transitions, the time variable time is updated to the value of the next timeout, that is, the minimum of the timeout variables. Since timeout automata models give rise to an infinite state space, verification of such models is usually based on infinite bounded model checking techniques such as for example provided by SAL' s inf-bmc tool. In the above example, the value of startup_time is given by the value of the variable time obtained when all components have reached the synchronous state.

A slightly modification of the above lemma allows one to compute the worst-case startup time for a given cluster consisting of n nodes and redundant links. This is done by parameterizing the *timely_startup* lemma by a variable *par_startup*, and using the model-checking algorithm to compute the value for this variable.

```
timely_startup: LEMMA system |- G(startup_time<=@par_startup);
```

By analyzing different cluster sizes and different degrees of fault, the worst-case startup time was computed to be $7 \cdot \tau$_round + $5 \cdot \tau$_slot, where *τ_round* denotes the duration of a round, and *τ_slot* the duration of a slot [44]. This lemma was proven for 5 nodes in the presence of a faulty node with fault degree of 6 in 4480 seconds showing the feasibility of such analysis during development.

5.2 Dependability of the Development Process and Robustness of MBD

Simulink or SCADE are often used in MBD. Because SCADE has been described in detail in public literature and Honeywell uses HiLiTE in production, we present an alternative tooling approach called HiLiTE for achieving process assurance. HiLiTE (Honeywell Integrated Lifecycle Tools & Environment) [10,11] has been used for engine and flight control MBD testing support during production. Differences between HiLiTE and SCADE are described in [10]. HiLiTE leverages a domain-specific block library that describes and augments Simulink with independent concise analytical representation and test vector augmentation. The capabilities of HiLiTE are:

- Auto generation of test cases and vectors from Matlab Simulink and StateFlow models
- In-depth semantic analysis of models for design consistency and robustness
- Auto generation of code from Matlab Simulink and StateFlow models

HiLiTE analyzes the design for soundness and robustness (like divide-by-zero, overflow/underflow, deactivated blocks, un-testable conditions) and verifies that the object code as implemented on the target processor complies with functional behavior specified with the by-product of code coverage hence addressing DO-178b [35] objectives (Section A-4.2,3,5; A-6.3,4,5; A-7.4,5,6,7) in an automated manner.

In the following, HiLiTE's test generation is briefly described followed by example model evaluations of non-functional property model. Fig. 1 presents logic gates and a library block under test called *ConfirmSec*. The low-level requirement of this block are a timer that expires (*Timeout = 1*), if input *Confirm* has been *1* for as many seconds as the value of input *TimeLimit*. *Timeout* is *0* if input *Confirm* is *0* and in all other cases (timeout not yet expired).

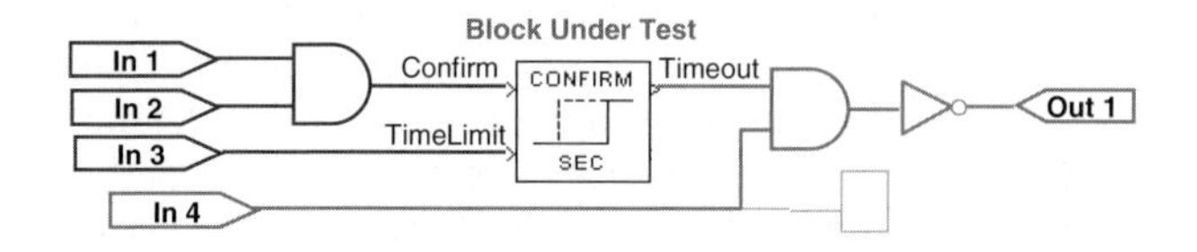

Fig. 1. Example Model for Test Generation. Block ConfirmSec

Fig. 2 depicts a test case template for the *ConfirmSec* block, where rows depict vector values to be applied at inputs of the blocks and expected values of block outputs in consecutive, contiguous time steps of the model. HiLiTE's test generation performs a backward data flow search from the block under test through intermediate blocks to find values to be applied at model inputs (In1, In2, In3) that leads to values required by the template at the block under test. In addition forward data flow is performed to allow externally-visible model output, that the block under test produced that expected value at its output. More details of the test generated and the approach and description and discussion of the achieved coverage can be found in [10,11]. Such a test approach assures correctness of the translation of model to target.

Rate = 50 Hz

Time Steps

No. of Time Steps	Block Under Test			comment
	Confirm	TimeLimit	Timeout	
1	0	Range.mid	0	reset timer
TimeLimit * Rate – 1	1	Range.mid	0	1 cycle before
1	1	Range.mid	1	timer expires
1	1	Range.mid	1	1 cycle after

Fig. 2. Test case template for ConfirmSec

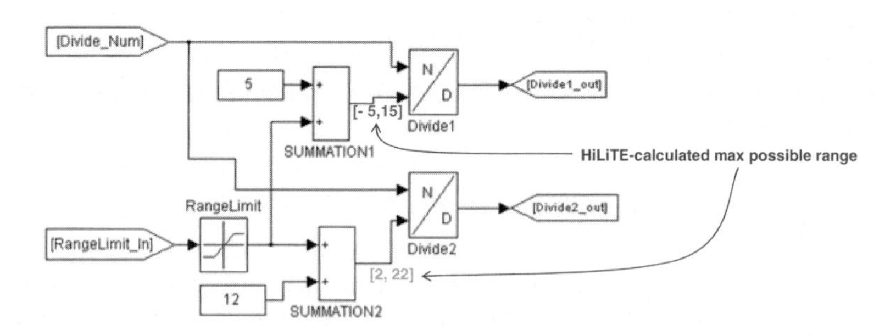

Fig. 3. Achieving robustness of models: Range checking of HiLiTE can detect potential divide-by-zero vulnerabilities

In addition HiLiTE performs analysis targeting robustness and soundness. Fig. 3 presents an example were HiLiTE used range checking and build-in assertions checking for divide-by-zero vulnerabilities to find a potential divide-by-zero in the platform code related to block *Divide1*.

HiLiTE can automatically detected unbounded counter patterns (as found by the connected blocks *plusOne*, *Counter*, *delay* in the model depicted in Fig. 4) by detecting counter semantics in models. This brief description of HiLiTE shows how non-functional requirements of models and process assurance can be achieved via a template and block-based model augmentation approach.

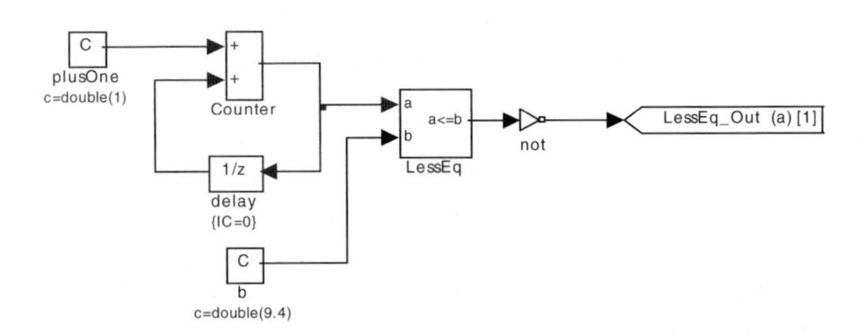

Fig. 4. Achieving robustness of models: detection of unbounded counter patterns by HiLiTE

5.3 Quantitative Dependability and Timing Assessment

Vestal et al. [48] describe the specification of an avionics IMA in MetaH and an automated error model to fault tree translation and follow-on quantitative assessment of the architecture using a COTS fault tree solver. Vestal et al. [47,48] provides an example avionics timing analysis and investigation of an IMA as well as theory of end-to-end timing based assessment of asynchronous distributed systems.

5.4 Schedulability

Recent work has shown the adequacy of SAL for schedulability analysis of IMA systems [49,50]. SAL's model checkers can be efficiently used to automatically compute schedulers that minimize the transmission latency, by encoding the task and message scheduling problem as a satisfiability problem with linear arithmetic constraints and tusing SAL's bounded model checker for finding the shortest schedule. We are currently investigating this line of work for IMA applications.

6 Summary and Conclusions

This paper presents a large variety of non-functional requirements (NFR) in avionics that are often treated as functional requirements. NFRs are reflected in the architectural approach of software, hardware, and systems very similar to functional requirements. The work presented is new as it provides a dense list of NFR for avionics and its trends. It also provides known exemplary formal capturing and analysis approaches. The mentioned requirements are by no means complete, but paint a picture of the breadth capability needed of a potential holistic tool chain that would capture, manage, and analyze non-functional and functional requirements, and avionics architectures. The authors hope to encourage system and tool designers to take on the work presented and integrate it into their approaches of NFR representation and analyses.

Acknowledgement

We would like to thank Devesh Bhatt, principle investigator of HiLiTE, for his MBD examples and input.

References

1. ARINC, Aircraft Data Network, Part 7, Avionics Full Duplex Switched Ethernet (AFDX) Network, ARINC 664 part 7 (June 2005)
2. ARINC, Electronic Distribution of Software, ARINC report 666 (May 17, 2002)
3. ARINC, Electronic Distribution of Software, ARINC Report 666A (May 24, 2005)
4. ARINC, Multi-Transmitter Data Bus ARINC 629 Part 1-2 (1999)
5. ARINC, Avionics Application Standard Software Interface. ARINC 653 (2003)
6. ARINC. Electronic Distribution of Software (EDS) Working Group (March 5, 2008)
7. Avižienis, A., Laprie, J.C., Randell, B., Landwehr, C.: Basic concepts and taxonomy of de and secure computing. IEEE Trans. on Dependable and Secure Comp. 1(1), 11–33 (2004)
8. Bate, I., Hawkins, R., McDermid, J.: A contract-based approach to designing safe systems. In: Proc. of the 8th Australian Workshop on Safety Critical Systems and Software, Canberra, Australia, vol. 33, pp. 25–36 (2003)
9. Baumann, R.: Soft Errors in Advanced Computer Systems. IEEE Design and Test of Computers, 258–266 (2005)
10. Bhatt, D., Hall, B., Dajani-Brown, S., Hickman, S., Paulitsch, M.: Model-based development and the implications to design assurance and certification. In: 24th Digital Avionics Systems Conference (October 2005)
11. Bhatt, D., Hickman, S., Schloegel, K., Oglesby, D.: An Approach and Tool for Test Generation from Model-Based Functional Requirements. In: Proc. of the Intl. Workshop on Aerospace Software Engineering (May 2007)
12. Binns, P., Englehart, M., Jackson, M., Vestal, S.: Domain-specific software architectures for guidance, navigation and control. Int. Journal of Software Engineering and Knowledge Engineering 6(2), 201–227 (1996)
13. Briere, D., Traverse, P.: Airbus A320/A330/A340 Electrical Flight Controls: A Family of Fault-Tolerant Systems. F TCS 23 (1993)
14. Butler, R.W., Finelli, G.B.: The infeasibility of quantifying the reliability of life-critical real-time software. IEEE Trans. on Software Engineering 19(1), 3–12 (1993)
15. de Moura, L., Owre, S., Rueß, H., Rushby, J., Shankar, N., Sorea, M., Tiwari, A.: Tool presentation: SAL2. In: Alur, R., Peled, D.A. (eds.) CAV 2004. LNCS, vol. 3114, pp. 496–500. Springer, Heidelberg (2004)
16. Dutertre, B., Sorea, M.: Modeling and Verification of a Fault-Tolerant Real-time Startup Protocol using Calendar Automata. FORMATS/FTRTFT, 199–214 (2004)
17. Glinz, M.: On Non-Functional Requirements. In: Proc. of IEEE Int. Requirements Engineering Conference, pp. 21–26 (2007)

18. Hall, B., Paulitsch, M., Benson, D., Behbahani, A.: Jet Engine Control Using Ethernet with a BRAIN. 44th AIAA/ASME/SAE/ASEE Joint Propulsion Conference & Exhibit. AIAA Paper No AIAA-2008-5291. Hartford, CT, USA (July 2008)
19. Hecht, H.: Why prognostics for avionics. In: Proc. of Aerospace Conf. IEEE, Los Alamitos (2006)
20. Heitmeyer, C.L., Jeffords, R.D., Labaw, B.G.: Automated consistency checking of requirements specifications. ACM Trans. on SW Eng. and Method. 5(3), 231–261 (1996)
21. Jacob, J.M.: High assurance security and safety for digital avionics. In: Proc. of the 23rd Digital Avionics Systems Conference, Vol. 2, pp.8.E.4 - 8.1–9 (24-28 October 2004)
22. Johnson, D.P.: Assessing the Security of Airborne Networks. Aerospace Safety- Design, Maintenance/Operations, and Safety/Security. SAE Doc.No 2007-01-3784 (2007)
23. Knight, J.C., Leveson, N.G.: An Experimental Evaluation of the Assumption of Independence in Multi-version Programming. IEEE Trans. on Software Engineering SE-12(1), 96–109 (1986)
24. Malan, R., Bredemeyer, D.: Defining Non-Functional Requirements. white paper (accessed May 2008) (August 3, 2001), http://www.bredemeyer.com
25. McWha, J.: Development of the 777 flight control system. AIAA Guidance, Navigation, and Control Conference (August 2003)
26. Morris, J., Koopman, P.: Representing Design Tradeoffs in Safety Critical Systems. In: Proc. of 2005 Workshop on Architecting Dependable Systems, pp. 1–5 (2005)
27. Object Management Group (OMG). A UML Profile for MARTE: Modeling and Analysis of Real-Time Embedded systems, Version Beta 2 (June 8, 2008)
28. Owens, B.D., Herring, M.S., Dulac, N., Leveson, N.G., Ingham, M.D., Weiss, K.A.: Application of a Safety-Driven Design Methodology to an Outer Planet Exploration Mission. In: IEEE Aerospace Conference. Big Sky, MT (March 2008)
29. Paech, B., Dutoit, A., Kerkow, D., von Knethen, A.: Functional requirements, non-functional requirements and architecture specification cannot be separated – A position paper. REFSQ (2002)
30. Paulitsch, M., Morris, J., Hall, B., Driscoll, K., Latronico, E., Koopman, P.: Coverage and the use of cyclic redundancy codes in ultra-dependable systems. In: Proc. of Int. Conf. on Dependable Systems and Networks (DSN), 28 June - 1 July 2005, pp. 346–355 (2005)
31. Pop, P., Eles, P., Peng, Z.: Schedulability-Driven Communication Synthesis for Time Triggered Embedded Systems. In: 6th Int. Conf. on Real-Time Computing Systems and Applications (RTCSA 1999), Hong Kong, December 13-15, 1999, pp. 287–294 (1999)
32. Powell, D.: Failure mode assumptions and assumption coverage. In: Proc. of FTCS 1992, pp. 386–395. IEEE Computer Society Press, Los Alamitos (1992)
33. Royalty, C.: Keep the User in Mind: Operational Considerations for Securing Airborne Networks, Aerospace Safety- Design, Maintenance/Operations, and Safety/Security. SAE Doc. No 2007-01-3785 (September 2007)
34. RTCA SC-164. Audio Systems Characteristics and Minimum Operational Performance Standards for Aircraft Audio Systems and Equipment Systems and Equipment, Wash. D.C., RTCA Inc. (1993)
35. RTCA SC-167/EUROCAE WG-12, DO-178B/ED12B Software Considerations in Airborne Systems and Equipment Certification, Wash. D.C., RTCA Inc. (1992)
36. SAE, Certification Considerations for Highly-Integrated Or Complex Aircraft Systems, SAE Doc. No ARP4754 (November 1996)
37. SAE, Guidelines and Methods for Conducting the Safety Assessment Process on Civil Airborne Systems and Equipment, SAE Doc. No ARP4761 (December 1996)

38. SAE, Guidelines for Time-Limited-Dispatch (TLD) Analysis for Electronic Engine Control Systems, SAE Doc. No ARP5107 Ref. B (November 2006)
39. SAE, SAE Architecture Analysis Design Language (AADL) Doc.AS5506/1 (June 2006)
40. Shawlee, W., Humphrey, D.: Aging avionics- what causes it and how to respond. IEEE Trans on Components and Packaging Technologies 24(4), 739–740 (2001)
41. Sifakis, J.: A Framework for Component-based Construction. In: 3rd IEEE Int. Conf. on Software Engineering and Formal Methods (SEFM 2005), pp. 293–300 (September 2005)
42. Sorea, M., Steiner, W.: Classification and analysis of failure modes for time-triggered systems. In: Proceedings of FeT (2007)
43. Srivastava, D., Narasimhan, P.: Architectural Support for Mode-Driven Fault Tolerance in Distributed Applications. In: Proc. of the 2005 workshop on Architecting Dependable Systems, St. Louis, Missouri, USA, pp. 1–7 (2005)
44. Steiner, W., Rushby, J., Sorea, M., Pfeifer, H.: Model checking a fault-tolerant startup algorithm: From design exploration to exhaustive fault simulation. In: DSN 2004 (2004)
45. Steiner, W.: Startup and Recovery of Fault-Tolerant Time-Triggered Communication. PhD Thesis, Technische Universität Wien (2004)
46. Tovar, E., Vasques, F.: From Task Scheduling in Single Processor Environments to Message Scheduling in a PROFIBUS. In: IPPS/SPDP Workshops, pp. 339–352 (1999)
47. Vestal, S.: Real-Time Sampled Signal Flows through Asynchronous Distributed Systems. In: IEEE Real-Time and Embedded Technology and Applications Symp. (2005)
48. Vestal, S., Stickler, L., Kune, D.F., Binns, P., Lamba, N.: Architecture Specification and Automated Timing and Safety Analysis for a Large Avionics System (June 16, 2004), `http://la.sei.cmu.edu/aadl/documents/AADL-MetaH%20for%20LAS.pdf`
49. Voss, S.: Scheduling in time-triggered networks. In: Meersman, R., Tari, Z., Herrero, P. (eds.) OTM-WS 2007, Part II. LNCS, vol. 4806, pp. 1081–1091. Springer, Heidelberg (2007)
50. Voss, S., Sorea, M., Echtle, K.: Symbolic Scheduling in Time-Triggered Systems (in preparation, 2008)
51. Wilkinson, C., Haselrick, B., Paulitsch, M., Hall, B.: Transitioning Aerospace Electronic Systems from Reactive to Proactive Obsolescence Management. IEEE Trans. on Components and Packaging Technologies (2008)
52. Wittenmark, B., Nilsson, J., Törngren.: Timing Problems in Real-Time Control Systems. In: Proc. of American Control Conf., June 21-23, vol. 3, pp. 2000–2004 (1995)
53. Xu, L., Ziv, H., Richardson, D., Alspaugh, T.A.: An architectural pattern for non-functional dependability requirements. SIGSOFT Softw. Eng. Notes 30(4), 1–6 (2005)
54. Zetter, K.: FAA: Boeing's New 787 May Be Vulnerable to Hacker Attack. wired.com (April 1, 2008)

A Simulation Approach for Performance Validation during Embedded Systems Design

Zhonglei Wang[1], Wolfgang Haberl[1], Andreas Herkersdorf[1], and Martin Wechs[2]

[1] Technische Universität München
Arcisstraße 21, 80290 München, Germany
zhonglei.wang@tum.de, haberl@in.tum.de, herkersdorf@tum.de
[2] BMW Forschung und Technik GmbH
Hanauer Straße 46, 80992 München, Germany
martin.wechs@bmw.de

Abstract. Due to the time-to-market pressure, it is highly desirable to design hardware and software of embedded systems in parallel. However, hardware and software are developed mostly using very different methods, so that performance evaluation and validation of the whole system is not an easy task. In this paper, we propose a simulation approach to bridge the gap between model-driven software development and simulation based hardware design, by merging hardware and software models into a SystemC based simulation environment. An automated procedure has been established to generate software simulation models from formal models, while the hardware design is originally modeled in SystemC. As the simulation models are annotated with timing information, performance issues are tackled in the same pass as system functionality, rather than in a dedicated approach.

For designing real-time systems, although performance evaluation based on simulation cannot provide guarantees of safety, it can provide realistic performance values to validate whether the performance requirements are really satisfied or not and show how pessimistic the static analysis is. Further, the simulative approach is also able to provide the developers an insight into the system architecture to help find bottlenecks of the system. We use the simulative approach as a complement of static analysis and combine them in an integral development cycle.

1 Introduction

During embedded systems development, it is a critical issue to manage non-functional requirements concerning performance, security, power consumption and so on. Among these, performance is one of the most important factors to be considered. If performance requirements cannot be met, this could lead to system failure. This is especially true for safety critical systems. Since performance problems detected at later development phases may result in considerable changes in the whole system, including hardware platform and software architecture, it is necessary to handle performance issues from early development phases until system implementation.

T. Margaria and B. Steffen (Eds.): ISoLA 2008, CCIS 17, pp. 385–399, 2008.

Today, many embedded systems are multiprocessor or distributed systems, where applications are partitioned into several tasks and allocated to a set of processors or processing elements, which are interconnected and cooperate to realize the system functionality. A good example for a distributed system is an automotive network, which consists of several buses that connect the electronic control units (ECU) as well as sensors and actuators. Most such embedded systems are designed for applications in a specific domain and require both, the software and the hardware system, to be adapted to the applications. Regarding traditional system development methods, software design starts after the hardware platform is ready for use. Due to the time-to-market pressure it is desirable to develop both hardware and software in a tightly coupled loop.

However, the methods for hardware and software development are quite different, which makes performance estimation of the whole embedded system difficult. Today, model driven development (MDD) approaches are increasingly used to deal with the ever-growing complexity of software, while the current industry practice for hardware platform design is mostly based on simulation. Among system level design languages (SLDL), SystemC is the most frequently used one in both academia and industry and has become a standard for system level design space exploration [1]. An ideal co-development process should provide an efficient way to bridge the gap between MDD processes for software development and SystemC based simulative approaches for hardware design.

1.1 Overview of SystemC

SystemC supports modeling systems at different levels of abstraction, from system level to register-transfer level, and allows to co-simulate software and hardware components within a single framework. Essentially, it is a C++ class library featuring methods for building and composing SystemC elements. In order to model concurrent system behavior, SystemC extends C++ with concepts used by hardware modeling languages, like VHDL and Verilog.

TLM (transaction-level modeling) [2,3] is a widely used modeling style in SystemC. In this modeling style, communication architectures are modeled as channels, which provide interfaces to functional units. Modeling effort can be reduced, if different communication architectures support a common set of abstract interfaces. Thus, communication and computation can be modeled separately.

The OSCI (Open SystemC Initiative) Transaction Level Working Group has defined seven levels of abstraction supported by SystemC [3]: algorithmic (ALG), communicating processes (CP), communicating processes with time (CP+T), programmer's view (PV), programmer's view with time (PV+T), cycle accurate (CA) and register transfer level (RTL). A system can be modeled at a high level of abstraction, for example ALG, and refined stepwise to a lower level of abstraction, which might be RTL, where simulation is more accurate but simulation time increases.

1.2 A Model Driven Development Process

In a MDD process, design starts at high levels of abstraction and captures a system's functionality in a formal model. The resulting design can be formally reasoned about, for example using formal verification, and implementation code can be generated, all supported by automated tools.

In our MDD process, we chose COLA [4], the Component Language, as the formal basis and have developed an automatic deployment process for hard real-time systems design, using non-functional requirements as a guidance for automatic allocation and scheduling of the modeled tasks. The modeling framework and the deployment process will be introduced in Section 2.

The current MDD process supports software modeling down to the implementation on a concrete platform, retaining correctness with respect to the model. Still the following problems remain to be solved:

- Static scheduling and schedulability analysis are based on calculations employing worst case execution times of the tasks as a basis. This can avoid underestimation and guarantees safety of the system, but is often overly pessimistic, especially when applied to event-triggered systems. The formal model that static analysis is based on cannot accurately capture dynamic effects, such as resource contentions and varying communication delays.
- In the current process the modeled tasks are targeted to a given platform, which is assumed to be existing. However, if the hardware architecture is still under design, the execution time and resource usages cannot be estimated precisely. This might result in erroneous deployment. On the other hand, if software development starts after the hardware system is ready, the time-to-market would be delayed and the hardware system were designed without evaluation using the real application.
- The last but not the least problem is that static analysis can only answer "yes or no" questions, that is, it can only tell us whether the tasks are schedulable on the given platform or not. It cannot provide an insight into the system and thus cannot give important information for detection of performance bottlenecks and system improvement.

The mentioned problems not only exist in our process but generally in static analysis centric design methods. We will present an approach to tackle these problems in this paper.

1.3 An Overview of the Proposed Approach

Concerning the facts discussed above we propose a simulative approach, which bridges the gap between SystemC-based design methods and the COLA-based MDD process for real-time software development. The advantage of our simulative approach, compared to static analysis, is that, on the one hand it delivers more realistic values and, on the other hand hardware details which might be neglected by the abstract perspective of static analysis are taken into account. In contrast, static analysis has the advantage that it is able to guarantee feasible designs under hard real-time performance requirements. Our approach combines the two design methods in an integral hardware/software co-development process that makes use of the advantages of both methods. In this co-development process, the COLA-based MDD process is used for behavior modeling and automatic deployment. Simulation is used for system level hardware design decisions and performance evaluation of the whole system. The simulation results give us detailed performance statistics to validate whether all the performance requirements are satisfied and how pessimistic the static analysis is, and also to provide information for system enhancement. If some requirements are not satisfied, we can generate enough information to find performance bottlenecks to decide which parts of the system should be improved. In this way, hardware design and software development are tightly coupled and the exploration cycle is repeated to achieve high performance of the whole system.

As discussed, static analysis and simulation are complementary approaches to manage performance requirements. Static analysis uses given performance requirements as constraints to find an optimal allocation and scheduling, while simulation evaluates a design to check if the requirements are satisfied. In our view, the design space exploration is finished, when both approaches indicate the satisfaction of the performance requirements. To establish such a desired simulation approach, we investigated the following aspects:

- Automatic generation of software simulation models from COLA models.
- A well-suited technique for estimation and representation of software performance in the simulation models.
- Automatic construction of simulators using existing simulation components.

In addition, we have also considered coverage-based test case generation for reduction of simulation time.

1.4 Organization

The rest of the paper is organized as follows: Section 2 gives a brief introduction to modeling concepts of COLA and also presents the COLA based development process. Section 3 describes the proposed simulation approach. Following this, Section 4 contains a detailed description of the generation process of software simulation models and a performance estimation technique. The way of building simulators is presented in Section 5. Section 6 concludes this paper.

2 The COLA-Based MDD Process

In the following we will detail on the COLA language and the development process established thereon. The described concept allows for consistent modeling and preservation of the model's semantics down to the executable system.

2.1 Modeling Concepts of COLA

COLA is a component-based modeling language especially targeted at embedded control systems. It offers a graphical representation to specify the functional behavior of the modeled application. Being a synchronous formalism, COLA follows the *hypothesis of perfect synchrony* [5]. Basically, this asserts that computation and communication occur instantly in a system, i.e. take no time. Components in a synchronous data flow language then operate in parallel, processing input and output signals at discrete instants of time. This discrete uniform time-base allows for a deterministic description of concurrency by abstracting from concrete implementation details, such as physical bus communication, or signal jitter. To take the resulting models to the designated hardware platform, automated code generation is supported by our established tool chain [6,7].

COLA offers several advantages in a tool-backed MDD process. There, not only behavioral modeling is sought for, but several views onto the complete system must be distinguished. Following the nomenclature of Pretschner et al. [8], behavioral models form the *logical architecture.* The description of the target hardware platform and other non-functional requirements then comprise the *technical architecture.* The latter is usually excluded in the modeling formalisms, or rather, focused on with a lack of description of the logical layer. This kind of lower abstraction is applied, e.g. in the Metropolis project [9] and the CARAT toolkit [10].

The basic language element of COLA is the *unit.* Units can be composed hierarchically, or occur in terms of *blocks* that define the basic (arithmetic) operations of a system. Each unit has a set of typed *ports* describing the interface, called *signature of the unit* in COLA, and which are categorized into input and output ports. Units can be used to build more complex components by building a *network* of units and by defining an interface to such a network. The individual connections of (sub-) units in a network are called *channels* and connect an output port with one or more suitably typed input ports.

In addition to the hierarchy of networks, COLA provides a decomposition into *automata* (i. e., finite state machines, similar to Statecharts [11]). If a unit is decomposed into an automaton, each state of the automaton is associated with a corresponding sub-unit, which determines the behavior in that particular state. This definition of an automaton is therefore well-suited to partition complex networks of units into disjoint *operating modes* (cf. [12]), whose respective activation depends on the input signals of the automaton.

The collection of all units forms a COLA *system*, which models the application, possibly including its environment. Such a system does not have any unconnected input or output ports as there would be no way to provide input to systems. For effective communication with the environment, *sources* and *sinks* provide connectors to the underlying hardware.

2.2 Development Process

As mentioned already, COLA is ideally applied in a development process that employs modeling, model analysis, formal verification, automatic hardware and software synthesis and automated deployment to a concrete platform within a well integrated tool chain. The whole development cycle from feature modeling down to implementation is done in a single formalism. An overview of the COLA based process is illustrated in Figure 1.

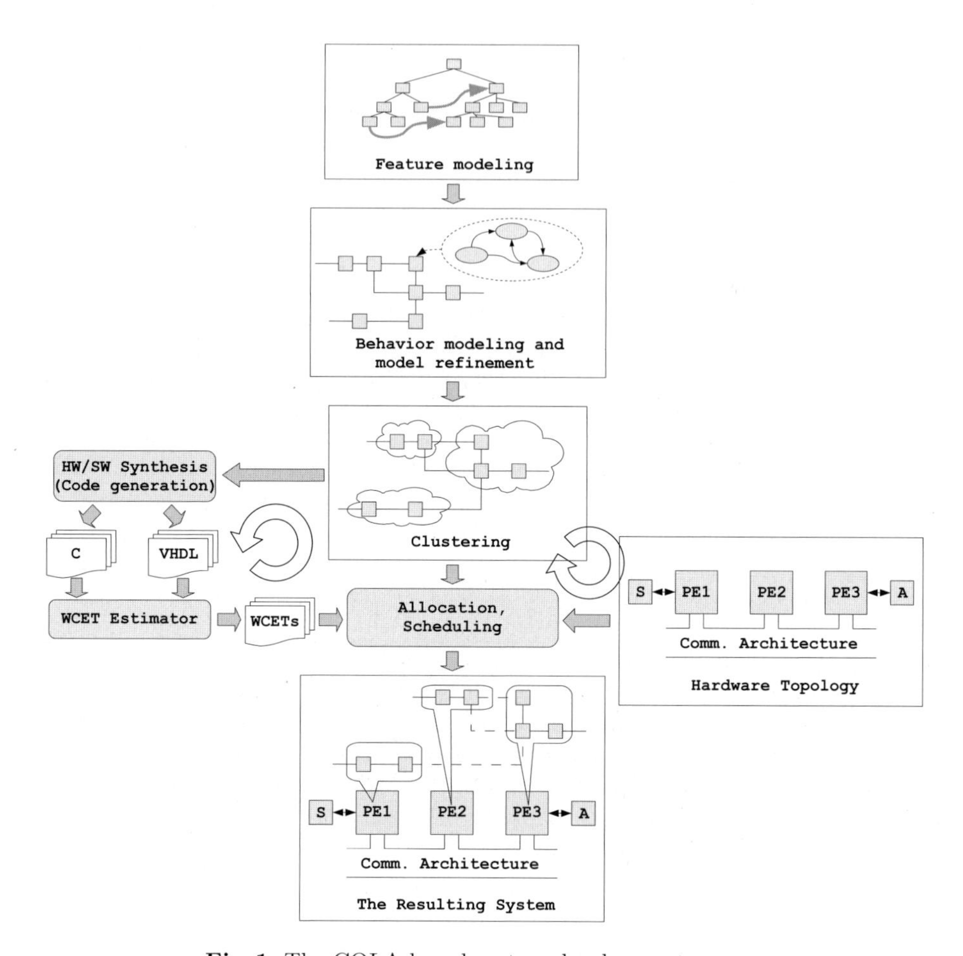

Fig. 1. The COLA-based system development process

Feature Modeling: In the requirement phase, the system features and how these features interact with each other should be captured in a *feature tree*. In COLA a feature tree is described by networks and automata, connected by untyped channels. The hierarchical nature of COLA networks allows for decomposition of features into sub-features.

Functional Modeling and Model Refinement: The leaves of the feature tree set the starting points for modeling the system's functionality. The feature model is converted to a functional model throughout several steps of model transformation and rearrangement. The resulting high-level models are further refined until all designated functionality of the system is covered. As both modeling and model refinement are performed using the easily understandable COLA graphical representation, human faults can be significantly reduced. Further, thanks to COLA's formal semantics, the models correctness can be checked by formal verification. Another advantage of COLA modeling concepts is the model reusability because of its composability nature. In order to guarantee the compatibility between components in different contexts and runtime safety, type checking and type inference are supported by automated tools [13].

Deployment Process: In oder to reduce human design effort and retain the model's correctness down to the implementation on a concrete platform, an automatic deployment process is highly desired. Our deployment process contains the following steps:

- Clustering: Before allocation, units of the functional model are grouped into *clusters*, depending on performance constraints as well as other important non-functional requirements. A cluster is the model representation of a task from an operating system's point of view and is the basic element in the deployment process. For more details on clustering, please refer to [14].
- Performance estimation: During this step execution times, including worst- (WCET) and best-case execution times (BCET), and resource usages for each cluster are estimated. These non-functional properties are based on generated C code and back-annotated to clusters for later use.
- Allocation: Allocation is the process of assigning tasks to available computing resources with respect to non-functional requirements. To tackle this challenge we have developed an algorithm, which takes cluster architecture and hardware topology as its input and tries to find an optimal allocation under certain non-functional constrains.
- Scheduling: Scheduling is aimed at determining execution order of tasks while minimizing the overall completion time of the system. The role of schedulability analysis is to determine whether there is a scheduling plan that satisfies the given performance requirements. More information on scheduling can be found in [15].

Implementation: After finding a proper design that fulfills the requirements, C code is generated [6] and compiled for execution on the target platform. To satisfy the communication demands of the modeled system, we developed a configurable middleware [16] fulfilling this duty. Sometimes, it is also necessary to implement some tasks in hardware [7], when higher performance is required.

3 Simulation Environment

As already discussed, it is our goal to establish a simulation framework for performance validation of the whole system design including application software, hardware and service layers between software and hardware. The service layers typically include a real-time operating system (RTOS) and a middleware. As SystemC is considered as the most suitable SLDL for our purpose, the simulator is implemented on top of the SystemC simulation kernel.

As both software behavior and hardware architecture can be formalized into COLA models, our approach allows for automatic generation of software simulation models, hardware topology and deployment information. An overview of

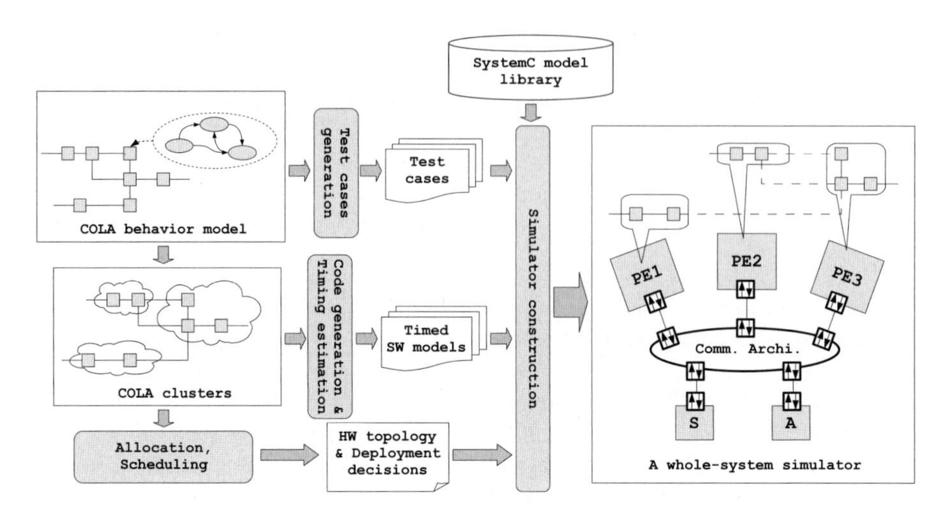

Fig. 2. The process of creating a simulator

the approach of creating a sample simulator is given in Figure 2. The following required steps are depicted in the figure:

- Software simulation models are automatically generated from COLA clusters. Each model corresponds to one cluster. During the generation process, a timing estimation tool is called to predict the execution time for each basic block of the cluster and to carry back the timing information into the software model. Thus, the software model runs on the host machine instead of an instruction set simulator. Still, the temporal behavior of the target execution is accurately simulated.
- Because the hardware model in COLA is an abstraction of the real hardware and only contains information required for allocation and scheduling, such as processing speed of a processing unit and bandwidth of a bus, hardware simulation models cannot be generated directly through model transformations. However, the basic configuration information including hardware topology, allocation of clusters and scheduling information can be generated and stored in an XML file. A tool reads this file and combines existing simulation components to construct a simulator. Therefore, before a simulator can be built, hardware designers should spend effort to establish a SystemC model library, which contains simulation models of the system components in question. For example bus models of Flexray and CAN should be included in the library for an automotive system design.
- The choice of test cases is very important. A poorly selected set of test cases might lack corner cases or might even contain redundant test cases. Using several test cases that cover the same execution path cannot provide any additional information but wastes time. In other words, an ideal test generator should generate the smallest set of test cases to cover the whole *test space*. Several established test case generation methods can be used with

our approach. They generate test cases either by model checking (e.g. [17]) or directly from C code (e.g. [18]). To use the former method, COLA models can be transformed into Promela code and checked using the SPIN model checker [19].

A detailed description of test case generation is out of the scope of this paper. We rather focus on the first two working steps and give a more detailed introduction to them in the following sections.

4 Software Simulation Model Generation

Software simulation model generation is a key factor to bridge the gap between hardware design and software development. To allow for a combination of hard- and software simulation components in SystemC, the software models have to be encapsulated in SystemC modules. Figure 3 depicts the generation process. First, C code is generated from COLA clusters. Then a timing estimation tool predicts the execution time for each basic block, annotates the timing information for the C code and finally encapsulates the code into a SystemC module. The C code generated in this step can be regarded as a temporary representation that is used only for timing estimation. After the design space exploration the same code generator is used to generate C code for the production system.

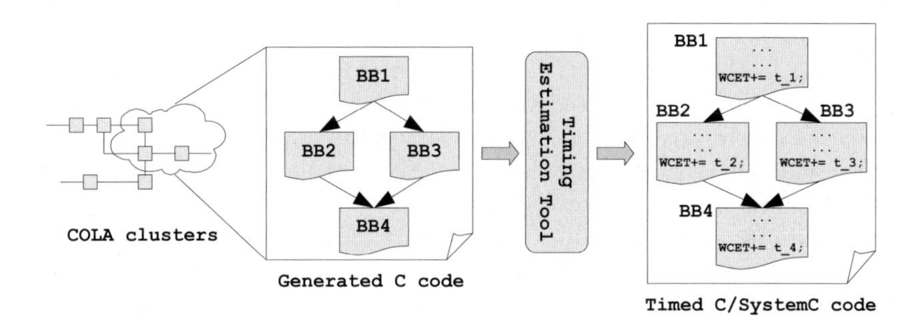

Fig. 3. Software simulation model generation

4.1 C Code Generation

The code generation relies on a template-like set of translation rules. As COLA has a slender syntax, the number of translation rules is small. The translation rules are well documented in [6]. We just give an overview here.

For each composite unit found in the given COLA system, the code generator creates a C function with an appropriate signature, where variables defined for inputs and outputs of the unit are included. The body of a generated C function implements the related unit's behavior. For a network, this means that the generated function for each sub-unit included in the network is called. Of course the sequence of calls has to preserve the order induced by semantics of the data flow. To realize a channel that is being written to by a unit and read by the descendant one, a variable is used to pass data from one function call to the next. For an automaton, the code describing the behaviors of its contained states are organized in a switch-case construct. Which case is to be executed depends on the stored automaton's state. The guards for the outgoing transitions of the active state are evaluated. Depending on the result of this evaluation, either the actual state stays active or a following one is activated.

4.2 Timing Estimation

The C code generated by the code generator is subsequently input to the timing estimation tool. The execution time of a program is influenced by several factors including execution path and low level timing effects due to microcontrollers' features like pipeline, cache and branch predictor. It is a goal of the simulation to provide dynamic performance values, which resemble to the system performance of real executions. Therefore, during the timing estimation we do not bound execution paths like WCET analysis, but rather keep the execution paths, and hence execution times, dependent on concrete input data derived from a test case generator. Thus, the estimation pessimism of a static analysis tool is avoided.

The low-level timing effects can be categorized into local timing effects and global timing effects. Pipeline effects are a typical example of local timing effects. When loading instructions into a pipeline, adjacent instructions affect each other but remote instructions do not affect their respective execution. Local timing effects can be accurately estimated in the scope of a basic block using either static timing analysis or simulation. Whereas, global timing effects are highly context-related and different execution paths set different context scenarios for a basic block. A cache access or branch instruction will affect future cache accesses or branch predictions, so the cache and branch prediction effects are global timing effects. They have to be estimated at run time.

We propose to use static analysis to estimate the local timing effects in order to reduce overhead of run-time simulation. In embedded software, an instruction is often repeated many times either because it is in a loop or because the task is triggered many times in an application. During static analysis, timing estimation is performed only once for each instruction related to the timing effect, while the run-time simulation must be repeated as often as the instruction is executed. Thus static analysis generates significantly less effort in this case.

For global timing effects, a dynamic estimation method is proposed in our previous work [20]. We insert function calls into the source code to send run-time data to a data cache simulator and a branch predictor simulator for load/store instructions and branch instructions, respectively. The simulators are driven by the run-time data to analyze the dynamic behaviors of the respective instructions related to the global timing effects.

The instruction cache effect is a special case of global timing effects. Instruction cache accesses are not as context-related as other global timing effects except for the instructions in a loop body. If there are no nested loops used and instructions in a loop body are analyzed for the first iteration and for the later

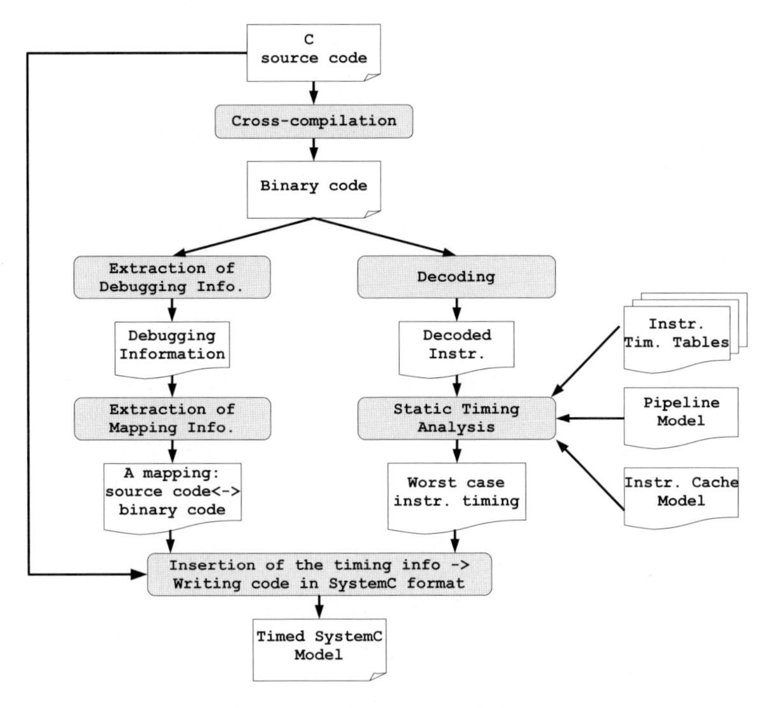

Fig. 4. Performance estimation framework

iterations separately, the instruction cache effect can also be estimated by static timing analysis in the scope of a basic block. This approximation will not reduce estimation accuracy too much.

The work of timing estimation and back-annotation is supported by a tool. Figure 3 gives an overview of the work flow of the timing estimation tool. Its working steps are introduced in the following:

- Cross-compilation: the generated C code is cross-compiled into target binary code with debugging information included. We use the GCC (GNU compiler collection) compilers, which support lots of processors commonly used. The generated binary code is in ELF (executable and linkable format), which is a standard binary format for Unix and Unix-like systems.
- Timing analysis: From the binary file, two pieces of important information are to be extracted: the low-level instruction timing and the information describing the mapping between source code and binary code. As already discussed, a hybrid method is used to estimate the execution time: pipeline analysis and instruction cache analysis are done statically and timing effects of data cache and branch predictor are simulated at run time.
- Extraction of the mapping information: We extract the DWARF's line table from the binary file. DWARF is a common debugging data format and is associated with ELF. DWARF's line table provides the mapping between source code lines and the target machine instructions generated from these lines. The mapping information is stored in a specific data structure to facilitate later use.

– Back-annotation: The tool reads a basic block of source code and finds the corresponding binary instructions by checking the mapping information. The individual instruction timings are cumulated and inserted into the source code. Finally the C code is rewritten in SystemC format, thus allowing for a timed simulation in SystemC.

5 Simulator Construction

As already mentioned, SystemC supports system modeling at seven levels of abstraction. However, COLA is more suitable for modeling at the ALG (algorithmic) and CP (communicating processes) levels than SystemC, because the artifacts of COLA can be formally reasoned about, resulting in less errors contained in the modeled systems. In our approach, the system modeling in SystemC starts from the PV+T (programmer's view with time) level. As described in the last section, software simulation models at the PV+T level are generated form COLA models at the CP level, skipping modeling at the CP+T (communicating processes with time) and PV (programmer's view) levels. Although COLA provides mechanisms for modeling hardware platforms, this hardware model is very abstract and cannot be employed to generate simulation models through model transformation. Therefore the platform simulation components must be specified by hardware designers as library elements. The components of the COLA hardware model are mapped to corresponding platform simulation components. This mapping information can be generated from the hardware topology captured in COLA. In addition, the information about allocation decisions and scheduling is also generated from the COLA hardware model and can be used to construct an executable whole-system simulator.

At the PV+T level platform simulation models include typically communication architectures and service layers:

– Communication architecture: It gives a structural view of a bus or network. For each transaction, the message length is defined and the sending order of the messages is determined by a specific mechanism, e.g. by priorities of the senders. The communication architecture can be further refined to the cycle accurate level, where the communication is triggered by a clock, and its timing behavior is accurately modeled.
– RTOS model: In real-time systems, there is commonly an RTOS running on each node, liable for scheduling and dispatching the tasks running on the node and for providing an abstraction of the underlying hardware to the running applications. In our approach, a scheduler is modeled first to realize the scheduling determined by the schedulability analysis. In the next refinement step, the scheduler model is replaced by an RTOS model, which captures the influences of the target RTOS on the timing behaviors of the tasks more accurately. Similar RTOS models are introduced in [21,22].

– Middleware model: To assemble hardware and software simulation models, the software has to be adapted to specific TLM APIs provided by the hardware platform model. As a result, the code for interaction with the underlying platform highly depends on the TLM APIs, which however may vary during the development. This is rather inconvenient for software developers. To allow for platform independent software development a middleware model that provides a set of abstract services supported by different platforms is used. It can not only be used in the transaction-level modeling but also be refined and implemented on a real hardware platform as we described in [16].

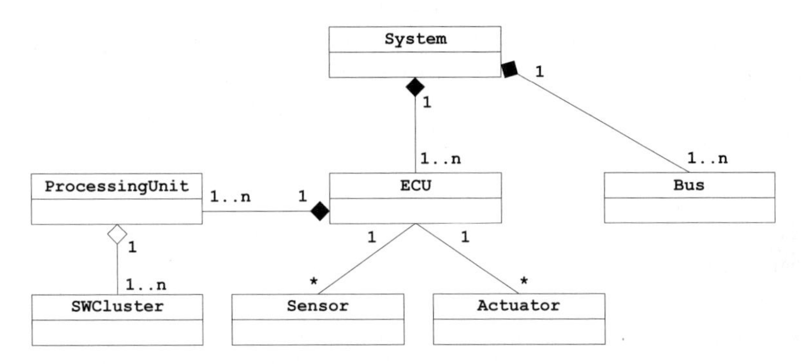

Fig. 5. Platform meta-model

Figure 5 shows a class model of the COLA platform meta-model. In the meta-model most information for simulator construction is covered, such as hardware topology and allocation decisions. The scheduling will be determined in the schedulability analysis of our process. This information is transformed into an XML file. The simulator construction tool parses the XML file and employs the existing simulation components to build a simulator.

6 Conclusion

In this paper we have presented a simulation approach for evaluation of the performance of embedded systems in a holistic manner. This approach combines model driven software development and simulation based hardware systems design. We chose COLA as the formal basis of our exemplified MDD process. From COLA clusters, the presented tool generates software simulation models extended with timing information. We showed the use of a hybrid performance estimation technique, which combines static timing analysis and simulation. The generated software simulation models can be connected with hardware simulation models afterwards. The whole simulator is built according to a configuration file which is generated from the COLA hardware model and contains hardware topology, allocation and scheduling information. This allows for a semantically correct simulation of the modeled system, thus leading to realistic results. With the performance statistics obtained from the simulation, the system components can be evaluated to find performance bottlenecks in the system for improvement.

For soft real-time systems design, this simulation approach is iterated for design space exploration. Yet, for hard real-time systems design, static analysis is desirable to guarantee feasible designs under hard real-time performance requirements. In this context, the simulation is used as a necessary complement of the static analysis to validate the analysis results. It is able to check whether the performance requirements are really satisfied by the designs found by the static analysis and how pessimistic the analysis is.

At the time of writing this paper, the whole framework is not yet completed, but most of the tools such as the code generator, the timing estimator and the tool for scheduling have been implemented. The COLA-based MDD process has also been established. We are currently implementing the tools for automatic construction of the simulation model and for test case generation. Subsequently, we will validate the efficiency of the proposed approach by using the simulator with a case study.

References

1. Institute of Electrical and Electronics Engineers: IEEE Std 1666 - 2005 IEEE Standard SystemC Language Reference Manual. IEEE Std 1666-2005 (2006)
2. Cai, L., Gajski, D.: Transaction level modeling: an overview. In: Proceedings of the 1st IEEE/ACM/IFIP international conference on Hardware/software codesign and system synthesis (CODES+ISSS 2003), pp. 19–24 (2003)
3. Donlin, A.: Transaction level modeling: flows and use models. In: Proceedings of the 2nd IEEE/ACM/IFIP international conference on Hardware/software codesign and system synthesis (CODES+ISSS 2004), pp. 75–80 (2004)
4. Kugele, S., Tautschnig, M., Bauer, A., Schallhart, C., Merenda, S., Haberl, W., Kühnel, C., Müller, F., Wang, Z., Wild, D., Rittmann, S., Wechs, M.: COLA – The component language. Technical Report TUM-I0714, Institut für Informatik, Technische Universität München (September 2007)
5. Benveniste, A., Caspi, P., Edwards, S.A., Halbwachs, N., Le Guernic, P., de Simone, R.: The synchronous languages 12 years later. Proceedings of the IEEE 91(1) (January 2003)
6. Haberl, W., Tautschnig, M., Baumgarten, U.: Running COLA on embedded systems. In: Proceedings of The International MultiConference of Engineers and Computer Scientists, Hongkong, China (March 2008) (accepted)
7. Wang, Z., Merenda, S., Tautschnig, M., Herkersdorf, A.: A model driven development approach for implementing reactive systems in hardware. In: Proceedings of International Forum on Specification and Design Languages (FDL 2008) (September 2008)
8. Pretschner, A., Broy, M., Krüger, I.H., Stauner, T.: Software engineering for automotive systems: A roadmap. In: Future of Software Engineering (FOSE 2007), Los Alamitos, CA, USA, pp. 55–71. IEEE Computer Society, Los Alamitos (2007)
9. Balarin, F., Watanabe, Y., Hsieh, H., Lavagno, L., Passerone, C., Sangiovanni-Vincentelli, A.L.: Metropolis: An integrated electronic system design environment. IEEE Computer 36(4), 45–52 (2003)

10. Bondarev, E.R.V., Chaudron, M., de With, P.H.N.: Carat: a toolkit for design and performance analysis of component-based embedded systems. In: Lauwereins, R., Madsen, J. (eds.) DATE, pp. 1024–1029. ACM, New York (2007)
11. Booch, G., Rumbaugh, J., Jacobson, I.: The Unified Modeling Language User Guide. Addison-Wesley, Reading (1998)
12. Bauer, A., Broy, M., Romberg, J., Schätz, B., Braun, P., Freund, U., Mata, N., Sandner, R., Ziegenbein, D.: AutoMoDe — Notations, Methods, and Tools for Model-Based Development of Automotive Software. In: Proceedings of the SAE 2005 World Congress, Detroit, MI. Society of Automotive Engineers (April 2005)
13. Kühnel, C., Bauer, A., Tautschnig, M.: Compatibility and reuse in component-based systems via type and unit inference. In: Proceedings of 33rd EUROMICRO Conference on Software Engineering and Advanced Applications, Lübeck, Germany, pp. 101–108 (2007)
14. Kugele, S., Haberl, W.: Mapping Data-Flow Dependencies onto Distributed Embedded Systems. In: Proceedings of the 2008 International Conference on Software Engineering Research & Practice (SERP 2008), Las Vegas Nevada, USA (July 2008)
15. Cheng, A.M.K.: Real-Time Systems: Scheduling, Analysis, and Verification. John Wiley & Sons, Chichester (2002)
16. Haberl, W., Baumgarten, U., Birke, J.: A Middleware for Model-Based Embedded Systems. In: Proceedings of the 2008 International Conference on Embedded Systems and Applications (ESA 2008), Las Vegas, Nevada, USA (July 2008)
17. Rayadurgam, S., Heimdahl, M.: Coverage based test-case generation using model checkers. In: Proceedings of the Eighth Annual IEEE International Conference and Workshop on Engineering of Computer Based Systems (ECBS 2001), pp. 83–91 (2001)
18. Holzer, A., Schallhart, C., Tautschnig, M., Veith, H.: FShell: Systematic Test Case Generation for Dynamic Analysis and Measurement. In: Proceedings of the 20th International Conference on Computer Aided Verification (CAV 2008), Princeton, NJ, USA, pp. 209–213 (July 2008)
19. Holzmann, G.J.: The SPIN Model Checker: Primer and Reference Manual. Addison-Wesley Professional, Reading (2003)
20. Wang, Z., Sanchez, A., Herkersdorf, A.: SciSim: A Software Performance Estimation Framework using Source Code Instrumentation. In: Proceedings of the 7th International Workshop on Software and Performance (WOSP 2008), Princeton, NJ, USA (June 2008)
21. Yu, H., Gerstlauer, A., Gajski, D.: RTOS scheduling in transaction level models. In: Proceedings of the International Symposium on System Synthesis, pp. 31–36 (October 2003)
22. Moigne, R.L., Pasquier, O., Calvez, J.P.: A generic rtos model for real-time systems simulation with systemc. In: Proceedings of the conference on Design, automation and test in Europe (DATE 2004) (2004)

Optimizing Automatic Deployment Using Non-functional Requirement Annotations

Stefan Kugele[1,2], Wolfgang Haberl[1], Michael Tautschnig[2], and Martin Wechs[3]

[1] Institut für Informatik
Technische Universität München
Boltzmannstr. 3, 85748 Garching b. München, Germany
[2] Institut für Informatik
Technische Universität Darmstadt
Hochschulstr. 10, 64289 Darmstadt, Germany
[3] BMW Forschung und Technik GmbH
Hanauer Straße 46, 80992 München, Germany

Abstract. Model-driven development has become common practice in design of safety-critical real-time systems. High-level modeling constructs help to reduce the overall system complexity apparent to developers. This abstraction caters for fewer implementation errors in the resulting systems. In order to retain correctness of the model down to the software executed on a concrete platform, human faults during implementation must be avoided. This calls for an automatic, unattended deployment process including allocation, scheduling, and platform configuration.

In this paper we introduce the concept of a *systems compiler* using non-functional requirements (NFR) as a guidance for deployment of real-time systems. The postulated requirements are then used to optimize the allocation decision, i. e., the process of mapping model entities to available computing nodes, as well as the subsequent generation of schedules.

1 Introduction

By far the largest part of computer systems today is used in embedded systems (98%) [1]. These are integrated in laundry machines, medical systems, cars, and aircrafts, just to name a few. In this paper we focus on large scale distributed embedded systems, built up from dozens or even hundreds of computing nodes, interconnected by various bus systems. Such systems contain or constitute life-critical electronic resources. Faults, of any kind, thus may be fatal. Even if not fatal, they bare large warranty costs for the designers and integrators of the product. The design methodology described in this paper tries to reduce the error rate of problems resulting from *implementation errors*. We do not consider bugs in specifications or byzantine software failures due to hardware errors, but extensions proposed to alleviate such issues may well be integrated.

Today, model driven development (MDD) is an established means of tackling the enormous complexity involved in designing distributed embedded systems. The large scale prohibits engineers from grasping the entire system at once.

T. Margaria and B. Steffen (Eds.): ISoLA 2008, CCIS 17, pp. 400–414, 2008.

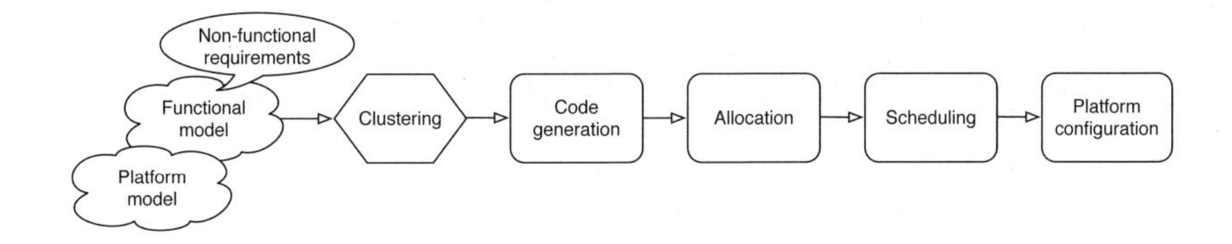

Fig. 1. Systems compilation steps

Rather, a hierarchy of abstractions is applied to attain manageability at each given level of abstraction. Pretschner et al. [2] for example consider three layers of abstraction: a model of *system features* (requirements), a *logical view* (system behavior), and a *technical architecture* (description of the target platform).

At higher levels of abstraction, even full formal verification, e.g., using model checking, can be applied to guarantee adherence to a set of properties. Then, proper behavior at model level may be guaranteed. In case of embedded real-time systems, however, the target platform to operate on likely invalidates several assumptions made at model level, or exposes properties that are not captured by functional/behavioral modeling. We call such properties *non-functional requirements*, which includes the description of the target platform, or supplier specific artifacts (see Section 3).

The complexity of the modeled system not only necessitates proper abstractions, but also calls for automation to take a model to an executable object, and later to a functional integrated system. An automated translation likely reduces errors and further guarantees reproducible results, and thus improves overall quality. Such an automatism, however, must be made aware of all requirements concerning the translation, which to a large extend involves non-functional requirements.

In this paper we describe concepts and implementation, both for specification of non-functional requirements and the automated translation from behavioral models down to the effective runnable. The process of translation is best compared to that of a software compiler. Given a functional model, usually as a piece of source code, a runnable entity is produced. Compiler and linker will be given all constraints imposed by the operating system and the target hardware platform to obtain an appropriate piece of software. Apart from the straightforward translation, a fundamental job of today's compilers is optimization in terms of size and execution speed.

In embedded systems, we will call this process *systems compilation*, since the compilation will be accomplished for the overall system model where the involved software and hardware components may be of various types. Here, both translation and optimization are by no means straightforward. As per translation, a heterogenous heap of models and requirements must be considered to obtain a valid runnable entity (cf. [3]). Today, a certain level of black magic performed by engineers is required to fit the software and hardware components into the targeted vehicle. In this paper, additional non-functional requirements are considered with the objective of a cost optimized system.

In Figure 1 we outline the process of automated systems compilation as described in this paper. We propose non-functional requirements be annotated to the functional models. The obtained executables are tailored towards the specific platform and require no further manual intervention.

1.1 Related Work

Annotation of non-functional requirements and a notation of platform capabilities was described by Dinkel and Baumgarten [4]. Their goal, however, was the dynamic system reconfiguration at run-time. We not only model these non-functional requirements and capabilities, but describe a fully automatic deployment process. This process ranges from a system design modeled in the language COLA (Component Language) [5], to determination of optimal allocation with respect to an optimization goal and pre-runtime scheduling.

Wuyts and Ducasse instrument components, with non-functional requirements, specified in Comes (a general Component Meta-Model) [6]. In Comes, components are seen as black boxes annotated with properties. This may be sufficient for allocation and scheduling, but lacks the information necessary for model-checking and other verification techniques. In COLA, each level of abstraction—from a very high-level system design down to the low implementation level—offers a white-box view and therefore provides all necessary information.

The UML profile MARTE (Modeling and Analysis of Real-Time and Embedded Systems) [7] is currently in the course of standards definition. Therefore, Espinoza et al. proposed an annotation of UML models with non-functional properties [8]. UML, however, is a general purpose language, which does not cater for the specific needs of the sub-domains of embedded systems design, like automotive or avionics industry. In [1], Broy objects and favors the use of domain specific languages and architectures to improve the state of the art. We present COLA as such a domain specific language, which, in contrast to UML, also features a unique formal semantics.

Moreover, Matic et al. [9] take platform specifications, e.g., power modes of the micro-controller, into account, as well as application specific information like periods of tasks, in order to generate an optimal scheduling. Compared to our approach, their work starts from having tasks to schedule. Our approach, however, supports an integrated development process of distributed hard real-time systems from requirements engineering (system features) over the design phase to the actual code generation, task allocation and scheduling in a consistent modeling formalism. Furthermore, we optimize an objective function subject to certain constraints stemming from non-functional requirements.

Regarding the overall design process, the DECOS project [10] is closest to our approach. Unlike COLA, however, they do not use a consistent modeling formalism, but rather resort to various techniques.

1.2 Organization

The rest of the paper is structured as follows. The next section gives a brief introduction to the Component Language (COLA). In Section 3, we discuss different non-functional requirements. Section 4 introduces the platform model used throughout this paper with its annotated requirements and capabilities. The optimized automatic deployment process is described in Section 5. Allocation and scheduling are mentioned as well as the concluding platform configuration. Finally, conclusions of the presented work are given in Section 6.

2 COLA—The Component Language

During the past years, synchronous data-flow languages have become increasingly popular tools for the description and design of safety-critical embedded control-systems. Like MATLAB/Simulink [11], the industry standard CASE-tool, or SCADE by Esterel Technologies (A380, FCS) [12], COLA uses data-flow networks to describe complex automotive and avionics systems. Approaches for model-based development and design for embedded control systems based on the synchronous paradigm have been described in [13, 14]. In synchronous data-flow languages, components work in parallel with respect to data dependencies and process their input and output values at *clock ticks*, i. e., discrete time points. In COLA, similar to other approaches following the *hypothesis of perfect synchrony* [15] it is assumed that communication of data via connections—in COLA, they are called *channels*—as well as computation of data-flow networks elapse infinitely fast and therefore take no time. In this paper we use the synchronous data-flow language COLA, which supports both a graphical and textual syntax and is based on a rigorous semantics.

The key concept of COLA are *units*. Units are at the very heart of the COLA syntax definition because all COLA models are built up by units and form data-flow networks. A unit itself can further be decomposed into sub-units in a hierarchical fashion and build up complex *networks*. The lowest level of those hierarchical networks consist only of so-called *basic blocks* that provide basic arithmetic and comparison operators. Environmental interaction is given via typed *ports*. In addition to basic blocks and networks, units can be decomposed into *automata*, i. e., finite state machines similar to Statecharts [16]. The behavior in each state is again determined by units corresponding to each of the

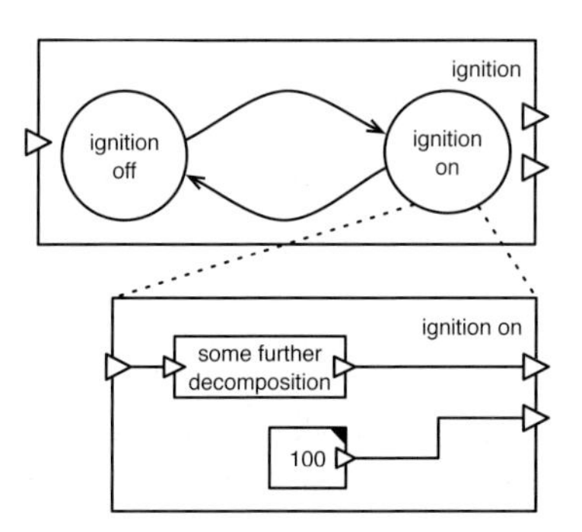

Fig. 2. Fictive ignition modeled in COLA using operating modes

states. This capability is well suited to express disjoint system modes, also called *operating modes* (cf. [13,17,18]). Figure 2 shows a COLA system implementing parts of an ignition with its states ignition on and ignition off. The state ignition on is further decomposed in this example. Furthermore, COLA includes a special unit, called *delay*, to retain data for one clock tick. In this way, memories and feedback-loops can be realized.

To make distributed execution of COLA models possible, a partitioning into runnable software components has to be accomplished. These components are referred to as *clusters* in the context of COLA.

3 Non-functional Requirements

In requirements engineering of software systems, we distinguish *functional* and *non-functional* requirements. Functional requirements cover all requisites necessary for the correct evaluation of the specified algorithms, i. e., the mathematical functions. These mainly depend on the availability of input data. Contrariwise, non-functional requirements cover all additional demands, which are specified for a piece of software and which do not directly influence the resulting output data. They are measurable such that their compliance can be checked.

In this paper, we further distinguish two kinds of non-functional requirements: first, non-functional requirements that are essential for a correct operation of the specified system are considered. If at least one of these requirements is not satisfied, an error-free operation of the overall system cannot be guaranteed. Second, we consider non-functional requirements that are not necessary for the system to operate, but rather improve a system's quality regarding timely execution (i. e., preservation of deadlines), resource usage, redundancy, etc. Some possible quality requirements are given in ISO 9126. For example, it could be beneficial to allocate safety-critical tasks onto processors on different, redundant electronic control units (ECU). Another requirement might be to allocate all tasks implemented by the same third-party supplier onto the same ECU, resulting in a simplified maintenance process.

We use the terms *processor* and *processing unit* interchangeably and mean a CPU or DSP without RAM, ROM, etc., whereas an *ECU* may include several processors, RAM, ROM, and is connected to sensors, actuators and buses (cf. Figure 4).

The NFRs mentioned here are intended to show the use of our methodology. Of course, more than the discussed NFRs can be taken into account and easily integrated in both the described model and the used allocation and scheduling algorithms.

3.1 Essential Non-functional Requirements

In the following, we briefly outline those NFRs that are *essential* for a correct operation of the overall system.

Computing power: Each cluster needs a certain amount of computing power for execution. This amount is annotated to the cluster embodying its worst-case requirement. Hence this requirement can be checked against the given platform. If more clusters are allocated onto a single processing unit than it can handle, not all clusters are guaranteed be be evaluated.

Memory: Similarly to computing power, a cluster needs a minimum amount of available memory. Two forms of memory are consumed: first, the binary file generated for a cluster has to be stored in the permanent storage (ROM) of the ECU. Second, the code generated for the cluster has demands regarding the RAM available during execution.

Power state: Typically, embedded systems are bound to limited power supply. Hence huge efforts are put into research and development of power saving technologies. For distributed embedded systems like cars, this can be achieved through the definition of different power states. According to the actual state of the car, e.g. locked, ignition off, ignition on, a varying number of ECUs might be active. Other nodes are shut down at the same time to avoid a waste of power.

To distinguish power states, a state hierarchy is given. Each power state defines the set of ECUs running in it. Each higher state contains the same ECUs, and at least one additional more. Therefore the relation $S_0 \subset S_1 \subset S_2 \subset S_3$ indicates four power states which S_0 being the lowest state and S_3 being the highest state in that example.

3.2 Auxiliary Non-functional Requirements

In addition to the mentioned essential NFRs, we also address *auxiliary* NFRs. These are not necessary for correct operation, but raise further demands on the system that, e.g., lower its cost or improve its efficiency.

Supplier: Large scale embedded systems are often the result of a cooperation of several partners in industry. When defining a model for the whole system, the definition of work packages for the different team partners is desirable. These could consist of several clusters each in case of COLA. To allow for this partitioning the designated partner can be annotated to each cluster of the model. The supplier information can then be used to allocate tasks implemented by a single supplier exclusively onto the same ECU(s). This approach enables the partners to retain their current work-sharing where each partner implements a piece of hardware, e.g., an ECU, together with the corresponding software.

Redundancy: Dealing with safety-critical hard real-time systems, demands for the implementation of error correcting techniques in case of a system node's failure emerge. A frequently used technique for error masking is the use of redundant software components, specified using clusters in our case. The specification of a redundancy requirement defines the number of redundant cluster copies to use in the system, i. e., on how many different ECUs a cluster should be deployed.

Processor architecture: If a cluster's implementation is dependent on a specific processor's capabilities, e.g. a digital signal processor (DSP), the cluster has to be placed accordingly. This might be necessary for implementations of algorithms requiring a large amount of processing power without violating given deadlines.

Cost: From an economical point of view, one of the most important NFRs are costs. In the automotive domain, for example, manufacturers operate in a highly competitive mass market with strong cost pressure. Therefore, the major part of the presented optimization approach is guided by costs. In this paper cost is seen from the manufacturer's point of view. In some cases it may be beneficial to assemble more processors than needed to fulfill the desired functionality, only to reduce the overall system costs. It is due to the optimization process to decide on the most economic solution.

4 Requirements and Capabilities Meta-models

In order to allow for an automatic transformation of the modeled COLA system into an executable system, algorithms for allocation and scheduling of clusters are needed. Their evaluation is influenced by the NFRs specified in the COLA model. Thus each cluster of the COLA model may be annotated with several NFRs. In the following we detail on the meta-model for specification of cluster requirements and platform capabilities.

Requirements Specification. Cluster requirements are captured as annotations in the system model. These annotations occur in two forms: first, annotations like power states, call frequency, etc. can be set. The values given for these requirements are fixed independent of the processor the cluster is deployed.

Second, cluster requirements annotations that are specific for each processing unit the cluster is deployed to, can be defined. For example, consider the number of computing cycles and the memory consumption. In contrast to simple NFRs, these requirements are specific for each processor on an ECU, because the values differ for the processor architecture, memory segmentation, etc. used on the ECU in question. Therefore, these values have to be defined for each possible allocation target. Thus these requirements are given for the cluster as a set of

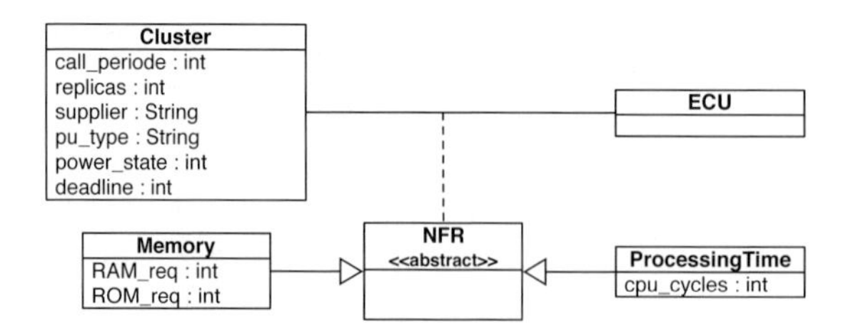

Fig. 3. Cluster annotation model

tuples, each tuple consisting of the addressed node and the according value of the requirement for that node. A class diagram of the meta-model for clusters and their requirement annotations is given in Figure 3. As depicted, the requirements presented in Section 3 are covered in this meta-model. Simple annotations are added to the clusters as attributes. In order to allow for a matching of these requirements and the platform capabilities, a unit for the requirement has to be chosen for each value. For example, the redundancy requirement for a cluster is specified by giving the number of needed copies. Other values may be represented by sets, e.g., the specification of clusters implemented by a single supplier. Besides these simple requirements, node specific requirements are covered by the meta-model. As their values differ according to each node the cluster might be deployed to, the requirements are stored in an association class. Therefore, distinct values are stored for each possible cluster allocation onto a system's node. A complete list as well as an explanation for the attributes covered in Figure 3 is given in Table 1.

Capabilities Specification. In order to calculate allocation and scheduling decisions, the capabilities of the platform have to be given. These capabilities are stored as an extension of the platform model, which include hardware, software and other aspects. The algorithms described in Section 5 rely on the availability of this information. While most capabilities are used as constraints for choosing valid allocation and scheduling schemes, the cost attribute has to be handled

Table 1. Table of NFRs and capabilities

Requirement	Unit	Description
cpu_cycles	(ID, cycles)	The amount of processing cycles needed is specific for every processor in question. Thus the value is specified as a tuple mapping the processor ID to a number of cycles.
RAM_req	kByte	The dynamic memory demand during task execution.
ROM_req	kByte	The memory needed for binary file storage.
power_state	Name	Name of the lowest power state in which this task is active.
supplier	Name	The name of the supplier implementing this cluster.
replicas	Instances	The number of copies distributed over the system for redundancy reasons.
pu_type	Set<Arch.>	The names of valid processor architectures.
deadline	ms	Specifies a deadline within a cluster has to be executed.
Capability	**Unit**	**Description**
cost	Euro	The cost generated by using this hardware component.
ROM_cap	kByte	The amount of permanent memory available on the node.
RAM_cap	kByte	The working memory available on the node.
os_overhead	ms	For every called task, a certain amount of operating system overhead is generated for dispatching, memory management, etc.
power_state	State	An ECU is active in the specified power state and all higher power states.
supplier	Name	The name of the supplier building this piece of hardware.
pu_arch	Name	Processing units differ by their respective processor architecture. Thus general purpose processors, DSPs and others can be distinguished.
proc_cycles	Cycles/ms	To state the amount of processing power available, the number of cycles per milliseconds is given.

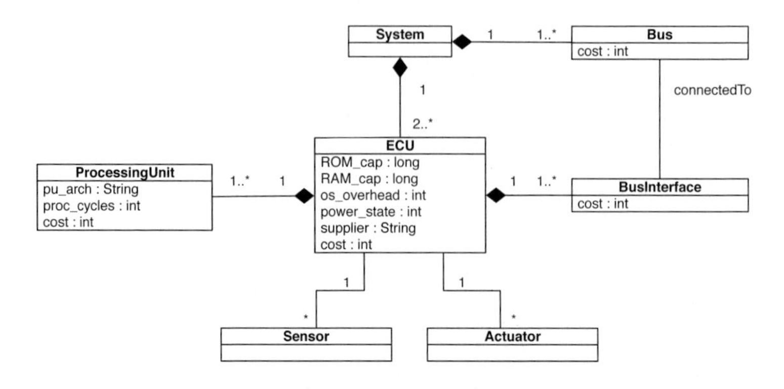

Fig. 4. Platform model

differently. It allows for an optimization of the resulting allocation and scheduling plan by calculating the most economic system architecture.

The complete list of platform model attributes, and an explanation of these, is given in Table 1. The attributes are taken from the COLA platform meta-model, which can be seen in Figure 4.

5 Deployment Process

The aim of a fully automatic deployment process is bridging the gap between the system description—in our case, in a model-based fashion—and the target platform without a need for human interaction. As the system is modeled without taking distribution aspects into account, a division of software components into cluster—the model representation of software tasks—and an allocation of these onto processing units is defined. A clustering is derived from an optimized software architecture w.r.t. reusability, maintainability, design guidelines, documentation and others (cf. [19]).

Subsequently, a static schedule for the tasks on each node is defined and the appertaining C code is generated. Finally, the execution platform has to be configured, regarding addressing of messages, buffer allocation, etc. In the following, we will briefly introduce these steps.

5.1 Allocation

Our approach focuses on an *optimized* automatic deployment process for embedded hard real-time systems w.r.t. a set of given non-functional requirements. In Section 4, we introduced a meta-model for annotating systems with NFRs. These requirements are now taken into account by the presented allocation algorithm. Similar to Zheng et al. [20] and Matic et al. [9] we use an integer linear programming (ILP) approach and therefore chose a similar nomenclature. In addition to Zheng et al., Metzner and Herde [21] who are using a SAT-based approach for the task allocation problem, our approach takes non-functional requirements during the deployment process into account. Before listing a set of constraints and defining the optimization function, we introduce the notation used in this section.

Notation. Let T denote the set of all clusters (tasks), and let P be the set of all processing units. In the following, we use the indicator variable $a_{t,p}$ where $t \in T$ is a task and $p \in P$ is a processing unit to indicate where a task is deployed to:

$$a_{t,p} = \begin{cases} 1 & \text{if task } t \text{ is allocated to processor } p \\ 0 & \text{otherwise.} \end{cases}$$

Furthermore, as abbreviating notation for the set $\{t \mid t \in T \wedge \phi(t)\}$, where ϕ is some predicate over model attributes, we write $t_{|\phi}$, e.g., $p_{|\mathsf{supplier}=s} \equiv \{p \mid p \in P \wedge \mathsf{supplier}(p) = s\}$. Variable names written in sans serif font refer to attributes of the platform model shown in Figure 4 and the cluster annotation model depicted in Figure 3, respectively.

In the following, we refer to several sets of model artifacts: ECU (electronic control units), P (processing units), PA (processor architectures), T (tasks), PS (power states), and S (suppliers).

Constraints

1. The following essential NFRs have to be met:
   (a) Computing power: For all processing units $p \in P$ it holds

$$\sum_{t \in T} a_{t,p} \cdot (\mathsf{cpu\_cycles}(t,p) + \mathsf{os\_overhead}(p)) \cdot \varrho \leq \mathsf{proc\_cycles}(p)$$

   where ϱ defines the number of task invocations per time unit.
   (b) Memory consumption: For all ECUs $e \in ECU$ it holds

$$\sum_{p \in \mathsf{proc}(e)} \sum_{t \in T} a_{t,p} \cdot \mathsf{RAM\_req}(t,p) \leq \mathsf{RAM\_cap}(p)$$

$$\sum_{p \in \mathsf{proc}(e)} \sum_{t \in T} a_{t,p} \cdot \mathsf{ROM\_req}(t,p) \leq \mathsf{ROM\_cap}(p)$$

   where $\mathsf{proc}(e)$ returns a set of processors present at ECU e.
   (c) Power states: For all power states $ps \in PS$ and all tasks $t_{|\mathsf{power\_state}=ps}$ it holds:

$$\sum_{p_{|\mathsf{power\_state} \geq ps}} a_{t,p} = N$$

2. Auxiliary non-functional requirements:
   (a) Supplier: For all suppliers $s \in S$ and all tasks $t_{|\mathsf{supplier}=s}$ holds:

$$\sum_{p_{|\mathsf{supplier}=s}} a_{t,p} = N$$

(b) Redundancy: Each cluster has to be deployed onto N processing units. If no redundancy annotation is given, then $N = 1$, otherwise $N = \mathsf{replicas}(t)$. This holds for all tasks $t \in T$.

$$\sum_{p \in P} a_{t,p} = N$$

(c) Processor architecture: For all processor architectures $pa \in PA$ and all tasks $t_{|\mathsf{pu\_arch}=pa}$ it holds:

$$\sum_{p_{|\mathsf{pu\_arch}=pa}} a_{t,p} = N$$

(d) Communication costs: Inter- and intra-processor communication may be important in a real-time system to guarantee certain deadlines. We introduce indicator variables $a_{t_i,p_u}^{t_j,p_v}$ which are 1, if task task t_i is deployed onto processor p_u and task t_j onto processor p_v, and 0 otherwise. It holds: $a_{t_i,p_u}^{t_j,p_v} \iff a_{t_i,p_u} \wedge a_{t_j,p_v}$. Formulated as linear constraints we get for all $1 \leq i,j \leq |T|$ and $1 \leq u,v \leq |P|$:

$$-a_{t_i,p_u} - a_{t_j,p_v} + a_{t_i,p_u}^{t_j,p_v} > -2 \quad \text{and} \quad -2\, a_{t_i,p_u}^{t_j,p_v} + a_{t_i,p_u} + a_{t_j,p_v} \geq 0$$

These indicator variables are then multiplied by measured costs for inter- and intra-ECU communication. These costs include, amongst others, the communication frequency. Both, indicator variables and costs form the basis for a possible metric in the optimization function.

(e) Costs: Hardware is an important expense factor. Hence unused components like controllers, buses and connection interfaces are only assembled if for example the costs for future extensions are then reduced. If a bus is exclusively used by unnecessary nodes, i. e., no tasks are mapped onto them, it can be economized. This scenario, which is representative for similar dependencies, can be expressed as follows:

$$\forall t \in T\ \forall p \in P \quad -a_{t,p} + c_p > -1$$

where $c_p \in \{0,1\}$ indicates that the expense for processor p has to be taken into account during the optimization process. This decision implies that costs for the involved connection interfaces etc. have to be considered:

$$\forall p \in P \quad -c_p + c_b > -1$$

where $c_b \in \{0,1\}$ is an indicator for the costs due to processor p being connected to the bus b via a connection interface.

(f) Fixed allocation for some other reason: If a task $t \in T$ has to be allocated onto a special processor p, then $a_{t,p} = 1$ has to be added as constraint.

All the mentioned constraints, and other conceivable constraint extensions have to be fulfilled such that it is possible to find an (optimal) solution. Additional requirements include for example maintainability, extensibility and locality of input/output hardware. Maintainability demands for a placement of related tasks onto the same or a small number of ECUs. This results in fewer system nodes involved in software maintenance activities. Considering future functionality improvements, it may be beneficial to include some spare system capacity. This can be achieved by introducing dummy clusters. Regarding bus communication, it is convenient to place tasks involved in environmental interaction on the ECU the respective sensors and actuators are connected to. To allow for optimization, in the following an objective function is given.

Optimization Function. Beside the given constraints, it is mandatory to define an optimization function. It consists of the two main components *costs* and *metrics*. Costs characterize actual expenses whereas metrics subsume non-functional optimization factors like memory, CPU time, or communication costs.

$$\begin{array}{ll}\textsf{minimize} & \\ \textsf{s.t.} & \sum_j \lambda_j \cdot cost_j + \sum_k \mu_k \cdot metric_k\end{array}$$

E.g., the costs for processors $cost_{proc}$ sum up to: $cost_{proc} = \sum_{p \in P} c_p \cdot \kappa_p$, where κ_p is the cost per unit obtained from the bill of material (BOM). By setting an upper and a lower bound for $cost_j$ and $metric_k$, outliers during optimization are avoided. Metrics can be gained in a similar way. The distinct but fixed weightings λ_j and μ_k enable to characterize OEM's optimization criteria. Criteria for this parameter selection will be subject to subsequent work. Hereby, statistical processes as well as methods from financial mathematics are involved.

5.2 Scheduling

In this paper we describe a static, i. e., offline approach, which is comparable to the work of Schild and Würz [22], but in contrast, our approach optimizes the result w.r.t. costs and other metrics.

To realize the modeled system, the assumption we made on the logical architecture—the complete system is evaluated in zero time and operate at discrete ticks—is replaced by deadlines specified in the model. As long as all active clusters are evaluated and all their deadlines are met, the time assumption can be seen as fulfilled. Hardware interaction has to be handled in a specific way to converge towards the synchrony assumption. Assuming this hypothesis, all sensors and actuators are read from or written to, respectively, at the same instant of time. In a car, however, this cannot be achieved, as a parallel reading of several sensors connected to the same ECU is technically impossible. For example, consider the four wheel speed sensors providing rotation values used for the electronic stability control task. A lag in reading times beyond a certain threshold would lead to malfunction. Therefore, we propose a scheduling cycle starting with reading all sensors, subsequent execution of application tasks, and finally the writing of all actuators. This conforms to the described scenario as close as possible. Figure 5 illustrates such a scheduling cycle. The generation of schedules is—among other prerequisites—guided by the causal order of clusters.

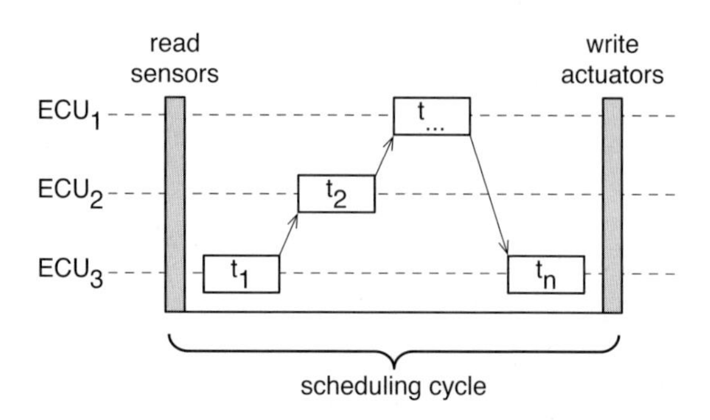

Fig. 5. Scheduling cycle

This causality can be derived from the data-flow defined in the COLA model and depicted in a *cluster dependency graph* (CDG), as described in [19].

Since allocation and scheduling are separated, the scheduler already knows about task distribution. This separation may result in a worse result compared to a combined approach, but seems to be more feasible. The challenge remains to find an optimal schedule for the complete system, preserving the model semantics. The objective is to minimize:

$$f : \sum_{t \in T} tc(t)$$

where $tc(t)$ defines the *completion time* of task t taken from the set of all tasks T. Our algorithm is implemented in a way that all tasks of the distributed system are scheduled to have their completion times as early as possible w.r.t. possible data dependencies. This procedure causes a compaction of tasks at the beginning of the schedule cycle. The possibly remaining cycle time can be used in future extensions to schedule aperiodic and sporadic tasks.

5.3 Platform Configuration and Execution

Subsequent to scheduling, C code for the modeled system is generated. As mentioned before, a cluster is the model representation of a task. Thus a single source file is generated for each cluster by our code generator [23]. The automatic generation of code guarantees the conformance of the C code to the COLA model.

Comparing the overall system model designed in COLA and its realization in software, obviously a mapping from COLA channels to communication between tasks has to be defined. In a distributed system this may be local communication as well as bus communication. The data dependencies are captured in a task graph [19] in the COLA modeling process. It is our intention to allow for a flexible distribution of tasks without defining static communication addresses. This is realized using a communication middleware for all task interactions as well as task state storage. Additionally, the middleware is responsible for the dispatching of tasks according to the calculated schedule. The dispatching plan, as well as the task to address mapping is generated unattended, and therefore avoids manual faults. We employ our middleware [24] for mapping channels to communication.

6 Conclusions

In this paper, we introduced an integrated model-driven development process for embedded real-time systems. We outlined the necessary steps for getting from a functional system design modeled with COLA to a runnable entity. The metaphor of a systems compiler best describes this process. First, the model is cut into clusters which are subsequently allocated onto the available processing units. Afterwards, an optimal schedule for the complete system is calculated. By annotating the model with non-functional requirements, we were able not only to find a feasible solution, but even an optimal solution for both task allocation and task scheduling, respectively, w.r.t. the given NFRs. The unattended platform configuration tops the process off. Using this deployment process, an adaptive cruise control system (ACC) was realized on the LEGO Mindstorms platform as well as a parking assistance using several interconnected gumstix microcontrollers with a RTOS installed.

References

1. Broy, M.: Automotive software and systems engineering (panel). In: MEMOCODE, pp. 143–149 (2005)
2. Pretschner, A., Broy, M., Krüger, I.H., Stauner, T.: Software engineering for automotive systems: A roadmap. In: FOSE 2007, pp. 55–71 (2007)
3. Henzinger, T.A., Sifakis, J.: The discipline of embedded systems design. IEEE Computer 40(10), 32–40 (2007)
4. Dinkel, M., Baumgarten, U.: Modeling nonfunctional requirements: a basis for dynamic systems management. SIGSOFT Softw. Eng. Notes 30(4), 1–8 (2005)
5. Kugele, S., Tautschnig, M., Bauer, A., Schallhart, C., Merenda, S., Haberl, W., Kühnel, C., Müller, F., Wang, Z., Wild, D., Rittmann, S., Wechs, M.: COLA – The component language. Technical Report TUM-I0714, Institut für Informatik, Technische Universität München (September 2007)
6. Wuyts, R., Ducasse, S.: Non-functional requirements in a component model for embedded systems. In: SAVCBS 2001 (2001)
7. Object Management Group: Uml profile for modeling and analysis of real-time and embedded systems (marte). OMG document: ptc/07-08-04 (2007)
8. Espinoza, H., Dubois, H., Gérard, S., Pasaje, J.L.M., Petriu, D.C., Woodside, C.M.: Annotating UML models with non-functional properties for quantitative analysis. In: MoDELS Satellite Events, pp. 79–90 (2005)
9. Matic, S., Goraczko, M., Liu, J., Lymberopoulos, D., Priyantha, B., Zhao, F.: Resource modeling and scheduling for extensible embedded platforms. Technical Report MSR-TR-2006-176, Microsoft Reasearch, One Microsoft Way, Redmond, WA, USA (2006)
10. Kopetz, H., Obermaisser, R., Peti, P., Suri, N.: From a federated to an integrated architecture for dependable embedded real-time systems. Technical Report 22, Technische Universität Wien, Institut für Technische Informatik, Austria (2004)

11. The MathWorks Inc.: Using Simulink (2000)
12. Berry, G., Gonthier, G.: The esterel synchronous programming language: design, semantics, implementation. Sci. Comput. Program 19(2), 87–152 (1992)
13. Bauer, A., Broy, M., Romberg, J., Schätz, B., Braun, P., Freund, U., Mata, N., Sandner, R., Ziegenbein, D.: AutoMoDe — Notations, Methods, and Tools for Model-Based Development of Automotive Software. In: Proceedings of the SAE 2005 World Congress, Detroit, MI. Society of Automotive Engineers (April 2005)
14. Caspi, P., Curic, A., Maignan, A., Sofronis, C., Tripakis, S., Niebert, P.: From simulink to SCADE/lustre to TTA: a layered approach for distributed embedded applications. In: LCTES, pp. 153–162. ACM, New York (2003)
15. Halbwachs, N., Caspi, P., Raymond, P., Pilaud, D.: The synchronous data-flow programming language LUSTRE. Proceedings of the IEEE 79(9), 1305–1320 (1991)
16. Booch, G., Rumbaugh, J., Jacobson, I.: The Unified Modeling Language User Guide. Addison-Wesley, Reading (1998)
17. IEEE: IEEE Std 830-1998: IEEE Recommended Practice for Software Requirements Specifications. Institute of Electrical and Electronics Engineers (1998)
18. Maraninchi, F., Rémond, Y.: Mode-automata: a new domain-specific construct for the development of safe critical systems. Science of Computer Programming 46(3), 219–254 (2003)
19. Kugele, S., Haberl, W.: Mapping Data-Flow Dependencies onto Distributed Embedded Systems. In: SERP 2008, Las Vegas, Nevada, USA (July 2008)
20. Zheng, W., Zhu, Q., Natale, M.D., Vincentelli, A.S.: Definition of task allocation and priority assignment in hard real-time distributed systems. In: RTSS 2007, Washington, DC, USA, pp. 161–170. IEEE Computer Society Press, Los Alamitos (2007)
21. Metzner, A., Herde, C.: Rtsat–an optimal and efficient approach to the task allocation problem in distributed architectures. In: RTSS, pp. 147–158 (2006)
22. Schild, K., Würtz, J.: Off-line scheduling of a real-time system. In: Proceedings of the 1998 ACM symposium on Applied Computing (January 1998)
23. Haberl, W., Tautschnig, M., Baumgarten, U.: Running COLA on Embedded Systems. In: IMECS 2008 (March 2008)
24. Haberl, W., Baumgarten, U., Birke, J.: A Middleware for Model-Based Embedded Systems. In: ESA 2008, Las Vegas, Nevada, USA (July 2008)

Experiences with Evolutionary Timing Test of Automotive Software Components

Florian Franz

BMW Group and Institute for Real-Time Computer Systems TU Munich
florian.franz@cdtm.de

Abstract. This paper reports our experiences in estimating the worst case execution time (WCET) of automotive software components with evolutionary testing (ET). The concept maximizes the runtime of software components (SWCs) with internal states by evolving the applied test sequences. We show that the use of timing tests is strongly facilitated by the automotive architecture framework AUTOSAR. A problem of the testing concept is the high temporal effort, that comes along with measuring the execution time of a test sequence on the target hardware. An analysis of the evolutionary testability shows, that the high number of input parameters makes it hard to find the maximum execution time. The WCET estimates obtained with genetic algorithms (GAs) are inferior compared with the results of random testing. GAs run into local optima in case of flat execution time profiles, whereas random testing keeps searching globally. Random testing is outperformed by extended GAs which are adaptive to the underlying optimization problem.

1 Introduction

The standard approach to determine the WCET is static analysis. This method provides the system architect with a conservative estimate of the WCET, that is larger than the actual value. It is an analytical technique that is especially useful for hard, safety-critical real time systems, where the execution time must be strictly bounded. However the static analysis has two major drawbacks. It often requires manual input, which is time-consuming and error-prone, and it tends to be overly pessimistic.

In case of soft real time systems, where missed deadlines do not have dramatic consequences, the application of static analysis often cannot be justified. To ensure sufficient quality, the timing of SWCs is examined with other methods. A common approach in the industry is to perform runtime tests on the target hardware for estimating the WCET. The benefit of measuring execution times on the target is, that it avoids the tedious and error-prone modeling of the processor. If the component is not split up for measuring, this so called dynamic analysis by definition leads to WCET estimates, that are below the actual value. The use of these optimistic estimates is problematic, because a system with too high actual computation times might be classified as sufficiently fast. In consequence, it is necessary to make sure that the gap between estimated and actual WCET

T. Margaria and B. Steffen (Eds.): ISoLA 2008, CCIS 17, pp. 415–429, 2008.

is small. The challenge for the dynamic test is to find input data that cause large runtimes.

The concept of the evolutionary timing test with GAs has been introduced by Wegener [1]. He interprets the problem of determining the maximum runtime of SWCs as an optimization problem. The WCET is searched by varying the input parameters of the examined SWC. An iteration of the heuristic search consists of a test case generations step and a start-to-end runtime measurement. In contrast to the concept from Bernat et al. the component is not divided into its basic blocks but measured as a whole [2]. This avoids the pessimism in the WCET estimate, which results from combining the basic block measurements conservatively. Wegener showed, that GAs are well-suited for estimating the WCET of SW components with no internal state [3].

We applied the concept for testing the WCET of state-based SW components in the serial-development process of automotive SW. The contribution of this paper is to adapt the evolutionary timing test for practical problems, to evaluate its performance and to examine the related work-effort. The paper is structured as follows. After a depiction of the basic concepts of evolutionary testing and AUTOSAR, we present our approach for testing state-based SWCs. In a next step our adaptations for testing AUTOSAR SWCs are described. In this context the benefits for evolutionary testing that arise from the AUTOSAR architecture are explained. After that, the genetic optimization concept is evaluated for SWCs of two electronic control units (ECUs) relative to random testing. On this basis the problem is analyzed in more depth and the optimization concept is refined to outperform the random test.

2 Related Work

2.1 Evolutionary Test of the WCET

This section briefly describes the basic concept for genetic WCET tests. More detailed information can be found in [1] and [5]. GAs are parallel optimization techniques, that apply the concepts of genetics and darwinism. A population of individuals evolves over generations by genetic changes and selection processes.

The individuals represent input data vectors of the examined SWC. The elements of the input data vectors form the genetic material which is evolved. Consequently the elements of the input data vector are called chromosomes. Basically the optimization heuristic performs a controlled search of the input space by changing and combining the chromosomes of individuals. Individuals that are close to the optimization goal are selected to replace other individuals. Applying this darwinistic technique GAs manage to be more goal oriented than pure random search. The genetic evolution of the individuals is based on the iterative execution of the steps fitness evaluation, selection, recombination, mutation, and replacement.

The fitness of the individuals corresponds to the start-to-end execution time that results from the input data vector. To obtain an individual's fitness the examined piece of software is executed with the corresponding input data vector.

In the next phase individuals with high fitness are selected for further evolution. This selection step makes sure that the GA concentrates on genetic material with high execution times and that no further resources are spent for examining search regions with low execution times.

In the recombination phase, the genetic material of two randomly selected individuals is merged. In this merging step the corresponding chromosomes of the two individuals are exchanged or interpolated. This operation allows a knowledge exchange between the selected individuals.

In the mutation phase a few chromosomes of the individuals are randomly changed. This local random search helps the algorithm to keep on searching for the global optimum.

The last step of the GA is the replacement operation where the genetically evolved population replaces the original population. At the beginning of the GA all individuals are initialized with random values. Then the individuals are genetically evolved until a termination criterion is reached. Potential termination criteria are the stagnation of the fitness or a reached maximum number of generations.

A combination of static WCET analysis and dynamic test has been presented in [6]. Puschner and Nossal developed a concept to prove the results of static WCET analysis by applying dynamic tests with GAs.

2.2 Runtime Test of AUTOSAR SWCs

The WCET estimations performed in this paper are done by testing application SWCs, that are based on the automotive architecture standard AUTOSAR [7,8]. An extension of the AUTOSAR model to capture timing properties more adequately has been presented in [9,10]. According to Scheickl and Rudorfer there are currently no known research activities, that estimate WCET values by applying information from the AUTOSAR model [9]. We close this gap by harvesting the benefits from AUTOSAR, which are depicted in section 4.3.

The aspects of AUTOSAR, which are relevant for the timing test shall be briefly reviewed. A major element of the AUTOSAR architecture is a middleware layer, which is called runtime environment (RTE). Above the RTE one can find application SWCs, which implement the abstracted functionality in an HW independent way.

A SWC communicates with other SWCs or underlying SW layers exclusively via its RTE interface. In consequence, a component‘s RTE interface captures the inputs and outputs of a SWC, which are relevant for performing WCET tests, completely. AUTOSAR requires a precise modeling of both the static interface of a SWC and the communication relationships between the SWCs. The RTE is the test interface, which we use for determining the temporal properties of the SWCs. The communication between two AUTOSAR SWCs via the RTE is pictured in figure 1.

An application SWC typically does not run directly in a task of the operating system (OS). Instead, the SWC is clustered in multiple runnable entities, that can be independently mapped to OS tasks with different periodicities. In

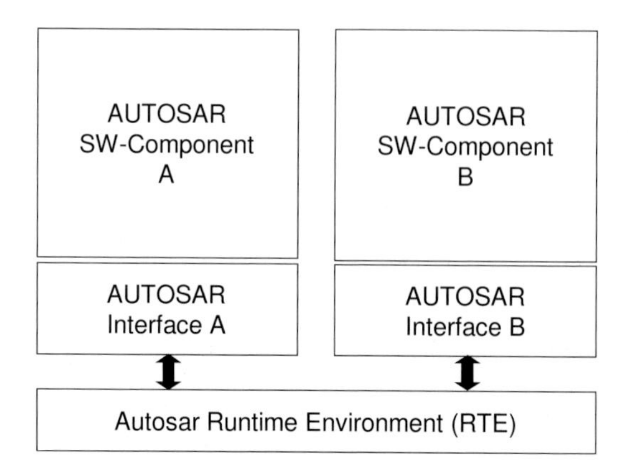

Fig. 1. AUTOSAR architecture with SWCs and RTE

consequence, multiple runnable entities of different SWCs can reside on the same OS task. The runnable entity is the unit under test, whose WCET is estimated within this paper. For a scheduling analysis of an ECU that is composed from several SWCs one is typically interested in the WCET of a complete task. Timing composability is given, because the analyzed ECUs do not contain sources of timing anomalies like caches [11]. Consequently the WCET of a task can be easily computed by adding up the WCETs of its contained runnable entities.

3 Adaptation of ET Concept for Test of State-Based Systems

3.1 State-Based Timing Test with Test Sequences

The basic concept for ET examines SWCs with no internal state by applying a test vector to all inputs. There are multiple concepts for extending ET to state-based systems [5]. One concept is to apply the evolutionary optimization concept to test sequences. This means that a separate test vector is applied to the inputs of the SWC in each temporal step of the test sequence. The problem of this approach is, that it can lead to a considerable enlargement of the search space.

Another approach is to perform separate WCET estimations for each system state. The drawback of this concept is, that it requires a mechanism to reach all system states. One possibility to cope with this, is to rely on already existing test sequences. Another way are special test input variables, which allow a tester to establish internal states.

None of these mechanisms to reach the internal system states was available or easy-to-implement for the SWCs that we examined. Consequently we decided to perform an evolutionary optimization of test sequences. By limiting the number of changed variables in each test step, we avoided an explosion of the search area.

3.2 Data Structure for Optimizing Test Sequences

To model test sequences we adapted the optimized data structure such, that it reflects the temporal properties. A generic structure is to describe a test case as a temporal sequence of test steps. A test step shall be defined such, that the examined runnable entity is executed once in every test step.

When evaluating a test sequence one runtime measurement is performed with every execution of the examined runnable. We define the fitness of a test sequence as the maximum execution time during its test steps.

The structure of the examined runnables corresponds to the simple task model from Kopetz [4]. The runnables do not contain synchronization operations, that may cause blockings. All relevant RTE variables are read in at the begin of the runnable‘s execution. Consequently an RTE variable that changes its value during the execution of a runnable does not impact the runnable, if the value changed after the atomic reading operation. Therefore the exact timestamps when input signals change are irrelevant for the operation of the runnables. For the optimized data structure this means, that it is sufficient to capture the values of the inputs at the discrete instants, when the atomic reading operations are performed. The reading operations are performed once per test step, and so the optimized data structure only needs to store the input values in the different test steps.

To avoid a data structure with unmanageable size, we made the simplification, that only one input changes its value in a single test step. The value of the other inputs remains like in the previous test step. Considering, that the examined runnables are called in short periods of few milliseconds, this assumption seems plausible for the SWCs that have been analyzed in this paper, as they mainly depend on physical input parameters and user interactions. The reduced data structure cannot analyze such applications correctly, that exhibit their WCET when all input parameters change at the same time. But without reducing the data structure one obtains large test sequences, which are hard to optimize. For instance, a component that is analyzed in 100 test steps would require a data structure with 10 000 elements, if it has 100 inputs that may change in every test step.

A refined reduction concept for the data structure limits the total number of variable alterations per test case by an upper boundary and allows an arbitrary number of input parameter changes per test step while the upper boundary is kept. The drawback of this approach is an inhomogeneous data structure, which makes it hard to define an effective crossover operator. This refined concept is subject to further research.

The simplified concept can be efficiently mapped to a data structure that only holds that single input parameter per test step, which will be changed. The advantage of just storing differential information is the avoidance of redundant data and the focus on the decisive information. The coding of a test sequence is illustrated in figure 2. In each of the three exemplary test steps S_i, one input I_j changes its value. As shown with I_1 one input can change its value multiple times. The value of an input is encoded as a bit string, whose size depends on the data range of the corresponding input parameter.

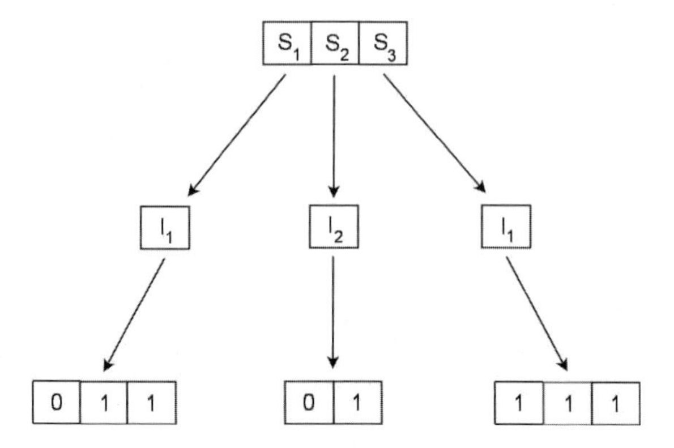

Fig. 2. Data structure for test sequence

The number of test steps which is used for ET has to be configured a priori by a system expert. In the best case, the largest time constant involved with the software component under test is modestly high, such that the test vector remains small. It is a limitation of the testing approach that processes which require a long time span to elapse cannot be tested efficiently. If the runtime test requires very many executions of the examined runnable, too much experimental time is spent.

A theoretical option is to work with a simulated system clock that is speeded up by software. We did not pursue this approach, as we found out that several SWCs do not only rely on the system clock but also on implicit timing information. An example is a function, which exploits the fact, that it is called every 5 milliseconds to deduct an internal timer. A speed up of the system time without of executing the runnable consistently distorts the behavior of the component under test. Without removing the internal timers from the tested SWCs it is not possible to reduce the experimental time by avoiding explicit executions of the runnables.

4 Evolutionary Test of AUTOSAR SWCs

4.1 Runnable Execution Pattern

As stated above, each SWC has its defined interface to the RTE, which we use for testing. The analyzed test objects are the runnables from which the SWCs are composed. The communication between the runnables of a SWC is typically via shared variables and not via the RTE. This means, that a tested runnable is not fully separated by the RTE test interface. The constellation is pictured in figure 3.

To utilize the formally specified RTE interface despite of this problem, it is required to execute not only the runnable whose maximum execution time is tested, but also the remaining runnables in the same SWC.

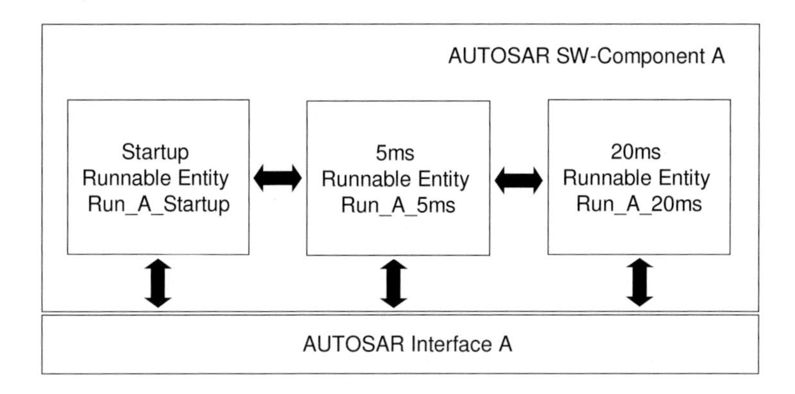

Fig. 3. Communication between runnables that compose a SWC

Fig. 4. Pattern of executed runnables

An example for this problem is the processing of vehicle configuration parameters. These constant parameters are often solely read in from the RTE in a startup runnable, which is only executed once in the boot up phase of the ECU. A runtime test of a second runnable within the same SWC does not take into account the impact of non-default configuration parameters, if the startup runnable has not been called beforehand.

Another example is the preprocessing of input data and the downsampling of the result in the same SWC. A 5ms runnable shall read in input data from the RTE and preprocess them. The result is stored in a shared variable, that is read by a 20 ms runnable. It is not possible to test the 20 ms runnable via the RTE interface sufficiently without of executing the 5ms runnable in advance.

To incorporate the interdependencies between runnables of the same SWC with different periodicities in the timing tests, we execute all runnables of a SWC in their designated temporal sequence. An example is pictured in figure 4.

In section 3.2 we stated, that only one input parameter changes its value per test step. An exception to this rule has been made for the startup runnable. Before the very first runnable is executed, a larger set of parameters is allowed to change their value to be different from default. Otherwise the input data of the startup runnable are very close to the default parameters for all generated test sequences. In the example with the vehicle configuration parameters this avoids, that the SWC is only tested with close-to-default configuration parameters.

4.2 Test Environment for AUTOSAR SWCs

The runtime test of SWCs requires a method to control the SWC on the target HW. We developed a dedicated testbed, that can be controlled via a serial connection, for running the tested SWC. The testbed allows a test control on a PC to set the input RTE variables and to trigger the execution of the runnables on the target HW. Moreover the testbed measures and provides the execution times of the executed runnables. To enable undisturbed measurements all interrupts are deactivated while a runnable is executed.

The runtime test of a test sequence with 250 test steps requires approximately 80 seconds. This is three orders of magnitude longer than the pure execution time on the target HW. The overhead can be reasoned with the time that is required for communicating with the testbed, for triggering the measurements and for configuring the input parameters. Another time-consuming aspect is the necessity to reset the SWC and the underlying HW between subsequent test sequences. This helps to avoid mutual interferences between separate test sequences.

The applied communication concept is considered bandwidth efficient, as we transmit identifiers instead of full names. We evaluated other concepts for operating the SWCs on the target, but we could not find a more efficient one. One approach is to control the runtime experiments with an interfaced embedded debugger.

4.3 Benefits of AUTOSAR for Evolutionary Timing Test

AUTOSAR provides the evolutionary timing test with the following benefits:

- **Homogeneous SW architecture**
  The AUTOSAR middleware enforces clear cut SWCs with a standardized (test-) interface.
- **Formal interface specification**
  Machine readable specification of the components and their interfaces avoids manual user input of the test interface, which is an error-prone and tedious task. From the specified interface the test stubs can be generated automatically.
- **Orientation of data flow specified**
  The AUTOSAR interface description specifies the direction of the data-flow. This makes it possible to differentiate between input and output parameters. Therefore the dimensionality of the search region for optimizing the input parameters can be cut roughly by factor two.
- **Range of values specified accurately**
  The value ranges that the RTE variables can have are specified in bit-accuracy. With this information the search region can be restricted further.
- **Periods of the cyclic runnables specified**
  This makes it possible to generate the runnable execution pattern from section 4.1 automatically.
- **HW independent source code allows test on PC and embedded system**
  The problem of high experiment duration when running the SWCs on the target HW will be avoided in the future by shifting the pre-analysis of generated test cases to a PC environment.

5 Evaluation of Genetic Optimization Concept

5.1 Tested SWCs

The tested SW components are in the domain of body- and comfort electronics. Examples for customer functions are central locking, power windows, terminal control, comfort access and interior light. The SWCs have been taken from real-life serial-development projects.

The complexity of the runnables RUN_{10} to RUN_{15} is illustrated in table 1. It lists the number of executable lines of code, the cyclomatic complexity, the knot count, the maximum nesting level and the number of input / output variables.

Table 1. Complexity of examined runnables

Runnable	RUN_{10}	RUN_{11}	RUN_{12}	RUN_{13}	RUN_{14}	RUN_{15}
Executable Lines of Code	2956	1710	1538	1995	2957	6553
Cyclomatic Complexity	448	271	273	292	442	1161
Knot Count	140	182	38	218	287	430
Maximum Nesting Level	34	6	13	9	8	7
Number of I/O variables	252	90	71	114	81	154

The complexity metrics for runtime-tested SWCs, that have been stated by Tlili et al. in [13], indicate that our examples are considerably more complex. In this study, the number of executable lines of code and the cyclomatic complexity, which corresponds to the number of decisions plus one, carry values that are roughly one order of magnitude higher. Also the knot count, that sums up the number of jump statements like break or continue, is clearly higher. The maximum nesting level from our examples is approximately twice as high as in [13]. The high number of inputs and outputs is a further metric that indicates the complexity of the examined SWCs.

5.2 Results of Genetic Optimization

This section discusses the results, which were obtained with the evolutionary timing test. The parameters, which were used in the evaluation are listed in table 2. This parameter set reached the best results in comparison with other parameterizations, that require the same total number of test steps. Considering the complexity of the problems, that contain up to 252 input / output variables, it is advisable to increase the testing effort by allowing a higher population size, more generations and test steps, if sufficient experimental time is available. With the selected configuration approximately 100 minutes are required to obtain the WCET estimate for a runnable. An increase of the testing time is not practicable within the scope of this paper, that requires numerous WCET experiments for analyzing different SWCs with miscellaneous algorithms. For the evaluation of a non-deterministic search algorithm's estimation accuracy, one requires multiple WCET test runs to reduce the impact of statistical outliers.

Table 2. Parameterization of GA

Parameter	Value
Population size	25
Number of generations	3
Selection scheme	Ranking (best 10 %)
Replacement scheme	Comma replacement
Elitism	Weak elitism
Number of test steps	250

The population size has been dimensioned to be larger than the number of generations. This reduces the impact of the randomly generated initial population on the estimation accuracy. Due to the low genetic testability, that will be shown in section 5.3, a deeper search with more generations obtains less accurate results, if the testing effort is hold constant.

The selection scheme performs a hard decision for the best 10% of the testcases. The replacement is such, that old generations are completely replaced by younger generations. The only exception is the case where the new generation's best individuum is inferior to the best individuum of the old generation. In this case, the weak elitism strategy conserves the best individuum of the old generation to ensure that the population does not develop negatively. The number of teststeps has been deducted from time constants of the SW components.

We tested the WCET of runnable entities from two ECUs, which shall be called ECU_1 and ECU_2. The results of the evaluation are pictured in the tables 3 and 4. They show the WCET estimations obtained with GAs relative to results of random testing for the runnables RUN_1 to RUN_{15}. Because of the random nature of the algorithms the results have been averaged over eight test runs. The fourth column shows the results of an improved GA concept, which will be explained in section 5.4. The highest WCET estimate, which has been ever obtained for a certain runnable with any of the algorithms is listed in the fifth column. We use this value as an estimation for the true WCET. For interpreting the performance of the algorithms, one has to reconsider that the results of the dynamic start-to-end test are below the actual worst case. This means that larger estimation results are closer to the actual WCET and therefore more accurate.

The experimental results have been divided into two groups by a horizontal line. For the runnables RUN_1 to RUN_6 and RUN_{10} to RUN_{13} the result of random testing is close to the largest WCET estimation ever obtained by different testing methods. This means, that there is little room for the GA to outperform random testing for these examples. For these examples the results of the GA are similar to the WCET estimations obtained with random testing. An exception is runnable RUN_6, where random testing even outperforms the GA.

A more significant gap between largest ever determined WCET and random testing can be found for the runnables RUN_7 to RUN_9 and RUN_{14} to RUN_{15}. For these runnables the estimated WCET of random testing tends to be more accurate than for the GA. The reason for this is the problem, that GAs run into local optima whereas random testing searches globally.

Table 3. WCET estimation with GAs relative to random testing for ECU 1

Component	Standard GA	Random test	GA with fitness landscape adaptation	Best WCET estimation
RUN_1	235 μs	235 μs	235 μs	235 μs
RUN_2	684 μs	684 μs	684 μs	684 μs
RUN_3	276 μs	277 μs	276 μs	277 μs
RUN_4	852 μs	852 μs	853 μs	855 μs
RUN_5	581 μs	583 μs	582 μs	585 μs
RUN_6	952 μs	974 μs	974 μs	977 μs
RUN_7	1084 μs	1076 μs	1091 μs	1095 μs
RUN_8	766 μs	797 μs	836 μs	1191 μs
RUN_9	5374 μs	5703 μs	8819 μs	14593 μs

Table 4. WCET estimation with GAs relative to random testing for ECU 2

Component	Standard GA	Random test	GA with fitness landscape adaptation	Best WCET estimation
RUN_{10}	224,4 μs	224,2 μs	224,3 μs	225,5 μs
RUN_{11}	61,7 μs	61,4 μs	61,5 μs	63,1 μs
RUN_{12}	76,0 μs	76,0 μs	76,0 μs	76,9 μs
RUN_{13}	88,8 μs	88,6 μs	88,9 μs	89,2 μs
RUN_{14}	112,4 μs	111,0 μs	111,8 μs	114,6 μs
RUN_{15}	203,1 μs	204,0 μs	207,1 μs	213,9 μs

An illustrative example where random testing is superior to GAs can be found in [15]. A more detailed analysis of the optimization problem in the next section analyzes the root cause for the inferior performance of GAs.

5.3 Quantification of Genetic Testability

In order to find out, why the GAs' performance in testing the WCET is inferior to random tests we analyze the genetic testability of our components under test. Gross has developed a concept to forecast the result quality of evolutionary timing tests by analyzing the control flow structure of the tested SWC [12]. We did not apply this concept, because it has been criticized in the literature to not capture all required dependencies [5] and because it requires considerable work effort to perform a syntax analysis of source code.

An alternative concept from the optimization literature is the so-called fitness-distance correlation (FDC) [14]. The FDC is the correlation between the individuals' distance to the global optimum and their fitness. A positive FDC means, that an individual which is far away from the global optimum tends to have a high fitness. A high positive FDC is disadvantageous for an optimization, because individuals, that have a high distance from the global optimum will be encouraged due to their high fitness. Analogously, a high negative FDC leads to optimization problems, that are more easily solved.

Table 5. Fitness-Distance Correlation for different runnables

Runnable	Fitness-Distance Correlation
RUN_1	- 0,08
RUN_2	0,0
RUN_3	0,0
RUN_4	+ 0,01
RUN_5	0,0
RUN_6	- 0,05
RUN_7	+ 0,09
RUN_8	- 0,12
RUN_9	- 0,10

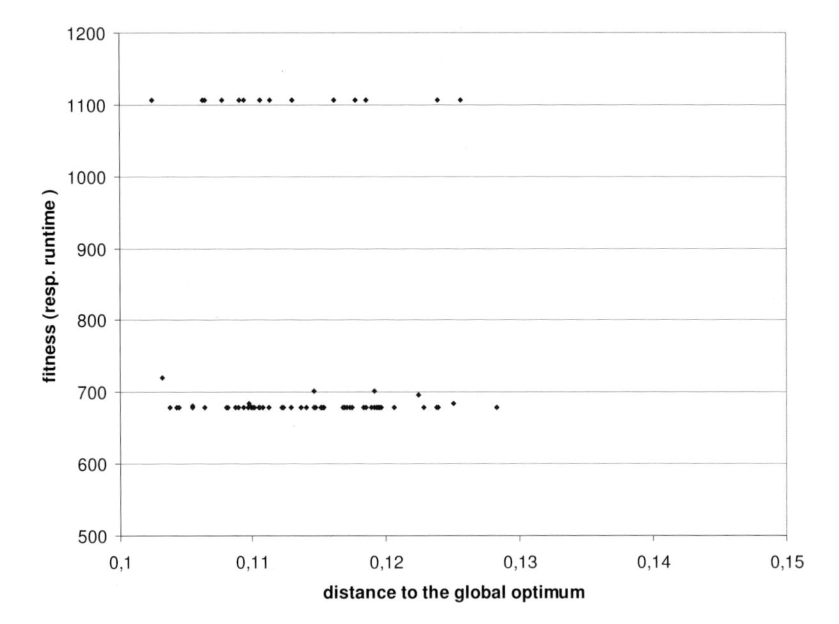

Fig. 5. Scatter plot of fitness and distance to global optimum for RUN_8

Jones and Forrest provide a decision boundary to classify genetic optimization problems [14]. If the FDC is above $+0,15$ the optimization problem is hard to solve with GAs, if it is below $-0,15$ it is easy to solve.

The global optimum, which is required for calculating the FDC, is unfortunately not known. To cope with this, we assumed that the maximum observed execution time from all experiments is close to the global optimum and took this value accordingly. The FDC values for the ECU ECU_1 are depicted in table 5.

One can observe, that the norm of the FDC value is below the decision-boundary $0,15$ for all examples. This means that there is only a weak relation between the distance to the optimization target and the fitness value. It cannot be classified, if the global optimum attracts or detracts the optimized individuals. The reason for this is the high dimensionality of the input data space. We presume a higher correlation between few runtime-decisive parameters and the resulting fitness. It was observed, that there is a high number of input parameters, which do not impact the fitness resp. the maximum runtime of a test sequence. However, these parameters have an impact on the distance from the optimal test sequence, which contains arbitrary values for irrelevant inputs. The resulting distortion leads to a low norm of the FDC.

A detailed profile of fitness and distance is depicted in figure 5, that shows a scatter plot for the runnable RUN_8. One can see that the fitness profile is very flat. This means, that the GA gets little guidance on the search for the maximum execution time. In this example the GA performs worse than random testing, if all individuals of the initial population have low fitness values around 700. This can be reasoned with the local search of the GA, that focuses on search regions around the best individuals of the population. The best individuals in this case do not provide guidance to the global optimum. In that example, random testing performs better, as it may find a test sequence whose fitness is above 1100 in every randomly generated test sequence.

5.4 Concept Refinement for Flat Fitness Profiles

This paragraph tries to refine the GA concept such, that it also performs good in case of flat fitness profiles. Section 5.3 showed, that random testing is superior in the case, where there is no learning potential from the current population. Our refined approach inserts a step that analyzes the fitness profile of the population before the selection phase. If the analysis finds out, that the GA has yet found interesting individuals the standard selection concept is performed, that selects individuals with high fitness for further optimization. If the analysis result shows that the current population contains only few or no interesting individuals, the population is enriched with random individuals. This adaptive concept makes it possible to exploit the advantages of both random testing and GAs. The algorithm flexibly adapts to the fitness profile of the test object by applying the appropriate strategy.

The result of GAs with fitness landscape adaptation can be found in the tables 3 and 4. For the runnables RUN_1 to RUN_6 and RUN_{10} to RUN_{14} the enhanced GA reaches the same estimation accuracy as random testing. In the remaining runnables the fitness adaptive GA outperforms random testing.

6 Conclusion

We developed a concept and reported our experiences in measuring the WCET of automotive SWCs by applying test sequences, that have been generated with GAs. For this purpose one can leverage the AUTOSAR architecture by using information that has been formally modeled. The RTE provides a test interface that makes it possible to test free-cut SWCs. The necessary adaptations to measure runtimes of runnables are in a reasonable extent. A drawback of the testing concept is the long time, that is required for measuring a complete test sequence on the target HW. In the future, we will increase the efficiency by pre-evaluating test sequences on the test PC. By examining the traversed control flow path, it is possible to avoid costly timing tests of paths, which are unlikely to increase the present WCET estimate.

We found out, that the estimation quality of standard GAs is below the performance of random tests for state-based SWCs with real-life complexity. This can be reasoned with the flat runtime profile and the difficulty of an optimization problem with many input parameters. The extended GA version, which adapts to the runtime profile of the examined SWC, performs better or equal relative to random testing for all examples.

References

1. Wegener, J., Sthamer, H.-H., Jones, B.F., Eyres, D.E.: Testing real-time systems using genetic algorithms. Software Quality Journal, 127–135 (1997)
2. Bernat, G., Colin, A., Petters, S.: WCET analysis of probabilistic hard real-time systems. In: Real-Time Systems Symposium (RTSS), Austin, USA (2002)
3. Mueller, F., Wegener, J.: A comparison of static analysis and evolutionary testing for the verification of timing constraints. In: IEEE Real-Time Technology and Applications Symposium, pp. 179–188 (1998)
4. Kopetz, H.: Real-Time Systems: Design Principles for Distributed Embedded Applications, 1st edn., vol. 75. Kluwer Academic Publishers, Dordrecht (1997)
5. Wegener, J.: Evolutionaerer Test des Zeitverhaltens von Realzeitsystemen. Shaker Verlag (2001)
6. Puschner, P., Nossal, R.: Testing the results of static worst-case execution time analysis. In: IEEE Real-Time Systems Symposium, pp. 134–143 (1998)
7. AUTOSAR consortium website, `http://www.autosar.org/`
8. Fennel, H., Bunzel, S., Heinecke, H., Bielefeld, J., Fuerst, S., Schnelle, K.-P., Grote, W., Maldener, N., Weber, T., Wohlgemuth, F., Ruh, J., Lundh, L., Sandèn, T., Heitkämper, P., Rimkus, R., Leflour, J., Gilberg, A., Virnich, U., Voget, S., Nishikawa, K., Kajio, K., Lange, K., Scharnhorst, T., Kunkel, B.: Achievements and Exploitation of the AUTOSAR Development Partnership Convergence 2006, Detroit (2006)
9. Scheickl, O., Rudorfer, M.: Automotive Real Time Development Using a Timing-augmented AUTOSAR Specification. In: Embedded Real Time Software (ERTS), Toulouse (2008)
10. Rudorfer, M., Ochs, T., Hoser, P., Thiede, M., Moessmer, M., Scheickl, O., Heinecke, H.: Realtime System Design Utilizing AUTOSAR Methodology. Elektronik Automotive (2007)
11. Reineke, J., Wachter, B., Thesing, S., Wilhelm, R., Polian, I., Eisinger, J., Becker, B.: A definition and classification of timing anomalies. In: 6th Intl. Workshop on Worst-Case Execution Time (WCET) Analysis (2006)
12. Gross, H.G.: Measuring Evolutionary Testability of Real-Time Software. PhD thesis, Univ. of Glamorgan, UK (2000)
13. Tlili, M., Sthamer, H., Wappler, S., Wegener, J.: Improving Evolutionary Real-Time Testing by Seeding Structural Test Data Evolutionary Computation (CEC 2006), pp. 885–891 (2006)

14. Jones, T., Forrest, S.: Fitness Distance Correlation as a Measure of Problem Difficulty for Genetic Algorithms. In: Proceedings of the Sixth International Conference on Genetic Algorithms (1995)
15. Borenstein, Y., Poli, R.: Fitness distribution and GA hardness. In: Yao, X., Burke, E.K., Lozano, J.A., Smith, J., Merelo-Guervós, J.J., Bullinaria, J.A., Rowe, J.E., Tiňo, P., Kabán, A., Schwefel, H.-P. (eds.) PPSN 2004. LNCS, vol. 3242, pp. 11–20. Springer, Heidelberg (2004)

Measurement-Based Timing Analysis*

Ingomar Wenzel, Raimund Kirner, Bernhard Rieder, and Peter Puschner

Institut für Technische Informatik,
Technische Universität Wien, Vienna, Austria

Abstract. In this paper we present a measurement-based worst-case execution time (WCET) analysis method. Exhaustive end-to-end execution-time measurements are computationally intractable in most cases. Therefore, we propose to measure execution times of subparts of the application code and then compose these times into a safe WCET bound.

This raises a number of challenges to be solved. First, there is the question of how to define and subsequently calculate adequate subparts. Second, a huge amount of test data is required enforcing the execution of selected paths to perform the desired runtime measurements.

The presented method provides solutions to both problems. In a number of experiments we show the usefulness of the theoretical concepts and the practical feasibility by using current state-of-the-art industrial case studies from project partners.

1 Introduction

In the last years the number of electronic control systems has increased rapidly. In order to stay competitive, more and more functionality is integrated into a growing number of powerful and complex computer hardware. Due to these advances in control systems engineering, new challenges for analyzing the timing behavior of real-time computer systems arise.

Resulting from the temporal constraints for the correct operation of such a real-time system, predictability in the temporal domain is a stringent imperative to be satisfied. Therefore, it is necessary to determine the timing behavior of the tasks running on a real-time computer system. Worst-case execution time (WCET) analysis is the research field investigating methods to assess the worst-case timing behavior of real-time tasks [1].

A central part in WCET analysis is to model the timing behavior of the target platform. However, manual hardware modelling is time-consuming and error prone, especially for new types of highly complex processor hardware. In order to avoid this effort and to address the portability problem in an elegant manner, a hybrid WCET analysis approach has been developed. Execution-time measurements on the instrumented application executable substitute the hardware timing model and are combined with elements from static static timing analysis.

There are also other approaches of measurement-based timing analysis. For example, Petters et al. [2] modifies the program code to enforce the execution of selected paths. The drawback of this approach is that the measured program and the final program cannot be the same. Bernat et al. [3] and Ernst et al. [4] calculate a WCET estimate from

* This work has been supported by the FIT-IT research project "Model-based Development of Distributed Embedded Control Systems (MoDECS)".

T. Margaria and B. Steffen (Eds.): ISoLA 2008, CCIS 17, pp. 430–444, 2008.

the measured execution times of decomposed program entities. While the last two approaches like our technique also partition the program for the measurements, they do not address the challenging problem of systematic generation of input data for the measurements. Heuristic methods for input-data generation have been developed [5] which alone are not adequate to ensure a concrete coverage for the timing measurements.

2 Basic Concepts

In this section, basic concepts for modeling a system by measurement-based timing analysis are introduced. These include modeling the program representation, the semantics, and the physical hardware.

2.1 Static Program Representation

A *control flow graph* (CFG) is used to model the control flow of a program. A CFG $G = \langle N, E, s, t \rangle$ consists of a set of nodes N representing *basic blocks*, a set of edges $E : N \times N$ representing the control flow, a unique entry node s, and a unique end node t. A *basic block* contains a sequence of instructions that is entered at the beginning and the only exit is at the end, i.e., only the last instruction may be a control-flow changing instruction. The current support for function calls is done by function inlining.

2.2 Execution Path Representation

We introduce *paths* in order to describe execution scenarios (Def. 1).

Definition 1. *Path / Execution Path / Sub-Path*
Given a CFG $G = \langle N, E, s, t \rangle$, *a* path π *from node* $a \in N$ *to node* $b \in N$ *is a sequence of nodes* $\pi = (n_0, n_1, ..., n_n)$ *(representing basic blocks) such that* $n_0 = a$, $n_n = b$, *and* $\forall\, 0 \leq i < n : \langle n_i, n_{i+1} \rangle \in E$ *. The length of such a path* π *is* $n + 1$.
An execution path *is defined as a path starting from* s *and ending in* t. Π *denotes the set of all* execution paths *of the CFG* G, *i.e., all paths that can be taken through the program represented by the CFG.*
A sub-path *is a subsequence of an* execution path.

If programs are analyzed the set of feasible paths, i.e., the set of paths that can be actually executed is of special interest (because exclusively the execution times of these paths can influence the timing behavior).

Our approach, based on model-checking, allows to check the feasibility of a path (see Def. 2). To ensure the termination of the analysis, the model checker is stopped if it cannot perform the analysis of a path within a certain amount of time. However, in this case the feasibility of the respective paths has to be checked manually.

Definition 2. *Feasibility of paths*
Given that the set of execution paths of a program P *is modeled by its CFG* G, *we call a path* $\pi \in G$ feasible, *iff there exist input data for program* P *enforcing that the control-flow follows* π. *Conversely, paths that are not feasible are called* infeasible. *Defining* Π *as the paths of the CFG and* Π^f *as the set of feasible paths, it holds that* $\Pi^f \subseteq \Pi$.

3 The Principle of Measurement-Based Timing Analysis

The *measurement-based timing analysis* (MBTA) method is a hybrid WCET analysis technique, i.e., it combines static program analysis with a dynamic part, the execution-time measurements. As shown in Figure 1, the following steps are performed [6]:

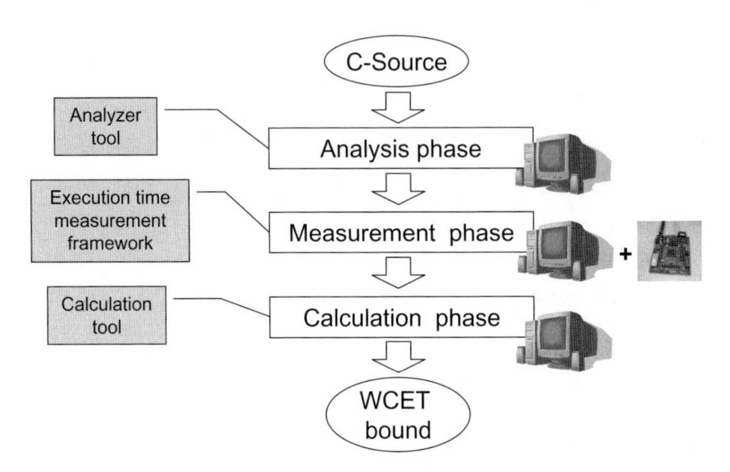

Fig. 1. The three phases of measurement-based timing analysis

1. Analysis Phase: First the source code is parsed and static analyzes extract path information. Then, the program is partitioned into segments, which are defined in Section 4. The segment size is customizable to keep the number of different paths for the later measurement phase tractable. To assess the execution time that a task spends within each of the identified program segments, adequate test data are needed to guide the program's execution into all the paths of a segment. These test data are generated automatically. Besides applying random test-data vectors and heuristics, bounded model checking for test-data generation is introduced.

As described in Section 4, when using model checking, we generate for each program segment and instrumented instance of the source-code.

In contrast to methods that work on object-code level, the C-code analysis ensures a high level of portability because ANSI C is a well established programming language in control systems engineering. Additionally, C is also used as output format of code generation tools like Real-Time Workshop (Mathworks Inc.) or TargetLink (dSpace GmbH).

2. Measurement Phase: The generated test data force program execution onto the required paths within the program segments. The measured execution times are captured by code instrumentations that are automatically generated and placed at program segment boundaries. The instrumented programs are executed and timed on the target platform.

3. Calculation Phase: The obtained execution times and path information are combined to calculate a final WCET bound. This calculation uses techniques from static WCET analysis. It utilizes the path information acquired in the *static analysis* phase. (see 1.)

In case of complex hardware where the instruction timing depends on the execution history, MBTA can still provide safe WCET bounds when using explicit state enforcement at the beginning of each segment to eliminate state variations. For example, the pipeline could be flushed or the cache content could be invalidated or pre-loaded.

The contributions of this measurement-based worst-case execution time analysis (MBTA) method are:

Avoidance of explicit hardware modelling. In contrast to pure static WCET analysis methods [1], this approach does not require to build a sophisticated execution-time model for each instruction type. In fact, the actual timing behavior of instructions within their context is obtained from execution-time measurements on the concrete hardware.

Automated test-data generation using model checking. This allows us to *completely* generate all required and feasible test data. In the first experiments we used symbolic model checking. Later, bounded model checking turned out to be superior wrt. model size and computation times.

Parametrizable complexity reduction. The control-flow graph partitioning algorithm allows a parameterizable complexity reduction of the analysis process (i.e., the number of required execution-time measurements and the size of the test data set can be chosen according to the available computing resources). On the reverse side, the accuracy of the analysis decreases by reducing the number of tests. This allows for an adaptation to user demands and available resources.

Modular tool architecture. The tool structure is completely modular. It is possible to improve the components for each step independently (e.g., the test-data generation mechanism, WCET bound calculation step).

Scalability of the analysis process. Execution-time measurements and test-data generation (that consume together around 98% of the total analysis time) can be executed highly parallel if multiple target machines respectively host computers are available.

In our implementation, the interface data passed between the three phases (i.e., extracted path information, the test data, and the obtained execution times) are stored in XML files.

4 Parameterizable Program Partitioning for MBTA

In the following sections, the main concepts of the measurement-based timing analysis approach [7] are described in detail. The proposed method is a hybrid approach that combines elements of static analysis with the dynamic execution of software.

After preparing the previously described CFG, the partitioning algorithm is invoked to split the CFG into smaller entities, so-called *program segments* (Definition 3). This segmentation is necessary, because when instead trying to use end-to-end measurements the number of paths in Π (the set of paths of the function subject to analysis) is in general intractable. Our segmentation is similar to that described by Ernst et al. [4]. However, we do not differ between segments of single or multiple paths, instead we use a path bound to limit segment size. In a second step, the paths within the program segments are explicitly enumerated in a data structure called *dtree* (coming from decision-tree).

Definition 3. *Program Segmentation (PSG)*
A program segment *(PS) is a tuple* $PS = \langle s, t, \Pi \rangle$ *where* s *is the start node and* t *is the respective end node.* Π *refers to the set of associated paths* $\pi_i \in \Pi$*. Further, each path of a segment has its origin in* s *and its end in* t*:*

$$\forall \pi = (n_1, ..., n_n) \in \Pi : n_1 = s \land n_n = t$$

The intermediate nodes of a path of a segment may not be equal to its start or end node:

$$\forall \pi = (n_1, n_2, ..., n_{n-1}, n_n) \in \Pi \ \forall 2 \leq i \leq n-1 : n_i \neq s \land n_i \neq t$$

The set of all program segments PS *of a program is denoted as* PSG*.*

Each program segment spawns a finite set of paths Π_j. For each of these paths we are interested in the set of feasible paths and the respective input data (test data) that force the execution of the code onto this path. This set is constructed by using a hierarchy of test-data generation methods. When decomposing a program into program segments, two important issues arise:

First, each program segment has to be instrumented for obtaining the execution times of its feasible paths. Each instrumentation introduces some overhead. Therefore, these instrumentations are not desired and their number should be minimized.

Second, the computational effort of generating input data increases with larger program segments sizes, especially when using model checking.

If no constraints are given, there are many different program segmentations possible. For instance, one extreme segmentation would be that for each CFG edge one program segment is generated, i.e., $PSG = \{PS_i \mid PS_i = \langle n_o, n_p, \{(n_o, n_p)\} \rangle \land (n_o, n_p) \in E\}$. The other end of the spectrum would be to put all nodes into one program segment, i.e., $PSG = \{PS\}$ with $PS = \langle s, t, \Pi \rangle$ and Π having a complete enumeration of all paths within a function (and its called functions).

A "good" program segmentation PSG is a program segmentation that balances *the number of program segments* and the *average number of paths per program segment.* These two "goals" are not independent. When the number of program segments is decreased, typically[1] the sum of paths increases and vice versa. A segmentation resulting in fewer program segments causes (i) less instrumentation effort and related overheads at runtime and (ii) higher computational resource needs during analysis because more paths have to be evaluated. In contrast, a segmentation into more program segments results in (i) higher instrumentation effort and (ii) faster path evaluation. This is because the larger a segment is, the more paths are inside a segment, but the less different segment boundaries have to be instrumented.

In practice, a reasonable combination of the number of paths per segment and the number of program segments has to be selected. The major limitation turned out to be the computational resources required to generate the input data for the paths (see Section 5).

4.1 Path-Bounded Partitioning Algorithm

The partitioning algorithm automatically partitions a CFG into program segments. As there is a functional relationship between the number of program segments and the

[1] The term "typically" is used because there are some exceptions at the boundaries. Examples for this are presented in Section 4.2.

overall number of sub-paths to be measured, we choose one factor and derive the other one. One possibility is to provide a target value for the maximum number of paths for each PS_j (denoted as *path bound* PB), i.e., ideally $|\Pi_j| \approx PB$.

The detailed description of the partitioning algorithm is given in [6]. Basically, the partitioning algorithm investigates the number of paths between dominated nodes and in case it is higher than PB a recursive decomposition is performed. Due to the short runtime of the partitioning algorithm (even for large code samples), it is possible to experiment with various values for PB and calculate the resulting number of paths within reasonable time ($< 1s$).

4.2 Example of Path-Bounded Program Partitioning

To demonstrate the operation of the MBTA framework, the C code example given in Figure 2(a) is used. The corresponding CFG is given in Figure 2(b).

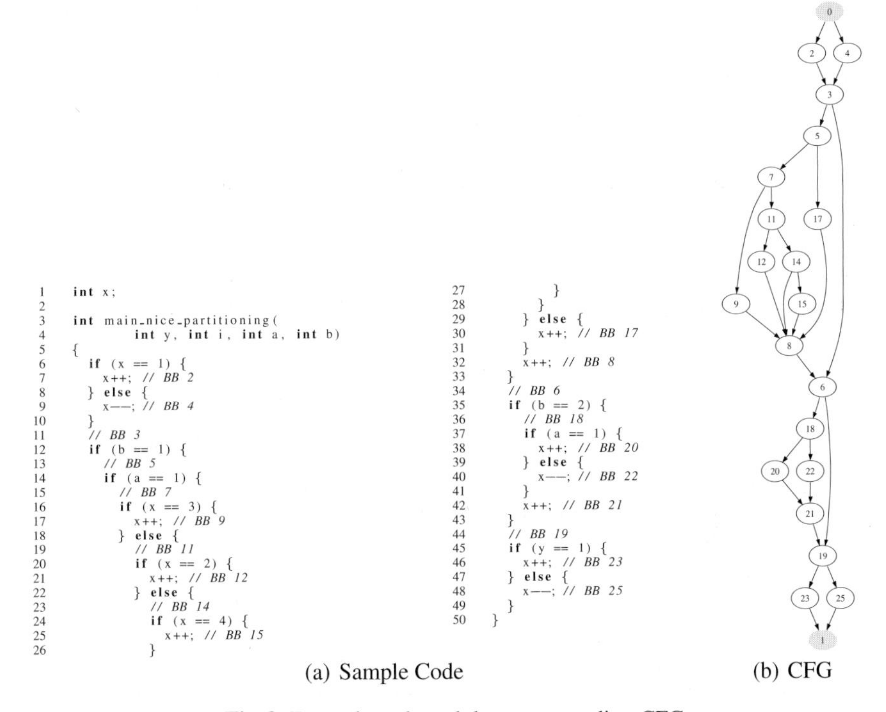

int x;
int main_nice_partitioning(
int y, int i, int a, int b)
{
if (x == 1) {
x++; // BB 2
} else {
x--; // BB 4
}
// BB 3
if (b == 1) {
// BB 5
if (a == 1) {
// BB 7
if (x == 3) {
x++; // BB 9
} else {
// BB 11
if (x == 2) {
x++; // BB 12
} else {
// BB 14
if (x == 4) {
x++; // BB 15
}
}
}
} else {
x++; // BB 17
}
x++; // BB 8
}
// BB 6
if (b == 2) {
// BB 18
if (a == 1) {
x++; // BB 20
} else {
x--; // BB 22
}
x++; // BB 21
}
// BB 19
if (y == 1) {
x++; // BB 23
} else {
x--; // BB 25
}
}
(a) Sample Code
(b) CFG

Fig. 2. Example code and the corresponding CFG

Assuming a path bound $PB = 5$, the partitioning algorithm constructs a segmentation with 6 program segments, i.e., $PSG = \{PS_0, PS_1, PS_2, PS_3, PS_4, PS_5\}$ with

$$\begin{aligned}
PS_0 &= (0, 3,\ \{(0, 2, 3),\ (0, 4, 3)\}),\\
PS_1 &= (3, 5,\ \{(3, 5)\}),\\
PS_2 &= (3, 6,\ \{(5, 7, 9, 8, 6),\ (5, 7, 11, 12, 8, 6),\ (5, 7, 11, 14, 8, 6),\\
&\qquad (5, 7, 11, 14, 15, 8, 6),\ (5, 17, 8, 6)\}),\\
PS_3 &= (3, 6,\ \{(3, 6)\}),\\
PS_4 &= (6, 19, \{(6, 18, 20, 21, 19),\ (6, 18, 22, 21, 19),\ (6, 19)\}),\\
PS_5 &= (19, 1, \{(19, 23, 1),\ (19, 25, 1)\}).
\end{aligned}$$

The partitioning results for PB being 5, 10, 20, and 100, respectively are summarized in Figure 3(a). Figure 3(b) shows the dependency of the number of segments ($|PSG|$) and the number of sub-paths ($\sum |\Pi_j|$) for each of these segmentations. This example illustrates that in general fewer program segments cause a higher overall number of paths to be considered.

Path Bound	|PSG|	#Paths ($\sum \|\pi_j\|$)
1	30	30
5	6	14
10	3	14
20	2	18
100	1	72

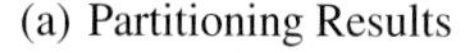

(a) Partitioning Results

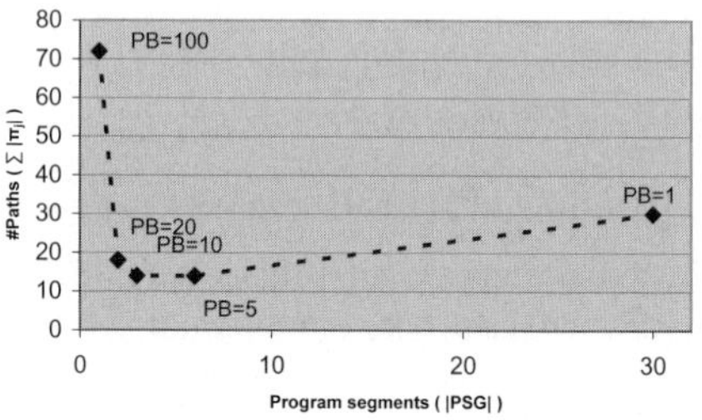

(b) Dependency between $|PSG|$ and $\sum |\Pi_j|$

Fig. 3. Dependency between number of segments ($|PSG|$) and number of sub-paths ($\sum |\Pi_j|$)

5 Automated Test-Data Generation

For each path that has been previously determined in the program segmentation step, we are interested in whether it is a feasible path. Feasible paths may contribute to the timing behavior of the application and thus have to be subject to execution-time measurements.

5.1 Problem Statement

As described previously the set of paths $\sum |\Pi_j|$ has to be executed to perform the execution-time measurements. Therefore, it is necessary to acquire for each path $\pi_i \in \Pi_j$ a suitable set of input-variable assignments such that the respective assignments at the function start causes exactly the control flow that follows π_i. In contrast, for *infeasible paths* their infeasibility has to be proven to know that they cannot contribute to the timing behavior of the program.

5.2 Test-Data Generation Hierarchy

When applying the method it turned out that the test-data generation process is the bottleneck of the analysis. Especially, model checking is very resource intensive. To improve performance we decided to use a combination of different methods for generating the input data. We start by using fast techniques and gradually use more formal and resource-consuming methods to cover the paths for which the cheaper methods did not found appropriate input data. Figure 4 shows the hierarchy of methods we apply. On the basic level test-data reuse is applied. This means that we reuse all existing test data for that application from previous runs. On the second level, pure random search is performed, i.e., all input variables are bound to random numbers. Third, heuristics like genetic algorithms can be used. Finally, all data that could not be found using the generation methods of level 1 to 3, are calculated by model checking. Especially, the infeasibility of paths can be proven only by model checking (at level 4). The actual

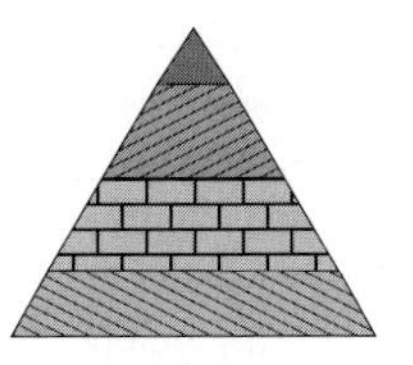

Fig. 4. Test-data generation hierarchy

computational effort spent on each of the levels is application dependent. If an application has many infeasible paths, model checking is required to show that each of these paths is really infeasible.

The key advantages of this hierarchical test-data generation approach are (i) that many test data are generated by fast strategies, only left over cases have to resort to expensive model checking; (ii) the correlation of test data and the covered path is known even when applying heuristics since we monitor the covered paths before doing the measurements; (iii) and complementary, model checking is used in the final phase of test data generation. This allows generating input data for a desired path whenever such a path is feasible or otherwise to prove that the path is infeasible.

5.3 Test-Data Generation Using Model Checking

The basic idea of performing test-data generation by model checking (level 4) is that the CFG (and the instructions in the nodes) are transformed into a model that can be analyzed by a model checker. For each $\pi_i \in \Pi_j$ to be analyzed a new model $model(\pi_i)$ is generated. This model is passed to a model checker $check(model(\pi_i))$ that yields a suitable variable binding in case a counter example can be found by the model checker. Otherwise, the function *check* returns that the path is infeasible.

When generating a model $model(\pi_i)$, an assertion is added stating that the particular path π_i cannot be executed within that model. Program code that does not influence the reachability of that path π_i is cut away (slicing) to reduce the size of the model. Then the model checker tries to prove this formally. Whenever the proof fails, the model checker provides a counter example that represents the exact input data that enforce an execution of the desired path π_i. However, if the assertion holds, the path is infeasible and therefore no input data do exist.

The current implementation does not support the analysis of loops. However, we work on loop unrolling to support loops.

Symbolic Model Checking vs. Bounded Model Checking. We implemented model checking backends for *symbolic model checking* and *bounded model checking* [8]. The model checker SAL [9] is used for symbolic model checking [9] and the model checkers SAL-BMC [9] and CBMC [10] are used for bounded model checking. In experiments, it turned out that bounded model checking supports (i) bigger applications in terms of lines of code and (ii) supports longer program segments (i.e., longer paths). Therefore, our MBTA uses the bounded model checker CBMC by default.

5.4 Example Application for Test-Data Generation

In this section we show the result of applying bounded model checking to find a specific path in the sample program of Figure 2. The paths for program segmentation PSG

described in Section 4.2 are represented as *dtree* data structure (Figure 5). This data structure is a tree which root node has the name of the CFG (name of subroutine). All immediate successor nodes denote a program segment. In the parentheses the starting basic-block node is denoted, e.g., PS_0 starts at basic block 0. Then, the succeeding nodes denote the intermediary basic blocks. The end nodes provide additional information corresponding to the path starting from the start node and leading to this end node, i.e., every end node represents one path within a program segment. This information consists of the data-set number and the model number. The data-set number identifies the input data to reach this path. When using model checking to generate the test data, the model number identifies the model $model(\pi_i)$ for path π_i. For instance, the model number of *model*(π_3) for path $\pi_3 = (5, 7, 9, 8, 6)$ equals 3.

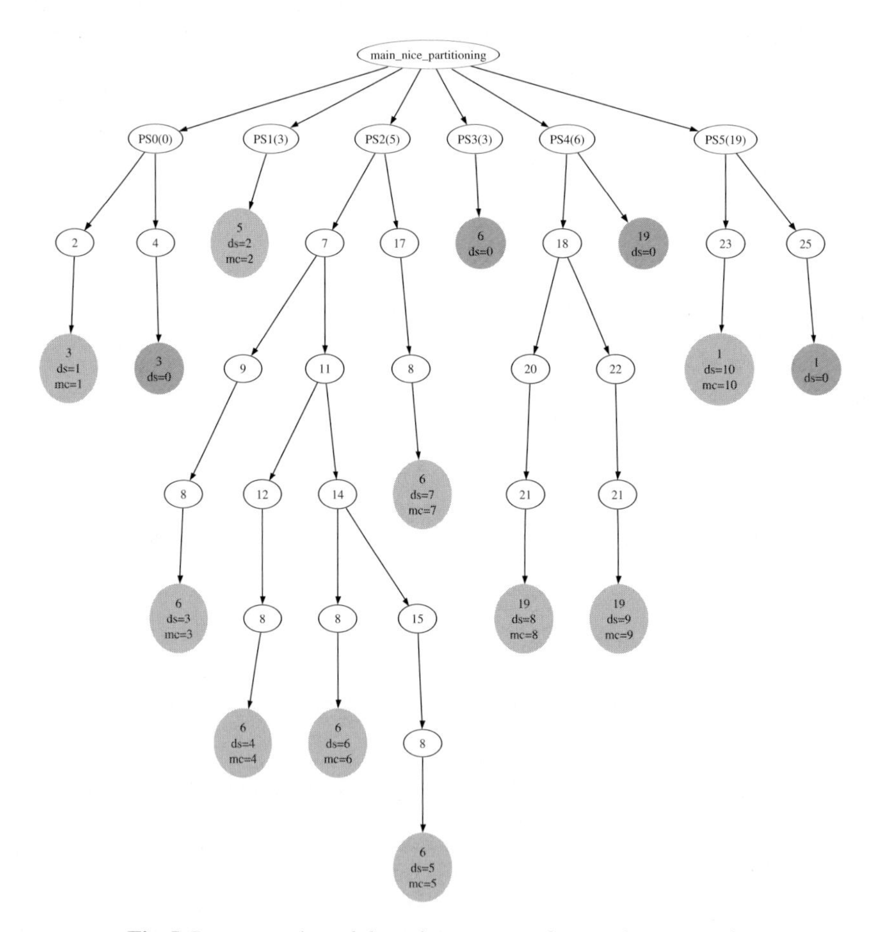

Fig. 5. Representation of *dtree* data structure for test-data generation

In Figure 6 the code of the automatically generated model for $\pi_3 = (5, 7, 9, 8, 6)$ is depicted. In the `main` function the program counter `mc_pc` is initialized. Next, the function subject to analysis is called with its respective parameters. Within the function, first all instructions preceding the PS are conserved, i.e., basic blocks BB0, BB2, BB4,

BB3. Starting with BB5, the *PS* entry node, cut off actions take place. These cut-off actions mean that the functional code of BB17 has been removed. Instead of this removed code additional exits have to be added. This avoids that other basic blocks modify the calculations and change the execution path.

Whenever code of basic blocks residing on the actual investigated path is executed, the program counter `mc_pc` of the model is increased. Thus, this increase is performed for basic blocks BB5, BB7, BB9, BB8 and BB6.

Finally, after returning to `main` the assertion `assert(mc_pc != 5)` ensures that $mc\_pc \neq 5$, i.e., path $\pi_3 = (5, 7, 9, 8, 6)$ cannot be executed.

In a standard program execution, this assertion would be raised whenever – depending on the currently assigned variable values – path π_3 is executed. However, when passed to a C model checker, the model checker tries to formally prove whether this assertion **always** holds. If not, the model checker provides a counter example containing variable bindings that violate the assertion. In this case, we get the data binding $\{x \leftarrow 4, y \leftarrow 0, i \leftarrow 0, a \leftarrow 1, b \leftarrow 1\}$. If the model checker affirms that the assertion holds, then we know that the path is infeasible. In case the model checker runs out of resources, the path has to be checked manually.

```
int mc_pc;
int x, local_y, local_i, local_a, local_b

int main_nice_partitioning(int y, int i, int a, int b)
{
  if (x == 1) {
    x++; // BB 2
  } else {
    x--; // BB 4
  }
  // BB 3
  if (b == 1) {
    mc_pc++;  /* BB 5 */              /* mc_pc increment */
    if (a == 1) {
      mc_pc++;  /* BB 7 */            /* mc_pc increment */
      if (x == 3) {
        mc_pc++;  /* BB 9 */          /* mc_pc increment */
        x++;
      } else {
        mc_pc = -1; /* BB 11 */       /* mc cut off */
        return 0;                     /* mc cut off */
      }
    } else {
      mc_pc = -1; /* BB 17 */         /* mc cut off  */
      return 0;                       /* mc cut off  */
    }
    mc_pc++; /* BB 8 */               /* mc_pc increment */
    x++;
  }
  mc_pc++; /* BB 6 */                 /* mc_pc increment */
  return 0;                           /* mc cut off  */
}

int main()
{
  mc_pc = 0;                          /* mc_pc reset */
  main_nice_partitioning(local_y, local_i, local_a, local_b);

  assert(mc_pc != 5);                 /* mc assertion */
}
```

Fig. 6. Automatically generated code for *model*(π_3) with $\pi_3 = (5, 7, 9, 8, 6)$

5.5 Complexity Reduction

When evaluating the paths $\bigcup \Pi_j \mid \Pi_j \in PSG$ that have to be analyzed with model checking, it is essential to apply a number of complexity reductions on the models.

For each path π_i the complexity reduction is performed in several steps:

1. All paths **after** a *PS* are cut off because they do not influence the control flow leading to a *PS* or inside a *PS*.
2. Paths **preceding** the *PS* are kept without modifications. This has practical reasons. Originally, it was intended to remove the preceding code. However, it turned out that this is not necessary immediately because the model checker can solve the problem within a reasonable amount of time. The advantage why this code remains unchanged is that more infeasible paths – namely from the global function view – can be determined. Thus, only feasible paths contribute to the timing information of the program segment.

3. Due to the **goal** of model checking (namely to check whether there exists a specific path), the model checker can perform optimizations on its own, e.g., program slicing [11] by removing unused variables (i.e., variables that do not influence the actual execution paths).

6 The Execution-Time Model of MBTA

The role of the *execution time model* is to provide the information to map execution times to instruction sequences. The use of the execution time model in MBTA is in principal the same as in static WCET analysis [1]. However, the main difference is that in MBTA the timing information is obtained by measurements instead of deriving it from the user manual and other sources as done in static WCET analysis.

The execution time measurements of MBTA in general require to instrument the code with additional instructions to signal program locations and/or store measurement results. Since the instrumentations change the analyzed object code, there are some requirements on the code instrumentations:

1. The impact of the instrumentation code on the execution time and code size should be small.
2. If the instrumented code used for MBTA is not the same as the final application code under operation, the code instrumentations should allow to determine an estimate on the change of the WCET of suitable precision between the instrumented code and the final application code. Fulfilling this requirement may be challenging in practice, e.g, when requiring precise safe upper bounds on complex target hardware.

6.1 Enforcing Predictable Hardware States

Besides the above quality criteria of code instrumentations, there is also a substantial potential of using code instrumentations: on complex hardware where the instruction timing depends on the execution history it is challenging to determine a precise WCET bound. Code instrumentations can be used to enforce an a-priori known state at the beginning of a program segment, thus avoiding the need for considering the execution history when determining the execution time within a program segment. For example, code instrumentations could be used to explicitly load/lock the cache, to synchronize the pipeline, etc.

6.2 Execution-Time Composition

After performing the execution-time measurements we know that each path $\pi \in \Pi_j$ is assigned its measured execution time $t(\pi)$. Now, the next step is to compose these measured execution times into a WCET estimate. In general, three different approaches are possible, which are explained in [1]. Using *tree-based methods*, the WCET is calculated based on the syntactic constructs. In *path-based* methods, a longest path search is performed. The *Implicit path enumeration technique* (IPET) models the program flow by (linear) flow constraints. After applying this calculation step, we get a final WCET estimate that is the overall result of the MBTA.

In order to illustrate this flexibility of choosing the calculation method, a path-based calculation method (longest path search) and IPET (using integer linear programming - ILP) have been implemented in our MBTA framework. It has been shown that it is possible to incorporate flow facts into the ILP model without restricting generality [6].

7 Experiments

We have implemented the described MBTA as a prototype. The **host system** of the framework has been installed on two systems, on Linux and also on Microsoft Windows XP with Cygwin. The quantitative results described in this section have been obtained using a PC system with an Intel Pentium 4 CPU at 2.8 Ghz and 2.5GB RAM running on a Debian 4.0 Linux system.

As **target system** we used a Motorola HCS12 evaluation board (MC9S12DP256). The board is clocked at 16Mhz, has 256kB flash memory, 4kB EEPROM, and 12kB RAM. It is equipped with two serial communication interfaces (SCI), three serial port interfaces (SPI), two controller area network (CAN) modules, eight 16bit timers, 16 A/D converters.

As a **measurement device** our frameworks can either use one of the counters of the HCS12 board or an external timer. The experiments reported here have been performed using a custom-built external counter device that is clocked at 200MHz. This device is connected via USB to the host system and by two I/O pins to the target hardware [6].

Application Name	Source	LOC	#BB	#Execution Paths
TestNicePartitioning	Teaching example	46	30	72
ActuatorMotorControl	Industry	1150	171	1.90E+11
ADCConv	Industry	321	31	144
ActuatorSysCtrl	Industry	274	54	97

Fig. 7. Summary of the used case studies

In order to study relevant program code, we investigated the code structure of applications delivered by industrial partners (Magna Steyr Fahrzeugtechnik, AVL List). It was decided to support code structures representing a class of highly important applications (safety-critical embedded real-time system). Figure 7 summarizes the **benchmark programs** used in the experiments (`LOC` = lines of code, `#BB` = number of basic blocks, `#ExecutionPaths` = number of *execution paths*) of the active application. The first benchmark has been written by hand as a test program in order to evaluate the MBTA framework. The second one has been developed using Matlab/Simulink in order to walk through all stages of a modern software development process. The last three benchmarks representing industrial applications from our industrial project partners have been the key drivers for the development of the MBTA framework.

7.1 Experiment with Model Checking for Automated Test-Data Generation

The goal of this experiment is to compare the performance of different model checkers for automatically generating test data. Figure 8 shows the analysis time of the different model checkers that have been introduced in Section 5.3. Please note that these figures do not state anything about the general quality of a model checker, as even in case of

	#Paths MC	Time Analysis [s]		
		CBMC	SAL	SAL BMC
TestNicePartitioning	63	11.2	109.6	259.3
ActuatorMotorControl	280	1202.2	N.A.[1]	N.A.[1]
ADCConv	136	65.2	7202.5	2325.5
ActuatorSysCtrl	96	32.7	507.4	491.3

[1] Model size is too big, memory error of the model checker (core dump)

Fig. 8. Comparison of required model-checking time to generate test data

test-data generation, the model-checker performance is of high sensitivity. Thus, the following interpretation is only valid for the concrete case study (model).

The main result gained from our experiment is that the CBMC model checker is well-suited for these types of problems. It boosts test data calculation by factors 10-20 over using symbolic model checking. Some applications cannot be analyzed using SAL at all.

7.2 Experiments with Automated Complexity Reduction

In this experiment we repeated the complexity reduction of the didactic sample code summarized in Figure 3 with the industrial case study `ActuatorMotorControl`. The results are given in Figure 9 using a logarithmic scale for the X-axis.

Path bound	|PSG|	#Paths ($\sum \|\pi_j\|$)
1	171	171
2	88	117
4	38	84
6	21	83
10	14	92
15	13	106
20	11	130
50	8	242
100	7	336
1000	5	1455

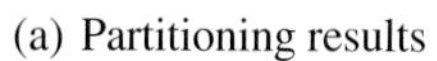

(a) Partitioning results

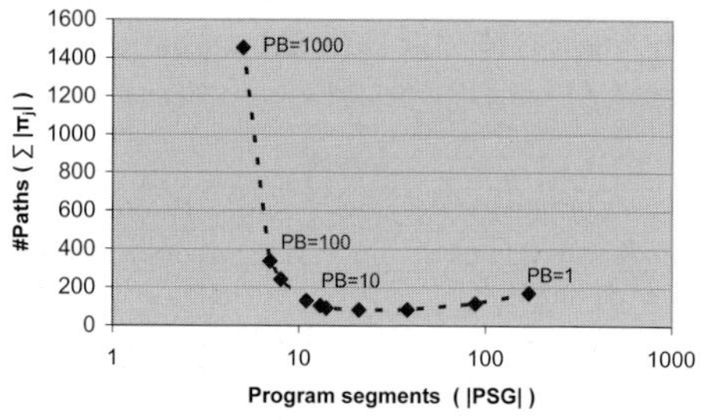

(b) Dependency between $|PSG|$ and $\sum |\Pi_j|$

Fig. 9. Program segmentation results for `ActuatorMotorControl`

Enumerating all $1.9 * 10^{11}$ different execution paths (see Figure 7) of the case study `ActuatorMotorControl` is practically intractable. Thus, partitioning into program segments is necessary. With a path bound $PB = 1$ each basic block of the program resides in a separate segment and with an unlimited path bound the whole program is placed in one segment. The partitioning results in Figure 9 show that there is a certain path bound for which the resulting number of sub-paths $\sum |\Pi_j|$ is minimal. When further increasing the path bound the number of program segments still decreases (which is profitable as it increases the precision of the measurements because the segments get larger). However, at the same time the number of sub-paths strongly increases, which increases the overall computational effort needed for test-data generation and execution-time measurements. Thus, the right path bound to be chosen depends on how much computational resources are available and how much precision is required.

7.3 Experiments with MBTA

Applying the MBTA on the case studies presented in Figure 7 using different values for the *path bound* leads to the results in Figure 10. "*#Paths Random*" gives the number of paths that have been already found by using random generation of test data and "*#Paths MC*" gives the remaining number of paths that had to be generated using model checking. "*Coverage (#Paths)*" represents the number of *feasible paths*. Note that if for a path bound PB=1 it implies that "*#Paths Random*" + "*#Paths MC*" $\neq$ "*Coverage (#Paths)*" it follows that the program contains *unreachable code*. Column "*WCET Bound*" shows the WCET estimate obtained with the MBTA framework.

"*Time (Analysis) [s]*" shows the time spent within the *analysis phase*. "*Time (ETM) [s]*" shows the time spent within the execution-time *measurement phase*, which includes also the compile and load time. "*Overall Time [s]*" is the sum of "*Time (Analysis) [s]*" and "*Time (ETM) [s]*". "*Time Analysis / Path MC [s]*" gives the average time required for using model checking (CBMC) to generate a single test vector for a sub-path. This number is quite significant, because the time required for test-data generation using model checking contributes most of the runtime of the *analysis phase* (except for very low path bounds). It has a rather small variation over different sub-paths of the same model. "*Time (ETM) / Covered Path [s]*" gives the average runtime needed to measure a single sub-path. "*#Paths / Program Segment*" shows the average number of *feasible paths* per program segment.

	Path Bound	#Paths ($\sum \lvert\pi_j\rvert$)	#Program Segments	#Paths Random	#Paths MC	Coverage (#Paths)	WCET Bound	Time (Analysis) [s]	Time (ETM) [s]	Overall Time [s]	Time Analysis / Path MC [s]	Time ETM / Covered Path [s]	#Paths / Program Segment
ActuatorMotorControl	1	171	171	165	6	165	N.A.	468	1289	1757	78.00	7.8	1.0
	10	92	14	63	29	68	3445	841	116	957	29.00	1.7	6.6
	100	336	7	57	279	89	3323	7732	62	7794	27.71	0.7	48.0
	1000	1455	5	82	1373	130	3298	41353	49	41402	30.12	0.4	291.0
ADCConv	1	31	31	31	0	31	872	24	192	216	N.A.	6.2	1.0
	10	17	3	8	9	9	870	31	22	53	3.44	2.4	5.7
	100	74	2	8	66	14	872	220	17	237	3.33	1.2	37.0
	1000	144	1	12	132	12	872	483	11	494	3.66	0.9	144.0
ActuatorSysCtrl	1	54	54	54	0	54	173	26	318	344	N.A.	5.9	1.0
	10	36	14	36	0	36	173	10	85	95	N.A.	2.4	2.6
	100	97	1	18	79	25	131	191	10	201	2.42	0.4	97.0
TestNicePartitioning	1	30	30	6	24	30	151	34	175	209	1.42	5.8	1.0
	5	14	6	4	10	14	151	15	39	54	1.50	2.8	2.3
	10	14	3	3	11	14	151	16	21	37	1.45	1.5	4.7
	20	18	2	2	16	15	150	22	16	38	1.38	1.1	9.0
	100	72	1	1	71	26	129	106	12	118	1.49	0.5	72.0

Fig. 10. Summarized experiments of case studies

The experimental results illustrate the tradeoff between precision and required analysis time. For the case study `TestNicePartitioning` the gained bound contains some pessimism due to the lack of flow facts that characterize path dependencies across program segment boundaries. However, it has been shown that it is possible to include additional flow information in the analysis in order to tighten the bound by increasing the program-segment size. For `ActuatorSysCtrl` the situation is similar. With increasing program-segment size (i.e., by choosing a higher path bound) the existing pessimism can be stepwise eliminated. Such variations do not exist for `ADCConv`. Here all obtained results are almost identical. `ActuatorMotorControl` indicates similar results. Whenever the path bound is increased, the WCET bound is tightened a little bit yielding a WCET bound of 3298 cycles (for a program segmentation having path bound 1000). However, the cost for this increase in precision is an analysis time of about 11.5

hours. The missing WCET bound (N.A.) for path bound PB=1 is caused by a limitation in the current tool implementation and is not a conceptional problem.

8 Conclusion

In this paper we presented the design and implementation results of MBTA, a fully automated WCET analysis process that does not require any user intervention. The input program is partitioned into segments, allowing the user to select a path bound for the size of the segments. Depending on this parameter, the analysis time ranges from a few seconds up to multiple hours. The bigger the chosen program-segment size, the more implicit flow information and hardware effects are incorporated into the timing model. Also, in this case the number of required instrumentations is low.

As a separate model (to be solved by the model checker) is used for each required path, this stage of the test-data generating process can be easily parallelized. The MBTA is easily retargetable to new target hardware due to its operation on a restricted set of ANSI-C code.

The MBTA allows to derive safe WCET estimates even on complex hardware. To achieve this, additional instrumentations are necessary to enforce predictable hardware states. The experimentation with such instrumentations and the analysis of program loops is considered future work.

References

1. Kirner, R., Puschner, P.: Classification of WCET analysis techniques. In: Proc. 8th IEEE International Symposium on Object-oriented Real-time distributed Computing, Seattle, WA, May 2005, pp. 190–199 (2005)
2. Petters, S.M.: Bounding the execution of real-time tasks on modern processors. In: Proc. 7th IEEE International Conference on Real-Time Computing Systems and Applications, Cheju Island, South Korea, pp. 12–14 (2000)
3. Bernat, G., Colin, A., Petters, S.M.: WCET analysis of probabilistic hard real-time systems. In: Proc. 23rd Real-Time Systems Symposium, Austin, Texas, USA, pp. 279–288 (2002)
4. Ernst, R., Ye, W.: Embedded program timing analysis based on path clustering and architecture classification. In: Proc. International Conference on Computer-Aided Design (ICCAD 1997), San Jose, USA (1997)
5. Puschner, P., Nossal, R.: Testing the results of static worst-case execution-time analysis. In: Proceedings of the 19th IEEE Real-Time Systems Symposium (RTSS 1998), pp. 134–143. IEEEP (1998)
6. Wenzel, I.: Measurement-Based Timing Analysis of Superscalar Processors. PhD thesis, Technische Universität Wien, Institut für Technische Informatik, Treitlstr. 3/3/182-1, 1040 Vienna, Austria (2006)
7. Wenzel, I., Kirner, R., Rieder, B., Puschner, P.: Measurement-based worst-case execution time analysis. In: Third IEEE Workshop on Software Technologies for Future Embedded and Ubiquitous Systems (SEUS), pp. 7–10 (2005)
8. Biere, A., Cimatti, A., Clarke, E., Zhu, Y.: Symbolic model checking without BDDs. In: Cleaveland, W.R. (ed.) TACAS 1999. LNCS, vol. 1579, pp. 193–207. Springer, Heidelberg (1999)
9. Moura, L.D., Owre, S., Ruess, H., Rushby, J., Shankar, N., Sorea, M., Tiwari, A.: SAL 2. In: Alur, R., Peled, D.A. (eds.) CAV 2004. LNCS, vol. 3114. Springer, Heidelberg (2004)
10. Clarke, E., Kroening, D., Lerda, F.: A tool for checking ANSI-C programs. In: Jensen, K., Podelski, A. (eds.) TACAS 2004. LNCS, vol. 2988, pp. 168–176. Springer, Heidelberg (2004)
11. Tip, F.: A survey of program slicing techniques. Journal of Programming Languages 3, 121–189 (1995)

ALL-TIMES – A European Project on Integrating Timing Technology*

Jan Gustafsson[1], Björn Lisper[1], Markus Schordan[2], Christian Ferdinand[3], Peter Gliwa[4], Marek Jersak[5], and Guillem Bernat[6]

[1] School of Innovation, Design, and Engineering, Mälardalen University, 721 23 Västerås, Sweden
[2] Vienna University of Technology, Argentinierstrasse 8/4/185.1, A-1040 Vienna, Austria
[3] AbsInt Angewandte Informatik GmbH, Science Park 1, 66123 Saarbruecken Germany
[4] Gliwa GmbH, Dollmannstr. 4, D-81541 München, Germany
[5] Symtavision GmbH, Frankfurter Str. 3 B, 38122 Braunschweig, Germany
[6] Rapita Systems Ltd., IT Centre, York Science Park, York, YO10 5DG, United Kingdom

Abstract. ALL-TIMES is a research project within the EC 7th Framework Programme. The project concerns embedded systems that are subject to safety, availability, reliability, and performance requirements. Increasingly, these requirements relate to correct timing. Consequently, the need for appropriate timing analysis methods and tools is growing rapidly. An increasing number of sophisticated and technically mature timing analysis tools and methods are becoming available commercially and in academia. However, tools and methods have historically been developed in isolation, and the potential users are missing a process-related and continuous tool- and methodology-support. Due to this fragmentation, the timing analysis tool landscape does not yet fully exploit its potential.

The ALL-TIMES project aims at: combining independent research results into a consistent methodology, integrating available timing tools into a single framework, and developing new timing analysis methods and tools where appropriate.

ALL-TIMES will enable interoperability of the various tools from leading commercial vendors and universities alike, and develop integrated tool chains using as well as creating open tool frameworks and interfaces. In order to evaluate the tool integrations, a number of industrial case studies will be performed.

This paper describes the aims of the ALL-TIMES project, the partners, and the planned work.

1 Introduction

ALL-TIMES (Integrating European Timing Analysis Technology) [1] is a research project within the EC 7th Framework Programme, with focus on correct

* This work was supported by the EU FP7 project ALL-TIMES (Integrating European Timing Analysis Technology, grant agreement no. 215068).

T. Margaria and B. Steffen (Eds.): ISoLA 2008, CCIS 17, pp. 445–459, 2008.

timing of real-time embedded systems. The project started in December 2007 and will go on for 2 years and 3 months. The subject of ALL-TIMES has wide industrial relevance and there is a significant body of European research and experience in this area including a number of hi-tech SMEs. Timing measurement/analysis is vital for improving the reliability, performance, and efficiency of embedded systems. It helps to reduce the overall system costs by validating timing requirements, reducing the cost of development, and reducing unit costs in production.

Existing tools (commercial and academic) provide a set of powerful analysis techniques. Nevertheless there is a growing need, addressed in the ALL-TIMES project, for the integration of existing timing measurement/analysis techniques with the latest academic results in this area.

1.1 Concept, and General Objectives

A large class of embedded systems have safety, availability, reliability and performance requirements. This class spans across several areas, including automotive, avionics, telecom, and space systems. Common for these systems is the need to guarantee their correct behaviour as well as the satisfaction of non-functional requirements, in particular regarding timing.

The cost for delivering products with latent errors is staggering. For example, warranty costs in the automotive industry run 2% - 5% of sales [2]. Such levels have tremendous impact on the profitability. Timing is an essential dimension, notably one of the most difficult to analyze, and one that is generally only addressed late in the design cycle. In the automotive industry 50% of warranty costs today can be traced to software and electronics problems [2], for which about one third are reported to be directly related to timing issues. Current trends in industry of increased size and complexity of systems make the timing problem much more difficult, and in the future, consequences could be more dire.

Engineering timing correctness into a system requires treating timing as a first-class citizen throughout the software development process, including early stages: not as a property that is only addressed at the latest stage of this process. Early stage means before all code is available and all system design decisions have been made.

1.2 Timing Analysis

Timing analysis can be divided into *code-level analysis* and *system-level analysis*. *Worst-case execution time* (WCET) *analysis* and *scheduling analysis* are two exemplary techniques for the respective levels. WCET analysis computes an upper bound to the longest execution time that a fragment of code (e.g., a task) takes to execute in the worst case. Scheduling analysis determines the end-to-end execution time of a set of tasks. Code-level analysis thus assumes an isolated view of a fragment of code, whereas system-level analysis takes the complete system (one Embedded Control Unit (ECU), or even several ECUs including their communication interfaces) into consideration.

1.3 The Problem

Industry faces a difficult task to improve the reliability, safety, performance and resource efficiency of systems with regard to timing. The take up by industry of research and development in timing analysis is still low. There are several aspects to this problem; we classify them in the following themes:

– interoperation, scale and automation;
– integration into build process;
– education, and dissemination of knowledge.

Interoperation, Scale and Automation. Current technologies lack strong interoperability with other timing tools and compilers, making the adoption effort much more significant. Standard formats for representation and interoperability with tools are needed. Early efforts in the ARTIST2 [3] and INTEREST [4] projects indicate promising technologies.

Furthermore, some of the current analysis techniques have serious scalability issues relating to the size of the programs to be analyzed. Finally, a major issue is the full automation of the analysis process (the magic one-button solution) that is a pre-requisite for integration of timing analysis tools into current build processes.

Integration into Build Process. Industries that do need timing analysis tend to be conservative by nature. The adoption of a new technology implies change, which demands clear demonstrable benefits in perspective, and may be costly. Thus, new technology may be slow to deploy and integrate into the end-customer process. Especially difficult is the integration of a new technology into a project in progress. Academic prototypes are not usable by large companies that require commercial quality tools with long-term support guarantees. This results in large lead times to get these technologies to market, and consequently in the loss of market opportunity. A second issue is the large number of evolved procedures and constraints, which can make it difficult to exploit a technology simply because required input data cannot be obtained, or because parameters yielding the biggest improvements cannot be changed. This project will address these issues by targeted pilot studies to demonstrate the added value that investing in timing analysis tools brings to customers.

Education, and Dissemination of Knowledge. The timing analysis expertise is fragmented over universities and small companies, and its ability to reach a wider audience is limited. Large companies know that they need timing analysis, and are aware of the risks and consequences of timing errors in their products. However, few have knowledge of the available solutions, and even fewer have the capacity and will to take up the technology.

The current level of engineers, as regards knowledge of timing issues, is not sufficient. A recent example is the failure to establish a timing model in the current AUTOSAR [5] standard. An ALL-TIMES partner (Symtavision) is heavily involved in this activity. On the other hand there have been a good number of success stories on companies adopting these technologies. Unfortunately, the dissemination of these results is slow, partially due to restrictive corporate publishing policies.

The rest of this article is organized as follows: We present the main objectives of the ALL-TIMES project in Section 2 and its expected results in Section 3. In Section 4, we list the ALL-TIMES partners and their respective roles in the project. In Section 5, we describe the work packages. Finally, in Section 6, we draw some conclusions.

2 Main Project Objectives

The two principal project objectives are:

- to integrate different timing measurement/analysis tools using an open tool framework, and
- to achieve 25% improvement in the design time pertaining to timing issues.

One of the overall objectives of the project is the provision of new integrated tool sets for timing measurement and analysis targeted at the embedded real-time systems market. This relates to the advancement of new analysis techniques for integrated scheduling analysis, WCET analysis and timing measurement. In particular, the project will deliver new methods for timing measurement and analysis at both the system level and the code level in an open framework. An important aspect is a precise characterization of industrial requirements regarding timing. The project will provide a detailed requirements study in the first project phase.

A demonstrable 25% improvement in design time of embedded systems development can be achieved by enabling a quick, safe, automatic and efficient mechanism for deriving timing data instead of conventional manual and laborious approaches. The tool integration and analysis development work in ALL-TIMES aims at this. The fulfilment of the objective will be estimated by interviewing engineers participating in case studies on the efforts required to obtain timing estimates, and the quality of the results.

3 Expected Results

The ALL-TIMES project will:

- interface the different analysis techniques (three code-level and two system-level techniques) that are represented in the project;
- provide an open interface to integrate additional timing measurement/analysis techniques and tools, aiming at becoming a de-facto standard;
- provide solutions for timing analysis/estimation in early design phases as part of design-space exploration and architecture optimization.

4 Partners, Their Tools, and Their Roles

Two partners in ALL-TIMES are university groups:

- The WCET group at Mälardalen University - MDH (coordinator) [6]
- The SATIrE group at Vienna University of Technology - TUV [7]

The other four partners are SMEs. They will contribute to the development, evaluation and exploitation of different parts of the project:

- AbsInt Angewandte Informatik GmbH - ABS [8]
- Gliwa GmbH - GLI [9]
- Symtavision GmbH - SYM [10]
- Rapita Systems Ltd - RPT [11]

The partners, and the tools they contribute to the project, are shortly described below. We also briefly indicate the tool integrations that may be considered.

4.1 Mälardalen University

The WCET group at Mälardalen University works with methods and tools for WCET analysis for real-time systems. Specifically, they have developed a tool (SWEET) for analysis of programs written in C. Its modular tool architecture consists of three major phases:

1. A flow analysis phase, where bounds on the number of times instructions can be executed are derived, given the program code and possible input values.
2. A low-level analysis phase, where bounds on time it might take to execute instructions are derived, given the program object code and the architectural features of the target hardware.
3. A WCET estimate calculation phase, where the costliest program execution path is found using information from the first two phases.

The analysis phases communicate their results through well-defined data structures. The current research topic of the Mälardalen group is flow analysis. An annotation language can be used to constrain input data values.

4.2 Vienna University of Technology

The researchers involved in this project in the compilers and languages group at TU Vienna are concerned with the design, implementation, and application of programming languages, program analysis and optimization, and tools for embedded systems. Specifically they have developed the Static Analysis Tool Integration Engine (SATIrE) and integrated components of different program analysis tools. The design philosophy of SATIrE is the integration of analysis tools such that the results can always be used by all other integrated tools, enabling the composition of arbitrary tool chains. A plug-in mechanism for user-defined components enables connections to other external tools. SATIrE offers the following integrated base components:

- EDG C/C++ Front End
- LLNL-ROSE C/C++ intermediate representation
- ROSE C++ Unparser
- Program Analysis Generator (PAG) from AbsInt
- Annotation Parser & Mapper
- Annotation Generator
- Generator & Parser for external representation of AST
- Loop Optimizer (part of LLNL-ROSE, ported from Fortran D)

SATIrE currently allows to address all features of C++ with Exceptions being the only open issue. It supports all features of EC++. For C most features including some dialects are supported. The mapping of analysis information through different intermediate levels is supported by user-defined analysis-information transformers.

Based on SATIrE, the WCET tool TuBound [12] is being developed for computing the worst-case execution time of C programs by static analysis. The TuBound approach combines source-level analysis and code-level analysis in the presence of compiler optimizations.

4.3 AbsInt Angewandte Informatik GmbH

aiT is AbsInt's family of WCET analyzer tools. aiT WCET Analyzers statically compute tight upper bounds for the worst-case execution times (WCET) of tasks in real-time systems. They directly analyze binary executables without any need for instrumentation, and take the intrinsic cache and pipeline behavior into account.

The analyzers employ abstract interpretation to determine estimations for the WCETs of basic blocks. Integer linear programming (ILP) is used to derive a worst-case program path and an overall WCET estimation from the basic block WCET estimations. A graphical user interface supports the visualization of the worst-case path and the interactive inspection of all pipeline and cache states at arbitrary program points.

aiT's results are valid for all inputs and each execution of a task. aiT can be run interactively via a graphical user interface (GUI). The fields in the GUI can be filled with appropriate values, which may be stored in a project file. Alternatively, an existing project file can be loaded. aiT can also be started in simple batch mode with a project file.

4.4 Gliwa GmbH

Gliwa develops debugGURU, which is a framework for measuring and debugging timing related aspects of embedded software. The target code gets instrumented to gather timing information at run-time. This information is either processed "on the fly" by the target or transferred to and interpreted/visualized by a PC. Since debugGURU supports various target interfaces such as CAN, Nexus or KWP2000, measuring is possible not only in a development environment but also "on the road".

There are several plug-ins available that are easy to integrate into a system which supports debugGURU, for example:

timeGURU measures reliable run-time information about tasks, interrupts, processes, and/or any piece of code.
memGURU monitor memory accesses and consumption
delayGURU examines how much time is left in a task or an interrupt for additional functionality, useful for example during the development of embedded systems.

4.5 Symtavision GmbH

SymTA/S, developed by Symtavision, stands for Symbolic Timing Analysis for Systems. SymTA/S focuses exclusively on system timing and performance. Detailed functionality is abstracted, and only those properties that impact timing are modeled. The main advantages of this approach are: efficient modeling; unrivalled analysis speed; applicability in early design phases (when functions have not even been implemented); flexibility and independence of specific hardware and software.

SymTA/S is not a single, monolithic tool but rather a flexible and extensible tool suite. SymTA/S performs scheduling analysis for CPUs with RTOSes, buses with arbitrating protocols, and systems consisting of multiple resources (CPUs and buses). SymTA/S calculates resource loads, worst-case response times for tasks scheduled on CPUs, worst-case transmission times for messages sent via shared buses, end-to-end latencies and compares these values against user-specified constraints, e.g., deadlines. Additionally, SymTA/S has powerful exploration and sensitivity analysis modules for optimization of electronic architectures and scheduling. SymTA/S can be used early on in architecture definition and contracting phases, and continuously throughout the design until timing is verified as part of sign-off.

The core package is the SymTA/S analysis engine. The analysis engine provides all the basic functions to design and analyze the timing in a system, regardless of the internal implementation of the resources. It focuses on the interfaces between resources, where input-output timing and buffering are of central concern.

For the analysis of individual resources, SymTA/S has an interface to component libraries. The analysis engine integrates these local resource performance models into a global, system-level analysis model, and solves it. The analysis engine together with one or more component libraries allows quick modeling, configuration, and analysis of the performance and timing – from a single resource all the way to a distributed system including complex functional and architectural dependencies.

4.6 Rapita Systems Ltd

RapiTime is a software toolkit that provides a unique solution to the problem of worst-case execution time analysis and performance profiling, a solution that works for complex software running on advanced embedded microprocessors.

RapiTime is a comprehensive performance analysis and WCET tool. It supports software written in C and Ada. It is compatible with industrial-scale programs from a few KBytes to millions of lines of code, and works with virtually every 8, 16, and 32-bit embedded microprocessor on the market, including those with advanced hardware features.

RapiTime contains the following main functions:

Performance Profiling. View high and low water marks, examine how different functions contribute to the average, longest, and shortest execution times, and locate performance bottlenecks at the root of throughput problems.

Code Coverage Analysis. Identify code coverage omissions, assess the coverage necessary for WCET analysis, check if the worst-case path has been followed during testing, and more.

Worst-Case Execution Time Analysis. Determine accurate worst case execution times, visualize the contribution of each function to the overall worst-case, examine worst-case execution frequencies, identify code on the worst-case path, and explore the variability in execution times due to hardware effects.

Targeted Optimization. Identify worst-case hotspots, select the best opportunities for optimization via advanced code metrics, see the difference between code that contributes the most on average, and code that contributes the most to the worst-case. Assess the headroom available to add new functionality.

Report Viewer. Eclipse-based, interactive access to data. Configurable views of worst-case, high water mark, and average-case behavior. Code metrics and comparisons. Search and sort facilities to highlight hotspots. Call-tree views of program structure and worst-case path. Graphical analysis of execution time distributions.

4.7 Possible Tool Integrations

Figure 1 indicates the possible integrations between timing analysis tools that may be considered within ALL-TIMES.

5 Work Packages

The project is divided into four work packages. We now briefly describe these.

5.1 Work Package 1: Requirements

The aim of this work package is to identify the particular requirements for ALL-TIMES. These requirements appear on two different levels:

- requirements on timing analysis tools in general, and
- requirements on interfaces between tools.

The first level requires an identification of relevant use cases. These will come from (potential) end-users of timing analysis technology, in particular in the avionics and automotive industry. The SME partners all have customers in these

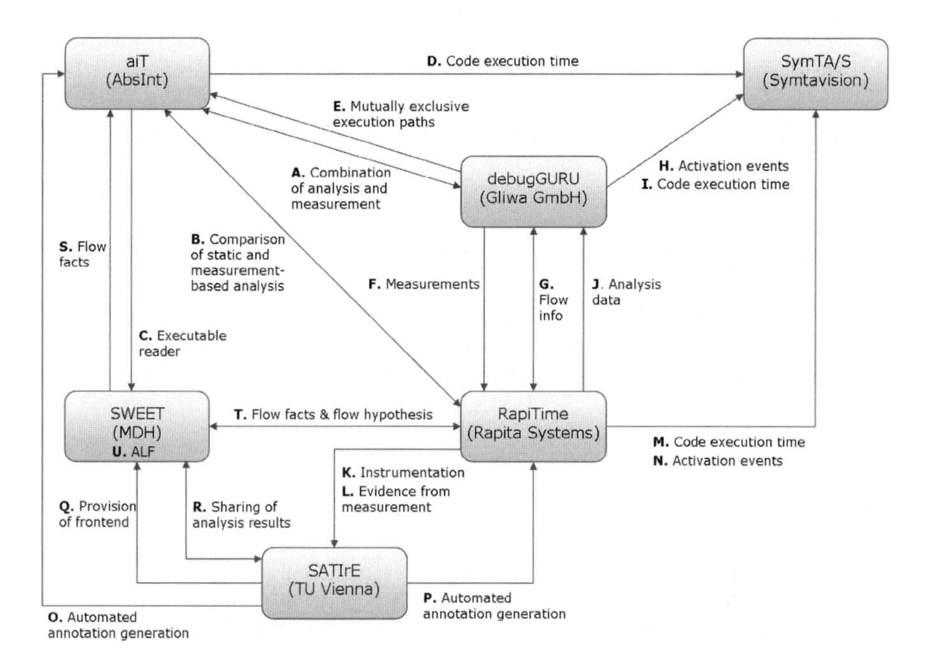

Fig. 1. Possible integrations between timing analysis tools

areas, and representative use cases will be collected from some of these. In this process, it is possible to apply the "Mälardalen model" (see Section 5.4), and involve M.Sc. students in the collection and analysis of use cases.

The second level is of a more technical nature, and requires close interaction between tool experts.

Identification of Use Cases. The project needs to focus on most promising use cases. Project partners already have visions and concepts for use cases during different design stages. These use cases can serve as a starting point for discussion with end users. In this process, those use cases that are both valuable from the end users' perspective, and realistic from the project partners' perspective, will be identified, elaborated, and prepared for implementation.

Along with the use cases, an initial evaluation of timing analysis tools will be conducted. This investigation will elaborate the strengths and weaknesses of the respective tools, for different use cases, leading to a methodology to decide on the right tool for a given development phase.

General Requirements on Timing Analysis Tools. An initial estimate of the most important factors influencing the choice/combination of timing analysis/performance verification tools includes:

– Criticality of timing constraints
– Design stage (early estimation vs. late verification)
– Established design flow and hence availability / type / quality of input data

This needs to be verified and refined based on the identified use cases. The identified use cases need to be refined into technical requirements and design steps. On system level, one crucial aspect is the availability of input data required for scheduling analysis. This data will come from the different tools and techniques present in this project. The combination of test-based, tracing, semi-formal and formal approaches will enable to identify and demonstrate best fits for each of these techniques. Aspects to be considered:

- Accuracy of analysis
- Ease of obtaining the required input data
- Refinement from early, abstract models to later, more detailed models
- Roundtrip engineering / product lines / product evolution
- Architecture alternatives
- Different contexts and corresponding system behavior
- Tool interface requirements

The requirements on the code- and system level tools, in order to communicate with each other, need to be examined. For code level tools, the various tool characteristics result in specific input requirements and possible output. Broad room in this examination will for example be given to the import of measurement data in analysis tools and the communication of the results of source level analysis to analyzers working on binary code, to list but a few. The requirements on the communication of timing estimates from code level to system level will also be examined.

As a starting point, existing tool integration technologies will be reviewed (e.g., the XML timing cookies developed in INTEREST [4] or AIR, the ARTIST2 Intermediate program Representation for WCET analysis tools [3]) to assess these w.r.t. possible adaptation/extension for ALL-TIMES purposes. An appropriate solution will be specified.

5.2 Work Package 2: System-Level Integration

This work package addresses reliable integration of multiple functions sharing a processor in a real-time system. For this, system-level analysis takes the complete system into consideration (whereas code-level analysis in Work Package 3 assumes an isolated view of a piece of code). The key to system-level integration is to assure schedulability of the system under all relevant conditions. The different timing analysis techniques in ALL-TIMES will be combined to determine system schedulability, with the goal to exploit the strengths of the different techniques, to avoid their weak points, and to overcome their limitations. The work package consists of three parts: interface, early-stage methodology and late-stage methodology. Here, early-stage and late-stage refer to design stages of a system that the user of an integrated tool chain is designing.

Development of the system-level tool interface will start in parallel with development of the early-stage system-level analysis methodology. The interface will then be refined and extended together with the development of the late-stage system-level analysis methodology. The rationale for this ordering (early stage before late stage) is the lack of detailed system information at an early stage. Therefore, a relatively simple interface will be sufficient, and the emphasis should be on speed and flexibility of the integrated tool chain. In the second step, the interface will be enriched to allow exchanging a larger variety of detailed system data available in later design stages.

System-level Interface Specification for Timing Analysis Techniques. An open interface to combine different timing analysis techniques (scheduling analysis, WCET analysis, simulation, test, tracing, ...) will be specified. The interface specification will be rich and flexible enough to allow combining timing analysis techniques in different ways depending on a specific design situation, to exchange data between tools at different levels of granularity and detail, and to iterate between different techniques for refinement of analysis results. Specifically, the interface must be suited for both early design stages and late design stages.

Early-Stage System-level Timing Analysis methodology. A methodology for system-level timing analysis will be developed that exploits the strengths of different timing analysis techniques (scheduling analysis, WCET analysis, simulation, test, tracing, ...) during early design stages. The goal is to enable a user of an integrated-tool chain-specific solution.

The methodology will include execution time estimation for software components on alternative processors as well as performance estimation using scheduling analysis and sensitivity analysis. The latter will allow a user to assess how much room there is for estimation errors and how much flexibility remains for later changes.

Late-Stage System-level Timing Analysis Methodology. A methodology for system-level timing analysis will be developed that exploits the strengths of different timing analysis techniques (scheduling analysis, WCET analysis, simulation, test, tracing, ...) during late design stages. The goal is to enable a user of an integrated-tool chain to verify system timing on a level of quality and reliability not achievable by any single technique.

The methodology will combine the various techniques:

- to determine worst-case response times and response jitter, response time distributions and other important performance measures of a system
- to obtain tight analysis bounds by considering correlations between functions and events in different system contexts and scenarios.

5.3 Work Package 3: Code-Level Tool Integration

Code-level analysis assumes an isolated view of a piece of code whereas system-level analysis takes the complete system into consideration. The ALL-TIMES project will consider three different approaches to code-level analysis: Measurement of execution time (GLI), measurement-based (or hybrid) analysis (RPT), and static analysis on binary level (ABS) and source/intermediate level (MDH, TUV). The focus of this work package is to combine these approaches in an optimal manner, to exploit the strengths of the different methods, to avoid their weak points, and to overcome their limitations.

Incorporating Time Measurement Data. The purpose of this work is to improve static analyzers by using the results of time measurements. This will be done in the following directions:

- Comparison of the statically computed longest path with measured data to identify the unwanted inclusion of error cases in the statically computed longest path. Once identified, the error cases can usually be excluded by a manual user annotation.
- Adaptation of the different tools to measurement methods with different number and position of measurements points in a program. For example, AbsInt's aiT can directly handle basic block measurements, but the results of less fine-grained measurement require some extensions. The result of this work will include a common format to specify all kinds of timing measurement results.

Source-level Analyses. The micro-architecture analysis has to consider the very details of a processor implementation and therefore works on the binary program representation. A tool like AbsInt's aiT also tries to determine auxiliary information such as upper bounds of loop iterations on the binary level. Yet better results usually can be expected from source code analyses. One of the goals of the project is to overcome the limitations of considering only one level.

Examples of analyses that can be promising on source level involve the determination of loop bounds and recursion depths, possible values of function pointers, (non-)accessed variables of a function/task, and path exclusions. Measurement-based WCET analyses can usually do without such analyses. Yet an important aspect is quality of the measured data. Analyses like the ones enumerated above can give hints on the reached coverage of measurements. The purpose of this work is to create analyses using an industrial strength front-end for C/C++, to integrate the results of source code analyses as performed by TUV's and MDH's tools into binary-level and measurement-based tools, and to develop a worst-case execution time estimator for programs in C/C++ source code. This estimator will use some parameters to configure a virtual processor so that it resembles real processors.

Code-level Timing Analysis in Early Design Stages. Code-level timing analysis currently requires executable code as well as a detailed model of the target processor for static analysis or actual hardware for measurements. This means that all current code-level techniques can be applied only relatively late in the design, when code and hardware (models) are already far developed. Yet timing problems becoming apparent only in late design stages may require a costly re-iteration through earlier stages. Thus, we are striving for the possibility to perform code-level timing analysis already in early design stages.

Choosing a suitable processor configuration (core, memory, peripherals, ...) for an automotive project at the beginning of the development is a challenge. In the high-volume market, choosing a too powerful configuration can lead to a serious waste of money. Choosing a configuration not powerful enough leads to severe changes late in the development cycle and might delay the delivery.

Currently, to a great extent this risky decision is taken based on gut feeling and previous experience. Our goal is to provide a family of tools to assist in the exploration of alternative system configurations before committing to a specific solution. Our approach requires that (representative) source code of (representative) parts of the application is available. This code can come from previous releases of a product or can be generated from a model within a rapid prototyping development environment.

To achieve the task, we will extend AbsInt's family of aiT WCET analyzers. aiT WCET analyzers statically compute tight upper bounds of worst-case execution times (WCET) of tasks in real-time systems, taking into account the cache and pipeline behaviour. They operate on binary executables and may take additional information in the form of user annotations. Through annotations the user provides information the tool needs to successfully carry out the analysis (e.g., loop bounds and recursion bounds that cannot be determined automatically, targets of computed calls or branches, etc.) or to improve precision.

aiT supports various cores and support is extended constantly. To be applicable in early design phases, the tool will be extended to make the cache and memory mapping completely parameterizable so that the user can experiment with different configurations. Furthermore, since performance guarantees at that stage are not as important as later in the development process, some precision will be traded against ease of use, speed and reduced resource needs. For example, source-code analysis will be integrated to enable certain information like unknown loop bounds to be determined from the source code, instead of asking the user for annotations.

Our early-phase code-level analysis will be integrated into the SymTA/S system-level architecture exploration analysis. The combination of code-level and system-level architecture exploration will lead to informed decisions with respect to which architectures are appropriate for an application.

5.4 Work Package 4: Validation and Dissemination

System- and Code-level Validation. The main purpose of the validation work is to compare and evaluate the different approaches to timing analysis subproblems and to develop a methodology for selecting the optimal method and tool for the work at hand. One important way to validate the methods developed within ALL-TIMES is to perform case studies together with industrial partners on selected problems. In this way, the ALL-TIMES methods and tools will be tested on industrial-strength systems, valuable feed-back from early users will be conveyed back to the developers, and end-user awareness will be raised early to solutions in the area of timing analysis.

The "Mälardalen Model". The main performers of the case studies will be students on MSc level, supervised by experts at the company and from the ALL-TIMES project.

During a number of years, Mälardalen University has been performing case studies to evaluate timing tools in industrial settings. The purposes of the case studies have been, amongst other things, to evaluate the tools and methods on "real" code to get feedback for research and development. Results and evaluations made in the reports have resulted in research reports [13] and spawned new research and development activities. An additional advantage of the model is that it brings timing analysis into education; the M.Sc. students themselves become proficient with the latest timing analysis technology. It also helps disseminating the technology: both directly, to companies participating in the case studies, and indirectly by the students bringing their competence into their respective workplaces after graduation.

The time spent by the MSc student is typically used in the following way:

- introduction to timing analysis (university) – one week
- study of state of the art (MSc student) – a few weeks
- education in the used tool(s) (tool vendor) – one week
- introduction to the company and its code (company) – one week
- applying timing analysis to the code (MSc student) – 2–3 months
- writing report and presenting results to the other partners (MSc student) – one month

The ALL-TIMES project partners have an extensive network of industrial partners that will be enrolled during the case studies.

Dissemination. Dissemination and exploitation of the results from ALL-TIMES is aiming at spreading awareness of timing analysis and knowledge of the solutions (tools and methods) proposed by ALL-TIMES. The targets of dissemination are professionals working in the area of embedded and real-time computer systems, the research community (including PhD students), undergraduate students at universities, and the interested public.

6 Conclusions

The ALL-TIMES project is an ambitious effort to enable interoperability of timing tools from leading commercial vendors and universities in the EC. The project will develop tool chains using open tool frameworks and interfaces. These integrated tool chains will be evaluated using case studies performed towards industrial end-user companies. The main goal will be a demonstrable improvement in the design time of embedded systems development.

References

1. ALL-TIMES: Homepage (2008), http://www.all-times.org
2. IBM: News Web page (April 2005), http://www.ibm.com/news/be/en/2005/05/3102.html
3. ARTIST2: Timing-Analysis Cluster homepage (2008), http://www.artist-embedded.org/artist
4. INTEREST: INTEREST (2008), http://www.interest-strep.eu/
5. AUTOSAR: Homepage (2008), http://www.autosar.org/

6. Mälardalen University: WCET project homepage (2008), http://www.mrtc.mdh.se/projects/wcet
7. SATIrE: SATIrE homepage (2008), http://www.complang.tuwien.ac.at/markus/satire
8. AbsInt: aiT tool homepage (2008), http://www.absint.com/ait
9. Gliwa: homepage (2008), http://www.gliwa.com/e/home.html
10. Symtavision: homepage (2008), http://www.symtavision.com/
11. Rapita: RapiTime WCET tool homepage (2006), http://www.rapitasystems.com
12. Prantl, A., Schordan, M., Knoop, J.: TuBound - a conceptually new tool for worst-case execution time analysis. In: Proceedings of the 8th International Workshop on Worst-Case Execution Time Analysis (July 2008)
13. Gustafsson, J., Ermedahl, A.: Experiences from applying WCET analysis in industrial settings. In: Proc. 10th IEEE International Symposium on Object/Component/Service-oriented Real-time Distributed Computing (ISORC 2007), Santorini Island, Greece (May 2007)

Weaving a Formal Methods Education with Problem-Based Learning

J Paul Gibson

Le Département Logiciels-Réseaux, IT-SudParis,
9 rue Charles Fourier, 91011 Évry cedex, France
paul.gibson@it-sudparis.eu
http://www-public.it-sudparis.eu/~gibson/

Abstract. The idea of weaving formal methods through computing (or software engineering) degrees is not a new one. However, there has been little success in developing and implementing such a curriculum. Formal methods continue to be taught as stand-alone modules and students, in general, fail to see how fundamental these methods are to the engineering of software. A major problem is one of motivation — how can the students be expected to enthusiastically embrace a challenging subject when the learning benefits, beyond passing an exam and achieving curriculum credits, are not clear? Problem-based learning has gradually moved from being an innovative pedagogique technique, commonly used to better-motivate students, to being widely adopted in the teaching of many different disciplines, including computer science and software engineering. Our experience shows that a good problem can be re-used throughout a student's academic life. In fact, the best computing problems can be used with children (young and old), undergraduates and postgraduates. In this paper we present a process for weaving formal methods through a University curriculum that is founded on the application of problem-based learning and a library of good software engineering problems, where students learn about formal methods without sitting a traditional formal methods module. The process of constructing good problems and integrating them into the curriculum is shown to be analagous to the process of engineering software. This approach is not intended to replace more traditional formal methods modules: it will better prepare students for such specialised modules and ensure that all students have an understanding and appreciation for formal methods even if they do not go on to specialise in them.

Keywords: Teaching Formal Methods, Computing Curriculum, Mathematics of Computer Science, Science of Software Engineering.

1 Introduction

In this paper we consider the problem of teaching formal methods at 3rd level institutions (universities, colleges, institutes of technology, etc.). We support the view that the best way to teach formal methods is not to teach the subject as

T. Margaria and B. Steffen (Eds.): ISoLA 2008, CCIS 17, pp. 460–472, 2008.

a stand-alone module or set of modules, but to try to integrate (weave) the formality throughout the whole curriculum. We propose a problem-based learning approach[1] (PBL)as the best way in which to weave the formal methods.

In the remainder of this introduction we review the notion of weaving formal methods, summarise the learning theory that lies behind problem-based learning (PBL), review PBL and introduce the core issue of finding good formal methods problems.

After the introduction, section 2 proposes some formal methods learning objectives, section 3 proposes a process — much like the software engineering process — by which formal methods can be woven through a curriculum, section 4 reviews some of the problems that we have found to be successful, and section 5 concludes with some brief observations.

We note that we try — where possible — to bring our own research back into all our teaching (undergraduate and postgraduate). Thus, much of our source material originates from our own research publications, which we cite. Of course, when teaching our students we ensure that they are also made aware of the work on which our own research is based. In the space of this paper we are unable to reference all this secondary material, although we do reference the research that is specific to teaching formal methods, where appropriate.

1.1 Weaving a Formal Methods Thread through a Curriculum: The Integration Problem

In 2000, Jeanette Wing wrote about weaving formal methods[2]:

> "Rather than treat formal methods solely as a separate subject to study, we should weave their use into the existing infrastructure of an undergraduate computer science curriculum. In so doing, we would be teaching formal methods alongside other mathematical, scientific, and engineering methods already taught. Formal methods would simply be additional weapons in a computer scientist's arsenal of ways to think when attacking and solving problems.
> My ideal is to get to the point where computer scientists use formal methods without even thinking about it. Just as we use simple mathematics in our daily life, computer scientists would use formal methods routinely."

She then goes on to identify the common core elements that need to be taught: state machines, invariants, abstract mappings, composition, specification, induction and verification. She states that tools are critical: model checkers, specification checkers and theorem provers. Specific courses where formal methods can be taught are identified as: introduction to programming, data structures and algorithms, programming principles, programming languages, compilers, software engineering, computer architecture, operating systems, networking, databases, and user interfaces. She concludes her paper by stating:

> "The biggest obstacle is getting "buy-in" from our colleagues: convincing co-instructors, curricula committees, and administrators that integrating

> formal methods unintru- sively is a good thing to do ... The nitty-gritty hard future work is in thinking of the examples to use in lectures, in designing appropriate homework and exam problems, and in making learning these concepts and tools enjoyable."

Eight years have passed since this paper was published and not much has changed. Formal methods continue to be taught in a stand-alone fashion and little progress has been made in fully integrating them into the computer science and software engineering (CS&SE) curricula.

More recently, Kiniry and Zimmerman discuss the use of "secret ninja" techniques[3] "to integrate applied formal methods into software engineering courses." They demonstrate that formal methods can be taught through "stealth" (without calling them formal methods) in a number of different courses; but note that this success would not have been possible without good tool suppport. Their work is founded mostly on applying the design-by-contract paradigm. This demonstrates that formal methods can and should be used in the teaching of software design; and this view is supported by other research[4].

We believe that there are many other practitioners of teaching formal methods by stealth throughout the world. The problem is that each has their own technique for better integrating formal methods into the specific part of the curriculum in which they teach. There is no consistent approach to this integration. In this paper we propose that good problems can be used to weave (integrate) formal methods in a consistent manner. However, before we look at PBL we review the learning theory upon which our claims are based.

1.2 Learning Theory

There are numerous complementary, and competing, theories of learning. The review by Hilgard and Bower published over half a century ago[5] is a good introduction to the foundations of learning theory. In this paper, we review the work of the researchers that have had most influence on our own research into teaching formal methods: Piaget, Bruner, Guildford, Gardner, Papert, Schoenfeld and Bloom.

Cognitive structure is the concept central to Piaget's theory. (See the work by Brainerd[6] for a good overview and analysis of Piaget's seminal contribution.) These structures are used to identify patterns underlying certain acts of intelligence, and Paiget proposes that these correspond to stages of child development. Piaget's most interesting experiments focused on the development of mathematical and logical concepts. However, his work predates the development of software engineering as a discipline.

Piaget's theory is similar to other *constructivist* perspectives of learning (e.g., Bruner [7]), which model learning as an active process where learners construct new concepts upon their current knowledge and previous experience. As a result of following this theory, teachers encourage students to discover principles by themselves: this is the foundation upon which problem-based learning is built.

Similarites can be seen between the constructivist view and the *theories of intelligence* such as proposed by Guildford's *structure of intellect* (SI) theory [8] and Gardner's *multiple intelligences*[9]. Typically, these theories structure the learning space in terms of practical problem solving skills.

Piaget's ideas also influenced the seminal work by Seymour Papert in the specific domain of computers and education[10]. Papert argues that children can understand concepts best when they are able to explain them algorithmicaly through writing computer programs.

We were also influenced by the domain of teaching mathematics. In particular, Alan Schoenfeld argues that understanding and teaching mathematics should be treated as problem-solving [11]. He identifies four skills that are needed to be successful in mathematics: proposition and procedural knowledge, strategies and techniques for problem resolution, decisions about when and what knoweldge and strategies to use, and a logical *world view* that motivates an individual's approach to solving a particular problem.

To conclude our review we mention Blooms taxonomy[12] of educational objectives which is a fundamental model of learning, providing a well-accepted foundation for research and development into the preparation of learning evaluation materials. It structures understanding into 6 distinct levels: Knowledge, Comprehension, Application, Analysis, Synthesis and Evaluation.

1.3 Problem Based Learning

While there is no universal definition of PBL we present definitions from the last three decades. PBL was defined by Barrows and Tamblyn[13] as "the learning which results from the process of working towards the understanding of, or resolution of, a problem. The problem is encountered first in the learning process". Woods defined it[1] as "an approach to learning that uses a problem to drive the learning rather than a lecture with subject matter which is taught." Torp and Sage define it[14] as "Focused, experiential learning (minds-on, hands-on) organised around the investigation and resolution of messy, real-world problems."

Thus, the guiding principle behind PBL is that the problem is the driving force behind the learning. Within the PBL environment the problem acts as the catalyst that initiates the learning process. It is said that this way of learning encourages a deeper understanding of the material, rather than surface learning, because it is the students who are actively *doing*. As the problem is such a critical component of the learning process it is imperative that one uses *good* problems. In 2001, Duch identified five characteristics of what makes a PBL problem *good*[15]:

1. Effective problems should engage the students' interest and motivate them to probe for deeper understanding.
2. PBL problems should be designed with multiple stages.
3. The problems should be complex enough that cooperation within a group will be necessary in order for them to effectively work towards a solution.
4. The problem should be open-ended.
5. The content objectives of the course should be incorporated into the problems.

One of the major obstacles to the implementation of PBL, within any discipline, is the lack of a good set of problems. However, good PBL problems usually do not appear in textbooks[16]. Clearing houses provide an avenue to allow for the sharing of problems, but unfortunately there is a lack of CS&SE problems[1].

1.4 Good Formal Methods Problems

It is known that the students initial reactions to a subject or topic is critical to them gaining an interest. The choice of problem is therefore critical. A good formal methods problem is one in which students will have the computer science knowledge necessary to solve the problem but need software engineering knowledge to learn how to apply the science, or students will identify (through software engineering knowledge) a possible solution to the problem whose suitability depends on some core computer science that they do not currently have. The problem should lead both types of student to appreciate the need for formality and rigour. Consequently, they build their own formal methods bridges that link the science with the engineering (but just happen to start the construction on opposite sides of the academic divide).

The high-level objective of helping bridge the gap between the science and engineering is laudable; however, it is much too abstract. We must refine this high-level objective into more concrete objectives against which our problems can be verified.

2 Formal Methods: Learning Objectives

Through our formal methods problems we can verify our high level objective of helping students to bridge the gap between computer science and software engineering by checking that the students who work on the problems are then:

- able to build better software,
- better at reasoning about problems that are to be solved using a computer,
- motivated and able to work with abstract models and conceptual tools,
- able to classify, and motivated to use, software development tools,
- knowledgable about the scientific foundations upon which the tools are built, and
- comfortable working with mathematics such as logic and set theory.

2.1 Improve Software (Development)

Software engineering is all about going from *what* to *how*, moving from abstract problems to concrete solutions. This involves design steps: decisions that are made in order to move a model away from an open (usually non-deterministic)

[1] There is an abundance of CS programming problems available; however, the vast majority of these problems place emphasis on the learning of a particular programming concept rather than problem solving.

description of requirements to a closed (usually deterministic) description of the implementation. Software engineering cannot, in practice, be done prescriptively (otherwise we would automatically generate solutions from problems); and it cannot be done in a purely ad-hoc fashion (otherwise we would not need software processes to manage the complexity of the systems and behaviour being modelled). Software engineering is a unique mix of science, engineering and art: the best practitioners know that each new problem requires a different balance between the potential chaos of innovation and the constraints imposed by order and structure.

Thus, engineering is not about finding the correct solution to a problem; it is about understanding the engineering compromises involved in choosing a solution from a large number of possibilities. In such a situation can we judge how well a software engineer is working by judging the quality of a single project on which they have worked? In practice, it is very difficult, if not impossible, to fairly evaluate whether the objective of improving the students' software development skills is being met by our PBL approach to teaching formal methods. O'Kelly and Gibson have discussed the issues that arise when trying to validate PBL in the context of teaching programming[17], and many of the issues that they identify are relevant when analysing whether the formal methods problems are teaching the students how to be better software engineers (i.e. engineer better software).

Anecdotal evidence suggests that the better students adopt formal engineering practices (like the specification of invariants) in projects on other courses which follow their work on the formal methods problems (without being told to do so). Furthermore, the software that these students produce is better than that produced by the other students. However, that should be no surprise as these are the better students!

2.2 Thinking about (Computational/Algorithmic) Thinking

In 2006 Wing discusses the importance of computational thinking in education[18]:

> "Computational thinking involves solving problems, designing systems, and understanding human behavior, by drawing on the concepts fundamental to computer science. Computational thinking includes a range of mental tools that reflect the breadth of the field of computer science."

She then goes on to discuss the characteristics of such thinking:

1. Conceptualizing, not programming;
2. Fundamental, not rote skill;
3. A way that humans, not computers, think;
4. Complements and combines mathematical and engineering thinking;
5. Ideas, not artifacts;
6. For everyone, everywhere.

Such computational thinking starts from a very early age[19] and should be exploited in the teaching of computer science (and formal methods) in schools[20].

Our experience shows that looking at simple formal methods problems with school children improves their ability to think computationally. Thus, we believe that this should also be true for university students.

2.3 Make Friends with Abstraction and Modelling: Conceptual Tools

One of the biggest problems in teaching software engineering is that students find it very difficult to work with models at different levels of abstraction. Through the formal methods problems, the students naturally discover that abstraction is a critical skill when searching the space of possible solutions. They then proceed to discover refinement — where they gradually add details to their abstract models in order to move them closer to a concrete solution. Students learn that nondeterminism is a very powerful mechanism. We first noticed this when we analysed how best to teach formal specification as part of requirements engineering[21].

2.4 Make Friends with Software for Software Engineering: Development Tools

The need for students to be able to use general software development tools is widely accepted by industry; but the importance of them being able to use formal methods tools is not. One used to be able to argue that formal methods were not used in industry because they were not mature enough — and therefore it would be difficult to motivate students to learn how to use them[22] — but this is no longer the case.

2.5 Understand the Scientific Foundations

In 2003, Curran discussed the balancing required between Computer Science (CS) and Software Education (SE) education[23]:

> "It is no longer clear whether SE topics reflect current industry needs or whether they are intended to lead and update industry practices. But regardless of who leads whom, without some sort of rapid, two-way communication, we run the risk of producing graduates who are out of touch, require much re-training, and have trouble competing. Industry might indicate that they need specific skills and knowledge from their CS employees, and that the special skills required of software engineers would be performed by software engineers, not by CS majors."

He concluded by stating:

> "...individual departmental goals for a degree in CS and the role of SE in the curriculum should be clearly understood so that a balance can be struck between academic topics and skills training."

We believe that PBL offers a natural solution to achieving this required balance and in using formal methods to bridge the gap between CS and SE.

More recently, Parnas and Soltys address the need for a "Basic Science for Software Developers"[24], stating:

> "The fundamental properties of computers are very important because they affect what we can and cannot do. Sometimes, an understanding of these properties is necessary to find the best solution to a problem. In most cases, those who understand computing fundamentals can anticipate problems and adjust their goals so that they can get the real job done. Those who do not understand these limitations, may waste their time attempting something impossible or, even worse, produce a product with poorly understood or not clearly stated capabilities. Further, those that understand the fundamental limitations are better equipped to clearly state the capabilities and limitations of a product that they produce. Finally, an understanding of these limitations, and the way that they are proved, often reveals practical solutions to practical problems. Consequently, "basic science" should be a required component of any accredited Software Engineering program."

They then suggest the curriculum for a theoretical computer science that would cover the required science of software engineering. The main topics proposed are:

1. Finite Automata (finite number of states, and no memory),
2. Regular Expressions,
3. Context-Free Grammars,
4. Pushdown Automata (like finite automata, except they have a stack, with no limit on how much can be stored in the stack),
5. Turing Machines (simplified model of a general computer, but equivalent to general computers)
6. Rudimentary Complexity.

We do not directly address the teaching of any of these theoretical computer science foundational topics in our problem based learning. Most of our problems can be (and are) extended to introduce the concepts of complexity, computability, correctness and common-sense — which we see as the fundamental computer science *boundaries* that all software engineers should know about.

2.6 Be Comfortable with Mathematics

Habrias has written about the problems of teaching formal methods when the students do not have a good understanding of foundational mathematics such as logic and set theory[25]. Much of the literature on teaching formal methods directly addresses the need for firm mathematical foundations. We believe that the problem-based learning approach helps students with the mathematics because they learn the mathematical concepts in the context of their practical application.

3 A Software Engineering Approach to Constructing a Formal Methods Curriculum

Parnas makes a strong case that "Software Engineering Programmes are not Computer Science Programmes"[26]. He discusses the differences between traditional computer science programmes and most engineering programmes and argues that we need software engineering programmes that follow the traditional engineering approach to professional education.

He summarises the issue as follows:

> "Just as the scientific basis of electrical engineering is primarily physics, the scientific basis of software engineering is primarily computer science. Attempts to distinguish two separate bodies of knowledge will lead to confusion. ... Recognising that the two programmes would share much of their core material will help us to understand the real differences."

Future scientists will add to our "knowledge base" while future engineers will design trustworthy products. His position is that: "engineers learn science plus the methods needed to apply science".

However, we must now ask where formal methods fit into this pedagogic structure and whether our approach to teaching formal methods should change depending on our target audience: computer scientists or software engineers.

In our approach we see formal methods as the main bridge between computer science and software engineering. Without formal methods software engineering is not a true engineering discipline; and without formal methods computer science remains a mainly theoretical subject. Thus, teaching formal methods should not be seen as a problem to be solved; but it should be viewed as the answer to the fundamental question of how we can better educate computer scientists *and* software engineers.

Our problem based learning approach helps us to better adapt our teaching to our target audience. Our experience suggests that good problems are not good for only one type of students (engineering or science, or even arts and humanities). The best problems can be introduced to any of these students and through interacting with the problem (and with the guidance of the lecturer) the problem will dynamically evolve in order for particular learning objectives to be met. In general, engineering students will learn by trying to build solutions to the problems whilst science students will learn through trying to analyse them. Of course, the lecturer will be responsible for making sure that the students learn that these are complementary approaches and for finding the right balance for the particular type of student that is being taught.

We propose that each problem should be set up to meet a specific curriculum objective. Each problem would then have a life-cycle similar to that seen for software and services, with key stages being specification, design, implementation, testing and maintenance. Once a problem is meeting a specific objective then it can be refined to incorporate other objectives. These objectives may be the responsibility of a single lecturer as part of a single module; but good problems will evolve to survive across different modules. In our experience this is most likely to happen when a single lecturer is responsible for multiple modules (where problems can be shared). However, in order to better weave our formal methods objectives through the curriculum we have to be able to also work with colleagues who do not teach formal methods but do teach other CS&SE modules.

We propose four complementary approaches to this weaving process. Firstly, look at the problems that are being used in other modules and incorporate them into a dedicated formal methods module. Secondly, offer to extend such problems (to meet the formal methods objectives) as part of the original modules in which the problems were taught. Thirdly, offer to extend your existing formal methods problems so that they incorporate learning objectives of colleagues teaching other modules. Fourthly, invite colleagues to participate in the PBL teaching in your own formal methods module(s).

We note that this integration should probably be done in an incremental fashion as we may end up replicating the feature interaction problem[27] at the level of the requirements (learning objectives). To extend our analogy of a problem as being a service, with additional learning objectives as features, we can consider the curriculum to be a system of collaborating services. As our curriculum evolves we maintain the system by updating our problem set: adding new problems, removing unsuccessful problems and evolving successful problems. As with large, complex, software systems the best way to manage this process is to have a clearly documented set of requirements and procedures in place to map these requirements through to the final implemented system (via the design).

We propose that the underlying architecture of the curriculum should be service-oriented in the sense that the main structure should support the evolution of the underlying objectives and the problems that are used to meet these objectives. In the next section we briefly review some of the problems that we have used to meet particular learning objectives. All these problems have been successfully shared across different modules (and different years) in the curriculum.

4 Weaving Formal Methods with Problem Based Learning

In each of the following subsections we briefly review a problem that we have used to teach formal methods within other parts of the CS&SE curriculum. In all cases, these problems have been used at different institutions and in different countries (Ireland, France and USA). Furthermore, they have all been used to teach students at different stages of their academic lives (school, undergraduate and postgraduate).

4.1 Example 1: Stacks and Queues

Stacks and queues are normally taught as part of an algorithms and data structures module. We have found them very useful as a design problem and have used them to teach formal design techniques[4]. We have also used them in teaching about testing, fault tolerance and dependable distributed systems.

4.2 Example 2: E-Voting

The e-voting case study has already been used in the teaching of formal methods [28] where they describe how they have developed a single teaching tutorial, making use of an electronic voting system (EVS), to complement an existing model checking course.

In our work we have used our published research on using formal methods in the verification of safety critical properties[29,30,31,32] as the starting point for problems presented to CS&SE undergraduates (from 1st year to 4th year), and to postgraduates specialising in software engineering. The problem has been re-used in teaching the following modules: introduction to programming, object oriented programming, data structures and algorithms, HCI, testing, requirements and design, rigorous software process, software process improvement.

4.3 Example 3: Sorting and Searching

Sorting and searching are such fundamental computations that it is difficult to imagine a CS&SE module in which they cannot be used as the foundation for a good problem. We have used sorting and searching problems to teach about refinement and correctness-by-construction[22,20] to school children and post-graduates. We also use them to teach about complexity and parallel programming. Finally, we use them in our teaching of models of computation where we consider non-standard computers such as optical computers.

4.4 Example 4: Games, Puzzles and Intelligence

Some of the games that we have used in our PBL teaching include TicTacToe[33], Connect4, and the 15-puzzle. TicTacToe is particularly good when trying to formalise the rules of the game and prove that a particular artificial player respects the rules. We also use it as a simple example of how easy it is for a model checker to automatically examine all possible states of the game. The 15-puzzle is very good when reasoning formally about optimizations as refinements. All these examples have been used in a software process course and all have been used in a module on object oriented design.

4.5 Example 5: Feature Interactions in Telephones

Everyone (who you could possibly wish to teach formal methods to) has an understanding of what you can do with a telephone; even if very few know how it works. It provides an excellent example of modelling and abstraction that can be used with all students. Even students who have never studied computer science usually end up drawing a state machine in order to explain their understanding. For CS&SE students this is a good point at which to introduce features and feature interactions[34]. With respect to formal methods, we use this problem to illustrate the limitations of model checking and the use of theorem provers. We also use it to let students discover the need for models for reasoning about temporal properties such as fairness. This problem has also been used in the teaching of object oriented programming and in the teaching of HCI.

5 Conclusions

We have had some success in weaving formal methods into our CS&SE curriculum by evolving problems that can be shared between modules and that meet multiple learning objectives. There is still much work to be done in adopting a problem-oriented approach to curriculum development. The hardest task is to convice certain colleagues that this approach works: many of them ask for strong evidence that is currently impossible to provide.

We believe that the future of software engineering as a discipline is dependent on students being exposed to formal methods throughout their academic lives. We propose that PBL is a good teaching approach for achieving this aim.

References

1. Woods, D.R.: Problem-based Learning: how to gain the most from PBL. Waterdown, Ontario (1996)
2. Wing, J.M.: Invited talk: Weaving formal methods into the undergraduate computer science curriculum. In: Rus, T. (ed.) AMAST 2000. LNCS, vol. 1816, pp. 2–9. Springer, Heidelberg (2000)
3. Kiniry, J.R., Zimmerman, D.M.: Secret ninja formal methods. In: Cuellar, J., Maibaum, T.S.E., Sere, K. (eds.) FM 2008. LNCS, vol. 5014, pp. 214–228. Springer, Heidelberg (2008)
4. Gibson, J.P., Lallet, E., Raffy, J.L.: How do I know if my design is correct? In: Formal Methods in Computer Science Education (FORMED), pp. 59–69 (March 2008)
5. Hilgard, E.R., Bower, G.H.: Theories of Learning. Prentice Hall, Englewood Cliffs (1956)
6. Brainerd, C.: Piaget's Theory of Intelligence. Prentice Hall, Englewood Cliffs (1978)
7. Bruner, J.S.: Toward a theory of instruction. Belknap Press of Harvard University, Cambridge (1966)
8. Guilford, J.P.: The Nature of Human Intelligence. McGraw-Hill, New York (1967)
9. Gardner, H.: Frames of mind: the theory of multiple intelligence. Basic Books, New York (1983)
10. Papert, S., Sculley, J.: Mindstorms: children, computers, and powerful ideas. Basic Books, New York (1980)
11. Schoenfeld, A.H.: Mathematical Problem Solving. Academic Press, Orlando (1985)
12. Bloom, B.S., Engelhart, M.D., Furst, E.J., Hill, W.H., Krathwohl, D.R.: Taxonomy of educational objectives Handbook 1: cognitive domain. Longman Group Ltd., London (1956)
13. Barrows, H., Tamblyn, R.: Problem-Based Learning: An Approach to Medical Education. Springer Publishing Company, New York (1980)
14. Torp, L., Sage, S.: Problems as Possibilities: Problem-Based Learning for K16 Education. Association for Supervision and Curriculum Development (ASCD), Alexandria (2002)

15. Duch, B.: Writing Problems for Deeper Understanding, pp. 47–53. Stylus Publishing, Sterling (2001)
16. Tien, C., Chu, S., Lin, Y.: Four phases to construct problem-based learning instruction materials. In: PBL In Context Bridging work and Education, pp. 117–133. Tampere University Press (2005)
17. O'Kelly, J., Gibson, J.P.: PBL: Year one analysis — interpretation and validation. In: PBL In Context — Bridging Work and Education (2005)
18. Wing, J.M.: Computational thinking. Commun. ACM 49(3), 33–35 (2006)
19. Gibson, J.P., O'Kelly, J.: Software engineering as a model of understanding for learning and problem solving. In: ICER 2005: Proceedings of the 2005 international workshop on Computing education research, pp. 87–97. ACM, New York (2005)
20. Gibson, J.P.: Formal methods - never too young to start. In: Formal Methods in Computer Science Education (FORMED), pp. 149–159 (March 2008)
21. Gibson, J.P.: Formal requirements engineering: Learning from the students. In: Australian Software Engineering Conference, pp. 171–180. IEEE Computer Society, Los Alamitos (2000)
22. Gibson, J.P., Méry, D.: Teaching formal methods: Lessons to learn. In: Flynn, S., Butterfield, A. (eds.) IWFM. Workshops in Computing, BCS (1998)
23. Curran, W.S.: Teaching software engineering in the computer science curriculum. SIGCSE Bull. 35(4), 72–75 (2003)
24. Parnas, D.L., Soltys, M.: Basic science for software developers. In: Workshop on Formal Methods in the Teaching Lab (FM-Ed 2006), pp. 9–14 (August 2006)
25. Habrias, H.: Teaching specifications, hands on. In: Formal Methods in Computer Science Education (FORMED), pp. 5–15 (March 2008)
26. Parnas, D.L.: Software engineering programmes are not computer science programmes. Ann. Software Eng. 6, 19–37 (1998)
27. Gibson, J.P.: Feature requirements models: Understanding interactions. In: Dini, P., Boutaba, R., Logrippo, L. (eds.) Feature Interactions in Telecommunications Networks IV (FIW 1997), pp. 46–60. IOS Press, Amsterdam (1997)
28. Miller, A., Cutts, Q.: The use of an electronic voting system in a formal methods course. In: Workshop on Formal Methods in the Teaching Lab (FM-Ed 2006), pp. 3–8 (August 2006)
29. Gibson, J.P., McGaley, M.: Verification and maintenance of e-voting systems and standards. In: 8th European Conference on e-Government, pp. 283–290 (July 2008)
30. Cansell, D., Gibson, J.P., Méry, D.: Refinement: A constructive approach to formal software design for a secure e-voting interface. Electr. Notes Theor. Comput. Sci. 183, 39–55 (2007)
31. Cansell, D., Gibson, J.P., Méry, D.: Formal verification of tamper-evident storage for e-voting. In: Software Engineering and Formal Methods (SEFM 2007), pp. 329–338. IEEE Computer Society, Los Alamitos (2007)
32. Gibson, J.P.: E-voting and the need for rigorous software engineering — the past, present and future. In: Julliand, J., Kouchnarenko, O. (eds.) B 2007. LNCS, vol. 4355, p. 1. Springer, Heidelberg (2006)
33. Gibson, J.P.: A noughts and crosses java applet to teach programming to primary school children. In: PPPJ 2003: Proceedings of the 2nd international conference on Principles and practice of programming in Java, pp. 85–88. Computer Science Press, Inc., New York (2003)
34. Gibson, D.J.P.: Méry,: Formal modelling of services for getting a better understanding of the feature interaction problem. In: Bjorner, D., Broy, M., Zamulin, A.V. (eds.) PSI 1999. LNCS, vol. 1755, pp. 155–179. Springer, Heidelberg (2000)

Encouraging the Uptake of Formal Methods Training in an Industrial Context
(Extended Abstract)

Michael G. Hinchey

Lero–the Irish Software Engineering Research Centre
University of Limerick
Ireland
mike.hinchey@lero.ie

1 Introduction

I recently had occasion to revisit a collection of papers edited by myself and Jonathan Bowen published way back in 1995. The collection, *Applications of Formal Methods* [1], sprung from the obvious need in the formal methods community for detailed examples, insights from industrial best practice, and experience reports.

At the time, this was very necessary. As one of the contributors to the collection, David Lorge Parnas, succinctly pointed out [2]:

> Unfortunately, in spite of many years of effort, and hundreds of papers, industrial applications of formal (mathematical) methods remain rather rare. One notices that the same examples of applications are cited repeatedly. These cases serve as "existence proofs", proofs that the methods can work, but, if one visits typical programming shops, one rarely finds anyone who has used these methods. Existence proofs are not proofs of practicality.

Birthday books and steam boiler case studies, quite prevalent at the time, were useful to introduce the notations, and, as Parnas pointed out, did serve to demonstrate that formal methods could be used, but would their usage be practical in an industrial context? Could practitioners be convinced to use such techniques? And, more importantly, could practitioners (as opposed to academics) successfully apply such techniques in practice?

Several other articles appeared prior to this collection describing successful formal methods projects (e.g., [3] and [4]), and others have appeared since, but what was different about our collection was that the experiences were described by the practitioners themselves rather than being a summary of experiences, and that the collection described actual projects rather than different approaches to the same (often unrealistic) case study.

Notwithstanding, the collection spawned a couple of articles by Jonathan and myself, using the examples given in the collection to illuminate advice and guidance for practical application. The papers, *Ten Commandments of Formal Methods* [5] and a follow up to Anthony Hall's *Seven Myths of Formal Methods* [6], imaginatively entitled *Seven More Myths of Formal Methods* [7], are quite widely used in both academic and industrial formal methods training courses, and it is very gratifying to find that at least some of the advice given in the papers has been useful to some.

T. Margaria and B. Steffen (Eds.): ISoLA 2008, CCIS 17, pp. 473–477, 2008.

While I have relaxed my stance to some extent over the years (see, for example, [8]), I am still a fervent believer in the value of formal methods, and indeed in the necessity of more rigorous approaches when dealing with particular classes of application, or in critical domains. Nevertheless, formal methods have not become as popular as we had once hoped they would, and many successful software developments have avoided their usage. In the last few years, attempts to champion formal methods in both government and industry, as well as other technologies related to software assurance [9], has provided some insights into why there is reluctance to engage in formal methods training, or why that training has not been so successful.

2 Impediments to Formal Methods Training

Re-reading Parnas' article [2], I was pleased to see that again he had succinctly hit on at least part of the problem:

> When new methods do not catch on, there are two obvious possible explanations. Either the methods are not yet good enough, or practitioners are too conservative, unwilling to learn, and resistant to change. In most cases there is truth in both explanations. The best known formal methods clearly work, but it is equally clear that they require a lot of tedious writing of expressions that are difficult to read. In fact, some of the methods are so tedious that people take short-cuts and make mistakes.

After more than a quarter of a century of development, and more than a decade since Parnas' article, we can hardly describe formal methods as "new methods", and we can certainly discount the fact that they are "not yet good enough", as evidenced by various success stories. However, it is still certainly true that practitioners are loath to take them on-board, in part because of exaggerated claims that were erroneously made by proponents in the past [8] and in part because of misconceptions that they are difficult to use, etc. [6, 7].

As one would expect, if many (or most) practitioners feel that formal methods are impractical, or are unlikely to embrace their usage, for whatever reasons, then they are unlikely to be interested in formal methods training. However, it is only through training that practitioners will understand what formal methods can do for them, and see that they are applicable in their particular circumstances. While it must be conceded that formal methods are not suitable for all, or in all circumstances, there are many more cases where they would be useful than in which they are currently exploited. Essentially we have a chicken-and-egg problem: practitioners must truly understand formal methods and be extensively trained in their usage if they are to adopt them and exploit them in their work. However, they will often be reluctant to engage in formal methods training courses because they cannot see their value or fear that they will not provide sufficient return for the effort of learning the notation and coming to grips with the concepts.

Personal experience in the transfer of technologies related to software assurance (including, but not exclusively, formal methods) in a government agency [9] has helped me highlight four areas that I feel are essential for formal methods training to be successful:

1. There must be sufficient evidence that the technology is valid and worth the effort of learning.
2. The technology must be mature and immediately applicable in the given context.
3. There must be sufficient support for adoption of the technology, including, but not limited to, installation support, training, and tools.
4. There must be sufficient consideration of the people involved, their constraints, experience, strengths and deficiencies and of those who *need* to be involved.

2.1 Evidence of Successful Use

I have been dismayed at the number of times practitioners of my acquaintance have refused to consider a particular technology (not just formal methods) that others have strenuously advised them to consider.

In part, this can be attributed to a reluctance to take on board a new technology with a substantial learning curve and the risk that the practitioners may take longer to adapt to the technology than the time available in the project. Often, however, it is due to a refusal to be convinced that the technology will reduce the level of effort, or improve the final product, to a level that justifies the investment (both financially and in terms of time and effort).

What was most convincing for practitioners was evidence that the technology had previously reduced costs or lead-times, reduced complexity, or substantially improved the product *in their own organization* or in a substantially similar organization, or in developing a substantially similar product.

2.2 Technology Maturity

The maturity of a technology and its readiness for immediate deployment is a significant factor. While many of the mainstream formal methods have been around for quite some time, many have evolved and spawned variants and extensions, often for good reason, but which means that notations and tools are evolving, and that continuous training and updating is required.

We applied the concept of a *Technology Readiness Level (TRL)*, commonly used in the organization, to determine how prepared various technologies and tools were for use within the organization. Contributing to the TRL were such factors as stability of the approach and solidity of the associated tools, appropriate documentation, availability of training materials, and experience of previous application. While this is a rather subjective measure, based on nothing more than our own insights, it was clear that those technologies that were highest on the scale were those that had the greatest successes and were most likely to be used again. The difference in experience of those applying a low-to-mid-TRL technology and those applying a high-TRL technology was dramatic. In most cases there was a direct correlation between the TRL and the likelihood of success of the project. From the point of view of training, the technology (formal methods, or otherwise) needs to be well-established, reasonably fixed in its notation and approach, and well-supported in order to be feasible.

2.3 Support

Just as successful application of formal methods (or any technology transfer) requires adequate support, support is vital for formal methods training to be successful.

It is all but pointless attempting to introduce a method that does not have sufficient tool support and a body of examples, exercises and illustrative case studies relevant to the environment. Support is required not just for training, but also in installation and set-up. We have seen too many projects suffer serious delays in getting tools installed and operational, even to the point where the success of the project was compromised. This is particularly true of expensive tools that might be customized for a customer or adapted and used by a small number of customers. More mass-market tools typically were easier to install and to get hands-on experience with quickly, and greater levels of support were often available.

Tools are certainly vital to the industrial application of formal methods and the availability of easy-to-use, easy-to-setup and interactive tools makes formal methods training a lot easier. Support must also come in the guise of financial support: good training is often expensive, but the difference between good training and mediocre training is dramatic and what may seem like fiscal prudence can often be detrimental to the project.

2.4 People

Rogers holds that any successful technology transfer must match well with the norms and practices of the receiving organization [10], and that has been our experience [9]. Equally, when planning training, it is essential to consider the characteristics, strengths, and weaknesses of the personnel, their modes of operation, and how the subject of the training matches with the individuals within the organization.

More importantly, it is essential to remember that the transfer of any technology benefits greatly from the participation of a team member who will "champion" that technology and address many of the issues raised in the previous sections. We found this to be very true in our software assurance technology transfer [9], and it matches well with Rogers' principles [10]. Jim Foley of Georgia Tech says that technology transfer is a contact sport (by now a phrase that many people have purloined); formal methods training *is* technology transfer. There is truly no substitute for having an enthusiastic member of a development team when transitioning a new technology. Likewise, having a member of the training group who is enthusiastic about the new technology, principles, or new principles being presented to them, is invaluable in ensuring the success of the training program.

3 Conclusion

While those of us working in the field are committed in our belief that formal methods have much to offer in system development, and that they have advanced to a point where they are industrially applicable, they are still not well understood and suffer from misconceptions about how difficult they are to work with. Essential to overcoming these misconceptions is the development of solid training programs within industry to educate developers and their management about the benefits of these techniques.

The uptake of formal methods training within industry is predicated on providing evidence that the techniques do indeed work in real-life complex applications on an industrial scale, ensuring that the methods we try to train people in are truly mature with mature supporting tools and materials. And lastly, but not least, we must remember the human dimension not only in training, but in any system development process, and exploit that asset to ensure success.

Acknowledgement. This work was supported in part by Science Foundation Ireland grant 03/CE2/I303_1 to Lero—the Irish Software Engineering Research Centre (www.lero.ie).

References

1 Hinchey, M.G., Bowen, J.P. (eds.): Applications of Formal Methods. Prentice Hall International Series in Computer Science, Hemel Hempstead (1995)
2 Parnas, D.L.: Using Mathematical Models in the Inspection of Critical Software. In: [1], pp. 17–31
3 Gerhart, S., Craigen, D., Ralston, T.: Experience with Formal Methods in Critical Systems. IEEE Software 11(1), 21–28 (1994)
4 Gerhart, S., Craigen, D., Ralston, T.: Regulatory Case Studies. IEEE Software 11(1), 30–39 (1994)
5 Bowen, J.P., Hinchey, M.G.: Ten Commandments of Formal Methods. Computer 28(4), 56–63 (1995)
6 Hall, J.A.: Seven Myths of Formal Methods. IEEE Software 7(5), 11–19 (1990)
7 Bowen, J.P., Hinchey, M.G.: Seven More Myths of Formal Methods. IEEE Software 12(4), 34–41 (1995)
8 Hinchey, M.G.: Confessions of a Formal Methodist. In: Proc. of the 7th Australian Workshop on Safety Critical Systems and Software, Adelaide, Australia (2002)
9 Hinchey, M.G., Pressburger, T., Feather, M.S., Markosian, L., Deadrick, W.: Software Assurance Research Infusion: the NASA Experience. In: Proc. ISoLA 2006, Paphos, Cyprus, October 2006. IEEE Computer Society Press, Los Alamitos (2006)
10 Rogers, E.M.: Diffusion of Innovations, 5th edn. Free Press, New York (2003)

Computer-Supported Collaborative Learning with Mind-Maps*

Dmitrij Koznov[1] and Michel Pliskin[2]

[1] Saint-Petersburg State University, Software Engineering Department, Universiteskij pr. 28, 198504, St. Petersburg, Russia
dkoznov@yandex.ru
[2] Comapping, Blaagaardstraede 8FDK-4000, Roskilde, Denmark
pl@tepkom.ru

Abstract. Collaborative learning is a set of various approaches in education that involve joint intellectual effort by students or students and teachers. It opposed to the traditional 'direct transmission' model, in which learners are assumed to be passive, receptive, isolated receivers of knowledge and skills delivered by an external source. Today Computer-Supported Collaborative Learning (CSCL) is actively developed to support collaborative learning process with the help of modern information and communication technologies. Mindmaps is one of the wide-known learning technique which can be used in CSCL. In this paper we present new mindmaps Web-based tool Comapping, which provides a wide variety of ways to organize collaborative processes in education. We also describe our experiments with applying the CSLC-paradigm using Comapping while teaching Software Engineering in Saint Petersburg State University.

Keywords: Computer-Supported Collaborative Learning, Collaborative Learning, Mind maps, SADT, Author/Commenter Cycle Review Process.

1 Introduction

Mind maps [1] are a popular technique having been widely used in the education area for several decades by now. It is used both on its own and as a part of other methodologies like active learning [2] and others. Mind maps are extremely efficient when working individually on learning material as they emphasize human creative skills, improve memory and are generally proved useful in all kinds of intellectual activities. There are a number of software mindmapping solutions on the market now (please refer to [3] for a complete listing). However, use of a mindmapping in collaborative learning is not too widely recognized at the moment. At the same time, mind maps are proved to be a great tool for different kinds of collaborative work between both the teacher and the student and inside a group of students.

Computer-supported mind maps are efficient in organizing all kinds of collaborative processes in various areas: business, education, science and more. A mind map

* Educational experiments with Comapping tools described in this paper were partially funded by Hewlett-Packard and RFFI (grant 08-01-08342).

T. Margaria and B. Steffen (Eds.): ISoLA 2008, CCIS 17, pp. 478–489, 2008.

can easily be sent by email to friends and colleagues and revise it later according to their comments. Some of mindmapping tools: MindMeister, mind42 and others have lots of extra advanced collaboration features. However, all of them lack the ability to handle large diagrams efficiently and visually clearly, which is an essential thing for most educational uses.

This article is focused on how to apply mind maps in Computer-Supported Collaborative Learning (CSCL) [4]. We are going to introduce a software application named Comapping[1], being a pure online mindmapping application. Comapping has numerous advanced collaboration features like real-time collaborative editing, live indication of other users' position, and efficient support for large maps. We are also presenting the results of our experiments to use Comapping-based mind maps to set up efficient collaborative learning processes in Software Engineering Department of Mathematics and Mechanics Faculty of Saint-Petersburg State University.

2 Background

2.1 Computer-Supported Collaborative Learning

Briefly, CSCL is focused on how collaborative learning supported by technology can enhance peer interaction and work in groups, and how collaboration and technology facilitate sharing and distributing of knowledge and expertise among community members [4]. Collaborative learning is in an education process when two or more people learn or attempt to learn something together [5]. There are many interpretation of this concept and it now mostly seen as a general framework unifying lots of different educational methods, approaches and techniques.

It is not easy to decide when and where to start CSCL history. Collaborative learning is the subject of study in a wide variety of disciplines such as developmental psychology (e.g., sociocognitive conflict), social psychology (person perception, motivation, group processes), sociology (status, power and authority), cognitive psychology (how learning occurs, learning outcomes) and sociocultural perspectives (cultural influence on interaction, mediation of learning) [6].

2.2 Mind Maps

The approach was suggested by Tony Buzan in 1970 as an efficient way to work with arbitrary information. The idea is to use a very simple diagramming notation: the central (primary) object is drawn in the middle, and secondary and further objects clarifying the meaning of the central one are put around it and connected together. This makes a radial structure suitable to analyze and understand large amounts of data. The approach is widely used in education, business, psychology and other areas. There are also a number of software tools implementing the approach. More information can be found in [1, 3].

2.3 Mindmapping Tools

In this section we are going to give a brief overview of current online mindmapping solutions and will try analyze them a bit from collaboration learning perspective. This

[1] www.comapping.com

overview is not supposed to be 100% comprehensive as there are more and more applications appearing nearly every day, and it does not seem feasible to cover all of them, but we are going to cover the basic trends and most often used examples.

First, let us list the features we consider most important for collaboration.

Pure online application in a modern highly-heterogeneous cross-platform world, the only reasonable way to communicate is to use online applications. Desktop applications are just not the way to go anymore because the complexity they bring makes the real learning and communication complicated up to useless.

Live collaboration is the key feature for collaboration. It allows people to edit a single map simultaneously in real time, to share maps, and therefore to communicate efficiently.

Export & import to/from other formats allows convert move the data quickly between applications (both online and desktop), providing easy ways to back up, store and integrate data.

Automatic intelligent layout of different kinds as shared maps tends to become large, users need an efficient way to work with these large maps efficiently. As screen space is always limited, applications need efficient ways to handle the problem, leading to different kinds of automatic map layout engines.

Smart printing paper copies are still very important in academic world, and intelligent printing seems to be one of key features.

Based on these criteria we can summarize the popular online mindmapping solutions in the Table 1. We consider the following online applications: MindMeister, Mindomo, Mind42[2], comparing them with Comapping[3].

Table 1. Online mindmapping solutions

Feature/Tools	MindMeister	Mindomo	Mind42	Comapping
Pure online application	YES	YES	YES	YES
Live collaboration	YES	NO	YES	YES
Export/Import	YES	YES	YES	YES
Intelligent auto-layout	Partial	Partial	Partial	YES
Smart printing	NO	NO	NO	YES

As we can see, most tools are quite similar in terms of basic functionality. We can only mention Mindomo not having online collaboration and Comapping's unique auto-layout and smart printing features.

2.4 Author/Commenter Cycle Review Process SADT/IDEF

In this section we describe wide-known collaborative technique to elaborate visual models which we use for collaborative mindmapping development. This is author/Commenter cycle review process SADT/IDEF [7] in 70s, which was introduced in SADT and after that formalized in EDEF-standards [8] in 90s.

[2] MindMeister – www.mindmeister.com, Mindomo – www.mindomo.com, Mind42 – www.mind42.com

[3] For more information concerning mindmapping tools we would recommend [3].

SADT (Structural Analysis and Design Technique) method is to perform structural analysis of a software system allowing to reduce the number of expensive errors by structuring the knowledge about the system as well as improving the communication between developers and users or customers. SADT was used in ICAM (Integrated Computer-Aided Manufacturing) of US AirForce leading to adopting some part of it as IDEF0 standard and wide adoption of this standard in the US military industry. SADT is not used in software development now, but it is still in active use for business process modeling.

Author/Commenter cycle review process is one of SADT/EDEF. In order to build a usable description of a system in question, we need to evaluate the models quickly by experts and future users. The two primary roles here are author and commenter - the second one being the domain expert. Author is interviewing the commenter to get the necessary information. He is then fixing commenter's comments in the model. The models are thus created in an iterative way until considered ready by the experts.

3 Comapping

3.1 Overview

Comapping (www.comapping.com) is a next-generation collaborative online mind-mapping application. Its basic purpose is to allow users to create, edit and share mind maps. Comapping introduces features like easy drag'n'drop, smooth animation, support for large maps with smart auto-focusing feature, and more. Tree-like notation (left-to-right mindmapping) is proved better for computer-based mindmapping when

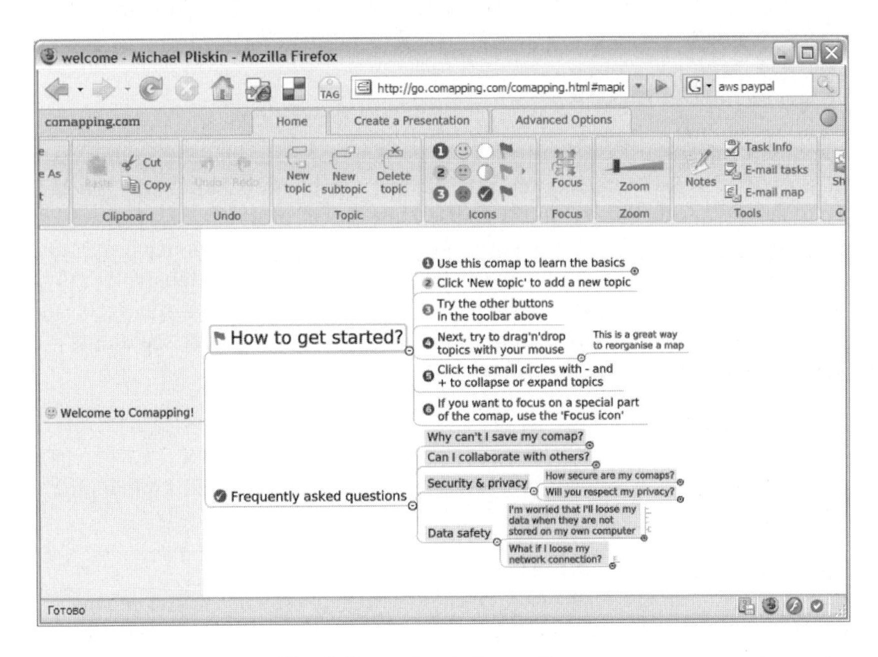

Fig. 1. Example mind map diagram

combined with auto-layout algorithm as it is easier to read and understand than the center-based one, and the intuitive power of the center-based approach goes away when map is no longer static as it is on paper. An example mind map in Comapping is presented in Fig. 1.

Comapping has the following extra features to ease collaboration and active learning:

1. **Pure online application**. This allows users to avoid the hassle of installing the application locally and taking care of mind maps stored as local files as they are kept on the server instead. The application also has built-in communication tools eliminating the need to use external e-mail and/or chat software like Microsoft Outlook or Skype. Users can also work offline for a while if the connection goes down as all their data will be automatically copied to server once it is up again.
2. **Real-time collaborative map editing.** The system allows sharing maps to any number of users, as well as notifying users about map changes. These changes are then highlighted on a map with the detailed information about who and when made each individual change. Other users can they review the changes and leave comments making Comapping a great tool for professors to review their students' work.
3. **Smart, convenient and flexible printing.** Allows a professor to print a number of maps quickly and then review them offline. Multiple printing options (such as fit to page, fit to multiple pages, print parts of map) makes it possible to review even large maps and models with just a sheet of paper.
4. **User-friendliness and ease of use.** People (especially students) do not normally need a user manual or any other documentation everything is intuitive and self-explanatory.
5. **Export/import features.** Ability to insert mind maps into PowerPoint presentations and interoperability with other popular software is a key thing for collaboration as well[4].

3.2 Implementation Details

Technically, Comapping is implemented as an Adobe Flash application on the client and as a Apache/Neko[5] application on the server. The client is built using the Model-View-Controller design pattern and is coded using haXe[6] programming language. Due to the nature of Flash virtual machine, the client is using functional programming concepts like high-order functions and pattern-matching pretty extensively, allowing for simple code performing the complicated tasks. The server is a relatively simple stateless HTTP request processor (providing therefore an excellent scalability), coupled with a database engine.

3.3 Usage Examples

In this section we present several projects done by students using the Comapping tool. These projects include:

---

[4] Reader can try Comapping for free to evaluate it herself. The service has an one month free trial.

[5] http://www.nekovm.org

[6] http://www.haxe.org

- An UML quiz designed by students
- A plan of an article to be written by PhD student and his supervisor.

As you can see from the screenshots below, the tool helps to structure the problem, split it into subproblems, and go on with this process for as long as needed. At the same time, other peers can review/augment/comment the work done, and thus perform the task together efficiently.

In case of UML quiz Comapping was used to present a lot of information in a nice group discussion-friendly way. A high-level overview of the quiz is presented on Fig. 2. You can see the first level completely and three more levels of the main branch. The quiz itself appeared to be large and deeply structured, and therefore we needed a tool to create an outline for it and then navigate, change and review this outline easily.

Fig. 3 shows how Comapping can display large models: you can see one of deep levels "focused" allowing the user to concentrate on it and its details, and the left grey area shows the context preventing the reviewer from getting lost in a large diagram.

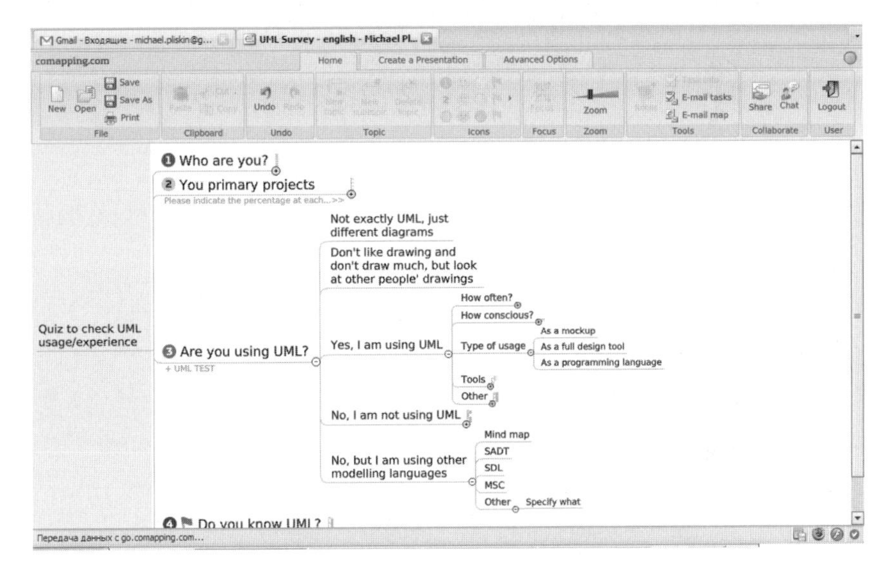

Fig. 2. UML Usage/experience survey

The second example (see Fig. 4) solves a different task. A student has written an article which contained all the necessary information, but the structure was not adequate and sometimes it was not focused properly. The supervisor then restructured the article using a paper-based mind map, and then the student was offered to re-do this mind map in Comapping. The original paper-based mind map was intentionally not very accurate, and some parts were even made unreadable. The supervisor wanted to make the student understand the plan better while converting, actually to make her own new plan using the original one only as inspiration. The obvious reason is that student will need to write a new article according to the plan, and working on your own plan is a lot more efficient compared to working on someone else's plan. The result has been reviewed several times and was finally successfully converted to a ultimately published good article. The definite conclusion is that the traditional paper-based review loop would take a lot more time and effort for the both parties, and especially for the supervisor, as explaining your position about a heavily detailed and complicated problem to someone else without the right tool is a very difficult task.

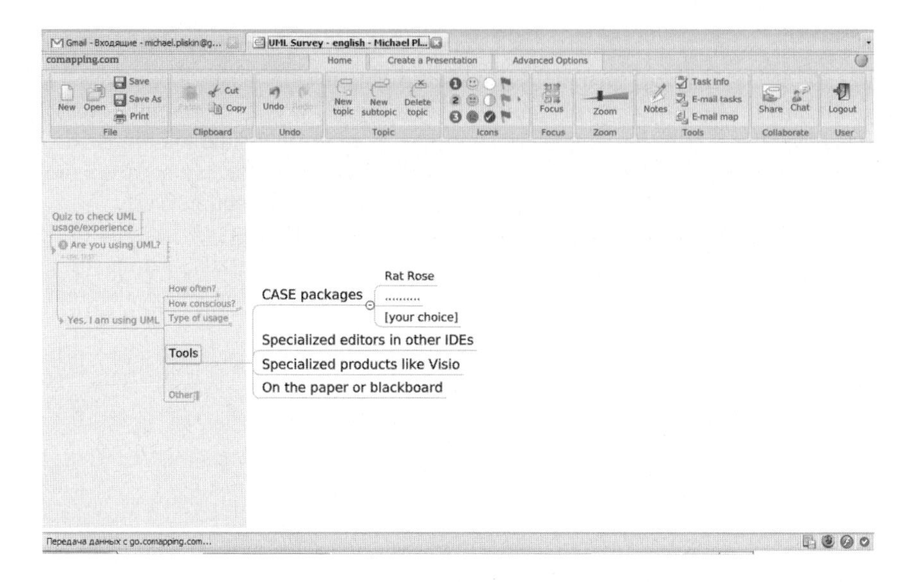

Fig. 3. Details of UML quiz

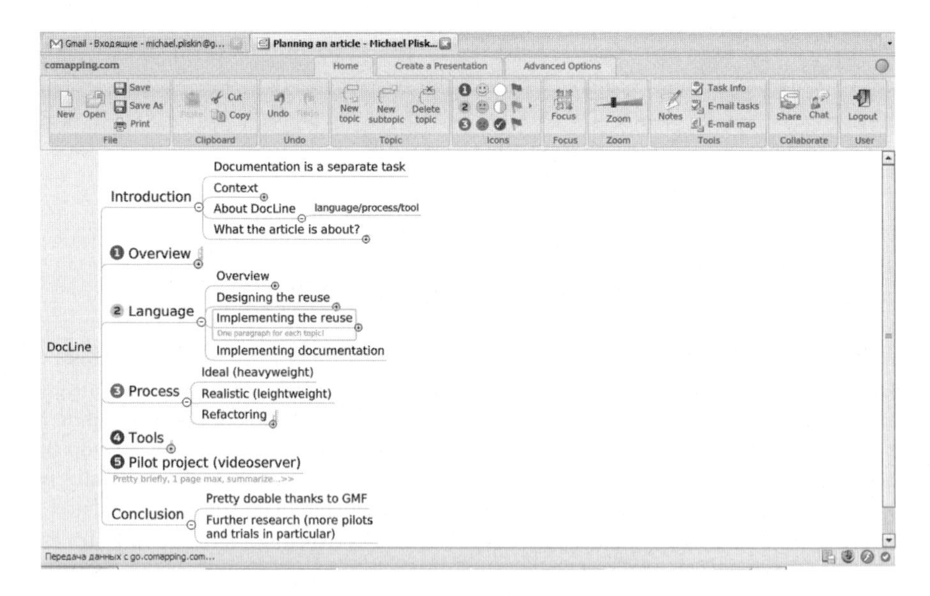

Fig. 4. Planning an article

Fig. 5 shows the real-time collaboration on the mind map of article along with the share dialog used to invite more people to collaborate. You can see also how the tool indicates what other users are doing on a map currently, allowing for even more efficient collaboration and group work (mark «Dmitrij Koznov» near the node «Implementation documentation»).

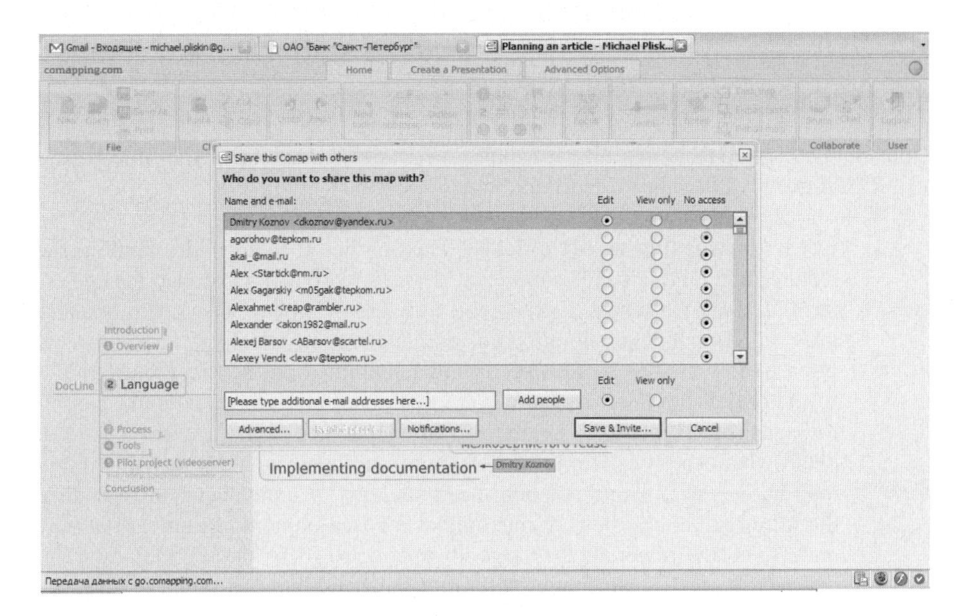

Fig. 5. Collaboration on the article plan

4 Education Experiments with Comapping

4.1 Starting Points

The basic purpose of our experiments was to make collaborative learning processes in Software Engineering Department of Saint-Petersburg State University more efficient and make students more active, involved and committed. This basically applies to seminars, lectures and writing papers of all kinds (term papers, Bachelor, Master and PhD thesis). We realized that the current learning processes are mainly focused on teachers, while students are mostly playing a passive role.

Having looked deeper on the problem, it is easy to realize that most teaching courses consist of two levels. The first level is focused on basic concepts, notions and facts, and requires student mostly to remember some amount of information. The second level is a next step and is focused on understanding, analyzing and (later) practical usage of the knowledge given. This essentially means that while the first level is pretty similar for all students and is perfectly measurable using traditional tools like tests, exams, and simple assignments. The second level, if passed for a student, leads to very student-specific results which are far more difficult to measure using traditional tools. After passing the second level, student comes with her own understanding and point of view on the area, which might differ significantly from what was given on the lectures and how the teaches thinks about it. This is an essential thing for practical application of knowledge given, and thus is especially important in highly practical areas like for instance Software Engineering.

The problem we are facing then is how to induce and then evaluate student achievements on the second level. We found the mind maps in general and Comapping tool in particular are of a great help here.

4.2 Issues and Solutions

Comapping allowed us to organize learning process more efficiently. The following is a quick summary of the most important things we tried.

1. **Get a measurable result quickly.** This applies to both understanding the lectures and talking to the supervisor. It occurred that a mind map created after a lecture or a talk is a very good measure of what does student actually understand about the subject. Oral communication which is normally used often merely creates an illusion of understanding, and the real picture might reveal only much later. As opposed to that, mind maps created on the spot allow teachers to measure the understanding fast and easily and to explain in detail what exactly is wrong and where to improve. Carefully designed mind map-based assignments not only need students to remember and reproduce the information, but they are much more focused on demonstrating how they understand the material. It is a good practice to focus on relations between different topics or concepts, preferably the ones that are implied from the course material but were not explicitly mentioned. Mind maps then allow to check students on a number of topics much quicker than an oral examination could take (of course sacrificing the quality compared to oral exam). We use this approach for regular tests at the beginning of a lecture to check how the last lecture is understood and in exams. The exam itself worked more like an intensive seminar in this case and could last for several hours, and the best thing was to run a group process, when everybody were working on the same task, but with completely different results.
2. **Organize the iterative collaboration between teacher and students.** There are a lot of situations (on seminars, exams, etc.) when teacher and student intensively communicate with each other. And very often this communication occurs in iterative manner: student gets some information from supervisor and should think over it. In this case mind maps are a good mean for student to reflect her current level of understanding of a subject and for supervisor to check this level and make corrections or comments. Comapping collaborative features allowed us to organize this work into iterations with intermediate reviews by teacher. We used Author/Commenter cycle review process SADT/IDEF by adopting the iterative author-commenter collaboration improving the same mind map. Student is normally acting as author, and teacher is normally a commenter. And thanks to online nature of Comapping we were able to perform this communication over the Internet easily.

3. **Improve paper writing efficiency.** Many students experience considerable difficulties creating there term papers and all kinds of thesis. On the other hand, it is often a time-consuming work for a supervisor to review the papers multiple times during their preparation. Comapping allowed to go from iterative reviews to iterative planning: instead of rewriting the real text many times, a student together with his supervisor is working on a detailed plan of paper. Tree-like expandable structure of Comapping Mind maps with text nodes allows focusing and discussing individual aspects or abstraction layers of a paper while still keeping the overall concept in mind. Online collaborative features allow to use the Internet to share results and notes. As a practical note, mind map-based plans of articles and other writings work best if kept small to fit in just 1 page. This allows for viewing them as a whole and at once without checking the details on different pages. It is similar to One Page Method [9] which is used business meetings (in project management, research areas etc.) to focus one a given topic. Ability to the problem as a whole is a must when dealing with complicated information[7].

   The best way to apply mind maps and Comapping is not from the very beginning but when some part of real work is already done and the author now has to understand its meaning and write the text. At this point, the information is usually abundant, not scarce, and thus the author needs to realize what she is focusing on and what has to be left aside. Mind maps are of great help here, but the most important things are not the maps themselves but the thoughts and understanding they in fact induce.
4. **Organize a student groupwork.** Someone just creates a map and shares with everybody including the teacher. Other people are then making changes (all at once or one-by-one as agreed beforehand). The teacher can easily see how actively each individual student is working by looking at her changes, and she can also make her own changes into the shared map. We also use Author/Commenter cycle review process SADT/IDEF. Students are rotating as authors, and teacher and other students are commenters. Each next author has to improve the work of the previous ones, not to start everything from scratch. In order to achieve that the group aligned itself and developed a shared vision before make the initial mind map.
5. **Make the results of students' work publicly available.** Assignments and results made in Comapping appear to be a great material for further teaching. We have the whole libraries of mind maps on different subjects.

4.3 Problems

However, we've also met some problems while using mind maps and Comapping.

1. We have found out that we have to teach our students how to make good maps (not how to use Comapping).

[7] Reducing a complicated phenomenon to a compact rule is the basic principle of western science. It is also applied in using drawings in construction and engineering, visual modeling, (SADT [7], UML [10], etc.), in software engineering.

2. Sometimes it is more efficient to make maps on paper instead of Comapping. Moreover, we have also used other diagrams (for instance, UML [10]). These changes are often necessary to adapt to specific requirements of some students or courses. For instance, as we are teaching Software Engineering, it was often making sense to use the classical diagramming notations of this domain.
3. Another problem we observed sometimes is that students and teachers often tend to focus on designing and improving the maps themselves (in multiple review-comment-fix cycles). The problem here is to keep focusing on the content, not the form. Sometimes we found ourselves spent a great deal of time making a great map which does not make any sense at all.

5 Conclusions

Our experiments involved about 200 students totally during one academic year. We taught two courses and several seminars using mind maps with Comapping. There are about 30 students that used Comapping to create their term papers and Bachelors/Masters/PhD thesis. We've noticed booming efficiency of collaborative learning processes and student activity, and the entire education process seems to have become more creative and interesting. We are going to continue this experiment, and we do believe that the key thing here is not only to create and facilitate the common approach to use mind maps in Computer-Supported Collaborative Learning, but to stimulate the creative work of both students and teachers. Each course, each lecture, each student can be taught in a highly customized way based on these basic ideas and principles.

We're also going to improve and develop Comapping further to make it better for educators. This includes a bunch of new features (like better notes, support for equations and maths, and many more) as well as co-operating with major educational institutions and industry leaders to promote Comapping usage actively in education area.

References

1. Buzan, T.: The mind map book, 2nd edn. BBC Books, London (1995)
2. Willis, C.L., Miertschin, S.L.: Mind maps as active learning tools. Journal of Computing Sciences in Colleges 21(4), 266–272 (2006)
3. http://mindmapping.typepad.com/
4. Lehtinen, E., Hakkarainen, K., Lipponen, L., Rahikainen, M., Muukkonen, H.: Computer-supported collaborative learning: A review of research and development (The J.H.G.I Giesbers Reports on Education, 10). University of Nijmegen, Department of Educational Sciences, Netherlands (1999)
5. Dillenbourg, P.: Introduction: What do you mean by collaborative learning? In: Dillenbourg, P. (ed.) Collaborative Learning: Cognitive and computational approaches, pp. 1–19. Elsevier Science, Amsterdam (1999)
6. O'Donnell, A.M., Hmelo-Silver, C.E., Erkens, G. (eds.): Collaborative learning, reasoning, and technology. Erlbaum, Mahwah (2006)
7. Marca, D.A., McGowan, C.L.: SADT Structured Analysis and Design Technique. McGraw-Hill, New York (1988)

8. Integration Definition For Function Modeling (IDEF0). Draft Federal Information Processing Standards Publication 183, 79 p. (1993)
9. Koznov, D.V.: Visual Modeling and Software Project Management. In: Krivulin, N. (ed.) Proceedings of 2nd International Workshop New Models of Business: Managerial Aspects and Enabling Technology, Saint-Petersburg, pp. 161–169 (2002)
10. UML 2.0 Infrastructure Specification (September, 2004), http://www.omg.org/

Agile IT: Thinking in User-Centric Models

Tiziana Margaria[1] and Bernhard Steffen[2]

[1] Chair Service and Software Engineering, University of Potsdam, Germany
margaria@cs.uni-potsdam.de
[2] Chair of Programming Systems, TU Dortmund, Germany
steffen@cs.uni-dortmund.de

Abstract. We advocate a new teaching direction for modern CS curricula: extreme model-driven development (XMDD), a new development paradigm designed to continuously involve the customer/application expert throughout the whole systems life cycle. Based on the 'One-Thing Approach', which works by successively enriching and refining one single artifact, system development becomes in essence a user-centric orchestration of intuitive service functionality. XMDD differs radically from classical software development, which, in our opinion is no longer adequate for the bulk of application programming – in particular when it comes to heterogeneous, cross organizational systems which must adapt to rapidly changing market requirements. Thus there is a need for new curricula addressing this model-driven, lightweight, and cooperative development paradigm that puts the *user process* in the center of the development and the *application expert* in control of the process evolution.

1 Motivation

Industrial practice is characterized by vaguely defined but urgent IT needs: following pressure, external (by the market or by changed regulations), or internal (by a merger, or for improvement), it is clear that things (be they products, applications, or the own IT landscape) must be changed, but how? Answering this question is typically impossible before major parts of a realization are in place. This is due to the fact that only concrete artifacts provide a sufficiently stable ground for a common understanding between the involved stakeholders. Moreover, only when the customer has a tangible understanding of the options, he can effectively criticize and decide. One observes over and over again that in today's practice this kind of criticism starts only after a first release of a system, and that it continues during the whole life cycle. This observation makes *agility a* if not *the* central requirement for industrial system design.

During the last decade, we developed an extreme version of model-driven development (XMDD) [18], which is designed to continuously involve the customer/application expert throughout the whole system's life cycle. Technically, this is achieved following our 'One-Thing Approach' [19,27], which works by enriching and refining one single artifact: user-level models are successively refined from the user perspective until a sufficient level of detail is reached, where elementary services can be implemented solving application-level tasks. Thus, in essence, system

T. Margaria and B. Steffen (Eds.): ISoLA 2008, CCIS 17, pp. 490–502, 2008.

development becomes user-centric orchestration of intuitive service functionality. The realization of the individual services should typically be simple, often based on functionality provided by third-party and standard software systems.

XMDD differs radically from classical software development, which is in our opinion in fact no longer adequate for the bulk of application programming. This holds in particular when it comes to heterogeneous, cross organizational systems which must adapt to rapidly changing market requirements. Accordingly, a need arises for new curricula that address these issues as rigorously and methodologically as is today the case for classical software development.

The paper addresses cornerstones for such a curriculum while reflecting on our experience with XMDD. This concerns in particular the following 6 questions:

- How to structure solutions from the application perspective (user-centric modelling).
- How to validate the application logic (animation-based requirement validation and model checking).
- How to find an adequate level, where application modelling is handed over to the implementation of (elementary) services. Essentially this can be seen as an identification of the domain language.
- How to deploy their complex aggregations and compositions.
- How to monitor solutions at run time.
- How to adapt existing solutions according to new requirements.

The following section structure is meant as a guideline for organizing a corresponding course/curriculum. Depending on the level of specialization and the background of the audience, this can be dealt with in a lecture, in a course, or in a specialization topic as series of in-depth courses complemented by projects and seminars.

It starts with a motivation, by pointing at one of the most annoying technical hurdles in application development (Sec. 2), before it presents XMDD, our new approach to address, in particular, this issue in Sec. 3. The two subsequent sections then address in Sec. 4 the three major dimensions important to grasp XMDD and in Sec. 5 a corresponding development framework. The two final sections sketch three application scenarios (Sec. 6) and present our conclusions and perspectives (Sec. 7).

2 Technical Hurdles: Compatibility and Interoperability

Already today's systems require an unacceptable effort for deployment, which is typically caused by incompatibilities, feature interactions, and the sometimes catastrophic behavior of component upgrades, which no longer behave as expected. This gets even worse when considering heterogeneous, cross organizational systems, whose components and interfaces typically evolve independently. Thus it is almost impossible to keep up with the required pace of changing market requirements.

Responsible for this situation is mainly the level on which systems are technically composed: even though high level languages and even model driven development are used for component development, the system-level point of view is not yet adequately supported. In fact, in particular the deployment of a heterogeneous systems is still a matter of assembly-level search for the reasons of incompatibility, which may be due to minimal version changes, slight hardware incompatibilities, or simply to hideous bugs, which come to surface only in a new, collaborative context of application. Integration testing and the quest for 'true' interoperability are indeed major cost factors and major risks in a system implementation and deployment.

The hardware industry faced similar problems with even more dramatic consequences already a decade ago: hardware is in fact by nature far more difficult to patch, making failure of compatibility a real disaster. It is therefore the trend since the late '90s to move beyond VLSI towards Systems-on-a-Chip (SoC) in order to guarantee larger integration in both senses: physically, by compacting complex systems on a single chip instead of physically wiring them on a board, but in particular also projectually, i.e. integrating the components well before the silicon level, namely at the design level. Rather than combining chips (the classical way), hardware engineers started years ago to combine directly the component's designs and to directly produce (in their terms, synthesize) system-level solutions which are homogeneous at the silicon level. Interestingly, they solve the problem of compatibility by moving it to a *higher level of abstraction* and going towards more homogeneous final products.

The next section presents XMDD, a paradigm for application development that is conceptually closely related to the sketched SoC approach.

3 XMDD: Extreme Model-Driven Development

At the larger scale of system development, moving the problem of compatibility to a higher level of abstraction means moving it to the modelling level (see

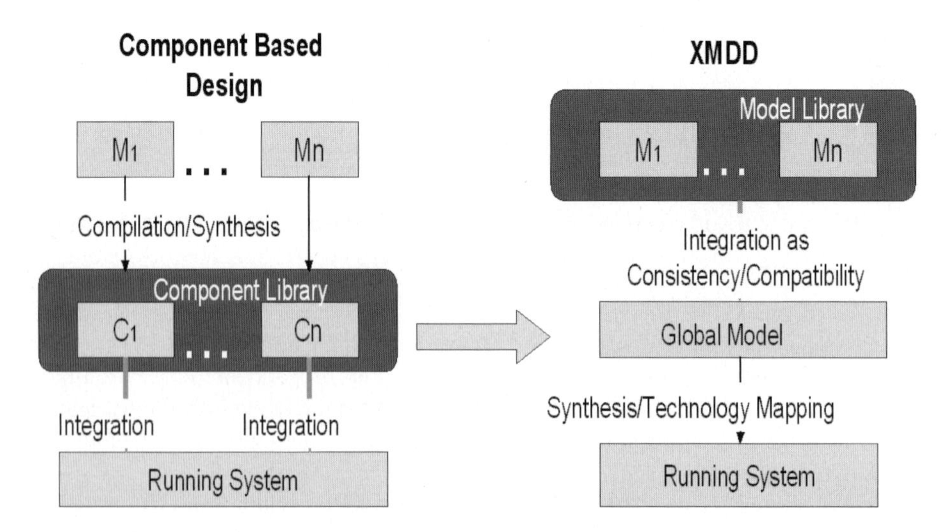

Fig. 1. The XMDD Process

Fig. 1): rather than using the models, as usual in today's Component Based Development paradigm, just as a means of specification, which

- need to be compiled to become a 'real thing' (e.g., a component of a software library),
- must be updated (but typically are not), whenever the real thing changes
- typically only provide a local view of a portion or an aspect of a system,

models should be put into the center of the design activity, becoming *the* first class entities of the *global* system design process. In such an approach, as shown on the right side of Fig. 1,

- libraries should be established on the model level: building blocks should be (elementary) models rather than software components,
- systems should be specified by model combinations (composition, configuration, superposition, conjunction...), viewed as a set of constraints that the implementation needs to satisfy,
- global model combinations should be compiled (synthesized, e.g. by solving all the imposed constraints) into a homogeneous solution for a desired environment, which of course includes the realization of an adequate technology mapping,
- system changes (upgrades, customer-specific adaptations, new versions, etc.) should happen only (or at least primarily) at the model level, with a subsequent global recompilation (re-synthesis),
- optimizations should be kept distinct from design issues, in order to maintain the information on the structure and the design decisions independently of the considerations that lead to a particular optimized implementation.

With this *extreme* style of *model-driven development* (XMDD), which strictly separates compatibility, migration, and optimization issues from model/functionality composition, it would be possible to overcome the problem of incompatibility between

- (global) models and (global) implementations, which is guaranteed and later-on maintained by (semi-) automatic compilation and synthesis, as well as between
- system components, paradigms, and hardware platforms: a dedicated compilation/synthesis of the considered *global* functionality for a specific platform architecture avoids the problems of incompatible design decisions for the individual components.

In essence, delaying the compilation/synthesis until all parameters are known (e.g. all compatibility constraints are available), may drastically simplify this task, as the individual parts can already be compiled/synthesized specifically for the current global context. In a good setup, this should not only simplify the integration issue (rather than having to be open for all eventualities, one can concentrate on precisely given circumstances), but also improve the efficiency of the compiled/synthesized implementations.

In fact, XMDD has the potential to drastically reduce the long-term costs due to version incompatibility, system migration and upgrading, and lower risk factors like vendor and technology dependency. Thus it helps protecting the investment in the software infrastructure. We are therefore convinced that this aggressive style of model-driven development will become the development style at least for mass customized software in the future.

In particular we believe that XMDD, even though being drastically different from state of the art industrial system design, which is very much driven right from the beginning by the underlying hardware architecture, will change accordingly: technology moves so fast, and the varieties are so manifold that the classical platform-focussed development will find its limits very soon.

4 Central Issues to Be Addressed

In order to fully leverage the XMDD potential, a number of issues need to be addressed:

- design of adequate modelling patterns,
- adaptations of analysis, verification and compilation techniques and tools to the XMDD setting, and
- realization of automatic deployment procedures.

A lecture should discuss these issues in the context of related technologies.

4.1 Heterogeneous Landscape of Models

One of the major problems in software engineering is that software is multi-dimensional: it comprises a number of different (loosely related) dimensions, which typically need to be modelled in different styles in order to be treated adequately. Important for simplifying the software/application development is the reduction of the complexity of this multi-dimensional space, by placing it into some standard scenario. Such reductions are typically application-specific. Besides simplifying the application development they also provide a handle for the required automatic compilation and deployment procedures.

Typical among these dimensions, often also called **views**, are

- the *(user) process view*, which describes the dynamic behavior of the system. How does it behave under which circumstance,
- the *architectural view*, which expresses the static structure of the software (dependencies like nesting, inheritance, references). This should not be confused with the architectural view of the hardware platform, which may indeed be drastically different. - The charm of the OO-style was that it claimed to bridge this gap,
- the *exception view*, which addresses the system's behavior under malicious or even unforeseen circumstances,
- the *timing view*, addressing real time aspects,
- the various *thematic views* concerned with roles, specific requirements, and other aspect-like points of view.

Of course, UML already tries to address all these facets in a unifying way, but we all know that UML is currently rather a heterogeneous, expressive sample of languages, which lacks a clear notion of (conceptual) integration like consistency and the idea of global dynamic behavior. Such aspects are currently dealt with independently, e.g. by means of concepts like *contracts* [1] (or more generally, and more complicated, via business-rules oriented programming like e.g. in [12]). The latter concepts are also not supported by systematic means for guaranteeing consistency. In contrast, XMDD views these heterogeneous specifications (consisting of essentially independent models) just as constraints which must be respected during the compilation/synthesis phase (see also [25]).

Another recently very popular approach is Aspect Oriented Programming (AOP) [13,2], which sounds convincing at first, but does not seem to scale for realistic systems. The programmer treats different aspects separately in the code, but has to understand precisely the weaving mechanism, which often is more complicated than programming all the system traditionally. In particular, the claimed modularity is only in the file structure but not on the conceptual side. In other words, in the good case one can write down the aspects separately, but understanding their mutual global impact requires a deep understanding of weaving, and, even worse, of the result of weaving, which very much reminds of an interleaving expansion of a highly distributed system.

4.2 Formal Methods and Tools

There are numerous formal methods and tools addressing validation, ranging from methods for correctness-by-construction/rule-based transformation, correctness

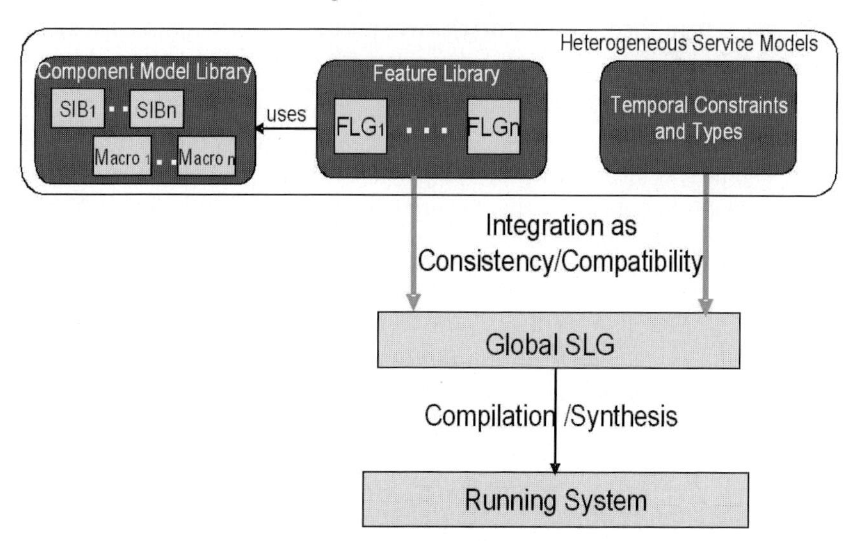

Fig. 2. The XMDD Process in the jABC

calculi, model checkers, and constraint solvers to tools in practical use like PVS [24], Bandera [6], SLAM [5] to name just a few. On the compiler side there are complex (optimizing) compiler suites, code generators, and controller synthesizers, and other methods to support technology mapping. A complete account of these methods would be far beyond the purpose of this paper. Here it is sufficient to note that there is already a high potential of technology waiting to be used.

4.3 Automatic Deployment and Maintenance Support

At the moment, this is the weakest point of the current practice: the deployment of complex systems on a heterogeneous, distributed platform is typically a nightmare, the required system-level testing is virtually unsupported, and the maintenance and upgrading very often turn out to be extremely time consuming and expensive, de facto responsible for the slogan "never change a running system".

Still, also in this area there is a lot of technology one can build upon: the development of Java and the JVM or the .net activities are well-accepted means to help getting models into operation, in particular, when heterogeneous hardware is concerned. Interoperability can be established using CORBA, RMI, RPC, Web services, complex middleware etc, and there are tools for testing and version management. Unfortunately, using these tools requires a lot of expertise, time to detect undocumented anomalies and to develop patches, and this for every application to be deployed.

In order to get a good feeling for the potential of XMDD, a corresponding curriculum should place the discussion of these three issues in a concrete setting, allowing extensive hands-on experience on all these aspects and addressing the 6 issues identified in Sect. 1.

The next section sketches the jABC [10,27], a framework designed to support systematic development according to the XMDD paradigm. jABC provides:

1. a *heterogeneous landscape of models*, to be able to capture all the particularities necessary for the subsequent adequate product synthesis. This concerns the system specification itself, the platforms it runs on together with their communication topology, the required programming style, exceptions, real time aspects, etc.
2. a rich collection of *flexible formal methods and tools*, to deal with the heterogeneous models, their consistency, and their validation, compilation, and testing.
3. *automatic deployment and maintenance support* that are integrated in the whole process and are able to provide 'intelligent' feedback in case of late problems or errors.

5 The jABC as an XMDD Environment

The jABC, developed at METAFrame Technologies in cooperation with the TU Dortmund is intended to promote the XMDD-style of development in order to move the responsibility and control of application development for certain classes of applications towards the application expert. Already in its current version the jABC supports an agile and cooperative development of service-oriented systems along the lines of the One-Thing Approach. Technically it comprises in the following way the three features discussed above (Fig. 2):

1. *Heterogeneous landscape of models*: the central model structure of the ABC are hierarchical Service Logic Graphs (SLGs)[17,16]. SLGs are flow chart-like graphs. They model the application behavior in terms of the intended process flows, based on coarse granular building blocks called SIBs (Service-Independent Building blocks) which are intended to be understood directly by the application experts [17] – independently of the structure of the underlying code, which, in our case, is typically written in Java/C/C++. The component models (SIBs or hierarchical subservices called GraphSIBs), the feature-based service models called Feature Logic Graphs (FLGs), and the Global SLGs modelling applications are all hierarchical SLGs.
   Additionally, the jABC supports model specification in terms of
   (a) two modal logics, to abstractly and loosely characterize valid behaviors (see also [11]),
   (b) a classification scheme for building blocks and types, and
   (c) high level type specifications, used to specify compatibility between the building blocks of the SLGs.
   The granularity of the building blocks is essential here, as it determines the level of abstraction of the whole reasoning: the verification tools directly consider the SLGs as formal models, the names of the (parameterized) building blocks as (parameterized) events, and the branching conditions as (atomic) propositions. Thus the jABC focusses on the level of *component composition* rather than on component construction: its compatibility, its type correctness, and its behavioral correctness are under formal methods' control [16].
2. *Formal methods and tools*: the ABC comprises a high-level type checker, two model checkers, a model synthesizer, a compiler for SLGs, an interpreter, and a view generator. The model synthesizer, the model checkers and the type checker take care of the consistency and compatibility conditions expressed by the four kinds of constraints/models mentioned above.
3. *Automatic deployment and maintenance support*: an automated deployment process, system-level testing [21], regression testing, version control, and online monitoring [7] support the phases following the first deployment.
   In particular the automatic deployment service needs some meta-modelling in advance. In fact, this has been realized using the jABC itself. Also the testing services and the online monitoring are themselves strong formal methods-based [22] and have been realized via the jABC.

The jABC can be regarded as a first framework for XMDD. It is designed to continuously involve the customer/application expert throughout the whole systems life cycle according to the 'One-Thing Approach' [19].

In order to be effective, it is important that a corresponding course provides a tangible experience of this approach, which works by enriching and refining one single artifact. User-level models are successively refined from the user perspective up to a level, where elementary services can be implemented solving application-level tasks.

Students should see (and appreciate) how, accordingly, the composition and coordination of components as well as their maintenance and version control happen in the jABC exclusively at the modelling level, and how the compilation to running source code (mostly Java and C++) and deployment of the resulting applications are fully automatic.

6 XMDD Case Studies in jABC

The XMDD paradigm has been successfully used in several contexts, at different abstraction levels. The following selection briefly illustrates how the jABC uniformly supports all the abstraction levels, from the requirements/design with non-IT experts in Sec. 6.1, to application design in Sec. 6.2, to middleware-level configurations in Sec. 6.3.

6.1 Requirements and Specification: Supply Chain Management

In [9] we concentrate on the collaborative design of complex embedded systems in the jABC, that has proven to be effective and adequate for the team cooperation with *non-IT personnel*. Concretely, we show how our approach to model-driven collaborative design was applied to the requirement and specification phase of part of IKEA's P3 Document Management Process (part of a new Supply Chain Management system), where it complemented the Rational Unified Process development process already in use. Central contribution of this approach is two-dimensional support of consistency at the user process level:

- *vertical consistency* of models, e.g. across abstraction layers, as well as
- *horizontal model consistency*, which is needed e.g. across organizational borders within a same abstraction level.

In this particular case we had to bridge between various business process specifications provided by business analysts on one side and use case/activity diagram views needed as specifications by the IT designers on the other side. Based on the One-Thing Approach, horizontal consistency was guaranteed by maintaining the global perspective throughout the refinement process, down to the code level, and vertical consistency by the simple discipline for refinement.

6.2 Application Construction: The SWSC Mediation Scenario

A case study that demonstrates a wide span of XMDD features, from the design by modelling to the deployment and test, is our solution with jABC of the Mediation scenario of the Semantic Web Service Challenge, as described in [14]. There, we show how we solved the Mediation task (a benchmark scenario of the

Challenge, described in [23]) in a model driven, service oriented fashion using the jABC framework for model driven development and its jETI extension [26] for seamless integration of remote (Web) services. In particular we illustrate

- how atomic services and orchestrations are modelled in the jABC,
- how legacy services and their proxies are represented within our framework, and how they are imported into our framework,
- how the mediator arises as orchestrations of the testbed's remote services and of local services,
- how vital properties of the Mediator are verified via model checking in the jABC, and
- how jABC/jETI orchestrated services are exported as Web services.

Besides providing a solution to the mediation problem, this also illustrates the *agility* of jABC-based solutions, since in the Challenge each scenario comprises a set of problems that come in different levels that build onto each other. One of the central assessments is in fact the ability of a methodology and of the corresponding technologies and tools to leverage on the first-level solutions to accommodate the changes/extensions required by the subsequent levels with minimal intrusion (in the solution and platforms) and effort (of a modeller/programmer).

6.3 Middleware Services: MaTRICS

In [4] we present how we realize in jABC the remote configuration and fault tolerance of the Online Conference Service (OCS) [15] with our service oriented framework MaTRICS [3]. MaTRICS is our model-based service-oriented platform for remote intelligent configuration and management of systems and services and is built on top of the jABC, thus it inherits the XMDD perspective. Providing with low overhead high-availability mechanisms for complex applications that run on distributed platforms is one of the central services offered by MaTRICS. Our solution lets the services untouched and uses the open source cluster management software *heartbeat* [8,20] to provide the high availability features. We showed there how jABC's XMDD approach supports the management services at, or close to, the middleware and operating system level, providing a user-friendly level of service models (implemented as SLGs according to the XMDD paradigm) for the monitoring (sensing of correct functionality) and the reconfiguration/service migration (actuating the changes on the cluster by steering heatbeat functionality). This in contrast with the usual, script-based, heartbeat working manner, which is strictly code-based.

Reexamining the 6 issues mentioned in Sec. 1, in this case study we

- structure the high-availability solution from the application perspective, for an application-level definition and management of the high-availability services well above the scripting level (user-centric modelling),
- enable the model-level validation of the application logic (animation-based requirement validation and model checking), opposed to the sole testing possible in a script-based solution,

- we find an adequate, higher and more declarative level, where application modelling is handed over to the implementation of (elementary) services. In fact, the library of services provided by MaTRICS has been extended by a new, reusable collection that internally uses heartbeat. This establishes a higher-level domain-specific language and service library for high-availability monitoring and enforcement,
- automatically deploy the new services, which are complex aggregations and enhanced compositions of the middleware services they embed,
- being jABC artifacts, the new high-availability services and test cases are themselves monitorable at run time,
- they are easily adaptable according to new requirements and to new platforms.

7 Conclusions and Perspectives

We have advocated a new teaching direction for modern CS curricula: extreme model-driven development (XMDD), a new development paradigm designed to continuously involve the customer/application expert throughout the whole systems' life cycle. XMDD puts the user process in the center of the development and the application expert in control of the process evolution. It differs radically from classical software development, which, in our opinion is no longer adequate for the bulk of application programming – in particular, when it comes to heterogeneous, cross organizational systems which must adapt to rapidly changing market requirements.

Of course, XMDD will never replace genuine software development, as it assumes techniques to be able to solve problems (like synthesis or technology mapping) which are undecidable in general and therefore not automatable. On the other hand, more than 90% of the software development costs that arise worldwide concern a rather primitive software development level – as during routine application programming or software updates – where there are no technological or design challenges. There, the major problem faced is software quantity rather than achievement of very high quality, and automation should be thus largely possible. XMDD is intended to address (a significant part of) this 90% 'niche', which is certainly important enough to justify an adequate coverage in future CS curricula.

Moreover, we are convinced that this expertise will be of growing importance for most of the interdisciplinary B.Sc. and M.Sc. curricula that focus on a combination of computer science with another discipline, like bio-informatics, commercial information technology, and various degrees that bridge management/economy and CS. These professional profiles address much less the production of code and the algorithmic skills than the capability of abstraction from IT-specific issues and bridging towards the users' perspective, mostly for users with a different background, in their own terms.

References

1. Andrade, L.F., Fiadeiro, J.L.: Architecture Based Evolution of Software Systems, `http://www.atxsoftware.com/publications/SFM.pdf`
2. AspectJ Website, `http://eclipse.org/aspectj/`
3. Bajohr, M., Margaria, T.: MaTRICS: A Service-Based Management Tool for Remote Intelligent Configuration of Systems. Innovations in Systems and Software Engineering (ISSE) 2(2), 99–111 (2005)
4. Bajohr, M., Margaria, T.: High Service Availability in MaTRICS for the OCS. In: Proc. ISoLA 2008, 3rd Int. Symp. on Leveraging Applications of Formal Methods, Verification, and Validation, Chalkidiki (GR), October 2008. CCIS, vol. 17. Springer, Heidelberg (2008)
5. Ball, T., Cook, B., Das, S., Rajamani, S.: Refining approximations in software predicate abstraction. In: Jensen, K., Podelski, A. (eds.) TACAS 2004. LNCS, vol. 2988, pp. 338–340. Springer, Heidelberg (2004)
6. Corbett, J., Dwyer, M., Hatcliff, J., Robby.: Bandera: A Source-level Interface for Model Checking Java Programs. In: Proc. ICSE 2000, 22nd Int. Conf. on Software Engineering, pp. 762–765 (2000)
7. Hagerer, A., Hungar, H., Niese, O., Steffen, B.: Model Generation by Moderated Regular Extrapolation. In: Kutsche, R.-D., Weber, H. (eds.) FASE 2002. LNCS, vol. 2306, pp. 80–95. Springer, Heidelberg (2002)
8. Heartbeat, Open Source High Availability Software, `http://www.linux-ha.org`
9. Hörmann, M., Margaria, T., Mender, T., Nagel, R., Steffen, B., Trinh, H.: The jABC Approach to Rigorous Collaborative Development of SCM Applications. In: Proc. ISoLA 2008, 3rd Int. Symp. on Leveraging Applications of Formal Methods, Verification, and Validation, Chalkidiki (GR), October 2008. CCIS, vol. 17. Springer, Heidelberg (2008)
10. Jörges, S., Kubczak, C., Nagel, R., Margaria, T., Steffen, B.: Model-Driven Development with the jABC. In: Bin, E., Ziv, A., Ur, S. (eds.) HVC 2006. LNCS, vol. 4383, pp. 92–108. Springer, Heidelberg (2007)
11. Jonsson, B., Margaria, T., Naeser, G., Nyström, J., Steffen, B.: Incremental requirement specification for evolving systems. Nordic Journal of Computing 8(1), 65 (2001); In: Proc. of Feature Interactions in Telecommunications and Software Systems (2000)
12. JRules, ILOG, `http://www.ilog.com/`
13. Kiczales, G., Lamping, J., Mendhekar, A., Maeda, C., Videira Lopes, C., Loingtier, J.-M., Irwin, J.: Aspect-Oriented Programming. In: Akşit, M., Matsuoka, S. (eds.) ECOOP 1997. LNCS, vol. 1241, pp. 220–242. Springer, Heidelberg (1997)
14. Kubczak, C., Margaria, T., Steffen, B., Nagel, R.: Service-oriented Mediation with jABC/jETI. In: Semantic Web Services Challenge Results from the First Year (Semantic Web and Beyond). Springer, Heidelberg (2008)
15. Margaria, T., Karusseit, M.: Community Usage of the Online Conference Service: an Experience Report from three CS Conferences, 2nd IFIP Conference on e- commerce, e-business, e-government (I3E 2002). In: Towards the Knowledge Society - eCommerce, eBusiness and eGovernment, Lisboa (P), 7-9 Oct. 2002, pp. 497–511. Kluwer Academic Publishers, Dordrecht (2002)
16. Margaria, T., Steffen, B.: Lightweight Coarse-grained Coordination: A Scalable System-Level Approach. STTT, Int. Journal on Software Tools for Technology Transfer (2003)

17. Margaria, T., Steffen, B.: METAFrame in Practice: Design of Intelligent Network Services. In: Olderog, E.-R., Steffen, B. (eds.) Correct System Design. LNCS, vol. 1710, pp. 390–415. Springer, Heidelberg (1999)
18. Margaria, T., Steffen, B.: From the How to the What. In: Proc. VSTTE 2005, Verified Software—Theories, Tools, and Experiments, IFIP Working Conference, Zurich, October 2005. LNCS, vol. 4171. Springer, Heidelberg (2005)
19. Margaria, T., Steffen, B.: Business Process Modelling in the jABC: The One-Thing Approach. In: Cardoso, J., van der Aalst, W. (eds.) Handbook of Research on Business Process Modeling. IGI Global (2009)
20. Marowsky-Bre, L.: A new cluster resource manager for heartbeat. In: UKUUG LISA/Winter Conf. on High-Availability and Reliability, Bournemouth, UK (2004)
21. Niese, O., Margaria, T., Hagerer, A., Nagelmann, M., Steffen, B., Brune, G., Ide, H.: An automated testing environment for CTI systems using concepts for specification and verification of workflows. Annual Review of Communication. In: Int. Engineering Consortium (IEC), Chicago, USA, vol. 54, pp. 927–936 (2001)
22. Niese, O., Steffen, B., Margaria, T., Hagerer, A., Brune, G., Ide, H.: Library-based design and consistency checks of system-level industrial test cases. In: Hussmann, H. (ed.) FASE 2001. LNCS, vol. 2029, pp. 233–248. Springer, Heidelberg (2001)
23. Petrie, C., Zaremba, M., Lausen, H., Komazec, S., Küster, U.: SWS Challenge Scenarios. In: Semantic Web Services Challenge Results from the First Year (Semantic Web and Beyond). Springer, Heidelberg (2008)
24. Shankar, N., Owre, S.: Principles and Pragmatics of Subtyping in PVS. In: Bert, D., Choppy, C., Mosses, P.D. (eds.) WADT 1999. LNCS, vol. 1827, pp. 37–52. Springer, Heidelberg (2000)
25. Steffen, B.: Unifying models. In: Reischuk, R., Morvan, M. (eds.) STACS 1997. LNCS, vol. 1200, pp. 1–20. Springer, Heidelberg (1997)
26. Steffen, B., Margaria, T., Braun, V.: The Electronic Tool Integration platform: concepts and design. In: [28], pp. 9–30
27. Steffen, B., Narayan, P.: Full Life-Cycle Support for End-to-End Processes. IEEE Computer 40(11), 64–73 (2007)
28. Special Section on the Electronic Tool Integration Platform. Int. Journal on Software Tools for Technology Transfer 1(1+2) (November 1997)

Specialization and Instantiation Aspects of a Standard Process for Developing Educational Modules

Ellen Francine Barbosa and José Carlos Maldonado*

University of São Paulo – ICMC/USP
Av. do Trabalhador São-Carlense, 400 – P.O. Box 668
São Carlos (SP) Brazil – 13560-970
{francine,jcmaldon}@icmc.sc.usp.br

Abstract. Educational modules can be seen as relevant mechanisms to improve the learning processes in general. The goal is to produce quality educational products, capable of motivating the learners and effectively contribute to their knowledge construction process. Despite their relevance, none of the initiatives to address the problem of creating educational modules considers a systematic process for developing them. The establishment of a well-defined set of guidelines and supporting mechanisms should ease the distributed and cooperative work to create, reuse and evolve educational modules, taking also into account the impact on the learning process. In this work we present a standardized process we have established aiming at creating well-designed, highly flexible and configurable educational modules. We focus on the aspects of process specialization and instantiation, illustrating the practical application of the instantiated process by the development of an educational module for teaching the fundamentals of software testing. Particularly, the availability of learning facilities, allied to the development of testing tools, should facilitate the apprenticeship of specific testing theories and skills, promoting better dissemination conditions to the practical evaluation and application of testing strategies, both in academic and industrial sets. The produced module has been applied and preliminarily evaluated in terms of the learning effectiveness. The results obtained give us some evidences on the practical use of the standard process as a supporting mechanism to the development of effective educational modules.

1 Introduction

Several initiatives on using new computing technologies have been investigated in order to facilitate the learning process in general [7,12,13,15,19,22]. The challenge is to provide ways to establish quality educational products, capable of motivating the students and effectively contribute to their knowledge construction processes in active learning environments. Also, there is a need for a global

* The authors would like to thank the Brazilian funding agencies (FAPESP, CAPES, CNPq) and to the QualiPSo Project for their support.

T. Margaria and B. Steffen (Eds.): ISoLA 2008, CCIS 17, pp. 503–518, 2008.

education, capable of crossing international, cultural and social borders in order to prepare the students for the global market [3].

Educational modules, which consist of concise units of study delivered to students by using technologies and computational resources [3,2,1], can be explored in this perspective. Basically, they should provide: (1) effective support to traditional learning approaches; (2) effective support to non-traditional environments, motivating the transition from lecture-based to active learning; and (3) transferability to different institutions and learning environments.

Similar to software products, educational modules require the establishment of systematic development processes to produce reliable and quality products [3]. Despite its relevance, none of the initiatives to address the problem of creating educational modules considers a systematic process for developing them. In short, the development of such modules can involve developers from different domains, working on multi-disciplinary and heterogeneous teams, geographically dispersed or not. They should cooperate, sharing data and information regarding the project. Furthermore, there is a need for adaptability and reusability - educational modules should be seen as independent units of study, subject to be adaptable and reusable in different educational and training scenarios, according to parameters such as the learner's profile, instructor's preferences, learning goals and course length, among others.

Motivated by this scenario, we have investigated the establishment of a systematic process for developing educational modules, aiming at providing a well-defined set of guidelines and supporting mechanisms to create, reuse and evolve them. The Standard Process for Developing Educational Modules [3] is based on ISO/IEC 12207, taking into account issues of content modeling [21,2], practices from instructional design [11], and aspects of distributed and cooperative work [20]. As part of the standard, we have also proposed an integrated modeling approach for developing educational content – *IMA-CID* (Integrated Modeling Approach – Conceptual, Instructional and Didactic) [2]. In our research line, at the very end, we intend to provide a context for "open learning materials", which could facilitate the cooperation and use in different institutions and learning environments and effectively support new learning approaches.

In this paper, we focus on aspects of the standard process specialization and instantiation. We illustrate the practical application of our instantiated process by the development of an educational module for teaching the fundamentals of software testing. We consider the testing area since it is one of the most relevant activities to guarantee the quality of the software under development [24] but, at the same time, it is a difficult topic to learn or teach without the appropriate supporting mechanisms [14]. Since our proposed mechanisms are domain-independent, in short-term we intend to explore them into the development of educational modules for other testing-related topics, such as formal methods (involving, for instance, FSM-based testing [25]), and the integrated teaching of programming and testing [4]. Particularly, the availability of learning facilities, allied to the development of testing tools, would promote better dissemination conditions to the practical evaluation and application of testing strategies, both in academic and industrial contexts. Educational modules for other Software Engineering sub-areas (e.g., requirement analysis, maintenance), Computer Science areas (e.g., databases, distributed systems), and general areas (e.g., mathematics, physics, biology) can also be produced.

The remainder of this paper is organized as follows. In Section 2 we summarize the supporting mechanisms we have proposed in the context of educational modules – a standard process for developing educational modules and an approach for modeling educational content. Aspects of the standard process specialization and instantiation are discussed in Section 3. In Section 4 we illustrate the application of the instantiated process for developing an educational module for the software testing domain. We focus on the content modeling activity and on the results from preliminary evaluations on the effectiveness of the produced modules we have conducted. Finally, in Section 5 we summarize our contributions and discuss the perspectives for further work.

2 Developing Educational Modules

Educational modules are concise units of study, composed by theoretical and practical content which can be delivered to learners by using technological and computational resources [3,2,1]. For theoretical content, we use books, papers, web information, slides, class annotations, audio, video, and so on. Practical content is the instructional activities and associated evaluations, as well as their resulting artifacts (e.g., executable programs, experimental studies, collaborative discussions). Theoretical and practical content are integrated in terms of learning materials. Learning environments, presentation tools and mechanisms to capture classroom lectures and to support discussion spaces and collaborative work are examples of the required infrastructure for delivering the learning materials.

2.1 The Standard Process

The Standard Process for Educational Modules is based on the International Standard ISO/IEC 12207, tailored to the context of educational modules by including aspects of content modeling [2,21], practices from instructional design [11], and issues of distributed and cooperative work [20].

Basically, the standard establishes a set of processes that can be employed to acquire, supply, develop, deliver, operate, and maintain educational modules. Three categories of processes are defined: (1) the primary processes deal with the main activities and tasks performed during the life cycle of an educational module; (2) the supporting processes support other processes and contribute to the success and quality of the development project, and (3) the organizational processes are employed by an organization to establish, implement and improve an underlying structure made up of associated life cycle processes and personnel. Figure 1 shows the general structure of the standard. In dashed rectangles are the processes adapted from the ISO/IEC 12207. In dotted rectangles are the processes adapted from the standard process for geographically dispersed

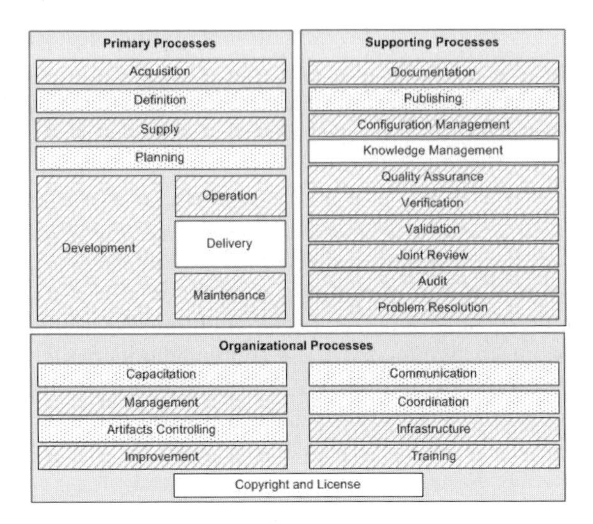

Fig. 1. Main Structure of the Standard Process for Educational Modules

working groups [20]. In white rectangles are the processes specifically developed to the context of teaching and learning.

In the establishment of the primary processes we have considered the main principles and practices from instructional design. In short, the goals of instructional design are achieved by means of five phases: Analysis, Design, Development, Implementation, and Evaluation. These phases correspond to the ADDIE Model, which serves as the basis for the most of the approaches for instructional design [11]. These practices are spread out through the activities and tasks related to the primary processes. For instance, the *Operation* and *Delivery* processes address issues of the implementation phase of the ADDIE Model. Supporting and organizational processes are established in a similar way.

2.2 The *IMA-CID* Approach

Particularly, in the case of the *Development Process*, besides the practices of instructional design, aspects from educational content modeling are also explored [2,21]. Content modeling plays a fundamental role into the development process of educational modules. It helps the author to determine the main concepts to be taught, providing a systematic way to structure the relevant parts of the subject knowledge domain. Also, how the content is structured impacts on the effectiveness, reusability, evolvability and adaptability of the module.

In spite of its relevance, few approaches are specifically designed for modeling educational content. Actually, the establishment of models for representing such content involves several different issues. For instance, we have to consider the specific characteristics related to the knowledge domain, to define the practical tasks and the evaluation mechanisms that will be applied to students, and to establish pedagogical sequences for presenting the modeled information. Since there is not a set of predefined requirements for content modeling, each model deals with different perspectives that can be suitable for a given learning scenario but inadequate for others [2].

In this sense, we have proposed *IMA-CID* (*Integrated Modeling Approach – Conceptual, Instructional and Didactic*) [2,1] – an integrated approach for modeling educational content. *IMA-CID* is composed by a set of models, each one dealing with specific aspects of the development of educational content: (1) the *conceptual model* corresponds to a high-level description of the knowledge domain, representing the main concepts and the relationships among them; (2) the *instructional model* characterizes what kind of additional information (e.g., facts, principles, procedures, examples, and exercises) can be used to develop learning materials; and (3) the *didactic model* characterizes the prerequisites and sequences of presentation among conceptual and instructional elements.

We have also introduced the idea of *open specifications*, which provide support for the definition of dynamic contexts of learning [2]. Depending on aspects such as audience, learning goals and course length, distinct ways for presenting and navigating through the same content can be required. An open specification allows to represent all sequences of presentation in the same didactic model. So, from a single model, several versions of the same content can be generated according to different pedagogical aspects. Moreover, when an educational module is implemented based on an open specification (*open implementation*), its navigation paths can be defined by the user, in "execution time", based on the learner's understanding and feedback, for instance.

3 Standard Process Specialization and Instantiation

The standard process is responsible for the establishment of a unique development structure to be adopted and followed by the entire organization [3,1]. However, changes in organizational procedures, educational paradigms and principles, learning requirements, development methods and strategies, as well as the size and complexity of the projects, among other aspects, impact the way an educational module is produced. To be adopted in particular projects, the processes should be defined case by case, considering specific features of each project.

Process specialization and instantiation have also been explored in order to apply the standard process into specific learning environments and organizations. In short, the definition of a process for developing a given educational module should consider its adequacy to: (1) the involved technologies, supporting mechanisms and budget; (2) the domain of the educational application; (3) the characteristics of the module; (4) the maturity level of the development team; and (5) the characteristics of the organization. As a result, processes into different levels of abstraction are defined. The main aspects of the standard process instantiation and specialization as well as its application for developing an educational module for the software testing domain are discussed next.

3.1 Specializing the Standard Process

In the same line as the CMMI Model for software development, a capability maturity model for educational modules development – the *CMMI/Educational* – has been proposed and used as a supporting mechanism to the standard process specialization [3,1]. The main goals are to guaranteeing that distributed projects can be developed with unlike maturity level teams and improve each working group capability.

The *CMMI/Educational* is adapted from CMMI for the context of teaching and learning. A capability maturity model for geographically dispersed software development [20] is also considered to establishing the tasks and practices related to the distributed and collaborative creation of the modules. Both continuous and staged representations are addressed.

Similar to the staged representation of CMMI, *CMMI/Educational* establishes five maturity levels. Two new process areas (PAs) are included at Level 2: *Distributed Knowledge Management* and *Distributed Infrastructure Management.* At Level 3, three new PAs are established: *Knowledge Evolution Management, Domain Experts Interaction* and *Distributed Monitoring and Management of Educational Modules Utilization.* At Level 4, we include the PA of *Quantitative Management of Educational Modules Utilization.* Finally, at Level 5, we define a new practice – *Change Management of Educational Paradigms and Principles* –, included as part of the PA *Organizational Innovation and Deployment.* For instance, the PA of *Knowledge Evolution Management* is responsible for: (1) identifying, choosing and evaluating the new information related to the subject knowledge domain; and (2) establishing and maintaining the supporting mechanisms to systematically integrate the new information into the module.

By determining the correspondence between the standard process aspects and the PAs of the capability maturity model, we can identify the process categories that would require more attention and generate the standard process specializations. The specialization of a given maturity level is generated by excluding the activities of higher levels. So, the specialization of the second level does not contain the activities of the third, fourth and fifth levels. Instead, it contains only the activities related to the PAs of Level 2.

3.2 Instantiating the Standard Process

An instance of a process should take in account the development and organizational environment; it may address specific features of a particular project. Process instantiation consists of the selection and allocation of development methods and techniques as well as human, technological and computational resources.

In order to illustrate the standard process instantiation we consider its application in a specific type of educational projects. Basically, these projects should be conducted in an academic institution, involving the development of educational modules to be used in traditional classes. The produced modules can be applied either as part of an one-semester course, in the academic institution; as a short-course, a tutorial or an invited talk, in scientific events; or as a training course, at industrial organizations.

We have defined, among others: (1) the human resources and their roles in the process; (2) the produced and consumed artifacts; (3) the life cycle model and development methods and techniques; and (4) the automated tools and supporting mechanisms for the process. Regarding the human resources and their roles in the process, the following actors have been defined to compose the development team:

– *Domain expert*: Provides support and clears doubts related to the establishment of components and relevant parts of the educational module. Plays a fundamental role in content modeling, particularly to constructing the conceptual model and to determining the knowledge categories. Also, performs the instructional validation of the module.

– *Project manager*: Assigns activities, integrates results, specifies the module's metadata, and defines the validation mechanisms to be adopted.

– *Team coordinator*: Coordinates the development team, fostering the communication between team members and the project manager.

– *Version manager*: Responsible for maintaining the different versions of the module.

– *Developer*: Responsible for the module development. Several different roles can be assigned to him/her: (1) *analyst*, responsible for specifying the module requirements and, also, for its validation; (2) *instructional designer*, responsible for modeling the educational content and for designing the module interface; (3) *implementer*, responsible for implementing the module, i.e., for editing the content, for integrating the multimedia components, for verifying and for testing the module; (4) *operator*, responsible for providing the operational support for the module users; and (5) *maintainer*, responsible for the maintaining the module.

– *Technician*: Establishes and manages the technological and computational resources used in the project. Provides technical support to the development and delivery of the educational module.

– *Instructor*: Responsible for establishing the instructional needs, for delivering the module and for monitoring its use. Also, can help on verification and validation activities.

Figure 2 illustrates the relationship among team members as well as the main roles assigned to them. Notice that different roles can be assigned to the same person. On the other hand, several persons can be assigned to the same role. Produced and consumed artifacts are also illustrated.

As the life cycle model to be adopted through the projects we chose the ADDIE Model [11]. It is specifically designed for the development of educational products, establishing mechanisms for the systematic application of practices and principles of instructional design. For modeling the educational content, we chose the *IMA-CID* approach [2].

In terms of technological and computational resources, tools and mechanisms to automate and support the instantiated process should be selected according to the roles they would play in the context of each specific project. Two basic

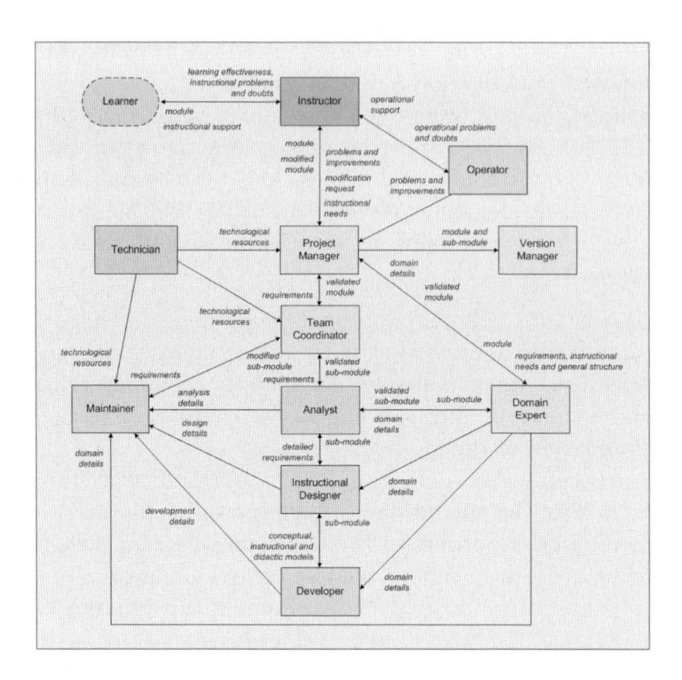

Fig. 2. Development Team and Assigned Roles

categories of tools should be analyzed. *Authoring tools* support the creation of the educational content, taking into account representation, integration and management aspects of the subject knowledge domain. We consider as authoring tools: (1) tools for modeling the educational content; (2) tools for knowledge integration; and (3) tools for editing the content.

Educational tools consist of the required infrastructure for integrating the learning materials and for delivering/publishing them to the learners. They are also responsible for providing support to perform practical tasks and evaluations. We consider as educational tools: (1) presentation tools, which support delivery of learning materials; (2) collaborative tools, which support collaborative work and augment communication and discussion among instructors and learners; (3) evaluative tools, which support the evaluation of learner's performance; and (4) capture tools, which provide ways to transform the content of a traditional lecture into browsable, searchable and extensible digital media that serves both short- and long-term educational goals. One essential activity during the instantiation process is the identification and analysis of supporting tools to the standard process. The results of this activity constitute the alternatives to instantiating the standard process. Therefore, each instance of the standard process establishes a specific set of automated tools and supporting mechanisms to be applied. In our instantiated process, we adopted specific tools – *WebCT* [15] and *Moodle* [22], and generic tools – web and *PowerPoint* (when the use of educational tools is not required) as presentation tools. As a collaborative tool, we adopted *CoWeb* [12]. As the infrastructure for capturing the classes, we chose the *eClass* environment [7]. As a support for authoring the educational content, we adopted generic editing tools: *Word*, *PowerPoint*, *FrontPage*, *Visio*, *LaTeX*. To support communication between the members of the development team we chose electronic mail and *CoWeb*.

Taking into account the supporting tools to the standard process and the requirements of the project under development (software testing educational module for traditional classes) we then define the instantiated process to a particular project, since each project may require itself specific tools and related mechanisms. Notice that some constraints are to be considered. For instance, the *IMA-CID* models had to be manually developed since the existent modeling tools do not incorporate the extensions required to construct them. Thus, the development of automated tools for the *IMA-CID* models is one of the research lines we intend to further explore.

4 Applying the Instantiated Process

In this section we illustrate the application of the instantiated process for developing an educational module for the software testing domain. Based on the instantiated process, we have conducted the following tasks:

- *Determination of the current state of learning* (Definition Process): This task consists of identifying the lack of knowledge and skills observed when teaching a certain topic. The main problems are identified based on the previous experience of the instructor. Considering the testing domain, for instance, we have identified problems related to the characterization of testing goals and limitations, testing steps and phases, testing requirements, testing criteria, testing tools, among others.
- *Definition of learning goals and related skills* (Definition Process): From the problems and needs previously identified, the main goals to be reached by using the module can be established. For the testing module, we intended to provide a broad, deep view on the testing activity, addressing both theoretical and practical aspects. The idea was to provide a good knowledge on the main testing techniques, criteria and strategies, as well as skills on their practical application by using testing tools.
- *Definition of the module structure* (Planning Process): This task consists of identifying the materials that have already been developed for the subject domain as well as other sources of information related to the topic. From this investigation and from the learning goals previously identified, the module structure can be established. For software testing, besides the existent material we had, we took into account the Computing Curricula of ACM [17] and the recommendations of SWEBOK (Software Engineering Body of Knowledge) [16]. The module was divided in 16 sub-modules, three of them designed for motivating, illustrating and practicing the concepts addressed into the other sub-modules. The module structure was defined in terms of a conceptual map. For the sake of space, this structure is not presented here. Details can be found in [1].

– *Establishment of the development team* (Planning Process): The development team of the testing module was composed by three members: (1) the teacher of the testing course, acting as the domain expert as well as the instructor of the module; (2) a graduate student, performing the roles of project manager, version manager, coordinator and developer; and (3) an undergraduate student, acting as developer and technician.

– *Determination of methodologies, standards and tools* (Planning Process): The methodologies, standards and tools adopted into the development of the module should be in agreement with those established in the instantiated process. So, as the development methods and techniques we selected ADDIE Model [11] and *IMA-CID* approach. As the metadata standard we adopted IEEE LOM (Learning Object Metadata) [18]. As the automated support, we adopted: *Word*, *PowerPoint*, *FrontPage*, *Visio*, *LaTeX*, *WebCT*, *Moodle*, *CoWeb*, and *e-Class*. Additionally to the authoring and educational tools, specific tools for the subject knowledge domain of the educational module were also considered. For the testing domain, we chose *Proteum* [9], and *PokeTool* [8] as the testing tools to be adopted. The main goal was to enable the application of basic testing concepts in realistic situations, fostering training scenarios and promoting exchange of technology between industry and academia.

– *Audience analysis* (Development Process): This task consists of determining the target audience for the module under development. The audience of the testing module is composed by graduate and undergraduate students, as well as professionals from industry. Although each group of learners can require different ways for presenting and navigating through the module, the content is essentially the same. So, the module should be as flexible as possible in order to be suitable to different profiles without having to modify its structure significantly. As pre-requirements for the testing module, the learners should have basic knowledge on data structures and programming languages, as well as general knowledge on software development techniques, methodologies and paradigms. Also, the learners must be motivated for doing practical assignments in cooperation with other students, for presenting and discussing their ideas using collaborative tools, and for researching related topics on the web.

– *Content modeling* (Development Process): This task consists of modeling the content related to the educational module. In Section 4.1 we specifically address the content modeling by applying the *IMA-CID* approach.

– *Interface design* (Development Process): This task consists of specifying and designing the module interface. In our project, we adopted the *ADV's* (Abstract Data Views) proposed as part of the OOHDM Model [23]. The dynamic aspects of the module were specified by means of *ADV Charts*, representing the transformations at the interface level and their impact on presenting the information items and instructional elements.

– *Implementation, integration and testing* (Development Process): The implementation and integration tasks consist of translating the content models and the interface previously designed to an implementation environment in order to construct the educational module. The testing module was developed according to the characteristics of open specification/implementation [2], by using general editing tools, as established by the instantiated process. Concepts, facts, principles, procedures, examples and exercises were modeled and implemented as a set of slides, integrated to HTML pages, text documents, learning environments and testing tools. Regarding the testing task, the module was evaluated according to the following perspectives: (1) standard verification, checking the module against the interface standards established; (2) editorial verification, checking the module against grammar errors; and (3) functional verification, checking the module against logical errors through the navigation.

– *Delivery* (Delivery Process) and *Identification of problems and improvements* (Delivery Process): These tasks consist of applying and evaluating the produced module. As a result, it is possible to determine the module strengths and weaknesses, identifying the needs for further improvements. In Section 4.2 we discuss the preliminary evaluations we have conducted on the testing module.

4.1 Content Modeling

IMA-CID was applied as part of the development of the educational module for software testing. The *IMA-CID* models were constructed for each one of the 16 sub-modules that composes the module. For the sake of space, here we focus on the didactic model, named *HMBS/Didactic*, developed for a particular subject of the *testing techniques* sub-module – the mutation analysis criterion [10].

HMBS/Didactic is based on the HMBS (Hypertext Model Based on Statecharts) Model [26]. In short, HMBS uses the structure and execution semantics of Statecharts to specify both the structural organization and the browsing semantics of hyperdocuments. Figure 3 illustrates part of the *HMBS/Didactic*[1]. It corresponds to an *open specification*, in which all possible sequences of presentation among the modeled objects are represented. Aiming at representing open specifications, we extended HMBS with the notion of *DD* (Dynamically Defined) *states*. Basically, all OR substates of a *DD* state (OR_{DD}) are totally connected to each other, i.e., from any substate of a *DD* state X, we can reach all other substates of X. For the sake of legibility, transitions and events are implicitly represented. We also established an hierarchy of *DD*-superstates – leaving a *DD* state X can active the OR_{DD} states from the hierarchy of *DD*-superstates of X.

Consider, for instance, the `MutationAnalysisDetails` state. By exploring the notion of *DD* states, the `MutationAnalysisDetails` substates (OR_{DD} states) – `MutantOperator`, `MutantGeneral`, `MutationScore`, `Application` and `ApproachesGeneral` – are all connected to each other by implicit transitions, which are responsible for establishing the navigation paths among them. From `MutantOperator` we can get to the states `MutantGeneral`, `MutationScore`, `Application` and `ApproachesGeneral` (and vice versa). Similarly, consider the `Mutant` state. From `Mutant` we are able to get to `MutantClassification` (and vice versa). Actually, both states are substates of `MutantGeneral` (*DD* state) and, therefore, they are connected to each other by means of implicit transitions.

[1] Explanatory and exploratory were not considered.

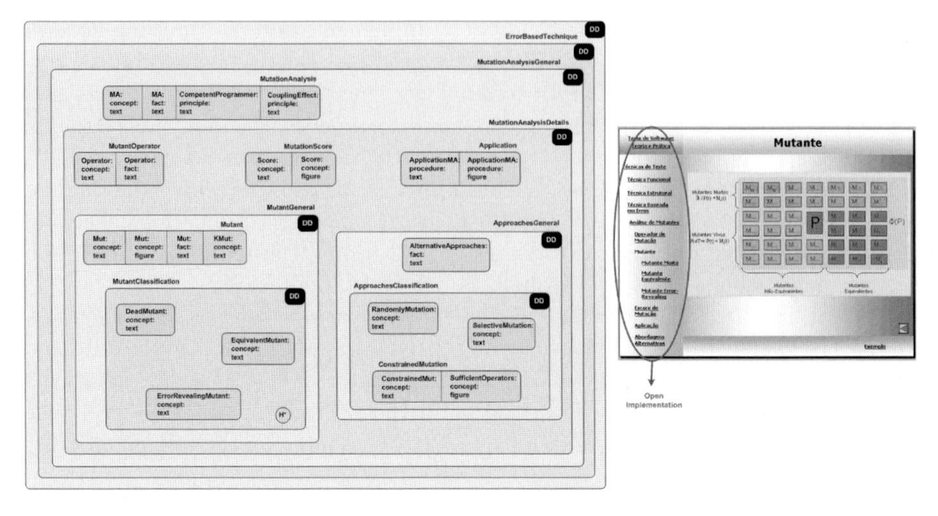

Fig. 3. Didactic Model / Slides for Mutation Analysis: Open Specification

We can also explore the idea of an hierarchy of DD-superstates. For instance, consider the sequence (MutantGeneral, MutationAnalysisDetails, MutationAnalysisGeneral, ErrorBasedTechnique, TestingTechnique, SoftwareTesting_TheoryPractice) as the hierarchy of DD-superstates of the Mutant state. According to this hierarchy, from Mutant we can reach all OR_{DD} states of MutationAnalysisDetails. To define the full set of states we can reach from Mutant, the same analysis should be carried out for all states of the hierarchy of DD-superstates of MutantGeneral. Notice that we cannot get to the states AlternativeApproaches and ApproachesClassification from the Mutant state. Indeed, ApproachesGeneral does not pertain to the hierarchy of DD-superstates of Mutant.

Besides the open specification, a *partially open specification* and a *close specification* were also considered in order to define the didactic model for mutation analysis. Basically, in a partially open specification, while some sequences of presentation can be established in "execution time", others are previously defined by the domain expert and/or the instructor during the development of the module. Indeed, instead of having just implicit transitions, the idea is to make some of them be explicitly represented in the didactic model. On the other hand, in a close specification all sequences are predefined, that is, just a fixed sequence of presentation is available in the module. In this case, the transitions would be explicitly represented.

Notice the sequences of presentation derived from partially open specifications and from close specifications represent subsets of the total set of sequences established by an open specification. The decision on which kind of specification to use should be based on the users (learners and instructors) as well as on the expected characteristics of the module. For instance, one strength of open specifications is the flexibility to navigate the material according to the feedback and questions of the audience. On the other side, the instructor has to make sure to achieve the objectives of the lessons in order to keep the learners localized. Indeed, while for less experienced instructors a close specification (and implementation) seems to be the better choice, for the most experienced ones, an open specification would be an adequate alternative too.

4.2 Evaluating the Educational Module for Software Testing

Figure 4 shows the main components of the testing module and their integration. The module was produced by applying the instance of the standard process we have defined. The content was modeled according to the *IMA-CID* approach.

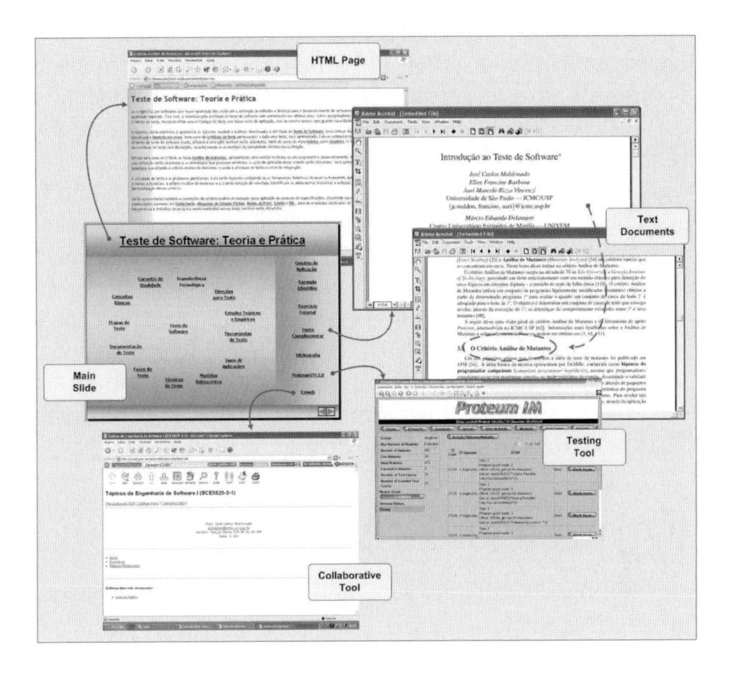

Fig. 4. Educational Module for Software Testing

To provide a preliminary evaluation on the effectiveness of the testing module, it was applied as part of a three-hour short-course on software testing for a group of about 60 undergraduate students with previous knowledge of software engineering. We focused on theoretical aspects of software testing, providing an introductory perspective on the subject. Practical aspects were illustrated but, due to time constraints, there was no direct participation by the audience on using any of the materials. The effects of our approach were informally evaluated by applying a voluntary survey to the students after they had finished the course. The survey covered the students' attitude toward: (1) content, regarding the concepts, additional information, examples and exercises used in the module; (2) usability, in terms of the interface of the module; (3) navigational aspects; and (4) general aspects about the module. In general, we could observe a positive attitude toward the flexibility provided by the produced module. Furthermore, instructor's responses were also observed by his comments after using the module. The possibility of having defined the sequences of navigation through the module during the "execution time", based on the learner's understanding and feedback, was a significant point highlighted.

We also applied the testing module in two one-semester undergraduate courses at ICMC/USP. The main goal of both courses were to explore the fundamentals of V&V. The module was delivered in expositive classes, exploring the theoretical aspects of testing activities and related supporting tools. At the end of each class, practical exercises were proposed. Aiming at evaluating the module, we have replicated an extended version of the Basili & Selby experiment [6], originally used for comparing V&V techniques, now considering the educational context. The experiments in each course involved 36 (9 teams) and 52 (13 teams) students, respectively. The results were mainly analyzed in terms of the students' ability and uniformity on: (1) detecting existent faults; (2) generating test cases; and (3) covering the test requirements. They gave us very preliminary evidences on the learning effectiveness provided by the module produced. Details can be found in [5].

The results obtained so far provide some evidences on the practical use of the standard process and the *IMA-CID* approach as supporting mechanisms to the development of effective educational modules. However, it is important to conduct more systematic and controlled experiments to validate our ideas. Such experiments have already been planned for the next term, involving different courses on software testing, offered to graduate and undergraduate students at ICMC/USP as well as to professionals from local industries. Both students and instructors' attitudes toward the module should be evaluated.

5 Conclusions and Further Work

The main contribution of this paper is to motivate the use of systematic processes and modeling mechanisms for creating well-designed, highly flexible and configurable educational modules. Such modules would provide: (1) effective support to traditional learning approaches; (2) effective support to non-traditional environments, motivating the transition from lecture-based to active learning; and (3) transferability to different institutions and learning environments.

Process specialization and instantiation have been explored in order to apply the standard process we have proposed into specific learning environments and organizations. Indeed, changes in organizational procedures, educational paradigms and principles, learning requirements, development methods and strategies, as well as the size and complexity of the projects, among other aspects, impact the way an educational module should be produced. To be adopted in particular projects, the process should be defined case by case, considering specific features of each project. As a result, processes into different levels of abstraction are defined. The main aspects of the standard process instantiation and specialization as well as its application for developing an educational module for the software testing domain were discussed.

As a further work, we intend to focus on the development of educational modules to be applied in non-traditional environments, motivating the transition from lecture-based to active learning. The input of learners in the very early stages of the module development, similarly to the participative approach in software development, is another point to be further investigated. Particularly for the testing domain, the availability of distance learning facilities and testing tools would promote better learning and dissemination conditions to the practical evaluation and application of testing strategies, both in academia and industry.

We are also motivated to keep evolving and evaluating the mechanisms we have proposed in future offerings of testing courses. We are now working on the development of an educational module for the integrated teaching of testing and programming foundations in introductory Computer Science courses [4]. The idea is to gradually introduce the testing fundamentals while the programming concepts are being taught to the students. Since the proposed mechanisms can be applied to different domains, we are also interested in using them to develop and evaluate educational modules for other areas and broader projects.

At the very end, we intend to establish a culture for "open educational modules" so that the use and evolution of them by a broader community would be better motivated and become a reality. The existence of a well-defined process to systematize the development of educational modules and, at the same time, flexible enough to be adaptable to different knowledge domains and development teams, is a relevant issue to be addressed in crossing international, cultural and social borders in order to prepare the learners to be successful in a global market, with diverse groups of people.

References

1. Barbosa, E.F.: Uma Contribuição ao Processo de Desenvolvimento e Modelagem de Módulos Educacionais. PhD thesis, ICMC-USP, São Carlos, SP (March 2004) (in Portuguese)
2. Barbosa, E.F., Maldonado, J.C.: An integrated content modeling approach for educational modules. In: IFIP 19th World Computer Congress – International Conference on Education for the 21st Century, Santiago, Chile, pp. 17–26 (August 2006)
3. Barbosa, E.F., Maldonado, J.C.: Towards the establishment of a standard process for developing educational modules. In: 36th Annual Frontiers in Education Conference (FIE 2006), San Diego, CA, p. 6. CD-ROM (October 2006)
4. Barbosa, E.F., Silva, M.A.G., Corte, C.K.D., Maldonado, J.C.: Integrated teaching of programming foundations and software testing. In: 38th Annual Frontiers in Education Conference (FIE 2008), Saratoga Springs, NY, p. 6 (October 2008) (to appear)
5. Barbosa, E.F., Souza, S.R.S., Maldonado, J.C.: An experience on applying learning mechanisms for teaching inspection and software testing. In: 21st Conference on Software Engineering Education and Training (CSEET 2008), Charleston, SC, pp. 189–196 (April 2008)
6. Basili, V., Selby, R.W.: Comparing the Effectiveness of Software Testing Strategies. IEEE Transactions on Software Engineering SE-13(12), 1278–1296 (1987)
7. Brotherton, J.A., Abowd, G.D.: Lessons learned from eClass: Assessing automated capture and access in the classroom. ACM Transactions on Computer-Human Interaction 11(2), 121–155 (2004)

8. Chaim, M.L.: PokeTool – Uma ferramenta para suporte ao teste estrutural de programas baseado em análise de fluxo de dados. Master's thesis, DCA/FEEC/UNICAMP, Campinas, SP (April 1991) (in Portuguse)
9. Delamaro, M.E., Maldonado, J.C., Mathur, A.P.: Interface mutation: An approach for integration testing. IEEE Transactions on Software Engineering 27(3), 228–247 (2001)
10. DeMillo, R.A., Lipton, R.J., Sayward, F.G.: Hints on test data selection: Help for the practicing programmer. IEEE Computer 11(4), 34–43 (1978)
11. Dick, W., Carey, L., Carey, J.O.: The Systematic Design of Instruction, 5th edn. Longman (2001)
12. Dieberger, A., Guzdial, M.: CoWeb – experiences with collaborative web spaces. In: Lueg, C., Fisher, D. (eds.) From Usenet to CoWebs: Interacting with Social Information Spaces. Springer, Heidelberg (2003)
13. Downes, S.: Learning objects: Resources for distance education worldwide. International Review of Research in Open and Distance Learning 2(1) (July 2001)
14. Edwards, S.H.: Improving student performance by evaluating how well students test their own programs. Journal on Educational Resources in Computing 3(3), 24 (2003)
15. Goldberg, M.W., Salari, S., Swoboda, P.: World Wide Web - Course Tool: An environment for building WWW-based courses. Computer Networks and ISDN Systems 28(7–11), 1219–1231 (1996)
16. IEEE Computer Society. Guide to the Software Engineering Body of Knowledge: Trial version (1.0) (May 2001), http://www.swebok.org/
17. IEEE Computer Society and Association for Computing Machinery. Computing Curricula – Computer Science Volume, Final Report (December 2001), http://www.computer.org/education/cc2001/
18. IEEE Learning Technology Standards Committee. Learning Object Metadata (LOM) (June 2002)
19. John, W.C., Toto, R., Lim, K.Y.: Introducing Tablet PCs: Initial results from the classroom. In: 36th Annual Frontiers in Education Conference (FIE 2006), San Diego, CA, p. 6. CD-ROM (October 2006)
20. Maidantchik, C.L.L., Rocha, A.R.: Managing a worldwide software process. In: Workshop on Global Software Development – International Conference on Software Engineering (ICSE 2002), Orlando, FL (May 2002)
21. Mayorga, J.I., Verdejo, M.F., Rodríguez-Artacho, M., Calero, M.Y.: Domain modelling to support educational web-based authoring. In: TET 1999 Congress, Norway (June 1999)
22. Moodle, D.G.: Moodle – a free, open source course management system for online learning (2006), http://moodle.org/
23. Schwabe, D., Rossi, G.: The object-oriented hypermedia design model. Communications of the ACM 38(8), 45–46 (1995)
24. Shepard, T., Lamb, M., Kelly, D.: More testing should be taught. Communications of the ACM 44(6), 103–108 (2001)
25. Simão, A.S., Ambrósio, A.M., Fabbri, S.C.P.F., Amaral, A.S., Martins, E., Maldonado, J.C.: Plavis/FSM: an environment to integrate FSM-based testing tools. In: XIX Simpósio Brasileiro de Engenharia de Software (SBES 2005) – Sessão de Ferramentas, Uberlândia, MG, pp. 1–6 (October 2005)
26. Turine, M.A.S., Oliveira, M.C.F., Masiero, P.C.: Designing structured hypertext with HMBS. In: VIII International ACM Hypertext Conference (Hypertext 1997), Southampton, UK, pp. 241–256 (April 1997)

A Formal Framework for Modeling Context-Aware Behavior in Ubiquitous Computing

Isabel Cafezeiro[1], José Viterbo[2], Alexandre Rademaker[2], Edward Hermann Haeusler[2], and Markus Endler[2]

[1] Departamento de Ciência da Computação
Universidade Federal Fluminense
Rua Passo da Patria, 156 - Bloco E - 3 andar, Boa Viagem
24210-240 – Niterói – Brasil
[2] Departamento de Informática
Pontifícia Universidade Católica do Rio de Janeiro
Rua Marquês de São Vicente 225, Gávea
22453-900 – Rio de Janeiro – Brasil

Abstract. A formal framework to contextualize ontologies, proposed in [3], provides several ways of composing ontologies, contexts or both. The proposed algebra can be used to model applications in which the meaning of an entity depends on environment constraints or where dynamic changes in the environment have to be considered. In this article we use this algebra to formalize the problem of interpreting context information in ubiquitous systems, based on a concrete scenario. The main goal is to verify, on one hand, how the formal approach can contribute with a better understanding of the fundamental concepts of ubiquitous computing and, on the other hand, if this formal framework is flexible and rich enough to adequately express specific characteristics of the concrete application domain and scenario.

1 Introduction

In the last years, Ubiquitous Computing has been the focus of much research, most of which in topics related to system's development. Despite that, until now, very few works can be found on formal models for this area, where the main challenge is to precisely model — and reason about — the interactions between a system and its environment, and the fact that this environment can change in unpredictable ways.

In particular, context-awareness, i.e. the ability of applications to detect changes in their environment and to adapt their behavior accordingly, has soon become the paramount programming paradigm for such systems. As a consequence, more recently, many researchers have attempted to define, classify or model the notions of context and context-awareness. Nevertheless, most of these definitions are informal and thus lack a solid, mathematical foundation. Therefore, according to several authors [1,5], there is still demand for a comprehensive

T. Margaria and B. Steffen (Eds.): ISoLA 2008, CCIS 17, pp. 519–533, 2008.

formal framework for understanding and working with ubiquitous and context-aware computing.

For such a framework to be useful, however, it should ideally: (a) closely reflect the intrinsic characteristics of ubiquitous systems, clearly describing their relevant issues, and (b) provide means of describing (and solving) concrete application problems by allowing a suitable interpretation adaptated from the results of the underlying theory.

In [3] we have proposed a formal framework to contextualize ontologies, providing several ways of composing ontologies, contexts or both. This algebra is suitable for modeling applications in which the meaning of an entity depends on environment constraints or where dynamic changes in the environment should be considered. It emphasizes the relationships of contexts with entities — considering that contexts are essential to assign meaning to entities — and supports new forms of representing context for applications that consider dynamic changes of the environment. In this article we use this algebra to formalize the problem of interpreting context information in ubiquitous computing systems.

Through this experiment we intend to show not only how the formal approach may contribute with a precise understanding of the concepts and fundamental problems of a specific application domain, but also, how a concrete application domain can be used to assess the flexibility and expressiveness of a formal language. We believe that this is essential for reducing the gap between the theoretical framework and its possible applications, and for validating its mechanisms in a concrete and complex application domain.

The formal framework considered here is founded in Category Theory [4,8]. Along this article, though, we avoided the use of the categorical terminology, preseting concepts in an informal way. In [2] and [3] the reader can find the formalization of the algebra and associations between categorical concepts and the ontology terminology.

This article is organized as follows. In Section 2 we describe other efforts to formalize ubiquitous and context-aware systems. In Section 3 we discuss the algebra of contextualized ontologies. In Section 4 we describe ubiquitous environments and present a specific scenario. In Section 5 we apply the algebra to formalize the ontologies discussed in this scenario. Finally, in Section 6 we present our conclusions.

2 Related Work

In the last few years, some research has been undertaken towards formalizing ubiquitous and context-aware computing. Roman et al [6,10] have proposed Context UNITY, a dialect of Mobile UNITY with constructs that allow the reasoning about the manipulation of context, as well as the interaction of systems with the context. Their goal was to specify applications that use flexible mechanisms for defining individual contexts, which are transparently maintained as the environment evolves. In their approach, context is defined from the perspective of each component and hence, not every component sees the same context. On one hand, the variable-assignment-notation of Context UNITY — used to express context definitions and resolutions — is quite expressive, but on the other hand, it is quite complex to be used for larger and more sophisticated context-aware applications.

A completely different approach is pursued in [15], where the authors present an extension of the classical action system formalism with the notion of context. In their formalism it is possible to prove some system properties using standard action system proof techniques. What the authors call a *Context-Aware Action System* is built from a parallel or prioritized composition of simpler action system components, where the context dependency of each component is expressed as a collection of relations that constrain when the computation of the component can take place, and how its internal actions are affected by the context variables. By applying their formalism in two small — but concrete — context-aware examples (i.e. a reminding and a messaging service), they show that their formal framework can be helpful to modularly describe systems and infer some simple context-aware properties.

Birkedal et al [1] investigated the modeling of context-aware systems using Bigraphical Reactive System (BRS) Models (i.e. graphical models of mobile computation that emphasize both locality and connectivity and a set of reaction rules that rewrite bigraphs to bigraphs. According to the authors, the main goals of the theory of Bigraphical Reactive Systems are to model ubiquitous systems on one hand, and to be a meta-theory encompassing existing calculi for concurrency and mobility (such as CCS, π-calculus) on the other hand. Hence, this work tried to push forward the first goal. Interestingly, however, the main finding was that naively modeling context-aware systems as BSRs is very complex and awkward. Instead, they have proposed a model named *Plato-graphical* model, where the system's perceived context and the actual context are represented as distinct but overlapping BRSs. Using their formalism they described a simple location-aware printing service, and concluded that the resulting model was very well suited for modeling the location-aware systems.

Our proposal differs from Context UNITY, but can serve as a model for the later. In fact, UNITY has a precise Category Theoretic based semantics that fits quite well in our approach and allows a better comparison between the approaches. While Context UNITY puts the context information inside the specification (by means of the *context* section), our approach maps the specification into each of the environments listed in this very context section. Therefore, one can say that our approach is structurally and semantically richer than Context UNITY. On the other hand, the approach using Context-Aware Action System is more related to the way current context-aware systems are designed, i.e. in which some of their actions are triggered, or inhibited, by specific conditions of the environment. Hence, this approach is much more related to an operational view of systems (e.g. syncronous composition on sequential processes) than ours, but which can be adequately interpreted as categorial co-limits induced by the actions alphabet. Finally, the approach based on Bigraphical Reactive Systems, as long as it serves as a model for process algebras in a true-concurrency style of semantics, can be regarded as being at a similar level of abstraction as ours. However, since the bigraphical representation model seems to lack compositionality, we believe that our approach is more adequate for modeling complex systems.

3 The Algebra of Contextualized Ontologies

The algebra of contextualized ontologies is designed for applications in which additional information is required in order to describe an entity. This information, that we call *context*, may be some kind of meta-data or any information related to — but not particular to — that entity. This is the case of ubiquitous computing applications [14]. Under this paradigm, information concerning either physical or computational environment is a relevant part of the application. Besides, the overall information available for an application — i.e. the context where it is imersed — constantly suffers dynamic changes.

This algebra is based on two basic features: *(i)* a uniform representation of entities and context and *(ii)* the emphasis on the relationship. Concerning *(i)*, we use ontologies for representing both entities and contexts. This enhances the flexibility of the framework avoiding to determine *a priori* the role of an ontology: an ontology may represent an entity, a context or even both an entity and a context. Concerning *(ii)*, the framework puts the focus on the *relationship* among the components of a systems and not on the components themselves. In this way, the internal constitution of an entity is hidden, and descriptions are built in a modular and reusable way. The benefits of emphasising relationships are similar to those well known in systems constructions since the 70's: *Every module (...) is characterized by its knowledge of a design decision which it hides from all others. Its interface or definition was chosen to reveal as little as possible about its inner workings* [9]. The combination of *(i)* and *(ii)* makes possible the reuse of descriptions in a wide sense. Also, as it is the relationship that determines, at any time, the role of an ontology as entity or context the meaning of the subject being described is given by a net of relationships, what enables more accurate descriptions.

3.1 Contextualized Ontologies

By ontology we refer to a structure composed by concepts organized in a taxonomy, relations that determine non-taxonomical relationships, and logical axioms that set restrictions among relationships. The axioms are given in some expressive language whose model-theoretic semantics provides meaning.

Contextualized Ontologies are described as structures that persist a link between two ontologies. The source of the link is the entity and the target is the context. By *structure preserving* we mean that the context respects the hierarchical structure and the ontological relations of the entity. In other words, the entity is coherent with respect to its context. Formally, this means that if an ontology O has a relation $f(c_1, c_2)$ where c_1, c_2 are concepts of the ontology. Then a link $F : O \rightarrow O'$ from O to a context O' is such that $F(f(c_1, c_2)) = F(f)[F(c_1), F(c_2)]$.

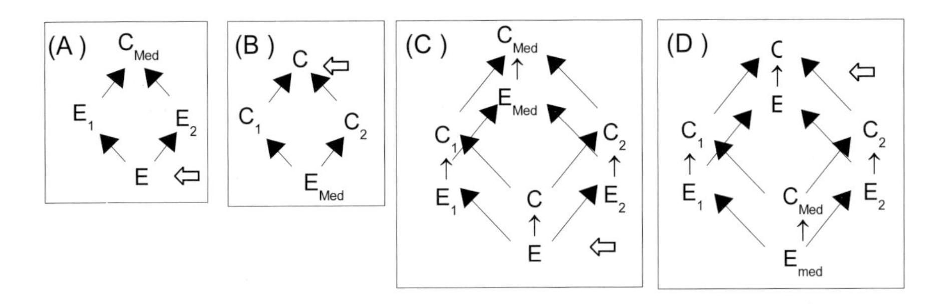

Fig. 1. (A) Entity Integration. (B) Context Integration. (C) Relative Intersection. (D) Collapsed Union.

In order to avoid violating internal constitution of entities, few constraints must be stated about links: *(i)* there is an identity link for any entity or context, that maps the entity/context to itself. Thus the entity may be viewed as a (non-informative) context of itself; *(ii)* an entity is called *domain* of a link, while a context is called *codomain* of a link; *(iii)* links can be composed in an associative way if the codomain of the first is the domain of the second. The notation of a triple (entity, link, context), also represented by $e \rightarrow c$, will be used any time we want to identify the ontologies that act as entity or context in a contextualized ontology. We will use the symbol "$\circ$" to denote the associative composition of contextualized ontologies.

In the sequel we present modular constructs that can be applied to contextualized entities, in order to coherently combine entities, contexts or both. We divide the operations in three classes: Entity Integration, Context Integration and Combined Integration. We use the term "component" to refer to concepts or relations of ontologies[1].

Entity Integration. (Fig. 1-A) Operations in this class have the purpose of integrating entities (E_1 and E_2) that share the same context:$E_1 \rightarrow C_{Med} \leftarrow E_2$. As entities are coherent with respect to their context, the integration has the context as mediator. The result is a new entity (E) contextualized by the original ones (and by transitivity, by the original context C_{Med}). The entity integration performs the semantic intersection of the entities under the mediation of the context, that is, the new entity will embody all, and nothing more than, information of the original entities that is mapped in the same component of the context.

Context Integration. (Figure 1-B) These operations consider situations where a single entity E_{Med} has more than one context ($C1$ and $C2$) : $C_1 \leftarrow E_{Med} \rightarrow C_2$. The context integration produces a new context $C_1 \rightarrow C \leftarrow C_2$ that combines

[1] The reader aware of Category Theory will note that in the following discussion one is considering a category of Ontologies $\mathcal{O}$ and the operations just described correspond to limits and colimits taken in $\mathcal{O}$ itself and $\mathcal{O}^{\rightarrow}$ respectively.

information of the original context preserving the coherence with the entity. This operation can be used in situations where a single entity can be viewed in many ways, according to the considered context. The integration performs the amalgamated union of contexts, collapsing components that are images of the same component in the original entity.

Combined Integration. This class of operations embodies two subclasses: relative intersection and collapsed union. They consider the need to integrate the contextualize ontology as a whole, whithout making distintion between entity or context.

Relative Intersection. (Figure 1-C) Is the intersection of two contextualized ontologies mediated by a third contextualized ontology. It produces a new contextualized ontology having just the components of the originals that are mapped in the mediator.

Collapsed Union. (Figure 1-D) Is the amalgamated union of two contextualized ontologies mediated by a third contextualized ontology. It produces a new contextualized ontology having all components of the original but collapsing those components of the original that are image of the same component of the mediator.

4 Ubiquitous Computing

Ubiquitous computing is a particularly interesting and challenging domain for applying the formal algebra described in Sect. 3. In the vision of ubiquitous computing, computer systems will seamlessly be incorporated into our everyday lives, providing services and information anytime and anywhere [14]. Compared to traditional distributed systems, ubiquitous systems feature increased dynamism and heterogeneity. The underlying ubiquitous computing infrastructures are more complex and bring into the foreground issues such as user mobility, device disconnections, join and leave of devices, heterogeneous networks, as well as the need to integrate the physical environment with the computing infrastructure [7].

As a fundamental requirement, ubiquitous applications must be capable of responding to dynamic changes in their environments with minimal human interference. Users should be able to take full advantage of the local capabilities within a given environment and be able to seamlessly roam between several environments, despite variations of the computing and communication resources' availability (e.g. available wireless bandwidth, residual energy, location-specific services, etc). Hence, ubiquitous computing systems strongly rely on context data, which is used to trigger adaptations at different levels, such as at communication protocols, middleware services, or the user interface.

In ubiquitous systems, ontology has been widely adopted for representing context information. The use of ontologies has not only the advantage of enabling the reuse and sharing of common knowledge among several applications [11], but also of allowing the use of logic reasoning mechanisms to deduce high-level contextual information [13]. In the following subsection we describe a simple scenario, which illustrates the use of context in a ubiquitous environment, and highlights some concepts such as location-specific context, reasoning, heterogeneous contexts and semantic mediation. The numbers in italics between brackets are used to identify situations that will be further referred in Sect. 5.

4.1 Scenario

We consider two universities in Brazil, for instance, PUC-Rio and UFF, which are collaborating in some research projects, e.g. the UbiForm Project. Silva is a professor and researcher who works at the CS Department of PUC-Rio, and is also participating in the UbiForm Project. Silva carries with him his smart phone, which host some context-aware applications that respond to different situations, according to his preferences and to environment conditions.

When he arrives at PUC-Rio, an Ambient Management Service (AMS) registers his smart phone (SMP_{Silva}) and detects that it belongs to him. The system verifies that Silva works there as a professor and sets his workspace *(1)*. This service also informs other members of Silva's team about Silva's arrival *(2)*. A Personal Agenda application running on SMP_{Silva} contacts the context infrastructure with a request to be notified about the beginning of each event involving the whole project team, based on the project schedule and the location *(3)*. Another application on SMP_{Silva}, a Configuration Management Service (CMS), requests to be notified whenever Silva is in a room in which an activity (e.g. a technical presentation, a brainstorm session) has started, so that it may set the smart phone to blocked mode, and as soon as the activity ends, switch it back to the ring mode. But if Silva's wife sends him a message during the meeting, the phone should vibrate, so that he can discreetly check the message's subject *(4)*.

From this example, we may see that the ubiquitous services described above rely on a wide variety of context information to trigger their actions. While the Ambient Management Service and the Personal Agenda must be aware of the context information that describes Silva's role and location in the organization, the Configuration Management Service also takes into consideration Silva's personal preferences. Thus, to be able to apply the rule described, we notice that the context that fully describes the user Silva comprises not only the context that describes his role at PUC-Rio (location of Silva and his device in the organization), or in the UbiForm Project (schedule of activitues), but also the context that describes Silva's personal preferences and features (the one calling is Silva's wife). When Silva is at home or somewhere else — e.g. at an Airport *(5)* —, the Configuration Management Service will be imersed in an different overall context. In such cases, formalization may help to describe and understand how different contexts form a specific combined view.

Now supposing that Silva is visiting UFF with several other researchers and, as usually, he carries with him his smart phone running the same context-aware services. Their purpose is to have joint workshops about the collaboration project. When Silva arrives at UFF, the Wi-Fi and GPS enabled SMP_{Silva} connects to the network, and using the current GPS data, queries a location service to find out that its owner (Silva) is at UFF *(6)*. It then determines that this university is a partner institution of PUC-Rio; obtains the IP address of the AMS at UFF and registers with it, indicating the user's identity and preferences. The Ambient Management Service registers SMP_{Silva} and identifies that the device belongs to Silva, a visiting professor from PUC-Rio. The system verifies that Silva is involved with the collaboration project and sets a workspace for him *(7)*. Notice that when the Personal Agenda and the Configuration Management Service interact with the Ambient's local context provider at UFF, although Silva is identified as a visitor at that institution, he can still be perceived as a professor from PUC-Rio. Hence, supposing that only professors can have access to printers at UFF, when setting Silva's workspace, AMS will recognize this access permission and configure the printer setup utility at his operating system to use the locally available printers *(8)*. In addition to this, suppose that AMS would make available to Professor Silva the publications of UFF which are related to his production. For this, AMS should also be aware of Professor Silva's production, i.e. list of publications. Once more, we identify that one of the main requirements of ubiquitous systems is the ability to adapt services/behaviors to the current context view. Again, formalization may be useful to describe a relation between different contexts in the form of a resulting aligned view.

5 Formalizing the Application

5.1 High Level Diagrams

In this section, we refer to the numbers that appear in Sect. 4.1 to draw high level diagrams of the situations described in the scenenario. Consider that *Silva*, *PUC*, *UFF*, *UbiForm Project* and *Airport* are ontologies that, describe, respectively, personal information about Professor Silva, PUC-Rio and UFF administrative organization, and information about the UbiForm Project and a given Airport. These ontologies are not contextualized. Their contexts will appear as we proceed in the construction of the formal model.

We start at *(1)*, when the Ambient Management Service (AMS) registers Professor Silva's smart phone. This process concerns the integration of the ontologies *Silva* and *PUC* with respect to the smart phone of Professor Silva. We construct a very simple ontology: SMP_{Silva} to be contextualized in $Silva$ and PUC. This means that concepts and relations of SMP_{Silva} will be linked into correspondents of $Silva$ and PUC, respecting the structure of the ontologies. SMP_{Silva} will act as mediator of $Silva$ and PUC in a context integration $Silva \overset{AMS}{\longleftarrow} SMP_{Silva} \overset{AMS}{\longrightarrow} PUC$. The integration will result in a new ontology that we will name $SilvaAtPUC$.

It will embody all components of $Silva$, all components of PUC, and will have the images of concepts of the mediator SMP_{Silva} collapsed. Operating in

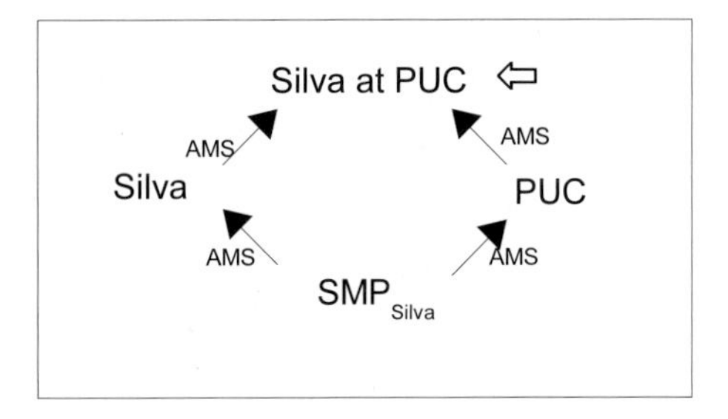

Fig. 2. Considering the ontologies of Professor Silva and PUC, AMS generates the ontology SilvaAtPUC

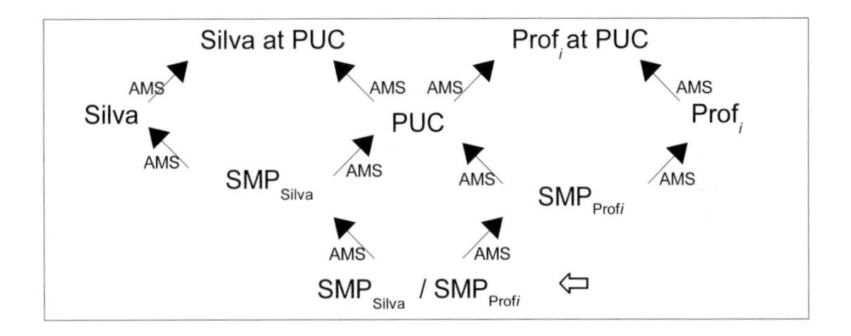

Fig. 3. AMS integrates SMP of Silva with SMP of professors

this integrated context (*SilvaAtPUC*), AMS will have enough information to identify the presence of Professor Silva at PUC (Fig. 2). A similar diagram can be considered for each member of the project that is present at the moment.

Then, in *(2)*, AMS informs other members of Silva's team about his arrival. Considering that, for any member $Prof_i$, a context integration $Prof_i \xleftarrow{AMS} SMP_{Prof_i} \xrightarrow{AMS} PUC$ has been generated, the entity integration of each SMP_{Prof_i} and SMP_{Silva} under the context of PUC will make the connection among the smart phones of the i professors of PUC and the smart phone of Professor Silva (Fig. 3). The resulting entity will be composed by the smart phone of each professor.

In *(3)*, the Personal Agenda (PA) of Silva's smart phone contacts the UbiForm Project Agenda to be notified about scheduled activities. The entity integration $SMP_{Silva} \xrightarrow{PA} UbiFormProject \xleftarrow{PA} SMP_{Prof_i}$ embodies the synchronization of the professors' agendas with respect to the UbiForm Project agenda. In the resulting ontology the Personal Agenda can process information about events in which all professors i and Silva take part (Fig. 4).

In *(4)* the Configuration Management Service (CMS) (running on SMP_{Silva}) requests the UbiForm Project Agenda to be notified when any activity is about to start. AMS is aware of the location of Professor Silva at PUC, and hence of his presence in a room where a project activity is taking place. It also considers

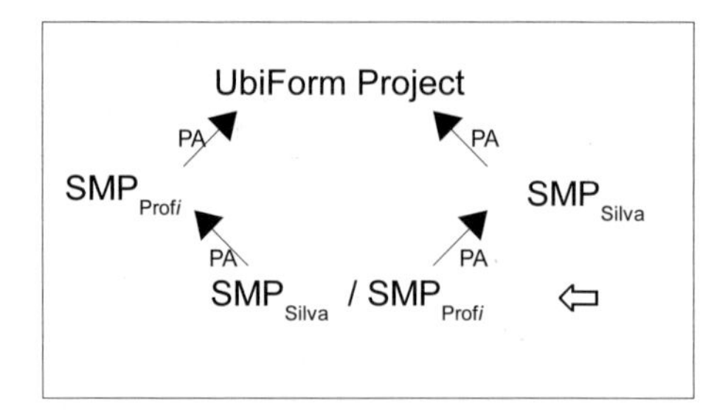

Fig. 4. Personal Agenda of Silva's smart phone contacts the UbiForm Project Agenda to be notified about scheduled activities, and to be synchronized with the other professor's agends

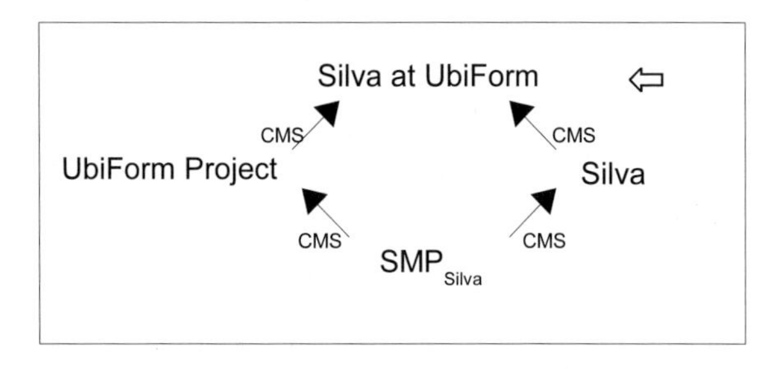

Fig. 5. CMS considers personal information about Silva and his physical position at the UbiForm

Silva's personal information in order to properly configure his phone alarm. This phone configuration could be represented by a rule — involving concepts associated to different contexts — that would trigger an adaptation for the CMS application:

$$\textbf{Device}(SMP_{Silva}) \wedge \textbf{isLocatedIn(?d,?r)} \wedge \textbf{inActivity(?r)} \wedge \textbf{PersonCalling(?p)} \wedge \\ \textbf{isWife(?p,``Silva'')} \Rightarrow \textbf{setVibrate}(SMP_{Silva})$$

A context integration $UbiFormProject \overset{CMS}{\longleftarrow} SMP_{Silva} \overset{CMS}{\longrightarrow} Silva$ results in a context $SilvaAtUbiForm$ which combines personal information about Silva and the present UbiForm activity in which he is involved (Fig. 5). Similar situation occurs when Silva is somewhere else, e.g. as at the airport *(5)*. The context integration $Airport \overset{CMS}{\longleftarrow} SMP_{Silva} \overset{CMS}{\longrightarrow} Silva$ results in the context *SilvaAtAirport* wherein the CMS can configure his phone alarm according to his contextual preferences.

Later, Professor Silva is visiting UFF *(6)*, where he is registered as a visitor researcher. Within the context $SilvaAtUFF$ that results from integration $Silva \overset{AMS}{\longleftarrow} SMP_{Silva} \overset{AMS}{\longrightarrow} UFF$, AMS can properly set the professor's workspace. But some of Silva's permissions for the use of resources come from the fact that he is a Professor at PUC *(7)*. Thus, information about Silva's

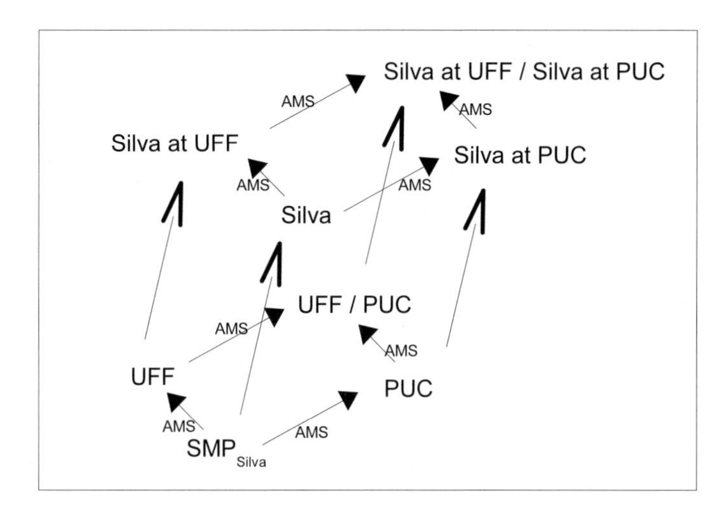

Fig. 6. Each face of the cube shows a context integration. The cube can also be considered as the collapsed union of the contextualized entities $UFF \rightarrow SilvaAtUFF$, $PUC \rightarrow SilvaAtPUC$ mediated by $SMP_{Silva} \rightarrow Silva$.

status at PUC must also be taken into account for setting access permissions properly. The context integration $UFF \overset{AMS}{\longleftarrow} SMP_{Silva} \overset{AMS}{\longrightarrow} PUC$ generates a context where AMS can find information about Silva as a PUC professor and as a UFF visitor researcher in the joint project UFF/PUC (base square of Fig. 6). The context integration $SilvaAtUFF \overset{AMS}{\longleftarrow} Silva \overset{AMS}{\longrightarrow} SilvaAtPUC$ generates a context where AMS can find not only information about Silva as a PUC professor or as a UFF visitor researcher, but also personal information about Silva (top square of Fig. 6). Note that Fig. 6 also pictures a combined integration: the collapsed union of the contextualized entities $UFF \rightarrow SilvaAtUFF$, $PUC \rightarrow SilvaAtPUC$ mediated by $SMP_{Silva} \rightarrow Silva$.

5.2 A Zoom into Ontologies and Morphisms

Since a detailed description of the whole scenario would exceed the space limitation of this paper, we selected only two diagrams of the previous subsection to illustrate how this framework provides the required information to adapt services or behaviors according to the context changes. First, we consider a situation in which information coming one context enables decisions about an entity in a different context. For instance, *(8)*, Professor Silva is allowed to use the printer at UFF as a consequence of the fact that, at PUC, he is a professor. AMS also makes available to Professor Silva the publications of UFF which are related to his production. The permission to print could be represented as a rule that would set an access permission in a ubiquitous regulation service, such as in [12]:

$$\textbf{Person(?p)} \wedge \textbf{worksAt(?p,“PUC-Rio”)} \wedge \textbf{playsRole(?p,“Professor”)} \Rightarrow \textbf{hasAccess(?p,“Printer”)}$$

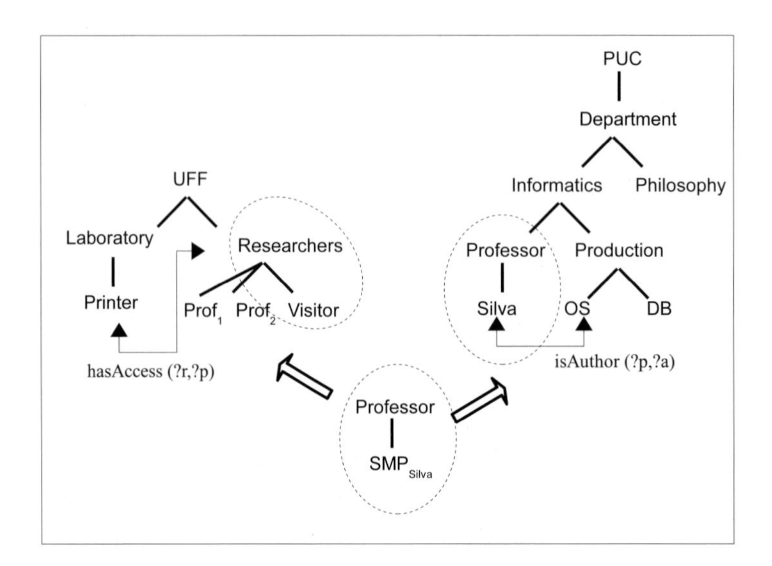

Fig. 7. Alignment of UFF and PUC under the mediation of SMP_{Silva}. The mediator captures the fact that Silva is a professor and properly map this information in the ontology of UFF.

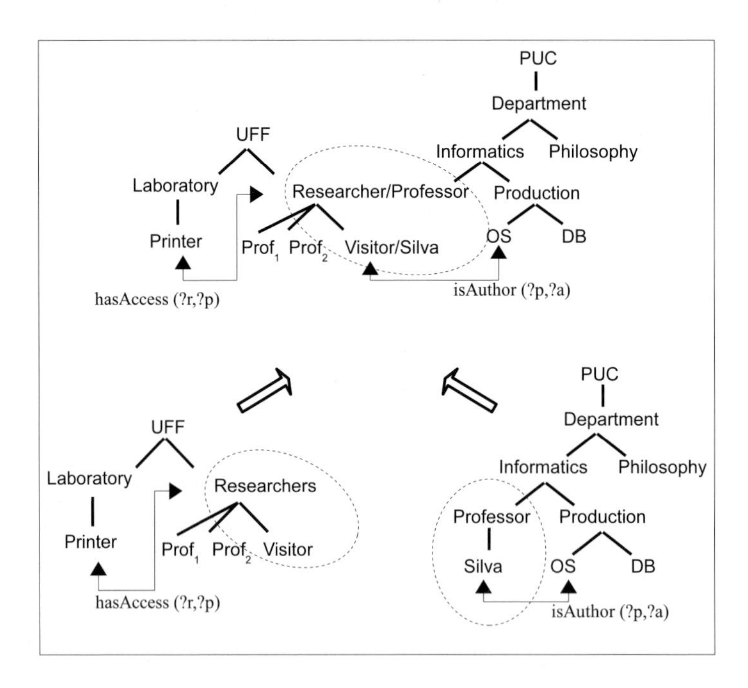

Fig. 8. The context integration of the alignment of figure 7: the relation *hasAcces(Researcher, Printer)* holds for Professor Silva and Printer and information about Professor Silva's production is avaiable

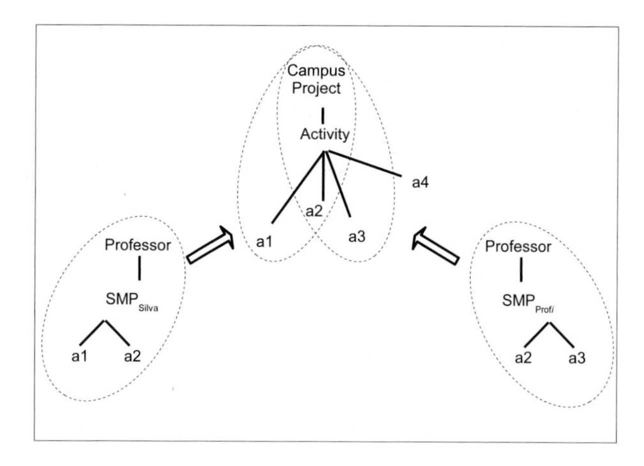

Fig. 9. The alignment of SMP of Professor i and SMP of Professor Silva with respect to the agenda of the UbiForm Project

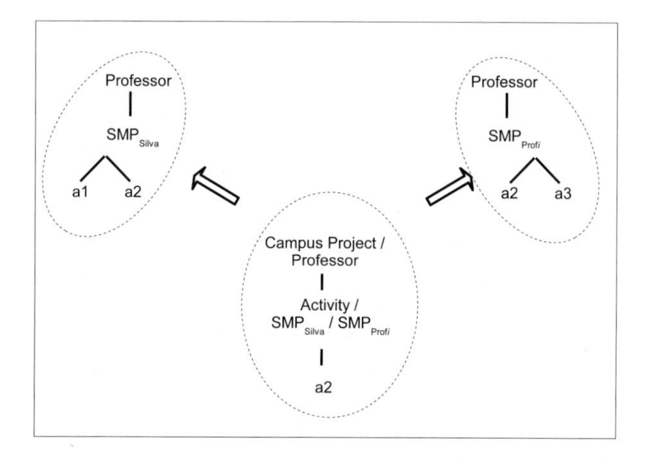

Fig. 10. Integration of agendas: Silva and Professor i will be present at Event 2

Considering the base square of Fig. 6, the mediator SMP_{Silva} of the context integration $UFF \overset{AMS}{\longleftarrow} SMP_{Silva} \overset{AMS}{\longrightarrow} PUC$ must capture the fact that Silva is a professor and properly map this information into the ontology of UFF. Figure 7 depicts the ontology for UFF and PUC and shows this alignment. Note that, as the concept *Professor* at *PUC* is related to *Researcher* at *UFF*, the relation *hasAccess(?p, ?d)* will hold for Professor Silva and Printer in the resulting context (in Fig. 8). Also, note that, in this resulting context information about Professor Silva's production is avaiable to be used by AMS. Secondly, we show how the integration can filter information in order to affect just a selected set of entities. We consider the situation *(3)*, where the Personal Agenda of Silva's smart phone contacts the UbiForm Project Agenda to be notified about events.

Diagram of Fig. 4 pictures this situation, showing the integration of SMP of Professor i and SMP of Professor Silva under the context of the UbiForm Project. Figure 9 shows the alignment of SMP of Professor i and SMP of Professor Silva with respect to the context of the UbiForm Project. Figure 10 shows the resulting entity, in which appears only the events that both take part.

6 Conclusions

In this article, we used an algebra of contextualized ontologies to formalize the problem of interpreting context information in ubiquitous systems based on a concrete scenario. The main goal was to verify not only the contributions of this formal approach for better understanding of the fundamental concepts of ubiquitous computing, but also the adequability, expressiveness and flexibility of this approach to express specific characteristics of the concrete application domain and scenario.

Before using a formal model, method or language for a specific problem domain, it is worth thinking about the expected benefits versus the required efforts of this endeavor. In fact, formalization usually helps to develop a better understanding of the problem domain and its scope, as well as clearly define the major concepts involved. Ontologies strongly contributes in this sense, enabling modular and reusable taxonomical descriptions and enhancing the expressive power through the use of logic reasoning mechanisms. The algebra of contextualized ontologies enforce these benefits, having modularity and reuse as fundamental requirements, over which the operations to compose and decompose ontologies are defined. In the algebra, the alignment of ontologies is naturally supported as initial step of integration. As a result, the use of the algebra becomes very close to the usual way of handling ontologies.

One should also be aware of the limitations and potential risks of applying formal methods to a concrete problem. When we use a formal model for any subject we always abstract from some issues or entities which apparently seem less relevant. In real systems these issues might well have a significant impact on the real system's behavior, and should ideally be accounted for. Hence, whenever we develop a formal model of a system, there is always a trade-off between the model's degree of realism, its complexity and its underlying set of applicable basic results. The possibility of adopting levels of abstraction, however, contributes to reduce the gap between the formal approach and the real system. High level diagrams considering just entities and contexts give an abstract view of formalizations. Ontologies and mappings come later, in refinement steps introducing more details gradually.

References

1. Birkedal, L., Debois, S., Elsborg, E., Hildebrandt, T., Niss, H.: Bigraphical Models of Context-aware Systems. Technical Report TR-2005-74, The IT University of Copenhagen (November 2005)
2. Cafezeiro, I., Haeusler, E.H.: Semantic interoperability via category theory. In: Conferences in Research and Practice in Information Technology, vol. 83 (2006)

3. Cafezeiro, I., Rademaker, A., Haeusler, E.H.: Ontology and Context. In: Proceedings of CoMoREA 2008, pp. 53–62 (2008)
4. Goldblatt, R.: Topoi: The Categorical Analysis of Logicser. Ser Studies in Logic and the Foundations of Mathematics. North Holland, Amsterdam (1979)
5. Henricksen, K., Indulska, J.: Developing context-aware pervasive computing applications: Models and approach. Pervasive and Mobile Computing 2(1), 37–64 (2006)
6. Julien, C., Payton, J., Roman, G.-C.: Reasoning About Context-Awareness in the Presence of Mobility. In: Proc. of the 2nd Int. Workshop on Foundations of Coordination Languages and Software Architectures (FOCLASA 2003), Marseille, France (September 2003)
7. Kindberg, T., Fox, A.: System software for ubiquitous computing. Pervasive Computing Magazine (2002)
8. MacLane, S.: Categories for the Working Matematician. Springer, Berlin (1997)
9. Parnas, D.: On the criteria to be used in decomposing systems into modules. Communications of the ACM (December 1972)
10. Roman, G.-C., Julien, C., Payton, J.: A Formal Treatment of Context Awareness. In: Wermelinger, M., Margaria-Steffen, T. (eds.) FASE 2004. LNCS, vol. 2984, pp. 12–36. Springer, Heidelberg (2004)
11. Shehzad, A., Ngo, H.Q., Pham, K.A., Lee, S.Y.: Formal modeling in context aware systems. In: Proceedings of the First International Workshop on Modeling and Retrieval of Context (September 2004)
12. Viterbo, J., Endler, M., Briot, J.-P.: Ubiquitous service regulation based on dynamic rules. In: Proceedings of the 13th IEEE International Conference on Engineering of Complex Computer Systems (ICECCS 2008), Belfast, pp. 175–182. IEEE Computer Society Press, Los Alamitos (2008)
13. Wang, X.H., Zhang, D.Q., Gu, T., Pung, H.K.: Ontology based context modeling and reasoning using OWL. In: Proc. of 2nd IEEE Conf. Pervasive Computing and Communications (PerCom 2004), Workshop on Context Modeling and Reasoning, Orlando, Florida, March 2004, pp. 18–22. IEEE Computer Society Press, Los Alamitos (2004)
14. Weiser, M.: The computer for the twenty-first century. Scientific American 265(3), 94–104 (1991)
15. Yan, L., Sere, K.: A Formalism for Context-Aware Mobile Computing. In: Proceedings of the IEEE 3rd International Workshop on Algorithms, Models and Tools for Parallel Computing on Heterogeneous Networks (HeteroPar), Cork, Ireland (July 2004)

Contexts and Context Awareness in View of the Diagram Predicate Framework

Uwe Wolter[1] and Zinovy Diskin[2]

[1] Department of Informatics, University of Bergen, Norway
[2] Department of Computer Science, University of Toronto, Canada

Abstract. The paper presents a formal model of *entities* and of *contexts with entry points*, and a formal description of the scenarios *an entity enters a context* and *an entity works in a context*. Our model is defined within the Diagram Predicate Framework and therefore is automatically generic since any instantiation of the framework results in a special modeling technique including schema-based, graph-based, object-oriented or ontology-based techniques.

1 Introduction

Inter-operation and integration of systems (electronic devices, communication networks, software applications and users) built on different platforms and principles is a major problem in ubiquitous context-aware computing. Precise modeling of interfaces and communication protocols of these components, and the architectures of systems built from the component, is a key to approaching the problem. Importance of modeling is well recognized by the community, and many modeling approaches were proposed – see, for example, the survey [SLP04], where the modeling approaches are classified by the data modeling language used for specifying contextual information. In more detail, the following groups are distinguished: Key-value pairs, Markup schemas, Graphical models like UML- or ER-, or ORM-diagrams, Logic-based models and Ontology-based models. This heterogeneity of modeling approaches is not accidental and reflects an extreme heterogeneity of ubiquitous computing. However, a particular modeling language L that is good and natural for some class of systems and applications can be "foreign" for another class of systems and applications and hence does not facilitate effective design decisions for them. In addition, unfortunate consequences of the situation when a community speaks different languages are well known for a (very) long time. The problem calls for *generic* modeling techniques admitting many different instantiations, and this is where the present paper is intended to contribute.

The Diagram Predicate Framework (DPF) is a generic specification format (still under development) aimed at and providing rigorous and formal foundations for a variety of modeling techniques used in Software Engineering (SE), particularly, encompassing those ones mentioned above. The underlying mathematical theory is presented in [DW08], and its applications to conceptual modeling and

T. Margaria and B. Steffen (Eds.): ISoLA 2008, CCIS 17, pp. 534–547, 2008.

object-oriented design can be found in [DK03, Dis03, DED08] respectively. The authors of the present paper are newcomers in the area of ubiquitous and context-aware computing, and well recognize the danger of one more implementation of the known pattern: "if you have a hammer (DPF in this case), then everything is a nail". Still we hope that our first attempt to approach the problems in the area may be helpful for both sides and may open fruitful communication and collaboration.

The paper is organized as follows. In section 2 we discuss the quidelines and requirements for the formal model we need to build; it serves as an informal motivation for the formalities to follow further. Section 3 combines an informal discussion and analysis of modeling techniques with a stepwise introduction of the basic concepts of the DPF. A precise formal model of entities entering a context is presented in Section 4. The final Section 5 summarizes what we have gained so far and formulates some open problems and questions for future research.

2 Entities and Contexts, I: An Informal Discussion

The starting point of our discussion is the following requirement specification [End05]:

> When a user enters a new context, it is desirable that the applications on his devices be able to adapt to the new situation, and the environment be able to adapt its services to the presence of the new user.

To make things not too complicated, we will not distinguish between "a user", "his devices", and "an application on his devices". We will just talk about "entities". We will also use the term "context" instead of "environment".

By analyzing the requirement specification we can formulate the following **guidelines and requirements** for the development of our formal model:

1. There is a kind of asymmetry: An entity is somehow "smaller" than a context. Moreover, the context is a service provider for the entities, not the other way round.
2. A context may be entered by different entities and there may be different kinds of entities allowed to enter a context.
3. For each kind of entity there is a special package of services offered by the context, and these services are only available after an entity has entered and the services have been adapted to this entity.
4. A context is a system for its own, even if no entities have been entered the context yet. We will refer to this system as the *context kernel.*
5. There are special points where an entity can enter a context. And for each of those *entry points* it should be specified what kinds of entities are admitted to enter the context at this point.
6. After an entity has successfully entered a context, a new system is established integrating the context and the entity in a certain way. And this integrated system offers adapted services for the entity.

These considerations are schematically described by an informal diagram in Fig. 1. In this diagram, nodes (clouds and ovals) denote complex structures (think of UML- or ER-diagrams or FOL theories), and arrows are directed relationships between them (think about mappings between the correspondign structures).

Oval $\mathcal{A}$ represents the "admission requirements" specifying what entities are allowed to enter a context. Cloud $\mathcal{C}(\mathcal{P})$ denotes a context structure $\mathcal{C}$ with a designated substructure $\mathcal{P}$ considered as a "place" where an entity will be placed within the context after it got admission. Oval $\mathcal{E}$ is an entity and the existence of an arrow m from $\mathcal{A}$ to $\mathcal{E}$ indicates that $\mathcal{E}$ satisfies the "admission requirements". Cloud $\mathcal{C} + \mathcal{E}$ with inserted entity structure denotes then the resulting system "entity $\mathcal{E}$ working in context $\mathcal{C}$ at place $\mathcal{P}$".

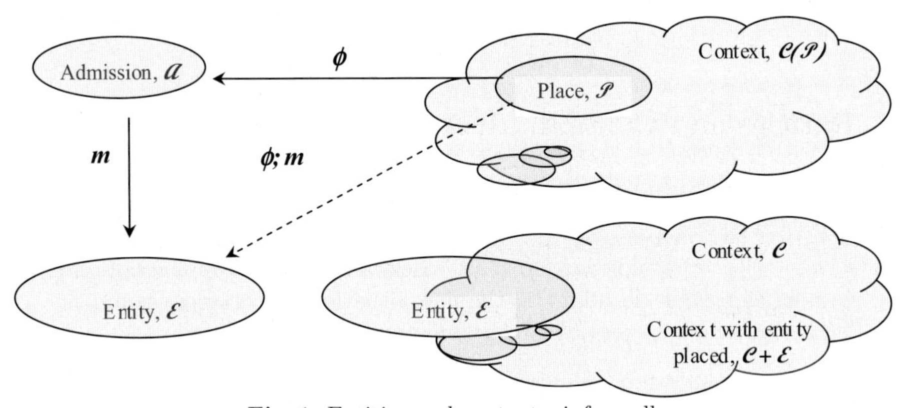

Fig. 1. Entities and contexts, informally

The goal of the rest of the paper is to make the diagram precise and formal. That is, we need to define in a formal way what the structures (nodes) in questions are, and what the mappings (arrows) between them are. Importantly, we aim at generic formal definitions of nodes and arrows (which can be instantiated with different modeling formalisms mentioned above) rather than a particular formalism. That is, we want to make the diagram in Fig. 1 a formal specification pattern, which encompasses modeling formalisms employed in the area of ubiquitous context-aware computing in a uniform way.

3 The Diagram Predicate Framework

The Diagram Predicate Framework (DPF) is based on Graph Theory and Category Theory (CT). It borrows its main ideas from both categorical and first-order logic, and adapts them to software engineering needs. Actually, it has emerged as generalization and extension of the *sketch* formalism invented in CT in the 60s. Therefore we have used the term "generalized sketch framework" in earlier and more theoretically oriented publications [Dis97, DK03, DW08]. However, since the term "sketch" is normally associated with an informal drawing rather than a formal specification, lately we decided to use instead the term "Diagram Predicate Framework".

We are going to introduce, step by step, the basic concepts of our framework and give their formal definitions. A few simple illustrating examples, and additional formal details and results, can be found in [DW08].

3.1 The Syntax

To refer to things like "a UML class diagram", "an ER-diagram", "a database scheme", "an ontology", ..., we will use the term *model*. Let us start by asking: What is a model? How can we define the concept of model in a generic formal way?

The first observation is that all these models are (or at least can be) graphically presented by one or another kind of "diagram". The basic components of those "diagrams" are nodes and arrows. Thus we can formulate our

Observation 1: A model has an underlying "carrier graph" G.

To allow for multiple arrows between nodes we work with the following definition of graphs:

Definition 1 (Graph). *A* ***graph*** $G = (G_0, G_1, sc, tg)$ *is given by a set* G_0 *of nodes, a set* G_1 *of arrows, and two maps* $sc, tg : G_1 \to G_0$ *assigning to each arrow its* ***source*** *and* ***target****, respectively. We usually write* $f : x \to y$ *or* $x \xrightarrow{f} y$ *to indicate that* $sc(f) = x$ *and* $tg(f) = y$.

A graph $G=(G_0, G_1, sc^G, tg^G)$ *is* ***subgraph*** *of a graph* $H=(H_0, H_1, sc^H, tg^H)$, $G \sqsubseteq H$ *in symbols, iff* $G_0 \subseteq H_0$, $G_1 \subseteq H_1$, *and* $sc^G(f) = sc^H(f)$, $tg^G(f) = tg^H(f)$ *for all* $f \in G_1$. □

The next observation is that nodes in G are usually classified as classes, data types, entities, relationships or, say, tables. Arrows in G are usually classified as associations, references, containment's, attributes or, say, isA-arrows. Moreover, arrows between certain kinds of nodes are allowed and between other kinds of nodes they are not allowed. So, each modeling technique puts typing requirements on their models, which can be formally expressed in the following way.

Observation 2: Each modeling technique comes along with a *type graph* T and the models have to conform to the corresponding typing requirements, that is, for each model there has to be a graph homomorphism $t : G \to T$.

Definition 2 (Graph Homomorphism). *A* ***graph homomorphism*** $\varphi : G \to H$ *is a pair of maps* $\varphi_0 : G_0 \to H_0$ *and* $\varphi_1 : G_1 \to H_1$ *such that for each arrow* $f : x \to y$ *of* G *we have* $\varphi_1(f) : \varphi_0(x) \to \varphi_0(y)$ *in* H, *i.e., we have* $sr^H(\varphi_1(f)) = \varphi_0(sr^G(f))$ *and* $tg^H(\varphi_1(f)) = \varphi_0(tg^G(f))$ *for all* $f \in G_1$.

The ***composition*** $\varphi;\psi : G \to K$ *of two graph homomorphisms* $\varphi : G \to H$ *and* $\psi : H \to K$ *is defined component-wise*

$$\varphi;\psi = (\varphi_0, \varphi_1);(\psi_0, \psi_1) \stackrel{def}{=} (\varphi_0;\psi_0, \varphi_1;\psi_1).$$

Remark 1 (Inclusions). Note, that $G \sqsubseteq H$ iff the inclusion maps $in_i : G_i \hookrightarrow H_i$, $i = 0, 1$ define a graph homomorphism $in = (in_0, in_1) : G \hookrightarrow H$.

Moreover, most modeling techniques allow us to enrich our models with constraints, for example, multiplicities or general OCL constraints in UML, key constraints for relational data schemas, weak entity constraints for ER-diagrams. Those constraints concern single arrows in G or special configurations of arrows in G:

Observation 3: Each modeling techniques provides a collection of constraints where each kind of constraint is defined by a name and by a "pattern" describing where in our models constraints of this kind are allowed to appear.

Observations 3 and 1 lead us to the following definitions:

Definition 3 (Signature). *A* ***signature*** $\Sigma = (\Pi, \alpha)$ *is given by a set* Π *of* ***predicate labels (symbols)*** *and a function* α *assigning to each label* $P \in \Pi$ *its* ***arity graph*** $\alpha(P)$*.*

Definition 4 (Models). *A* Σ***-model*** $\mathcal{S} = (G^{\mathcal{S}}, \mathcal{S}(\Pi))$ *consists of a graph* $G^{\mathcal{S}}$ *and a set* $\mathcal{S}(\Pi)$ *of* ***constraints*** (P, d) *with* $P \in \Pi$ *a label and* $d : \alpha(P) \to G$ *a graph homomorphism.*[1]

A Σ*-model* $\mathcal{S} = (G^{\mathcal{S}}, \mathcal{S}(\Pi))$ *is* Σ***-submodel*** *of a* Σ*-model* $\mathcal{T} = (G^{\mathcal{T}}, \mathcal{T}(\Pi))$, $\mathcal{S} \sqsubseteq \mathcal{T}$ *in symbols, iff* $G^{\mathcal{S}} \sqsubseteq G^{\mathcal{T}}$ *and* $\mathcal{S}(\Pi) \subseteq \mathcal{T}(\Pi)$*.*

Remark 2 (Graphs). All definitions in this paper are based on graphs and graph homomorphisms, but we can easily vary them in case we need or want to use other structures than graphs (see [DW08]).

Remark 3 (Meta-modeling). The mechanism of typing, as formulated in Observation 2, can be naturally integrated into the definition of signatures and models. We will not treat this aspect here since we don't want to burden the exposition too much. It is worth mentioning that the typing mechanism can be extended within our formalism to a full "meta-modeling mechanism".

The motivational discussion in Section 2 has shown that we will need morphisms to formalize the concepts of context and context awareness.

Definition 5 (Model Morphisms). *A* Σ***-model morphism*** $f : \mathcal{S} \to \mathcal{S}'$ *between two* Σ*-models* $\mathcal{S} = (G^{\mathcal{S}}, \mathcal{S}(\Pi))$ *and* $\mathcal{S}' = (G^{\mathcal{S}'}, \mathcal{S}'(\Pi))$ *is a graph homomorphism* $f : G^{\mathcal{S}} \to G^{\mathcal{S}'}$ *preserving constraints, i.e., for all constraints* $(P, d : \alpha(P) \to G^{\mathcal{S}}) \in \mathcal{S}(\Pi)$ *we have that* $(P, d; f : \alpha(P) \to G^{\mathcal{S}'}) \in \mathcal{S}'(\Pi)$*.*

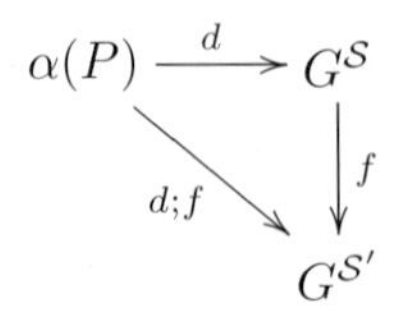

[1] In CT those graph homomorphisms are usually called diagrams. But, to avoid potential confusion in this community we decided for another term.

Remark 4 (Submodels). Note, that $\mathcal{S} \sqsubseteq \mathcal{T}$ iff the inclusion graph homomorphism $in : G^{\mathcal{S}} \hookrightarrow G^{\mathcal{T}}$ defines a Σ-model morphism $in : \mathcal{S} \hookrightarrow \mathcal{T}$.

Later we will need to construct pushouts of model morphisms. The pushout exists for any span of model morphisms and is obtained by first constructing the pushout of the corresponding span of graph homomorphisms and then putting together the constraints from the two target models of the span. In our applications here, one model morphism will be always an inclusion and in this case the pushout can be constructed essentially by complements and disjoint unions. The following definition gives a concrete description of such a "combination of models".

Definition 6 (Combined Model). *Let be given a Σ-model $\mathcal{S} = (G^{\mathcal{S}}, \mathcal{S}(\Pi))$, two Σ-models $\mathcal{L} = (G^{\mathcal{L}}, \mathcal{L}(\Pi))$, $\mathcal{R} = (G^{\mathcal{R}}, \mathcal{R}(\Pi))$ such that $\mathcal{L} \sqsubseteq \mathcal{R}$, and a Σ-model morphism (**match**) $m : \mathcal{L} \to \mathcal{S}$. Then the **combination of $\mathcal{S}$ and $\mathcal{R}$ via m** results in a Σ-model $\mathcal{C} = (G^{\mathcal{C}}, \mathcal{C}(\Pi))$ and in a Σ-model morphism $m^* : \mathcal{R} \to \mathcal{C}$ such that $\mathcal{S} \sqsubseteq \mathcal{C}$ and $m; \sqsubseteq = \sqsubseteq; m^*$.*

$$\begin{array}{ccc} \mathcal{L} & \xrightarrow{\sqsubseteq} & \mathcal{R} \\ {\scriptstyle m}\downarrow & & \downarrow{\scriptstyle m^*} \\ \mathcal{S} & \xrightarrow{\sqsubseteq} & \mathcal{C} \end{array}$$

Thereby the underlying graph $G^{\mathcal{C}}$ is defined as follows

$$G_i^{\mathcal{C}} \stackrel{def}{=} G_i^{\mathcal{S}} \cup \{(m, x) \mid x \in G_i^{\mathcal{R}} \setminus G_i^{\mathcal{L}}\} \quad i = 0, 1.$$

$$sc^{G^{\mathcal{C}}}(f) \stackrel{def}{=} \begin{cases} sc^{G^{\mathcal{S}}}(f) \quad , \text{if } f \in G_1^{\mathcal{S}} \\ m_0(sc^{G^{\mathcal{R}}}(g)), \text{if } f = (m, g), sc^{G^{\mathcal{R}}}(g) \in G_0^{\mathcal{L}} \\ (m, sc^{G^{\mathcal{R}}}(g)), \text{if } f = (m, g), sc^{G^{\mathcal{R}}}(g) \notin G_0^{\mathcal{L}} \end{cases}$$

$$tg^{G^{\mathcal{C}}}(f) \stackrel{def}{=} \begin{cases} tg^{G^{\mathcal{S}}}(f) \quad , \text{if } f \in G_1^{\mathcal{S}} \\ m_0(tg^{G^{\mathcal{R}}}(g)), \text{if } f = (m, g), tg^{G^{\mathcal{R}}}(g) \in G_0^{\mathcal{L}} \\ (m, tg^{G^{\mathcal{R}}}(g)), \text{if } f = (m, g), tg^{G^{\mathcal{R}}}(g) \notin G_0^{\mathcal{L}} \end{cases}$$

The graph homomorphism $m^* : G^{\mathcal{R}} \to G^{\mathcal{C}}$ is given for $i = 0, 1$ by

$$m_i^*(x) \stackrel{def}{=} \begin{cases} m_i(x), \text{if } x \in G_i^{\mathcal{L}} \\ (m, x), \text{if } x \in G_i^{\mathcal{R}} \setminus G_i^{\mathcal{L}} \end{cases}$$

And further we have $\quad \mathcal{C}(\Pi) \stackrel{def}{=} \mathcal{S}(\Pi) \cup \{(P, d; m^*) \mid (P, d) \in \mathcal{R}(\Pi) \setminus \mathcal{L}(\Pi)\}.$

Note, that $m^* : G^{\mathcal{R}} \to G^{\mathcal{C}}$ defines indeed a Σ-model morphism $m^* : \mathcal{R} \to \mathcal{C}$: For all $(P, d) \in \mathcal{L}(\Pi)$ we have $(P, d; m^*) = (P, d; m)$ due to the definition of m^* and thus $(P, d; m^*) = (P, d; m) \in \mathcal{S}(\Pi) \subseteq \mathcal{C}(\Pi)$ since $m : \mathcal{L} \to \mathcal{S}$ is a Σ-model morphism. For all $(P, d) \in \mathcal{R}(\Pi) \setminus \mathcal{L}(\Pi)$ we obtain directly $(P, d; m^*) \in \mathcal{C}(\Pi)$ due to the definition of $\mathcal{C}(\Pi)$.

For our later discussions we will use the notation $\mathcal{S} +_m \mathcal{R}$ for the combined model Σ-model $\mathcal{C}$ defined in Definition 6.

3.2 The Semantics

This subsection is devoted to things like "an object diagram for a given class diagram" and "a state of a database". That is, we address the question: What is an "instance" of a model $\mathcal{S} = (G^{\mathcal{S}}, \mathcal{S}(\Pi))$?

The common idea is that a node in $G^{\mathcal{S}}$ stands for a set of "objects", "data", "rows", ..., and that an arrow in $G^{\mathcal{S}}$ represents a (multi valued) map between those sets. One possibility to formalize this idea is to consider instances as graphs O together with a graph homomorphism $\tau : O \rightarrow G^{\mathcal{S}}$ where a node x in $G^{\mathcal{S}}$ represents the set $\tau^{-1}(x) \subseteq O_0$.[2] Given an instance $\tau : O \rightarrow G^{\mathcal{S}}$, we have to check whether the constraints in $\mathcal{S}$ are satisfied. This requires that our modeling technique has a fixed semantics for its constraints, and we are not concerned how this semantics is defined: by set theory, by first-order logic or by a "validation procedure".

Definition 7 (Semantics of Signatures). *A* ***semantic interpretation*** *of a signature $\Sigma = (\Pi, \alpha)$ is a mapping $[\![..]\!]$, which assigns to each predicate symbol $P \in \Pi$ a set $[\![P]\!]$ of graph homomorphisms $\iota : I \rightarrow \alpha(P)$ called the* ***valid instances of*** *P.*

To check if a graph homomorphism $\tau : O \rightarrow G^{\mathcal{S}}$ satisfies a constraint $d : \alpha(P) \rightarrow G^{\mathcal{S}}$ we need only to consider the part of O affected by this constraint. The restriction of O to this part is described in CT by the so-called "pullback" construction, which in this case can be seen as a generalization of the inverse image construction.

The construction of the pullback of a co-span of graph homomorphisms is based on a componentwise construction of the pullbacks of the corresponding co-spans of maps between sets of nodes and sets of arrows, respectively (in analogy to the construction of pushouts in Definition 6). Therefore, it may be enough to present here a concrete pullback construction for maps:

Definition 8 (Pullback of Maps). *The* ***pullback*** *of a co-span $A \xrightarrow{f} C \xleftarrow{g} B$ of maps is given by the following commutative diagram of maps*

$$\begin{array}{ccc} B|_f & \xrightarrow{f^*} & B \\ {\scriptstyle g|_f}\downarrow & & \downarrow{\scriptstyle g} \\ A & \xrightarrow{f} & C \end{array}$$

with

$$B|_f \stackrel{def}{=} \{(b:a) \mid a \in A, b \in B, f(a) = g(b)\}$$

and $g|_f(b:a) \stackrel{def}{=} a$ and $f^*(b:a) \stackrel{def}{=} b$ for all $(b:a) \in B|_f$.

[2] This kind of semantics could be called "fibred" in contrast to "indexed". The interested reader may have a look into [WD07] where the relation between both kinds of semantics is discussed in more detail.

Remark 5 (Pullback). Note, that the notation $(b : a)$ can be read as "b in the role a". In case, f injective non of the b's can play different role's. That is, in this case we could just define $B|_f$ as the inverse image $g^{-1}(f(A)) \subseteq B$ thus f^* becomes an inclusion and $g|_f(b)$ will be the unique a such that $f(a) = g(b)$.

Now, we have everything at place to define what an instance of a model is:

Definition 9 (Instances). *An* ***instance*** *of a Σ-model $\mathcal{S} = (G^{\mathcal{S}}, \mathcal{S}(\Pi))$ is given by a graph O and a graph homomorphism $\tau : O \to G^{\mathcal{S}}$ such that $\tau|_d \in [\![P]\!]$ for all constraints (P, d) in $\mathcal{S}(\Pi)$.*

$$\begin{array}{ccc} O|_d & \xrightarrow{d^*} & O \\ {\scriptstyle \tau|_d}\downarrow & & \downarrow{\scriptstyle \tau} \\ \alpha(P) & \xrightarrow{d} & G^{\mathcal{S}} \end{array}$$

By Inst($\mathcal{S}$) we denote the set of all instances of the model $\mathcal{S}$.

Following the intuition that a model morphism embeds a "small model" into a "big model", it is natural to expect that any instance of the "big model" can be reduced to an instance of the "small model". The pullback construction indeed provides this kind of semantic transformation opposite to the direction of the syntactic translation:

Proposition 1 (Reduction of Instances). *Every Σ-model morphism $f : \mathcal{S} \to \mathcal{S}'$ induces a map*

$$[\![f]\!] : Inst(\mathcal{S}') \to Inst(\mathcal{S}) \quad with \quad [\![f]\!](\tau) \stackrel{def}{=} \tau|_f$$

for all instances $\tau : O \to G^{\mathcal{S}'}$ of $\mathcal{S}'$.

$$\begin{array}{ccc} O|_f & \xrightarrow{f^*} & O \\ {\scriptstyle \tau|_f}\downarrow & & \downarrow{\scriptstyle \tau} \\ G^{\mathcal{S}} & \xrightarrow{f} & G^{\mathcal{S}'} \end{array}$$

In our discussion of entities and contexts in the next section, we will need one more concept – the concept of a method. A method changes the state of a system and for our later discussion we don't need to know how methods are actually defined or implemented. It will be enough to work with the following abstract definition:

Definition 10 (Methods). *An $\mathcal{S}$-method for a Σ-model $\mathcal{S} = (G^{\mathcal{S}}, \mathcal{S}(\Pi))$ is a map $\mu : Inst(\mathcal{S}) \to Inst(\mathcal{S})$.*

A given modeling technique can be described by defining a corresponding signature of diagram predicates and a semantic interpretation of the signature. The DPF also allows us to describe transformations between modeling techniques and the integration of modeling techniques. However, for our present discussion of entities and contexts, , we will restrict ourselves to the homogeneous setting. That is, for the rest of the paper we are working with a fixed signature $\Sigma = (\Pi, \alpha)$ and a fixed semantic interpretation $[\![..]\!]$ of Σ.

4 Entities and Contexts, II: A Formal Model

Following the guidelines of Section 2, we will develop now, step by step, our formal model of entities and contexts, and of what it means that an entity enters a context.

4.1 A Context with an Entry Point

Entities and Context Kernel: An **entity** is given by a Σ-model $\mathcal{E} = (G^{\mathcal{E}}, \mathcal{E}(\Pi))$ and a set $OP_{\mathcal{E}}$ of $\mathcal{E}$-methods attached to the entity. In the same way, the **context kernel** is given by a Σ-model $\mathcal{C} = (G^{\mathcal{C}}, \mathcal{C}(\Pi))$ and a set $OP_{\mathcal{C}}$ of $\mathcal{C}$-methods attached to the context kernel.

Entry Points: An **entry point** is given by "admission requirements", that is, by a Σ-model $\mathcal{A} = (G^{\mathcal{A}}, \mathcal{A}(\Pi))$ specifying what kinds of entities are allowed to enter the context at this point. Moreover, we have a **place**, that is, a Σ-submodel $\mathcal{P} \sqsubseteq \mathcal{C}$ together with a Σ-model morphism $\phi : \mathcal{P} \to \mathcal{A}$, thus the span

$$\mathcal{A} \xleftarrow{\phi} \mathcal{P} \xrightarrow{\sqsubseteq} \mathcal{C}$$

of Σ-model morphisms describes where an entity will be placed within the context after entering at this point.

The question may arise why we are proposing a span of arrows instead of a single arrow. Here are two possible answers:

- In case of a single arrow from $\mathcal{A}$ to $\mathcal{C}$ the admission requirements would be part of the context kernel, and this seems to be not a good design decision.
- An entity may not have a "fixed place" in the context after entering, and this can be modeled by choosing $\mathcal{P}$ to be the empty model.

Service packages: According to our guidelines each entry point should offer a special package of services. Services provide the interaction between the context and an entity that has entered the context at a certain entry point. Therefore it is quite natural to model the package of services, offered at entry point $(\mathcal{A}, \phi, \mathcal{P})$, by a set $SERV_{\mathcal{A}}$ of $(\mathcal{A}+_{\phi}\mathcal{C})$-methods attached to the combined Σ-model $\mathcal{A}+_{\phi}\mathcal{C}$.

Putting the pieces together we obtain a formal model of a system **"context with entry point"**. And the configuration of this system can be described by the following pushout diagram of Σ-models and Σ-model morphisms together with attached sets of methods:

$$\begin{array}{ccccc} \mathcal{P} & \xrightarrow{\sqsubseteq} & \mathcal{C} & \leftarrow\cdots & OP_{\mathcal{C}} \\ \downarrow \phi & & \downarrow \phi^* & & \\ \mathcal{A} & \xrightarrow{\sqsubseteq} & \mathcal{A} +_{\phi} \mathcal{C} & \leftarrow\cdots & SERV_{\mathcal{A}} \end{array}$$

Of course, we can also model a context with arbitrary many entry points, where the same place may have different admission requirements and/or we may have different places with the same admission requirements.

4.2 An Entity Enters a Context

How can we describe now the scenario that an entity enters a context at a certain entry point?

Admission: Only those entities fulfilling the admission requirements $\mathcal{A}$ are allowed to enter a context at entry point $(\mathcal{A}, \phi, \mathcal{P})$. That is, an entity $\mathcal{E}$ is admitted to enter this point if a Σ-model morphism $m : \mathcal{A} \to \mathcal{E}$ can be established. This involves two steps: First, a matching graph homomorphism $m : G^{\mathcal{A}} \to G^{\mathcal{E}}$ has to be found. Second, it has to be checked if the constraints in $\mathcal{A}$ are translated by m into constraints (commitments) in $\mathcal{E}$.

The configuration of the system **"entity $\mathcal{E}$ got admission at entry point $(\mathcal{A}, \phi, \mathcal{P})$ via m"** can be described by the following diagram:

$$\begin{array}{ccccccc} & & \mathcal{P} & \xrightarrow{\sqsubseteq} & \mathcal{C} & \dashleftarrow & OP_{\mathcal{C}} \\ & & \downarrow{\scriptstyle \phi} & & \downarrow{\scriptstyle \phi^*} & & \\ OP_{\mathcal{E}} & \dashrightarrow \mathcal{E} \xleftarrow{m} & \mathcal{A} & \xrightarrow{\sqsubseteq} & \mathcal{A} +_{\phi} \mathcal{C} & \dashleftarrow & SERV_{\mathcal{A}} \end{array}$$

Adaption of Services: Due to our requirements the context has "to adapt its services to the presence of the new entity". This means that we have to make out of the set $SERV_{\mathcal{A}}$ of "service templates" a set $SERV_{\mathcal{A}}^{m}$ of services adapted to $\mathcal{E}$, that is, of $(\mathcal{E} +_{\phi;m} \mathcal{C})$-methods that will be attached then to the combined Σ-model $\mathcal{E} +_{\phi;m} \mathcal{C}$. Note, that due to general properties of pushouts the Σ-models $\mathcal{E} +_{\phi;m} \mathcal{C}$ and $\mathcal{E} +_{m} (\mathcal{A} +_{\phi} \mathcal{C})$ are equivalent (isomorphic).

In such a way, the configuration of the system **"entity $\mathcal{E}$ placed in context $\mathcal{C}$ at place $\mathcal{P}$ via $\phi; m$"** can be described by the following pushout diagram of Σ-models and Σ-model morphisms together with attached sets of methods:

$$\begin{array}{ccccccc} & & \mathcal{P} & \xrightarrow{\sqsubseteq} & \mathcal{C} & \dashleftarrow & OP_{\mathcal{C}} \\ & & \downarrow{\scriptstyle \phi;m} & & \downarrow{\scriptstyle (\phi;m)^*} & & \\ OP_{\mathcal{E}} & \dashrightarrow & \mathcal{E} & \xrightarrow{\sqsubseteq} & \mathcal{E} +_{\phi;m} \mathcal{C} & \dashleftarrow & SERV_{\mathcal{A}}^{m} \end{array}$$

In case, $\mathcal{A}$ can provide admission to a set of of places one of these places $\phi_i : \mathcal{P}_i \to \mathcal{A}$ has to be chosen and the entity will be placed at place $\mathcal{P}_i$ via $\phi_i; m$.

Internal States: We need also to consider the internal states of this system and of its components. Every component has a "local state" but what is a "global state", that is, a state of the whole system?

Our system can only be considered as an integrated whole, if the local states are related/coordinated in a certain way: A quadruple

$$(\tau_{\mathcal{E}}, \tau_{\mathcal{P}}, \tau_{\mathcal{C}}, \tau) \in Inst(\mathcal{E}) \times Inst(\mathcal{P}) \times Inst(\mathcal{C}) \times Inst(\mathcal{E} +_{\phi;m} \mathcal{C})$$

of local states constitutes a global state if, and only if,

$$[\![(\phi;m)^*]\!](\tau) = \tau_{\mathcal{C}},\ [\![\sqsubseteq]\!](\tau) = \tau_{\mathcal{E}},\ \text{and}\ [\![\phi;m]\!](\tau_{\mathcal{E}}) = [\![\sqsubseteq]\!](\tau_{\mathcal{C}}) = \tau_{\mathcal{P}}.$$

The commutativity of the square of Σ-model morphisms ensures that any local state τ of the $(\mathcal{E} +_{\phi;m} \mathcal{C})$-component represents such a global state, namely, the state:

$$([\![\sqsubseteq]\!](\tau), \tau_{\mathcal{P}}, [\![(\phi;m)^*]\!](\tau), \tau)\ \text{with}\ \tau_{\mathcal{P}} \stackrel{def}{=} [\![\phi;m]\!]([\![\sqsubseteq]\!](\tau)) = [\![\sqsubseteq]\!]([\![(\phi;m)^*]\!](\tau)).$$

Note that, in such a way, the adapted services in $SERV_{\mathcal{A}}^m$ are indeed always changing the global state since they are $(\mathcal{E} +_{\phi;m} \mathcal{C})$-methods.

A pair $(\tau_{\mathcal{E}}, \tau_{\mathcal{C}}) \in Inst(\mathcal{E}) \times Inst(\mathcal{C})$ of local states of the $\mathcal{E}$-component and of the $\mathcal{C}$-component, respectively, will be called **$\mathcal{P}$-coordinated** if $[\![\phi;m]\!](\tau_{\mathcal{E}}) = [\![\sqsubseteq]\!](\tau_{\mathcal{C}})$. The crucial fact is that any $\mathcal{P}$-coordinated pair $(\tau_{\mathcal{E}}, \tau_{\mathcal{C}})$ of local states represents also a global state since $\tau_{\mathcal{E}}$ and $\tau_{\mathcal{C}}$ can be "amalgamated" into a state $\tau_{\mathcal{E}} +_{\phi;m} \tau_{\mathcal{C}}$ of the $(\mathcal{E} +_{\phi;m} \mathcal{C})$-component such that

$$[\![(\phi;m)^*]\!](\tau_{\mathcal{E}} +_{\phi;m} \tau_{\mathcal{C}}) = \tau_{\mathcal{C}} \quad \text{and} \quad [\![\sqsubseteq]\!](\tau_{\mathcal{E}} +_{\phi;m} \tau_{\mathcal{C}}) = \tau_{\mathcal{E}}.$$

This is ensured by general results concerning the interplay of pushout and pullback constructions sometimes referred to as "van-Kampen square" [EEPT06, WD07].

Synchronization: At the moment when the entity enters the context, the present local states of the entity and of the context will be, in general, not $\mathcal{P}$-coordinated. We have to synchronize the entity and the context. That is, we have to apply $\mathcal{E}$-methods from $OP_{\mathcal{E}}$ to the present state $\tau_{\mathcal{E}}$ of the entity and/or to apply $\mathcal{C}$-methods from $OP_{\mathcal{C}}$ to the present state $\tau_{\mathcal{C}}$ of the context such that the resulting states $\tau'_{\mathcal{E}}$ and $\tau'_{\mathcal{C}}$ are $\mathcal{P}$-coordinated.

After synchronization the entity and the context constitute an integrated whole and the entity can start to work in the context.

4.3 An Entity Working in a Context

Any method anywhere in an integrated system will change the global state of the system. As discussed in Subsection 4.2, this is the case for the adapted services in $SERV_{\mathcal{A}}^m$. But, what about the methods in $OP_{\mathcal{E}}$ and $OP_{\mathcal{C}}$ attached to the entity and the context kernel, respectively?

An application of such a method can change the local state of the place and thus may violate the coordination between the local state of the entity and the local state of the context kernel. To ensure $\mathcal{P}$-coordination during the time, the entity is working in the context, we will need additional control mechanisms. We discuss three possible mechanisms:

1. **Avoidance of conflicts beforehand:** Before the entity starts to work all methods in $OP_{\mathcal{E}}$ and $OP_{\mathcal{C}}$ that can potentially change the local state of $\mathcal{P}$ are made unavailable and can not be applied as long as the entity is working in the context.

2. **Avoidance of conflicts at run time:** In case the application of a method $\mu \in OP_{\mathcal{E}}$ in a present local state $\tau_{\mathcal{E}}$ of the entity $\mathcal{E}$ would change the present local state $\tau_{\mathcal{P}} = [\![\phi; m]\!](\tau_{\mathcal{E}})$ of place $\mathcal{P}$, that is, if $[\![\phi; m]\!](\tau_{\mathcal{E}}) \neq [\![\phi; m]\!](\mu(\tau_{\mathcal{E}}))$, the entity is not allowed to apply the method. In the same way the context kernel is not allowed to apply a method if the local state of the place would be changed. Note, that this mechanism may turn methods in $OP_{\mathcal{E}}$ and $OP_{\mathcal{C}}$ into partial methods.
3. **Adaptation to changes:** If the application of a method $\mu \in OP_{\mathcal{E}}$ in a present local state $\tau_{\mathcal{E}}$ of the entity $\mathcal{E}$ changes the present local state $\tau_{\mathcal{P}} = [\![\phi; m]\!](\tau_{\mathcal{E}}) = [\![\sqsubseteq]\!](\tau_{\mathcal{C}})$ of the place $\mathcal{P}$, the context kernel may be able to adapt to this change. That is, the change from $\tau_{\mathcal{P}}$ to $\tau'_{\mathcal{P}} = [\![\phi; m]\!](\mu(\tau_{\mathcal{E}}))$ may trigger a change of the local state of the context kernel into a state $\tau'_{\mathcal{C}}$ such that $[\![\sqsubseteq]\!](\tau'_{\mathcal{C}}) = \tau'_{\mathcal{P}}$. A change of the local state of the place caused by a method applied by the context kernel may be adapted by the entity in a similar way. (A side remark: In case the other component can not adapt to a change the system runs into a deadlock or falls apart.)

Any of these control mechanisms or any combination of them makes out of the set $OP_{\mathcal{E}}$ of $\mathcal{E}$-methods and the set $OP_{\mathcal{C}}$ of $\mathcal{C}$-methods a set $OP^m_{\mathcal{E}}$ and a set $OP^m_{\mathcal{C}}$ of $(\mathcal{E} +_{\phi;m} \mathcal{C})$-methods. The methods are still attached to the entity and the context kernel, respectively, but the effect of the methods has been "globalized".

In such a way, the final running system **"entity $\mathcal{E}$ working in context $\mathcal{C}$ at place $\mathcal{P}$"** can be visualized by the following diagram:

$$
\begin{array}{ccccccc}
 & & \mathcal{P} & \xrightarrow{\sqsubseteq} & \mathcal{C} & \leftarrow\cdots & OP^m_{\mathcal{C}} \\
 & & {\scriptstyle \phi;m}\downarrow & & \downarrow{\scriptstyle (\phi;m)^*} & & \\
OP^m_{\mathcal{E}} & \cdots\rightarrow & \mathcal{E} & \xrightarrow{\sqsubseteq} & \mathcal{E} +_{\phi;m} \mathcal{C} & \leftarrow\cdots & SERV^m_{A}
\end{array}
$$

5 Conclusion

We have developed a generic formal model of *entities* and of *contexts with entry points* within the Diagram Predicate Framework (DPF). We have also described in a precise formal way two important scenarios: *an entity enters a context* and *an entity works in a context*. The model is generic in the sense that it can be instantiated for different modeling techniques by choosing an appropriate signature and semantics for this signature. Our overall claim and vision is that, in principle, all modeling techniques used in Software Engeneering can be described in this way as instances of the DPF. The latter is especially appropriate for a natural formalization of object-oriented diagrammatic modeling. On the other hand, according to [End05], object-oriented and ontology-based models are most suited for modeling context for ubiquitous computing. Therefore, we hope that the DPF, being extended and rearranged in a suitable way, can provide an appropriate formal framework for modeling context-aware systems.

There are, at least, two directions of further work.

Development of the DPF. Beside the announced meta-modeling features we are also working on a generic graph based logic for our framework.

The concept of *method* used in the present paper is a very abstract one. We have started to study how those methods can be actually defined and we have to integrate corresponding definition mechanisms into DPF. Natural candidates for those mechanisms are the various variants of graph transformations [EEPT06], and we have to investigate how to adapt and to extend them for use in the DPF. Those mechanisms should allow us to describe, in a uniform and formal way,

- the "adaption of services" and, especially,
- the idea of a "service template",
- the "avoidance of conflicts", and
- the "triggering of changes".

Context Model. The announced extension of our model by allowing different entry points should be discussed and worked out in detail. Moreover, it seems to be a reasonable effort to develop an "algebra of entities and contexts". Such an "algebra" would emerge as a generalization and/or adaptation of similar approaches like the "algebra of modules" in [EM90], the "algebra of architectural connectors" in [Fia05], and the "algebra of contextual ontologies" in [CHR08].
Acknowledgement. We are very thankful to Edward Hermann Haeusler for challenging us to investigate if our DPF can contribute to meet the "urgent need of formal models for modeling context" as it is stated in the Call for Papers. Critical comments of the anonymous referees were helpful in improving the initial version of the paper and shaping it to its current form (still far from being what we would like to have). The first author was partially supported by the Norwegian NFR project SHIP/VERDIKT, and the second author by Bell Canada through the Bell University Labs and the Ontario Centres of Excellence.

References

[CHR08] Cafezeiro, I., Haeusler, E.H., Rademaker, A.: Ontology and context. In: Sixth Annual IEEE International Conference on Pervasive Computing and Communications (PerCom 2008), Hong Kong, 17-21 March 2008, pp. 417–422. IEEE Computer Society, Los Alamitos (2008)

[DED08] Diskin, Z., Easterbrook, S., Dingel, J.: Engineering Associations: From Models to Codeand Back through Semantics. In: Paige, R.F., Meyer, B. (eds.) 46th International Conference, Tools, Objects, Components, Models and Patterns EUROPE 2008. LNBIP, vol. 11, pp. 336–355. Springer, Heidelberg (2008)

[Dis97] Diskin, Z.: Towards algebraic graph-based model theory for computer science. Bulletin of Symbolic Logic 3, 144–145 (1997); Presented (by title) Logic Colloquium 1995

[Dis03] Diskin, Z.: Mathematics of UML: Making the Odysseys of UML less dramatic. In: Kilov, H., Baclawski, K. (eds.) Practical Foundations of Business System Specifications, pp. 348–381. Kluwer Academic Publishers, Dordrecht (2003)

[DK03] Diskin, Z., Kadish, B.: Variable set semantics for keyed generalized sketches: Formal semantics for object identity and abstract syntax for conceptual modeling. Data & Knowledge Engineering 47, 1–59 (2003)

[DW08] Diskin, Z., Wolter, U.: A Diagrammatic Logic for Object-Oriented Visual Modeling. ENTCS (accepted, 2008)

[EEPT06] Ehrig, H., Ehrig, K., Prange, U., Taentzer, G.: Fundamentals of Algebraic Graph Transformations. EATCS Monographs on Theoretical Computer Science. Springer, Berlin (2006)

[EM90] Ehrig, H., Mahr, B.: Fundamentals of Algebraic Specification 2: Module Specifications and Constraints. EATCS Monographs on Theoretical Computer Science, vol. 21. Springer, Berlin (1990)

[End05] Endler, M.: Context awareness (2005) (Summary)

[Fia05] Fiadeiro, J.L.: Categories for Software Engineering. Springer, Berlin (2005)

[SLP04] Strang, T., Linnhoff-Popien, C.: A Context Modeling Survey. In: 1st Int. Workshop on Advanced Context Modeling, Reasoning and Management (2004)

[WD07] Wolter, U., Diskin, Z.: From Indexed to Fibred Semantics – The Generalized Sketch File. Technical Report Report No 361, Department of Informatics, University of Bergen (October 2007)

The Use of Adaptive Semantic Hypermedia for Ubiquitous Collaboration Systems

Patricia Seefelder de Assis[1] and Daniel Schwabe[2]

[1] Instituto Politécnico, Campus Regional de Nova Friburgo – Universidade Estadual do Rio de Janeiro (UERJ) – Caixa Postal 97.282 – 28.610-974 – Friburgo – RJ – Brazil
[2] Departamento de Informática – Pontifícia Universidade Católica do Rio de Janeiro (PUC-Rio) – Caixa Postal 38.097 – 22.453-900 – Rio de Janeiro – RJ – Brazil
patricia@iprj.uerj.br, dschwabe@inf.puc-rio.br

Abstract. Adaptation techniques often consider applications developed for single users and static scenarios. With the evolution of collaborative environments and the widespread use of mobile technologies, adaptation must take into account the use of systems at any time, anywhere and in a collaborative way. This work suggests a way to extend the Adaptive Semantic Hypermedia Design Model to include these new dimensions.

Keywords: Adaptivity, modeling, group modeling, collaboration, ubiquitous computing, ubiquitous user modeling.

1 Introduction

The evolution of communication technologies has enabled developing collaborative computer environments. Collaboration allows participants to exchange information as well as to produce ideas, simplify problems and resolve tasks. According to [7], the contribution of the team as a whole could be less than the sum of its parts without appropriate attention to group process. Hence, group interaction should be improved so that group performance surpasses the sum of individual performances. Focusing the group on the core issues and facilitating group interaction can lead to better collaboration.

In addition, the progress of mobile technologies offers wireless access to information (from the World Wide Web or other systems) from virtually anywhere at any time (ubiquitous computing). Besides the increasing availability of data and computing resources on portable devices and mobile environments, we are witnessing a new trend appointed by some as "cloud computing". One definition for cloud computing is that it is "a computing paradigm in which tasks are assigned to a combination of connections, software and services accessed over a network"[1]. The idea that applications may run somewhere on the "cloud" (whether an internal corporate network or the public Internet) seems as a way to do "business on the road".

With computing technology becoming pervasive, not only environmental factors, but also information access will become increasingly integrated into normal environments.

[1] http://searchsoa.techtarget.com/sDefinition/0,,sid26_gci1287881,00.html; last access: May/08.

T. Margaria and B. Steffen (Eds.): ISoLA 2008, CCIS 17, pp. 548–560, 2008.

A general-purpose architecture for adaptation in hypermedia systems, using the Adaptive Semantic Hypermedia Design Model (ASHDM), together with the Hypermedia Development Environment (HyperDE) [15] extended to include adaptation is presented in [1].

The ASHDM is composed by the following models: *Conceptual* (Domain) (DM), *Adaptation* (AM), *Navigation* (NM), *Interface* (Presentation) (IM), *Integration*[2] (to integrate domains) and *Adaptation Context*[3] (ACM), and provides a framework that facilitates the analysis of what is adapted, based on what the adaptation occurs (including the granularity of time) and how the adaptation is achieved. The ACM generalizes the idea of User Model and User Context Model. The proposed architecture is model-driven and ontology-based, so data and model may be handled in the same way.

Roughly speaking, we can say that data from the Adaptation Context Model and from the Domain Model are used by the Adaptation Model to alter the Navigation and Presentation Models providing content adaptation, navigation adaptation and presentation adaptation. For more details, see [1].

The original proposal was developed for a single user. In this work the proposal is reviewed considering the anywhere and any time collaborative use of systems.

2 Adaptive Ubiquitous Collaboration Systems

With respect to adaptation, computer systems should operate differently depending on the situation they are being used. Whether the user is alone or in a group; the system architecture; domain; systems approach (e.g. pedagogical, commercial); type of tasks as well as goals to achieve are examples of what should be taken into account when providing adaptation.

Adaptation is often based on User Modeling technologies. In order to tailor applications to a group, a model to represent group characteristics and their evolution is also necessary. It is important to have in mind that groups are made of individuals. Adaptivity cannot be based only on a group model. Each user (member) should be modeled as well. According to [9], mappings from individual models to group models are not linear and straightforward. One issue appointed by [2] is the compromise between what should be considered for the user as an individual and as a group member. People may behave differently when in a group. Besides, conflicts and contradictions may appear when modeling a group. Another issue is how to preserve the privacy from the members while sharing their information that is useful to the group.

Thus we can say that group adaptation is influenced by the kind of relationship among the members (group composition; how they happen to work together; if the group is a virtual community, a workgroup and so on); the available collaboration resources as well as the duration and quality of interaction (when and how the members communicate with each other).

Pervasive systems that can adapt to changing environments and availability of resources must be aware of their context since they sense and react to it. Context awareness also plays a crucial role for communities since users or groups of users can

[2] In fact, the Integration Model is not defined because we consider that integration of domains can be done through our Navigation Model.

[3] By context we mean the situation in which the application is used.

interact with each other, through interconnected smart devices, to accomplish collaborative tasks. The degree of participation of a single user may dynamically change in relation to the distance from the place where practices occur and in relation with the ability of gathering the right information at the right time, and in a proper way.

It is worth to note that context-aware systems must be able to deal with uncertain context information. A context-aware system senses its context via a network of sensors working together. Sensors are inherently inaccurate, or they could report inaccurately because they come up against a phenomenon for which they have not been designed. In addition, the resolutions, accuracies and formats of these sensors can differ from each other and thus the resulting sensed values could have conflicts and ambiguities. Another source of uncertainty is that high-level context information is deduced from low-level sensor data and the underlying reasoning systems still have limitations. There is also a gap of time between context acquisition and use of context. Therefore adaptation should take into account parameters like accuracy, confidence and ambiguity.

Two main aspects that should be considered with regard to mobility are:

- Device: new products are announced nearly every day. The number and variety of smart devices may lead to an overcharge of complex or irrelevant interaction. Moreover, this diversity of devices, all differing in fundamental ways (operating system, CPU, memory, interaction modality and screen size), may hinder adaptation to the various device contexts. Nevertheless, according to [5], the screen size of the device typically correlates with the computational resources like memory and processor and the type of wireless connection since the size of the screen determines the available space for the other parts (as the screen size grows there is more space in the back of the unit for other parts. Consequently small screens lead to less computational resources and vice versa). Moreover, the size of the screen determines the types of possible interactions.
- Network: a wireless network is essential for mobile computing. However, the Quality of Service (QoS) supported by individual networks can vary considerably and wireless networking may be an unsatisfactory experience when faced with the reliability and performance of fixed network applications. Strategies of pre-caching may be used to give the illusion of low latency and high bandwidth.

Considering the dynamic nature of the end-users' situation, the possibility of finding out a user's status at any given time provides for better adaptation. Though capturing all aspects of a user's context is impractical, it is feasible to capture the main aspects of a user's current situation to adapt the behavior of an application appropriately.

To deal with all of this, the Ambient Intelligence (AmI) paradigm seems to be an interesting line of research. AmI (or "intelligent" pervasive computing [16]) "turns a networked system of smart devices and sensors into an environment acting as a global interface between users and information systems" [18]. A key point for AmI environments is to provide adaptation thus reducing configuration effort and irrelevant user solicitation.

Agents, through their collaborative nature, inherent intelligence and awareness of their environment (and themselves), are particularly suitable for modeling the complex and dynamic situations that frequently arise in mobile computing. Intelligent agents are an attractive and viable option for realizing AmI applications due to their autonomous nature, ability to react to external events, as well as an inherent capability to be proactive in fulfilling their objectives. The ability to adapt and respond to unexpected events is enhanced with a mobility capability and reasoning facilities that more advanced agents have.

Usually, agents are colligated in a Multi-Agent System (MAS). Not only artificial agents but human users as well - together with their various types of interaction and collaboration - are materialized in MAS in a single software system [16]. Each individual agent has its own responsibilities but also collaborates with other agents to achieve complex tasks, An Agent Communications Language (ACL), shared and understood by all agents, provides for the collaboration between agents and is the basis for agents' autonomic behavior. ACL is a high-level semantic language that supports complex interactions between entities. This is essential then AmI environments deal with heterogeneous information from physical sensors, services or users preferences

One of the main properties of MAS is that it provides decentralized control, based on distributed autonomous entities, making it possible to design applications that are highly flexible, scalable and adaptive. Depending on current conditions, groups of agents are able to create and reconfigure application dynamically.

MAS can be seen as a society of agents with capacities and roles. This metaphorical system representation, similar to a human society, when interacting with users facilitates their understanding and control of the system's behavior.

The incorporation of autonomic principles into the design of Multi-Agent Systems is a way to overcome the complexity of pervasive environments. Autonomic implies a number of fundamental features including: self-configuring, self-healing, self-optimizing and self-protecting [14].

The agent-based and multi-agent system paradigm is an effective approach for modeling Collaborative Ubiquitous Environments (CUEs) since the relevant entities in pervasive computing systems are autonomous components capable of establishing high-level interactions with each other. These entities should be cooperative (i.e., able to collaborate one with each other according to coordination patterns that define who is involved in a task and with which role) and context-aware (i.e., able to perceive and share information about the context in order to adapt themselves).

Next we present an example scenario to give a hint of how adaptation in CUE can improve the use of systems. Then we review the ASHDM considering these new dimensions of collaboration and ubiquity.

3 Example Scenario

Larry, Helen, and Paul work together on a budget to present to a client. Larry is the manager; Helen is responsible for collecting prices in several countries and Paul analyzes prices, exchange rates, taxes and delivery conditions to find the best offer. It is a big client and they work according to the any time and anywhere paradigm to get the most effective proposal. Thus, on her way home, Helen's mobile notifies her about a great computer offer. Meanwhile Paul is notified about a significant decrease on the exchange rate. Larry decides that it is worth updating the proposal. Though working on the same document, each of them sees a different output, according to their context. Helen cannot see graphics because she is working on a small-screen device. The system decides the kind of communication according to the bandwidth: when she enters a high bandwidth zone, the system shows also a VOIP option. Otherwise, she may only communicate through textual chat. Paul has a help text besides the document because he isn't familiar with the system.

When they close the proposal, Helen sends a print command to her printer at home so that everything is ready when she passes by to pick her baggage and leave to meet the client.

As a manager, Larry has access to high-level information through links shown in a different color. According to his preferences, when the group works on the same environment, using the same screen, the system may hide these links or show them as disabled. When on the same environment, the help screen is shown because at least one member of the group is not proficient in using the system. As Paul gets accustomed with the system the help text becomes less and less detailed.

This small example gives only a taste of how a system can adapt itself according, for example, to individual or group preferences, bandwidth and kind of device. The parameters are captured at real-time giving more agility to the decisions.

4 ASHDM Reviewed

4.1 Conceptual Model

The Conceptual Model is considered to be any ontology defined for the Semantic Web that uses concepts and relationships between them to represent the real world. This representation is supposed to be application-independent, and it may overlap with the UM (see section 3.4.).

The use of ontologies is appropriate to represent information in pervasive computing [19].

4.2 Navigation Model

Navigational objects are considered to be views over conceptual objects. These views are based on user's tasks and user's profile. The Navigation Model is specified by an ontology-based vocabulary that defines navigational classes, links, navigational contexts, access structures and landmarks. Views are defined by mapping a conceptual ontology into this navigational ontology.

The Navigation Model can be understood as an Integration Model in the sense that navigational views can be constructed over conceptual ontologies defined for different domains. We can extend the idea to integrate information from a diverse range of sources thus concerning pervasive computing that is by nature open and extensible. However cooperating parties may use different ontologies, which can be ambiguous. It is necessary to define a mapping disambiguation policy.

4.3 Interface Model

The Interface Model (IM) represents the interaction between users and system through Abstract and Concrete Widgets Ontologies, and the mapping from abstract to concrete as proposed by [13]. Essentially, this interaction occurs through events that can be "activators" (Button/Link); "exhibitors" (Image/Label) and "capturers" (widgets such as CheckBox, ComboBox, RadioButton or an element composed by Link).

These ontologies were designed to be easily extensible in order to incorporate new technologies. They will be reviewed to incorporate the many different interaction interfaces that characterize pervasive computing environments and to account for entities like agents and mobile technology.

4.4 Adaptation Context Model

This is the core model with respect to adaptation. This section is organized as follows: first we present our point of view about the correlation between domain, user and context; then we present a User Model Schema; next we present ideas about group modeling and, finally, we consider the use in pervasive systems.

Usually, Adaptive Hypermedia Systems (AHSs) are used for domains where the user exists as an individual and is typically modeled by a class in the domain model. So the User Model (UM) may contain an overlay model representing the relationship between the user and the domain concepts. This relationship is in the sense of knowing or having a previous experience with the modeled concept (e.g.: in the e-learning domain, to represent what the user – or student - knows about the subject matter and in e-commerce domain, this relationship may represent if the user – or customer - already bought a given product). In these cases, the adaptation depends on the *domain user* or simply, *user*. In the examples above, user is modeled by the "student" or "customer" classes in the domain model.

Sometimes, however, there is no need to consider the user as an individual for adaptation purposes. If the adaptation is based on the bandwidth, or on display size, or on the place where it occurs, and so on, the result of the adaptation is the same for every *adaptation user* or *meta-user*.

We consider that the *meta-user* is represented by a UM which is a component of a general adaptation context. A User Representation (UR) is used to model the representation of the *user* in the particular domain (e.g., "student" or "customer"), and may be related to other domain concepts (overlay model).

To avoid redundancy, we need to unify the data in the UM and in the UR. A simple way of doing this is by inheritance. In ASHDM the UR is defined as a subclass of the UM metaclass. Thus the UR may have its own attributes as well as the attributes inherited from UM.

The unified user information has to be integrated with other context and domain data. We use the notion of view to create a virtual context with all needed information.

Figure 1 shows an example of a virtual museum with a class `User` that has five attributes: `ID` (identifier), `name`, `address`, `birthday` and `favorites` (to record the rooms selected by the user). The ACM contains the attribute `display`, the UM also stores `ID` and `name`, together with `cognitive style` and `presentation preferences`. The overlay attribute `history` represents rooms already visited by the user. For adaptation, the Context View has the attributes: `age`, `interest categories`, `history` and `display`. The `interest category` could be inferred from `age`, for example.

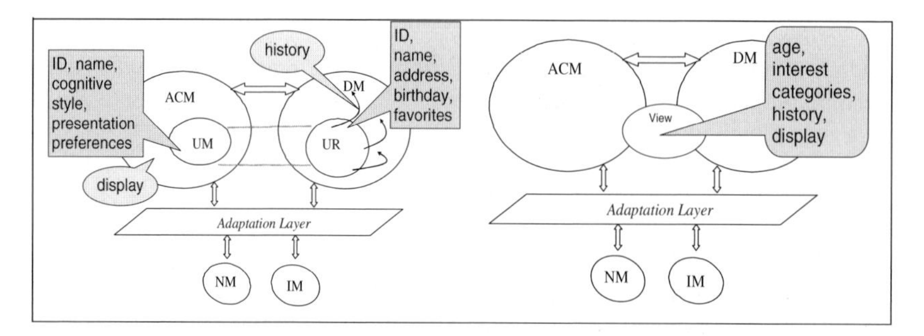

Fig. 1. Example of Adaptation Context View

4.4.1 User Model Schema

Research in user modeling area states that the User Model should be independent from AHSs, facilitating the tasks of constructing and maintaining the UM and enabling the reuse of the model. Application from the same domain or from similar domains could cooperate using the same part of the UM [12]. The semantics of a UM must be known, and the identification of which part is domain-independent and which one is common for all domains must be done in order to share a UM [12].

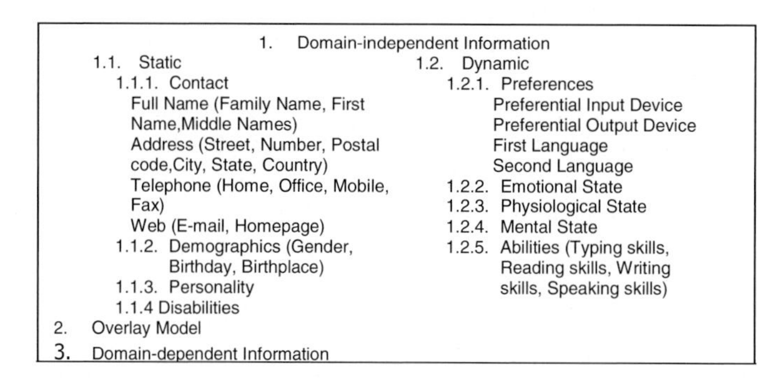
1. Domain-independent Information
- 1.1. Static
  - 1.1.1. Contact
    - Full Name (Family Name, First Name,Middle Names)
    - Address (Street, Number, Postal code,City, State, Country)
    - Telephone (Home, Office, Mobile, Fax)
    - Web (E-mail, Homepage)
  - 1.1.2. Demographics (Gender, Birthday, Birthplace)
  - 1.1.3. Personality
  - 1.1.4 Disabilities
- 1.2. Dynamic
  - 1.2.1. Preferences
    - Preferential Input Device
    - Preferential Output Device
    - First Language
    - Second Language
  - 1.2.2. Emotional State
  - 1.2.3. Physiological State
  - 1.2.4. Mental State
  - 1.2.5. Abilities (Typing skills, Reading skills, Writing skills, Speaking skills)

2. Overlay Model
3. Domain-dependent Information

Fig. 2. User Model Structure: Domain-independent Information

The use of ontologies helps to structure the UM, but which information should be represented in the UM, and which one in the DM is an open question. As far as the adaptation mechanism is concerned, it actually makes no difference where (UM or DM) the data is stored, because the adaptation context view joins all this information. However, structuring user-related data independently from the domain may enable reuse across domains and applications.

We consider that information useful for any application independently from the domain-specific semantic, such as preferred input device, should be stored in the UM, Preferences and data about the user which do not make sense for all domains – such as performance, preferred musical style, learning style, salary and so on – are classified as Domain-dependent information and should be stored in the DM. However, since the domain ontology may be arbitrary, it must be considered that some user information may be represented in the domain ontology. For example, IMS LIP [10], a typical UR used in the DM of educational applications, stores user identification information, which in principle should be in the UM. On the other hand, it is possible to obtain domain-dependent data from ontologies like IMS LIP by eliminating all user-related classes that do not have a "knowledge meaning". This is possible because the use of metamodels and ontologies enable the definition of a metarule that queries the ontology definition e.g., "retrieve all resources whose domain belongs to user-class and whose property is not 'knows'".

We propose a modular structure for the UM divided in three main categories: Domain-independent data; Overlay model, and Domain-dependent data. The general idea is based on GUMO (General User Model Ontology) [8]. The proposal, presented in Figure 2, is only a core structure. New information may be added as needed, and some information may be ignored in some applications.

In the proposed structure, static information is used for customization, as it does not change during system use. Contact information is mostly used for administrative tasks. Demographic and Personality are information suitable for most domains, although not all applications have mechanisms to deal with it.

Whereas GUMO models the five senses and the ability to walk and speak, we assume them as default. The absence of one or more of them is modeled as a deficiency. Information about emotional, physiological and mental states as well as some abilities is theoretically suited for all domains, although only specific applications deal with it. Furthermore, such user characteristics are difficult, if not impossible, to extract automatically, making them less likely to be used in most applications. We include them only for completeness.

In many domains, adaptation is based not only on user and environment characteristics, but also on relations between the user model and the domain model. The existence of a relationship between the user model and the domain concepts is usually represented in an Overlay Model. As we said, this relationship is in the sense of knowing or having a previous experience with the modeled concept.

This schema proposes a way to organize the UM so that the UM core together with some modules could be shared between applications of the same kind and same domain. This structure also allows the definition of metarules that select rules according to the model properties. For example, "if the UM has the property nationality, include news about the user's country".

This modular structure satisfies the requirements proposed by [11]: (a) different views of the UM may be available for each adaptive application, which will define only the UM components it needs; (b) a user may define which parts of the UM will be available to which applications; (c) users may want to have their personal data stored locally and may choose which data will be outside his/her direct control.

We consider the proposed UM as a task ontology that can be integrated with the application domain ontology. According to [3], "task ontology" defines a vocabulary for modeling a structure inherent to problem solutions for all tasks in a domain-independent way whereas the vocabulary defined for "domain ontology" specifies object classes and relationships that exist in certain domains.

4.4.2 Group Modeling

When groups are taken into account, before creating the virtual context, a pseudo-user is modeled to summarize the attributes of the members, according to system's features and group's characteristics. How this is done depends on the Adaptation Engine being used. In a homogeneous group, the average value of all elements of the group may be used. Otherwise, a value of the most dominant element (according to some governance criteria) can be chosen.

The attributes of the pseudo-user do not overlay the individual ones and can have different meanings. The knowledge and mistakes of the pseudo-user, for example, could represent the success or failure of the group in some task, while the values inferred at the individual level remains (in the overlay model, for example). On the other hand, if a pseudo-user has some skill (or background), it could mean that at least one group member has it. Attributes such as age or gender may be set considering the group uniformity level. Preferences can reflect some governance criteria.

In the above example: `age` could be replaced by an average age (when the members of the group have similar ages), by a number that represents a dominant age (when visiting a museum, the age of each member may differ a lot and a child may have a stronger influence) or by null indicating that the age should not be taken into account because of large age disparities between group members; `history` could store places visited by at least one member, by the majority of the members or by all members, according to the governance criteria, for example.

We consider that the pseudo-user is a kind of group modeling. The Group Model (GM) itself can be used to represent data inherent to the group like the kind of relationship between members; the nature of interactions among members and so on. There is a need for an association class between a User and a Group to represent attributes of a user with respect to the group, such as the role played by the user within the group.

4.4.3 Pervasive Computing

Typical pervasive computing environments are characterized as having large amounts of continuously changing contextual information. Dynamic adaptation to the changing environment can be achieved due context reasoning. The use of ontologies (to represent context data) and ontology reasoning mechanisms makes context reasoning more powerful and precise.

Typical ontologies for such systems are location, agent (describe actors in a system), temporal and activity (to model actions that can be performed by agents). According to [19], "these concepts permeate all of pervasive computing, while common peripheral or task specific contexts may be introduced for specific applications (such as music, weather, and settings of the room)".

Since uncertainty must be taken into account when dealing with pervasive systems, concepts like accuracy, confidence, uncertainty and provenance should be considered with respect to context data and represented as part of their ontological description.

4.5 Adaptation Model

The Adaptation Model is inspired by the AHAM reference model [4] and consists of a set of rules that define how the adaptation must be performed.

AM uses rules following PRML (Personalization Rules Modeling Language) [6], where <body> may represent an action, or an action associated to a condition:

```
When event do         When event do          When event do
      <body>                action              If condition then action
endWhen               endWhen                endWhen
```

In ASHDM, `events` are interactions between users and systems, represented in the Interface Model (see 3.3). `Actions` may adapt the content, navigation or presentation and may also update the ACM, including the UM. `Conditions` refer to the parameters for adaptation (based on what the adaptation occurs).

When considering collaborative and pervasive environments, `events` may also be interactions between users or triggered by agents. GM, pseudo-user and context ontologies will also be updated as a result of `Actions`.

As we will see in the next section, HyperDE is model-driven and rules may be used to adapt the models themselves or their instances. Therefore, the use of adaptation rules together with HyperDE enables the meta-adaptation where the kind of adaptation may also be adapted according to several parameters.

5 Implementation Architecture

The HyperDE environment, extended with adaptation mechanisms was chosen to implement the ASHDM, since it is a framework and development environment for hypermedia application, driven by ontologies. Figure 3 shows the general HyperDE architecture.

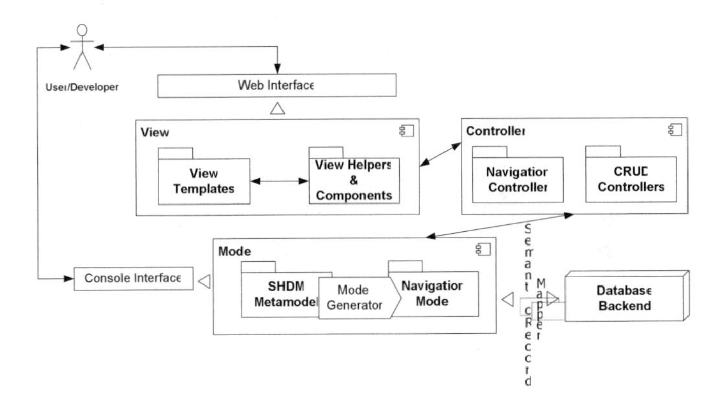

Fig. 3. HyperDE General Architecture

HyperDE allows program code to be passed as function parameter (closure). Thus, hooks may be defined to associate adaptation rules to the control, model or view layers, according to the desired adaptation type. PRML rules conditions usually test attribute values according to aspects on which the adaptation is based, whereas actions alter content, navigation or presentation and may also update the models. The presentation adaptation as proposed by ASHDM has not yet been implemented, since HyperDE currently does not use the abstract and concrete ontologies proposed by [13] (for more details see [1]). Therefore, whereas events from PRML rules are captured by the IM in the ASHDM Adaptation Model, in HyperDE they are captured by the control layer.

When an `event` is detected, the control layer is activated. Rules are executed, if it is the case. Then the control layer triggers events at the model layer passing the parameters needed to instantiate the models, i.e., which metaclass will be instantiated and with which values. If the metaclass has associated rules, they will be executed (conditional instantiation) and the result is the adapted application navigation model. Next, the control layer activates (selects) the view to render the application. This selection may be conditional and the CSS code associated to the view may change if existing associated rules alter them. The adapted page is then presented to the user.

As an example we can consider a collaborative task to be done by a group of four students. When one of them connects to the learning environment, all other members are warned. The kind of message depends on the connection and device being used. For example, a student in a desktop receives the name and hour of connection while other with a cell-phone sees only a sign. Animations may be shown only for students with a high bandwidth and so on.

6 Conclusions and Future Work

Adaptive Hypermedia techniques have been employed to suit Hypermedia Systems to individual needs in order to make the use of such systems more efficient. Now, these techniques should be employed considering groups of users and ubiquitous computing. Ubiquitous Collaboration Systems poses many challenges. This work highlights the most important open questions and shows that it is possible to extend the ASHDM to suit such kind of systems.

The proposed model is a general-purpose one thus being useful to the several domains where adaptation applies. Besides, it defines distinct semantic models and the interrelationships between them. Adaptation can be done on the models as well as on their relationships favoring the meta-adaptation. The proposed implementation architecture is model-driven and adaptation can be directly obtained by altering these models or their instances through rules defined as part of the Adaptation Model.

The use of ontologies provides a common vocabulary for models and data contributing to a modular architecture and to the implementation of the meta-adaptation. According to [17], ontology-based models are a promising context modeling approach for ubiquitous computing environments. They provide a formal way to model context into well-structured terminologies, and also support formal reasoning mechanisms. Moreover, the need for adaptable and reconfigurable applications strongly calls for a modular design approach [18]. Therefore, ASHDM being ontology-based and driven by models fits well to CUEs.

Adaptation is not user-centered on ASHDM. The idea is that the UM can be considered as a component of a general ACM. The introduction of a pseudo-user class to represent the relevant attributes of the elements of a group - according to a Group Model and rules defined by an Adaptation Engine - facilitates the mapping from individuals features to a composed profile.

Context-awareness is an inherent property of the proposed architecture. The notion of using a view to create a Virtual Context helps to put together what should be considered in Adaptive Systems.

It was shown that ASHDM suits the CUEs due its ontology-based and modular nature. On the other hand, the AmI paradigm seems to be a good alternative to deal with context-awareness and dynamic environments. Further work should be done to show how to effectively integrate AmI principles into ASHDM.

In the same way, the MAS paradigm as an option to realize AmI applications and model CUEs needs to be further explored and incorporated into ASHDM.

More example scenarios should be developed and case studies need to be implemented in order to evaluate the proposed ideas.

Additional research should be done in order to show how ASHDM may fit other projects, involving context-awareness and adaptation, under development.

Acknowledgement. The authors were partially supported by a grant from CNPq.

References

1. Assis, P.S., Schwabe, D., Nunes, D.A.: ASHDM Model Driven Adaptation and Meta Adaptation. In: Wade, V.P., Ashman, H., Smyth, B. (eds.) AH 2006. LNCS, vol. 4018, pp. 213–222. Springer, Heidelberg (2006)
2. Barra, M.: Distributed Systems for Group Adaptivity on the Web. In: Brusilovsky, P., Stock, O., Strapparava, C. (eds.) AH 2000. LNCS, vol. 1892, pp. 396–402. Springer, Heidelberg (2000)
3. Chen, W., Mizoguchi, R.: Learner Model Ontology and Learner Model Agent. In: Kommers, P. (ed.) Cognitive Support for Learning Imagining the Unknown, pp. 189–200. IOS Press, Amsterdam (2004)
4. De Bra, P., Brusilovsky, P., Houben, G.J.: Adaptive Hypermedia: From Systems to Framework. ACM Computing Surveys 31(4) (1999), http://www.cs.brown.edu/memex/ACM_HypertextTestbed/papers/25.html
5. Deters, R.: Pervasive Computing Devices for Education. In: Proceedings of the Workshop on International Conference on AI and Education, Multi Agent Architectures for Distributed Learning Environments, San Antonio, Texas, pp. 49–54 (2001)
6. Garrigós, I., Gómez, J., Barna, P., Houben, G.J.: A Reusable Personalization Model in Web Application Design. In: International Workshop on Web Information Systems Modeling (WISM 2005) (Held in conjunction with ICWE 2005), Sydney, Australia (2005)
7. Goodman, B.A., Drury, J., Gaimari, R.D., Kurland, L., Zarrella, J.: Applying User Models to Improve Team Decision Making. MITRE Sponsored Research Final Report (2006), http://www.mitre.org/work/tech_papers/tech_papers_07/06_1351/06_1351.pdf
8. Heckmann, D., Schwartz, T., Brandherm, B., Schmitz, M., von Wilamowitz Moellendorff, M.: GUMO The General User Model Ontology. In: Proceedings of UM 2005: International Conference on User Modeling, Edinburgh, UK (2005), http://www.gumo.org
9. Hoppe, U., apud Winter, M., McCalla, G.: An Analysis of Group Performance in Terms of the Functional Knowledge and Teamwork Skills of Group Members. In: Hoppe, U., Verdejo, F., Kay, J. (eds.) Artificial Intelligence in Education, pp. 261–268. IOS Press, Amsterdam (2003)
10. IMS Learner Information Packaging Best Practice & Implementation Guide. Final Specification, V. 1.0 (2001), http://www.imsglobal.org/profiles/lipbest01.html

11. Kay, J., Kummerfeld, R.J., Lauder, P.: Personis: a server for user models. In: De Bra, P., Brusilovsky, P., Conejo, R. (eds.) AH 2002. LNCS, vol. 2347, pp. 203–212. Springer, Heidelberg (2002)
12. Kuruc, J.: Sharing a User Model between Several Adaptive Hypermedia Applications, IIT SRC (2005), http://www.fiit.stuba.sk/iit-src/38-kuruc.pdf
13. Moura, S.S.: Desenvolvimento de interfaces governadas por ontologia para aplicações hipermídia, Dissertação de Mestrado, PUC Rio (2004)
14. Muldoon, C., O'Hare, G.M.P., O'Grady, M.J.: Collaborative Agent Tuning: Performance Enhancement on Mobile Devices. In: Dikenelli, O., Gleizes, M.-P., Ricci, A. (eds.) ESAW 2005. LNCS (LNAI), vol. 3963, pp. 241–258. Springer, Heidelberg (2006)
15. Nunes, D.A.: HyperDE um Framework e Ambiente de Desenvolvimento dirigido por Ontologias para Aplicações Hipermídia. MSc.Dissertation, PUC Rio. HyperDE (2005), http://server2.tecweb.inf.pucrio.br:8000/projects/hyperde/trac.cgi/wiki
16. Seghrouchni, A.E.F., Breitman, K., Sabouret, N., Endler, M., Charif, Y., Briot, J.P.: Ambient Intelligence Applications: Introducing the Campus Framework. In: Proc. of the 13th IEEE International Conference on Engineering of Complex Computer Systems (ICECCS 2008), Belfast, pp. 165–174 (2008) ISBN 0 7695 3139 3
17. Strang, T., Linnhoff Popien, C.: A context modeling survey. In: Proceedings of the Workshop on Advanced Context Modelling, Reasoning and Management as part of UbiComp 2004, Nottingham/England (2004)
18. Vallée, M., Ramparany, F., Vercouter, L.: A Multi Agent System for Dynamic Service Composition in Ambient Intelligence Environments Doctoral Colloquium – Pervasive, Munich, Germany (2005)
19. Ye, J., Coyle, L., Dobson, S., Nixon, P.: Ontology based models in pervasive computing systems. The Knowledge Engineering Review 22(4), 315–347 (2007)

The Use of Formal Ontology to Specify Context in Ubiquitous Computing

Karin K. Breitman[1] and Michael G. Hinchey[2]

[1] PUC-Rio, Computer Science Department
Rua Marquês de São Vicente 225 - 22453-900, Rio de Janeiro, RJ, Brazil
karin@inf.puc-rio.br
[2] Lero-the Irish Software Engineering Research Centre
International Science Centre, University of Limerick, Ireland
mike.hinchey@lero.ie

Abstract. Although context-awareness is a central paradigm for the implementation of ubiquitous systems, it still lacks adequate representation models, methods and tools that support the development of such systems. Particularly, in order to secure interoperability and allow device interaction, software applications are required to provide unambiguous data and device representation models. In this paper we argue in favor of the use of formal ontology as the tool to formalize the notion of context, describe the interplay between systems and environments and, ultimately, enable verification. Ontologies allow machines to process and integrate devices intelligently, enable quick and accurate search, facilitate communication between a multitude of heterogeneous devices and enable reasoning [22].

1 Introduction

In the last few years emergent technologies, such as 3rd generation mobile phones, WiFi computers and Bluetooth devices are being combined to create what is known as ubiquitous computing infrastructures - systems that are accessible from anywhere, at any time, and with (almost) any electronic device. Ubiquitous computing is leveraging new business models and encouraging new ways of working. Ubiquitous and mobile collaboration systems are creating a demand for new conceptualizations, models, methodologies, and support technologies to fully explore its potential.

The methods, tools and technologies required to support these new ways of working are still under investigation. It is very likely that concepts and technologies from a variety of related fields, such as workflow systems, software engineering, formal methods, human computer interaction, semantic web and ontology engineering, will need to be revisited and made adequate "for consumption" in ubiquitous computing systems. In this paper we focus in the issue of formalizing the notion of context and context awareness, i.e., the ability of a system to sense the current environment and autonomously adapt in order to reach optimal operation, control its general behavior and provide interface adequately with its users. We argue in favor of the use of formal ontology. In particular we favor a specific family of representation, those that use the W3C recommended ontology language, OWL.

T. Margaria and B. Steffen (Eds.): ISoLA 2008, CCIS 17, pp. 561–571, 2008.

The rest of this paper is divided as follows. In section 2 we discuss the use of ontologies in computer science, in sections 3 and 4 we discuss ontology implementation languages RDF and OWL. In section 5 we define the notions of context and context awareness in ubiquitous computing. In section 6 we revisit some ubiquitous computing environments and discuss how they acquire and represent context, from an ontological point of view. In section 7 we present our concluding remarks.

2 Ontologies

The word ontology comes from the Greek *ontos* (being) + *logos* (word). It was introduced in philosophy in the nineteenth century by German philosophers to distinguish the study of being as such from the study of various kinds of beings in the natural sciences. As a philosophical discipline:

The subject of Ontology is the study of the categories of things that exist or may exist in some domain. The product of such a study, called an ontology, is a catalogue of the types of things that are assumed to exist in a domain of interest D from the perspective of a person who uses a language L for the purpose of talking about D. The types in the ontology represent the predicates, word senses, or concept and relation types of the language L when used to discuss topics in the domain D. [21]

In computer science, ontologies were adopted in artificial intelligence to facilitate knowledge sharing and reuse [7, 4] Today, their use is becoming widespread in areas such as intelligent information integration, cooperative information systems, agent-based software engineering and electronic commerce. Ontology is defined in Guarino [8] as "an artifact, constituted by a specific vocabulary used to describe a certain reality, plus a set of explicit assumptions regarding the intended meaning of the vocabulary." Ontologies are conceptual models that capture and make explicit the vocabulary used in semantic applications, thereby guaranteeing communication free of ambiguities.

To ensure effective information sharing among devices, ontologies need to be expressive enough to establish a common terminology that guarantees consistent interpretation. We adopt the ontology structure $\mathcal{O}$ proposed by Maedche [12]. According to the author, an ontology can be described by a 5-tuple consisting of the core elements of an ontology, i.e., concepts, relations, hierarchy, a function that relates concepts non-taxonomically and a set of axioms. The elements are defined as follows:

$\mathcal{O} := \{\mathcal{C}, \mathcal{R}, \mathcal{H^C}, rel, \mathcal{A^O}\}$ consisting of :

- Two disjoint sets, $\mathcal{C}$ (concepts) and $\mathcal{R}$ (relations)
- A **concept hierarchy**, $\mathcal{H^C}$: $\mathcal{H^C}$ is a directed relation $\mathcal{H^C} \subseteq \mathcal{C} \times \mathcal{C}$ which is called concept hierarchy or taxonomy. $\mathcal{H^C}(\mathcal{C}_1, \mathcal{C}_2)$ means $\mathcal{C}_1$ is a subconcept of $\mathcal{C}_2$
- A **function** $rel: \mathcal{R} \rightarrow \mathcal{C} \times \mathcal{C}$ that relates the concepts non taxonomically
- A set of ontology **axioms** $\mathcal{A^O}$, expressed in appropriate logical language.

Each concept in the ontology is represented by two types of description, as opposed to dictionaries, lexicons, glossaries and thesauri, that provide a monolith description. The first type is the denotation, the intended meaning, of the ontological concept. The denotation is equivalent to a description found in a typical dictionary. The second type of description is the connotation of the ontological concept, that is, additional meaning provided by the composition with other concepts ($\mathcal{C}$) or relations ($\mathcal{R}$) in the ontology. The connotation of an ontology concept describes how a concept relates to others in the ontology, composing new meanings. Those are represented using both taxonomical (hierarchical) relationships of the type $\mathcal{H}^{\mathcal{C}}$ and non taxonomical ones (rel: $\mathcal{R} \rightarrow \mathcal{C} \times \mathcal{C}$). This representation has a parallel in the work of Umberto Eco, in which he defines a system of codes based on signs, denotations, connotations and a set of rules (the set of relationships that relate signs to denotations and connotations) [6,1].

Most existing ontology representation languages can be mapped to the structure discussed above [12]. It is important to note, however, that because first-order logic is known to be intractable, we restrict to description logic based ontology languages as the paradigm formal system. Briefly, description logic models the application domain by defining the relevant concepts of the domain and then using these concepts to specify properties of objects and individuals occurring in the domain. In the next two sections we discuss two ontology implementation languages that translate to description logics. It is not our intent to make a lengthy discussion, but rather to highlight the features that are important to the formalization of context awareness in ubiquitous computing environments.

3 Ontology Implementation Languages: RDF

The *Resource Description Framework* (RDF) is a general-purpose language for representing information in the Web. It is particularly intended for representing metadata about Web resources, but it can also be used to represent information about objects that can be identified on the Web, even when they cannot be directly retrieved from the Web. To some extent, RDF is a lightweight ontology language to support interoperability between applications that exchange machine-understandable information on the Web.

RDF has a very simple and flexible data model, based on the central concept of the RDF statement. We also consider the concept of vocabulary as part of the RDF data model, due to its relevance to ontology modeling. RDF offers three equivalent notations: RDF triples, RDF graphs, and RDF/XML. An *RDF statement* (or simply a *statement*) is a triple *(S, P, O),* where

- *S* is a URIref[1], called the *subject* of the statement
- *P* is a URIref, called the *property* (also called the *predicate*) of the statement, that denotes a binary relationship
- *O* is either a URIref or a literal, called the *object* of the statement; if *O* is a literal, then *O* is also called the *value* of the property *P*

Let ***s*** be the resource identified by the URIref *S*. We also say that ***s*** *has a P property of O*, or that ***s*** *has a P property with value O.*

[1] A *Uniform Resource Identifier* (URI) is a character string that identifies an abstract or physical resource on the Web. A *URI reference* (URIref) denotes the common usage of a URI, with an optional *fragment identifier* attached to it and preceded by the character "#".

Literals are character strings that represent datatype values. Literals may not be used as subjects or properties in RDF statements.

A *vocabulary* is a set of URIrefs and is therefore synonymous with an XML namespace. Note that, because a vocabulary is a set, each URIref must be unique within a vocabulary. A vocabulary *V* is frequently specified in two alternative ways. The first alternative uses qualified names to define *V* as follows.

- Select a fixed URIref `U` and a prefix `p` for it
- Define a set of qualified names with prefix `p`
- Define *V* as the set of URIrefs represented by such qualified names

A set ***R*** of RDF statements should be understood as expressing the conjunction of the statements. The URIrefs used in the RDF statements in ***R*** may be taken from *native* vocabularies, that is, vocabularies defined exclusively for ***R***, or from *imported* vocabularies, that is, vocabularies defined elsewhere.

RDF provides an extension that allows for modeling simple ontologies, containing classes and properties, and hierarchies, known as the *RDF Vocabulary Description Language 1.0: RDF Schema* (RDF Schema or RDF-S).

In RDF Schema, a *class* is any resource having an `rdf:type` property whose value is the qualified name `rdfs:Class` of the RDF Schema vocabulary. A class *C* is defined as a *subclass* of a class *D* by using the predefined `rdfs:subClassOf` property to relate the two classes. The `rdfs:subClassOf` property is transitive in RDF Schema.

A *property* is any instance of the class `rdfs:Property`. The `rdfs:domain` property is used to indicate that a particular property applies to a designated class, and the `rdfs:range` property is used to indicate that the values of a particular property are instances of a designated class or, alternatively, are instances (i.e., literals) of an XML Schema datatype. A comprehensive account of RDF and RDF Schema can be found in Manola and Miller [13].

RDF however, is criticized as an ontology language because it lacks expressiveness [10]. In the RDF Schema logical connectives such as negation, disjunction and conjunction are not provided, thus restricting the expressive power of the ontology.

4 Ontology Implementation Languages: RDF and OWL

The *Web Ontology Language* (OWL) describes classes, properties, and relations among these conceptual objects in a way that facilitates machine interpretability of Web content. OWL is the result of the Web Ontology Working Group (now closed) and descends from DAML+Oil, which is in turn an amalgamation of DAML and OIL.

OWL is defined as a vocabulary, just as are RDF and RDF Schema, but it has a richer semantics. Hence, an ontology in OWL is a collection of RDF triples, which uses such vocabulary. The definition of OWL is organized as three increasingly expressive sublanguages: *OWL Lite* (offers hierarchies of classes and properties, and simple constraints with enough expressive power to model thesauri and simple ontologies), *OWL DL* (increases expressiveness and yet retains decidability of the classification problem) *and OWL Full* (complete language, without limitations, but it ignores decidability issues).

OWL Full can be viewed as an extension of RDF, whereas OWL Lite and OWL DL are extensions of restricted forms of RDF.

RDF is more expressive than OWL Lite and OWL DL exactly because the RDF data model imposes no limitations on how resources (URIrefs) can be related to each other. For example, in RDF, a class can be an instance of another class, whereas OWL DL and OWL Lite require that the sets of URIrefs that denote classes, properties, and individuals be mutually disjoint. Therefore, care must be taken when translating from RDF to OWL Lite or OWL DL.

OWL DL offer constructs to specify complex class descriptions and to define class restrictions and axioms, as summarized in Table 1.

Table 1. Class constructors used in OWL

Term	Set Theory	DL	Description
owl:Thing	U	$\top$	the set of all individuals
owl:Nothing	$\varnothing$	$\bot$	the empty set
owl:oneOf	$\{x_1,\dots,x_n\}$		the set of $x_1,\dots,x_n$
rdfs:subClassOf	$A \subseteq B$	$A \sqsubseteq B$	A is a subset of B
<owl:Restriction> ... R ... </owl:Restriction>	$\{x / R\}$		the set of all things satisfying R
owl:equivalentClass	$A = B$	$A \equiv B$	A is equal to B
owl:intersectionOf	$A \cap B$	$A \sqcap B$	A intersection B
owl:unionOf	$A \cup B$	$A \sqcup B$	A union B
owl:complementOf	$\sim B$ $A \sim B$	$\neg B$ $A \sqcap \neg B$	complement of B w.r.t. U complement of B w.r.t A
owl:disjointWith	$A \cap B = \varnothing$	$A \sqcap B \equiv \bot$	A and B are disjoint

OWL allows the description of a class C to include a restriction R on the individuals that may belong to C. The specification of R is always based on some property P of C and, as such, R is called a *property restriction* (in the sense of a restriction defined with the help of a property). In set-theoretic notation, this is equivalent to saying that C is subjected to a restriction of the form $C \subseteq \{x / R\}$.

Note that the above set inclusion allows the existence of individuals that satisfy R and yet are not in C. In other words, R defines a necessary, but not sufficient, condition for an individual to be in C.

In OWL notation, a class definition with a restriction has the following pattern.

```
1. <owl:Class rdf:about=C >
2.        ...
3.        <rdfs:subClassOf>
4.            <owl:Restriction>
5.                <owl:onProperty rdf:resource=P>
6.                ... declaration of restriction R...
7.            </owl:Restriction>
8.        </rdfs:subClassOf>
9.        ...
10. </owl:Class>
```

Set Theory: $C \subseteq \{x / R\}$

Lines 4 to 7 define the (unnamed) class of all things that satisfy R, and line 3 indicates that C is a subclass of such a (unnamed) class. The pattern in lines 3 to 8 may be repeated to define multiple restrictions for the same class.

Restriction declarations may be of three types: quantified restrictions; cardinality restrictions; and value restrictions (also called filler information).

A *quantified restriction* may be an existential or a universal restriction, declared with the help of `owl:someValuesFrom` and `owl:allValuesFrom`, respectively. An *existential restriction* for C, P, and D requires that every instance c of C must have at least one occurrence of property P whose value is an instance of D. An existential restriction therefore corresponds to a description logic inclusion of the form $C \sqsubseteq \exists P.D$.

A *universal restriction* for C, P, and D requires that, for every instance c of C, if c has an occurrence of a property P whose value is d, then d must be an instance of D. Note that a universal restriction does not require c to have at least one occurrence of property P. A universal restriction therefore corresponds to a description logic inclusion of the form $C \sqsubseteq \forall P.D$.

For example, assume that we have two classes, `Conf` and `EuropeanCity`, whose instances represent conferences and cities in Europe, respectively, and a property, `heldIn`, which maps conferences into cities. We may then define a new class, `heldInEuropeConf`, and restrict it to contain only individuals that are conferences held at least once in a European city as follows

```
1. <owl:Class rdf:about="heldInEuropeConf">
2.    <rdfs:subClassOf rdf:resource="Conf"/>
3.    <rdfs:subClassOf>
4.       <owl:Restriction>
5.          <owl:onProperty rdf:resource="heldIn"/>
6.          <owl:someValuesFrom rdf:resource="EuropeanCity"/>
7.       </owl:Restriction>
8.    </rdfs:subClassOf>
9. </owl:Class>
```

Set Theory: $\texttt{heldInEuropeConf} \subseteq \texttt{Conf} \cap \{x / \exists y(\texttt{heldIn}(x, y) \wedge y \in \texttt{EuropeanCity})\}$

Description Logic: $\texttt{heldInEuropeConf} \sqsubseteq \texttt{Conf} \sqcap \exists \texttt{heldIn.EuropeanCity}$

Lines 4 to 7 define the (unnamed) class of all things with at least one occurrence (there may be more than one) of the `heldIn` property whose value is an instance of the `EuropeanCity` class. Lines 2 and 3 indicate that the `heldInEuropeConf` class is a subclass of the intersection of this (unnamed) class and the `Conf` class. Note that the OWL fragment in lines 1 to 9 does not guarantee that `heldInEuropeConf` contains all individuals that are conferences held at least once in a European city (that is, it is a necessary, but not sufficient condition).

A full account of OWL and its sub languages can be found in Dean and Schreiber (2004) and in McGuinness and Harmelen (2004).

5 Context Awareness

Context can be defined as any information which characterizes the state of a resource (of a device), of a user or of an environment. In particular, we are interested in handling the following types of context information [2,3]:

- System context: data about the mobile device's and the network resources, including device capabilitie, currently free memory, CPU utilization, battery level, connectivity status, connectivity parameters (such as IP address, mask, current wireless (Wifi) access point, etc.
- Physical context: data about a device's or an environment's symbolic location (as opposed to its geographic position), city, country, and data collected from sensors, such as temperature, noise, luminosity, acceleration, etc.
- Time context: information such as hour of the day, day of the week, week of the year, month, year, etc.
- User context: data that indicate the user's role, profile, preferences, activity, etc. Compared to the other types of context information, this is the only kind of information which can not be inferred automatically and requires some user intervention.

Finding an adequate, machine processable, conceptual representation for the notion of concept is fundamental in securing interoperability in ubiquitous computing environments. The chosen conceptual model should enable devices to communicate with each other with users by means of ad-hoc wireless networking, enable users to control and interact with the environment in natural (voice, gesture) and personalized ways (preferences, context), thus providing users with an environment that offers services when and if needed. Of course such representation should be expressive enough as to help in identifying, choosing and activating such services.

Additionally, the representation should allow for reasoning. Context data in ubiquitous environments is uncertain and, most of the time, imperfect. Reasoning, in this case, is used to detect possible errors, inconsistencies and verify data. Reasoning is also fundamental for any kind of context-oriented decision-making, e.g. system adaptations according to user-provided or learned decision rules.

Context reasoning in ubiquitous computing is very complex due to the dynamic, imprecise and ambiguous nature of context data, the need to process large volumes of data, and the fact that reasoning needs to be performed in a decentralized, cooperative way amongst several entities. Approaches to context reasoning include ontological, rule-based, distributed and probabilistic reasoning [22]. In this paper we focus on ontological reasoning. In the next section we discuss the adoption of formal ontology in ubiquitous computing environments.

6 Use of Formal Ontology in Ubiquitous Computing Environmopents

In this section we discuss some ubiquitous computing environments in respect to how they acquire and formalize context, their use of ontology and reasoning.

The multi agent CoBrA infrastructure provides a framework that supports software agents, services and device interaction [3]. It is built around a context broker component, responsible for providing an export schema to represent and mediate context information and use inference to detect and correct data inconsistencies. Context is acquired using a library of procedures over a set of predefined sensors.

The infrastructure makes use of the CoBrA (COBRA-ONT) and SOUPA ontologies. The first is used by software agents as the means to exchange context knowledge. The second, SOUPA, is a standard ontology for supporting pervasive and ubiquitous computing applications. CoBrA's context reasoning is backed by the Jena rule engine, the Java Expert System Shell (JESS) and the Theorist system. The reasoning for interpreting context information uses two different rule-based systems. Jena rule-based reasoners are used for OWL ontology inferences and the JESS rule engine is used for interpreting context using domain specific rules.

The CHIL project developed a middleware infrastructure capable of acquiring context information using software agents [20]. Context information is obtained from sensors by software agents and made accessible to other agents of the performed through special *Proxy agents,* that are responsible for interfacing with the agent framework. Mechanisms for modeling composite contextual information and describing networks of situation states are also available.

A general-purpose vocabulary comprising multi-sensor smart spaces and context-aware applications is provided via the CHIL ontology [16]. Inference is based on the notion of a *network of situation states*. According to this approach, a situation is considered as a state description of the environment expressed in terms of entities and their properties. Changes to individual or relative properties of specified entities correspond to events that signal a change in the situation.

The Context-Aware Middleware Ubiquitous Robotic Companion System (CAMUS) is a context-aware infrastructure for the development and execution of a network-based intelligent robot system [11]. In CAMUS, a sensor framework processes input data from various sources such as physical sensors, applications and user commands and transfers them to the Context Manager component through the event system.

CAMUS implements four different abstraction level ontologies: common, domain, infrastructure and specific domain ontologies. The common ontology provides the high-level knowledge description to context-aware applications. The *domain ontology layer* is a specialization of the *common ontology layer* and provides domain specific knowledge to context-aware applications. The next, more specific layer, is composed of the *infrastructure domain ontology* and a set of *specific domain ontologies* for the application. The *infrastructure domain ontology* is the schema of the context model that is represented and managed in the context-aware system. The *specific domain ontology* provides descriptions of specific services, for example, a presentation service. Ontology reasoning in CAMUS is done using RACER [9], that offers inference support to the discovery of subsumption/instance relationships and consistency verification of context knowledge base. First order, temporal, higher order, fuzzy logic reasoners are also available.

The distributed semantic service framework, OWL-SF [15], supports the design of ubiquitous context-aware systems considering both the distributed nature of context information and the heterogeneity of devices that provide services and deliver context. It uses OWL to represent high-level context information, that is encapsulated in Super Distributed Objects (SDOs) [18]. An SDO may be sensors, devices, user's interfaces (GUIs) or services.

Each functional entity implemented as OWL-SDO has to be described using its own ontology containing terminological knowledge that enables the automatic classification of the object into appropriate service categories. Reasoning is achieved using the RACER OWL-DL reasoner [9].

The Campus framework supports the development of multi- agent, context aware, pervasive computing applications [19,22]. Campus is designed to provide the necessary infrastructure for ubiquitous computing environments. Based on multi agent system technology, Campus provides an infrastructure to develop innovative context aware applications that accommodate an ample spectrum of mobile and fixed devices. The support for semantic interoperability, offered by the communication and coordination layer, allows for the discovery, exchange and collaboration among hybrid devices, regardless of proprietary representations of information. Context is acquired using MoCA (*Mobile Collaboration Architecture*), a service-oriented architecture that supports the development of context-aware applications and services for mobile computing [17]. Besides a small and simple set of APIs to build such systems, MoCA provides efficient services to collect, store and distribute context information associated with mobile devices

The Campus ontology serves as a knowledge base for the framework implementation, i.e., provides the necessary semantics to allow high level exchanges, including brokering, negotiation and coordination amongst software agents. It contains precise definitions for every relevant concept in the framework e.g, it defines that a service is described by a tuple containing its name, a parameter list, a capability list, the communication port number, and protocol. Ontology reasoning in Campus, as well as in CAMUS and OWL-SF is done using the RACER inference mechanism [9].

7 Conclusions

In this paper we argued that formal ontology is most adequate to represent the notion of context in ubiquitous computing because they are semantically richer, i.e., provide greater power of expression than more traditional software modeling techniques such as taxonomies, entity relationships or OO. Also, ontologies organize conceptual knowledge using a complex and accurate representations that are above and beyond hierarchical approaches. Moreover, if written using the OWL ontology language discussed in sections ***, they also present the following advantages

- can be verified/classified with the aid of Inference Mechanisms, e.g. RACER and FaCT:
- consistency checks
- classification
- new information discovery
- use a XML/RDF syntax that allows them to be automatically manipulated and understood by most resources on the Internet
- capture and represent finely granulated knowledge
- are modular, reusable and code independent - ontology driven applications are specified separately from the ontology itself. Changes to the ontology donot impact the code or vice versa

- can be combined with emerging rule languages, such as the semantic web rule language (SWRL)

We surveyed a few ubiquitous computing environments, with special regards to their use of ontology and reasoning mechanisms. We conclude that, at some level, they support the use of formal ontology to represent important concepts. More importantly, most make use of inference to aid the classification of new concepts and to verify overall consistency.

References

1. Carnap, R.: The Methodological Character of Theoretical Concepts. In: Feigl, H., Scriven, M. (eds.) Minnesota Studies in the Philosophy of Science, vol. I. University of Minnesota Press, Minneapolis (1956)
2. Chen, H.: An Intelligent Broker Architecture for Pervasive Context-Aware Systems. PhD thesis, Department of Computer Science, University of Maryland, Baltimore County
3. Chen, H., Finin, T., Joshi, A.: An ontology for context-aware pervasive computing environments. Special Issue on Ontologies for Distributed Systems, Knowledge Engineering Review
4. Davies, J., Fensel, D., Harmelen, F.V. (eds.): Towards the Semantic Web: Ontology Driven Knowledge Management. John Wiley & Sons, New York (2003)
5. Dean, M., Schreiber, G. (eds.): OWL Web Ontology Language Reference. W3C Recommendation (February 10, 2004), `http://www.w3.org/TR/owl-ref/`
6. Eco; Umberto - A theory of Semiotics. Indiana University Press, Bloomington (1979)
7. Fensel, D.: Ontologies: A Silver Bullet for Knowledge Management and Electronic Commerce. Springer, New York (2001)
8. Guarino, N.: Formal ontology and information systems. In: Proceedings of the First International Conference on Formal Ontologies in Information Systems, FOIS 1998, Trento, Italy, pp. 3–15 (1998)
9. Haarslev, V., Möller, R.: RACER system description. In: Goré, R.P., Leitsch, A., Nipkow, T. (eds.) IJCAR 2001. LNCS (LNAI), vol. 2083. Springer, Heidelberg (2001)
10. Heflin, J., Hendler, J.: A Portrait of the Semantic Web in Action. IEEE Intelligent Systems, 54–59 (March/April 2001)
11. Kim, H., Cho, Y., Oh, S.: CAMUS: A Middleware Supporting Context-aware Services for Networkbased Robots. In: IEEEWorkshop on Advanced Robotics and Social Impacts (2005)
12. Maedche, A.: Ontology Learning for the Sematic Web. Kluwer Academic Publishers, Dordrecht (2002)
13. Manola, F., Miller, E. (eds.): RDF Primer. W3C Recommendation(February 10, 2004), `http://www.w3.org/TR/rdf-primer/`
14. McGuinness, D.L., Harmelen, F.V. (eds.): OWL Web Ontology Language Overview. W3C Recommendation (February 10, 2004), `http://www.w3.org/TR/owl-features/`
15. Mrohs, B., Luther, M., Vaidya, R., Wagner, M., Steglich, S., Kellerer, W., Arbanowski, S.: OWL-SF – a distributed semantic service framework. In: Proceedings of the Workshop on Context Awareness for Proactive Systems (CAPS 2005), Helsinki, pp. 67–77 (2005)
16. Pandis, I., Soldatos, J., Paar, A., Reuter, J., Carras, M., Polymenakos, L.: An ontology-based framework for dynamic resource management in ubiquitous computing environments. In: Proceeding of the 2nd International Conference on Embedded Software and Systems, Northwestern Polytechnical University of Xi'an, PR China, pp. 16–18 (December 2005)

17. Sacramento, V., Endler, M., Rubinsztejn, H.K., Lima, L.S., Gonçalves, K., Nascimento, F.N., Bueno, G.: MoCA: A Middleware for Developing Collaborative Applications for Mobile Users IEEE Distributed Systems Online, vol. 5(10) (October 2004) ISSN 1541-4922
18. Sameshima, S., Suzuki, J., et al.: Platform Independent Model and Platform Specific Model for SDOs. Final recommended specification, OMG (2004)
19. Seghrouchni, A.E.F., Breitman, K.K., Sabouret, N., Endler, M., Charif, Y., Briot, J.P.: Ambient Intelligence Applications: Introducing the Campus Framework. In: Proc. of the 13th IEEE International Conference on Engineering of Complex Computer Systems, vol. 1, pp. 165–174. IEEE Computer Society Press, Los Alamitos (2008)
20. Soldatos, J., Dimakis, N., Stamatis, K., Polymenakos, L., Crowley, J.L.: A breadboard architecture for pervasive context-aware services in smart spaces: middleware components and prototype applications. Pervasive and Ubiquitous Computing 11, 193–212
21. Sowa, J.F.: Knowledge Representation: Logical, Philosophical and Computational Foundations. Brooks/Cole, Pacific Grove, CA, USA (1999)
22. Viterbo, J., Mazuel, L., Charif, Y., Endler, M., Sabouret, N., Breitman, K.K., Seghrouchni, A.E.F., Briot, J.P.: Ambient Intelligence: Management of Distributed and Heterogeneous Context Knowledge. In: Dargie, W. (ed.) Context-Aware Self managing Systems. CRC Studies in Informatics series. CRC Press, Chapman & Hall

High Service Availability in MaTRICS for the OCS

Markus Bajohr and Tiziana Margaria

Chair Service and Software Engineering, Universität Potsdam
August Bebel Str. 89, 14482 Potsdam, Germany
{bajohr,margaria}@cs.uni-potsdam.de

Abstract. Internet services are becoming an integral part of our daily environment. Nobody sees the background of the configuration of the services and its backend systems, but it is expected that critical services, like flight booking systems, online banking, etc. are resilient against server and service faults. Therefore those services often run in a cluster on several machines in an Active/Standby configuration in a clustered mode.

We present how we realize remote configuration and fault tolerance of the Online Conference Service (OCS) with our service oriented framework MaTRICS. Our solution lets the services untouched and uses the cluster management software *heartbeat* to provide high availability.

1 Motivation

Continuous and reliable operation of services is of central importance, yet services like web, mail, etc. are still commonly provided by single servers hosting them. The availability of such services can be increased by redundant installation on several machines, possibly distributed at different locations. In case of a service fault of the active machine we need a mechanism for switching a redundancy machine to active. Providing such mechanisms at low overhead is one of the services offered by MaTRICS [1], our model-based service-oriented platform for remote intelligent configuration and management of systems and services.

MaTRICS allows remotely connected users (here, service or system administrators) to test and modify the configuration of any service provided on (application) servers, like email-, news- or web-servers. MaTRICS can seamlessly manage configuration processes on heterogeneous software and hardware platforms, which are performed from a variety of peripherals unmatched in today's practice, including lightweight mobile terminals like SMS or PDAs.

In this paper, we describe how a high availability architecture based on heartbeat [5, 12, 15] enhances MaTRICS with a number of test- and reconfiguration services ready to be parameterized and executed. We have realized this for our continuously running instances of the Online Conference Service (OCS) [6, 7, 8], a complex collaborative decision support system implemented as an internet service. The OCS proactively helps authors, Program Committee chairs, Program Committee members, and reviewers to cooperate efficiently during the distributed process of selecting a conference program. The important characteristic is

T. Margaria and B. Steffen (Eds.): ISoLA 2008, CCIS 17, pp. 572–586, 2008.

that the service is customizable and flexibly reconfigurable online at any time, for each role, for each conference, and for each user. The OCS has been successfully used for over 100 computer science conferences, mostly with LNCS proceedings [8]. Springer's cluster for OCS has thus evident high availability and high performance requirements: totalling at any time over 2000 users worldwide, the services are active and used in a 24x7 way, for weeks. Remote access to and monitoring of the services and of the server cluster at any time, also *during non-working hours* are therefore of vital importance. Those operations could be traditionally carried out only inside the local network, sometimes even only on the console.

We now manage the installation of new (conference-specific) instances of the OCS on a high availability cluster and administrative tasks like starting/stopping or updating the services with MaTRICS. MaTRICS also monitors every service and in case of a fault, it starts an intelligent reconfiguration process of the backend server systems to guarantee the reliable continuous operation of the OCS. Via the notification management of the MaTRICS framework we can generate notifications for each communication channel, like SMS, EMail, SIP, etc.

MaTRICS provides a scalable and model-driven solution to the problem of accessing, stopping, reconfiguring, and restarting application servers, web servers, databases, memory, and process monitors at any time over a large variety of communication channels. The proposed solution requires limited capabilities and has a non-invasive footprint in terms of flexibility (e.g., access rights management) and mobility (e.g., personal communication channels). Every process definition is modelled at the service logic level in the jABC [11,17], and then verified wrt. properties with jABC's integrated model checker GEAR [4]. This game based model checker allows us to formally verify essential process properties in a flexible *what-if* scenario.

In the following, we summarize the MaTRICS framework from an architectural point of view (Sect. 2) and the design concept of heartbeat (Sect. 3), then in Sect. 4 we show its integration in MaTRICS. Sect. 5 shows the server- and network-architecture of the cluster hosting over 100 parallel running instances of the OCS. Sect. 6 deals with our model-based service design style to design availability test services for the OCS, which directly interacts with heartbeat. Finally, Sect. 7 draws the conclusions and sketches how we may extend the current capabilities to support also high-availability hardware and middleware solutions.

2 The MaTRICS Framework

As described in [1], MaTRICS is a distributed system for the remote intelligent configuration of server systems that offers

- an architecture for the platform independent management and platform dependent execution of *configuration tasks*, which comprise in our vocabulary installation, update, upgrade, reconfiguration of system and application software packages

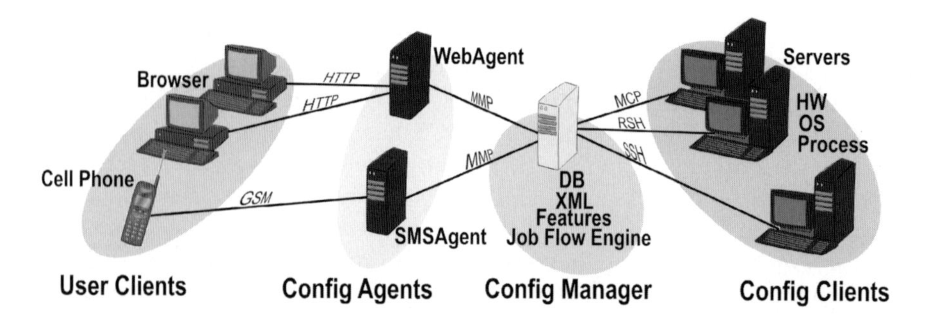

Fig. 1. The High-level Architecture of MaTRICS

- facilities for carrying out these configuration tasks from thin, mobile clients (like phone, fax, PDAs)
- and an environment for the *eXtreme Model Driven Design* [10] of all the configuration tasks, meaning that the models for those tasks are executable and also amenable to formal analysis and verification.

A physical server system usually provides a number of services, each coming with an own configuration format that depends on the version number of a service and the underlying operating system, and is stored in different files distributed over the file system. Updating a service thus results in an adaptation of the old configuration to the new one, which requires the execution of a set of activities, expressible by means of a *configuration workflow*. Its distributed architecture is shown in Fig. 1.

- *Users* access the MaTRICS from their thin terminals via protocol-specialized agents called `ConfigAgents`.
- `ConfigAgents` serve as protocol adapters between the client-specific protocols and the `ConfigManager`.
- `ConfigClients` are the servers to be configured. They communicate with the `ConfigManager` via standard protocols, like SSH or RSH.
- Any modification of the configuration of a `ConfigClient` is caused by user activities (sent to the `ConfigManager` via the `ConfigAgent` adaption) that require the execution of configuration workflows on that client. This is done by the `ConfigManager`'s `JobFlow-Engine`.

2.1 The ConfigManager

The `ConfigManager` is the heart of MaTRICS. It is conceptually organized in the following components (see Fig. 2), called layers due to their sequential use in the lifetime of a request/grant cycle:

- a **Communication layer** handles the `ConfigAgents`. It communicates over the MaTRICSManagerProtocol (`MMP`) the presentation data for the user clients in a uniform XML format, realized by the `AgentProtocolManager`. The `ConfigAgent` transforms them for appropriate display on the user's client.

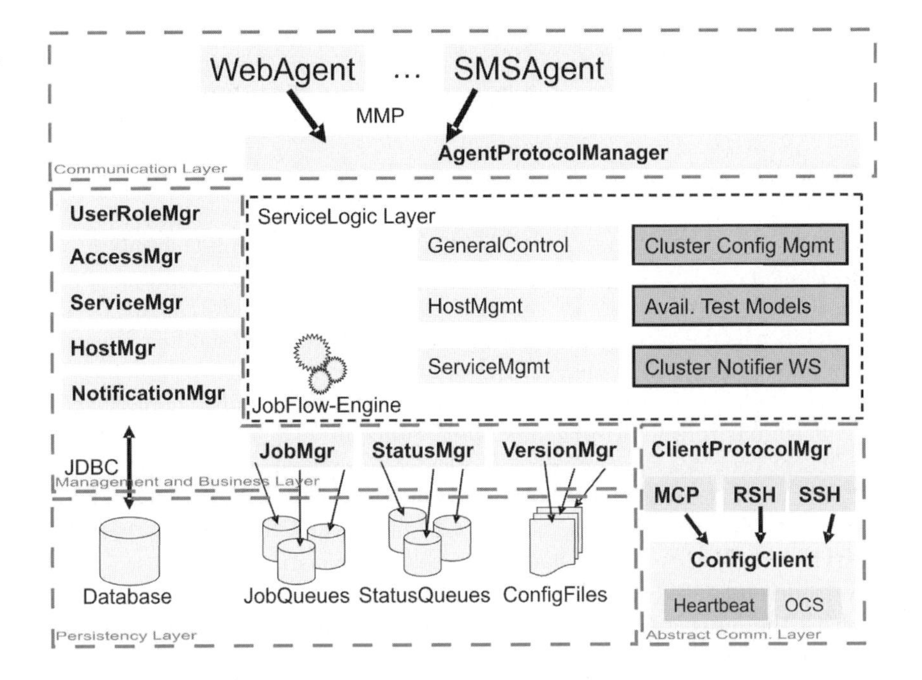

Fig. 2. The Core of MaTRICS: The ConfigManager

- a **Coordination and ServiceLogic layer** handles the configuration services and contains the basic services. For example, the `Cluster Configuration Management` service enables the configuration of heartbeat and the service availability management components. As any (configuration) service within the MaTRICS, also these are built via ServiceLogicGraphs (`SLG`).
- a **Management- and Business layer** contains the core components shared by all sessions and services. They provide a standardized interface for the coordination layer and the basic services of the MaTRICS.
- a **Persistency layer** for backend services, like database, queues, or file system.
- an **Abstract communication layer** takes care of the heterogeneity of protocols and formats for the `ConfigClients`. The `ClientProtocolManager` provides methods for processing jobs from the job flow engine, translating the jobs into the `ConfigClient`'s shell language.
- the **Notification layer** contains a notification management for sending messages to users on different communication channels, like SMS, EMail or SIP.

2.2 Model Based Design of MaTRICS Services

In MaTRICS, every workflow for a service is accurately defined by an operational *model* that contains its business logic, including alternatives, special cases, and exception handling. This model, expressed as *Service Logic Graph* (SLG) [9,17] is formally defined as a deterministic finite state automaton, and it is automatically analyzable via model checking. Configuration workflows are executed in the `ConfigManager`, the centralized core component of MaTRICS.

3 Hearbeat

Heartbeat [5,12,15] is a fundamental part of the High-Availability Linux project. It provides core cluster management services, including membership, communication, resource monitoring, and management services, IP address takeover etc. The machines in the cluster communicate with each other by sending "heartbeat packets" about twice a second. Heartbeat runs scripts on the primary node to bring the applications up and shut them down (on the standby nodes). In that way, it is similar to a multi-machine "init" process.

Heartbeat provides a generic peer-to-peer solution for high availability by running availability tests on the services (called resources). If a test fails, heartbeat starts its failover mechanisms, defined by rules called constraints, to activate the service on another node. Heartbeat reads its constraint database for every cluster node and takes the applications from the failed node over to the cluster node with the highest score. The failed node is marked with a failcount, which excludes its from the score calculation. For our purpose we have defined three constraints for every cluster group:

- Applications shall run on the preferred node: Score = 100
- Never run applications on unreachable nodes: Score = $-\infty$
- Run applications on nodes marked standby. For every standby node there is a constraint with Score = 10

The goal of heartbeat is that the defined services, called resources, can be run on every defined cluster node and heartbeat takes care to start and stop a service. Thereby heartbeat guarantees that a service runs only on one node, the one with the highest score. Sets of services can be arranged by resource groups. This means that all services of a resource group have to move in its defined order to another cluster node if any of these services is faulty.

The configuration of resource groups and resources is done by the bundled manager programs, like cibadmin. This information is stored in the cluster information base (CIB), a set of XML-based files for every cluster node. Modifications of the CIB are done by its manager programs in form of XML-based fragments. This kind of configuration is very complex and error-prone. Furthermore the stability of a cluster can be affected by invalid XML snippets.

In this context MaTRICS plays three roles:

1. it is used to configure the cluster with its cluster nodes and resources,
2. it watches over the cluster state and stores all cluster changes in its own history database,
3. finally, it monitors heartbeat by executing special test models, see Sect. 6.

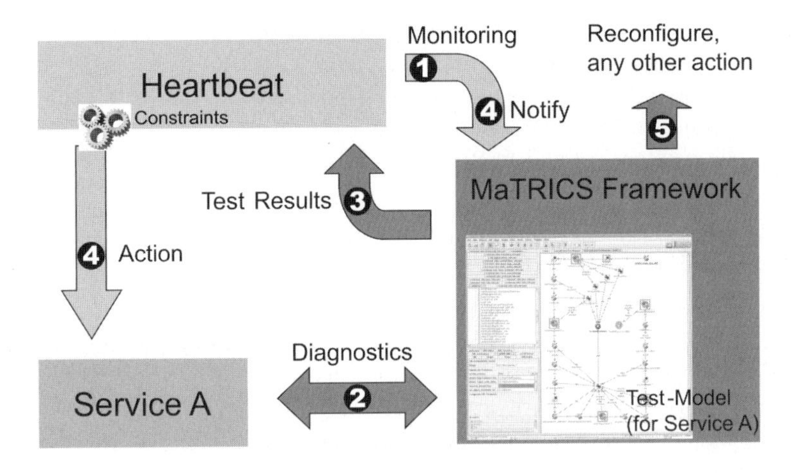

Fig. 3. The Interaction of Heartbeat and MaTRICS

Accordingly, for the integration there are some problems to solve:

- Executing the heartbeat manager programs for modifying the CIB
- Receiving the actual state of a cluster and its resources
- Monitoring a resource by our test models.

4 Heartbeat Integration in MaTRICS

Fig. 3 shows the high level architecture of the heartbeat integration in MaTRICS. The constraints and resources with their actions for Service A in heartbeat's CIB have to be defined via scripts in OCF- or LSF-format [13]. Similar scripts are also used for the monitoring and management process of a service.

Instead of using those scripts, we delegate the *monitoring process of heartbeat* (1) to the MaTRICS framework. For every service we define a specific testcase model in the jABC: it describes the test workflow (here for service A) to be executed for monitoring. The advantage is that the jABC test cases are more precise than the heartbeat OCF-/LSF-scripts. For example, a fault of service A can only be detected by heartbeat if the entire service is down. It is also difficult to design a test case in an OCF-/LSF-script to detect a service fault if only a component of service A does not work properly.

MaTRICS periodically connects to the service and runs the test cases described by the test model (2). The results are validated and returned back to heartbeat (3). If the test results detect a fault heartbeat runs the actions defined in the corresponding OCF-script (4), e.g. stop the resource on actual node and start it on another node. Thereby heartbeat sends a notification about the cluster changes to MaTRICS (4). MaTRICS retrieves the actual cluster state from one cluster node and updates its cluster history database. At need MaTRICS can invoke any other action, like notifying the system administrator (5).

In this configuration the ConfigManager is the central point of failure, because if it is itself down the heartbeat daemons cannot get the test results. We solve this problem by enhancing our own OCF-scripts with a connection that checks the ConfigManager. If it is unreachable the heartbeat daemons run only a simple check on the service, defined in its OCF-scripts, like doing a HTTP-request to the first page of an internet service.

4.1 Enhancing the ConfigManager

Fig. 2 shows the core components of the ConfigManager. The configuration and monitoring workflows for heartbeat are designed in the Service Logic Layer (gray components).

The `Cluster Configuration Management` service, discussed in Sect. 4.3, describes the configuration process of a heartbeat cluster. It allows dynamic modifications on existing clusters, like adding or removing resources, groups and constraints.

The `Cluster Notifier WebService` is a webservice for receiving notifications from the heartbeat cluster processes. It is called by the external OCF-/LSF-scripts from the heartbeat daemons, described in Sect. 4.2. The logic of this service is specified by its Service Logic Graph, see Fig. 4.

In addition, the service tests invoked by the heartbeat daemons are designed by Service Logic Graphs, too. In Sect. 6 we present a test model for the OCS, an internet service for managing scientific conferences.

4.2 Receiving the Actual Cluster State

Notifications from heartbeat can be received in MaTRICS either by adapting all scripts with transmit statements to MaTRICS, or by delegating the transmit statements to special virtual primitives. We prefer the second solution because we want to be independent and not resort to modifying scripts by other providers. Every primitive of a resource is included in an ordered group with a beginning virtual primitive `VPB` and a corresponding ending virtual primitive `VPE` that notify MaTRICS. The cluster state is only changed after the execution of primitive `P`, while `VPB` and `VPE`, as virtual primitives, only notify MaTRICS before and after a change of the cluster. These notifications are used in MaTRICS for updating its cluster history.

To get the current cluster state the service of Fig.4 is executed. The notification for MaTRICS is done by a HTTP request, which contains an authentication and a cluster identifier. `VPB` and `VPE` are OCF-scripts, which are directly executed from the shell environment of the heartbeat daemons. The generation of a HTTP request can be done by invoking wget.

The SLG of Fig. 4 is the notifier webservice for MaTRICS, which is accessed by its URL from external programs, like the OCF-scripts `VPB` or `VPE`. This service is also executed periodically every n minutes by a thread of the ConfigManager: cluster changes are refreshed automatically without sending a notification from the scripts. Heartbeat operations are indicated by "hearts" icons.

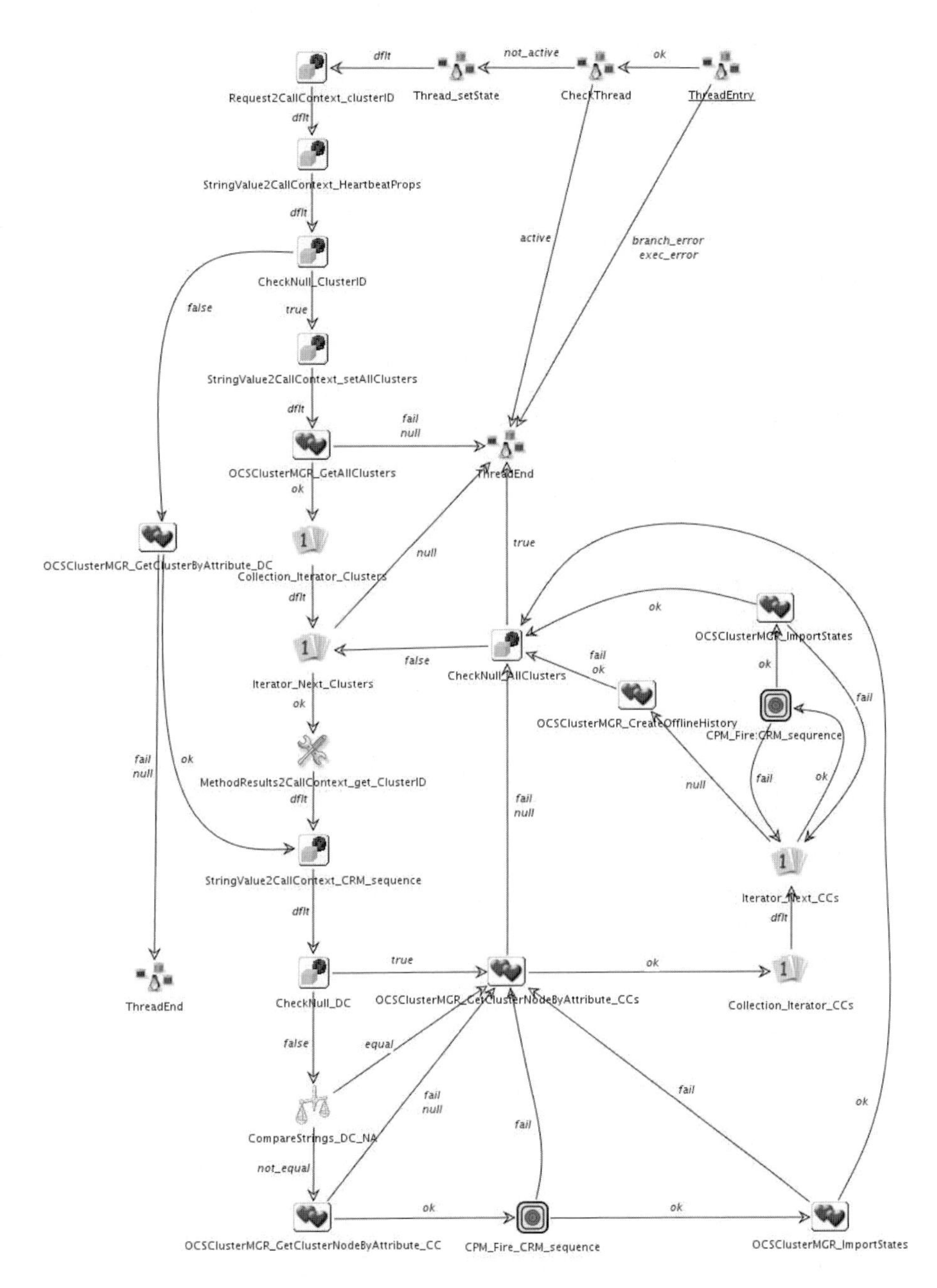

Fig. 4. MaTRICS Service Get_heartbeat_cluster_state

The start node `ThreadEntry` (at the top right) initializes the service and checks the authorization of the request. It is then checked if the request transmitted a clusterID. If not, the cluster information for all running clusters must be read by iteration over each cluster. Otherwise it takes the left path to

OCSClusterMGR_GetClusterByAttribute_DC, which gets the Designated Coordinator (DC), the master node of the cluster, from the ClusterManager, the core component of the Cluster Configuration Management service.

First of all the DC should connected, because this node must be always reachable. If the DC was set (CheckNull_DC), the connection to the ConfigClient representing the DC can be established. The connection to the ConfigClient is done by the CPM_Fire_CRM_sequence. This node is a GraphSIB, which represents another model: we use hierarchical structures in our models.

The connection method (SSH, RSH, Telnet, etc.) is transparent for the service and is handled by the ClientProtocolManager, the core connection library of the ConfigManager. In the GraphSIB CPM_Fire_CRM_sequence the cluster monitor tool of heartbeat crm_mon is called. The results are handed over to OCSClusterMGR_ImportStates, which parses the input and stores the results into the MaTRICS cluster history database.

The service is terminated by ThreadEnd if it is called with a valid clusterID (CheckNull_AllClusters). Otherwise the next clusterID is read from the set of clusters (Iterator_Next_Clusters) to get the next cluster state.

Two special cases need specific handling: if no valid DC is given and if all cluster nodes are down.

- If no valid DC can be detected by the ClusterManager, a connection to another cluster node of the cluster has to be established. Therefore OCSClusterMGR-_GetClusterNodeByAttribute_CCs returns all members of the cluster. For each member the crm_mon command has to be executed by the GraphSIB CPM_Fire_CRM_sequence. If the result could not be parsed or stored into the database the next ConfigClient is chosen.
- The cluster is offline if the actual cluster state could not be read from any node of the cluster. Then the cluster history has to be updated to offline by OCSClusterMGR_CreateOfflineHistory.

4.3 Configuring and Managing Heartbeat

With MaTRICS, we want to provide an easy to use interface for the configuration and management of a heartbeat cluster. The main configuration of heartbeat is stored in the configuration files ha.cf and authkeys. These files must once be adapted to the own cluster and network architecture.

The definition of resources, groups and constraints has to be defined into the Cluster Information Base, an XML file. For modifications of the CIB during runtime, heartbeat provides a special update mechanism for distributing the CIB to each cluster node. Therefore a update of the CIB has to be done by invoking the CIB-admin scripts of the heartbeat package.

The Cluster Configuration Management service of MaTRICS stores the configuration of the CIB in its own format. We use a relational database design, which stores the clusternodes, resources, resourcegroups and constraints in separate tables. The initial CIB XML-File is generated from this database and all modifications are done by creating XML snippets, which are deployed

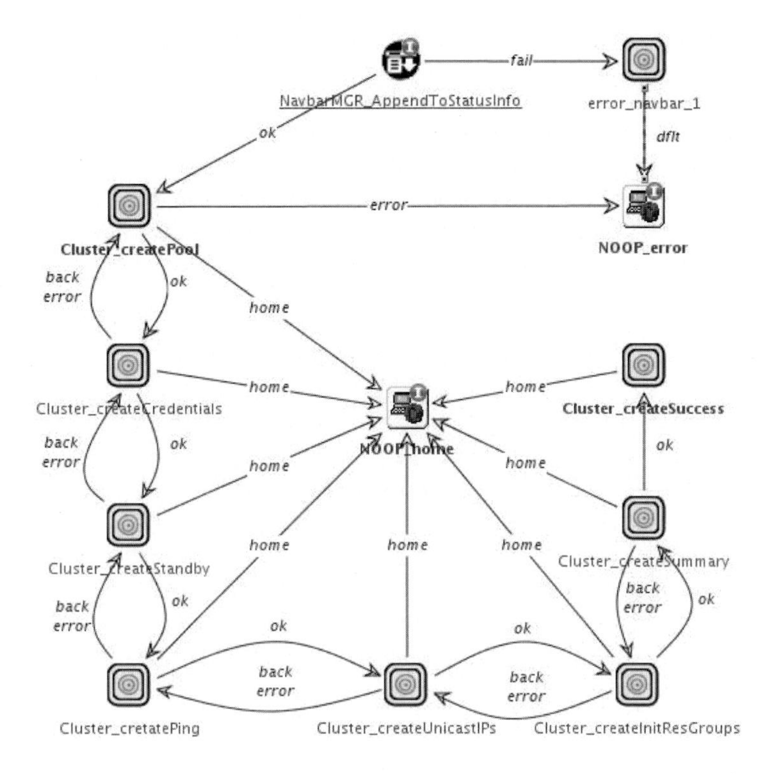

Fig. 5. High Level Service Logic Graph for the Cluster Creation Workflow

to the cluster by invoking the CIB-admin scripts. This has the advantage that the cluster configuration can be done in the database without deploying them to the cluster, so that every configuration step can be undo. After a successful configuration and validation it can be deployed to the cluster.

The deployment/configuration process in MaTRICS is carried out by the MaTRICS JobFlow-Engine. We call one configuration process a task, which contains a set of jobs, local or remote.

Remote jobs describe a single execution on the destination machine in a high level job-language. This job-language will be transformed into the machine's specific language, for example in bash for Linux/Solaris systems and RPC for Windows systems.

In contrast, local jobs are executed in the ConfigManager runtime and are designed by Service Logic Graphs. This has the advantage that the execution of a task is decoupled from the creation time, so that configurations can be done for ConfigClients, which are offline. A task begins its execution if all ConfigClients are in a consistent state and are online. In addition the JobFlow-Engine checks the execution of every job and starts a rollback for a task, if one job of a task fails. The undo-operations must be defined for all jobs.

Fig. 5 shows the high level workflow for the initial creation of a heartbeat cluster over a Web interface. `NavbarMGR_AppendToStatusInfo` sets the MaTRICS progress bar. Here we heavily use hierarchy: several GraphSIBs (those with the green circle) contain a separate SLG that realizes reusable functionality. The initial cluster creation workflow is designed in a wizard concept, so that one can switch between the pages (back- and error-edges). On the last page a summary of all entered values will be displayed (Cluster_createSummary) and if the user confirms, the cluster configuration is stored into the database (Cluster_createSuccess). Then the execution is returned to the upper model. NOOP_home is an end node too, entered if the user interrupts the wizard.

5 Application: High Availability for the OCS Cluster

This technology is now in operative use for the cluster that hosts in Dordrecht (NL) Springer Verlag's Online Conference Service. The OCS is implemented as an internet service running in a Tomcat Servlet-Container. For each conference there is a separate OCS instance that runs in an own Tomcat container. This way faults of one servlet container only affect one conference. On the other hand, it requires more memory and CPU-power for providing the servlet containers. Every OCS instance stores the conference data in an own database. These databases are hosted on one or more database servers. The OCS itself has no high-availability mechanisms at the application level for testing its vitality. For example, if the connection to the database server fails or the servlet container dies, the hosted conference is down.

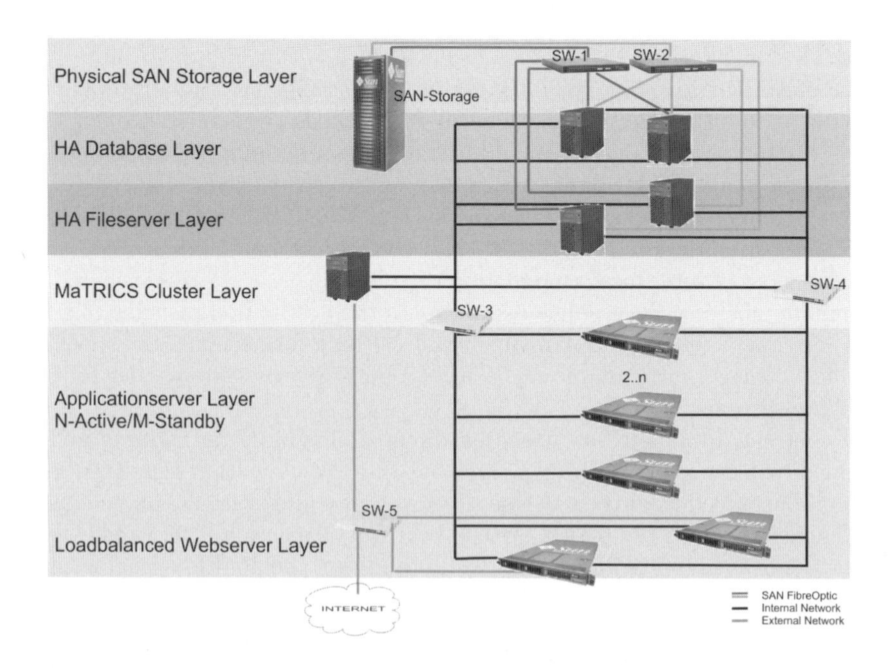

Fig. 6. Architecture of the Cluster for the OCS

Fig. 6 shows the server- and network-architecture of a high-availability cluster for hosting over 100 parallel running instances of the OCS. To protect the cluster against hardware faults, we supply the database- and file-servers by a storage area network (SAN) with multipath hostbus adapters (orange and red wires). If one component (SW-1, SW-2, red/orange wires) dies, there is already a path to the SAN-Storage. The same is done for the ethernet network (black/green wires). For the internal network, we have two different segments connected to the switches SW-3 and SW-4. This requires two network interface cards for the servers running in a bounding mode. The OCS instances runs in its Tomcat containers on the application servers of the Application server Layer in a n-Active/m-Standby mode. Therefore one (or more) of these servers runs as a standby server, ready to assume any Tomcat container of other application servers. Tomcat containers are defined as resources of heartbeat, and are monitored by MaTRICS. To guarantee a consistent files ystem for every application server, we use two NFS-servers connected to the SAN. These NFS-servers run in an Active/Standby configuration and mount the cluster file system GFS, which permits a concurrent read- and write-access to the file system. In case of a fault, it is important to migrate the locking information of the active NFS-server to the standby NFS-server, which is normally stored under /var/lib/nfs. The easiest way of ensuring this is to use the same GFS filesystem. The failover procedure is managed by heartbeat.

The HA Database Layer consists of two PostgreSQL database servers serving the same databases running in a Master/Slave configuration. We use a replication mechanism provided by Slony-I [16]. Thereby changes of the master database are propagated to its slave databases. If the master database dies, one of the slave databases has to become master, and take control of the faulty database server.

Each conference service is accessed via an own URL. To distribute the load of the web servers we use a load balancing technique implemented in the DNS. The web servers run in an n-Active configuration and tunnel the HTTP-requests to the application servers by the AJP-13 protocol.

In this context, MaTRICS runs on a dedicated machine which is connected to all networks. It manages the configuration of the servers and the OCS instances, it monitors the OCS instances, and triggers heartbeat for a failover procedure.

6 Defining Availability Test Models

The availability test workflows are provided to the MaTRICS users as abstract *services* that we call test models. Normally test models are designed specifically for a target service (one application, like the OCS). Accordingly they form a service family, because they are specialized to that service logic. Every test model is executed by the MaTRICS runtime environment, which provides the designer of the test models with a huge set of predefined functionalities (called SIBs) for connecting to a service and defining a test case, like database access, etc.

Login Availability for the OCS. The test model of Fig. 7 checks the availability of the user login procedure into the OCS. At the end-user level the

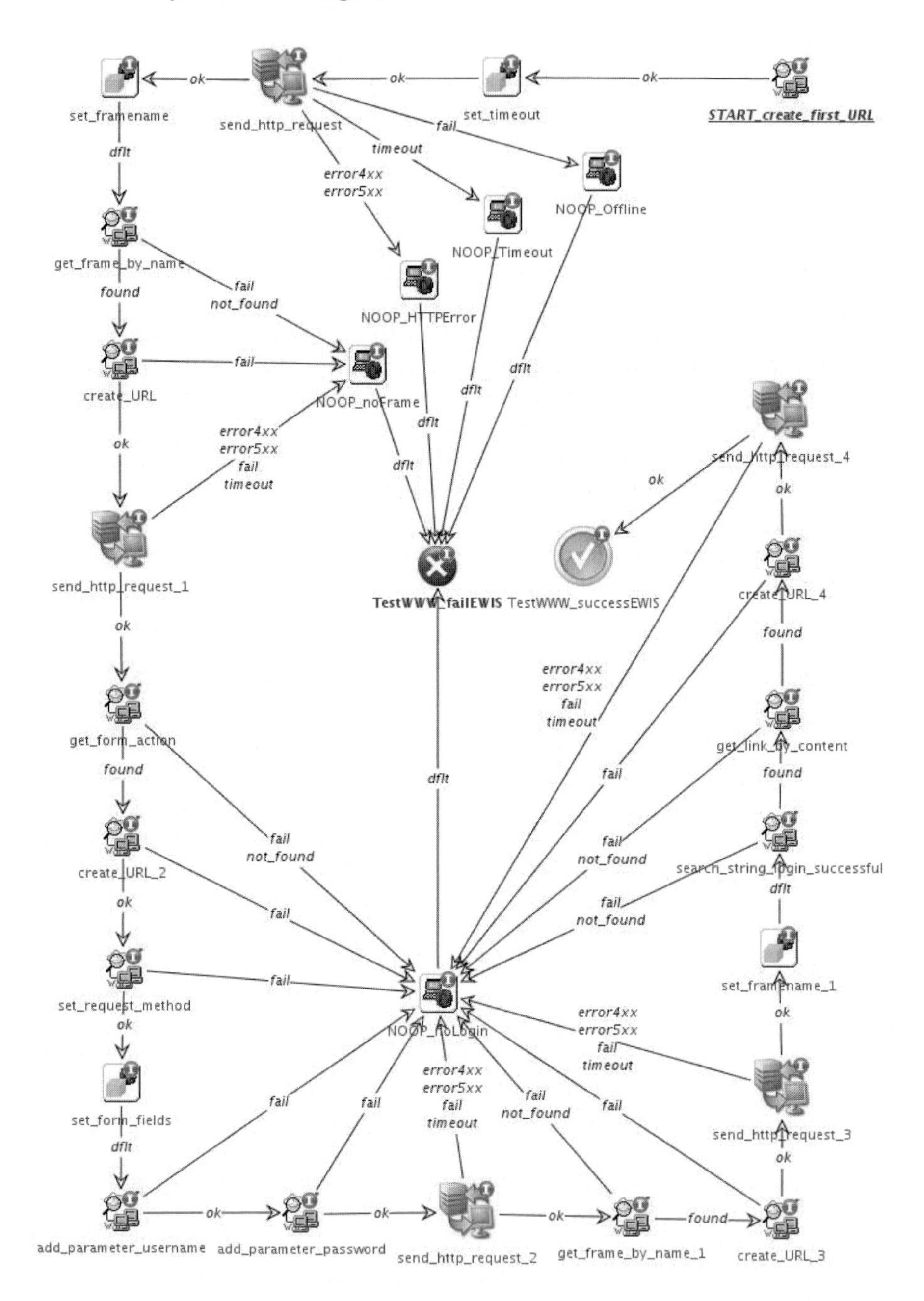

Fig. 7. Test Model for the OCS: the Login Procedure

functionality is very simple: after a successful login the user logs out. However, this test case guarantees a working database for the OCS and a working business logic. Just sending a HTTP request to the first page of the OCS a would not detect a database fault in the business logic, because the response is answered correctly without connecting to the database. The middleware-level availability test model is therefore more complex.

The test model begins with the creation of the HTTP-request to the login page of the OCS. All HTTP-interactions are done by the SIBs beginning with `send_http_request`. The HTTP-response sent by `send_http_request` contains the frameset for the navigation and the login page. Then a new HTTP-request for the login page is sent by `send_http_request_1`. The HTTP-response is parsed and a valid OCS username and password are sent by the next request (`send_http_request_2`). We expect to be returned a frameset for the personalized navbar and content page. `send_http_request_3` sends a request for the navbar. Upon successful login the navbar shows the username, so `search-_string_login_successful` searches for it. If it is found, `get_link_by_content` follows the URL or link for the logout. If the logout was successful (`send_http_request_4`) the test is passed and the terminal state `TestWWW_successEWIS` is reached. In all other cases the test fails and `TestWWW_failEWIS` is entered.

7 Conclusions and Future Work

We have shown that we can exploit the MaTRICS model-driven remote intelligent configuration and management of servers and of services not only for normal operation, but also to extend by the cluster management software heartbeat, that we use to provide high availability in an Active/Standby operation for every service managed by MaTRICS.

The advantages of the model-driven MaTRICS approach are manyfold:
MaTRICS drastically lowers the entrance hurdle for system operators to configure, provide and update server software and services. Since all the necessary features are provided as workflows in a platform-independent way, also less skilled or occasional users can perform (even remotely, from thin clients) complex operations. In addition, configuration workflows are validated before applying changes to the running servers, and monitored during execution.

Concerning service availability, we have delegated the generic high availability features to the cluster management software heartbeat, and use MaTRICS as an orchestration framework which enhances heartbeat by fine granular test processes. Actions, for example start/stop- or failover of resources are controlled by MaTRICS, so that complex operations like the reconfiguration of systems can be triggered. We have implemented this for the monitoring process for the OCS instances hosted on a high availability cluster.

We are going to extend the current MaTRICS to provide high availability in a n-Active/m-HotStandby scenario, that allows a service switching without losing any context information. This is done by Checkpoint services, which are integral part of high availability middleware and platforms, like e.g. Fujitsu-Siemens' RTP-PRIMECLUSTER solution [2,3] or the OpenSAF [14] project.

Acknowledgement. We thank Daniel Da Silva Lopes for the help in programming of several components for the heartbeat management service in MaTRICS.

References

1. Bajohr, M., Margaria, T.: MaTRICS: A Service-Based Management Tool for Remote Intelligent Configuration of Systems. Innovations in Systems and Software Engineering (ISSE) 2(2), 99–111 (2005)
2. Fujitsu Siemens Computers: Reliable Telco Platform, http://www.fujitsu-siemens.fr/products/software/cluster_technology/rtp4.html
3. Fujitsu Siemens Computers: PRIMECLUSTER, http://www.fujitsu-siemens.fr/products/software/cluster_technology/primecluster/
4. GEAR - A Game based Model Checking Tool, http://jabc.cs.uni-dortmund.de/modelchecking/
5. Heartbeat, Open Source High Availability Software, http://www.linux-ha.org
6. Lindner, B., Margaria, T., Steffen, B.: Ein personalisierter Internetdienst für wissenschaftliche Begutachtungsprozesse, GI-VOI-BITKOM-OCG-TeleTrusT Konferenz Elektronische Geschäftsprozesse (eBusiness Processes), Universität Klagenfurt (September 2001), http://syssec.uni-klu.ac.at/EBP2001/
7. Margaria, T.: Components, Features, and Agents in the ABC. In: Ryan, M.D., Meyer, J.-J.C., Ehrich, H.-D. (eds.) Objects, Agents, and Features. LNCS, vol. 2975, pp. 154–174. Springer, Heidelberg (2004)
8. Margaria, T., Karusseit, M.: Community Usage of the Online Conference Service: an Experience Report from three CS Conferences. In: 2nd IFIP Conf. on e-commerce, e-business, e-government (I3E 2002), Lisboa (P), pp. 497–511. Kluwer, Dordrecht (2002)
9. Margaria, T., Steffen, B.: Lightweight Coarse-grained Coordination: A Scalable System-Level Approach. STTT, Special Section on Formal Methods in Industrial Critical Systems, of the Int. Journal on Software Tools for Technology Transfer 5(2-3), 107–123 (2004)
10. Margaria, T., Steffen, B.: From the How to the What. In: VSTTE 2005, IFIP WG 2.3 Working Conf. on Verified Software: Tools, Techniques, and Experiments, Zürich (CH), October 2005. LNCS. Springer, Heidelberg (2005)
11. Margaria, T., Steffen, B.: Service Engineering: Linking Business and IT. IEEE Computer, 53–63 (2006)
12. Marowsky-Brée, L.: A new cluster resource manager for heartbeat. In: UKUUG LISA/Winter Conf. on High-Availability and Reliability, Bournemouth (UK) (2004)
13. The Open Cluster Framework (OCF), http://opencf.org
14. OpenSAF, The Open Service Availability Framework, http://www.opensaf.org
15. Robertson, A.: The Evolution of the Linux-HA Project, UKUUG LISA/Winter Conference High-Availability and Reliability, Bournemouth, UK (2004)
16. Slony-I, Enterprise-level replication system, http://www.slony.info
17. Steffen, B., Margaria, T., Nagel, R., Jörges, S., Kubczak, C.: Model-Driven Development with the jABC. In: Bin, E., Ziv, A., Ur, S. (eds.) HVC 2006. LNCS, vol. 4383, pp. 92–108. Springer, Heidelberg (2007)

Supporting Requirements Definition and Quality Assurance in Ubiquitous Software Project

Rodrigo O. Spínola, Felipe C.R. Pinto, and Guilherme H. Travassos

PESC-COPPE/UFRJ
Cx. Postal 68.511, CEP 21945-970, Rio de Janeiro, RJ, Brasil
{ros,felipecrp,ght}@cos.ufrj.br

Abstract. The development of ubiquitous software project demands the use of specific software technologies to deal with the inherent complexity of this type of project. Despite the advances in the software engineering field, the building of ubiquitous software still represents a grand challenge. For instance, secondary and primary studies indicated the existence of 13 ubiquity characteristics that can influence ubiquitous software projects. Therefore, in this paper we describe these ubiquity characteristics organized into a body of knowledge regarding ubiquitous computing and used to characterize ubiquitous software projects. Besides, an ongoing research concerned with supporting ubiquity requirements definition and verification (checklist based inspection) activities is also introduced.

Keywords: Ubiquitous Computing, Requirements Engineering, Software Quality, Experimental Software Engineering.

1 Introduction

The increasing complexity and exposure to new risks can prevent traditional software technologies to keep their effectiveness when used to develop ubiquitous software projects. This is due to the different software characteristics involved in the engineering of such projects that must be considered for assuring the delivering of quality products [4, 11, 13].

Into this software engineering context, some development challenges such as quality, time and budget constraints can be made explicit by answering questions such as: (1) What (new) software technologies are necessary to deal with the software ubiquity characteristics?; (2) What are the risks associated with ubiquitous software projects?; (3) What quality characteristics software engineers should have in mind when accomplishing ubiquitous software projects? (4) How to support the requirements definition and quality assurance activities in ubiquitous software projects?

Additionally, answering these questions can represent big challenges because:

- Ubiquitous computing (ubicomp) represents a multidisciplinary and new research intensive knowledge area [11]. Consequently, we can observe a constant evolution of ubicomp concepts in software related areas such as computer networks, signal processing, optimization, and artificial intelligence among others;

T. Margaria and B. Steffen (Eds.): ISoLA 2008, CCIS 17, pp. 587–603, 2008.

- A small number of papers evidencing the use of software engineering principles to support the development of ubiquitous software projects can be currently found in the technical literature, making hard identifying the ubiquity characteristics influence in software projects.

These challenges combined with our experience on dealing with software projects involving requirements regarding ubiquity motivated us to try to understand what could be the ubiquity characteristics influence in the software development life cycle. The difficult on dealing with this new software category requirements have driven us to think about how to enlarge the usual body of knowledge regarding the development of conventional software projects to also embrace ubicomp applications.

Sakamura [13] states that the creation of ubiquitous software applications is hard and can involve several ubiquity characteristics. It was also observed by Spínola et al. [14], which identified and evaluated 10 relevant characteristics concerned with ubiquitous software, such as service omnipresence, invisibility, context sensitivity, adaptable behavior, experience capture, service discovery, function composition, spontaneous interoperability, heterogeneity of devices and fault tolerance by undertaking a systematic literature review. In complement, information regarding functional and restrictive factors concerned with the main issues when developing ubiquitous software projects have been described. At this point, a functional factor is concerned with the facts or situations related to functional requirements. A restrictive factor is concerned with the facts or situations related to non- functional requirements.

This information can be useful when a software engineer is looking for software technologies to use in the software projects. For instance, some software requirements technologies can be used to deal with one or other ubiquity characteristic [26, 27, 28, 21, 20, 19, 10, 8, 2]. However, their use in ubiquitous software projects can be limited due to the lack of knowledge on how to apply them when ubiquity characteristics are combined into the project.

Aiming at providing support for software developers in characterizing and developing ubiquitous software projects, this paper describes an on-going research towards the creation of a framework to support software technologies concerned with the definition and quality assurance of ubiquity requirements. The first target is represented by organizing knowledge regarding ubiquitous software projects through secondary and primary studies and making it available to the practitioners. It is intended to support development activities concerned with ubiquity requirements specification and validation (checklist based inspection). So, a set o facilities is going to be available supporting:

- To choose relevant ubiquity characteristics for the software project (level of relevance can depend on the application domain or project's requirements);
- To identify the ubiquity requirements (functional) through a list of functional factors regarding each selected ubiquity characteristic;
- To define the ubiquity requirements, by guiding the software engineer to properly detail all requirements accordingly the selected ubiquity characteristic; and,
- To assure the ubiquity requirements quality, by providing checklists that can make the software engineer able to inspect whether all expected ubiquity features were appropriately captured by the requirements specification.

This paper is organized in eight sections, including this Introduction. In the following section, the definition of ubicomp and its characteristics are discussed. In sequence, the results of a detailed analysis for each ubiquitous characteristic considering its functional and restrictive factors are presented. Then, we present an approach to characterize applications considering their ubiquity adherence level. We also present some results obtained with the use of the characterization approach. In sequence, the evaluation of the concepts involving ubiquitous computing previous discussed is presented. After that, some concepts about requirements engineering and related works are analyzed. In the following section, the proposed framework is explained. Finally, we summarize the main contributions of this paper and future perspectives of this research.

2 Ubiquitous Computing Characteristics

Weiser introduced the area of ubiquitous computing and put forth a vision of people and environments augmented with computational resources providing information and services when and where desired [17]. Weiser's vision also described a proliferation of devices at varying scales, ranging in size from hand-held "inch-scale" personal devices to "yard-scale" shared devices. That is, the computer is integrated into the environment in such a way that its use becomes non intrusive. This definition set the origin of the term Ubiquitous Computing and, although it is important for presenting a new computing paradigm, we believe it is not currently complete at all. This positive lack of completeness reflects its importance and innovation at that time, and how fast technology has evolved.

Therefore, an investigation towards an updated definition of ubiquitous computing seems to be necessary. So, this section intends to present the reached results of a systematic review whose goals were the field understanding and describing an up-to-date ubiquitous computing definition that could support our research: (Q0) What is ubiquitous computing?; (Q1) How ubiquitous computing is currently being presented?; (Q2) What characteristics do define applications for ubiquitous computing?

To accomplish this systematic review, it was elaborated and accomplished a research protocol. The items below define the main characteristics of this protocol:

- Keywords: ubiquitous computing, pervasive computing, ubiquitous application, ubiquitous system, ubiquitous software, pervasive application, pervasive system, pervasive software, feature, requirement, characteristic, definition, characterization, and concept.
- Paper sources: IEEE Portal, ACM Digital Library, INSPEC, and EI COMPENDEX. These digital libraries have been chosen by convenience because they were fully available to the researchers.
- Example of a search string (Q0 only) for ACM Digital Library:
  +"ubiquitous computing" abstract:concept abstract:definition abstract:characteristc
  +"pervasive computing" abstract:concept abstract:definition abstract:characteristic
- Inclusion and exclusion criteria: These criteria define statements that must be true for the paper be included in the selected papers set. They must be available on the internet, be written in English, provide a ubiquitous definition (Q0 only), report

current applications regarding ubiquitous computing concepts (Q1 only), report software application (applications concerned with supporting software are not considered) and present characteristics associated with ubiquitous systems (Q2 only).
- Preliminary studies selection process: each returned publication must have its abstract and introduction analyzed by two researchers and, based on the inclusion and exclusion criteria, they select it or not to a more thorough analysis.

To summarize, following the research protocol 41 papers among 751 were selected to extract information. These papers supported the identification of an updated ubiquitous computing definition besides a set of concepts characterizing ubiquitous software projects, as described below.

Ubiquitous computing is present when computational services or facilities become available to the people in such a way that computer is no longer visible nor needed to be used as an essential tool to access these services or facilities. The services or facilities can materialize themselves at any time or place, transparently, through the use of common daily devices. To make it happens it is desired that systems composing this domain take into consideration the following characteristics (an illustrative scenario aiming at providing our interpretation is also provided):

- **Service Omnipresence (SO):** It allows users to move around with the sensation of carrying computing services with them;
  - Scenario: An employee is taking part in a business meeting but needs to leave it. However, it also needs monitoring the meeting progress to report its results for the manager. When the employee leaves the meeting's room, the distance conference managing software can be activated on the smartphone. Thus, the employee will have access to the meeting everywhere when it is moving around.
- **Invisibility (IN):** The ability of being present in daily use objects, weakening, from user's point of view, the sensation of explicit use of a computer and enhancing the perception that objects or devices can provide services or some kind of "intelligence". Thus, it demands natural interfaces to facilitate a richer variety of communications capabilities among humans and computer systems. The goal of these natural interfaces is to support common forms of human expressions and leverage more of our implicit actions in the world [23];
  - Scenario: a personal health care system that must be constantly monitoring some health variables without patients' intervention.
- **Context Sensitivity (CS):** Ubiquitous systems should have mechanisms to collect information from the environment where it is being used;
  - Scenario: a system to control a refrigerator should be constantly monitoring the temperature to keep the device in the ideal state for products conservation.
- **Adaptable Behavior (AB):** The ability of dynamically to adapt itself accordingly the offered environment services, respecting its limitations;
  - Scenario: By identifying the bandwidth reduction to the point of harming the audio and video transmission, the video conference management software should reduce the audio and video quality allowing the normal communication flow between the conference participants.

- **Experience Capture (EC):** Ubiquitous systems should have mechanisms to support the capturing and registering of experiences for later use;
  - o Scenario: A software for ambient intelligence can identify common user behaviors, for example: when arrives at home, the user turns on the room light, heats water for coffee, turns on the tub and sets the water temperature to 28 ° C. The software can manage these activities as soon as it identifies the user arrives at home without repetitive user's commands.
- **Service Discovery (SD):** This characteristic states that ubicomp systems should have mechanisms to support pro-active discovery of services, which should be according to the environment where it is being used in order to find new services or information to achieve some desired target;
  - o Scenario: A smartphone software can identify services provided by a supermarket to support the purchase of products by the customer, such as a map with promotions and products location.
- **Function Composition (FC):** To be able to creating a service required by the user based on available basic services;
  - o Scenario: A user needs to have a spreadsheet view and generate a PDF file with the view outcome and these services are not available on the workstation. The software can identify the necessary services and makes them available for use.
- **Spontaneous Interoperability (SI):** The ability to change partners during its operation and according to its movement;
  - o Scenario: A person is moving and the software, running on a PDA, is playing a task-intensive processing. During the moving, the software can interact with other devices in the environment for temporary allocation of processing.
- **Heterogeneity of Devices (HD):** It provides application mobility among heterogeneous devices. That is, the application could migrate among devices and adjust itself to each one of them;
  - o Scenario: A software for stock market monitoring allows the access to all its functionalities through a workstation at the office. However, in other organizational unit only a PDA is available. In this situation, the software should migrate part of its features to be accessed by a PDA in a way that a user could continue to access the necessary information.
- **Fault Tolerance (FT):** The ability to self adapt when facing environment's faults (for example, on-line/off-line availability).
  - o Scenario: ubiquitous systems are liable to a large number of events that can cause system failure, such as, sensors with hardware problem, network failure, among others.

At this point, it is important to notice that the ubicomp definition captures the conditions where we can access computerized resources in a ubiquitous way. Besides, ubiquitous systems have a well-defined scope, and this scope is influenced by the ubiquity characteristics set present in the application. We believe it happens because ubiquity can be considered a system property and it can be also partially achieved. Thus, a system can implement completely or partially the functionalities associated with the ubiquity characteristics.

3 Functional and Restrictive Factors Related to Ubicomp Characteristics

The ubiquity characteristics previously mentioned are still described in high abstraction level, making hard to understand how they could influence the software functionalities or restrict the software design possibilities. Therefore, it is important to make explicit functional and restrictive information for each one of the ubiquity characteristics. For this, a complementary systematic literature review was undertaken. Its goal was to answer the question: what are the functional and restrictive factors associated with each one of the ubiquitous software characteristics?

The research protocol previously mentioned (section 2) was reused and evolved to support this study. The items below define the main variations:

- Keywords: ubiquitous computing, pervasive computing, functional requirement, functionality, feature, characteristic, non-functional requirement, quality requirement, invisibility, context sensitivity, adaptable behavior or task dynamism, capture of experiences, service discovery, spontaneous interoperability, device heterogeneity and fault tolerance.
- Paper sources: IEEE Portal and ACM Digital Library. These digital libraries have been chosen for the sake of simplicity (reduction in the number of search strings) and full availability to the researchers.
- Example of a search string for the IEEE Portal: (('pervasive computing' <or> 'ubiquitous computing') <in> metadata) <and> ((('functional requirement' <or> functionality <or> feature <or> characteristic) <or> 'non-functional requirement' <or> 'quality requirement')) <in>metadata) <and> ('computer everywhere')
- Inclusion and exclusion criteria: the papers must be available on the internet, the papers must be written in English and the papers must provide information regarding functional and/or restrictive factors associated with each ubiquitous characteristic.
- Preliminary studies selection process: each returned publication must have its abstract and introduction analyzed by one researcher and, based on the inclusion and exclusion criteria, to be selected or not to a more thorough analysis. Conflicts will count with a second researcher to help on the inclusion decision.

To summarize, 59 papers among 599 were selected to extract information following the research protocol. Using the acquired data, it was possible to identify 168 factors (123 functional and 45 restrictive) (the complete set of functional and restrictive factors can be found at http://www.cos.ufrj.br/~ros/ubforms.html). Moreover, it was also possible to group the factors accordingly their meaning and conceptual linkage, associating each factor to just one group of factors. For example, for the “Context Sensitivity” characteristic, the factors “Contextualize obtained information” and “Store information” can be grouped into the “Context Information Management” factor group.

The grouping made easier the analysis process due to the great number of factors found by the systematic literature review. Table 1 summarizes quantitatively the reached results. The first column shows the ubiquity characteristics. The second and third columns show how many studies were found regarding each characteristic, in absolute and percentage values respectively considering the set of selected papers for analysis. The fourth and fifth columns show how many functional and restrictive factors were found for each ubiquity characteristic, respectively. At the last column, it is presented the percentage distribution of factors per characteristic.

From Table 1 it is possible to observe that, for all ubiquity characteristics but service discovery and fault tolerance, the focus is concentrated in the functional factors. This observation is based on the fact that the number of identified functional factors is greater than the number of restrictive factors. Besides, it can represent an indication that more researches on ubicomp have been made with the purpose of investigating how ubiquitous software projects can be defined in terms of functionalities. However more investigation is necessary to understand this behavior.

Table 1. Ubiquity Characteristics and correspondingly amount of functional/restrictive factors

Ubiquity Characteristic	**Presence**	**% of 59**	**Functional**	**Restrictive**	**% of 168**
Service Omnipresence (SO)	28	47,5	9	1	6,0
Invisibility (IN)	26	44,0	8	2	6,0
Context Sensitivity (CS)	56	94,9	22	8	17,9
Adaptable Behavior (AB)	52	88,1	24	8	19,0
Experience Capture (EC)	11	18,6	7	0	4,2
Service Discovery (SD)	28	47,5	13	13	15,5
Function Composition (FC)	19	32,2	18	5	13,7
Spontaneous Interoperability (SI)	21	35,6	10	2	7,1
Heterogeneity of Devices (HD)	18	30,5	9	3	7,1
Fault Tolerance (FT)	11	18,6	3	3	3,6
Total of factors			**123**	**45**	

4 Characterizing Ubiquitous Software Projects

Ubiquitous software projects can exhibit different levels of adherence to the ubiquity characteristics and their respective factors (these different levels of adherence can be a consequence of the application domain and project's requirements, for instance) [14]. It seems that the comprehension about how these ubiquity characteristics are usually explored in software projects can be important to support the proposal of new software engineering technologies regarding the development of ubiquitous software projects.

Therefore, taking into account the concepts previously described, we have designed a checklist and proposed an approach to support the characterization of software projects accordingly their ubiquity adherence level. Basically, this characterization approach is composed by three steps: (1) Identifying the presence of the functional and restrictive factors of each ubiquity characteristic considering the ubiquitous software project requirements set; (2) Assessing the adherence level of each ubiquity characteristic for the software project based on the presence/absence of each correspondent functional and restrictive factor; (3) Representing the ubiquity adherence level for the system through using the values obtained in the step 2 to generate a graph.

To support the steps 2 and 3, it has been built a spreadsheet-based form to calculate the adherence level for each ubiquity characteristic. Fig. 1 shows a fragment of the proposed checklist. Basically, as the user fills in the Status column, the Factor Group Adherence Level and Characteristic Adherence Level columns can be calculated for each group of factors and the ubiquitous computing characteristic, respectively. In the final step, the evaluated percentage values of the Ubiquity Characteristics Adherence Level column are used to draw a graph representing the software project ubiquity adherence level. For instance, Fig. 2 (left graph) represents the obtained graph when applying this checklist to the ubiquitous application presented in [16]. We can notice that a real ubiquitous software project can differ from the captured ubiquitous scenario (sections 2 and 3) observing the left and right graph presented on Fig. 2.

Characteristic	Characteristic Adherence Level	Factor Group	Factor Group Adherence Level	Factor	Status
Service omnipresence	70%	Mobility	50%	User section management	✓
				To deal with the user's mobility	✗
				When moving the services, these should continue operand starting from the point that it processing was interrupted for the migration of the functionality	✓
				To support the mobility among domains and inside of a same domain	✗
		Service management	67%	Each device should contain a container to allocate services	✓
				Each device should manage the services allocated in it container	✗
				To organize services according to the context	✓
		Service publish	100%	To publish the existence of the service for other devices / applications	✓
				To maintain the registry of services published in cache to increase the performance in a new services publish	✓
		Restrictive Factor	100%	Each service should be generic enough to continue executing while alterations happen in the environment	✓

Fig. 1. A checklist fragment to characterize ubiquitous software projects

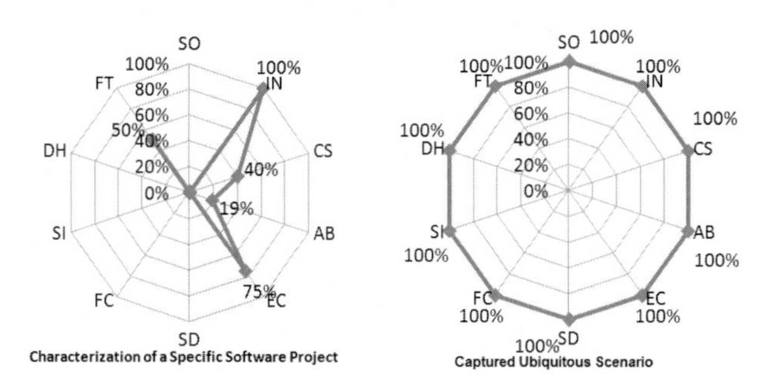

Fig. 2. Example of ubiquity characteristics and their adherence levels

This checklist has also been used to characterize 12 different ubiquitous software projects [1, 3, 5, 6, 7, 9, 12, 15, 16, 18, 29, 30]. A detailed description of the characterization process and its results can be found in [22]. An interesting behavior could be observed: if the number of factors identified for each ubiquity characteristic increases or decreases, the same happens with the number of factors implemented in the software projects. This behavior can indicate: a) there is a natural gap between the state-of-the-art and state-of-the-practice; b) ubiquitous software projects can capture those ubicomp characteristics differently. However, an exception to this behavior was observed regarding the Function Composition characteristic. None of the 12 ubiquitous software projects reported to deal with any of the 23 factors regarding the FC characteristic. This behavior was not expected because this ubiquity characteristic has been considered required in about 32.2% of the analyzed papers from the second systematic review (section 3). A possible explanation could be the difficulty to deal with the inherent complexity regarding the composition of functions in software. As stated before, more investigation is necessary to also understand this behavior.

An additional observed behavior is regarding the focus on some specific ubiquity characteristics. It seems that ubiquitous software projects pay more attention to the invisibility, context sensitive and adaptable behavior characteristics. The other ones seem to appear as isolated initiatives, even considering the analyzed projects represent examples in the years' range 2000-2007, where some technological evolution took place. We did not found any feasible explanation for this behavior. However, some questions could be raised:

- Does this behavior represent a natural gap between the state-of-the-art and state-of-the-practice that deserves further investigation?
- Is there a need to evaluate the set of identified ubiquity characteristics and their functional and restrictive factors?

Some feasible answers to these two questions could be, respectively:

- The set of identified ubiquity characteristics and their functional and restrictive factors make sense, and the distance between the state-of-the-art and state-of-the-practice is natural and relates to the technology evolution;
- There are some adjustments that must be applied to the set of identified ubiquity characteristics and their correspondingly functional and restrictive factors.

One could consider the answers can make sense. However, further investigation is necessary, what leads us to consider the ubiquity characteristics and their associated factors evaluation directly in the field. Therefore, we considered to survey ubicomp researchers which is described in the next section.

5 Evaluating Ubicomp Concepts through a Survey

The goal of this study was to **analyze** the previously described ubiquity characteristics, their factors, and group of factors extracted from the technical literature **with the purpose of** characterizing **with respect to** their applicability and scope **into the context of** ubiquitous software projects **from the point of view of** software engineering researchers working with the research and development of ubiquitous software projects.

This study was planned to survey ubicomp researchers considering the following questions regarding the previously described set of ubiquity characteristics and functional and restrictive factors:

- Is there any additional ubiquity characteristic that is not present in the initial set that should be included?
- Is there any ubiquity characteristic present in the initial set that should be excluded?
- Is there any additional ubiquity characteristic factor group or factor that is not present in the initial set that should be included?

- Is there any ubiquity characteristic factor group or factor present in the initial set that should be excluded?
- Are the ubiquity characteristics and their associated factors and factor groups applicable to characterize ubiquitous software projects?

This survey has already been planned and executed, in a first moment, considering the Brazilian researcher's population. The choice of the subjects was based on the CNPq's (National Council for Scientific and Technological Development) Research Groups Search Directory considering those ones which list ubicomp as one of their research interests. The subjects were contacted by e-mail (at total 60 ubicomp researchers have been invited), and the questionnaire was also sent by e-mail. The questionnaire was organized to be filled in three steps:

1) Characterization of the subjects' background and skills. In this step the subjects were asked about his/her personal data (name, email), academic degree, experience level on software project development (in years), and the number of executed software projects per ubicomp characteristic;
2) Identification of the ubiquity characteristics that should be included/excluded/kept in the initial set. The subject can confirm which ubiquity characteristics are important to characterize ubiquitous software projects, input additional characteristics that he/she considers important, or exclude some characteristics of the initial set;
3) Identification of the ubiquity characteristic factor groups and factors that should be included/excluded/kept in the initial set. For each factor group and factor, the subject can confirm their importance, input additional factor groups or factors not included in the initial set that he/she considers important, or exclude some of them.

At the end, 10 subjects (about 17% of the invited researchers) answered the questionnaire (8 of them PhDs). Table 2 shows the researchers' skill level for each ubiquity characteristic where: (1) **H**igh: researches and has taken part of more than two software projects considering the ubiquity characteristic; (2) **M**edium: researches and has taken part of one or two software projects considering the ubiquity characteristic. (3) **L**ow: just researches about the ubiquity characteristic; (4) **N**one: does not research neither has taken part of a software project with the ubiquity characteristic.

For the analysis stage, each subject had a different weight according to his/her background and skill level. Researchers with higher experience/skill level had greater weight. After the weights definition, the answers from all subjects were evaluated for each evaluated ubicomp characteristic, factor group, and factor. It is important to notice that, except the fault tolerance characteristic, all others have been evaluated by at least one researcher with high skill level.

The results allowed us to evolve the initial set of ubiquity characteristics, factors and their factor groups. Basically, the changes were: (1) Inclusion of three additional ubiquity characteristics: scalability, quality of service, and privacy and trust; (2) Reorganization of the ubiquity characteristics considering the two perspectives: functional and restrictive; (3) Exclusion of three functional factors.

Table 2. Researchers' skill level

ID	Academic Degree	SO	IN	CS	AB	EC	SD	FC	SI	DH	FT
R01	M.Sc.	H	M	H	M	H	M	M	L	N	L
R02	M.Sc.	H	H	H	H	M	M	M	M	M	M
R03	Ph.D.	L	L	M	M	L	M	M	M	N	L
R04	Ph.D.	H	L	L	L	L	L	L	L	L	L
R05	Ph.D.	H	M	H	H	L	M	M	L	H	N
R06	Ph.D.	H	M	H	M	L	L	L	L	H	L
R07	Ph.D.	M	M	H	H	H	M	L	M	M	L
R08	Ph.D.	M	M	L	H	H	H	M	M	N	N
R09	Ph.D.	L	L	H	H	H	N	M	M	M	M
R10	Ph.D.	H	L	L	H	M	L	H	H	N	N

The initial ubiquity characteristics set organization before and after survey execution is shown in Fig. 3. Before survey execution, 10 ubiquity characteristics were identified by the systematic literature reviews (sections 2 and 3). The survey execution allowed us to observe that those 10 characteristics can also be structured considering the two different perspectives: functional and restrictive. This new categorization seems to make sense because there are characteristics that are clearly related with non-functional software aspects and they can bring some constraints on how the functional characteristics are implemented. Moreover, 3 new restrictive ubiquity characteristics were identified: scalability, quality of service, and privacy and trust. Additionally, the fault tolerance characteristic was included into the ubicomp restrictive characteristics group.

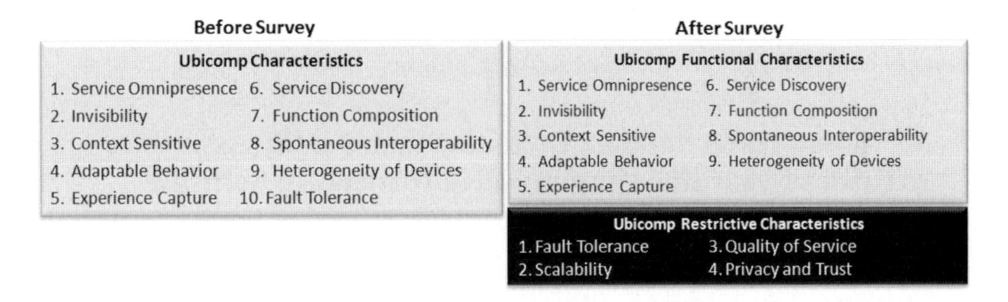

Fig. 3. Ubicomp characteristics definition before and after survey execution

These findings allowed us to evolve the set of knowledge regarding ubiquitous software projects and their characteristics. At this point in time, it was able to define a body of knowledge regarding ubicomp, to provide a conceptual framework to guide new researchers and practitioners in the ubiquitous software projects development, and, to evaluate the proposed checklist. Considering the obtained qualitative data, researchers suggested the importance of supporting software engineering activities regarding ubiquitous software projects, mainly those related with requirements specification and project planning.

6 Ubicomp and Requirements Engineering

The results obtained in our research regarding software development in general increased our interest in the challenges related with ubicomp requirements engineering. We are particularly interested on software technologies to support activities regarding requirements definition and quality assurance considering the ubicomp scenario. Well specified requirements can be considered a success factor to deliver software products with the expected quality and following the project budget [25]. It should not be different when dealing with ubiquitous software projects.

For this, we accomplished an ad-hoc literature review influenced by the systematic review principles. The review goal was to identify the existence of approaches supporting requirements definition and verification activities regarding the ubiquity characteristics (section 5). The following sources of information were analyzed: IEEE and ACM Digital Library, Ubicomp Proceedings and International Requirements Engineering Conference Proceedings. Additionally, one paper [2] analyzing the bibliography reference on the selected papers has been identified.

This review resulted in the selection of nine papers [2, 8, 10, 19, 20, 21, 26, 27, 28] to extract information. All of them presented requirements definition techniques or examples of requirements definition. Among them, the approach proposed by Chiu et al. [27] presents a set of steps to support activities regarding requirements elicitation and specification that could be used in a more general way. However, in the paper it is limited to the context sensitivity characteristic.

The other proposals have a more limited scope. Two of them just show how the requirements of a ubiquitous system are defined [21, 28]. In both cases, the requirements are only listed and textually detailed in the paper without any elaborated description about the technique supporting their definition and verification. Finally, it is important to notice that it was not found any quality assurance technique regarding ubiquity requirements for ubiquitous software projects.

7 A Framework to Support Definition and Quality Assurance Activities Regarding Ubiquity Requirements in Software Projects

Hereafter, we are going to present a framework proposal to support activities regarding the definition of ubiquity requirements and their verification and validation. It represents an on-going research aiming at the establishment of a software technology to deal with all nine ubicomp functional characteristics (section 5). We recognize the importance of non-functional requirements for software development. However, the decision regarding initially research support for functional requirements about ubiquitous software projects is due to the fact that ubicomp researches currently are more focused on the functional requirements of software [14].

The proposed framework is composed by a set of facilities associated with ubiquity requirements definition, verification, and validation activities. Fig. 4 shows the supported facilities (white boxes), their relationship with requirements activities, and their respective consumed/produced artifacts (gray boxes). It also shows that framework facilities are based on the ubicomp body of knowledge previously discussed and acquired through secondary and primary studies (systematic reviews and survey).

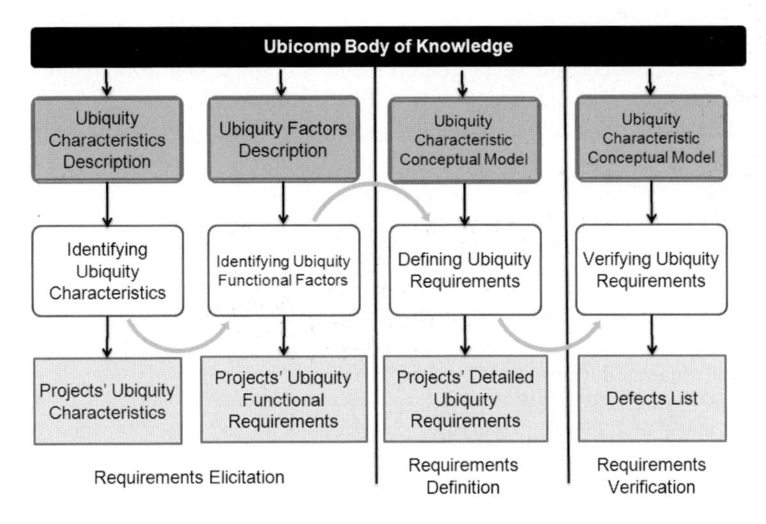

Fig. 4. Overview of the framework

In the next three subsections, we will present how the framework intends to provide a complementary set of facilities that is not given by the conventional software engineering techniques to properly deliver ubiquitous software products in the context of requirements activities.

7.1 Requirements Elicitation

Requirements elicitation is the practice of obtaining the requirements of a system from users, customers and other stakeholders [25]. In the context of this work, we are concerned with ubiquity requirements for software projects. In order to support this activity, the proposed framework has two facilities:

Identifying ubiquity characteristics. This facility intends to help the requirements analyst to identify the ubiquity characteristics that should be considered in the software project. Therefore, for each ubiquity characteristic, a set of questions was defined to help identifying which one of them should be included in the software. The definition of these questions was intended to be the system user because these questions are part of a checklist that guides the user interview activity. As the requirements analyst gets the answers from users, s/he registers in the checklist if the ubiquity characteristic is desired or not.

Identifying ubiquity functional factors. Once the software ubiquity characteristics have been defined, its functional requirements can be identified.

Therefore, a functional factors list associated to the defined ubicomp functional characteristics (section 5) was used to create a complementary checklist. Again, the checklist was defined in a way that it could be used for requirements gathering activities. Thus, based on the identifying ubicomp characteristics step, the checklist is dynamically organized with specific questions considering the selected ubiquity characteristics. For each corresponding functional factor (section 3), the requirements analyst identifies if it is or not necessary.

In the final step, for each selected factor, the requirements analyst is requested to define the correspondent functional requirement. It is important to notice that a ubiquity functional factor is not necessarily a functional requirement. However, it can motivate the definition of a specific functional requirement for the software project.

7.2 Requirements Definition

The next step regards supporting the requirements analyst to detail each identified functional requirement. For this, firstly, the analyst can group the functional requirements (because the relationship between the functional requirements and requirements specification[1] is M:N). Next, a set of information to be defined by the analyst is presented for each requirement that will be detailed.

This information can be different for each ubiquity characteristic and its associated factors. For each ubiquity characteristic, a conceptual model based on their respective functional factors was defined in a way that the models could capture their most relevant concepts and relationships. Based on this information, it was possible to define what must be captured to define requirements in accordance with the ubicomp characteristics.

7.3 Requirements Verification

This step is provided to assure the specified requirements quality. It is supported by an additional checklist that guides the reviewer through the reading of the generated requirements document and helps him to identify possible defects.

For the checklist construction, nine conceptual models (relating to the nine ubicomp functional characteristics and their corresponding factors) were elaborated to capture the most relevant concepts and relationships. These models, besides providing a better way to understand the ubiquity characteristics, allow the definition of what needs to be specified in the requirements to completely cover the chosen ubiquity characteristic.

For instance, from the conceptual model for context sensitivity ubicomp characteristic it is possible to exemplify questions that will compose the verification checklist, such as: (1) Do all information have a data source attached to it?; (2) Are the available devices associated with the context in which they should work?; (3) Is the context information of each available data source described?; (4) Are all information classified in one of the four perspectives: physical, infra-structure, system or user information?

At the end of this step, a list of defects can be created and used to improve the requirements specification quality.

8 Conclusions and Further Works

According to Weiser (1991), computers should be embedded into the environment in such way that their use becomes natural and transparent. This prospective scenario represents new research challenges in many areas like computer network, signal processing, optimization, and artificial intelligence. Particularly, from the point of view of software engineering, these challenges can effectively be observed on the development of different software technologies, such as methodologies, software processes, testing approaches, and quality assurance techniques.

---

[1] Requirements and use case descriptions.

In this paper we intended to present a framework proposal to support the definition and quality assurance activities regarding ubiquity requirements on ubiquitous software projects. We believe it represents an important step towards the development of increased quality ubiquitous software projects.

The context sensitivity characteristic was chosen as the first one to be included into this framework. This decision was based on the fact that this characteristic seems to be the more investigated by the research community [14].

Moreover, to facilitate the development of this framework, it was important to execute a comprehensive and systematic literature review. It results allowed us to obtain a set of ubiquity definitions and characteristics reflecting the concepts of ubicomp used currently by the scientific community. Thus, this paper also presents contributions as: (1) an updated definition for ubiquitous computing and ubicomp systems; (2) a set of ubiquity characteristics to achieve ubicomp on software projects; (3) the identification of functional and restrictive factors for each ubiquity characteristic; (4) a checklist to characterize ubiquitous software projects using the ubiquity characteristics as a way to evaluate its ubiquity adherence level, and (5) identifying which ubiquity characteristics have been currently considered on ubicomp software projects. All these results were reached using the scientific method represented through systematic literature reviews and knowledge evaluation using surveys.

Finally, it is important to reinforce that the creation of ubiquitous software applications is a hard task [13]. Based on that, as the identification of ubiquity characteristics and factors can provide better understanding of ubicomp, this research can represent an important step to deal with this kind of software and also creating subsidies to support other project development phases, including planning and design.

This work is still in progress. The next steps include: (1) Replicating the survey considering a broader audience, which will allow to observe the feasibility of the initial results; (2) Evolving the definition of the framework to support activities of definition and quality assurance regarding ubiquity requirements specification for ubiquitous software projects; (3) Creating an initial version of an infrastructure to support the framework activities mentioned above; (4) Experimentally evaluate the infrastructure and improving it according to the experimental study results.

Acknowledgments. The authors would like to thank CAPES, CNPq, FAPERJ for the financial support to this work and Dr. Karin Breitman for her valuable comments and motivation. This work has been developed as part of the Experimental Software Engineering and Science in Large Scale CNPq Project (475459/2007-5) and FAPERJ research activities.

References

1. Ali, J.A., Won-Sik, Y., Jai-Hoon, K., We-Duke, C.: U-kitchen: application scenario. In: Proc. of the Second IEEE Workshop on Software Technologies for Future Embedded and Ubiquitous Systems 2004, May 11-12, 2004, pp. 169–171 (2004)
2. Cheng, B.H.C., Berry, D.M., Zhang, J.: The four levels of requirements engineering for and in dynamic adaptive systems. In: 11th Int. Work. on Requirements Engineering Foundations for Software Quality. Co-located with CAiSE 2005, Porto, Portugal (June 2005)

3. Bossen, C., Jorgensen, J.B.: Context-descriptive prototypes and their application to medicine administration. In: Proc. of the Conference on Designing interactive systems: processes, practices, methods, and techniques 2004, pp. 297–306 (2004)
4. Ducatel, K., Bogdanowicz, M., Scapolo, F., Leijten, J., Burgelman, J.-C.: Ambient Intelligence: From Vision to Reality. IST Advisory Group Draft Rep., Eur. (2003)
5. Hatala, M., Wakkary, R., Kalantari, L.: Rules and Ontologies in Support of Real-time Ubiquitous Application. Journal of Web Semantics, 5–22 (2005)
6. Joel, S., Arnott, J.L., Hine, N.A., Ingvarsson, H., Rentoul, R., Schofield, S.: A framework for analyzing interactivity in a remote access field exploration system. SMC(3), 2669–2674 (2005)
7. Kientz, J.A., Boring, S., Abowd, G.D., Hayes, G.R.: Abaris: Evaluating Automated Capture Applied to Structured Autism Interventions. In: Proc. of the 7th Int. Conference on Ubiquitous Computing, Tokyo, Japan, September 11-14 (2005)
8. Jorgensen, J.B., Bossen, C.: Requirements Engineering for a Pervasive Health Case System. In: 11t IEEE Int. Requirements Engineering Conference 2003, pp. 55–64 (2003)
9. Lee, S.H., Chung, T.C.: System Architecture for Context-Aware Home Application. In: Proceedings of the Second IEEE Workshop on Software Technologies for Future Embedded and Ubiquitous Systems, May 11-12, 2004, pp. 149–153 (2004)
10. Goldsby, H., Cheng, B.H.C.: Goal-Oriented Modeling of Requirements Engineering for Dynamically Adaptive Systems. In: 14t IEEE Int. Requirements Engineering Conf., September 11-15, 2006, pp. 345–346 (2006)
11. Niemela, E., Latvakoski, J.: Survey of requirements and solutions for ubiquitous software. In: Proceedings of the 3rd International Conference on Mobile and Ubiquitous Multimedia, pp. 71–78 (2004)
12. O'Neill, E., Kindberg, T., Schieck, A.F., gen, J.T., Penn, A., Fraser, D.S.: Instrumenting the city: developing methods for observing and understanding the digital cityscape. In: Dourish, P., Friday, A. (eds.) UbiComp 2006. LNCS, vol. 4206, pp. 315–332. Springer, Heidelberg (2006)
13. Sakamura, K.: Challenges in the Age of Ubiquitous Computing: A Case Study of T-Engine, An Open Development Platform for Embedded Systems. In: Proceedings of the 28th International Conference on Software Engineering, pp. 713–720 (2006)
14. Spínola, R.O., Silva, J.L.M., Travassos, G.H.: Checklist to Characterize Ubiquitous Software Projects. In: XXI Simpósio Brasileiro de Engenharia de Software, João Pessoa. Anais do XXI Simpósio Brasileiro de Engenharia de Software. Porto Alegre: Sociedade Brasileira de Computação, 2007. vol. 1, pp. 39–55 (2007)
15. Tahti, M., Rauto, V., Arhippainen, L.: Utilizing context-awareness in office-type working life. In: Proc. of the 3rd Int. Conf. on Mobile and Ubiquitous Multimedia 2004, College Park, Maryland, pp. 79–84 (2004)
16. Vainio, A.M., Valtonen, M., Vanhala, J.: Learning and adaptive fuzzy control system for smart home. In: Proc. of the AmI.d 2006, September 20-22, pp. 28–47 (2006)
17. Weiser, M.: The Computer for the 21st Century, pp. 94–104. Scientific American (1991)
18. Zhou, P., Nadeem, T., Kang, P., Borcea, C., Iftode, L.: EZCab: A Cab Booking Application Using Short-Range Wireless Communication. In: Third IEEE International Conference on Pervasive Computing and Communications PerCom 2005, 8-12 March 2005, pp. 27–38 (2005)
19. Hong, D., Chiu, D.K.W., Shen, V.Y.: Requirements Elicitation for the Design of Context-aware Applications in a Ubiquitous Environment. In: Proceedings of the 7th international conference on Electronic Commerce, Xi'an, China, pp. 590–596 (2005)

20. Xiang, J., Liu, L., Qiao, W., Yang, J.: SREM: A Service Requirements Elicitation Mechanism based on Ontology. In: 31st Annual International Computer Software and Applications Conference, 2007. COMPSAC 2007, 24-27 July 2007, vol. 1, pp. 196–203 (2007)
21. Cherif, A.R., Hina, M.D., Tadj, C., Levy, N.: Analysis of a New Ubiquitous Multimodal Multimedia Computing System. In: Proceedings of the 9th IEEE International Symposium on Multimedia, pp. 161–168 (2007)
22. Spínola, R.O., Silva, J.L.M., Travassos, G.H.: Characterizing Ubicomp Software Projects through a Checklist. In: WPUC 2007 - I Workshop on Pervasive and Ubiquitous Computing, 2007, Gramado; Proceedings of WPUC 2007, vol. 1, pp. 1–6. Sociedade Brasileira de Computação, Porto Alegre (2007)
23. Abowd, G.D., Mynatt, E.D.: Charting Past, Present and Future Research in Ubiquitous Computing. ACM Transactions on Computer-Human Interaction (TOCHI) 7(1), 29–58 (2000); Special issue on human-computer interaction in the new millennium, Part 1
24. Biolchini, J., Mian, P.G., Natali, A.C.C., Travassos, G.H.: Systematic Review in Software Engineering. Technical Report ES 679/05. COPPE/UFRJ (2005)
25. Pfleeger, S.: Software Engineering: Theory and Practice, 2nd edn. Prentice Hall, Englewood Cliffs (2007)
26. Bo, C., Xiang-Wu, M., Jun-Liang, C.: An Adaptive User Requirements Elicitation Framework. In: Proceedings of the 31st Annual International Computer Software and Applications Conference (COMPSAC 2007), vol. 2, pp. 501–502 (2007)
27. Chiu, D., Hong, D., Cheung, S.C., Kafeza, E.: Towards Ubiquitous Government Services through Adaptations with Context and Views in a Three-Tier Architecture. In: Proc. of the 40th Hawaii Int. Conf. on System Sciences, January 2007, p. 94 (2007)
28. Cheng, J., Goto, Y., Koide, M., Nagahama, K., Someya, M., Utsumi, Y., Sshionoiri, A.: ENQUETE-BAISE: A General-Purpose E-Questionnaire Server for Ubiquitous Questionnaire. In: IEEE Asia-Pacific Services Computing Conference, 11-14 December, pp. 187–195 (2007)
29. Kindberg, T., Barton, J., Becker, G., Caswell, D., Debaty, P., Gopal, G., Frig, M., Krishnan, V., Morris, H., Schettino, J., Serra, B., Spasojevic, M.: People, places, things: Web presence for the real world. In: Third IEEE Workshop on Mobile Computing Systems and Applications, pp. 19–28 (2000)
30. Nawyn, J., Intille, S., Larson, K.: Embedding Behavior Modification Strategies into Consumer Electronic Devices: A Case Study. In: Proc. of the 8th Int. Conference on Ubiquitous Computing (2006)

Squeeze All the Power Out of Your Hardware to Verify Your Software!

Jiří Barnat and Luboš Brim*

Faculty of Informatics, Masaryk University
Brno, Czech Republic

Abstract. The computer industry is undergoing a paradigm shift. Chip manufacturers are shifting development resources away from single-processor chips to a new generation of multi-processor chips, huge clusters of multi-core workstations are easily accessible everywhere, external memory devices, such as hard disks or solid state disks, are getting more powerful both in terms of capacity and access speed. This fundamental technological shift in core computing architecture will require a fundamental change in how we ensure the quality of software. The key issue is that verification techniques need to undergo a similarly deep technological transition to catch up with the complexity of software designed for the new hardware. In this position paper we would like to advocate the necessity of fully exploiting the power offered by the new computer hardware to make the verification techniques capable of handling next-generation software.

1 Introduction

The computing power of computers has increased by a factor of a million over the past couple of decades. As a matter of fact, the development effort, both in industry and in academia, has gone into developing bigger, more powerful and more complex applications. In the next few decades we may still expect a similar rate of growth, due to various factors such as continuing miniaturization, parallel and distributed computing.

With the increase in complexity of computer systems, it becomes even more important to develop formal methods for ensuring their quality and reliability. Various techniques for automated and semi-automated analysis and verification have been successfully applied to real-life computer systems. However, these techniques are computationally demanding and memory-intensive in general and their applicability to extremely large and complex systems routinely seen in practice these days is limited. The major hampering factor is the state space explosion problem due to which large industrial models cannot be efficiently handled unless we use more sophisticated and scalable methods and a balance of the usual trade-off between run-time, memory requirements, and precision of a method.

* This work has been partially supported by the Grant Agency of Czech Republic grant No. 201/06/1338 and the Academy of Sciences grant No. 1ET408050503.

T. Margaria and B. Steffen (Eds.): ISoLA 2008, CCIS 17, pp. 604–618, 2008.

A lot of attention has been paid to the development of approaches to battle the state space explosion problem. Many techniques, such as abstraction, state compression, state space reduction, symbolic state representation, etc., are used to reduce the size of the problem to be handled allowing thus a single old-fashioned single-processor computer to process larger systems. All these methods can be therefore characterized as "reduction" techniques.

Verification and analysis methods that are tailored to exploit the capabilities of the new hardware architectures are slowly appearing as well. These "platform-dependent" techniques focus on increasing the amount of available computational power. These are, for example, techniques to fight memory limits with efficient utilisation of external I/O devices, techniques that introduce cluster-based algorithms to employ aggregate power of network-interconnected computers, or techniques to speed-up the verification on multi-core processors.

The idea of exploiting hard disks or parallel computers in verification already appeared in the very early years of the formal verification era. However, inaccessibility of cheap parallel computers with sufficiently fast external memory together with negative theoretical complexity results excluded these approaches from the main stream in formal verification. The situation changed dramatically during the past several years. The computer progress over the past two decades has measured several orders of magnitude with respect to various physical parameters such as computing power, memory size at all hierarchy levels from caches to disk, power consumption, physical size and cost. In particular, the focus of novel computer architectures in parallel and distributed computing has shifted away from unique massively parallel systems competing for world records towards smaller and more cost effective systems built from personal computer parts. In addition, recent shift in the emphasis of research on parallel algorithms to pragmatic issues has provided practically efficient algorithms for solving computationally hard problems. As a matter of fact, interest in platform-depended verification has been revived.

2 Running Example: Enumerative LTL Model-Checking

Model checking is one of the major techniques used in the formal verification [17]. It builds on an automatic procedure that takes a model of the system and decides whether it satisfies a given property. In case the property is not satisfied, the procedure gives a counterexample, i.e. a particular behaviour of the model that violates the verified property.

In order to demonstrate, overview and advocate the advantages we can gain by exploiting the new hardware possibilities in more technical setting, we consider one particular verification problem, namely *enumerative LTL model checking*. Similar conclusions can be drawn for other verification problems as well.

An efficient procedure to decide LTL model checking problem is based on automata and was introduced in [41]. The approach exploits the fact that every set of executions expressible by an LTL formula is an ω-regular set and can be described by a *Büchi automaton*. In particular, the approach suggests to express all system executions by a *system automaton* and all executions not satisfying the formula by a *property* or *negative claim automaton*. These automata are combined into their synchronous product in order to check for the presence of system executions that violate the property expressed by the formula. The language recognised by the *product automaton* is empty if and only if no system execution is invalid.

The language emptiness problem for Büchi automata can be expressed as an *accepting cycle detection problem* in a graph. Each Büchi automaton can be naturally identified with an *automaton graph* which is a directed graph $G = (V, E, s, A)$ where V is the set of vertices ($n = |V|$), E is a set of edges ($m = |E|$), s is an initial vertex, and $A \subseteq V$ is a set of accepting vertices. We say that a cycle in G is accepting if it contains an accepting vertex. Let $\mathcal{A}$ be a Büchi automaton and $G_{\mathcal{A}}$ the corresponding automaton graph. Then $\mathcal{A}$ recognises a nonempty language iff $G_{\mathcal{A}}$ contains an accepting cycle reachable from s. The LTL model-checking problem is thus reduced to the accepting cycle detection problem in the automaton graph.

The optimal sequential algorithms for accepting cycle detection use depth-first search strategies to detect accepting cycles. The individual algorithms differ in their space requirements, length of the counter example produced, and other aspects. For a recent survey we refer to [40]. The well-known *Nested DFS* algorithm is used in many model checkers and is considered to be the best suitable algorithm for enumerative sequential LTL model checking. The algorithm was proposed by Courcoubetis et al. [18] and its main idea is to use two interleaved searches to detect reachable accepting cycles. The first search discovers accepting states while the second one, the nested one, checks for self-reachability. Several modifications of the algorithm have been suggested to remedy some of its disadvantages [23]. Another group of optimal algorithms are *SCC-based algorithms* originating in Tarjan's algorithm for the decomposition of the graph into strongly connected components (SCCs) [39]. While Nested DFS is more space efficient, SCC-based algorithms produce shorter counterexamples in general. For a survey we refer to [21]. The time complexity of these algorithms is linear in the size of the graph, i.e. $\mathcal{O}(m + n)$, where m is the number of edges and n is the number of vertices.

The effectiveness of the *Nested DFS* algorithm is achieved due to the particular order in which the graph is explored and which guarantees that vertices are not revisited more than twice. In fact, all the best-known algorithms rely on the same exploring principle, namely the *postorder* as computed by the DFS. It is a well-known fact that the postorder problem is P-complete and, consequently, e.g. a scalable parallel algorithm which would be directly based on DFS postorder is unlikely to exist.

An additional important criterion for a model checking algorithm is whether it works *on-the-fly*. On-the-fly algorithms generate the automaton graph gradually as they explore vertices of the graph. An accepting cycle can thus be detected before the complete set of vertices is generated and stored in memory. On-the-fly algorithms usually assume the graph to be given *implicitly* by the function F_{init} giving the initial vertex and by the function F_{succ} which returns immediate successors of a given vertex.

3 Get New Algorithms!

POSITION STATEMENT:
Recent architectural shift means that it is no longer possible to benefit from hardware progress, without introducing algorithmic changes to our tools. New algorithms have to be designed.

In many cases the algorithms as used traditionally are not appropriate to be adopted to the new hardware architectures. This can be demonstrated by LTL model checking algorithms as mention above. All the efficient algorithms build on depth-first search exploration of the state space. However, there is no known way to compute DFS postorder when using hard disks or parallel architectures efficiently. New algorithms, often radically different, have to be invented to replace the classical ones.

We will support this argument by presenting two different algorithms for accepting cycle detection (LTL model checking). Sequential complexity of these algorithms is worse than those based on DFS, but both allow to solve the LTL model-checking problem on new hardware architectures much more efficiently as will be exemplified later in the paper. Here we consider only two such algorithms. One is the MAP algorithm [13,14], the other one is the enumerative OWCTY algorithm [15]. For a survey on these and other algorithms we refer to [2].

Algorithm Based on Topological Sort

The main idea behind the OWCTY algorithm comes out from the fact that a directed graph can be topologically sorted if and only if it is acyclic. The core of the accepting cycle detection algorithm is thus in application of the standard linear topological sort algorithm to the input graph. Failure in topologically sorting the graph means the graph contains a cycle.

The algorithm performs a cycle detection that is based on the recursive elimination of vertices with zero predecessors. At first, the algorithm computes *reachibilty* to remove vertices from which no accepting state is reachable (these cannot belong to any accepting cycle) and computes the number of immediate predecessors for every reachable vertex. Then the algorithm *eliminates* vertices whose predecessor count drops to zero. During vertex elimination, the predecessor count is decreased for all immediate successors of the eliminated vertex.

The algorithm does not work on-the-fly and the entire automaton graph has to be generated first. Also, the algorithm does not immediately give the accepting cycle, it only checks for its *presence* in the graph. However, the counter-example is easily generated using two additional linear graph traversal, like BFS.

Time complexity of the algorithm is $\mathcal{O}(h \cdot m)$ where h is the height of the corresponding quotient graph (the graph of strongly connected components). Here the factor m comes from the computation of *Reachability* and *Elimination* functions and the factor h relates to the number of external iterations. In practice, the number of external iterations is very small (up to 40-50) even for very large graphs. This observation is supported by experiments in [22]. Similar results are communicated in [35] where heights of quotient graphs were measured for several models. As reported, 70% of the models have heights smaller than 50.

A positive aspect of the algorithm is its extreme effectiveness for *weak automaton graphs.* A graph is weak if in each strongly connected component all the states are accepting or none of them is. For weak graphs only one iteration of the algorithm is necessary to decide accepting cycles, the algorithm works in linear time and is thus optimal. The studies of temporal properties [19,16] reveal that verification of up to 90% of LTL properties leads to weak automaton graphs.

Maximal Accepting Predecessors Algorithm

The main idea behind the MAP algorithm is based on the fact that each accepting vertex lying on an accepting cycle is its own predecessor. The algorithm that would be directly derived from such an idea requires expensive storing of all proper accepting predecessors for each (accepting) vertex. To remedy this, the algorithm stores only a single representative accepting predecessor for each vertex. We presuppose a linear ordering $\prec$ of vertices (given e.g. by their memory representation) and choose the *maximal accepting predecessor.* For a vertex u we denote its maximal accepting predecessor in the graph G by $map_G(u)$. Clearly, if an accepting vertex is its own maximal accepting predecessor ($map_G(u) = u$), it lies on an accepting cycle. Unfortunately, the opposite does not hold in general. It can happen that the maximal accepting predecessor for an accepting vertex on a cycle does not lie on the cycle. This is exemplified on the graph given in Fig. 1. The accepting cycle $\langle 2, 1, 3, 2 \rangle$ is not revealed due to the greater accepting vertex 4 outside the cycle. However, as vertex 4 does not lie on *any* cycle, it can be safely deleted (marked as non-accepting) from the set of accepting vertices and the accepting cycle still remains in the resulting graph. This idea is formalised as a *deleting transformation.* Whenever the deleting transformation is applied to the automaton graph G with $map_G(v) \neq v$ for all $v \in V$, it shrinks the set of accepting vertices by those vertices that do not lie on any cycle. As the set of accepting vertices can change after the deleting transformation has been applied, maximal accepting predecessors must be recomputed. It can happen that even in the graph $del(G)$ the maximal accepting predecessor function is still not sufficient for cycle detection. However, after a finite number of iterations consisting of computing maximal accepting predecessors followed by application of the deleting transformation an accepting cycle is certified. For an automaton graph without accepting cycles the repetitive application of the deleting transformation results in an automaton graph with an empty set of accepting vertices.

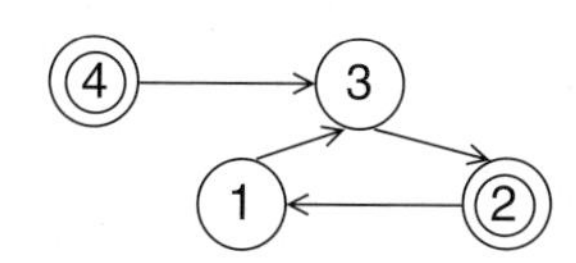

Fig. 1. Undiscovered cycle

Time complexity of the algorithm is $\mathcal{O}(a^2 \cdot m)$, where a is the number of accepting vertices. Here the factor $a \cdot m$ comes from the computation of the *map* function and the factor a relates to the number of iterations. Unlike the OWCTY algorithm, the MAP algorithm works on-the-fly.

Experimental evaluation of this algorithm demonstrated that accepting cycles were typically detected in a very small number of iterations. On the other hand, if there is no accepting cycle in the graph, the number of iterations is typically very small comparing to the size of the graph (up to 40-50). Thus, the algorithm exhibits nearly linear performance in practice.

4 Squeeze the Juice Out of Your Hard Disk!

POSITION STATEMENT:
External memory devices provide a viable computational alternative in analysing and verifying very large systems. With special external memory efficient techniques we can touch verification problems that are far beyond the capabilities of pure RAM approaches.

Hard disk has traditionally been regarded as a hopelessly slow cousin to RAM. However, the bandwidth of commodity disks today is on the order of 100MB/s. Is this enough to consider disk-based computation a way to increase working memory and achieve results that are not otherwise economical?

For external memory devices, the goal is to develop algorithms that minimize the number of I/O operations an algorithm has to perform to complete its task. This is because the access to information stored on an external device is orders of magnitude slower than the access to information stored in the main memory. Thus the complexity of I/O efficient algorithms is measured in the number of I/O operations only.

Using operating system's virtual memory often slows down the performance dramatically. A lot of effort has been therefore put into research on special I/O efficient algorithms, in particular graph algorithms. A distinguished technique that allows for an I/O efficient implementation of a graph traversal procedures is the so called *delayed duplicate detection* [31,34,38]. A traversal procedure has to maintain a set of visited vertices to prevent their re-exploration. Since the graphs are large, the set cannot be completely kept in the main memory and must be stored on the external memory device. When a new vertex is generated it is checked against the set to avoid its re-exploration. The idea of the delayed duplicate detection technique is to postpone the individual checks and perform them together in a group for the price of a single scan operation.

Unfortunately, the delayed duplicate detection technique is incompatible with the depth-first search (DFS) of a graph [20]. Therefore, the first approaches to I/O efficient LTL model checking have focused on the state space generation and verification of safety properties only. The very first I/O efficient algorithm for state space generation has been implemented in Murφ [38]. Later on, several heuristics for the state space generation were suggested and implemented in various verification tools [26,29,32]. The first attempt to verify more than safety properties has been described in [30]. The approach uses the random search to find a counterexample to a given property, it is thus incomplete in the sense that it is not able to prove validity of the property.

A *complete* I/O efficient LTL model checker was suggested in [20] (we refer to it as IO-EJ) where the problematic DFS-based algorithm was avoided by the reduction of the accepting cycle detection problem to the reachability problem [10,37] whose I/O efficient solution was further improved by using the directed (A^*) search and parallelism. The algorithm works in the on-the-fly manner meaning that only the part of the state space is constructed, which is needed in order to check the desired property. The reduction transforms the graph so that the size of the graph after the transformation is asymptotically quadratic with respect to the original one. As the external memory algorithms are meant to be applied to large graphs, the quadratic increase in the size of the graph is significant. This is especially the case when the model is valid and the entire graph has to be explored to prove the absence of an accepting cycle. The approach is thus mainly useful for finding counterexamples (*falsification*) in the case a standard verification tool fails due to the lack of memory.

Another complete I/O efficient LTL model checking algorithm (IO-OWCTY) has been proposed in [5]. The algorithm builds on the topological sort algorithm described in Section 3. Remember that this algorithm does not rely on the DFS postorder, hence is compatible with the delayed duplicate detection technique.

The algorithm uses BFS to traverse the graph and basically maintains three data structures: a set of vertices that await processing (*open set*), a set of vertices that have been processed already (*closed set*), and a set of *candidates*, i. e., vertices for which the corresponding check against the closed set has been postponed. The way in which vertices are manipulated is depicted in Fig. 2(a). A vertex from the open set is selected and its immediate successors are generated. The newly generated vertices are checked against the candidate set, to ensure that information stored in the candidate set is properly updated. Also, if there is a need for further processing of some vertices, they are inserted back into the open set along with all necessary information for the processing. As the check is not done directly against the closed set, this is the point where duplicates might appear.

Candidates are flushed to disk to resolve duplicates using a *merge* operation under two different circumstances: either the open set runs empty and the algorithm has to perform a merge to get new vertices into it, or the candidate set is too large and cannot be kept in memory anymore. The merge operation performs the duplicate check of candidate vertices against closed vertices, and inserts those vertices that require further processing into the open set.

A weak point of the IO-OWCTY algorithm is that the merge operation is performed every time the algorithm empties the set of open vertices, which happens at least after every BFS level. Often a single BFS level contains a relatively small number of vertices, in comparison to the full graph. Processing them means that the merge operation has to traverse a large disk file, which is costly.

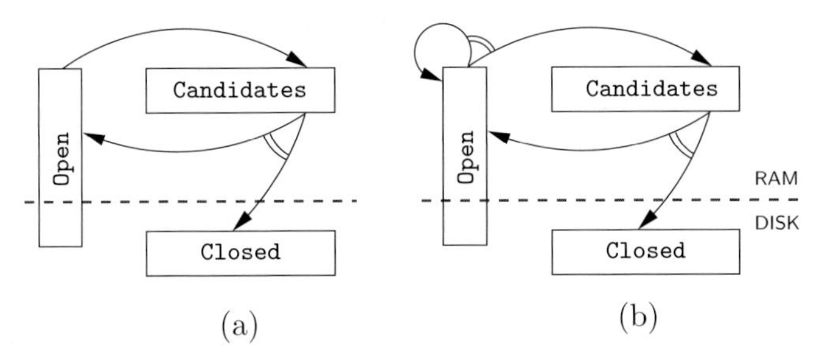

Fig. 2. Vertex work flow: (a) I/O search algorithm with delayed duplicate detection, (b) I/O search algorithm with delayed duplicate detection and revisiting

In [6] a different algorithm (IO-MAP) to fight this inefficiency was suggested. This algorithm builds on the maximal accepting predecessors algorithm as described in Section 3. The distinguished feature of the algorithm is that it allows more BFS levels to be explored at once without destroying the correctness of the algorithm (the algorithm is termed *revisiting resistant*). The substantial modification in the vertex work flow of an I/O efficient algorithm is depicted in Fig. 2(b). A vertex, when generated, is inserted not only into the set of candidates, but also into the open set. This causes some of the vertices stored in the candidate set to be revisited. I.e., the "visit" procedure is performed repeatedly for a vertex *without* properly updating its associated information in the closed set residing in external memory. Note that some graph algorithms, like topological sort, may exhibit incorrect behavior in this case. There is another very important difference between IO-OWCTY and IO-MAP, namely the latter works on-the-fly.

To demonstrate how I/O efficient LTL model checking algorithms compare, we conclude with some experimental measurements. All the models and their LTL properties are taken from the BEEM project [36]. The results are listed in Table 1. We noticed that just before an unsuccessful termination of IO-EJ due to exhausting the disk space, the BFS level size still tended to grow. This suggests that the computation would last substantially longer if sufficient disk space would have been available. For the same input graphs, the algorithms IO-OWCTY and IO-MAP manage to perform the verification using a few Gigabytes of disk space only.

Evaluation on models with valid properties demonstrates that IO-MAP is able to successfully prove their validity, while IO-EJ fails. The IO-MAP with its revisiting resistant techniques is able to outperform IO-OWCTY in many cases. We observed that specifically in cases with high h_{BFS}, e.g., Rether(16,8,4),P2, time savings are substantial. A notable weakness of IO-OWCTY is its slowness on models with invalid properties. It does not work on-the-fly, and is consequently outperformed by IO-EJ in the aforementioned class of inputs. The algorithm IO-MAP does not share IO-OWCTY's drawbacks, and in fact it outperforms both, IO-OWCTY and IO-EJ on those inputs. This can be attributed to their on-the-fly nature (on all our inputs, a counter example, if existing, has been found during the first iteration).

Table 1. Run times in `hh:mm:ss` format and memory consumption on a single workstation for I/O LTL algorithms. "OOS" means "out of space".

	IO-EJ		IO-OWCTY		IO-MAP	
Experiment	Time	Disk	Time	Disk	Time	Disk
Valid Properties						
Lamport(5),P4	(OOS)		02:37:17	5.5 GB	02:37:56	8.5 GB
MCS(5),P4	(OOS)		03:27:05	9.8 GB	04:13:21	11 GB
Peterson(5),P4	(OOS)		18:20:03	26 GB	15:24:29	27 GB
Phils(16,1),P3	(OOS)		01:49:41	6.2 GB	02:19:20	8.1 GB
Rether(16,8,4),P2	53:06:44	12 GB	07:22:05	3.2 GB	00:39:07	6.3 GB
Szymanski(5),P4	(OOS)		45:52:25	38 GB	29:09:12	39 GB
Invalid Properties						
Anderson(5),P2	00:00:17	50 MB	07:14:23	3.3 GB	00:00:01	4 MB
Bakery(5,5),P3	00:25:59	5.4 GB	68:23:34	38 GB	00:00:23	54 MB
Szymanski(4),P2	00:00:50	203 MB	00:20:07	253 MB	00:00:02	4 MB
Elevator2(7),P5	00:01:02	130 MB	00:00:25	6 MB	00:00:01	3 MB

5 Squeeze the Juice Out of Your Parallel Computer!

POSITION STATEMENT:
Forget about old-fashioned desktop computers! Nowadays, there is a powerful personal parallel supercomputer sitting in front of you. To get as much as possible from it, your software needs to get parallelized.

Parallel computers in principle come in two flavours. As shared-memory, in which multiple computing units share a single global large piece of memory, and as distributed-memory, in which every computing unit is equipped with its own local (not necessarily small) amount of memory.

Until recently, improvements in hardware architecture have been providing verification tools with performance increases mostly for free – without any need for implementational or algorithmic changes in the tools. However, this trend appears to be diminishing in favour of increasing parallelism in the system – which is nowadays much cheaper and easier to implement than it is to build computers with even faster sequential operation. However, this architectural shift means that it is no longer possible to benefit from hardware progress, without introducing algorithmic changes to our tools. This is what we are striving for – providing algorithms able to exploit such parallel architectures and offering an implementation that can be deployed in practical situations.

To gain the maximum of a parallel computer we have to use suitable parallel algorithms. Despite rare situations, where the problem is embarrassingly parallel, we need to do more than just adopt the best sequential algorithm to a parallel machine. As for LTL model checking, both the Nested DFS and the Tarjan's algorithm are inconvenient for parallel systems as they essentially rely on a depth first search postorder of vertices. Unfortunately, no optimal scalable technique is known that would allow to compute the postorder while not eliminating the parallel processing at the same time. As a result, theoretically unoptimal, but parallel and scalable algorithms are used in practice. This is because despite the purely theoretical asymptotic worst case complexity, there are many other, often more practical, aspects that render an algorithm suitable for solving the LTL model checking problem. For example, both the algorithms presented in Section 3 can be of use.

While these parallel algorithms perform single parallel computation on a bunch of computation units that communicate intensively to achieve their common goal, a different approach might be to decompose the problem into subproblems and solve these subproblems independently combining just the individual results at the end of parallel computation.

This type of parallel processing was considered also for enumerative LTL model checking [1]. In the automata-based approach to LTL model checking the product automaton originates from synchronous product of the property and system automata. Hence, vertices are ordered pairs. An interesting observation is that every cycle in a product automaton graph emerges from cycles in the system and the property automaton graphs. As the property automaton is typically quite small, it can be pre-analysed. In particular, it is possible to identify *all* strongly connected components of the property automaton graph. The decomposition of the property automaton can be then used to identify independent subgraphs of the graph to be searched for the presence of an accepting cycle. If a part of the product automaton graph respects the decomposition of the property automaton graph into strongly connected components, no cycle can cross the boundaries of the part. If every part is processed by a single computation node only, multiple Nested DFS algorithms localized to individual parts of the graph may be employed to detect the presence of an accepting cycle in the whole graph.

Another interesting information can be drawn from the property automaton graph decomposition. Maximal strongly connected components can be classified into three categories [33]:

Type F: (*Fully Accepting*) Any cycle within the component contains at least one accepting vertex. (There is no non-accepting cycle within the component.)
Type P: (*Partially Accepting*) There is at least one accepting cycle and one non-accepting cycle within the component.
Type N: (*Non-Accepting*) There is no accepting cycle within the component.

Realising that a vertex of a product automaton graph is accepting only if the corresponding vertex in the property automaton graph is accepting it is possible to characterise types of strongly connected components of product automaton graph according to types of components in the property automaton graph. Classification of components into types N, F, and P is useful for parallel processing as dedicated algorithms may be applied to process parts of the graph of different types. In [15] it was shown that the OWCTY algorithm is in fact optimal in the case the graph of property automaton contains only components of type N

and F. Moreover, the same authors claimed that most LTL properties that are verified in practice are of this type [16].

A different example of dividing the given task into independent subtasks is nicely demonstrated on the parallel version of the MAP algorithm. It can be easily seen that an accepting cycle can be formed from vertices with the same maximal accepting predecessor only. A graph induced by the set of vertices having the same maximal accepting predecessor is called *predecessor subgraph.* It is clear that every strongly connected component (hence every cycle) in the graph is completely included in one of the predecessor subgraphs. Therefore, after applying the deleting transformation, the new *map* function can be computed separately and independently for every predecessor subgraph. This allows for speeding up the computation (values are not propagated to vertices in different subgraphs) and for an efficient parallelisation of the computation.

Shared-Memory LTL Model Checking

Both platforms have been considered in the context of model checking. Much of the extensive research on the parallelization of model checking algorithms for followed initially the distributed-memory programming model and the algorithms were parallelized for networks of workstations, largely due to easy access to networks of workstations. However, it is the shared-memory environment that is paid more attention in the last several years. This is because multicored CPUs made it easily available to general public.

It is in principle possible to take a distributed-memory parallel algorithm and simply run it on a multi-core machine as it is (which is possible, e.g. due to multi-core implementation of MPI). The result will be disappointing however. In Fig. 3 this is demonstrated on the bad scaling of the OWCTY algorithm. Adaptations taking into account specifics of the shared-memory architecture must be taken into account. Of course the very first attempt is to fully exploit the shared-memory for sharing data among individual threads. It is a little bit surprising that using shared hash table to avoid contention does not necessarily lead to better performance. For LTL model-checking on multi-core machines it seems to be best to use partitioned hash-tables (similarly to distributed-memory) which give better cache locality and to tune the parallel algorithm using techniques like efficient concurrent memory allocation and deallocation or lock-free and wait-free data structures for interactions [7].

The pioneering work is [28], where Holzmann and Bosnacki proposed an extension of the SPIN model checker for dual-core machines. Proposed algorithms keep their linear time complexity and the liveness checking algorithm supports full LTL. The algorithm for checking safety properties is capable of running on an arbitrary number of CPU cores, whereas the liveness checking algorithm, which is based on the original SPIN's nested DFS, is limited to dual-core systems.

The paper [4] was the first one on multi-core LTL model-checking, focused on bringing distributed-memory algorithms to shared memory. It has discussed implementation techniques that have allowed to improve scalability of those algorithms on multi-core machines. In [7] the results have been further extended in the direction of different hash table and work distribution options.

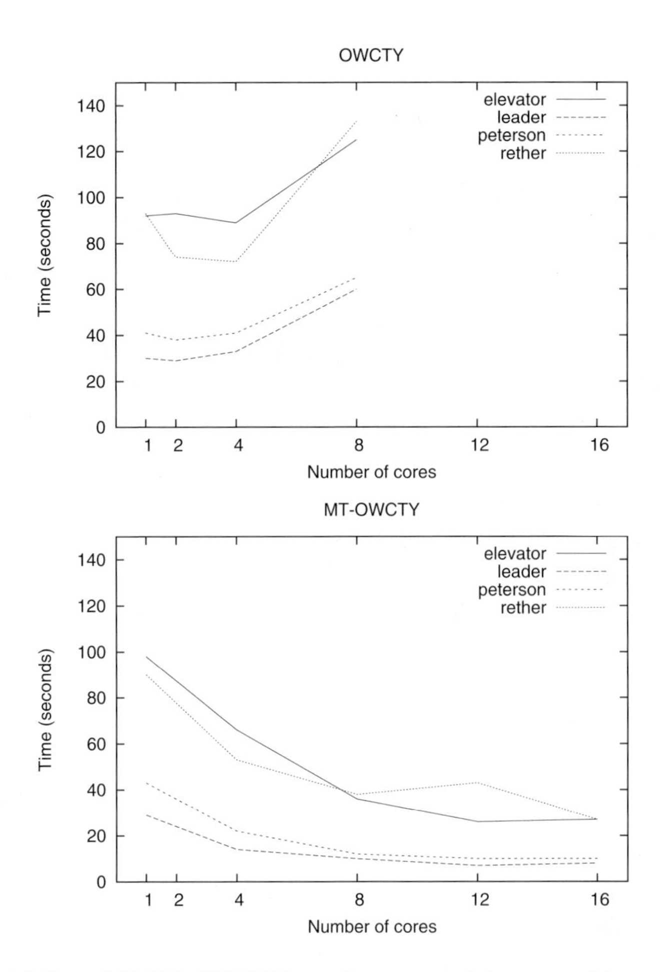

Fig. 3. Scalability of "MPI" OWCTY running on a multi-core machine and the tuned MT-OWCTY version

Distributed Memory LTL Model Checking

The standard parallel platform for distributed-memory computing is a network of workstations, a cluster for short. Cluster-based algorithms perform their computation simultaneously on multiple computation nodes that are allowed to communicate and synchronise themselves by means of message passing. The advantage of this environment is not only the aggregate computation speed achieved by parallel processing, but also the aggregate amount of memory the platform can provide. Cluster-based algorithms proved their usefulness in verification of large-scale systems in many studies. They have been successfully applied to symbolic model checking [24,25], analysis of stochastic [27] and timed [8] systems, equivalence checking [11] and other related problems [9,12].

6 Conclusion

Platform-dependent verification is a newly emerging field. Extending the techniques as they are known from the sequential world adds significant complications and often requires entirely new approaches. We need to change our attitude in designing practical solutions for verification on the new hardware architectures. The key steps for their effective deployment in industry and real applications is to design appropriate algorithms, use algorithm engineering techniques and effects of the memory hierarchy, as well as implications of communication complexity, and heuristics. The new demand for platform-dependent verification algorithms that are of practical utility has raised the need to replace the traditional sequential approach.

Despite significant progress in platform-depended verification that we have encountered during the last several years, practically useful platform-dependent verification tools are still to be developed. There are only a few of them, mostly of academic nature. In the area of LTL model-checking, the parallel distributed-memory verification tool DiVinE [3] has recently been released in its multi-core version – slightly ahead of the release of the multi-core version of SPIN. There are also many open questions and problems that naturally arise when we consider the new technological platform. An example is the following open problem: Is there a scalable parallel algorithm for accepting cycle detection whose sequential complexity is linear and the algorithm works on-the-fly?

References

1. Barnat, J., Brim, L., Černá, I.: Property Driven Distribution of Nested DFS. In: Proceedings of the 3rd International Workshop on Verification and Computational Logic (VCL 2002 – held at the PLI 2002 Symposium). University of Southampton, UK, Technical Report DSSE-TR-2002-5 in DSSE, pp. 1–10 (2002)
2. Barnat, J., Brim, L., Černá, I.: I/O Efficient Accepting Cycle Detection. In: Damm, W., Hermanns, H. (eds.) CAV 2007. LNCS, vol. 4590, pp. 281–293. Springer, Heidelberg (2007)
3. Barnat, J., Brim, L., Černá, I., Moravec, P., Ročkai, P., Šimeček, P.: DiVinE – A Tool for Distributed Verification (Tool Paper). In: Ball, T., Jones, R.B. (eds.) CAV 2006. LNCS, vol. 4144, pp. 278–281. Springer, Heidelberg (2006)
4. Barnat, J., Brim, L., Ročkai, P.: Scalable Multi-core LTL Model-Checkin. In: Bošnački, D., Edelkamp, S. (eds.) SPIN 2007. LNCS, vol. 4595, pp. 187–203. Springer, Heidelberg (2007)
5. Barnat, J., Brim, L., Šimeček, P.: I/O Efficient Accepting Cycle Detection. In: Damm, W., Hermanns, H. (eds.) CAV 2007. LNCS, vol. 4590, pp. 281–293. Springer, Heidelberg (2007)
6. Barnat, J., Brim, L., Šimeček, P., Weber, M.: Revisiting Resistance Speeds Up I/O-Efficient LTL Model Checking. In: Ramakrishnan, C.R., Rehof, J. (eds.) TACAS 2008. LNCS, vol. 4963, pp. 48–62. Springer, Heidelberg (2008)
7. Barnat, J., Ročkai, P.: Shared Hash Tables in Parallel Model Checking. ENTCS 198(1), 79–91 (2008)

8. Behrmann, G., Hune, T.S., Vaandrager, F.W.: Distributed Timed Model Checking — How the Search Order Matters. In: Emerson, E.A., Sistla, A.P. (eds.) CAV 2000. LNCS, vol. 1855, pp. 216–231. Springer, Heidelberg (2000)
9. Bell, A., Haverkort, B.R.: Sequential and distributed model checking of petri net specifications. Int. J. Softw. Tools Technol. Transfer 7(1), 43–60 (2005)
10. Biere, A., Artho, C., Schuppan, V.: Liveness Checking as Safety Checking. Electr. Notes Theor. Comput. Sci. 66(2) (2002)
11. Blom, S., Orzan, S.: A Distributed Algorithm for Strong Bisimulation Reduction Of State Spaces. Int. J. Softw. Tools Technol. Transfer 7(1), 74–86 (2005)
12. Bollig, B., Leucker, M., Weber, M.: Parallel Model Checking for the Alternation Free μ-Calculus. In: Margaria, T., Yi, W. (eds.) TACAS 2001. LNCS, vol. 2031, pp. 543–558. Springer, Heidelberg (2001)
13. Brim, L., Černá, I., Moravec, P., Šimša, J.: Accepting Predecessors are Better than Back Edges in Distributed LTL Model-Checking. In: Hu, A.J., Martin, A.K. (eds.) FMCAD 2004. LNCS, vol. 3312, pp. 352–366. Springer, Heidelberg (2004)
14. Brim, L., Černá, I., Moravec, P., Šimša, J.: How to order vertices for distributed ltl model-checking based on accepting predecessors. Electronic Notes in Theoretical Computer Science 135(2), 3–18 (2006)
15. Černá, I., Pelánek, R.: Distributed Explicit Fair cycle Detection (Set Based Approach). In: Ball, T., Rajamani, S.K. (eds.) SPIN 2003. LNCS, vol. 2648, pp. 49–73. Springer, Heidelberg (2003)
16. Černá, I., Pelánek, R.: Relating Hierarchy of Temporal Properties to Model Checking. In: Rovan, B., Vojtáš, P. (eds.) MFCS 2003. LNCS, vol. 2747, pp. 318–327. Springer, Heidelberg (2003)
17. Clarke Jr., E.M., Grumberg, O., Peled, D.A.: Model Checking. MIT Press, Cambridge (1999)
18. Courcoubetics, C., Vardi, M., Wolper, P., Yannakakis, M.: Memory efficient algorithms for the verification of temporal properties. In: Clarke, E., Kurshan, R.P. (eds.) CAV 1990. LNCS, vol. 531, pp. 233–242. Springer, Heidelberg (1991)
19. Dwyer, M.B., Avrunin, G.S., Corbett, J.C.: Property Specification Patterns for Finite-State Verification. In: Proc. Workshop on Formal Methods in Software Practice, pp. 7–15. ACM Press, New York (1998)
20. Edelkamp, S., Jabbar, S.: Large-Scale Directed Model Checking LTL. In: Valmari, A. (ed.) SPIN 2006. LNCS, vol. 3925, pp. 1–18. Springer, Heidelberg (2006)
21. Esparza, J., Schwoon, S.: A note on on-the-fly verification algorithms. In: Halbwachs, N., Zuck, L.D. (eds.) TACAS 2005. LNCS, vol. 3440, pp. 174–190. Springer, Heidelberg (2005)
22. Fisler, K., Fraer, R., Kamhi, G., Vardi, M.Y., Yang, Z.: Is there a best symbolic cycle-detection algorithm? In: Margaria, T., Yi, W. (eds.) TACAS 2001. LNCS, vol. 2031, pp. 420–434. Springer, Heidelberg (2001)
23. Geldenhuys, J., Valmari, A.: Tarjan's algorithm makes on-the-fly LTL verification more efficient. In: Jensen, K., Podelski, A. (eds.) TACAS 2004. LNCS, vol. 2988, pp. 205–219. Springer, Heidelberg (2004)
24. Grumberg, O., Heyman, T., Ifergan, N., Schuster, A.: Achieving speedups in distributed symbolic reachability analysis through asynchronous computation. In: Borrione, D., Paul, W. (eds.) CHARME 2005. LNCS, vol. 3725, pp. 129–145. Springer, Heidelberg (2005)
25. Grumberg, O., Heyman, T., Schuster, A.: Distributed Model Checking for μ-calculus. In: Berry, G., Comon, H., Finkel, A. (eds.) CAV 2001. LNCS, vol. 2102, pp. 350–362. Springer, Heidelberg (2001)

26. Hammer, M., Weber, M.: To Store Or Not To Store Reloaded. In: Brim, L., Haverkort, B.R., Leucker, M., van de Pol, J. (eds.) FMICS 2006 and PDMC 2006. LNCS, vol. 4346, pp. 51–66. Springer, Heidelberg (2007)
27. Haverkort, B.R., Bell, A., Bohnenkamp, H.C.: On the Efficient Sequential and Distributed Generation of Very Large Markov Chains From Stochastic Petri Nets. In: Proc. 8th Int. Workshop on Petri Net and Performance Models, pp. 12–21. IEEE Computer Society Press, Los Alamitos (1999)
28. Holzmann, G.J., Bosnacki, D.: The design of a multicore extension of the spin model checker. IEEE Transactions on Software Engineering 33(10), 659–674 (2007)
29. Jabbar, S., Edelkamp, S.: I/O Efficient Directed Model Checking. In: Cousot, R. (ed.) VMCAI 2005. LNCS, vol. 3385, pp. 313–329. Springer, Heidelberg (2005)
30. Jones, M., Mercer, E.: Explicit State Model Checking with Hopper. In: Graf, S., Mounier, L. (eds.) SPIN 2004. LNCS, vol. 2989, pp. 146–150. Springer, Heidelberg (2004)
31. Korf, R.: Best-First Frontier Search with Delayed Duplicate Detection. In: AAAI 2004, pp. 650–657. AAAI Press / The MIT Press (2004)
32. Kristensen, L., Mailund, T.: Efficient Path Finding with the Sweep-Line Method Using External Storage. In: Dong, J.S., Woodcock, J. (eds.) ICFEM 2003. LNCS, vol. 2885, pp. 319–337. Springer, Heidelberg (2003)
33. Lafuente, A.L.: Simplified distributed LTL model checking by localizing cycles. Technical Report 00176, Institut für Informatik, University Freiburg, Germany (July 2002)
34. Munagala, K., Ranade, A.: I/O-Complexity of Graph Algorithms. In: SODA 1999, Philadelphia, PA, USA, pp. 687–694. Society for Industrial and Applied Mathematics (1999)
35. Pelánek, R.: Typical structural properties of state spaces. In: Graf, S., Mounier, L. (eds.) SPIN 2004. LNCS, vol. 2989, pp. 5–22. Springer, Heidelberg (2004)
36. Pelánek, R.: BEEM: Benchmarks for Explicit Model Checkers. In: Bošnački, D., Edelkamp, S. (eds.) SPIN 2007. LNCS, vol. 4595, pp. 263–267. Springer, Heidelberg (2007)
37. Schuppan, V., Biere, A.: Efficient Reduction of Finite State Model Checking to Reachability Analysis. International Journal on Software Tools for Technology Transfer (STTT) 5(2–3), 185–204 (2004)
38. Stern, U., Dill, D.L.: Using Magnetic Disk Instead of Main Memory in the Murphi Verifier. In: Vardi, M., Y. (ed.) CAV 1998. LNCS, vol. 1427, pp. 172–183. Springer, Heidelberg (1998)
39. Tarjan, R.: Depth First Search and Linear Graph Algorithms. SIAM Journal on Computing, 146–160 (January 1972)
40. Vardi, M.: Automata-Theoretic Model Checking Revisited. In: Cook, B., Podelski, A. (eds.) VMCAI 2007. LNCS, vol. 4349, pp. 137–150. Springer, Heidelberg (2007)
41. Vardi, M.Y., Wolper, P.: An automata-theoretic approach to automatic program verification. In: Proc. IEEE Symposium on Logic in Computer Science, pp. 322–331. Computer Society Press (1986)

Static Partial-Order Reduction of Concurrent Systems in Polynomial Time

Robert Mittermayr and Johann Blieberger

Institute of Computer-Aided Automation
Vienna University of Technology
Austria

Abstract. We present an algorithm for attacking the state explosion problem in analyzing multithreaded programs. Our approach employs partial-order reduction and static virtual coarsening. It uses information on shared variables to generate and interleave blocks of statements.

Our algorithm performs polynomially as long as the number of shared variables is constant.

1 Introduction

With the advent of multi-core processors scientific and industrial interest focuses on multithreaded applications. Examples like [3] show that writing even small multithreaded programs can be a tedious task.

For safety-critical systems or robust embedded systems, software has to be provably correct. So, in order to incorporate concurrently executing threads in safety-critical systems, these concurrent programs have to be proved to be correct. Verifying concurrent programs is challenging because the number of thread interleavings grows exponentially in the number of statements of the program. All state-of-the-art methods, such as model-checking, suffer from this so-called *state explosion problem*.

The main contributions of this paper are a theoretical analysis of interleavings, an algorithm for the static reduction of interleavings needed to be taken into account in order to generate the state space, and a worst-case estimation of this algorithm.

The remainder of the paper is organized as follows. In Section 2 the state explosion problem is discussed theoretically. An algorithm for reducing the amount of interleavings without losing any computational results is presented in Section 3. The worst-case behavior of the presented algorithm is presented in Section 4. In Section 5 an example shows how the algorithm works. Related work is discussed in Section 6. Finally, we conclude the paper and outline possible future work in Section 7.

2 Interleavings and the State Explosion Problem

For the analysis of multithreaded software in general it is very important to analyze all possible execution sequences. This ensures that each possible state

T. Margaria and B. Steffen (Eds.): ISoLA 2008, CCIS 17, pp. 619–633, 2008.

is reached. In this section we will start with an example which introduces the problem in practice. The simple example will be followed by a theoretical analysis of the state explosion problem.

As a motivating example consider

$$P\colon (\underbrace{x{:=}4}_{a}; \underbrace{x{:=}x+3}_{b}) \parallel (\underbrace{x{:=}2}_{c}; \underbrace{x{:=}(x*x)+1}_{d}) .$$

Program P may result in six states. All possible final states of program P are depicted in Table 1. Please note that we define all statements in this paper to be atomic.

Table 1. Computation results

Order	x
a b c d	5
a c b d	26
a c d b	8
c a b d	50
c a d b	20
c d a b	7

For enumerating the number of interleavings for n threads $(t_1, t_2, \ldots, t_n)$ where each t_i has k_i statements (where $1 \leq i \leq n$) the multinomial theorem can be applied. This results in

$$\binom{k_1+k_2+k_3+\cdots+k_n}{k_n}\cdots\binom{k_1+k_2+k_3}{k_3}\cdot\binom{k_1+k_2}{k_2} = \frac{(k_1+k_2+k_3+\cdots+k_n)!}{k_1!k_2!k_3!\ldots k_n!}$$

interleavings.

Lemma 1 (Number of Interleavings). *Given n threads $(t_1, t_2, \ldots, t_n)$ where each t_i has k_i statements, the number of interleavings is given by*

$$\frac{\left(\sum_{i=1}^{n} k_i\right)!}{\prod_{i=1}^{n} k_i!}. \tag{1}$$

□

Lemma 1 shows how simple it is to get astronomically high numbers of interleavings. If we have 20 statements in each of three threads we get $\frac{(60!}{(20!)^3} \approx 5 \times 10^{26}$ interleavings.

In order to find the maximum of Eq. (1) we have to maximize

$$\frac{k!}{\prod_{i=1}^{n} k_i!} \tag{2}$$

where $k = \sum_{i=1}^{n} k_i$. In the following we use the gamma function $\Gamma(x)$ (cf. [1]) to replace the integer factorial by a real-valued function. Note that $\Gamma(m+1) = m!$.

In order to find the extreme value of Eq. (2) we employ the logarithmic derivative of Eq. (2) which simplifies the calculations significantly.

The derivative of

$$log(k!) - \sum_{i=1}^{n} log(\Gamma(k_i + 1)) + \lambda(\sum_{i=1}^{n} k_i - k)$$

with respect to k_i is

$$-\frac{\Gamma'(k_i + 1)}{\Gamma(k_i + 1)} + \lambda = 0,$$

where $1 \leq i \leq n$. This is valid for all k_i, in particular for $i = s$ and $i = t$, i.e.,

$$\frac{\Gamma'(k_s + 1)}{\Gamma(k_s + 1)} = \frac{\Gamma'(k_t + 1)}{\Gamma(k_t + 1)}.$$

Using the digamma function $\psi(x) = \frac{\Gamma'(x)}{\Gamma(x)}$ (cf. [1]) we can write

$$\psi(k_s + 1) = \psi(k_t + 1).$$

Because $\psi(x)$ is monotonically increasing for $x \geq 0$ (cf. e.g. [1]) we get

$$k_s = k_t, \text{ for all } 1 \leq s, t \leq n$$

which implies $k_i = k/n$, provided that n divides k $(n|k)$.

Thus we have proved the following lemma.

Lemma 2. *For a given number of statements k, the worst-case number of interleavings appears if all n threads have the same number of statements. In this case the number of interleavings is given by*

$$\frac{k!}{\left((\frac{k}{n})!\right)^n} \tag{3}$$

where $n|k$. □

In the following we write $k = \beta \cdot n$. If the number of statements per thread $\beta \geq 1$ is fixed, Formula (3) can be estimated by Stirling's approximation $m! = (\frac{m}{e})^m \sqrt{2\pi m}(1 + O(\frac{1}{m}))$ as $m \to \infty$ (cf. e.g. [1]) giving

$$\frac{(\beta\, n)!}{(\beta!)^n} \sim n^{\beta\, n + \frac{1}{2}}\, (2\pi\beta)^{-\frac{n}{2}+\frac{1}{2}},\ (n \to \infty). \tag{4}$$

For $\beta \in \{5, 10, 15, 20, 25, 30\}$ the characteristics of this formula are depicted in Fig. 1. This case describes the practical case when there is e.g. an Ada task type defining tasks with β statements.

In Fig. 2 the behavior of a variable number of statements per thread $2 \leq \beta \leq 200$ and a variable number of threads $1 \leq n \leq 40$ is depicted in logarithmic scale. Please note that the functions depicted in Fig. 1 and 2 are actually defined for natural numbers only. The same applies for the figures in Section 4.

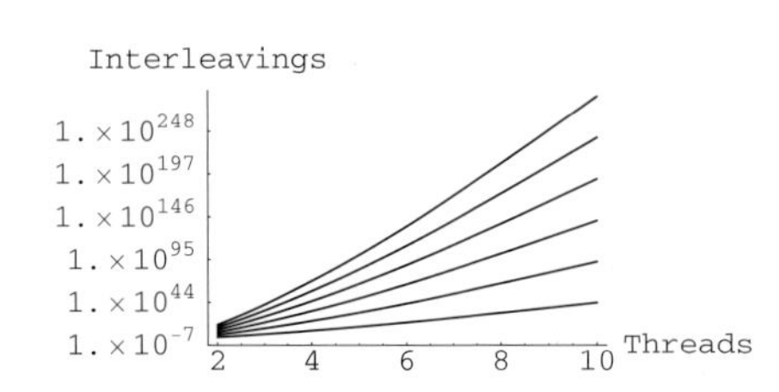

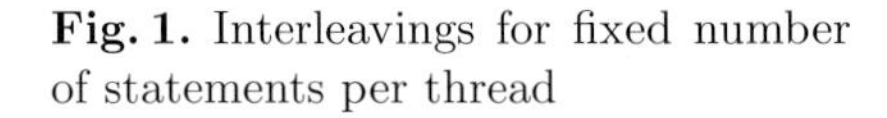
Fig. 1. Interleavings for fixed number of statements per thread

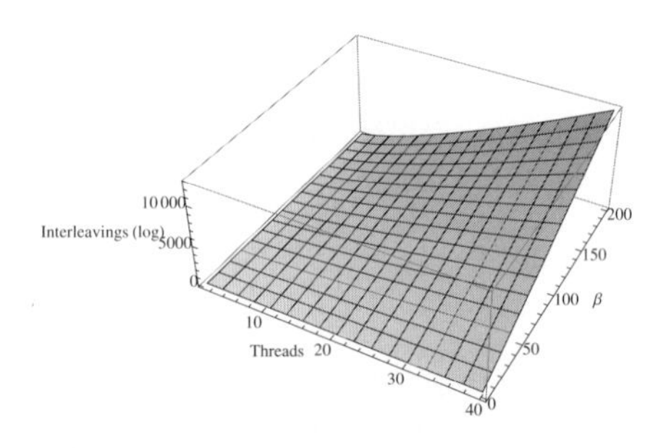

Fig. 2. Interleavings for a variable number of threads and statements per thread

3 Algorithm

In this section we present an algorithm for reducing the amount of interleavings without losing possible resulting states. We achieve this by building blocks of statements. We combine a *virtual coarsening* approach similar to [2,16] with a partial order relation of blocks of statements. The correctness of virtual coarsening has been proved in [2].

We say that a statement *accesses* a variable v if the statement reads or writes the variable v. A variable is said to be shared if more than one thread accesses it. The set of shared variables is denoted by V. We refer to the set of threads with T.

Definition 1. *A* block *is a list of consecutive statements and contains at most one statement accessing shared variables. If the number of blocks is minimized, we call the resulting list of consecutive blocks* minimum block list.

We define a strict partial order relation "$<$" between blocks that is irreflexive, asymmetric, and transitive. Let bl_i and bl_j be blocks. Then $bl_i < bl_j$ holds iff there exists an execution sequence of the underlying program such that bl_i preceeds bl_j.

We distinguish between two kinds of strict partial order relations, intra-thread and inter-thread orders. Intra-thread orders define orders of blocks within a thread and inter-thread orders define an ordering between blocks of different threads.

Both relations can be represented by graphs. We call such graphs *partial order graphs* or *PO graphs* for short.

Let $t(bl_i) = t_j$ when bl_i is part of thread t_j, where $1 \leq j \leq n$ and $1 \leq i \leq b$. Let $a(v_i) = \{bl_j \mid \exists$ *statement s in* bl_j *which accesses* $v_i\}$. Let $a(v_i, t_j) = \{bl_k \mid \exists$ *statement s in* bl_k *which accesses* v_i *and* $t(bl_k) \neq t_j\}$. In addition, we define $SV(bl_i) = \{v_j \mid$ where block bl_i contains a statement which accesses the shared variable $v_j\}$. Let the number of shared variables be r and further let $b^{(v_j)}$ denote the number of blocks accessing shared variable v_j (over all threads).

The algorithm consists of the following six steps:

Find shared variables. This step fills the set V.

Build minimum block list.

Generate partial orders for the blocks accessing the same shared variables.

Construct PO graphs

Apply topological sorting to each PO graph. This step results in exactly one order of blocks for any PO graph constructed in the previous step.

Compute the state space of the program by executing the blocks in the orders calculated in the previous step.

The algorithm is presented in more detail below.

```
ALGORITHM ()
1  List[] blocks := new List[1..n]
2  List[][] blocks_var := new List[1..r][1..n]
3  List[] finalInterThreadOrderedBlocks
4  ListOfListOfPartialOrders combinedInterThreadOrderedBlocks
5  FINDSHAREDVARIABLES()
6  BUILDBLOCKS()
7  GENERATEORDERS()
8  CONSTRUCTPOGRAPHS()
9  TOPOLOGICALSORTING()
10 COMPUTESTATESPACE()
```

```
GENERATEORDERS ()
1  GENERATEINTRATHREADORDERS
2  GENERATEINTERTHREADORDERS
3  COMBINEINTERTHREADORDERS
```

```
GENERATEINTRATHREADORDERS ()
1  for each thread t_i ∈ T do
2     for each pair bl_j, bl_{j+1} ∈ blocks[i] do
3        DEFINE bl_j < bl_{j+1}
4     endfor
5  endfor
```

```
BUILDBLOCKS ()
1  for each thread t_i ∈ T do
2     boolean firstBlock := true
3     Block actualBlock := new Block()
4     blocks[i].add(actualBlock)
5     for each statement s ∈ t_i do
6        if s accesses v ∈ V then
7           if not firstBlock then
8              actualBlock := new Block()
9              blocks[i].add(actualBlock)
10          else
11             firstBlock := false
12          endif
13       endif
14       append s to actualBlock
15    endfor
16 endfor
```

```
GenerateInterThreadOrders()
1   int b_var_k
2   for each thread t_i ∈ T do
3      for each bl_j ∈ blocks[i] do
4         for each v_k ∈ SV(bl_j) do
5            blocks_var[k][i].add(bl_j)
6         endfor
7      endfor
8   endfor
9   for each v_k ∈ V do
10     b_var_k := b^(v_k)
11     Block[] interThreadOrderedBlocks := new Block[1..b_var_k]
12     Interleave_rec(blocks_var[k], interThreadOrderedBlocks, 1, k)
13  endfor
```

```
Interleave_rec (List[] blks, Block[] interThrdOrdBlks, int block_nr, int var_nr)
1   for each i ∈ {1...n} do
2      if blks[i].count() > 0 then
3         interThrdOrdBlks[block_nr]:=blks[i].getHead()
4         if block_nr = b_var_k then
5            finalInterThreadOrderedBlocks[var_nr].add(new List(interThrdOrdBlks))
6         else
7            List[] local_blks:=blks.clone()
8            local_blks.removeHead()
9            interleave_rec(local_blks, interThrdOrdBlks, block_nr + 1, var_nr)
10        endif
11     endif
12  endfor
```

```
CombineInterThreadOrders()
1   GenerateCombinations_rec(0, new ListOfPartialOrders())
```

```
GenerateCombinations_rec (int cur_var, ListOfPartialOrders ordersTillNow)
1   for each interThreadOrderedBlocks ∈
2         finalInterThreadOrderedBlocks[cur_var] do
3      ListOfPartialOrders ordersToUse := ordersTillNow.clone()
4      for each pair bl_i, bl_{i+1} ∈
5            finalInterThreadOrderedBlocks[cur_var][interThreadOrderedBlocks] do
6         Define bl_i < bl_{i+1} and add it to ordersToUse
7      endfor
8      if cur_var < r then
9         GenerateCombinations_rec(cur_var+1,ordersToUse)
10     else
11        combinedInterThreadOrderedBlocks.add(ordersToUse)
12     endif
13  endfor
```

```
ConstructPOGraphs ()
1  for each concreteOrders ∈ combinedInterThreadOrderedBlocks do
2     use PO graph generated from intra-thread orders for a new PO graph
3     for each PO(b_i, b_j) ∈ concreteOrders do
4        add directed edge from node_{b_i} to node_{b_j}
5     endfor
6     add PO graph to the set of resulting PO graphs
7  endfor
```

Each of the steps (except the first one) uses information generated in the previous steps. Note that we generate the reduced state space without generating the original state space as an intermediate result. This is of course important because if the original state space would be generated it would abandon the achieved reductions. In addition, note that our approach, in its current version, needs no human modeling or specification input.

The initial exponential growth of interleavings in terms of the number of statements can be reduced to an exponential growth in terms of the number of shared variables. In a lot of cases this approach enables static analysis of multithreaded programs.

If a statement accesses two or more different shared variables, it may happen that conflicting partial order relations appear. If e.g. a statement s_1 in block bl_1 which is part of thread t_1 reads variable x and writes variable y, whereas statement s_2 in block bl_2 which is part of thread t_2 writes the shared variable x and reads the variable y then the algorithm generates the following inter-thread orders

$$\begin{pmatrix} bl_1 < bl_2 \\ bl_2 < bl_1 \end{pmatrix} \times \begin{pmatrix} bl_1 < bl_2 \\ bl_2 < bl_1 \end{pmatrix}.$$

This results in a cyclic directed graph[1]. Topological sorting can detect this and the algorithm can be aborted for such contradictory partial orders. In the above example the algorithm aborts two times and only the two orders $bl_1; bl_2$ and $bl_2; bl_1$ are being generated.

The presented algorithm acts on the assumption that all threads are running at the same time. In addition, it is assumed that every statement s_1 of a thread t_1 may happen in parallel to every statement s_2 of another thread t_2 (cf. e.g. [4]). This assumptions assure the completeness of the approach. On the other hand this conservative approach may lead to false positives.

Please note that currently we are not handling conditionals, loops, and procedure calls. This will be future work.

4 Worst-Case Analysis

In this section we assume that each statement only accesses one single shared variable. Note however that this is no real constraint because statements accessing several shared variables can be replaced by simpler statements accessing only one single shared variable by introducing artificial (local) variables.

[1] Note that duplicate partial orders can be ignored during PO graph construction.

In addition to the definitions in previous sections let $b_i^{(v_j)}$ denote the number of blocks in thread i accessing shared variable v_j.

To derive the worst-case complexity of the approach from Section 3, a multivariate extreme value calculation can be employed. The following expression, which denotes the number of graphs generated, has to be maximized

$$\prod_{j=1}^{r} \sum_{i=1}^{n} b_i^{(v_j)} \left(b^{(v_j)} - b_i^{(v_j)} \right). \tag{5}$$

In addition, we have the following constraint

$$\sum_{i=1}^{n} b_i^{(v_j)} = b^{(v_j)}.$$

Differentiating

$$\prod_{j=1}^{r} \sum_{i=1}^{n} b_i^{(v_j)} \left(b^{(v_j)} - b_i^{(v_j)} \right) + \lambda_1 \left(\sum_{i=1}^{n} b_i^{(v_j)} - b^{(v_j)} \right)$$

with respect to $b_i^{(v_j)}$, we get for all $1 \le i \le n$ and $1 \le j \le r$

$$b^{(v_j)} - 2\, b_i{}^{(v_j)} + \lambda_1 = 0. \tag{6}$$

Summing up (6) for $i = 1, 2, \ldots, n$, we have $n\, b^{(v_j)} - 2\, b^{(v_j)} + n\, \lambda_1 = 0$, which implies $\lambda_1 = \frac{2-n}{n}\, b^{(v_j)}$. Inserting this into (6), we obtain

$$b_i^{(v_j)} = \frac{b^{(v_j)}}{n}. \tag{7}$$

Inserting (7) into (5), we get

$$\prod_{j=1}^{r} b^{(v_j)} \left(b^{(v_j)} - \frac{b^{(v_j)}}{n} \right) = \prod_{j=1}^{r} \left[\left(b^{(v_j)} \right)^2 \left(1 - \frac{1}{n} \right) \right] =$$

$$\left(1 - \frac{1}{n} \right)^r \prod_{j=1}^{r} \left(b^{(v_j)} \right)^2 \tag{8}$$

which has to be maximized under the constraint

$$\sum_{j=1}^{r} b^{(v_j)} = b. \tag{9}$$

Differentiating

$$\left(1 - \frac{1}{n} \right)^r \prod_{j=1}^{r} \left(b^{(v_j)} \right)^2 + \lambda_2 \left(\sum_{j=1}^{r} b^{(v_j)} - b \right)$$

with respect to $b^{(v_j)}$ we obtain

$$\left(1-\frac{1}{n}\right)^r 2\, b^{(v_j)} \prod_{\substack{1\leq l\leq r\\ l\neq j}} \left(b^{(v_l)}\right)^2 + \lambda_2 = 0$$

which implies

$$\lambda_2 = -\frac{2}{b^{(v_j)}}\left(1-\frac{1}{n}\right)^r \prod_{l=1}^{r}\left(b^{(v_l)}\right)^2. \tag{10}$$

Now, (10) is valid for all v_j, in particular for $j = s$ and $j = t$, i.e.,

$$\frac{2}{b^{(v_s)}}\left(1-\frac{1}{n}\right)^r \prod_{l=1}^{r}\left(b^{(v_l)}\right)^2 = \frac{2}{b^{(v_t)}}\left(1-\frac{1}{n}\right)^r \prod_{l=1}^{r}\left(b^{(v_l)}\right)^2$$

which implies $b^{(v_s)} = b^{(v_t)}$ for all s, t. By using Eq. (9) we get

$$b^{(v_j)} = \frac{b}{r}. \tag{11}$$

By inserting Eq. (11) into Eq. (8) we have proved the following theorem.

Theorem 1 (Number of PO Graphs). *The number of PO graphs with b nodes for n threads and r shared variables is bounded above by*

$$\prod_{j=1}^{r}\left(\left(\frac{b}{r}\right)^2\left(1-\frac{1}{n}\right)\right) = \left(\frac{b}{r}\right)^{2r}\left(1-\frac{1}{n}\right)^r \leq \left(\frac{b}{r}\right)^{2r}. \tag{12}$$

□

From Theorem 1 we know an upper bound of the number of graphs with b nodes. Because topological sorting hast to be applied for every graph our algorithm has the following worst-case behavior

$$O\left(b\left(\frac{b}{r}\right)^{2r}\left(1-\frac{1}{n}\right)^r\right). \tag{13}$$

This shows that if $r = O(1)$ the algorithm behaves polynomially.

A simple computation shows that the extreme value of (13) appears if

$$r = \frac{b}{e}\sqrt{1-\frac{1}{n}},$$

where e denotes the base of the natural logarithm.

Corollary 1 (Worst-Case Value of r). *For a given pair (n, b), Eq. (12) has its maximum at $r = (b/e)\cdot\sqrt{1-1/n}$. For $n \to \infty$ this results in $r \to b/e$.* □

By using Corollary 1 the extreme value of (13) is bounded above by

$$O\left(b\left(\frac{e}{\sqrt{1-\frac{1}{n}}}\right)^{2\frac{b}{e}\sqrt{1-\frac{1}{n}}}\left(1-\frac{1}{n}\right)^{\frac{b}{e}\sqrt{1-\frac{1}{n}}}\right)=$$

$$O\left(b\left(e^{\frac{2}{e}}\right)^{b\sqrt{1-\frac{1}{n}}}\right)=O\left(b\left(e^{\frac{2}{e}}\right)^{b}\right).$$

Hence we summarize our results in the following theorem.

Theorem 2. *The worst-case timing behavior of the algorithm presented in Section 3 is*

$$O\left(b\left(e^{\frac{2}{e}}\right)^{b}\right)$$

where b denotes the number of blocks of the underlying program and $e^{\frac{2}{e}} = 2.087\ldots$. □

This concludes that our approach from Section 3 behaves exponentially in the worst-case.

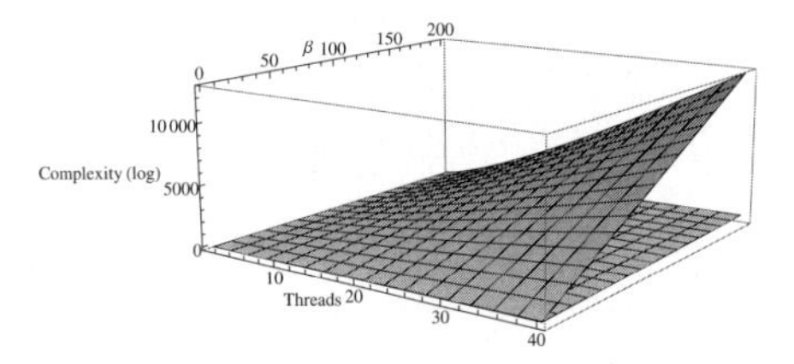

Fig. 3. Comparison

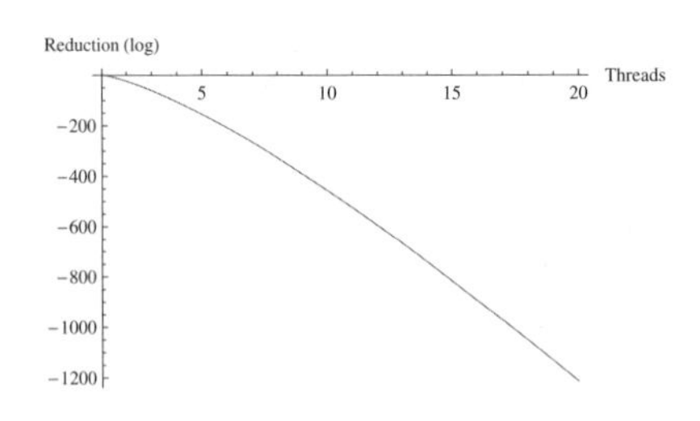

Fig. 4. Reduction for 50 blocks per thread

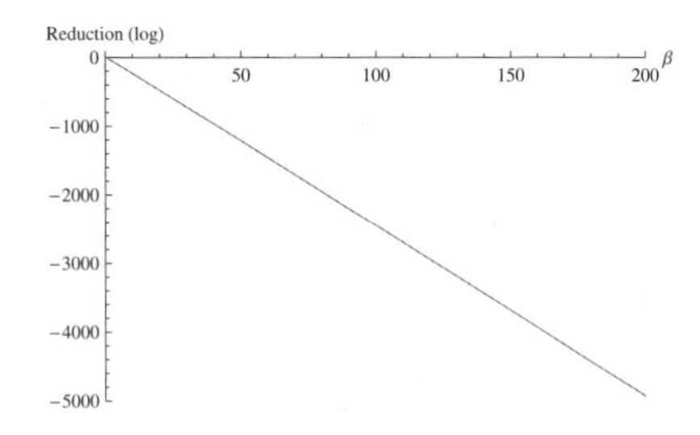

Fig. 5. Reduction for 20 threads with each β blocks

For the remaining part of this section it is assumed that each block consists of 5 statements. In Fig. 3 the curves of Fig. 2 and our worst-case are compared. The achieved reduction of the complexity is for $n = 20$ and $\beta = 200$ at least 10^{4923}.

Please keep in mind that this is still the worst-case behavior of our algorithm where $r = (b/e) \cdot \sqrt{1 - 1/n}$, i.e., for practical settings we expect an even higher reduction.

Large values of n and/or b lead to more reduction. Figure 4 depicts the reduction in the worst-case for $\beta = 50$ in dependence of n ranging from 1 to 20. Figure 5 shows the achieved reduction in worst-case settings for $n = 20$ in dependence of β ranging from 1 to 200.

5 Example

If each of the three threads in Figure 6 has 20 statements then we have $\beta = 20$ and $n = 3$. The possible interleavings on a statement level (cf. Eq. (4)) are $\frac{(\beta\, n)!}{(\beta!)^n} = \frac{60!}{(20!)^3} \approx 5 \times 10^{26}$.

If only the shown statements access the shared variables `e` and `f` we get with our algorithm one block for each of the first two threads, namely bl_1 and bl_2, respectively. Because the third thread accesses both of the two variables two blocks are being generated, namely bl_3 and bl_4.

By interleaving these blocks (cf. Lemma 1) we obtain $\frac{4!}{1!1!2!} = 12$ different interleavings. Although this is already an enormous reduction, it can still be improved. This is due to the fact that only orders of blocks concerning the same shared variables are relevant. We express this by using the notation of inter-thread orders.

Only the orders of bl_1 and bl_3 and, similarly, the orders of bl_2 and bl_4 are relevant. To express all possible combinations GenerateInterThreadOrders of our algorithm generates

$$\begin{pmatrix} bl_1 < bl_3 \\ bl_3 < bl_1 \end{pmatrix} \times \begin{pmatrix} bl_2 < bl_4 \\ bl_4 < bl_2 \end{pmatrix}.$$

The third thread contains an intra-thread order $bl_3 < bl_4$. Because of this the initial PO graph for every concrete interleaving (in this example) looks like the

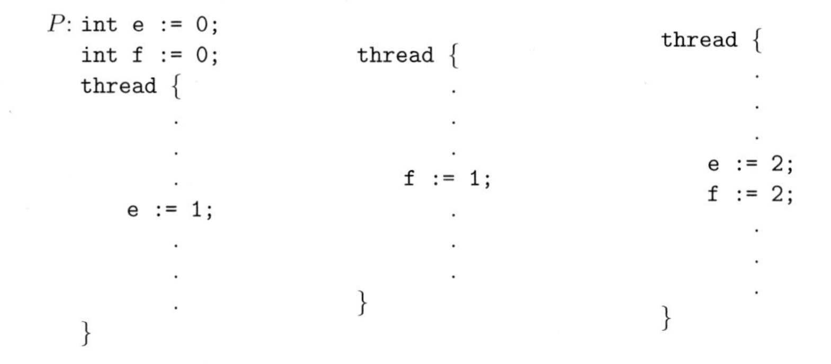

Fig. 6. Example with 3 threads

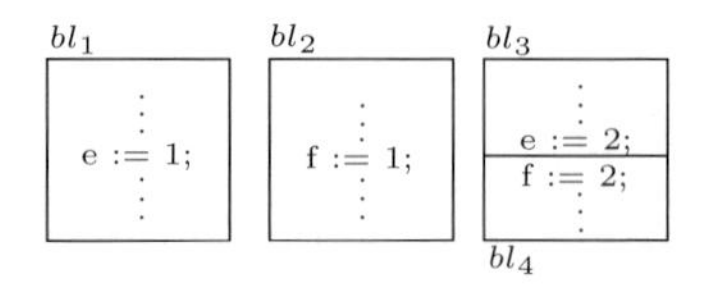

Fig. 7. Blocks for Example 6

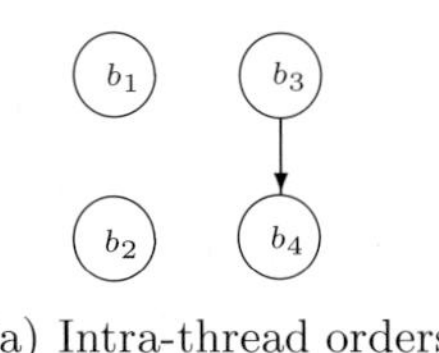

(a) Intra-thread orders

ON	inter-tread order
1	$bl_1 < bl_3, bl_2 < bl_4$
2	$bl_1 < bl_3, bl_4 < bl_2$
3	$bl_3 < bl_1, bl_2 < bl_4$
4	$bl_3 < bl_1, bl_4 < bl_2$

(b) Inter-thread orders

Fig. 8. Partial orders

one depicted in Fig. 8(a). In the following this graph is now used as a basis for every PO graph constructed by our algorithm. For every pair of the above inter-thread orders, a PO graph is being constructed. Table 8(b) shows the resulting partial orders with an assigned order number (ON) for ease of reference. By adding the partial orders of one order number to the PO graph in Fig. 8(a) results in a new graph. The four different PO graphs shown in Fig. 9 are being generated if this is done for every line in Table 8(b).

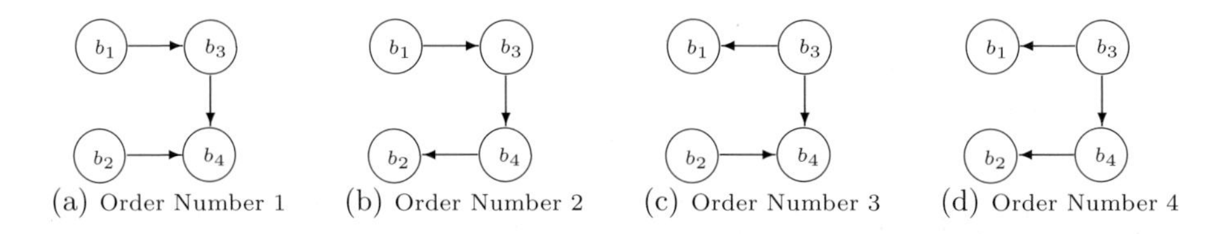

(a) Order Number 1 (b) Order Number 2 (c) Order Number 3 (d) Order Number 4

Fig. 9. PO Graphs

Sorting the nodes in each PO graph using *topological sorting* leads to four computations. Each computation gives a unique result[2]. This means we get four interleavings which compute all possible results for the shared variables `e` and `f`. For the PO graphs from Fig. 9(a), 9(b), 9(c), and 9(d) we get $bl_1; bl_3; bl_2; bl_4$, $bl_1; bl_3; bl_4; bl_2$, $bl_3; bl_1; bl_2; bl_4$, and $bl_3; bl_1; bl_4; bl_2$, respectively. The results are shown in Table 2. Please note that some orders of blocks depend on how topological sorting is implemented, in particular, when there are two or more possible block arrangements[3]. In this case two or more interleavings build an equivalence class (cf. [2]). For verification purposes only one exemplar in this equivalence

[2] Unless two different computations result in an identical state by chance.

[3] Nevertheless, this has no effect on the computed results.

Table 2. Computation Results

ON	Order	e	f
1	$bl_1; bl_3; bl_2; bl_4$	2	2
2	$bl_1; bl_3; bl_4; bl_2$	2	1
3	$bl_3; bl_1; bl_2; bl_4$	1	2
4	$bl_3; bl_1; bl_4; bl_2$	1	1

class needs to be computed. For example topological sorting of the PO graph in Fig. 9(a) can also result in $bl_1; bl_2; bl_3; bl_4$. This is due to the fact that the order of bl_2 and bl_3 is irrelevant concerning the resulting state of the shared variables `e` and `f`. With our approach exactly one of the possible interleavings is being computed. This helps to achieve an enormous reduction in the number of interleavings.

6 Related Work

Early reduction algorithms can be found in [14]. In [18] (Chapters 6 and 7) Valmari gives a good survey of models and approaches used so far. Due to space limitations we cite only some fundamental approaches and techniques in the following.

Virtual Coarsening. The idea is that in a concurrent program only the ordering of actions visible to other threads is important. This reduction can be made without loss of information [2,16].

Stubborn Sets. In [17,18] the theory of stubborn sets, which is based on commutativity, is presented. Two versions, weak and strong, are distinguished. The weak theory is more complicated and more difficult to implement, but it leads to better reduction results. This method tries to "save effort by postponing the investigation of structural transitions to future states..." [18].

Sleeping and Persistent Sets. In [6,7] sleeping sets and persistent sets are presented. Sleeping sets capture information of the past of the search. This information is being used to avoid unnecessary transitions. "...sleep sets avoid the investigation of transitions that have been investigated in the past states." [18]. Persistent sets can be seen as an enhancement of stubborn sets. The semantic model was inspired by Mazurkiewicz's traces [11].

Ample Sets. Ample sets are persistent sets satisfying additional conditions sufficient for LTL model checking [15]. Minea [12] uses also ample sets, but with a less restrictive independence relation.

Symmetric Reduction. A system may contain several identical components that are coupled to each other. Symmetric reduction tries to find such symmetries. Its complexity is proved to be the same as that of the graph isomorphism problem [9].

Dynamic Partial-Order Reduction. An approach somehow similar to ours, but dynamic in its nature, can be found in [8].

There is a lot of work building on the papers mentioned above. Some combine several approaches to achieve better results. A short overview of other techniques e.g. binary decision diagrams (BDDs), unfolding method, data independence, and Holzmann's supertrace can be found in [18]. In order to perform a more precise commutativity analysis a static and dynamic object escape analysis is being incorporated in [5]. Information about locks is being collected. This approach improves the performance of partial-order techniques on shared-memory programs.

CHESS [13], a concurrency unit testing tool, exhaustively explores the thread schedules of a concurrent program within a budget of c preemptions. Model checking techniques are being used in order to systematically generate all interleavings for a given scenario.

In [10] it is shown that for unidirectional bitvector problems in analyzing parallel programs with shared memory it is sufficient to perform a linear scan of each thread rather than to analyze all possible interleaving sequences.

7 Conclusion

We have presented an algorithm for attacking the state explosion problem in analyzing multithreaded programs. Our approach employs partial-order reduction and static virtual coarsening. It uses information on shared variables to generate and interleave blocks of statements. The number of interleavings compared to the original setting is reduced significantly.

Our algorithm performs polynomially as long as the number of shared variables is constant. However, its worst-case behavior is exponential.

We have already implemented the algorithm and tested it on hand-crafted examples. An interface to an existing compiler or parser will be a future step.

We are currently working on an operational semantics which should enable the justification of our work. Furthermore, we are planning to support conditionals and loops.

References

1. Abramowitz, M., Stegun, I.A.: Handbook of Mathematical Functions with Formulas, Graphs, and Mathematical Tables. Dover, New York (1964)
2. Ashcroft, E.A., Manna, Z.: Formalization of Properties of Parallel Programs. In: Meltzer, B., Michie, D. (eds.) Proc. of the Sixth Annual Machine Intelligence Workshop 1970, Edinburgh, pp. 17–41. University of Edinburgh Press (1971)
3. Ben-Ari, M., Burns, A.: Extreme Interleavings. IEEE Concurrency 6(3), 90–91 (1998)
4. Burgstaller, B., Blieberger, J., Mittermayr, R.: Static Detection of Access Anomalies in Ada95. In: Pinho, L.M., González Harbour, M. (eds.) Ada-Europe 2006. LNCS, vol. 4006, pp. 40–55. Springer, Heidelberg (2006)
5. Dwyer, M.B., Hatcliff, J., Robby, Ranganath, V.P.: Exploiting Object Escape and Locking Information in Partial-Order Reductions for Concurrent Object-Oriented Programs. Formal Methods in System Design 25(2-3), 199–240 (2004)

6. Godefroid, P.: Partial-Order Methods for the Verification of Concurrent Systems – An Approach to the State-Explosion Problem. In: Godefroid, P. (ed.) Partial-Order Methods for the Verification of Concurrent Systems. LNCS, vol. 1032. Springer, Heidelberg (1996)
7. Godefroid, P.: On the Costs and Benefits of Using Partial-Order Methods for the Verification of Concurrent Systems. In: Peled, D.A., Pratt, V.R., Holzmann, G.J. (eds.) POMIV 1996: Proc. of the DIMACS workshop on Partial Order Methods in Verification, pp. 289–303. AMS Press, Inc., New York (1997)
8. Gueta, G., Flanagan, C., Yahav, E., Sagiv, M.: Cartesian Partial-Order Reduction. In: Bošnački, D., Edelkamp, S. (eds.) SPIN 2007. LNCS, vol. 4595, pp. 95–112. Springer, Heidelberg (2007)
9. Junttila, T.: On The Symmetry Reduction Method For Petri Nets and Similar Formalisms. PhD thesis, Helsinki University of Technology (2003)
10. Knoop, J., Steffen, B., Vollmer, J.: Parallelism for Free: Efficient and Optimal Bitvector Analyses for Parallel Programs. ACM Transactions on Programming Languages and Systems 18(3), 268–299 (1996)
11. Mazurkiewicz, A.: Introduction to Trace Theory. In: Diekert, V., Rozenberg, G. (eds.) The Book of Traces, pp. 3–41. World Scientific Pub. Co., Inc., Singapore (1995)
12. Minea, M.: Partial Order Reduction for Verification of Timed Systems. PhD thesis, Carnegie Mellon University, Pittsburgh, PA, USA (1999)
13. Musuvathi, M., Qadeer, S.: Iterative Context Bounding for Systematic Testing of Multithreaded Programs. SIGPLAN Not. 42(6), 446–455 (2007)
14. Overman, W.T.: Verification of Concurrent Systems: Function and Timing. PhD thesis, University of California, Los Angeles (1981)
15. Peled, D.: Combining Partial Order Reductions with On-the-fly Model-Checking. In: Dill, D.L. (ed.) CAV 1994. LNCS, vol. 818, pp. 377–390. Springer, Heidelberg (1994)
16. Pnueli, A.: Applications of Temporal Logic to the Specification and Verification of Reactive Systems: A Survey of Current Trends. In: Rozenberg, G., de Bakker, J.W., de Roever, W.-P. (eds.) Current Trends in Concurrency. LNCS, vol. 224, pp. 510–584. Springer, Heidelberg (1986)
17. Valmari, A.: Eliminating Redundant Interleavings During Concurrent Program Verification. In: Odijk, E., Rem, M., Syre, J.-C. (eds.) PARLE 1989. LNCS, vol. 366, pp. 89–103. Springer, Heidelberg (1989)
18. Valmari, A.: The State Explosion Problem. In: Reisig, W., Rozenberg, G. (eds.) APN 1998. LNCS, vol. 1491, pp. 429–528. Springer, Heidelberg (1998)

An Extensible Space-Based Coordination Approach for Modeling Complex Patterns in Large Systems[⋆,⋆⋆]

Eva Kühn, Richard Mordinyi, and Christian Schreiber

Vienna University of Technology, Institute of Computer Languages,
Space Based Computing Group and Complex Systems Design and Engineering Lab,
Argentinierstr. 8, A-1040 Wien
{eva,richard,cs}@complang.tuwien.ac.at

Abstract. Coordination is frequently associated with shared data spaces employing Linda coordination. But in practice, communication between parallel and distributed processes is carried out with message exchange patterns. What, actually, do shared data spaces contribute beyond these? In this paper we present a formal representation for a definition of shared spaces by introducing an "extensible tuple model", based on existing research on Linda coordination, some Linda extensions, and virtual shared memory. The main enhancements of the extensible tuple model comprise: means for structuring of spaces, Internet- compatible addressing of resources, more powerful coordination capabilities, a clear separation of user data and coordination information, support of symmetric peer application architectures, and extensibility through programmable aspects. The advantages of the extensible tuple model (XTM) are that it allows for a specification of complex coordination patterns.

1 Introduction

The coordination theory was founded by Malone and Crowston and described as "managing dependencies between activities". In [16] it is argued that coordination makes sense only if tasks are interdependent. Additionally, the theory suggests that standardized coordination mechanisms can be applied to specific coordination problems. Ciancarini therefore describes a generic coordination model [4] as a triple of {E, M, L}. It suggests to have a clear separation between the specification of the communication entities of a system and the specification of their interactions or dependencies. In the model, {E} stands for either physical or logical entities to be coordinated. These can be data (structures), software processes, services, agents, or even human beings interacting

⋆ We would like to thank Stefan Craß, Geri Joskowicz, Hans Moritsch, Gernot Salzer, Thomas Scheller, Vesna Sesum-Cavic, and Ralf Westphal for their helpful discussions on this topic.

⋆⋆ The project is partly funded by TripCom (IST-4-027324-STP project, http://www.tripcom.org) and CAPI (project at TU-Vienna) of the Institute of Computer Languages.

T. Margaria and B. Steffen (Eds.): ISoLA 2008, CCIS 17, pp. 634–648, 2008.

with computer-based systems. {M} represents the coordination media (i.e. communication channels) serving as a connector between the entities and enables communication, which is a mandatory prerequisite for direct coordination [26,6]. Such coordination media may be message-passing systems, pipes, tuple spaces etc. {L} specifies the coordination laws between the entities defining how the interdependences have to be resolved and therefore, semantically define the coordination mechanisms.

From the point of view of designing a language for distributed systems the idea of associative communication based on a shared data space is one of the most interesting paradigms [3]. This is because a shared space allows to clearly separate the issue of controlling coordinating communication entities from the issue to control a single entity. A Tuple Space [22] is an example of this kind of languages. It is a well-known coordination model such as Linda [8], JavaSpaces [7] and TSpaces [15]. Tuple spaces are flat and unstructured multisets of tuples that can be accessed via very basic output, read, and input operations.

In the tuple space approach processes communicate with the other entities in the environment by writing tuples (ordered sequences of data) into the tuple space. Sharing of data via spaces [2] is not a novel paradigm. It comes from parallel processing and was later considered for distributed environments. Due to its high-level abstraction of communication by simply reading and writing data from/into a shared space this paradigm fits to growing dynamics and collaboration in the network [29]. The processes interested in retrieving information useful for coordinating their activities perform blocking **rd** or **in** operations specified via a template. In case several tuples match the template of a data-retrieval operation, only one of them is selected non-deterministically.

The limitation of current tuple space implementations is that they support template-matching only. This is problematic if any other form of coordination is needed, like FIFO. In such cases the coordination entity itself has to manage ordering of the tuples the right way and agree about it with other entities. Thus, the implementation of the coordination entity must contain functionalities that a coordination media should provide. However, queries involving relational comparison operators cannot be implemented with template matching. The proposed approach aims to describe a generic and extensible coordination model based on tags, upon which any kind of coordination laws can be modeled, starting with simple ones like FIFO and KEY, to more complex concurrent collection patterns, and finally also patterns that as e.g. described in [9] also cope with distributon. The extensible coordination approach is realized by means of the coordination media XVSM (extensible virtual shared memory) [25], [14] clearly separating the responsibilities between coordination middleware and entity again. The reason for adding additional forms of coordination laws to a space coordination medium are based on our experiences with programming real applications:

- Developers consider Linda template matching as too unstructured in comparison to query facilities offered by databases. Being forced to pack coordination information into tuple content is a drawback [17].

- Autonomous business partners require a programming language and platform neutral API specification that allows coordination across the Internet. E.g., JavaSpaces [7] exhibits only a Java based API specification.
- For future Web2.0 scenarios, a crucial requirement will be to hide the differences between communication within an enterprise and across enterprise borders.

Experiences gathered with such applications within large systems are e.g. GONG with near-time database replication [12] using the Corso [11] virtual shared memory for load-balancing and network bandwidth optimization, the SVSDM [19], [18] used for the efficient distribution of working packages to mobile agents of an insurance company and in catastrophic scenarios [14], the RealSafe project for reliable data distribution and retrievement in the traffic telematics area, and the project SWIS [24] in cooperation with Frequentis AG[1] focusing on efficient and reliable clustering of network nodes and communication between those. These systems contain complex patterns like replication, notification, or fifo coordination. Therefore, this paper details in section 4 the way how such patterns are implemented with the introduced model.

In the following, the classic "tuple spaces model" referring to Linda and JavaSpaces is termed "TSM", and the "extensible tuple model" as proposed in this paper is called "XTM".

2 Structuring the Coordination Space

Motivated by numerous works that extend the original TSM, we propose an extension of the TSM called XTM (extensible tuple model) for modeling data and coordination in the shared space in a more structured way, and a formal notation for the XTM. The goal is to define a system with a minimal feature set that is extensible, can be configured upon request to meet complex collaboration requirements, and has a well-defined semantics. Briefly, the main concept in XTM is a shared container that manages data items called entries (generalizing tuples in TSM). Both, container and entry are modeled by means of an xtuple (extensible tuple). The operations on a container comprise addition, and (destructive) selection of entries. In this paper we show the query language of the XTM; the operational semantics are only sketched informally.

2.1 Xtuple and Entry

An xtuple (extensible tuple, or XT for short) is either an n-tuple "$\langle E1, \ldots, En \rangle$" which is an ordered list of entries Ei (i = 1..n) with the property that its arity n can change (expand or shrink) through addition and destructive selection of entries, or empty ("$\langle\rangle$"). Entries within an xtuple can be accessed using "XT[j]" where j is the position of the entry. An entry is a multi-set of tags. A tag is a pair that consists of a name and a value. The value of a tag can be accessed using

[1] http://www.frequentis.com

"get(name, E)" where name is the name of the tag and E the entry. Each entry in an xtuple always has one implicit tag representing a unique position number ("$P") for access. The numbering within an xtuple starts with 1. However, the position number is not an immutable part of the entry, it may change if entries are added to or removed from the xtuple, and it is automatically stripped from the entry, if the entry is removed from the xtuple. Entries have no identity. The fact that entry E has a position number with value "i" is denoted as: "$P=i".

Example 1. (xtuple)

- "⟨[payload=hello, $P=1], [payload=space, $P=2], [payload=2008, $P=3]⟩" is an xtuple with 3 entries containing the payloads "hello", "space", and "2008" plus their position number tags.
- "⟨⟩" is an empty xtuple.
- Let E be [payload=eva], then "get(payload, E)" returns the value of the tag payload.

2.2 Container and Container Referencing

A container is a pair consisting of (1) a container-name which is a URL [14] that can be addressed via the Internet, and (2) an xtuple. For a container that is represented by the pair (C, xtuple), its xtuple can be accessed via "*C".

A container-name is used by **read**, **take** and **write** operations to retrieve the container's xtuple at the peer site where the container is hosted. A distributed data space is a collection of such referenceable containers.

2.3 Structuring of Containers

Entries constitute either proxies for structured user data to be processed jointly, or coordination data for the interaction of processes.

2.4 Entry Addition

When an entry is added to an xtuple XT, it is appended to the end of the XT and the position number reflects the order in which the entries have been added.

Example 2. (entry addition)

- E1 = "[payload=jens, pin=12, title=prof]".
  XT1 = "⟨[payload=chris, $P=1, pin=78, title=ms]⟩".
  Adding E1 to XT1 obviously yields "⟨[payload=chris, $P=1, pin=78, title=ms], [payload=jens, $P=2, pin=12, title=prof]⟩".

2.5 (Destructive) Entry Selection

For (destructive) selection of entries from an xtuple XT using **read** or **take**, an XQ (xtuple query) is introduced. Selected entries are copied into a new xtuple that represents the result of the (destructive) selection; take is destructive and also removes the selected entries from XT.

An XQ is a single-XQ (SXQ) or a composition of SXQs using the binary operator "|" which is left-associative and not commutative. A SXQ has the syntax, where "name" refers to the name of a tag:

- name *relational-operator* value (relational comparison)
- name $\in [value^1\text{–}value^k]$ (range)
- name $\in [value^1, \ldots, value^k]$ (enumeration)
- name *function* (name, *template*) (matching function)

Beyond tag selection using relational comparison operator, range or enumeration definitions, also a *match-maker* function can be given, which denotes a user-definable function. Its argument represents a template that is matched with the value of the name and results into success or fail.

The execution semantics is that each SXQ (from left to right) of an XQ = SXQ_1 | ... | SXQ_n is applied to each entry in the xtuple XT in entry position order. If successful, a new xtuple results to which the next SXQ is applied, a.s.o. The basic idea behind this mechanism is that streaming becomes possible, as each SXQ can be decided by each single entry. In contrast to databases, no join and aggregation operators are supported. The SXQs can work concurrently and can be seen as filters that pump the information from one stage to the other, comparable with the staged driven architecture (SEDA) approach [28], [27] that is known to scale well. Figure 1 depicts the execution of an XQ. The first SXQ, SXQ_1, is applied to the input xtuple XT creating an xtuple (XT') that contains all entries which fulfil the SXQ. XT' is then the input for the next SXQ, SXQ_2. This process is repeated for all SXQs of the XQ. After the last SXQ_n has been executed the resulting xtuple (RXT) contains all entries which fulfil the XQ.

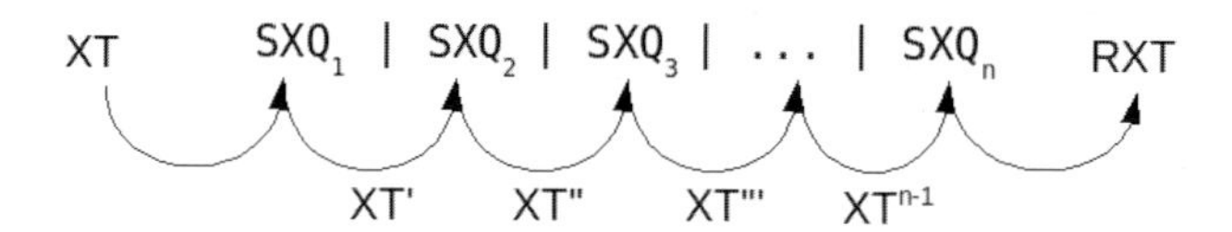

Fig. 1. Execution semantic of an XQ

An entry fulfills an XQ, if it fulfills all SXQs of the XQ. An entry fulfills a SXQ:

- If the SXQ is a relational comparison, or a range or enumeration query and if the entry has at least one tag with the given name the value of which fulfills the SXQ. For a relational comparison, or a range query the result could be 0,1,... entries, whereas for an enumeration query at least one entry must be found for each value contained in the enumeration. Note that $ is used to denote the arity of the xtuple and can be used in query expressions.
- If the SXQ is a match-maker function and a user-defined match-maker function exists with same name as the match-maker function name, which applied to the denoted tag's value of the entry returns success. This means that the entry must possess at least such a tag. The parameters of the user defined match-maker function are the name of the value to which it is to be applied, and the template.

The result of an application of a SXQ contains all entries that fulfill the XQ and that are currently contained in the xtuple to which it is applied. An XQ is used by **read** and **take** for selection and is executed in one atomic step. If later on entries are added to the xtuple that would also fulfill the XQ, they are not considered any more.

Example 3. (fullfillment).

- Entry "[payload=A, a=5]" fulfills the XQ "a∈[1 – 100]".
- Entry "[payload=B, b=5]" fulfills the XQs "b∈[3, 5]", and "b=∗". Note: with "=" the usage of ∗ as wildcard is allowed.
- Entry "[payload=C, c=1, d=2]" fulfills the XQ "d∈[2 – 4] | c=1".

If a SXQ cannot be fulfilled, the **read** or **take** is delayed (except if there are contra-dictionary SXQs in which case it fails), and next time will retry from the beginning, i.e. with the left-most SXQ. E.g. selection from XT = "⟨[payload=100, link=left], [payload=200, link=right]⟩" using XQ = "link∈[next]" will delay.

Example 4. (SXQ, XQ)
Selections that could cause a delay are marked with "D"; "n" is the arity of the XT to which the XQ is applied; column "nres" denotes number of result entries.

XQ:	select from XT:	nres:	delay:
$P ∈ [1,...,10]	the first 10 entries	10	D
pin ∈ [1 – 10]	all entries with a tag named "pin" with value between 1 and 10	$0, 1, \ldots, n$	
pin ∈ [1,. . . ,10]	all entries with a tag named "pin" with value between 1 and 10; at least one entry must be found for each given value	$10, 11, \ldots, n$	D
payload ∈ linda((chris,*,*)) | pin ≤ 50	all entries that represent students with name "chris" and that have a pin that is ≤ 50	$0, 1, \ldots, n$	
P ∈ [1 – 10] | label ∈ [4 – 5]	the up to 10 entries in XT, from these select all that have a label with value "4" or "5"	$0, 1, \ldots, 10$	
l1 = green | l2 = blue | payload ∈ (ralf,author,∗) | x ∈ [5,6] | $P ∈ [1,2]	all entries that have a tag with name l1 and value="green", and that have a tag with name l2 and value="blue", and that have a palyoad tag that is a tuple with arity="3" with first arg="ralf" and second arg="author", and that have a tag with name x and value="5" and one with value="6" (note: entries for both keys must be found), and select two entries in position order	2	D
P ∈ [1 – $]	all, possibly 0 entries	0,1,. . .,n	

3 Core Container Functionality

A container exhibits a lean API which is defined by means of an XML protocol [5]. No connect operation is required as each operation refers to an Internet-addressable resource. Each peer application runs an embedded space runtime. Each protocol message also carries a context parameter not shown below, in which system or user defined parameters can be passed: e.g. security tokens, execution states etc. In the following, the protocol messages[2] defining the basic core container functionality, and their operational semantics are only informally described:

***i*-tx-create (S, ttl):** creates a local transaction at the peer's site denoted by the URL "S" which refers to the URL of a peer runtime representing a local space; "*i*" stands for isolation-level and is either "e" or "c": An exclusive transaction ("e") locks every container it accesses exclusively, whereas a concurrent transaction ("c") allows concurrent readers and writers using pessimistic locking at entry level. The "ttl" parameter sets a time-to-live value for the entire transaction in seconds; if expired the transaction is automatically rolledback. The answer protocol message contains the newly created transaction reference ("tx") which is a URL, too.

tx-commit (tx), tx-rollback (tx): commits or rollbacks a transaction given by its URL "tx". The answer is the termination result of the transaction.

create-container (S, C, tx): creates a container with the name "C" in a space referenced by its URL "S", within a transaction.

destroy-container (C, tx): destroys a container with a given name "C" within a transaction.

***read-op* (C, XQ, tx, to, AC):** (destructively) selects entries from a container (with URL "C") with optional transaction "tx" and timeout "to" parameters; "*read-op*" stands for either take or read. If tx is null, an implicit tx is assumed that immediately commits. A timeout > 0 indicates that this operation might block and retry within the given timeout if no answer is found. Answer to a **take** or **read** message is a **write** message (see below) that writes the selected entries into container "AC". Typically AC will be located at the requestor's site and can e.g. be intercepted by a pre-write aspect (see below) that calls a callback method or wakes up some waiting thread. "AC" can be null, in this case the result is not written anywhere. A take operation with "AC" set to null corresponds to a delete operation and can be used to save network bandwidth. Note that we describe a protocol; a binding can be provided for any programming language which can use this protocol to implement a blocking read/take or an asynchronous callback.

write (C, E, tx, to): adds entry E to container C.

bulk-write (C, <E1, E2, ..., Ek>, tx, to): appends k entries E1, E2, ..., Ek—given by means of an xtuple—to container C in the order of the xtuple.

[2] The protocol is implemented in XML which allows the XTM to be used by any programming language binding.

A main concept of the XTM are *aspects* to extend the space dynamically through user defined actions, i.e. a script or method call that are injected into any of the above operations at a certain ipoint (interception point). This is comparable to reactions in LIME [20], [21]; the difference is that aspects are called before (pre) a certain operation is invoked on a container, immediately afterwards (post), or if the operation is committed (on-commit); whereas reactions are called when a tuple matching a certain pattern is found in a tuple space.

def-aspect (C, ipoint, priority, program, tx, ttl): creates an aspect and in the answer message sends a URL (aspect identifier "aid") to identify it. Program is an xtuple containing the single lines of the script to be executed. The ttl parameter specifies its life time.

undef-aspect (aid, tx, to): removes an aspect given by its URL.

The order of aspect action execution is resolved by a priority parameter. Cf. join points in aspect oriented programming which allow triggering of code before, after, or instead of method execution [10]. This concept has been proven useful for collaborative space-based applications at application level [13] and is now proposed to be integrated into the space core.

With aspects, the behaviour of a container can be changed creating a shareable "abstract data type" based on a container. Orca [1] showed that "having users define their own operations has many advantages". Orca supports shared, replicated objects that can be read and updated using blocking and non-blocking read/write operations. However, in Orca no dynamic "programming" of the space is possible.

Aspects can also be used to implement reactions on state changes [20], [21]: e.g. if a certain entry is written to, or taken from a container.

An action has access to parameters and relevant data of the original method it intercepts and depends on its ipoint. E.g. a pre-write action has access to 5 parameters referencable by $0, $1, . . . , $4: with $0=context, $1=C, $2=entry, $3=tx, and $4=to; a post-write-on-commit action or a post-write action has: $0=context, $1=C, $2=entry, $3=tx, and $4=to. For the bulk-write ipoints, $2=xtuple with the written entries. Read ipoints have the following arguments: $1=C, $2=XQ, $3=tx, $4=to and $5=CA.

The return value of an aspect determines the control flow: "ok" implies normal continuation; "skip" in a pre-ipoint skips all further pre-actions and the original method action, continuing with the first post-action, if given; "skip" in a post-action skips all further post-actions; "fail" causes the entire operation to fail; "reschedule" causes the operation to be delayed until a corresponding event occurs upon which it is rescheduled, as long as the timeout condition is fulfilled; and "remove-me" causes the aspect to be removed. Execution states are implicitly passed via context parameter.

The main goal was to keep the set of operations of the XTM minimal and extensible so that higher-level APIs for more advanced data structures and collections can be bootstrapped on top of it. For the extensibility aspects are introduced. The core container functionality like read, write and take is influenced by the Linda model. All of these support bulk-data to optimize the network behaviour and to enable the implementation of iterators. Basic transaction functionality is obviously essential and transactions have therefore already been suggested by other spaces like JavaSpaces (pessimistic concurrency control) and Corso (optimistic concurrency control). The XTM provides pessimistic concurrency control.

4 Extending the Functionality

With help of the XTM functionality, more complex coordination laws can be defined and "injected" into the space without changing the protocol. This can be for example FIFO selection, or more complex access patterns like a time bounded cache, notifications and iterators, or other vertical features like replication. Also more complex coordination laws can be defined this way, like e.g. a container supporting multiple coordinations simultaneously.

In the following code snippets, "result ← message" stands for: "send message, execute it, and extract result from the answer message of the protocol".

4.1 FIFO Coordination

Example 5. (FIFO coordination) Define a new SXQ named **FIFO(n)** that selects n entries in FIFO order and that can be used by **read** or **take** operations:

FIFO(n) ::= $P∈[1,...,n]

4.2 Notification

In this section two realisations of a notification mechanism are shown. At least two containers are normally involved in a notification in XTM. The container on which the notification is registered and a container which stores the information of the fired notifications (the notification container). A notification is realized by analysing the operations executed on a container using an aspect. The aspect decides whether the notification has to be fired or not. For example, a notification could fire when a template matches newly written entries, a certain amount of entries has been written, or when entries have been read. In case of the notification has to be fired, the aspect writes the required information into the notification container. From this container a user can take the information for further computation (waking up a thread, calling a callback method, ...). The information written to the notification container can be customized for the needs of an application. For instance, the entry which caused the notification to fire, a token which indicates that the notification fired or any other information can be written by the aspect.

Example 6 defines a notification similar to the JavaSpace [7] notification. It fires when a newly written entry matches a given template. The new entry which caused the notification to fire is not passed to the application. The application is only informed that something new has been written.

First, a container (TC) is created which stores the template and an aspect is created which handles the firing of the notification. The aspect simply executes a read operation on the TC after each (committed) write operation using the payload of the new entry as template. This is possible because it is assumed that the used match-maker function (LINDA) can handle the inversion of the template and the payload. The answer of the read operation is written into the notification container (in this case the answer of the read operation is always the template because it is the only entry in the TC).

This example could be extended supporting multiple templates by writing more then one template into the TC. The user can distinguish which template caused the notification to fire by analysing the data in the NC.

Example 6. (JavaSpace notification)

create-Notification(site, C, CN, template) :=
create-container(site, TC, null)
write(TC,$\langle$[*payload* = *template*]$\rangle$, null, 0)
def-aspect(C, post-write-on-commit, *priority*,
$\langle$ read(TC, LINDA(payload, get(payload, \$2), null, 0, NC) $\rangle$,
null, INFINITE)

Example 7 defines another notification flavour which is very similar to the first one. Instead of informing the application that something happened, the entry which caused the notification to fire is written to the notification container. To realize this an aspect is added to the container on which the notification shall be registered. When a new entry is written, the aspect creates a new container containing the new entry. Afterwards, a take operation is executed on the new container using the template passed during creation of the notification. The result of the take operation is written to the NC (when the take operation can be fulfilled the entry matches the template and therefore the notification has to fire). Finally, the container created by the aspect is destroyed to avoid unnecessary garbage.

Example 7. (Notification which returns the data)

create-Notification(site, C, CN, template) :=
def-aspect(C, post-write-on-commit, *priority*,
$\langle$ create-container (site, C', null)
write(C', $\langle$\$2$\rangle$, null, 0)
take(C', LINDA(payload, template), null, 0, NC)
destroy-container(C') $\rangle$,
null, INFINITE)

4.3 Read Iterator

Example 8. (iterator) Define an iterator that (1) first reads all existing entries from a container and then (2) asynchronously copies all prospectively inserted entries into a container "CN" from which these entries can be collected with

take. (2) is achieved by means of an aspect. The aspect writes all entries written to C into the answer container CN.

The reading of all data (1) and the aspect definition (2) must be done in one exclusive tx to avoid data loss.

read-iterator (site, C, CI) ::=
  tx ← e-tx-create (site, INFINITE)
  read (C, FIFO($), tx, CI)
  def-aspect (C, post-write-on-commit, *priority*,
    ⟨ write (CI, $2, $3, $4) ⟩,
    tx, to, INFINITE);
  tx-commit (tx);

To keep the above examples simple, bulk-operations are not considered. The required extensions are straight forward and can be done analogously to the specification of the replication shown in the next section.

4.4 Single Master Replication

Finally we show a pattern for a single master replication. One peer site is the owner of the master copy of the container (MC), and other sites can create replica containers RC_1,. . .,RC_k from M. From each RC_i in turn new replicas RC_{i1},. . .,RC_{ik} can be created a.s.o. as depicted in figure 2.

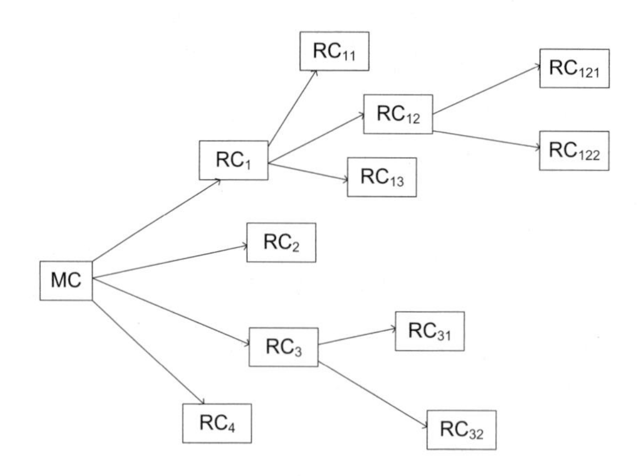

Fig. 2. Single Master Replication

Each RC shall be an identical copy of the MC. It represents a cache from which peers can read in order to reach a scalable system, and to improve availability and performance. If a peer wants to write to a local RC, then there are two scenarios in the pattern: (a) this is forbidden, and (b) the writing is allowed but internally redirected to the container from which the RC was created. If RC is not a direct ancestor of MC, then the re-direction is done in a cascading way. In the following examples we show the re-direction as a "write-through" operation that is perfomed synchronoulsy. A variant that calls the aspect in a fire-and-forget way would allow for an asynchronous behaviour.

The newly defined extended API is termed **create-single-master-replica-container (MC, RC)**. The name RC must not yet be used. A new container is created and published under the name RC, all entries contained in MC are copied into RC (called *first sync*) and an aspect is injected into MC that listens on changes and transfers and applies them to RC. For this, an on-change-iterator is defined that performs the following actions in an atomic step (see figure 9):

1. Create aspects on MC for the post-ipoints of all operations that perform changes on a container—i.e. write, bulk-write, and take—to report the information about the change into a container called RSC (see below) that is passed to the API as argument and that serves to collect the changes for each peer replica, in the form of a *command entry.* The command entry has the form [op=*command*, changed=*entries*], and otherwise [op=*command*, inserted=*entries*], where *command* is either delete or insert. For the replication scenario, it is assumed that each entry that is inserted into MC possesses a unique id with tag-name "guid". So in order to be a capable MC, it must possess an aspect that is injected upon container creation and that adds this tag to each newly written entry.
2. Copy all entries E1,...,Ek of MC into RSC as a command entry of the form [op=bulk-write, inserted=⟨E1,...,Ek⟩].

Example 9. **on-change-iterator (MC, RSC, tx) ::=**
read (MC, FIFO($), tx, INFINITE, RSC)
def-aspect (MC, post-take, 1, ⟨ write (RSC, [cmd=delete, changed= *$5], $3, $4) ⟩, tx, INFINITE, INFINITE)
def-aspect (MC, post-write, 1, ⟨ write (RSC, [cmd=insert, changed= $2], $3, $4) ⟩, tx, INFINITE, INFINITE)
def-aspect (MC, post-bulk-write, 1, ⟨ write (RSC, [cmd=delete, changed= *$2], $3, $4) ⟩, tx, INFINITE, INFINITE)

We can now implement the replication to perform (see figure 10) the following steps atomically, where we assume that the RSC shall be created at the site of the MC:

1. Create a new container termed *replication subscription container* RSC for RC. RSC can be located at either the site of MC, or RC, or at any third site. In the first case, this refers to a "pull" situation, and in the second case it implements a "push" scenario.
2. Create an on-change-iterator for this new replica on MC.
3. Periodically fetch the changes in SRC and apply them to RC. Note that this could also lead to variants of the pattern where the fetching is done e.g. at certain times, at certain events (using an aspect), or taking only a certain amount of changes in one step etc.

Example 10. **create-single-master-replica-container (MC, RC) ::=**

```
tx ← tx-create (MC-site, INFINITE)
create-container (MC-site, RSC, tx)
on-change-iterator (MC, RSC, tx)
tx-commit (tx)
periodically do:
    create-container (RC-site, TEMPC)
    take (RSC, $P = 1 , tx, INFINITE, TEMPC)
    if(get(cmd, *TEMPC[1]) == delete)
        take(RC, guid=entry.guid, null, 0, null)
    else
        write(RC, get(changed, *TEMPC[1]), null, 0)
    destroy-container (TEMPC)
```

For case (a) where updates are forbidden on a RC, upon creation of the RC pre-aspects must be set on every change operation that simply return an exception without calling the original operation. For case (b), these aspects are implemented differently in that they re-direct the operation as is to the direct ancestor container from which the replica RC was created.

5 Conclusion

Reliable, near-time, on-line collaboration will require a different architectural style than a "store & forward" oriented one. Bi-directional access to arbitrary data structures that go beyond fifo queues are needed to ease collaboration.

In this paper we have presented a formal notation called the extensible tuple model (XTM) that can serve to model the TSM (tuple space model) as well as essential enhancements of it. XTM allows for a clear specification of complex coordination patterns. Examples are shown for FIFO coordination, two different notification patterns, an iterator pattern, and a replication pattern with some variants. The main proposed extensions are a better structuring of the space, more powerful coordination capabilities, a clear separation of user data and coordination information, support of symmetric peer application architectures, a well- defined semantics of bulk-operations (read/take of multiple entries), and a protocol that makes it usable in the Internet. The model has been implemented by the XVSM system and is available as an open source implementation [25].

XTM is extensible with respect to the following three points: (1) The behavior of a container, which is the core shared data structure in the XTM, can be programmed dynamically using aspects. This way, arbitrary abstract data types can be created which resemble shared collections for queues, dictionaries, maps, trees etc. Using aspects, notifications and iterators in different flavors can be realized with a well-defined semantics. (2) The possibility to include coordination tags into an entry can be used to extend the container by other higher-level user defined selectors, e.g. stack, random access, vector, least recently used, priorities, role based scheduling etc. (3) The XTM query language can be extended by the definition of match-maker functions, e.g. for supporting RDF or XML based query facilities.

The described model in this paper has been used to implement the open source XVSM implementation called MozartSpaces [23]. In our future work we will use this model for verification and analyzation of space implementations as described in section 4. Additional future work will also deal with further extensions of the XTM query language, and a model for the operational semantics of the XTM.

References

1. Bal, H.E., Kaashoek, M.F., Tanenbaum, A.S.: Orca: a language for parallel programming of distributed systems. IEEE Transactions on Software Engineering 18(3), 190–205 (1992)
2. Carriero, N., Gelernter, D.: Linda in context. Commun. ACM 32(4), 444–458 (1989)
3. Ciancarini, P.: Distributed programming with logic tuple spaces. New Gen. Comput. 12(3), 251–284 (1994)
4. Ciancarini, P.: Coordination models and languages as software integrators. ACM Comput. Surv. 28(2), 300–302 (1996)
5. Ecker, S.: Communication protocols in XVSM - design and implementation. Master's thesis, Vienna University of Technology, E185/1 (2005)
6. Franklin, S.: Coordination without communication. Technical report, Inst. For Intelligent Systems, Univ. of Memphis (April 2008)
7. Freeman, E., Arnold, K., Hupfer, S.: JavaSpaces Principles, Patterns, and Practice. Addison-Wesley Longman Ltd., Essex (1999)
8. Gelernter, D.: Generative communication in linda. ACM Trans. Program. Lang. Syst. 7(1), 80–112 (1985)
9. Hohpe, G., Woolf, B.: Enterprise Integration Patterns: Designing, Building, and Deploying Messaging Solutions. Addison-Wesley Longman Publishing Co., Inc., Boston (2003)
10. Kiczales, G., Lamping, J., Menhdhekar, A., Maeda, C., Lopes, C., Loingtier, J.-M., Irwin, J.: Aspect-oriented programming. In: Akşit, M., Matsuoka, S. (eds.) ECOOP 1997. LNCS, vol. 1241, pp. 220–242. Springer, Heidelberg (1997)
11. Kühn, E.: Virtual Shared Memory for Distributed Architecture. Nova Science Publishers (2001)
12. Kühn, E.: The zero-delay data warehouse: mobilizing heterogeneous database. In: Proceedings of the 29th international conference on Very large data bases (VLDB 2003), pp. 1035–1040 (2003)
13. Kühn, E., Fessl, G., Schmied, F.: Aspect-oriented programming with runtime-generated subclass proxies and net dynamic methods. Journal of NET Technologies 4, 1801–2108 (2006)
14. Kühn, E., Riemer, J., Mordinyi, R., Lechner, L.: Integration of XVSM spaces with the web to meet the challenging interaction demands in pervasive scenarios. Ubiquitous Computing And Communication Journal (UbiCC), special issue on Coordination in Pervasive Environments 3 (2008)
15. Lehman, T.J., McLaughry, S.W., Wycko, P.: T-spaces: The next wave. In: HICSS (1999)
16. Malone, T.W., Crowston, K.: The interdisciplinary study of coordination. ACM Comput. Surv. 26(1), 87–119 (1994)
17. Martin, D., Wutke, D., Scheibler, T., Leymann, F.: An eai pattern-based comparison of spaces and messaging. In: Proceedings of the 11th IEEE International Enterprise Distributed Object Computing Conference (EDOC 2007), Washington, DC, USA, p. 511. IEEE Computer Society Press, Los Alamitos (2007)

18. Mor, M., Mordinyi, R., Riemer, J.: Using space-based computing for more efficient group coordination and monitoring in an event-based work management system. In: The Second International Conference on Availability, Reliability and Security (ARES 2007), pp. 1116–1123 (April 2007)
19. Mordinyi, R.: Shared virtual space distribution manager - SVSDM - design and implementation. Master's thesis, Vienna University of Technology, E185/1 (2005)
20. Murphy, A.L., Picco, G.P., Roman, G.-C.: Lime: A coordination model and middleware supporting mobility of hosts and agents. ACM Trans. Softw. Eng. Methodol. 15(3), 279–328 (2006)
21. Picco, G.P., Murphy, A.L., Roman, G.-C.: Lime: Linda meets mobility. In: ICSE 1999: Proceedings of the 21st international conference on Software engineering, pp. 368–377. IEEE Computer Society Press, Los Alamitos (1999)
22. Semini, L., Montangero, C.: A refinement calculus for tuple spaces. Science of Computer Programming 34(2), 79–140 (1999)
23. MozartSpaces WebSite (2008), http://www.mozartspaces.org
24. SWIS WebSite (2008), http://www.isis.tuwien.ac.at/node/4841
25. XVSM WebSite (2008), http://www.xvsm.org
26. Weigand, H., van der Poll, F., de Moor, A.: Coordination through communication. In: Proc. of the 8th International Working Conference on the Language-Action Perspective on Communication Modelling (LAP 2003), pp. 1–2 (2003)
27. Welsh, M., Culler, D.: Overload management as a fundamental service design primitive. In: EW10: Proceedings of the 10th workshop on ACM SIGOPS European workshop, pp. 63–69. ACM Press, New York (2002)
28. Welsh, M., Culler, D., Brewer, E.: Seda: an architecture for well-conditioned, scalable internet services. SIGOPS Oper. Syst. Rev. 35(5), 230–243 (2001)
29. Zhen, L., Parashar, M.: Comet: a scalable coordination space for decentralized distributed environments. In: Second International Workshop on Hot Topics in Peer-to-Peer Systems (HOT-P2P 2005), 21 July 2005, pp. 104–111 (2005)

On the Design of Knowledge Discovery Services Design Patterns and Their Application in a Use Case Implementation

Jeroen de Bruin[1], Joost N. Kok[1], Nada Lavrac[2], and Igor Trajkovski[3]

[1] LIACS, Leiden University, Leiden, The Netherlands
[2] Jozef Stefan Institute, Ljubljana, Slovenia
[3] New York University Skopje, Skopje, Macedonia

Abstract. As service-orientation becomes more and more popular in the computer science community, more research is done in applying service-oriented applications in specific fields, including knowledge discovery. In this paper we investigate how the service-oriented paradigm can benefit knowledge discovery, and how specific services and the knowledge discovery process as a whole should be designed. We propose a model for the design of a service-oriented knowledge discovery process, and provide guidelines for the types of functionalities it requires. We also provide a case design to show the application and benefits of the proposed model and design pattern in practise.

1 Introduction

Knowledge Discovery (KD) in data can be a very intensive process in terms of computation and data transport, but also because the construction of a KD process can be quite difficult and time-consuming. Over time, many have tried to find ways to improve the quality of KD processes, for example by making them faster, easier to construct and/or less data intensive. When new technologies appear, it is interesting to see how they can be applied to improve performance in these areas.

In this paper we take a look at the Service Orientation (SO) paradigm and in what ways it can benefit KD. The SO paradigm allows users to design applications (in this context we will see a KD process as an application) in terms of individual components than can be connected to each other through standardized communication. These components can be either locally or remotely available, and can be found through public lookup facilities. The potential of the SO paradigm can make KD processes easier, faster, more understandable.

The focus of the SO paradigm has primarily been on bussiness components and the construction of distributed corporate applications, but SO seems to become quite predominant in the scientific world as well. In this paper we explore the benefits and drawbacks of the SO paradigm in KD, mainly focussing on the design of a KD service and process. We support the design theories by a small case study of two components, which are combined together to form a KD process.

T. Margaria and B. Steffen (Eds.): ISoLA 2008, CCIS 17, pp. 649–662, 2008.

This paper is organized as follows: In Section 2 we discuss diverse work related to service-oriented knowledge discovery, work that we used to generate ideas for research and that we compared to our own ideas. In Section 3 we discuss SO technology, thereby discussing standards and potential advantages in a scientific context. In Section 4 we discuss the design of the case study, and provide guidelines in the design of KD processes and indiviual components. In Section 4 we discuss the case study trial runs and give a few statistics in terms of performance compared to other implementations. Finally, in Section 5 we draw some conclusions on the implications of the use of SO in KD, and discuss some future work.

2 Related Work

Over the last few years distributed KD has become increasingly more popular, which generated research incentives in diverse fields of technology. In [DBG+06] distributed data mining is proposed by using peer-to-peer networks. The authors sketch a high-level introduction to peer-to-peer data mining and give some pointers and requirements for methods, as well as a theoretical example. However, a comparison with other techniques lacks, as does technological depth or formal models. The authors of paper [AC06] focus on the area of text mining, and give criteria and requirements which need to be supported by good text mining tools. While they focus on their tool being embedded in other applications and address issues such as security and statelessness, they seem to only brush the topic of service orientation and web services as part of the tool, and present restrictions and not solutions. In [CZW+06] the authors take a view quite similar to ours, but use Business Process Execution Language for Web Services (BPEL4WS) to achieve stateful long running interactions, and focusses on data security through gaussian models, while our focus lies on the design principles of web services itself within service-oriented knowledge discovery. Finally, [GJF06] describes a framework in which web services are used for knowledge discovery in databases, and describes the framework indepth, as well as supported algorithms, but not the web service design and construction methodology, and thus serves as a useful complement to this paper.

3 Background

In this section we discuss the SO paradigm, and present its benefits with respect to KD processes. We also discuss current standards in the SO paradigm. These standards will be used in the design and implementation of the use case, which will be presented in Section 3 and Section 4.

The SO paradigm is expressed in a Service-Oriented Architecture (SOA)[Gro]. A SOA is a layered architectural style that supports SO, where SO is a way of thinking in terms of services and service-based development and the outcomes of services. In practise, SOA is a distributed architecture that allows a user to build an application by means of composing individual components that potentially

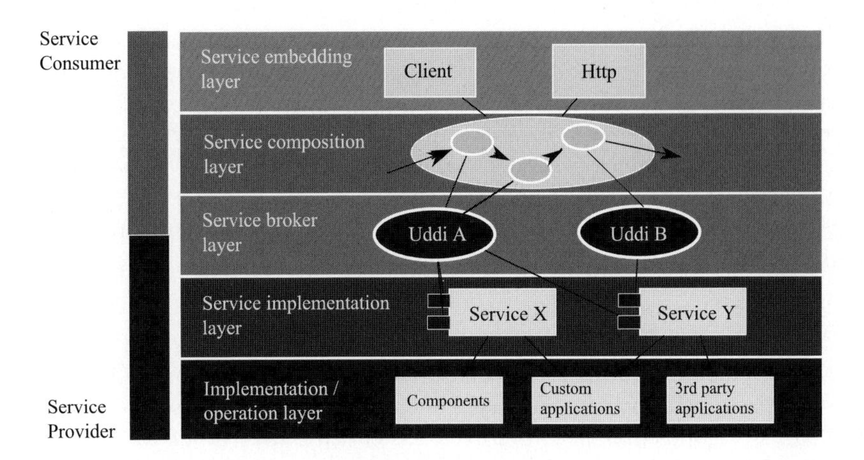

Fig. 1. SOA Layers

exist across separate (physical or logical) domains. These components are called web services [HD06] An overview of SOA is shown in Figure 1

Without going into too much detail, there are a few key points in Figure 1 that we would like to draw attention to. First, notice how in the service provider layers service components can consist of not only custom software, but also existing solutions. This is possible because of the standardized messaging and interface formats that are part of the SOA specification. SOA incorporates a methodology that is called design by contract [Mey92]. In this methodology, implementation is decoupled from a program's interface, whereby and interface is an annotation of the service's functionality that serves as a contract between the service user and the service provider.

A widely used standard for defining web service interfaces is the Web Service Description Language (WSDL) [W3Cb]. WSDL is an XML-based standard that describes for each web service how the service handles incoming messages, what type of service it is, what kind of parameters it supports, and how the service interface is connected to the underlying implementation. We discuss WSDL in more detail in the next section.

Another area of interest are the service consumer layers. Notice that applications are no longer *constructed* but instead *composed* by putting together individual web services. This composability is partly the merit of the standardized interfaces, but also because SOA is message-oriented; communication between individual components proceeds through the use of uniformly defined messsages. A standard that is often used for web service message transport is the Simple Object Access Protocol (SOAP)[W3Ca], which is an XLM-based message format and transport protocol. Using both standardized ways of accessing and messaging makes an application decomposable into distinct, uniformly accessable units of computation and processing, which allows for remote computing.

Finally, the last point of interest is the middle layer called the services layer. In this layer the interfaces of the web services are offered to the consumers who search for their underlying functionality. For a user it is impossible to know the location of each service, and similarly for a provider it is impossible to know the location of all its users. To meet both demands, the Universal Description Discovery and Integration (UDDI)[Dra] facility was created, which is a registry for web services offered by service providers containing all WSDL documents corresponding to interfaces of those services.

With all these protocols, standards and facilities in place, there are a plethora of advantages to be gained in the KD context. We summarize a few below:

- **Easier KD process setup**
  A scientist usually perceives a KD process as a workflow where data is continually modified in discrete computational steps. By using SOA and web service composition, the scientist's mental model is more closely approached. Process composition becomes even easier with the use of tools that offer a GUI like Taverna [MyG]. By offering the scientist an environment that matches his conceptual model of a KD process, the process becomes easier to understand and compose.
- **Easier KD process modification**
  Since web service interfaces are decoupled of their implementation, a user only needs to rely on the interface. If another webservice is available that adheres to the interface, that service could replace the forementioned one in a process without the need for any additional modification by the user.
- **Increased component availability**
  When a scientist searches for the solution of a specific step in his KD process, it might occur that an implementation is hard to find. With the UDDI in place, a scientist has a central location where specific solutions can be found. This reduces the time of process setup, and increases the chances of finding a solution.
- **Increased Performance**
  Since SOA and all related protocols are platform-independent technologies, each platform can potentially support it. This makes it easier for the service provider to use an implementation environment that is best suited for the web service, perhaps on specialized hardware which normally would not be available to the users. Moreover, if two services can be executed independently and are located on different physical domains, they can be executed in parallel.

4 Service-Oriented KD Design

In this section we discuss the SO design model and patterns that we used to create the case study, and examine how these SO principles influence individual services and KD processes on a whole. First we discuss WSDL a bit more and explain how the standard influenced the design of the web service. After that, we discuss a design model for SO KD processes. Finally, we present guiding principles for individual KD service design, which were also used to design the use case.

4.1 WSDL and Design Implications

There are many views on the design of a KD process, ranging from a global view stating what functionality a service in a process has and what standard to use to design and implement it, to microdetails such as what message format to use. Since the use case was designed by using WSDL, this influences our further design of a web service and a KD process as a whole. In this paper we focus on the different operation types that are defined in WSDL, and its influence on the design of KD process and a KD service:

- **Request/Response**
  In this case, the client sends a message to the service, and the service sends a message to the client in response. This is the message equivalent of a function call.
- **Solicit/Response**
  This is the reverse case of the Request/Response type. The service sends a message to the client, and the client sends a message to the service in response. This is often used when a service needs to poll clients.
- **Client messenger**
  Here, the client sends a message but does not expect a message in return.
- **Server notification**
  Server notification is the exact opposite of the client messenger type. In this case, the service sends a notification to the client without expecting or waiting for an answer.

As we shall see in the remainder of this section, operation types have an inpact on the entire KD process, so selecting the right type of operation is important in order to obtain a process with optimal performance.

4.2 KD Process Design

A KD process can be seen as a workflow, whereby data flows from one unit of processing to another. Conceptually we try to map these unists of processing to web services. How successful this can be done depends on the understanding of the process and the functional discreteness of individual steps. We see the design of a KD process as a three-dimensional challenge containing the Logical, Funtional and Relational views, that al influence each other. We propose the following KD process design model for SO that incorporates all these views, which is illustrated in Figure 2 and described below. By applying this model in the design of an SO KD process, a better understanding of the process is achieved, which leads to a better design, until both understanding and design are optimal.

- **Logical view**
  In this view, the entire KD process is being examined to identify all services and relations in the process. This logical view is not only guided by the designer's expertise, but also on the services already available, for example,

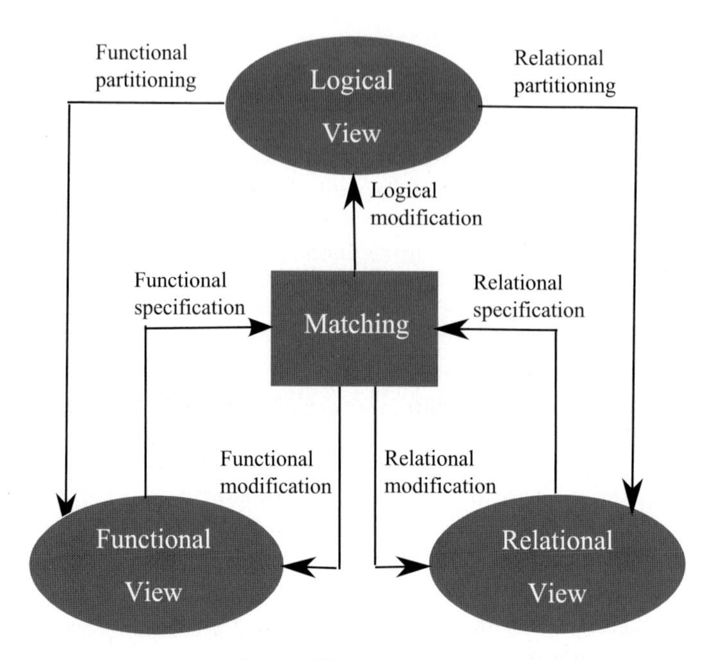

Fig. 2. KD process in SO

services built earlier or services publicly available through a UDDI. Ideally all services fit together perfectly and are all available, but this is rarely the case. Therefore, choices have to be made if readily available services should be used, and how the unavailable process parts should be logically partitioned. Since different partitionings of a KD process yields different services and relations, the partitioning will affect the functionalities of each service as well as the relations among them.

- **Functional view**
  For each service identified all functionalities are recorded. These functinalities will serve as a guideline for interface design and operation type selection, and will determine the nature of the relations with other functionalities. In this stage similarities between services and dissimilarities within services can be uncovered on the basis of functionality, leading to a possible joining or splitting of services.
- **Relational view**
  In this aspect of design, relations should be identified for each service with other functionalities in other services. These relations should be annotated in two dimensions: direction and usage type. The direction indicates if messages will be flowing from a service or to a service, the usage type indicates if the relation is used only once, or continually until processing is done. Both dimensions will influence the functionality of a service, the operation type of the functionality's interface, and the content and format of the messages that will be transported. Similarities and dissimilarities in relations amongst services might also lead to a revision of the service partitioning.

- **Matching**
  This dimension is the feedback step of the model, and matches the outcome of all other phases to one another. It serves as a feedback phase for the design, and indicates if service partitionings, functionalities or relations should be modified or adapted in case of a mismatch.

4.3 KD Service Design

In this part we focus on the functionality design of a KD service, and how the design choices are expressed in the WSDL operation types.

As stated earlier, KD processes can be very time-consuming, especially when large data volumes are involved. This means that any error may result in the loss of a great amount of time. Therefore, individual KD services should be designed for interaction; A scientist should get regular feedback on the progress of the process, and should at all time be able to interact with the process.

We also mentioned that a KD process is often perceived as a workflow, a sequence of computational steps whereby data flows from one step to another. This does not mean, however, that one step should be completed in order for the next step to begin; the results that come from these actions sometimes can already be transferred to the next process phase without waiting for the service to finish processing all the data. To optimize performance as well, KD services functionality should be designed for streaming data where possible.

Having observed the facts stated above, we divided the functionalities of a KD service into three categories: Initialization, Feedback and Enactment. This classification forms a guideline for the design of a service's functionality using WSDL.

- **Initialization**
  Procedures designed in this class are expected to handle a continuous stream of messages that initialize this part of the experiment. Client messagers are usually best suited for these functions, unless initialization requires critical feedback, in which case Request/Response should be used.
- **Feedback**
  In this category methods need to be designed that provide feedback to the service client. Both Notification or Solicit/Response method types can be used here, depending on if the feedback is used purely for informative purposes or if it is used to steer an interactive experiment through client intervention. Feedback is often provided iteratively, sending messages whenever an event occurs.
- **Enactment**
  This category combines the actual functionalities of the service with the feedback functionalities that report on the service's progress. Since an experiment usually is expected to return a result, a Request/Response type method is usually chosen. However, if one does not need to wait on this service in order to continue with other processing steps, a combined Client messager and Server notification procedure could be used to let the service run asynchronously. Note that enactment can be done both atomically or iteratively, as we will see in the next section.

5 Use Case

In this section we present the use case. For our case study we implemented a KD scenario described in [TZTL06]. In this scenario two classes of leukemia are compared with each other. The microarray dataset from Golub et al. [GST+99] is processed to identify differentially expressed genes per class, based on a threshold score computed by the student's t-test. This set of differentially expressed genes, together with a selection of their non-differentially expressed counterparts (both expressed in Entrez id's [MOPT05]), are then annotated with terms from the Gene Ontology (GO)[GO]. In the final step these annotations, together with information about interaction amongst genes, are combined to find subgroups. We extended this scenario to also include the Kyoto Encyclopedia of Genes and Genomes (KEGG)[KEG] ontology, and used a tree-like rule miner that induces rules on the basis of maximal subsets that satisfy the user-defined support constraints.

We designed the use case using the model discussed in the previous section and compared it to the original design. Both implementations are done in C-sharp that use a C++ .Net back-end, using WSDL as an interface definition language, and use SOAP as transport protocol. All services and algorithms are performed on Microsoft Windows XP using an Intel Centrino duo processor 1.66GHz, and 1GB of main memory.

5.1 Use Case Process Design

- **Logical view**
  In the use case we identified two different web services that are used together to provide one composite service. The first service is the **GeneSelector** service that is used to compute a t-scores for all genes in the microarray data, and place it either in the differential or non-differential collection. The second service is the **GeneRuleInducer** service which takes the two lists and produces rules that describe subsets of these lists that share the same terms in the GO and KEGG ontology, which are also provided in the rule.

- **Functional view**
  Per service we identify functionalities divided in the three forementioned categories.
  - **GeneSelector**
    Initilialization functionalities
    * *Probe mapper*: Each row of the microarray data is annotated per probe and not per gene, so probes need to be mapped to entrez gene id's.
    * *Class mapper*: Each column of the microarray data is annotated with a label and not a class, so labels need to be mapped to classes.
    * *Cutoff initializer*: Initialises the t-score cutoff value for genes.

Feedback functionalities
  * *Probe Feedback*: When a probe does not match any gene, a message is sent to inform on this.
  * *Class Feedback*: When a label does not match a class, a message is sent.

Enactment functionalities
  * *T-test calculator*: With help of both mappings, t-test value for a gene per class is computed and compared with the supplied cutoff.

- **GeneRuleInducer**
  Initilialization functionalities
  * *Gene loader*: Loads genes and their scores in the ontology tree-mining structure.
  * *Support constraint initializer*: Initilaizes the minimum and maximum support constraints.
  * *Ontology loader*: Loads the ontology in a tree-structure.
  * *Gene to ontology mapper*: Loads the data that maps gene id's to ontology keys.
  * *Gene interaction mapper*: Loads the data that specifies interaction between genes.

  Feedback functionalities
  * *Gene List feedback*: When something is wrong with one of the lists, the user is sent a message that specifies the problem and the performed action.
  * *Rule feedback*: Presents periodical feedback on the progress of the rule miner.

  Enactment functionalities
  * *Rule miner*: Using the internal tree-structure of the ontologies which are annoted with differential and non-differential genes, rules are uncovered that satisfy the minimal differential support constraint and the maximal non-differential support constraint.

– **Relational view**
Here we specify relations and if they are iterative or not. Iterative relations are denoted with *.
Client to GeneSelector relations
- *Probe map input*: Message containing probe and gene id's. Only needs to be supplied once.
- *Class map input*: Message containing classes and labels. Only needs to be supplied once as well.
- *Cutoff input*: Message containing the user-defined t-score cutoff.
- *Data input**: Message containing a probe identifier and expressions per label.

GeneSelector to Client relations

- *Probe map feedback output**: Message that returns a problem with the probe mapping.
- *Class map feedback output**: Message that returns a problem with the class mapping.

GeneSelector to GeneRuleMiner

- *Data return output**: Message that returns the score of the gene and if it's in the differential set or not.

Client to GeneRuleMiner

- *Differential support input*: Message that supplies the cutoff for the minimal number of differential genes a rule has to support.
- *Non-differential support input*: Message that supplies the cutoff for the maximal number of non-differential genes a rule may to support.

- *Enactment input*: Message that enacts the mining process.

GeneRuleMiner to Client

- *Gene list feedback output**: Message specifying feedback if anything goes wrong loading the specified lists.
- *Rule miner output*: Message that returns rules uncovered by the algortihm.

A complete overview of service connectivity and data flow is presented in Figure 3. Note that only those functionalities that require interaction with the user or another service are displayed.

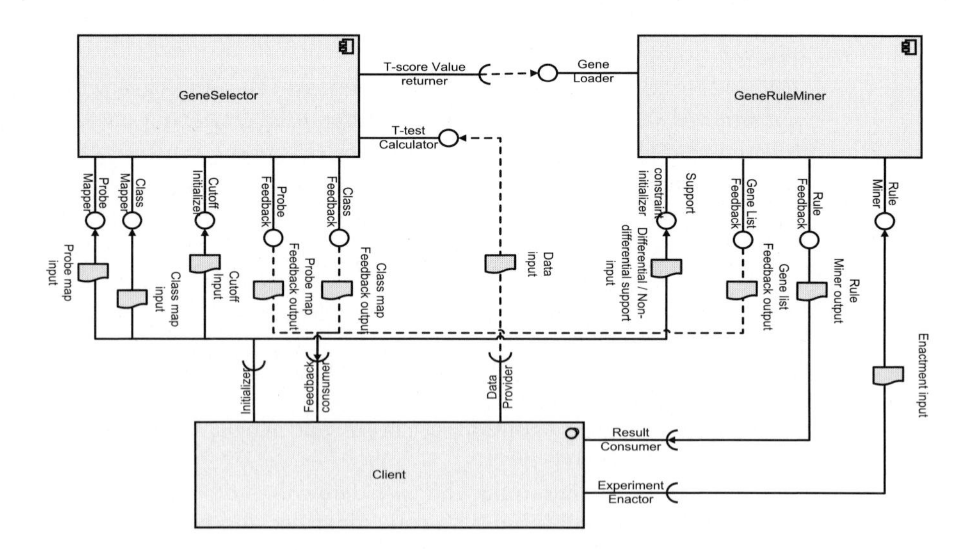

Fig. 3. SO KD use case design

5.2 Use Case Process Comparison

The original process was divided in the same service partitioning as the one that our model yielded, but processing of individual services was done one by one, and results did not transfer before processing was completed. Furthermore, in the original implementation feedback was not supplied upon occurence of the event, but as a return value after processing, which is a less interactive way. A complete list of differences per service are listed in Table 1 and Table 2

Table 1. Design differences in GeneSelector service

Category	Original process	Use case process
Service feedback	as return values	iterative on occurence of event
Service initialization	Supplied as a whole	Iterative data supply
Service processing	all	per element
Service outputs	at end of processing	continuous outputting per element

Table 2. Design differences in GeneRuleMiner service

Category	Original process	Use case process
Service feedback	as return values	iterative on occurence of event
Service initialization	Supplied as a whole	Iterative data supply
Service processing	all	all
Service outputs	at end of processing	at end of processing

Table 3. Benchmarks of the original process

Phase	Cutoff 15	Cutoff 10	Cutoff 8
GeneSelector initialization	74	69	73
GeneSelector processing	1331	1291	1328
GeneRuleMiner initialization	3388	7122	13318

Table 4. Benchmarks of the re-designed use case

Phase	Cutoff 15	Cutoff 10	Cutoff 8
GeneSelector initialization	73	69	74
GeneSelector processing	1260	1228	1257
GeneRuleMiner initialization	2139	5841	11998

Finally, we took some benchmarks for the performance of the original process and the re-designed use case. As input for the selector we took respectively cutoffs of t-score 15, 10 and 8. For the GeneRuleMiner, we took supports of minimally 10% differential genes and maximally 5% non-differential genes. Results of the original process are displayed in Table 3, and those of the re-designed use case are in Table 4. Note that the measurements of each phase in the table indicate after how much time since the *process* started this phase ended. All measurements

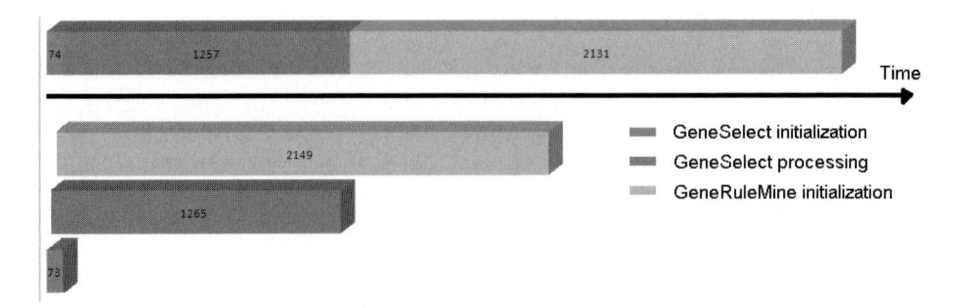

Fig. 4. Benchmark comparison of t-score 15 cutoff process

are averages over 50 consecutive runs, and are in milliseconds. Since in the GeneRuleMiner processing is no speedup to be gained due to the return of all results at once, we only show the benchmarks of the phases preceeding the GeneRuleMiner processing phase.

To make the difference between the original process and the re-designed use case more clear, consider Figure 4. Here, the cutoff 15 scenario was worked out more thoroughly. The top part displays how the original process parts consecutively get processed. The bottom part shows how the re-designed process part iteratively get processed in parallel where possible.

6 Conclusions and Future Work

In this paper we discussed the design of KD processes in an SO environment. We discussed the SO technology and related standards, and showed how KD processes can benefit from SO technology; It makes process setup and modification easier, increases component availability, and can have a positive inpact on performance.

By designing a SOKD process workflow using a design model that combines logical, functional and relational views, a better understanding of a KD process can be gained iteratively due to the matching and mismatching of entities in these views, whereby each iteration yields a better SOKD process design and a closer match of relations, services and functionality. An important factor that influences the partioning of services are the services already available, thereby promoting software reuse.

When designing individual services in KD, interaction and feedback are importants aspects to keep in mind. Interaction and regular feedback are important for the scientist to steer the KD process in a correct way, for KD processes are often time-consuming and thus any process incorrectly set up could possibly result in a considerable loss of time. Another important aspect is performance through paralellization. Since web services can be distributed across different logical or physical platforms, their execution could possibly proceed in a parallel fashion. To support paralellism, streaming data is preferred over monolithic data transport where possible. By combining these aspects and the functionality types in WSDL, we created a guideline for the design of a KD service's functionality that is otimized for streaming data where possible and incorporates the need for feedback.

To illustrate the merits of SO and our developped design model and guidelines, we implemented a use case according to our model, and compared it to a web service implementation using monolithical data transfer and periodical step-by-step execution. In some cases, processing times for the initialization of a process were reduced up to 37%, and with 22% on average.

The design principles stated in this paper are but a minor step to incorporating SO technology in the field of KD. However, by assuring that the design of a KD process and individual services is optimized for feedback and paralellism, a researcher can enact a process and conclude it successfully with minimal error and maximal performance. For further research we would need to study more use cases to ensure the research principles have maximum support in the KD scientific field. Furthermore, this design needs to be supported by grapical workflow tools that support iterative relationships instead of just monolithical data transport.

References

[AC06] Adeva, J.J.G., Calvo, R.A.: Mining text with pimiento. IEEE Internet Computing 10(4), 27–35 (2006)

[CZW+06] Cheung, W.K., Zhang, X.-F., Wong, H.-F., Liu, J., Luo, Z.-W., Tong, F.C.H.: Service-oriented distributed data mining. IEEE Internet Computing 10(4), 44–54 (2006)

[DBG+06] Datta, S., Bhaduri, K., Giannella, C., Wolff, R., Kargupta, H.: Distributed data mining in peer-to-peer networks. IEEE Internet Computing 10(4), 18–26 (2006)

[Dra] Uddi Open Draft. Uddi version 2.0 api specification

[GJF06] Guedes, D., Meira Jr., W., Ferreira, R.: Anteater: A service-oriented architecture for high-performance data mining. IEEE Internet Computing 10(4), 36–43 (2006)

[GO] The gene ontology, http://www.geneontology.org/

[Gro] The Open Group. Definition of soa, version 1.1, http://opengroup.org/projects/soa/doc.tpl?gdid=10632

[GST+99] Golub, T.R., Slonim, D.K., Tamayo, P., Huard, C., Gaasenbeek, M., Mesirov, J.P., Coller, H., Loh, M.L., Downing, J.R., Caligiuri, M.A., Bloomfield, C.D., Lander, E.S.: Molecular classification of cancer: class discovery and class prediction by gene expression monitoring. Science 286(5439), 531–537 (1999)

[HD06] Hasan, J., Duran, M.: Expert Service-Oriented Architecture in C# 2005, 2nd edn. Apress, Berkely (2006)

[KEG] Kegg: Kyoto encyclopedia of genes and genomes, http://www.genome.jp/kegg/

[Mey92] Meyer, B.: Applying design by contract. IEEE Computer 25(10), 40–51 (1992)

[MOPT05] Maglott, D., Ostell, J., Pruitt, K.D., Tatusova, T.: Entrez gene: gene-centered information at ncbi. Nucleic Acids Res. 33 (Database issue) (January 2005)

[MyG] MyGrid. Taverna workbench 1.7, http://taverna.sourceforge.net/

[TZTL06] Trajkovski, I., Zelezný, F., Tolar, J., Lavrac, N.: Relational subgroup discovery for descriptive analysis of microarray data. In: Berthold, M., R., Glen, R.C., Fischer, I. (eds.) CompLife 2006. LNCS (LNBI), vol. 4216, pp. 86–96. Springer, Heidelberg (2006)

[W3Ca] The World Wide Web Consortium W3C. Soap version 1.2 part 0: Primer (second edn.), http://www.w3.org/TR/2007/REC-soap12-part0-20070427/

[W3Cb] The World Wide Web Consortium W3C. Web services description language (wsdl) 1.1, http://www.w3.org/TR/wsdl

The ASK System and the Challenge of Distributed Knowledge Discovery

Andries Stam

Almende BV, Rotterdam, The Netherlands
andries@almende.org

Abstract. ASK is an industrial software system for connecting people to each other. The system uses intelligent matching functionality and learning mechanisms in order to find effective connections between requesters and responders in a community. Currently, Almende investigates ways to connect multiple distributed configurations of ASK to each other and to different existing systems. Thereby, we face the issue of how to derive knowledge about connections between people in such distributed heterogeneous settings. In this paper, we introduce ASK, indicate its future development and discuss the imposed challenges.

1 Introduction

ASK has been developed by Almende [1], a Dutch research company focusing on the application of self-organisation techniques in human organisations and agent-oriented software systems. The system is marketed by ASK Community Systems [2]. ASK provides mechanisms for matching users requiring information or services with potential suppliers. Based on information about earlier established contacts and feedback of users, the system learns to bring people into contact with each other in the most effective way. Typical applications for ASK are workforce planning, customer service, knowledge sharing, social care and emergency response. Customers of ASK include the European mail distribution company TNT Post, the cooperative financial services provider Rabobank and the world's largest pharmaceutical company Pfizer. The amount of people using a single ASK configuration varies from several hundreds to several thousands.

Currently, ASK configurations are deployed on a per-customer basis in a centralized manner. Developments in information and communication services, however, call for more openness and distribution of the services of ASK. Future versions of ASK likely include the possibility to connect multiple ASK configurations to each other or to different knowledge intensive systems, or even the creation of personal ASK configurations which maintain personal data and information about the connectivity with colleagues or clients. These possibilities inherently imply the distribution of data and put a challenge on the acquisition of knowledge for single or even multiple overlapping communities.

T. Margaria and B. Steffen (Eds.): ISoLA 2008, CCIS 17, pp. 663–668, 2008.

In this paper, we indicate future developments envisioned for ASK and expected challenges related to distributed knowledge discovery and management. We have set up the paper as follows. In Section 2, we provide an overview of the ASK system. In Section 3, we indicate current research initiatives at Almende and future development directions regarding ASK, and discuss the challenges regarding distributed knowledge discovery. We summarize in Section 4.

2 An Overview of the ASK System

The primary goal of the ASK system is to connect people to other people in the most effective way. The system acts as a *mediator* in establishing the contacts: people can contact the system via various media like telephone or email, and the system itself is also able to contact people via those media. In determining the *effectiveness* of contact establishment, multiple aspects play a role. For example, the rating of *human knowledge and skills* is important in cases where people request contact with specialists or service providers. In these cases, the ASK system is able to ask participants for feedback on the quality of service after the contact. This feedback can be used for optimization of subsequent requests of the same kind. A different role is played by *time schedules*, which indicate when certain people can be reached for certain purposes. The ASK system differentiates between regular plannings and ad-hoc schedules caused by sudden events or delays. Different *communication media* play another role. In most ASK configurations, voice communication (phone, VoIP) is the primary communication medium used, but different media like email and SMS are supported by ASK as well. Moreover, people can own various phone numbers and email addresses, for which they can indicate preferences and time or service dependent usage constraints. The ASK system is able to exploit knowledge about the reacheability of people via specific media, for example in the context of emergency response systems, where people must be contacted within a certain time window. In general, learning from past experiences of all kinds and forecasting based on these experiences plays a crucial role in ASK.

The software of ASK can be technically divided into three parts: the *web front-end*, the *database* and the *contact engine* (see Figure 1). The *web front-end* acts as a configuration dashboard, via which typical domain data like users, groups, phone numbers, mail addresses, interactive voice response menus, services and scheduled jobs can be created, edited and deleted. This data is stored in a *database*, one for each configuration of ASK. The feedback of users and the knowledge derived from earlier established contacts are also stored in this database. Finally, the *contact engine* consists of a quintuple of components *Reception*, *Matcher*, *Executer*, *Resource Manager* and *Scheduler*, which handle inbound and outbound communication with the system and provide the intelligent matching and scheduling functionality.

The "heartbeat" of the contact engine is the *Request loop*, indicated with thick arrows. Requests loop through the system until they are fully completed. The *Reception* component determines which steps must be taken by ASK in order

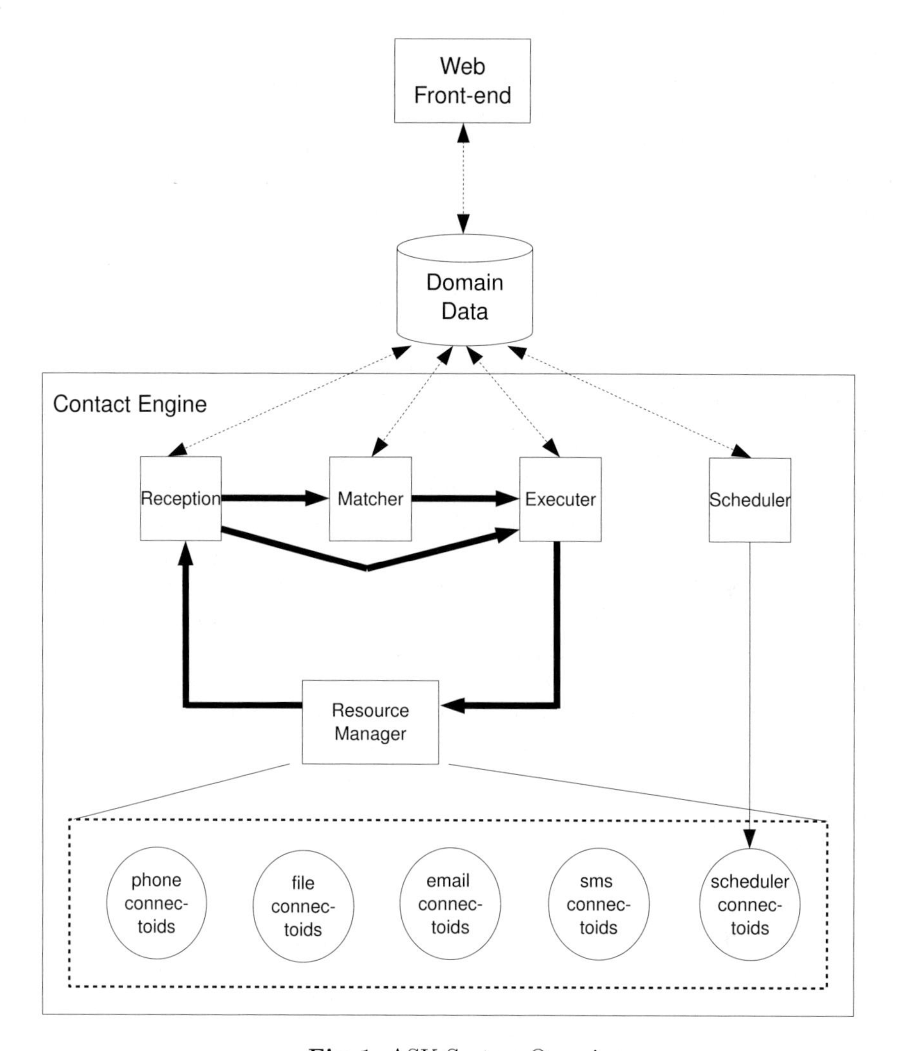

Fig. 1. ASK System Overview

to fulfil (part of) a request. The *Matcher* component searches for appropriate participants for a request. The *Executer* component determines the best way in which the participants can be connected. ASK clearly separates the medium and resource independent request loop from the level of media-specific resources needed for fulfilling the request, called *connectoids* (e.g., a connected phone line, a sound file being played, an email being written, an SMS message to be sent). The *Resource Manager* component acts as a bridge between these two levels. Finally, a separate *Scheduler* component schedules requests based on job descriptions in the database. In the next paragraphs, we discuss in more detail those components which create and exploit knowledge in ASK: the *Reception*, the *Matcher* and the *Scheduler* component.

Reception. The major role of the Reception component is to determine which action should be taken by the ASK system based on a request. To give an example, if a request is received containing an incoming call event from a certain telephone number, the Reception component can decide to present a specific interactive voice response (IVR) menu to the caller, depending on the current date and time, number of the caller and the number being called. The caller is then able to provide information about the request, by selecting submenus or actions via dual-tone multi-frequency (DTMF) dial tones. A request could also originate from the scheduler, for example if the ASK system calls a user in order to ask for feedback or for availability as an ASK responder for a certain time period. The reception component is responsible for performing updates to the contents of the database in terms of adding previously unknown telephone numbers, adding feedback from users or changing schedules of responders.

Matcher. The Matcher component tries to find matching users for a request. For example, a person calling the ASK system could ask for a connection with a specialist on a certain topic. Matching can be complicated, since the preferences and time schedules of the requester and candidate responders must be taken into account, as well as feedback about earlier contacts. The Matcher tries to find several candidate responders and selects between them using one of four possible methods:

1. Round Robin: the Matcher randomly selects a responder from the set of candidates available.
2. Last Spoken: the Matcher selects the responder that was selected previously.
3. Rating: the Matcher uses feedback provided by the requester about potential responders and selects the one with the highest rating.
4. Friendly Rating: the Matcher again selects based on the received ratings, but occasionally randomly selects a different responder in order to provide them with the opportunity to improve their rating.

Scheduler. The Scheduler component realizes the execution of various types of scheduled jobs. Typical jobs are: contacting requesters and responders to obtain feedback about earlier connections, or contacting potential responders for availability. In executing these jobs, the Scheduler component keeps track of the time schedules and preferences of users. The Scheduler itself does not take part in the request loop: its messages enter the request loop as if they come from outside the system. Jobs for the Scheduler can be put into the database manually via the web front-end, or automatically, as the result of the execution of requests in the contact engine.

3 The Future of ASK

As we indicated in the introduction, future customers will require increasing agility with regard to the integration of new communication technologies, customer specific extensions and existing information systems in ASK. Another requirement is that of autonomic run-time scalability: the ability of the software to adapt its configuration by distribution and replication, as to achieve better load balancing without human intervention. Almende aims at even more dynamism in future configurations of ASK. Matching and scheduling functionality can be diversified and provided by multiple distributed interacting components, acting upon several distributed data sources. Matching can then be performed not only within a single community, but also across various indirectly related communities. In addition to the existing customer-specific configurations of ASK, personal contact managers can be set up to maintain personal data and knowledge about the connectivity with colleagues, clients, or service providers.

As a consequence, the current ASK system will be changed and extended considerably in the near future. Such changes can be realized in a more reliable way when combined with the use of *formal methods* for the modeling, analysis and testing of software. Currently, Almende is involved in the EU FP6 project *Credo*: Modeling and analysis of evolutionary structures for distributed services (IST-33826). In the context of this project, several formal methods and techniques are applied to the ASK system, in its current shape and with various extensions. For example, we use the modeling language Creol [5] to model the functionality of the ASK system, at a high level of abstraction, for analysis and verification purposes. Communication within and between ASK components is reorganized into communication via REO Circuits [3], as a means to achieve better compositionality through exogenous coordination and to enable dynamic reconfiguration. The mechanism of dynamic reconfiguration has been promoted by Almende in earlier research on the Common Hybrid Agent Platform (CHAP) [6]. Furthermore, we apply Task Automata [4] for the verification of timing and scheduling issues, like the completion of requests and the execution of scheduler jobs in the system.

The future scenarios we envision, and for which we are now taking the first steps, also pose high requirements on the capabilities of the ASK system to derive knowledge from inherently distributed data:

- How can efficient matching be performed in a distributed setting? Efficiency is especially important in the case of phone communication.
- How can we cope with conflicts, redundancy or dependencies in time schedules and availability data stored in different databases at different places?
- How can we exploit the updated contents from one database in the context of another database? In particular, how can we use customer feedback provided in one context to improve matching in another context?
- How can we enable cross-community knowledge discovery and at the same time keep personal contact information private and secure?

4 Summary

In this paper, we presented the ASK system, a system for effectively connecting people to each other. The system implements an intelligent matching mechanism which uses knowledge derived from past experiences. Our aim is to evolve ASK into a system in which this knowledge will be inherently distributed over various community-wide and personal databases. Formal methods play a crucial role in the modeling and verification of such an evolving system. In addition, future configurations of the ASK system certainly need to incorporate efficient techniques for distributed knowledge discovery.

References

[1] Almende website, http://www.almende.com
[2] ASK community systems website, http://www.ask-cs.com
[3] Arbab, F.: Reo: a channel-based coordination model for component composition. Mathematical. Structures in Comp. Sci. 14(3), 329–366 (2004)
[4] Fersman, E., Krcal, P., Pettersson, P., Yi, W.: Task automata: Schedulability, decidability and undecidability. Inf. Comput. 205(8), 1149–1172 (2007)
[5] Johnsen, E.B., Owe, O.: An asynchronous communication model for distributed concurrent objects. Software and Systems Modeling 6(1), 35–58 (2007)
[6] Valk, J., Larsen, J.P., van Tooren, P., ter Mors, A.: Channel-based architecture for dynamically reconfigurable networks. In: BNAIC, pp. 246–253 (2005)

A Scenario Implementation in R for SubtypeDiscovery Examplified on Chemoinformatics Data

Fabrice Colas[1], Ingrid Meulenbelt[2], Jeanine J. Houwing-Duistermaat[3], Margreet Kloppenburg[4], Iain Watt[5], Stephanie M. van Rooden[6], Martine Visser[6], Johan Marinus[6], Edward O. Cannon[7], Andreas Bender[8], Jacobus J. van Hilten[6], P. Eline Slagboom[2], and Joost N. Kok[1,2]

[1] LIACS, Leiden University, The Netherlands
{fcolas,joost}@liacs.nl
[2] MOLEPI, LUMC, The Netherlands
{I.Meulenbelt,P.Slagboom@}lumc.nl
[3] MEDSTATS, LUMC, The Netherlands
J.J.Houwing@lumc.nl
[4] Rheumatology dept., LUMC, The Netherlands
G.Kloppenburg@lumc.nl
[5] Radiology dept., LUMC, The Netherlands
I.Watt@lumc.nl
[6] Neurology dept., LUMC, The Netherlands
{S.M.van_Rooden,M.Visser,J.Marinus,J.J.van_Hilten}@lumc.nl
[7] UCMSI, University of Cambridge, United Kingdom
Eoc21@cam.ac.uk
[8] LACDR, Leiden University, The Netherlands
bendera@lacdr.leidenuniv.nl

Abstract. We developed a methodology that both facilitates and enhances the search for homogeneous subtypes in data. We applied this methodology to medical research on Osteoarthritis and Parkinson's Disease and to chemoinformatics research on the chemical structure of molecule profiles. We release this methodology as the R SubtypeDiscovery package to enable *reproducibility* of our analyses. In this paper, we present the package implementation and we illustrate its output on molecular data from chemoinformatics. Our methodology includes different techniques to process the data, a computational approach repeating data modelling to select for a number of subtypes or a type of model, and additional methods to characterize, compare and evaluate the top ranking models. Therefore, this methodology does not solely cluster data but it also produces a complete set of results to conduct a subtype discovery analysis.

1 Introduction

In medical research, it is of interest to identify subtypes of diseases like Osteoarthritis (OA) and Parkinson's Disease (PD) that present clinical heterogeneity; we can do so by searching for homogeneous clusters in values of markers

T. Margaria and B. Steffen (Eds.): ISoLA 2008, CCIS 17, pp. 669–683, 2008.

that reflect the severity of the disease. In chemoinformatics, various databases list and classify molecules, therefore, it is of interest to search for characteristic subgroups of molecules that exhibit particular features on the molecule's chemical structures.

To this aim, we developed a methodology mimicking a cluster analysis process: from data preparation to cluster evaluation. In particular, it implements various data preparation techniques to facilitate the analysis given different data processing [1]. It also features a computational approach that repeats data modelling in order to select for a number of subtypes or a type of model. Additionally, it defines a selection of methods to characterize, compare and evaluate the top ranking models.

The outline of the rest of the paper is as follows. We first describe the three studies on which we carried a SubtypeDiscovery analysis. Second, we detail data preparation issues with methods to answer them, as well as our preferred clustering approach. Third, we report additional methods to select, characterize, compare and evaluate cluster results. Finally, as the search for subtypes appears in many areas, we abstract from the application we have done up to now and make it available as the R SubtypeDiscovery package, which we discus in the last section. Illustrations of our methodology throughout this paper are from medical research on OA and PD (somewhat restricted due to confidentiality) and to a public chemoinformatics data set embedded in our package.

2 Experimental Data

Osteoarthritis. OA is a disabling common late onset disease of the joints characterized by cartilage degradation and the formation of new bone. These investigations will assess whether the spread of the disease across different joint sites is stochastic or follows a particular pattern depending on the underlying disease aetiology. At joint locations like the hands, hips, knees, and the spine, Radiographic characteristics of OA (ROA) was assessed by physicians who graded OA severity on a 4-points scale $\{0, 1, 2, 3, 4\}$, which is referred to as the Kellgren and Lawrence scale, see [2,3] for an account of previous research. Such ROA was ascertained at 45 locations. We carried our cluster analysis on 422 participants who issue from 211 families. We dropped out 13 participants either because they missed ROA scores or because the family sibship already involved two members.

Parkinson's Disease. PD is a progressive neurological disorder that is characterized by problems with movement: stiffness, slowness of movement, and trembling. However, patients have also several other problems not related to movement. Among the PD patients, there is marked heterogeneity, both in presence and severity of different impairments and in other variables like age at onset or family history. Better knowledge of different subtypes of PD will help to understand and facilitate the search for the aetiology of PD and to characterize patients with different progression profiles. The severity of PD is assessed on scales developed specifically for PD [4]. Participants are evaluated on 17 scores reflecting cognitive, autonomic, motor problems and some additional aspects of the disease.

The participants have a baseline measurement and are followed-up over 3 years with an interval of a year. Here, we do not consider the longitudinal aspect of the data and we proceed to our analysis on 1152 profiles from the 4 years.

Chemoinformatics public data set (wada2008). Originally generated by Edward O. Cannon, the data set is composed of substances taken from the 2008 WADA (World Anti-Doping Agency) Prohibited List together with molecules having similar biological activity and chemical structure from the MDL Drug Data Report database. Those molecules may belong to ten different activity classes: the β blockers, anabolic agents, hormones and related substances, β-2 agonists, hormone antagonists and modulators, diuretics and other masking agents, stimulants, narcotics, cannabinoids and glucocorticosteroids. This list of molecules was imported into Molecular Operating Environment (MOE) from which all 184 two dimensional descriptors were calculated. The `wada2008` data set is similar to the `wada2005` which was previously published in [5].

3 Data Preparation and Clustering

We aim to identify homogeneous and *reliable* subtypes. Hence, cluster results should be reproducible and the clusters should characterize true underlying patterns, not the incidental ones. We discuss in this section the removal of the *time* dimension in OA and PD data sets, the *reliability* and *validity* of cluster results and we recall the main ideas behind model based clustering.

Data preparation. As data preparation can influence largely the result of data analyses, our methodology includes various methods to transform and process data, e.g. computing the z-scores of variables to obtain scale-invariant quantities, normalizing according to L_2, L_1, max and centering with respect to the $mean, median, min$. Alternatively, we may want to remove the time dimension in the data because we do not want to model clusters only characterized by the time, e.g. see Fig. 1. Indeed, in the overal severity of OA and PD, respectively age or disease duration which we further refer to as the *time*, are known to play a major role. Therefore, to model for clusters without the *time* dimension, we first perform regressions on the *time* for each variable and next, we search for clusters on the residual variance. If we denote by α and β the estimated intercept and coefficient vectors of the regression, by $\mathbf{X}$ the OA and PD data where x_{ij} refers to measurement j of observation i then, we express the regression as

$$x_{ij}(t_i) = \alpha_j + \beta_j g(t_i) + \varepsilon_{ij}, \quad (1)$$

$$\varepsilon_{ij} = x_{ij}(t_i) - \alpha_j - \beta_j g(t_i). \quad (2)$$

The ε_{ij} refers to the residual variation and $g(t) \in \{log(t), \sqrt{t}, t, t^2, exp(t)\}$ because the time effect is not necessarily linear. Additionally, residuals ε_{ij} should distribute normally around zero for each variable j as illustrate Fig. 2. In previous experiments [1], we assessed the *reliability* of cluster results for the different adjustments. We found that cluster results were most stable for a logartihmic age effect in OA and a square root disease duration in PD.

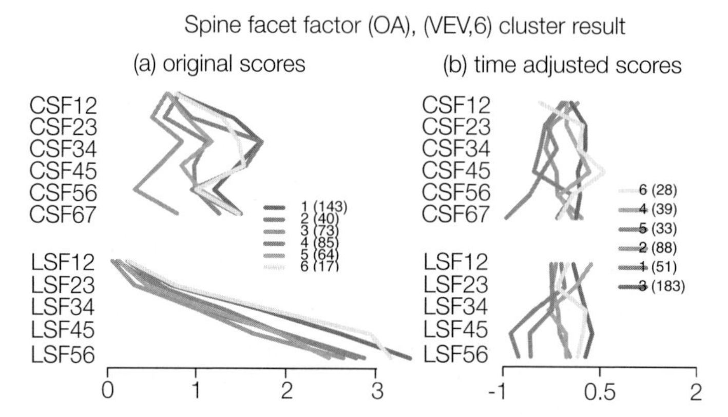

Fig. 1. For OA, we report result extracts of two cluster analyses on the spine facets factor with a VEV model having six mixtures. In (a), the modeling is on the original ROA scores, i.e. between $[0, 4]$ and in (b), on the time adjusted scores, i.e. z-scores. This illustrates how the time can influence the cluster result when its dimension is not removed in the data. Additionally, we also remark the variable ordering which mimicks the disposition of the cervical and lumbar vertebrae, from top to bottom.

The reliability and validity of a cluster result. Targeting our analysis to medical research, hierarchical clustering or k-means [6] do not match our expectation in terms of *reliability* and *validity*. First, in terms of *reliability*, cluster results should be consistent when we repeat the analysis. However, as we repeat twice k-means for instance, solutions may differ because of the different starting values. Second, both algorithms depend on distance measures which do not mimic the data distribution of the clusters. To be valid, clusters should be understandable, which is not evident with distance-based defined clusters, and especially non-euclidean distances. They should also be distinguishable, which becomes an issue as the modeling proceeds in high dimensions because distance-based algorithms are sensitive to the curse of dimensionality [7]. Another aspect that hampers especially hierarchical clustering concerns the numerous parameters that can only be set subjectively [8].

To be fair, *reliability* issues also exist for clustering by mixture of Gaussians because it relies on the EM-algorithm (Expectation Maximization) which iteratively optimizes the model likelihood. As a matter of fact, different starting values for EM may lead to different cluster results. Therefore, an important issue concerns the sensibility to different starting values of the mixture modelling. Fraley and Raftery systematically initiate their EM-algorithm by a model based hierarchical clustering [9]. This choice ensures the reproducibility of the cluster results because two repeats of the mixture modelling will initiate EM equally. Regarding the *validity* issue, mixture modelling not only reports the estimated center of each mixture but also estimates its covariance structure. Therefore, it also yields certainty and uncertainty estimates of the cluster membership.

In our experiments, we use the model based clustering framework developed by Fraley and Raftery [9,10,11,12]. As shown in [13], the framework relies on the

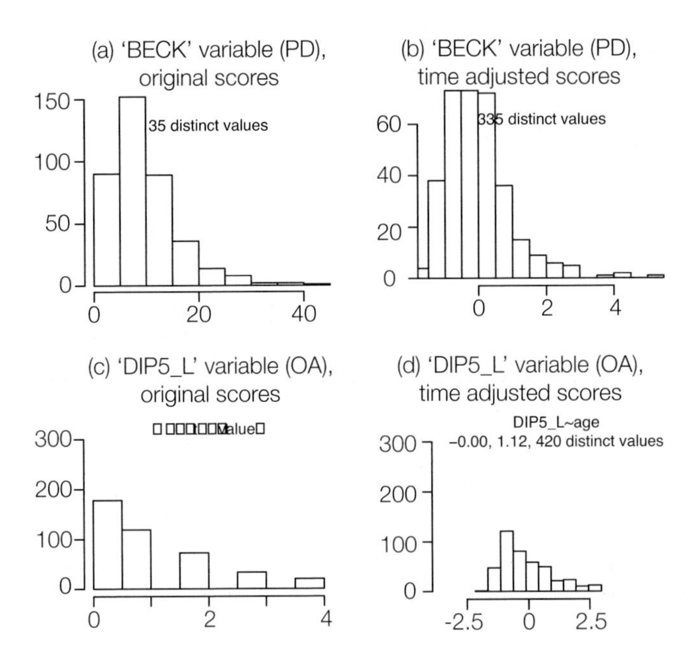

Fig. 2. These four figures illustrate the original and the time-adjusted data distributions of variables DIP5_L and beck, which respectively pertain to OA and PD analyses. Such histograms are obtained when plotting a data set class (`cdata`) of the R SubtypeDiscovery package. To be valid, the residuals ε_{ij} of the regression on the time should distribute normally around zero for each variable j.

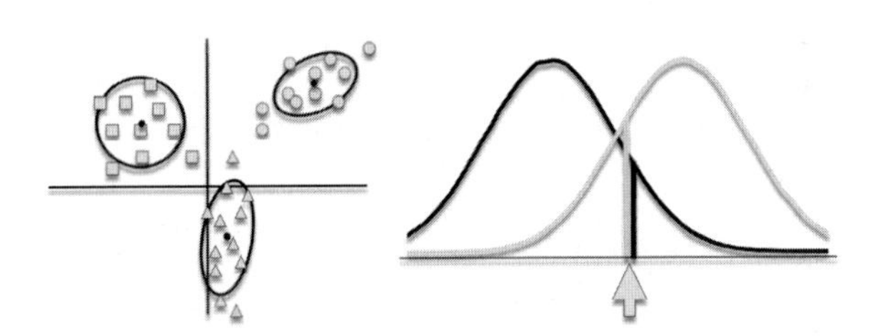

Fig. 3. On the left, we illustrate a simple modelling with three mixtures in two dimensions which are defined by their center μ_k and their geometry Σ_k, $k = 1, 2, 3$. On the right, we illustrate two mixtures on a single dimension. The gray is most likely and determines the cluster membership. The black is less likely and informs on the clustering uncertainty.

concept of reparameterization of the covariance matrix which enables to select and adapt the level of complexity of the covariance by controlling its geometry as Fig. 3 illustrate on an elementary example.

For instance, a particular model may conjecture an equal data distribution for all mixtures, while another may simply neglect the estimation of the covariates in the model. Hence, the analysis offers a range of models that involve varying number of parameters to estimate.

Clustering by mixture of Gaussians. We describe clustering by mixture modelling, which is also illustrated in Fig. 3. We start by defining the likelihood function of a mixture of Gaussians by

$$\mathcal{L}_{MIX}(\theta, \tau|\mathbf{x}) = \prod_{i=1}^{N} \sum_{k=1}^{G} \tau_k \phi_k(\mathbf{x}_i|\mu_k, \Sigma_k), \quad (3)$$

where $\mathbf{x}_i$ represents the ith of N observations, G is the number of components and τ_k the probability that an observation belongs to the kth component so that $\tau_k \geq 0$ and $\Sigma_{k=1}^{G} \tau_k = 1$. Then, the likelihood of an observation $\mathbf{x}_i$ to belong to the kth component takes the form

$$\phi_k(\mathbf{x}_i|\mu_k, \Sigma_k) = \frac{\exp\{-\frac{1}{2}(\mathbf{x}_i - \mu_k)^T \Sigma_k^{-1}(\mathbf{x}_i - \mu_k)\}}{\sqrt{det(2\pi\Sigma_k)}}. \quad (4)$$

The reparameterization proceeds by eigenvalue decomposition of $\Sigma_k = D_k \Lambda_k D_k^T$. It depends on the eigenvector matrix D_k which determines the orientation of the principal components, and on the diagonal matrix Λ_k of the eigenvalues. Further, the matrix Λ_k is rewritten $\Lambda_k = \lambda_k A_k$ with A_k the geometrical shape and λ_k the largest eigenvalue. In practice, Fraley and Raftery control Σ_k's structure using the three parameters λ_k, A_k and D_k with values in I, E, V, standing respectively for identical, equal and variable. In words, λ_k refers to the relative size or the *scale* of the kth mixture which may be equal for all mixtures (E) or vary (V). While A_k specifies the *geometrical shape* which may limit the mixtures to spherical shapes (I), to equally elongated shapes for all mixtures (E), or to varying ones (V). D_k characterizes the principal orientations of the covariance which may simply coordinate along the axes (I) and therefore neglect estimation of the covariates. But when considering covariates, we may select an equal orientation for all mixtures (E) or a different one (V).

For a given number of mixtures and a covariance model, the EM-algorithm is used to estimate the model parameters. It alternates iteratively between Expectation to estimate for each observation its cluster membership likelihood, and Maximization to optimize the model parameters that maximize the likelihood. Then the iterative process stops as likelihood improvements become very small. Moreover, an important concern with EM relates to the starting point of the algorithm. Fraley and Raftery propose to initialize EM with a model based hierarchical clustering, though another common strategy consists to start EM from several random points and to observe the sensibility of the cluster results to these changes. In our analyses we repeat model estimation given different starting points and then, we use the starting point that leads to the most likely model.

4 Methods to Select, Characterize, Compare and Evaluate Cluster Results

As we cluster data by models that use different spatial-shapes, we need a method that, first, helps select the most likely cluster results. Second, we need to report their essential characteristics to compare them. Further, as we analyse data from medical research, we also consider the clinical relevance of the clusters as an important feature. In this section we discus these different aspects.

BIC analysis. The larger the number of parameters, the more likely it is that our model may overfit the data which restricts its generality and comprehensiveness. To select the most likely model, Kass and Raftery [14] prefer the Bayesian Information Criterion (BIC) to the Akaike Information Criterion (AIC) because it approximates the Bayes Factor; we use the BIC in our analyses, $BIC = -2\log\mathcal{L}_{MIX} + \log(N \times \sharp params)$. We further approach computationally by repeating the data modeling, the problem of selecting a number of clusters and a type of model. Thus, our BIC score analysis reports in first place a BIC table aggregating the best scores given all repeats, several rankings on: the models, the number of clusters and the starting values and last, tables reporting regular statistics on the BIC score like the *mean*, standard deviation, *median*, 2.5 and 97.5% quantiles.

Characterizing clusters using visual-aids. To check the effect of changing experimental settings of cluster model (complexity / number of clusters) in OA and PD analysis having 45 and 17 variables, we need efficient visualization tools to see the prominent characteristics of the cluster results under different viewpoints. So, influenced by Tukey [15] and Tufte [16,17] for scientific data visualization and by Brewer's suggestions for color selection in geography [18], we selected three visual-aids, heatmaps [19], parallel coordinates [20] and dendrograms [8].

Micro array analysis commonly uses heatmaps to display and cluster data. However, by depending on hierarchical clustering, heatmaps require to set many parameters rather subjectively. As it works on distance measures, the variables should be scale-free and comparable, which may be awkward with non scale-homogeneous variables. On top of that, calculating distances on correlated variables mostly reveals patterns on the principal dimensions. We can illustrate this on the OA data by considering a large joint factor that consists of hips and knees and another one that consists of the spine joints. Simply because there are only four variables in the first factor and about 20 in the second, the spine weigh more than the large joints in the distance. So, simple distances lack sensitivity to manifest changes in the small principal dimensions. We propose instead to use the heatmaps to illustrate only the cluster centers, see Fig. 6.

In fact, as hip left and right pertain to the hips in OA or, in PD, as both urinary and cardiovascular problems reflect autonomic symptoms, we can often group variables into main factors. Reasonably, we may expect variables to correlate in each factor. Standard heat maps do not exploit the grouping of the variables which impairs the potential comprehesion of the cluster results.

Table 1. For each sum score l, we consider a middle value δ_l such as the data set *mean* or *median*. For cells A and B, we use it to count how many observations i in the cluster S_k have a sum score above and below its value. For cells C and D, we proceed to a similar count but on the rest of the observations $i \in \{S - S_k\}$.

	$x_i < \delta_l$	$x_i \geq \delta_l$
$i \in S_k$	A	B
$i \in \{S - S_k\}$	C	D

In parallel coordinates, we can use this information to arrange and order variables accordingly, e.g. see Fig. 1. We use a different color for each cluster and we characterize its center (μ_k) by connected lines between the variable-axis as is illustrated for OA in Fig. 1. In particular, we remark that a disposition is used of the cervical and lumbar spinal joints which mimicks the natural ordering of these joints from top to bottom. Also note that the differences between the cluster results in the left and in the right illustrate particularly well the effect of adjusting for a time effect in OA. It calls attention to how much the time influences the modelling when we do not adjust for it. Finally, besides the center of each cluster, we could report additional statistics such as the 2.5% and 97.5% quantiles or the median.

In spite of the many disadvantages of hierarchical clustering, yet, we find it a useful complement to the color images and parallel coordinates because we like to report dendrograms that illustrate the similarity between the center profiles and between the variables. While a dendrogram on the cluster centers may help order the clusters by pattern similarity, dendrogram on the variables may provide a rudimentary factor analysis. In fact, both dendrograms provide additional comprehension for the cluster result.

Characterizing and comparing cluster results by table-charts. In complement to visual-aids, we use table-charts that report the main cluster characteristics using the *log of the odds* and that allow cross-comparison between cluster results using regular association tables. From these tables, the χ^2-statistic is calculated to draw a single association measure in terms of the *Cramer's V* nominal association coefficient. Then, as a way to assess the *reproducibility* of cluster results, we also report the generalization estimates of common machine learning algorithms which we train on the clustered data.

So, to identify the cluster characteristics, we rely on the *log of the odds* that we compute on factors summing variables of a main group, e.g. spine for OA, autonomic disorders for PD, or atom and bond counts in chemoinformatics. Thus for OA, we group variables by main joint site such as spine facets, spine lumbars, hips, knees, distal and proximal interphalengeal joints, for PD, by impairment domain such as cognitive, motricity and autonomic disorders and by class of molecular descriptors in chemoinformatics. Then, on these main factors, we compute the *odd* of a cluster data distribution as compared to the one of the data set. In practice, people might refer to the *log of the odds* as the cross-product because we calculate it from tables similar to Table 1.

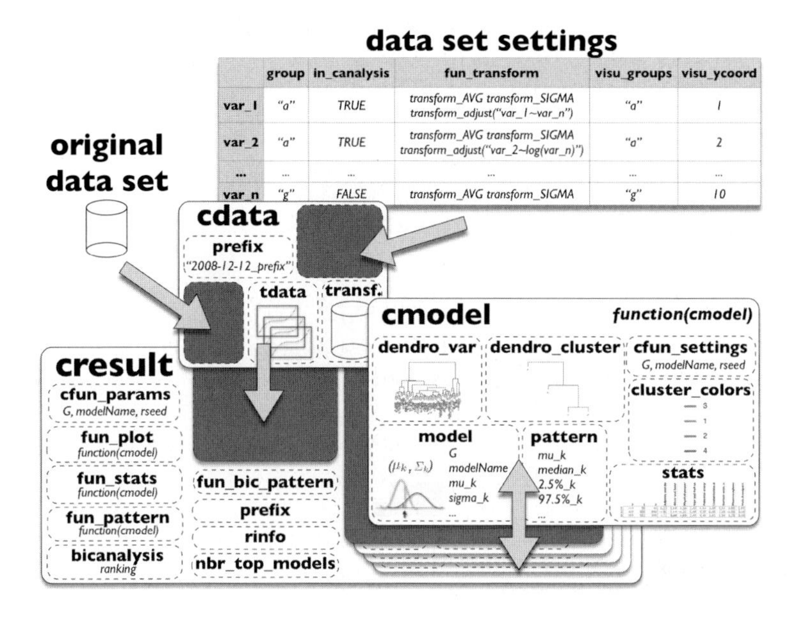

Fig. 4. We illustrate the main three classes of our package: the data `cdata`, the cluster model `cmodel` and the set of cluster results `cresult`. In particular, the data set preparation (`cdata`) uses `set_cdata()` which takes as input the raw data and the `settings` that describe the data transformation.

And as a result, we express the log of the odds of a cluster k on a factor l as

$$logodds_{kl} = \log \frac{A \times D}{B \times C}. \tag{5}$$

Concerning association tables, they are useful to illustrate the joint distribution of two variables. Here, we use them to compare cluster membership between two cluster results. When the table exhibits many empty cells, then the cluster results associate particularly. However, an even joint distribution on all cells would illustrate two cluster results which relate little. Next, as a single number summary of these association tables, we report the *Cramer's V* symmetric coefficient of nominal association which is defined by

$$V = \sqrt{\frac{\chi^2}{n \times m}}, \tag{6}$$

where n is the sample size and $m = min(rows, columns) - 1$. Therefore, the *Cramer's V* derives from χ^2 statistics and it takes values in $[0, 1]$. The outcome, one stands for completely correlated variables and zero for stochastically independent ones. The more unequal the marginals, the more V will be less than one. Finally, *Cramer's V* can be regarded as a percentage of the maximum possible variation

```
library(SubtypeDiscovery)
data(wada2008)
data(wada2008_settings)

# CDATA
cdata1  <- set_cdata(data=wada2008
    , prefix="WADA2008_Sample_Analysis"
    , settings=wada2008_settings)
cdata2 <- get_cdata_princomp(cdata1)
# CRESULT
x <- set_cresult(cdata=cdata2, nbr_top_models=5, cfun=fun_mbc_em,
   fun_plot=list(plot_parcoord=get_plot_fun(type="plot_parcoord"),
      plot_legend=get_plot_fun(type="plot_legend"),
      plot_image=get_plot_fun(type="plot_image"),
      plot_dendro_cluster=get_plot_fun(type="plot_dendro_cluster")),
   fun_pattern=list(mean=patternMean),
   fun_stats=list(oddratios=get_fun_stats(fun_name="oddratios",
      fun_midthreshold=mean), auuc=get_fun_stats(fun_name="auuc")),
   cfun_settings=list(modelName=c("EII","VII","EEI","VEI",
      "EVI","VVI"), G=3:6, rseed=6013:6023))

# MODELLING, BIC ANALYSIS, PLOT, PRINT, WRITE MODELS
x <- analysis(x)
```

Fig. 5. Sample analysis on the package public chemoinformatics data: `wada2008`

between two variables. In Table 2, we illustrate our table-charts which embeds in the top left an association table and the *Cramer's V* coefficient in its lowest row.

We perform unsupervised cluster analyses, therefore, it is important to know whether the cluster result generalizes, e.g. in the case of medical research to the total patient population. Therefore, we assess the cluster result *learnability* using naive Bayes, linear Support Vector Machines or one nearest neighbor as a baseline. To evaluate these algorithms, we rely on the classifier accuracy estimated by repeating ten times on a training-test split with 70% of the observations in the training set and 30% in the test set. In particular, we discard the variability depending on the cluster membership probability by preserving the cluster proportions of the original sample in every training and test set. This stratified sampling is coherent with the practice in machine learning because we primarily aim to compare algorithms but, e.g. in medical research, we might prefer to include the variability inherent to the cluster proportions.

Evaluating the clinical relevance of clusters. Finally, when conducting a subtype discovery analysis, a key concern is the cluster evaluation. For that purpose, we implemented a simple mechanism to add study-specific evaluation procedures of the clusters. In OA for instance, as the study involves siblings pairs, we defined two statistical tests that assess the level of familial aggregation in each subtype and its significance. Our first test relies on a risk ratio which we refer to as the λ_{sibs}, whereas the second test makes use of a χ^2-test of goodness of fit. In chemoinformatics, we simply rely on a regular χ^2-test of independence between the human-affected molecule "class" and the cluster result.

Table 2. Given all repeats, we report tables with the best BIC scores, the starting values leading the most likely model, the ranking of the models given a number of clusters and vice versa and the cross comparison of cluster results (VVI, 6, 6022) and (VVI, 6, 6016). Then, on factor A/d, A/B, C.1, C.2, KHK, Q, Pha., Phys., numbers above 1 and below -1 illustrate high odd ratios especially characterizing a subtype, whereas the association table and the *Cramer's V* measure (65%) illustrate the level of association between the results.

	EII	**VII**	**EEI**	**VEI**	**EVI**	**VVI**
3	-172857.6	-137398.7	-173010.0	-120257.3	-133262.9	-109035.2
4	-173025.8	-131224.6	-173178.1	-114099.2	-129299.2	-104159.8
5	-173194.1	-127733.5	-173346.4	-109503.1	-126058.9	-99545.5
6	-173362.1	-124697.7	-173514.5	-105724.1	-122780.8	**-93887.8**

	EII	**VII**	**EEI**	**VEI**	**EVI**	**VVI**
3	6013	6013	6013	6022	6017	6014
4	6013	6013	6013	6023	6017	6017
5	6016	6019	6016	6018	6020	6017
6	6016	6022	6016	6016	6024	**6022**

	EII	**VII**	**EEI**	**VEI**	**EVI**	**VVI**
3	**1**	4	**1**	4	4	4
4	2	3	2	3	3	3
5	3	1.9	3	2	2	2
6	4	**1.1**	4	**1**	**1**	**1**

	3	**4**	**5**	**6**
EII	5	5	5	5
VII	3.7	3.8	3.9	4
EEI	6	6	6	6
EVI	3.3	3.3	3.1	3
VEI	1.8	2	2	2
VVI	**1.3**	**1**	**1**	**1**

	1	2	4	6	3	5	**A/d**	**A/B**	**C.1**	**C.2**	**KHK**	**Q**	**Pha.**	**Phy.**
2	824					227	- .4	- .8	.93	Inf	**-1.3**	**-2.6**	**-1.6**	**-1.4**
5	15	13	7	42	494	446	.8	**1.5**	**-1.5**	.5	**1.7**	0.5	**1.5**	**1.4**
1		193				243	- .3	- .9	.8	Inf	- .9	**-3.3**	- .8	.0
3	177					55	**-3.8**	-Inf	Inf	- .5	-Inf	-Inf	-Inf	-Inf
4		5	156	60	27		.9	**1.6**	**-1.3**	**-2.3**	**1.5**	**2.1**	**2.0**	**2.1**
6				53			-Inf	-Inf	Inf	-Inf	-Inf	Inf	-Inf	-Inf
A/d	- .9	- .6	.4	**1.4**	- .0	.6								
A/B	**-1.5**	- .6	**1.2**	**1.1**	**1.4**	.1								
C.1	**1.5**	.7	- .8	**-1.3**	**-1.2**	- .2								
C.2	**1.2**	Inf	- .7	-7.8	Inf	**2.7**								
KHK	**-1.9**	- .9	1.0	**1.4**	**1.5**	.2								
Q	**-3.7**	**-1.5**	.8	**5.5**	- .0	- .7								
Pha.	**-2.2**	- .6	**1.2**	**1.4**	**1.5**	.0								
Phys.	**-2.1**	**-1.1**	**1.8**	**1.1**	**1.4**	.5								
χ^2	0													
V	65%													

log of the odds

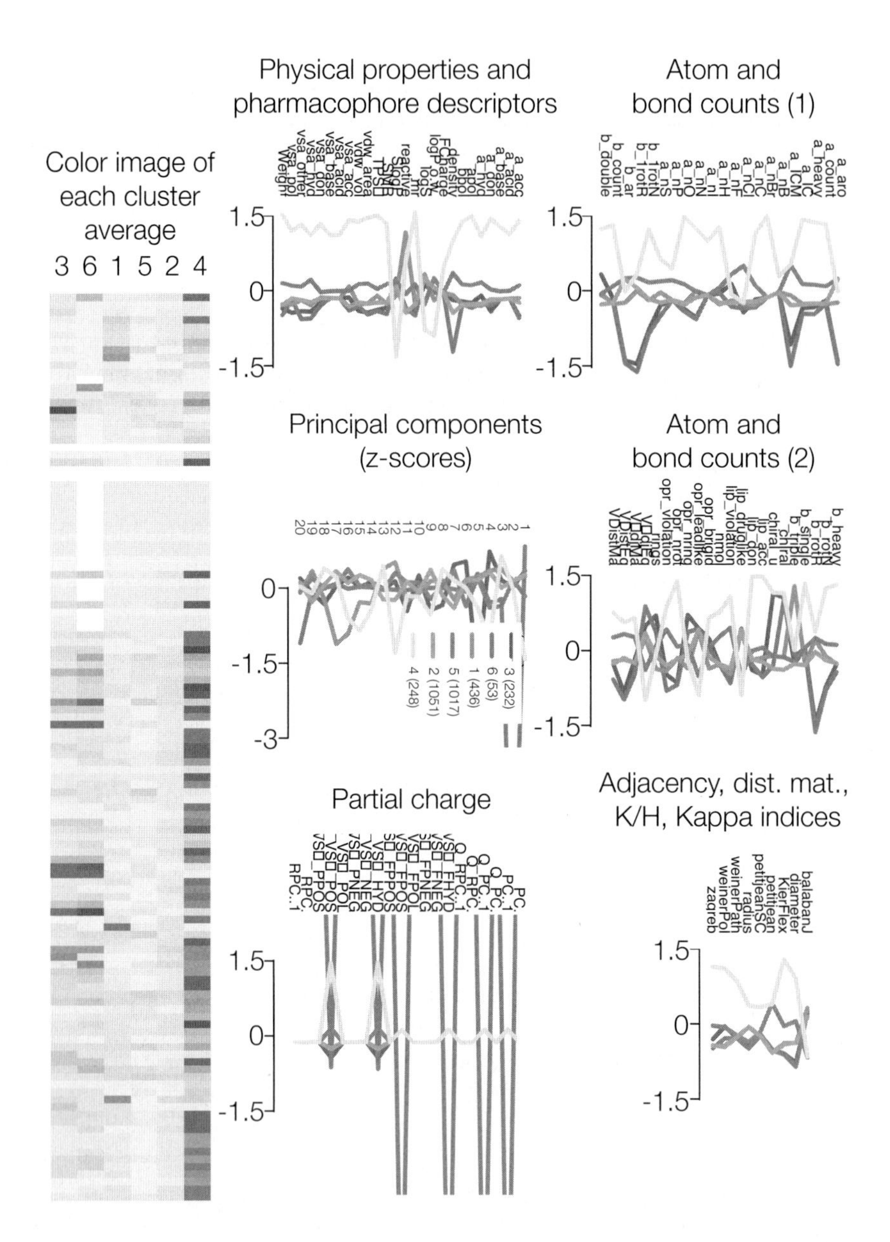

Fig. 6. This Figure exhibits a color image illustrating the six average pattern of (VVI, 6, 6022). It also characteristizes the different subtypes on all variables which we grouped by factor. The plot-scale refers to the z-scores with 95% of the values that should fit within $[-2, 2]$. In this Figure, the yellow subtype with (248) molecules displays an especially high profile on most descriptors. In the contrary, the blue (53) and red (232) subtypes show comparatively low profiles. These two subtypes differentiate on the Partial charge factor where we may account the blue zigzag pattern to the type of the variables which are scores.

For the λ_{sibs} risk ratio, we characterize each individual as proband or sibling depending on whether this individual was the first sibling involved in the study or not. This test quantifies the risk increases of the second sibling given the characteristics of the proband. For instance, a $\lambda_{sibs} = 1$ means that the risk does not increase and that the cluster membership of the proband does not influence the one of his sibling. On the other hand, if $\lambda_{sibs} = 2$, then the risk increases two-fold. Finally, a λ_{sibs} shows significant as its 95% confidence interval exceeds 1. In the following, we describe formally the λ_{sibs} and we derive its confidence interval analytically by the delta method. Defining two siblings as s_1 and s_2 with s_1 the proband, considering the probability of a sibling to belong to a group S_k as $P(s_i \in S_k)$ with $i \in \{1, 2\}$, or for short $P(s_i)$, then, the conditional probability that the second sibling is in S_k provided that the first sibling is also in S_k is referred to as $P(s_2|s_1)$. The λ_{sibs} expresses as

$$\lambda_{sibs}(S_k) = \frac{P(s_2|s_1)}{P(s_2)} = \frac{P(s_1, s_2)}{P(s_1)P(s_2)} = \frac{P(s_1, s_2)}{P(s)^2}. \quad (7)$$

Further, as we consider the population infinite with $P(s_1) = P(s_2) = P(s)$, we derive the confidence interval by the delta method on $\lambda_{sibs} = \hat{\alpha}/\hat{\beta}$ with $\hat{\alpha} = P(s_1, s_2)$, $\hat{\beta} = P(s)$ and the hat denoting quantities estimated from the data. The variances and covariance of $\hat{\alpha}, \hat{\beta}$ have the form $\sigma_\alpha^2 = \hat{\alpha}(1-\hat{\alpha})/n_i$, with n_i the sibship size, $\sigma_\beta^2 = \hat{\beta}(1-\hat{\beta})/N$, with N the number of observations and $cov(\hat{\alpha}, \hat{\beta}) = \hat{\alpha}(1-\hat{\beta})/N$. To obtain the final form of the variance of λ_{sibs}, we take the first order Taylor approximation of λ_{sibs}, move its zeroth derivative to the left and raise both members to the square so that

$$\sigma_\lambda^2 = \frac{1}{\hat{\beta}^4}\left(\sigma_\alpha^2 - 4cov(\hat{\alpha}, \hat{\beta})\hat{\beta}\lambda + 4\sigma_\beta^2\lambda\right). \quad (8)$$

We also implemented a simple χ^2 test of goodness of fit to assess for familial aggregation. This test counts the pairs of siblings in each group and compares them to the ones expected when cluster membership would be random. Defining N as the number of individuals, S being a random draw of size $|S|$, then, the probability of an individual i to belong to S is $P(i \in S) = |S|/N$. Considering a second individual j independent of i, the joint probability that both i and j belong to S expresses as $P(i, j \in S) = P(i \in S)P(j \in S) = (|S|/N)^2$. Denoting by $E(i, j \in S)$ the expected number of sibling pairs under random cluster membership which relies on $N/2$ (the total number of pairs), then $E(i, j \in S) = P(i, j \in S)^2 N/2$. Finally, we report the Grand Total of the χ^2 test as

$$GrandTotal = \sum_{k=1}^{G} \frac{(O(i, j \in S_k) - E(i, j \in S_k))^2}{E(i, j \in S_k)} = \sum_{k=1}^{G} \chi_k^2, \quad (9)$$

where k indices over the different clusters and χ_k^2 refers to the separate χ^2 statistics of each cluster. The number of degrees of freedom is $df = G - 1$, G the number of clusters.

5 The Package, Its Implementation and a Sample Analysis

Package design. The implementation articulates around three main classes: the data set `cdata`, the cluster model `cmodel` and the set of cluster results `cresult`. Their entity-relationship cardinalities is as follows: a `cresult` describes a SubtypeDiscovery analysis, it holds a data set `cdata` and it holds several cluster models `cmodel`. In Fig. 4, we illustrate `cdata` requiring an input data set and a description of how it should be interpreted into `settings`. We also describe the relation between `cdata`, `cmodel` and `cresult`.

Plotting a `cdata` class gives for each variable its boxplot, histogram and information like, e.g. its empirical mean or standard deviation. Regards `cresult`, plotting can be restricted to a queried `cmodel` or, by default, it plots all of them. We illustrate such plot for the top-ranking model (VVI, 6, 6022) in Fig. 6. Finally, a print on a `cresult` generates a report that includes the different table charts from the BIC analysis and those focusing on the top-ranking cluster results characterististics, two-by-two comparison, and evaluation. We report some of the most important table-charts in Table 2.

6 Concluding Remarks

We developed a methodology that facilitates and enhances the search for more homogeneous subtypes with application to medical research and chemoinformatics. This methodology involves techniques to prepare data, a computational approach repeating data modelling to select for a number of clusters or a particular model, as well as other methods to characterize, compare and evaluate the most likely models. Therefore, our methodology does not solely cluster data but it also produces a complete set of results to conduct a subtype discovery analysis: from data preparation to cluster evaluation. In this context, to enable *reproducibility* of our analyses, we release and documented this methodology as the R SubtypeDiscovery package. We presented its implementation in this paper and we illustrated its application with examples from OA and PD research as well as chemoinformatics.

Acknowledgements. This work has been supported by the Netherlands Bioinformatics Centre (NBIC) through its research program BioRange, the Michael J Fox Foundation, PD-subtypes program. The Leiden University Medical Centre, the Dutch Arthritis Association and Pfizer Inc. and Groton, CT, USA support the GARP study (OA).

References

1. Colas, F., Meulenbelt, I., Houwing-Duistermaat, J., van Rooden, S., Visser, M., Marinus, H., van Hilten, B., Slagboom, P.E., Kok, J.N.: Stability of clusters for different time adjustments in complex disease research. In: 30th Annual International IEEE EMBS Conference (EMBC 2008), Vancouver, British Columbia, Canada (August 2008)

2. Meulenbelt, I.: Genetic predisposing factors of osteoarthritis. PhD thesis, Universiteit van Leiden (1997)
3. Riyazi, N.: Familial osteoarthritis, risk factors and determinants of outcome. PhD thesis, Universiteit van Leiden (2006)
4. Neurology Department: SCales for Outcomes in PArkinson's Disease-PROfiling PARKinson's Disease. Leiden University Medical Center, Leiden, The Netherlands
5. Cannon, E.O., Nigsch, F., Mitchell, J.B.O.: A novel hybrid ultrafast shape descriptor method for use in virtual screening. Chemistry Central Journal 2 (2008)
6. Hastie, T., Tibshirani, R., Friedman, J.: The Elements of Statistical Learning, Data Mining, Inference, and Prediction. Springer Series in Statistics. Springer, Heidelberg (2001)
7. Beyer, K., Goldstein, J., Ramakrishnan, R., Shaft, U.: When is "nearest neighbor" meaningful? In: Beeri, C., Bruneman, P. (eds.) ICDT 1999. LNCS, vol. 1540, pp. 217–235. Springer, Heidelberg (1998)
8. Sneath, P.H.A., Sokal, R.R.: Numerical Taxonomy, The Principles and Practice of Numerical Classification. Books in Biology. W. H. Freeman and Company, New York (1973)
9. Fraley, C., Raftery, A.E.: MCLUST: Software for model-based cluster analysis. Journal of Classification 16, 297–306 (1999)
10. Fraley, C., Raftery, A.E.: Model-based clustering, discriminant analysis and density estimation. Journal of the American Statistical Association 97, 611–631 (2002)
11. Fraley, C., Raftery, A.E.: Enhanced software for model-based clustering, density estimation, and discriminant analysis: MCLUST. Journal of Classification 20, 263–286 (2003)
12. Fraley, C., Raftery, A.E.: MCLUST version 3 for R: Normal mixture modeling and model-based clustering. Technical Report 504, University of Washington, Department of Statistics (September 2006)
13. Banfield, J.D., Raftery, A.E.: Model-based Gaussian and non-Gaussian clustering. Biometrics 49, 803–821 (1993)
14. Kass, R.E., Raftery, A.E.: Bayes factors. Journal of the American Statistical Association 90(430) (1995)
15. Tukey, J.W.: Exploratory Data Analysis. Addison-Wesley, Reading (1977)
16. Tufte, E.R.: The Visual Display of Quantitative Information. Graphics Press, Cheshire (1983)
17. Tufte, E.R.: Envisioning Information. Graphics Press, Cheshire (1990)
18. Brewer, C.A.: 7. In: Color Use Guidelines for Mapping and Visualization, pp. 123–147. Elsevier Science, Tarrytown (1994)
19. Eisen, M.B., Spellman, P.T., Brown, P.O., Botstein, D.: Cluster analysis and display of genome-wide expression patterns. Proceedings of National Academy of Science USA 95, 11863–14868 (1998)
20. Inselberg, A.: The plane with parallel coordinates. The Visual Computer 1(2), 69–91 (1985)
21. R Development Core Team: R: A Language and Environment for Statistical Computing. R Foundation for Statistical Computing, Vienna, Austria (2008) ISBN 3-900051-07-0

Requirements for Ontology Based Design Project Assessment

Axel Hahn[1], Stephan große Austing[1], Stefan Häusler[2], and Matthias Reinelt[1]

[1] University of Oldenburg
26111 Oldenburg, Germany
{hahn,austing,reinelt}@wi-ol.de
[2] OFFIS – Institute for Information Technology
26121 Oldenburg, Germany
haeusler@offis.de

Abstract. Ontologies are formal knowledge representation. Looking at ontologies in more detail can offer concealed details on the ontology or the conceptualized domain. This requires technologies for ontology analysis. By analysing the use case of R&D management this paper identifies typical metrics on ontologies and evaluates metric calculation mechanisms.

Keywords: Ontology Analysis, Business Metrics.

1 Introduction

"An ontology is a [...] conceptualization of a domain" This is the usual definition from Gruber referenced in academic publications [1]. While an ontology represents the domain, analysing the ontology helps to analyse the domain itself. This is the main hypothesis e.g. in conceptual metrics [2], ontology based business intelligence [3], knowledge assessment and last but not least the authors work on R&D management. This requires suitable tools for ontology analysis e.g. by metrics.

To confirm the hypothesis and to contribute to the day by day challenge of R&D project management in industry, the use case of R&D output measurement is used in this paper to derive requirements on analysing ontologies and their contained domain knowledge. R&D projects are lacking conclusive methods to measure output to evaluate progress and productivity [4]. Ontology can be used to describe the output of R&D projects independent from data models used by the design tools to store their results and from the different engineering disciplines.

This paper starts with examples of ontology based analysis followed by the use case product design project performance assessment.

By studying this use case, technical requirements for ontology analysis are identified followed by an evaluation of existing approaches for ontology or graph analysis regarding these requirements. This paper closes with a summary.

2 Using Ontologies for Domain Assessment

Ontologies conceptualize a domain of interest [1]. Most Ontology languages like OWL implement descriptive logics like *SHIQ* [5]. A formal representation of domain

T. Margaria and B. Steffen (Eds.): ISoLA 2008, CCIS 17, pp. 684–692, 2008.

knowledge allows answering questions using the knowledge base the ontology provides. By assuming the formal representation covers all relevant aspects of the domain of interest, an analysis of the ontology can help to understand the domain itself.

In literature numerous examples are found to use conceptual analysis with and without formal ontologies. This is done by numerical analysis and/or reasoning.

One example not using formal ontologies but modelling technologies is conceptual software metrics, [2]. But metrics like counting the lines of code proved weak soon [6]. Measuring the amount of "conceptual" artefacts showed more realistic in evaluation of the software system regarding complexity or in estimating the development effort. This evaluated and counted artefacts can be use cases or requirements in the early design phases, functions (function point analysis) or model entities in object oriented design [7].

These methods analyse models that represent the software system under development. Ontologies can be used to analyse the suitability and expressiveness of the modelling techniques. The work of Fettke and Loos describes the modelling technology and the area of interest (e.g. process models for enterprise modelling) with BWW ontologies [8] and count the concepts and mismatch of both domains [9]. Opdahl and Henderson-Sellers apply the same approach on UML models [10]. Typical metrics are the comparison of the ontology which describes the concepts of the subject of interest and the ontology which covers the concepts of the modelling technology by counting of similar concepts versus different concepts to conclude about the similarity.

While the mentioned examples cover the analysis of models and their capabilities, ontologies can be used to analyse the domain of interest directly, too. In [3] numerous applications in business systems analysis are described. They use Bunge-Wand-Weber (BWW) ontologies to describe business systems as proposed by Wand and Weber in [11]. The used metrics include simple counting of concepts, properties or statements or simple further processing (like (number of BWW – events) divided by (BWW states) in [12]).

Another application of the usage of metrics on ontologies is quality assessment of the ontologies themselves. Gomez-Peres and Locano-Tello do an analysis of ontologies to measure the suitability of an ontology [13]. These researchers adopt the idea of weighted decisions trees (Analytic Hierarchy Processes) [14]. So they use a more complex analysis that uses weighted criteria while counting ontology entities for calculation of metrics.

While there is no general or formal prove on the conclusiveness of metrics on ontologies the examples show that this approach is followed in a number of domains to analyse complex and non formalized systems to detect new knowledge. None of the cited publications stress the required methods and tools to perform the ontological analysis technically.

As introduced in the next chapter, the approach of ontology based investigation can be applied on R&D projects e.g. in product design.

3 Analysis of Engineering Projects

The development of modern products is a challenging task that requires the cooperation of domain experts from programmer to project manager. Each of these groups contributes with their specific expertise to the project by externalizing their knowledge and thus creating an integrated product model. This model consists of partial models from different domains on different levels of abstraction. Ontologies enable us to describe these models in a common language. Furthermore relations between partial models can be stated without loss of semantics. The knowledge intensive process of product development can become tangible on the basis of ontologies and thus measurable. With a holistic description of product development at hand, the question is for metrics that will provide a knowledge gain regarding the business goals.

In our use case the GQM method by Basili et al. [15] (see figure 1 below) is used to substantiate the business goal of product development performance improvement into related questions. Then metrics are defined that give quantified answers to these question so that progress towards the business goal becomes measurable. These metrics depend on the domain and the company or even the department.

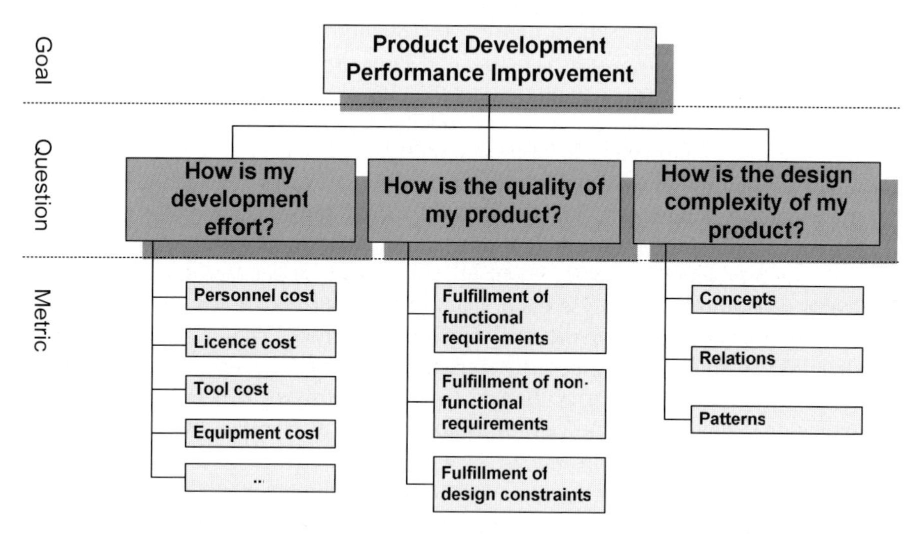

Fig. 1. GQM Tree for "Product Development Performance Improvement"

To achieve the business goal of product development performance improvement, it is needed to measure the actual performance and find weak parts of the process where optimization is needed. This procedure of process optimization is based on the Capability Maturity Model Integration (CMMI) [16] where companies with CMMI Level 4 have quantitative control of their processes and companies with CMMI Level 5 use the results to optimize their process.

Productivity and performance respectively is defined as the ratio between effort and result. That is why there are three main questions that must be considered in product development performance measurement shown in figure 1:

What Is My Development Effort?

The effort put into a product development is the accumulation of all resources that were spent on the project. These resources like personnel, licences, tools and equipment have to be evaluated in monetary terms and then summed up into a single cost value. The project management model provides the basis for these calculations.

How Is the Design Complexity of My Product?

A simple approach to quantify the product is to measure product model properties like lines of code. As mentioned before metrics on a conceptual level e.g. number of program classes or geometric features proved more valuable for this task. However these metrics are often influenced by the individual modelling preferences of the developer. In some cases a large product model may even be an indicator for bad modelling. To overcome these issues we evaluate the knowledge that is externalized in the product models instead. Ontologies give us a formal description of the concepts and relations in the specific domain and therefore a model for automatic analysis.

Similar to conceptual metrics concepts provides the basis for complexity evaluation. An artefact can belong to an arbitrary number of concepts with different weightings and the basic complexity is given as the sum of these weightings. Furthermore relations can add to an artefact complexity. In some cases the amount of relations like dependency and inheritance can be the most important complexity factor in development. In [17] we presented an ontology-based framework which is able to capture these relations.

To estimate the knowledge necessary to create the artefacts we will have to take a second look at the relation graph. A larger model may be caused by the multiplication of sub-components that are placed into the model without or with little modifications. To evaluate the extent of reuse similar patterns in a product model graph have to be detected. The complexity of similar artefacts has to be lowered accordingly. On the other hand certain patterns like a cycle can add to the artefacts that are part of these patterns. An analysis must be able to detect these and increase the complexity value accordingly. Finally the complexity of the product must be calculated by aggregating the complexity values from the artefacts to the level of the product.

How Is the Quality of My Product?

One factor to quantify the output (the result) of one or more process steps is the quality of the product. A widely accepted definition of quality is the degree to which the product conforms to its requirements (see e.g. [18][19] or ISO 9000-2005).

In figure 1 we distinguish between three different requirement types that must be taken into account in product quality estimation.

Firstly, the design has to be functionally correct. Therefore, the fulfilment degree of each functional requirement based on the current verification status is an input factor for quality. The estimation of the current verification status is based on measurable metrics that must be defined for the specific domain. For that reason we just show the aggregated fulfilment degrees in figure 1. Secondly, the overall quality may suffer from failing physical design constraints as e.g. area, power or timing in integrated circuit development. Thus, physical constraints have to be considered in a quality evaluation as well, if the product under development is a physical one. Finally, non-functional quality requirements have to be evaluated. Some examples are e.g. maintainability or reusability. The assessment of these quality requirements is based on measurable product characteristics, as it is done in various works on software quality (see e.g. [20][21][22]).

In [23] the authors proposed a method for development accompanied quality monitoring that describes the quality assessment process and the modelling of requirements and quality characteristics using ontologies in detail. For the analysis of requirement fulfilment degrees there are two steps needed. Firstly, it is needed to calculate the actual value for the quality characteristic under consideration, secondly a requirements fulfilment degree must be assessed based on the actual value, a given target value and optional tolerance limits. Resulting requirement fulfilment degrees are aggregated to quality values.

4 Requirements

In this section six requirements for ontology based project assessment are stated:

1. Descriptions of **aggregation operators** and **conditional querying**. Operators like sum, average or count as well as the possibility to formulate conditions (as in SQL for relational databases) are required. This is needed to count instances of a certain concept with specific relations and properties. Furthermore, it is often needed to form the average or the sum of product properties on component level to the product level.
2. Description of **mathematical operators and functions**. Mathematical operators are needed to describe quality models and metrics to calculate an actual value. This value is used in an assessment function to calculate a requirement fulfilment degree.
3. Description of **non-continuous functions**. To assess a requirement fulfilment degree, a comparison of the calculated actual value, the target value and given tolerance limits is needed.

Fig. 2 demonstrates an example for a non-continuous assessment function. The fulfilment value is 1 if quality is over an upper limit and respectively 0 if the quality is below a lower limit. Between these limits the quality is defined by a linear function.

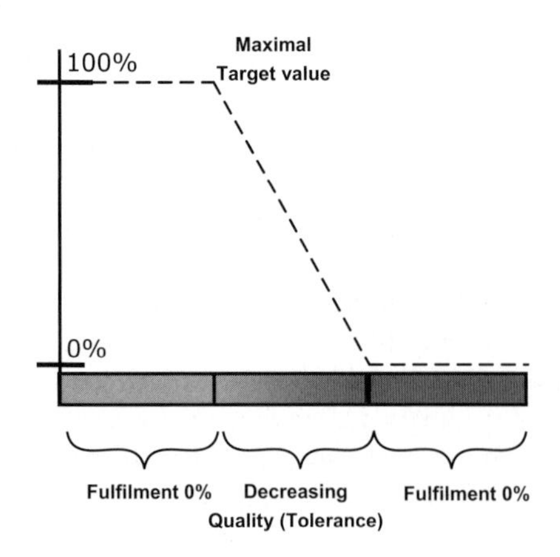

Fig. 2. Example for a linear requirement fulfillment assessment function

4. **(Fuzzy-) Classification** for non-functional requirement fulfilment. In some use cases qualify qualification of requirement fulfilment degrees is needed. Especially for (quality-) requirements a percentage value has less expressiveness. To give managers a quick overview about the development status and current quality of a product, it would be better to state that the maintainability of the product is 'average' or 'good' instead of 77%. Both crisp as well as fuzzy classification mechanisms are thinkable.
5. Detection of **graph patterns and similar patterns**. To fully analyse a graph known patterns must be recognized as they may play an important role like in the complexity analysis. Similar patterns can be evaluated by defining a distance metric on two artefacts depending on the comparison of their graph neighbourhoods. Not a requirement derived from the use case but important to other application is the detection of unknown pattern in sense of data-mining. Since this is a complex and wide field we will not further regard this kind of analysis.
6. To ensure that every user is able to perform such analyses some kind of "semantic graph Excel" is needed if a single query would become too complex. **Usability** is the keyword to allow flexible definition of functional calculations by non experts.

5 Ontology Analysis and Metrics

To see how the aforementioned requirements can be realized we took a look at current developments in this area.

Tools like Protégé [24] are able to retrieve information out of an ontology using a query language. The official W3C Recommendation for querying an ontology (=RDF graph) is SPARQL [25]. With SPARQL querying graph patterns along with their conjunctions and disjunctions is possible. It also supports extensible value testing and constraining queries by source RDF graph. The following figure shows the SPARQL query tab of Protégé.

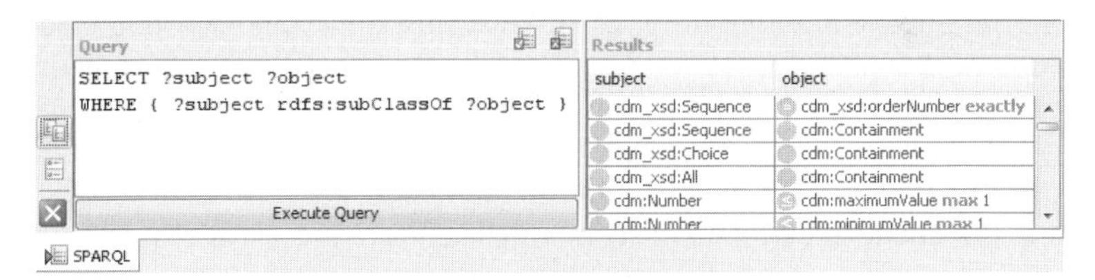

Fig. 3. Protégé 3.4 SPARQL query tab

Aggregate functions (COUNT, SUM, MIN, MAX, …), associated machinery (GROUP BY, HAVING, …) or an update language are currently not part of the recommendation. Nevertheless, current SPARQL processors like Jena's ARQ [26] go beyond SPARQL syntax and support these features (req. 1+2).

Thanks to ontology evolution and analysis a lot of graph metrics have been determined. While Protégé together with the visualization plug-in Jambalaya [27] only support basic metrics (see figure 3) tools like OntoQA [28] (measurement of ontology quality), AKTiveRank [29] (ontology ranking) or OntoCAT [30] (ontology evaluation for re-usage) offer a wider range of graph-based metrics. These can be used for the detection of graph and similar patterns (req. 5).

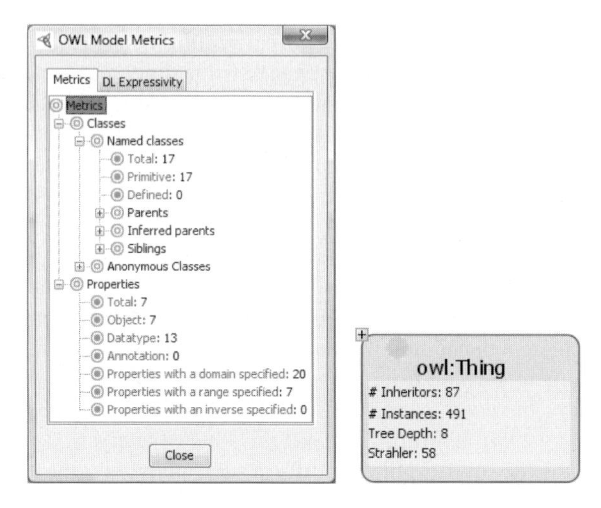

Fig. 4. Protégé 3.4 and Jambalaya metrics view

The main problem of all these query languages und metric tools is that they work isolated and only for their purposes. This means that e.g. it is neither possible to re-use results of a graph metric in a SPARQL query, nor combine several queries to an aggregated function. The lack of generality of the current solutions requires an enhanced user-friendly (req. 6) query engine to fulfil these requirements. Especially requirements 3 and 4 depend on this.

6 Summary

Ontologies formally represent a specific part of the world. Can we gain knowledge on the world from analysing an ontology? At least this is an approach followed by numerous researchers. A quantitative analysis of ontologies requires tools to both query and to calculate metrics on graphs. This paper collects a number of requirements for ontology based analysis of R&D projects. It turned out that at least popular tools and techniques like Protégé incl. plug-ins and SPARQL do not provide a proper basis to fulfil all requirements mentioned in section 4. Therefore the set of requirements form the basis for the development of an analyse engine for ontologies.

References

[1] Gruber, T.R.: Towards Principles for the Design of Ontologies Used for Knowledge Sharing. In: Guarino, N., Poli, R. (hrsg.) Formal Ontology in Conceptual Analysis and Knowledge Representation. Kluwer Academic Publishers, Deventer (1993), `http://citeseer.ist.psu.edu/gruber93toward.html`

[2] Genero, M., Piattini, M., Calero, C.: Metrics for Software Conceptual Models. Imperial College Press, London (2005)

[3] Green, P., Rosemann, M.: Business Systems Analysis with Ontologies. Idea Group Publishing, Hershey (2005)

[4] Ellis, L.: Evaluation of R&D Processes: Effectiveness Through Measurements. Artech House, Boston (1997)
[5] Horrocks, I., Patel-Schneider, P.F., van Harmelen, F.: From SHIQ and RDF to OWL: The making of a webontology language. Journal of Web Semanitcs 1 (2003)
[6] Anselmo, D., Ledgarf, H.: Measuring Productivity in the Software Industry. Communications of the ACM 46 (2003)
[7] Zuse, H.: Object-oriented Software Measures. In: Proceedings of the Third International Software Metrics Symposium. IEEE Computer Society Press, Los Alamitos (1996)
[8] Kayed, A., Colomb, R.M.: Using BWW model to evaluate building ontologies in CGs formalism. Information Systems 30, S.379–S.398 (2005)
[9] Fettke, P., Loos, P.: Ontological Evaluation of Scheer's Reference Model for Production Planning and Control Systems - Outline. Modellierung, S.317–S.318 (2004)
[10] Opdal, L., Henderson-Sellers, B.: Ontological Evaluation of the UML using the Bunge-Wand-Weber Model. Softw. Syst. Model, 43–47 (2006)
[11] Wand, Y., Weber, R.: Mario Bunges's ontology as a formal foundation for information system concepts. In: Studies on Mario Bunge's Treatise, Rodopi, Atlanta (1990)
[12] Fettke, P., Loos, P.: Ontological Analysis of Reference Models. In: Business Systems Analysis with Ontologies. Idea Group Publishing, Hershey (2005)
[13] Gomez-Perez, A., Lozano-Tello, A.: Applying the ONTOMETRIC Method to Measure the suitability of Ontologies. In: Bsuiness Systems Analysis with Ontologies. Idea Group Publishing, Hershey (2005)
[14] Saaty, T.: How to Make a Decision: The Analytic Hierarchy Process. European Journal of Operational Research 48 (1990)
[15] Basili, V.R., Caldiera, G., Rombach, H.D.: Goal Question Metric Approach. In: Encyclopedia of Software Engineering, pp. S.528–S.532. John Wiley & Sons, Chichester (1994)
[16] CMMI Product Team, CMMI for Development (2006)
[17] Hahn, A., große Austing, S., Strickmann, J.: Metrics - The Business Intelligence Side of PLM. In: Garetti u.a., M. (ed.) Product Lifecycle Management: Assessing the industrial relevance, pp. S.11–S.20. Inderscience Enterprises Limited (2007)
[18] Crosby, P.: Quality is Free. Reissue Edition, Signet, Stuttgart
[19] Gilmore, H.: Product Conformance Cost. Quality Progress, S. 16–S.19 (1974)
[20] Deutsch, M., Willis, R.: Software Quality Engineering. Prentice-Hall, Englewood Cliffs (1988)
[21] Nance, R.: Software Quality Indicators: An Holistic Approach to Measurement. In: Proc. 4th Annual Software Quality Workshop. Alexandria Bay, New York (1992)
[22] Boehm u.a., B.: Characteristics of Software Quality. a Characteristics of Software Quality. North-Holland, New York (1978)
[23] Häusler, S., Hahn, A., Poppen, F.: Real-Time Quality Estimation to Enable Process Evaluation in Integrated Circuit Development. In: Proceedings of the First International Engineering Management Conference in Europe. IEEE, Los Alamitos (2008)
[24] The Protégé Ontology Editor and Knowledge Acquisition System, `http://protege.stanford.edu/`
[25] SPARQL Query Language for RDF, `http://www.w3.org/TR/rdf-sparql-query/`
[26] ARQ - A SPARQL Processor for Jena, `http://jena.sourceforge.net/ARQ/`
[27] Jambalaya | The CHISEL Group, University of Victoria, `http://www.thechiselgroup.org/jambalaya`

[28] Tartir u.a., S.: OntoQA: Metric-Based Ontology Quality Analysis. In: Proceedings of IEEE Workshop on Knowledge Acquisition from Distributed, Autonomous, Semantically Heterogeneous Data and Knowledge Sources (2005)

[29] Alani, H., Brewster, C., Shadbolt, N.: Ranking Ontologies with AKTiveRank. In: Cruz, I., Decker, S., Allemang, D., Preist, C., Schwabe, D., Mika, P., Uschold, M., Aroyo, L.M. (eds.) ISWC 2006. LNCS, vol. 4273. Springer, Heidelberg (2006)

[30] Cross, V.V., Pal, A.: OntoCAT: An Ontology Consumer Analysis Tool and Its Use on Product Services Categorization Standards. In: Hepp, M., Tempich, C. (hrsg.) SEBIZ, E.P.B. Simperl (2006), http://CEUR-WS.org

[31] http://dblp.uni-trier.de/db/conf/semweb/sebiz2006.html#CrossP06

Organizing the World's Machine Learning Information

Joaquin Vanschoren[1], Hendrik Blockeel[1], Bernhard Pfahringer[2], and Geoff Holmes[2]

[1] Computer Science Dept., K.U. Leuven, Leuven, Belgium
[2] Computer Science Dept., University of Waikato, Hamilton, New Zealand

Abstract. All around the globe, thousands of learning experiments are being executed on a daily basis, only to be discarded after interpretation. Yet, the information contained in these experiments might have uses beyond their original intent and, if properly stored, could be of great use to future research. In this paper, we hope to stimulate the development of such learning experiment repositories by providing a bird's-eye view of how they can be created and used in practice, bringing together existing approaches and new ideas. We draw parallels between how experiments are being curated in other sciences, and consecutively discuss how both the empirical and theoretical details of learning experiments can be expressed, organized and made universally accessible. Finally, we discuss a range of possible services such a resource can offer, either used directly or integrated into data mining tools.

1 Introduction

Research in machine learning and exploratory data analysis are, to a large extent, guided by the collection and interpretation of performance evaluations of machine learning algorithms. As such, studies in this area comprise extensive experimental evaluations, analyzing the performance of many algorithms on many datasets, or many preprocessed versions of the same dataset. Unfortunately, the results of these experiments are usually interpreted with a single focus of interest, and their details are usually lost after publication or not publicly accessible.

Sharing this information with the world would greatly benefit research in these fields, fostering the reuse of previously obtained results for additional and possibly much broader investigation. To realize this in practice, we examine how to collect learning experiments in public repositories and, more importantly, how to organize all this information so that it is both easily accessible and useful. The former implies that the repository should be searchable, allowing easy retrieval of specific results. To achieve the latter, results should be kept in context, relating them to known theoretical properties of the included methods and datasets.

One could envisage many creative uses of such a resource. In machine learning research, pooling the results of many studies would significantly increase the amount of available experimental data, enabling much larger studies aimed at finding fundamental insights into the dynamics of learning processes and offering

T. Margaria and B. Steffen (Eds.): ISoLA 2008, CCIS 17, pp. 693–708, 2008.

well-founded answers to open questions. Furthermore, meta-level information about algorithms and datasets available in the repository puts those results in context, bringing all information together in one platform for meta-analysis. For instance, one could investigate how different data properties affect algorithm performance, making it easier to study how algorithms could be improved, or conversely, which preprocessing steps or parameter settings might be advisable on certain types of data. Furthermore, it offers a forum for negative results, creating a comprehensive map of learning approaches showing what has have been tried before and what was achieved. Finally, in algorithm development, empirical evaluations often use the same benchmark datasets. This means many experiments are needlessly repeated, while the cost of setting up and running them often limits the range of datasets, algorithms and parameter settings that can be explored. Reusing prior experiments would free up resources better used to test a wider range of conditions, thus yielding more generalizable results.

Conversely, in exploratory data analysis, practitioners faced with a specific problem will try different preprocessing and modeling techniques to gain a deeper understanding of the data at hand. In this case, even though each dataset is unique, a searchable repository of previous experiments could be used to gain from previous experience. For instance, one might check whether logistic regression is feasible on data with many attributes, and thus whether a feature selection step might be useful. Furthermore, one could search for similar datasets and the methods that were particularly successful on it, or automatically mine for meta-rules describing the usability of a particular method. Last but not least, the formalized description of experimental results and theoretical knowledge would allow integration into larger data mining assistance tools and web services.

The concept of experiment repositories has been introduced earlier [3,4]. In this paper, we aim to provide a bird's-eye view of their possibilities and the challenges that need to be addressed before their full potential can be exploited. For those challenges that have been discussed before, we offer pointers to the available literature and suggest improvements. For those that are new, we propose solutions, but also point out directions for further research.

In Section 2 of this paper, we first look at existing approaches towards building experiment repositories in various scientific disciplines. Next, in Section 3, we propose a language to describe and share learning experiments, and in Section 4, we discuss how to automatically organize all this information in a searchable database. Finally, Section 5 uses the resulting repository to show how it can assist the development and application of learning algorithms, either used directly as an online service, or integrated into data mining tools. Section 6 concludes.

2 Previous Work

Many scientific disciplines store experimental data as a means of collaboration between different research groups or to make sure experiments are not needlessly repeated, most notably in fields like high-energy physics where experiments are expensive. Still, most fields lack common standards for experiment description.

2.1 Bioinformatics

Bioinformatics has led the way in describing and collecting experimental data [5]. Probably the best known application can be found in the emergence of microarray databases[1] [14]. The need for reproducibility, as well as recognition of the potential value of microarray results beyond the summarized descriptions found in most papers, have led to the creation of public repositories of microarray data [6]. Submitting experimental data in these repositories has become a condition for publication in several journals [2].

In establishing common standards for describing microarray data, significant progress has been made to ensure that such data can be properly managed and shared. In particular, a set of guidelines was drawn up regarding the required Minimal Information About a Microarray Experiment (MIAME [5]), a MicroArray Gene Expression Markup Language (MAGE-ML [14]) was conceived so that data could be uniformly described and shared between projects, and an ontology (MO [14]) was designed to provide common descriptors required by MIAME for capturing core information about microarray experiments.

Other, more specific projects go even further. The Robot Scientist [13], a fully automated scientific discovery system, expresses all physical aspects of experiment execution and even describes the hypotheses that are under investigation and what has been learned from past experiments.

2.2 Machine Learning

Creating experiment repositories for machine learning inevitably calls for the development of common standards to describe and share learning experiments, and many lessons may be learned from the bioinformatics community. First, similar to the MIAME guidelines, learning experiment descriptions should at least contain the information needed to reproduce the experiment. Such a set of guidelines is described in [4], covering what should minimally be known about the algorithms, datasets and experimental procedures. It also proposes a database schema to store classification experiments, which we shall develop further in Sect. 4.1 to, in addition, capture preprocessing steps and to allow for a more flexible description of different learning tasks besides classification.

3 A Language for Sharing Machine Learning Information

To enable a free exchange of experimental results, it would be useful to have a common description language. As such, learning experiments could be described in a unified way, without having to know how they are physically stored, while allowing them to be automatically verified, uploaded to, retrieved from, and transfered between any existing experiment repository, even if these repositories are implemented differently or distributed geographically. However, as new learning approaches are being developed at a constant rate and new learning

[1] A microarray records the expression levels of thousands of genes.

tasks often put new twists on classical problems, such a format should easily extend to capture new types of learning experiments.

To further the development of such standards, we propose an XML-based markup language, dubbed ExpML, that can be used to describe most classification and regression experiments[2]. An important benefit of XML is that it is hierarchical and extensible. It adapts to experiments of various complexities by extending the description of any aspect of a learning experiment as much as needed. In this section, we first provide a formal definition of this language, after which we will illustrate it with an example.

3.1 ExpML Definition

The XML Schema Definition (XSD) below creates an XML vocabulary for describing machine learning experiments and governs which elements should appear, in what order, and the information they should contain. It ensures that experiments are uniquely defined, and that each of its elements (algorithms, kernels, (preprocessed) datasets, evaluation metrics, etc.) are described in sufficient detail. To capture both (theoretical) meta-information about the experiments and the (empirical) settings and results, it distinguishes between element *definitions* and element *instantiations*. Definitions make sure the element is uniquely defined and can hold known properties and descriptions, while instantiations declare a specific configuration, e.g. including specific parameter settings.

Main Structure. We highlight the most important parts of the language definition[3], full definitions are available online at `http://expdb.cs.kuleuven.be/`. As the following excerpt shows, each description starts with an arbitrary number of definitions.

```
<xs:element name="expml">
  <xs:complexType>
    <xs:sequence>
      <xs:element name="definition" nobounds>
        <xs:complexType>
          <xs:choice>
            <xs:element name="algorithm" type="algorithmFull"/>
            <xs:element name="kernel" type="algorithmFull"/>
            <xs:element name="dataset" type="datasetFull"/>
            <xs:element name="preprocessor" type="algorithmFull"/>
            <xs:element name="evalmethod" type="algorithmFull"/>
            <xs:element name="metric" type="metricFull"/>
            <xs:element name="environment" type="environmentFull"/>
          </xs:choice>
        </xs:complexType>
      </xs:element>
```

Next, an arbitrary number of experiments may be defined, starting with the exact setup, i.e. which instantiations of algorithms, datasets and evaluation procedures are used. Next, we state the results of the evaluation, the predictions generated by the model for each target variable and the used computational environment[4]. Finally, experiments can be labeled to provide additional information.

[2] This language was used in practice to upload all experiments mentioned in Sect. 4.2.

[3] We use 'nobounds' as a shorthand for 'minOccurs="0" maxOccurs="unbounded"'.

[4] Although model description formats exist [8], they are not yet included here.

```
<xs:element name="experiment" nobounds>
  <xs:complexType>
    <xs:sequence>
      <xs:element name="setting">
        <xs:complexType>
          <xs:all>
            <xs:element name="algorithm" type="algorithmInst"/>
            <xs:element name="dataset" type="dataInst"/>
            <xs:element name="evalmethod" type="evalMethodInst"/>
          </xs:all>
        </xs:complexType>
      </xs:element>
      <xs:element name="evaluation" type="evaluationType"/>
      <xs:element name="prediction" type="predictionType" maxOccurs="unbounded"/>
      <xs:element name="environment" type="xs:string"/>
      <xs:element name="label" type="nameValue" nobounds/>
    </xs:sequence>
  </xs:complexType>
</xs:element>
</xs:sequence>
</xs:complexType>
</xs:element>
```

Definitions. The definitions for new elements should allow them to be properly used and easily retrieved. This includes descriptions of an algorithm's parameters, whether and how a dataset was preprocessed, how an evaluation metric is calculated and details about the environment used. Most elements can also be annotated further using *properties*, such as dataset and algorithm characterizations or computational benchmarks. Moreover, the required attributes of the elements state the minimal information needed to ensure reproducibility, and whether the definition updates a previous one.

```
<xs:complexType name="algorithmFull">
  <xs:complexContent>
    <xs:sequence>
      <xs:element name="parameter" type="parameterFull" nobounds/>
      <xs:element name="property" type="propertyType" nobounds/>
    </xs:sequence>
    <xs:attributeGroup ref="algoInfoFull"/>
  </xs:complexContent>
</xs:complexType>
<xs:complexType name="parameterFull">
  <xs:complexContent>
    <xs:sequence>
      <xs:element name="description" type="xs:string"/>
      <xs:element name="default" type="xs:string"/>
      <xs:element name="property" type="propertyType" nobounds/>
    </xs:sequence>
    <xs:attribute name="name" type="xs:string" use="required"/>
  </xs:complexContent>
</xs:complexType>
<xs:complexType name="datasetFull">
  <xs:complexContent>
    <xs:sequence>
      <xs:element name="preprocessor" type="preprocInst" nobounds/>
      <xs:element name="classindex" type="xs:integer" minOccurs="0"/>
      <xs:element name="property" type="propertyType" nobounds/>
    </xs:sequence>
    <xs:attributeGroup ref="dataInfo"/>
  </xs:complexContent>
</xs:complexType>
<xs:complexType name="metricFull">
  <xs:complexContent>
    <xs:all>
      <xs:element name="name" type="xs:string"/>
      <xs:element name="formula" type="xs:string"/>
```

```
      <xs:element name="description" type="xs:string"/>
    </xs:all>
  <xs:attribute name="isUpdate" type="xs:boolean"/>
  </xs:complexContent>
</xs:complexType>
<xs:complexType name="environmentFull">
  <xs:complexContent>
    <xs:sequence>
      <xs:element name="cpu" type="xs:string"/>
      <xs:element name="memory" type="xs:string"/>
      <xs:element name="property" type="propertyType" nobounds/>
    </xs:sequence>
    <xs:attribute name="name" type="xs:string" use="required"/>
    <xs:attribute name="isUpdate" type="xs:boolean"/>
  </xs:complexContent>
</xs:complexType>
<xs:attributeGroup name="algoInfo">
  <xs:attribute name="name" type="xs:string" use="required"/>
  <xs:attribute name="libname" type="xs:string"/>
</xs:attributeGroup>
<xs:attributeGroup name="algoInfoFull">
  <xs:attributeGroup ref="algoInfo"/>
  <xs:attribute name="version" type="xs:string" use="required"/>
  <xs:attribute name="libversion" type="xs:string"/>
  <xs:attribute name="url" type="xs:anyURI" use="required"/>
  <xs:attribute name="isUpdate" type="xs:boolean"/>
</xs:attributeGroup>
<xs:attributeGroup name="dataInfo">
  <xs:attribute name="name" type="xs:string" use="required"/>
  <xs:attribute name="url" type="xs:anyURI" use="required"/>
  <xs:attribute name="isUpdate" type="xs:boolean"/>
</xs:attributeGroup>
```

Instantiations. Inside an experiment, instantiations describe a specific application of the defined elements. While their attributes point to the general definition, they additionally define the element's individual configuration. For algorithms, this includes setting parameters or meta-parameters, encapsulating other algorithms (base-learners) or kernels. Datasets, on the other hand, can be instantiated by a number of nested preprocessing steps, which in turn may have parameter settings as well, as does the evaluation method.

```
<xs:complexType name="algorithmInst">
  <xs:complexContent>
    <xs:sequence>
      <xs:element name="parameter" type="metaParInst" nobounds/>
    </xs:sequence>
    <xs:attributeGroup ref="algoInfo"/>
  </xs:complexContent>
</xs:complexType>
<xs:complexType name="dataInst">
  <xs:complexContent>
    <xs:sequence>
      <xs:element name="preprocessor" type="preprocInst" nobounds/>
      <xs:element name="classindex" type="xs:integer" minOccurs="0"/>
    </xs:sequence>
    <xs:attributeGroup ref="dataInfo"/>
  </xs:complexContent>
</xs:complexType>
<xs:complexType name="preprocInst">
  <xs:complexContent>
    <xs:sequence>
      <xs:element name="parameter" type="metaParInst" nobounds/>
    </xs:sequence>
    <xs:attributeGroup ref="algoInfo"/>
```

```
  </xs:complexContent>
</xs:complexType>
<xs:complexType name="evalMethodInst">
  <xs:complexContent>
    <xs:sequence>
      <xs:element name="parameter" type="nameValue" nobounds/>
    </xs:sequence>
    <xs:attributeGroup ref="algoInfo"/>
  </xs:complexContent>
</xs:complexType>
<xs:complexType name="nameValue">
  <xs:complexContent>
    <xs:attribute name="name" type="xs:string" use="required"/>
    <xs:attribute name="value" type="xs:string" use="required"/>
  </xs:complexContent>
</xs:complexType>
<xs:complexType name="metaParInst">
  <xs:complexContent>
    <xs:extension base="nameValue">
      <xs:sequence minOccurs="0">
        <xs:element name="algorithm" type="algorithmInst" minOccurs="0"/>
        <xs:element name="kernel" type="algorithmInst" minOccurs="0"/>
      </xs:sequence>
    </xs:extension>
  </xs:complexContent>
</xs:complexType>
```

Results. The result of an experiment encompasses the outcomes of an arbitrary selection of evaluations metrics (depending on the task), and predictions for each data instance. In the case of classification tasks, the latter may also hold probabilities for each class.

```
<xs:complexType name="evaluationType">
  <xs:complexContent>
    <xs:sequence>
      <xs:element name="metric" maxOccurs="unbounded">
        <xs:complexType>
          <xs:attribute name="name" type="xs:string" use="required"/>
          <xs:attribute name="value" type="xs:string" use="required"/>
        </xs:complexType>
      </xs:element>
    </xs:sequence>
  </xs:complexContent>
</xs:complexType>
<xs:complexType name="predictions">
  <xs:complexContent>
    <xs:sequence>
      <xs:element name="instance" maxOccurs="unbounded">
        <xs:complexType>
          <xs:sequence>
            <xs:element name="prob" maxOccurs="unbounded">
             <xs:complexType>
               <xs:attribute name="prediction" type="xs:string" use="required"/>
               <xs:attribute name="value" type="xs:string" use="required"/>
             </xs:complexType>
            </xs:element>
          </xs:sequence>
        <xs:attribute name="nr" type="xs:integer" use="required"/>
        <xs:attribute name="prediction" type="xs:string" use="required"/>
        </xs:complexType>
      </xs:element>
    </xs:sequence>
    <xs:attribute name="target" type="xs:string"/>
  <xs:complexContent>
</xs:complexType>
```

3.2 An Example Description

As an illustration, we could use this language to define a new algorithm, run it on a preprocessed classification problem, and store the generated results:

```
<algorithm name="Bagging" version="1.31.2.2" libname="weka"
     libversion="3.4.8" url="http://www.cs.waikato.ac.nz/ml/weka/"
     classpath="weka.classifiers.meta.Bagging">
  <parameter name="P">
    <description>Size of each bag as percentage of data set size</description>
    <default>100</default>
    <property name="suggested_min" value="20"/>
     ...
  </parameter>
  ...
  <property name="class" value="ensemble">
  <property name="handles_classification" value="true">
  ...
</algorithm>
...
<experiment>
  <setting>
    <algorithm name="Bagging" version="1.31.2.2" libname="weka">
      <parameter name="P" value="90"/>
      <parameter name="O" value="false"/>
      <parameter name="I" value="40"/>
      <parameter name="W" value="algorithm">
        <algorithm name="NaiveBayes" version="1.16" libname="weka"/>
      </parameter>
    </algorithm>
    <dataset name="pendigits-90%">
      <preprocessor name="RemovePercentage" version="1.3" libname="weka">
        <parameter name="P" value="10"/>
        <dataset name="pendigits" url="http://archive.ics.uci.edu/ml/">
           <classIndex>-1</classIndex>
        </dataset>
      </preprocessor>
      <classIndex>-1</classIndex>
    </dataset>
    <evalmethod name="CrossValidation" version="1.53" libname="weka"
         libversion="3.4.8">
      <parameter name="nbfolds" value="10"/>
      <parameter name="randomseed" value="1"/>
    </evalmethod>
  </setting>
  <evaluation>
    <metric name="build_cputime" value="5.67"/>
    <metric name="build_memory" value="17929416"/>
    <metric name="mean_absolute_error" value="0.030570337062541805"/>
    <metric name="root_mean_squared_error" value="0.1596060779229l556"/>
    <metric name="predictive_accuracy" value="0.8570778748180494"/>
    <metric name="kappa" value="0.8411692914743762"/>
    <metric name="confusion_matrix" value="
        [[0,1,2,3,4,5,6,7,8,9],[1021,0,0,0,2,0,3,0,51,4],[1,883,...],...]]"/>
    ...
  </evaluation>
  <predictions target="0">
    <instance nr="00000" prediction="8">
      <prob prediction="0" value="1.8761967426234115E-5"/>
       ...
      <prob prediction="8" value="0.9991914442703987"/>
      <prob prediction="9" value="3.2190267582597184E-31"/>
    </instance>
    ...
  </predictions>
  <environment>machine14</environment>
  <label spec="type" value="classification"/>
</experiment>
```

In this case, we first added the 'Bagging' algorithm with all the necessary information, descriptions of its parameters and some basic properties. Next, we added an experiment using an instantiation of this algorithm with specific parameter values. Since this is an ensemble algorithm, one of these parameters encapsulates another (parameterless) algorithm, viz. 'NaiveBayes'. The dataset we investigate is 'pendigits', preprocessed by feeding it into the 'RemovePercentage' preprocessor with the stated parameters. The generated model is evaluated using the 10-fold cross-validation technique. The results of this evaluation are stated next, using several evaluation metrics, and are followed by predictions for all the instances, including the probabilities for each class.

3.3 Future Work

While this language is designed to capture a large variety of contemporary classification and regression experiments, it will still need to be developed further. First of all, learning algorithms definitions are still quite limited. It would be instrumental to develop an ontology that models various learning techniques and their relationships. Also, learning tasks in machine learning, such as clustering, link discovery and mining relational data are very different, and might require different 'flavours' of this basic language to suit their needs. Alternatively, an ontology of machine learning techniques could be envisaged to work towards a unified format. Interesting approaches towards building such an ontology can be found in [10] and [1]. Finally, although the language allows the description of sequences of preprocessing steps, more work is needed to capture more complex data mining workflows.

4 Organizing Experimental Data

For all this information to be accessible and useful, it still needs to be stored in an organized fashion. Inserting it into a database seems a good solution [3], allowing powerful query possibilities (SQL) and easy integration into software tools. Ideally, such databases would evolve with the description language to be able to capture future extensions. There may be several interconnected databases, using the common language to transfer stored experiments, or conversely, some databases may be set up locally for sensitive, or preliminary data.

In this section, we focus on designing a database conforming to the structure of the language described previously, thus capturing the basic organization of machine learning experiments. This leads to the schema shown in Fig. 1.

4.1 Anatomy of an Experiment Database

Basically, an `Experiment` consists of a `Learner` run on a `Dataset` using a certain `Machine`, and the resulting `Model` is evaluated with a certain `Evaluation Method`. These are depicted in Fig. 1 by the dashed lines. Each of these components can be defined and instantiated over several other tables. An `Experiment` is stored as a specific combination of component instances.

More specifically, a *learner instance* points to a learning algorithm (`Learner`), which can be characterized by any number of features, and its specific parameter settings. For `Ensemble` learners, parameters can point to other learner instances, and additional records are kept to facilitate querying. A dataset instance is defined by the original dataset and a number of preprocessing steps, which can in turn be described further, including all the involved parameters. The evaluation method (e.g. cross-validation) can also be instantiated. Finally, the evaluation results of each experiment are stored for each employed evaluation metric, and for predictive models, the (non-zero probability) predictions returned for each data instance are recorded as well.

This database is publicly accessible at `http://expdb.cs.kuleuven.be/`. The website also hosts ExpML definitions, the available tools for uploading experiments, a gallery of SQL queries (including the ones used in the next section), and a query interface including visualization tools for displaying returned results.

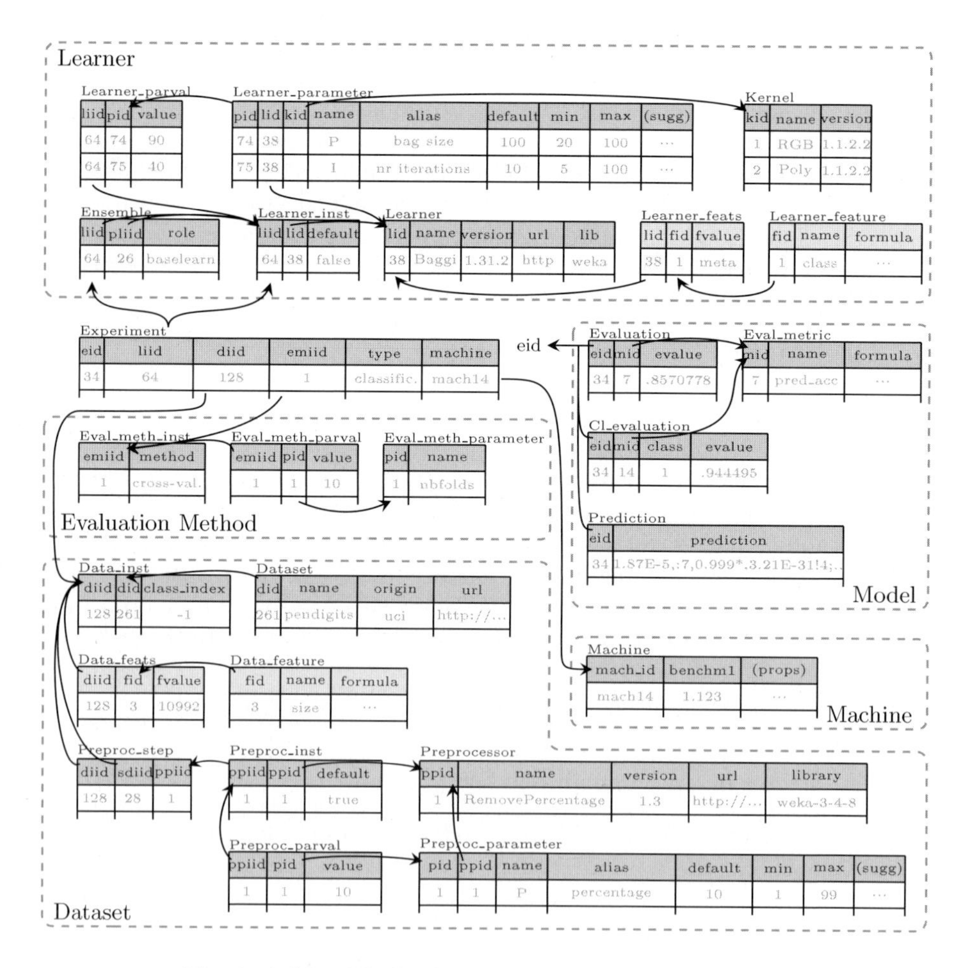

Fig. 1. A (simplified) schema for an experiment database

4.2 Populating the Database

To fill this database with experiments, we focused on supervised classification. We extended the WEKA platform[16] to output experiments in the format described above, and developed an interface to the database to automatically interpret and store the experiments.

The repository currently holds about 500,000 experiments, using 54 well-known classification algorithms (from WEKA), 86 commonly used classification datasets taken from the UCI repository, and 2 preprocessing methods (also from WEKA). We ran all algorithms, with default parameter settings, on all datasets. Furthermore, the algorithms SMO (an SVM trainer), MultilayerPerceptron, J48 (C4.5), OneR, Random Forests, Bagging and Boosting were varied over their most important parameter settings[5]. For all randomized algorithms, each experiment was repeated 20 times with different random seeds. All experiments were evaluated with 10-fold cross-validation, using the same folds on each dataset, and a large subset was additionally evaluated with a bias-variance analysis.

5 Services of Experiment Repositories

The principled way of annotating algorithms, data, and entire experiments provides a much needed formal grounds for the development of data mining "web services" which allow on-demand retrieval of theoretical and empirical data about learning techniques, and which could then be automatically orchestrated into real data mining processes. In this section, we illustrate some of the possible services offered by an experiment database, either by directly querying the database, or by integrating it in larger data mining tools.

5.1 Public Database Access

All information stored in an experiment database can be accessed directly by writing the right database query (e.g. in SQL), providing a very versatile means to investigate a large number of experimental results, both under very specific and very general conditions. To further facilitate access to this information, a graphical query interface could hide the complexity of SQL queries. We focus here on the different services allowed by querying, a wider range of interesting queries is discussed in [15].

Experiment Reuse. As mentioned earlier, when evaluating a new algorithm, one could use the repository to retrieve previously stored results. For instance, to query for the results of all previous algorithms on a specific dataset, we simply ask for all experiments on that dataset and select the algorithm used and the performance recorded. Fig. 2 shows the result on dataset "letter". It is immediately clear how previous algorithms performed, how much variation is caused by parameter tuning, and what the effect is of various ensemble techniques.

[5] For the ensemble methods, all non-ensemble learners were used as possible base-learners, each with default parameter settings.

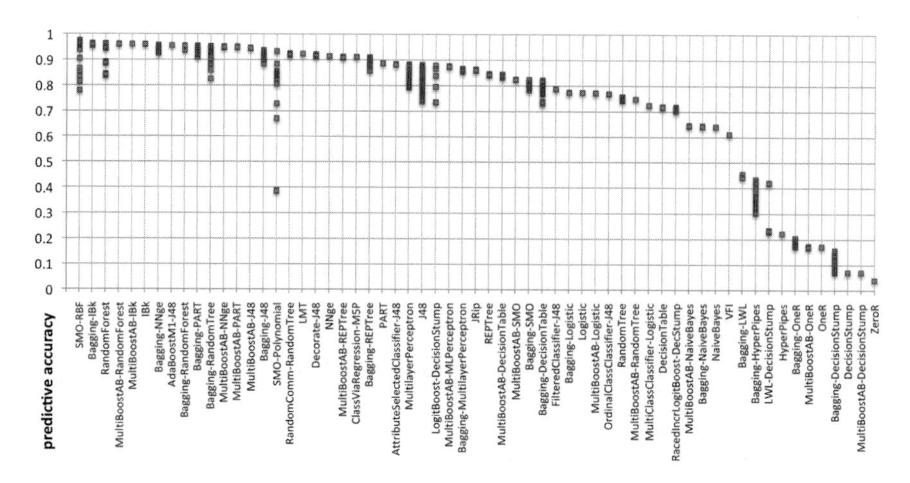

Fig. 2. Performance of all algorithms on dataset 'letter', with base-learners and kernels

Hypothesis Testing. Writing queries also provides a fast way to explore the stored data and check hypotheses about any aspect of learning performance. For instance, to see if the variation in the SMO-RBF data from the previous query is caused by a specific parameter, we can 'zoom in' the SMO-RBF data (adding a constraint) and include the value of the 'gamma' parameter (selecting an extra field), yielding Fig. 3. When expanding the query towards several datasets, one can see that the optimal value of that parameter depends heavily on the dataset used, and more specifically on its number of attributes (indicated in brackets)[6].

When analyzing a dataset, one might be interested in how the dataset size affects the performance of an algorithm. Asking for the performance of algorithms on various downsampled versions of a dataset yields the learning curves shown in Fig. 4. Such queries may be useful to decide which algorithm to use based on the amount of available data or, conversely, how much data to collect.

Finding Fundamental Insights. Pooling data from different sources enables us to perform studies that would be impossible, or very expensive to setup from scratch, but that may bring very general insights into learning performance. For instance, one could perform a general comparison of all algorithms (selecting optimal parameter settings) on the UCI datasets. Following a technique used by [7], we compare over a range of different evaluation metrics, using SQL aggregation functions to normalize each performance value between baseline and optimal performance, yielding Fig. 5 as the result of a single query. Note that this query can simply be rerun as new algorithms are introduced over time. A complete discussion of the results can be found in [15].

Ranking. It is also possible to rank algorithms by writing a query. For instance, to investigate whether some algorithms consistently rank high over various

[6] As discussed in [15], this reveals that on data with many attributes, it is better to use small gamma values, suggesting ways to improve the algorithm implementation.

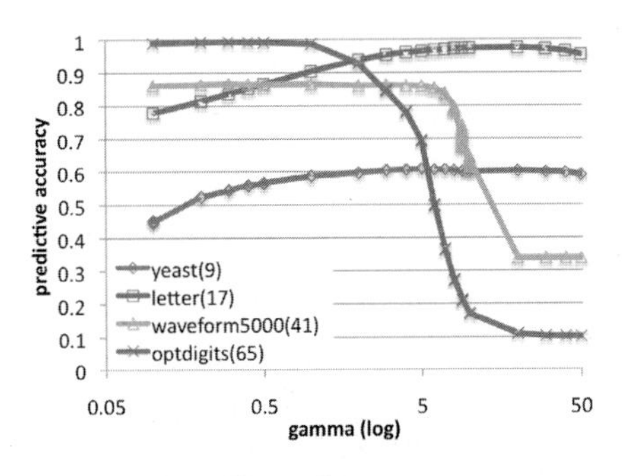

Fig. 3. The effect of parameter gamma of the RBF-kernel in SVMs

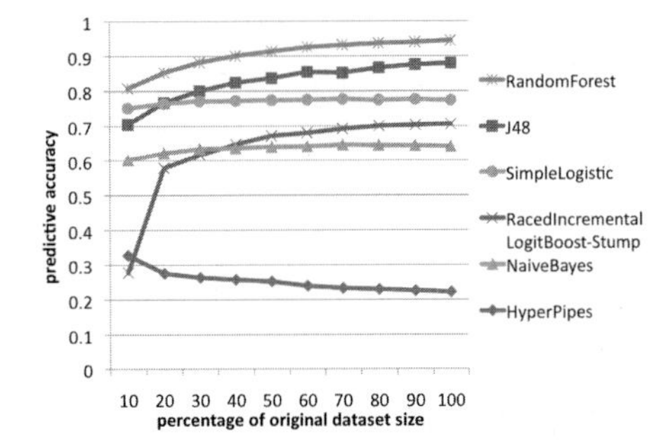

Fig. 4. Learning curves on dataset 'letter'

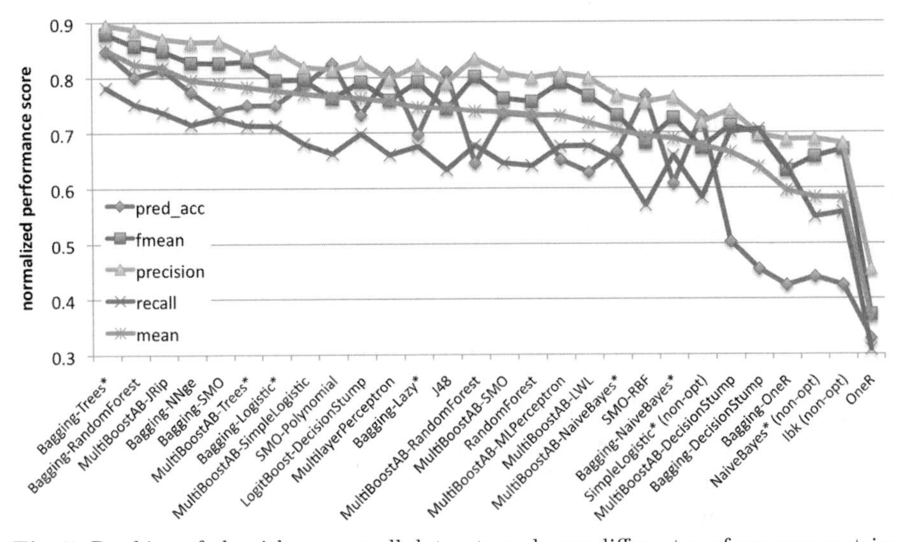

Fig. 5. Ranking of algorithms over all datasets and over different performance metrics. Similar algorithms are compacted in groups, indicated with an asterix (*).

problems, we can query for their average rank (based on optimal parameter settings) over all datasets. Using the Friedman ranking and the Nemenyi test to find the critical difference (the minimal rank gap for algorithms to perform significantly different)[9], we yield Fig. 6 for learning approaches in general, and Fig. 7 for algorithms with specific base-learners and kernels. This shows that indeed, some algorithms rank significantly higher on average than others on the UCI datasets.

Other Uses. There are many more uses that can be thought of. For instance, much more could be studied when looking at the stored predictions: we could investigate which instances of a dataset are significantly hard to predict for most algorithms (and why), whether specific combinations of classifiers perform very well, or whether a vote over every single algorithm would result in good

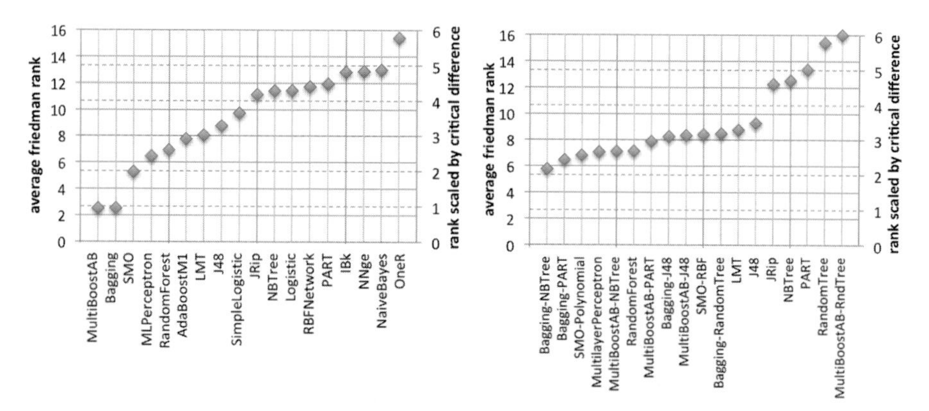

Fig. 6. Average rank, general algorithms **Fig. 7.** Average rank, specific algorithms

performance. Given the large amount of experiments, it could also be very interesting to mine the repository and look for patterns in algorithm performance.

5.2 Integration in Data Mining Tools

Besides being queried directly, an experiment database could also be a valuable resource when integrated in a variety of data mining tools. One application would be to avoid unnecessary computation. When performing a large set of experiments, the tool could automatically consult the experiment database to see if some experiments can be reused. Furthermore, one could parallelize the execution of experiments by uploading unfinished experiments to the database and have several computers checking for unfinished experiments to run.

The tool could also automatically export experiments into a local or global experiment repository. Local repositories could typically be used for studies where datasets are not (yet) publicly available or where algorithms are still under development, offering a means to automatically organize all experiments for easier analysis. The experiments (or a selection thereof) could still be shared at a later point in time by transferring them to global repositories.

Finally, one could integrate experiment databases and inductive databases [11], creating repositories with much more powerful querying capabilities [3].

6 Conclusions

Sharing machine learning experiments and organizing them into experiment repositories opens up many opportunities for machine learning research and exploratory data analysis. While such repositories have been used in other sciences, most notably in bio-informatics, they have only recently been introduced into machine learning. To stimulate the future development of these repositories, we have discussed how they can be created and used in practice, and what challenges remain to be addressed to realize their full potential. To allow the free exchange of learning experiments, we have proposed an XML-based description language capturing a wide range of experiments. Next, we have used the same inherent structure to implement a database to capture and automatically organize learning experiments, improving upon earlier suggestions. Finally, we gave an overview of possible services that such a resource could offer, either by querying it to retrieve relevant information, or by integrating it into data mining tools. It is likely that many more creative uses remain to be discovered.

Acknowledgements

Hendrik Blockeel is Postdoctoral Fellow of the Fund for Scientific Research - Flanders (Belgium) (F.W.O.-Vlaanderen), and this research is further supported by GOA 2003/08 "Inductive Knowledge Bases".

References

1. Allison, L.: Models for machine learning and data mining in functional programming. Journal of Functional Programming 15(1), 15–32 (2005)
2. Ball, C.A., Brazma, A., Causton, H., Chervitz, S., Edgar, R., et al.: Submission of Microarray Data to Public Repositories. PLoS Biol. 2(9), e317 (2004)
3. Blockeel, H.: Experiment databases: A novel methodology for experimental research. In: Bonchi, F., Boulicaut, J.-F. (eds.) KDID 2005. LNCS, vol. 3933, pp. 72–85. Springer, Heidelberg (2006)
4. Blockeel, H., Vanschoren, J.: Experiment databases: Towards an improved experimental methodology in machine learning. In: Kok, J.N., Koronacki, J., López de Mántaras, R., Matwin, S., Mladenič, D., Skowron, A. (eds.) PKDD 2007. LNCS (LNAI), vol. 4702, pp. 6–17. Springer, Heidelberg (2007)
5. Brazma, A., Hingamp, P., Quackenbush, J., Sherlock, G., et al.: Minimum information about a microarray experiment (MIAME): toward standards for microarray data. Nature Genetics 29, 365–371 (2001)
6. Brazma, A., Parkinson, H., Sarkans, U., Shojatalab, M., et al.: ArrayExpress–a public repository for microarray gene expression data at the EBI. Nucleic Acids Research 31(1), 68–71 (2003)
7. Caruana, R., Niculescu-Mizil, A.: An empirical comparison of supervised learning algorithms. In: Airoldi, E.M., Blei, D.M., Fienberg, S.E., Goldenberg, A., Xing, E.P., Zheng, A.X. (eds.) ICML 2006. LNCS, vol. 4503, pp. 161–168. Springer, Heidelberg (2007)
8. The Data Mining Group: The Predictive Model Markup Language (PMML), version 3.2, `http://www.dmg.org/pmml-v3-2.html`
9. Demšar, J.: Statistical Comparisons of Classifiers over Multiple Data Sets. Journal of Machine Learning Research 7, 1–30 (2006)
10. Džeroski, S.: Towards a General Framework for Data Mining. In: Džeroski, S., Struyf, J. (eds.) KDID 2006. LNCS, vol. 4747, pp. 259–300. Springer, Heidelberg (2007)
11. Imielinski, T., Mannila, H.: A database perspective on knowledge discovery. Communications of the ACM 39(11), 58–64 (1996)
12. Perlich, C., Provost, F., Siminoff, J.: Tree induction vs. logistic regression: A learning curve analysis. Journal of Machine Learning Research 4, 211–255 (2003)

13. Soldatova, L.N., Clare, A., Sparkes, A., King, R.D.: An ontology for a Robot Scientist. Bioinformatics 22(14), 464–471 (2006)
14. Stoeckert, C., Causton, H., Ball, C.: Microarray databases: standards and ontologies. Nature Genetics 32, 469–473 (2002)
15. Vanschoren, J., Pfahringer, B., Holmes, G.: Learning From The Past with Experiment Databases. Working Paper Series 08/2008, Computer Science Department, University of Waikato (2008)
16. Witten, I.H., Frank, E.: Data Mining: Practical Machine Learning Tools and Techniques, 2nd edn. Morgan Kaufmann, San Francisco (2005)

Workflow Testing

R. Breu[1], A. Lechner[2], M. Willburger[1,2], and B. Katt[1]

[1] Research Group "Quality Engineering", Universität Innsbruck
Institut für Informatik, A-6020 Innsbruck, Austria
[2] world-direct/eBusiness Solutions GmbH, A-6073 Sistrans/Innsbruck
ruth.breu@uibk.ac.at, alexander.lechner@world-direct.at,
mathias.willburger@student.uibk.ac.at, basel.katt@uibk.ac.at

Abstract. The increased use of workflow management systems and orchestrated services has created the need for frameworks supporting the quality assurance of workflows. In this paper we present WorkflowInspector, a prototype of a workflow test framework for the Windows Workflow Foundation.

1 Introduction

Business processes are part of every company. Workflow management systems like the Windows Workflow Foundation provide new techniques to model these processes as workflows. Typical usage scenarios are ordering systems, payroll or hiring applications.

What is still missing are applications to monitor and test these workflows. So far all workflow applications have to be tested manually. In fact, the developer has to test all application features according to a test script.

The main intention for developing the WorkflowInspector in a cooperation of the research group Quality Engineering and world-direct was to enable developers to perform automated test suites of arbitrary Windows Workflow Foundation workflows. The test runs, as well as the related data, are stored in a test database. Hence, the workflow execution may be reviewed in detail afterwards. The graphical visualization possibilities of the application enable also other usage scenarios. For instance, they allow an early involvement of the software when communicating with the customer. It is possible to demonstrate basic application flows without the need to create input forms even if user input is required. The integrated graph view can be used to present workflows without utilization of any third-party software.

2 Windows Workflow Foundation

The Windows Workflow Foundation (WF) was launched by Microsoft as early beta at the end of 2005. It combines a programming model, engine and tools to build workflow enabled applications [1]. As part of the .NET 3.0 framework it is free of charge. With the introduction of this technology Microsoft aims for the following targets [2]:

T. Margaria and B. Steffen (Eds.): ISoLA 2008, CCIS 17, pp. 709–723, 2008.

- Build up a common workflow platform for all windows applications.
- Support for multiple workflow types (e.g. sequential workflows, state machines).
- A model driven development of workflows.
- Introducing reusable workflow elements and extensibility points.

2.1 Architecture and Features

The Windows Workflow Foundation framework comprises a *Base Activity Library*, a *Runtime Engine*, several *Runtime Services* and a *Visual Designer*. As it is not a standalone application it is executed inside a *Host Process*. A host can be any type of .NET software, such as console applications, web applications, web services or the Sharepoint Portal Server. They all provide a variety of different services to workflow applications [3] like for example: *workflow management* (e.g. creation/distruction), *scalling of workflows* (e.g. the usage of multiple CPUs in cluster) or *security management*. The Workflow Foundation introduces two different workflow models: sequential workflows and event driven state mailmachines. They are described in the following (*for further details please refer to [4]*):

2.2 The Sequential Workflow Model

A sequential workflow executes a set of consecutive activities. It does not move on to the next activity until the prior one is executed completely. The tasks can be processed with little or no user interaction. Even though the workflow may include branches, loops and external events, its steps are predictable in the majority of cases [4]. Sequential workflows are ideal to model business processes. If data needs to be read from a source, processed and written into another data sink this workflow type fits best. A typical example for a sequential workflow can be seen in Figure 1. The workflow includes basic elements like branching (*ifElseActivity*) and looping (*whileActivity*). Furthermore several code activities are included (*codeActivity1*, *codeActivity2* and *codeActivity3*).

2.3 The State Machine Workflow Model

State machine workflows are useful if the workflow includes a lot of user interaction. The important choices of the application flow are made outside the system. This enables the user to gain more control over the workflow. In fact, state machines have a single starting point (*initial state*) and a set of end points (*accepting states* or *terminal states*). The states in between are controlled by events to occur while the machine is in a specific state. A change from one state into another is called *transition*. In contrast to sequential workflows state machines in the most cases are non-deterministic.

State machine workflows consist of *State* activities which basically act as containers for sequential workflows. Figure 2 shows an example for a state machine which models an ordering process. The internal activities and performed steps cannot be seen in this type of illustration.

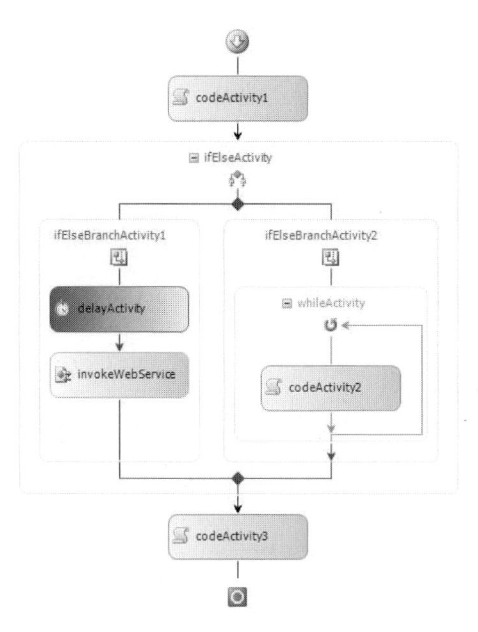

Fig. 1. Sequential workflow

3 Workflow Testing

There exist several approaches for testing traditional source code, e.g. unit testing. Some of these methods can directly be mapped to workflow tests. Like in traditional testing workflow tests are used to measure the quality of the developed process.

3.1 Test Considerations

Usually regular source code testing requires the generation of drivers and stubs [5]. A similar approach has to be taken into account when testing workflows. A simulation of interaction partners is mandatory. According to [6] this is due to the following reasons:

1. Some of the dependent partner processes may still be under development, e.g. GUI components.
2. Some processes may be developed by third-party companies. Because of this it is difficult to obtain the source code of the process. Moreover, also the specific application environment for the process would have to be simulated.
3. Sometimes simulated processes are preferred due to less effort of implementation.

For WorkflowInspector a test architecture that implements of the following features was derived:

- An implementation of several test algorithms which can be applied to workflow executions.
- A generic way to interact with workflows, i.e. simulating interaction partners.

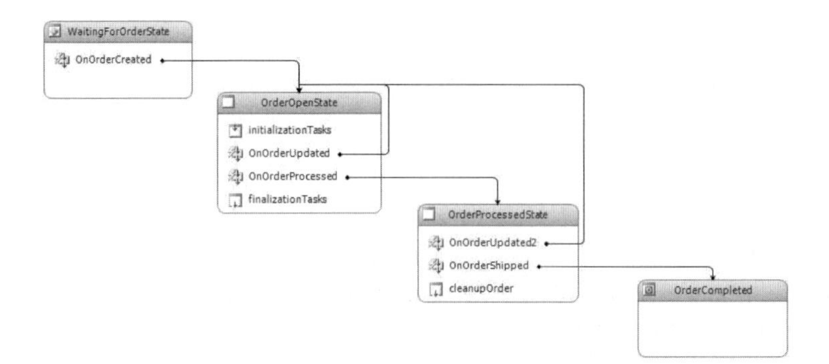

Fig. 2. Ordering state machine workflow

3.2 Test Types

Basically there exist two test approaches: blackbox and whitebox tests. The difference lies in location of the *Point of Observation (PoO)* and the *Point of Control (PoC)*. On one hand, Blackbox testing assumes an external view of the test object, i.e. the software under test. So there is no information about the internal structure of the executed code or workflow. One can only see the behavior from outside. Additionaly to PoO, PoC is also outside. The tester has no possibility to change parameters of the execution except the definition of input values. On the other hand the whitebox test can be seen as a "glass box". It is a structural test method because the internal structure (e.g. source code, data flow, control flow) can be seen by the tester. Both, PoC and PoO, are inside the object under test

A fundamental requirement for the development of a test environment for Windows workflows was to not alter existing workflow definitions. WorkflowInspector therefor is developed as external application which does not interfere with the source code. This on the other hand brings also a disadvantage. The source code of the workflow is not accessible for the application. This is because it is encapsulated inside an assembly. Hence, there is no possibility to check which statement in the source code is actually executed. On the other hand it is possible to use a tracking service to track the execution. However, only the actually executed activity and not the nested code is visible. A work-around for this problem is to track also the error stack trace of the .NET runtime. It provides the complete error history once the workflow fails.

Concluding, WorkflowInspector's test method can be seen as "gray-box" test.

In the following the coverage test types are described which are implemented to give some metrics about the workflow executions.

- *Activity Converage* A full activity coverage is reached if all activities in the workflow are executed at least once. This may already happen if only one TestRun was executed. Never covered activities are hints for uncovered source code.

- *Branch Coverage* To obtain full branch coverage all edges of the workflow's control flow graph of the workflow have to be covered at least once. The branch coverage test includes the activity coverage test.
- *Path Coverage* If the workflow contains loops the tests described so far are not sufficient. A path coverage covers all possible paths through the whole workflow. This may get complex as every integrated loop, i.e. while, increases the amount of paths depending on its exit condition. Within complex workflows or state machines it is nearly impossible to reach 100% path coverage. Therefor a boundary interior test is introduced. This means only a selected amount of loops is performed.

3.3 Test Structure

Workflow tests as used within WorkflowInspector consist of two parts: A *TestRun* describes a single workflow execution. All related data (i.e. execution steps, user input, application output) is stored into a database for later use. A *TestRun* can also be seen as one test case. However, there may exist more *TestRuns* which represent the same test case. The user input has actually to be provided manually during the TestRun. A *TestSuite* is a set of TestRuns including also the information about the workflow itself. In fact, the workflow assembly name and all referenced assemblies are stored. Furthermore, some preconditions and/or postconditions may be set. They enable the developer to define some basic parameters which have to be fulfilled before and after the workflow execution, respectively.

3.4 Test Execution

A Windows Workflow Foundation workflow is always part of an executable application, i.e. the workflow host. It cannot be executed by itself. Therefor the whole application has to be deployed and executed in order to test it. Two concepts were taken into account [7]:

1. *Simulated testing*: The workflow may use some kind of debug API to interact with the other components. For instance, the API should be able to intercept calls to Web services and handle them locally. Furthermore, it should be able to send data back to the workflow under test.
2. *Real-life testing*: All service partners are replaced by mocks. In other words, they are replaced by own web service implementation simulating the behavior of the original ones. This also means that the workflow under test has to be altered. In fact, all references to external services are changed to references to the local mocks.

As the second approach brings the disadvantage that the workflow has to be altered, WorkflowInspector implements a mixture of both. First, it provides an integrated runtime to the workflow. This means that the workflow may be tested independently of the application where it is included. Thus, the execution flow can be tracked without any changes to the source code . Second, WorkflowInspector intercepts the communication with external services. Once a user interaction or input is required it displays an input form on the screen. On the one hand this is an advantage because workflows do not have to be altered for testing purposes. However the tester has to have certain technical knowledge about the systems the workflow is interacting with.

3.5 Test Results

WorkflowInspector provides detailed information about the TestSuite to the user. At first all recorded data is displayed. Hence, the user may review the exact workflow executions. Moreover, all points of failure are displayed with time and cause of the error.

If additionally a coverage test is applied, the test results are given in percentage values. For example activity coverage of 100% indicates each workflow activity has been executed at least once.

4 Workflow Inspector

4.1 Software Features

In this section the main features of our tool are described. To get an overview of the capabilities of WorkflowInspector a summary of all components is given.

- *Testing of State Machine Workflows* WorkflowInspector is basically designed to test state machine workflows. However, as state machines always include nested sequential workflows, these may automatically be tested, too. However, extracting sub-workflows might cause errors because of the possible non-determinism of the state machines, hence it is not supported.
- *Workflow Tracking* WorkflowInspector supports the recording of all workflow execution data. It includes a generic configuration of the Microsoft tracking service. Hence, no workflow needs to be altered for testing purposes. Once it is loaded into the application it can be used with the tracking service. So the assemblies may directly be deployed as soon as the testing is complete.
- *Implemented Test Types* The prototype version supports activity, branch and path coverage tests which can be executed individually. The latter one is implemented as boundary interior test to avoid infinite looping.
  The test results enable detailed insight in the covered actions and executed paths to support an optimization of the workflow. They speed up the error finding process, too.
- *Manual Input of Test Data* WorkflowInspector provides a generic way to interact with all kinds of workflows. Usually a custom user interface or input form for each workflow has to be created. It enables the user to input data and manipulate the flow of the application. This step can be omitted using WorkflowInspector in the following way.

Whenever external data is required to resume the workflow execution, WorkflowInspector deals with the form creation. It produces an input form which is displayed on-screen. The form contains all parameters which are needed to continue. It should be noted that this feature allows to use WorkflowInspector not only for testing purposes. Presentations of the basic workflow functionality become manageable already at specification time. Workflows which barely contain the mandatory execution steps may be executed. No time has to be spent on the creation of user interfaces until the latest possible moment in the project progress. Thus, the development can completely be focused on creating a stable application core and clear workflow definitions.

- *Data and Workflow Display via a Win32 GUI* WorkflowInspector inherits the full graphical notion of the designer used by Visual Studio. This enables developers to continue their work without having to be familiar with new notions.
- *Graph Visualization* The application additionally provides a new view of the workflow not used within Visual Studio. It includes a graph conversion algorithm which generates directed graphs using Windows Workflow Foundation workflow assemblies. On the one hand this is useful for the developer. It provides a better overview of the whole system, even if nested activities are used. On the other hand the graph representation can be used for presentation purposes. Workflows can be displayed on an abstraction level not showing any specific implementation information.
- *Error Reconstruction* A challenge when testing software in general is the communication of error reasons between testers and developers. Testers have to provide a full documentation of execution steps to provoke a designated error. WorkflowInspector supports this communication by saving the complete execution history, as well as all user inputs. Furthermore the error stack trace is stored.
- *Pre- and Postcondition Validation* To verify that TestRuns fulfill specified basic conditions WorkflowInspector provides a simple validation mechanism. By use of boolean operations constraints for all public workflow parameters may be defined. They can be verified after the TestRun execution.

4.2 System Integration

Figure 3 illustrates the integration of WorkflowInspector into the development infrastructure of our industrial partner. The designed workflows are being executed on an application server which is used as a web server at the same time (1). Physically it does not matter if the two servers are installed on the same or on different computers. To simplify matters they are shown as one object. The workflow runtime in which the workflows live is installed on the application server. Additionally, a Windows service is installed. It acts as host for the runtime. It is also responsible for workflow management, e.g. correct workflow instantiation and termination. In contrast a user interface is installed on the web server. It can be accessed via network, i.e. intranet or Internet. In the current

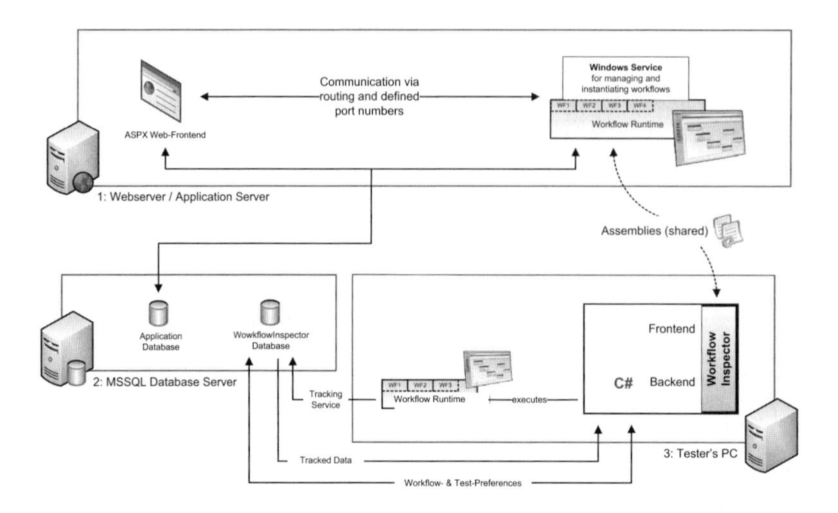

Fig. 3. Involved system components

illustration it is represented by an ASPX[1] website. However, it may also be a Win32 GUI on a remote PC depending on the customer's needs. The next component involved is the database server (2). It stores the individual application objects, e.g. order items. therefor Microsoft SQL 2005 server is used.

The elements described so far are completely independent from WorkflowInspector or the tested workflows. Hence, there is no interference of the approved and already deployed workflows.

The WorkflowInspector database is located on the same server as the database of the application. It comprises information about workflow executions and test management. It must be pointed out that two independent databases have to be used to avoid interference.

Finally the tester's PC is the one where WorkflowInspector is installed (3). Like almost every Win32 application it consists of graphical frontend and logical backend components. Furthermore, WorkflowInspector hosts its own workflow runtime. This enables the tester to execute workflows independent from the application server within some kind of sandbox, i.e. in a secure environment.

The only components shared between the application server and the tester's PC are the workflow assemblies. However, they are never used by both parties at the same time. The slashed line in Figure 3 only indicates that the assemblies can directly be deployed on the application sever once the testing is complete.

4.3 Integration of WorkflowInspector in the Development Process Model

WorkflowInspector emphasizes on designing and testing workflows in early stages of application development cycle to allow small iterations in the application development. Indeed, the software also supports developers in bringing their

[1] ASPX is the file format for ASP.NET Web applications (cf. [8]).

development process to agile methods. The main focus lies on the introduction of automated test phases to reduce testing and maintenance time.

Figure 4 shows an optimized timeline for projects using WorkflowInspector. The illustration is generally speaking still designed according to the waterfall model. However, there are major modifications to support an iterative and incremental development which are described in the following.

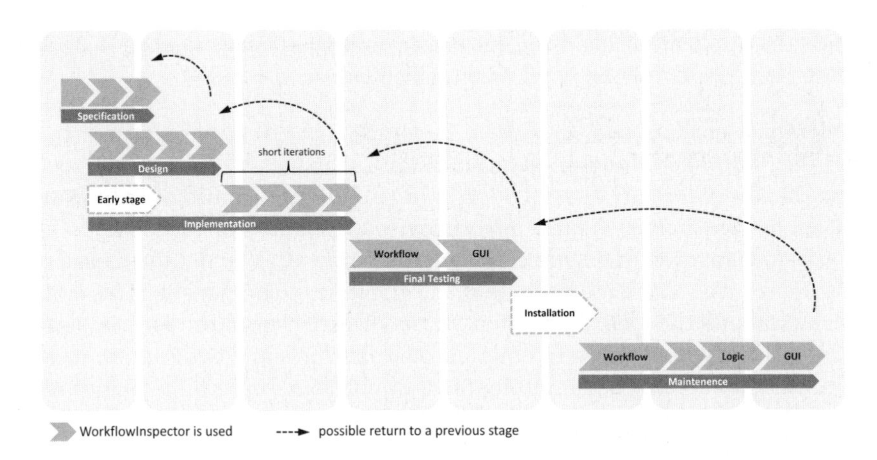

Fig. 4. Improved project timeline with usage of WorkflowInspector

WorkflowInspector is basically designed for developers and testers. Though, its clear graphical presentations also enable customers to understand the processes without complete knowledge of the technical background. Therefore WorkflowInspector may already be introduced at specification time. Workflow examples can be created to demonstrate the Windows Workflow Foundation abilities to the customer. Moreover, also basic processes without business logic of the final application may be executed. Different scenarios can also be discussed with the client. The big advantage of it is that the core framework is used, which also will come into operation in the final application. Thus, specification, design and implementation are partially merged. In other words, the communication with the customer is improved and early workflow prototypes may be reused without loss of development time.

Next, the main implementation starts in arbitrary many iterations. There is still no need to create a user interface yet. Due to the capabilities of WorkflowInspector to provide generic input forms, the final interface may be created as late as possible. This also reduces maintenance time.

In every iteration the changed workflow can be tested immediately. Workflow errors or unused paths due to changes in the system may be discovered at once. However, the business logic has to be tested using conventional testing frameworks for source code such as for example NUnit (cf. [9]).

The final task shown in Figure 4 is maintenance. Even by improving the development process some servicing tasks may still be necessary. However,

WorkflowInspector reduces the time of correcting errors or implementing new features. This is again because every change can be tested immediately.

4.4 Logical Application Architecture

Figure 5 shows the interaction of the single components used within WorkflowInspector.

Once the application has been initialized and the GUI is loaded (1-3) there are three main parts of the application which can be used:

1. *Workflow Loading and Execution* A workflow is loaded or executed by use of the *Workflow Manager*. It initiates and manages all workflows executed by the *Workflow Runtime*. The *Workflow Manager* is also able to perform some finalization tasks after a workflow was executed or terminated. These tasks may involve for example application notification or database clearance. Moreover, the manager has a built-in monitoring component. The monitor knows about the exact execution status of each workflow. This is useful if the workflow needs user interaction or waits for some external application event. The monitor then automatically informs all observing parties about the actual workflow status. Finally, the *Workflow Runtime* is connected to the *Tracking Service* to write data into the database.

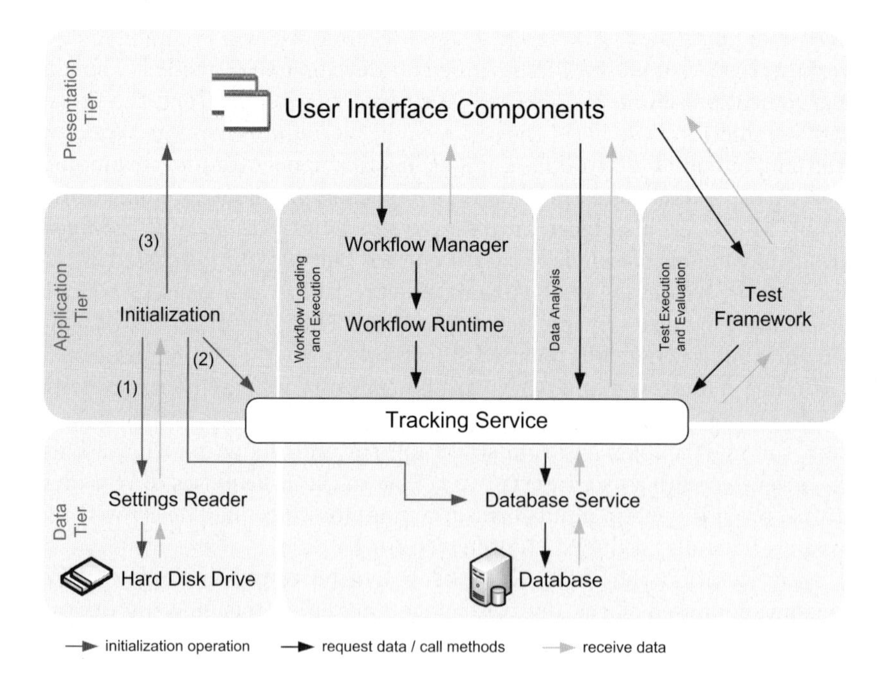

Fig. 5. Logical components diagram

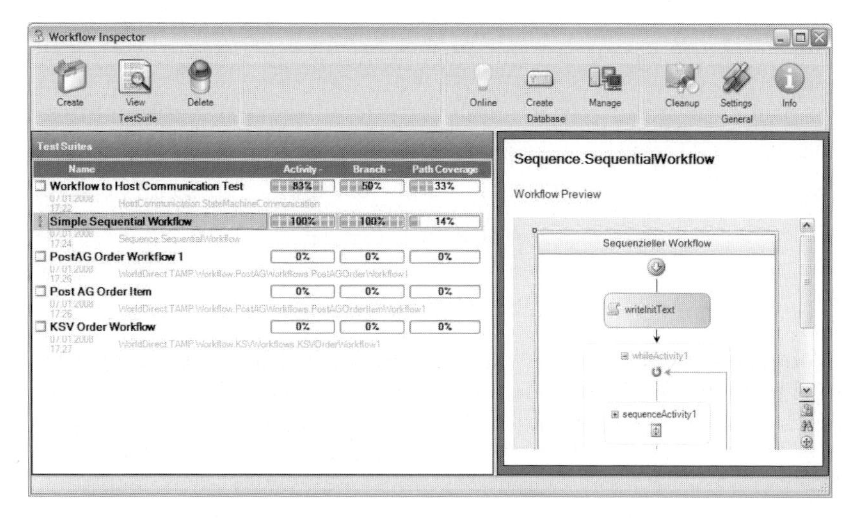

Fig. 6. WorkflowInspector workbench

2. *Data Analysis* One of the main features of WorkflowInspector is the possibility to display tracked data in a user friendly way and as detailed as possible. This is done by extensive use of graphical features such as graph or tree representations.

   The section called *Data Analysis* shows the communication between the *GUI* and the *Tracking Service*. There are no additional components of the application tier involved in this process as the main challenge is to prepare all tracked data for visualization purposes. This is done by the user interface components directly.
3. *Test Execution and Evaluation* The last part deals with test execution and evaluation. The *Test Framework* queries all data about existing workflow executions using the *Tracking Service*. After applying tests and preparing the data for graphical display the values can be processed by the *GUI*. The test results are saved back to the database.

4.5 Usage Example

After WorkflowInspector is started, the main screen is displayed (cf. Figure 6). The window is divided in two main sections: 1) *TestSuite Overview* shows all actual workflows under test (WUT). They are represented by a unique workflow name and an arbitrary TestSuite name. If there have been applied some tests the percentage of the test coverage is shown in the form of progress bars beside the test name. 2) *Graphical Representation* of the workflow as it was defined by the developer. In fact, even the arrangement of the single workflow components is equal in case a layout file is provided with the workflow assembly.

Adding a New TestSuite. When a new TestSuite is added, several preferences may be set. First, a workflow assembly has to be selected. If there are some

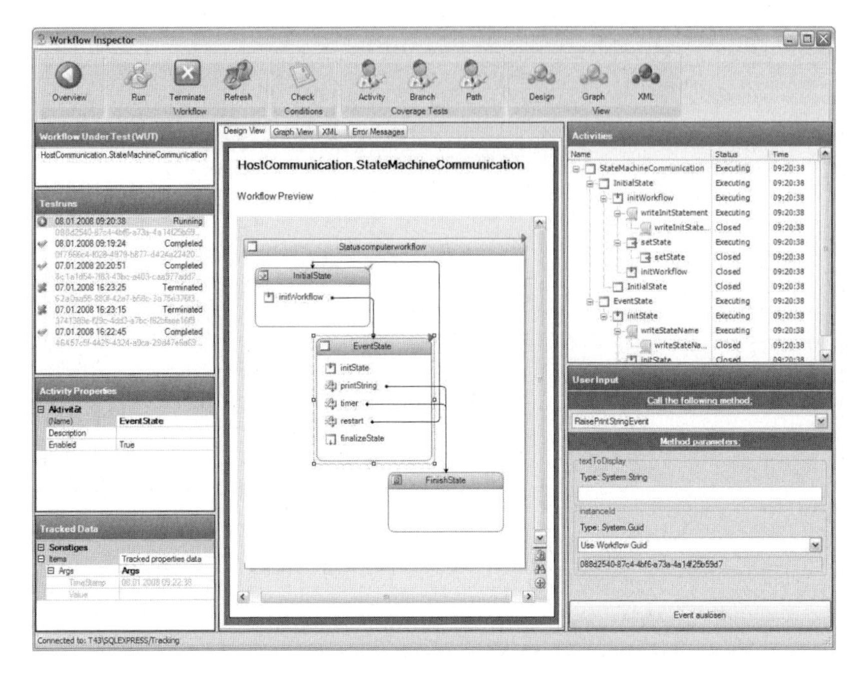

Fig. 7. Detailed TestRuns view

additional assemblies needed more file explorer windows will be displayed. Next, some pre- and postconditions for the test can be set.

Detailed TestRuns View. Once the TestSuite is saved a detailed TestRuns view can be accessed. It shows all details about the single workflow executions. The window is partitioned into several sections (cf. Figure 7). 1) *Workflow Under Test (WUT)* contains the full workflow name to avoid misunderstandings. 2) *TestRuns* shows all TestRuns executed. A green play button indicates that the TestRun is actually running. If a green check mark shows up the TestRun was completed successfully. In contrast a red cross indicates a failure and terminated workflow. 3) *Activity Properties and Tracked Data* shows the properties of each activity of the workflow. These can either be predefined values by the Windows Workflow Foundation or custom parameters like for example looping conditions. To review the execution process and to find possible errors the single execution steps and its properties are displayed. 4) *Activities* enable the user to see every single step of the workflow execution ordered by execution time. If an error occurs while the workflow is executed the activities are marked with *Failure* and so is the parent workflow. 5) *User Input* used every time a user interaction is needed, the application generates a user form depending on the required input data. This enables developers to execute workflows without having to code a user interface. 6) *Design View* is the center part of the *TestRuns View* which is used to display the workflow graphical representation already known from the *Main Screen* or the window to add a new TestRun. And finally the *Graph View* provides a complete new graphical representation. Here the workflow is

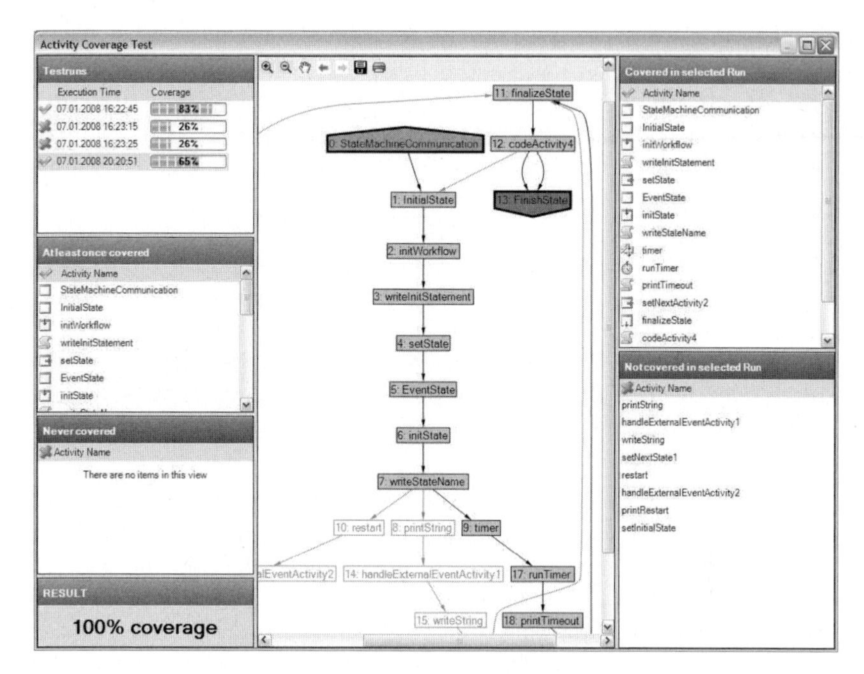

Fig. 8. Activity coverage test result window

shown as directed graph. For sequential workflows this simply means a different formatting of the single components. However, with state machine workflows, the nested activities are converted into a "flat" sequential representation. This enables developers, testers and also end users to get a better overview of the whole system and its complexity by use of a single picture.

WorkflowInspector has a built-in algorithm that transforms all types of workflows into directed graphs (cf. Figure 8).

4.6 Perform Coverage Tests

A coverage test may be applied to a TestSuite which contains at least one TestRun. As representative example the activity coverage test result window is shown (cf. Figure 8).

The center of the window shows the *Graph View* of the workflow. All executed activities are marked in blue. The transitions are represented by black arrows which connect the single activities. Not executed activities and transitions are displayed in gray color. The result window is divided into several sections which itemize the test results. *TestRuns* shows all workflow executions and their activity coverage using a progress bar. The graph view changes when selecting a different TestRun. *Covered in the selected run* shows all activities which were executed in the TestRun which is selected in the *TestRuns* section. *Not covered in the selected run* shows all activities not covered during the selected TestRun. *At least once covered* shows the activities which were at least once executed during **all** workflow executions of this TestSuite. *Never covered* shows all activities which were never executed during *all* workflow executions of this Test-Suite. *RESULT* shows the overall activity coverage calculated from the *At least once covered* and *Never covered* values. The test execution leads also to a change of the progress bar percentage value in the *Main Screen*.

5 Conclusion

In this paper a new approach to test Windows Workflow Foundation based workflows was presented. At the moment WorkflowInspector is the only application available providing the presented functionality. It enhances the overall development process as described in the following. The arguments are adapted from iterative development models, e.g. V-Model XT (cf. [10]), and conventional unit testing techniques (cf. [11]).

5.1 Advantages

1. *Increased Project Quality* WorkflowInspector increases the quality of software. It allows the developer to perform automated tests of the application core (i.e. the workflow) as often as possible. Errors may be detected immediately after changes in the workflow definition have been made. Even though software bugs may not be fully eliminated, their amount can be reduced noticeably. Hence, WorkflowInspector is a useful extension of conventional source code testing methods.
2. *Tests Allow to check Refactoring* By using workflow tests it is possible to change parts of the workflow throughout the lifetime of the application. This refers for example to the readability of the workflow definition, documentation or naming conventions for activities and events. Once some changes have been performed, WorkflowInspector may be used to check immediately if the behavior of the workflow is still identical.
3. *Shifting Focus* The focus of the application development is shifted from maintenance to specification, design and implementation. Hence, the appearance of bugs is reduced.
4. *Improvement of the Communication Between All Involved Parties* The visualization capabilities are one of the major advancements all involved parties benefit from. The workflow developer, head of development, head of testing, testers and users are able to discuss on the basis of the same illustrations. The possibility of executing rudimentary workflows allows to demonstrate application flows even at specification time. This for example supports the customers' understanding of the Windows Workflow Foundation application design. Thus, specific needs may be expressed more precisely. In addition, customers are able to track the whole workflow and application development in every iteration.

5.2 Benefits of the Usage of WorkflowInspector at World-Direct

Workflow Inspector has been developed in the context of a research cooperation between the University of Innsbruck and world-direct. The tool is used in development projects of world-direct for testing and evaluating workflows and is extended continuously. Currently, world-direct is developing plug-ins for a deeper integration of the software in the development framework.

References

1. Microsoft: Microsoft. NET Framework 3.0 (2007) (Accessed on 2007-03-01) , http://www.netfx3.com/
2. Aschenbrenner, K.: Windows Workflow Foundation - Designer für effektive Workflows. dotnetpro 1, 78–85 (2006)
3. Kanjilal, J.: An Introduction to Windows Workflow Foundation (2006) (Accessed on 2008-01-21), http://aspalliance.com/1074_An_Introduction_to_Windows_Workflow_Foundation
4. Allen, S.: Windows Workflow Foundation - Practical WF Techniques and Examples using XAML and C#. Packt Publishing (2006)
5. Pressman, R.S.: Software Engineering: A Practitioner's Approach, 6th edn. McGraw-Hill Higher Education, New York (2004)
6. Li, Z., Sun, W., Jiang, Z.B., Zhang, X.: BPEL4WS Unit Testing: Framework and Implementation. In: Proceedings of the IEEE International Conference on Web Services (ICWS 2005), vol. 1, pp. 103–110. IBM China Research Lab (2005)
7. Mayer, P., Lübke, D.: Towards a BPEL unit testing framework. In: Proceedings of the 2006 workshop on Testing, analysis, and verification of web services and applications, Portland, Maine, University of Hannover, FG Software Engineering, pp. 33–42. ACM Press, New York (2006)
8. Microsoft: The Official Microsoft ASP.NET Site (2008) (Accessed on 2008-01-29), http://www.asp.net/
9. NUnit.org: NUnit (2007) (Accessed on 2008-01-21), http://www.nunit.org
10. Koordinierung und Beratungsstelle der Bundesregierung für Informationstechnik in der Bundesverwaltung: V-Modell XT 1.2.1 Dokumentation. Technical report, Bundesminsterium des Innern (2007)
11. Burke, E.M., Coyner, B.M.: Java Extreme Programming Cookbook, 1st edn. O'Reilly, Sebastopol (2003)

The jABC Approach to Rigorous Collaborative Development of SCM Applications

Martina Hörmann[1], Tiziana Margaria[2], Thomas Mender[1], Ralf Nagel[3], Bernhard Steffen[3], and Hong Trinh[1]

[1] IKEA IT Germany GmbH, Werne, Germany
[2] Chair of Service and Software Engineering, Institute for Informatics, University of Potsdam, Germany
margaria@cs.uni-potsdam.de
[3] Chair of Programming Systems, University of Dortmund, Germany
{ralf.nagel,steffen}@cs.uni-dortmund.de

Abstract. Our approach to the model-driven collaborative design of IKEA's P3 Delivery Management Process uses the jABC [9] for model driven mediation and choreography to complement a RUP-based (Rational Unified Process) development process. jABC is a framework for service development based on Lightweight Process Coordination. Users (product developers and system/software designers) easily develop services and applications by composing reusable building-blocks into (flow-) graph structures that can be animated, analyzed, simulated, verified, executed, and compiled. This way of handling the collaborative design of complex embedded systems has proven to be effective and adequate for the cooperation of *non-programmers* and *non-technical people*, which is the focus of this contribution, and it is now being rolled out in the operative practice.

1 The Setting: The P3 Challenge

Shipping goods beyond country boundaries using various means of transportation requires an enormous organizational effort. IKEA is currently redesigning the whole IT lansdscape around its world-wide delivery management process. This ongoing project involves a major effort by teams distributed world-wide and spanning various corporations.

This paper addresses the design of an integrated document management system for this process, provided by IKEA IT Germany. In this system,

- the document management system sits in the background, essentially as a controller/executor serving the overall delivery process.
- its reliability is business critical. In particular this requires the integration of flexible mechanisms for fault tolerance.
- it is realized as a network of platforms, ranging from pure data management to systems steering the loading and unloading of vehicles or monitoring the progress of a shipment.

T. Margaria and B. Steffen (Eds.): ISoLA 2008, CCIS 17, pp. 724–737, 2008.

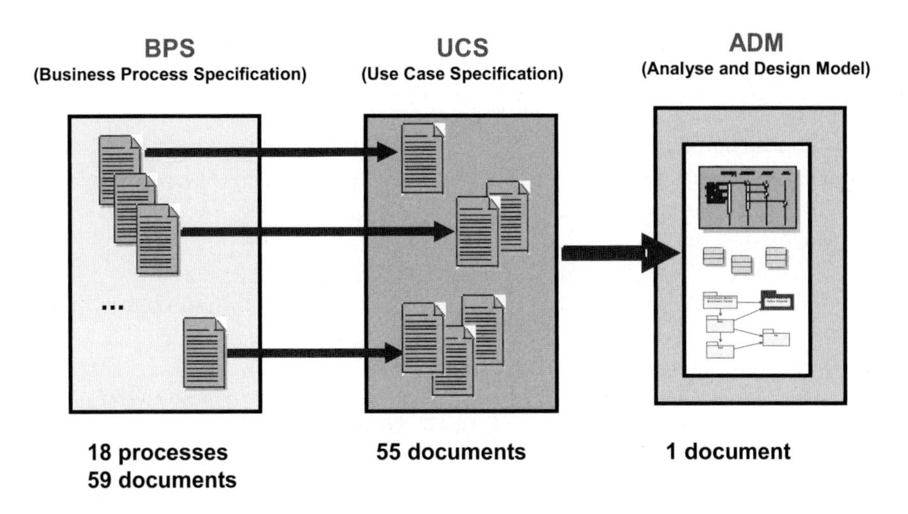

Fig. 1. The IKEA IT working method within P3: RUP workflow

In this paper, we show how our approach to the model-driven collaborative design of IKEA's P3 Document Management Process uses the jABC [9] for model driven mediation and choreography to complement a RUP-based (Rational Unified Process) development process.

As shown in Fig. 1, the development process in use at IKEA is the state-of-the-art Rational Unified Process (RUP). Requirement modelling tools are Microsoft Word for a large number of requirement documents produced by non-technical project members, together with Rational products (Rose) for Use cases and for the subsequent analysis and design model. The development modelling language is UML (Unified Modelling Language).

Although a widely recognized development best practice, RUP with UML turned out not to adequately cover the needs of P3: while the whole project addresses processes, most of the models support primarily a static view instead of a behavioral description. This leads to a number of deficiencies:

- *Vertically*, it fails to consistently connect the different levels of abstraction. E.g., there is no clear connection between the Use cases, which are the entry point to UML, and the Business Process Specifications provided by the business analysts (which, in our case, are spread in 59 word documents describing 18 processes).
- *Horizontally*, it fails to consistently connect the different models at the same level. E.g., the mutual dependencies between the many Use case are not addressed.

As an obvious consequence, the impact of changes to an individual process model remains totally undetected.

We introduced the jABC-based process modelling approach to P3 in order to complement the RUP modelling in a way that compensates for the mentioned deficiencies. In particular, this made it possible to check consistency vertically, horizontally, and over changes.

Addressing non-IT users
There are three large areas of related work, which, in fact, can be seen as the three main facets of our approach: model-driven design, service oriented computing, and business process modelling. The main differences to our jABC-based approach can be sketched quite easily: the first two areas view the world from the technological/IT perspective. They do not (directly) address the applications experts. Business process modelling, in contrast, supports the business expert, but leaves the classical bunsines/IT gap when it comes to the realization. The following elaboration is not comprehensive, but addresses the main characteristics of these three areas, which

Numerous techniques, models, and diagrams have been proposed by the UML-community to capture different kinds of requirements, and there have been attempts to address the mutual consistency between these artefacts. Examples of such approaches are GMT [5] and Fujaba [7]. However, these attempts are technically involved, requiring knowledge of technical modelling, UML, and programming, and typically address only very specific aspects. Thus they are not yet ready for a wider systematic use in practice, and require significant computer science knowledge. In particular, they are inadequate for a use by non-IT people, like business analysts because they are tied to the IT perspective. Rather than reflecting the user process, these models specify IT-based solutions. This is true e.g. for the whole Rational suite, also at the platform independent modelling levels.

Service-oriented computing virtualizes platforms and functionality and establishes a new kind of reuse. In particular in combination with standards like e.g. in Web Services, this is rather promising. Still, the methodology is not yet at a level accessible by application experts. The required knowledge about the syntax is awkward, the provided frameworks and tools are still quite unreliable, due to too many layers that must work together perfectly, and are outside of the responsibility of the user and of the developer, and still require too much knowledge about e.g., middleware and interface specification, including formalism like WSDL. This is an agreed result from the experience of two years of Semantic Web Service Challenge: lessons learned that explicitely address this point are summarized in a specific Chapter of the book [22] and in [15].

Finally, there exist also many approaches to business process modelling and workflow management, typically supported for analysis by techniques like simulation. However, they lack (intuitive) verification techniques for end-to-end processes, and they are not adequately linked to the realization process: the known cultural gap between business and IT remains unresolved. The BPEL [3] approach might look like an exception here, as it comes with dedicated execution engines which support the execution of the process models themselves - and indeed, this approach is the most similar to ours. However, BPEL engines typically fail in practice (in particular, when cross platform/organizational processes are concerned), as they are focussed on Web Services, and largely proprietary. The focus on the sole Web service technology, e.g. excludes their application in business scenarios comprising the processing of high data volumes, or (legacy) functionality not available as Web Services. Moreover, BPEL (like BPNM) can not really be regarded as a language for non IT people.

Putting non-IT experts in the center means that in particular, roles and rights, or permissions can be controlled (defined, modified, monitored) by the business expert without requiring any IT support, on easily understandable models. These models are then successively refined in our jABC-based approach up to a level where the basic functionalities can be implemented as simple services. The code for these services is typically rather small, just combining results of some calls to APIs or Web Services, and can be semi-automatically generated to a large extent. The quality of these services has to be guaranteed by the providers, according to some service-level agreement. Thus typical implementation issues, like e.g., connecting to data bases or executing a transaction on an ERP system, are virtualized for the jABC, i.e., not in the focus here, and delegated to other parties. Moreover concerns like e.g. high availability, roll back, and the management of session and long running transactions do also not belong to the top-level modelling framework. They are captured by our execution engine, which also comprises the functionality of the popular BPEL engines like Active BPEL [1].

This radically service-oriented approach puts the emphasis on the business process and hands the control over to the IT only at the level of elementary services. Thus the business side is and remains process owner much longer than in usual model-driven approaches. Thus changing requirements at the business side can mostly be treated in the business process model, typically without requiring IT support. On the other hand, platform migration may happen simply by exchanging the service implementations, and therefore transparent to the business user.

We call this approach 'One-Thing Approach' (OTA, [26]), as there is in fact only one artefact during the whole systems' life cycle. This artefact is successively refined in various dimensions in order to add details concerning roles, rights, permissions, performance constraints, simulation code (to animate the models), productive code, pre/post conditions, etc.., with the effect that all stakeholders, including the application expert, can follow the progress from their perspective (view): initially, application experts may e.g. only browse the documentation and annotate the models, but as soon as some simulation code is available, they may start playing with the system in order to check and enforce an adequate user experience. The user experience gets the more realistic the further the development progresses. This continuous involvement of the application expert allows one to control the harm of the classical business/IT gap, because misconceptions and misunderstandings become immediately apparent.

In the following we will briefly sketch the basic concepts of the jABC Modelling framework (Sect. 2), before we enter the main part of the paper, the presentation of our document management process (Sect. 3), which focusses on the consistency and the execution-oriented features of the jABC. Finally we give some conclusions.

2 Basic Concepts of the jABC Modelling Framework

jABC [9,10] is a framework for service-oriented model driven development based on Lightweight Process Coordination [17]. Predecessors of jABC have been used since 1995 to design, among others, industrial telecommunication services [20], Web-based distributed decision support systems [11], and test automation environments for Computer-Telephony integrated systems [8].

jABC allows users to easily develop services and applications by composing reusable building-blocks into (flow-)graph structures. This development process is supported by an extensible set of plugins that provide additional functionality in order to adequately support all the activities needed along the development lifecycle like e.g. animation, rapid prototyping, formal verification, debugging, code generation, and evolution. It does not substitute but rather enhance other modelling practices like the UML-based RUP (Rational Unified Process, [24]), which are in fact used in our process to design the single components.

Lightweight Process Coordination offers a number of advantages that play a particular role when integrating off-the-shelf, possibly remote functionalities.

- **Simplicity.** jABC focuses on application experts, who are typically non-programmers. The basic ideas of our modelling process have been explained in past projects to new participants in less than one hour.
- **Agility.** We expect requirements, models, and artefacts to change over time, therefore the process supports evolution as a normal process phase.
- **Customizability.** The building blocks which form the model can be freely renamed or restructured to fit the habits of the application experts.
- **Consistency.** The same modelling paradigm underlies the whole process, from the very first steps of prototyping up to the final execution, guaranteeing traceability and semantic consistency.
- **Verification.** With techniques like model checking and local checks we support the user to keep the models consistent throughout their evolution modify his model. The basic idea is to define local or global properties that the model must satisfy and to provide automatic checking mechanisms.
- **Service orientation.** Existing or external features, applications, or services can be easily integrated into a model by wrapping the existing functionality into building blocks that can be used inside the models.
- **Executability.** The model can have different kinds of execution code. These can be as abstract as textual descriptions (e.g. in the first animations during requirement capture), and as concrete as the final runtime implementation.
- **Universality.** Thanks to Java as platform-independent, object-oriented implementation language, jABC can be easily adopted in a large variety of technical contexts and of application domains.

The central advantage of this approach is that it is intuitive and expressive enough to enable all the stakeholders (business experts, process modelers, designers, software developers, quality assurer, and the like) to participate throughout the whole system life cycle, and each at the own level of expertise. For this the basic modelling in terms of hierarchical flow graphs (SLGs, see Sect. 3) can be enriched on demand in a consistent fashion to comprise concurrency, roles and rights, permissions, exception handling, etc.. The control for all these enrichments stays with the responsible expert:

- roles and rights or permissions are under the full control of the business expert,
- exception handling has more flavors, like e.g.:
  - the application side, like dealing with disease and replacement of personnel. This has to be explicitly modelled as a process within the jABC by the application expert.
  - the technical side, like dealing with a broken server. This is a matter of implementation, but may also be taken care of by the platform by means of technology for high availability. In fact, we have also realized a process-based high availability solution within the jABC for this purpose, which needs to be set up by the platform expert.
  - transaction safety. This is typically under the responsibility of the service providers. In cases where a whole subprocess needs to be rolled back, the corresponding roll back process needs to be modelled in a similar fashion as the high availability process. However, in contrast to the high availability case, where a certain safe state has to be reestablished, roll back requires application knowledge, as it is typically not possible to simply undo executed process steps. - This is quite similar as e.g. in solutions for BPEL.
- Validation and monitoring are quite complex, and in the hands of more than one stakeholder, as they involve application knowledge, as well a different kinds of technical knowledge about logics, tools, etc.. Still, also their impact can be viewed in a stake holder-specific fashion in order for the stakeholders to be able to check whether their understanding and intention is still maintained.

The (application) process-specific part of all these facets is kept in one single model, the reason for us to call our approach 'One-Thing-Approach' [14,26]. This makes it possible for all the stakeholders to be able to check at any time the progress of development from their view point. In particular, it is possible that partially implemented processes can be executed in mixed mode: some parts might still be navigated just by documentation browsing, others animated in simulation mode, and even other really run using productive code. Such heterogeneous situations appear dominantly in later phases of the process life cycle, where the impact of modifications must be investigated. The one-thing-approach serves in these cases for early, realistic experimental feedback.

The model is a Service Logic Graph, initially very coarse and successively refined in our jABC-based approach to a level where the basic functionalities can be implemented as simple services. It is important that this refinement is done from the application point of view: all the models are meant to reflect (sub) processes supporting concrete users of the system under development. This reduces the business/IT gap, moves it to a later phase of the conception/design,

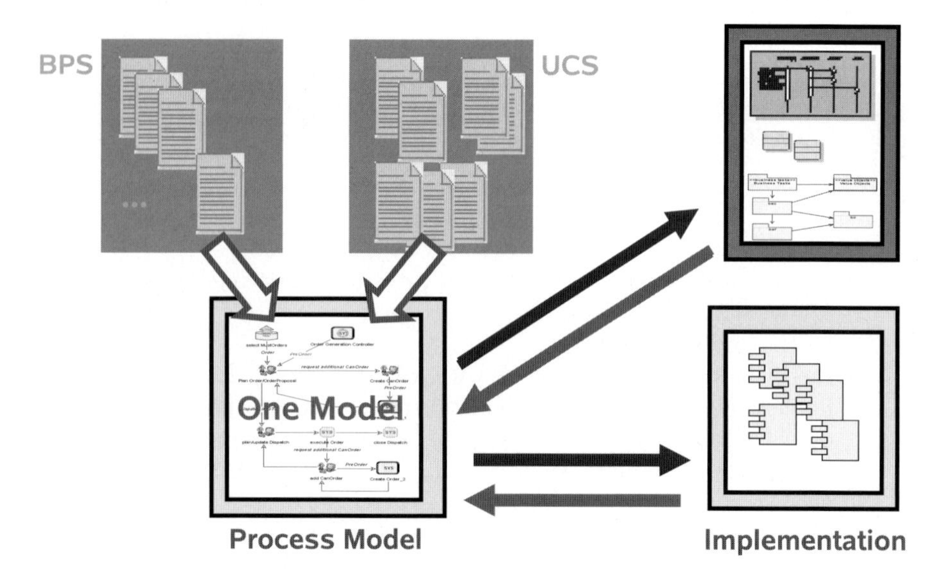

Fig. 2. The One Model Approach in the jABC

and gives a maximum of freedom for business process evolution. It also lowers the dependency from standard software, as the required elementary services are typically supported by many providers.

This radically service-oriented approach makes changing requirements at the business side a business process modelling activity, typically not requiring any IT support. On the other hand, platform migration may happen simply by exchanging the service implementations, and therefore it becomes transparent to the business user.

We now illustrate some of the impact of the One-Thing-Approach along the concrete Document Management Process case study.

3 Designing the Document Management Process

A central requirement to the jABC process-oriented models was the capability to bridge the gap between the high-level descriptions of the whole project, typically produced by business analysts with no UML or technical background, and the detailed models usable by programmers and engineers at implementation time.

As shown in Fig. 1, we had a set of 114 distinct yet interrelated documents that described the high-level requirements and specifications for the new system. In the course of the projects, these documents were condensed into a single, hierarchical jABC model (see Fig. 2), which was annotated with the essential parts of the original documents, and which was immediately animatable and executable. This was done internally at IKEA, with consultancy by the jABC team.

In jABC, every functionality used within an application or service is encapsulated within a Service-Independent Building Block (SIB). In fact, we use SIBs to

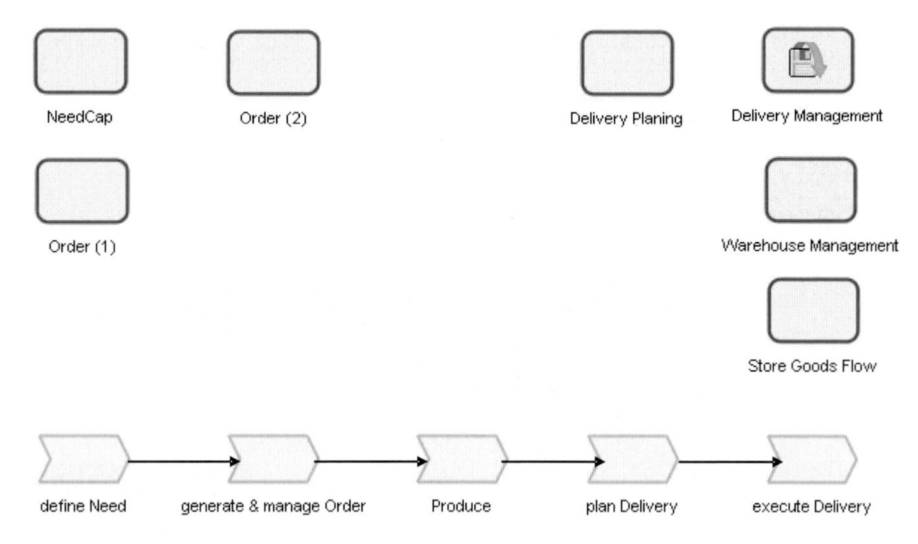

Fig. 3. The P3 Business Process Overview designed within the jABC

form the workflow of the P3 within a Service Logic Graph (SLG), jABC's way of defining processes. A SIB could contain a single functionality, or also whole subgraphs (another SLG), thus serving as a macro that hides more detailed and basic steps.

3.1 The Global Workflow

Using graph SIBs we are able to model the big picture workflow exactly as described by the business analysts: the process flow at the bottom of Fig. 3 shows the top-level phases of the supply chain process as modelled by business experts and as familiar to managers. Each phase is composed of specific processes, which are here drawn vertically on top of it. In particular, to the Execute Delivery phase are associated the processes Delivery Management, which describes the transport of goods, as well as Warehouse Management, and Store Goods Flow for the in-store logistics and warehousing. The Delivery Management process is already refined, as indicated by the graph SIB icon. Its refinement is the SLG on the left side of Fig. 4.

3.2 The Delivery Management Workflow

In Fig. 4 we see the top-level flow of the Delivery Management process. The Delivery Management SLG shows the typical structure of these processes, which makes explicit their embedded system character. On the left we see a high-level process for the shipment of the ordered goods, and on the right separate functionality for the associated document management, with an event driven communication that is highly deadline-sensitive. The document management runs on an own platform (hardware and software). In fact it is under the responsibility of a distinct group

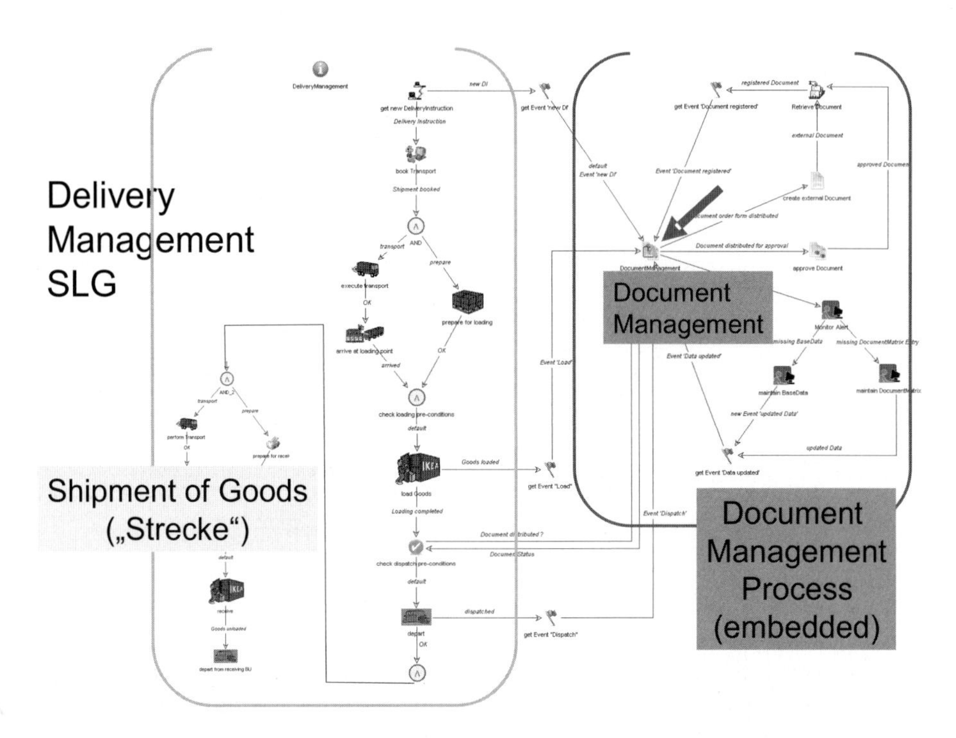

Fig. 4. The Delivery Management Workflow designed within the jABC

of designers and of a distinct operation team. The document management process executes in parallel with the shipment process, but additionally to producing its own deliverables (the shipment documents), it monitors and controls the shipment process. As such, the shipment process de facto behaves like a business and time critical controlled system, and the document manager as its controller.

3.3 The Document Management Workflow

The Document Management process shown in Fig. 5(left), which refines the SIB at the tip of the arrow in Fig. 4, is the basis for the successive implementation of the event driven embedded document management system. It contains functionality to set up and administer the lists of shipment documents associated with each shipment order, it manages the deadlines and the human-in-the-loop functionality and exceptions, and it contains a dedicated event manager, the Execute Event SIB, that runs in parallel to the document management functionality.

The Execute Event SIB, shown in Fig. 5(right), is itself still hierarchical: it has a subgraph Create Document List for creating the document list, and several occurrences of the Handle Document document handler. These more detailed processes are hidden in this subgraph, and can be expanded at need to the required level of detail.

At this stage of development, most SIBs just contain the calls to animation and simulation code. This is sufficient to animate the specifications and to show

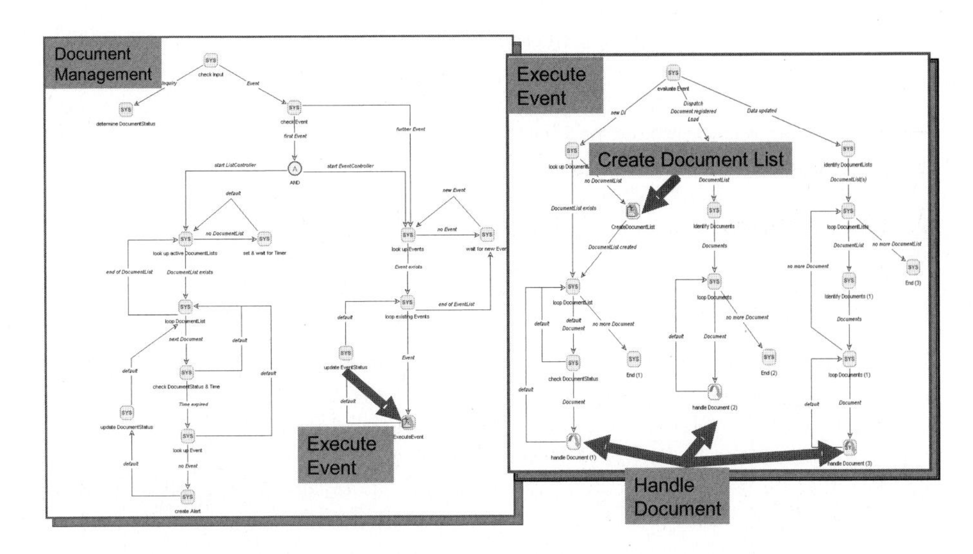

Fig. 5. The Document Management and the Execute-Event SLGs

the interplay of the different functionalities, in particular concerning the interoperability and cooperation of the shipment and document delivery subprocesses, which are under the responsibility of different teams.

Later on these SIBs will be further refined and finally implemented by software components, like Java classes or external web services provided by external systems and applications.

3.4 Workflow Granularity

The top-level worklow designed within the jABC shown in Fig. 3 is rather simple: it is for instance cycle free. The loops needed by the detailed tasks can be modelled in different ways, mostly depending on the desired abstraction of the workflow:

- they can be modelled within the implementation code of the specific SIBs, e.g., as iterations over variables. This is desirable, if there is no need to reason (or prove anything) about that behaviour at the modelling level, which is considered an implementation issue.
- if we are interested in the loop behaviour, we can refine the SLG of the workflow and model the (relevant) loops at the workflow level, either for the whole process, or just inside specific graph SIBs if that portion of the workflow needs specific attention.
- In principle, workflows can be refined up to the detail of single statements, if is desired.

Successive analysis of the code can help also in cases where the workflow has not been refined to the very end.

In this case, we ended with a successive refinement of the processes in 5 levels[1]. The overall business logic contained in the many documents was captured and expressed, without one line of code, resulting in the individuation of several shared subprocesses, that were isolated and capsuled in devoted models and reused several times.

The models, even at intermediate stages of design, were immediately executable as animated traces in the jABC, via the Tracer plugin.

3.5 Workflow Execution

After designing the workflow, by means of the tracer plugin we are able to animate, simulate or interpret it (depending on the kind of executable code associated with the SIBs: mock code, simulation code, or real implementation).

In this concrete case, the execution of the first design phase stepped through the processes and displayed the original document passages where these steps were described. Already this proved to be very valuable in the light of consistency checking, since multiple sources provided by different author teams could be examined next to each other and in the business logic context. Several imprecisions were this way unveiled.

Further levels of execution concerned simulation code and real implementation code.

3.6 Workflow Validation and Verification

Our approach also supports model checking-based [4,23] verification of compliance to business rules at the process level, to guarantee the satisfaction of certain properties. That way we are able to build *certified* business processes. A knowledge base of such properties or constraints greatly improves the overall quality and reliability of the processes.

SLGs are semantically interpreted as Kripke Transition Systems (KTS), a generalization of both Kripke structures and labelled transition systems [21] that allows labels both on nodes and edges. Nodes in the SLG represent activities (or services, or components, depending on the application domain). The edges directly correspond to the SIB branches: they describe how to continue the execution depending on the result of the previous activity. More formally, a KTS is defined as follows:

A KTS $(V, AP, Act, \rightarrow)$ consists of a set of nodes V and a set of atomic propositions AP describing basic properties for a node. The interpretation function $I : V \rightarrow 2^{AP}$ specifies which propositions hold at which node. A set of action labels Act is used to designate the edges. The possible transitions between nodes are given through the relation $\rightarrow \subseteq V \times Act \times V$ [21,2].

Model checking [4,23] is a powerful approach to automatic verification of models, as it provides an effective way to determine whether a given system model is consistent with a specified property. The jABC framework incorporates this

[1] We are not allowed to expose here more detail on the real concrete processes.

technique via a core plugin called GEAR [2]. Intuitively, any system modelled as SLG can be verified with this plugin: SLGs can be seen as KTS including atomic propositions and actions. Specifications of a model can be defined using appropriate formalisms, in the case of GEAR these are temporal logics, for example CTL (Computation Tree Logic) or the modal μ-calculus [12].

An example of such business rule is the following:

> A truckload can only `depart` if the `Bill of Consignment` and the `Load Approval` are ready. If it is a `Non-EU delivery` additionally the `Custom Documents` must be available:

$$\neg\mathsf{Departure}\ \mathbf{U}\ (\mathsf{BillOfConsignment}\ \wedge\ \mathsf{LoadApproval}\ \wedge\ (\mathsf{NonEUDelivery}\ \Rightarrow\ \mathsf{CustomDocuments}))$$

In these formulas, Departure, BillOfConsignment, etc are atomic propositions that hold in particular nodes of the model, while **U** is the *until* operator. These atomic propositions can be gained in different ways. In the simplest case they are annotated to the nodes manually by the user.

3.7 Code Generation

We can also generate source code for the SLGs by invoking one of the jABC code generators, offered by the Genesys plugin. Genesys is itself a service-oriented framework for the high-level construction of certified code generators. They differ in the structure and efficiency of the generated code, but all of them allow getting a running application that is independent of the jABC. In this case, the target platform is Java, for which we have a number of code generators (from the extruder to pure Java) that allow to fine-tune the degree of independence of the final code from jABC's structure and environment. The two extremes are the Extruders, that use the execution engine of our framework that provides features like thread and event handling, and Pure Generators, that fall back to the most basic engine provided by a platform, like e.g. the Java Runtime Environment (JRE).

3.8 Workflow Evolution

The whole process of designing the solution to the P3 redesign challenge can be solved with little initial coding effort by instantiating existing template SIBs (like the SYS SIB used here) and graphically designing and configuring the workflows at the SLGs level. In fact, this is already also sufficient to support a flexible change management, an important requirement for the second project phase.

4 Conclusions and Perspective

In this paper, we have shown how our approach to model-driven collaborative design was used for IKEA's P3 Document Management Process, where it complements the Rational Unified Process development process already in use. Central contribution is the support of the *vertical* consistency of models, e.g. across abstraction layers, as well as of the *horizontal* model consistency, which is needed e.g. across organizational borders within a same abstraction level. In this particular case we had to bridge e.g., between various business process specifications provided by business analysts and Use case/activity diagram views needed by the designers, keeping adequate track of the dependencies. With our techniques we were able to immediately detect so many of these dependencies which had been overseen before that it was decided to restart the modelling in our framework in order to avoid these problems by design.

Scenarios like this are ideal candidates for applying the one-thing-approach for end-to-end processes as described in [26]. There, horizontal consistency is guaranteed by maintaining the global perspective throughout the refinement process down to the code level, and vertical consistency by the simple discipline for refinement. Thus this holistic approach goes beyond state of the art approaches, as e.g. represented by IDEs like Eclipse and NetBeans [27], which do not support the business process level, as well as beyond process modelling tools like ARIS [6], which fail to capture the later phases of development. Also combinations of these techniques are not sufficient, as they introduce gaps when moving from one technique to the other. In contrast, in our one-thing-approach, changes at the business process level are immediately done on the 'one thing', and therefore immediately executable, as long as no new functionality is added that requires coding.

References

1. Active BPEL execution engine, `http://www.activevos.com/community-open-source.php`
2. Bakera, M., Renner, C.: GEAR - A Model Checking Plugin for the jABC framework (2007), `http://www.jabc.de/modelchecking/`
3. BPEL specifications website, `http://www.ibm.com/developerworks/library/specification/ws-bpel/`
4. Clarke, E.M., Grumberg, O., Peled, D.A.: Model Checking. MIT Press, Cambridge (2001)
5. Davis, J.: GME: Generic Modeling Environment, Demonstration session. In: OOPSLA, Anaheim, CA, pp. 82–83. ACM, New York (2003)
6. Davis, R.: ARIS Design Platform: Advanced Process Modelling and Administration. Springer, Heidelberg (2008)
7. Fujaba homepage, `http://wwwcs.uni-paderborn.de/cs/fujaba/index.html`
8. Hungar, H., Margaria, T., Steffen, B.: Test-Based Model Generation for Legacy Systems. In: IEEE International Test Conference (ITC), Charlotte, NC, September 30 - October 2 (2003)
9. jABC Website, `http://www.jabc.de`
10. Jörges, S., Kubczak, C., Nagel, R., Margaria, T., Steffen, B.: Model-Driven Development with the jABC. In: Bin, E., Ziv, A., Ur, S. (eds.) HVC 2006. LNCS, vol. 4383. Springer, Heidelberg (2007)

11. Karusseit, M., Margaria, T.: Feature-based Modelling of a Complex, Online-Reconfigurable Decision Support Service. In: WWV 2005. 1st Int'l Workshop on Automated Specification and Verification of Web Sites, Valencia, Spain, March 14-15 (2005); Post Workshop Proc. appear in ENTCS
12. Kozen, D.: Results on the Propositional mu-Calculus. Theoretical Computer Science 27, 333–354 (1983)
13. Margaria, T.: Web Services-Based Tool-Integration in the ETI Platform. SoSyM, Int. Journal on Software and System Modelling 4(2), 141–156 (2005)
14. Margaria, T.: Service Is in the Eyes of the Beholder. IEEE Computer 40(11), 33–37 (2007)
15. Margaria, T.: The Semantic Web Services Challenge: Tackling Complexity at the Orchestration Level. In: ICECCS 2008, 13th IEEE Intern. Conf. on Engineering of Complex Computer Systems, Belfast, UK, April 2008, pp. 183–189. IEEE CS Press, Los Alamitos (2008)
16. Margaria, T., Nagel, R., Steffen, B.: Remote Integration and Coordination of Verification Tools in jETI. In: Proc. ECBS 2005, 12th IEEE Int. Conf. on the Engineering of Computer Based Systems, Greenbelt, USA, April 2005, pp. 431–436. IEEE Computer Soc. Press, Los Alamitos (2005)
17. Margaria, T., Steffen, B.: Lightweight coarse-grained coordination: a scalable system-level approach. STTT 5(2–3), 107–123 (2004)
18. Margaria, T., Steffen, B.: From the How to the What. In: Proc. VSTTE 2005, Verified Software—Theories, Tools, and Experiments, IFIP Working Conference, Zurich. LNCS, vol. 4171. Springer, Heidelberg (2005)
19. Margaria, T., Steffen, B.: Service Engineering: Linking Business and IT. In: IEEE Computer, issue 60th anniv. of the Computer Society, pp. 53–63. IEEE Press, Los Alamitos (2006)
20. Margaria, T., Steffen, B., Reitenspieß, M.: Service-Oriented Design: The Roots. In: Benatallah, B., Casati, F., Traverso, P. (eds.) ICSOC 2005. LNCS, vol. 3826, pp. 450–464. Springer, Heidelberg (2005)
21. Müller-Olm, M., Schmidt, D.A., Steffen, B.: Model-Checking: A Tutorial Introduction. In: Cortesi, A., Filé, G. (eds.) SAS 1999. LNCS, vol. 1694, pp. 330–354. Springer, Heidelberg (1999)
22. Petrie, C., Lausen, H., Zaremba, M., Margaria, T. (eds.): Semantic Web Services Challenge: Results from the First Year (Semantic Web and Beyond). Springer, Heidelberg (to appear, November 2008)
23. Queille, J.-P., Sifakis, J.: Specification and verification of concurrent systems in CESAR. In: Proc. 5th Colloquium on International Symposium on Programming, pp. 337–351. Springer, London (1982)
24. Rational Unified Process, `http://www-306.ibm.com/software/awdtools/rup/`
25. Semantic Web Services Challenge: Challenge on Automating Web Services Mediation, Choreography and Discovery, `http://www.sws-challenge.org/`
26. Steffen, B., Narayan, P.: Full Life-Cycle Support for End-to-End Processes. IEEE Computer 40(11), 64–73 (2007)
27. SUN Microsystems's NetBeans IDE, `www.netbeans.org`

Gesper: Support to Capitalize on Experience in a Network of SMEs*

Maura Cerioli[1], Giovanni Lagorio[1], Enrico Morten[2], and Gianna Reggio[1]

[1] DISI–Dipartimento di Informatica e Scienze dell'Informazione,
Università di Genova, Via Dodecaneso 35, 16146 Genova, Italy
{cerioli,lagorio,reggio}@disi.unige.it
[2] Softeco Sismat S.p.A.
WTC Tower - Via De Marini 1, 16149 Genova, Italy
enrico.morten@softeco.it

Abstract. Small and medium enterprises (SMEs) are the most affected by the exponentially increasing complexity of the average software system: not losing the grip on the new technologies may turn out to be an unsustainable drain on productive effort, as their developers need to devote a substantial part of their time to learning instead of producing.

In order to support continuous education and gathering/reusing solutions, SMEs need a tool supported management of experience and knowledge, providing problem-driven searches.

We describe the experience gained in designing and developing *Gesper*, a tool for knowledge sharing that provides semantic searches based on ontologies. This tool has been tailored to the needs of SMEs and a prototype implementation has been built using free and open source tools.

Introduction

The complexity of the average software system is increasing each year, making production and maintenance more and more difficult. Indeed, such a fast growth may be sustained only thanks to the constantly improved technologies and methodologies for software development. Therefore, it is mandatory for software producers to keep their personnel and processes always updated.

Unfortunately, not losing the grip on the new technologies may turn out to be an unsustainable drain on the productive effort, requiring developers to devote a substantial part of their time to learning instead of producing. This is particularly true for small and medium enterprises (SMEs in the following), where the (human) resources are scant and the budget small.

Thus, many SMEs give up on a well planned effort. But, in order to keep in contact with the evolution of tools, methodologies and technologies, they rely on a plethora of ill assorted knowledge gathering efforts, like individual learning initiative, endeavors by team members to somehow cope with the new tools and

* This research has been supported by the Parco Scientifico e Tecnologico della Liguria s.c.p.a. - POS. N. 23 Avv. 2/2006.

T. Margaria and B. Steffen (Eds.): ISoLA 2008, CCIS 17, pp. 738–752, 2008.

technologies required by challenging projects, and acquisitions of new personnel, with a different cultural background. Then, the bits and pieces of knowledge so randomly acquired and the information about the availability of reusable assets produced by a team are expected to spontaneously spread through the personnel. But, relying on this person-to-person schema of knowledge dissemination has two main flaws. First of all, the person having the crucial bit of information for one project may be currently tied up into another one and hence not assignable to the lacking team. Thus, the knowledge cannot be accessed and shared at the required moment, even if it is available inside the SME. Moreover, the availability of the expertise (reusable resource) may be unknown to the people needing it, because they are not sufficiently familiar with the expert (the team that produced it). The obvious solution to these problems is to have a more formalized management of experience, knowledge, and resources available within the SME [1] allowing the needed information to be found without having to rely on the social network. However, any formal process has its costs and to keep them as low as possible, the best solution is to support the required activities by a tool. Though some approaches and software systems support knowledge management and collaborative working (see e.g., [3,14]), none of them is satisfactory for the management of the enterprise knowledge and experience in a SME. Indeed, in most cases those systems are specialized for a restricted kind of experience or documents in a particular phase of the development, like, for instance, the tools for code management (see, e.g., *Eclipse* [7]). The more general systems are usually expensive and complex, being designed for the application in large companies, and they require a difficult and time-consuming tailoring. Moreover, quite often such tools are capable of supporting only a specific process model and are difficult, or altogether impossible, to adapt to those in use in a given SME. To the best of our knowledge, ViSEK [8] is the tool whose aim is closest to ours. However, ViSEK is a wide-spectrum portal targeting a public sharing of knowledge and resources on software engineering. Instead, we need to model a more sophisticated mechanism, where resources are owned by individual SMEs, which can decide to keep some of them private, share some others with their partners, and even publish a few, possibly in a restricted version. Therefore, a fine-grained visibility policy has to be provided. Thus, the production of a new system appears to be the only viable solution to the problem. In this paper we describe a prototype of such a system, called *Gesper*, from GEStione dell'ESPERienza (Experience Management), which is currently under development by a group of SMEs and the Department of Computer Science (DISI) of the University of Genova.

The requirements and the design of the resources managed by Gesper are discussed in Section 1. Section 2 is devoted to the architecture and a sketch of the implementation. At the end we briefly discuss our results and further work.

[1] Public information can quite easily found on the internet by using tools like Google. The challenging problem is how to search data, which the SME wants to keep private.

1 Experience Management in a Network of SMEs

Designing a tool for managing experiences and knowledge for a cluster of cooperating SMEs has been more challenging from the viewpoint of its integration in the productive process and policies than technically. In the following subsections we discuss Gesper requirements and the part of design that is implied by them.

1.1 High-Level Requirements of Gesper

In order to help the SMEs to keep up with the ever-evolving challenges of software production, we have identified a few strategic points to be tackled.

First of all, the tool shall manage *easy to access* information, resources and experiences, making them immediately expendable assets of the enterprise. Notice that experiences, being memorized in the system (as opposed to inside the head of the person who actually made them) will be available independently of the career choices of the experience originators. Ideally, people will access the system to solve a specific problem and will get the correct resources, which could be references to experts, hints or carefully documented explanations of the solution(s) found by other people in previous projects, tutorials, web references and so forth. In Subsection 1.2 we will illustrate the conceptual model of managed resources. It is worth noting, however, that the main requirements are parametric on this model, being more concerned with searches and resource lifecycle, which are independent from the structure of the managed resources. Thus, most part of the requirement analysis and design of the tool discussed here, also applies to other contextes where the resources are differently modelled.

As we argued, the resources to be hoarded and searched should have not only a structure making immediate to extract knowledge from them, but also a clear connection to the problems they refer to, so that the search can be problem-driven, avoiding most false positives. To support this *semantic* search, resources should be indexed using a common dictionary including the most relevant terms of the problem domain. Thus, technically we need an ontology describing the problem domain, so that the resources may be indexed by keywords chosen from this ontology. Notice that the ontology is a configuration parameter of the system and, though Gesper is based on an ontology for software development, discussed in Subsection 2.1, it could be adapted to a different application domain to support the management of experience for another market.

A second important point is the integration of the managed resources into the company organization. This, on the one hand, means that they need to have a well-defined lifecycle. That is, newly inserted resources have to get an approval in order to become visible to users other than who has inserted them. In this way, for instance, a practitioner writes the first draft and submits it while a person more expert in company policies checks that the form agrees with the documentation standards and that security concerns about private data disclosures are met. This two-steps process also helps junior or newly hired staff to learn the company practices by comparing their original draft to the published version. Moreover, the resource will be updated or declared obsolete by an analogous review process, so that the repository will not be cluttered by useless information. On the other hand, the integration requires the resources to have different levels of visibility, so that the results of a query will depend on who is performing it, possibly granting more privileges to employees of the SME owning the system than to those working for partner companies, and limiting guest access to public data.

Finally, the efforts to document the development process required, for instance, by a quality plan should not be duplicated in order to capitalize on the experience gained during the development. Therefore, the information that can be retrieved from project documents, people curricula, etc should be automatically acquired, pending the check and approval of a human supervisor, of course. Even in the cases when structured knowledge cannot be (semi)automatically extracted from existing documents, it may still be convenient to integrate them in Gesper, to make them searchable in a problem-driven fashion and have their lifecycle managed by the tool. Indeed, such documents may provide a solution, albeit indirect, for some problem missing better answers by structured resources, and they have almost no extra production costs.

So far, we have discussed the requirements of Gesper from the viewpoint of an individual SME. However, the tool should also address the needs of a *cluster* of SMEs, supporting their cooperation. To this aim, the main requirement is the capability of sharing resources in a limited and controlled form, providing different levels of visibility, in order to let each company have full control of its own resources. Gesper is actually designed as a *federation* of instances. Thus, each company in the cluster owns an instance, installed on some local server, containing its own resources. On such server, internal and external users may perform queries with the assigned privileges. The cluster also owns an instance, which is populated with the resources, suitably restricted, of all the individual SMEs, in order to provide a centralized search point. To guarantee that no unwanted disclosures take place, the instance of each company exports a restricted view of its resources to the global instance.

1.2 Conceptual Model of Experience

A central point of the system design is the choice of which resources will be managed by the system, that is, which kinds of resource will possibly be the results of problem-driven searches. Indeed, modelling this aspect captures one of the tailoring needs for the system to be usable by a specific SME.

Figure 1 shows the fragment of UML [16] class diagram describing the resources at a high abstraction level. The root of the conceptual model is the class Resource, representing any kind of managed resource. All the results of a search in the system will be of a type extending Resource. Its attributes and relationships, hence, are those needed by the system to represent resources with a realistic lifecycle in the context of a cluster of companies and to use them for problem-driven searches. Indeed, resources are *tagged* by keywords described by the ontology, so that the *semantic* search is possible. The results of a search are briefly presented by just showing their name and a short description, for the user to decide if a closer examination is worthwhile. Depending on the role of

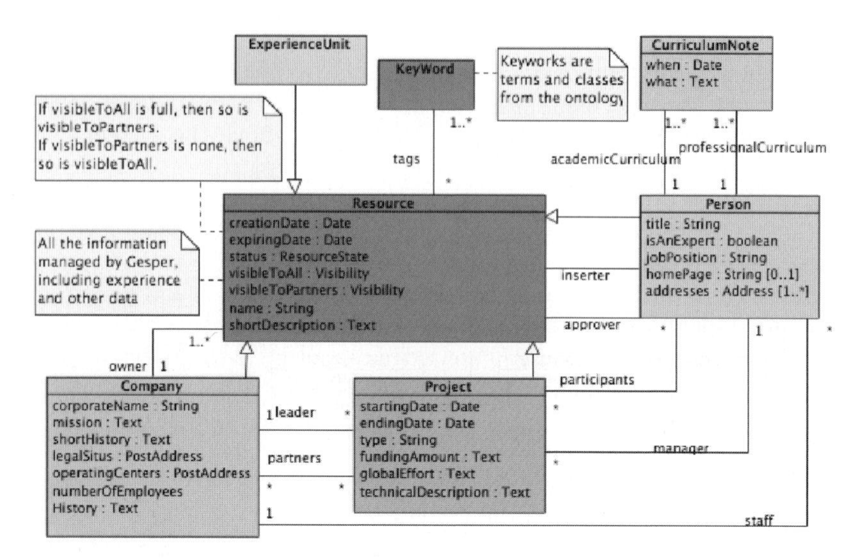

Fig. 1. Conceptual model of resources

the user, who can be an employee of the company owning the resource, or of a partner company, or just any guest, the level of visibility of the resource can be full (that is, the user can see all the details), or restricted (that is, only the name and the short description are shown), or none at all, corresponding to an exclusion of that resource from the search results. For the owning company, the visibility level is always full. However, not everybody in the company staff has the complete control of the resource. In particular, two (possibly coinciding) roles are identified for those entitled to editing: the employee who has submitted the draft of the resource and the manager for approval of the resource. Indeed, each resource has a status, which can be *draft*, *automatically inserted* (hence more prone to contain errors), *approved*, and *obsolete*. The last value is automatically set by the system when the resource has passed its expiring date and can be reset by the approver, who is responsible for all aspects of the resource lifecycle.

Resources are specialized in order to capture different kinds of elements somehow representing knowledge.

The class Person has a flag for distinguishing experts, who can appear as results of a query if their expertise matches the search parameters. Persons who are not flagged as experts may still be represented within Gesper, because they are related to some other resource, for instance they work for the company or are involved in some project, yet, they will not be yielded as results of any query. It is interesting to note that during the requirement elicitation the SMEs involved as clients refused to have the keywords and the expert flag automatically extracted from the curricula of a person. Indeed, our clients want to keep the full control on who should be contacted as expert on a given topic. Thus, Gesper allows an employee to have a deep knowledge of some area, as recorded in his/her curriculum, and yet not appear as an expert of that topic so that (s)he will not be bothered with requests for help from his/her colleagues.

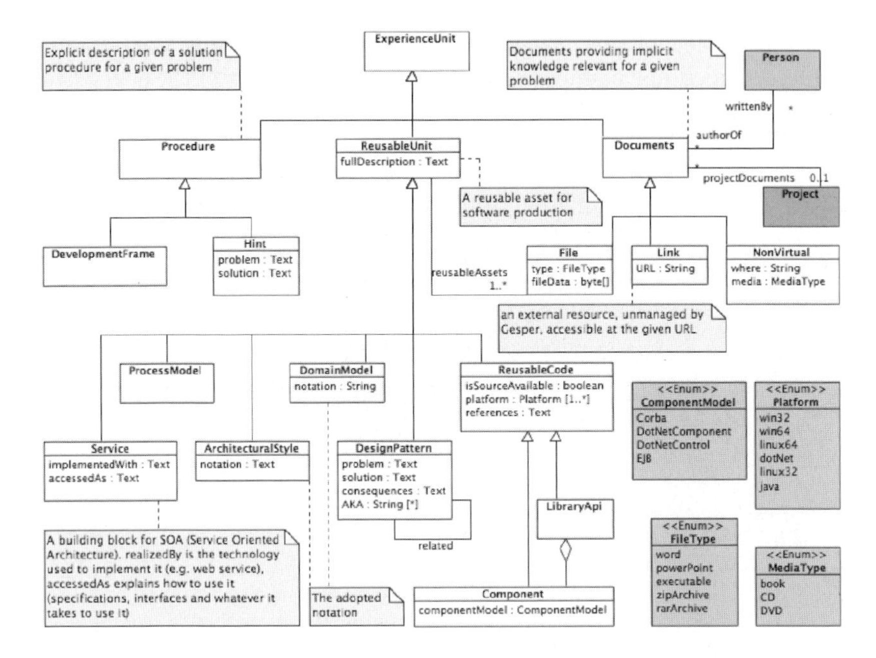

Fig. 2. Conceptual model of resources representing experience

The class Project classifies not only the projects that involves, or involved, the SME owning this installation of Gesper, but also those of partner companies and those which some known expert participated in. Projects are valuable resources, for instance, for solving problems in the area of locating prospective partners in future projects or support of people experienced in the bureaucracy of a specific form of funding. Moreover, projects are a natural source of implicit knowledge in the form of the produced documents, which can be managed as elements of a special subclass of ExperienceUnit.

The class Company has as elements the SME owning this installation of Gesper, owning all the resources inserted by its employees, and the other companies in the SME cluster, the partners in some project, and so on.

The most interesting specialization of Resource is the class ExperienceUnit, which captures the knowledge, both in implicit and explicit forms, accumulated through the experience of the SME, its employees and partners. In Figure 2 we detail the descendants of ExperienceUnit.

The first level of specialization distinguishes the experience units in categories, accordingly to how the user can put the experience to practical use. Indeed, we have Procedure, representing resources that directly describe a procedure to solve a problem, like, for instance, hints and solution for specific problems formalized as *problem frames* (see, e.g., [4]), ReusableUnit, whose instances are reusable assets to be directly imported and used in the software development, like, for instance, models, code or design patterns [9], and Document, which indirectly provide knowledge, like, for instance, files managed by Gesper itself, or external files, or even physical documents, e.g. books, CDs and DVDs.

The deeper levels of specializations have been only partially worked out and should be extended in a commercial tool. While a large part of the specialization tree having Resource as root could be reused in the model of another system of experience management for SME in different areas, the design of the categories of reusable units and procedures is mostly specific of SMEs in the ICT field and should be reworked for a different application.

1.3 Main Usage Scenarios

Let us briefly describe the usage scenarios concerning the core business of Gesper. As they are quite intuitive, we here summarize them mostly in natural language. However, they were all fully developed as use cases and we propose one of them in full details to let the reader get the gist of Gesper documentation.

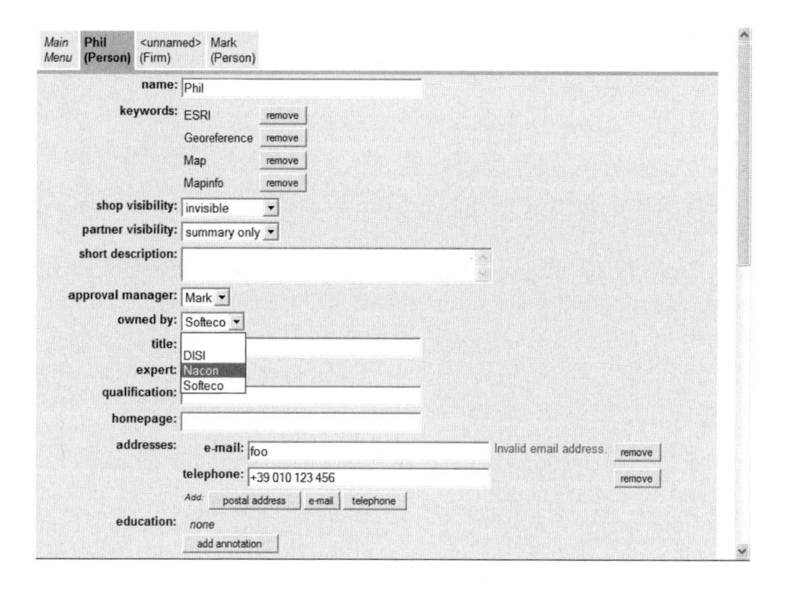

Fig. 3. Screenshot of the *Wizard*

When appropriate, the use cases are complemented by sketches of the corresponding GUI, to give the clients a better understanding of the expected interactions with the system.

In general, the user interface shall be as simple and intuitive as possible. It will show a graphical view and a tree representation of the ontology, to allow selecting keywords for resource searching and indexing, together with a research panel and, possibly, several editing/creating resource forms in separate tabs. The capability of inserting and/or editing multiple resources at the same time will be extremely useful when, while editing a resource, say the person *Phil* (as in the example shown in the screenshot in Figure 3), the user notices that the resource should be linked to another that has not been entered yet. Suppose, for instance, that the resource the user is inserting is *owned by ACME*, a firm which is not in the repository. Since the firm is not yet present, its name does not show up in the combo box corresponding to the relation *owned by*. Thanks to the tab-based interface, the user can open another tab to create the new firm, say *ACME*, and save it in the repository. Because the combo boxes are automatically updated, the user can then go back to editing the resource he/she was inserting, choose *ACME* from the combo box and seamlessly continue his/her work.

Resource insertion use case

Name Resource insertion
Primary actors Internal User (IU)
Supporting actors None
Description IU adds a new resource to the system
Triggers None
Pre-conditions IU is logged in the system
Normal flow *Course of actions*

1. IU chooses to create a new resource (specifying its kind).
2. Gesper creates an empty edit tab for the new resource.
3. IU correctly fills in the fields with the resource data:
   - selecting keywords from the ontology using indifferently the graphic view or the tree representation
   - choosing values from lists for enumeration types and resources.
4. IU saves the resource
5. Gesper automatically provides the values *draft* for the *status*, *IU* for the *inserter*, and the *current date* for the *creation date*; then it saves the new resource in the repository.

Post-conditions The repository contains the new resource
Additional requirements None
Notes and issues Data editing and creation will be supported by the GUI using:

- Combo boxes for fields admitting a finite (and reasonably small) set of values (see, e.g., the visibility tags in Figure 3).
- Combo boxes for enumerating resources that could be linked with the one the user is inserting or editing. Furthermore, these combo boxes will be views on the repository, automatically updated when something changes (see, e.g., the `owned by` field in Figure 3).
- Instant field validation, warning the users by means of not obtrusive hints and forbidding to save inconsistent data (see, e.g., near the `e-mail` field in Figure 3).
- The graphical and tree representations of the ontology for selecting the keywords for the resource (not present in the fragment in Figure 3).

Automatic insertion of a documental resource. Logged users can choose to insert a document using the *Automatic-Input*, to have the ontology keywords automatically extracted by the tool.

Users select a document file in their (local) system specifying the template[2] it adheres to; for instance, that for *meeting minutes*. Then, the tool parses the document, searching for ontology keywords to be associated with the resource. Gesper completes the other data automatically as for manual insertion and saves the new resource with state *automatically inserted*.

Edit and approval of a resource. Managers can review, edit and approve resources. Gesper provides, to logged managers, a list of draft resources to be reviewed. When one of these resource is selected by a manager, Gesper opens an edit tab where the resource can be edited and, optionally, approved.

Searching. From the search page, users can insert a search string, choose which kinds of resources they are interested in, and start the search. Gesper shows the list of the matching resources and allows to refine the search string manually or using input from either (or both) representations of the ontology.

When the search string contains one keyword from the ontology, the graphic view of the ontology is centered on that (and the same one is selected on the tree representation). Otherwise, if more keywords are present, then the user is asked to choose the one to use as centering point of the ontology representations.

2 Gesper Architecture and Implementation

In this section we sketches Gesper architecture and briefly discuss the most interesting implementation details.

It is interesting to note that a large part of the architecture has been almost completely fixed by the decision, at the level of requirements, of using already available open-source and freeware software. Thus, the design phase has focused mainly on the definition of the ontology, discussed in Subsection 2.1.

2.1 Ontology

The choice of the ontology is an important part of the customization of Gesper. Indeed, the ontology plays the role of dictionary for the keywords used to tag the resources and hence to direct the searches. Thus, changing the ontology effectively changes the applicative domain (within the limits imposed by the modelled resources).

An acceptable ontology for Gesper should encompass not only the concepts used in software development, covering both the technologies and the processes, but also those specific of the applicative domains targeted by the SMEs using the system. Clearly, if all the aspects are fully developed, the ontology risks growing too much, becoming unmanageable. Therefore, we needed a carefully designed ontology that, on the one hand, spreads on different domains, from software engineering to, say, national healthcare organizations and industrial

[2] Gesper has to be customized for the templates defined in a particular SME, for instance by its QA plan. In the prototype we used templates of one of the client SMEs.

automation, and on the other hand, cut down to only those terms actually used by the interested SME. For instance, cutting down the software engineering terminology to those development processes actually used. Thus, we did not find a satisfactory ontology among the *plethora* of those somehow related to software development (see e.g., [1,15,13,20,19] and [5] for further references), as they were missing the domain specific parts. Moreover, we were not able to combine several ontologies on different domains to get what we needed, as merging the interesting ontologies would have produced a too large result and required careful work to avoid duplicates of concepts on the overlapping areas.

Therefore, we designed the ontology provided with the prototype in a collaborative way with the help of software developers working in several different SMEs, in particular those playing the role of Gesper clients. The current version is still incomplete, with only the major areas fully developed and should be improved in a realistic tool.

The design process of the ontology consisted of two steps.

First we discussed the categories with the aid of a visual model of the ontology, realized in UML, describing the infrastructure of the ontology. The model captures the classes used to categorize the concepts and their relationships, including subtyping, in an immediate way, very easy to understand. Thus, it provided an invaluable support to the several brainstorming meetings needed to finalize its structure. By design, all classes of the ontology contain either individual elements, that is, are leaves of the hierarchy, or only subclasses. In this phase, we also decided which part of the ontology to detail and use to index the resources in the prototype.

The second step of the process was the selection of the individual instances of the leaf classes and the links among those individuals, that is the instances of the relations between classes. This further analysis has been conducted in an asynchronous and concurrent way, starting from a textual file generated from the model and containing the structure of the ontology, that is the list of the classes and their relationships. Then each group involved in the design added to its own copy of the file the interesting instances and their links in fixed format and positions, so that the result could be automatically processed. The resulting files were merged and the complete file was used, on the one hand, to automatically import the ontology into Protégé (see, e.g., [18]), by a Protégé plug-in we have developed for this purpose, and, on the other hand, to update the UML model, by adding the class instances to it.

Finally, the Protégé project was exported in OWL [17] format to be used as a configuration parameter of Gesper. While in the current prototype the ontology is a fixed resource of the tool, an industrial strong tool should allow users to update and extend the ontology as needed. This aim could be easily achieved, for instance, by integrating the Protégé editor within Gesper.

The root level of the ontology is depicted in Figure 4. Notice that classes at this level describe the standard concepts of any software development process and are quite stable in time. On the contrary, the elements of the class `Applicative Domain` have been produced by analyzing the current projects of the involved

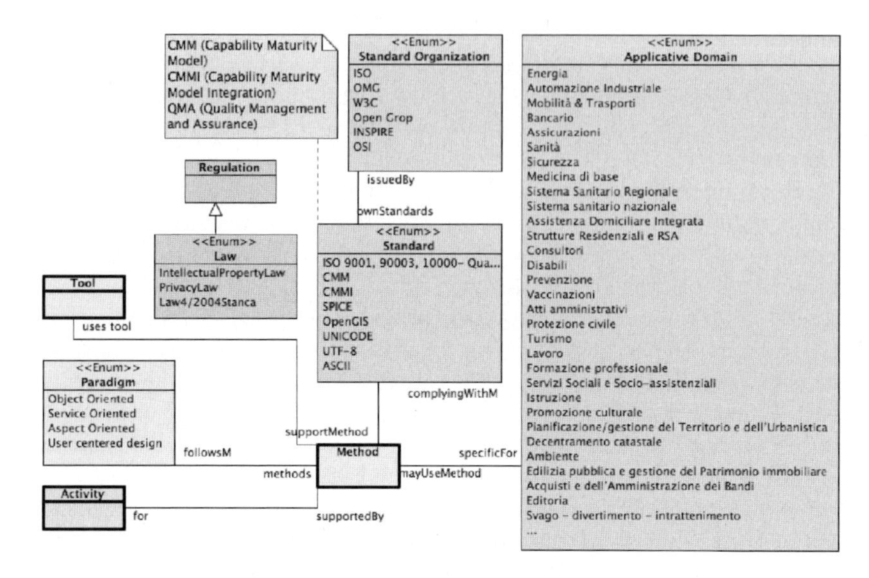

Fig. 4. Ontology: the Root View

SMEs. Thus, they are specific of the prototype and should be changed for a different productive district. Moreover, even for the same group of users they will change when the client portfolio of the SMEs evolves.

To give just the intuition of the complexity of the final ontology, Figure 5 depicts the fragment of diagram related to the applicative domain and the GIS.

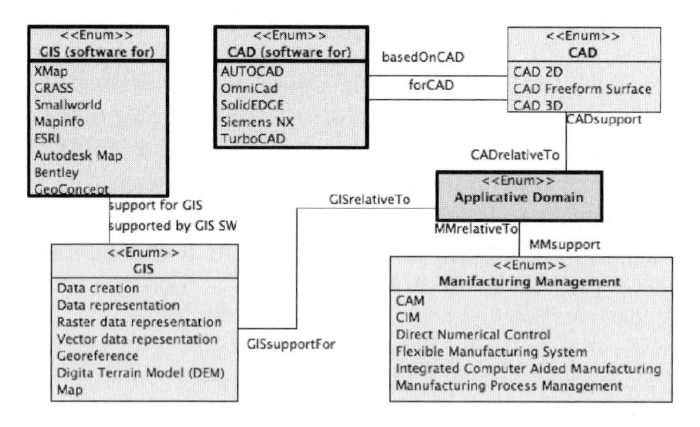

Fig. 5. Ontology: the Applicative Domain View

2.2 Gesper Architecture

The architecture of Gesper consists of several independent modules, detailed below, that work on the *content repository*, providing services like data input, searches and analysis. Figure 6 contains a schematic view of the whole Gesper

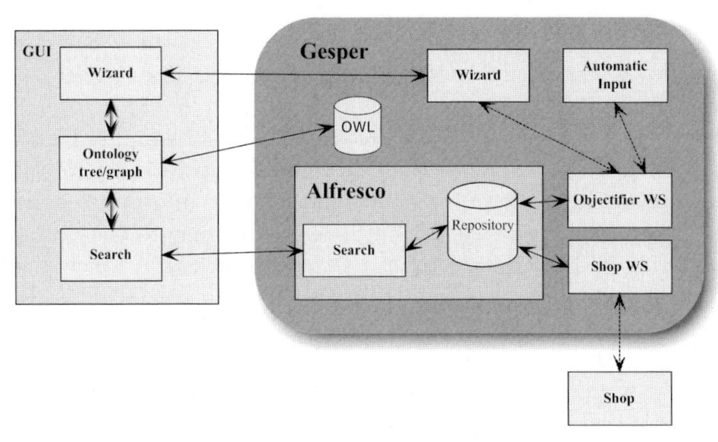

Fig. 6. Gesper architecture

architecture. The box on the left, *GUI*, represents a generic client, which, in the current prototype, is a graphical user interface hosted inside a web browser. The big rounded box represents an instance of a *Gesper server*, that is, a single node of a *federation*, owned by a SME, that hosts a resource repository and its services. Finally, the box on the bottom right, *Shop*, represents the central node of the federation, which gathers (summarized) data from all the other nodes of the federation and presents a view of this data to the public.

The implementation of Gesper relies on free tools and platforms; at its core we find *Alfresco* [2], a Java-based open source ECM (Enterprise Content Management) providing document management and search facilities. Alfresco offers its functionalities via Web Services and the Java Content Repository API. Moreover, Alfresco includes a web application allowing users to manage the document repository through any web browser. This web application has been customized and enriched to seamlessly work with the Gesper modules interacting with users.

At the moment there are eight modules: *Wizard* and *Automatic-Input* handle data input, *Ontology-Tree* and *Ontology-Graph* allow to navigate the ontology, *Search*, as the name implies, performs searches and *Shop* aggregates some data to showcase the public results and resources of a Gesper federation. Finally, *ObjectifierWS* and *ShopWS* are two auxiliary modules providing simple interfaces to Alfresco; the former maps Java objects to and from the Alfresco repository and the latter allow *Shop* to perform predefined queries.

Some modules run only on clients (for instance, *Ontology-Tree*) or on the server (e.g., *ObjectifierWS*), but most of them consists of a client part, which is a GUI for the users, and a server part, which interacts with the repository.

Let us detail the tasks of each module.

Although both *Wizard* and *Automatic-Input* handle data input, the former presents the users a user-friendly interface to input/edit resources and handle their lifecycles, while the latter performs offline batch acquisitions of (electronic) documents, inferring their metadata by scanning their contents.

Wizard exploits AJAX technology using the *GWT (Google Web Toolkit)* [10] that makes it easier to write high-performance AJAX applications. Using GWT, web applications can be developed in the Java programming language, using full-featured Java integrated development environments, and then compiled into highly optimized JavaScript.

Automatic-Input relies on the Java library *DUO* [6], a wrapper for *UNO* [21], to read Word `.doc` and Open Office `.odt` documents. As mentioned before, *Automatic-Input* needs to read the document contents in order to extract their metadata. The module searches for *keywords*, belonging to the ontology, and other information in fixed, but customizable, positions. For instance, the module can extract the participant list from the minutes of a meeting. This is achieved by using document *templates*, specifying the locations, inside documents, where important metadata can be found and extracted. The prototype handles two templates, one for meeting minutes and the other for development quality plans.

Ontology-Tree and *Ontology-Graph* allow the users to navigate through the ontology. The former presents the entire (linearized) hierarchy of classes and their instances in a tree-based way; the hierarchy has to be linearized because every class can have any number of parents in the ontology. The view offered by *Ontology-Tree* is best suited when the user is an expert, knows the relations between the concepts, and, basically, knows "what to look for" (that is, where are the exact keywords (s)he is looking for in the logical hierarchy). In these cases the tree view offers the quickest access to any part of the ontology. However, when the user is not an expert or needs advice on what entities are related to what is current looking for, the tree based view is not particularly helpful, because it does not represent any relationship but inheritance: in these cases the *Ontology-Graph* kicks in. The *Ontology-Graph* offers a graph view where nodes represent classes and instances, and edges represent relations among those. The view is initially centered on a particular node and, to avoid cluttering the display, only the selected node (the one the view is centered on) and its *directly related* nodes are shown. Users can navigate the ontology by re-centering the view on another area simply by clicking on the node they want to center the view on. The use of this module is best suited for exploratory queries and for navigating through the ontology, in order to gather ideas. Both ontology modules consists of a server-side part, written in Java, and a client-side part written in Javascript. The server components rely on *Jena* [11] for reading the ontology, stored as an OWL [17] file. *Ontology-Graph* uses *jsViz* [12] to render the graphs.

The *Search* enriches the built-in search capabilities of Alfresco with *semantic* searches, exploiting *Ontology-Tree* and *Ontology-Graph* on the client side, and a small layer of custom code, on top of Alfresco search module, on the server side.

The *Shop* provides the users nicely formatted reports summarizing the public data of all nodes inside a federation. *Shop* uses its server side counterpart, *ShopWS*, to query the Alfresco repository. This latter module has been explicitly designed with information security in mind, so it allows to run only queries that have been previously checked and approved. This avoid any leak of sensitive information that could be, innocently or maliciously, gathered by running generic queries run on the repository.

3 Conclusions and Further Work

We have presented the insight gained by our experience of design and development of a tool for managing experiences and knowledge in a small network of SMEs. In order to contain the development costs, the use of open-source and free software was required from the very beginning. This choice has greatly influenced the design and the architecture of Gesper.

The most original features of Gesper are, on the one hand, the presentation of knowledge in a problem-driven style supported by a *semantic* search based on an *ad-hoc* ontology and, on the other hand, the management of resources directly representing knowledge, as opposed to documents from which the knowledge may be extracted, as it is in most cases.

Being a prototype, Gesper could be improved on a number of aspects, besides a better implementation of the current features.

First, the role of administrator should be supported by tools to manage the ontology, the users, and the templates to be used in the automatic acquisition of documents. The former two activities are currently performed by functionalities of respectively Protégé and Alfresco, which could be integrated in Gesper, possibly making this improvement not much expensive. The ontology maintanance is prioritary, because of the quick changes of the applicative domain, requiring the users to update constantly the terminology used to tag the resources.

A second aspect needing improvement is the management of the Gesper federation and, in particular, how to avoid resource duplications. Indeed, currently if two SMEs share a resource, for instance a document of a joint project, two totally independent instances of the resource exist, in the content management system of each company. Though a better approach to sharing is obviously needed (and solutions could be probably borrowed from the peer-to-peer field), privacy policies and dynamic aspects (for instance employees changing the company they work for) make modelling the federative aspects quite challenging.

An extremely challenging add-in to Gesper, would be to automatically extract knowledge from experience while it takes place, by means of a small wizard helping the users to take notes of the relevant points during their normal workflow, or of watchers, able to record the principal steps taken during procedures, or to compute the resources used for some activity, to help future estimates.

Last, but not least, we need to analyze the user feedback to understand the acceptance of the tool and see how to prioritize its improvements.

References

1. Garcìa, F., Bertoa, M.F., Calero, C., Vallecillo, A., Ruiz, F., Piattini, M., Genero, M.: Towards a consistent terminology for software measurement. Information & Software Technology 48(8), 631–644 (2006)
2. Alfresco, `http://www.alfresco.com/`
3. Basili, V., McGarry, F.: The Experience Factory: How to Build and Run One. In: Proceedings of the 1997 (19th) International Conference on Software Engineering. IEEE publishing, Los Alamitos (1997)

4. Choppy, C., Reggio, G.: A UML-based approach for problem frame oriented software development. Information and Software Technology 47(14), 929–954 (2005)
5. Calero, C., Ruiz, F., Piattini, M.: Ontologies for Software Engineering and Software Technology. Springer, Berlin (2006)
6. OpenOffice.org UNO/Java wrapper, http://sourceforge.net/projects/duo-wrapper
7. Eclipse - an open development platform, http://www.eclipse.org/
8. Feldmann, R.L., Pizka, M.: An on-line software engineering repository for Germany's SME - an experience report. In: Henninger, S., Maurer, F. (eds.) LSO 2003. LNCS, vol. 2640, pp. 34–43. Springer, Heidelberg (2003)
9. Gamma, E., Helm, R., Johnson, R., Vlissides, J.M.: Design Patterns: Elements of Reusable Object-Oriented Software. Addison-Wesley, Reading (1995)
10. Google Web Toolkit, http://code.google.com/webtoolkit/
11. Jena – a semantic web framework for Java, http://jena.sourceforge.net/
12. jsViz, http://code.google.com/p/jsviz/
13. OpenCyc, http://www.opencyc.org/
14. Kim, G., Lee, M., Lee, J., Lee, K.: Design of SPICE experience factory model for accumulation and utilization of process assessment experience. In: Proceedings of Third ACIS International Conference on Software Engineering Research, Management and Applications. IEEE publishing, Los Alamitos (2005)
15. Mendes, O., Abran, A.: Issues in the development of an ontology for a emerging engineering discipline. In: Chu, W.C., Juristo Juzgado, N., Wong, W.E. (eds.) Proceedings of the 17th International Conference on Software Engineering and Knowledge Engineering (SEKE 2005), Taipei, Taiwan, Republic of China, July 14-16, 2005, pp. 139–144 (2005)
16. OMG. UML superstructure specification v. 2.1.2 (2007), http://www.omg.org/spec/UML/2.1.2/
17. OWL Web Ontology Language, http://www.w3.org/TR/owl-features/
18. Protégé, http://protege.stanford.edu/
19. Lin, S.S., Liu, F.H, Loe, S.F.: Building a knowledge base of IEEE/EAI 12207 and CMMI with ontology. In: Proceedings of Sixth International Protégé Workshop, Manchester, England, July 7–9 (2003)
20. Tansalarak, N., Claypool, K.T.: XCM: A component ontology. In: Proceedings of Workshop on Ontologies as Software Engineering Artifacts (OOPSLA), October 24–28 (2004)
21. Open Office UNO - Universal Network Objects, http://udk.openoffice.org/

Directed Generation of Test Data for Static Semantics Checker

M.V. Arkhipova and S.V. Zelenov

Institute for System Programming of the Russian Academy of Sciences
{maryn,zelenov}@ispras.ru
http://www.unitesk.com

Abstract. We present an automatic method, named SemaTESK[1], for generation of test sets for a translator front end. We focus on the validation and verification of static semantics checker. Most the know methods for semantics test generation produce test suites by filtering a pre-generated set of random texts in the target language. In contrast, SemaTESK allows to generate tests for context conditions directly. It significantly reduces generation time and allows reaching completeness criteria defined in the paper. The presented method to specify static semantics allows to formalize informal requirements described in normative documents (e.g. standard). The method includes SRL notation for compact formal specification of context conditions and STG tool for efficient generation of test suite from SRL specification.

The SemaTESK method has been used in a number of projects, including testing static semantics checkers of C and Java.

Keywords: Automated test data generation, context condition, grammar, specification based testing, static semantics.

1 Introduction

Formal languages are widely used in many areas of IT: Programming languages are the main instruments in software development; query languages are used to manage databases; markup languages are used in various document processing systems (e.g. browsers, text processors), etc. Translator is a program that converts text written in a formal language into some appropriate form. For example, a compiler translates a program into an executable form, a DBMS translates a query written in a high level query language (e.g. SQL) into sequence of low level operations on DB, a browser translates an information page into drawing commands, etc. Defects in a translator break entities resulting from translation: their properties differs from what is specified in the language specification. For example, defects in executable entities induced by erroneous compiler are hard to detect and find a workaround, thus correctness of executables obtained from an incorrect compiler is always a doubt. Validation and verification of a translator is an important activity for dissemination of the translator in industry.

[1] *SemaTESK* stands for "Semantics Testing Kit".

T. Margaria and B. Steffen (Eds.): ISoLA 2008, CCIS 17, pp. 753–768, 2008.

Validation and verification of translators is always complicated. The main source of difficulties is complexity of input and output: the input is a document with a furcated syntax structure and rich set of context constraints imposed by the language specification, the output is written in machine or intermediate language and possesses similar or even higher degree of complexity. The usual way to cope with complications of translator validation and verification is decomposition the validation and verification task into several subtasks that in total cover the whole functionality of the translator. Typical translator includes the following set of functions:

1. analysis of syntax correctness and parsing of input text;
2. checking static semantics[2] of the input;
3. generation of the output.

In this paper, we focus on the task of validation and verification of static semantics checker. We treat *static semantics* as a synonym to *context conditions*. Within this paper a static semantics checker is a boolean function of the form $f : S(L) \to B$, where $S(L)$ is a set of syntactically correct strings in the given formal language L, and $B = \{true, false\}$. $f(s)$ takes a value of $true$ if string s satisfies all context conditions of language L and takes a value of $false$ if string s violates at least one of the context conditions of the language L.

We use testing [1] based on formal specifications and models [2] as the primary tool for validation and verification. In the course of testing, one checks a software under test for quality on some specially created test input data. There is the following problem: The set of test data should be representative, so that results of the testing do reflect real quality of a software under test. Another problem is: Usually, there are too many situations that should be tested. So, it is practically impossible to create tests by hand. Usage of formal description of a software under test allows both formulating appropriate test completeness criteria and generating tests automatically.

1.1 Related Approaches

The most traditional way to specify language properties uses grammar of some appropriate kind.

In order to generate semantically correct tests, the approaches presented in works [3,4,5] use grammars in the form of extended BNF supplied with special code fragments that incorporate semantics-related information: *actions* contain some calculations, *guards* are used to check conditions that allow generating corresponding part of test. However, such form of a grammar[3] is not a specification of a language. It rather seems like a program for generating tests.

---

[2] Given a formal language, a *static semantics* describes properties of the language that may be checked at compile-time (such as scoping and static typing constraints), whereas a *dynamic semantics* describes run-time properties of the language ("meaning" of language constructs).

[3] Sirer and Bershad in [5] call it a *production grammar*.

Boyapati et al. [6] presents the Korat test data generator. This generator uses a specification of desired test data in the form of Java-method that checks correctness of data structure, and parameters that restrict the set of all possible test data to some finite set. Khurshid and Marinov [7] presents the TestEra framework for specification-based testing of Java programs. Specifications are first-order logic formulae written in Alloy declarative language [8]. TestEra also requires a bound that limits the size of the test cases to be generated. Unfortunately, both Korat and TestEra can not be provided with a domain-specific completeness criteria. They generate *all* non-isomorphic structures that match given restrictions. Besides, in the case of semantics checker testing, it is practically impossible to have a (either reference or "under test") checker written in Java.

Daniel et al. [9] present a method for automated testing of refactoring engines. In order to generate tests for some refactoring, one should develop corresponding generator on the basis of specific ASTGen library. The main disadvantage of this approach is that test data generators are developed manually.

Harm and Lämmel [10,11] present approaches to automated test data generation for static semantics checker based on usage specification of semantics in the form of attribute grammars (AG) [12]. Kalinov et al. [13] suggest another approach to this task that uses specification in the form of Gurevich's ASM [14]. The authors of these approaches consider various test coverage criteria for static semantics checker testing and suggest corresponding automated test generators that work as follows: First, the generator creates a set of syntactically correct sentences; Next, the generator checks semantical correctness of every generated sentence with the help of appropriate interpreter of AG or ASM specification of semantics; All semantically incorrect sentences are rejected.

Thus, in those approaches, specification of semantics is used only for the following purposes: To formulate coverage criteria and to check semantical correctness of generated sentences. Tests generation is syntax-directed. In other words, specification of semantics is not used to generate semantically correct sentences directly. In general case, the generation process is very time-consuming: Generator has to create millions of syntactically correct sentences in order to obtain several hundreds of semantically correct tests. In papers [11,15], the authors of these approaches suggest some optimizations of generation process: They try to reveal semantic incorrectness of subsentences of generated sentences "as soon as possible".

Here we proceed with discussion of AG-related approaches. Similar arguments are also applicable to approaches based on ASM. AG is suitable for developing checkers, but it seems not suitable for directed generation of tests. One can treat an AG specification of language semantics as a predicate P over abstract syntax trees. In order to create semantically correct test, one should find a tree t such that $P(t) = true$. To do this, the AG-related approaches construct syntactically correct trees t and check value $P(t)$ for every t.

We believe that more effective way to generate semantically correct tests is to use an algorithm that directly creates some solutions of the equation $P(t) = true$. The form of classical AG is the main obstacle to solve this equation. AG is a very powerful tool. However, it has several essential weaknesses that are shown in the following example.

Example 1. Let us consider some procedural programming language that requires separate statements for variable declarations and assignments. There are two context conditions:

1. All names of variables declared in one procedure must be different;
2. Name of an assigned variable must be declared in the same procedure.

In the classical AG approach, the corresponding part of attribute grammar for this language looks as follows:

```
1: Procedure ::= ( Stmt )*
2:  { attribute SymbolTable vars;
3:     attribute Boolean ok;  };
4: Stmt ::= VarDecl | Assignment | ... ;
5: VarDecl ::= ''var'' <name:ID>
6:  { Procedure.ok &= !Procedure.vars.has( name );
7:     Procedure.vars.add( name );  };
8: Assignment ::= <name:ID> ''='' ...
9:  { Procedure.ok &= Procedure.vars.has( name );  };
```

In this grammar, there is the symbol table `vars` declared in the `Procedure` rule that collects information about names of variables declared in one procedure. The table is updated in the `VarDecl` rule and checked in the `VarDecl` and `Assignment` rules. The checking results are stored in the boolean attribute `ok` declared in the `Procedure` rule.

This example uncovers the following weaknesses of classical AG:

- The attributes declared in the `Procedure` rule are sort of *global variables*, which yields well known *problems in maintenance* of a grammar.
- In order to formalize *a context condition*, one has to write many lines of code in *several different parts* of a grammar: For example, the second context condition (see above) is formalized in four lines (2, 3, 7, and 9) that relate to three different rules. This yields very *weak traceability*.

We suppose that the weaknesses stated above do not allow creating semantically correct tests directly on the basis of a language semantics description in AG form. Indeed, a generator must be very intelligent to understand what it should do in order to resolve a context condition.

In this paper, we present the SemaTESK method aimed at automated generation of tests for static semantics checkers. The SemaTESK method is based on UniTESK approach [16,17] that belongs to the family of specification-based approaches to testing. The SemaTESK method includes an appropriate language called SRL[4]. The purpose of SRL is to write formal specifications of static semantics in a form that is suitable for directed generation of tests. The SemaTESK method is supported by a test case generator called STG[5] that allows automated generating of tests on the basis of static semantics specifications written in SRL.

[4] *SRL* stands for "Semantics Relation Language".
[5] *STG* stands for "Semantic Tests Generator".

The remainder of the paper is organized as follows. In Section 2 we present the SRL language. In Section 3 we formulate completeness criteria. In Section 4 we describe the STG generator. In Section 5 we show several application examples and discuss benefits of the SemaTESK method. Section 6 contains some discussion. In Section 7 the paper is concluded.

2 Semantics Relation Language

2.1 Peculiarities of SRL

We start with the following example:

Example 2. The context condition "Name of an assigned variable must be declared in the same procedure" from Example 1 written in SRL looks as follows:

```
one-to-many relation DeclareAssignedVarName {
  ordered  equal
  target Assignment {name}
  source VarDecl {name}
  context: same Procedure  }
```

One can read this *context condition descriptor* as follows: If there is an occurrence of `Assignment` in a sentence, then there must exist an occurrence of `VarDecl` in the `same Procedure` such that the attribute `name` of the `VarDecl` is `equal` to the attribute `name` of the `Assignment`, the `Assignment` must be in succession to the `VarDecl` (i.e. the `Assignment` and `VarDecl` must be `ordered`), and the `name` declared in *one* `VarDecl` may be used in *many* `Assignments` (cf. `one-to-many` keyword).

This example shows the following peculiarities of SRL:

- The static semantics of a language are formalized as context condition descriptors over an attributed context-free grammar. We do not relate a context condition descriptor to a particular grammar production rule, as in AG, since in many cases it is difficult to choose pertinent production rule (e.g. in Example 2, do the context condition relates to `Assignment`? or to `VarDecl`? or to `Procedure`? As Example 1 shows, in the AG-related approach, different parts of code of this context condition relate to all those three rules!).
- One context condition from a language specification expressed in a natural language corresponds to one block of code (i.e. context condition descriptor) written in SRL. This yields efficient traceability.
- Context condition descriptors have a form of "item declaration — item usage" relations[6]. The core of a context condition descriptor is a pair of constructions started with keywords `target` and `source`. Generally speaking, for any occurrence of `target` (i.e. an item usage), there must exist an appropriate occurrence of `source` (i.e. an item declaration) that meets the context condition.

[6] The practice shows, that in the majority of cases, context conditions are managed to be specified in such manner but, when it is necessary, context condition specification can be appended by Java code.

At present, both the SRL language and the STG generator are still evolving. Every new application of the STG generator uncovers new ways the generator could be improved "if only SRL had this new feature". Nevertheless, the underlying principle of SRL remains firm, and this is the subject of the rest of this section.

2.2 The Form of Underlying Grammar

In order to formalize a context-free grammar, we use the TreeDL[7] language [18]. The purpose of TreeDL is to describe structure of abstract syntax trees. TreeDL allows describing structure of tree nodes that includes specification of children nodes and additional attributes.

Example 3. The context-free part of the grammar presented in Example 1 may be described in TreeDL as follows:

```
node Procedure { child Stmt* statements; }
abstract node Stmt {}
node VarDecl : Stmt { child ID name; }
node Assignment : Stmt { child ID name; ... }
node ID { attribute string value; }
```

The TreeDL form of a grammar has the following advantages over BNF:

- All children and attributes in one node are named; So, each child or attribute can be unambiguously addressed.
- One can add some additional (e.g. semantics related) attributes into nodes.

2.3 Context Condition Descriptor

The main atomic object of a language semantics description written in SRL is a *context condition descriptor* (CCD). Every CCD specifies a relation between two nodes called *source* and *target* in the following sense: A structure of a target node depends on a structure of a source node. In most cases, one can treat target node as a usage of an item and a source node as a declaration of that item. In Example 2, source and target nodes are described by their types:

```
target Assignment {...}
source VarDecl {...}
```

This description means that for the CCD under consideration, any node of type `Assignment` may be a target and any node of type `VarDecl` may be a source. In general case, source and target nodes may be described more accurate (see Subsection 2.4). In fact, a CCD specifies a relation between some subtrees of source and target nodes. Those subtrees are described in braces that follows node descriptions. In Example 2, the CCD specifies a relation between the field `name` of a source node and the field `name` of a target node:

```
target Assignment {name}
source VarDecl {name}
```

[7] *TreeDL* stands for "Tree Description Language".

One can treat such subtrees as *arguments* of a CCD. Dependency between the arguments is specified by means of describing an appropriate dependency kind. SRL provides several keywords to specify dependency between source and target. Those keywords cover almost all context conditions of typical programming languages (see Subsection 2.5). In Example 2, the keyword `equal` is used in the CCD in order to specify that the arguments must be equal.

In some cases, a context condition is restricted to have source and target in some specific context. For instance, in Example 2, both assignment and variable declaration must be in the same procedure. A context is specified in CCD by means of `context` keyword. There are two variants of a context specification.

- If both source and target should be located in the same subtree with the root node of type `<RootNodeType>`, then the following construction is used:

```
context: same <RootNodeType>
```

- If source and target must be in different subtrees with roots of (possibly) different types, then the following construction is used:

```
context: differ source_context <SourceRootNodeType>
                target_context <TargetRootNodeType>
```

If a source node of a CCD must precede the target node, then the CCD should be marked by `ordered` keyword (cf. Example 2). Otherwise, it should be marked by `unordered` keyword.

In order to specify, how many nodes may relate to each other by a dependency imposed by a CCD, one should describe a relation type of the CCD (see Subsection 2.6). In Example 2, the relation type is specified by the keyword `one-to-many` that means that a name declared in *one* `VarDecl` may be used in *many* `Assignments`.

Here we proceed with detailed description of some SRL constructions used in CCDs.

2.4 Node Description

Source and target nodes are specified by paths over an abstract syntax tree. Such a path has a form of chain $e_1.\cdots.e_n$ of path elements e_i separated by dots. Each path matches a corresponding set of nodes. Such a set is defined inductively as follows. Let S_0 be an empty set, and S_k ($k = 1,\ldots,n$) be a set of nodes that match a path $e_1.\cdots.e_k$. The set S_k ($k = 1,\ldots,n$) depends on S_{k-1} and the kind of the element e_k.

There are the following kinds of path elements:

- `<NodeType>` — if $k = 1$, then such an element matches all nodes N such that type of N is `<NodeType>`; If $k > 1$, then it matches all nodes N such that N is a child of type `<NodeType>` some node from S_{k-1}.
- `<fieldName>` — matches all nodes N such that N is a value of a child or an attribute named `<fieldName>` in some node from S_{k-1}.

– `parent` — matches all nodes N such that N is the parent of some node from S_{k-1}.
– `^<ParentNodeType>` — matches all nodes N such that N is the nearest parent node of type `<ParentNodeType>` for some node from S_{k-1}.
– `target` — matches the target of the current CCD (valid only in path that specifies a source node).
– `context` — matches the context of the current CCD (valid only if context has the "`same`" form).
– `source_context` and `target_context` — match context of the source and the target nodes of the current CCD correspondingly (valid only if context has the "`differ`" form).

Example 4. For trees described in Example 3, the node description `Assignment.name` specifies all names of all assignments, the node description `Assignment.^Procedure.VarDecl` specifies all variable declarations contained in procedures that contain an assignment.

2.5 Dependency Kind

SRL provides the following keywords for specifying a kind of dependency between arguments of a CCD:

– `equal` — means that values of the arguments of the CCD must be equal (more precisely, subtrees that have the arguments of the CCD as roots must be isomorphic).
– `unequal` — means that values of the arguments of the CCD must be different (more precisely, subtrees that have the arguments of the CCD as roots must not be isomorphic).
– `present` — means that if the `source`-related argument of the CCD exists, then the `target`-related argument of the CCD must exist as well.
– `absent` — means that if the `source`-related argument of the CCD exists, then the `target`-related argument of the CCD must not exist.
– `compatible` — means that the `source`-related argument of the CCD must be compatible (in a sense of type compatibility in programming languages, see Subsection 2.7) with the `target`-related argument of the CCD (in this case, the arguments of the CCD must describe types; see Example 6 below).

We understand that in some cases, a dependency imposed by some context condition may have a kind that differs from the kinds listed above. In such a case, one should use the keyword `custom` and provide some additional program code that implements processing the CCD in the test generator (this subject is beyond the scope of this paper, see [19] for details). Practice shows that in a such complex language as Java, there are only two context conditions (of about 300) that requires usage of the `custom` keyword[8].

[8] Those context conditions relates to semantics of method signature.

2.6 Relation Type

Relation type of a CCD specifies, how many nodes may relate to each other by a dependency imposed by the CCD. SRL provides the following keywords for specifying a relation type:

- The keyword `one-to-many` means that *one* source node may correspond to *many* target nodes, such that for any occurrence of a target node, there must exist an appropriate occurrence of a source node that meets the context condition (see Example 2).
- The keyword `many-to-many` means that *many* source nodes may correspond to *many* target nodes, such that any occurrence of a target node and any occurrence of a source node (that differs from the occurrence of the target node) must meet the context condition.
- The keyword `one-node` means that a context condition is imposed on *one node* (more precisely, it is imposed on a subtree that has this node as the root). Such a node is specified as a target node, and location of a source node is addressed relatively to the target node (i.e. `source` construction of a CCD starts with `target`).

Example 5. The context condition "All names of variables declared in one procedure must be different" from Example 1 written in SRL looks as follows:

```
many-to-many relation DifferentVarNames {
  unordered  unequal
  target VarDecl {name}
  source VarDecl {name}
  context: same Procedure  }
```

Example 6. Let the `Assignment` statement from Example 1 has an `Expression` in its RHS. Let us consider the following corresponding TreeDL description:

```
node Assignment : Stmt { child ID name; child Expression rhs; attribute Type lhs_type; }
abstract node Expression { attribute Type type; }
```

In order to describe semantics of types, we add the attribute `lhs_type` to the `Assignment` node and the attribute `type` to the `Expression` node. Thus, the context condition "A variable of one type can store only a value of a compatible type" written in SRL looks as follows:

```
one-node relation AsgnTypes {
  unordered  compatible
  target Assignment {rhs.type}
  source target {lhs_type}  }
```

2.7 Type Compatibility

Given a programming language, the semantics of the language usually has a significant part that relates to semantics of types. Semantics of types is generally reduced to conditions of type compatibility in different contexts.

In SRL, compatible types are specified as follows. Given a language under consideration, one should specify a partially ordered set of types of the language imposed by the compatibility relation. Such a set should be specified by means of chains of linearly ordered subsets. In order to specify a chain of types that are compatible from left to right, one should enumerate the types of the chain in an SRL `typeset` construction.

Example 7. Let us consider a language that contains the following types: `short`, `int`, and `long`. For this language, type compatibility may be specified by the following chain of types:

```
typeset PrimitiveTypes { PrimitiveType.SHORT, PrimitiveType.INT, PrimitiveType.LONG }
```

In this example, constructions `PrimitiveType.SHORT` and the others are the possible values of node attributes that describe types of expressions (cf. the attributes `lhs_type` and `type` in Example 6).

The SRL language also allows describing compatibility of user-defined types. This requires usage of some features of SRL that are beyond the scope of this paper (see [19] for details).

3 Completeness Criteria

3.1 Semantically Correct Tests

Given an SRL specifications, one can formulate the following naive completeness criterion for semantically correct tests: *All CCDs from the specification must be covered* with respect to the following definition:

Definition 1. *A CCD is considered covered iff a test set contains a sentence, such that the corresponding abstract syntax tree contains two nodes that match a pair of the source and the target of the CCD.*

Example 8. Suppose that the language from Example 1 allows using nested blocks in a procedure. A compiler developer will say that the following situations are different for a static semantics checker, whereas they cover the same context condition:

```
                        {
{                         var A;
  var A;                  {
  A = 1;                    A = 1;
}                         }
                        }
```

Thus, the criterion “All CCDs” is not sufficient for good testing, and one can improve it by the following way: *All CCDs from the specification must be covered with all possible environments of source and target nodes* with respect to the following definition:

Definition 2. *An environment of a node in an abstract syntax tree is a chain of nodes on the path from the node under consideration to the root of the tree.*

3.2 Semantically Incorrect Tests

Another important task in testing static semantics checkers is to test that a checker rejects incorrect sentences. Given a test that violates some context conditions, one may expect that a static semantics checker rejects this test and provides some appropriate diagnostics. If the test violates several different context conditions, then in general case it is difficult to predict the corresponding diagnostics since a checker under test may exit immediately after detecting only one violated context condition. Thus, we suggest generating such tests that each test violates only one context condition. Suppose that we can generate tests that do meet static semantics. In order to generate tests that violates some context condition, we suggest to generate tests that meet negation of this context condition.

Definition 3. *Given a CCD R, a negation $\tilde{R}$ of R is a CCD such that the following condition holds: if a sentence meets $\tilde{R}$, then the sentence violates R.*

Example 9. An example of negation for the CCD "Name of an assigned variable must be declared in the same procedure" from Example 2 looks as follows:

```
many-to-many relation DeclareAssignedVarName_neg {
  ordered  unequal
  target Assignment {name}
  source VarDecl {name}
  context: same Procedure  }
```

Let S be a specification of a language semantics written in SRL, and $R \in S$. Let us consider the following *R-negation* of the specification: $\tilde{S}^{(R)} = \{\tilde{R}\} \cup S \backslash \{R\}$. One can summarize the above discussion by the following completeness criterion for semantically incorrect tests: *For each CCD R, all negations $\tilde{R}$ must be covered in $\tilde{S}^{(R)}$ with all possible environments of source and target nodes.*

4 Semantic Tests Generator

The purpose of SRL is to describe a language semantics in a form that is suitable for automated generation of tests for static semantics checker. In the method SemaTESK we present in this paper, the test case generator STG generates test sets that meet the completeness criteria formulated above (see Section 3). STG takes a corresponding language grammar in TreeDL and a context conditions specification in SRL. The core of STG is the engine that builds syntax trees according to the grammar and the context conditions. Text builder maps generated trees to concrete documents in the given language. Text builder traverses syntax tree and creates textual elements that correspond to generated syntax nodes. Before we briefly formulate the algorithm of test generation used in STG engine (see [19] for details), let us give the following definitions.

Definition 4. *A subtree of an abstract syntax tree is called a syntactically complete tree if it corresponds to some syntactically correct sentence.*

Definition 5. *A context condition corresponding to some target node and described in some CCD over an abstract syntax tree is resolved if the tree contains all necessary elements (nodes and attributes) in required contexts such that the tree with this target node match the CCD.*

Definition 6. *An abstract syntax tree is called semantically complete if it corresponds to some semantically correct sentence.*

Definition 7. *Given a CCD, a subtree of an abstract syntax tree is called a prime tree if it contains nodes that match specifications of source and target nodes of the CCD.*

One can treat a prime tree for some CCD as a tree that contains only the source node and the target node with their environments. All context conditions in any semantically complete tree are resolved.

The STG generator applies the following algorithm to each CCD from the specification of a language semantics:

1. Given a CCD, the generator creates a set of all possible prime trees[9] (with respect to the given value of the recursion depth).
2. For each prime tree t_{prime}, the generator creates a minimal[10] syntactically complete tree t that contains t_{prime} as a subtree.
3. Given a syntactically complete tree t, the generator tries to create the corresponding semantically complete tree $\bar{t}$ (see below).
4. If the generator successfully creates the tree $\bar{t}$, then it prints its text in the formal language under consideration.

The STG generator uses both attribute dependency graph and syntax tree for stepwise directed creation of tests that meet context conditions. Given a syntax tree obtained at the previous step, the generator searches the tree for unresolved context conditions and, in order to resolve them, creates additional subtrees in the tree. Given a syntactically complete tree t, the STG generator tries to create the corresponding semantically complete tree by the following algorithm:

1. The generator searches the tree t for unresolved CCDs; If all CCDs are resolved, then t is semantically complete.
2. In order to resolve the CCDs found on the previous step, the generator tries to modify the tree by the following rules:
   a) the prime subtree t_{prime} is always invariant;
   b) if for some one-to-many CCD, there is no a source node in the tree, then the generator walks the tree and tries to add new subtree containing a node that match the specification of a source node in the CCD;

[9] This set consists of prime trees that contain source nodes and target nodes (w.r.t. the CCD) in all various possible combinations of environments.

[10] All lists are instantiated with minimal possible size; alternatives are instantiated to the simples variant, e.g. empty or terminal, etc.

   c) if a dependency kind of some CCD requires that the tree must contain some specific node that currently does not exists in the tree, then the generator tries to add new such node (like in rule 2.b).
3. If the generator could not resolve the previously found unresolved CCDs, then the tree is rejected; Otherwise, go to the step 1 of this algorithm, since the tree has been changed in the step 2 and may contain new unresolved CCDs.

5 Case Studies

The SemaTESK method has been approved in the following projects:

- testing IPMP-21 message header processors [20];
- testing the C front-end of the GCC compiler;
- testing the CTESK translator [21] developed in ISP RAS.
- testing the JavaTESK translator [22] developed in ISP RAS.

Some properties of the languages under test are presented in Table 1.

Table 1. Properties of languages under test

Language	Number of CCDs	Size of specification	Tests generated
IPMP-21 XML	4	28 lines	54
C	85	1019 lines	about 10000
Java	278	3350 lines	about 32000

The main purpose of the pilot project on testing IPMP-21 was to demonstrate feasibility of SemaTESK approach to static semantics formalization for the generation of semantically correct XML documents. The purpose of the pilot project on testing GCC was to demonstrate feasibility of SemaTESK approach to static semantics formalization of a complex programming language.

The SemaTESK method has been successfully approved in specifying semantics of C for testing the CTESK translator [21] and in specifying semantics of Java for testing the JavaTESK translator [22]: several bugs have been found in the semantics checkers of translators that had been thoroughly tested before by means of manually developed tests.

We consider a static semantics checker as a boolean function. In SemaTESK, we use an automatic test oracle to run generated semantically correct tests. The oracle considers a test run successful if a semantics checker under test returns true for the given test input. In practice, the true value means that work of the semantics checker completes without any error messages about context conditions violations. To run generated semantically incorrect tests we also use the automatic test oracle that considers a test run successful if a semantics checker under test returns false for the given test input. In practice, the false value means that the semantics checker completes with error messages about some context conditions violations.

Let us estimate benefits from using the SemaTESK method. Suppose that one test for a static semantics checker contains about 10–30 lines of code. Here are the approximate numbers of lines that should be manually written in order to create 10 tests by means of different methods (the estimations are based on the Table 1 and the assumption stated above):

- Manual development – about 100–300 of manually written lines per 10 tests.
- The SemaTESK method – about 1–2 of manually written lines per 10 tests.

Thus, the effort for development of tests by means of the SemaTESK method is about hundred times less than the effort for manual test development.

6 Discussion

We have developed the SemaTESK method just for directed generation of test data for static semantics checkers of formal languages. We doubt whether the presented ideas can be used for generation of efficient static semantics checkers.

We have applied SemaTESK to testing checkers of programming languages most of all. At present, the method is still evolving. Every new application of it may require to improve both SRL and STG. We believe that the method is applicable to testing checkers of formal documents content, telecommunications messages, DB queries, etc as well.

It is of interest to note that the most promising way of SemaTESK use is a generation of tests sets for language dialects under development. Because it is rather simple to change specifications of language dialects and thus the amount of handwork required to make language specification matching current state is reduced. On the other hand, if some context conditions change, then it is much easier to modify several CCDs in a corresponding SRL specifications than to revise all manually written tests that concern the changed context conditions.

7 Conclusions

This paper presents the SemaTESK method that implements specification-based testing approach for static semantics checker testing. The SemaTESK method provides the SRL language for writing formal specifications of static semantics in the form that yields efficient traceability and is suitable for semantics-directed automated generation of tests. The SemaTESK method is supplied by the corresponding test case generator STG that allows generating test sets that meet appropriate completeness criteria formulated on the basis of SRL specifications of a language under test. The STG generator takes SRL specifications as an input and automatically produces both semantically correct and semantically incorrect (with unambiguously stated kind of an incorrectness) tests.

The SemaTESK method has been used in several case studies including testing static semantics checker of such a complex programming languages as C and Java. Obtained practical results prove effectiveness of the SemaTESK method.

References

1. Beizer, B.: Software Testing Techniques, 2nd edn. van Nostrand Reinhold (1990)
2. Petrenko, A.: Specification based testing: Towards practice. In: Bjørner, D., Broy, M., Zamulin, A.V. (eds.) PSI 2001. LNCS, vol. 2244, pp. 287–300. Springer, Heidelberg (2001)
3. Duncan, A., Hutchison, J.: Using attributed grammars to test designs and implementation. In: Proceedings of the 5th international conference on Software engineering, pp. 170–178 (1981)
4. Guilmette, R.F.: TGGS: A flexible system for generating efficient test case generators (1995)
5. Sirer, E.G., Bershad, B.N.: Using production grammars in software testing. In: Second Conference on Domain-Specific Languages, pp. 1–13 (1999)
6. Boyapati, C., Khurshid, S., Marinov, D.: Korat: Automated testing based on java predicates. In: Proc. of International Symposium on Software Testing and Analysis (ISSTA) (2002)
7. Khurshid, S., Marinov, D.: Testera: Specification-based testing of java programs using sat. Automated Software Engineering Journal 11(4), 403–434 (2004)
8. Jackson, D.: Alloy: a lightweight object modelling notation. ACM Trans. Softw. Eng. Methodol. 11(2), 256–290 (2002)
9. Daniel, B., Dig, D., Garcia, K., Marinov, D.: Automated testing of refactoring engines. In: ESEC/FSE, pp. 185–194 (2007)
10. Harm, J.: Automatic test program generation from formal language specifications. Rostocker Informatik-Berishte 20, 33–56 (1997)
11. Harm, J., Lämmel, R.: Two-dimensional approximation coverage. Informatica 24(3) (2000)
12. Paakki, J.: Attribute grammar paradigms – a high-level methodology in language implementation. ACM Computing Surveys 27(2), 196–255 (1995)
13. Kalinov, A., Kossatchev, A., Posypkin, M., Shishkov, V.: Using ASM specification for automatic test suite generation for mpC parallel programming language compiler. In: Proceedings of Fourth International Workshop on Action Semantic, AS 2002, BRICS note series NS-02-8, pp. 99–109 (2002)
14. Gurevich, Y.: Abstract state machines: An overview of the project. In: Seipel, D., Turull-Torres, J.M.a. (eds.) FoIKS 2004. LNCS, vol. 2942, pp. 6–13. Springer, Heidelberg (2004)
15. Kossatchev, A., Kutter, P., Posypkin, M.: Automated generation of strictly conforming tests based on formal specification of dynamic semantics of the programming language. Programming and Computing Software 30(4), 218–229 (2004)
16. Bourdonov, I., Kossatchev, A., Kuliamin, V., Petrenko, A.: Unitesk test suite architecture. In: Eriksson, L.-H., Lindsay, P.A. (eds.) FME 2002. LNCS, vol. 2391, pp. 77–88. Springer, Heidelberg (2002)
17. ISP RAS: UniTESK Technology Web-site, `http://www.unitesk.com/`
18. Demakov, A.V.: TreeDL: Tree Description Language, `http://treedl.sourceforge.net/treedl/treedl_en.html`
19. Arkhipova, M.V.: Automated Generation of Tests for Semantics Analysers in Translators. PhD thesis, Moscow, Russia (in Russian) (2006)

20. ISO/IEC JTC1/SC29/WG11: IPMP: Intellectual Property Management and Protection in MPEG Standards,
http://www.chiariglione.org/mpeg/standards/ipmp/
21. ISP RAS: CTESK: toolkit for testing applications developed in C,
http://www.unitesk.com/content/category/7/14/33/
22. ISP RAS: JavaTESK: Toolkit for testing applications developed in Java,
http://www.unitesk.com/content/category/7/28/74/

Event-Based Approach to Modelling Dynamic Architecture: Application to Mobile Ad-Hoc Network

Christian Attiogbé

LINA - UMR CNRS 6241 - University of Nantes
F-44322 Nantes Cedex, France
Christian.Attiogbe@univ-nantes.fr

Abstract. We describe an event-based approach to specifiy systems with dynamically evolving architecture; the study is illustrated with the structuring and routing in Mobile Ad-hoc Network. The resulting specification is augmented with desired properties and then analysed using theorem proving and model checking tools.

Keywords: Specification, Verification, Dynamic Architecture, Event B.

1 Introduction

Distributed systems modelling, design, analysis and implementation are difficult engineering tasks. They still pose challenging specification and analysis difficulties. To master them one needs specific languages, methods and tools.

The general motivation of our work is the need for practical methods, techniques and tools to help the developers in specifying and analysing asynchronous systems with dynamically evolving architecture. They are systems composed of several processes (multi-process) but their number and their structure may be varying in the time. In this article we focus on the systematic specification and analysis of these multi-process systems with evolving structure. We use Mobile Ad-hoc Networks (MANET) as application domain. The expression *dynamic architecture* refers to the evolving structure of such systems.

The contribution of this work is twofold: *i)* an event-based method to guide the specification and analysis of multi-process systems that have dynamic architecture; *ii)* a proof of concept on mobile ad-hoc network modelling and analysis.

The remainder of the article is organised as follows: in the section 2 we describe the main features of dynamic architectures and we present our specification method. Section 3 provides an overview of the used tools (Event B and Pro B). Section 4 presents the modelling and analysis of MANET. Finally Section 5 concludes the article.

2 Modelling Dynamic Architecture

In many specification contexts, one has to deal with dynamic configuration of the system architecture : an example is the growing number of client processes that participate in a resource allocation system and that interact with the resource server.

T. Margaria and B. Steffen (Eds.): ISoLA 2008, CCIS 17, pp. 769–781, 2008.

2.1 Features of Multi-process Systems

Two main features characterise systems with dynamic architecture: *structuring* and *interaction.*

The structure of a classical centralised software system is based on the composition of several sub-systems or processes. They are often parallely composed to enable synchronisation and communication. Unlikely, decentralised systems with dynamically evolving architecture have unfixed but varying structure. They cannot be structured with parallel operators that compose a fixed number of processes; they have an ad-hoc structure related to the number of involved processes.

Interaction is supported by communication and synchronisation between a group of processes currently involved in the cooperation to achieve given goals (the ones defined at the global system level). A group communication is then needed for systems with dynamic architecture. But the structure of the group, hence the architecture of the system, is varying; processes may join or leave the group at any time. The interaction among the processes that compose the system is based on message passing. A process of a group may send/receive messages to/from other processes of the group. Regarding approaches such as finite state automata, multi-process systems are often dealt with by considering the composition or reasoning on an arbitrary high number of processes. However, it is a biased solution to the problem of dynamic architecture.

2.2 Related Specification Approaches

State Transitions or FSM Approach. Capturing a process behaviour is intuitive but state transition systems lack high level structures for complex processes. Handling an undefined, variable number of processes is not tractable; dealing with several instances of the same processes is not possible; synchronisation of processes should be made explicit.

Process algebras. (such as CCS [16], CSP[18], LOTOS[15]) generalise state transition approaches and are widely used to model interacting processes; herein the behaviours of elementary processes are described and then the parallel composition operators are used to combine the processes. Therefore the architecture of a system is also a static composition of a finite number of processes. The π−calculus [17] permits the description of evolving structures of processes but new processes are generated from existing ones with the name passing mechanisms; the π−calculus is also not yet well supported by tools.

Handling dynamic behaviour of processes and their architecture is not well treated with the above classical approaches. Event-based approaches provide solutions, they do not consider a specific configuration of communicating processes. Events may be guarded and their occurrence may impact on any process of the current system architecture.

B System Approach. The Event B approach is an event-based one where communicating asynchronous systems are modelled with the interleaved composition of their behaviours viewed as event occurrences. A difficult concern is that of the completeness with respect to event ordering (liveness concerns): did the specification cover all the possible evolution (event sequences) expressed in the requirement? Indeed one can have a consistent system (with respect to the stated invariant) which does not meet the desired behavioural requirements. This is particularly challenging for dynamically evolving systems.

Therefore rigorous guidelines are needed to help in discovering and expressing the desired behaviours of a system with dynamic architecture; liveness properties help to cover the related completeness aspect. The approach [5] that is used here combines a process-oriented view (at low level) and an event-based one (at global level); it copes with the specification of the dynamically interacting processes and deals with the limitations described above. As an experimental framework we use the Event-B method.

2.3 The Specification Method: Overview

The used specification method is summarised as follows.

- Structuring aspects: each identified *type of process* P_i that may participate in the global system model is specified by considering its space state S_i and the events E_i with their description Evt_i that leads its behaviour and the events to join and leave the system. Note that some events are common to several processes; they handle interaction ans sharing aspects.

$$P_i \mathrel{\widehat{=}} \langle S_i, E_i, Evt_i \rangle$$

  At this low level, a process-oriented view is consider to discover the needed events for a process behaviour.
- Interaction aspects: as far as communication is concerned we use guarded events, message passing and ordering event occurrences; the processes synchronise and communicate through the enabling/disabling of the guards of their events. An event is used to model a process which is waiting for a data; it may be blocked until the availability of the data (enabling the event guard), which is the effect produced by another process event. Consider for example the case of processes exchanging messages, one process waits for the message and the other process sends the message. An abstract channel modelled as a set, is used to wait for a message or to deposit it. Hence the interaction between the processes are handled using common abstract channels. By the way, the communication is achieved in a completely decoupled way to favour dynamic structuring.
- All the described processes are combined by a fusion operation that merges state spaces and the events of the processes into a single global system S.

$$S \mathrel{\widehat{=}} \biguplus_i \langle S_i, E_i, Evt_i \rangle$$

In the following the method is illustrated with the MANET system using B abstract system.

3 Overview of the Used Materials

In this study we use the Event B method as the practical framework of our specification method of the MANETs. Prior to the formal specification we provide an overview of the Event B method[2,4] and the related Pro B tool[13].

3.1 Overview of Event B

Within the Event B framework, asynchronous systems may be developed and structured using *abstract systems* [2,4]. *Abstract systems* are the basic structures of the so-called *event-driven* B, and they replace the *abstract machines* which are the basic structures of the earlier *operation-driven* approach of the B method[1]. An *abstract system* [2,4] describes a mathematical model of a system behaviour[1]. It is made mainly of a state description (constants, properties, variables and invariant) and several *event* descriptions. Abstract systems are comparable to Action Systems [7]; they describe a nondeterministic evolution of a system through guarded actions. Dynamic constraints can be expressed within abstract systems to specify various liveness properties [4,10]. The state of an abstract system is described by variables and constants linked by an invariant. Variables and constants represent the data space of the system being formalised. Abstract systems may be refined like abstract machines [10,3].

Data of an Abstract System. At a higher level an abstract system models and contains the data of an entire system, be it distributed or not. Abstract systems have been used to formalise the behaviour of various (including distributed) systems [2,9,10,3]. Considering a global vision, the data that are formalised within the abstract system may correspond to all the elements of the distributed system.

Events of an Abstract System. Within B, an event is considered as the observation of a system transition. Events are spontaneous and show the way a system evolves. An event e is modelled as a *guarded substitution*: $e \mathrel{\widehat{=}} eG \Longrightarrow eB$ where eG is the event *guard* and eB the event *body* or *action*.

An event may occur or may be observed only when its guard holds. The action of an event describes, with generalised substitutions, how the system state evolves when this event occurs. Several events may have their guards held simultaneously; in this case, only one of them occurs. The system makes internally a nondeterministic choice. If no guard is true the abstract system is blocking (deadlock).

An event has one of the general forms (Fig. 1) where gcv denotes the global constants and variables of the abstract system containing the event; bv denotes the bound variables (variables bound to ANY). $P_{(bv,gcv)}$ denotes a predicate P expressed with the variables bv and gcv; in the same way $GS_{(bv,gcv)}$ is a generalised substitution S which models the event action using the variables bv

[1] A system behaviour is the set of its possible transitions from state to state beginning from an initial state.

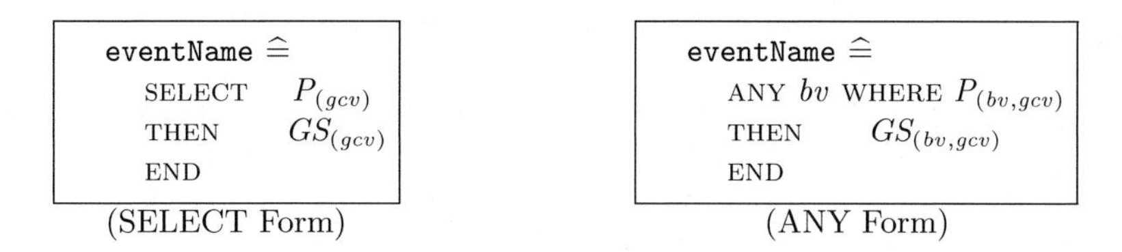

Fig. 1. General forms of events

and gcv. The SELECT form is a particular case of the ANY form. The guard of an event with the SELECT form is $P_{(gcv)}$. The guard of an event with the ANY form is $\exists(bv).P_{(bv,gcv)}$.

Semantics and Consistency. The semantics of a B model described as an abstract system relies on its invariant and is guaranteed by proof obligations (POs). The *consistency* of the model is established by such proof obligations:

i) the initialisation U should establish the invariant I: $[U]I$;
ii) each event of the given abstract system should preserve the invariant of the model.

The proof obligation of an event with the ANY form (Fig. 1) is:

$$I_{(gcv)} \wedge P_{(bv,gcv)} \wedge \mathsf{term}(GS_{(bv,gcv)}) \Rightarrow [GS_{(bv,gcv)}]I_{(gcv)}$$

where $I_{(gcv)}$ stands for the invariant of the abstract system.

The predicate $\mathsf{term}(GS_{(bv,gcv)})$ expresses that the event should terminate. The deadlock-freeness should be established for an abstract system: the disjunction of the event guards should be true. The event-based semantics of an abstract system A is the event traces of A ($traces(A)$); the set of finite event sequences generated by the evolution of A. The B method is supported by the theorem provers Atelier-B [12] and B-Toolkit [6] which are industrial tools. Public domain tools such as B4free[2] and ProB[3] are available.

3.2 Overview of ProB

The ProB tool [13,14] is an animator and a model checker for B specifications. It provides functionalities to display graphical view of automata. It supports automated consistency checking of B specifications (an abstract machine or a refinement with its state space, its initialisation and its operations). The consistency checking is performed on all the reachable states of the machine. The ProB also provides a constraint-based checking; with this approach ProB does not explore the state space from the initialisation, it checks whether applying one of the operation can result in an invariant violation independently from the initialisation.

The ProB offers many functionalities. The main ones are organised within three categories: *Animation*, *Verification* and *Analysis*. Several functionalities

[2] B4free is one of the tool dedicated to Event B: `www.B4free.fr`

[3] ProB `www.stups.uni-duesseldorf.de/ProB/`, is a free model checker for B.

are provided for each category but here, we just list a few of them which are used in this article.

In the *Verification* category, the following functionalities are available:

Temporal Model Checking: starting from a set of initialisation states (initial nodes), it systematically explores the state space of the current B specification.

LTL Model Checking: this functionality enables one to check the specification against a given LTL property.

In the *Analysis* category we consider the following functionality:

Compute Coverage: the state space (the nodes) and the transitions of the current specification are checked, some statistics are given on deadlocked states, live states[4], covered and uncovered operations.

The ProB tool is used in our study to help in discharging consistency proof obligations (invariant violation) and to check liveness properties.

4 Modelling the MANET System

The study of MANET (Mobile Ad-hoc Network)[11] is an active and challenging field as this type of network is rapidly growing and supporting small and medium size applications such as mobile services sharing, wireless peer-to-peer systems, etc. We chose the field of MANET for this work because it is a challenging field in the frontier of computer networks and software engineering. Especially, communication protocols, which are specific software systems, should be correct to ensure the (quality of) services deployed on networks. From the software system point of view, the MANET system is a typical asynchronous system with dynamically evolving architecture, it is decentralised. Moreover, its properties (dynamicity, mobility, correctness, etc) need a combined use of several verification techniques (namely a multifacet analysis).

4.1 Overview of Mobile Ad-Hoc Network

A mobile ad-hoc network [11] is a network formed by wireless mobile nodes (called ad-hoc nodes) which are the users equipments or devices. A MANET has no dedicated network infrastructure, but each node serves as a part of the network and acts a *router* to forward messages or packets since there is no router dedicated to that task.

A mobile ad-hoc network is formed only when a group of users put together their resources to enable and perform communications; hence a mobile ad-hoc network is dynamically created and may also desappear quickly.

In a MANET, the nodes communicate either by exchanging directly or via intermediate nodes. Technically they use ISM band[5] and more generally Wireless LAN technologies. Each node is equipped with one or more radio interfaces with specific transmission features. The *transmission range* of a node is the transmission area accessible from this node. All the nodes in this range are

[4] The already computed states.

[5] They are radio system frequency initially dedicated to industrial, scientific and medical usage.

accessible directly (one hop); they are called the neighbours. To address a known node which is not in its transmission range, the sender node sends its packet to one of the neighbour nodes which is closer to the destination node (according to the transmission ranges). Each node may communicates directly or indirectly using relay nodes (multi-hop), with other nodes that are outside the sender range.

Dynamic Aspect. One of the main features of a MANET is its dynamic aspect: the structure or topology of the network is frequently changing. A node may join or leave the net at any time, changing the net topology. The structure or topology of the net is then highly dynamic.

Mobility Aspect. The ad-hoc nodes may move at any time and very frequently due to their mobile nature; consequently this impacts not only on the net topology but also on its quality; there may be route changes, information loss, partitions of the network into different networks, etc. As far as routing is concerned, in classical infrastructure-based network, there are one or several nodes called routers that are in charge of routing packets between nodes. For this purpose the routers and the nodes are equipped with a routing table where there is the information about how to join a given destination node or a network identified with an Internet Address (IP address).

In the scope of MANET, efficient routing protocols development is a challenging concern. A message or packet sent to a node reaches it unless the net is partitionned. The destination node of a packet is either in the range of the sender node or it is in the range of an intermediate node that is closer to the destination node or that is itself the destination. Concerning the time, it is assumed to be discrete and divided into frames. A node has a set of neighbour nodes during a frame. During a frame a node may be iddle, it also may send messages, receive messages, forward the received messages. Before sending a message to a destination, a source node *sn* which does not have the destination node address, sends a route request to get this destination address. The request travels through the net possibly with multi-hop and reaches the destination which sends back it address. When the address is received by *sn* the latter can send its message to the right destination address.

4.2 Formal Specification of MANET

In our study, a MANET is viewed as an evolving global system. Formally, it is a set of nodes with a connection relationship: a configuration. The evolution of the MANET is viewed as the combined evolution of the nodes, hence a sequence of configurations; going from a configuration to another is observed as an event and it depends on the actions performed by the net nodes.

Specifying Node Processes. A node is modelled as a process using Event B. Each node has some features: an identifier, a location, an IP address, a connection relation that indicates its neighbours, etc. Accordingly we have the S_i part of the node. A set of events (E_i) with the associated behaviours (Evt_i) defines the process behaviour which leads the evolution of the system. Any node may initiate a message for a given destination, send a message, receive a message, forward a message, leave a net (a transmission range). The behaviour described by these events is observed only when a net exists; that means the net structuring events are related to those needed for the routing. Also we deal with the creation of a network by nodes which have a given range, other nodes may join or leave this range. Therefore, in the B model, we link the range of a node with a given abstract network.

Event B Specification of MANETs. The MANET is formed by the nodes (already defined with S_i, E_i, Evt_i). The formal specification of a MANET is a set of possible sequence of configurations of the considered nodes. Concerning the structuring aspect, we describe the configuration by *state variables* (hence a state space) resulting from the fusion of the node state variables; the sequence of configurations is modelled through the enabling of *events* which possibly modify the state space. Concerning the evolution of the entire MANET system, we consider the events of the nodes and also the common events related to the entire system network (*ie* the management of ranges). All the network is dynamic, the nodes leave and join it at any time, new ranges appear, others disappear, etc.

Moreover, from the methodological point of view, we have considered two aspects in the Event B specification of MANET: the structuring of the networks (the configuration related to the net topology) and the routing in the networks.

As far as routing is concerned we consider one of the widely studied routing protocol of MANET: *Ad-hoc On demand Distance Vector* (AODV) [11].

Therefore a part of our B specification is related to the structuring and another part is about the routing protocol.

Specifying the MANET Structure. The structuring of a MANET is achieved using a set of state variables and an invariant that describes the nodes and their current configurations:

INVARIANT

$nodes \subseteq NODE \wedge ranges \subseteq RANGE \wedge messages \subseteq MSG$

$\wedge\ rangNodes \in ranges \leftrightarrow nodes \wedge reqMsg \in nodes \leftrightarrow messages$

$\wedge\ inReqMsg, inRspMsg \in nodes \leftrightarrow messages$

$\wedge\ waitReqMsg \in nodes \leftrightarrow messages$

$\wedge \cdots$

The evolution of the system depends on the set of events that define the nodes and the specific system events: the observation of a net creation (*newRange*); an existing net may disappear if there is no more connected nodes (*rmvRange*). The other events considered for the network structuring are summarised in the table Tab. 1;

The combination of the two categories of events forms an abstract MANET specification which is the reference model for the specification. It describes a system composed of node processes and abstract MANET networks. The evolving of the system architecture is based on the fact that the event guards depends on the variables $nodes, messages, \cdots$ which in turn depend on current event. This is illustrated by the non-deterministic form of the event specifications:

$$\texttt{event} \mathrel{\widehat{=}} \text{ANY } sn \text{ WHERE } sn \in nodes \text{ THEN ... END}$$

Table 1. Network structuring events

Event	Description
newRange	A new network range appears
joinRange	A node joins a range
leaveRange	A node leaves a net range
newNode	A new node appears
newMsg	A node initiate a message

Specifying the AODV Routing Protocol. Within the Ad-hoc On demand Distant Vector (AODV) protocol, each node acts as a router, contributes to construct routes and forward messages to other nodes. There are two phases of the protocol: route discovery and route maintenance. Route discovery is achieved by exchanging Route Request (RREQ) and Route Response (RREP) messages. The algorithm of the nodes is as follows: when a node desires to set up a route to a destination node, it broadcasts a RREQ message to its neighbours (the nodes in its range). The RREQ/RREP messages have the following main parameters: the source node Id, the destination node Id, the number of hop.

When a node *nd* receives a RREQ message, *i)* either *nd* is itself a destination and *nd* responds with a RREP or *nd* is an active route to the searched destination node then *nd* responds with a route information using the RREP message; *ii)* otherwise *nd* broadcasts the RREQ further with the hop count of RREQ increased by 1. When a node *nd* receives a duplicate RREQ, it drops the message. The routing of message is symmetric when a node receives a RREP message. The Event B specification comprises the events related to the routing protocol described above. These events are listed in the table Tab. 2.

Table 2. Routing events

Event	Description
sndRREQ	Route Request sending
fwdRREQ	Route Request forwarding
rcvRREQ	Route Request receiving
sndRREP	Route Response sending
fwdRREP	Route Response forwarding
rcvRREP	Route Response receiving

The B specification of a MANET is then an abstract system equipped with these events (see Fig. 2).

We give in the following (see Fig. 3) the specification of the `sndRREQ` event to illustrate the specification principle. Here, any node (*sn*) may send a message (*msg*) that it has already prepared ($msg \in reqMsg[\{sn\}]$) to all the nodes in its range (*otherNodesInRange*). Exchanged messages are modelled using abstract channels (*inRepMsg*,*repMsg*).

The other events are specified in quite the same way. Therefore the complete specification enables us to model the dynamic evolution of the MANET (as

```
SYSTEM MANET
SETS NODE, RANGE, MSG /* abstract sets */
VARIABLES
   nodes, ranges, messages, ··· /* state variables*/
INVARIANT   /* state space predicate
   nodes ⊆ NODE ∧ ranges ⊆ RANGE
∧ messages ⊆ MSG ∧ rangNodes ∈ ranges ↔ nodes
∧ ···
INITIALISATION
   nodes, ranges, messages, rangNodes := ∅, ∅, ∅, ∅
|| ···
```

```
EVENTS
   newNODE ≙ ···
;  newRANGE ≙ ···
;  joinRange ≙ ···
;  leaveRange ≙ ···
;  newMsg ≙ ···
;  sndRREQ ≙ ···
;  rcvRREQ ≙ ···
;  fwdRREQ ≙ ···
;  newRespMsg ≙ ···
;  sndRREP ≙ ···
;  rcvRREP ≙ ···
END
```

Fig. 2. Structure of the abstract system

```
sndRREQ ≙   /* route request from sn to dn */
ANY sn, msg WHERE
   sn ∈ nodes /* source */
   ∧ msg ∈ MSG ∧ msg ∈ messages
   ∧ msg ∈ reqMsg[{sn}] /* a msg initiated by nd */
THEN
   LET otherNodesInRange
   BE otherNodesInRange = {ndi | ndi ∈ nodes
   ∧ ndi ≠ sn ∧ rangNodes⁻¹(sn) = rangNodes⁻¹(ndi)}
   IN   inReqMsg :=
           inReqMsg ∪ (otherNodesInRange ∗ {msg})
      || reqMsg := reqMsg − {(sn ↦ msg)}
   END
END
```

Fig. 3. Specification of the sndRREQ event

Fig. 4. Evolution and various dynamic interactions

illustrated in Fig. 4) and the routing protocol via dynamically interacting variable number of node processes.

4.3 Analysis of the Specified MANET System

A multifacet analysis with a reference abstract model is performed on the MANET system. For this purpose two different tools are used but they cover different facets of the analysis: B4free and ProB [13]. Both tools use one common input specification: the B reference model previously specified; this ensures consistency of verification and feedbacks.

Consistency and Refinement of System. The previously described abstract system is proved consistent (see Sect.3.1) using the B4free tool. Then it is refined; more details are added to the state space and the event specifications; for instance we consider the management of the IP addresses of the nodes and exchanged messages. Unlike in the abstract system where a packet destination is nondeterministically selected, in the refinement the nodes and the messages have IP addresses, therefore, the receiver node is checked against the destination IP address. The resulting refined system is also proved correct with respect to consistency using the B4free tool. However to accomplish the proofs, we combine the use of B4free and ProB. That is, when a proof obligation is not discharged by B4free, we model-check the specification and discover possible errors by displaying and analysing the displayed error state. Accordingly the feedback is propagated in the reference model and we iterate. This multifacet analysis approach helps here to make precise the correct ordering of the events: the simulation functionalities and the listing of uncovered operations help to correct the B abstract system. This aspect is very important because, an abstract system proved correct, may have an incomplete or even a wrong behaviour if for example we have an event which is never enabled. Using the multifacet approach, helps us to get a complete analysis. The ab. 3 shows a ProB experiment result where one deadlock is detected after the exploration of 31257 nodes and 1168 transitions ; all operations (the B events) are covered, with the indicated occurrences.

Table 3. Analysis results

NODES	
invariant_violated	: 0
deadlocked	: 1
live	: 2521
explored_transitions	: 1168
open	: 28735
total	: 31257
TOTAL_OPERATIONS	
44110	

COVERED_OPERATIONS	
initialise_machine	: 1
newRANGE	: 225
rcvRREP	: 14
sndRREP	: 29
newRespMsg	: 300
sndRREQ	: 1829
rcvRREQ	: 1697
newNODE	: 10487
joinRange	: 7411
leaveRange	: 9721
newMsg	: 11042
fwdRREQ	: 1354
UNCOVERED_OPERATIONS	

The state corresponding to the deadlock is carefully analysed. We discover that it corresponds to a situation (net partitioning) where there are nodes with some packets to be transmitted but no node in the current net range. This corresponds to a real-life situation which is due to the dynamic aspect of the MANET and the mobility of nodes. A feedback is then propagated in the Event B specification. To confirm that, the model is corrected by strengthening the guard of message initiation by the hypothesis of non-emptiness of the net range. Thus the analysis of the model runs without errors[6]. In the real-life situation, this corresponds to the fact that after a while the net may be reconstituted with other nodes.

Liveness Properties Analysis. Many properties of the MANET routing protocol are well-expressed using LTL formula which is not supported by the B4free tool. We express these liveness properties with the ProB LTL formalism. Then we extend the Event B abstract system with these LTL properties; the resulting specification is model-checked.

The following are illustrations of some checked properties.

$\mathbf{P}_1$. A route request is always followed by a response:
$G(e(sndRREQ) \Rightarrow F(e(sndRREP)))$ false

$\mathbf{P}_2$. A route request may be followed by a response:
$e(sndRREQ) \Rightarrow F(e(sndRREP))$ true

$\mathbf{P}_3$. A route request may be finally received:
$F(e(sndRREQ) \Rightarrow X(e(rcvRREQ)))$ true

We come to the conclusion that our model of the MANET extended with the stated properties, is correct with respect to these properties.

5 Conclusion

We presented the main features of decentralised system with dynamically evolving architecture; we showed that these features are not well handled with classical state-oriented approaches and accordingly we presented a method that deals with them using event-based approach. The composition of processes used to model the system components is completely decoupled to favour the evolving of the system architecture. The method which combines a process-oriented view (at low level) and an event-based one (at global level) was illustrated with the specification and the analysis of a MANET system. The proof is given that the specified system with dynamic architecture may be studied with respect to safety and liveness properties. For this purpose the Event B tools are used. There are several works on dynamic and self-managing component architectures, [8] presents a survey; most of them use a process-algebra oriented approach, focus on the changes on defined architectures and define rules to perform reconfiguration. Compared with these works our event-based approach adds distribution and mobility of processes and no predefined reconfiguration rules are needed, instead we consider the behaviour of process types. Ongoing works are about the scalability of our approach; we consider precisely two aspects, one is the analysis of Mobile Linux codes (drivers) for embedded systems by considering their abstractions, the other one is the strengthening of message passing aspects and the refinement of our specifications into executable codes for physical devices.

[6] The experiment result tables, not displayed here, show 0 deadlocked states for hundreds of explored states and transitions.

References

1. Abrial, J.-R.: The B Book. Cambridge University Press, Cambridge (1996)
2. Abrial, J.-R.: Extending B without Changing it (for developping distributed systems). In: Habrias, H. (ed.) Proc. of the 1st Conf. on the B method, France, pp. 169–190 (1996)
3. Abrial, J.-R., Cansell, D., Mery, D.: Formal Derivation of Spanning Trees Algorithms. In: Bert, D., et al. (eds.) ZB 2003. LNCS, vol. 2651, pp. 457–476. Springer, Heidelberg (2003)
4. Abrial, J.-R., Mussat, L.: Introducing Dynamic Constraints in B. In: Bert, D. (ed.) B 1998. LNCS, vol. 1393, pp. 83–128. Springer, Heidelberg (1998)
5. Attiogbé, C.: Multi-process Systems Analysis using Event B: Application to Group Communication Systems. In: Liu, Z., He, J. (eds.) ICFEM 2006. LNCS, vol. 4260, pp. 660–677. Springer, Heidelberg (2006)
6. B-Core. B-Toolkit, UK (consulted, 2007), www.b-core.com
7. Back, R., Kurki-Suonio, R.: Decentralisation of Process Nets with Centralised Control. In: Proc. of the 2nd ACM SIGACT-SIGOPS Symp. on Principles of Distributed Computing, pp. 131–142 (1983)
8. Bradbury, J.S., Cordy, J.R., Dingel, J., Wermelinger, M.: A survey of self-management in dynamic software architecture specifications. In: WOSS 2004: Proceedings of the 1st ACM SIGSOFT workshop on Self-managed systems, pp. 28–33. ACM, New York (2004)
9. Butler, M., Walden, M.: Distributed System Development in B. In: Habrias, H. (ed.) Proc. of the 1st Conference on the B method, France, pp. 155–168 (1996)
10. Cansell, D., Gopalakrishnan, G., Jones, M., Mery, D.: Incremental Proof of the Producer/Consumer Property for the PCI Protocol. In: Bert, D., P. Bowen, J., C. Henson, M., Robinson, K. (eds.) B 2002 and ZB 2002. LNCS, vol. 2272, pp. 22–41. Springer, Heidelberg (2002)
11. Chlamtac, I., Conti, M., Liu, J.: Mobile Ad hoc Networking: Imperatives and Challenges. Ad Hoc Networks 1(1), 13–64 (2003)
12. ClearSy. Atelier B V3.6. Steria, Aix-en-Provence, France, (consulted, 2007), www.clearsy.com
13. Leuschel, M., Butler, M.: ProB: A Model Checker for B. In: Araki, K., Gnesi, S., Mandrioli, D. (eds.) FME 2003. LNCS, vol. 2805, pp. 855–874. Springer, Heidelberg (2003)
14. Leuschel, M., Turner, E.: Visualizing Larger State Spaces in ProB. In: Treharne, H., King, S., C. Henson, M., Schneider, S. (eds.) ZB 2005. LNCS, vol. 3455, pp. 6–23. Springer, Heidelberg (2005)
15. Lotos, I.: A Formal Description Technique Based on The Temporal Ordering of Observational Behaviour. In: IOS - OSI, Geneva (1988); International Standard 8807
16. Milner, R.: Communication and Concurrency. Prentice-Hall, Englewood Cliffs (1989)
17. Milner, R., Parrow, J., Walker, D.: A Calculus of Mobile Processes. Journal of Information and Computation 100 (1992)
18. Roscoe, A.: The Theory and Practice of concurrency. Prentice-Hall, Englewood Cliffs (1998)

Trusted Theorem Proving: A Case Study in SLD-Resolution

Konstantine Arkoudas and Olin Shivers

MIT Computer Science and Artificial Intelligence Lab
Northeastern University College of Computer and Information Science
arkoudas@csail.mit.edu, shivers@ccs.neu.edu

Abstract. Prolog's implementation of SLD-resolution furnishes an efficient theorem-proving technique for the Horn-clause subset of first-order logic, and makes for a powerful addition to any automatic or semi-automatic verification system. However, due to the complexity of SLD-resolution, a naive incorporation of a Prolog engine into such a system would inordinately increase the overall trusted base. In this paper we show how to integrate this procedure in a disciplined, trusted manner, by making the Prolog engine justify its results with very simple natural deduction reasoning. In effect, instead of taking SLD-resolution as a *primitive* inference rule, we express it as a *derived* inference rule in terms of much simpler rules such as conditional elimination.

This reduction is an example of a general methodology for building highly reliable software systems called *certified computation*, whereby a program not only produces a result r for a given input x but also *proves* that r is correct for x. Such a proof can be viewed as a *certificate* for the result r, and can significantly enhance the latter's credibility: if we trust the axioms and inference rules used in the proof, we can trust the result. We present a complete implementation of a certifying Prolog interpreter that relies only on three exceptionally simple inference rules: conditional elimination, universal specialization, and conjunction introduction.

1 Introduction

The key concern in formal verification is trust. The *trusted base* of a digital system S, or $TB(S)$ for short, can be understood roughly as the totality of propositions whose truth must be taken for granted if we are to be justified in accepting the correctness of S. This base consists of two main parts: a body of theoretical principles subserving the operation of S; and a set of software and hardware components whose operation must be assumed to be correct if we are to be justified in believing that the operation of S is correct. For example, if S is an implementation of the simplex algorithm, then $TB(S)$ includes a body of mathematical theory (the theory of linear programming), as well as assumptions about the actual software and hardware involved in the implementation. In particular, we must assume the soundness of the theory on which the algorithm is based (and the soundness of the algorithm itself); and we must also assume that

T. Margaria and B. Steffen (Eds.): ISoLA 2008, CCIS 17, pp. 782–796, 2008.

the particular program which we are using is a correct implementation of that algorithm. In addition, the trusted base recursively includes the trusted bases of all the software and hardware components mediating the implementation, most notably the compiler of the language in which the algorithm is implemented, the underlying operating system, and the actual hardware on which the implementation runs. However, since they tend to be invariant over many different pieces of software, in practice these recursive inclusions of nested trusted bases tend to be disregarded.

Now suppose we use a verification technology V (involving, e.g., theorem proving, model checking, proof checking, or any combination thereof) to verify that some system S has some desired property. What reason do we have for believing the result of the verification? In particular, why should we believe the verification of S any more than S itself? Indeed, it is often overlooked that V itself has a trusted base, $TB(V)$. The trusted base of V includes both a body of theory and a set of software and hardware systems which rely on that theory. Now, if the trusted base of V is *larger* than the trusted base of the system S whose correctness we are trying to verify, then the verification exercise will not buy us anything. This can happen if the theory on which V rests is inordinately complicated or insufficiently understood; or if the implementation of V contains bugs; or both. Typically the theoretical concerns are minimal because the logics on which these verification systems rest (e.g. first-order or higher-order logic) have been extensively investigated over long periods of time. The practical concerns about implementation bugs, however, are more serious. Clearly, the larger the code base of a verification system, the higher the probability that it contains errors.

For instance, if we are using a theorem prover T written in 50,000 lines of C code to verify a string-matching algorithm M written in 200 lines of code, something is clearly amiss. Of course, one could argue that the prover T has been successfully used in many other projects before, and hence our confidence in it is considerably larger than our confidence in M. But that is mere inductive evidence. All it says is that the prover T has been well-tested. So why not do the same for M, instead of verifying it formally? That is, why not simply test M thoroughly until our confidence in it becomes just as solid as our confidence in T? That would certainly be a lot easier than formal verification. The answer, of course, is that we are looking for some sort of assurance that is qualitatively more compelling than the type of inductive evidence we can get from testing and experience. And such assurance will not be forthcoming if the best we can do is point out that T has been extensively tested in the past. A more promising possibility suggests itself: Perhaps the theorem prover T itself has been formally verified! But then the same questions arise anew. What system T' was used to verify T? What theory did T' rely on? How large was the code base implementing T'? And so on.

One way to avoid the regress is to engineer T so that it provably relies on a very simple and well-understood logic $\mathcal{L}$, comprising a small number of inference rules and axioms, in such a way that any computation of T that results in a theorem p is guaranteed to correspond to a proof of p in $\mathcal{L}$. Perhaps the most common way of achieving this is to endow the system with a metalanguage, so that any computation of T consists essentially of two stages, the first *analytic* and the second *synthetic*: (a) a proof search in $\mathcal{L}$, encoded in the said metalanguage; and, assuming that a proof is found, (b) the execution or evaluation of that proof. The main feature of this approach, which was pioneered by LCF [5] and later HOL [6], is that the user can write arbitrarily complicated tactics, and yet the system is structured in such a way that it can never go wrong, i.e., it can never result in a false theorem, because ultimately all outputs of type "theorem" are obtained by putting together a proof in $\mathcal{L}$ during stage (b) above.

However, this guarantee is theoretical: It only tells us that the theoretical commitments of T are fairly minimal, i.e., those of $\mathcal{L}$. In practice we still have to trust that the particular implementation of T which we are using is free of errors. This is non-trivial, since the metalanguage of T is likely to include sophisticated computational mechanisms for proof search. But we can do better here. We can avoid trusting the implementation of T by decoupling its general (total) correctness from the correctness of its specific results, by having T output the proof that was put together during the synthetic stage (b) above. That proof can then be checked independently by a proof checker for $\mathcal{L}$, which will presumably be much smaller and simpler than T.

An interesting variation of this idea is the notion of certified computation [2], whereby instead of verifying a digital system S in a trusted theorem prover T, we directly implement S *in* T. An implementation of this sort not only produces a result r for a given input x, but also *proves* that r is correct for x. Such a proof can be viewed as a *certificate* for the result r, and can greatly enhance the latter's credibility: If we trust the axioms and inference rules used in the proof, we can trust the result.

In what follows we will illustrate this methodology by developing a certified implementation of SLD-resolution. Prolog's implementation [13] of the SLD-resolution technique of logic programming [9] furnishes an efficient theorem-proving tool for the Horn-clause subset of predicate logic, and makes for a powerful addition to any general-purpose theorem prover. But Prolog's execution model is too complex to be used as a trusted primitive. A naive incorporation of a Prolog engine into a theorem prover would greatly increase the prover's trusted base: We would need to trust the engine's implementation of unification, backtracking, substitution operations, and a good deal of other non-trivial code. Here we show how to implement this technique in a trusted manner, by making the Prolog engine justify its results using extremely simple reasoning. In effect, instead of taking SLD-resolution as a primitive inference rule, we show how to express it as a derived inference rule in terms of much simpler rules such as modus ponens.

Strictly speaking, it is not necessary to use a provably sound programmable logical framework for certified computation. In principle, the proof search could be performed in any language whatsoever, as long as every output is ultimately backed up by a proof (certificate) in $\mathcal{L}$. However, our discussion will demonstrate that the use of a rich logical framework can greatly facilitate both the analytic stage of proof search and the generation of the proof. In fact, as we will see, the second stage does not have to be explicitly programmed at all. In the type of logical framework we will be considering, the generation of the proof is automatic, i.e., stage (b) is always followed by the successful conclusion of stage (a).

The particular logical framework that we use is Athena [1], a programmable theorem-proving system in the tradition of HOL, i.e., in which every proof search is guaranteed to result in a valid theorem. However, unlike HOL-like systems, Athena is based on a much more intuitive block-structured Fitch-style system of natural deduction, instead of a sequent calculus. This style of proof is known to have the closest resemblance to informal mathematical reasoning [11]. Moreover, unlike the Isar front end for Isabelle [15], Athena's block-structured style of natural deduction is not just a veneer for a sequent calculus, but is instead reflected in the native syntax and semantics of the system. In particular, a block-structured natural deduction format is used not only for writing proofs, but also for writing tactics—or *methods*, in Athena's terminology. Methods in this style are considerably easier to write; complicated proof-search algorithms can be expressed succinctly and fluidly. As a result, methods are widely used in Athena (see, e.g., [3,12]). Our implementation was also facilitated by several high-level features offered by Athena, such as sophisticated pattern matching, built-in backtracking mechanisms, first-class proof continuations, anonymous methods, and a combination of state with lexical scoping and higher-order methods and functions. We also leveraged Athena's built-in support for terms and propositions, including substitutions and unification. As a result, the entire implementation takes less than one page of code, even though it achieves a dramatic trust reduction. Specifically, it expresses SLD-resolution in terms of only three exceptionally simple inference rules: modus ponens, conjunction introduction, and universal specialization.

2 SLD Trees

In what follows Horn clauses will be called *rules* (or sometimes *axioms*), and will be represented by Athena propositions of the form

$$(\forall x_1) \cdots (\forall x_n) [P_1(x_1, \ldots, x_n) \wedge \cdots \wedge P_k(x_1, \ldots, x_n) \Rightarrow R(x_1, \ldots, x_n)] \quad (1)$$

for $n \geq 0$, $k \geq 1$, where $R(x_1, \ldots, x_n)$ and each $P_i(x_1, \ldots, x_n)$ are atomic propositions that may have free occurrences of $x_1, \ldots, x_n$; no variables outside $x_1, \ldots, x_n$ may occur in these atoms. We will refer to the atoms

$$P_1(x_1, \ldots, x_n), \ldots, P_k(x_1, \ldots, x_n) \quad (2)$$

as the *antecedents* of the rule, and to the atom $R(x_1, \ldots, x_n)$ as its *conclusion*. The conjunction of the antecedents, $P_1(x_1, \ldots, x_n) \wedge \cdots \wedge P_k(x_1, \ldots, x_n)$, will be called the *body* of the rule. By a *fact* we will mean a rule whose antecedent is the sole atom *true*. A *query* is simply an atomic proposition. For any rule $\mathcal{R}$ of the form (1), we define $Ant(\mathcal{R})$ as the list of its antecedents (given in the order of (2)). It is convenient to stipulate that $Ant(\mathcal{R}) = []$ whenever $\mathcal{R}$ is a fact. The symbol $\oplus$ will denote the binary operation of list concatenation.

We can now give a partial formulation of the problem as follows (a more precise problem statement will be given shortly): Define a binary tactic `solve` that takes a list of rules $[\mathcal{R}_1, \ldots, \mathcal{R}_n]$ and a list of queries $[Q_1, \ldots, Q_m]$ and produces a theorem of the form $Q'_1 \wedge \cdots \wedge Q'_m$ that is a ground instance of the proposition $Q_1 \wedge \cdots \wedge Q_m$; in other words, such that

$$\theta(Q_1 \wedge \cdots \wedge Q_m) = Q'_1 \wedge \cdots \wedge Q'_m$$

for some substitution θ that maps the free variables of $Q_1, \ldots, Q_m$ to ground terms. (Of course `solve` may also fail or get into an infinite loop.) Thus the second argument to `solve` represents our queries and the first argument represents the "logic program"—a list of rules $[\mathcal{R}_1, \ldots, \mathcal{R}_n]$ of the form described above. These rules should be in the assumption base at the time when `solve` is invoked. The order in which the rules appear in the given list is important. The rules should be given in the order in which they would be listed in a Prolog program. This might affect termination. Further, `solve` should not use any axioms other than the given rules and no primitive methods other than simple introduction and elimination rules for the propositional connectives and quantifiers.

By a *computation rule* we will understand any unary computable function $\mathcal{C}$ that takes an arbitrary non-empty list of queries L and produces a triple $\langle L_1, G, L_2 \rangle$ consisting of a query list L_1, a single query G, and another query list L_2 such that $L_1 \oplus [G] \oplus L2 = L$. Hence, the triple $\langle L_1, G, L_2 \rangle$ represents a decomposition of L into a prefix L_1, a *selected goal* G, and a suffix L_2. Every deterministic interpreter of logic programs must fix a computation rule. Prolog makes a particularly simple choice: the selected goal is always the first element of the given query list. Therefore, using our definitions, for any given $L = [G_1, \ldots, G_k]$, $k > 0$, Prolog's computation rule returns the triple $\langle [], G_1, [G_2, \ldots, G_k] \rangle$.

For the remainder of this section fix a set of function symbols $\mathcal{F}$ and a disjoint set of relation symbols $\mathcal{R}$, with each $f \in \mathcal{F}$ and $p \in \mathcal{R}$ having a unique non-negative arity, and a countably infinite set of variables $\mathcal{V}$, disjoint from $\mathcal{F}$ and $\mathcal{R}$. We assume that $\mathcal{V}$ is totally ordered by some computable binary relation $\prec$, and we will use v as a metavariable ranging over $\mathcal{V}$. The Herbrand universe $Terms(\mathcal{F}, \mathcal{V})$ of terms built over $\mathcal{F}$ and $\mathcal{V}$ is defined as usual. A substitution θ is defined as any function from $\mathcal{V}$ to $Terms(\mathcal{F}, \mathcal{V})$ that is the identity almost everywhere, except for some finite subset of $\mathcal{V}$ known as the "support" of θ. A substitution with support $\{x_1, \ldots, x_n\}$ that maps each x_i to t_i is often written as $\{x_1 \mapsto t_1, \ldots, x_n \mapsto t_n\}$. Every substitution $\theta : \mathcal{V} \rightarrow Terms(\mathcal{F}, \mathcal{V})$ has a unique homomorphic extension $\overline{\theta} : Terms(\mathcal{F}, \mathcal{V}) \rightarrow Terms(\mathcal{F}, \mathcal{V})$. For a list of terms $L = [t_1, \ldots, t_n]$, we define $\overline{\theta}(L) = [\overline{\theta}(t_1), \ldots, \overline{\theta}(t_n)]$. A binary *composition* operation $\circ$ on substitutions is defined as

$$\sigma \circ \theta = \lambda\, v \in \mathcal{V} \,.\, \overline{\sigma}(\theta(v)).$$

It is well-known that the set of all substitutions forms a monoid under $\circ$ [14].

We say that n terms $t_1, \ldots, t_n$ are *unifiable* iff there is a substitution θ such that $\overline{\theta}(t_1) = \cdots = \overline{\theta}(t_n)$. There are efficient unification algorithms [8] that take any finite number of terms and produce the most general possible substitution that unifies them, if the terms are unifiable at all. The substitutions returned by such algorithms are called *mgus* ("most general unifiers") and have a number of nice properties such as idempotence.

With variables, terms, and relation symbols at our disposal, propositions are defined as usual—we have atoms, propositional combinations, and quantifications. The application of a substitution $\theta = \{x_1 \mapsto t_1, \ldots, x_n \mapsto t_n\}$ to a proposition P, which we will denote simply as $\theta\, P$, is also defined as usual: every free occurrence of x_i within P is replaced by t_i.[1] If L is a list of propositions $[P_1, \ldots, P_n]$, we write $\theta(L)$ to denote $[\theta P_1, \ldots, \theta P_n]$. Finally, let V' be a finite subset of V and let P be a proposition of the form $(\forall\, x_1) \cdots (\forall\, x_k)\, Q$, $k \geq 0$, where Q contains no variables outside $x_1, \ldots, x_k$. Setting $\theta = \{x_1 \mapsto z_1, \ldots, x_k \mapsto z_k\}$, where z_i is the least variable (according to the ordering $\prec$) outside the set $\{x_1, \ldots, x_k\} \cup V' \cup \{z_1, \ldots, z_{i-1}\}$, for $i = 1, \ldots, k$, we define *the V'-instance of P* as the proposition $(\forall\, z_1) \cdots (\forall\, z_k)\, \theta\, Q$. Thus the V'-instance of P is simply a (uniquely defined) freshly renamed copy of P, with the fresh variables being taken outside V' and of course also outside the variables that occur in P.

Furthermore, fix a computation rule $\mathcal{C}$ and let a logic program $\mathcal{P}$ be given as a list of $n > 0$ rules $\mathcal{R}_1, \ldots, \mathcal{R}_n$, let $V_{\mathcal{P}}$ be the set of all and only those variables that occur in some rule $\mathcal{R}_i$, and consider a list of goals L. We define the *SLD-tree* of L, denoted $SLDT(L)$, as explained below. The nodes of the tree will be lists of goals, with L at the root. Every edge in the tree will be decorated with a pair of the form $\langle \widehat{\mathcal{R}_i}, \theta \rangle$, comprising an instance $\widehat{\mathcal{R}_i}$ of $\mathcal{R}_i$, for some $i \in \{1, \ldots, n\}$, and a substitution θ. For any node M in the tree, we will write $Var(M)$ for the set of all and only those variables that occur in the unique path leading from the root to M.[2] More precisely, $SLDT(L)$ is defined as follows:

1. The root of $SLDT(L)$ is L.
2. Suppose that a node of $SLDT(L)$ is a list of goals M. If M is empty, then the node is a leaf—there are no children. Otherwise, let $\mathcal{C}(M) = \langle M_1, G, M_2 \rangle$, and suppose that there is an $i \in \{1, \ldots, n\}$ such that the selected goal G unifies with the conclusion of $\widehat{\mathcal{R}_i}$ under some mgu θ, where $\widehat{\mathcal{R}_i}$ is the $(V_{\mathcal{P}} \cup Var(M))$-instance of $\mathcal{R}_i$. Then M has a child $M' = \theta(M_1 \oplus Ant(\widehat{\mathcal{R}_i}) \oplus M_2)$, joined to M by an edge labeled with the pair $\langle \widehat{\mathcal{R}_i}, \theta \rangle$. We refer to $\widehat{\mathcal{R}_i}$ and θ as the *resolving rule* and *substitution* of M'; i is called the *index* of M'.

We will assume that the children of every node are totally ordered in accordance with their indices: A node L_1 precedes one of its siblings L_2 iff the index of L_1 is strictly smaller than that of L_2. Since an index i indicates that the child was obtained by resolving the selected goal of its parent list with an instance of the ith

[1] In general we might first have to rename P via alphabetic conversion to avoid variable capture, but this will not be an issue here.

[2] Where a variable is understood to occur in a path if it occurs either in a node (a list of goals) on the path, or in one of the objects attached to an edge along the path.

rule in the program, this ordering entails that a depth-first traversal of $SLDT(L)$ examines the given rules from top to bottom. In tandem with a computation rule that always selects the first goal in a list of queries, this means that a depth-first search of $SLDT(L)$ gives us the operational semantics of Prolog.

There are two kinds of finite branches in a SLD-tree: *success branches*, ending in leaves that contain the empty list of goals; and *failure branches*, ending in leaves that contain non-empty goal lists whose selected goal cannot be resolved with any rule. There may be infinite branches as well.

Given a list of queries L, a Prolog interpreter performs a depth-first search of $SLDT(L)$. If the search does not diverge, there are two possibilities. If there is a success branch, the result is the composition of all the resolving substitutions found along the edges of the leftmost success branch, with the composition proceeding from top to bottom. If there is no success branch, then failure is reported. Of course the search might diverge if there is an infinite path to the left of the leftmost success branch.

A precise formulation of the problem can now be given thus: Define a binary method `solve` that takes a logic program $\mathcal{P}$ (represented as a list of Horn clauses in the manner described earlier) and a list of goals $L = [G_1, \ldots, G_k]$ (represented as a list of atoms, as discussed earlier), and behaves as follows. If a depth-first search of $SLDT(L)$ diverges before discovering any success branches, `solve` should also diverge. Otherwise, if there is a success branch, then the theorem produced by `solve` should be $\theta\,(G_1 \wedge \cdots \wedge G_k)$, where θ is the composition of all substitutions found along the leftmost success branch; else if there are no success branches, `solve` should fail.

3 Proof Construction

Suppose that our initial list of queries is $L = [G_1, \ldots, G_k]$, and that a depth-first search on the SLD-tree of this list eventually discovers a success branch that yields a substitution θ as the final result. Since SLD-resolution is sound, this means that the conjunction $\theta\,(G_1 \wedge \cdots G_k)$ follows logically from the given Horn clauses—provided our implementation is correct.

How can we *prove* that the result $\theta\,(G_1 \wedge \cdots G_k)$ follows from the program's axioms using simple natural deduction reasoning only? The answer becomes straightforward once we study the structure of SLD-trees. We will traverse the success branch backwards, visiting every edge along the way from the leaf to the root. Writing [**US**], [**MP**], and [$\wedge$-**I**] as respective abbreviations for universal specialization, conditional elimination (modus ponens), and conjunction introduction, here is what we do for each such edge connecting a parent M to a child N:

1. Invariant: every atom in the list $\theta(N)$ has already been proven.
2. Let $\mathcal{R} = (\forall\, v_1) \cdots (\forall\, v_m)\, P$, $m \geq 0$, be the resolving rule attached to the current edge. Perform m successive applications of [**US**] on $\mathcal{R}$, instantiating v_1 with $\theta(v_1), \ldots, v_m$ with $\theta(v_m)$. The resulting theorem will be either of the form $true \Rightarrow B$ or of the form

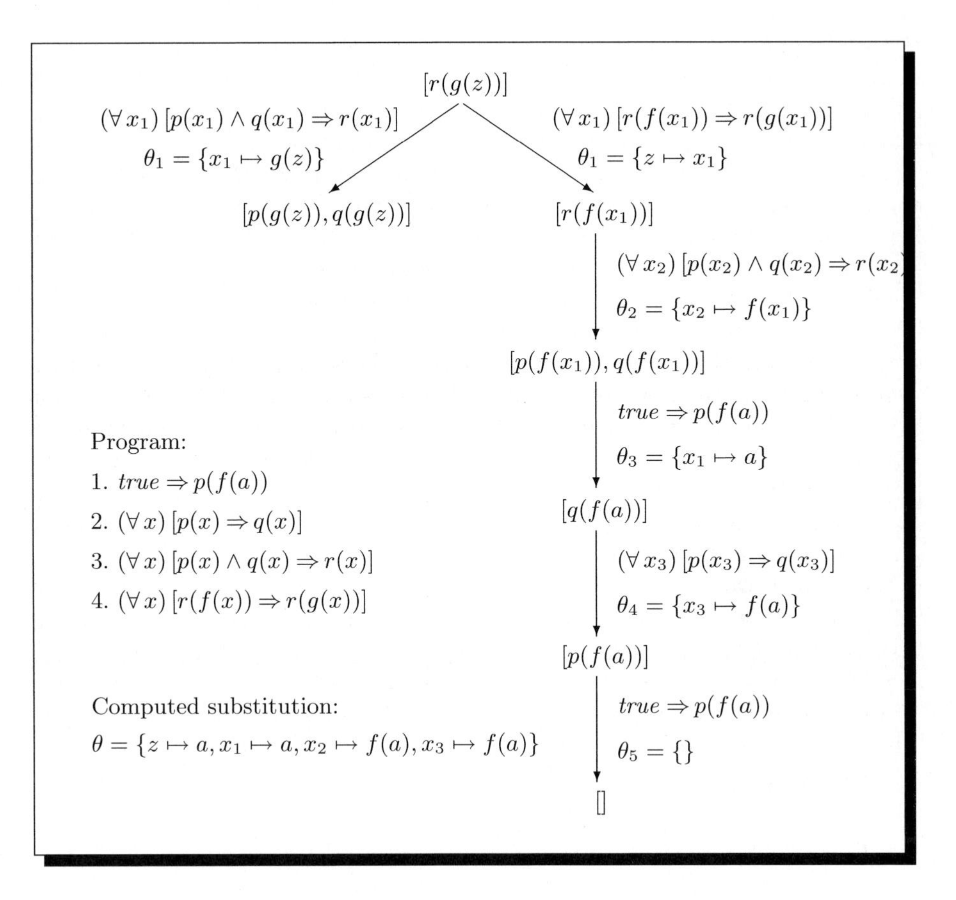

Fig. 1. The SLD-tree of the query $r(g(z))$, for the program shown on the left

$$A_1 \wedge \cdots \wedge A_l \Rightarrow B. \tag{3}$$

In the first case, apply [**MP**] on *true* $\Rightarrow B$ and *true* to obtain B. In the second case we claim that, inductively, the atoms $A_1, \ldots, A_l$ have already been proven previously. This follows from the foregoing invariant because, by the way SLD-trees are constructed, the atoms $A_1, \ldots, A_l$ are members of $\theta(N)$. Accordingly, use [$\wedge$-**I**] to obtain the conjunction $A_1 \wedge \cdots \wedge A_l$, and then use [**MP**] on (3) and the said conjunction to obtain B.

3. Invariant: every atom in the list $\theta(M)$ has now been proven.
4. Continue with the next edge, if there is one.

The second invariant follows from the first, because, with the exception of B, every goal H_i in $\theta(M)$ is also in $\theta(N)$, so the first invariant guarantees that H_i has already been proven. Hence, once we also establish B via modus ponens, we will have proven every member of $\theta(M)$. Graphically:

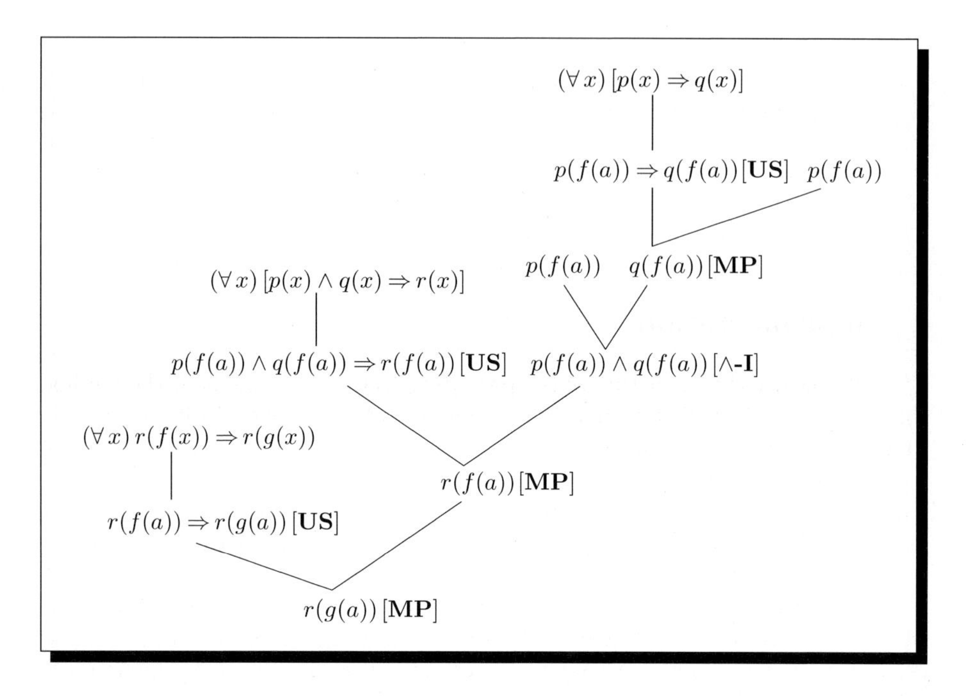

Fig. 2. A conventional proof tree deriving the atom $r(g(a))$

$$\theta(M) = [\underline{B}, H_1, \ldots, H_p]$$

$$\downarrow \qquad \text{Specialized resolving rule: } A_1 \wedge \cdots \wedge A_l \Rightarrow B$$

$$\theta(N) = [\overline{A_1, \ldots, A_l}, H_1, \ldots, H_p]$$

To start things off, the top invariant is vacuously true at the beginning of the algorithm. Upon conclusion, the bottom invariant guarantees that every atom in $\theta(L) = [\theta G_1, \ldots, \theta G_k]$ has been deduced, so at that point we can simply use conjunction introduction to infer the desired $\theta G_1 \wedge \cdots \wedge \theta G_k = \theta(G_1 \wedge \cdots \wedge G_k)$.

As an example, suppose that our first-order language comprises two unary function symbols f and g, one constant symbol a, and three unary relation symbols p, q, and r. Further, suppose that our set of variables is $\mathcal{V} = \{x, y, z, x_1, x_2, x_3, x_4, \ldots\}$, ordered as listed. Now consider the following logic program:

1. $\mathit{true} \Rightarrow p(f(a))$
2. $(\forall x)\,[p(x) \Rightarrow q(x)]$
3. $(\forall x)\,[p(x) \wedge q(x) \Rightarrow r(x)]$
4. $(\forall x)\,[r(f(x)) \Rightarrow r(g(x))]$

Assuming Prolog's computation rule, the SLD-tree of the query $r(g(z))$ is shown in Figure 1. The leftmost branch is a failure branch, while the second branch is a success branch, resulting in the theorem $r(g(a))$, obtained by applying the computed substitution to the original goal $r(g(z))$. Using the foregoing algorithm, we can prove this result as shown in Figure 2. The deduction of Figure 2 is depicted in classic proof-tree style, where a leaf represents a premise and an interior node represents an intermediate lemma, obtained through the application of some n-ary inference rule to the n children of the node. The proposition at the root represents the conclusion of the entire deduction. Note that the leaves of the tree in Figure 2 consist only of program axioms, while the only inference rules used at interior nodes are [**US**], [**MP**], and [$\wedge$-**I**].[3]

4 Implementation

We will now use the algorithm of the preceding section to implement the method `solve` that was specified earlier. The implementation appears in its entirety in Figure 3. (The reader who is unfamiliar with the details of the language can consult Arvizo (2002) for a brief presentation of its syntax and semantics.) The main method in Figure 3 is `solve`, as specified earlier, aided by two auxiliary methods `try-matches` and `resolve`, and two functions, `match-conclusion-of` and `get-matches`.

The function `match-conclusion-of` tries to match an atomic goal G with the conclusion of some rule ("`axiom`") P. First a freshly renamed version P' of P is obtained, and then the conclusion of P' is unified with the goal G. If the unification successfully produces some mgu θ, then the pair $[P', \theta]$ is returned. Thus the result of `match-conclusion-of` comprises the two pieces of data that appear on an SLD-tree edge: a resolving rule and a resolving substitution. We will refer to the pair $[P', \theta]$ as a *match*. If the unification fails, then `match-conclusion-of` returns `false`. The function `get-matches` returns a list of all the matches between an atomic goal and a list of rules, as determined by `match-conclusion-of`. This list could be empty if the goal does not match the conclusion of any of the rules, which would cause the prover to fail. If the rule list constitutes a logic program, then the left-to-right processing ensures that we examine the rules in the given order.

The method `try-matches` takes a list of matches of the form $[[P_1, \theta_1], \ldots, [P_n, \theta_n]]$ and a binary method `process-match`, which we will refer to as a *match handler*, and sequentially applies `process-match` to P_i and θ_i, for $i = 1, \ldots, n$, until such an application succeeds or until there are no more matches, in which case a failure occurs.

The core of `solve` is the internal method `prove`, which performs the analysis (search) of the SLD-tree. This can be thought of as the method that we invoke at a given node M of the SLD-tree in order to expand the search one level deeper. It takes three arguments:

1. the goal list of M;
2. the current substitution θ (this is the composition of all the substitutions above M, i.e., all the substitutions that can be found on the path leading from the root of the SLD-tree to M); and

[3] To save space, the axiom $true \Rightarrow p(f(a))$ was written simply as $p(f(a))$.

```
(define (match-conclusion-of axiom goal)
  (let ((renamed-axiom (rename axiom)))
    (match renamed-axiom
      ((forall (some-list vars) (if _ concl))
         (match (unify goal concl)
           ((some-sub theta) [renamed-axiom theta])
           (_ false)))
      (_ false))))

(define (get-matches goal axioms)
  (letrec ((search (function (axioms results)
                     (match axioms
                       ([] (rev results))
                       ((list-of axiom more)
                          (let ((res (match-conclusion-of axiom goal)))
                            (match res
                              (false (search more results))
                              (_ (search more (add res results))))))))))
    (search axioms [])))

(define (try-matches matches process-match)
  (dmatch matches
    ((list-of [axiom unifying-sub] rest-matches)
      (try (!process-match axiom unifying-sub)
           (!try-matches rest-matches process-match)))))

(define (resolve P usub goals prove theta M)
  (dmatch P
    ((forall (some-list vars) (if (and (some-list ants)) _))
      (dlet ((new-goals (usub (join ants goals))))
        (!prove new-goals (compose-subs usub theta)
           (method (sub) (dbegin (!mp (!uspec-list P (sub vars)) (!conj-intro (sub ants)))
                                 (!M sub))))))))

(define (solve axioms queries)
  (dletrec ((prove (method (goals theta M)
                     (dmatch goals
                       ([] (!M theta))
                       ((list-of goal more-goals)
                          (!try-matches (get-matches goal axioms)
                                        (method (P usub)
                                          (!resolve P usub more-goals prove theta M))))))))
      (!prove queries {} (method (theta) (!conj-intro (theta queries))))))
```

Fig. 3. Athena implementation of a trusted Prolog interpreter

3. a proof continuation, represented as a unary method `M`, that will be used for the synthetic task of putting the proof together. This continuation is increasingly stacked as we move down the tree, and is finally unwound once we reach a successful leaf node (i.e., an empty goal list), at which point it is invoked with the final substitution as its argument.

If the first argument given to `prove` is the empty goal list, then we have reached the end of a success branch and we simply invoke the proof continuation with the current substitution, which, at this point, is the final computed substitution—the composition of all the substitutions along the path from the root to the present leaf. Otherwise we select the first goal `goal` from the list (in accordance with Prolog's computation rule), and we call `try-matches` on (a) all the matches between `goal` and the various program rules, and (b) a match handler, expressed as an anonymous method, that takes a resolving rule `P` and a resolving substitution `usub` and calls `resolve` on `P`, `usub`, and the rest of the goals `more-goals`, as well as the method `prove` itself, the current substitution `theta`, and the current continuation `M`. The method `resolve` will then recursively call `prove` with:

1. a new goal list, obtained by prepending the antecedents of the resolving rule `P` to `more-goals` and applying the resolving substitution `usub` to the resulting list;
2. a new current substitution, obtained by composing the resolving substitution `usub` with `theta`, and
3. a new anonymous proof continuation, obtained by stacking the necessary applications of `mp`, `uspec-list`, etc. (as described in Section 3) to `M`. Observe the form of the new continuation:

```
(method (sub) (dbegin (!mp (!uspec-list P (sub vars))
                           (!conj-intro (sub ants)))
                      (!M sub)))
```

   The key point here is that the new continuation invokes `M` in the tail position of the `dbegin`, which ensures that the assumption base is threaded linearly—so that the conclusion of the modus ponens will be available throughout the evaluation of `(!M sub)`.

5 Extensions and Improvements

5.1 Obtaining the Final Substitution

Clients of `solve` might wish to be given access to the final substitution θ that is computed internally during a successful call to `solve`. Although a client could easily obtain the values of θ for the query variables by matching the theorem produced by `solve` against the conjunction of the queries, it would be easier and more efficient if `solve` itself somehow passed θ out, so that anyone who was interested in it could immediately get it. But methods can only produce propositions, so `solve` cannot directly return a substitution along with its theorem. We can easily get around this through a judicious use of side effects. We can supply `solve` with a third argument, a cell, which can then be assigned to contain the final substitution:

```
(define (solve axioms queries sub-cell)
  (dletrec ((prove (method (goals theta M)
                     (dmatch goals
                       ([] (!M theta))
                       ((list-of goal more-goals)
                          (!try-matches (get-matches goal axioms)
                                        (method (P usub)
                                          (!resolve P usub more-goals
                                                    prove theta M))))))))
      (!prove queries {} (method (theta)
                           (dbegin (set! sub-cell theta)
                                   (!conj-intro (theta queries)))))))
```

The rest of the code is unaffected by this change.

5.2 Multiple Solutions

Prolog engines are capable of discovering not just one success branch but all of them, by performing a potentially exhaustive depth-first search of the SLD-tree. In practice this is usually implemented as follows: first, the substitution determined by the leftmost success branch is displayed, and then every time the user presses the "enter" key the substitution determined by the next success branch is computed and displayed, until the entire tree has been scanned. This is a powerful feature of logic programming, and it is natural to ask whether we can simulate it in our framework.

It turns out we can implement this quite succinctly owing to the powerful combination of higher-order methods, lexical scoping, and state. We will supply `solve` with an extra argument, a cell that will be assigned to contain a method of zero arguments (a "proof thunk"). After `solve` returns, every time we invoke the contents of that cell we will obtain the theorem determined by the next success branch, until there are no more solutions. As a very simple sample use of this new version of `solve`, consider a program consisting of the three facts `(p a)`, `(p b)`, and `(p c)`, listed in that order. The query `(p ?X)` should give rise to three theorems, obtained by consecutively instantiating `?X` with `a`, `b`, and `c`. Supposing that `tc` is a cell, the initial call `(!solve axioms [(p ?X)] tc)` will derive the theorem `(p a)`, and also, as a side effect, put an appropriate thunk in `tc`. Then invoking that thunk with the method call `(!(ref tc))` will produce the theorem `(p b)`. (Because a phrase such as `(!(ref tc))` is, syntactically speaking, a deduction, the soundness theorem of Athena guarantees that its result will be a logical consequence of the assumption base.) One more invocation `(!(ref tc))` will derive `(p c)`, and any additional invocations after that point will fail.

The thunk cell supplied to `solve` will be passed on to `try-matches`, which will be responsible for modifying it appropriately:

```
(define (solve axioms queries thunk-cell)
  (dletrec ((prove (method (goals theta M)
                     (dmatch goals
                       ([] (!M theta))
                       ((list-of goal more-goals)
                          (!try-matches (get-matches goal axioms)
                                        (method (P msub)
                                          (!resolve P msub more-goals
                                                    prove theta M))
                                        thunk-cell))))))
    (!prove queries {} (method (theta) (!conj-intro (theta queries))))))
```

All `try-matches` now has to do is form a thunk containing its own recursive call on the remaining matches and put that thunk into the given cell. The second arm of the `try` now becomes a simple invocation of the thunk:

```
(define (try-matches matches process-match thunk-cell)
  (dmatch matches
    ((list-of [axiom unifying-sub] rest)
      (dlet ((thunk (method ()
```

```
                (!try-matches rest process-match thunk-cell)))
          (_ (set! thunk-cell thunk)))
      (try (!process-match axiom unifying-sub)
          (!thunk))))))
```

Observe that the same `thunk-cell` is passed as an argument to the recursive call to `try-matches` in the body of the thunk. This is crucial in order for the cell to be appropriately updated every time its contents are called. The rest of the code is unaffected.

6 Conclusions

We have shown how to define Prolog's implementation of SLD-resolution in terms of a very small number of very simple inference rules. More precisely, we have extended the usual execution model of SLD-resolution to make it justify its operation by producing formal proofs of correctness using only one introduction and two elimination rules for natural deduction. Such proofs can be verified by exceptionally simple proof checkers.

In particular, we presented a complete implementation of SLD-resolution as a trusted Athena method. We are not aware of any other published implementations of SLD-resolution engines as trusted theorem-proving tactics[4]. We discussed our implementation in detail, and demonstrated that Athena's proof-search mechanisms allow for concise and fluid definitions of complex inference strategies.

The present work can be regarded as an application of certified computation [2], a general methodology for producing reliable software. This technique is different from conventional program verification. Program verification is static and total: we prove once and for all that an algorithm will always give correct results, no matter what input we supply to it. In the case of SLD-resolution, for instance, this has been done in the Calculus of Constructions (Coq) [7]. Certified computation, by contrast, is dynamic and partial: The correctness proof is performed at runtime, and pertains only to a particular result obtained for a particular input; no claims are made about other inputs and outputs. Thus certified computation provides a weaker guarantee than program verification. However, it is still a very useful guarantee—if and when we get a result, we can be assured that it is a correct result. That is particularly important in theorem-proving applications.

Moreover, total verification usually demands a much greater effort than certified computation. For instance, more than 600 lemmas had to be formulated and proved for the aforementioned correctness proof of SLD-resolution in Coq. By contrast, our certifying implementation fits in one page of code. Another important difference is that static proofs such as the one in Coq usually verify an abstract model of a software system, not actual code; whereas in certified computation the produced theorem refers to the actual result obtained in real time.

[4] Isabelle has a built-in notion of resolution which is used to perform Prolog-style derivations in Section 14 of "Introduction to Isabelle" [10]. However, no actual implementation of SLD-resolution in terms of simpler rules is given.

References

1. Arkoudas, K.: Athena, http://www.pac.csail.mit.edu/athena
2. Arkoudas, K., Rinard, M.: Deductive runtime certification. Electronic Notes on Theoretical Computer Science (ENTCS) 113(3), 45–63 (2005); 2004 Workshop on Runtime Verification, Barcelona, Spain
3. Arkoudas, K., Zee, K., Kuncak, V., Rinard, M.: Verifying a file system implementation. In: Davies, J., Schulte, W., Barnett, M. (eds.) ICFEM 2004. LNCS, vol. 3308, pp. 373–390. Springer, Heidelberg (2004)
4. Arvizo, T.: A virtual machine for a type-ω denotational proof language. MS thesis, MIT (2002), ftp://publications.ai.mit.edu/ai-publications/2002/AITR-2002-204.pdf
5. Gordon, M.J., Miller, A.J., Wadsworth, C.P.: Edinburgh LCF. LNCS, vol. 78. Springer, Heidelberg (1979)
6. Gordon, M.J.C., Melham, T.F.: Introduction to HOL, a theorem proving environment for higher-order logic. Cambridge University Press, Cambridge (1993)
7. Jaume, M.: A full formalization of SLD-resolution in the calculus of inductive constructions. Journal of Automated Reasoning 23(3-4), 347–371 (1999)
8. Knight, K.: Unification: A multidisciplinary survey. ACM Computing Surveys 21(1), 93–124 (1989)
9. Lloyd, J.W.: Foundations of Logic Programming. Springer, Berlin (1984)
10. Paulson, L.C.: Introduction to Isabelle. Technical Report 280, CUCL (1993)
11. Pelletier, F.J.: A Brief History of Natural Deduction. History and Philosophy of Logic 20, 1–31 (1999)
12. Salcianu, A., Arkoudas, K.: Machine-checkable correctness proofs for intraprocedural dataflow analyses. Electronic Notes on Theoretical Computer Science (ENTCS) 141(2), 53–68 (2005); Fourth International Workshop on Compiler Optimization Meets Compiler Verification (COCV), Edinburgh, Scotland
13. Sterling, L., Shapiro, E.: The Art of Prolog, 2nd edn. MIT Press, Cambridge (1994)
14. Wechler, W.: Universal Algebra for Computer Scientists. Springer, Heidelberg (1992)
15. Wenzel, M.: Isar — a generic interpretative approach to readable formal proof documents. In: Proceedings of the 1999 conference on theorem proving in higher-order logic, pp. 167–183 (1999)

High Level Analysis, Design and Validation of Distributed Mobile Systems with CoreASM

R. Farahbod, U. Glässer, P.J. Jackson, and M. Vajihollahi

Software Technology Lab
School of Computing Science
Simon Fraser University
B.C., Canada
{roozbehf,glaesser,pjj,monav}@cs.sfu.ca

Abstract. System design is a creative activity calling for abstract models that facilitate reasoning about the key system attributes (desired requirements and resulting properties) so as to ensure these attributes are properly established prior to actually building a system. We explore here the practical side of using the *abstract state machine* (ASM) formalism in combination with the CoreASM open source tool environment for high-level design and experimental validation of complex distributed systems. Emphasizing the early phases of the design process, a guiding principle is to support freedom of experimentation by minimizing the need for encoding. CoreASM has been developed and tested building on a broad scope of applications, spanning computational criminology, maritime surveillance and situation analysis. We critically reexamine here the CoreASM project in light of three different application scenarios.

1 Introduction

In this paper, we explore the practical side of using the *abstract state machine* (ASM) formalism [1] combined with the CoreASM modeling suite [2] for high-level design and experimental validation of distributed mobile systems. Design is a creative activity calling for abstract models that facilitate the use of analytical means for reasoning about the key system attributes so as to ensure that these attributes are well understood and properly established prior to actually building a system. More specifically, computational modeling of behavioral aspects in the early phases of the development lifecycle is meaningful not only for analyzing complex functional requirements and resulting dynamic properties but also for exploring design alternatives and for validating design decisions. The systems we consider here are characterized by their decentralized control structures, their intricate interaction patterns and their concurrent and reactive behavior that is best described in terms of discrete mathematics and computational logic. Mathematical precision in the early design phases is essential to uncover and eliminate design flaws and weaknesses that often go unnoticed otherwise.

The ASM formalism and underlying abstraction principles are known for their versatility in semantic modeling of algorithms, architectures, languages,

T. Margaria and B. Steffen (Eds.): ISoLA 2008, CCIS 17, pp. 797–814, 2008.

protocols and apply to virtually all kinds of sequential, parallel and distributed systems. Widely recognized applications include semantic foundations of popular programming languages, like JAVA [3], C# [4] and Prolog [5], industrial system design languages, like SDL [6], VHDL [7] and SystemC [8], embedded control systems [9], Web services [10], network architectures [11], wireless networks [12], among others (see also the ASM Research Center at `www.asmcenter.org`). A driving factor in many of these applications is the desire to systematically reveal abstract architectural and behavioral concepts inevitably present in every system design, however hidden they may be, so that the underlying *blueprint* of the functional system requirements becomes clearly visible and can be checked and examined by analytical means based on human expertise.

Emphasizing the early phases of the development lifecycle, a guiding principle is to support freedom of experimentation by minimizing the need for encoding. CoreASM is an Open Source project for the development of a succinct, *extensible and executable ASM language* with supporting tool environment (implemented in Java and readily available at www.coreasm.org) that supports the evolutionary nature of design as a product of creativity. To minimize encoding in mapping the problem space to a formal model, it allows writing highly abstract and concise specifications—starting with mathematically-oriented, abstract and untyped models, gradually refining them down to more concrete versions with a degree of detail and precision as needed. It supports interactive development of sequential, synchronous parallel and distributed (asynchronous) ASM computation models, making them executable on real machines. The CoreASM *engine*, the heart of the CoreASM tool suite, is based on an extensible architecture supporting various kinds of extensions (as will be explained in Section 3.2) through *plug-ins* [13].

CoreASM has been developed and tested for several years, building on a broad scope of applications in the private and public sector spanning computational criminology[1], maritime surveillance and situation analysis. We reexamine here the practicability of using CoreASM for requirements analysis, design specification and rapid prototyping (experimental validation) of high-level executable models in light of three systems engineering projects that have been carried out at SFU's Software Technology Lab in close collaboration with industrial partners, Defence R&D Canada, SFU's Institute for Canadian Urban Research Studies and the Royal Canadian Mounted Police. One may argue that many of the aspects addressed here likely carry over to an even broader scope of systems.

Section 2 outlines the core ASM concepts prior to the CoreASM language and tool architecture being introduced in Section 3. Next, three application case studies, each of which using CoreASM in a major role but in a diverse context, are presented in Section 4. Based on the resulting work, Section 5 summarizes lessons learned from the practical experience with CoreASM in terms of what works best and what is missing. Section 6 concludes the paper.

[1] Computational criminology is a rapidly growing field that explores the use of computer science methods in different stages of studying complex criminal phenomena.

2 Abstract State Machines

This section briefly outlines the basic concepts for modeling behavioral aspects of distributed systems as abstract machine *runs* performed by a distributed ASM. The underlying notions of concurrency, reactivity and time are described using common abstractions and structures from computational logic and discrete mathematics. For further details, we refer to [1,14,15].

A distributed ASM, or DASM, defines the concurrent and reactive behavior of a collection of autonomously operating computational agents that cooperatively perform distributed computations. Intuitively, every computation step of the DASM involves one or more agents, each performing a single computation step according to their local view of a globally shared machine state. The underlying semantic model regulates interactions between agents so that potential conflicts are resolved according to the definition of *partially ordered runs* [11].

A DASM M is defined over a given vocabulary V by its program P_M and a non-empty set I_M of initial states. V consists of some finite collection of symbols for denoting the mathematical objects and their relation in the formal representation of M, where we distinguish *domain symbols*, *function symbols* and *predicate symbols*. Symbols that have a fixed interpretation regardless of the state of M are called *static*; those that may have different interpretations in different states of M are called *dynamic*. A state S of M results from a valid interpretation of all the symbols in V and constitutes a variant of a first-order structure, one in which all relations are formally represented as Boolean-valued functions.

Concurrent control threads in an execution of P_M are modeled by a dynamic set AGENT of computational *agents*. This set may change dynamically over runs of M, as required to model a varying number of computational resources. Agents interact with one another, and typically also with the operational environment of M, by reading and writing shared locations of a global machine state.

P_M consists of a statically defined collection of agent programs $P_{M_1}, ..., P_{M_k}$, $k \geq 1$, each of which defines the behavior of a certain *type* of agent in terms of state transition rules. The canonical rule consists of a basic update instruction of the form

$$f(t_1, t_2, ..., t_n) := t_0,$$

where f is an n-ary dynamic function symbol and each t_i $(0 \leq i \leq n)$ a term. Intuitively, one can perceive a dynamic function as a finite function table where each row associates a sequence of argument values with a function value. An update instruction specifies a *pointwise* function update: an operation that replaces a function value for specified arguments by a new value to be associated with the same arguments. In general, rules are inductively defined by a number of well defined rule constructors, allowing the composition of complex rules for describing sophisticated behavioral patterns.

A computation of M, starting with a given initial state S_0 from I_M, results in a finite or infinite sequence of consecutive state transitions of the form

$$S_0 \xrightarrow{\Delta_{S_0}} S_1 \xrightarrow{\Delta_{S_1}} S_2 \xrightarrow{\Delta_{S_2}} \cdots,$$

such that S_{i+1} is obtained from S_i, for $i \geq 0$, by firing Δ_{S_i} on S_i, where Δ_{S_i} denotes a finite set of updates computed by evaluating P_M over S_i. Firing an update set means that all the updates in the set are fired simultaneously in one atomic step. The result of firing an update set is defined if and only if the set does not contain any conflicting (inconsistent) updates.

M interacts with its operational environment—the part of the external world visible to M—through actions/events observable at external interfaces, formally represented by externally controlled functions. Intuitively, such functions are manipulated by the external world rather than agents of M. Of particular interest are *monitored functions*. Such functions change their values dynamically over runs of M, although they cannot be updated internally by agents of M. A typical example is the abstract representation of global system time. In a given state S of M, the global time (as measured by some external clock) is given by a monitored nullary function *now* taking values in a linearly ordered domain $\mathsf{TIME} \subseteq \mathsf{REAL}$. Values of *now* increase monotonically over runs of M.

3 The CoreASM Project

CoreASM is an open source project[2] focussing on design and development of an extensible executable specification language based on abstract state machines together with a surrounding tool environment that supports *high-level design in application-domain terms*, and *rapid prototyping of executable abstract specifications*. The CoreASM environment consists of a *1)* platform-independent extensible engine for executing the language, *2)* various plugins that extend the language and the behavior of the engine, and *3)* a set of applications that utilize the engine, such as an IDE for interactive visualization and control of simulation runs (see Fig. 1). The engine comes with a sophisticated and well defined interface, called Control API, thereby enabling future development and integration of complementary tools, e.g., for model checking and automated test generation.

The design of CoreASM is novel and the underlying design principles are unprecedented among the existing executable ASM languages, including the most advanced ones: Asmeta [16], AsmL [17], the ASM Workbench [18], XASM [19], and AsmGofer [20]. In contrast to CoreASM, all the above languages build on predefined type concepts rather than the untyped language underlying the theoretical model of ASMs; none of these languages comes with a run-time system supporting the execution of distributed ASM models; only Xasm is designed for systematic language extensions and in that respect is similar to our approach; however, the Xasm language itself diverts from the original definition of ASMs and seems closer to a programming language. In addition, CoreASM is the only one that is entirely specified in ASM terms.

The rest of this section provides an overview of the CoreASM project. An in-depth introduction to the architecture of the CoreASM engine and its extensibility mechanisms is provided in [2,13].

[2] CoreASM is available at `http://www.coreasm.org`

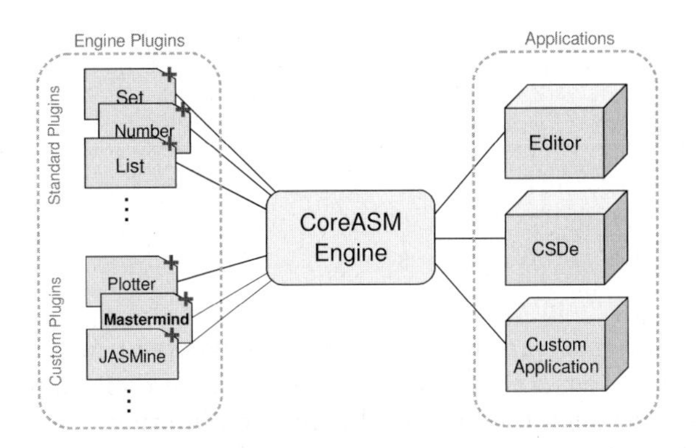

Fig. 1. CoreASM engine extended by plugins and custom applications

3.1 The CoreASM Engine

The CoreASM engine consists of four basic components: a *parser*, an *interpreter*, a *scheduler*, and an *abstract storage*. The interpreter, the scheduler, and the abstract storage work together to simulate an ASM run. The engine interacts with the environment through a single interface, called the *control API*, which provides various operations such as loading a CoreASM specification, starting an ASM run, or performing a single step.

The parser reads a CoreASM specification and provides the interpreter with an annotated parse tree for each program (in the case of multiple agent types). The interpreter then evaluates the programs by examining the rules, generating update sets. The abstract storage maintains the data model of the abstract state. In addition to the current state of the simulated machine, it also keeps a history of its previous states. To evaluate a program, the interpreter interacts with the abstract storage in order to obtain values from the current state and generates updates for the next state. The role of the scheduler is to orchestrate the whole execution process. For distributed ASMs, it selects the set of agents that will contribute to the next computation step and coordinates the execution of those agents. The scheduler also handles cases of inconsistency of update sets.

3.2 Engine Plugins

The design of CoreASM is streamlined towards flexible extensibility of the language definition and its underlying execution engine. In principle, there are three basic dimensions being considered for extending and altering CoreASM through the use of plugins, respectively related to: (i) data structures, (ii) control structures, and (iii) the execution model[3]. The possibility of conveniently extending data structures as needed is the most prominent one, extensively discussed in the theoretical ASM literature, e.g. in [21]. Control structures can be extended with

[3] The execution model refers to the dynamic features of the CoreASM engine, including the simulation process, scheduling policies, and exception handling.

respect to new syntactic constructs that either provide new semantics or only add syntactic sugar (i.e., the semantics of which can be expressed by means of in-language transformations). Finally, the need for altering or extending the execution model is justified by pragmatic considerations such as debugging purposes, analyzing program execution, or introducing additional scheduling policies.

Most of the functionality of the engine is implemented through plugins to a minimal kernel. This kernel contains only the bare essentials, that is, all that is needed to execute only the most basic ASM:

- the concepts of *functions* and *universes* are native to the kernel, as they are needed to define the state of an ASM;
- universes are represented through their characteristic functions, hence *booleans* are also included in the kernel;
- the special value *undef* is contained in the kernel;
- an ASM program is defined by a finite number of rules, hence the domain of *rules* is included in the kernel as well.

It should be noted that the kernel includes the above mentioned domains, but not all of the 'expected' backgrounds. While, for example, the domain of booleans (that is, true and false) is in the kernel, boolean algebra ($\wedge$, $\vee$, $\neg$, etc.) is not, and is instead provided through a background plugin. In the same vein, while universes are represented in the kernel through set characteristic functions, the background of finite sets is implemented in a plugin, which provides expression syntax for defining them, as well as an implicit representation for storing sets in the abstract state, and implementations of the various set theoretic operations (e.g., $\in$) that work on such an implicit representation.

The kernel includes only the most basic control structures (transition rules), such as assignment. This particular choice is motivated by the fact that without updates established by assignments there would be no way of specifying how the state should evolve. All other rule forms (e.g., **if**, **choose**, **forall**), as well as sub-machine calls and macros, are implemented as plugins which, when needed, can be loaded separately or together in form of a standard library.

Finally, there is a single scheduling policy implemented in the kernel—the pseudo-random selection of an arbitrary subset of agents—which is sufficient for multi-agent ASMs where no assumptions are made on the scheduling policy.

3.3 CoreASM in Eclipse

The CoreASM engine in its current implementation is a Java component and requires a user interface to interact with the engine, e.g., to pass specification files to the engine and to control its simulation run by manipulating parameters. There are two user interfaces available for the engine: a powerful yet simple command-line tool called Carma, and a graphical interactive development environment in the Eclipse platform[4], known as the CoreASM Eclipse Plugin. The CoreASM plugin for Eclipse extends the Eclipse platform to support dynamic syntax highlighting and interactive execution of CoreASM specifications.

[4] http://www.eclipse.org

3.4 Control State Diagrams

One practical class of abstract state machines are Control State ASMs. These ASMs can be represented as a directed graph, where nodes consist of control states interspersed optionally with conditions and/or rules. Conditions direct the flow of execution; rules denote actions taken as part of state transitions. The expressive flexibility of this type of ASM is demonstrated by their capacity for representing many classical automata such as various extensions of finite state machines [1]. Since, by definition, they can be depicted graphically, they are a sound foundation for the visual modeling of this particular class of ASMs.

The Control State Diagram editor (CSDe) is a software tool for creating and modifying Control State ASMs. It is distributed as a plugin for the Eclipse software development suite. The plugin allows the user to work with Control State Diagrams (CSDs) using a point-and-click schema. Both the simplicity of CSDs and the intuitiveness of the graphical interface work together to allow users to confidently contribute to the design, regardless of their technical background. For the purpose of increase expressiveness, we permit multiple conditions and rules between control states as well as the turbo ASM mechanism [1] of sequential behavior within a rule block, in addition to the usual parallelism.

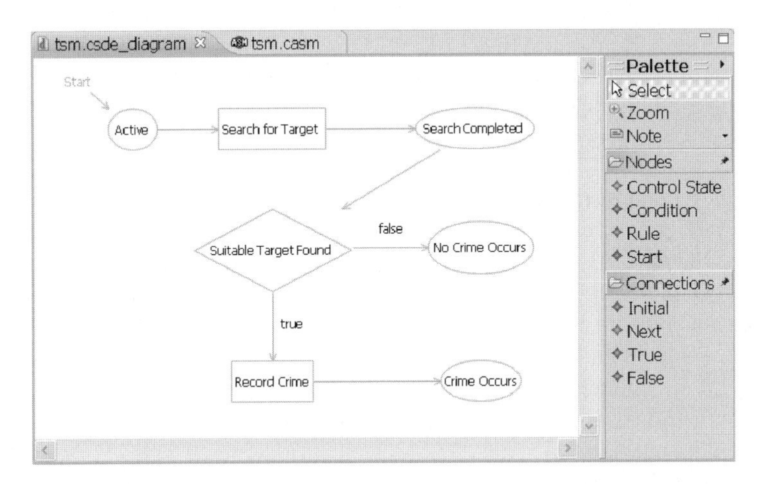

Fig. 2. CSDe: A Control State Diagram editor plugin for the Eclipse development environment, with automatic translation to CoreASM code

The plugin is also capable of automatically transforming diagrams into CoreASM code. Since a CSD may not include the initial system state or other information required to run as program, it is possible that the CoreASM file generated is not directly executable. However, the resulting code acts as a foundation for further development of the structure under consideration. This automated translation from a diagram into code improves the ease of transition from high-level design towards subsequent stages of development.

The versatility of CSDe offers an efficient way to perform the early phases of design and validation in a manner that is non-technical yet still fundamentally formal. In most projects, domain experts and technical specialists must work together to come up with a valid design. However, the specialized knowledge that makes such a collaboration so useful also acts as an obstacle to communication, since they may not share a common vocabulary. CSDe circumvents these issues by providing a clear and precise method for working with ideas at a high-level. By describing concepts in a straightforward, visual manner, all project members should be able to participate fully, regardless of their background.

3.5 Model Checking CoreASM Specifications

The CoreASM engine facilitates experimental validation of ASM models first and foremost by allowing to explore behavioral aspects with computational means in an interactive fashion. However, experimental validation without model checking cannot formally verify the correctness of a system with respect to all of its possible behaviors. In order to provide model checking support for CoreASM, we developed a tool called CoreASM2Promela that utilizes the CoreASM engine to translate CoreASM models into equivalent Promela models which can be verified using the Spin model checker.[5] From a high level perspective, the steps in the translation and verification process are as follows: (i) a CoreASM specification is loaded and parsed by the CoreASM engine, producing an abstract syntax tree; (ii) the tree is translated into Promela; (iii) Spin is invoked to generate a verifier of the Promela model, producing C code; (iv) the C code is compiled, generating a custom verifier of the CoreASM specification; (v) the verifier is run, producing a counter example if the property being checked does not hold.

In order to properly translate CoreASM specifications into Promela models, we needed to extend the CoreASM language by two new plug-ins, namely the *Signature Plugin* and the *Property Plugin*, to support declaration of function signatures and specification of LTL properties as part of CoreASM specifications. A comprehensive specification of these plug-ins is provided in [23].

We have successfully used CoreASM2Promela to model check several non-trivial ASM specifications; the details of the case studies and a comprehensive discussion of the results are presented in [23]. However, there are certain limitations in model checking abstract ASM specifications using Spin. For example, as Spin can only check finite models, the translation scheme is limited to CoreASM specifications which have finite states. Thus, the translation supports only static universes and enumerated backgrounds.

3.6 A Simple CoreASM Example

This section borrows the Railroad Crossing example of [1] to illustrate the syntax of CoreASM and its application in modeling industrial systems. Due to the space limitations, a simplified version of the example and the model are presented.

[5] Spin is a widely used automata based model checker that has been used extensively in the design of asynchronous distributed systems [22].

A system controls a gate at a railroad crossing. There are multiple tracks on which trains can travel in both directions. There are sensors on the tracks that can detect if a train is *coming* or if it is currently *crossing*. The gate is controlled by two signals *open* and *close*. We want the gate to be closed if a train is crossing (safety), and to be open otherwise (liveness).

When a train is detected as *coming*, it takes at least d_{min} seconds for it to arrive at the crossing. The gate takes d_{close} seconds to be closed and d_{open} to get opened. Thus we have $WaitTime = d_{min} - d_{close}$ seconds to start closing the gate. Hence, we maintain a *deadline* for every track t to indicate the maximum allowable time we have before we safely close the gate with regard to t.

Based on this view, we define the following domains and functions in the signature section of our CoreASM specification of the controller:

```
enum Track = {track1, track2, tack3}
enum TrStatus = {empty, coming, crossing}
enum Direction = {open, close}
enum GateState = {opened, closed}
```

```
function deadline : Track -> TIME
function trStatus : Track -> TrStatus
function dir : -> Direction
function gate : -> GateState
```

The track control program (`TrackControl` below) is then a parallel execution of two main rules: 1) for all tracks, calculating the deadlines, sending a closed signal if needed, and clearing passed deadlines; 2) keeping the gate open if it is safe to do so. The detailed definitions of the rules `SetDeadline` and `SignalOpen` together with the predicate `safeToOpen` are provided on the right hand side:

```
rule TrackControl =
   forall x in Track do
      SetDeadline(x)
      SignalClose(x)
      ClearDeadline(x)
   SignalOpen
```

```
rule SetDeadline(a) =
   if trStatus(a)=coming and deadline(a)=infinity then
      deadline(a) := now + waitTime

rule SignalOpen =
   if dir=close and safeToOpen then dir := open

derived safeToOpen = forall tx in Track holds
      trStatus(tx)=empty or (now + dopen)<deadline(tx)
```

4 Case Studies

This section presents three case studies from three diverse application contexts to reexamine the practicability of using CoreASM for requirements analysis, design specification and rapid prototyping of abstract system models in the early design phases. The particular choice made here is meant to illustrate by example the wide scope of application domains for CoreASM above and beyond classical software system design problems, like the design of Web service architectures [10]. The three examples presented here result from projects that have been carried out at SFU's Software Technology Lab in close collaboration with industrial partners, Defence R&D Canada, SFU's Institute for Canadian Urban Research Studies and the Royal Canadian Mounted Police.

4.1 The Mastermind Project

Mastermind is a pioneering project in computational criminology, employing formal modeling and simulation as tools to investigate offender behavior in an urban environment. The project aims at developing computational models of criminal activity patterns, with a special focus on spatiotemporal characteristics of crime, potentially involving multiple offenders and multiple targets. The Mastermind project utilizes the ASM method and the CoreASM tool suite to address the specific requirements of developing computational models and analysis tools for the study of crime in a collaborative research environment.

Crime is understood to be comprised of four main elements: the law, the offender, the target and the location [24]. We construct a multi-dimensional model of crime in order to study the interaction of these elements. Our focus is on the concepts of environmental criminology, which argues that in spite of their complexity, criminal events can be understood in the context of people's movements in the course of everyday routines [24]. Through movement within a given environment, possible offenders, characterized as *agents*, develop mental maps of the places they know (*awareness space*) and the places they regularly visit (*activity space*). At its core, Mastermind captures the essence of the Crime Pattern theory, i.e. crime occurs when a motivated individual encounters a suitable target [24]. Figure 2 captures this behavior in terms of a Control State ASM.

The main building block of Mastermind is a robust *ASM ground model* [25] developed through several iterations required for checking the validity of the model with respect to the understanding of domain experts. The process of establishing the key properties, determining the right level of abstraction, and ensuring the validity of the model was greatly facilitated using the simple graphical notation provided by CSDe and the ability to run experiments on abstract models in early stages of design using the CoreASM engine.

The ground model has been further refined into more concrete models with specific details systematically added, an example of which is the simulation model of Mastermind implemented in Java. The Java version provides a responsive user interface and a simulation environment based on real-world Geographical Information System (GIS) data and captures the navigation behavior of offenders with a high degree of detail and complexity. We have also refined the CoreASM executable ground model to run more controlled experiments, which allows for a structured analysis of theories in a hypothetical world. These simple and comprehensible models provides domain experts with full control over the variables under study and their interdependence. Both versions also provide visualization features which are a priority for criminology publications. Figure 3 shows snapshots of both implementations of Mastermind. The visualizations show agents' movement between activity nodes, the formation of their activity spaces and the effects on crime hotspots. The CoreASM model is meant to study concepts at a higher level of abstraction, using a simple grid structure in the example. In contrast, the Java version runs on the real road network of downtown Vancouver, including Stanley Park, and captures a finer degree of detail and complexity.

It is important to emphasize the role of the CoreASM tool environment in facing the challenges of two major phases of our project, namely *formalization* and *validation*. In an interdisciplinary research project, the communication problem is

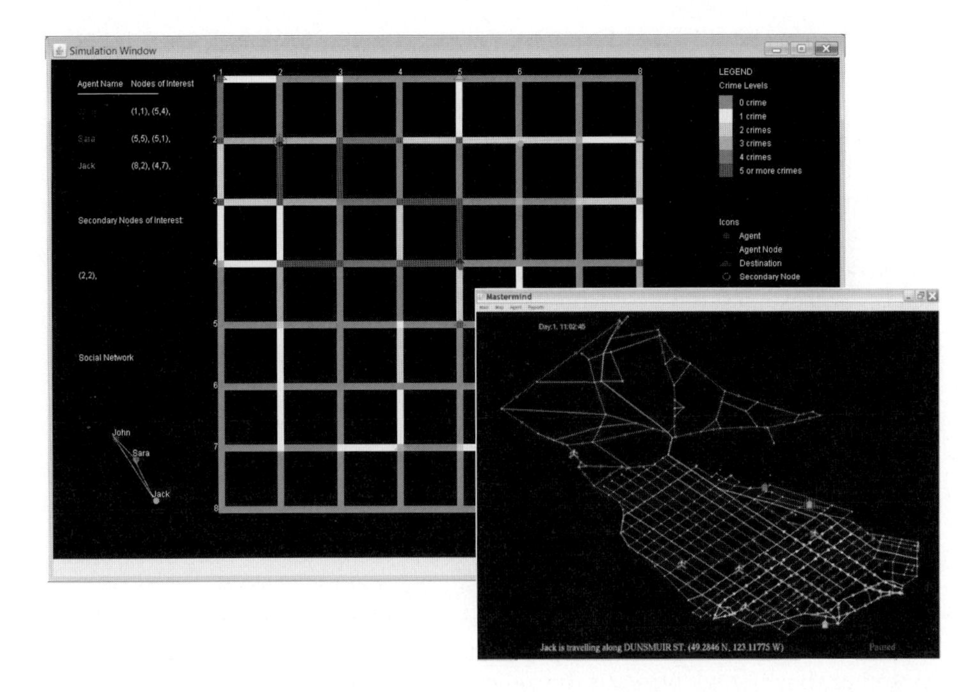

Fig. 3. The CoreASM & Java implementations of Mastermind. The Java version (in front) aims at using computational power to simulate the dynamic interaction of a variety of factors, including a street network based on real world data. The CoreASM version (behind) is more abstract, focusing exclusively on specific elements.

intensified, imposing serious challenges in ensuring a correct transformation from domain knowledge to computational artifacts. This difficulty is compounded due to differences between academic disciplines in terms of approach and underlying assumptions, not to mention the fact that real-life events, such as crime events, are not usually thought of in a discrete, mathematical manner. To this end, diagrams created by CSDe greatly facilitate an interactive design process where domain experts are able to directly check and correct a design.

Secondly, it is important to compare the utility of the full-fledged Mastermind simulation model in Java with the simpler, more abstract CoreASM model. The complexity of the Java version and the fact that it is considered as a black-box by domain experts introduces limitations on its academic usage. On the other hand, the CoreASM program code is easier for non-programmers to read, and is well-suited for designing *controlled* experiments. Taking advantage of the highly flexible plugin architecture offered by CoreASM, we were able to rapidly develop the Mastermind Plugin to address the specific needs of criminologists, especially with respect to visualizing the results. In other words, the Mastermind Plugin encapsulates the mathematical structure of the ASM model in a comprehensible and familiar format for domain experts. This greatly facilitates communication with domain experts and analysis of the results for validation purposes.

The results of our work on the Mastermind project have been well-received both by the researchers in academia and law enforcement officials. For more details on the project and the results, we refer to our publications [26,27], and also the project website at `www.stl.sfu.ca/projects/mastermind`

4.2 Dynamic Resource Configuration & Management Architecture

Dynamic Resource Configuration & Management Architecture (DRCMA) is a highly adaptive and auto-configurable multi-layer network architecture for distributed information fusion. The primary goal of DRCMA is to address large volume surveillance challenges, assuming a wide range of different sensor types operating on multiple mobile platforms for intelligence, surveillance and reconnaissance. The focus is on network enabled operations to efficiently manage and improve employment of heterogeneous sets of surveillance and patrolling resources, their information fusion engines and their networking capabilities under dynamically changing and essentially unpredictable conditions. We build on realistic application scenarios adopted from the design and development of the CanCoastWatch system [28,29].

The overall design objective of DRCMA is a highly robust and scalable network architecture that supports reconfigurable applications and self-organizing structures, flexibly adapting to dynamically changing resource requirements as well as changes in the availability of resources. Global mission goals are to be operationalized into local tasks performed by semi-autonomously operating resource units that can handle basic adjustments and realignments of resources automatically. The architectural design emphasizes a hierarchical command and control structure.

Missions injected into the system are complex tasks, each of which needs to be transformed into a collection of constituent elementary tasks, so as to map these tasks onto the available resources. Complex tasks therefore are decomposed in one or more steps into simpler ones until all of the resulting tasks are of elementary type, meaning that each of them can directly be assigned to a *physical resource* capable of performing the task. Physical resources refer to individual resource entities that exist in the physical environment. Depending on the level of abstraction, a physical resource may either identify a group of sensor platforms or a single sensor platform or even an individual sensor unit on a sensor platform.

Logical resources represent clusters of resources formed by aggregating two or more physical and/or logical resources, each with a certain range of capabilities, into a higher level resource with a greater capacity for performing complex operations. Resource clusters operate semi-autonomously to increase robustness and to reduce control and communication overhead by making local decisions regarding the realignment and reorganization of resources within the cluster. Dynamic reconfiguration of clusters is performed in an ad hoc manner using 'plug and play' mechanisms. Resources may join or be removed from a cluster on demand and depending on their capabilities, geographic location, cost aspects and other characteristics.

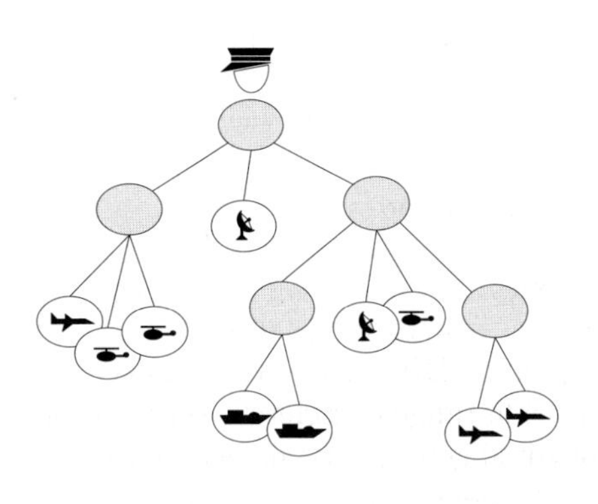

(a) Hierarchical structure of logical and physical nodes in DRCMA

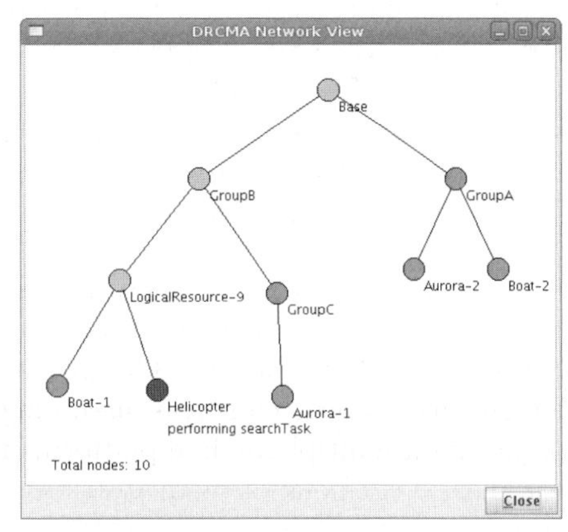

(b) Snapshot of a search & rescue scenario using the DRCMA model in CoreASM

Fig. 4. Dynamic Resource Configuration & Management Architecture

The DRCMA model is described in abstract functional and operational terms in form of an executable distributed abstract state machine specification, using the CoreASM modeling environment [2,30]. This description of the underlying design concepts provides a concise yet precise blueprint for reasoning about key system attributes at an intuitive level of understanding, supporting requirements specification, design analysis, validation and, where appropriate, formal verification of system properties prior to actually building the system. A basic graphical user interface (see Fig. 4) has also been developed in Java to provide a live view of the resource network and its command and control hierarchy during the simulation of scenarios, using the JASMine plugin[6] of CoreASM [31].

Building an abstract yet executable model of DRCMA in CoreASM enabled us to experiment with the model and validate design decisions at a fairly high level of abstraction. In subsequent steps, we will extend and further refine the DRCMA model into a comprehensive architecture for adaptive distributed information fusion. The result will be a prototype for testing, experimental validation and machine-assisted verification of the key system attributes prior to actually building the system. In conclusion, the proposed design approach facilitates a seamless transition across the three dimensions of modeling discrete dynamic systems: conceptual, mathematical and computational.

4.3 Decision Support for Situation Analysis

Situation Awareness is essential for conducting decision-making activities. It is the perception of elements in the environment, comprehension of their meaning, and projection of their status in the near future [32]. Agents develop an understanding of a situation based on a discrete perception and evaluation of events

[6] JASMine is a CoreASM plugin that provides the means to access Java objects and classes from inside an ASM specification.

as they unfold over time and forecast their anticipated evolution in the future. Situation Analysis (SA) is defined as a process, the examination of a situation, its elements, and their relations, to provide and maintain a state of situation awareness for the decision maker [33].

The rationale for establishing a formal semantic foundation for the design of situation analysis and decision support systems is discussed in detail in [34]. Inspired by recent work at Defence R&D Canada at Valcartier that proposes the use of Interpreted Systems for Situation Analysis [35,36], a systematic approach combining Abstract State Machines and Interpreted Systems seems appealing, as each of the two semantic modeling frameworks has its particular focus and strength, complementing each other in several respects. They both share common abstraction principles for describing distributed system behavior based on an abstract operational view of multiagent systems. Additionally, pragmatic considerations regarding practical needs for system design and development are relevant to support the systematic refinement of abstract specifications into executable models serving as a basis for rapid prototyping and experimental validation of decision support systems.

In a preliminary study [37], we illustrated the similarities between the two frameworks using a simple surveillance scenario originally presented in [36]. In order to put the abstract model into practice and to realize what is practically feasible, we used the CoreASM modeling suite to produce an executable model of the scenario through refinement of the abstract rules and functions of the model. Such a refinement, with the goal of producing an executable model, is interesting in two aspects: *a)* it helps in finding ambiguities, missing pieces and loose-ends of the model and forces the system analyst/modeler to think clearly about the main concepts and their definitions, and *b)* it supports experimental validation through execution (simulation).

Our work demonstrates how one can benefit from using ASMs, and in particular CoreASM, to model a multiagent system while still being able to apply and extend the Interpreted Systems approach of [36] for situation analysis. For example, by combining Interpreted Systems and multiagent ASMs, situation analysis queries can not only be analyzed using the proposed methods in [36], but they can also be examined either by explicitly encoding the queries as computable functions in the model and running the executable model, or by applying the available model checking techniques for ASM [23,38].

5 Lessons Learned

Arguably, there is something appealing about the ASM approach to modeling behavioral aspects of distributed and mobile systems in abstract mathematical terms making this formal framework a sensible choice for interactive design and validation of concurrent and reactive behavior. In light of practical needs, two natural questions come to mind: *what works best* and *what is missing*?

Comprehensive answers to these questions exceed the scope of this paper; rather we highlight here certain aspects that turned out to be most relevant in the ASM applications described in Section 4, where we also draw from our previous experience in other application contexts, specifically semantic foundations for industrial specification and design languages, such as BPEL [10], SDL [6] and VHDL [7], and distributed network architectures [12,11].

Starting from the general observation that *abstract machine* models neatly reflect a systems engineering view by building on common abstraction principles, we feel that there is much more to it than just the machine concept. A typical challenge in the early phases of architectural design is lack of a thorough understanding of the functional requirements, resulting in vague descriptions and fuzzy architectural concepts. Striving for more clarity and regularity while exploring the design space and comparing competing design alternatives, any encoding should not only be minimal but also be as direct and intuitive as possible, so as to not add extra weight to the overall problem scope. Serving practical needs, the relatively simple semantic foundation of the ASM framework contributes a great deal to the ease of using this approach as a precise analytical means for communicating ideas and for reasoning about design decisions and their consequences. Viewing states as first-order structures, or simply as abstract *mathematical data structures*, being manipulated by concurrently operating computational agents greatly simplifies things when complexity kicks in. Also, a virtually minimal *instruction set* for describing state transition behavior based on an untyped language, combined with flexible refinement techniques [25], naturally facilitates experimentation by supporting design for change. Finally, the ability to freely choose and mix common modeling styles, e.g. declarative, functional and operational, depending on what appears most suitable in a given application context, is invaluable. In short, the ASM formalism offers much of the freedom that comes with using pseudocode as a design language—just that pseudocode does usually not have a precise (unambiguous) meaning and thus is not executable.

CoreASM aims at preserving the very idea of ASM modeling, as outlined above, so that the salient features carry over to an *executable* ASM language for rapid prototyping of distributed system models. We argue that this goal has widely been accomplished, not only pertaining to desirable characteristics of abstract mathematical models, such as conciseness, simplicity and intelligibility, but also with regard to methodological guidelines and best practices for ASM modeling [25] that directly apply to CoreASM as well. Virtually, there is no difference between the core of an abstract state machine model and its executable version in CoreASM. However, to make a 'pure' abstract model machine-executable, one often has to add some minor details. CoreASM aims to shorten the gap by providing a comprehensive set of abstract data structures and by facilitating the development of application-specific plugins that provide abstract concepts, domain-specific data structures, and whatever standard means are expected to be available in a given application context.

Finally, not everything is perfect. Some open issues have not been sufficiently addressed by the CoreASM project primarily focusing on mathematical modeling, especially requirements and design specification, and experimental validation, rather than formal verification. A proper formal specification, such that the validity of the initial formalization step can be established, is a prerequisite for any meaningful approach to formal verification. On the other hand, machine-assisted verification is supported by the current implementation of CoreASM only in the form of rudimentary model checking [23]. More sophisticated interfaces to existing model checking tools are needed to fully exploit the potential that leading model checkers provide. Likewise, there is currently no support for automatic code generation from CoreASM models. The CoreASM engine is reasonably fast and efficient for interactive modeling & experimental validation; nonetheless, there is room for improving performance by generating Java or C++ code. Automatic text case generation for conformance testing, comparable to Spec Explorer [39] is a work in progress, but not yet available. No doubt, more work needs to be done to close these gaps in the future. Having more sophisticated data structures, as well as debugging tools and state space visualizers would greatly assist the modeling and design process, especially when dealing with complex control flows. Also, further improvements to the CoreASM IDE to provide enhanced coding assistance features, such as easy navigation between different layers of abstraction and refinements, would be of real value in building complex models. In order to add to the convenience and utility of the CoreASM tool set, we consider these improvements as subjects of our future work.

6 Concluding Remarks

CoreASM has been developed and tested at SFU's Software Technology Lab in collaboration with international partners, especially at the University of Pisa, over the past three years. Among all the existing ASM tool environments (see [2] for an overview and further discussion), it stands out as being closest to the spirit of abstract state machines in the aforementioned sense and the only one that directly supports distributed ASM computation models, making such models directly executable on real machines. Based on solid experience gained through the practical use of CoreASM in a number of diverse application domains, we feel that the current implementation works well, serving practical needs of high-level system modeling and rapid prototyping, including reverse engineering applications. So far, there have been several hundred downloads of the tool suite. We are always seeking critical feedback from external users and are grateful for the many comments we received.

References

1. Börger, E., Stärk, R.: Abstract State Machines: A Method for High-Level System Design and Analysis. Springer, Heidelberg (2003)
2. Farahbod, R., Gervasi, V., Glässer, U.: CoreASM: An Extensible ASM Execution Engine. Fundamenta Informaticae, 71–103 (2007)
3. Stärk, R., Schmid, J., Börger, E.: Java and the Java Virtual Machine: Definition, Verification, Validation. Springer, Heidelberg (2001)
4. Börger, E., Fruja, N.G., Gervasi, V., Stärk, R.F.: A High-level Modular Definition of the Semantics of C#. Theoretical Computer Science 336, 235–284 (2005)

5. Börger, E.: A Logical Operational Semantics for Full Prolog. Part I: Selection Core and Control. In: Börger, E., Kleine Büning, H., Richter, M.M. (eds.) CSL 1989. LNCS, vol. 440, pp. 36–64. Springer, Heidelberg (1990)
6. Glässer, U., Gotzhein, R., Prinz, A.: The Formal Semantics of SDL-2000: Status and Perspectives. Comput. Networks 42, 343–358 (2003)
7. Börger, E., Glässer, U., Müller, W.: Formal Definition of an Abstract VHDL 1993 Simulator by EA-Machines. In: Delgado Kloos, C., Breuer, P.T. (eds.) Formal Semantics for VHDL, pp. 107–139. Kluwer Academic Publishers, Dordrecht (1995)
8. Müller, W., Ruf, J., Rosenstiel, W.: An ASM Based SystemC Simulation Semantics. In: Müller, W., et al. (eds.) SystemC - Methodologies and Applications. Kluwer Academic Publishers, Dordrecht (2003)
9. Börger, E., Riccobene, E., Schmid, J.: Capturing Requirements by Abstract State Machines: The Light Control Case Study. Journal of Universal Computer Science 6, 597–620 (2000)
10. Farahbod, R., Glässer, U., Vajihollahi, M.: An Abstract Machine Architecture for Web Service Based Business Process Management. Intl. Journal of Business Process Integration and Management 1, 279–291 (2007)
11. Glässer, U., Gurevich, Y., Veanes, M.: Abstract Communication Model for Distributed Systems. IEEE Trans. on Soft. Eng. 30, 458–472 (2004)
12. Glässer, U., Gu, Q.P.: Formal Description and Analysis of a Distributed Location Service for Mobile Ad Hoc Networks. Theoretical Comp. Sci. 336, 285–309 (2005)
13. Farahbod, R., Gervasi, V., Glässer, U., Ma, G.: CoreASM plug-in architecture. In: Proceedings of the Dagstuhl Seminar on Rigorous Methods for Software Construction and Analysis (LNCS Festschrift). Springer, Heidelberg (to be published, 2008)
14. Gurevich, Y.: Evolving Algebras 1993: Lipari Guide. In: Börger, E. (ed.) Specification and Validation Methods, pp. 9–36. Oxford University Press, Oxford (1995)
15. Farahbod, R., Glässer, U.: Semantic Blueprints of Discrete Dynamic Systems: Challenges and Needs in Computational Modeling of Complex Behavior. In: New Trends in Parallel and Distributed Computing, Proc. 6th Intl. Heinz Nixdorf Symposium, January 2006, pp. 81–95. Heinz Nixdorf Institute (2006)
16. Gargantini, A., Riccobene, E., Scandurra, P.: A Metamodel-based Simulator for ASMs. In: Proc. of the 14th Intl. Abstract State Machines Workshop (2007)
17. Microsoft FSE Group: The Abstract State Machine Language (2003) (Last visited June 2003), `http://research.microsoft.com/fse/asml/`
18. Del Castillo, G.: Towards Comprehensive Tool Support for Abstract State Machines. In: Hutter, D., Traverso, P. (eds.) FM-Trends 1998. LNCS, vol. 1641, pp. 311–325. Springer, Heidelberg (1999)
19. Anlauff, M.: XASM – An Extensible, Component-Based Abstract State Machines Language. In: Gurevich, Y., Kutter, P.W., Odersky, M., Thiele, L. (eds.) ASM 2000. LNCS, vol. 1912, pp. 69–90. Springer, Heidelberg (2000)
20. Schmid, J.: Executing ASM Specitications with AsmGofer (Last visited September 2005) (2005), `http://www.tydo.de/AsmGofer/`
21. Blass, A., Gurevich, Y.: Background, Reserve, and Gandy Machines. In: Clote, P.G., Schwichtenberg, H. (eds.) CSL 2000. LNCS, vol. 1862, pp. 1–17. Springer, Heidelberg (2000)
22. Holzmann, G.J.: The Model Checker SPIN. IEEE Trans. Software Eng. 23, 279–295 (1997)
23. Ma, G.Z.: Model Checking Support for CoreASM: Model Checking Distributed Abstract State Machines Using Spin. Master's thesis, Simon Fraser University, Canada (2007)

24. Brantingham, P.J., Brantingham, P.L.: Patterns in Crime. Macmillan Publishing Company, New York (1984)
25. Börger, E.: Construction and Analysis of Ground Models and their Refinements as a Foundation for Validating Computer Based Systems. Formal Aspects of Computing 19, 225–241 (2007)
26. Brantingham, P.L., Kinney, B., Glässer, U., Jackson, P., Vajihollahi, M.: Mastermind: Computational Modeling and Simulation of Spatiotemporal Aspects of Crime in Urban Environments. In: Liu, L., Eck, J. (eds.) Artificial Crime Analysis Systems: Using Computer Simulations and Geographic Information Systems, Information Science Reference (2008)
27. Brantingham, P.L., Glässer, U., Kinney, B., Singh, K., Vajihollahi, M.: A Computational Model for Simulating Spatial Aspects of Crime in Urban Environments. In: Jamshidi, M. (ed.) Proc. of 2005 IEEE Intl. Conf. on Systems, Man and Cybernetics, pp. 3667–3674 (2005)
28. Wehn, H., et al.: A Distributed Information Fusion Testbed for Coastal Surveillance. In: Proc. of the 10th Intl. Conf. on Information Fusion (2007)
29. Farahbod, R., Glässer, U., Wehn, H.: CanCoastWatch Dynamic Configuration Manager. In: Proc. of the 14th Intl. Abstract State Machines Workshop (2007)
30. Farahbod, R., Glässer, U.: Dynamic Resource Management for Adaptive Distributed Information Fusion in Large Volume Surveillance—Phase One. Technical Report SFU-CMPT-TR-2008-08, Simon Fraser University (2008)
31. Farahbod, R., Gervasi, V.: JASMine: Accessing Java Code from CoreASM. In: Proceedings of the Dagstuhl Seminar on Rigorous Methods for Software Construction and Analysis (LNCS Festschrift) (to be published, 2008)
32. Endsley, M.R.: Theoretical Underpinnings of Situation Awareness: A Critical Review. In: Endsley, M.R., Garland, D.J. (eds.) Situation Awareness Analysis and Measurement, LEA (2000)
33. Bossé, É., Roy, J., Ward, S.: Models and Tools for Information Fusion (2007)
34. Bossé, É., Jousselme, A.L., Maupin, P.: Situation Analysis for Decision Support: A Formal Approach. In: Proc. of the 10th Intl. Conf. on Information Fusion (2007)
35. Maupin, P., Jousselme, A.L.: A General Algebraic Framework for Situation Analysis. In: Proc. of the 8th Intl. Conf. on Information Fusion, Philadelphia, PA (2005)
36. Maupin, P., Jousselme, A.L.: Interpreted Systems for Situation Analysis. In: Proc. of the 10th Intl. Conf. on Information Fusion, Quebec city, Canada (2007)
37. Farahbod, R., Glässer, U., Bossé, E., Guitouni, A.: Integrating Abstract State Machines and Interpreted Systems for Situation Analysis Decision Support Design. In: Proc. of the 11th Intl Conf. on Information Fusion (Fusion 2008) (2008)
38. Gargantini, A., Riccobene, E., Rinzivillo, S.: Using Spin to Generate Tests from ASM Specifications. In: Abstract State Machines 2003, pp. 263–277. Springer, Heidelberg (2003)
39. Veanes, M., Campbell, C., Grieskamp, W., Schulte, W., Tillmann, N., Nachmanson, L.: Model-Based Testing of Object-Oriented Reactive Systems with Spec Explorer. In: Hierons, R.M., Bowen, J.P., Harman, M. (eds.) FORTEST. LNCS, vol. 4949, pp. 39–76. Springer, Heidelberg (2008)

Optimizing the System Observability Level for Diagnosability*

Laura Brandán Briones, Alexander Lazovik, and Philippe Dague

LRI, Univ.Paris-Sud, CNRS, Parc Club Orsay Université,
4 rue Jacques Monod, bât G, Orsay, F-91893, France
{laura.brandan,alexander.lazovik,philippe.dague}@lri.fr

Abstract. A system model is *diagnosable* when every fault can be unambiguously detected from its observable events. Diagnosability is a desirable system property, enabling large and complex systems to be designed with automatic fault detection and isolation mechanisms.

In this paper we study the relation between a system's level of observability and its diagnosability. We provide both necessary and sufficient conditions on the observable events maintained by the system in order to be diagnosable. We concentrate on two problems: First, we show how to transform a diagnosable system into another one which is still diagnosable but also has a minimal level of observability. Second, we show how to transform a non-diagnosable system into a diagnosable by subsequently increasing the level of observability.

Finally, we expand our framework with several extensions, dealing with distinguishability, predictability and extended fault models.

1 Introduction

The design of automatic fault detection mechanisms for systems is an important task, and has been studied for several years. Due to the increasing reliability requirements imposed on autonomous systems, particularly mission-critical ones, many sophisticated methods have been proposed. These methods enable the accurate analysis of faults, and, in particular, their diagnosability.

A system model is *diagnosable* when every fault can be unambiguously detected from its observable events within a predefined (finite) amount of steps. Typically, the detection of faults is performed by systematically monitoring the system, e.g., by receiving information from sensors, or by inspecting the system logs.

However, when a system is being set up, a problem appears, as it is unclear how much observability is necessary in order to keep the system diagnosable. In practice, this problem is made evident by doubts of the form "how many sensors should be installed?" or "how many events should be monitored?".

In particular, when trying enhance an existing legacy system so that it becomes diagnosable, one may ask "How many new sensors or monitors should be installed in order to provide diagnosability?". Conversely, and more sublty, if the legacy system is already diagnosable one may wonder if "Are there too many sensors or monitors, making unnecessary and redundant the collected information?".

* This research has been funded by the EU through the FP6 IST project 516933 WS-Diamond and the tenure of an ERCIM "Alain Bensoussan" Fellowship Programme.

T. Margaria and B. Steffen (Eds.): ISoLA 2008, CCIS 17, pp. 815–830, 2008.

This paper gives the most efficient system observability (list of observable events) that keeps the system diagnosable. We build on top of the work of Lin [10], which shows that the most efficient system observability is not unique. Our contribution is twofold: First, we give an algorithm that keeps a system diagnosable but with a minimal set of observable events. Second, we present an algorithm that builds the optimal set of observable events to ensure diagnosability in a given system.

In practice, it is often the case (e.g., in already existing legacy systems) that one is not allowed to modify the running system in any way except the level and intensity of the observations (e.g., sensors or logs of the system). Accordingly, all algorithms in this paper are allowed to only transform the degree of observability of the system, but not change anything else in the considered system; its structure (i.e., its transitions, events and states) remain untouched.

In order to deal with faults in an uniform and generic way, we adapt a notion of *signature* from Continuous Systems (CS) that accounts, intuitively, with all the situations when faults occur.

In Continuous Systems, the diagnosis of systems is often performed on a snapshot of observables, i.e., an evaluation of observable variables at a given moment of time. In the case that the observation implies a fault occurrence the observation is called a *signature*.

However, for the discrete event systems (DES) we consider, the diagnosis of systems is made typically in a more dynamic fashion, i.e., with different observations being recorded for a period of time. Therefore, we redefine and adapt the concept of signature in this setting.

We propose a definition of signatures for DES, which allows us to deal with different fault situations in a uniform way, and enables us to provide:

1. An efficient method for reducing and expanding the observability of a given system.
2. An extra layer between the actual fault model and the algorithms, which makes possible to develop algorithms independent from the actual nature of the faults.

Using signatures we build a general framework perfectly suited to our purpose of reducing and expanding observability. Moreover, it's easily extensible to a wide range of problems:

- Distinguishability, where it is important to differentiate types of faults.
- Predictability, where the fault is predicted rather than detected *a posteriori*.
- Extended fault model, where a fault is formed by a specific faulty sequence of events, (but each event in isolation is not a fault).

We focus on defining and developing the foundational concepts of our theory, as opposed to considering issues related to the practical application of the proposed techniques, which we leave for future work (e.g., the application of our framework to real cases [16]).

1.1 Organization of the Paper

The next section provides basic definitions, e.g., label transition system and diagnosability. Section 3 introduces the notion of signatures and correct behaviours. The framework for reducing and expanding observability is presented in Section 4. Section 5 describes briefly a prototype implementation tool. Extensions of the framework are provided in Section 6; and Section 7 overviews the related work. Finally, we draw conclusions in Section 8.

2 Discrete Event Systems

Preliminaries. Let L be any set. Then with L^* we denote the set of all finite sequences over L, with L^∞ we denote the set of all infinite sequences over L and with L^ω we denote the set of all finite and infinite sequences over L. The empty sequence is denoted by ε. For $\sigma, \rho \in L^\omega$, we say that σ is a *prefix* of ρ and write $\sigma \sqsubseteq \rho$, if $\rho = \sigma\sigma'$ for some $\sigma' \in L^\omega$ (then $\sigma' = \rho - \sigma$). If σ is a prefix of ρ, then ρ is a *continuation* of σ. We call σ a *proper prefix* of ρ and ρ a *proper continuation* of σ if $\sigma \sqsubseteq \rho$, but $\sigma \neq \rho$. We denote by $\mathcal{P}(L)$ the power set of L. Given $L' \subseteq L$ and σ a sequence over L^ω we denote by $\sigma_{L'}$ the restriction of σ over L'.

2.1 Labelled Transition Systems

Definition 1 (LTS). *A* labelled transition system, LTS, *is a tuple* $A = \langle Q, q^0, L, T\rangle$ *where*

- Q *is a finite set of states.*
- $q^0 \in Q$ *is the initial state.*
- L *is a finite set of events.*
- $T \subseteq Q \times L \times Q$ *is a finite branching transition relation.*

We denote the components of A *by* Q_A, q^0_A, L_A, *and* T_A. *We omit the subscript* A *if it is clear from the context.*

In Figure 1-(A) we represent $A = \langle Q, q^0, L, T\rangle$ a LTS where $Q = \{q_0, \cdots, q_5\}$, $q^0 = q_0$, $L = \{a, b, c, d, f\}$ and $T = \{(q_0, a, q_1), (q_1, f, q_3), \cdots, (q_5, c, q_4)\}$.

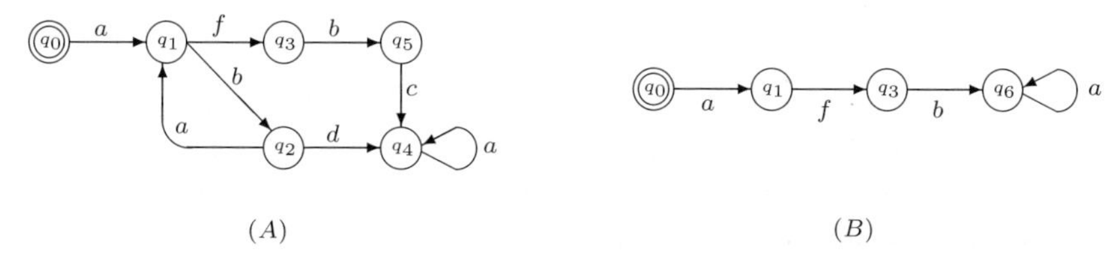

Fig. 1. LTSs

Definition 2 (path, trace, $|\sigma|$, $q \xrightarrow{\sigma} q'$, cycle, $\breve{\sigma}^k$). *Let* $A = \langle Q, q^0, L, T\rangle$ *be a LTS, then*

- *A* path *in* A *is a sequence* $\pi = q_0 a_0 q_1 \ldots$ *such that for all* i *we have* $(q_i, a_i, q_{i+1}) \in T$. *We denote with* $\mathsf{paths}(q)$ *the set of paths starting in* q. *We use* $\mathsf{paths}(A)$ *for* $\mathsf{paths}(q^0)$. *We denote with* $\mathsf{paths}(q, q')$ *the set of paths starting in* q *and ending in* q'. *We write* $q \rightarrow q'$, *if* $\mathsf{paths}(q, q')$ *is not empty and* $q \rightarrow$, *if there exists a state* q' *such that* $q \rightarrow q'$.

- *The* trace σ *of a path* π, *denoted* $\mathsf{trace}(\pi)$, *is the sequence* $\sigma = a_0 a_1 \ldots$ *of events in* L *occurring in* π. *We write* $\mathsf{traces}(A) = \{\mathsf{trace}(\pi) \mid \pi \in \mathsf{paths}(A)\}$ *for the set of traces in A, particularly we write* $\mathsf{traces}^{\infty}(A)$ *to denote the set of infinite traces in A. In case* σ *is finite, with* $|\sigma|$ *we denote the length of the trace* σ *and we define by* $\mathsf{last}(\sigma)$ *the last event of* σ.
- *We write* $q \xrightarrow{\sigma} q'$ *if the state* q' *can be reached from the state* q *via the trace* σ, *i.e., if there is a path* $\pi \in \mathsf{paths}(q, q')$ *such that* $\mathsf{trace}(\pi) = \sigma$.
- *A* cycle *is a non empty element in* $\mathsf{paths}(q, q)$ *for some state* q. *We denote by* $\mathsf{cycle}(A)$ *all the cycles in A.*
- *Given a trace* $\sigma \in \mathsf{traces}(A)$, *we denote by* $\breve{\sigma}$ *its postlanguage, i.e.,* $\breve{\sigma} = \{\rho \in \mathsf{traces}(A) \mid \sigma \sqsubseteq \rho\}$. *Moreover, for a given natural number* $k \in \mathbb{N}$ *we denote by* $\breve{\sigma}^k$ *its postlanguage with words with length equal or longer than* $|\sigma| + k$, *i.e.,* $\breve{\sigma}^k = \{\rho \in \breve{\sigma} \mid k \leq |\rho - \sigma|\}$.

We say that a LTS A is *live* if for all states there exists a transition initiated in that state, i.e.,

$$A = \langle Q, q^0, L, T\rangle \text{ is live} \quad \text{if and only if} \quad \forall\, q \in Q : q \rightarrow \tag{1}$$

Example, the LTSs from Figure 1-(A) (on the left) and 1-(B) (on the right) are live.

2.2 Observable LTSs with Faults

An *observable labelled transition system with faults* is a LTS that has its set of events subdivided into observable events (L_o) and unobservable events (L_u). Moreover, there exists a subset of L_u that represents fault events (L_f).

Definition 3 (observable LTS(L_f)). *An* observable labelled transition system with faults, *denoted LTS*(L_f), *is a tuple* $A(L_u) = \langle Q, q^0, L, T, L_u, L_f\rangle$ *where* $\langle Q, q^0, L, T\rangle$ *is a LTS and*

- *The set of events* L *is partitioned into a set of* observable events, L_o, *and a set of* unobservable events, L_u, *with* $L = L_o \cup L_u$ *and* $L_o \cap L_u = \emptyset$.
- *There is a subset of the unobservable events, called the* fault events, *denoted* L_f.

An observable LTS(L_f) is about hiding the faults and some other events. From now on, we refer to LTS(L_f) as to observable LTS(L_f) unless we state the opposite.

For example, Figure 1-(A) also represents a LTS(L_f) with: $L_u = \{f\}$ and $L_f = \{f\}$.

Definition 4 (observable trace, traces^f**,** $\mathsf{traces}^{f,k}$**,** $f \in \sigma$**).** *Let* $A(L_u) = \langle Q, q^0, L, T, L_u, L_f\rangle$ *be a LTS*(L_f), *then:*

- *The* observable trace *of a trace* σ, *denoted* σ_{L_o}, *is the sequence* $a_0 a_1 \ldots$ *of events in* L_o *occurring in* σ.
- *We denote by* $\mathsf{traces}^f(A)$ *the set of traces in A that end with a fault, i.e.,* $\mathsf{traces}^f(A) = \{\sigma \in \mathsf{traces}(A) \mid \sigma \in L^* L_f\}$.
- *Given a natural number* $k \in \mathbb{N}$ *we denote by* $\mathsf{traces}^{f,k}(A)$, *the set of traces* σ *such that there exists another trace* ρ *that ends in a fault and* σ *extends* ρ *with* k *or more events, i.e.,* $\mathsf{traces}^{f,k}(A) = \{\sigma \in \mathsf{traces}(A) \mid \exists\, \rho \in \mathsf{traces}^f(A) \wedge \sigma \in \breve{\rho}^k\}$.
- *Given a trace* σ, *we write* $f \in \sigma$ *to denote that* σ *has a fault, i.e.,* $\sigma \in L^* L_f L^{\omega}$.

We say that a LTS(L_f) A is *convergent* if it does not have cycles with non-observable events, i.e.,

$$A \text{ is } \textit{convergent} \quad \text{if and only if} \quad \forall\, \pi \in \mathsf{cycle}(A) : \exists\, a \in L_o : a \in \pi \qquad (2)$$

2.3 Diagnosability

The diagnosability of a system means that its model, supposed to be a LTS(L_f), can be unambiguously diagnosable, where a diagnosable LTS(L_f) is defined as being able to detect a fault occurrence within a finite number of steps based only on the observable traces.

Definition 5 (diagnosability). *Let* $A = \langle Q, q^0, L, T, L_u, L_f \rangle$ *be an observable LTS*(L_f)*, then* A *is* diagnosable *if the following holds;* $\exists\, n \in \mathbb{N} : \forall\, \rho \in \mathsf{traces}^{f,n}(A)$:

$$\textit{if} \quad \alpha \in \mathsf{traces}(A) : \rho_{L_o} = \alpha_{L_o} \quad \textit{then} \quad f \in \alpha.$$

The previous definition is a reformulation of the known Sampath [14] diagnosability definition, for the case with only one type of fault[1]. For example, the LTS(L_f) from Figure 1-(A), with $L_u = \{f\}$ is convergent and diagnosable.

Property 1. *Let* $A = \langle Q, q^0, L, T, L_u, L_f \rangle$ *be an observable LTS*(L_f)*, then* A *is* diagnosable *if the following holds;* $\exists\, n \in \mathbb{N} : \forall\, \rho \in \mathsf{traces}^{f,n}(A)$: *if* $\alpha \in \mathsf{traces}(A)$: $\rho_{L_o} = \alpha_{L_o}$ *then* $\forall\, \alpha' \in \mathsf{traces}^{\infty}(A) : \alpha \sqsubseteq \alpha' : f \in \alpha'$*.(Its proof can be found in [4].)*

Remark 1: For a given L_u, if the LTS$(L_f)A(L_u)$ is diagnosable, then $\forall\, L'_u : L_f \subseteq L'_u \subseteq L_u$, the LTS$(L_f)$ $A(L'_u)$ is diagnosable. Moreover, a LTS$(L_f)A(L)$ is never diagnosable (from the moment it has at least one correct trace and one faulty trace).

3 Observability and Signatures

3.1 Observability

Some systems can be non diagnosable even when all events, except fault events, are observable. We denote such systems *necessarily non diagnosable*. A more interesting situation is when a system is diagnosable with faults being the only unobservable events. We denote such systems *possibly diagnosable*. To distinguish if there exists an observability degree, for a particular system, that makes it diagnosable, we propose thus the following definition.

Definition 6 (necessarily non/possibly diagnosable). *A LTS*(L_f) A *is called:*

- Necessarily non diagnosable *if the LTS*(L_f) $A(L_f)$ *is not diagnosable.*
- Possibly diagnosable *if the LTS*(L_f) $A(L_f)$ *is diagnosable.*

Assumptions. From now on, we assume that all LTS(L_f) A, that we work with, are live, convergent and possibly diagnosable.

---

[1] In Section 6.1 we extend our approach to several types of faults.

3.2 Signatures in DES

In this section we introduce the notion of *signatures* that originally comes from continuous systems [15]. In this work we adopt *signatures* to represent faults executions for DES. A *signature* is a regular expression that denotes the set of traces with faults.

The *observable correct behaviour*, denoted **c**, is defined by the regular expression (with only observable events) that denotes all correct infinite traces, i.e., infinite traces that do not have faults.

Definition 7 (observable correct behaviour). *Given a LTS*(L_f) A *we define its* observable correct behaviour *as*

$$\mathbf{c} = \{\sigma \in L_o^\omega \mid \sigma \in \mathsf{traces}^\infty(A) : f \notin \sigma\}$$

In contrast with the observable correct behaviour, the *observable signature* is the regular expression that denotes all observable prefixes of faulty traces that are not prefix of an element of the observable correct behaviour.

To define observable signatures we use $\mathsf{traces}^{\mathbf{z}}$ to denote the set of all traces with exactly **z** events after the first occurrence of a fault. In [12] it is shown, that for an exhaustive diagnosability check, it is necessary to check traces of a maximal length $\frac{|Q|^2-|Q|}{2}$ (and, therefore we can choose $\mathbf{z} \leq \frac{|Q|^2-|Q|}{2}$), what is often impractically high. In practice, to build a correct signature, one is sometimes forced to set an upper bound for the length of faulty traces.

Definition 8 (observable signature). *Given a diagnosable LTS*(L_f) $A = \langle Q, q^0, L, T, L_u, L_f\rangle$, *its* observable signature *is defined as*

$$\mathbf{r} = \{\sigma \in L_o^* \mid \exists\, \alpha \in \mathsf{traces}^{\mathbf{z}}(A) : \sigma \sqsubseteq \alpha_{L_o} : \nexists\, \sigma' \in \mathbf{c} : \sigma \sqsubseteq \sigma'\}$$

Note that the observable correct behaviour is not the complement of the observable signature: there exist traces that do not belong to either class.

Remark 2: A consequence of the diagnosability definition (Definition 5) is that A being diagnosable ensures that **r** is not empty (from the moment A contains at least one fault) with a $\mathbf{z} = \frac{|Q|^2-|Q|}{2}$.

Following the example from Figure 1-(A), with $L_u = \{f\}$ we find $\mathbf{c} = a(ba)^*bda^\infty$, and with $\mathbf{z} = 4$, we have $\mathsf{traces}^{\mathbf{z}} = \{a(ba)^*fbca^2\}$. Thus, we obtain the observable signature $\mathbf{r} = a(ba)^*bc + a(ba)^*bca + a(ba)^*bca^2$.

In particular, we let observable signatures represent traces that do not have faults, but are prefixes of faulty traces. In Figure 1-(B) we represent a diagnosable system that is bound to have a fault with $L_u = L_f = \{f\}$. We obtain $\mathbf{c} = \emptyset$ because there is no infinite trace without fault. In addition, with $\mathbf{z} = 4$, we have $\mathsf{traces}^{\mathbf{z}} = \{afbaaa\}$ then we have $\mathbf{r} = a + ab + aba + aba^2 + aba^3$.

4 Reducing and Expanding Observability

4.1 Reducing the Observability

In this section we find a minimal set of observable events that still keeps the system diagnosable. We do it by reducing the set of observable events as much as possible still maintaining the diagnosability property.

The observable signature defined in Definition 8 describes the observable part of traces with faults or traces that certainly will produce a fault. Although, for the following proofs we use a more restricted version of signature, called *long signature*, denoted $\mathbf{lr}$. Long signatures do not contain traces that are prefix of another one, i.e.,

$$\mathbf{lr} \;=\; \{\sigma \in L_o^* \,|\, \sigma \in \mathbf{r} \wedge \nexists\, \sigma' \in \mathbf{r} : \sigma \sqsubset \sigma'\} \tag{3}$$

For example, our previous signature $\mathbf{r} = a(ba)^*bc + a(ba)^*bca + a(ba)^*bca^2$ is converted to the long signature $\mathbf{lr} = a(ba)^*bca^2$.

Moreover, for a trace σ we abuse the notation: $\sigma \in \mathbf{r}$, $\sigma \in \mathbf{lr}$, and $\sigma \in \mathbf{c}$ to denote that the observable trace of σ (i.e., σ_{L_o}) is in $\mathbf{r}$ or $\mathbf{c}$ respectively.

Structural differences, written $A \not\equiv B$, relate two sets of traces that do not have any trace in common, nor any prefix of a trace that belongs to the other set, except of the ε trace. Formally, structural differences are defined as follows.

Definition 9 (structural differences ($\not\equiv$)). *Let A and B be sets of traces, then*

$$A \not\equiv B \quad \textit{means} \quad (\forall\, \sigma \in A : \forall\, \sigma \sqsubseteq \sigma' : \sigma' \notin B) \wedge (\forall\, \sigma \in B : \forall\, \sigma \sqsubseteq \sigma' : \sigma' \notin A)$$

Lemma 1. *Let $A(L_u) = \langle Q, q^0, L, T, L_u, L_f \rangle$ be a diagnosable LTS(L_f), then if $a \in L_o : \mathbf{lr}_{L_o \setminus \{a\}} \not\equiv \mathbf{c}_{L_o \setminus \{a\}}$ and $A(L'_u) = \langle Q, q^0, L, T, L'_u, L_f \rangle$, with $L'_u = L_u \cup \{a\}$ is convergent then $A(L'_u)$ is diagnosable, and not diagnosable otherwise.*

The proof of this lemma can be found in an extended version of this paper in [1].

In the example from Figure 1-(A) with long signature: $\mathbf{lr} = a(ba)^*bca^2$ and correct behaviour: $\mathbf{c} = a(ba)^*bda^\infty$; using Lemma 1, we may drop the event c from the observable events, and the system remains diagnosable for $L_u = \{f, c\}$ and $L_o = \{a, b, d\}$.

We can easily convert back long signature into signature allowing any prefix of a trace in a long signature that is not a subtrace of a correct behaviour. For example, starting from the long signature $\mathbf{lr} = a(ba)^*bca^2$ from the system $A(L_u)$ with $L_u = \{f\}$, $L_o = \{a, b, c, d\}$, and correct behaviour $\mathbf{c} = a(ba)^*bda^\infty$ we obtain $\mathbf{r} = a(ba)^*bc + a(ba)^*bca + a(ba)^*bca^2$.

Theorem 1. *Let $A(L_u) = \langle Q, q^0, L, T, L_u, L_f \rangle$ be a diagnosable LTS(L_f), then we obtain a minimal set of observable events by repeatedly applying Lemma 1, $L'_o \subseteq L_o$ such that $A(L'_u) = \langle Q, q^0, L, T, L'_u, L_f \rangle$ is diagnosable, with $L'_u = L \setminus L'_o$.*

The proof for Theorem 1 is as follows. First, we derive the signature and correct behaviour from the diagnosable system A. Second, we obtain the long signature from the signature of the system. Third, we repeatedly apply Lemma 1 for all observable events until there does not exist any events in the observable events that can be converted to unobservable. Finally, we obtain back the signature from the last long signature that we obtained.

The above procedure can be performed according to different orders, depending on which observable events we choose to turn into unobservable ones. Note, that there always exists a minimal order w.r.t. the amount of observable events. The algorithm itself for reducing the observability is shown in Algorithm 1. It provides an algorithmic view for Lemma 1 and Theorem 1. Given a system, its observable events and observable signature, the algorithm returns a minimal set of observable events. It works in the following way. In line 3, it reduces the observable signature according with (3). In line 5-7, the algorithm chooses the set S with maximal cardinality, which is built by functions $checkUnObSet$ and $checkUnObserve$. The functions form the set S by iteratively reducing the set of observable events as far as observable signature for $\mathbf{lr}$ and observable correct behavior $\mathbf{c}$ are still distinguishable, in the same way as it was defined by Lemma 1.

In the following example we show how we obtain the minimal set of observable events for the system A from Figure 1-(A). Starting from $A(L_u) = \langle Q, q^0, L, T, L_u, L_f \rangle$ with $L_u = \{f\}$, $L_o = \{a, b, c, d\}$, $\mathbf{r} = a(ba)^*bc + a(ba)^*bca + a(ba)^*bca^2$ and $\mathbf{c} = a(ba)^*bda^\infty$. Then, (i) we obtain $\mathbf{lr} = a(ba)^*bca^2$; (ii) we convert d into unobservable, having $\mathbf{lr} = a(ba)^*bca^2$ and $\mathbf{c} = a(ba)^*ba^\infty$; (iii) we convert b into unobservable, having $\mathbf{lr} = aa^*ca^2$ and $\mathbf{c} = aa^*a^\infty = a^\infty$; and (iv) we reconstruct the signature as $\mathbf{r}' = aa^*c + aa^*ca + aa^*ca^2$. It is easy to note that $A(L'_u) = \langle Q, q^0, L, T, L'_u, L_f \rangle$ with $L'_u = \{f, d, b\}$, $L_o = \{a, c\}$ is diagnosable.

Algorithm 1. Reducing the observability

1: **Input:** System A, obs. events L_o, obs. correct behavior $\mathbf{c}$, obs. signature $\mathbf{r}$
2: **Output:** Minimal set of obs. events L'_o

3: $\mathbf{lr}$ = reduceToLongSignature($\mathbf{r}$)
4: $S_{max} = \emptyset$
5: **for all** $S \subseteq L_o$ **do**
6:   **if** checkUnObSet($A, S, \mathbf{c}, \mathbf{lr}$) $\wedge\ |S_{max}| < |S|$ **then**
7:     $S_{max} = S$
8:   **end if**
9: **end for**
10: **return** $L_o \backslash S_{max}$

11: **function** checkUnObSet(A, S, $\mathbf{c}$, $\mathbf{lr}$)
12:   **with** $a \in S$ **do**
13:     **if** isConvergent(A, $L_o \backslash a$) $\wedge$ checkUnObserve($\mathbf{c}$, $\mathbf{lr}$, a) **then**
14:       **return** checkUnObSet(A, $S \backslash a$, $\mathbf{c} - \{a\}$, $\mathbf{lr} - \{a\}$)
15:     **end if**
16:   **return** $S = \emptyset$

17: **function** checkUnObserve($\mathbf{c}$, $\mathbf{lr}$, a)
18:   **for all** $\sigma \in (\mathbf{c} - \{a\})$ **do**
19:     **for all** $\sigma' \in$ prefix(σ)$\wedge$ ($|\sigma'| \leq |\mathbf{lr}|$) **do**
20:       **if** $\sigma' \in (\mathbf{lr} - \{a\})$ **then**
21:         **return false**
22:       **end if**
23:     **end for**
24:   **end for**
25:   **return true**

Algorithm 2. Expanding the observability

1: **Input:** System A, obs. events L_o
2: **Output:** Minimal set of obs. events L'_o

3: **for all** $\sigma \in \mathsf{traces}^{f,n} \wedge |\sigma| \leq \mathbf{z}$ **do**
4:   **for all** $\alpha \in \mathsf{traces}(A)$: $\alpha_{L_o} = \sigma_{L_o} \wedge f \notin \alpha$ **do**
5:     $S_{\sigma\alpha} = \{O \mid \sigma_{L_o \cup O} \neq \alpha_{L_o \cup O} \wedge f \notin O\}$
6:   **end for**
7: **end for**
8: $S = \emptyset$
9: **for all** $S_{\sigma\alpha}$ **do**
10:   $S = \{B' \cup B'' \mid (B', B'') \in S \times S_{\sigma\alpha}\}$
11:   **for all** $B_i, B_j \in S, B_i \subseteq B_j$ **do**
12:     $S = S - B_j$
13:   **end for**
14: **end for**
15: **return** $L_o \cup B_{min}$, where $B_{min} \in S \wedge |B_{min}| = min|B|, B \in S$

4.2 Expanding the Observability

In this section we present the algorithm to transform a non-diagnosable system into a diagnosable one, expanding its set of observable events.

We assume that the system is possibly diagnosable (Definition 6). Thus, if we consider the system with all events as observable, except faults, then the system is diagnosable. We define $S_{\sigma\alpha}$ as a set of sets of events that distinguish traces σ and α. So, in a possibly diagnosable system with two traces σ and α with the same observability such that one has a fault, and afterwards it has at least n events, and the latter one without a fault, we define $S_{\sigma\alpha}$ as a set of sets of events (not from L_f) that makes σ and α distinguishable.

Definition 10 **($S_{\sigma\alpha}$).** *Let $A(L_u)$ be a possibly diagnosable LTS(L_f), then* $\forall\ \sigma, \alpha \in \mathsf{traces}(A) : \sigma \in \mathsf{traces}^{f,n}(A) \wedge f \notin \alpha : \sigma_{L_o} = \alpha_{L_o}$, *we define*

$$S_{\sigma\alpha} = \{O \in L_o \backslash L_f \mid \sigma_{L_o \cup O} \neq \alpha_{L_o \cup O}\}$$

where n is the bound, given by the diagnosability definition, for the system $A(L_u)$.

Considering the system presented in Figure 1-(A), with $L_o = \{a, b\}$, $L_u = \{c, d, f\}$; $\sigma = afbca$ and $\alpha = aba$ (so $\sigma_{L_o} = aba$ and $\alpha_{L_o} = aba$) we have $S_{\sigma\alpha} = \{\{c\}, \{c, d\}\}$. Now, with $\sigma' = abafbca$ and $\alpha' = ababda$, we obtain $S_{\sigma'\alpha'} = \{\{c\}, \{d\}, \{c, d\}\}$.

A *minimal distinguishable set*, denoted by S, represents a set that includes at least one set for all $S_{\sigma\alpha}$.

Definition 11 **(S).** *S is a* minimal distinguishable set, *if it has minimal cardinality and for all $S_{\sigma\alpha}$ with* $\sigma, \alpha \in \mathsf{traces}(A) : \sigma \in \mathsf{traces}^{f,n}(A) \wedge f \notin \alpha : \sigma_{L_o} = \alpha_{L_o}$, *there exists $B \in S_{\sigma\alpha} : B \subseteq S$.*

For the example shown in Figure 1-(A) we have $S = \{c\}$.

Theorem 2. *Let $A(L_u) = \langle Q, q^0, L, T, L_u, L_f \rangle$ be a possible diagnosable but non-diagnosable LTS(L_f), and let S defined as in Definition 11, then $A(L'_u) = \langle Q, q^0, L, T, L'_u, L_f \rangle$ is diagnosable, with $L'_u = L_u \backslash S$.*

The proof of this theorem can be found in an extended version of this paper in [1].

The algorithm is provided in Algorithm 2. It transforms the system into a diagnosable one without changing its structure (set of transitions, events or states) and only by expanding its observability. Moreover, the algorithm finds a minimal set of events that should be added to the initial set of observable events. The algorithm itself is based on the definitions and the theorem above: lines 3-5 refer to Definition 10, lines 9-12 refer to Definition 11 and Theorem 2. Note, that in line 3 we use $\mathbf{z}$ to limit the maximum length of σ. For an exhaustive search $\mathbf{z}$ has to be equal to $\frac{|Q|^2-|Q|}{2}$. In practice it is often possible to provide a better bound (e.g., [12]). Note that, depending on the initial L_o, L'_o is not necessarily a minimal set of observable events that makes the system diagnosable. However, the minimality can always be reached by applying the algorithm presented in Section 4.1 from $L_o = L \backslash L_f$.

In our example from Figure 1-(A) starting with $L_o = \{a, b\}$, following Algorithm 2 we obtain $S = \{c\}$. Thus, we obtain $A(L'_u) = \langle Q, q^0, L, T, L'_u, L_f \rangle$ with $L'_o = \{a, b, c\}$. In contrast, as we already pointed out in Section 4.1, the minimal set of observable events for this diagnosable system is $L_o^{min} = \{a, c\}$.

5 Implementation

We implemement the Algorithms, presented in Section 4, using constraint satisfaction techniques. The idea behind the implementation are the following.

LTS signature and correct behaviour are represented as set of constraints over variables representing states and labelles. Additional constraints are also added to represent the structural difference relation between signature and correct behavior. A valid assignment represents a trace in the LTS, which is modeled by both, signature and correct behavior. Wich makes signature and correct behavior to be not structually different. Therefore, having a solution to the generated constraint problem means that with that given level of observability the system is not diagnosable. The described encoding represents an efficient implementation of the $checkUnObserve$ function from Algorithm 1, and the condition at line 4 from Algorithm 2.

Our implementation uses as a constraint solver Choco [2]. Choco is a Java library for constraint satisfaction problems (CSP), constraint programming (CP) and explanation-based constraint solving (e-CP). In the scenarios that we are interested, users may wish to know why certain solutions are preferred to others. Explanation-based constraint programming is a viable approach to solve such problems. This is one of the reasons that lead us to Choco, as Palm is an explanation-based constraint system built on top of it.

The initial evaluation of the implementation, based on the examples available in [16], showed that the system finds an optimal observability level for diagnosable systems with up to 2000 states. However, these are just preliminary results, and more considerate and careful evaluation is planned to be done in future work.

The implementation itself, together with evaluation tests, can be fund in `http://www.dit.unitn.it/~lazovik/pmwiki/index.php?n=Research.Diag`.

6 Extended Models

In this section we introduce various extensions to the diagnosability model that we presented in Section 2.3. Within the framework defined in Section 3, it is possible to reuse algorithms from Theorem 1 and Theorem 2, and, in the same time, take into account several extensions: distinguishability, predictability, and extended fault models. In the following sections we show what has to be modified in the proposed model and algorithms to deal with each particular case.

6.1 Distinguishability

The problem of *distinguishability* arises when we are interested in distinguishing different types of faults rather than in a simple indication whether a fault occurred or not.

In this section we partition the set of faults (subset of the unobservable events) into classes of faults, i.e., $\Pi_f = \{L_{f_1}, \cdots, L_{f_m}\}$, where L_{f_i} represents faults with type f_i.

Definition 12 (observable LTS(Π_f)). *An* observable labelled transition system LTS(Π_f) with fault types, *denoted by* Π_f*,* $A(L_u) = \langle Q, q^0, L, T, L_u, \Pi_f\rangle$ *is a LTS*(L_f)*, where the set of* fault events *(*L_f*) is partitioned into* $\Pi_f = \{L_{f_1}, \cdots, L_{f_m}\}$*, i.e.,* $L_f \subseteq L_u$*,* $L_f = L_{f_1} \cup \cdots \cup L_{f_m}$ *and* $\forall\, i \neq j : L_{f_i} \cap L_{f_j} = \emptyset$.

So an observable LTS(Π_f) is a normal LTS with a clear distinction between observable and unobservable events and inside the unobservable events there is a subset of fault events subdivided into classes.

Definition 13 **(traces^{fi}, traces^{fi,k}, $f_i \in \sigma$).** *Let* $A = \langle Q, q^0, L, T, L_u, \Pi_f \rangle$ *be a LTS*(Π_f)*, then:*

- *Given a type of fault* f_i*, we denote by* traces$^{fi}(A)$ *the set of traces in* A *that end with a fault of type* f_i*, i.e.,* $\text{traces}^{fi}(A) = \{\sigma \in \text{traces}(A) \mid \sigma \in L^* L_{f_i}\}$.
- *Given a type of fault* f_i *and a natural number* $k \in \mathbb{N}$ *we denote by* traces$^{fi,k}(A)$*, the set of traces* σ *such that there exists another trace* ρ *that ends in a fault of type* f_i *and* σ *extends* ρ *with length longer or equal to* k*, i.e.,* $\text{traces}^{fi,k}(A) = \{\sigma \in \text{traces}(A) \mid \exists\, \rho \in \text{traces}^{fi}(A) \wedge \sigma \in \check{\rho}^k\}$.
- *Given a trace* σ*, we write* $f_i \in \sigma$ *to denote that* σ *has a fault of type* f_i*, i.e.,* $\sigma \in L^* L_{f_i} L^\omega$.

As follows, we re-define diagnosability and observable signatures for LTS(Π_f).

Definition 14 **(diagnosability in LTS(Π_f)).** *Let* $A(L_u) = \langle Q, q^0, L, T, L_u, \Pi_f \rangle$ *be a LTS*(Π_f)*, then the set* traces(A) *is diagnosable if the following holds;*

$$\forall\, 1 \leq i \leq m : \exists\, n_i \in \mathbb{N} : \forall\, \rho \in \text{traces}^{fi,n_i}(A) : \textit{if}\ \alpha \in \text{traces}(A) : \rho_{L_o} = \alpha_{L_o}\ \textit{then}\ f_i \in \alpha.$$

Definition 15 **($\mathbf{r}^i$).** *Given a diagnosable LTS*(Π_f) A *and* f_i *a fault type;* $\mathbf{r}^i$ *is the* observable signature of f_i *if it observable prefixes of traces contans a fault of type* f_i *that are not prefix of a correct trace.*

$$\mathbf{r}^i = \{\sigma \in L_o^* \mid \exists\, \alpha \in \text{traces}^{f_i,n_i}(A) : \sigma \sqsubseteq \alpha_{L_o} : \nexists\, \sigma'' \in \mathbf{c} : \sigma \sqsubseteq \sigma''\}$$

Definition 16 **(signature in LTS(Π_f)).** *Given a LTS*(Π_f) A *and* $\mathbf{r}^1, \cdots, \mathbf{r}^m$ *the set of observable signatures for fault types* $f_1 \cdots f_m$*, we define the* observable signature of A*:*

$$\mathbf{r} = \mathbf{r}^1 + \cdots + \mathbf{r}^m$$

Now we can reformulated Lemma 1 with respect to different faults.

Lemma 2. *Let* $A(L_u) = \langle Q, q^0, L, T, L_u, \Pi_f \rangle$ *be a diagnosable LTS*(Π_f)*, then if* $a \in L_o : \mathbf{r}_{L_o \backslash \{a\}} \not\equiv \mathbf{c}_{L_o \backslash \{a\}}$ *and* $\forall\, i \neq j : {\mathbf{r}^i}_{L_o \backslash \{a\}} \not\equiv {\mathbf{r}^j}_{L_o \backslash \{a\}}$ *then* $A(L'_u) = \langle Q, q^0, L, T, L'_u, \Pi_f \rangle$*, with* $L'_u = L_u \cup \{a\}$*, is diagnosable.*

With this new lemma, Theorem 1 remains true. Moreover, if we redefine Definition 10 and Definition 11 as follows, also Theorem 2 remains true.

Definition 17 **($S_{\sigma\alpha}$, S in LTS(Π_f)).** *Let* $A(L_u)$ *be a possibly diagnosable LTS*(Π_f)*, then* $\forall\, 1 \leq i \leq m : \forall\, \sigma, \alpha \in \text{traces}(A) : \sigma \in \text{traces}^{f_i,n_i}(A) \wedge f_i \notin \alpha : \sigma_{L_o} = \alpha_{L_o}$*, we define*

- $S_{\sigma\alpha} = \{B \subseteq L_u \backslash L_f \mid \sigma_{L_o \cup B} \neq \alpha_{L_o \cup B}\}$.
- *S is a minimal cardinality set, such that* $\forall\, S_{\sigma\alpha} : \exists\, B \in S_{\sigma\alpha} : B \subseteq S$.

6.2 Predictability

In some cases, e.g., in mission critical scenarios, it is important to achive the prediction of a possible fault situation rather than a post-fault detection. For such scenarios we have to ensure that the fault is predictable, and we come to the problem of *predictability*. Predictability study is not new, it was first introduced in [4]. However, in [4] authors investigate only case of strongly predictable systems, ignoring the notion of safe predictability.

However, since predictability is about future, and future is non-deterministic, we have two types of predictability: safe predictability and strong predictability. *Safe predictability* refers to an observation of a sequence of events that may *potentially* end in a fault; while *strong predictability* refers to cases that will end in a fault (when the fault is unavoidable).

Definition 18 (Safe predictability). *A LTS*(L_f) $A(L_u) = \langle Q, q^0, L, T, L_u, L_f \rangle$ *is* safely predictable *if the following holds;* $\forall\, \sigma \in \mathsf{traces}^f(A)$ *if* $\exists\, \alpha \in \mathsf{traces}(A) : f \notin \alpha \wedge \sigma_{L_o} = \alpha_{L_o}$ *then* $\exists\, \alpha' \in \mathsf{traces}(A) : \alpha \sqsubset \alpha' \wedge f \in \alpha'$.

Definition 19 (Strong predictability). *A LTS*(L_f) $A(L_u) = \langle Q, q^0, L, T, L_u, L_f \rangle$ *is* strongly predictable *if the following holds;* $\forall\, \sigma \in \mathsf{traces}^f(A)$ *if* $\exists\, \alpha \in \mathsf{traces}(A) : f \notin \alpha \wedge \sigma_{L_o} = \alpha_{L_o}$ *then* $\forall\, \alpha' \in \mathsf{traces}^\infty(A) : \alpha \sqsubset \alpha' \wedge f \in \alpha'$.

In our example, from Figure 1-(A), let assume we have $L_o = \{a, b\}$. Then, the system is safely predictable, since whenever we observe events a we know that we have the possibility to have a fault in the future. However, the system is not strongly predictable, since there is no sequence of observable events that unambiguously predicts f occurrence. On the other hand, the example from Figure 1-(B) is clearly strongly predictable with a list of observable events like $L_o = \{a\}$.

Within the defined framework, as in [4,5] where similar results are presented, strong predictability implies diagnosability and safe predictability.

Property 2. *Strong predictability implies diagnosability. It follows immediately from Property 1.*

Property 3. *Strong predictability implies safe predictability.*

A *predictability signature* is defined as a set of observable events that, if occurred, always or potentially (depends on the type of predictability) bring the execution to a fault event.

Definition 20 (safe/strong predictable signatures). *Given a* $A(L_u) = \langle Q, q^0, L, T, L_u, L_f \rangle \in$ *LTS*(L_f)*, then:*

- *If A is* safe predictable *then its observable-safe-predictable-signatures (*safe_**pr***) is*

$$safe\_\mathbf{pr} = \{\sigma \in L_o^* \mid \exists\, \sigma' \in \mathsf{traces}^f(A) : \sigma_{L_o} \sqsubseteq \sigma'_{L_o}\}$$

- *If A is* strong predictable *then its observable-strong-predictable-signatures (*strong_**pr***) is*

$$strong\_\mathbf{pr} = \{\sigma \in L_o^* \mid \forall\, \sigma' \in \mathsf{traces}^\infty(A) : \sigma_{L_o} \sqsubseteq \sigma'_{L_o} : f \in \sigma'\}$$

We can apply the previous algorithms directly for strong predictable systems.

Property 4. *Given a strong predictable system* $A(L_u) = \langle Q, q^0, L, T, L_u, L_f \rangle \in$ *LTS*(L_f) *with* **c** *as its correct behaviour (Definition 7) and strong_***pr** *as its strong-predictable-signatures (Definition 20), then:*

(i) The algorithm presented in Theorem 1 reduces the set of observable events correctly, keeping the system strong predictable.
(ii) The algorithm presented in Theorem 2 expands the set of observable events correctly, keeping the system strong predictable.

We also can apply the algorithms for safe predictable systems, but it is necessary to adapt the notion of *observable correct behaviour.*

Definition 21 (secure correct behaviour). *Given a system $A(L_u) \in LTS(L_f)$ we define the* observable secure correct behaviour *as*

$$\mathbf{sc} = \{\sigma \in L_o^\omega \mid \sigma \in \mathsf{traces}^\infty(A) : f \notin \sigma \wedge (\forall\, \alpha \sqsubseteq \sigma : \nexists\, \alpha \sqsubseteq \alpha' : f \in \alpha')\}$$

This definition is an adaptation of that of observable correct behaviour (Definition 7 in Section 3.2). The idea is analogous to the previous one; the main novelty here is that subtraces of correct traces can never be part of observable-safe-predictable-signatures. In this way we still keep the structural difference between correct behaviours and signatures.

Property 5. *Given a safe predictable system $A(L_u) = \langle Q, q^0, L, T, L_u, L_f\rangle \in LTS(L_f)$ with* **sc** *as its secure correct behaviour (Definition 21) and safe_***pr** *as its safe-predictable-signatures (Definition 20), then:*

(i) The algorithm presented in Theorem 1 reduces the set of observable events correctly, keeping the system safe predictable.
(ii) The algorithm presented in Theorem 2 expands the set of observable events correctly, keeping the system safe predictable.

We leave the properties in this section without proofs, since the proofs are analogous to Theorem 1 and Theorem 2.

6.3 Extended Fault Model

In this section we define an extended fault model, where a fault is formed by a specific fault sequence of events, that are not faults by themselves. Consider an example of driving a vehicle, where driving having doors open is a fault, while in most other situations it is an absolutely legal and expected action. In this case, the fault is defined not by a faulty event but rather by a sequence of events that forms a fault. Furthermore, a fault sequence can contain any arbitrary events that do not contribute to the fault. For the vehicle example, we may have something occurred between opening the door and driving, and still, if the door is open, we shoul not drive. We define this problem as diagnosability problem in an *extended fault model.*

In the extended fault model the fault is defined as a sequence of events. The fault is considered to be occurred when the last event of the sequence occurs. Besides, events in the sequence are not required to occur one after another one, we may have other events happening in the meantime. An *extended fault* is defined by a sequence of events, denoted ρ_f. The set of *fault executions* is then defined as $\{\sigma \mid \rho_f \subseteq \sigma\}$, where $\rho_f \subseteq \sigma$ means that the events from ρ_f happened in σ in order but not necessarily consecutively. So, if $\rho_f = ab$ then the trace $\sigma = cacbe$ is $\subseteq$ with respect to ρ_f. We denote by ρ_f^l the last event of the fault sequence ρ_f, i.e., $\rho_f^l = \mathsf{last}(\rho_f)$.

Definition 22 (Diagnosability with an extended fault model). *An extended fault model system A is called* diagnosable *with respect to to a fault sequence ρ_f and a set of observable events L_o if $\exists\, n \in \mathbb{N} : \forall\, \sigma \in \mathsf{traces}^{\rho^l_f, \mathbf{z}}(A)$ if $\alpha \in \mathsf{traces}(A) : \sigma_{L_o} = \alpha_{L_o}$ then $\rho_f \in \alpha$.*

A signature of an extended fault, in a diagnosable system A, is defined by a set of observable traces that contain the extended fault, i.e., $\mathbf{r} = \{\sigma_{L_o} \mid \rho_f \in \mathsf{traces}^{\rho^l_f, n}(A)\}$.

Theorem 1 and Theorem 2 remain true also for diagnosability with extended fault model, since definitions, theorems and proofs, obtained in Section 4, work at the level of signatures, without representing the nature of signatures explicitly.

In our example we can assume that an extended fault of the system is $\rho_f = fb$, meaning that the system execution a fault if a b event is performed after a f event. It is easy to see that the system is diagnosable for the following set of observable events: $L_o = \{a, c, d\}$. Applying Theorem 1, we may reduce the set to $L_o = \{a, c\}$. From the other side, from a set of observable events $L_o = \{a, b\}$ (which makes the system not diagnosable), we may expand it to a set $L_o = \{a, b, c\}$ using Theorem 2.

7 Related Work

Diagnosability study for DES is not new, of course. In [14] diagnosability is precisely defined and an algorithm for checking it is provided. The literature contains many other treatments of diagnosablity. We will not attempt to survey that work here.

The diagnosability problem treated in this paper is slightly related to the problem of model checking. However, there is an important difference. Model checking algorithms verify if the (possibly infinite) executions of a system satisfy a given property. Merely, it checks if there is a fault in the system, while diagnosability verifies if the existing faults are detectable. However, there is some work, that shows how diagnosability can be represented as a model checking problem [3].

In this paper we go beyond diagnosability checking, we discuss different levels of observability for diagnosable in DES. There are different styles of representing lavels of observability in DES (see, for instance [11]), where the attention is limited to investigate how the system observability level affects its diagnosability. In contrast, in [8] optimal sensor selection is addressed. Moreover, in [17] it is proven that finding the optimal (minimal) set of sensors (in our case observable events) for a diagnosable system is a NP problem. We improve those works introducing the notion of *signature* to abstract from the underlying failure model. Signatures originally come from continuous systems [15]. We adopt them to represent fault executions in DES.

In active diagnosis [13], the controller is designed to take into account the issues of diagnosability. Similar problems are also tackled in planning, where a planner can decide on the most appropriate actions to deal with faults (e.g., [9]). However, our approach makes no assumption on whether the system has control over its events, making the system being "passively" diagnosable. Furthermore, in [10] to diagnose a fault is to be able to identify in which state or set of states the system is. In contrast, we do not require information about states, we require only to be certain that a fault has occurred.

Our notions of predictability are closely related to the work in [4,5], where the problem of predicting occurrences of a fault is addressed. We expand those works with definitions of *safe predictability* and *strong predictability*. Additionally, we define the signature concept for these two definitions and show how our framework can be applied to predictability.

More broadly, this paper is partly a contribution to the formal study of extending the fault models (Section 6). There are two related paper on this topic. One of them is [7] where faults are described as a formula in linear temporal logic. The other is [6] where a notion of a supervision pattern is introduced to allow more complicated pattern-based models of failures.

8 Conclusion and Future Work

In is paper we discussed different levels of observability for diagnosable DES. We mainly studied two approaches: first, we transform a diagnosable system into one with minimal observability and still diagnosable. Second, we transform a non-diagnosable system into diagnosable by increasing its observability. We present two algorithms that implement our approaches and we illustrat our propositions with an intuitive example through all the paper. We describe briefly a prototype implementation tool. Also, we provided several extensions to the problem of reducing and expanding the observability. Furthermore, the provid a framework that deals with both classical faults and an extended fault model, as well as with other extensions in a uniform way.

In future work we plan to further investigate various extensions to the diagnosability problem and see if our framework can be extended to deal with new types of problems. Also, we plan to evaluate the proposed algorithms against some real cases within the WS-Diamond project [16] and extend our framework to go distributed making it faster and more efficient.

The important issue of fault isolation and control is ignored within the framework presented in the paper. In the future we plan to extend the proposed approach with controllable actions that allow us to isolate faults or, at least, perform some compensation activities to repair the system from the occurred faults.

References

1. Brandán-Briones, L., Lazovik, A., Dague, P.: Optimal observability for diagnosability. In: DX 2008 (2008)
2. Choco. Constraint programming system, `http://choco.sourceforge.net/`
3. Cimatti, A., Pecheur, C., Cavada, R.: Formal verification of diagnosability via symbolic model checking. In: IJCAI, pp. 363–369 (2003)
4. Genc, S., Lafortune, S.: Predictability in discrete-event systems under partial observation. In: IFAC, Beijing, China (August 2006)
5. Jéron, T., Marchand, H., Genc, S., Lafortune, S.: Predictability of sequence patterns in discrete event systems. In: IFAC World Congress, Seoul, Korea (July 2008)
6. Jéron, T., Marchand, H., Pinchinat, S., Cordier, M.-O.: Supervision patterns in discrete event systems diagnosis, pp. 262–268 (2006)
7. Jiang, S., Kumar, R.: Failure diagnosis of discrete-event systems with linear-time temporal logic specifications. IEEE Trans. on Automatic Control 49(6), 934–945 (2004)
8. Jiang, S., Kumar, R., Garcia, H.: Optimal sensor selection for discrete-event systems with partial observation, pp. 369–381

9. Lazovik, A., Aiello, M., Papazoglou, M.: Planning and monitoring the execution of web service requests. Journal on Digital Libraries (2005)
10. Lin, F.: Diagnosability of discrete event systems and its applications. Discrete Event Dynamic Systems: Theory and Applications 4(2), 197–212 (1994)
11. Nau, D., Ghallab, M., Traverso, P.: Automated task planning. Theory and practice. Morgan Kaufmann, San Francisco (2004)
12. Rintanen, J.: Diagnosers and diagnosability of succinct transition systems. In: IJCAI, pp. 538–544 (2007)
13. Sampath, M., Lafortune, S., Teneketzis, D.: Active diagnosis of discrete-event systems. IEEE Trans. on Automatic Control 40, 908–929 (1998)
14. Sampath, M., Sengupta, R., Lafortune, S., Sinnamohideen, K., Teneketzis, D.: Diagnosability of discrete-event systems. IEEE Trans. on Automatic Control 9(40), 1555–1575 (1995)
15. Travé-Massuyés, L., Cordier, M.-O., Pucel, X.: Comparing diagnosability in cs and des. In: 17th Int. W-p on Principles of Diagnosis (DX 2006), pp. 55–60 (2006)
16. WS-Diamond. Web services - DIAgnosability, MONitoring and Diagnosis project, http://wsdiamond.di.unito.it/
17. Yoo, T., Lafortune, S.: Np-completeness of sensor selection problems arising in partially observed discrete-event systems, pp. 1495–1499

Weaving Authentication and Authorization Requirements into the Functional Model of a System Using Z Promotion

Ali Nasrat Haidar and Ali E. Abdallah

E-Security Research Centre
London South Bank University
103 Borough Road
London SE1 0AA, UK
{ali.haidar,a.abdallah}@lsbu.ac.uk

Abstract. The use of Z in software development has focused on specifying the functionality of a system. However, when developing secure system, it is important to address fundamental security aspects, such as authentication, authorization, and auditing. In this paper, we show an approach for building systems from generic and modular security components using promotion technique in Z. The approach focuses on weaving security component into the functionality of a system using *promotion* technique in Z. For each component, Z notation is used to construct its state-based model and the relevant operations. Once a component is introduced, the defined local operations are promoted to work on the global state. We illustrate this approach on the development of a "secure" model for a conference management system. With this approach, it is possible to specify the core functionalities of a system independently from the security mechanisms. Authentication and authorization are viewed as components which are carefully integrated with the functional system.

Keywords: Z specification, Security Requirements, Authentication, Authorization, Weaving Security into Functional Models, Z Promotion.

1 Introduction

The use of formal specification Z [15] in software development has focused on specifying the functionality of a system [16,7,4,10]. However, when developing secure systems, it is important to address fundamental security aspects, such as authentication and authorization [3]. The construction of complex distributed applications is often done by integrating previously-existing software components [13]. This raises an important question: how to integrate security requirements into software design. Although, it is well documented that security needs to be integrated into the software design process, few are able to describe an approach to achieve this goal [11].Current methodologies fail to provide evidence of integrating successfully security concerns throughout the whole development process [6].

T. Margaria and B. Steffen (Eds.): ISoLA 2008, CCIS 17, pp. 831–846, 2008.

The primary aim of this paper is to show an approach for building systems from generic and modular security components using promotion technique in Z [15,8]. The main emphasis of this approach is on "weaving" security components (authentication and authorization) into the functionality of a system using *promotion* technique in Z. The approach consists of two phases. In the first phase, the global system is divided into a number of modular components. For each component, Z notation is used to construct its state-based model and the relevant operations. Once a component is introduced, the defined local operations are promoted to work on the global state. As a result, a more complex system is constructed by appropriate composition of the states of the constituent components, but addresses all security requirements needed by the system. This approach is illustrated by a case study of a Web-based Conference Management System. The global system is divided into several components namely: the functional conference component without any security features, the authentication component, and the authorization component which is based on the parameterized Role Based Access Control (RBAC) model [2].

The remainder of the paper is organized as follows. Section 2 gives an overview of a conference management system and a state based model of it. Section 3 briefly presents a formal model for a simple authentication component by showing: a state based model of the component and some basic operations on it. Section 4 describes the authorization component and the $RBAC$ mechanism and shows a state based model in Z. Section 5 introduces *promotion* and shows how the security components are integrated with the conference system. Section 6 is the conclusion.

2 Conference Management System

A Web-based conference management component allows authors to electronically submit conference papers and abstracts using the Web. Authors wishing to submit papers need to register their personal details and acquire credentials (username/password). We assume that this is done by the "submitter" of the paper. The submitter uploads the papers, enters the co-authors details (if any) and indicates useful keywords. When the submission deadline of papers is reached, the chair of the conference assigns the submitted papers to reviewers according to a set of constraints and preferences. For instance, papers can be assigned based on the reviewers' topic preferences. Constraints include cases where a conflict of interest would arise such as a paper is assigned to be reviewed by its own author. The papers, authors and reviewers' details, papers reviews' reports and decisions are the main assets that should be protected in this system. A brief outline of the main informal requirements of the system is as follows.

- Authors can submit/withdraw their own paper online; read own paper review report.
- Reviewers can view paper(s) and submit review reports for the paper(s) assigned to them respectively.

– Chair can view all submitted papers; assign paper(s) to reviewers according to a set of constraints; view all paper reviews reports; notify authors whether their paper was accepted or rejected.

2.1 State-Based Model of the Conference Component

Let *UserID, PaperID, Review, Topic, Title, Name, Email, File* be abstract types for denoting the set of all usernames, papers' identifiers, review reports, papers' topics, papers' titles, users' and organizations' names, email addresses, and papers' files respectively.

$$[UserID, PaperID, Topic, Review, Title, Name, Email, File]$$

A new data type, denoted *User_Details*, maintains useful information about users which may consist of entities such as name, organization, and email. This type can be described in Z as follows:

User_Details
$name : Name$
$organization : Name$
$email : Email$

Conference reviewers can be modeled as follows:

ConfReviewer
$user : UserID \pfun User\_Details$
$reviewers : \mathbb{P}\ UserID$

$reviewers \subset \mathrm{dom}\ user$

The *Paper_Details* data type captures relevant information about submitted papers. This may typically consists of a title, a set of authors, a set keywords, and a file.

Paper_Details
$paperTitle : Title$
$authors : \mathbb{P}\ User\_Details$
$keywords : \mathbb{P}\ Topic$
$file : File$

Each conference has at least one chair and can also have several chairs. This is modeled as a schema *ConfChair*.

ConfChair
$user : UserID \pfun User\_Details$
$chairs : \mathbb{P}\ UserID$

$chairs \subset \mathrm{dom}\ user$

The core functionality of a conference component is to maintain a set of registered users who can be submitters, reviewers or chairs; a set of submitted papers; and some mechanisms for associating papers with authors, reviewers and reviewers' reports. Users and papers can be dynamically added and removed. The abstract state of a conference consists of the following components:

- *paper*, a partial function that associates each submitted paper with its corresponding details.
- *user*, a partial function that associates each registered user with the corresponding details.
- *submitter*, a partial function that associates each paper with a unique author for the purpose of correspondence.
- *assigned_reviewers*, a relation that associates papers with their allocated reviewers.
- *paper_reviews*, associates each paper with the review reports submitted by its assigned reviewers.

The core conference component is divided into two components namely: *ConfSubmission* that deals with papers' submission and *ConfReview* that deals with paper reviews:

ConfSubmission

$$paper : PaperID \nrightarrow Paper\_Details$$
$$user : UserID \nrightarrow User\_Details$$
$$submitter : PaperID \nrightarrow UserID$$
$$\operatorname{dom} paper = \operatorname{dom} submitter \wedge \operatorname{ran} submitter \subseteq \operatorname{dom} user$$

The invariant ensures that the set of submitted papers is the same as the set of papers stored on the system, and that all submitters are registered users of the system.

ConfReview

$$reviewers : \mathbb{P}\, UserID$$
$$paper : PaperID \nrightarrow Paper\_Details$$
$$assigned\_reviewers : PaperID \leftrightarrow UserID$$
$$paper\_reviews : PaperID \rightarrow (UserID \nrightarrow Review)$$
$$\operatorname{dom} assigned\_reviewers \subseteq \operatorname{dom} paper$$
$$\operatorname{ran} assigned\_reviewers \subseteq reviewers$$
$$\forall p : PaperID \bullet \operatorname{dom}(paper\_reviews(p)) \subseteq assigned\_reviewers(\!|\, \{p\} \,|\!)$$

The invariant states that the papers are only assigned to reviewers, and reviewers can only submit reports on the papers assigned to them. The conference component can then be described as a conjunction of the above components as follows.

$$Conf \mathrel{\widehat=} ConfSubmission \wedge ConfReview \wedge ConfReviewer \wedge ConfChair$$

When a conference is initialized, it contains no papers or authors. The conference system will have a chair(s) and reviewers.

$$\begin{array}{|l}
\multicolumn{1}{l}{_\ ConfInit\ ____________________} \\
Conf' \\
\hline
users' = \{john, ali, mark, denise\} \land \\
chairs' = \{john\} \land reviewers' = \{ali, mark, denise\} \land \\
paper' = \emptyset \land submitter' = \emptyset \land assigned_reviewers' = \emptyset \land paper_reviews' = \emptyset \\
\hline
\end{array}$$

2.2 Conference Component Operations

We consider three operations on the conference component namely: *SubmitPaper*, *View* and *Withdraw* paper.

A successful *SubmitPaper* operation requires that the *paper_id* is not in the domain of *paper* relation:

$$\begin{array}{|l}
\multicolumn{1}{l}{_\ SubmitPaper0\ ____________________} \\
\Delta Conf \\
uname? : UserID \\
fullpaper? : Paper_Details \\
paper_id! : PaperID \\
\hline
paper_id! \notin \mathrm{dom}\, paper \\
paper' = paper \oplus \{paper_id! \mapsto fullpaper?\} \\
submitter' = submitter \oplus \{paper_id! \mapsto uname?\} \\
assigned_reviewers' = assigned_reviewers \\
paper_reviews' = paper_reviews \\
\hline
\end{array}$$

A successful *View* paper operation requires an existing *paper_id* as input and provides the corresponding paper as output:

$$\begin{array}{|l}
\multicolumn{1}{l}{_\ View0\ ____________________} \\
\Xi Conf \\
paper_id? : PaperID \\
fullpaper! : Paper_Details \\
\hline
paper_id? \in \mathrm{dom}\, paper \land fullpaper! = paper(paper_id?) \\
\hline
\end{array}$$

A successful *withdraw* operation requires only that the *paper_id* in question exists:

$$\begin{array}{|l}
\multicolumn{1}{l}{_\ Withdraw0\ ____________________} \\
\Delta Conf \\
paper_id? : PaperID \\
\hline
paper_id? \in \mathrm{dom}\, paper \\
paper' = \{paper_id?\} \lhd paper \\
submitter' = \{paper_id?\} \lhd submitter \\
assigned_reviewers' = \{paper_id?\} \lhd assigned_reviewers \\
paper_reviews' = \{paper_id?\} \lhd paper_reviews \\
\hline
\end{array}$$

More operations can be described such as *SubmitReview* and *AssignReviewer* operations. Because of space restriction the details could not be included in this paper.

Let *Report* be a data type, the values of which are messages indicating whether an operation has been successful or has failed.

$$Report ::= Success \mid Failure \mid Access\_Granted \mid Access\_Denied$$

A failed operation upon the conference state will produce a report as output.

$$\begin{array}{|l} \textit{InvalidPaperId} \\ \hline \Xi Conf \\ paper\_id? : PaperID \\ r! : Report \\ \hline \end{array}$$

An error may arise because the *paper_id* doesn't exist,

$$\begin{array}{|l} \textit{PaperIdNotInUse} \\ \hline InvalidPaperId \\ \hline paper\_id? \notin \operatorname{dom} paper \wedge r! = Failure \\ \hline \end{array}$$

or because the specified *paper_id* is in use:

$$\begin{array}{|l} \textit{PaperIdInUse} \\ \hline InvalidPaperId \\ \hline paper\_id? \in \operatorname{dom} paper \wedge r! = Failure \\ \hline \end{array}$$

A successful operation will always produce a report with the same value:

$$\begin{array}{|l} \textit{Op\_Success} \\ \hline r! : Report \\ \hline r! = Success \\ \hline \end{array}$$

The conference operations will then be modelled as follows:

$$SubmitPaper \mathrel{\widehat=} (SubmitPaper0 \wedge Op\_Success) \vee PaperIdInUse$$
$$View \mathrel{\widehat=} (View0 \wedge Op\_Success) \vee PaperIdNotInUse$$
$$Withdraw \mathrel{\widehat=} (Withdraw0 \wedge Op\_Success) \vee PaperIdNotInUse$$

3 Authentication Component

Authentication is required for a large class of distributed applications, such as e-banking, e-commerce, and e-government. Authentication aims at verifying the identity of an entity [3]: a human user or an application acting on behalf of a user. Several mechanisms for authentication exist: username/password pairs, digital certificates, and IP-based authentication [3]. Here we consider the username/password authentication mechanism since it is widely used. We assume that passwords are stored in encrypted form in an authentication table. To be authenticated, any users must show knowledge of a valid username/password pair that matches an entry in the authentication table.

3.1 Formal Specification of the Authentication Component

Let *UserID, Data* be abstract types for denoting the set of all usernames, passwords, and encrypted passwords respectively.

$$[UserID, Data]$$

The state of the authentication server comprises: a set of registered users; a partial function *at* that associates each *userID* with one encrypted password; and a partial function *encrypt* that is used to encrypt/hash clear text passwords. The invariant ensures that every registered user must have a password. The model can be described in *Z* as follows:

$$\begin{array}{|l} \hline AuthenticationCredential \\ \hline registered\_users : \mathbb{P}\ UserID \\ at : UserID \pfun Data \\ encrypt : Data \pfun Data \\ \hline registered\_users = \operatorname{dom} at \\ \hline \end{array}$$

3.2 Authentication Component Operations

We consider the following operations on the *AuthenticationCredential* system namely: *Login*, *ChangePassword*, *AddCredential*, *RemoveCredential* and *Logout.*

A successful *Login* operation requires a username and a password as inputs, then checks whether the pair matches an entry in the authentication table:

$$\begin{array}{|l} \hline Login0 \\ \hline \Xi AuthenticationCredential \\ username? : UserID \\ pwd? : Data \\ \hline encrypt(pwd?) = at(username?) \\ \hline \end{array}$$

A successful *ChangePassword* operation replaces the old password for the specified *username* with a new password after checking that the old password supplied by a user matches an entry in the authentication table:

$$\begin{array}{|l} \hline ChangePassword0 \\ \hline \Delta AuthenticationCredential \\ username? : UserID \\ oldpwd? : Data \\ newpwd? : Data \\ \hline encrypt(oldpwd?) = at(username?) \land at' = at \oplus \{username? \mapsto encrypt(newpwd?)\} \\ \hline \end{array}$$

A successful *AddCredential* operation allows a new user to acquire new credentials: *username* and *password* by adding a new record to the authentication table. The operation has a precondition that is the chosen *username?* most not be in the domain of authentication table *at*.

$$\begin{array}{|l}
\textit{AddCredential0} \\
\Delta \textit{AuthenticationCredential} \\
\textit{username?} : \textit{UserID} \\
\textit{pwd?} : \textit{Data} \\
\hline
\textit{username?} \notin \operatorname{dom} \textit{at} \wedge \textit{at}' = \textit{at} \cup \{\textit{username?} \mapsto \textit{encrypt}(\textit{pwd?})\}
\end{array}$$

RemoveCredential operation takes a *username* as an input and removes this identity from the set of registered users. This operation only succeeds if the username exists in the domain of the authentication table.

$$\begin{array}{|l}
\textit{RemoveCredential0} \\
\Delta \textit{AuthenticationCredential} \\
\textit{username?} : \textit{UserID} \\
\hline
\textit{username?} \in \operatorname{dom} \textit{at} \wedge \textit{at}' = \{\textit{username?}\} \lhd \textit{at} \wedge \\
\textit{registered_users}' = \textit{registered_users}' \setminus \{\textit{username?}\}
\end{array}$$

A failed operation upon the state of the state of the Authentication component state will produce a report as output.

$$\begin{array}{|l}
\textit{InvalidUserId} \\
\Xi \textit{AuthenticationCredential} \\
\textit{username?} : \textit{UserID} \\
\textit{r!} : \textit{Report}
\end{array}$$

An error may arise because the *username* doesn't exist,

$$\begin{array}{|l}
\textit{UserIDNotInUse} \\
\textit{InvalidUserId} \\
\hline
\textit{username?} \notin \operatorname{dom} \textit{at} \wedge \textit{r!} = \textit{Failure}
\end{array}$$

or because the specified *username* is in use,

$$\begin{array}{|l}
\textit{UserIDInUse} \\
\textit{InvalidUserId} \\
\hline
\textit{username?} \in \operatorname{dom} \textit{at} \wedge \textit{r!} = \textit{Failure}
\end{array}$$

or the combination of username and password is wrong:

$$\begin{array}{|l}
\textit{InvalidCredential} \\
\Xi \textit{AuthenticationCredential} \\
\textit{username?} : \textit{UserID} \\
\textit{pwd?} : \textit{Data} \\
\textit{oldpwd?} : \textit{Data} \\
\textit{r!} : \textit{Report} \\
\hline
\neg\, (\textit{encrypt}(\textit{oldpwd?}) = \textit{at}(\textit{username?})) \wedge \textit{r!} = \textit{Failure}
\end{array}$$

The authentication component operations will then be modelled as follows:

$$Login \mathrel{\widehat=} (Login0 \land Op\_Success) \lor InvalidCredential$$

$$ChangePassword \mathrel{\widehat=} (ChangePassword0 \land Op\_Success) \lor UserIDNotInUse$$

$$AddCredential \mathrel{\widehat=} (Withdraw0 \land Op\_Success) \lor UserIDInUse$$

$$RemoveCredential \mathrel{\widehat=} (RemoveCredential0 \land Op\_Success) \lor UserIDNotInUse$$

It is assumed here that the committee members and the chairs are registered users. The initial state of the authentication component is described as follows:

$$\begin{array}{l}
\textit{AuthenticationCredentialInit} \\
\hline
\textit{AuthenticationCredential}' \\
\hline
registered_users' = \{ali, mark, john, denise\} \\
at' = \{(ali, pwdx), (mark, mrk3000), (john, wnd1980), (denise, dnz2000)\}
\end{array}$$

4 Authorization Component

Authorization determines whether or not a user is allowed to perform a given action on a resource, for example viewing or withdrawing a paper. There are several mechanisms for enforcing access control such as Access Control Lists (ACL) and Role Based Access Control (RBAC) [3]. *RBAC* focuses on the roles that users perform within an organization. Permissions are assigned to roles rather than given directly to users and users of the system are allocated to roles.

4.1 A Simple Formal RBAC Model

The model assumes the existence of the following given types:

$$[ROLE, PRINCIPAL, OPERATION, OBJECT, TASK]$$

to denote the set of all possible roles, usernames (also known as principal in RBAC), operations, and objects, and tasks respectively.

The state of the core RBAC model comprises a set of known principals, *Principals*, a set of recognized roles, *Roles*, and a set of valid tasks, *Tasks*. The core RBAC model is characterised by two relations: *PrincipalRoles*, that assigns roles to each principal; and *RolePermissions*, that relates permitted tasks to each role. The whole model can be described in Z using the following scheme. For full details of this model the reader is referred to [2].

Core_RBAC

$$
\begin{array}{l}
Roles : \mathbb{P}\, ROLE \\
Principals : \mathbb{P}\, PRINCIPAL \\
Tasks : \mathbb{P}\, TASK \\
PrincipalRoles : PRINCIPAL \leftrightarrow ROLE \\
RolePermissions : ROLE \leftrightarrow TASK \\
\hline
Principals \subseteq \mathrm{dom}\, PrincipalRoles \\
\mathrm{ran}\, PrincipalRoles \subseteq Roles \\
Roles \subseteq \mathrm{dom}\, RolePermissions \\
\mathrm{ran}\, RolePermissions \subseteq Tasks
\end{array}
$$

One important property that needs to be considered in this system is Conflict of interest - where a principal is not allowed to assume simultaneously two specific roles that are considered to have conflicting interests to the organization [2]. This is called the principle of *separation of duties* [14]. To clarify this principle, consider a user u with the role $submitter(u, p)$. This user should not be able to review his/her own paper, in other words, the user should not also hold the role of $reviewer(u, p)$.

SoD_RBAC

$$
\begin{array}{l}
Core\_RBAC \\
ConflictRoles : ROLE \leftrightarrow ROLE \\
\hline
\forall\, u : Principals \bullet (PrincipalRoles(\!|\ \{u\}\ |\!) \times PrincipalRoles(\!|\ \{u\}\ |\!)) \cap ConflictRoles = \emptyset
\end{array}
$$

The major strength of this *RBAC* model is in the simplicity of its authorization semantics. A request initiated by a principal u to perform a task t is granted by the access monitor if and only if:

$$(u?, t?) \in (PrincipalRoles \mathbin{;} RolePermissions)$$

The whole access monitor can be captured as follows:

SoD_RBAC_AccessMonitor

$$
\begin{array}{l}
\Xi SoD\_RBAC \\
u? : PRINCIPAL \\
t? : TASK \\
rep! : REPORT \\
\hline
(u?, t?) \notin (PrincipalRoles \mathbin{;} RolePermissions) \Rightarrow rep! = Access\_Denied \\
(u?, t?) \in (PrincipalRoles \mathbin{;} RolePermissions) \Rightarrow rep! = Access\_Granted
\end{array}
$$

One of the main benefits of *RBAC* is consistency; two users (UserID) with the same roles must have exactly the same permissions. However, this is not desirable because some tasks needs to be performed on objects related to the

UserID only and not on other objects. Consider the case where two users occupy the same role *Submitter* in the conference component. Submitters can withdraw their own paper(s) and only read review report of a paper(s) they submitted. In order to accurately express authorization requirements we use a parameterized RBAC model as described in [1]. The authorization space in the core *RBAC* model is enlarged as desired by adding parameters to roles, objects and/or permissions, as appropriate. In our case, the parameter needed to provide a fine grained access control to the assets is the *UserID*. Therefore, finer roles can be introduced such as $Submitter(u)$, where u denotes a user drawn from *UserID*. An Authenticated user u holding the role $Submitter(u)$ can perform the operations view and withdraw only on papers submitted by u.

4.2 Initialising RBAC

In the conference system, the set principals is the same as the set of registered users, which has an initial value, $registered\_users'$. Hence,

$$Principals' = \{ali, mark, john, denise\}$$

We show in the following sections how this component can be combined with the conference component in order to have the same set of usernames in both component.

The right hand side of each initialization refers to variable in the state of the conference system *Conf*. The set of identified roles is initialised as follows:

$$Roles' = \{Chair(u) \mid u : Conf.chairs\} \cup \{Submitter(u,p) \mid (p,u) : Conf.submitter\} \cup$$
$$\{Reviewer(u,p) \mid (p,u) : Conf.assigned\_reviewers\} \cup$$
$$\{Authenticated(u) \mid u : \mathrm{dom}(Conf.user)\} \cup \{Unauthenticated\}$$

The set of relevant tasks is:

$$\begin{aligned} Tasks' = \{&Login, ChangePassword(u), View(p), Withdraw(p),\\ &AddCredential, SubmitPaper, ReadReview(p), Assign\_review, Notify(u,p)\}\end{aligned}$$

The role *Unauthenticated* is the only role allocated to a user who is not successfully authenticated (anonymous users).

$$anonymous \in UserID \bullet (anonymous, \{Unauthenticated\}) \in PrincipalRoles'$$

The roles allocated to an authenticated user u can be calculated as follows:

$$PrincipalRoles'(u) = \{Chair(u) \mid c : Conf.chairs \land c = u\} \cup$$
$$\{Submitter(u,p) \mid p : Conf.submitter^{-1}(u)\} \cup$$
$$\{Reviewer(u,p) \mid p : Conf.assigned\_reviewers^{-1}(u)\} \cup \{Authenticated(u)\}$$

With regards to permissions, the only tasks that are permitted to the *Unauthenticated* role are to register (add user credential and details) or to login.

Please note that the role $Reviewer(u, p)$ involves submitting a review report for a particular paper p.

Permission is the authorization for a role to perform a set of tasks according to a security policy. The set of permissions for each role is calculated as follows:

$$\begin{array}{l} RolePermissions' = \{(Unauthenticated \mapsto \{Login, AddCredential\}), \\ (Authenticated(u) \mapsto \{ChangePassword(u), SubmitPaper, Logout\}), \\ (Submitter(u,p) \mapsto \{View(p), Withdraw(p), ReadReview(p)\}), \\ (Reviewer(u,p) \mapsto \{View(p), SubmitReview(p), ReadReview(p)\}), \\ (Chair(u) \mapsto \{View(p), ReadReview(p), AssignReviewer(r,p), AddReviewer, Notify(u,p)\} \\ \mid u \in UserID, r \in reviewers \wedge p \in PaperID\} \end{array}$$

The set of roles that can cause conflict of interest can be defined as follows. The submitter of a paper p cannot review p:

$$\begin{array}{l} ConflictRole' = \\ \{(Submitter(u,p) \mapsto Reviewer(u,p) \mid u \in reviewers \wedge p : PaperID), \\ (Submitter(u,p) \mapsto Chair(u) \mid u \in chairs \wedge p : PaperID)\} \end{array}$$

Another conflict would occur when the chair submits a paper to the conference. The chair should not be able to assign the paper to a reviewer because the reviewer should always remain anonymous to the author of the paper. There are other conflicts that can occur, such as a reviewer should not be able to review a paper submitted by an author(s) from the same institution.

For this initialisation to be valid a healthiness condition on this initialisation is to ensure that the invariant of the state holds.

5 Promotion

Promotion [15] is a technique used in Z to compose specifications. It enables integrating a local state with a global state, when the local state is treated as a data type in the global state. In our case, the data type *AuthenticationCredential* is used in defining the state of a conference *Conf*. This data type is used in conjunction with its operations: *Login*, *ChangePassword* and *AddCredential*. Given any particular username/password, these local operations only affect the state of *AuthenticationCredential*, which is independent from the conference component.

5.1 Promoting Authentication

The conference component can be integrated with the authentication component by conjunction of the two schemas, as shown below. The result is a new schema denoted "*A_Conf*" that means conference with authentication mechanism.

$$\begin{array}{|l} \multicolumn{1}{l}{A\_Conf} \\ \hline Conf \\ AuthenticationCredential \\ \hline \mathrm{dom}\ users \subseteq registered\_users \\ \hline \end{array}$$

The invariant ensures that all conference users must be registered users. The local state is described by $AuthenticationCredential$, the global state is described by A_Conf, and the promotion is characterised by the schema:

$$
\begin{array}{l}
\textit{PromoteCredential} \\
\hline
\Delta A\_Conf \\
\Delta AuthenticationCredential \\
\hline
\theta AuthenticationCredential = \langle\!| registered\_users \leadsto registered\_users, at \leadsto at |\!\rangle \\
\theta AuthenticationCredential' = \langle\!| registered\_users \leadsto registered\_users', at \leadsto at' |\!\rangle \\
\hline
\end{array}
$$

which explains the relationship between local and global states. The operations on the global state can now be defined using this promotion:

$$
\begin{array}{l}
PromoteLogIn \mathrel{\widehat{=}} \exists\, AuthenticationCredential \bullet Login \land PromoteCredential \\
PromoteChangePwd \mathrel{\widehat{=}} \exists\, \Delta AuthenticationCredential \bullet \\
\quad ChangePassword \land PromoteCredential \\
PromoteAddCred \mathrel{\widehat{=}} \exists\, \Delta AuthenticationCredential \bullet \\
\quad AddCredential \land PromoteCredential \\
PromoteRemoveCred \mathrel{\widehat{=}} \exists\, \Delta AuthenticationCredential \bullet \\
\quad RemoveCredential \land PromoteCredential
\end{array}
$$

5.2 Promoting Authorization

We stipulate that a request by a user u to perform a task on the global system will have the following form: $request =< u, op\_name, inputbindings >$, where $u \in UserID$, op_name is an operation on the conference system with its inputs.

In the SoD_RBAC authorisation model, tasks are calculated and defined on the system. These tasks are static. However, new tasks can be generated and revoked dynamically during the lifetime of the system. For example, consider the $SubmitPaper$ operation. After successful execution of this operation by a user u, new tasks are generated, such as $< View, pid >$, $< Withdraw, pid >$, and $< SubmitReview, pid >$ where pid is the identity of the newly submitted paper.

According to the SoD_RBAC model, any task of the form $< op\_name,$ $inputbindings >$ will be accepted by the system. For example, $< View, 1000 >$ is a valid task if the $paperid = 1000$ may not exist on the conference system. Given an initial state of the conference system, a model can be generated that only allows valid tasks to be accepted by linking the input binding to the state. If the conference system has the following papers $paperid = \{100, 101, 102\}$, then a valid operation would be $< View, 100 >$, $< View, 1001 >$, or $< View, 102 >$. A user requesting to perform the task $< View, 108 >$ will not be accepted because the paper 108 is not in the system.

The conference with authentication can now be integrated with the authorization component by conjunction of the two schemas, which results in the new

"*A_A_Conf*" that means conference with authorization mechanism. The invariant ensures that all users of the conference system will be assigned to role(s) in the authorisation component.

A_A_Conf
A_Conf
SoD_RBAC

$$\mathrm{dom}(PrincipalRoles \lhd \{reviewer(u,p) \mid u \in UserID \land p \in PaperID\}) \subseteq reviewers$$
$$\land\ \mathrm{dom}(PrincipalRoles \lhd \{submitter(u,p) \mid u \in UserID \land p \in PaperID\}) \subseteq \mathrm{dom}\ users$$
$$\land\ \mathrm{dom}(PrincipalRoles \lhd \{chair(u,p) \mid u \in UserID \land p \in PaperID\}) \subseteq chairs$$

$$Tasks' = \{Login, AddCredential, SubmitPaper, Assign\_reviewer\} \cup \bigcup_{p \in \mathrm{dom}\ paper, u \in \mathrm{dom}\ user} \{Changepassword(u), View(p), Withdraw(p), Notify(p)\}$$

Two types of requests are considered:

1. requests by an *authenticated* user;
2. and, requests by an *unauthenticated* user.

In the first case the user u will be allocated the role "Unauthenticated", as shown in the RBAC initialisation. The only operations permitted are: *Login* and *AddCredential*. Any other operation will be denied.

In case the user is authenticated, the request is first evaluated by the access monitor. Depending on the access monitor decision, if the decision is grant then operation is then forwarded to the conference component part. The task will only be performed if the precondition pre (op) is satisfied. Otherwise, the task will fail and error report is returned (i.e. incorrect input). If the decision is deny, then the the task will fail and the operation op will not be forwarded to the conference system.

6 Related Work

As stated in the introduction, very little work has been done on integrating security requirements into the design process of a complex system. However, the literature provides some approaches towards this goal. In [5], the authors present an approach based on using the notion of minimal refinement as a method for the stepwise addition of requirement in a model. Other approaches are based on extending the semi-formal Unified Modelling Language (UML) to include security requirements. In [9], the author proposes an extension of UML, UMLsec, to include modelling of security features namely:confidentiality and access control. The authors in [12] propose an approach based on SecureUML for modelling access control policies and how these policies can be integrated into a model-driven software development process. In [11] the authors propose an informal way for integrating security into the software life cycle.

7 Conclusion

In this paper we have introduced a rigorous formal approach using promotion technique in **Z** for weaving security into the functionality of a system. We have shown how authentication and role-based authorization can be viewed as independent components which could be integrated with a functional system. The strength of this approach lies in its attempts to separate functional requirements from the requirements of certain security aspects. A simple example illustrating this approach to integrate authentication, authorization, and functional operations within a conference system was illustrated.

References

1. Abdallah, A.E., Khayat, E.J.: A Fornal Model for Parameterized Role Based Access Control. In: Martinelli, F. (ed.) Formal Aspects in Security and Trust, pp. 233–247. Kluwer, Dordrecht (2004)
2. Abdallah, A.E., Khayat, E.J.: Formal Z Specifications of Several Flat Role-Based Access Control Models. SEW 0, 282–292 (2006)
3. Gollmann, D.: Computer Security, 2nd edn. Wiley, Chichester (2005)
4. Evans, A.: Specifying & verifying concurrent systems using z. In: Naftalin, M., Bertrán, M., Denvir, T. (eds.) FME 1994. LNCS, vol. 873, pp. 366–380. Springer, Heidelberg (1994)
5. Gorogiannis, N., Ryan, M.: Minimal refinements of specifications in model and termporal logics. Form. Asp. Comput. 19(1), 35–62 (2007)
6. Mouratidis, H., Giorgini, P., Manson, G.: Integrating Security and Systems Engineering: Towards the Modelling of Secure Information Systems. In: Eder, J., Missikoff, M. (eds.) CAiSE 2003. LNCS, vol. 2681, pp. 63–78. Springer, Heidelberg (2003)
7. Heiner, M., Heisel, M.: Modeling safety-critical systems with z and petri nets. In: Felici, M., Kanoun, K., Pasquini, A. (eds.) SAFECOMP 1999. LNCS, vol. 1698, pp. 361–374. Springer, Heidelberg (1999)
8. Houston, I.S.C., Josephs, M.B.: Specifying distributed CICS in Z: accessing local and remote resources. Formal Aspects of Computing 6(5), 569–579 (1994)
9. Jürjens, J.: Umlsec: Extending UML for secure systems development. In: Jézéquel, J.-M., Hussmann, H., Cook, S. (eds.) UML 2002. LNCS, vol. 2460, pp. 412–425. Springer, Heidelberg (2002)
10. Knight, J.C., Kienzle, D.M.: Preliminary experience using z to specify a safety-critical system. In: Proceedings of the Z User Workshop, London, UK, pp. 109–118. Springer, Heidelberg (1992)
11. Futcher, L., von Solms, R.: SecSDM: A Model for Integrating Security into the Software Development Life Cycle. In: Fifth World Conference on Information Security Education. IFIP International Federation for Information Processing, vol. 237, pp. 41–48. Springer, Heidelberg (2007)
12. Lodderstedt, T., Basin, D.A., Doser, J.: Secureuml: A UML-based modeling language for model-driven security. In: Jézéquel, J.-M., Hussmann, H., Cook, S. (eds.) UML 2002. LNCS, vol. 2460, pp. 426–441. Springer, Heidelberg (2002)
13. Nissanke, N.: Component security - issues and an approach. COMPSAC (2), 152–155 (2005)

14. Sandhu, R.S., Coyne, E.J., Feinstein, H.L., Youman, C.E.: Role-based access control models. IEEE Computer 29(2), 38–47 (1996)
15. Woodcock, J., Davies, J.: Using Z Specification, Refinement, and Proof. C.A.R Hoare series editor. Prentice Hall International, Englewood Cliffs (1996)
16. Zafar, N.A.: Modeling and formal specification of automated train control system using z notation. In: Multitopic Conference, 2006. INMIC 2006, December 23-24, 2006, pp. 438–443. IEEE, Los Alamitos (2006)

Simple Gedanken Experiments in Leveraging Applications of Formal Methods

Raymond Boute

INTEC — Ghent University, Belgium
boute@intec.UGent.be
http://www.funmath.be

Abstract. As experience in established engineering disciplines shows, the most (maybe only) effective way for leveraging formal methods (FM) into daily practice is by developing mathematical modeling abilities. Laying a solid theoretical basis early is best assisted by simple example problems with minimal technical content. It is shown how simplicity still allows covering all practical aspects of FM and even finding new insights because, as in basic science, simple problems lead to a variety of gedanken experiments. Of the wide realm of opportunities, three are illustrated: (a) microsemantics in algorithmic problem solving and reasoning about invariants, (b) experimenting with data abstractions to capture informal statements faithfully, (c) expressing puzzles involving procedures, possibly with nondeterminism and multiple loops, by simple mathematics. The proper rôle of software tools in leveraging FM is discussed alongside.

1 Introduction

Wider context and motivation. "Professional engineers can often be distinguished from other designers by the engineers' ability to use mathematical models to describe and analyze their products" is a characterization by Parnas [20] considered evident since many centuries in established engineering disciplines.

In software "engineering", this basic characteristic is still too often neglected. Worse, the growth of software design into a mature discipline is hampered by mathphobic trends in CS education and in design support tools.

The educational study by Kelemen et al. [16,22] uses American data, yet reflects the European situation equally well. Some engineering schools make their CS curriculum a refuge for mathphobic students to increase student count. Instead of devoting the scarce teaching resources to solid fundamentals [19], they are wasted on trendy topics that students can equally well pick up on their own.

Design support tools often advertise with "hiding the math", tacitly implying that software problems are easy and mathematics renders things difficult. In reality, the difficulty is in the problems, and mathematics evolved to facilitate problem solving. Yet, the illusion of an easier shortcut is kept alive by the periodic appearance of yet another acronymic "method", delaying the maturity of software engineering by "hiding" the most powerful intellectual tool available.

T. Margaria and B. Steffen (Eds.): ISoLA 2008, CCIS 17, pp. 847–861, 2008.

The reason why this stagnation seems to entail little penalty is that IT and computing have created a huge amount of useful, well-paid but mainly routine tasks requiring little or no reasoning and design skills. Of course, catering for these needs does not satisfy the needs at the engineering level.

Rationale. Reconciling the crucial role of mathematics in engineering with the given background of students and professionals is possible only by lowering the threshold without compromising the level. As observed by Parnas [19] and Lamport [18], a viable approach is focusing on mathematics that is not specialistic (particular to CS) but widely applicable throughout engineering.

Computing Science has given formal logic a more prominent role, but *practically useful* formal logic [15] emerged only recently by the calculational style [13]. This style has proven its wider applicability in discrete math [14] and in general engineering mathematics [5]. As intimated by many researchers [18,20], predicate calculus is the pivotal element. Enabling engineers to calculate with quantifiers as fluently as they were taught to do with derivatives and integrals opens the gate to unification [4,5,6]. However, this is already the second step.

Indeed, in leveraging formal methods as well as in curriculum design, foundations must be laid first. Making the abstraction threshold passable requires a variety of conceptual and application problems and illustrations. To also learn taking advantage of abstraction, the initial application domains are best chosen in non-technical areas to avoid distraction by domain-specific issues.

An aside about software tools. For the same reason, mathematics should come before software tools, both in order of importance and in time. Indeed, software tools are always limited by implementation restrictions imposed by the current state of the art. For instance, there is huge gap in application domains and, more importantly, styles between tools used in software design and those in "classical" engineering (e.g., MATLAB/Simulink). This indicates that a general software tool covering all of engineering mathematics is still a far-away ideal.

Hence using a tool as an initiation vehicle imparts a very narrow perspective. A better approach is starting with unifying mathematical foundations, in which variety of tools can be embedded as needed. In such a setting, tools based on a language close to mathematics[1], such as TLA$^+$ [17], are readily suited for illustration purposes without wasting valuable time on "learning the tool".

The power of simple example problems. Suitable foundations and predicate calculus as a unifying factor are covered sufficiently elsewhere [14,4,5,6]. Here we concentrate on the rôle of simple example problems, rather than domain-dependent "engineering" problems, for conceptualization and illustration. As observed in [7], both the professional and recreational mathematics literature abounds with a wide variety of "puzzles" that are ideal for that purpose.

That simple problems are indeed suited for illustrating the many issues that may arise in formal methods is not evident. This is because the typical solutions

[1] Some advocate (imperative) programming notation, claiming that "the average programmer thinks in language X". Given that X is *not* suited for thinking (without formal semantics), this reflects poorly on the thinking of the average programmer.

presented in the literature just “forge ahead” towards the solution in a “look how clever” attitude, whereas the opportunities for leveraging applications of formal methods reside in the process, namely systematic formulation and reasoning.

This paper demonstrates such opportunities by some selected simple gedanken experiments, discovering useful new insights along the way.

Gedanken experiments and the FM issues raised. (as considered in this paper)

a. Simple mathematical modeling for procedures: The wider context [4,5] is mathematical and (hence) declarative. Yet, many puzzles are stated procedurally while asking for an essentially declarative solution. This is the reverse of program design (which goes from specification to procedure), and therefore particularly instructive as it contributes to the diversity of views. Here is an example [9].

A school has 1000 students and an array of 1000 lockers, all initially closed. All students walk along the row one after the other, and the kth *student inverts the state of every* k^{th} *locker, that is: opens the locker if it was closed and vice versa. How many lockers are open in the end?*

Classical mathematics has no formalism for procedures, which partly explains why typical solutions make a large jump from the informal procedural statement to the mathematical equations from which the final solution is derived. Programming languages, however, can express procedures, and hence formalize the procedure stated verbally in a puzzle. Such a formalization for the preceding example, assuming `K` students and an array `L` of `N` lockers, is

```
for k in 1..K
do (for n in 1..N do if (k divides n) then inv (L n) fi od) od
```

Still, this reduces only the gap between informal and formal problem statements as procedures, but the gap between procedures and mathematical equations leading to the desired final solution is thereby made all the more visible.

The bridge from programs to equations is mathematical semantics or any formalism to derive, from a program text, mathematical equations expressing the program's behavior. This view on mathematically modeling a procedure is analogous to an electronics engineer modeling a circuit by deriving, from the circuit diagram, mathematical equations expressing the circuit's behaviour.

To be suitable at an elementary level, the formalism should be lightweight, matching the perceived simplicity of the puzzles. We choose microsemantics [7], extended in this paper with *state expressions* and reasoning about *invariants.*

b. Expressing procedures mathematically by relations in a genuine specification language: This opens a refreshing view for students raised in the tradition of C++ or Java [21]. We choose the language TLA$^+$ and the tool TLC [17].

Although TLA$^+$/TLC is designed for different purposes (specification, model checking), the closeness to mathematics is appealing qua style and especially educational for students to counterbalance the restrictiveness of program notation. Additionally, it is instructive to use tools beside their design goals, as borne out by very favorable experience with LabVIEW, meant for instrumentation and measurement [2], but neat for illustrating topics in discrete mathematics [4].

c. Data abstraction and style experiments: We experiment with TLA$^+$/TLC (i) at the transition between informal and formal statements, trying to make the renderings as faithful as possible [7], (ii) at the implementation level, bringing the formulas within the automatic handling capabilities of TLC while preserving declarative elegance. It was instructive finding that some TLA$^+$ definitions in [17] were not accepted by TLC and designing replacements (presented in this paper).

Educational observations. Students like computer tools, some because they feel relieved from thinking, some because they like seeing things "happen" on a screen (the video game syndrome). Style exercises provide an antidote against superficiality by requiring to formalize and prove relationships between specifications. Also, TLC checks invariants, which helps students early on to gain confidence with thinking in such terms.

Using a diversity of formalisms is found a bit taxing by some students. However, having diverse forms of expression is helpful in linking informal and formal statements. Second, diversity is a fact of life to which students should be accustomed from the start. Of course, this must be done gradually and gently, and the earlier the start, the smoother the slope can be made. For both aspects, a unifying formalism in which this diversity can be embedded is invaluable [5,6].

Overview. Section 2 recalls microsemantics [8] and extends it with state expressions and reasoning about invariants. Section 3 starts from a simple puzzle with a nondeterministic procedure to explore ways of formulating it in TLA$^+$ with minimal prerequisites and via different abstractions. Section 4 shows how Funmath [3,5] extends the palette of expressiveness, showing its use in reasoning about TLA$^+$ specifications and matching them to TLC. In section 5 the earlier locker puzzle is used to show how nested loops can be expressed in TLA$^+$.

This is much material for one paper, so the sections are not ready-to-use modules. Yet, they provide enough information for FM-aware lecturers to embed such experiments in introductory courses preparing for "heavier" FM.

2 Microsemantics, State Expressions and Invariants

This lightweight formalism uses only the most basic concept in formal mathematics, namely *substitution*, as in [14, Chapter 1]. Nothing more is assumed.

2.1 Refreshing the Principles [8]

Substitution. Substituting expression d for variable v in expression e is written $e[^v_d$. Generalizing v and d to tuples is obvious, e.g., using $\stackrel{s}{=}$ for syntactic equality,

$$(x + 3 \cdot y)[^{x,\, y}_{a \cdot y,\, z+1} \stackrel{s}{=} a \cdot y + 3 \cdot (z + 1) \quad .$$

Multiple substitution differs from successive substitution, as seen by elaborating $(x + 3 \cdot y)[^x_{a \cdot y}[^y_{z+1}$. Clearly, $e[^v_c[^w_d$ stands for $(e[^v_c)[^w_d$ as $e([^v_c[^w_d)$ makes no sense.

Program equations. The *state* is the tuple matching the program variables, each with its declared type. We let s be the tuple of the variable names themselves.

A *command* c is modeled as a function from states to states, defined by an axiom of the form $c\,s = e$, as usual for functions in mathematics. Such an axiom is *instantiated* [14] as $(c\,s = e)[^s_d \overset{\mathsf{s}}{=} c\,d = e[^s_d$.

Basic commands are *assignment* (v := e), *composition* (c ; c'), *selection* (if b then c else c' fi), for commands c and c' and boolean expression b.

$$(v \texttt{ := } e)\; s = s[^v_e \qquad (1)$$
$$(c \texttt{ ; } c')\; s = c'\,(c\,s) \qquad (2)$$
$$(\texttt{if } b \texttt{ then } c \texttt{ else } c' \texttt{ fi})\; s = b \mathbin{?} c\,s \dagger c's \quad . \qquad (3)$$

We used a *conditional expression* of the form $b \mathbin{?} e_1 \dagger e_0$, read as "if b then e_1 else e_0" and formalized by the axiom $(b \mathbin{?} e_1 \dagger e_0) = e_b$ where b is 0 or 1.

The following are *derived* commands, definable via the basic ones.

$$\texttt{skip} = (v \texttt{ := } v) \qquad \text{(as a basic command, } \texttt{skip}\,s = s\text{)} \qquad (4)$$
$$(\texttt{if } b \texttt{ then } c \texttt{ fi}) = (\texttt{if } b \texttt{ then } c \texttt{ else skip fi}) \qquad (5)$$
$$(\texttt{while } b \texttt{ do } c \texttt{ od}) = (\texttt{if } b \texttt{ then } (c \texttt{ ; while } b \texttt{ do } c \texttt{ od) fi}) \qquad (6)$$

Microsemantics is minimalist, using just a program notation and substitution. The full machinery of semantics can be presented at a more advanced stage.

A note on assignment. This is an excerpt from the guidelines in [8]. It concerns only assignment, in view of a substitution issue that seems puzzling at first.

Consider an example with variables x and y, so the state s is (x, y). For the assignment x := x + y, clearly (x := x + y) $(x, y) = (x+y, y)$. Instantiating this result yields (x := x + y) $(2, 3) = (5, 3)$, as one would expect.

Generally, instantiating $c\,s = e$ by $[^s_d$ yields $c\,d = e[^s_d$. Hence, for Axiom (1),

$$(v \texttt{ := } e)\; d = (s[^v_e)[^s_d \quad . \qquad (7)$$

Warning: it is tempting to shortcut $(s[^v_e)[^s_d$ as $d[^v_e$. For (x := x + y) $(2, 3)$ this would amount to $(2, 3)[^x_{x+y}$, which is clearly incorrect.

Microsemantics in bootstrapping FM. In [8] it is shown how microsemantics can be used to bootstrap FM concepts such as (a) syntax, axiomatics, semantics, pragmatics; (b) equational reasoning; (c) lambda calculus; (d) propositional and predicate logic; (e) induction; (f) relations; (g) specification and design.

2.2 State Expressions and Invariants in Microsemantics

Motivation. In *Algorithmic Problem Solving*, Backhouse presents a collection of puzzles, including the following "Chocolate Bar Problem" [1, page 5].

A rectangular chocolate bar is divided into squares by horizontal and vertical grooves, in the usual way. It is to be cut into individual squares. A cut is made by taking a single piece and cutting along one of the grooves. (Thus each cut splits one piece into two pieces.). How many cuts in total are needed to completely cut the chocolate into all its pieces?

Observing that each cut increases the number of cuts by one and the number of pieces by one, the effect of making a cut is captured by the assignment

$$\texttt{p, c := p + 1, c + 1.} \tag{8}$$

To calculate the effect of an assignment ls `:=` rs on an expression E, [1] suggests $E[ls := rs]$, the expression obtained by replacing all occurrences of the variables in E listed in ls by the corresponding expression in the list of expressions in rs, and illustrates this by expressing the effect of (8) on $p - c$ as

$$(p - c)\,[p, c := p + 1, c + 1] = (p + 1) - (c + 1) = p - c. \tag{9}$$

This happens to be correct. However, it may tempt some students into making incorrect generalizations, for instance when successive assignments are involved. The simplest example is `x := y ; y := x` with the following erroneous calculation of the effect on the expression x.

$$\begin{aligned} x\,[x := y\,; y := x] &= \langle\text{Composition}\rangle\ (x\,[x := y])\,[y := x] \\ &= \langle\text{Substitution}\rangle\ y\,[y := x] \\ &= \langle\text{Substitution}\rangle\ x. \end{aligned} \tag{10}$$

This is clearly wrong, but some students may be confused as to why substitution gave a correct result in example (9) but not in (10). The central question is how to do such calculations correctly in general. This is shown next, noting that for substitution we usually write $[^{v}_{e}$ rather than $[v := e]$ to save horizontal space.

State expressions in microsemantics. A *state expression* is an expression with state variables. The *expansion* of a state expression g in a state d (tuple of state expressions) is $g[^{s}_{d}$, written $\mathcal{X}\,g\,d$ when convenient. The state after executing command c with initial state s is $c\,s$, for which the expansion of g is $\mathcal{X}\,g\,(c\,s)$.

If c is the assignment `v := e`, then $c\,s = s[^{v}_{e}$ and hence

$$\mathcal{X}\,g\,(c\,s) = g[^{s}_{c\,s} = g[^{s}_{s[^{v}_{e}} = g[^{v}_{e},$$

which explains why (9) happens to be correct. However, writing $c\,s$ assumes that the state before executing c is s. If the state before executing c is an arbitrary state d, for instance as the result of a preceding assignment, then we must calculate $\mathcal{X}\,g\,(c\,d)$, which equals $\mathcal{X}\,g\,(s[^{v}_{e}[^{s}_{d})$ and does not simplify to $g[^{v}_{e}$.

A correct version of the calculation (10) is the following.

$$\begin{aligned} &\mathcal{X}\,x\,((\texttt{x := y ; y := x})\,(x, y)) \\ &= \langle\text{Composition}\rangle\ \mathcal{X}\,x\,((\texttt{y := x})\,((\texttt{x := y})\,(x, y))) \\ &= \langle\text{Assignment}\rangle\ \mathcal{X}\,x\,((\texttt{y := x})\,(y, y)) \\ &= \langle\text{Assignment}\rangle\ \mathcal{X}\,x\,((x, y)[^{y}_{x}[^{x,y}_{y,y}) \\ &= \langle\text{Substitution}\rangle\ \mathcal{X}\,x\,(y, y) \\ &= \langle\text{Expansion}\rangle\ x[^{x,y}_{y,y} \\ &= \langle\text{Substitution}\rangle\ y \end{aligned}$$

Invariants in microsemantics. The rôle of state expressions in [1] is their use as invariants. We say that a state expression g is *invariant* under a command c iff $\mathcal{X}\, g\,(c\, d) = \mathcal{X}\, g\, d$ for any arbitrary state d. For this, it is necessary and sufficient that $\mathcal{X}\, g\,(c\, s) = g$, based on purely syntactic arguments.

However, $\mathcal{X}\, g\,(c\, s) = g$ need not be seen as a purely syntactic equality, since this would be too strict for practical use. Mathematical equality also allows using domain-dependent calculation rules, e.g., arihmetic[2]. An illustration:

$$\begin{aligned} &\mathcal{X}\,(p-c)\,(\texttt{(p, c := p + 1, c + 1)}\,(p,c)) \\ &\quad = \langle\text{Assignment}\rangle\ \mathcal{X}\,(p-c)\,(p+1, c+1) \\ &\quad = \langle\text{Exp., subst.}\rangle\ (p+1)-(c+1) \\ &\quad = \langle\text{Arithmetic}\rangle\ p-c\ . \end{aligned}$$

For an iteration of the form `while` b `do` c `od`, we may define g to be a *loop invariant* iff $b \Rightarrow \mathcal{X}\, g\,(c\, s) = g$.

3 Analyzing Procedural Puzzles in TLA+ anf TLC

3.1 Rôle of Procedural Puzzles

An example: the coffee bean puzzle. At various places on the web, one finds the following puzzle, most likely originating from David Gries.

Consider a coffee can which contains an unknown number of brown beans and an unknown number of white beans. Repeat the following process until exactly one bean remains. Select two beans from the can at random. If they are both the same color, throw them both out, but insert another brown bean. If they are different colors, throw the brown one away, but return the white one. What can you deduce about the color of the last bean as a function of the initial number of black and white beans? Hint: find a useful invariant maintained by the process.

Here is the usual informal solution: the obvious invariant is the parity (i.e., being even or odd) of the number of white beans, so the one remaining bean is white iff the original number of white beans was odd.

End of story? Far from it: for making such puzzles relevant to formal methods, one must dig considerably deeper.

Procedural puzzles as a preamble to formal methods. As argued in [7], the value of such puzzles as a preamble to formal methods is not in finding "quickie" informal solutions, but in the careful formalization of the informal statement and the systematic derivation of solutions.

For puzzles stated as procedures, the steps are: (a) translating the informal description into a formal language, (b) analyzing the result mathematically.

Step (a) includes making the statement more precise. For instance, the task stated in the example starts by taking beans. How about an empty can?

[2] The extent to which the distinction between '$=$' and '$\overset{s}{=}$' should be kept explicit is a matter of educational optimization. Since '$\overset{s}{=}$' is the stronger, replacing it by '$=$' is safe, but loses information.

Equally important, and more challenging, is aiming at a close rendering of the informal text.

Faithful renderings: the inversion criterion. How faithfully an informal text is formalized is to some extent a matter of taste. However, there is a reasonable working criterion: how well can the informal statement be reconstructed from the formalized one? For obvious reasons, we call this the *inversion criterion*.

The essence of faithful renderings is in using proper abstractions. Here "proper abstraction" does *not* mean: away from the problem (to the contrary), but: away from the restrictions due to the specification language or its implementation.

Hence the crucial limiting factor is the expressiveness of the language. For instance, the statement of the bean problem indicates that nondeterministic choice must be supported. However, as we shall see, more is needed.

3.2 Formal Renderings of the Coffee Bean Puzzle

This section is derived from a set of exam questions, recast here in a form suited for an article. The interested lecturer can easily do the inverse recasting.

Formalization in the Guarded Command Language. Here is a possible rendering in Dijkstra's Guarded Command Language [10,12].

```
do w + b > 1 -> if w >= 2 -> w := w - 2 ; b := b + 1
                [] b >= 2 -> b := b - 1
                [] w >= 1 and b >= 1 -> b := b - 1   fi od
```

It deserves at least two relevant criticisms.

First, since this language supports nondeterminism only via an `if`-statement, the random choice in the problem statement had to be "forced" into this shape.

Second, this rendering starts directly with numbers, which is coding-oriented and hence not a proper abstraction: the inversion criterion is far from being met.

Still, this program provides a nice and simple exercise for proving termination and invariants in a short classroom session or in an exam. For this purpose, we recommend the "checklist" given in [14] and proven in detail in [6].

Low-level formalization in TLA$^+$. Figure 1 is formalizes the beans puzzle in TLA$^+$ [17] in a low-level representation, that is: using numbers.

The central definition in this module is *CBnxt*. The example shows how to express procedural specifications by relations. Even before becoming proficient in formal calculation with relations, beginning students soon get some feeling for this different style of expression as compared to C++ or Java.

On the other hand, here is some style criticism. Note how the "meaningful identifiers" (*SlctAnyTwo* etc.) create the illusion of a faithful rendering [11], but the real test by the inversion criterion is after replacing these identifiers with their definitions a few lines earlier. All that remains then is some mumbo-jumbo with numbers, far removed from the problem statements. This is where data abstraction enters the picture, as illustrated in the following paragraph.

MODULE *Nob*

EXTENDS *Naturals*, *TLC*

VARIABLES w, b, ws
$s \triangleq \langle w, b, ws \rangle$
CONSTANTS — defined in the module to avoid updating the config file.
Initial contents, modeled by number W of white and B of brown beans.
$W \triangleq 5$ Parameter value example
$B \triangleq 3$ Parameter value example

$$CBini \triangleq \land w = W \land b = B \land w \geq 0 \land b \geq 0 \land w + b > 0$$
$$\land Print(\langle \text{"Initial number of white beans"}, w \rangle, \text{TRUE})$$
$$\land Print(\langle \text{"Initial number of brown beans"}, b \rangle, \text{TRUE})$$
$$\land ws = 0$$

$$CBinv \triangleq \land w\%2 = W\%2 \land w \geq 0 \land b \geq 0 \land w + b > 0$$

$SlctAnyTwo \triangleq w + b \geq 2 \land ws' = \text{CHOOSE } k \in 0 \,..\, w : k \leq 2 \land 2 - k \leq b$
Note: $ws =$ number of white beans in the sample; $bs = 2 - ws$ is implicit.
$AllSame \triangleq \neg(ws' = 1)$
$brown \triangleq 0$ Possible value for r in $Rplcby(r)$
$white \triangleq 1$ Possible value for r in $Rplcby(r)$
$Rplcby(r) \triangleq \land w' = w - ws' + r \land b' = b - (2 - ws') + (1 - r)$
$JstOneLft \triangleq w + b = 1$

$$CBfin \triangleq \land \text{UNCHANGED } s$$
$$\land Print(\langle \text{"Final number of white beans"}, w \rangle, \text{TRUE})$$
$$\land Print(\langle \text{"Final number of brown beans"}, b \rangle, \text{TRUE})$$

$$CBnxt \triangleq \lor (SlctAnyTwo \land \text{IF } AllSame \text{ THEN } Rplcby(brown) \text{ ELSE } Rplcby(white))$$
$$\lor (JstOneLft \land CBfin)$$

$$CB \triangleq CBini \land \Box[CBnxt]_s$$

THEOREM $CB \implies \Box CBinv$

Fig. 1. Numbers of beans

Formalization in TLA$^+$ using bags. Figure 2 uses the data structure *Bags* to model both the contents of the can c and the bean sample bs.

The central definition *CBnxt* is unchanged w.r.t. figure 1 mainly for educational reasons: emphasizing what is different, without possibly distracting other changes. However, replacing the "meaningful identifiers" with their definitions a few lines earlier now results in a procedure specification meeting the inversion criterion. The only difference is that the generic data abstraction is called a "bag" whereas the problem statement talks about a "can". For instance,

$$bs' = \text{CHOOSE } p \in SubBag(c) : size(p) = 2$$

reads as: "[the sample] bs' comes from choosing any subbag from c of size 2".

MODULE *Bob*

$\text{EXTENDS } Naturals, FiniteSets, Bags, TLC$

Some auxiliary operators

$size(B) \triangleq BagCardinality(B)$

$IsBag(B) \triangleq B \in [\text{DOMAIN } B \rightarrow \{n \in Nat : n > 0\}]$

$SingBag(e) \triangleq [x \in \{e\} \mapsto 1]$

$IsBagOf(B, S) \triangleq IsBag(B) \land \text{DOMAIN } B \subseteq S$

$Homog(B) \triangleq IsBag(B) \land Cardinality(\text{DOMAIN } B) \leq 1$

$\text{VARIABLES } c, bs$

$s \triangleq \langle c, bs \rangle$

CONSTANT — defined in the module to avoid updating the config file.

Initial contents of the can, modeled as a bag.

$C \triangleq [wt \mapsto 53, br \mapsto 35]$ Parameter value example

---

$white \triangleq$ "wt"

$brown \triangleq$ "br"

$Beans \triangleq \{white, brown\}$

$CBini \triangleq \land c = C \land IsBagOf(c, Beans) \land c \neq EmptyBag$
$\quad \land Print(\langle$"Initial number of white beans"$, CopiesIn(white, c)\rangle, \text{TRUE})$
$\quad \land Print(\langle$"Initial number of brown beans"$, CopiesIn(brown, c)\rangle, \text{TRUE})$
$\quad \land bs = EmptyBag$

$CBinv \triangleq \land CopiesIn(white, c)\%2 = CopiesIn(white, C)\%2$
$\quad \land IsBagOf(c, Beans) \land c \neq EmptyBag$

$SlctAnyTwo \triangleq size(c) \geq 2 \land bs' = \text{CHOOSE } p \in SubBag(c) : size(p) = 2$

$AllSame \triangleq Homog(bs')$

$Rplcby(r) \triangleq c' = c \ominus bs' \oplus SingBag(r)$

$JstOneLft \triangleq size(c) = 1$

$CBfin \triangleq \land \text{UNCHANGED } s$
$\quad \land Print(\langle$"Final number of white beans"$, CopiesIn(white, c)\rangle, \text{TRUE})$
$\quad \land Print(\langle$"Final number of brown beans"$, CopiesIn(brown, c)\rangle, \text{TRUE})$

$CBnxt \triangleq \lor (SlctAnyTwo \land (\text{IF } AllSame \text{ THEN } Rplcby(brown) \text{ ELSE } Rplcby(white)))$
$\quad \lor (JstOneLft \land CBfin)$

$CB \triangleq CBini \land \Box[CBnxt]_s$

$\text{THEOREM } CB \implies \Box CBinv$

Fig. 2. Bag of beans

4 Intermezzo: More Experimenting with Styles

In experimenting with TLA$^+$, Funmath [3,5] turns out to be a very good formalism for reasoning about TLA$^+$ function definitions. Here we illustrate two issues: styles of definition for matching informal description, and styles of definition for making definitions acceptable to TLC while preserving elegance and clarity. We start with the latter for the sake of continuity with the preceding section.

4.1 Defining Functions on Abstract Data Structures

Whereas TLA$^+$ as a language imposes no restrictions beyond its syntax, TLC accepts only definitions that do not require exploring infinite structures.

```
---------------------------- MODULE SBagsC ----------------------------
LOCAL INSTANCE Naturals
IsABag(B) ≜ B ∈ [DOMAIN B → {n ∈ Nat : n > 0}]
SetToBag(S) ≜ [e ∈ S ↦ 1]
BagIn(e, B) ≜ e ∈ DOMAIN B
EmptyBag ≜ SetToBag({})
CopiesIn(e, B) ≜ IF BagIn(e, B) THEN B[e] ELSE 0
B1 ⊕ B2 ≜ [e ∈ (DOMAIN B1) ∪ (DOMAIN B2) ↦ CopiesIn(e, B1) + CopiesIn(e, B2)]
B1 ⊖ B2 ≜ LET B ≜ [e ∈ DOMAIN B1 ↦ CopiesIn(e, B1) − CopiesIn(e, B2)]
          IN   [e ∈ {d ∈ DOMAIN B : B[d] > 0} ↦ B[e]]
LOCAL Sum(f) ≜ LET DSum[S ∈ SUBSET DOMAIN f] ≜
                     LET elt ≜ CHOOSE e ∈ S : TRUE
                     IN   IF S = {} THEN 0 ELSE f[elt] + DSum[S \ {elt}]
               IN   DSum[DOMAIN f]
B1 ⊑ B2 ≜ (DOMAIN B1) ⊆ (DOMAIN B2) ∧ ∀ e ∈ DOMAIN B1 : B1[e] ≤ B2[e]
SubBag(B) ≜ LET AllBagsOfSubset ≜
                  UNION {[SB → {n ∈ Nat : n > 0}] : SB ∈ SUBSET DOMAIN B}
            IN   {SB ∈ AllBagsOfSubset : ∀ e ∈ DOMAIN SB : SB[e] ≤ B[e]}
BagCardinality(B) ≜ Sum(B)
------------------------------------------------------------------------
```

Fig. 3. The *Bags* module from *Specifying Systems* compressed

For instance, figure 3 shows the basic *Bags* module from [17, page 343]. A pleasant feature of TLA$^+$ is using mathematical rather than programming notation. Hence readers with a minimal general mathematical background (no specialist familiarity with some programming language) should be able to understand these definitions with a little bit of study.

Consider, however, the definition of *SubBag* in figure 3, a function used in the *Bob* module (fig. 2). When model checking *BoB* using TLC, an error message indicated that the definition in figure 3 leads TLC to exploring the natural numbers. Leslie Lamport was so kind to send a replacement module.

Meanwhile, as an exercise, the author independently developed his own variant using the concepts of Funmath, in particular the Generalized Functional Cartesian Product [4,5], which is our "workhorse" for function typing. Omitting the design considerations, here is the definition. For any set-valued function T,

$$\times T = \{f : \mathcal{D}\,T \to \bigcup T \mid \forall x : \mathcal{D}\,T \cap \mathcal{D} f \,.\, f\,x \in T\,x\} \quad . \tag{11}$$

As an example, T may be a tuple of sets, as in $A \times B \times C = \times(A, B, C)$, or be denoted by (function) abstractions, as in $\times T = \times x : \mathcal{D}\,T \,.\, T\,x$.

The set of subbags of a given bag B is built as follows. The domain of any subbag of B is a subset of $\mathcal{D}\,B$, say S. A little reflection shows that the set of subbags of B with domain S is $\times\, s : S\,.\,1\,..\,B\,s$ and hence the set of all subbags of B is the union of these sets as S ranges over all subsets of B, that is:

$$SubBag\,B = \bigcup S : \mathcal{P}\,(\mathcal{D}\,B)\,.\,\times\, s : S\,.\,1\,..\,B\,s \tag{12}$$

where $\mathcal{P}\,X$ is the powerset of set X. Expanding $\times\, s : S\,.\,1\,..\,B\,s$,

$$\begin{aligned} &\times\,(s : S\,.\,1\,..\,B\,s) \\ &= \langle\text{Def. } \times\,(11)\rangle\ \{b : S \to \bigcup(s : S\,.\,1\,..\,B\,s) \mid \forall\, s : S\,.\,b\,s \in 1\,..\,B\,s\} \\ &= \langle\text{Calculations}\rangle\ \{b : S \to 1\,..\,nlub\,(B\,s \mid s : S) \mid b \sqsubseteq B\} \end{aligned}$$

where $nlub$ is the l.u.b. operator for $\mathbb{N}$ under $\leq$. We omit detail in "calculations". Substituting in (12) and translating the result into TLA$^+$ yields the following replacement for $SubBag$ in fig. 3, bringing it within the capabilities of TLC.

$$\begin{aligned} snlub(Snat) \;&\triangleq\; \text{IF } Snat = \{\} \text{ THEN } 0 \\ &\qquad\qquad \text{ELSE CHOOSE } n \in Snat : \forall\, m \in Snat : n \geq m \\ SubBag(B) \;&\triangleq\; \text{UNION } \{\{b \in [S \to 1\,..\,snlub(\{B[s] : s \in S\})] : b \sqsubseteq B\} \\ &\qquad\qquad : S \in \text{SUBSET DOMAIN } B\} \end{aligned}$$

4.2 Defining TLA$^+$ Functions at a More Abstract Level

Once more we address faithful formalization of informal statements, recalling an example from [7], and showing an interesting improvement.

Here is the informal statement: *Given a sequence of symbols, replace successive appearances of the same symbol* (aptly called *stuttering* in the context of [17]) *by a single appearance of that symbol.*

It is informative letting students formalize this as a homework assignment.

Lamport's formal specification [17] is not evident and covers infinite sequences only. A formula that reflects the intuitive simplicity of the specification is designed in [7]. An even simpler formula is the following: for any sequence β,

$$\natural\,\beta \;=\; +\!\!+\, n : \mathcal{D}\,\beta\,.\,(n > 0 \wedge \beta\,(n-1) = \beta\,n)\;?\;\varepsilon \mid \tau\,(\beta\,n)\quad, \tag{13}$$

where $+\!\!+$ is the concatenation operator, ε the empty sequence and $\tau\,e$ the sequence of length one containing just the element e.

5 Handling Nested Loops in TLA$^+$ and TLC

This is another experiment using a tool outside its normal application range.

Recalling the locker puzzle from the introduction, the procedural description is translated into TLA$^+$ as shown in figure 4. Observe how the control part for k and n is concentrated in one conjunction. This was straightforward (and possible) because the specification requires no other state changes in between.

```
---------------------------- MODULE SalC ----------------------------
EXTENDS Naturals, TLC
----------------------------------------------------------------------
VARIABLES k, n, a
s ≜ ⟨k, n, a⟩
  CONSTANTS —— defined in the module to avoid updating the config file.
  Initial contents, modeled by number K of students and N of lockers.
K ≜ 20 Parameter value example
N ≜ 16 Parameter value example
A ≜ [i ∈ 1 .. N ↦ 0] Initial array of lockers, all initially closed

LOCAL sum(f) ≜ LET asum[S ∈ SUBSET DOMAIN f] ≜
                       LET e ≜ CHOOSE x ∈ S : TRUE
                       IN  IF S = {} THEN 0 ELSE f[e] + asum[S \ {e}]
                   IN  asum[DOMAIN f]
LOCAL Divides(j, m) ≜ j ≠ 0 ∧ ∃ i ∈ 1 .. m : m = i * j
----------------------------------------------------------------------
SLini ≜ ∧ k = 1 ∧ n = 1 ∧ a = A
         ∧ Print(⟨"Number of students", K⟩, TRUE)
         ∧ Print(⟨"Number of lockers", N⟩, TRUE)
SLfin ≜ ∧ UNCHANGED s
         ∧ Print(⟨"Number of open lockers", sum(a)⟩, TRUE)
Invert(f, i) ≜ [f EXCEPT ![i] = 1 − @]
SLnxt ≜ IF k ∈ 1 .. K THEN ∧ a' = (IF Divides(k, n) THEN Invert(a, n) ELSE a)
                            ∧ IF n < N THEN n' = n + 1 ∧ k' = k
                                       ELSE n' = 1 ∧ k' = k + 1
                  ELSE SLfin
SL ≜ SLini ∧ □[SLnxt]_s
----------------------------------------------------------------------
```

Fig. 4. The locker procedure in TLA$^+$

Since this is rather restrictive, we also considered a more general situation, and developed a general template module. Although the normal limits for a paper prevent its description here, full details are available from the author. We hope that others will find this an interesting playground.

Here is a final note on TLA$^+$ and TLC. As mentioned, one of the most valuable features is the difference in style from languages like C++ or Java [21]. On the other hand, students weaned on speed rather than thought will be disappointed by the "execution" time TLC may take. It should be made clear that model checking is quite different from the usual notion of execution, but on the other hand allows a more thorough verification in many ways.

6 Conclusions

We have argued that domain-independent problems provide a better starting point for leveraging applications of FM than embarking directly on domain-specific "engineering" problems where the technicalities make separation of concerns more difficult. Not only does walking come before running in the learning process, but even the more advanced or more ambitious designers may gain by some reflection: *reculer pour mieux sauter.*

We also demonstrated how, contrary to first intuition, very simple problems provide sufficiently rich ramifications to illustrate all conceptual aspects of FM.

At the same time, we explored a diversity of style exercises aimed at capturing informal statements or specifications elegantly and faithfully in a formal setting. As an antidote against the superficiality of a purely tool-oriented initiation to formal methods, we indicated along the way numerous handles to more advanced topics and proof obligations appropriate for later stages in the familiarization with FM. We refer to Parnas [19,20] and Spolsky [21] for some valuable insights about the topics and attitudes to be found in a genuine CS education.

References

1. Backhouse, R.: Algorithmic Problem Solving. Lecture Notes, University of Nottingham (2007), `http://www.cs.nott.ac.uk/~rcb/G51APS/aps.ps`
2. Bishop, R.: LabVIEW 8 Student Edn. Prentice-Hall, Englewood Cliffs (2006)
3. Boute, R.: Functional Mathematics: a Unifying Declarative and Calculational Approach to Systems, Circuits and Programs — Part I. Course notes, Ghent University (2002), `http://www.funmath.be/`
4. Boute, R.: Concrete Generic Functionals: Principles, Design and Applications. In: Gibbons, J., Jeuring, J. (eds.) Generic Programming, pp. 89–119. Kluwer, Dordrecht (2003)
5. Boute, R.: Functional declarative language design and predicate calculus: a practical approach. ACM Trans. Prog. Lang. Syst. 27(5), 988–1047 (2005)
6. Boute, R.: Calculational semantics: deriving programming theories from equations by functional predicate calculus. ACM Trans. Prog. Lang. Syst. 28(4), 747–793 (2006)
7. Boute, R.: Using Domain-Independent Problems for Introducing Formal Methods. In: Misra, J., Nipkow, T., Sekerinski, E. (eds.) FM 2006. LNCS, vol. 4085, pp. 316–331. Springer, Heidelberg (2006)
8. Boute, R.: Microsemantics as a Bootstrap in Teaching Formal Methods. In: Boca, P., Duce, D. (eds.) Teaching Formal Methods: Practice and Experience (December 2006)
9. Dahlke, K.: Fun and Challenging Math Problems for the Young, and Young At Heart, `http://www.eklhad.net/funmath.html`
10. Dijkstra, E.W.: A Discipline of Programming. Prentice-Hall, Englewood Cliffs (1976)
11. Dijkstra, E.W.: To hell with meaningful identifiers, EWD 1044. University of Texas at Austin, Web (February 1989), `http://www.cs.utexas.edu/users/EWD/ewd10xx/EWD1044.PDF`
12. Dijkstra, E.W., Scholten, C.S.: Predicate Calculus and Program Semantics. Springer, Heidelberg (1990)
13. Dijkstra, E.W.: How Computing Science created a new mathematical style, EWD 1073. University of Texas at Austin, (March 1990), `http://www.cs.utexas.edu/users/EWD/ewd10xx/EWD1073.PDF`
14. Gries, D., Schneider, F.: A Logical Approach to Discrete Math. Springer, Heidelberg (1993)

15. Gries, D.: The need for education in useful formal logic. IEEE Computer 29, 29–30 (1996)
16. Kelemen, C., Tucker, A., Henderson, P., Bruce, K., Astrachan, O.: Has our Curriculum Become Math-Phobic (an American Perspective). In: 5th Ann. Conf. on Innovation and Technology in Computer Science Education (July 2000), http://citeseer.ist.psu.edu/kelemen00has.html
17. Lamport, L.: Specifying Systems: The TLA+ Language and Tools for Hardware and Software Engineers. Addison-Wesley, Reading (2002), http://research.microsoft.com/users/lamport/tla/book.html
18. Lamport, L.: All I really need to know I learned in high school. In: 2004 CoLogNET/FME Symposium on Teaching Formal Methods, Ghent (November 2004)
19. Parnas, D.L.: Education for computing professionals. IEEE Computer 23(1), 17–22 (1990)
20. Parnas, D.L.: Predicate Logic for Software Engineering. IEEE Trans. SWE 19(9), 856–862 (1993)
21. Spolsky, J.: The Perils of Java Schools. In: Joel on Software (December 2005), http://www.joelonsoftware.com/articles/ThePerilsofJavaSchools.html
22. Tucker, A.B., Kelemen, C.F., Bruce, K.B.: Our Curriculum Has Become Math-Phobic. ACM SIGCSEB, SIGCSE Bulletin 33 (2001), http://citeseer.ist.psu.edu/tucker01our.html

Composition of Web Services Using Wrappers

Ali Nasrat Haidar and Ali E. Abdallah

E-Security Research Centre
London South Bank University
103 Borough Road
London SE1 0AA, UK
{Ali.Haidar,A.Abdallah}@lsbu.ac.uk

Abstract. Web services (WSs) compositions deal with specifying how to assemble a complex WS system from elementary services. These services can be provided on the Web by third parties as WSs, COTS, or bespoke components. Wrappers are becoming the norm for customising existing components in order to integrate them into larger WS systems. In many cases, using a component "as-is" is very unlikely to occur. A component has to be customized because of, for example, incompatibilities between the interfaces of components that need to communicate with one another, need for extra security features, or, blocking unneeded functionality. This paper presents an approach for modeling several wrapping techniques that can be used for composing WS application using Hoare's CSP process algebra.

1 Introduction

A Web Service (WS) is a communicating system that is specifically designed to support interoperable machine to machine interactions over the Internet. The ultimate objective of WSs is to enable the construction of complex distributed applications by discovering and composing small, modular and reusable services available throughout the Internet [6]. A WS component's interface is described in the Web Service Description Language (WSDL) [6], and communication with other components is performed using standard SOAP [6] messages. WSs compositions deal with specifying how to assemble (integrate) a complex WS system from elementary services in order to provide new and more sophisticated functionality [1]. A typical example of WS composition is encountered when buying a holiday package from an online travel agency such as *Expedia.co.uk* [5]. This service can involve different elementary services combined together, such as various airlines flight searching services, online booking services, payment WSs offered and developed by various providers on the Web in different programming languages. There are several proposals for expressing orchestration of WSs compositions, such as Business Process Execution Language (WS-BPEL) [7], and Web Services Choreography Description Language (WS-CDL) [9]. These standards assume that the components to be composed already have standard WSDL interfaces, which is not the general case. This is because WSs can also

T. Margaria and B. Steffen (Eds.): ISoLA 2008, CCIS 17, pp. 862–865, 2008.

be built by reusing pre-existing components such as bespoke components which are developed inhouse, or Component-off-the-shelf (COTS) [8] provided by third parties, such as shopping carts.

When a designer identifies the various components of a complex system, the next step is to compose these components in order to construct the global system. Ideally, the intention is to use each of the identified components "as it is". However, it is well documented in the literature [2,3] that "as-is" reuse is very unlikely to occur, and in many cases, a reused component has to be customized in some way to match the global application's requirements. Customization can be needed due to, for example, incompatibilities between the interfaces of components that need to communicate with one another, need for extra security features, or, blocking unneeded functionality provided by the component. Components are usually specified as black boxes, so that components consumers can use them without knowing their internal details. The interface of a component is the only information available to the designer on how a component can be connected with other components. Thus, they are crucial for components composition.

One of the most currently used component customization technique is *wrappers* [1]. A wrapper is a specialized component inserted between a component and its environment to deal with requests coming to and/or replies from the wrapped component [1]. Components are placed within a wrapper and all interactions with the component are done through the wrapper. The wrapper hides the details of the interface of the component from external clients and acts as an interface between its caller and the wrapped component. It enables a component to have a new interface so that it can interact with a new component.

There are several wrapping techniques that can be used to customise components in order to compose them into a complex WS system. Because of page restriction, only a simple conversion wrapper is presented and modeled in CSP notation [4]. CSP offers constructs to compose components in various ways in terms of sequential, parallel, and conditional combinations, which can lead to composing complex WSs. This approach makes it easier to reason about the specified WS systems built from communicating components.

2 Simple Conversion Wrapper Example

A known problem when reusing a component is that the protocols and data format used by a component do not match the protocols and data format used by the global system [10]. For example, a component can be designed to be used with *RPC* protocol, whereas the global system is intended to use *SOAP* protocol. A wrapper can be used in this case to intercept incoming messages, which can be *SOAP* requests, and convert them to RPC calls. Outgoing messages from the component are also intercepted and converted to *SOAP* replies.

Consider a component described by the process *COMP* that has the following interface: $\alpha COMP = \{a, b, c, d\}$ as shown in Figure 1. The process *COMP* receives requests on interfaces a and b and outputs replies on interfaces c and d respectively. Let V and W denote the processes corresponding to the conversion

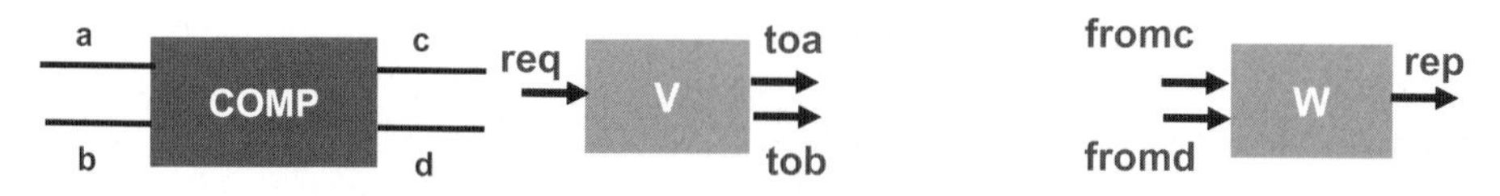

Fig. 1. Component and Converters

components respectively. Process V is used for converting messages coming from the environment to messages that can be interpreted by the component to be wrapped. Process W is used for converting messages coming from the component to messages that can be interpreted by the environment. The alphabets of processes V and W are: $\alpha V = \{req, toa, tob\}$ and $\alpha W = \{fromc, fromd, rep\}$.

On channel *req* the process V receives the incoming requests from the environment in one format, then, parses the request and transmits it in a new format to the appropriate component's interface. In this case, the request is transmitted to either a (or b) on channels *toa* (and *tob* respectively). On channel *fromc* (*fromd* respectively) the process W receives outputs from the component's channel c (d respectively), and on channel *rep* it outputs messages coming from the component to the environment. The conversion wrapper can now be defined as the CSP process *WRAPPER* that is a parallel composition of processes V and W, by renaming their interfaces as follows:

$$WRAPPER = V[in/req, a'/toa, b'/tob] \parallel W[out/rep, c'/fromc, d'/fromd]$$

Where in, out are the external interface of the wrapper, and a', b', c', d' are the names on the internal wrapper interface that will be connected with the component. As a result, the interface of the wrapper is: $\alpha WRAPPER = \{in, out, a', b', c', d'\}$. $V[in/req, a'/toa, b'/tob]$ means that the old channel *req* is renamed as in, *toa* is renamed as a', and *tob* is renamed as b'. This is known as *renaming* in CSP, which enables connecting two processes by renaming events from both processes to a common name. By renaming the internal interface of the wrapper to that of the component, the two becomes connected as follows: $WRAPPER[a/a', b/b', c/c', d/d'] \parallel COMP$.

The newly wrapped component is then modeled by the CSP process *WRAPPED_COMP*, where the internal interface of the wrapper is hidden form the environment:

$$WRAPPED\_COMP = (COMP \parallel WRAPPER) \setminus \{\alpha COMP\}.$$

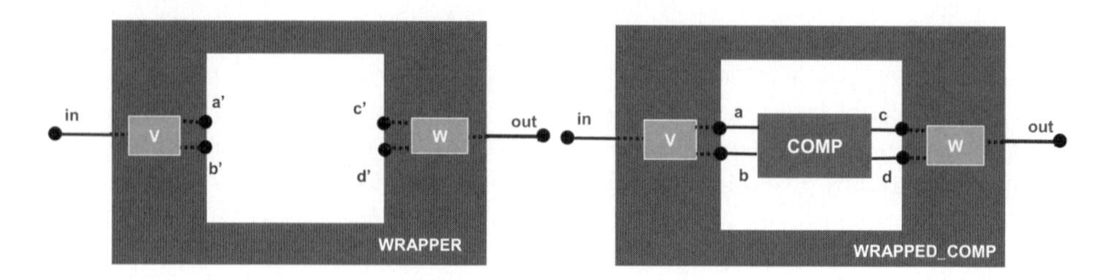

Fig. 2. Conversion Wrapper and a Wrapped component

3 Conclusion and Future Work

This paper presents a CSP approach that can be used to model wrapping techniques for composing complex WSs from reusable components. This approach can help in designing complex WSs compositions with rigor and precision. In the future several models for large class of used wrappers can be devised, such wrapping asynchronous components. A robust WS system can be designed by wrapping the functional part with an authorisation wrapper, and then, by adding authentication wrapper around it.

References

1. Alamri, A., Eid, M., El Saddik, A.: Classification of the state-of-the-art dynamic web services composition techniques. International Journal of Web and Grid Services 6(6), 148–166 (2006)
2. Srivastava, B., Koehler, J.: Web Service Composition — current solutions and open problems. In: ICAPS 2003 (2003)
3. Brant, J., Foote, B., Johnson, R.E., Roberts, D.: Wrappers to the rescue. In: ECCOP 1998 Proceedings of the 12th European Conference on Object-Oriented Programming, London, UK, pp. 396–417. Springer, Heidelberg (1998)
4. Hoare, C.A.R.: Communicating Sequential Processes. Prentice Hall, Englewood Cliffs (1985)
5. Expedia Corporation, `http://www.expedia.co.uk`
6. Kuno, H., Mchiraju, V., Alonso, G., Casati, F.: Web Services: Concepts, Architectures and Applications. Springer, Heidelberg (2004)
7. OASIS. Business Process Execution Language for Web Services Version 2.0. OASIS Standard (April 2007), `http://docs.oasis-open.org/wsbpel/2.0/CS01/wsbpel-v2.0-CS01.pdf`
8. Semancik, S.K., Conger, A.M.: The standard autonomous file server, a customized, off-the-shelf success story. In: Dean, J., Gravel, A. (eds.) ICCBSS 2002. LNCS, vol. 2255, pp. 234–244. Springer, Heidelberg (2002)
9. W3C. Web Services Choreography Description Language Version 1.0. Working draft (May 2004), `http://www.w3.org/TR/2004/WD-ws-cdl-10-20040427/`
10. Nakano, Y., Yamato, Y., Takemoto, M., Sunaga, H.: Method of creating web services from web applications. In: SOCA 2007: Proceedings of the IEEE International Conference on Service-Oriented Computing and Applications, Washington, DC, USA, pp. 65–71. IEEE Computer Society, Los Alamitos (2007)

Author Index

Printing: Mercedes-Druck, Berlin
Binding: Stein+Lehmann, Berlin